American Heritage®

DICTIONARY OF

AMERICAN QUOTATIONS

American Heritage®

DICTIONARY

OF AMERICAN

QUOTATIONS

Selected and Annotated by

MARGARET MINER

AND HUGH RAWSON

PENGUIN REFERENCE

PENGUIN REFERENCE
Published by the Penguin Group
Penguin Books USA Inc., 375 Hudson Street, New York, New York 10014, U.S.A.
Penguin Books Ltd, 27 Wrights Lane, London W8 5TZ, England
Penguin Books Australia Ltd, Ringwood, Victoria, Australia
Penguin Books Canada Ltd, 10 Alcorn Avenue, Toronto, Ontario, Canada M4V 3B2
Penguin Books (N.Z.) Ltd, 182–190 Wairau Road, Auckland 10, New Zealand

Penguin Books Ltd, Registered Offices: Harmondsworth, Middlesex, England

First Published in 1997 by Penguin Reference,
an imprint of Penguin Books USA Inc.

1   3   5   7   9   10   8   6   4   2

American Heritage and the eagle logo are registered trademarks of Forbes Inc.
Their use is pursuant to a license agreement with Forbes Inc.

LIBRARY OF CONGRESS CATALOGING IN PUBLICATION DATA
The American Heritage dictionary of American quotations/selected and
annotated by Margaret Miner and Hugh Rawson.
p.   cm.
Includes indexes.
ISBN 0-670-10002-1
1. Quotations, American—Dictionaries.   I. Miner, Margaret.
II. Rawson, Hugh.
PN6081.A623   1996
081'.03—dc20   96-8046

This book is printed on acid-free paper.
♾

Printed in the United States of America
Set in Trump Medieval
Designed by Victoria Hartman

For our nieces and nephews
Peter, Caroline, Robert, James, Rachel
Laura, Jennifer, Zoë, Peter

Acknowledgments

While this dictionary is the product of wide reading in books, newspapers, and magazines, as well as tuning in to radio and television, and following up the suggestions of friends, it nevertheless is true that no collection of this sort can be assembled without also consulting other dictionaries of quotations both to ensure comprehensive coverage and to verify our own findings.

General works that we found to be particularly valuable, aside from our own *New International Dictionary of Quotations* (Dutton, 2nd ed., 1993), which served as a starting point for this new book, included *Bartlett's Familiar Quotations* (16th ed., Justin Kaplan, ed., Little, Brown and Co., 1992); *A New Dictionary of Quotations on Historical Principles from Ancient and Modern Sources* (H. L. Mencken, Knopf, 1942); *Respectfully Quoted* (Suzy Platt, ed., Library of Congress, 1989); and the *International Thesaurus of Quotations* (Rhoda Thomas Tripp, ed., Thomas Y. Crowell Co., 1970).

Dictionaries dealing specifically with American quotations that we used included *American Quotations* (Gorton Carruth and Eugene Ehrlich, Wings Books, 1992); *The New York Public Library Book of 20th-Century Quotations* (ed. by Stephen Donadio et al., Warner Books, 1992); *A Dictionary of American Proverbs* (Wolfgang Mieder, editor in chief, Oxford University Press, 1992); *Words to Make My Children Live: A Book of African American Quotations* (Deirdre Mullane, Anchor Books, 1995); *The Oxford Dictionary of American Legal Quotations* (Fred R. Shapiro, Oxford University Press, 1993); and *American Sayings* (Henry F. Woods, Duell, Sloan and Pearce, 1945).

Other specialized dictionaries of help to us included *A Dictionary of Military and Naval Quotations* (Robert Debs Heinl, Jr., United States Naval Institute, 1966); *The Mystery Lovers' Book of Quotations* (Jane E. Horning, Mysterious Press, 1988); *The New Quotable Woman* (Elaine

Partnow, Facts on File, 1992, and its predecessors, *The Quotable Woman from Eve to 1799*, 1985, and *The Quotable Woman, 1800–1981*, 1982); *Nobody Said It Better!* (Miriam Ringo, Rand McNally, 1980); and *The Travellers' Dictionary of Quotations* (Peter Yapp, Routledge & Kegan Paul, 1983).

For checking attributions for quotations, we frequently consulted *They Never Said It* (Paul F. Boller, Jr., and John George, Oxford University Press, 1989) and *Nice Guys Finish Seventh* (Ralph Keyes, Harper-Collins, 1992).

Especially fertile sources of quotations, aside from back issues (into the 1950s) of *American Heritage* magazine, included *Looking Far West* (ed. by Frank Bergon and Zeese Papanikolas, Meridian, 1978); *The Heritage of America* (ed. by Henry Steele Commager and Allan Nevins, Little, Brown and Co., 1939); *A Documentary History of the United States* (Richard D. Heffner, Mentor, 5th edition, 1991); and *The Faber Book of America* (ed. by Christopher Ricks and William L. Vance, Faber and Faber, 1992).

Other references that were kept close at hand when preparing notes for quotations included *The Reader's Encyclopedia* (William Rose Benét, Thomas Y. Crowell Co., 2nd ed., 1965); *The Reader's Encyclopedia of American Literature* (Max J. Hertzberg, ed., Thomas Y. Crowell Co., 1962); *The Penguin Dictionary of Contemporary American History* (Stanley Hochman and Eleanor Hochman, Penguin Reference Books, 1997); *The Reader's Encyclopedia of the American West* (Howard R. Lamar, ed., Thomas Y. Crowell Co., 1977); *Folk Song USA* (Alan Lomax, ed., Plume, 1975); *The Oxford History of the American People* (Samuel Eliot Morison, Oxford University Press, 1965); and *Safire's New Political Dictionary* (William Safire, Random House, 1993). For dating of quotations from films, we consider the annually published *Leonard Maltin's Movie & Video Guide* (Signet) to be authoritative.

Many individuals also helped in various ways, including Kerry Acker; Cathleen Anderson; Anonymous, editor at *Soap Opera Digest*; Brenda Bailey at the Mark Twain Project, the University of California at Berkeley; David Barrett at *Golf* magazine; Tim Beard, librarian at the Minor Memorial Library in Roxbury, Connecticut; Douglas Brinkley; Jesse Cohen; Robert Creamer; Harold Davis at the Brownville Mills health store in Brownville, Nebraska; Elizabeth Dunn, librarian at the Hartman Center, Duke University; Jody Goggins at Wendy's International; Shaughan Lavine; the late Andrew Lytle; Arthur Maisel; Leonard Maltin; Joyce Melito, librarian at Saatchi & Saatchi Advertising in New York City; Dr. Albert Meloni at the Institute for American

Indian Studies in Washington, Connecticut; Henry Price, our copy editor; Noel Rae; Virginia Rodriguez at the *Washington Post;* Jeff Rovin; Betty Synnestvedt, assistant librarian at Minor Memorial Library in Roxbury, Connecticut; physicist John A. Wheeler of Princeton University; Robert Spencer Wilson, literary editor of *Civilization* magazine; Catherine Rawson and Nathaniel Rawson for help with indexing; Byron Preiss, president, and Michael Sagalyn, executive editor, at Byron Preiss Visual Publications, Inc.; and an extra thanks, for duty far above and beyond the call of normal family obligations, to William Fuller.

Introduction

Who is this American, this new man?
—J. HECTOR ST. JOHN DE CRÈVECOEUR

A morsel of genuine history is so rare a thing as to be always valuable. —THOMAS JEFFERSON

By necessity, by proclivity, and by delight, we all quote. —RALPH WALDO EMERSON

The *AMERICAN HERITAGE Dictionary of American Quotations* weaves together the three strands picked out by de Crèvecoeur, Jefferson, and Emerson: It is a collection, organized along historical lines, of more than five thousand memorable quotations on more than five hundred aspects of American life and culture. As the millennium draws to a close, this book offers a unique way of looking back to see how far we have traveled.

From ADVERTISING to MASSACHUSETTS to ZEAL, from the AMERICAN REVOLUTION to MARRIAGE to THE WEST, the *AMERICAN HERITAGE Dictionary of American Quotations* records our national experience as viewed by Americans from all walks of life—presidents and generals, pioneers and poets, entertainers and lawyers, athletes and Native American chiefs. John and Abigail Adams, Spiro Agnew, Yogi Berra, P. T. Barnum, Al Capone, Rachel Carson, and Clarence Darrow are here, along with the Roosevelts (Teddy, FDR, and Eleanor), Gertrude Stein, Sojourner Truth, John Updike, John Wayne, Woodrow Wilson, Malcolm X, and Brigham Young. And so are such foreign observers of the American scene as Alexis de Tocqueville, Harriet Martineau, Charles Dickens, and Rudyard Kipling. We also have counted as Americans a few foreigners who have spent appreciable parts of their working lives in this country, such as W. H. Auden, while retaining our claim on Americans who have spent most of their lives abroad, such as T. S. Eliot.

Quotations have been chosen not only for their historical significance but with an eye to their future utility. A great many of the entries in this book convey insights that transcend the immediate situations—often moments of stress and conflict—in which the words were written or spoken. They range from the brave reply of John Paul Jones, "I have not yet begun to fight," when asked to surrender his ship; to Jefferson's warning, "Our liberty depends on the freedom of the press, and that cannot be limited without being lost," to Thoreau's perception that "A man more right than his neighbors constitutes a majority of one," to Lincoln's "A house divided against itself cannot stand," to Mae West's admission that "I used to be Snow White—but I drifted," to Jim Henson's witty admonition (wearing his Miss Piggy mask) "Never eat more than you can lift."

The *AMERICAN HERITAGE Dictionary of American Quotations* is arranged to give readers at least three chances to find the quotations they want—through the main text, which is organized by subject; through the keyword index at the back of the book, and through the author index. Thus, Emerson's famous quote about building a better mousetrap, "If a man can write a better book, preach a better sermon, or make a better mousetrap than his neighbor . . . the world will make a beaten path to his door," is filed in the main text under EXCELLENCE. But the reader may also find the quote (which does not actually appear in Emerson's writings, by the way) in the keyword index under "mousetrap." Finally, by consulting the author index under Emerson, the reader also will be led back to the right quote in the EXCELLENCE category. Birth and death dates as well as authors' names, pseudonyms, and titles also are given in the author index.

The subject categories are listed alphabetically in the main text, with the principal topics printed in boldface capital letters along the left-hand margin of the page. Thus:

ABOLITION

ACTION & DOING

ADVENTURE

and so on, through to

WYOMING

YOUTH

ZEAL

Most subject categories also include references to related topics. These are printed in small-cap letters along the right-hand margin of the text. For example:

ACTION & DOING   *See also* ADVENTURE; BOLDNESS & INITIATIVE;
                                  DANGER & DANGEROUS PEOPLE; DECISION;
                                  ROOSEVELT, THEODORE; WORK & WORKERS

Within the subject categories, quotations are arranged in chronological order. They also are numbered, a new sequence beginning on each page. Thus, Emerson's mousetrap quote, the third quote on page 177 is listed in the keyword and author indexes as 177:3. Following each quotation is the name of the author ("Anonymous" if unknown), the title and date of the source, and, in many instances, a note from the editors. [The notes are printed in square brackets, like this sentence.]

The extensive annotations, together with the chronological method of arranging quotations within subject categories, constitute the chief features that distinguish the *AMERICAN HERITAGE Dictionary of American Quotations* from other collections of quotations. The notes—approximately thirty percent of the entries are annotated—set the quotations in historical context, provide additional information about the writer or speaker, and give earlier and later examples of similar turns of phrase. Many of the notes also cite other sources for attributions and refer the reader to related topics.

In addition, the notes assess questions of authenticity and originality in the case of quotations that have been commonly attributed to the wrong person, "improved" in some way over the years, or simply made up out of whole cloth. An example of the first sort is "Put all your eggs in one basket—and watch that basket," commonly credited to Mark Twain, who included the line in *Pudd'nhead Wilson*. But did he originate it? Actually, as noted in WISDOM, WORDS OF, Twain was given this advice, and in these very words, at dinner on the night of April 6, 1893, by a canny Scotsman: Andrew Carnegie.

Other quotations have become famous because they sound as though they *should* have been said or because they support patriotic interpretations of the past. Thus, Patrick Henry's ringing "give me liberty or give me death" has been repeated in schoolbooks for generations. Strangely, however, neither Washington nor Jefferson, who were present when Henry made this presumably memorable declaration, mentioned it in their own writings. Their silence is suspicious. The quotation, it turns out, comes from a biography of Henry that was published more than forty years after the event. The same biographer also added considerable sheen to Henry's "if this be treason, make the most of it," neglecting to mention that the orator went on to beg the pardon of his listeners if in the heat of moment he had said more than he had intended.

Spurious quotes are just as useful as real ones for making points, of course, and may be repeated unknowingly over and over again. The authority of LINCOLN in particular, as noted in the entry on the sixteenth president, often is invoked by citing him as the source for words he never said. Thus, Ronald Reagan quoted Lincoln at the 1992 Republican national convention as having said, "You cannot strengthen the weak by weakening the strong. You cannot help the wage earner by pulling down the wage payer. You cannot help men permanently by doing for them what they could and should do for themselves." But these solid, conservative sentiments actually came from the pen of a Rev. William John Henry Boetcker in 1916.

This dictionary's second distinctive feature, the chronological method of organization within subjects, helps show how Americans' understanding and views have developed over time on such diverse topics as EDUCATION and the ENVIRONMENT, the MEDIA and MILITARY STRATEGY, THE PRESIDENCY and GEORGE WASHINGTON. Thus, under FREEDOM, Patrick Henry precedes Davy Crockett, who precedes Thoreau, who precedes, among others—and moving forward in time—Lincoln, Harriet Tubman, Oliver Wendell Holmes, Jr., Franklin D. Roosevelt, and Martin Luther King, Jr. The section on THE WEST begins optimistically with Thoreau in 1836 ("Eastward I go only by force; but westward I go free") and concludes with Wallace Stegner in 1991 ("Ghost towns and dust bowls, like motels, are western inventions"). WOMEN ranges forward from Abigail Adams, writing to her husband in 1776 ("Men of sense of all ages abhor those customs which treat us only as vassals of your sex") to Gloria Steinem, addressing Yale students more than two hundred years later ("Some of us are becoming the men we wanted to marry"). Where exact dates of quotations are not known, we have placed them in approximate chronological order; in cases where quotations are drawn from later publications, the year dates are printed within brackets instead of parentheses.

The chronological arrangement also allows one to follow the progress of the AMERICAN REVOLUTION, THE CIVIL WAR, WORLD WAR I, WORLD WAR II, and other events and related sequences, such as FOREIGN POLICY, national elections (*see* POLITICAL SLOGANS), and WATERGATE. Thus, the section on the Civil War begins with William Seward's prewar warning (1858) of an "irrepressible conflict," then encapsulates key moments in the conflict, from Confederate General Bernard Bee's rallying cry at the first Battle of Bull Run in 1861, "See, there is Jackson, standing like a stone wall," to Lincoln's complaint in 1862, "If

McClellan is not using the army, I should like to borrow it for a while," to Sherman's 1864 signal, "Hold out, relief is coming" (often erroneously reported as "Hold the fort. I am coming"). And this section concludes with postwar observations by Mark Twain, "In the South, the war is what A.D. is elsewhere; they date from it" (1883), and Gertrude Stein, "There will never be anything in America more interesting than the Civil War, never" (1937).

This dictionary's notes and method of organization suit it for browsing as well as for reference. Both readers with an interest in history and those searching for apt quotations are likely to make many happy discoveries here. Anyone who is disappointed by not finding a favorite quotation is invited to submit it, along with the necessary source details, to the editors in care of the publisher so that it can be considered for inclusion when the dictionary is revised.

American Heritage®

DICTIONARY OF

AMERICAN QUOTATIONS

ABOLITION

See RACES & PEOPLES; SLAVERY

ACTION & DOING

See also ADVENTURE; BOLDNESS & INITIATIVE;
DANGER & DANGEROUS PEOPLE; DECISION;
ROOSEVELT, THEODORE; WORK & WORKERS

All great and honorable actions are accompanied with great difficulties.   1
—WILLIAM BRADFORD,
History of Plymouth Plantation,
written 1630–1651
[Bradford, longtime governor of the colony—he was reelected thirty times—
referred here to the dangers that the Pilgrims foresaw in leaving Holland in
1620 for a new land. His history (to 1646) disappeared during the American
Revolution, but was discovered in a library in London in 1855 and subsequently returned to Massachusetts.]

It is wonderful how much may be done if we are always doing.   2
—THOMAS JEFFERSON, letter to Martha Jefferson, May 5, 1787

I leave this rule for others when I'm dead,   3
Be always sure you're right—then go ahead.
—DAVID CROCKETT, his motto from the War of 1812,
in his *Narrative of the Life of David Crockett*, 1834

Always do what you are afraid to do.   —MARY MOODY EMERSON,   4
motto
[She was the aunt of Ralph Waldo Emerson, and a famous eccentric: just four-
feet, three-inches tall, she slept in a coffin-shaped bed. She had, however, a
large spirit, and was an expansive, sophisticated religious thinker. She inspired
her nephew to trust his own ideas, enthusiasms, and perceptions.]

In this country . . . men seem to live for action as long as they can and sink   5
into apathy when they retire.   —CHARLES FRANCIS ADAMS,
diary, April 15, 1836

1   Let us, then, be up and doing,
With a heart for any fate;
Still achieving, still pursuing,
Learn to labor and to wait.
                        —HENRY WADSWORTH LONGFELLOW,
                            A Psalm of Life, 1839
[See also Longfellow at HUMANS & HUMAN NATURE.]

2   But do your thing, and I shall know you.
                        —RALPH WALDO EMERSON, *Self-Reliance*,
                            in *Essays: First Series*, 1841
[The hippies of the 1960s may have stumbled independently upon the motto
"do your own thing," since the phrase here was changed by an editor to "do
your own work" in the 1903 edition of Emerson's writings; it has appeared that
way in all subsequent collections. Or possibly young people in the 1960s were
influenced by Chaucer, who used the expression a number of times in *The
Canterbury Tales*, e.g., from "The Clerk's Tale": "Ye been oure lord; dooth
with youre owene thyng."]

3   Something attempted, something done
Has earned a night's repose.
                        —HENRY WADSWORTH LONGFELLOW,
                            The Village Blacksmith, 1842

4   The reward of a thing well done, is to have done it.
                        —RALPH WALDO EMERSON,
                            Nominalist and Realist,
                            in *Essays: Second Series*, 1844

5   What the Puritans gave the world was not thought but action.
                        —WENDELL PHILLIPS, *The Pilgrims*,
                            speech, Dec. 21, 1855

6   I find the great thing in this world is not so much where we stand, as in what
direction we are moving: to reach the port of heaven, we must sail sometimes
with the wind and sometimes against it—but we must sail, and not drift, nor
lie at anchor.   —OLIVER WENDELL HOLMES, SR.,
                            The Autocrat of the Breakfast-Table, 1858

7   As we are, so we do; and as we do, so is it done to us; we are the builders of our
fortunes.   —RALPH WALDO EMERSON, *Worship*,
                            in *The Conduct of Life*, 1860
[See also Emerson on when "duty whispers" at YOUTH.]

8   I am only one,
But still I am one.
I cannot do everything,
But still I can do something;
And because I cannot do everything
I will not refuse to do the something that I can do.
                        —EDWARD EVERETT HALE,
                            Lend a Hand, c. 1871
[Hale founded the first Lend a Hand Club in Boston; see CHARITY & PHILAN-
THROPY.]

9   I am a verb.   —ULYSSES S. GRANT, letter to his physician,
                            John H. Douglas, July 1885
[For God as a verb, see R. Buckminster Fuller at GOD.]

'Tis the motive exalts the action;
'Tis the doing, and not the deed.   —MARGARET JUNKIN PRESTON,
      The Proclamation of Miles Standish,
      c. 1875

1

It is better to light one candle than to curse the darkness.   2
      —CHRISTOPHER SOCIETY, motto
[Adlai Stevenson praised Eleanor Roosevelt for lighting a candle and warming the world; see VIRTUE.]

Carry a message to Garcia.   —ELBERT HUBBARD, *A Message to Garcia,*   3
      March 1899
[Similar to "Just do it." Hubbard's article, which appeared in his magazine, *The Philistine,* called on young men "to be loyal to a trust, to act promptly, concentrate their energies, do a thing—'carry a message to Garcia.'" He was referring to the exploits of Lt. Andrew Summers Rowan of the U.S. Army Bureau of Intelligence, who, under orders from Pres. William McKinley, made his way into Cuba in 1898 to deliver a message to Gen. Calixto Garcia y Iniguez, the leader of a revolt against Spanish rule. See also SPANISH-AMERICAN WAR. Rowan received the Distinguished Service Cross for this achievement.

Hubbard, a strange mixture of reformer, huckster, and businessman, died in 1918 on the *Lusitania,* which was torpedoed in the Irish sea. He and Alfred Vanderbilt were the most famous victims.]

Get action. Seize the moment. Man was never intended to become an oyster.   4
      —THEODORE ROOSEVELT, to his children, quoted in
      David McCullough, *Mornings on Horseback* [1981]

It is not the critic who counts, not the man who points out how the strong man   5
stumbles, or where the doer of deeds could have done better. The credit belongs to the man who is actually in the arena; whose face is marred by dust and sweat and blood; who strives valiantly; who errs and comes short again and again, because there is no effort without error and shortcoming; but who does actually strive to do the deeds; who knows the great enthusiasms, the great devotions; who spends himself in a worthy cause; who, at the best, knows in the end the triumph of high achievement; and who, at the worst, if he fails, at least fails while daring greatly, so that his place shall never be with those cold and timid souls who know neither victory nor defeat.
      —THEODORE ROOSEVELT, speech, the Sorbonne,
      Paris, France, April 23, 1910
[Included in Roosevelt's *The Strenuous Life,* 1926, with the title *Citizenship in a Republic.*]

Life is action and passion.   —OLIVER WENDELL HOLMES, JR.,   6
      speech, to Harvard Law School alumni,
      New York City, Feb. 1916
[More at LIFE.]

Do the hardest thing in the world for you. Act for yourself. Face the truth.   7
      —KATHERINE MANSFIELD, *Journal,* Oct. 14, 1922

The country needs and, unless I mistake its temper, the country demands bold,   8
persistent experimentation. It is common sense to take a method and try it. If it fails, admit it frankly and try another. But above all, try something.
      —FRANKLIN D. ROOSEVELT, speech, Oglethorpe University,
      Atlanta, Ga., May 22, 1932

1   The difficult we do immediately. The impossible takes a little longer.
                                        —U.S. ARMY SERVICE FORCES, motto, World War II
    [A number of military groups have used a variant of this motto. One early
    source is Anthony Trollope, "The difficult is done at once; the impossible
    takes a little longer," *Phineas Redux*, 1873. Even earlier, French finance min-
    ister Charles-Alexandre de Calonne is said to have replied to a request from
    Marie-Antoinette, which she acknowledged would be "difficult," "If it is only
    difficult, it is done; if it is impossible, we shall see."]

2   He started to sing as he tackled the thing
    That couldn't be done, and he did it.   —EDGAR A. GUEST, *It Couldn't Be Done*,
                                        in *The Collected Works of Edgar A.
                                        Guest*, 1934

3   How do you know what you're going to do until you do it? The answer is, you
    don't. It's a stupid question.   —J. D. SALINGER,
                                        The Catcher in the Rye, 1951

4   Watch what we do, not what we say.   —JOHN MITCHELL, remark
                                        reported in the press, July 1969
    [This is the usual rendering; but in *Respectfully Quoted*, published by the Li-
    brary of Congress, the remark is given as, "You will be better advised to watch
    what we do instead of what we say." Attorney General Mitchell was talking to
    civil rights workers protesting the Nixon administration's policies.]

5   It can be done!   —COLIN POWELL,
                                        My American Journey, 1995
    [This is Gen. Powell's fourth maxim, leading many to wonder if this popular
    former chairman of the Joint Chiefs of Staff was referring here to a run for the
    presidency. Later in the year, he declined the opportunity. For another maxim
    from his list, see OPTIMISM & PESSIMISM.]

ADVENTURE   *See also* DANGER & DANGEROUS PEOPLE

6   I live only in the moment in this strange unmortal space, crowded with beauty,
    pierced with danger.   —CHARLES LINDBERGH,
                                        Spirit of St. Louis, 1954
    [His transatlantic flight was in 1927. A saying of his, recorded in Carl Sandburg's
    The Proverbs of a People, in *Good Morning, America*, 1928, was: "There must
    be pioneers, and some of them get killed." See also Amelia Earhart at COURAGE.]

7   To boldly go where no man has gone before.
                                        —GENE RODDENBERRY, *Star Trek* lead-in, 1966–69
    [More fully, "These are the voyages of the starship *Enterprise*. Its five-year mis-
    sion: to explore strange new worlds, to seek out new life and new civilizations,
    to boldly go where no man has gone before."]

ADVERSITY   *See* ANXIETY & WORRY; BAD TIMES; TROUBLE

ADVERTISING, ADVERTISING SLOGANS, & PUBLICITY

8   Secure the shadow ere the substance fade.
                                        —ANONYMOUS, advertising slogan from
                                        the 1840s promoting photography
    [The reference is to the widespread custom of taking daguerreotype portraits of

dead people, children especially. Requests for such portraits became an important source of income for many of the itinerant "professors" of photography who fanned out across the nation in the mid 1840s. By the next decade, photographic supply houses offered framing mats in black and daguerreotype cases with sentimental designs for deathbed portraits, according to William Welling's *Photography in America: The Formative Years, 1839–1900.*]

Only a woman can understand a woman's ills.   1
                                        —LYDIA E. PINKHAM, slogan for
                                        her Vegetable Compound, c. 1875
[The tonic was patented in 1876. The "sure cure" contained almost 18 percent alcohol, as well as some herbal extracts, according to Gerald Carson, *American Heritage,* June 1971. For another appeal to women, see Shirley Polykoff's copy for Miss Clairol at QUESTIONS & ANSWERS.]

The advertisements in a newspaper are more full of knowledge in respect to   2
what is going on in a state or community than the editorial columns are.
                                        —HENRY WARD BEECHER,
                                        Proverbs from Plymouth Pulpit, 1887

You press the button, we do the rest.   —GEORGE EASTMAN,   3
                                                         c. 1889
[Eastman wrote this copy for his fabulously successful Kodak camera, which he patented in September 1888. He coined the name *Kodak,* too; it was catchy, he thought.
   Starting in 1889, when the camera went on the market, Kodak campaigned to have shutterbugs send their film to its plant in Rochester, N.Y., for developing and printing. Within a year, the company was processing 6,000 to 7,000 negatives a day. The Kodak rapidly became known the world round, as witness this verse from the 1893 Gilbert and Sullivan operetta *Utopia, Limited.* Two demure English girls are singing: "To diagnose / Our modest pose / The Kodaks do their best: / If evidence you would possess / Of what is maiden bashfulness, / You only need a button press— / And we do all the rest."]

Half the money I spend on advertising is wasted, and the trouble is, I don't   4
know which half.   —JOHN WANAMAKER, quoted in David Ogilvy,
                                Confessions of an Advertising Man [1963]
[See also a similar, anonymous quote from the 1980s at DOCTORS & MEDICINE.]

99 44/100 per cent pure.   —HARLEY PROCTER,   5
                                        slogan for Ivory soap, 1904
[Procter & Gamble's most famous claim for its most famous product was based on the theory that pure soap consists of nothing but fatty acids and alkali. Chemical analysis of Ivory showed that it contained 0.11 percent uncombined alkali, 0.28 percent carbonates, and 0.17 percent mineral matter, a total of 0.56 percent of impurities, or, stated positively, that it was 99 44/100 percent pure. Mr. Procter also was responsible for dreaming up the Ivory name (trademarked July 18, 1879) while attending church in Cincinnati. His inspiration was the reading of the 45th psalm, eighth verse: "All thy garments smell of myrrh, and aloes, and cassia, out of the ivory palaces, whereby they have made thee glad."]

They all laughed when I sat down at the piano, But oh!, when I began to play.   6
                                        —JOHN CAPLES, legendary ad copy
                                        for mail-order piano lessons, 1925
[Zelda Fitzgerald followed her famous comment on the power of advertising (see below) with a specific reference to Caples's copy: "I *still* believe," she

wrote, "that one can learn to play the piano by mail and that mud will give you a perfect complexion."]

1   Quick, Henry, the Flit!   —Dr. Seuss (Theodor Seuss Geisel),
                                               ad copy for the Flit account of Standard Oil
                                               of New Jersey, 1928
[The wife of advertising executive H. K. McCann happened to see a cartoon in which freelancer Geisel used this line. This led to his being hired as the artist for the account, which greatly improved his financial status. Flit, by the way, was a spray to kill flying insects.]

2   We are living in an age of publicity. It used to be only saloons and circuses that wanted their name in the paper, but now it's corporations, churches, preachers, scientists, colleges, and cemeteries.   —Will Rogers, *Daily Telegrams*,
                                               June 23, 1931

3   We grew up founding our dreams on the infinite promise of American advertising.
                                   —Zelda Fitzgerald, *Save Me the Waltz*, 1932
[True, too true, despite the best efforts of a few naysayers, such as Judge William Jay Gaynor, who while campaigning for mayor of New York City in 1909, delivered a speech to the Advertising Men's League, in which he unpolitically quoted *The Merchant of Venice*; "Oh what a goodly outside falsehood hath!" Judge Gaynor was equally frank on almost all occasions, but, in a rare triumph for plain speaking, he won the election. Unfortunately, a year later, he was shot and seriously wounded by a disgruntled city employee. See also Gaynor under Language & Words.]

4   I think that I shall never see
    A billboard lovely as a tree.
    Indeed, unless the billboards fall,
    I'll never see a tree at all.   —Ogden Nash, *Song of the Open Road*,
                                               in *Happy Days*, 1933

5   Within This Vale
    Of Toil and Sin
    Your Head Grows Bald
    But Not Your Chin
    Burma-Shave   —Allan G. Odell,
                                               advertising jingle, c. 1940
[Starting in 1925, and peaking in the early 1950s, Burma-Shave jingles amused American motorists. Each line in a jingle appeared on a small sign, with the signs set about one hundred feet apart. Burma Vita Inc. was an Odell family business, and the copy was produced first by the Odells and later by the public in nationwide contests. The jingle above was Mr. Odell's favorite. Another popular one was "Henry the Eighth / Sure Had Trouble / Short-Term Wives / Long-Term Stubble / Burma-Shave." And again mining the distant past: "Pity All / The Mighty Caesars / They Pulled / Each Whisker Out / With Tweezers / Burma-Shave."]

6   Hey, quit kicking sand in my face.   —Charles Roman, ad for the
                                               Charles Atlas Company, from c. 1930
[In this ad, which in various versions appeared in comic books and magazines for years, a "ninety-seven pound weakling" is bullied by a big fellow at the beach, but, after a course of muscle building, he defeats the bad guy. The story is based on a true event: In 1909, Angelo Siciliano, age 15, took his girl to the beach at Coney Island, and a lifeguard kicked sand in his face. The young man

developed a course of "dynamic tension" exercises that worked wonders, and he changed his name to Charles Atlas. His fortune was made when he teamed up with advertiser Charles Roman, and in 1929 opened a mail-order body-building business. See also Atlas at HEALTH.

In 1991, Pres. George Bush described Iraqi dictator Saddam Hussein as "a classic bully who thinks he can get away with kicking sand in the face of the world."]

The art of publicity is a black art; but has come to stay, and every year adds to   1
its potency.   —LEARNED HAND, speech at
                                          the Elizabethan Club, May 1951
[For another, more lighthearted quote on deception through publicity, see Joseph Levine at THE PEOPLE, in the note to Lincoln's remark on fooling the people.]

The trouble with us in America isn't that the poetry of life has turned to prose,   2
but that it has turned to advertising copy.
                         —LOUIS KRONENBERGER, *The Spirit of the Age*,
                              in *Company Manners*, 1954

Doing business without advertising is like winking at a girl in the dark. You   3
know what you are doing, but nobody else does.
                           —STEUART HENDERSON BRITT, quoted in the
                                New York Herald Tribune, Oct. 30, 1956
[Britt was an educator, editor, and ad consultant.]

Do you sincerely want to be rich?   —BERNARD CORNFELD,   4
                                                        saying, c. 1956
[The flamboyant Cornfeld used this tag line to recruit sales people and investors for his vast and shaky Investors Overseas Services. His mutual-fund empire collapsed in 1970.]

The deeper problems connected with advertising come less from the un-   5
scrupulousness of our "deceivers" than from our pleasure in being deceived, less from the desire to seduce than from the desire to be seduced.
                              —DANIEL J. BOORSTIN, *The Image*, 1962

A pseudo event . . . comes about because someone has planned, planted, or in-   6
cited it. Typically, it is not a train wreck or an earthquake, but an interview.
                                                        —*Ibid.*

As advertising blather becomes the nation's normal idiom, language becomes   7
printed noise.   —GEORGE WILL, *Personality Against Character*,
                          July 1, 1976, in *The Pursuit of Happiness
                          and Other Sobering Thoughts* [1978]

Where's the beef?   —CLIFF FREEMAN, Dancer Fitzgerald Sample agency,   8
                                    slogan for Wendy's, Jan. 1984
[Television commercials for Wendy's hamburger chain featured 82-year-old actress Clara Peller with a small burger, presumably from a Wendy's competitor. After lifting the top of the bun, she incredulously poses this question to two friends, who appear amazed at the beeflessness of non-Wendy's hamburgers. The query was soon applied in all sorts of contexts, most famously by Democratic presidential candidate Walter Mondale with respect to his opponent in the Democratic primaries, Gary Hart.]

1   [A press agent:] A man of a few thousand well-chosen words.
—IRVING RUDD, *The Sporting Life*, 1990
[Rudd, a veteran sports press agent, is absolutely not a PR person. He explains that in the sports world in the 1930s and 1940s, "You were a press agent or a publicity man. Period." His view of PR people: "They're posturing phonies." For other unminced words from Rudd, see under INSULTS.]

2   It keeps going, and going, and going.   —CHIAT/DAY, slogan for
Energizer batteries, 1989

["It" is the Energizer pink bunny.]

ADVICE   *See also* WISDOM, WORDS OF

3   The advice of the elders to young men is very apt to be as unreal as a list of the hundred best books.   —OLIVER WENDELL HOLMES, JR.,
speech, Boston, Jan. 8, 1897

4   He had only one vanity; he thought he could give advice better than any other person.   —MARK TWAIN, *The Man That Corrupted Hadleyburg*, 1899

5   *Advice, n.* The smallest current coin.   —AMBROSE BIERCE,
The Devil's Dictionary, 1906

6   A good scare is worth more to a man than good advice.
—EDGAR WATSON HOWE, *Country Sayings*, 1911

7   The Miss Lonelyhearts are the priests of twentieth-century America.
—NATHANAEL WEST, *Miss Lonelyhearts*, 1933
[In this brilliant novel, Miss Lonelyhearts, putative author of a newspaper advice column, is in reality a troubled male writer.]

AFRICA   *See* NATIONS

AFRICAN-AMERICANS   *See* RACES & PEOPLES

AGES   *See also* CHILDREN; GENERATIONS; MIDDLE AGE & MIDLIFE CRISIS;
OLD AGE; YOUTH

8   Youth is the time of getting, middle age of improving, and old age of spending.
—ANNE BRADSTREET, *Meditations Divine and Moral*, 1644

9   Consider well the proportions of things. It is better to be a young June-bug than an old bird of paradise.   —MARK TWAIN, *Pudd'nhead Wilson's Calendar*,
in *Pudd'nhead Wilson*, 1894

10 The first half of life consists of the capacity to enjoy without the chance; the last half consists of the chance without the capacity.
—MARK TWAIN, letter to Edward L. Dimmit, July 19, 1901

11 Youth condemns; maturity condones.
—AMY LOWELL, *Tendencies in Modern American Poetry*, 1917

12 The young man who has not wept is a savage, and the old man who will not laugh is a fool.   —GEORGE SANTAYANA, *Dialogues in Limbo*, 1925

From birth to age eighteen, a girl needs good parents. From eighteen to thirty- 1
five, she needs good looks. From thirty-five to fifty-five, she needs a good personality. From fifty-five on, she needs good cash.
 —SOPHIE TUCKER, attributed, 1953
[*Bartlett's* reports that Tucker said this at age sixty-nine. Ralph Keyes in *Nice
Guys Finish Seventh* notes that the passage has also been attributed to novelist Kathleen Norris. Tucker, however, was a nationally recognized expert on
aging; she was known as "The Last of the Red Hot Mamas," from the title of a
Jack Yellen song that she introduced in 1928. See under HEALTH for her pre-
scription for longevity.]

ALABAMA
See also CITIES (Birmingham; Mobile)

Alabama . . . seems to have a bad name even among those who reside in it. 2
 —J. S. BUCKINGHAM, *The Slave States of America*, 1839
[Buckingham was an English traveler and writer.]

I came from Alabama with my banjo on my knee. 3
 —STEPHEN FOSTER, *Oh! Susanna*, 1848

As I have walked in Alabama my morning walk, 4
I have seen where the she-bird the mocking bird sat on her nest in
 the briers hatching her brood.
I have seen the he-bird also,
I have paused to hear him near at hand inflating his throat and
 joyfully singing. —WALT WHITMAN, *Starting from Paumanok*,
 in *Leaves of Grass*, 1881

Once upon a time, stars fell on Alabama, changing the land's destiny. 5
 —CARL CARMER, *Stars Fell on Alabama*, 1934
[The reference is to a memorable, pre–Civil War meteor shower.]

When I get to be a composer 6
I'm gonna write me some music about
Daybreak in Alabama.
And I'm gonna put the purtiest songs in it
Rising out of the ground like a swamp mist
And falling out of heaven like soft dew.
 —LANGSTON HUGHES, *Daybreak in Alabama*, 1940

Motto

Andemus iura nostra defendere. 7
We dare defend our rights.

ALASKA
See also CITIES (Nome)

Seward's folly. —ANONYMOUS, popular name 8
 for Alaska, 1867
[Also, "Seward's icebox." Secretary of State William H. Seward was the leading
advocate for acquisition of Alaska. He signed the agreement with Russia by
which the U.S. took over the vast territory for $7.2 million—about two cents
an acre.]

1   It is proposed to pay $7,200,000 for a country where none but malefactors will ever live, and where we are likely to be at constant war with the savages.
—CADWALLADER C. WASHBURN, debate on whether
to appropriate funds for the acquisition of Alaska,
U.S. House of Representatives, 1867

2   A practical race of intrepid navigators will swarm the coast, ready for any enterprise. . . . Commerce will find new arms, the country new defenders, the national flag new hands to bear it aloft.
—CHARLES SUMNER, speech in favor of ratifying treaty
with Russia to acquire Alaska, U.S. Senate, 1867

3   This is the law of the Yukon, that only the strong shall thrive;
That surely the weak shall perish, and only the fit survive.
Dissolute, damned and despairful, crippled and palsied and slain,
This is the Will of the Yukon—Lo, how she makes it plain!
—ROBERT W. SERVICE, *The Law of the Yukon*,
in *Songs of a Sourdough*, 1907
[Reprinted as *The Spell of the Yukon*, 1915.]

4   Some say God was tired when he made it [the land of Alaska];
Some say it's a fine land to shun;
Maybe; but there's some as would trade it
For no land on earth—and I'm one.
—ROBERT W. SERVICE, *Songs of a Sourdough*, 1907

5   And those who have undergone [life in Alaska] claim that in the making of the world God grew tired, and when He came to the last barrowload, "just dumped it anyhow," and that was how Alaska happened to be.
—JACK LONDON, *Gold Hunters of the North*,
in *Revolution and Other Essays*, 1910

6   This Alaska is a great country. If they can just keep from being taken over by the U.S., they got a great future.   —WILL ROGERS, *Daily Telegrams*,
August 13, 1935
[Rogers and aviator Wiley Post died two days later in a plane crash near Point Barrow, Alaska.]

7   The forty-ninth star twinkles. The Senate can make it shine.
—HOUSTON PRESS, editorial on statehood for Alaska, 1958

8   You are no longer an Arctic frontier. You constitute a bridge to the continent of Asia and all its people.   —DWIGHT D. EISENHOWER, speech,
Anchorage, Alaska, June 12, 1960

9   A handful of people clinging to a subcontinent.
—JOHN MCPHEE, *Coming into the Country*, 1977

10   Alaska's forests are the most welcoming I know. There are no ticks, no snakes, no poison ivy in Alaska.   —CHARLES KURALT,
Charles Kuralt's America, 1995

Motto

11   North to the future.

ALCOHOL & DRINKING

See also FOOD, WINE, & EATING;
LAST WORDS (Dylan Thomas)

I am sure the Americans can fix nothing without a drink. If you meet, you   1
drink; if you part, you drink; if you make acquaintance, you drink. . . . They
drink because it is hot; they drink because it is cold. If successful in elections,
they drink and rejoice; if not, they drink and swear; they begin to drink early in
the morning; they leave off late at night; they commence it early in life, and
they continue it, until they drop down into the grave.
—FREDERICK MARRYAT, *A Diary in America*, 1839

It's a long time between drinks.   —JOHN MOTLEY MOREHEAD,   2
c. 1843
[The remark was immortalized by Robert Louis Stevenson, who, in his comic
story *The Wrong Box*, attributed it to a governor of South Carolina in conversation with a governor of North Carolina. But Stevenson mixed up his states.
Morehead was governor of North Carolina from 1841 to 1845. Tradition has
it that the remark was made to James H. Hammond, governor of South
Carolina, who had come to Raleigh to demand the surrender of a North Carolinian who was wanted for a crime in South Carolina. When Morehead
declined, Hammond became furious, threatening to call up his militia and to
take the fugitive by force of arms. "Governor, what do you say?" demanded
Hammond. To which Morehead replied, "I say, Governor, that it is a long time
between drinks." The discussion continued, cordially so to speak, and Hammond and Morehead eventually parted on good terms. The fugitive was never
returned.]

Better sleep with a sober cannibal than a drunken Christian.   3
—HERMAN MELVILLE,
Moby-Dick, 1851

4

A slave to the demon rum.   —TIMOTHY SHAY ARTHUR, *Ten Nights
in a Barroom and What I Saw There*, 1854
[This phrase, which may have originated with Arthur, was commonly used in
the 19th-century temperance movement, with "rum" standing for all alcoholic drinks. Arthur, an editor, was not a teetotaler or prohibitionist; temperance was his message. This popular story was made into a play, which enjoyed
success both as a serious drama and, later, as a comic offering.]

5

Let me know what brand of whiskey Grant uses. For if it makes fighting generals like Grant, I should like to get some of it for distribution.
—ABRAHAM LINCOLN, to a Congressional delegation, 1863
[Grant's enemies in Congress had approached Lincoln, saying that Grant was a
drunk and should be demoted. Grant had trouble with the bottle before the war
but apparently stayed sober during it, despite rumors to the contrary, and Lincoln stuck with him, though perhaps not in such witty terms. The remark was
recorded by Chaplain John Eaton, who was told about the meeting with the
congressmen by Lincoln, but the president himself denied making it. According to Ralph Keyes's *Nice Guys Finish Seventh*, Lincoln thought the story
might have been inspired by an anecdote about George II who, when told that
Gen. James Wolfe was mad, is said to have retorted, "If General Wolfe is mad,
I hope he bites some of my other generals." In any case, Lincoln was by nature
forgiving toward drinkers. In 1842, in a speech on February 22 to the Springfield (Ill.) Washingtonian Temperance Society, he said: "I believe, if we take
habitual drinkers as a class, their heads and their hearts will bear an advanta-
geous comparison with those of any other class."]

1   Father, dear father, come home with me now;
The clock in the steeple strikes one;
You promised, dear father, that you would come home
As soon as your day's work was done.   —HENRY CLAY WORK, *Come Home,*
Father, temperance song, 1864

2   The first course was whiskey, the second whiskey, the third whiskey, all the
courses were whiskey, but still they called it supper.
    —OSCAR WILDE, letter describing a dinner with miners
in Leadville, Colo., April 13, 1882
[On the same evening, Wilde spotted a sign calling for restraint toward the piano player; see ART: MUSIC.]

3   The cocktail is a pleasant drink;
It's mild and harmless—I don't think.
When you've had one, you call for two,
And then you don't care what you do.   —GEORGE ADE,
The Sultan of Sulu, 1902

4   They got between the people and its beer.   —ALFRED HENRY LEWIS,
The Boss, 1903
[A character in Lewis's novel pinpoints the fatal error of turn-of-the-century re-
formers. In an article on political machines in *American Heritage,* June 1969,
William Shannon notes that while Theodore Roosevelt, head of the New York
City police board, was prowling the streets at night searching for saloon viola-
tions, the populace was singing that great vaudeville hit, *I Want What I Want*
When I Want It!.]

5   There are two things that will be believed of any man whatsoever, and one of
them is that he has taken to drink.   —BOOTH TARKINGTON, *Penrod,* 1914

6   Gimme a whiskey—ginger ale on the side. And don't be stingy, baby.
    —EUGENE O'NEILL, *Anna Christie,* 1921
[This is Anna's opening line, and in 1930, when the play was made into a
movie, Garbo had the lead, and it was her first appearance in a film with sound.
"Garbo Talks!" the publicity posters boasted. She talked in German, too—in a
version of the film that was shot at the same time and released abroad. The
German line was, *"Whiskey, aber nicht zu knapp!"*]

7   [Prohibition:] A noble experiment.
    —HERBERT HOOVER, attributed
[This is the popular short form of comments by Hoover on the prohibition of
alcohol enacted in the Eighteenth Amendment. In a letter to Sen. William E.
Borah of Idaho, dated February 28, 1928, Hoover wrote, "Our country has deliberately undertaken a great social and economic experiment, noble in motive
and far-reaching in purpose." He repeated the thought in accepting the Republican presidential nomination on August 11.]

8   The wine had such ill effects on Noah's health that it was all he could do to
live 950 years.   —WILL ROGERS, in Alex Ayres, ed.,
The Wit and Wisdom of Will Rogers [1993]

9   Three highballs, and I think I'm St. Francis of Assisi.
    —DOROTHY PARKER, *Just a Little One,*
in *Laments for the Living,* 1930
[See also Parker at SIN, VICE, & NAUGHTINESS.]

Candy   1
Is dandy
But liquor
Is quicker.   —OGDEN NASH, *Reflections on Ice-Breaking,*
                                        in *Hard Lines,* 1931

There is something about a Martini,   2
Ere the dining and dancing begin.
And to tell you the truth,
It's not the vermouth—
I think that perhaps it's the gin.
                                     —OGDEN NASH, *A Drink with Something
                                        in It,* in *The Primrose Path,* 1935

You ought to get out of those wet clothes and into a dry martini.   3
                                     —MAE WEST, *Every Day's a Holiday,* 1937
[Tony Augarde, editor of *The Oxford Dictionary of Modern Quotations,* came
up with this early citation for a quip usually associated with Robert Benchley.
Benchley himself attributed the line to his friend Charles Butterworth, who
spoke it in this Mae West movie, addressing Charles Winninger. In the 1942
movie *The Major and the Minor,* written by Billy Wilder and Charles Brackett,
Benchley says to Ginger Rogers, "Why don't you get out of that wet coat and into
a dry martini?" Alexander Woollcott has also been credited with the thought.]

God created alcohol.   —WILLIAM CARLOS WILLIAMS, *Io Baccho!,* 1950   4

There is nothing more dangerous than a lengthy cocktail hour.   5
                                     —A. R. GURNEY, *The Cocktail Hour,* 1988

ALIENATION   *See also* MADNESS; SOLITUDE & LONELINESS

From childhood's hour I have not been   6
As others were—I have not seen
As others saw.   —EDGAR ALLAN POE, *Alone,*
                                        1829 [published 1875]

Call me Ishmael.   —HERMAN MELVILLE,   7
                                                    Moby-Dick, 1851
[The opening line of the novel, spoken by the hero. The name *Ishmael* stands
for *outcast,* deriving from the biblical Ishmael, who was the bastard son of
Abraham and the bondservant Hagar, and the older brother of Isaac. Ishmael
was disinherited and, with his mother, exiled to the wilderness.]

I would prefer not to.   —HERMAN MELVILLE,   8
                                                 Bartleby the Scrivener, 1856
[With these words, Bartleby repeatedly rejects—everything.]

Miniver Cheevy, child of scorn,   9
Grew lean while he assailed the seasons;
He wept that he was ever born,
And he had reasons.   —EDWIN ARLINGTON ROBINSON,
                                                Miniver Cheevy, 1910

Which of us is not forever a stranger and alone?   10
                   —THOMAS WOLFE, *Look Homeward, Angel,* foreword, 1929

1   I'm less than two months old and I'm tired of living.
—E. B. WHITE, *Charlotte's Web*, 1952

AMBITION & ASPIRATION

2   In the long run, men hit only what they aim at.
—HENRY DAVID THOREAU, "Economy," *Walden*, 1854

3   Hitch your wagon to a star.   —RALPH WALDO EMERSON, *Civilization*,
in *Society and Solitude*, 1870
[A Yankee version of the Latin proverb: *Ad astra per ardua*—"To the stars
through difficulties."]

4   The ripest peach is highest on the tree.
—JAMES WHITCOMB RILEY, *The Ripest Peach*

5   Aim High—Then Shoot.   —ANONYMOUS,
"work-incentive" poster, 1920s
[These inspirational posters were intended to evoke greater effort and company
loyalty.]

6   What Makes Sammy Run?   —BUD SCHULBERG,
novel title, 1941
[The story of Sammy Glick, a self-made, ruthlessly ambitious Hollywood success.]

AMBIVALENCE   *See* INDECISION

AMERICA   *See also* AMERICAN HISTORY: MEMORABLE MOMENTS;
& AMERICANS   CONSTITUTION, THE; DECLARATION OF INDEPENDENCE;
DEMOCRACY; MILITARY, THE; PATRIOTISM & THE FLAG;
RACES & PEOPLES; SERVING ONE'S COUNTRY; UNION, THE

7   Columbus did not find out America by chance, but God directed him at that
time to discover it; it was contingent to him, but necessary to God.
—ROBERT BURTON, *The Anatomy of Melancholy*, 1621

8   They knew they were pilgrims.   —WILLIAM BRADFORD, *History of
Plymouth Plantation*, written 1630–1651
[Bradford came to America on the *Mayflower* and was governor of the colony
at Plymouth for most of his adult life. His history, covering years 1620–46, led
to the use of the term *pilgrims* for the colonists. See also Bradford at ACTION &
DOING.]

9   We shall be as a city upon a hill.
—JOHN WINTHROP, *A Model of Christian Charity*,
sermon on board the *Arbella*, 1630
[Winthrop was leader of the Puritan group that founded the Massachusetts Bay
Colony. His full statement reads: "For we must consider that we shall be as a
city upon a hill. The eyes of all people are upon us, so if we shall deal falsely
with our God in this work we have undertaken, and so cause him to withdraw
his present help from us, we shall be made a story and a byword through the
world."]

Winthrop borrowed here from *Matthew* 5:14: "Ye are the light of the world. A city that is set on a hill cannot be hid."]

In the beginning all the world was America.   1
                    —JOHN LOCKE, *Two Treatises of Government*, 1690

Westward the course of empire takes its way;   2
The four first acts already past,
A fifth shall close the drama with the day:
Time's noblest offspring is the last.
                    —GEORGE BERKELEY, *On the Prospect of Planting Arts
                    and Learning in America*, 1726 [published 1752]
[Bishop Berkeley's thought was echoed in 1862 by Arthur Hugh Clough in *Say
Not the Struggle Nought Availeth:* "In front the sun climbs slow, how slowly, /
But westward, look, the land is bright." See also Horace Walpole below.
   Another famous English cleric who had something nice to say about the
New World was John Donne, who, c. 1595, penned the line: "O my America,
my new-found land!" America here is metaphoric, however, and the poem, *To
His Mistress Going to Bed*, was written in Donne's youth, before he became
one of the great religious poets of the English language. Likening his mistress
to America arose from the thought that the New World was a place of unlimited, yet-to-be explored promise.]

Yankee Doodle came to town   3
Riding on a pony,
He stuck a feather in his hat
And called it Macaroni.

Yankee Doodle keep it up,
Yankee Doodle dandy,
Mind the music and the step,
And with the girls be handy.

                                          —ANONYMOUS, c. 1755
[The song, with verses set to an old English tune, was originally aimed deri-
sively by British troops at colonial would-be soldiers. A British army surgeon,
Dr. Richard Shuckburgh, gave the old tune its title and possibly wrote down
some verses, which apparently were being improvised, often bawdily. The
American militiamen turned the tables militarily and musically, triumphantly
adopted the Yankee Doodle label, and sang the song for dispirited British forces
at Concord in 1775, and later in numerous victories. The most familiar version
of the words apparently was composed in 1776 by Edward Bangs, a Harvard
sophomore and Minute Man.
   Calling the hat and feather "Macaroni" is a reference to Italian leadership in
fashion. English dandies of the period were called "macaronies." See under
CONNECTICUT for the origin of *Yankee*, and under PATRIOTISM & THE FLAG for
George M. Cohan's Yankee Doodle.]

America is more wild and absurd than ever.   4
                    —EDMUND BURKE, letter to Lord Rockingham, Sept. 9, 1769
[Nevertheless, Burke's sympathies were with the American colonists in their
protests against the Stamp Act and other intrusions upon their traditional liberties.]

The next Augustan age will dawn on the other side of the Atlantic.   5
                    —HORACE WALPOLE, letter to Horace Mann, Nov. 24, 1774

1   Don't tread on me.
                                                        —ANONYMOUS,
                                                    American motto
[The motto appeared on the first official flag of the North American colonists—
the "Rattlesnake Flag"—raised by Lt. John Paul Jones on the flagship *Alfred*,
December 3, 1775.]

2   The cause of America is in a great measure the cause of all mankind.
                            —THOMAS PAINE, *Common Sense*, 1776

3   *E Pluribus Unum.*
     Out of many, one.   —ANONYMOUS, motto for the national seal,
                                        selected by committee, 1776
[The committee, which consisted of Thomas Jefferson, John Adams, and Benjamin Franklin, was appointed on July 4, 1776. The members may have had in
mind the classical history of the phrase; it was used by Virgil in the form *E
pluribus unus*. But more immediately, it was the motto of *Gentleman's Magazine*, which was published in England, but was popular here, too. This periodical reprinted selected newspaper articles, and was the first such publication to
describe itself as a magazine; the term was borrowed from the military, where
it was used to mean a storehouse, especially for ammunition. A Swiss artist,
Pierre Eugene du Simitière, who was employed by the committee, has been
credited with suggesting the motto in a design for the seal that the committee
did not, in fact, accept. See also Rev. Jesse Jackson below, p. 24.]

4   You cannot conquer America.
                        —WILLIAM PITT, speech, House of Lords, Nov. 18, 1777
[More at AMERICAN REVOLUTION.]

5   They [Americans] are the hope of this world. They may become its model.
                    —A. R. J. TURGOT, letter to Dr. Richard Price, March 22, 1778
[Turgot, French economist and finance minister, foresaw that the choice for his
nation was reform or revolution.]

6   I am willing to love all mankind, *except an American.*
                                    —SAMUEL JOHNSON, April 15, 1778,
                                quoted in James Boswell, *Life of Johnson*

7   What then is the American, this new man?
                            —MICHEL GUILLAUME JEAN DE CRÈVECOEUR
                                (pen name, J. Hector St. John),
                                Letters from an American Farmer, 1782

8   Here individuals of all nations are melted into a new race of men, whose labors
     and posterity will one day cause great changes in the world.
                                                        —*Ibid.*
[Israel Zangwill made famous the melting pot metaphor. See below, p. 21.]

9   Indeed, I tremble for my country when I reflect that God is just.
                        —THOMAS JEFFERSON, *Notes on the State of Virginia*, 1781–85
[Jefferson was speaking of the injustice in slavery. More at FREEDOM.]

10   I wish the bald eagle had not been chosen as the representative of our coun-
     try. . . . The turkey . . . is a much more respectable bird.
                            —BENJAMIN FRANKLIN, letter to Sarah Bache, Jan. 26, 1784
[More at NATURE: ANIMALS.]

A republic if you can keep it.   —BENJAMIN FRANKLIN, answer to the question,   1
"Well, doctor, what have we got, a republic
or a monarchy?" Sept. 18, 1787
[The dialogue was recorded by James McHenry, an aide to George Washington.
The conversation took place in Philadelphia. A Mrs. Powel posed the question.]

No human power can now stop the march of a nation destined to exert its in-   2
fluence all over the world, and perhaps to dominate it.
—DOMINIQUE DUFOUR DE PRADT,
*Des Colonies et de la Révolution
actuelle de l'Amérique,* 1817
[The Abbé de Pradt had been Napoleon's chaplain.]

Who reads an American book, or goes to an American play, or looks at an   3
American picture or statue?   —SYDNEY SMITH,
Edinburgh Review, 1820
[Rev. Smith's famous taunt dated rapidly, as Longfellow became a best-seller in
England, Poe was taken up by the French, and so on to the situation today, in
which American culture more than holds its own.]

Wherever the standard of freedom and independence has been unfurled, there   4
will [America's] heart, her benedictions, and her prayers be. But she goes not
abroad in search of monsters to destroy.   —JOHN QUINCY ADAMS,
June 4, 1821
[The resolve to stay home weakened in the 19th century. In the 20th, the question of when to try to destroy monsters abroad has been one of the great, re-
curring issues facing the nation. Adams predicted that if America became
involved in foreign wars, gradually the principle of force would replace love of
liberty. He concluded, "She might become dictatress of the world; she would
no longer be the ruler of her own spirit." Will Rogers noted irreverently, "If we
ever pass out as a great nation, we ought to put on our tombstone, 'America
died of the delusion that she had moral leadership,'" *The Autobiography of
Will Rogers,* 1949.]

The happy union of these states is a wonder; their Constitution a miracle; their   5
example the hope of liberty throughout the world.
—JAMES MADISON,
"Outline" notes, Sept. 1829
[Inscribed in Madison Memorial Hall of the Library of Congress.]

The whole people [Americans] appear to be divided into an almost endless va-   6
riety of religious factions.
—FRANCES TROLLOPE, *Domestic Manners of the Americans,* 1832
[She made this observation in 1828, according to *American Heritage,* June
1976.]

I know of no country, indeed, where the love of money has taken a stronger   7
hold on the affections of men.
—ALEXIS DE TOCQUEVILLE, *Democracy in America,* 1835
[See also Tocqueville at MONEY & THE RICH.]

America is a land of wonders, in which everything is in constant motion and   8
every change seems an improvement. . . . No natural boundary seems to be set
to the efforts of man; and in his eyes, what is not yet done is only what he has
not yet attempted to do.   —*Ibid.*

1   If destruction be our lot, we must ourselves be its author and finisher. As a nation of freemen, we must live through all time or die by suicide.
—ABRAHAM LINCOLN, speech, Young Men's Lyceum,
Springfield, Ill., Jan. 27, 1838
[On the suicide of democracies, see also John Adams at DEMOCRACY. Lincoln prefaced the comments above with the questions: "At what point shall we expect the approach of danger? . . . Shall we expect some trans-Atlantic military giant to step the ocean and crush us at a blow?" He answered, "Never! All the armies of Europe, Asia, and Africa combined with all the treasure of the earth . . . could not by force take a drink from the Ohio, or make a track on the Blue Ridge, in a trial of a thousand years."]

2   We are the nation of human progress, and who will, what can, set limits to our onward march?   —JOHN L. O'SULLIVAN, *The Great Nation of Futurity*,
in the *Democratic Review*, Nov. 1839
[O'Sullivan, one of the most influential journalists of his time, later summarized this imperialist vision in the phrase "manifest destiny"; see below. The "nation of human progress" quote is usually ascribed to him, although the piece was unsigned and some scholars have had doubts on the point. Incidentally, this essay also referred to America's mission to spread four freedoms through the world, later used by Franklin D. Roosevelt; see FREEDOM.]

3   Our manifest destiny to overspread and to possess the whole of the continent, which Providence has given us for the great experiment of liberty.
—JOHN L. O'SULLIVAN, editorial, *Morning News*,
New York City, Dec. 27, 1845
[O'Sullivan was writing in support of incorporating Oregon into the U.S. This editorial made the phrase "manifest destiny" famous. O'Sullivan had, however, used it earlier in the year: "Our manifest destiny is to overspread the continent allotted by Providence for the free development of our yearly multiplying millions," *Democratic Review*, July–August, 1845. And a year earlier, George Bancroft referred to "the manifest purpose of Providence, that the light of democratic freedom should be borne from our fires to the domain beyond the Rocky Mountains," in a letter of August 15, 1844, accepting the nomination as Democratic candidate for governor of Massachusetts, August 15, 1844. See also Walt Whitman at MEXICAN WAR, and THE FRONTIER; and William McKinley at HAWAII.]

4   Sail on, O Ship of State!
Sail on, O Union, strong and great!
Humanity with all its fears,
With all the hopes of future years,
Is hanging breathless on thy fate!   —HENRY WADSWORTH LONGFELLOW,
The Building of the Ship, 1849

5   We Americans are the peculiar, chosen people—the Israel of our time; we bear the ark of the liberties of the world.   —HERMAN MELVILLE, *White-Jacket*, 1850

6   We are the pioneers of the world; . . . In our youth is our strength; in our inexperience, our wisdom.   —*Ibid.*
[These energetic and optimistic comments came two years before the devastating reviews of *Moby-Dick*, which essentially brought Melville's writing to an end—forty years before his death. *Billy Budd*, which we regard as a classic, was found in manuscript form in an old suitcase and published in the 1920s.]

7   The United States themselves are essentially the greatest poem.
—WALT WHITMAN, Preface, *Leaves of Grass*, 1st ed., 1855

America has not yet settled down. She is an unfinished edifice.   1
                            —ALEXANDER HERZEN, *My Past and Thoughts*, 1855
[Herzen, a philosopher and revolutionary, had contradictory feelings about
America, but on balance did not favor emigrating there. He wrote, "America,
as Garibaldi said, is the 'land for forgetting one's own'; let those who have no
faith in their fatherland go there."]

The United States is . . . a warning rather than an example to the world.   2
                            —LYDIA MARIA CHILD, speech at the 25th anniversary of
                            the Massachusetts Anti-Slavery Society, 1857

This country, with its institutions, belongs to the people who inhabit it.   3
Whenever they shall grow weary of the existing government, they can exercise
their constitutional right of amending it, or their revolutionary right to dis-
member or overthrow it.
                            —ABRAHAM LINCOLN, First Inaugural Address, 1861

America means opportunity, freedom, power.   4
                            —RALPH WALDO EMERSON, *Public and Private Education*,
                            Nov. 1864, in *Uncollected Lectures* [1932]

I hear America singing, the varied carols I hear.   5
                            —WALT WHITMAN, *I Hear America Singing*, 1867
[For a parody of Whitman, see Peter De Vries at SEX.]

America is a country of young men.   —RALPH WALDO EMERSON, *Old Age*,   6
                            in *Society and Solitude*, 1870

I hate this shallow Americanism which hopes to get rich by credit, to get   7
knowledge by raps on midnight tables, to learn the economy of the mind by
phrenology, or skill without study, or mastery without apprenticeship.
                            —RALPH WALDO EMERSON,
                            Success, in *Society and Solitude*, 1870

I shall use the word America and democracy as convertible terms.   8
                            —WALT WHITMAN, *Democratic Vistas*, 1871

And at this day, though I have kind invitations enough to visit America, I could   9
not, even for a couple of months, live in a country so miserable as to possess no
castles.   —JOHN RUSKIN, *Fors Clavigera*, Vol. I, letter 10, 1871

Among the rank and file, [in] both armies [in the Civil War], it was very general   10
to speak of the different States they came from by their slang names. Those
from Maine were call'd Foxes; New Hampshire, Granite Boys; Massachusetts,
Bay Staters; Vermont, Green Mountain Boys; Rhode Island, Gun Flints; Con-
necticut, Wooden Nutmegs; New York, Knickerbockers; New Jersey, Clam
Catchers; Pennsylvania, Logher Heads; Delaware, Muskrats; Maryland, Claw
Thumpers; Virginia, Beagles; North Carolina, Tar Boilers; South Carolina,
Weasels; Georgia, Buzzards; Louisiana, Creoles; Alabama, Lizards; Kentucky,
Corn Crackers; Ohio, Buckeyes; Michigan, Wolverines; Indiana, Hoosiers; Illi-
nois, Suckers; Missouri, Pukes; Mississippi, Tad Poles; Florida, Fly Up the
Creeks; Wisconsin, Badgers; Iowa, Hawkeyes; Oregon, Hard Cases.
                            —WALT WHITMAN, *Slang in America*,
                            in *North American Review*, Nov. 1885
[Whitman certainly heard many of these names while serving as a volunteer
nurse in army hospitals, but, as reported by Howard Birss in *American Speech*

[(June 1932), his list was drawn from an unsigned article in the *Broadway Journal* of May 3, 1845.]

1   O beautiful for spacious skies,
    For amber waves of grain,
    For purple mountain majesties
    Above the fruited plain!
    America! America!
    God shed his grace on thee
    And crown thy good with brotherhood
    From sea to shining sea!
                                 —KATHARINE LEE BATES, *America the Beautiful*, 1893
    [The music was by Samuel Ward. See under PATRIOTISM & THE FLAG for *The Star-Spangled Banner* and *My Country 'Tis of Thee*.]

2   Whether they will or no, Americans must now begin to look outward.
                                 —ALFRED T. MAHAN, *The United States
                                 Looking Outward*, 1890, included in
                                 The Interest of America in Sea Power, 1897
    [Capt. Mahan's writings on the importance of sea power strongly influenced Theodore Roosevelt, who was assistant secretary of the navy before becoming president. Mahan was a frank imperialist. See also Roosevelt at THE MILITARY and SPANISH-AMERICAN WAR.]

3   This is a billion-dollar country.   —THOMAS BRACKETT REED, remark
                                 in defense of the national deficit, c. 1890
    [The administration of Republican president Benjamin Harrison, elected in 1889, ran up an unprecedented deficit of $1 billion. When the Democrats expressed alarm at this "raid on the Treasury," Speaker of the House Reed silenced them with the above comment.]

4   To the frontier the American intellect owes its striking characteristics: that coarseness and strength combined with acuteness and inquisitiveness; that practical, inventive turn of mind, quick to find expedients; that masterful grasp of material things, lacking in the artistic but powerful to effect great ends; that restless, nervous energy; that dominant individualism, working for good and for evil, and withal that buoyancy and exuberance which comes with freedom.   —FREDERICK J. TURNER, *The Significance of the Frontier
                                 in American History*, 1893
    [For more on this great historical essay, see THE FRONTIER.]

5   America has been another name for opportunity.   —*Ibid.*

6   The youth of America is their oldest tradition. It has been going on now for three hundred years.   —OSCAR WILDE, *A Woman of No Importance*, 1893

7   It was wonderful to find America, but it would have been more wonderful to miss it.   —MARK TWAIN, *Pudd'nhead Wilson's Calendar*,
                                 in *Pudd'nhead Wilson*, 1894

8   It is by the goodness of God that in our country we have those three unspeakably precious things: freedom of speech, freedom of conscience, and the prudence never to practice either of them.
                                 —MARK TWAIN, *Pudd'nhead Wilson's New Calendar*,
                                 in *Following the Equator*, 1897

Don't sell America short.   —JOHN PIERPONT MORGAN,   1
popularized version of favorite saying, 1890s
[Morgan's aphorism ran on the lines of "Don't be a bear (as opposed to a stock-market bull) on America." This was abbreviated to the version given here. The aphorism may have originated with J. P. Morgan's father, Junius Spenser Morgan.]

From the old-world point of view, the American had no mind; he had an eco-   2
nomic thinking-machine which could work only on a fixed line. The American mind exasperated the Europeans as a buzz-saw might exasperate a pine forest.
—HENRY ADAMS, *The Education of Henry Adams*, 1907

America is God's crucible, the great melting pot, where all the races of Europe   3
are melting and re-forming. . . . Germans and Frenchmen, Irishmen and En-glishmen, Jews and Russians—into the crucible with you all! God is making the American!   —ISRAEL ZANGWILL,
The Melting Pot, 1908
[The quote is from Act One of Zangwill's play. The image may have come from Michel Guillaume Jean de Crèvecoeur's *Letters from an American Farmer*, 1782; see above. See also RACES & PEOPLES, and for boiling rather than melting, Thomas Dewey on New York City under CITIES.]

Our country—this great republic—means nothing unless it means the triumph   4
of a real democracy, the triumph of popular government, and, in the long run, of an economic system under which each man shall be guaranteed the oppor-tunity to show the best that there is in him.
—THEODORE ROOSEVELT, *The New Nationalism*, 1910

America first.   5
—WOODROW WILSON, speech, April 20, 1915
[Pres. Wilson was defending not entering the war in Europe. He said, "Our whole duty, for the present, at any rate, is summed up in the motto, 'America first.' Let us think of America before we think of Europe, in order that Amer-ica may be fit to be Europe's friend when the day of tested friendship comes." See also WORLD WAR I.]

I believe in the United States of America as a government of the people, by the   6
people, for the people.   —WILLIAM TYLER PAGE, *The American Creed*,
adopted by the U.S. House of Representatives,
April 3, 1918
[See GETTYSBURG ADDRESS and GOVERNMENT for more on "government of the people."]

There can be no fifty-fifty Americanism in this country. There is room here for   7
only one hundred percent Americanism.
—THEODORE ROOSEVELT, speech, July 19, 1918
[See also Roosevelt on "hyphenated Americans" at FOREIGNERS. The influence of the World War made this sort of chauvinistic rhetoric widely acceptable. See also Roosevelt at PATRIOTISM & THE FLAG.]

[The] ordinary American crowd, the best-natured, best-dressed, best-behaving,   8
and best-smelling crowd in the world.
—EDWIN SLOSSON, 1920, quoted in David Nasaw,
The Rise and Fall of Public Amusements, Basic Books, 1994

1   The essential American soul is hard, isolate, stoic, a killer.
—D. H. LAWRENCE, *Cooper's Leatherstocking Novels*,
in *Studies in Classic American Literature*, 1922

2   Oh, America,
The sun sets in you.
Are you the grave of our day?   —D. H. LAWRENCE, *The Evening Land*,
in *Birds, Beasts, and Flowers*, 1923

3   The pure products of America go crazy.   —WILLIAM CARLOS WILLIAMS,
Spring and All, XVIII, 1923

4   The discovery of America was the occasion of the greatest outburst of cruelty
and reckless greed known to history.
—JOSEPH CONRAD, *Geography and Some Explorers*,
1924, in *Last Essays* [1926]

5   The chief business of the American people is business.
—CALVIN COOLIDGE, speech, Jan. 17, 1925
[See also Charles F. Wilson on General Motors and the U.S. at BUSINESS.]

6   The men the American people admire most extravagantly are the most daring
liars; the men they detest the most violently are those who try to tell the truth.
—H. L. MENCKEN, from Alistair Cooke, ed.,
The Vintage Mencken [1955]
[For Mencken on the questionable intelligence of the American people, see THE
PEOPLE.]

7   The American system of rugged individualism.
—HERBERT HOOVER, campaign speech, Oct. 22, 1928
[Hoover, campaigning in New York, said, "We were challenged with a peace-
time choice between the American system of rugged individualism and a European philosophy of diametrically opposed doctrines—doctrines of paternalism
and state socialism."
Hoover wrote later, in *The Challenge to Liberty*, 1934, that the phrase "rugged
individualism" had been used by American leaders for at least fifty years, but
added, "I should be proud to have invented it." The phrase referred, he wrote,
to "those God-fearing men and women of honesty whose stamina and character and fearless assertion of rights led them to make their own way in life."]

8   There is nothing wrong with wrong with Americans except their ideals. The
real American is all right; it is the ideal American who is all wrong.
—G. K. CHESTERTON, in *The New York Times*, Feb. 1, 1931

9   In America, public opinion is the leader.   —FRANCES PERKINS,
People at Work, 1934

10   In the United States there is more space where nobody is than where anybody
is. That is what makes America what is.
—GERTRUDE STEIN, *The Geographical History of America*, 1936

11   There are no second acts in American lives.
—F. SCOTT FITZGERALD,
The Last Tycoon, notes [1941]
[The unfinished book was published posthumously. Fitzgerald died in 1940.]

I believe that we are lost here in America, but I believe that we shall be found. 1
　　　　　　　　　　—THOMAS WOLFE, *You Can't Go Home Again*, 1940

The land was ours before we were the land's. 2
She was our land more than a hundred years
Before we were her people.　　　　　　　—ROBERT FROST,
　　　　　　　　　　　　　　　　　　　　The Gift Outright, 1941
[The poet read this verse at the inauguration of Pres. John F. Kennedy, Jan. 20,
1961. He had presented it first, twenty years earlier, to the Phi Beta Kappa Society at William and Mary College. Commenting on these lines, Wallace Stegner wrote that to become healthy as a people, we must "learn to be quiet part
of the time, and acquire the sense not of ownership but of belonging. . . . Only
in the act of submission is the sense of place realized and a sustainable relationship between people and earth established," *The Sense of Place*, 1986. For
similar thoughts see Aldo Leopold at ENVIRONMENT.]

God bless the USA, so large 3
So friendly, and so rich.　　　　　—W. H. AUDEN, *On the Circuit*, 1941

Of nothing [in the U.S.] are you allowed to get the real odor or savor. Every- 4
thing is sterilized and wrapped in cellophane.
　　　　　　　　　—HENRY MILLER, *The Air-Conditioned Nightmare*, 1945
[In the same essay, Miller described America as "prematurely old . . . a fruit
which rotted before it had a chance to ripen."]

The national vice is waste.　　—HENRY MILLER, *Dr. Souchon: Surgeon-Painter*, 5
　　　　　　　　　　　　　　in *The Air-Conditioned Nightmare*, 1945

O, let America be America again— 6
The land that has never been yet—
And yet must be—
The land where every man is free.
　　　　　　　　　—LANGSTON HUGHES, *Let America Be America*,
　　　　　　　　　　in *The Poetry of the Negro*, 1949

America never was America to me. 7
And yet, I swear this oath—
America will be!　　　　　　　　　　　　　　　　　—*Ibid.*

All races and religions: that's America to me. 8
　　　　　　　　　—EARL ROBINSON, quoted in *The New York Times*,
　　　　　　　　　　obituary [July 23, 1991]
[Robinson wrote the music for the Alfred Hayes poem *Joe Hill*, honoring the la-
bor organizer who was executed in 1915; see under CAPITALISM & CAPITAL V.
LABOR.]

America is a large, friendly dog in a very small room. Every time it wags its tail 9
it knocks over a chair.　　　　　　　—ARNOLD TOYNBEE,
　　　　　　　　　　　　　　　　BBC news summary, July 14, 1954

This land is your land, this land is my land, 10
From California to the New York island,
From the redwood forest to the Gulf Stream waters,
This land was made for you and me.　　　—WOODY GUTHRIE,
　　　　　　　　　　　　　　　　　　This Land Is Your Land, 1956

1   Americans are suckers for good news.
                    —ADLAI STEVENSON, speech, June 8, 1958

2   Our national flower is the concrete cloverleaf.
                    —LEWIS MUMFORD, cited in *Quote* magazine, Oct. 8, 1961

3   We started from scratch, every American an immigrant who came because he
wanted change. *Why are we now afraid to change?*
                    —ELEANOR ROOSEVELT, *Tomorrow Is Now*, 1963

4   Americans—like omelettes:
there is no such thing
as a pretty good one.   —W. H. AUDEN, *Marginalia*, 1965–1968

5   Solitude is un-American.   —ERICA JONG, *Fear of Flying*, 1973

6   We are a nation that has a government—not the other way around. And this
makes us special among the nations of the earth.
                    —RONALD REAGAN, First Inaugural Address, 1981

7   Our flag is red, white, and blue, but our nation is a rainbow—red, yellow,
brown, black, and white—and we're all precious in God's sight.
                    —JESSE JACKSON, Democratic National Convention,
                    San Francisco, July 17, 1984
[Rev. Jackson later named his political organization the National Rainbow
Coalition. And in the same speech, he suggested another metaphor: "America
is not like a blanket—one piece of unbroken cloth, the same color, the same
texture, the same size. America is more like a quilt, many pieces, many colors,
many sizes, all woven and held together by a common thread."]

8   The genius of America is that out of the many, we become one.
                    —JESSE JACKSON, Democratic National Convention,
                    Atlanta, Ga., July 20, 1988

9   We are a nation of communities . . . a brilliant diversity spread like stars, like
a thousand points of light in a broad and peaceful sky.
                    —GEORGE BUSH, presidential nomination acceptance speech,
                    Republican National Convention, New Orleans,
                    August 18, 1988.
[The thousand points of light may come from Thomas Wolfe's *The Web and
The Rock* (1939), as suggested by *Bartlett's*: "Instantly he could see the town
below now, coiling in a thousand fumes of homely smoke, now winking into a
thousand points of friendly light its glorious small design, its aching passionate assurances of walls, warmth, comfort, food, and love." Stanley and Eleanor
Hochman in *The Penguin Dictionary of Contemporary American History*
point to another passage that might have been familiar to Bush's speechwriter,
Peggy Noonan—C. S. Lewis's description of the birth of Narnia, the magic
kingdom in his classic trilogy for children, *The Chronicles of Narnia*: "One
moment there was nothing but darkness; next moment a thousand points of
light leaped out." Noonan herself, in her book *What I Saw at the Revolution*,
did not acknowledge either source, however. "I don't know," she wrote, "a
thousand clowns [a movie], a thousand days [the administration of Pres. John
Kennedy]—a hundred wasn't enough and a million is too many."
    This same speech included the instantly famous call for "a kinder, gentler,
nation"—see POLITICAL SLOGANS—and the pledge, "No new taxes"; see TAXES.]

There is nothing wrong with America that cannot be cured by what is right   1
with America.   —BILL CLINTON, Inaugural Address, Jan. 20, 1993

Americans are impatient with memory.   2
—JAMAICA KINCAID, *Alien Soil*,
in *The New Yorker*, June 21, 1993

America must be described in romantic terms. . . . America is a romance in   3
which we all partake.
—NEWT GINGRICH, *To Renew America*, 1995
[Speaker of the House Gingrich wrote here that he learned this lesson from a
Republican of an earlier generation, Sen. Henry Cabot Lodge.]

AMERICAN HISTORY: *See also* AMERICA & AMERICANS;
MEMORABLE   CONSTITUTION, THE; DECLARATION
MOMENTS   OF INDEPENDENCE; DEPRESSION, THE;
                                   FOREIGN POLICY; GETTYSBURG ADDRESS;
                                   PATRIOTISM & THE FLAG; POLITICAL SLOGANS;
                                   PRESIDENCY, THE; SERVING ONE'S COUNTRY;
                                   UNION, THE; entries for specific wars; WATERGATE

Lumbre! Tierra!   4
Light! Land!
—PEDRO YZQUIERDO, midnight, Oct. 11, 1492
[Yzquierdo, a seaman on the *Santa María*, probably saw a shaft of moonlight
on a Bahamian beach. Neither Yzquierdo nor the seaman on the *Pinta* who
spotted the island at 2:00 A.M., October 12, received the royal annuity offered
to the first member of the expedition to sight land. Columbus reported that
he had seen light about two hours before Yzqeuierdo did, and collected the
reward.]

Being thus arrived in a good harbor, and brought safe to land, they fell upon their   5
knees and blessed the God of Heaven, who had brought them over the vast and
furious ocean, and delivered them from all the perils and miseries thereof, again
to set their feet on the firm and stable earth, their proper element.
—WILLIAM BRADFORD, *Of Plymouth Plantation*,
covering years 1620–46, written 1630–51

No taxation without representation.   —ANONYMOUS,   6
slogan, 1765
[From early on, taxes have been one of the most emotional subjects in American political life; see TAXES. The issue in 1765 was the Stamp Act, by which the
English Parliament required that government stamps be used on newspapers
and legal documents.]

If this be treason, make the most of it.   7
—PATRICK HENRY, speech,
Virginia House of Burgesses, May 29, 1765
[Henry, in protesting the Stamp Act, reminded the burgesses that "Tarquin and
Caesar each had his Brutus, Charles I his Cromwell, and George III"—the
Speaker of the House interrupted, calling out "Treason!"—"may profit by their
example," Henry continued. "If this be treason, make the most of it." This, at
least, is how the speech was reconstructed a half century later by Henry's bi-
ographer William Wirt. Notes made by a French visitor to Williamsburg at the
time, but not discovered until 1921, suggest that Henry actually backed down

when interrupted by the Speaker, begging pardon of the House if "the heat of passin (as the anonymous Frenchman spelled it) might have lead (*sic*) him to have said something more than he intended." See also Henry at FREEDOM and PATRIOTISM & THE FLAG.]

1   Let every man do his duty, and be true to his country.
                    —ANONYMOUS, rallying cry, Boston Tea Party, Dec. 16, 1773
[The words were recorded by George Hewes in *A Retrospect of the Boston Tea Party*, 1834. Hewes participated in the tax protest, in which colonists boarded three merchant vessels in Boston harbor on the night of December 16, 1773, and dumped their cargoes of tea overboard. Hewes dressed as a Mohawk and carried a hatchet. Among the leaders of the protest were Samuel Adams and Paul Revere.]

2   The country shall be independent, and we will be satisfied with nothing short of it.
                    —SAMUEL ADAMS, March 1774
[For Adams's reaction upon hearing the exchange of gunfire at Lexington, see AMERICAN REVOLUTION. See also DECLARATION OF INDEPENDENCE.]

3   Give me liberty or give me death!   —PATRICK HENRY, speech,
                    Virginia Convention, March 23, 1775
[More at FREEDOM. For the words of Nathan Hale, who met death in the fight for liberty, see AMERICAN REVOLUTION.]

4   With a heart full of love and gratitude, I now take my leave of you. I most devoutly wish that your latter days may be as prosperous and happy as your former ones have been glorious and honorable.
                    —GEORGE WASHINGTON, farewell to his officers,
                    Fraunces Tavern, New York City, Dec. 4, 1783
[This was an emotional scene—Washington, Henry Knox, and others wept freely. Again, when Washington returned his commission to Congress at Annapolis on December 23, there was hardly a dry eye in the house.]

5   Millions for defense, but not one cent for tribute.
                    —ROBERT GOODLOE HARPER,
                    toast at Congressional dinner for
                    John Marshall, June 18, 1798, quoted in
                    the *American Daily Advertiser*, June 20, 1798
[Often attributed to Charles C. Pinckney, this quote is an elaboration of Pinckney's refusal to bribe three French officials to obtain French acceptance of his ambassadorship and a pledge to cease attacks on American shipping. Pinckney actually said, "Not a penny! Not a penny!" or possibly "No, no, not a sixpence" (sources vary).
     Pres. John Adams in 1797 had sent John Marshall and Elbridge Gerry to assist Pinckney in what became known as the X Y Z Affair, because the officials were not named. Robert Goodloe Harper, incidentally, was from South Carolina, as was Pinckney.]

6   We are all Republicans—we are all Federalists.
                    —THOMAS JEFFERSON, First Inaugural Address, 1801
[More at THE UNION.]

7   Entangling alliances with none.
                    —*Ibid.*
[More at FOREIGN POLICY.]

We have lived long, but this is the noblest work of our lives.   1
—ROBERT R. LIVINGSTON, on the signing of
the Louisiana Purchase, May 1803

[The agreement was an extraordinary bargain. For $15 million, the U.S. acquired from France the entire watershed of the Mississippi, including the present states of Louisiana, Arkansas, Oklahoma, Missouri, North and South Dakota, Iowa, Nebraska, Kansas, Minnesota, Colorado, Wyoming, and Montana. Livingston was Pres. Thomas Jefferson's minister to France, and he worked together with U.S. special envoy James Monroe. The French foreign minister, Charles Maurice de Talleyrand, negotiated on behalf of the emperor Napoleon. A revolt in Haiti and impending war with Great Britain had inspired France to propose the deal.]

Oh, say, can you see by the dawn's early light,   2
What so proudly we hailed at the twilight's last gleaming?
—FRANCIS SCOTT KEY,
The Star-Spangled Banner, Sept. 14, 1814

[More at PATRIOTISM & THE FLAG.]

I shall never surrender nor retreat.   —WILLIAM BARRETT TRAVIS,   3
commander of the Alamo,
Feb. 24, 1836

[Thus, Lt. Col. Travis replied to the demand that he surrender to the Mexican army under Gen. Antonio López Santa Anna. That army, numbering several thousand, had beseiged the fortified mission in San Antonio, Texas; some 183 men were trapped inside. But as Col. David Crockett noted in his *Alamo Journal* on February 23, 1836, "They'll find that they have to do with men who will never lay down their arms as long as they can stand on their legs." (This autobiographical fragment may not have been written by Crockett himself, but it is thought to portray the siege accurately.) On March 6, the Alamo was captured and all 183 defenders killed.

For more, see Crockett at FREEDOM. See also Crockett at BOASTS.]

Thermopylae had her messenger of defeat—the Alamo had none.   4
—THOMAS JEFFERSON GREEN, attributed

[Green apparently wrote this thought for a speech by Edward Burleson. The sentence was engraved on the first monument to the Alamo in Austin, as well as on the rebuilt monument.]

Remember the Alamo!   5
—SIDNEY SHERMAN, battle cry, April 21, 1836

[The saying is traditionally attributed to Col. Sherman, whose troops advanced at San Jacinto chanting this battle cry. One month earlier, Gen. Santa Anna, the president of Mexico, had conquered the Alamo, leaving no survivors. In the battle at San Jacinto, Texans led by Commander in Chief Sam Houston, captured Santa Anna. In the Treaty of Velasco, which Santa Anna was forced to sign, Mexico recognized the independence of Texas. See also MEXICAN WAR.]

Your petitioner therefore prays your Honorable Court to grant him leave to sue   6
as a poor person, in order to establish his right to freedom.
—DRED SCOTT, petition, July 1, 1847

[With this petition, Scott, a slave, initiated litigation that led to one of the all-time worst decisions in a major case before a high court. Scott was seeking his freedom on the grounds that his owner had taken him from Missouri to Wisconsin territory, where slavery was illegal and where Scott had married and started a family; subsequently Scott was taken back to Missouri. When the case reached the Supreme Court, Chief Justice Roger B. Taney, ruled: "They [slaves and their descendants] are not included and were not intended to be included under the word 'citizens' in the Constitution." He referred to slaves as "beings of an inferior order" and found that the court's duty was for all time to protect the rights of the property owner, i.e., slaveholder (*Dred Scott v. Sandford*, 1857). The ruling further inflamed the violent passions of the time, and brought civil war yet closer.]

1   A house divided against itself cannot stand. I believe this government cannot endure permanently half slave and half free.
                    —ABRAHAM LINCOLN, speech, Republican State Convention,
                              Springfield, Ill., June 16, 1858
    [More at THE UNION.]

2   I believe that to have interfered as I have done—as I have always freely admitted I have done—in behalf of His despised poor, was not wrong but right.
                    —JOHN BROWN, Oct. 31, 1859,
                    in James Redpath, *The Public Life of John Brown*, 1860
    [This was part of Brown's eloquent statement to the court on being sentenced to death for his raid on the arsenal at Harpers Ferry on October 16. He willingly took on the martyr's role, saying, "If it is deemed necessary that I should forfeit my life for the furtherance of the ends of justice and mingle my blood further with the blood of my children and with the blood of millions in this slave country whose rights are disregarded by wicked, cruel, and unjust enactments— I submit; so let it be done."
        Southerners were greatly relieved by the failure of Brown's raid; no slaves had come to join him, as he had hoped. Meanwhile, many Northerners looked upon him as a saint. Church bells tolled in the North on December 2 when he was hanged, and Henry Wadsworth Longfellow predicted in his diary: "This will be a great day in our history, the date of a new revolution—quite as much needed as the old one. . . . As I write, they are leading old John Brown to execution. . . . This is sowing the wind to reap the whirlwind, which will soon come." See also Brown at LAST WORDS.]

3   We must not be enemies. Though passion may have strained, it must not break our bonds of affection.   —ABRAHAM LINCOLN,
                              First Inaugural Address, March 4, 1861
    [More at PEACE.]

4   Thenceforward, and forever free.
                    —ABRAHAM LINCOLN, Preliminary Emancipation Proclamation,
                              Sept. 22, 1862
    [For the context, see SLAVERY.]

5   Fourscore and seven years ago, our fathers brought forth on this continent a new nation, conceived in liberty, and dedicated to the proposition that all men are created equal.   —ABRAHAM LINCOLN, Gettysburg Address,
                              Nov. 19, 1863
    [More at GETTYSBURG ADDRESS.]

6   With malice toward none, with charity for all, with firmness in the right, as God gives us to see the right, let us strive on to finish the work we are in.
                    —ABRAHAM LINCOLN, Second Inaugural Address, March 4, 1865
    [More at THE CIVIL WAR.]

Sic semper tyrannis! The South is avenged!   1
                    —JOHN WILKES BOOTH,
                         after shooting Pres. Abraham Lincoln, April 14, 1865
[The Latin saying used by Booth means "Thus always to tyrants," and is also
the Virginia motto.]

God reigns and the government at Washington still lives.   2
                    —JAMES A. GARFIELD, speech, New York City, April 15, 1865
[Rep. Garfield of Ohio was in New York on the day of Lincoln's death, and ad-
dressed the public from a balcony at the U.S. Customs house on Wall Street.
He later became president, and he, too, was assassinated.]

Let us have peace.   3
                    —ULYSSES S. GRANT,
                         presidential nomination acceptance speech, May 29, 1868

Dr. Livingstone, I presume?   —HENRY MORTON STANLEY, remark   4
                                            to David Livingstone, Nov. 10, 1871
[Stanley fled to America from Wales when he was fifteen, and took his sur-
name from the man who adopted him, Henry Stanley. He became a citizen and
a correspondent for the *New York Herald,* which assigned him to find Livingstone, the famed Scottish missionary and explorer in Africa, who had been
searching for the source of the Nile. After a dreadful journey, Stanley reached
the ailing Livingstone at Ujiji on Lake Tanganyika, scoring a journalistic coup
for the U.S. His query, which quickly became a catch phrase, was cited in his
book, *How I Found Livingstone.*]

Give me your tired, your poor,   5
Your huddled masses yearning to breathe free,
The wretched refuse of your teeming shore,
Send these, the homeless, tempest-tost to me:
I lift my lamp beside the golden door.
                    —EMMA LAZARUS, *The New Colossus:
                         Inscription for the Statue of Liberty,* 1883

You shall not crucify mankind upon a cross of gold.   6
                    —WILLIAM JENNINGS BRYAN, speech,
                         Democratic National Convention,
                         Chicago, July 8, 1896
[This "Cross of Gold" speech won Bryan the presidential nomination at age
thirty-six. He had developed the metaphor some years earlier, and used it to
great effect. More at ECONOMICS.]

Success. Four flights Thursday morning all against twenty-one mile wind.   7
                    —WILBUR WRIGHT & ORVILLE WRIGHT, telegram to their father,
                         from Kitty Hawk, N.C., Dec. 17, 1903
[More at SCIENCE: TECHNOLOGY.]

Perdicaris alive, or Raisuli dead.   —JOHN HAY, cablegram to   8
                                                    the Sultan of Morocco, 1904
[An early hostage crisis. Perdicaris, a Greek-American, was kidnapped by a Mo-
roccan outlaw, Achmed Ben Mohammed Raisuli, and held for $70,000 ransom.
Secretary of State Hay's ultimatum became a national rallying cry in the summer of 1904, when his cable was read at the Republican National Convention
in Chicago in June. "We want Perdicaris alive, or Raisuli dead," Hay had ca-

bled. The sultan, despite being in a semiwar with Raisuli, paid the ransom, and the hostage was freed.]

1   We stand at Armageddon, and we battle for the Lord.
—THEODORE ROOSEVELT, speech,
Republican National Convention, June 18, 1912
[Despite this ringing declaration, Pres. William Howard Taft won the nomination of the convention, after unseating seventy-two Roosevelt delegates. Roosevelt formed the Progressive Party and challenged Taft. Woodrow Wilson benefited from the split Republican vote and won the election.]

2   It must be a peace without victory. . . . Only a peace between equals can last.
—WOODROW WILSON, speech, U.S. Senate, Jan. 22, 1917
[Pres. Wilson was describing to the Senate his understanding of the kind of peace that would be acceptable to the warring European powers. His assessment proved prescient, as the eventual peace, a peace based on victory and defeat, lasted only twenty years—until the Nazi invasion of Poland. See also WORLD WAR I and WORLD WAR II.
On the other hand, some historians argue that the peace failed because the victory was not sufficiently complete; Germany had not been totally destroyed.]

3   The world must be made safe for democracy.
—WOODROW WILSON, speech to the U.S. Congress
asking for a declaration of war, April 2, 1917
[More at WORLD WAR I.]

4   A general association of nations must be formed under specific covenants for the purpose of affording mutual guarantees of political independence and territorial integrity to great and small states alike.
—WOODROW WILSON, "Fourteen Points" speech
to Congress, Jan. 8, 1918
[The reference here is to the League of Nations, established after World War I. It became moribund in the 1930s, unable to cope with German and Japanese military aggression. After World War II, the League was succeeded by the United Nations. See also FOREIGN POLICY and PEACE.]

5   We must stabilize and strive for normalcy.
—WARREN G. HARDING, presidential nomination
acceptance speech, July 22, 1920
[Use of the rare term *normalcy* instead of the more normal *normality* was one of the few memorable aspects of Harding's campaign. The call for a return to normalcy was a rejection of the idealism and internationalism of the Wilson years. Earlier in the year, on May 20, in a speech in Boston, Harding summed up his message in these words: "America's present need is not heroics, but healing; not nostrums, but normalcy; not revolution, but restoration; not experimentation, but equipoise."]

6   An opportunity as does seldom come to mortal man to free seventeen million from political slavery was mine.
—HENRY THOMAS BURN, speech,
Tennessee House of Representatives, August 1920
[On August 18, 1920, Rep. Burn, age twenty-three, broke a tie in the Tennessee legislature by casting a vote in favor of the Nineteenth Amendment, granting suffrage to women. See also Burn at PARENTS and TENNESSEE; and his mother, Febb Ensminger Burn, at WOMEN.]

We in America today are nearer to the final triumph over poverty than ever be- 1
fore in the history of a land. —HERBERT HOOVER, presidential
nomination acceptance speech,
Republican National Convention, 1928
[The great Wall Street crash was a year away.]

We offer one who has the will to win—who not only deserves success but com- 2
mands it. Victory is his habit—the happy warrior, Alfred Smith.
—FRANKLIN DELANO ROOSEVELT,
nominating New York governor Al Smith
as president, Democratic National Convention,
Houston, Texas, 1928
[The happy warrior, as he was known thereafter, lost to Herbert Hoover. The
epithet comes from the Wordsworth poem *The Character of the Happy Warrior*, which includes the lines: "Who is this happy warrior? Who is he / That
every man in arms should wish to be?" According to Henry F. Woods, in *American Sayings* (1945), Roosevelt had previously used the phrase in a eulogy for
Grover Cleveland in 1908.]

Wall St. Lays an Egg. —SIME SILVERMAN, headline, *Variety*, 3
Oct. 30, 1929
[More at THE DEPRESSION.]

I pledge you, I pledge myself, to a new deal for the American people. 4
—FRANKLIN D. ROOSEVELT,
presidential nomination acceptance speech,
Democratic National Convention,
Chicago, July 2, 1932
["The New Deal" became a popular label for Roosevelt's administration and
policies in the 1930s. The phrase had been used earlier in British as well as
American politics, but neither FDR nor the men who worked on his acceptance speech, Samuel Rosenman and Raymond Moley, attached particular importance to the words. The press latched onto them right away, however. What
first made the Democrats realize that they had tumbled onto an exciting catch
phrase, according to *Safire's New Political Dictionary*, was a cartoon drawn by
Rollin Kirby on the day of the speech of a bewildered but hopeful man, leaning
on a hoe, and watching an airplane labeled "New Deal" flying overhead. See
also POLITICAL SLOGANS.]

The only thing we have to fear is fear itself, nameless, unreasoning, unjustified 5
terror which paralyzes needed efforts to convert retreat into advance.
—FRANKLIN D. ROOSEVELT, First Inaugural Address,
March 4, 1933
[The heartening effect of these words on a worried people cannot be exaggerated. Many, perhaps most, who heard this speech feared that the nation was on
the brink of chaos and possibly revolution; see THE DEPRESSION. For the occasion, Roosevelt turned to rhetoric already proved effective. His predecessors
include Henry David Thoreau—see under FEAR—and the duke of Wellington,
"The only thing I am afraid of is fear." Going back further, similar comments
were made by Francis Bacon and Montaigne.
   Another moving passage in this inaugural speech drew on the Bible: In 1964,
Lyndon Johnson recalled that when Roosevelt "quoted from *Proverbs:* 'Where
there is no vision, the people perish,' it gave me an inspiration that has carried
me all through the years since."]

1   This generation of Americans has a rendezvous with destiny.
                    —FRANKLIN D. ROOSEVELT, presidential nomination acceptance
                        speech, Democratic National Convention, June 27, 1936
    [More at GENERATIONS.]

2   I see one-third of a nation ill-housed, ill-clad, ill-nourished.
                    —FRANKLIN D. ROOSEVELT,
                        Second Inaugural Address, Jan. 20, 1937

3   We must be the great arsenal of democracy.
                    —FRANKLIN D. ROOSEVELT,
                        fireside radio talk, Dec. 29, 1940
    [This speech marked the beginning of the end of U.S. neutrality in World War II.
    The president called upon Americans to support Great Britain with "the same
    resolution, the same sense of urgency, the same spirit of patriotism and sacri-
    fice as we would show were we at war." A week later, he recommended to
    Congress a lend-lease act that would give him the authority to send war mate-
    rials to those nations fighting fascism.
        The December 29 talk recalls Woodrow Wilson's appeal to Congress in 1917
    to make the world safe for democracy; see DEMOCRACY.
        Gorton Carruth and Eugene Ehrlich, in *American Quotations,* credit French
    statesman Jean Monnet with first using the "arsenal of democracy" metaphor,
    in conversation with Felix Frankfurter. Writing in *The New Yorker,* August 15,
    1994, Doris Kearns Goodwin credits presidential aide Harry Hopkins with sug-
    gesting the phrase to Roosevelt.]

4   We look forward to a world founded upon four essential human freedoms.
                    —FRANKLIN D. ROOSEVELT, the "Four Freedoms" speech,
                        a State of the Union message, Jan. 6, 1941
    [More at FREEDOM.]

5   Yesterday, December 7, 1941—a date which will live in infamy.
                    —FRANKLIN D. ROOSEVELT, message to Congress, Dec. 8, 1941
    [More at WORLD WAR II.]

6   Boys, if you ever pray, pray for me now.
                    —HARRY S. TRUMAN, remark to the White House press corps,
                        April 13, 1945
    [Truman had been sworn in as president the day before, just ninety minutes
    after Eleanor Roosevelt told him that her husband was dead. "I felt like the
    moon, the stars, and all the planets had fallen on me," Truman told the press.]

7   Let us not be deceived. We are today in the midst of a cold war.
                    —BERNARD BARUCH, speech, April 16, 1947
    [A year earlier, Winston Churchill had announced gloomily, "From Stettin in
    the Baltic to Trieste in the Atlantic, an iron curtain has descended across the
    Continent," speech, April 5, 1946. Baruch's line is said to have been written by
    journalist and political consultant Herbert Bayard Swope, according to Stanley
    and Eleanor Hochman in *The Penguin Dictionary of Contemporary American
    History.* For the end of the Cold War, see George Bush and Paul Tsongas below.
    See also COMMUNISM.]

8   I'm going to fight hard, and I'm going to give them hell.
                    —HARRY S. TRUMAN, campaign pledge, 1948
    [See also POLITICAL SLOGANS.]

Dewey Defeats Truman. —CHICAGO TRIBUNE,   1
banner headline, Nov. 3, 1948

[Bad guess.]

While I cannot take the time to name all the men in the State Department who   2
have been named as members of the Communist Party and members of a spy
ring, I have here in my hand a list of 205 that were known to the Secretary of
State [Dean Acheson] as being members of the Communist Party and are still
working and shaping the policy of the State Department.
—JOSEPH R. MCCARTHY, speech, Wheeling, W. Va., Feb. 9, 1950
[This accusation established the junior senator from Wisconsin as the chief
Communist hunter in the U.S., but McCarthy seemed not to sense its importance, judging by the odd forum in which the charge was first aired—The
Women's Republican Club of Ohio County, West Virginia. The speech derived
in part from remarks on January 26, 1950, by fellow Republican Richard M.
Nixon, a member of the House Committee on Un-American Activities. The
paper in McCarthy's hand apparently was a letter, more than three years old,
from former Secretary of State James F. Byrnes to a member of the House that
gave figures on security risks in general, not just Communists. McCarthy
never actually came up with a single name from his list, and the number
changed from 205 to 57 to 81, 10, 116, then 1, 121, and 106. It was four years
before McCarthy's authority was challenged; see Edward R. Murrow and
Joseph N. Welch below. See also COMMUNISM.]

When I joined the Army, even before the turn of the century, it was the fulfill-   3
ment of all my hopes and dreams. The hopes and dreams have long since vanished. But I still remember the refrain of one of the most popular barracks
ballads of that day, which proclaimed proudly that, "Old soldiers never die.
They just fade away." And like the old soldier of the ballad, I now close my
military career and just fade away—an old soldier who tried to do his duty as
God gave him the light to see that duty.
—DOUGLAS MACARTHUR, speech,
joint session of Congress, April 19, 1951.
[The general had just been relieved of duty by Pres. Truman for insubordination. The hugely popular MacArthur believed that to win the Korean War the
U.S. would have to move against Communist China, using nuclear weapons
and the Nationalist forces under Chiang Kai-shek. This undermined the president's international initiatives; moreover, MacArthur had posted mixed results as commander of the Korean action. Nevertheless, Truman's decision
was risky, and MacArthur's speech inspired such a wave of emotion nationwide that there was fear of a popular uprising in favor of the general that would
force his reinstatement and the impeachment or censure of the president. But
within a month, MacArthur did indeed begin to fade. See also Gen. Omar
Bradley at WAR. For more on the song, see under MacArthur at THE MILITARY.]

Pat doesn't have a mink coat. But she does have a good respectable Republican   4
cloth coat. —RICHARD M. NIXON,
"Checkers" speech, Sept. 23, 1952
[Nixon was the vice-presidential candidate on the ticket headed by Gen.
Dwight D. Eisenhower, when it was disclosed in the press that a group of California businessmen had quietly given him more than $18,000 for campaign
expenses. It had appeared that Eisenhower might drop his runningmate until
Nixon scored a public relations coup with a televised speech to the nation
stressing that his family was scratching along with little money. "Pat [his wife]
and I have the satisfaction that every dime that we've got is honestly ours," he

said. He did admit accepting a spotted spaniel from a man in Texas, adding emotionally—see below.]

1   And our little girl, Tricia, the six-year-old, named it Checkers. And you know, the kids love the dog, and I just want to say this right now, that regardless of what they do about it, we're going to keep it.

—*Ibid.*

[Checkers was not the only famous dog in American politics. Fala, short for Murray of Fallahill, Franklin D. Roosevelt's Scottie, was frequently in the news, and Pres. George Bush's dog Millie allegedly wrote a book with First Lady Barbara Bush. FDR memorably defended his pet in 1944, when Republican newspapers spread a rumor that the dog had been left by mistake on an Aleutian island and then retrieved at great expense to taxpayers. FDR bested his critics with humor. "I don't resent attacks," he said, "and my family doesn't resent attacks, but Fala does resent them. You know, Fala is Scotch, and being a Scottie, as soon as he learned that the Republican fiction writers . . . had concocted a story that I . . . had sent a destroyer back to find him . . . his Scotch soul was furious. He has not been the same dog since."

Then there was Speaker of the House Champ Clark of Missouri, who used a hillbilly-dog song in his 1912 campaign for the Democratic presidential nomination. The idea was to project a down-home image in contrast to Woodrow Wilson's elitist mien. Clark's song went in part: "Ev'ry time I come to town, / The boys keep kickin' my dawg aroun'; / Makes no dif'rence if he is a houn', / They've gotta quit kickin' my dawg aroun'." For another sample of Clark's populist politics, see his epitaph for himself at EPITAPHS & GRAVESTONES.]

2   We must not confuse dissent with disloyalty.

—EDWARD R. MURROW, *Report on Sen. Joseph R. McCarthy,*
in Murrow's *See It Now* documentary television series,
March 7, 1954

[This was the first major assault on McCarthyism. Even the popular and influential Murrow felt that he had to bide his time until McCarthy's excesses began to worry the American public. The program was considered risky, but Murrow told his audience, "Remember that we are not descended from fearful men, not from men who feared to write, to speak, to associate, and to defend causes which were, for the moment, unpopular." The fatal blow to McCarthy was struck three months later; see Joseph N. Welch below.]

3   We conclude that in the field of public education "separate but equal" has no place. Separate educational facilities are inherently unequal.

—EARL WARREN, *Brown v. Board of Education of Topeka,*
May 17, 1954

[This Supreme Court decision marked the end of state-sanctioned segregation in the U.S. Reflecting on the fortieth anniversary of *Brown,* U. S. Rep. John Lewis of Georgia, said, "This country is a different country now. It is a better country. We have witnessed a nonviolent revolution," speech at the John F. Kennedy Library, Washington, D.C., April 1994. The attorney for the plaintiffs was Thurgood Marshall, who was appointed to the Supreme Court himself in 1967. The victory was also a vindication of Justice John Marshall Harlan, who in a dissenting opinion in the case of *Plessy v. Ferguson,* 1894, said that segregation was "the badge of slavery." In 1992, a federal appeals court found that the Topeka Board of Education still was not in compliance with the Constitutional requirement to integrate its schools. See also THE CONSTITUTION; RACES & PEOPLES.]

Have you no sense of decency, sir, at long last? Have you no sense of decency? 1
          —JOSEPH N. WELCH, Army–McCarthy hearings, June 9, 1954
[Attorney Welch, representing the U.S. Army, addressed this remark to Sen. Joseph McCarthy in televised hearings conducted by the senator to ferret out alleged Communist subversives in the military. People in the hearing room cheered. From this moment, McCarthy's power, and McCarthyism itself, began to wane.]

Ask not what your country can do for you—ask what you can do for your 2
country.   —JOHN F. KENNEDY, Inaugural Address,
          Jan. 20, 1961
[More at SERVING ONE'S COUNTRY.]

We're eyeball to eyeball, and I think the other fellow just blinked. 3
          —DEAN RUSK, conversation, Oct. 24, 1962
[Secretary of State Rusk was speaking of Premier Nikita Khrushchev. This was in the midst of the Cuban missile crisis. Pres. John F. Kennedy had demanded that Russia remove its ballistic missiles from Cuba. The blink was scarcely perceptible on October 24. The nation seemed to be on the brink of nuclear war, and it was another four days before Khrushchev backed down, and everyone breathed easier. This quote is in *Bartlett's.*]

You won't have Nixon to kick around any more, because, gentlemen, this is 4
my last press conference.
          —RICHARD M. NIXON, after losing to incumbent Pat Brown
          in the 1962 California gubernatorial race
[It wasn't.]

Ich bin ein Berliner.   —JOHN F. KENNEDY, speech, West Berlin, 5
          June 26, 1963
[Delivered to a large crowd at city hall in West Berlin, this speech affirmed U.S. commitment to the embattled democracy. The full passage was: "All free men wherever they may live, are citizens of Berlin. And therefore, as a free man, I take pride in the words, *'Ich bin ein Berliner.'*" It is sometimes said—in *Bartlett's* sixteenth edition and elsewhere—that JFK made a linguistic faux pas in referring to himself as a "Berliner" because a "Berliner" also is a sort of jelly doughnut. But Reinhold Aman, a native speaker of German as well as an authority on the language of aggression, debunked this theory in *Maledicta XI,* maintaining that Kennedy's words were perfectly intelligible. And in fact, the declaration was greeted with overwhelming, almost riotous cheering, not puzzlement or snickers.]

Now is the time to make real the promises of democracy. *Now* is the time to 6
rise from the dark and desolate valley of segregation to the sunlit path of racial justice. *Now* is the time to open the doors of opportunity to all of God's children. *Now* is the time to lift our nation from the quicksands of racial injustice to the solid rock of brotherhood.
          —MARTIN LUTHER KING, JR., speech at the Lincoln Memorial
          in Washington, D.C., to 200,000 civil rights marchers,
          August 28, 1963
[For the incident that led to King's emergence as a civil rights leader, see Rosa Parks at RACES & PEOPLES.]

Let us not seek to satisfy our thirst for freedom by drinking from the cup of bit- 7
terness and hatred. . . . Again and again we must rise to the majestic heights of meeting physical force with soul force.   —*Ibid.*

1   No, no, we are not satisfied, and we will not be satisfied until justice rolls down like waters and righteousness like a mighty stream.

—*Ibid.*

[Here Dr. King drew on the Old Testament, *Amos,* 5:24: "Let judgment run down as waters, and righteousness as a mighty stream."]

2   I say to you today, my friends, that in spite of the difficulties and frustrations of the moment, I still have a dream. It is a dream deeply rooted in the American dream.

I have a dream that one day on the red hills of Georgia, the sons of former slaves and the sons of former slaveowners will be able to sit down together at the table of brotherhood.

—*Ibid.*

[The "I have a dream" passages were the highpoint of this great address. Not since the wartime talks of Winston Churchill and Franklin D. Roosevelt had a speech reached so many so memorably.]

3   I have a dream that my four little children will one day live in a nation where they will not be judged by the color of their skin but by the content of their character.

I have a dream that one day this nation will rise up and live out the true meaning of its creed: "We hold these truths to be self-evident; that all men are created equal."

I have a dream today.   —*Ibid.*

4   When we let freedom ring, when we let it ring from every village and every hamlet, from every state and every city, we will be able to speed up that day when all of God's children, black men and white men, Jews and Gentiles, Protestants and Catholics, will be able to join hands and sing in the words of the old Negro spiritual, "Free at last! Free at last! Thank God Almighty, we are free at last!"

—*Ibid.*

[The finale of the speech.]

5   This administration today, here and now, declares unconditional war on poverty in America. . . . It will not be a short or easy struggle, no single weapon or strategy will suffice, but we shall not rest until that war is won.

—LYNDON B. JOHNSON, State of the Union speech, Jan. 8, 1964

[The war went quite well, a key initiative being passage of the Economic Opportunity Act later that year. But Johnson became ever more deeply engaged in a second war, in Vietnam. And as it turned out, the nation could not afford both guns and butter.]

6   For in your time we have the opportunity to move not only toward the rich society and the powerful society, but upward to the Great Society.

—LYNDON B. JOHNSON, speech, University of Michigan,
Ann Arbor, May 22, 1964

[See also Johnson at POLITICAL SLOGANS.]

7   I would remind you that extremism in the defense of liberty is no vice. And let me remind you also that moderation in the pursuit of justice is no virtue.

—BARRY GOLDWATER,
presidential nomination acceptance speech,
Republican National Convention, July 16, 1964

[Reminiscent of Thomas Paine's "Moderation in temper is always a virtue, but moderation in principle is always a vice," *The Rights of Man,* 1791.]

That's one small step for [a] man, one giant leap for mankind.   1
                    —NEIL A. ARMSTRONG, disembarking from
                    the Apollo 11 Eagle moon lander, July 20, 1969
[More at SCIENCE: TECHNOLOGY.]

Houston, we've had a problem here. Houston, we've had a problem.   2
                    —JAMES A. LOVELL, JR., from Apollo 13, April 1970
[The problem was that an exploding oxygen tank on the space ship had
knocked out one engine and the main supply of electric power. The command
module was essentially incapacitated, and the three astronauts had to use the
lunar landing module for power and air.]

We, therefore, conclude that the right of personal privacy includes the abortion 3
decision, but that this right is not unqualified and must be considered against
important state interests in regulation.   —HARRY A. BLACKMUN,
                    Roe v. Wade, 1973

Read my lips: No new taxes.   4
                    —GEORGE BUSH, presidential nomination acceptance speech,
                    Republican National Convention, Aug. 18, 1988
[More at TAXES. Two other phrases stand out from this speech: "a thousand
points of light"—see AMERICA & AMERICANS; and "a kinder, gentler, nation"—
see POLITICAL SLOGANS.]

By the grace of God, America won the cold war.   5
                    —GEORGE BUSH, Jan. 28, 1992
[In contrast to the president, Democrat Paul Tsongas took a secular view of
this turn of events. See below.]

The cold war is over, and Japan won.   6
                    —PAUL E. TSONGAS, 1992
[The former senator from Massachusetts used this line to press his campaign
for the Democratic presidential nomination. He lost to Bill Clinton.]

AMERICAN REVOLUTION, 1775–83

See also AMERICAN HISTORY:
MEMORABLE MOMENTS; DECLARATION OF
INDEPENDENCE; INDEPENDENCE DAY

United we stand, divided we fall.   —ANONYMOUS, watchword of the   7
                    American revolutionaries
[See also John Dickinson's *Liberty Song* at UNITY.]

In the name of the Great Jehovah and the Continental Congress.   8
                    —ETHAN ALLEN, Fort Ticonderoga, May 10, 1775
[Allen's reply, so he said several years later, to the British officer at Fort Ticonderoga who asked by what authority he demanded the post's surrender. Other
Green Mountain boys had differing recollections. One said that Allen shouted,
"Come out of here, you damned old rat"; another that he threatened, "Come
out of there, you sons of British whores, or I'll smoke you out." Pioneer sociol-
ogist William Graham Sumner asserted in a lecture at Yale in the 1890s on the
expurgation of American history that Allen used the even stronger "Open up
here, you goddamned son of a bitch." If Allen did make some sort of reference
to Jehovah and the Continental Congress, he certainly exaggerated, as neither
had authorized his mission.]

1 There [in Charlestown] I agreed with a Colonel Conant and some other gentlemen that if the British went out by water, we [in Boston] would show two
lanterns in the North Church steeple; and if by land, one as a signal; for we
were apprehensive it would be difficult [for a messenger] to cross the Charles
River or get over Boston Neck.   —PAUL REVERE,
                                                  letter to Dr. Jeremy Belknap
[This describes the arrangement made on Sunday, April 16, 1775, with Col. Conant of the Charlestown Committee of Safety for a signal if and when British
troops moved out of Boston. Revere feared that when the moment came, the
British might post guards to prevent American couriers from leaving Boston
and spreading the word. The colonists had learned that the British hoped to arrest Samuel Adams and John Hancock, who were in hiding in Lexington, and
to seize ammunition and other supplies hidden at Concord. Their informer
may have been the American-born wife of Gen. Thomas Gage, the commander
of British troops in North America.
    As the troops prepared to go on active duty on the night of April 18, the rev-
olutionary leader Dr. Joseph Warren dispatched Revere and another courier,
William Dawes, to Lexington. See below for Longfellow's version of events.]

2 Stand your ground. Don't fire unless fired upon, but if they mean to have a war,
let it begin here!   —JOHN PARKER, order to his Minutemen,
                                       Lexington, Mass., April 19, 1775
[This is as recounted by Capt. Parker's grandson, and is probably a well-
polished rendition. The Minutemen had gathered on the town green. Parker's
order came just before the British opened fire.]

3 What a glorious morning for America!   —SAMUEL ADAMS, hearing the sound
                                           of gunfire at Lexington,
                                           April 19, 1775
[This exclamation, traditionally attributed to Adams, is on Lexington's town
seal. Emerson called the gunfire "the shot heard 'round the world"; see below.]

4 Don't fire until you see the whites of their eyes.
                        —WILLIAM PRESCOTT, battle of Bunker Hill, June 17, 1775
[Also attributed to Israel Putnam, but he was probably relaying the order from
Prescott, commander of the 1,500 colonial troops at Breeds Hill, near Bunker
Hill. The British, with twice the manpower, needed three tries to dislodge the
Americans.
    The order has continental precedents, including Prince Charles of Prussia at
Jägerndorf, May 23, 1745: "Silent till you see the whites of their eyes"; and
Frederick the Great at Prague, May 6, 1757: "No firing till you see the whites
of their eyes." Historian Robert M. Ketchum has described the order as a
"time-honored admonition," *American Heritage*, June 1973.]

5 I wish this cursed place was burned!
                                       —THOMAS GAGE, June 17, 1775
[Lt. Gen. Gage, at this early date, foresaw the disaster that would eventually
overtake his country's forces. He made this bitter exclamation upon learning
of his losses at Bunker Hill.]

6 The period of debate is closed. Arms, as a last resource, must decide the contest.   —TOM PAINE, *Common Sense*, 1776

7 Rebellion to tyrants is obedience to God.   —ANONYMOUS, motto on
                                                Thomas Jefferson's seal, c. 1776
[In a letter to Edward Everett written on February 24, 1823, Jefferson said that

he believed that this was the motto of one of the regicides of Charles I. That probably would have been John Bradshaw.]

The time is now near at hand which must probably determine whether Americans are to be freemen or slaves. . . . The fate of unborn millions will now depend, under God, on the courage and conduct of this army. Our cruel and unrelenting enemy leaves us no choice but a brave resistance or the most abject submission. We have therefore to resolve to conquer or die.
—GEORGE WASHINGTON, general orders, July 2, 1776

I only regret that I have but one life to lose for my country.
—NATHAN HALE, at the gallows in Artillery Park,
New York City (near Third Avenue and 66th Street),
Sept. 22, 1776
[Capt. Hale, age twenty-one, was a graduate of Yale College, known as an excellent orator with liberal views—his graduation speech addressed the importance of educating women. When urged not to be a spy, Hale replied with a classic defense of cloak-and-dagger work: "Every kind of service necessary to the public good becomes honorable by being necessary," letter to William Hull, September 10, 1776. Hale's famous pronouncement prior to his execution was probably part of a fairly long and spirited statement. Hale adapted a line from Joseph Addison's *Cato:* "What a pity is it / That we can die but once to serve our country." See also under Joseph Addison at FREEDOM. In the end, the British paid dearly for their treatment of Hale; see under Maj. John André below.]

These are the times that try men's souls. The summer soldier and the sunshine patriot will, in this crisis, shrink from the services of their country; but he that stands it NOW deserves the love and thanks of man and woman.
—THOMAS PAINE,
The American Crisis, Dec. 23, 1776
[Paine, an English immigrant but an ardent supporter of independence, had joined George Washington's beaten and discouraged army. With winter closing in, Paine exhorted the downcast troops to stand fast.]

Necessity, dire necessity, will, nay must, justify my attack.
—GEORGE WASHINGTON, attributed, Dec. 25, 1776
[Washington was preparing to attack Trenton the next day. The Americans were truly desperate for a victory, and they got one, surprising the Hessians posted at Trenton. These German mercenaries did not think that the Continental army would attack in the foul winter weather—and they were under the weather themselves, having celebrated Christmas with too much cheer. As the American countersign—the phrase that the Continentals would use to identify themselves to each other—Washington selected "Victory or Die."]

It is a common observation here [Paris] that our cause is *the cause of all mankind,* and that we are fighting for their liberty in defending our own.
—BENJAMIN FRANKLIN, letter to Samuel Cooper, 1777

I desired as many as could to join together in fasting and prayer, that God would restore the spirit of love and of a sound mind to the poor deluded rebels in America. —JOHN WESLEY, *Journal,* August 1, 1777

We beat them tonight or Molly Stark's a widow.
—JOHN STARK, August 16, 1777
[Another version is, "There, my lads, are the Hessians! Tonight our flag floats over yonder hill, or Molly Stark sleeps a widow." Col. Stark was addressing his men before the Battle of Bennington. He and Seth Warner commanded the

Green Mountain Boys, who shattered a column of Hessians sent by British general John Burgoyne to raid an American supply depot at Bennington. The action was one of numerous setbacks in the British Saratoga campaign, which was aimed at dividing the colonies along the line of the Hudson River. Burgoyne was marching south from Canada. His counterparts to the south never made it up to Albany as plannned. Burgoyne's surrender at Saratoga on October 17 marked a turning point in the Revolution.]

1   If I were an American, as I am an Englishman, while a foreign troop was landed in my country, I would never lay down my arms—never, never, never! You cannot conquer America.   —WILLIAM PITT, speech,
House of Lords, Nov. 18, 1777

2   I wish to have no connection with any ship that does not sail *fast;* for I intend to go *in harm's way.*   —JOHN PAUL JONES, letter, Nov. 16, 1778

3   I have not yet begun to fight.
—JOHN PAUL JONES, reply from the *Bonhomme Richard*
to the *Serapis,* Sept. 23, 1779.
[Reports of Captain Jones's exact words vary but the sense is the same. The savage battle took place on a moonlit night off Flamborough Head on the east coast of England. Seeing that the *Richard* had been badly damaged in the opening salvos, the British called for its surrender. Jones, his decks awash in blood, replied that he would fight on. He managed to cross in front of the *Serapis,* causing it to collide with his vessel, then lashed the two ships together, and continued the fight with cannon and small arms at point-blank range. In the end, the *Serapis* struck its colors. The *Richard* was in sinking condition, so the Americans returned to their home base in France in the *Serapis.* This is the only naval battle in which the winning captain has lost his ship and returned in a captured vessel. When Jones heard that the British captain had been knighted for his valor, he is said to have observed: "Should I have the good fortune to fall in with him again, I'll make a Lord of him."]

4   It will be but a moment's pang. I pray you bear witness that I met my fate like a brave man.   —JOHN ANDRÉ,
Oct. 2, 1780
[André, an attractive and talented young major in the British army, was hanged as a spy. The Americans were saddened, but his death seemed necessary as a response to the British execution of Nathan Hale; see above.]

5   We fight, get beat, rise and fight again.   —NATHANAEL GREENE,
letter to Chevalier de la Luzerne,
June 22, 1781
[The chevalier was the French ambassador to the American colonies, and Greene was writing about the campaign in the Carolinas, which weakened the British even as they seemed to be winning. On July 18, 1781, Greene described his strategy in a letter to Henry Knox: "There are few generals that have run oftener, or more lustily than I have done. But I have taken care not to run too far, and commonly have run as fast forward as backward, to convince the enemy that we were like a crab, that could run either way."]

6   The World Turned Upside Down.
—ANONYMOUS, song, traditionally said to have been played
by the British when surrendering to the Americans
and French at Yorktown, Oct. 19, 1781
[Contemporary accounts do not mention this particular tune; the tradition

seems to date to the 19th century. Music was an important part of the surrender ceremony, however. Ordinarily, a besieged army would be permitted to march out with colors flying and playing one of the victor's marching tunes when it surrendered. But the British had not allowed these honors of war to Americans in 1780, when Gen. Benjamin Lincoln surrendered at Charleston, S.C., following a six-week siege. Now, Washington insisted that the British march out of Yorktown with colors encased and playing their own or German music. This humiliating requirement probably explains the "indisposition" that kept Earl Cornwallis from participating in the ceremony. When Gen. Charles O'Hara, the British second-in-command, offered his sword to the American commander, Washington directed O'Hara to his own second, who on this occasion happened to be—proving, if there were any doubt, how the world had been turned upside down—Gen. Benjamin Lincoln.]

The old spirit of '76.   —THOMAS JEFFERSON,   1
                                      letter to James Monroe, 1793
[Archibald Willard's famous painting for the 1876 Centennial Exhibition in Philadelphia, *The Spirit of '76*, shows three generations of military musicians, playing drums and fife. Actually the first title was *Yankee Doodle*, but Willard subsequently came up with the more sentimental tag.]

The Revolution was effected before the war commenced. The Revolution was   2
in the hearts and minds of the people. . . . This radical change in the principles, opinions, sentiments, and affections of the people was the real American Revolution.   —JOHN ADAMS,
                            letter to Hezekiah Niles, Feb. 13, 1818
[Adams favored this view of the revolution. For example, in an earlier letter to Thomas Jefferson, he wrote: "The revolution was in the minds of the people," August 24, 1815.

The phrase "hearts and minds" has had a long life. For example, in 1906, Pres. Theodore Roosevelt told his young aide Lt. Douglas MacArthur that the secret of popularity with the people is "to put into words what is in their hearts and minds but not in their mouths"; cited by William Safire in his *New Political Dictionary*. More recently the Vietnam War was frequently described as a battle for the hearts and minds of the Vietnamese people; see Nixon at VIETNAM WAR, p. 510 below (note).]

By the rude bridge that arched the flood,   3
Their flag to April's breeze unfurled,
Here once the embattled farmers stood,
And fired the shot heard round the world.   —RALPH WALDO EMERSON,
                                 Concord Hymn, 1837
[Emerson wrote the hymn for the dedication of the monument at the battleground in Concord. Here, on April 19, 1775, at the bridge entering Concord, Minutemen stood up against 800 British troops and forced them to retreat to Charlestown.]

Listen, my children, and you shall hear,   4
Of the midnight ride of Paul Revere,
On the eighteenth of April, in Seventy-five,
Hardly a man is now alive
Who remembers that famous day and year.
                          —HENRY WADSWORTH LONGFELLOW,
                          The Landlord's Tale: Paul Revere's Ride,
                          in *Tales of a Wayside Inn*, 1863–1874

1   One if by land and two if by sea;
    And I on the opposite shore will be,
    Ready to ride and spread the alarm
    Through every Middlesex village and farm.   —*Ibid.*

2   The fate of a nation was riding that night.
                                                                 —*Ibid.*
    [See Paul Revere above. Thanks to this poem, he has become one of our most
    enduring heroes.]

ANGER   *See also* ARGUMENTS

3   Anger is never without a reason, but seldom with a good one.
                        —BENJAMIN FRANKLIN, *Poor Richard's Almanack*, 1753

4   We boil at different degrees.   —RALPH WALDO EMERSON, *Eloquence*,
                                                in *Society and Solitude*, 1870

5   When angry, count four; when very angry, swear.
                                    —MARK TWAIN, *Pudd'nhead Wilson's Calendar*,
                                        in *Pudd'nhead Wilson*, 1894
    [A takeoff from the proverbial, "When angry, count ten before you speak;
    if very angry, an hundred." This was one of ten rules included by Thomas Jef-
    ferson in a letter to Thomas Jefferson Smith, February 21, 1825. Re Twain's
    recommendation to swear, he also pointed out that "In certain trying circum-
    stances, urgent circumstances, desperate circumstances, profanity furnishes
    a relief denied even to prayer," quoted by his friend and biographer, Albert
    Bigelow Paine, in *Mark Twain, A Biography*, 1912.]

6   Speak when you are angry, and you will make the best speech you will ever
    regret.   —AMBROSE BIERCE,
                                                    The Devil's Dictionary, 1906
    [Bierce, a newspaperman, mixed aphorisms with cynical definitions. In 1906,
    his publisher insisted upon calling this collection of sayings *The Cynic's Word
    Book*, but since then, Bierce's own title has been used. The advice here is pru-
    dent, but Bierce was not a cautious person himself. He disappeared in Mexico
    during the revolution of 1913–14.]

7   Don't get mad, get even.   —JOSEPH PATRICK KENNEDY, saying, attributed

8   Never go to bed mad. Stay up and fight.
                        —PHYLLIS DILLER, *Phyllis Diller's Housekeeping Hints*, 1966

9   We are surrounded by the enraged.   —DIANE JOHNSON,
                                                    The Shadow Knows, 1974

10 I'm mad as hell, and I'm not going to take it any more.
                                    —PADDY CHAYEVSKY, *Network*, 1976
    [London-born actor Peter Finch spoke this line, in the role of an anchorman
    driven over the edge by the television industry. The line is repeated several
    times in the film, sometimes in the form "I'm not going to take this any
    more." Ultimately, crowds join him in shouting, "I'm mad as hell (etc.)," and
    the statement has become a sort of rallying cry for a populist, antigovernment
    political trend, particularly among white males. Finch died a year after the
    movie was released.]

ANIMALS   *See* NATURE: ANIMALS; AMERICAN HISTORY: MEMORABLE MOMENTS (Richard Nixon's "Checkers" speech)

ANSWERS   *See* QUESTIONS & ANSWERS

ANXIETY & WORRY   *See also* CALMNESS

How much pain have cost us the evils which have never happened!   1
    —THOMAS JEFFERSON, "A Decalogue of Canons
    for observation in practical life,"
    letter to Thomas Jefferson Smith, Feb. 21, 1825

The cares, that infest the day,   2
Shall fold their tents, like the Arabs,
And as silently steal away.   —HENRY WADSWORTH LONGFELLOW,
    The Day Is Done, 1845

[More at ART: MUSIC.]

Never hurry and never worry!   —E. B. WHITE,   3
    Charlotte's Web, 1952

[Charlotte the spider to Wilbur, an endangered pig.]

What, Me Worry?   —MAD MAGAZINE, motto of signature character,   4
    Alfred E. Newman, 1955,
    from an advertising slogan c. 1900

We are, perhaps uniquely among the earth's creatures, the worrying animal.   5
We worry away our lives, fearing the future, discontent with the present, unable to take in the idea of dying, unable to sit still.
    —LEWIS THOMAS, *The Medusa and the Snail*, 1979
[Dr. Thomas, described in his *New York Times* obituary as a "poet-philosopher of medicine," headed the Memorial Sloan-Kettering Cancer Center, and earlier served as dean of the medical schools of New York University and Yale University. He was best known for brilliant essays on biology, music, and life in general.]

APPEARANCES   *See also* BEAUTY; BODY & LOOKS; FASHION & CLOTHES; REALITY, ILLUSIONS, & IMAGES

All visible objects, man, are but as pasteboard masks. . . . Strike, strike through   6
the mask!   —HERMAN MELVILLE, *Moby-Dick*, 1851

You can't expect men not to judge by appearances.   7
    —ELLEN GLASGOW, *The Sheltered Life*, 1932
[Glasgow, a Pulitzer Prize–winning Southerner "was a major historian of our times," wrote Henry Seidel Canby, "who, almost single-handedly, rescued Southern fiction from the glamorous sentimentality of the Lost Cause."]

ARGENTINA   *See* NATIONS

ARGUMENTS   *See also* ANGER; CONFLICT; CONVERSATION; DIFFERENCES

'Tis by our quarrels that we spoil our prayers.   8
    —COTTON MATHER, *The Wonders of the Invisible World*, 1693

1   It were endless to dispute upon everything that is disputable.
—WILLIAM PENN, *Some Fruits of Solitude*, 1693

2   I never saw an instance of one of two disputants convincing the other by argument.   —THOMAS JEFFERSON, letter to John Taylor, June 1, 1798

3   I am not arguing with you—I am telling you.
—JAMES ABBOTT MCNEILL WHISTLER,
The Gentle Art of Making Enemies, 1890

4   All right, have it your own way—you heard a seal bark!
—JAMES THURBER, cartoon caption,
in *The New Yorker*,
Jan. 30, 1932
[A large, alert seal is leaning over the headboard of a double bed in which a middle-aged couple are at odds. The woman evidently heard a seal bark, and has said so. The man declines to dispute such a ridiculous claim.]

ARIZONA

5   It is my land, my home, my father's land, to which I now ask to be allowed to return. I want to spend my last days there, and be buried among those mountains.   —GERONIMO, letter to Pres. Ulysses S. Grant
from the reservation at Fort Sill, Okla., 1875

6   Come to Arizona where summer spends the winter.
—ANONYMOUS, booster slogan, c. 1935
[H. L. Mencken in his dictionary of quotations notes that local wits added, "And hell spends the summer." In *Roughing It* (1872), Mark Twain passes along a story he heard from humorist George Horatio Derby about a wicked soldier from Yuma, who dies and goes "to the hottest corner of perdition—and the next day he *telegraphed back for his blankets!*"]

7   The Grand Canyon is carven deep by the master hand; it is the gulf of silence, widened in the desert; it is all time inscribing the naked rock; it is the book of earth.   —DONALD CULROSS PEATTIE,
The Road of a Naturalist, 1941

8   Land of extremes. Land of contrasts. Land of surprises. Land of contradictions.
—FEDERAL WRITERS' PROJECT,
Arizona: The Grand Canyon State, 1956

9   Across the Colorado River from Needles, the dark and jagged ramparts of Arizona stood up against the sky, and behind them the huge tilted plain rising toward the backbone of the continent again.
—JOHN STEINBECK, *Travels with Charley*, 1962

10   It's a tough country.   —CHARLES KURALT,
Dateline America, 1979

Motto

11   *Ditat Deus.*
God enriches.

ARKANSAS

See also CITIES (Arkansas City)

All the trees, the year round, were as green as if they stood in orchards, and the　1
woods were open.　　　　—A KNIGHT OF ELVAS,
Narratives of the Career of Hernando de Soto
in the Conquest of Florida
[The anonymous author, who signed himself "A Gentleman of Elvas," accompanied De Soto on his expedition in 1539 to North America. This is a description from 1541 of what is now Arkansas.]

If I could rest anywhere, it would be in Arkansaw, where the men are of the real　2
half-horse, half-alligator breed such as grows nowhere else on the face of the
earth.　　　　—DAVID CROCKETT,
Narrative of the Life of David Crockett, 1834
[This alternate spelling of *Arkansas* was used in the title of *The Arkansaw Traveler*, a popular comedy disrespectful of the great state. Poor Arkansas suffered such abuse that some considered giving it a new name. This proposal was rejected in a famous apocryphal speech supposedly delivered in the Arkansas legislature about 1875. The hyperbolic speech has been passed down in a number of versions, some extremely raunchy. The speaker, sometimes identified as Sen. Cassius M. Johnson, concludes, "Change the name of Arkansaw? Hell, No!"]

[Re Arkansas:] Its airs—just breathe them, and they will make you snort like a　3
horse.　　　　—THOMAS B. THORPE, *The Big Bear of Arkansas*, 1841

I've met with ups and downs in life, and better days I've saw;　　　　4
But I never knew what mis'ry were, till I came to Arkansas.
　　　　—ANONYMOUS, *The State of Arkansas*,
19th century, in John A. and Alan Lomax,
Folk Song U.S.A. [1947]
[This song, probably dating from before the Civil War, is an early example of the humorous but unflattering treatment of Arkansas in popular culture. The speaker was a migrant worker, perhaps Irish, who couldn't wait to get out of the state and write this verse.]

Biggest fool I ever saw　　　　5
Came from the state of Arkansas;
Put his shirt on over his coat,
Button his britches up round his throat.
　　　　—ANONYMOUS, folk song, in Howard W. Odum,
Wings on My Feet [1929]

If I die in Arkansas,　　　　6
Jes' ship my body to my mother-in-law.　　　　—ANONYMOUS, folk song

So the duke said these Arkansaw lunkheads couldn't come up to Shakespeare;　7
what they wanted was low comedy—any maybe something rather worse than
low comedy, he reckoned.　　　　—MARK TWAIN,
The Adventures of Huckleberry Finn, 1885
[The duke made up some handbills for his show, with one line in capital letters: "LADIES AND CHILDREN NOT ADMITTED. 'There,' says he, 'if that line don't fetch them, I don't know Arkansaw!'"]

I've never seen nothin; I don't know nothin; I haint got nothin; and I don't want　8
nothin!　　　　—ANONYMOUS, Arkansas saying, c. 1930s

1 There is pretty strong characters down there [in Arkansas]. You can't redeem
'em, you just join 'em.   —WILL ROGERS, Alex Ayres, ed.,
                               The Wit and Wisdom of Will Rogers [1993]
[Rogers's wife was from Arkansas.]

2 Any time you tangle with an Arkansaw hillbilly or hillbillyess, you are going
to run second.   —*Ibid.*

Motto

3   *Regnat populus.*
                 The people rule.

ARMY   *See* MILITARY, THE; WAR

ART

4 Art is long, and Time is fleeting.   —HENRY WADSWORTH LONGFELLOW,
                                             A Psalm of Life, 1839
[An ancient saying expressed in a variety of ways, including the anonymous
traditional *Ars longa, vita brevis*—"Art is long, life is short." Hippocrates,
with reference to the difficulty of mastering the art of medicine in a short lifetime, wrote: "Life is short, art long, opportunity fleeting, experience treacherous, judgment difficult," *Aphorisms.*]

5 Art is power.   —HENRY WADSWORTH LONGFELLOW, *Hyperion,* 1839

6 Art is the gift of God, and must be used unto his glory.
                               —HENRY WADSWORTH LONGFELLOW,
                               Michael Angelo, 1872–1882, published, 1886

7 Art is a jealous mistress.   —RALPH WALDO EMERSON, *Wealth,*
                                        in *The Conduct of Life,* 1860

8 Art without life is a poor affair.   —HENRY JAMES, *The Art of Fiction,* 1888

9 It is art that *makes* life, makes interest, makes importance.
                               —HENRY JAMES, letter to H. G. Wells, July 10, 1915

10 Mrs. Ballinger is one of the ladies who pursue Culture in bands, as though it
were dangerous to meet it alone.   —EDITH WHARTON,
                                                           Xingu, 1916
[For Dorothy Parker on horticulture, see EDUCATION.]

11 Art is the stored honey of the human soul, gathered on wings of misery and
travail.   —THEODORE DREISER, *Life, Art, and America,* 1917

12 Authors and actors and artists and such
Never know nothing, and never know much.
Sculptors and singers and those of their kidney
Tell their affairs from Seattle to Sydney.
Playwrights and poets and such horses' necks
Start off from anywhere, end up at sex.
Diarists, critics, and similar roe

Never say nothing and never say no.
People Who Do Things exceed my endurance;
God, for a man who solicits insurance!
                              —DOROTHY PARKER, *Bohemia*, 1927

In everything that can be called art there is a quality of redemption.   1
                              —RAYMOND CHANDLER, *The Simple Art of Murder*, 1950

Music and art and poetry attune the soul to God.   2
                              —THOMAS MERTON, *No Man Is an Island*, 1955

This [the arts] is an area where we have lagged far behind other countries. We   3
have been so preoccupied with our industrial growth that we have thought of
little else. The culture of a nation is, after all, as important as its economy.
                              —ELEANOR ROOSEVELT, *My Day*, Feb. 27, 1957

This nation cannot afford to be materially rich and spiritually poor.   4
                              —JOHN F. KENNEDY, State of the Union address, 1963
[This is the inscription on the Kennedy Center for the Performing Arts in
Washington, D.C.]

Art is the objectification of feeling and the subjectification of nature.   5
                              —SUZANNE K. LANGER, *Mind:*
                              An Essay on Human Feeling, 1967

ART: AESTHETICS   *See also* ART: CRITICISM; ART:
                                   STYLE IN WRITING & EXPRESSION;
                                   ART: WRITING; BEAUTY; SIMPLICITY

The art of art . . . is simplicity.   —WALT WHITMAN,   6
                                   Preface, *Leaves of Grass*, 1855–92
[More at ART: STYLE IN WRITING & EXPRESSION.]

In art, economy is always beautiful.   —HENRY JAMES, in *Prefaces*   7
                                   (*The Altar of the Dead*), 1907–1909
[See also architect Mies Van der Rohe's motto under ART: ARCHITECTURE.]

The only way of expressing emotion in the form of art is by finding an "objec-   8
tive correlative"; in other words, a set of objects, a situation, a chain of events
which shall be the formula of that *particular* emotion.
                              —T. S. ELIOT, *Hamlet and His Problems*, 1919

Whatever is felt upon the page without being specifically named there—that,   9
one might say, is created. It is the inexplicable presence of the thing not
named, of the overtone divined by the ear but not heard by it, the verbal mood,
the emotional aura of the fact or the thing or the deed, that gives high quality
to the novel or the drama, as well as to poetry itself.
                              —WILLA CATHER, *The Novel Démeublé*, c. 1925
[For her title—"the novel de-furnished"—Cather drew on the elder Alexandre
Dumas. She credits him with the observation that "to make a drama, a man
needed one passion, and four walls."]

Our American professors like their literature clear and cold and pure and very   10
dead.   —SINCLAIR LEWIS, *The American Fear of Literature*,
                              Nobel Prize acceptance speech, Dec. 12, 1930

1 Art strives for form, and hopes for beauty.   —GEORGE BELLOWS,
                                                        quoted in Stanley Walker,
                                                        City Editor, 1934
[Bellows is best known for his paintings of boxing matches and other scenes of city life.]

2 Can you draw sweet water from a foul well?
                                    —BROOKS ATKINSON, review of *Pal Joey,*
                                        New York Times, 1940
[Atkinson, the most influential theater reviewer in the U.S., penned this often-quoted question as he wrestled with a classic critic's dilemma: what to say about a well-done work of which one disapproves. *Pal Joey,* based on a John O'Hara story, featured a sleazy hero and great songs by Richard Rodgers and Lorenz Hart.
    Atkinson could have consulted a senior colleague, George Jean Nathan, who said, "There is no such thing as a dirty theme. There are only dirty writers," *Testament of a Critic,* 1931.]

3 Less is more.   —LUDWIG MIES VAN DER ROHE,
                                            motto
[German-born architect Mies van der Rohe borrowed the aphorism from the 19th-century poet Robert Browning, who used it in *Andrea del Sarto.* Cellist Mstislav Rostropovich totally disagrees. His motto is, "More is more" (quoted in the television program *Kennedy Center Honors Performance,* Dec. 30, 1992). Bandleader Artie Shaw remarked, "I did all you can do with a clarinet, any more would have been less."
    See also Mae West at EXCESS. For another favorite Mies van der Rohe aphorism, see DETAILS & OTHER SMALL THINGS, note under Anonymous.]

4 True originality refocuses the attentive eye.
                            —LINCOLN KIRSTEIN, *What Ballet Is All About,* 1959

ART: ARCHITECTURE   *See also* SCIENCE: TECHNOLOGY
                                                        (for bridges)

5 Form ever follows function.   —LOUIS HENRI SULLIVAN, *The Tall Office*
                                        Building Artistically Considered,
                                    in *Lippincott's Magazine,* March 1896
["Form follows function" was the motto of the Bauhaus school of architecture and art. For a related principle, see Ludwig Mies van der Rohe at ART: AESTHETICS above.]

6 The physician can bury his mistakes, but the architect can only advise his client to plant vines.   —FRANK LLOYD WRIGHT,
                            in *The New York Times Magazine,* Oct. 4, 1953

7 Architecture begins where engineering ends.
                            —WALTER GROPIUS, speech, Harvard University,
                                quoted in Paul Heyer, ed.,
                                Architects on Architecture [1978]

8 Architecture is . . . life itself taking form.
                            —FRANK LLOYD WRIGHT, *An Organic Architecture,* 1970

ART: CRITICISM   *See also* ART: AESTHETICS; CRITICISM; INSULTS

Nature fits all her children with something to do: 1
He who would write and can't write can surely review.
                    —JAMES RUSSELL LOWELL, *A Fable for Critics*, 1848

The public is the only critic whose opinion is worth anything at all.   2
                    —MARK TWAIN, "A General Reply,"
                    The Galaxy magazine, Nov. 1870

Persons attempting to find a motive in this narrative will be prosecuted; per-   3
sons attempting to find a moral in it will be banished; persons attempting to
find a plot in it will be shot.   —MARK TWAIN, "Notice,"
                    Adventures of Huckleberry Finn, 1885
[In 1990, the first half of the handwritten manuscript turned up, with new material and changes. Originally, this "Notice" had not included the reference to
a moral. Twain scholar Victor Doyno speculated in *The New York Times* (May
16, 1995) that the reference was added after the narrative came to focus more
than first planned on the liberation of the slave Jim and Huck's hard lessons in
empathy and integrity.]

The practice of "reviewing" . . . in general has nothing in common with the art   4
of criticism.   —HENRY JAMES,
                    Criticism, 1893
[In *Prefaces*, 1907–1909, writing of his *Portrait of a Lady*, James elaborated:
"To criticize is to appreciate, to appropriate, to take intellectual possession, to
establish in fine a relation with the criticized thing and to make it one's own."]

I don't know anything about music, really, but I know what I like.   5
                    —GELETT BURGESS, "Bromide no. 1,"
                    in *Are You a Bromide?*, 1906
[Burgess was making fun of this cliché, so useful to the uninformed. He coined
this sense of *bromide*; see Burgess under DIFFERENCES.]

I have read your lousy review of Margaret's concert. I've come to the conclu-   6
sion that you are an eight-ulcer man on a four-ulcer job. . . . Someday, I hope to
meet you. When that happens, you'll need a new nose, a lot of beefsteak for
black eyes, and perhaps a supporter below.
                    —HARRY S. TRUMAN, to critic Paul Hume,
                    quoted in *Time* magazine, Dec. 18, 1950
[The president's hotheaded defense of his daughter's singing seemed to some
undignified, but others found it human and refreshing.]

[Critics are] essential to the theater: as ants to a picnic, as boll weevils in a cot-   7
ton field.   —JOSEPH L. MANKIEWICZ, *All About Eve*, 1950

Be kind and considerate with your criticism. . . . It's just as hard to write a bad   8
book as a good book.   —MALCOLM COWLEY, quoted by Ken Kesey,
                    The New York Times [Dec. 31, 1989]

Pleasure is by no means an infallible guide, but it is the least fallible.   9
                    —W. H. AUDEN, *The Dyer's Hand*, 1962

One cannot review a bad book without showing off.   —*Ibid.* 10

1   Interpretation is the revenge of the intellect upon art.
—SUSAN SONTAG, *Against Interpretation*, title essay, 1966

2   [Response to negative reviews:] I cried all the way to the bank.
—LIBERACE, *Liberace, An Autobiography*, 1973

3   Don't read the review, just measure it.
—SIDNEY JANIS, attributed, *New York Times*,
"Week in Review," Oct. 23, 1994
[Janis, an influential Manhattan gallery owner for several decades, did not think much of art reviewers.]

4   Critics ought now and then to hesitate.
—IRVING HOWE, *A Critic's Notebook* [1995]

ART: DANCE

5   One becomes . . . an athlete of God.   —MARTHA GRAHAM,
May 15, 1945

[More at GRACE. See also later Graham quotes below.]

6   When in doubt, twirl.   —TED SHAWN, saying, quoted by Edward Gorey
in *The New Yorker* [Nov. 9, 1992]

7   Dance is motion, not emotion.   —ALWIN NIKOLAIS, saying, quoted in
The New York Times [Jan. 24, 1993]

8   I just put my feet in the air and move them around.
—FRED ASTAIRE,
attributed in the quotation game *Daring "Passages,"*
cited in *The New York Times*, August 21, 1994

9   Dancing is just discovery, discovery, discovery.
—MARTHA GRAHAM, interview,
New York Times, March 31, 1985

10 Dance is the hidden language of the soul.   —*Ibid.*

11 Movement never lies.   —MARTHA GRAHAM, *Blood Memory*, 1991

ART: DRAMA   *See* ART: THEATER, MAGIC, & DRAMA

ART: MUSIC

12 Music is the universal language of mankind—poetry their universal pastime
and delight.   —HENRY WADSWORTH LONGFELLOW, *Outre-Mer;*
a Pilgrimage Beyond the Sea, originally,
The Schoolmaster, c. 1832

13 And the night shall be filled with music,
And the cares that infest the day,
Shall fold their tents like the Arabs,
And as silently steal away.   —HENRY WADSWORTH LONGFELLOW,
The Day Is Done, 1844

God sent his Singers upon earth
With songs of sadness and of mirth.   —HENRY WADSWORTH LONGFELLOW,
The Singers, 1849

1

The banging and slamming and booming and crashing were beyond belief.
—MARK TWAIN, describing a production of *Lohengrin*,
in *A Tramp Abroad*, 1879
[The states were rich in opera companies in the 19th century. But the quality
evidently fluctuated. In the same period, Josh Billings remarked, "I have seen
wimmin in opera, and also have seen them in fits, and I prefer the fits, for then
I know what tew do for them."]

2

Over the piano was printed a notice: Please do not shoot the pianist. He is doing his best.   —OSCAR WILDE, *Leadville* (Colo.),
in *Personal Impressions of America*, 1883
[For an understanding of why the piano player—and everyone else—was
at risk, check ALCOHOL & DRINKING for Wilde's description of the dinner
menu.]

3

Lift Ev'ry Voice and Sing.
—JAMES WELDON JOHNSON, poem title, 1900
[The poem became known informally as the Negro National Anthem.]

4

Opera's no business, it's a disease.   —OSCAR HAMMERSTEIN I, remark
to a reporter, c. 1906
[Theater magnate Hammerstein built the Manhattan Opera House in 1906
to compete with the Met. His opera house in Philadelphia went up two
years later. Alas, his wonderful Manhattan Opera Company lasted just four
seasons.]

5

When people hear good music, it makes them homesick for something they
never had, and never will have.   —EDGAR WATSON HOWE,
Country Town Sayings, 1911

6

If you don't like the blues, you've got a hole in your soul.
—ANONYMOUS, saying

7

Drum on your drums, batter on your banjos, sob on the long cool
winding saxophones.
Go to it, O jazzmen.   —CARL SANDBURG, *Jazz Fantasia*, 1920

8

Classic music is th' kind that we keep thinkin'll turn into a tune.
—FRANK MCKINNEY "KIN" HUBBARD, *Comments of
Abe Martin and His Neighbors*, 1923

9

I care not who writes the laws of a country so long as I may listen to its songs.
—GEORGE JEAN NATHAN, *The World in Falseface*, 1923

10

It Don't Mean a Thing If It Ain't Got That Swing.
—DUKE ELLINGTON, song title, 1932

11

Lady, if you got to ask, you ain't got it.
—THOMAS "FATS" WALLER,
response when asked to explain rhythm, attributed
[Similarly, Louis Armstrong is said to have replied, "Man, if you gotta ask,
you'll never know," when asked what jazz is.]

12

1 If, as is nearly always the case, music appears to express something, this is only an illusion and not a reality.   —IGOR STRAVINSKY, *An Autobiography*, 1936

2 Music heard so deeply
That it is not heard at all, but you are the music
While the music lasts.   —T. S. ELIOT, *Four Quartets:
The Dry Salvages*, 1941

3 Play it, Sam. Play "As Time Goes By."
—JULIUS EPSTEIN, PHILIP EPSTEIN, & HOWARD KOCH,
Casablanca, screenplay, 1942

4 Composers shouldn't think too much—it interferes with their plagiarism.
—HOWARD DIETZ, news reports, Dec. 31, 1974

5 There's no addiction like the eight o'clock curtain at the opera.
—RUDOLF BING, quoted in *The New York Times*
[March 7, 1995]
[Bing was general manager of the Metropolitan Opera in New York from 1950 to 1972.]

6 Form is rhythm on a larger scale.
—TOM HARRELL, quoted by Whitney Balliett,
The New Yorker, April 15, 1996
[Music critic Balliett ranks Harrell, a trumpeter, flugelhornist, and composer, among the best contemporary jazz artists. Harrell has overcome diagnosed schizophrenia with the help of medicine and musical genius.]

ART: PAINTING   *See* ART: VISUAL

ART: POETRY

7 You will never be alone with a poet in your pocket.
—JOHN ADAMS, letter to his son
John Quincy Adams, Dec. 19, 1793

8 Poetry their universal pastime and delight.
—HENRY WADSWORTH LONGFELLOW, *Outre-Mer*, c. 1832
[More at ART: MUSIC.]

9 I would define, in brief, the poetry of words as the rhythmical creation of beauty. Its sole arbiter is taste. . . . Unless incidentally, it has no concern whatever with duty or with truth.
—EDGAR ALLAN POE, review of Henry Wadsworth Longfellow's
Ballads and Other Poems, in *Graham's Magazine*,
April 1842, incorporated into *The Poetic Principle* [1850]

10 The experience of each new age requires a new confession, and the world seems always waiting for its poet.   —RALPH WALDO EMERSON, *The Poet*,
in *Essays: Second Series*, 1844

11 Poetry must be as new as foam, and as old as the rock.
—RALPH WALDO EMERSON, *Journal*, March 1845

To have great poets, there must be great audiences, too.   1
—WALT WHITMAN, "Ventures on an Old Theme,"
in *Notes Left Over*

Publishing a volume of poetry is like dropping a rose petal down the Grand   2
Canyon and waiting for the echo.   —DON MARQUIS, *The Sun Dial*,
New York *Sun* column, started 1912

Immature poets imitate; mature poets steal.   3
—T. S. ELIOT, *Philip Massinger*, 1920

The courage of the poet is to keep ajar the door that leads to madness.   4
—CHRISTOPHER MORLEY, *Inward Ho*, 1923

Poetry is the opening and closing of a door, leaving those who look through to   5
guess about what is seen during a moment.
—CARL SANDBURG, *Poetry Considered*,
in *The Atlantic Monthly*, March 1923

A poem should not mean   6
But be.   —ARCHIBALD MACLEISH, *Ars Poetica*, 1926

Genuine poetry can communicate before it is understood.   7
—T. S. ELIOT, *Dante*, 1929

Poetry atrophies when it gets too far from music.   8
—EZRA POUND, *How to Read*, 1931

Writing free verse is like playing tennis with the net down.   9
—ROBERT FROST, speech at Milton Academy
in Massachusetts, May 17, 1935

Poetry is the subject of the poem.   —WALLACE STEVENS, *The Man with*   10
the Blue Guitar, 1937
[In *A High-toned Old Christian Woman*, 1923, Stevens described poetry as
"the supreme fiction." In *Notes Toward a Supreme Fiction*, 1947, he wrote,
"You must become an ignorant man again / And see the sun again with an ignorant eye / And see it clearly in the idea of it." In accepting the National Book
Award in 1955, he said, "We can never have great poetry unless we believe that
poetry serves great ends." Also, "The poem is a nature created by the poet [and
should contain] the full flower of the actual, not the California fruit of the
ideal," Milton J. Bates, ed., expanded *Opus Posthumous*. And see below.]

A poem is a meteor.   11
—WALLACE STEVENS, *Adagia*, in *Opus Posthumous* [1957]

Poetry is a search for the inexplicable.   *—Ibid.*   12

The poet is the priest of the invisible.   *—Ibid.*   13

The figure a poem makes. It begins in delight and ends in wisdom. The figure   14
is the same as for love.   —ROBERT FROST, Preface, *Collected Poems*, 1939

Poetry is a way of taking life by the throat.   15
—ROBERT FROST, comment, quoted in *Bartlett's*
Familiar Quotations, 16th edition [1992]

1   There are so many ways to ruin a poem it's quite amazing good ones ever get
    written.   —JOHN BERRYMAN, remark to Philip Levine, 1954

2   It is difficult
    to get the news from poems,
    yet men die miserably every day
    for lack
    of what is found there.   —WILLIAM CARLOS WILLIAMS, *Asphodel,*
                                         That Greeny Flower,
                                         in *A Journey to Love,* 1955

3   When power narrows the areas of man's concern, poetry reminds him of the
    richness and diversity of his existence. When power corrupts, poetry cleanses.
                                         —JOHN F. KENNEDY, speech, Oct. 26, 1963

4   The only thing that can save the world is the reclaiming of the awareness of
    the world. That's what poetry does.
                                         —ALLEN GINSBERG, quoted in Helen Weaver,
                                         review of Ginsberg's *Collected Poems,*
                                         Litchfield County Times [May 31, 1985]

5   Poetry . . . is always unexpected, and always as faithful and honest as dreams.
                                         —ALICE WALKER, *We Have a Beautiful Mother,* 1991

ART: STYLE IN WRITING   *See also* ART: AESTHETICS; ART: WRITING;
& EXPRESSION   LANGUAGE & WORDS; SIMPLICITY; STYLE

6   The art of art, the glory of expression, and the sunshine of the light of letters,
    is simplicity.   —WALT WHITMAN, Preface, *Leaves of Grass,* 1855–92

7   Spartans, stoics, heroes, saints, and gods use a short and positive speech.
                                         —RALPH WALDO EMERSON, *The Superlative,*
                                         in *Lectures and Biographical Sketches,* 1883

8   As to the Adjective: when in doubt, strike it out.
                                         —MARK TWAIN, *Pudd'nhead Wilson's Calendar,*
                                         in *Pudd'nhead Wilson,* 1894

9   A successful book is not made of what is in it, but what is left out of it.
                                         —MARK TWAIN, letter to William Dean Howells, Feb. 23, 1897

10 He has lived heroic poetry, and he can, therefore, afford to talk simple prose.
                                         —WILLIAM DEAN HOWELLS, referring to a speech by Booker
                                         T. Washington at Madison Square Garden Concert Hall,
                                         in New York City, on Dec. 4, 1899

11 Omit needless words. Vigorous writing is concise. A sentence should contain
    no unnecessary words, a paragraph no unnecessary sentences, for the same rea-
    son that a drawing should have no unnecessary lines and a machine no unnec-
    essary parts.   —WILLIAM STRUNK, JR., *The Elements of Style,* 1918

12 His [Warren Harding's] speeches left the impression of an army of pompous
    phrases moving over the landscape in search of an idea.
                                         —WILLIAM G. MCADOO, quoted in Leon A. Harris,
                                         The Fine Art of Political Wit [1964]
    [More at WARREN G. HARDING, where there is also H. L. Mencken's characteriza-

tion of Harding's writing as "rumble and bumble, flap and doodle, balder and dash."]

Verbal felicity is the result of art and diligence and refusing to be false.   1
    —MARIANNE MOORE, quoted by Louise Bogan,
    College English, Feb. 1953

Good style . . . is unseen style. It is style that is felt.   2
    —SIDNEY LUMET, *Making Movies,* 1995

ART: THEATER, DRAMA, & MAGIC

Behind the curtain's mystic fold   3
The glowing future lies unrolled.
    —BRET HARTE, speech, opening of the California Theatre,
    San Francisco, Jan. 19, 1870

A man in the theatrical business is allowed more liberties than his business   4
brothers. His business demands it.
    —OSCAR HAMMERSTEIN I, explanation of his
    relationship with an opera singer known as the
    Texas Patti, quoted in *American Heritage* [Feb. 1973]

The Great Actor always must act. . . . Every last second of his life must be pose   5
and posture.   —LIONEL BARRYMORE, 1904,
    quoted in Gene Fowler,
    Good Night, Sweet Prince [1943]

If you have ever been an actor . . . why it just about ruins you for any useful   6
employment for the rest of your life.
    —WILL ROGERS, in Alex Ayres, ed.,
    The Wit and Wisdom of Will Rogers [1993]
[Rogers noticed that the same is true of politics: "Once a man wants to hold a public office, he is absolutely no good for honest work," *Weekly Articles,* March 22, 1925.]

Satire is what closes on Saturday night.   7
    —GEORGE S. KAUFMAN, saying, c. 1930,
    attributed in Howard Teichmann, *George S. Kaufman* [1972]
[See also James Thurber at HUMOR.]

I'd rather play a maid than be one.   8
    —HATTIE McDANIEL, response when criticized for playing the
    role of Mammy in the 1939 movie *Gone With the Wind,*
    quoted in *The New York Times,* "Editorial Notebook"
    [Oct. 19, 1994]
[McDaniel was the first African-American to win an Academy Award.]

There's No Business Like Show Business.   9
    —IRVING BERLIN, song title, *Annie Get Your Gun,* 1946

[Actor:] What is my motivation?   10
[Director George Abbott:] Your job.
    —GEORGE ABBOTT, quoted in *The New York Times,*
    obituary [Feb. 2, 1995]
[Abbott, a legend in his time—he worked until his death at age 107—was making fun of the fashionable Method school of acting, which encourages

actors to find motivation for their onstage performance in their offstage experience.]

1   Speak low and speak slow.   —JOHN WAYNE,
                                                       advice to young actors
[Cited by attorney Robert L. Shapiro in *The Champion*, magazine of the National Association of Criminal Defense Lawyers, Jan.–Feb. 1993. Shapiro recommended that lawyers use the same technique when talking to the press.]

2   Nobody can really *like* an actor   —ALFRED HITCHCOCK, quoted in Donald
                                            Spoto, *The Dark Side of Genius:*
                                            The Life of Alfred Hitchcock [1983]

3   You can make a killing in the theater, but not a living.
                                          —ROBERT ANDERSON, c. 1954
[Playwright Anderson, author of *Tea and Sympathy*, recalls that he wrote this often-quoted bon mot in an article for a Sunday edition of either the *New York Herald Tribune* or *The New York Times*. He had added, "and that killing is taxed at ninety percent." In subsequent lectures, however, he moderated the warning, promising that although you can't make a living, "you can make a life."]

4   [A play:] a snare for the truth of human experience.
                                          —TENNESSEE WILLIAMS, stage direction,
                                          Cat on a Hot Tin Roof, 1955

5   If Hitler's alive, I hope he's out of town with a musical.
                                          —LARRY GELBART, attributed
[Gelbart suffered through an agonizing Washington tryout of his musical *The Conquering Hero*. He is best known as coauthor with Burt Shevelov of the musical *A Funny Thing Happened on the Way to the Forum* (1962) and as writer of the *M.A.S.H.* television series.]

6   What if the world is some kind of—of *show!* . . . What if we are only talent assembled by the Great Talent Scout Up Above! The Great Show of Life! Starring Everybody! Suppose entertainment is the Purpose of Life!
                                          —PHILIP ROTH, *On the Air*, short story
[For a similar notion, see Ishmael Reed at THE UNIVERSE.]

7   The movie actor, like the sacred king of primitive tribes, is a god in captivity.
                                          —ALEXANDER CHASE, *Perspective*, 1966

8   If an actor has a message, he should call Western Union. An actor's job is to act, nothing more.   —HUMPHREY BOGART, quoted in Stephen Humphrey Bogart,
                                          In Search of My Father [1995]

9   The trouble with the theater is that it's no longer a way of life for an audience. It's just a way to kill an evening.   —JESSICA TANDY, comment, 1986,
                                          quoted in *The New York Times*,
                                          obituary [Sept. 12, 1994]

10 Theater was a verb before it was a noun.
                                          —MARTHA GRAHAM, *Blood Memory*, 1991
[For other verbs see Buckminster Fuller at GOD, and Ulysses S. Grant at ACTION & DOING.]

You can't be boring. Life is boring. The weather is boring. Actors must not be   1
boring.   —STELLA ADLER, *New York Times*, obituary [Dec. 22, 1992]

The mind is led on, step by step, to defeat its own logic.   2
—DAI VERNON, definition of magic,
New York Times, Feb. 19, 1994
[For another magician on reality and perception, see Jerry Andrus at REALITY,
ILLUSIONS, & IMAGES.]

ART: VISUAL   *See also* KNOWLEDGE (Walker Evans)

In a big picture you can see what o'clock it is, afternoon or morning, if it's hot   3
or cold, winter or summer, and what kind of people are there, and what they
are doing, and why they are doing it.
—THOMAS EAKINS, letter from Paris, c. 1866,
cited in *The New Yorker*, Dec. 26, 1995/Jan. 2, 1996

The supreme gift, after light, is scale.   4
—HELEN FRANKENTHALER, in Frank O'Hara,
Robert Motherwell, 1965

There are things nobody would see if I didn't photograph them.   5
—DIANE ARBUS, in *Diane Arbus*, 1972

A painting [is] a symbol for the universe.   6
—CORITA KENT, in *Newsweek*, Dec. 17, 1984

ART: WRITING   *See also* ART: STYLE IN WRITING &
EXPRESSION; BOOKS & READING

All writing comes by the grace of God.   7
—RALPH WALDO EMERSON, *Experience*, in *Essays:
Second Series*, 1844

Writing may be either the record of a deed or a deed. It is nobler when it is a   8
deed.   —HENRY DAVID THOREAU, *Journal*, Jan. 7, 1844

It is the business of the novel to picture daily life in the most exact terms   9
possible.   —WILLIAM DEAN HOWELLS,
interview with Stephen Crane, 1894
[Howells was a leader in the realist movement in fiction, a movement that inspired extensive controversy. Ambrose Bierce called realism "the art of depicting nature as seen by toads." Realist Henry James said that realism in fiction
meant being "bravely and richly, and continuously psychological." His brother
William, pointed out that without the work of minds, reality lacks meaning:
"Our minds are not here simply to copy a reality that is already complete.
They are here to complete it, to add to its importance by their own remodeling
of it." The subject is treated in David E. Shi's *Realism in American Thought
and Culture*, 1994. See also REALITY, ILLUSIONS, & IMAGES.]

If you steal from one author, it's plagiarism; if you steal from many, it's   10
research.   —WILSON MIZNER, attributed

1   Literature is news that stays news.   —EZRA POUND, *How to Read*, 1931

2   What I like in a good author is not what he says, but what he whispers.
        —LOGAN PEARSALL SMITH, *Afterthoughts*, 1931

3   I always say, keep a diary and some day it'll keep you.
        —MAE WEST, *Every Day's a Holiday*, 1937

4   No tears in the writer, no tears in the reader.
        —ROBERT FROST, Preface, *Collected Poems*, 1939

5   The art of fiction is dead. Reality has strangled invention. Only the utterly im-
    possible, the inexpressibly fantastic can ever be plausible again.
            —WALTER "RED" SMITH, report on the final game
            of baseball's National League playoff, 1951
    [Bobby Thomson, at bat for the Giants in the bottom of the ninth, his team
    down 4–2, with one out and two on, hit a home run—the "shot heard round the
    world"—to beat the Dodgers.]

6   One must be ruthless with one's own writing or someone else will be.
            —JOHN BERRYMAN, 1954
    [Poet Philip Levine, who studied with Berryman, reported this remark in *The
    New York Times Book Review*, Dec. 26, 1993.]

7   For a true writer, each book should be a new beginning where he tries again for
    something that is beyond attainment.
            —ERNEST HEMINGWAY, speech in acceptance of the
            Nobel Prize for literature, 1954

8   The writer's only responsibility is to his art.
            —WILLIAM FAULKNER, interview, *The Paris Review*, spring 1956

9   If a writer has to rob his mother, he will not hesitate; the *Ode on a Grecian
    Urn* is worth any number of old ladies.   —*Ibid.*

10 The most essential gift for a good writer is a built-in, shockproof shit detector.
    This is the writer's radar, and all great writers have had it.
            —ERNEST HEMINGWAY, in *The Paris Review*, spring 1958

11 Literary genius is not an equal opportunity employer.
            —SUSAN SONTAG, speech, 1968 International PEN Congress

12 We tell ourselves stories in order to live.
            —JOAN DIDION, *The White Album: A Chronicle of Survival
            in the Sixties*, in *New West*, June 4, 1979

13 There's nothing to writing. All you do is sit down at a typewriter and open a
    vein.   —WALTER "RED" SMITH, in *Reader's Digest*, July 1982

14 Being a great writer is not the same as writing great.
            —JOHN UPDIKE, in *The New Yorker*, May 20, 1985

15 If there is a book you really want to read but it hasn't been written yet, then
    you must write it.
            —TONI MORRISON
    [This has been attributed to Morrison in a number of sources, including *The
    New York Times*. She told this book's editors that she remembers only that she
    said it in a speech.]

Be aware that your reader is at least as bright as you are.   1
　　　　　　　—WILLIAM MAXWELL, maxim, quoted by Larry Woiwode,
　　　　　　　　　in *The New York Times Book Review*, August 14, 1988
[Maxwell, a novelist, edited fiction at *The New Yorker* magazine for forty
years.]

ASPIRATION

See AMBITION & ASPIRATION; DREAMS &
DREAMERS; IDEAS & IDEALS

ATHEISM

See also GOD

[The Bible] has noble poetry in it; and some clever fables; and some blood-   2
drenched history; and a wealth of obscenity; and upwards of a thousand lies.
　　　　　　　—MARK TWAIN, *Letters from Earth* [1962]

My atheism, like that of Spinoza, is true piety towards the universe, and denies   3
only gods fashioned by men in their own image, to be servants of their human
interests.　　　　　—GEORGE SANTAYANA, *On My Friendly Critics*,
　　　　　　　　　in *Soliloquies in England and Later Soliloquies*, 1922

In spite of all the yearnings of men, no one can produce a single fact or reason   4
to support the belief in God and in personal immortality.
　　　　　　　—CLARENCE DARROW, *Sign* magazine, May 1938

There are no atheists in the foxholes.　　　　—WILLIAM THOMAS CUMMINGS,   5
　　　　　　　　　field sermon, Bataan, 1942
[Father Cummings, a Maryknoll missionary and commissioned first lieutenant, courageously provided solace to the doomed American and Filipino
troops on the Bataan peninsula. He refused to leave when he had the chance,
and was taken prisoner when Bataan surrendered to the Japanese. He was included in the sixty-mile Death March that killed 14,000 of the 70,000 prisoners. See also WORLD WAR II.]

An atheist is a man who has no invisible means of support.   6
　　　　　　　—FULTON J. SHEEN, *Look* magazine, Dec. 14, 1955

AUSTRALIA

See NATIONS

AUTOMOBILES

See SCIENCE: TECHNOLOGY

AUTUMN

See NATURE: SEASONS

B

BAD TIMES

See also DEPRESSION, THE; MODERN TIMES; TROUBLE

1 Lost is our old simplicity of times,
The world abounds with laws, and teems with crimes.
—ANONYMOUS, from the *Pennsylvania Gazette*, Feb. 8, 1775,
borrowed from an earlier, unidentified London magazine

2 These are the times that try men's souls.
—THOMAS PAINE, *The American Crisis*, Dec. 1776
[More at AMERICAN REVOLUTION.]

3 Society seems everywhere unhinged, and the demon of blood and slaughter has
been let loose upon us. —HEZEKIAH NILES,
in *Niles' Weekly Register*, 1835
[The *Niles' Register* was a popular newsweekly. In the age of Jackson, the conflict between the privileged and the laboring classes was intense, and people feared that a revolution might erupt. See also below and under CAPITALISM & CAPITAL V. LABOR.]

4 In society as it is now constituted, monotony, uniformity, intellectual inaction, and torpor reign: distrust, isolation, separation, conflict, and antagonism are almost universal: very little expansion of the generous affections and feelings obtain. . . . Society is spiritually a desert.
—ALBERT BRISBANE,
article in *The Bay State Democrat*, Jan. 15, 1844.
[Brisbane was the nation's leading Fourierite, a perceptive anti-capitalist but not strong on solutions.]

5 This is an age of the world where nations are trembling and convulsed.
—HARRIET BEECHER STOWE, *Uncle Tom's Cabin*, 1852
[More at INJUSTICE.]

6 The age is dull and mean. Men creep,
Not walk. —JOHN GREENLEAF WHITTIER, *Line Inscribed to Friends Under
Arrest for Treason Against the Slave Power*, 1856

Can anybody remember when the times were not hard, and money not scarce? 1
—RALPH WALDO EMERSON, Works and Days,
in Society and Solitude, 1870

Never was there, perhaps, more hollowness at heart than at present, and here 2
in the United States.　　　　　—WALT WHITMAN, *Democratic Vistas*, 1871

The grass will grow in the streets of a hundred cities. 3
—HERBERT HOOVER, speech, Oct. 31, 1936
[More at ECONOMICS.]

The epidemic of world lawlessness is spreading. 4
—FRANKLIN D. ROOSEVELT, "Quarantine the Aggressors" speech,
Chicago, Oct. 5, 1937

I saw the best minds of my generation destroyed by madness, starving hysteri- 5
cal naked.
—ALLEN GINSBERG, *Howl*, 1956
[More at MADNESS.]

BARRIERS　　　　　　　　　　　　　　　*See* DIVISIONS & BARRIERS

BEAUTY
See also APPEARANCES; ART: AESTHETICS;
BODY & LOOKS

The perception of beauty is a moral test. 6
—HENRY DAVID THOREAU, *Journal*, June 21, 1852

With beauty before me, I walk 7
With beauty behind me, I walk
With beauty above and about me, I walk.
—ANONYMOUS, Navaho night chant, in Frank Bergon &
Zeese Papaniklas, *Looking Far West* [1978]
[More at NATURE.]

A beautiful woman is a practical poet. 8
—RALPH WALDO EMERSON, *Beauty*, in *The Conduct of Life*, 1860

Beauty as we feel it is something indescribable: what it is or what it means can 9
never be said.　　　　　—GEORGE SANTAYANA, *The Sense of Beauty*, 1896

The superior gratification derived from the use and contemplation of costly 10
and supposedly beautiful products is, commonly, in great measure, a gratification of our sense of costliness masquerading under the name of beauty.
—THORSTEIN VEBLEN, *The Theory of the Leisure Class*, 1899

A Pretty Girl Is Like a Melody.　　　　　　—IRVING BERLIN, 11
song title, *Ziegfeld Follies*, 1919

Beauty is momentary in the mind— 12
The fitful tracing of a portal;
But in the flesh it is immortal;
The body dies; the body's beauty lives.
—WALLACE STEVENS, *Peter Quince at the Clavier*, 1923

1   Beauty is everlasting
And dust is for a time.
                                                —MARIANNE MOORE,
                                                    In Distrust of Merits, 1941

2   I'm tired of all this business about beauty being only skin-deep. That's deep
enough. What do you want—an adorable pancreas?
                                —JEAN KERR, *Mirror, Mirror on the Wall*
                                I Don't Want to Hear One Word Out of You,
                                in *The Snake Has All the Lines*, 1960

BIGNESS   *See also* SMALLNESS; STRENGTH & TOUGHNESS

3   I think no virtue goes with size.
                                                —RALPH WALDO EMERSON,
                                                    The Titmouse, in *Poems*, 1847

4   The bigger they come, the harder they fall.
                                                —JOHN L. SULLIVAN, saying, c. 1900
[More at SPORTS.]

5   We must develop huge demonstrations, because the world is used to big, dramatic affairs. They think in terms of hundreds of thousands and millions and
billions . . . Nothing little counts.
                            —A. PHILIP RANDOLPH, speech, policy conference,
                        March on Washington Movement, Detroit, Sept. 26, 1942
[Randolph was the most influential African-American labor leader of his
time—and it was a time in which labor gained great power.]

BILL OF RIGHTS   *See* CONSTITUTION, THE

BIOLOGY   *See* SCIENCE: BIOLOGY & PHYSIOLOGY

BLACKS   *See* RACES & PEOPLES

BOASTING

6   I'm that same David Crockett, fresh from the backwoods, half-horse, half-
alligator, a little touched with the snapping-turtle; can wade the Mississippi,
leap the Ohio, ride upon a streak of lightning, and slip without a scratch down
a honey-locust; can whip my weight in wild cats—and if any gentleman
pleases, for a ten dollar bill, he may throw in a panther—hug a bear too close
for comfort, and eat any man opposed to Jackson.
                        —DAVID CROCKETT, in *Sketches and Eccentricities of
                            Col. David Crockett, of West Tennessee*, 1833
[Crockett served three terms in the House, 1827–31 and 1833–35, representing
a district in western Tennessee. His image as a backwoods hero was largely
self-created. He was so ugly, he said, that his grin would bring a coon down
from a tree—and once, mistaking a tree knot for a coon, he grinned the bark
right off the tree. He also had "the roughest racking horse, the prettiest sister,
the surest rifle, and the ugliest dog in the district" (speech, House of Representatives, cited in *Davy Crockett's Almanac*, 1837). Campaigning in 1827, and
short of funds to treat voters in the manner to which they were accustomed, he
bagged a coon and traded its skin to a Yankee vendor for a quart of rum. While
the voters drank up, Crockett snuck the skin from beneath the bar, then traded

it back for another quart. In this way, he obtained ten quarts of rum for the same skin, won the election, and earned his nickname as "the coonskin congressmen." After his death at the Alamo in 1836, Crockett quickly became a mythic figure; tall tales about him were popularized in a series of "Crockett" almanacs published through 1856.]

I'm a Salt River roarer! I'm a ring-tailed squealer! I'm a reg'lar screamer from the ol' Massassip'! WHOOP! I'm the very infant that refused his milk before his eyes were open, and called out for a bottle of old rye! I love the women, and I'm chockful of fight! I'm half wild horse and half cock-eyed alligator, and the rest of me is crooked snags an' red-hot snappin' turkle. I can hit like fourth-proof lightnin' an' every lick I make in the woods lets in an acre o' sunshine. I can out-run, out-jump, out-shoot, out-brag, out-drink, an' out-fight, rough-an'-tumble, no holts barred, ary man on both sides of the river from Pittsburgh to New Orleans an' back ag'in to St. Louiee. Come on, you flatters, you bargers, you milk-white mechanics, an' see how tough I am to chaw! I ain't had a fight for two days an' I'm spilein' for exercise. Cock-a-doodle-do!
   —MIKE FINK, his brag,
    in Walter Blair and Franklin J. Meine,
     Mike Fink, King of the Mississippi Keelboatmen [1933]
[Legends collected around Fink, who was a deadly shot, a diabolical practical joker, and "King of the Keelboatmen." These laborers floated cargos down the Mississippi River to New Orleans and laboriously poled and warped their way back, a round-trip that could take nine months. The notoriously rough, coarse, riotous keelboatmen gradually were displaced by steamboats. By 1823, Fink had left the river and was working for a fur company in Montana. While engaging in the frontier sport of shooting a tin whisky cup off another man's head, he killed the fellow, perhaps not accidentally. He then was shot to death himself by a friend of the man he had slain.]

Whoo-oop! I'm the original iron-jawed, brass-mounted, copper-bellied corpse-maker from the wilds of Arkansas! Look at me! I'm the man they call Sudden Death and General Desolation! Sired by a hurricane, dam'd by an earthquake, half-brother to the cholera, nearly related to the smallpox on my mother's side. Look at me! I take nineteen alligators and a bar'l of whiskey for breakfast when I'm in robust health, and a bushel of rattlesnakes and a dead body when I'm ailing. I split the everlasting rocks with my glance, and I squench the thunder when I speak! Whoo-oop! Stand back and give me room according to my strength! Blood's my natural drink, and the wails of the dying is music to my ear. Cast your eye on me gentlemen! and lay low and hold your breath, for I'm 'bout to turn myself loose!
   —ANONYMOUS, keelboatman's boast
    in Mark Twain, *Life on the Mississippi*, 1883
[Twain apprenticed as a steamboat pilot before the Civil War. By Twain's time, the keelboats were gone, and the men had become hands on steamboats or else tended the huge coal- and timber-carrying rafts that the steamboats shepherded downriver. The rough-talking tradition of Mike Fink remained very much alive, however.]

I come to this country riding a lion, whipping him over the head with a .45 and picking my teeth with a .38 and wearing a .45 on each hip, using a cactus for a piller, whe-ee-e! I'm a two-gun man and very bad man and won't do to monkey with. Whe-ee-o, I'm a bad man! Whoopee!
   —ANONYMOUS, cowboy yell, from B. A. Botkin,
    Tall Talk and Tall Tales of the Southwest,
    in *The New Mexico Candle* [June 18, 1933]

1   I'm wild and woolly
    And full of fleas;
    Ain't never been curried
    Below the knees.
    I'm a wild she wolf
    From Bitter Creek,
    And it's my time
    To h-o-w-l, whoop-i-e-e-ee.   —ANONYMOUS, cowboy boast, in *American*
                                    Ballads and Folk Songs [1934], collected and
                                    compiled by John A. Lomax and Alan Lomax

2   It ain't braggin' if you can do it.   —DIZZY DEAN, attributed

BODY & LOOKS

See also BEAUTY; HEALTH; MIND, THOUGHT, &
UNDERSTANDING (Dickinson); PHYSICAL FITNESS

3   If anything is sacred, the human body is sacred.
                        —WALT WHITMAN, *I Sing the Body Electric*, 1855

4   The Lord prefers common-looking people. That is the reason he makes so
    many of them.   —ABRAHAM LINCOLN, Dec. 23, 1863, quoted by John Hay,
                            Letters of John Hay and Extracts from His Diary,
                            C. L. Hay, ed. [1908, reprint 1969]
    [As Hay tells it, Lincoln reported that he'd had a dream in which he was in a
    crowd, and someone, recognizing him, had said, "He is a very common-
    looking man." The president responded with the above remark.]

5   My face, I don't mind it,
    Because I'm behind it;
    It's the people out front that I jar.   —WOODROW WILSON,
                                                    saying
    [Surely not original with Wilson, but since he was unaffected enough to use it,
    he deserves credit.]

6   The body dies; the body's beauty lives.
                        —WALLACE STEVENS, *Peter Quince at the Clavier*, 1923
    [More at BEAUTY.]

7   The strongest, surest way to the soul is through the flesh.
                        —MABEL DODGE, *Lorenzo in Taos*, 1932
    [The Lorenzo of the title is D. H. Lawrence.]

8   The human body is an instrument for the production of art in the human soul.
                —ALFRED NORTH WHITEHEAD, *Adventures of Ideas*, 1933

9   The body says what words cannot.   —MARTHA GRAHAM, interview,
                                            New York Times, March 31, 1985

BOLDNESS & INITIATIVE

See also ACTION & DOING; DECISION;
MILITARY STRATEGY; SPEED

10 Offense is the best defense.
                                                    —ANONYMOUS
    [Traced to the 1700s in Bartlett Jere Whiting, ed., *Early American Proverbs and*
    Proverbial Phrases, 1977.]

Take calculated risks. That is quite different from being rash.   1
    —GEORGE S. PATTON, letter to his son, June 6, 1944 [D day]

BOOKS & READING   *See also* ART: WRITING; CENSORSHIP; MEDIA

I cannot live without books.   —THOMAS JEFFERSON,   2
    letter to John Adams, June 10, 1815

Books are for nothing but to inspire.   —RALPH WALDO EMERSON,   3
    The American Scholar, 1837

There is then creative reading as well as creative writing.   —*Ibid.*   4

Read the best books first, or you may not have a chance to read them at all.   5
    —HENRY DAVID THOREAU, *A Week on the
Concord and Merrimack Rivers*, 1849

How many a man has dated a new era in his life from the reading of a book.   6
    —HENRY DAVID THOREAU, "Reading," *Walden*, 1854

Books must be read as deliberately and reservedly as they were written.   7
    —*Ibid.*

Books are the treasured wealth of the world and the fit inheritance of genera-   8
tions and nations.   —*Ibid.*

Never read any book that is not a year old.   9
    —RALPH WALDO EMERSON, *In Praise of Books*,
in *The Conduct of Life*, 1860

Some books are so familiar reading them is like being home again.   10
    —LOUISA MAY ALCOTT, *Little Women*, 1868

There is no frigate like a book   11
To take us lands away,
Nor any coursers like a page
Of prancing poetry.   —EMILY DICKINSON, poem no. 1263, c. 1873

The love of learning, the sequestered nooks,   12
And all the sweet serenity of books.   —HENRY WADSWORTH LONGFELLOW,
    Morituri Salutamus, 1875

Wear the old coat and buy the new book.   13
    —AUSTIN PHELPS, *The Theory of Preaching;
Lectures on Homilectics*, 1881

Wisdom is wealth, and every good book is equivalent to a wise head—the head   14
may die, but the book may live forever.
    —JOSEPH WHEELER, speech, U.S. House of Representatives,
      debate on constructing the Library of Congress, Feb. 1883
[Rep. Wheeler was a well-known Confederate cavalry commander.]

Camerado, this is no book,   15
Whoso touches this touches a man.   —WALT WHITMAN, *So Long!*,
    in *Leaves of Grass*, 1891–1892

1　"Classic." A book which people praise and don't read.
　　　　　　　　—MARK TWAIN, *Pudd'nhead Wilson's New Calendar*,
　　　　　　　　in *Following the Equator*, 1897

2　Literature is my utopia.　　　　HELEN KELLER, *The Story of My Life*, 1902

3　The mortality of all inanimate things is terrible to me, but that of books most
　of all.　　　　　　—WILLIAM DEAN HOWELLS, letter to Charles Eliot Norton,
　　　　　　　　April 6, 1903

4　No girl was ever ruined by a book.
　　　　　　　　　　—JAMES J. "JIMMY" WALKER, attributed
　[Walker, a ladies' man, was mayor of New York City from 1925 to 1932. See
　also Herman Melville at CENSORSHIP.]

5　People say that life is the thing, but I prefer reading.
　　　　　　　　　　—LOGAN PEARSALL SMITH, *Afterthoughts*, 1931

6　All good books are alike in that they are truer than if they really happened and
　after you have finished reading one you will feel that it all happened to you,
　and afterwards it all belongs to you.
　　　　　　　　　　—ERNEST HEMINGWAY *An Old Newsman Writes*,
　　　　　　　　in *Esquire*, Dec. 1934

7　All modern American literature comes from one book by Mark Twain called
　Huckleberry Finn.
　　　　　　　　　—ERNEST HEMINGWAY, *Green Hills of Africa*, 1935

8　People die, but books never die.
　　　　　　　　　　—FRANKLIN D. ROOSEVELT, speech to the American
　　　　　　　　Booksellers Association, April 23, 1942
　[He was speaking with reference to book burning in Nazi Germany.]

9　There are some people who read too much: bibliobibuli.
　　　　　　　　　　—H. L. MENCKEN, *Minority Report:
　　　　　　　　H. L. Mencken's Notebooks* [1956]

10　What really knocks me out is a book that, when you're all done reading it, you
　wish that the author that wrote it was a terrific friend of yours and you could
　call him up on the phone whenever you felt like it. That doesn't happen much,
　though.　　　　　　—J. D. SALINGER, *The Catcher in the Rye*, 1951

11　We shouldn't teach great books; we should teach a love of reading.
　　　　　　　　　　—B. F. SKINNER, quoted in Richard I. Evans,
　　　　　　　　B. F. Skinner: The Man and His Ideas

12　Some books are undeservedly forgotten; none are undeservedly remembered.
　　　　　　　　　　—W. H. AUDEN, *The Dyer's Hand*, 1962

13　What stories can do . . . is make things present.
　　　　　　　　　　—TIM O'BRIEN, *The Things They Carried*, 1990

BORES & DULLNESS

14　Speeches measured by the hour die with the hour.
　　　　　　　　　　—THOMAS JEFFERSON, letter to David Harding, April 20, 1824

Bore, n. A person who talks when you wish him to listen. 1
—AMBROSE BIERCE, The Devil's Dictionary, 1906

The godless are the dull and the dull are the damned. 2
—E. E. CUMMINGS, Proud of his scientific attitude,
in Poems, 1940

[Comment following a tedious speech]: Gentlemen, you have just been listen- 3
ing to that Chinese sage, On Tu Long.
—WILL ROGERS, in Alex Ayres, ed.,
The Wit and Wisdom of Will Rogers [1993]

The capacity of human beings to bore one another seems to be vastly greater 4
than that of any other animals. Some of their most esteemed inventions have
no other apparent purpose, for example, the dinner party of more than two, the
epic poem, and the science of metaphysics.
—H. L. MENCKEN, Minority Report:
H. L. Mencken's Notebooks [1956]

[See also Mencken at WORK.]

A healthy male adult bore consumes each year one and a half times his weight 5
in other people's patience. —JOHN UPDIKE, *Confessions of a Wild Bore,*
in Assorted Prose, 1965

BRAVERY See COURAGE; HEROES

BRAZIL See NATIONS

BUREAUCRACY See GOVERNMENT; MANAGEMENT
TECHNIQUES

BUSINESS See also CAPITALISM & CAPITAL V. LABOR;
ECONOMICS; MANAGEMENT TECHNIQUES; MONEY &
THE RICH; SECURITY & SAFETY [Iacocca]

Method goes far to prevent trouble in business: for it makes the task easy, hin- 6
ders confusion, saves abundance of time, and instructs those that have business depending, both what to do and what to hope.
—WILLIAM PENN, Some Fruits of Solitude, 1693

The creditors are a superstitious sect, great observers of set days and times. 7
—BENJAMIN FRANKLIN, Poor Richard's Almanack, 1737

No nation was ever ruined by trade. 8
—BENJAMIN FRANKLIN, Thoughts on Commercial Subjects

How impure are the channels through which trade hath a conveyance. How 9
great is that danger to which poor lads are now exposed, when placed on ship-
board to learn the art of sailing. —JOHN WOOLMAN, *Journal*, 1774

Merchants love nobody. —THOMAS JEFFERSON, letter to John Langdon, 1785 10

Banking establishments are more dangerous than standing armies. 11
—THOMAS JEFFERSON, letter to John Taylor, May 28, 1816

1   Corporations have neither bodies to be kicked nor souls to be damned.
—ANONYMOUS
[This aphorism, cited by Arthur Schlesinger, Jr., in *The Age of Jackson* (1945) is similar to Sir Edward Coke's pronouncement in the 17th century, "They (corporations) cannot commit treason, nor be outlawed nor excommunicated, for they have no souls," *Case of Sutton's Hospital.* See also Henry Demarest Lloyd below, p. 69.]

2   Every monopoly and all exclusive privileges are granted at the expense of the public, which ought to receive a fair equivalent.
—ANDREW JACKSON, veto of the bill to renew the charter of the Bank of the United States, 1832
[The battle over whether to continue the bank pitted the populist westerner Jackson against the privileged easterners who ran the bank for the benefit of the moneyed class—or at least Jackson was able to present the issue this way, and his veto propelled him to reelection. See also Daniel Webster below.]

3   As directors of a company, men will sanction actions of which they would scorn to be guilty in their private capacity. A crime which would press heavily on the conscience of one man, becomes quite endurable when divided among many.   —WILLIAM M. GOUGE, *A Short History of Paper Money and Banking in the United States,* 1833

4   Credit is the vital air of the system of modern commerce.
—DANIEL WEBSTER, speech in the U.S. Senate, March 18, 1834
[Webster was speaking in support of the Bank of the United States. See also Herbert Hoover under ECONOMICS, p. 158.]

5   A power has risen up in the government greater than the people themselves, consisting of many and various and powerful interests, combined into one mass, and held together by the cohesive power of the vast surplus in the banks.
—JOHN C. CALHOUN, speech, May 27, 1836
[*Bartlett's* comments that this passage is the origin of the phrase: "cohesive power of public plunder."]

6   Corporations will do what individuals would not dare to do.
—PETER C. BROOKS, remark to Edward Everett, July 15, 1845
[Arthur Schlesinger, Jr., in *The Age of Jackson* (1945), describes Brooks as the wealthiest man in Boston.]

7   Well, I've got just as much conscience as any man in business can afford to keep—just a little, you know, to swear by, as 't were.
—HARRIET BEECHER STOWE, *Uncle Tom's Cabin,* 1852

8   Trade curses everything it handles, and though you trade in messages from heaven, the whole curse of trade attaches to the business.
—HENRY DAVID THOREAU, "Economy," *Walden,* 1854

9   Through want of enterprise and faith men are where they are, buying and selling, and spending their lives like serfs.   —HENRY DAVID THOREAU, "Baker Farm," *Ibid.*

10   I *don't* believe in princerple,
But oh I *du* in interest.
—JAMES RUSSELL LOWELL, *The Biglow Papers,* "The Courtin'" in Series II, 1866

The dealers in money have always, since the days of Moses, been the danger-   1
ous class.   —PETER COOPER, c. 1875, quoted in Peter Lyon,
                              The Honest Man, in *American Heritage* [Feb. 1959]
[Cooper, the founder of Cooper Union in New York City, used to say that his
life fell into three parts: thirty years to get started, thirty years to gain a fortune, and thirty years to dispose of it wisely. In old age, he ran for president as
a radical protest candidate, heading the National Independent party, usually
called the Greenback party. See also under MONEY & THE RICH.]

The public be damned! I'm working for my stockholders.   2
                              —WILLIAM H. VANDERBILT, comment to a news reporter,
                              Oct. 2, 1882
[This impatient remark by the railroad tycoon was seized on immediately as a
summation of the attitude of the captains of industry toward the common people.]

When a man sells eleven ounces for twelve, he makes a compact with the   3
devil, and sells himself for the value of an ounce.
          —HENRY WARD BEECHER, *Proverbs from Plymouth Pulpit,* 1887

Monopoly is business at the end of its journey.   4
          —HENRY DEMAREST LLOYD, *Wealth Against Commonwealth,* 1894

Corporations have no souls, but they can love each other.   5
                                                                  —*Ibid.*
[Lloyd was an influential economist, journalist, reformer, and wit. For more on
the famous aphorism on corporations and souls, see under Anonymous above.]

There are two times in a man's life when he should not speculate: when he   6
can't afford it and when he can.   —MARK TWAIN, *Pudd'nhead Wilson's New
                              Calendar, in *Following the Equator,* 1897
[Twain didn't heed his own advice. He repeatedly invested in new ventures,
and repeatedly lost money, most notably in the case of a typesetting machine
that never quite worked. In *Pudd'nhead Wilson's Calendar (Pudd'nhead Wilson,* 1894), Twain wrote: "October. This is one of the peculiarly dangerous
months to speculate in stocks in. The others are July, January, September . . ."
and so on through the rest of the months.]

We demand that big business give people a square deal.   7
                              —THEODORE ROOSEVELT, 1901
[More at POLITICAL SLOGANS. At the turn of the century, politicians had to address the concentration of power and money in the hands of a few men and corporations, such as J. P. Morgan's U.S. Steel. Roosevelt lost the 1912 presidential
election to Woodrow Wilson, whose "New Freedom" program was tougher on
big business.]

Most men are the servants of corporations.   8
                              —WOODROW WILSON, *The Old Order Changeth,*
                              in *The New Freedom,* 1913
[The whole sentence reads: "There was a time when corporations played a very
minor part in our business affairs, but now they play the chief part, and most
men are the servants of corporations." See also below.]

The present organization of business was meant for the big fellows and was not   9
meant for the little fellows; it was meant for those who are at the top and was
meant to exclude those who are at the bottom; it was meant to shut out beginners, to prevent new entries in the race, to prevent the building up of com-

petitive enterprises that would interfere with the monopolies which the great
trusts have built up.   —*Ibid.*

1   Smoke and blood is the mix of steel.
                                    —CARL SANDBURG, *Smoke and Steel,* 1920

2   The chief business of the American people is business.
                                    —CALVIN COOLIDGE, speech, The American Society of
                                    Newspaper Editors, Washington, D.C., Jan. 17, 1925

3   No man's credit is as good as his money.
                                    —EDGAR WATSON HOWE, *Sinner Sermons,* 1926

4   The customer is always right.
                                    —CARL SANDBURG, *Good Morning, America,* 1928
    [The saying was also the motto of the London department store Selfridge's,
    founded by H. Gordon Selfridge.]

5   If it don't go up, don't buy it.   —WILL ROGERS, advice on selecting a stock,
                                    Daily Telegrams, Oct. 31, 1929

6   [Wall Street:] A thoroughfare that begins in a graveyard and ends in a river.
                                    —ANONYMOUS, traditional saying

7   You can't mine coal without machine guns.
                                    —RICHARD B. MELLON, testimony, U.S. Congress,
                                    quoted in *Time,* June 14, 1937

8   [The insurer] insures all people against all happenings of everyday life, even the
    worm in the apple or the piano out of tune.
                                    —WALLACE STEVENS, article on insurance, in Milton J. Bates, ed.,
                                    expanded *Opus Posthumous*
    [Stevens, one of our great poets, was also a lawyer for Hartford Accident and In-
    demnity Company.]

9   For years I thought what was good for our country was good for General Mo-
    tors and vice versa. The difference did not exist.
                                    —CHARLES E. WILSON, testimony, U.S. Senate
                                    Armed Services Committee, Jan. 15, 1953
    [Often quoted, perhaps somewhat unfairly, in the vice versa form: "What is
    good for General Motors is good for the country." GM Chairman Wilson made
    the remark in hearings on his nomination to be Secretary of Defense. See also
    Calvin Coolidge on the business of the American people at AMERICA & AMERI-
    CANS, and for another peek into thought processes in the auto industry, see Lee
    Iacocca at SECURITY & SAFETY.]

10 Ben, I want to say one word to you—just one word—plastics.
                                    —BUCK HENRY & CALDER WILLINGHAM,
                                    The Graduate, screenplay, 1967
    [Based on Charles Webb's novel.]

11 He's a businessman. I'll make him an offer he can't refuse.
                                    —MARIO PUZO, *The Godfather,* 1969
    [The Godfather, Don Corleone, devising a strategy to deal with a Hollywood
    producer.]

This administration is not sympathetic to corporations, it is indentured to 1
corporations.   —RALPH NADER,
                                   news conference, Oct. 3, 1972
[He was speaking of the Nixon administration. The remark was quoted the
next day in the *Washington Post.*]

Just remember this: If bankers were as smart as you are, you would starve to 2
death.   —HENRY HARFIELD, quoted in Martin Mayer,
                                   The Bankers, 1975
[Attorney Harfield, senior partner of Shearman & Sterling, said this in a tape-
recorded talk to a group of lawyers. Mayer used the comment as the epigraph
for his book on the banking business, which hardly was a favor to Mr. Harfield,
as Shearman & Sterling were the lead counsel for Citicorp bank.]

The bottom line is in heaven.   —EDWIN HERBERT LAND, shareholders' 3
                                   meeting, Polaroid Corp., April 26, 1977

There is no limit to what a man can do or where he can go, if he doesn't mind 4
who gets the credit.
                                   —ANONYMOUS, business aphorism
[The saying derives from the 19th-century classics scholar Benjamin Jowett of
Oxford University. He said, "The way to get things done is not to mind who
gets the credit of doing them." The quote is included in *Handbook of Business
Quotations,* Charles Robert Lightfoot, ed., 1991.]

When a person with experience meets a person with money, the person with 5
experience will get the money. And the person with the money will get some
experience.   —LEONARD LAUDER, speech,
                    Woman's Economic Development Corporation, Feb. 1985
[Lauder was speaking of the early years of the Estée Lauder Company, founded
by his mother.]

It is better to lose opportunity than capital.   6
                    —SUSAN M. BYRNE, *Wall Street Week in Review*
                    television show, Feb. 15, 1985

No one on his deathbed ever said, "I wish I had spent more time on my 7
business."   —PAUL E. TSONGAS,
                                   quoting a letter from a friend
[This thought, which made the rounds in the notoriously materialistic 1980s,
was passed on to Sen. Tsongas when, as a result of illness, he decided to retire
after his 1979–85 term as junior senator from Massachusetts. He subsequently
ran for the Democratic nomination for president in 1992, standing out as the
intellectual in the race eventually won by Bill Clinton. In May 1993, Clinton's
deputy legal counsel and personal attorney, Vincent Foster, used the same
theme in addressing the graduating class of the University of Arkansas: "No
one was ever heard to say on their deathbed, 'I wish I had spent more time at
the office.' . . . The office can wait. . . . If you find yourself getting burned out
or unfulfilled, unappreciated . . . then have the courage to make a change." On
July 20, Foster shot himself."]

CALIFORNIA

See also CITIES (Los Angeles, Oakland, San Francisco)

1 There is no part of earth to be taken up, wherein there is not some special likelihood of gold or silver. —RICHARD HAKLUYT, *The Famous Voyage of Sir Francis Drake*, 1589, in *Principal Navigations . . . of the English Nation*, 1598–1600

2 The men [of California] are thriftless, proud, and extravagant, and very much given to gaming; and the women have but little education, and a good deal of beauty, and their morality, of course, is none of the best.
—RICHARD HENRY DANA, JR., *Two Years Before the Mast*, 1840

3 This valley [the San Joaquin] is a paradise. Grass, flowers, trees, beautiful clear rivers, thousands of deer, elk, wild horses, wonderful salmon . . . thousands of different kinds of ducks here; geese standing around as if tame.
—CHARLES PREUSS, diary, March 27, 1844, in *Exploring with Fremont* [1958]
[Preuss was the cartographer on Fremont's first, second, and fourth expeditions.]

4 Satan, from one of his elevations, showed mankind the kingdom of California, and they entered into a compact with him at once.
—HENRY DAVID THOREAU, *Journal*, Feb. 2, 1852
[Thoreau was writing specifically of the discovery of gold in California.]

5 California can and does furnish the best bad things that are obtainable in America. —HINTON R. HELPER, *Land of Gold: Reality versus Fiction*, 1855
[More at CITIES (San Francisco).]

6 California annexes the United States.
—ANONYMOUS, May 1869
[This message was carried on a banner in the streets of San Francisco in celebration of the completion of the transcontinental railroad.]

The attraction and superiority of California are in its days. It has better days, 1
and more of them, than any other country.
—RALPH WALDO EMERSON, *Journal*, April–May 1871

These Californian scoundrels are invariably lighthearted; crime cannot over- 2
shadow the exhilaration of the outdoor life; remorse and gloom are banished
like clouds before this perennially sunny climate. They make amusement out
of killing you.
—CLARENCE KING, *Mountaineering in the Sierra Nevada*, 1872

All scenery in California requires distance to give it charm. 3
—MARK TWAIN, *Roughing It*, 1872

An enthusiastic writer declared the climate of California to be "eminently 4
favourable to the cure of gunshot wounds."
—G. A. SALA, *America Revisited*, 1882

When a tree takes a notion to grow in California nothing in heaven or on earth 5
will stop it.   —LILIAN LELAND, *Travelling Alone,*
A Woman's Journey Round the World, 1890

East is East, and West is San Francisco, according to Californians. Californians 6
are a race of people; they are not merely inhabitants of a state.
—O. HENRY, *A Municipal Report,*
in *Strictly Business*, 1910

It is a shame to take this country away from the rattlesnakes. 7
—D. W. GRIFFITH, attributed

Yes, I have walked in California, 8
And the rivers there are blue and white.
Thunderclouds of grapes hang on the mountains.
Bears in the meadows pitch and fight.
—VACHEL LINDSAY, *The Golden Whales of California, I:*
A Short Walk along the Coast, 1920

I met a Californian who would 9
Talk California—a state so blessed,
He said, in climate, none had ever died there
A natural death.   —ROBERT FROST, *New Hampshire*, 1923

California, Here I come.   —BUDDY DeSYLVA, song title, 1924   10

California is a tragic country—like Palestine, like every Promised Land.   11
—CHRISTOPHER ISHERWOOD, *Los Angeles* 1947,
in *Exhumations* [1966]
[For more from this essay see SECURITY & SAFETY.]

The land around San Juan Capistrano is the pocket where the Creator keeps all   12
his treasures. Anything will grow there.
—FRANCES MARION, *Westward the Dream*, 1948

Nothing wrong with southern California that a rise in the ocean wouldn't   13
cure.   —ROSS MacDONALD, *The Drowning Pool*, 1950

1 California's a wonderful place to live—if you happen to be an orange.
—FRED ALLEN, attributed,
in Robert Taylor, *Fred Allen* [1989]

2 It was the end of a continent. They didn't give a damn.
—JACK KEROUAC, *On the Road*, 1957

3 It's a scientific fact that for every year you live in California, you lose two points off your I.Q. It's redundant to die in L.A.
—TRUMAN CAPOTE, remark, 1975, quoted
in Jay Presson Allen's play *Tru* [1989]

4 Whatever starts in California unfortunately has a tendency to spread.
—JIMMY CARTER, remark, cabinet meeting,
March 21, 1977, quoted in Robert Shogun,
Promises to Keep: Carter's First 100 Days [1977]

Motto

5   *Eureka.*
I have found it.

CALMNESS   *See also* ANXIETY & WORRY

6 Calmness is always godlike.   —RALPH WALDO EMERSON, *Journal*, 1840

7 Keep cool: it will be all one a hundred years hence.
—RALPH WALDO EMERSON, *Representative Men*, 1850
[A proverbial saying having many variations, including: It will be all the same a hundred years hence.]

8 It's the still hog that eats the most.
—Daniel Drew, saying quoted in Peter Lyon, *The Honest Man*,
in *American Heritage* [Feb. 1959]
[A variant on a proverbial expression: "The stillest hog gets the most swill." Also, "The quiet hog drinks the most swill."
  Drew, dubbed ironically "Uncle Dan," knew his livestock. This non-avuncular sharpie made his first bundle by feeding his steers salt on the night before a sale. The next morning, the desperately thirsty animals would drink so much water that each might gain up to fifty pounds in weight. From this trick comes the phrase "watered stock." Drew was also called "the Great Bear." In the 1860s, with aides Jim Fisk and Jay Gould, he embarked on a marginally legal selling-short spree (starting with shares of the Erie Railroad, a company of which he was treasurer). Before his luck and fortune collapsed in 1870, he had ruined thousands and was almost universally hated.]

9 A relaxed man is not necessarily a better man.
—JENNY HOLZER, aphorism in exhibit at the
Solomon R. Guggenheim Museum, New York City, 1989

CAMPAIGN SLOGANS   *See* POLITICAL SLOGANS

CANADA   *See* NATIONS

CAPITALISM & CAPITAL V. LABOR

See also BUSINESS; ECONOMICS; MONEY & THE RICH; RICH & POOR, WEALTH & POVERTY; WORK & WORKERS

The feud between the capitalist and laborer, the house of Have and the house   1
of Want, is as old as social union, and can never be entirely quieted; but he who
will act with moderation, prefer fact to theory, and remember that everything
in this world is relative and not absolute, will see that the violence of the contest may be stilled.   —GEORGE BANCROFT, *To the Workingmen*
of Northampton, in the *Boston Courier,*
Oct. 22, 1834

Those who produce all wealth are themselves left poor. They see principalities   2
extending and palaces built around them, without being aware that the entire
expense is a tax upon themselves.
    —AMOS KENDALL, in the *Washington Globe,*
Nov. 7, 1834
[The early quotations in this section reflect Marxist insights prior to the
Communist Manifesto, 1848. In a letter dated March 5, 1852, Marx wrote:
"The honor does not belong to me for having discovered the existence either of classes in modern society or of the struggle between the classes. Bourgeois historians a long time before me expounded the historical development
of this class struggle, and bourgeois economists, the economic anatomy of
classes."]

These capitalists generally act harmoniously and in concert to fleece the   3
people.   —ABRAHAM LINCOLN, speech, Illinois legislature, Jan. 1837

What we object to is the division of society into two classes, of which one class   4
owns the capital, and the other performs the labor.
    —ORESTES BROWNSON, *The Laboring Classes,*
in the *Boston Quarterly Review,* July 1840

I am glad to see that a system of labor prevails in New England under which la-   5
borers can strike when they want to . . . I like the system that lets a man quit
when he wants to, and wish it might prevail everywhere.
    —ABRAHAM LINCOLN, speech, New Haven, Conn., March 6, 1860

Labor is prior to, and independent of, capital. Capital is only the fruit of labor,   6
and could never have existed if labor had not first existed. Labor is the superior
of capital, and deserves much the higher consideration. Capital has its rights,
which are as worthy of protection as any other rights.
    —ABRAHAM LINCOLN, first annual message
to Congress, Dec. 3, 1861
[The "party of Lincoln" tends to focus on the last sentence and pass over the
preceding thoughts.]

Join the union, girls, and together say, "Equal pay for equal work."   7
    —SUSAN B. ANTHONY, in *The Revolution* newspaper,
March 18, 1869

Labor disgraces no man; unfortunately, you occasionally find men disgrace   8
labor.   —ULYSSES S. GRANT, speech, Midland International
Arbitration Union, Birmingham, England, 1877

1   Capital is a result of labor, and is used by labor to assist it in further production. Labor is the active and initial force, and labor is therefore the employer of capital.   —HENRY GEORGE, *Progress and Poverty,* 1879

2   *Labor, n.,* One of the processes by which A acquires property for B.
—AMBROSE BIERCE, *The Devil's Dictionary,* 1906

3   Solidarity forever, for the Union makes us strong.
—RALPH CHAPLIN, International Workers
of the World song, c. 1908
[This was sung to the tune of *The Battle Hymn of the Republic.* In an article in the June 1967 *American Heritage,* Bernard A. Weisberger credits Chicago commercial artist Ralph Chaplin with this verse, which was taken over by the entire labor movement. Members of the International Workers of the World (IWW), popularly called "Wobblies," proselytized through music and had their own bard, Joe Hill, a singing organizer who came to be seen as a martyr in the cause of labor; see below. Their *I.W.W. Songs to Fan the Flames of Discontent* was known generally as "The Little Red Song Book." Other Wobbly songs were *Halleluja, I'm a Bum,* sung to the tune of *Revive Us Again,* and *I Dreamed I Saw Joe Hill Last Night;* see below.]

4   With all their faults, trade-unions have done more for humanity than any other organization of men that ever existed.
—CLARENCE DARROW, in *The Railroad Trainman,* Nov. 1909

5   After God had finished the rattlesnake, the toad, the vampire, he had some awful substance left with which he made a scab.
—JACK LONDON, *A Scab,* in *C.I.O. News* [Sept. 13, 1946]
[See also INSULTS.]

6   Don't waste any time mourning—organize!
—JOE HILL, telegram to William Dudley "Big Bill" Haywood,
Nov. 18, 1915
[Hill had been convicted of murdering two policemen in Salt Lake City, Utah, while robbing a grocery store. He was executed by firing squad the day after sending this message to Haywood, who was one of the founders of the International Workers of the World.
Scholars still argue over whether Hill was framed. Thirty thousand people attended his funeral. He was an activist and a musician and had written many of the IWW's favorite songs, including *The Preacher and the Slave,* in which he popularized (and possibly coined) the phrase "pie in the sky" in the ironic refrain: "You will eat, bye and bye, / In that glorious land above the sky; / Work and pray, live on hay / You'll get pie in the sky when you die." Today, Hill is remembered best for the song about him by Alfred Hayes and Earl Robinson; see below.]

7   There is no right to strike against the public safety by anybody, anywhere, any time.   —CALVIN COOLIDGE, telegram to Samuel Gompers,
Sept. 14, 1919
[This was a reply to a protest telegram sent by American Federation of Labor president Gompers. Coolidge, who was governor of Massachusetts, had called in troops to restore order during a strike by the Boston police, who were AFL union members. Coolidge's position was widely applauded and he won the Republican nomination for the vice presidency the next year. He succeeded to the presidency upon the death of Warren G. Harding in 1923.]

I dreamed I saw Joe Hill last night   1
Alive as you and me.
Says I "But Joe, you're ten years dead."
"I never died," says he.
> —ALFRED HAYES, *The Daily Worker*, Sept. 4, 1936

[The music was by Earl Robinson.]

Private enterprise is ceasing to be free enterprise.   2
> —FRANKLIN D. ROOSEVELT, message to Congress proposing
> investigation of monopolies, 1938

The trouble with the profit system has always been that it is highly unprof-   3
itable to most people.
> —E. B. WHITE, *One Man's Meat*, 1944

The object of liberalism has never been to destroy capitalism . . . only to keep   4
the capitalists from destroying it.
> —ARTHUR M. SCHLESINGER, JR., *The Age of Jackson*, 1945

Reflecting the values of the larger capitalistic society, there is no prestige   5
whatsoever attached to actually working. Workers are invisible.
> —MARGE PIERCY, *The Grand Coolie Damn*,
> in Robin Morgan, ed., *Sisterhood Is Powerful*, 1970

CARDS   *See* GAMES

CENSORSHIP   *See also* BOOKS & READING; FREE SPEECH;
PRESS, THE

Subject opinion to coercion: whom will you make your inquisitors? Fallible   6
men; governed by bad passions, by private as well as public reasons.
> —THOMAS JEFFERSON, *Notes on the State of Virginia*, 1781–85

It is error alone which needs the support of government. Truth can stand by   7
itself.   *—Ibid.*

Every suppressed or expunged word reverberates through the earth from side to   8
side   —RALPH WALDO EMERSON, *Compensation*,
in *Essays: First Series*, 1841

Those whom books will hurt will not be proof against events. Events, not   9
books, should be forbid.   —HERMAN MELVILLE, *The Encantadas*,
in *The Piazza Tales*, 1856

[See also Jimmy Walker at BOOKS & READING.]

We write frankly and freely, but then we "modify" before we print.   10
> —MARK TWAIN,
> *Life on the Mississippi*, 1883

[This is what we now call "self-censorship." Twain did much of his "modify-
ing" at the behest of his beloved wife, Libby. Sometimes he put things in just
for the fun of seeing her strike them out.]

The mind that becomes soiled in youth can never again be washed clean; I   11
know this by my own experience, and to this day I cherish an unappeasable bit-

terness against the unfaithful guardians of my young life, who not only permitted but compelled me to read an unexpurgated Bible through before I was
fifteen years old.   —MARK TWAIN, letter
                                        to Asa Don Dickinson, Nov. 21, 1905
[The letter to Mr. Dickinson, a Brooklyn Public Library staffer, was occasioned
by news that the head of the children's department at the BPL had banished
Tom Sawyer and Huckleberry Finn to the adult stacks because they were too
unrefined for younger readers. Twain claimed to be disturbed that children had
been permitted to read the books in the first place, asserting that he had written them "for adults exclusively" and that it always distressed him to hear
"that boys and girls had been allowed access" to works that might soil their
youthful minds, etc.]

1   Scenes of passion should not be introduced when not essential to the plot. In
    general, passion should be so treated that these scenes do not stimulate the
    lower and baser element.
                        —THE MOTION PICTURE PRODUCERS AND DISTRIBUTORS
                        OF AMERICA, INC., Code for the Industry, 1930

2   Sex perversion or any inference of it is forbidden. White slavery shall not be
    treated. Miscegenation is forbidden. . . . Scenes of actual childbirth, in fact or
    in silhouette, are never to be represented.
                                                                    —Ibid.

    [See also MARRIAGE for more from the Code.]

3   Did you ever hear anyone say "that work had better be banned, because I might
    read it and it might be very damaging to me"?
                                      —JOSEPH HENRY JACKSON, saying
    [Jackson was the editor of the San Francisco Chronicle.]

4   I know it when I see it.   —POTTER STEWART, concurring opinion,
                                              Jacobellis v. Ohio, 1964
    [This is the closest that Supreme Court Justice Stewart could come to defining
    "hard-core pornography"—the sentence runs in full "I know it when I see it;
    and the motion picture in this case is not that." The motion picture was Louis
    Malle's comparatively tame The Lovers. As Justice Arthur Goldberg opined,
    "The love scene deemed objectionable is so fragmentary and fleeting that only
    a censor's alert would make an audience conscious that something 'question-
    able' is being portrayed. Except for this rapid sequence, the film concerns itself
    with the history of an ill-matched and unhappy marriage—a familiar subject in
    old and new novels and in current television soap operas."
        The court, since then, has not done much better in its search for a definition
    of obscenity. The currently reigning test, from Miller v. California, 1973,
    hinges on such nebulous notions as "contemporary community standards,"
    and whether a work "taken as a whole" is "patently offensive" or lacks "seri-
    ous literary, artistic, political, or scientific value." Justice William J. Brennan
    finally threw up his hands, telling Nat Hentoff: "I put sixteen years into that
    damn obscenity thing. I tried and I tried, and I waffled back and forth, and I fi-
    nally gave up. If you can't define it, you can't prosecute people for it" (The New
    Yorker, March 12, 1990).]

5   Without censorship, things can get terribly confused in the public mind.
                    —WILLIAM C. WESTMORELAND, 1982, quoted in Stanley Hochman
                        & Eleanor Hochman, eds., The Penguin Dictionary
                        of Contemporary American History [1997]
    [More at VIETNAM WAR.]

Not everything's for children. Not everything's for everyone.   1

—ROBERT CRUMB, in the documentary *Crumb*
by Terry Zwigoff, 1995

[Counterculture cartoonist Robert Crumb commenting on the political incorrectness of his work.]

CHANCE   *See* LUCK

CHANGE   *See also* AMERICA & AMERICANS (Eleanor Roosevelt);
NEW THINGS; TRUTH (Robert Frost)

Things do not change; we change.   —HENRY DAVID THOREAU, *Journal,* 1850   2

I shall try to correct errors when shown to be errors and I shall adopt new views   3
as fast as they shall appear to be true views.

—ABRAHAM LINCOLN, reply to Horace Greeley,
August 19, 1862

[Greeley had asked Lincoln to make emancipation a government goal. Lincoln was still inching toward that decision. See SLAVERY.]

It is not best to swap horses while crossing the river.   4

—ABRAHAM LINCOLN,
comment, June 9, 1864

[The president addressed this proverbial remark to a delegation from the National Union League. He told the League members, "I do not allow myself to suppose that either the convention or the League have concluded to decide that I am either the greatest or best man in America, but rather that they have decided it is not best to swap horses while crossing the river, and have further concluded that I am not so poor a horse that they might not make a botch of it in trying to swap."

The metaphor apparently stems from a joke, popular in the 1840s, about an Irishman (or Dutchman) who was crossing a river with a mare and a colt. Falling off the mare, he grabbed the colt's tail. Observers on the riverbank shouted that he should take hold of the mare's tail as she was the stronger swimmer. The man declined the advice, yelling back that this was not a good time for him to swap horses.

"Don't change horses" made a good campaign slogan; see POLITICAL SLOGANS. Democrats later recycled this bit of folk wisdom in FDR's reelection campaigns of 1940 and 1944. They also gave it an ironic twist in 1932: with the nation's economy in shambles and Herbert Hoover running for reelection, the Dems maintained that the Republican motto must be, "Don't swap barrels while going over Niagara."]

There is one great basic fact which underlies all the questions that are discussed on the political platforms at the present moment. That singular fact is   5
that nothing is done in this country as it was done twenty years ago.

—WOODROW WILSON, *The Old Order Changeth,*
in *The New Freedom,* 1913

[The essay took its title from this sentence: "The old order changeth—changeth under our very eyes, not quietly and equably, but swiftly and with the noise and heat and tumult of reconstruction." Wilson was alluding to Lord Tennyson's, "The old order changeth, yielding place to new; / And God fulfills himself in many ways, / Lest one good custom should corrupt the world," *Idylls of the King,* "The Passing of Arthur."]

1   For the times they are a-changin'.
                    —BOB DYLAN, *The Times They Are A-changin'*, 1963

2   Change is the law of life. And those who look only to the past or the present
    are certain to miss the future.   —JOHN F. KENNEDY, speech,
                            Frankfurt, West Germany, June 25, 1963

CHARACTER   *See* GRACE; VIRTUE

CHARITY & PHILANTHROPY

3   We do not quite forgive a giver. The hand that feeds us is in some danger of be-
    ing bitten.   —RALPH WALDO EMERSON, *Gifts*, in *Essays: Second Series*, 1844

4   Philanthropy is almost the only virtue which is sufficiently appreciated by
    mankind.   —HENRY DAVID THOREAU, "Economy," *Walden*, 1854

5   Look up and not down;
    Look forward and not back;
    Look out and not in;
    Lend a hand.   —EDWARD EVERETT HALE,
                    motto of the Lend a Hand Society, formed 1891
    [Hale founded the first Lend a Hand Club in Boston in 1871, and the society,
    or league, of clubs formed twenty years later. Hale later became chaplain to
    the U.S. Senate, and is remembered for a remark on prayer and senators; see
    CONGRESS.]

6   The heart hath its own memory, like the mind,
    And in it are enshrined
    The precious keepsakes, into which are wrought
    The giver's loving thought.   —HENRY WADSWORTH LONGFELLOW,
                                    From My Arm-chair, 1879

7   Charity has in it sometimes, perhaps often, a savor of superiority.
                    —JAMES RUSSELL LOWELL, speech, Westminster Abbey,
                            London, England, Dec. 13, 1881

8   Do not give, as many rich men do, like a hen that lays her egg and then
    cackles.   —HENRY WARD BEECHER,
                    Proverbs from Plymouth Pulpit, 1887
    [A Yankee version of the biblical, "Therefore when thou doest thine alms, do
    not sound a trumpet before thee, as the hypocrites do," *Matthew* 6:2.]

9   Private beneficence is totally inadequate to deal with the vast numbers of the
    city's disinherited.   —JANE ADDAMS,
                    Twenty Years at Hull House, 1910
    [Addams founded Hull House in Chicago, the first social settlement house in
    the U.S. She was co-winner of the Nobel Peace Prize in 1931.]

10 Better to go down dignified
    With boughten friendship at your side
    Than none at all. Provide, provide!   —ROBERT FROST, *Provide, Provide*, 1936

11 Don't deprive yourself of the joy of giving.
                    —MICHAEL GREENBERG, motto, 1963
    [Greenberg put this motto into practice by giving gloves to the derelicts in and

around the Bowery in New York City. He began doing this in 1963, between Thanksgiving and Christmas, in memory of his father, from whom he had learned the motto. Upon his death in 1995, a cousin said he intended to continue "Gloves" Greenberg's work.]

Philanthropy is commendable, but it must not cause the philanthropist to overlook the circumstances of economic injustice which make philanthropy necessary.
    —MARTIN LUTHER KING, JR.,
Strength to Love, 1963

1

One thing I had in my mind, I'm never going to be the richest person in the cemetery.
    —FRANCES L. LOEB, announcing a gift of
$7.5 million to Vassar College, 1990
[This was just one of numerous gifts by a woman who devoted her life to philanthropy and good works.]

2

CHILDREN
See also YOUTH

Childhood knows the human heart.
    —EDGAR ALLAN POE, *Tamerlane*,
1827

3

There was never a child so lovely but his mother was glad to get asleep.
    —RALPH WALDO EMERSON, *Journal*, 1836
[Three years later in his journal, Emerson similarly noted, "As soon as a child has left the room his strewn toys become affecting."]

4

Children are all foreigners.
    —*Ibid.*, 1839

5

What a difference it makes to come home to a child!
    —MARGARET FULLER, letter to friends, 1849

6

"Do you know who made you?" "Nobody as I knows on," said the child, with a short laugh . . . "I 'spect I growed. Don't think nobody never made me."
    —HARRIET BEECHER STOWE, *Uncle Tom's Cabin*, 1852
[Topsy is speaking.]

7

Blessings on thee, little man,
Barefoot boy, with cheek of tan! . . .
From my heart I give thee joy—
I was once a barefoot boy!
    —JOHN GREENLEAF WHITTIER, *The Barefoot Boy*, 1856

8

A torn jacket is soon mended; but hard words bruise the heart of a child.
    —HENRY WADSWORTH LONGFELLOW, "Table-Talk,"
in *Driftwood*, 1857

9

We find delight in the beauty and happiness of children that makes the heart too big for the body.
    —RALPH WALDO EMERSON, *Illusions*,
in *The Conduct of Life*, 1860

10

Between the dark and the daylight,
When the night is beginning to lower,
Comes a pause in the day's occupations,
That is known as the Children's Hour.
    —HENRY WADSWORTH LONGFELLOW,
The Children's Hour, 1860

11

1   I hear in the chamber above me
    The patter of little feet.   —*Ibid.*

2   There was a little girl
    Who had a little curl
    Right in the middle of her forehead;
    And when she was good
    She was very, very good,
    But when she was bad she was horrid.   —HENRY WADSWORTH LONGFELLOW,
                                                There Was a Little Girl

3   A baby is an inestimable blessing and bother.
                          —MARK TWAIN, letter to Annie Webster, Sept. 1, 1876

4   Children troop down from heaven because God wills it.
                                                —PATRICK HAYES, 1921
    [Archbishop Hayes of New York City was doing battle with birth-control pio-
    neer Margaret Sanger.]

5   Childhood Is the Kingdom Where Nobody Dies.
                          —EDNA ST. VINCENT MILLAY,
                              title of poem in *Wine from These Grapes*, 1934

6   There's no such thing in the world as a bad boy, I'm sure of that.
                          —ELEANORE GRIFFIN and DORE SCHARY, *Boys Town*, 1938
    [The line is spoken by Spencer Tracy playing Father Flanagan.]

CHINA   *See* NATIONS

CHRISTMAS

7   How many observe Christ's birthday! How few, his precepts! O! 'tis easier to
    keep holidays than commandments.
                          —BENJAMIN FRANKLIN, *Poor Richard's Almanack*, 1732–1757

8   'Twas the night before Christmas, when all through the house
    Not a creature was stirring—not even a mouse;
    The stockings were hung by the chimney with care,
    In hopes that St. Nicholas soon would be there.
    The children were nestled all snug in their beds,
    While visions of sugar plums danced in their heads.
                          —CLEMENT C. MOORE, *The Night Before Christmas,*
                              in the *Troy Sentinel,* Dec. 23, 1823
    [This poem, first published anonymously as *A Visit from St. Nicholas,* made
    Dr. Moore world famous. He would have preferred to be known for his distin-
    guished work as a classical scholar, including his comprehensive *Hebrew and
    English Lexicon.* But instead he is beloved for creating the best Father Christ-
    mas, a combination of St. Nicholas and the Norwegian Kriss Kringle, who
    helped St. Nicholas by driving a sleigh pulled by reindeer. Children's book
    writer X. J. Kennedy observed in *The New York Times Book Review,* December
    5, 1993, that Moore's St. Nicholas was a great improvement over other con-
    tenders for top Christmas billing, such as Washington Irving's St. Nick, who
    went around in a wagon, "riding jollily among the treetops."
       Moore wrote the poem in 1822 as a Christmas present for his daughter, who
    was seriously ill.]

Now, *Dasher!* now, *Dancer!* now, *Prancer* and *Vixen!*   1
On, *Comet!* on, *Cupid* on, *Donner* and *Blitzen!*   —*Ibid.*

He had a broad face and a little round belly,   2
That shook when he laughed, like a bowlful of jelly.   —*Ibid.*

But I heard him exclaim, ere he drove out of sight,   3
"Happy Christmas to all and to all a good night."   —*Ibid.*

It came upon the midnight clear,   4
That glorious song of old,
From angels bending near the earth
To touch their harps of gold;
"Peace on the earth, good will to men
From Heaven's all-gracious King"—
The world in solemn stillness lay
To hear the angels sing.
                                        —EDMUND HAMILTON SEARS,
                                          Christmas Carol, 1850

I heard the bells on Christmas Day   5
Their old, familiar carols play,
And wild and sweet
The words repeat
Of peace on earth, good-will to men!   —HENRY WADSWORTH LONGFELLOW,
                                              Christmas Bells,
                                              in *Flower-de-Luce,* 1867

Christmas won't be Christmas without any presents.   6
                    —LOUISA MAY ALCOTT, *Little Women,* 1868

O little town of Bethlehem,   7
How still we see thee lie!
Above thy deep and dreamless sleep
The silent stars go by.   —PHILLIPS BROOKS,
                                      O Little Town of Bethlehem, 1868

Yes, Virginia, there is a Santa Claus. . . . Thank God! he lives, and he lives for-   8
ever. A thousand years from now, Virginia, nay ten times ten thousand years
from now, he will continue to make glad the heart of childhood.
                              —FRANCIS PHARCELLUS CHURCH, *The Sun,*
                                      editorial, New York City, Sept. 21, 1897
[Virginia O'Hanlon of 115 West Ninety-fifth Street had written: "Dear Editor,
I am eight years old. Some of my little friends say there is no Santa Claus. Papa
says, 'If you see it in *The Sun* it's so.' Please tell me the truth; is there a Santa
Claus?" Church, formerly a Civil War correspondent with *The New York
Times,* wrote a long, anonymous editorial reply of five paragraphs. After his
death in 1906, the paper made an exception to its rule of editorial anonymity
to reveal that he was the author of what is probably the most famous editorial
in journalistic history.]

Angels come down, with Christmas in their hearts,   9
Gentle, whimsical, laughing, heaven-sent;
And, for a day, fair Peace have given me.
                    —VACHEL LINDSAY, *Springfield Magical,*
                        in *The Sangamon County Peace Advocate,* Christmas, 1909
[More at CITIES (Springfield).]

1   A cold coming we had of it,
     Just the worst time of the year.   T. S. ELIOT, *Journey of the Magi*, 1927

2   I'm Dreaming of a White Christmas.
                      IRVING BERLIN, *White Christmas*, song in *Holiday Inn*, 1942
     [The song, one of the greatest hits of all time, made Bing Crosby a superstar.]

CITIES

3   When we get piled upon one another in large cities as in Europe, we shall be-
     come corrupt as in Europe, and go to eating one another as they do there.
                                              —THOMAS JEFFERSON, letter
                                              to James Madison, Dec. 20, 1787

4   Cities degrade us by magnifying trifles.   —RALPH WALDO EMERSON, *Culture*,
                                                 in *The Conduct of Life*, 1860

5   The thing generally raised on city land is taxes.
                      —CHARLES DUDLEY WARNER, *My Summer in a Garden*, 1870

6   The government of cities is the one conspicuous failure of the United States.
                                              —JAMES BRYCE,
                                              The American Commonwealth, 1888
     [Bryce served as ambassador from England to the U.S., and this book was prob-
     ably the most influential study of America by a foreigner since Tocqueville's
     Democracy in America. The first edition was suppressed here after the author
     included a supplementary chapter on New York City's Tweed Ring.]

7   Thine alabaster cities gleam.   —KATHARINE LEE BATES,
                                                  America the Beautiful, 1893
     [This is from the fourth verse. The first verse is given at AMERICA & AMERICANS.]

8   In Boston they ask, How much does he know? In New York, How much is he
     worth? In Philadelphia, Who were his parents?
                      —MARK TWAIN, *What Paul Bourget Thinks of Us*, 1895
     [Twain identifies this as a familiar joke.]

9   The Shame of the Cities.   —LINCOLN STEFFENS, book title, 1904

10   In the Big City a man will disappear with the suddenness and completeness of
     the flame of a candle that is blown out.
                      —O. HENRY, *The Sleuths*, in *Sixes and Sevens*, 1911

11   But look what we have built. . . . This is not the rebuilding of cities. This is the
     sacking of cities.   —JANE JACOBS, Introduction, *The Death and Life*
                                   of Great American Cities, 1961
     [In this passage from her classic analysis of how a generation of city planners
     and architects went wrong, Ms. Jacobs refers to low-income housing projects
     more dangerous than the slums they replace, "cultural centers that are unable
     to support a good bookstore," "civic centers that are avoided by everyone but
     bums, empty promenades that go nowhere," and "expressways that eviscerate
     cities."]

12   We will neglect our cities to our peril, for in neglecting them we neglect the
     nation.   —JOHN F. KENNEDY,
                                          speech to Congress, Jan. 30, 1962

The more intelligent the people of a city, the worse its government.   1
                   —JOHN KENNETH GALBRAITH, c. 1962
[Quoted in *Plain Tales from the Embassy*, excerpts from letters and quotes dating from Mr. Galbraith's tenure as ambassador to India, *American Heritage*, October 1969.]

A city on hills has it over flat-land places.   2
              —JOHN STEINBECK, *Travels with Charley*, 1962
[He had in mind San Francisco, but the thought holds true worldwide.]

Chicago is the great American city. New York is one of the capitals of the   3
world and Los Angeles is a constellation of plastic, San Francisco is a lady, Boston has become Urban Renewal, Philadelphia and Baltimore and Washington wink like dull diamonds in the smog of Eastern Megalopolis, and New Orleans is unremarkable past the French Quarter. Detroit is a one-trade town, Pittsburgh has lost its golden triangle, St. Louis has become the golden arch of the corporation, and nights in Kansas City close early. The oil depletion allowance makes Houston and Dallas naught but checkerboards for this sort of game. But Chicago is a great American city. Perhaps it is the last of the great American cities.   —NORMAN MAILER,
               Miami and the Siege of Chicago, 1968

The bureaucratized, simplified cities, so dear to present-day city planners and   4
urban designers . . . run counter to the processes of city growth and economic development.   —JANE JACOBS, *The Economy of Cities*, 1969

If you've seen one slum, you've seen them all.   5
     —SPIRO AGNEW, television interview, Detroit, Mich., Oct. 6, 1969
[Vice President Agnew's attack style of political comment was new in its day. He resigned in disgrace in 1973—for past corruption—an exit hurried along so that he would not be in a position to succeed Pres. Richard Nixon, who was already tottering from the Watergate scandal. For a similar comment on trees, see Ronald Reagan under ENVIRONMENT.]

AMERICAN CITIES

Albany, N.Y.

This large city lay in the landscape like an anthill in a meadow.
     —HARRIETT MARTINEAU, *Retrospect of Western Travel*, 1838   6

Joe: Now, you take Albany, New York.
Moe: No, *you* take Albany, New York.   —ANONYMOUS, vaudeville routine   7

Those who are in Albany escaped Sing Sing, and those who are in Sing Sing   8
were on their way to Albany.   —ELBERT HUBBARD, *The Roycroft Dictionary and Book of Epigrams*, 1923
[The comment is directed more toward Albany as a seat of government than Albany as a community.]

Amarillo & El Paso, Tex.

Why, El Paso and Amarillo ain't no different from Sodom and Gomorrah. On a   9
smaller scale, of course.   —DAVID O. SELZNICK, *Duel in the Sun*,
                 screenplay, 1946
[The line is Walter Huston's. Selznick, the movie's producer, worked from an Oliver H. P. Garrett adaptation of Niven Busch's novel.]

Amherst, Mass.

1   The Amherst heart is plain and whole and permanent and warm.
—EMILY DICKINSON, letter to J. K. Chickering, 1885

Arkansas City, Ark.

2   We asked a passenger who belonged there what sort of a place it was. "Well," said he, after considering, and with the air of one who wishes to take time and be accurate, "It's a hell of a place." A description which was photographic for exactness.   —MARK TWAIN, *Life on the Mississippi*, 1883

Atlanta

3   I heard it said that the "architecture" of Atlanta is rococola.
—John Gunther, *Inside U.S.A.*, 1947

Augusta, Ga.

4   A queer little rustic city called Augusta—a great broad street two miles long—old quaint looking shops—houses with galleries—ware-houses—trees—cows and negroes strolling about the side walks—plank roads—a happy dirty tranquillity generally prevalent.   —WILLIAM MAKEPEACE THACKERAY, letter
to Kate Perry, Feb. 14–16, 1856

5   I never saw so many cows in my life,—at least in the streets of an inhabited town.   —G. A. SALA, *America Revisited*, 1882

Aurora, Nev.

6   All quiet in Aurora. Five men will be hung in an hour.
—BOB HOWLAND, city marshal, message to James Nye,
governor of the Nevada Territory, in Albert Bigelow Paine,
Mark Twain, A Biography [1924]
[A ghost town today, Aurora's heyday as a silver-mining camp in the 1860s was brief because the veins of ore were shallow and quickly worked out.]

Austin, Tex.

7   It reminds one somewhat of Washington; Washington *en petit*, seen through a reversed glass.   —FREDERICK LAW OLMSTED,
A Journey Through Texas, 1857
[Olmsted designed Central Park in Manhattan and Prospect Park in Brooklyn, N.Y.]

Avon, N.Y.

8   This Avon flows sweetly with nothing but whiskey and tobacco juice.
—FRANCES TROLLOPE, *Domestic Manners
of the Americans*, 1832
[Frances Trollope was mother to the famous Anthony as well as the less famous Thomas, also a novelist and essayist. She was a frank travel writer, but had nice things to say about this country, too; see, for example, NATURE: SEASONS, and Memphis below.]

Baltimore

This is the dirtiest place in the world.   —JOHN ADAMS, diary, Feb. 8, 1777   1

Wonderful little Baltimore.   —HENRY JAMES, *The American Scene*, 1907   2

The old charm, in truth, still survives in the town, despite the frantic efforts of   3
the boosters and boomers.
                —H. L. MENCKEN, *Prejudices: Fifth Series*, 1926

Birmingham, Ala.

Birmingham is a new city in an old land.   4
                —CARL CARMER, *Stars Fell on Alabama*, 1934

Boston

This place abounds with pritty women who . . . are, for the most part, free and   5
affable as well as pritty. I saw not one prude while I was here.
                —ALEXANDER HAMILTON, August 16, 1744, *Itinerarium*
[Boston in its youth was easygoing. The writer, Hamilton, was not the Founding Father of the same name, but an Annapolis physician, who traveled more
than 1,600 miles during a four-month tour of the northern colonies.]

Boston State-house is the hub of the solar system.   6
                —OLIVER WENDELL HOLMES, SR.,
                The Autocrat of the Breakfast-Table, 1858
[The opinion that 19th-century Bostonians had of themselves also is reflected
in the remark that William Ewart Gladstone attributed to an anonymous citizen of the Athens of America, aka, the Hub of the Universe: "There are not ten
men in Boston equal to Shakespeare."]

We say the cows laid out Boston. Well, there are worse surveyors.   7
                —RALPH WALDO EMERSON,
                Wealth, in *The Conduct of Life*, 1860

A solid man of Boston.   8
A comfortable man with dividends,
And the first salmon and the first green peas.
                —HENRY WADSWORTH LONGFELLOW, *John Endicott*,
                in *The New England Tragedies*, 1868

I have learned enough never to argue with a Bostonian.   9
                —RUDYARD KIPLING, *From Sea to Sea*, 1885

And this is good old Boston,   10
The home of the bean and the cod,
Where the Lowells talk to the Cabots,
And the Cabots talk only to God.   —JOHN COLLINS BOSSIDY, toast at the
                Holy Cross alumni dinner, 1910
[The toast was updated in 1952 by Franklin Pierce Adams (known as F.P.A.). He
wrote: "And here's to the City of Boston, / The town of the cries and groans, /
Where the Cabots can't see the Kabotschniks, / And the Lowells won't speak
to the Cohns," *On the Aristocracy of Harvard, Revised*, in *F.P.A.'s Book of
Quotations*, 1952.]

1 It will make you or break you,
But never forsake you.
Southie is my home town.
—ANONYMOUS, *Southie Is My Home Town*, c. 1910
[This vaudeville song was the anthem of South Boston, sung by several generations of Irish politicians and their constituents.]

2 It is not age which killed Boston, for no cities die of age; it is the youth of other cities.   —W. L. GEORGE, *Hail Columbia*, 1921

3 the Cambridge ladies who live in furnished souls
are unbeautiful and have comfortable minds.
—E. E. CUMMINGS,
Realities, I, in *Tulips and Chimneys*, 1923

4 If you hear an owl hoot: "To whom" instead of "To who" you can make up your mind he was born and educated in Boston.
—ANONYMOUS, in *F.P.A.'s Book of Quotations*, 1952

5 I have just returned from Boston. It is the only sane thing to do if you find yourself up there.   —FRED ALLEN,
letter to Groucho Marx, June 12, 1953

6 This is a town where there are three pastimes: politics, sports, and revenge.
—LAWRENCE C. MOULTER,
in *The New York Times*, Feb. 17, 1993
[Moulter, president of the New Boston Garden Corporation, also called the community "dysfunctional."]

Buffalo, N.Y.

7 Buffalo gals, won't you come out tonight,
And dance by the light of the moon?
—ANONYMOUS, *Buffalo Gals*, c. 1848
[Though commonly associated with boatmen on the Erie Canal, this probably began as a minstrel song. Cool White, an early blackface performer, published *Lubly Fan, Woncha Come Out Tonight* in 1844, according to *Folksong U.S.A.*, by John A. and Alan Lomax. The words were changed to "New York gals," "Bowery gals," "Philadelphia gals," and so on, depending on where the troupes were playing, with the "Buffalo" variant eventually becoming the most popular, probably for poetic reasons.]

8 The street cars swing at a curve,
The middle class passengers witness low life.
The car windows frame low life all day in pictures.
—CARL SANDBURG, *Slants at Buffalo, New York*,
in *Cornhuskers*, 1918

9 Within the town of Buffalo
Are prosy men with leaden eyes.
Like ants they worry to and fro
(Important men in Buffalo.)
But only twenty miles away
A deathless glory is at play;
Niagara, Niagara . . .
—VACHEL LINDSAY, *Niagara*, 1917

Butte, Mont.

Butte, "a mile high, a mile deep," built on the "richest hill on earth," and gen- 1
erally described as the greatest mining camp ever known . . . has a certain
inferno-like magnificence, with lights appropriately copper-colored—I heard it
called "the only electric-lit cemetery in the United States."
> —JOHN GUNTHER, *Inside U.S.A.,* 1947

[Gunther rated Butte as "the toughest, bawdiest town in America, with the
possible exception of Amarillo, Texas."]

Cairo, Ill.

This dismal Cairo.   2
> —CHARLES DICKENS, *American Notes,* 1842

[He hated the place. The American fad for giving ancient names to their towns
dates to January 5, 1789, when the citizens of Vanderheyden's Ferry, N.Y.,
voted to change the name of their burg to Troy.]

Carson City, Nev.

My informants declared that in and about Carson a dead man for breakfast was 3
the rule; besides accidents perpetually occurring to indifferent or to peace-
making parties, they reckoned per annum fifty murders.
> —RICHARD BURTON, *The City of the Saints,* 1861

They shoot folks here somewhat and the law is rather partial than otherwise to 4
first-class murderers.   —ARTEMUS WARD, *Artemus Ward, His Travels,* 1865

Charleston, S.C.

There prevails here [Charleston] a finer manner of life, and on the whole, there 5
are more evidences of courtesy than in the northern cities.
> —JOHANN DAVID SCHOEPF, *Travels in the Confederation,*
> *1783–1784* [1911]

Streets unpaved and narrow, small wooden houses, from among which rise, in 6
every quarter of the town, stately mansions, surrounded from top to bottom
with broad verandahs, and standing within little gardens full of orange trees,
palmettos, and magnolias, are features which give Charleston an expression
belonging rather to the south of Europe than to the Teutonic cities of the
north. . . . In other respects, it is a noble monument of what human avarice can
effect.   —FRANCIS HALL, *Travels in Canada and the United States*
> *in 1816 and 1817,* 1818

[Lt. Hall, a British visitor, found the climate of Charleston unbearable in summer, but noted that the fortunes to be made in rice, and the availability of
slaves to cultivate the crop, led to the creation of the city.]

In . . . [Charleston] you actually have to pin a man to the mat before you can do 7
business with him.   —HENRY MILLER, *The Air-Conditioned*
> *Nightmare,* 1945

An old Charlestonian may think of his city first and last, his heart bound to the 8
palm-lined Battery, where echoes linger from the blasts of the guns his forebears trained on two meddling foreign powers—Great Britain and the United
States.   —WILLIAM FRANCIS GUESS, *American Panorama:*
> *East of the Mississippi,* 1960

Chicago

1   This is a great uninteresting place of 600,000 inhabitants.
                                    —MATTHEW ARNOLD, letter to Frances Arnold,
                                        his sister, Jan. 23, 1884
[But about two years later, Robert Browning noted in a letter to New York politician Chauncey M. Depew that in the whole world the place that "sends me the most intelligent and thoughtful criticism upon my poetry is Chicago."]

2   Perhaps the most typically American place in America.
                                    —JAMES BRYCE, *The American Commonwealth*, 1888

3   I have struck a city—a real city—and they call it Chicago. . . . I urgently desire never to see it again. It is inhabited by savages.
                                    —RUDYARD KIPLING, *American Notes*, 1891

4   SATAN (impatiently) to NEW-COMER. The trouble with you Chicago people is that you think you are the best people down here, whereas you are merely the most numerous.   —Mark Twain, *Pudd'nhead Wilson's New Calendar*,
                                        in *Following the Equator*, 1897

5   First in violence, deepest in dirt, lawless, unlovely, ill-smelling, irreverent, new; an overgrown gawk of a—village, the "tough" among cities, a spectacle for the nation.
                                    —LINCOLN STEFFENS, *The Shame of the Cities*, 1904
[Either Steffens mellowed or Chicago improved; see Steffens below.]

6   In the twilight, it was a vision of power.
                                    —UPTON SINCLAIR, *The Jungle*, 1906

7   Chicago is the product of modern capitalism, and, like other great commercial centers, is unfit for human habitation.
                                    —EUGENE DEBS, 1908, quoted in Kevin Tierney, *Darrow* [1979]

8   Hog butcher for the world,
    Tool maker, stacker of wheat,
    Player with railroads and the nation's freight handler;
    Stormy, husky, brawling,
    City of the big shoulders.   —CARL SANDBURG, *Chicago*, 1916

9   It's one of the most progressive cities in the world. Shooting is only a sideline.
                                    —WILL ROGERS, *Weekly Articles*,
                                        June 22, 1930

10 Chicago will give you a chance. The sporting spirit is the spirit of Chicago.
                                    —LINCOLN STEFFENS, *The Autobiography
                                        of Lincoln Steffens*, 1931

11 Chicago is a great American city. Perhaps it is the last of the great American cities.
                                    —NORMAN MAILER, *Miami and the Siege of Chicago*, 1968
[More at CITIES above.]

12 Chicago was a town where nobody could forget how the money was made. It was picked up from floors still slippery with blood.
                                    —NORMAN MAILER, *Ibid.*

The city that works. —ANONYMOUS, saying, called "recently traditional" [1]
in *The Economist*, March 3–9, 1979
[Incidentally, the name *Chicago* is from an Indian word, *Chicagou*, meaning "garlic creek."]

Cincinnati, Ohio

I am sure I should have liked Cincinnati much better if the people had not [2]
dealt so very largely in hogs. —FRANCES TROLLOPE, *Domestic Manners
of the Americans*, 1832
[On Main Street, said Mrs. Trollope, "the chances were five hundred to one against my reaching the shady side without brushing by a snout fresh dripping from the kennel." On a stroll outside the city, she found to her distress that she had to cross a brook reddened from a nearby slaughterhouse, while her feet "literally got entangled in pigs' tails and jawbones."]

Cincinnati is a beautiful city; cheerful, thriving, and animated. [3]
—CHARLES DICKENS, *American Notes*, 1842
[In a letter of April 15, 1842, Dickens wrote: "Cincinnati is only fifty years old, but is a very beautiful city; I think the prettiest place I have seen here, except Boston. It has risen out of the forests like an Arabian night city; it is well laid out; ornamented in the suburbs with pretty villas; and, above all, for this is a rare feature in America, has smooth turf-plots and well kept gardens."]

The Queen of the West. —HENRY WADSWORTH LONGFELLOW, [4]
Catawba Wine, 1854
[The nickname dates from the 1830s, but this poem validated it. The poem is a thank-you from Longfellow to Nicholas Longworth of Cincinnati, who had given Longfellow some Catawba wine from vineyards that Longworth had established on the Ohio River. The full stanza reads: "And this Song of the Vine, / This greeting of mine, / The winds and the birds shall deliver / To the Queen of the West, / In her garlands dressed, / On the banks of the Beautiful River," quoted in *American Heritage*, February 1975.]

I saw it first bathed in the mellow light of a declining sun. . . . hill beyond hill, [5]
clothed with the rich verdure of an almost tropical clime, slopes of vineyards just ready for the wine-press, magnolias with their fragrant blossoms, and that queen of trees, the beautiful ilanthus, the "tree of heaven," as it is called; and everywhere foliage so luxuriant that it looked as if autumn and decay could never come.
—ISABELLA BIRD, description of Cincinnati in 1855
[She, too, was a visitor from England.]

Lying along the right bank of the Ohio River, with its wooded banks on both [6]
sides and its graceful reaches as it winds its course below the city, it is one of the most beautiful sites for a town I have ever seen.
—RICHARD COBDEN, diary entry, 1859
[Cobden, an English reformer, also mentioned the famous pork market that so struck Frances Trollope, but he was not put off by it. The city had a host of other industries, but nevertheless did earn the nickname "Porkopolis." The Bird and Cobden comments here are from *American Heritage*, December 1956.]

Cleveland, Ohio

I know of no other metropolis with quite so impressive a record in the practi- [7]
cal application of good citizenship to government.
—JOHN GUNTHER, *Inside U.S.A.*, 1947

Columbia, S.C.

1 There is about it an air of neatness and elegance which betokens it to be the residence of a superior class of people.
—CHARLES MACKAY, *Travels in the United States in 1846–47*, 1850

[Mackay did complain that the town was in the middle of nowhere, and that the government buildings were uninteresting, "their dimensions being very limited, and their style of a simple and altogether unambitious description."]

Columbus, Ohio

2 Columbus is a town in which almost anything is likely to happen and in which almost everything has.   —JAMES THURBER, *More Alarms at Night*, in *My Life and Hard Times*, 1933

Concord, Mass.

3 The biggest little place in America.
—HENRY JAMES, *The American Scene*, 1907

Dallas & Forth Worth, Tex.

4 Dallas is a baby Manhattan; Fort Worth is a cattle annex.
—JOHN GUNTHER, *Inside U.S.A.*, 1947

Denver

5 There have been during my two weeks sojourn, more brawls, more fights, more pistol shots with criminal intent in this log city of one hundred and fifty dwellings, not three-fourths completed, not two-thirds inhabited, nor one-third fit to be, than in any community of no greater numbers on earth.
—HORACE GREELEY, *An Overland Journey from New York to San Francisco . . . in 1859*, 1860

6 Cash! why they create it here.   —WALT WHITMAN, *Specimen Days, 1879*, 1882

7 The air is so refined that you can live without much lungs.
—SHANE LESLIE, *American Wonderland*, 1936

Des Moines, Iowa

8 Des Moines has the largest per capita ice cream consumption in America.
The second largest gold-fish farm in the world is located within seventy miles of Des Moines.
The best pair of overalls made on the American Continent came from Iowa.
There is no group of two and a half million people in the world who worship God as Iowans do.   —ANONYMOUS (a professor at Iowa State College), quoted by H. L. Mencken, in *Americana*, 1925

9 In Des Moines, a man's eyes will light up at the mere mention of the word "corn."   —PHILIP HAMBURGER, *An American Notebook*, 1965

Detroit

10 The capital of the new planet—the one, I mean, which will kill itself off—is of course Detroit.   —HENRY MILLER, *The Air-Conditioned Nightmare*, 1945

You can slip up on Detroit in the dead of night, consider it from any stand-   1
point, and it's still hell on wheels.   —GEORGE SESSIONS PERRY,
Cities of America, 1947

Say nice things about Detroit!   2
—ANONYMOUS, sign outside downtown Detroit pizzeria,
quoted in *The New York Times*, August 23, 1995

Duluth, Minn.

Duluth! The word fell upon my ear with peculiar and indescribable charm, like   3
the gentle murmur of a low fountain stealing forth in the midst of roses, or the
soft, sweet accents of an angel's whisper in the bright, joyous dream of sleeping
innocence. Duluth! 'Twas the name for which my soul had panted for years, as
the hart panteth for water-brooks. But where was Duluth? Never in all my limited reading had my vision been gladdened by seeing the celestial word in print.
—J. PROCTOR KNOTT, speech, U.S. House of Representatives,
Jan. 27, 1871

Zenith City of the Unsalted Seas.   4
—*Ibid.*
[This uproarious half-hour speech by Rep. Knott of Kentucky turned the nation's attention to Duluth, an obscure, muddy village with a population of
about three thousand. Knott was attacking a bill proposing to donate federal
lands to build a railroad that would link Duluth, with its port on Lake Superior, to the St. Croix River in Wisconsin. His oration, which left his colleagues
weak with laughter, killed the railway bill, but made Duluth famous—for
which Knott was properly thanked at a banquet in his honor when he eventually visited "that terrestrial paradise."]

El Paso, Tex.

[*See also* **Amarillo & El Paso**]

The city of the four C's—Climate, Cotton, Cattle, Copper.   5
—JOHN GUNTHER, *Inside U.S.A.*, 1947

Fort Worth, Tex.

[*See* **Dallas & Fort Worth**]

Frankfort, Ky.

Frankfort is the capital of Kentucky, and is as quietly a dull town as I ever vis-   6
ited. . . . The legislature of the state was not sitting when I was there, and the
grass was growing in the streets.
—ANTHONY TROLLOPE, *North America*, 1862

Hoboken, N.J.

Reporter. Might beauty then be in both the lily and Hoboken?   7
Oscar Wilde. Something of the kind.
—OSCAR WILDE, Jan. 3, 1882,
cited in Richard Ellman, *Oscar Wilde*, 1987
[When Wilde arrived in New York to tour America, reporters began querying
him about the fine points of aesthetics even before he disembarked. This also
was the occasion of one of his most famous bon mots (not recorded until much
later). Asked when passing through customs if he had anything to declare, the
great Oscar replied, "I have nothing to declare except my genius."]

1   It's Heaven, Hell, or Hoboken.
—ANONYMOUS, 1917

[More at WORLD WAR I.]

Hollywood

[*See* **Los Angeles**]

Houston, Tex.

2   In Houston the air was warm and rich and suggestive of fossil fuel.
—JOHN GUNTHER, *Inside U.S.A.*, 1947

Kansas City, Mo.

3   Ev'rythin's up to date in Kansas City.
—OSCAR HAMMERSTEIN II, *Kansas City*, in *Oklahoma!*, 1943

Laredo, Tex.

4   As I walked out in the streets of Laredo,
As I walked out in Laredo one day,
I spied a dear cowboy wrapped up in white linen,
Wrapped up in white linen as cold as the clay.
—ANONYMOUS, *The Streets of Laredo*, or
The Cowboy's Lament, c. 1860
[Alan Lomax reports in *Folksong U.S.A.* that his collection of ballads includes
more than one hundred examples of this song, set in almost as many western
towns. In what may be the original version, an English ballad, the young man
dies, not of a gunshot wound but of syphilis. In an Irish version, sung in Cork
around 1790, the dying man is a soldier. In still other versions, it is a young
woman who has gone astray. From the last evolved the famous *St. James Infirmary Blues*, which begins: "I was down in St. James Hospital, / My baby there
she lay / Out on cold marble table. / Well, I looked and I turned away."]

Las Vegas

5   If you aim to leave Las Vegas with a small fortune, go there with a large one.
—ANONYMOUS, saying, c. 1950
[Gambling was legalized in Nevada in 1931 but did not become a major factor
in the state's economy until after World War II. The first plush casino was
opened December 26, 1946, by gangster Benjamin "Bugsy" Siegel, who called
it the Flamingo, after the nickname of his mistress, Virginia Hill. Six months
later he was killed in a mob hit (three rifle bullets to the head) while talking to
an associate in the living room of Hill's home in Beverly Hills.]

6   Vegas is the most extreme and allegorical of American settlements, bizarre and
beautiful in its venality and in its devotion to immediate gratification.
—JOAN DIDION, *Marrying Absurd*,
in *Slouching Towards Bethlehem*, 1968

Los Angeles

7   Nineteen suburbs in search of a metropolis.
—ALDOUS HUXLEY, *Americana*, 1925
[The still more sprawling "seventy-two suburbs in search of a city" has been
attributed to Dorothy Parker and Alexander Woollcott, among others.]

Thought is barred in this City of Dreadful Joy, and conversation is unknown.   1
—ALDOUS HUXLEY, *Jesting Pilate*, 1926

There are millions to be grabbed out here, and your only competition is idiots.   2
Don't let this get around.
—HERMAN MANKIEWICZ, cable to Ben Hecht, 1926,
quoted in *The New York Times* [Jan. 8, 1993]

A trip through a sewer in a glass-bottomed boat.   3
—WILSON MIZNER, characterization of Hollywood, pre-1933,
in Alva Johnson, *The Incredible Mizners* [1953]

A dreary industrial town controlled by hoodlums of enormous wealth.   4
—S. J. PERELMAN, quoted on radio following his death,
Oct. 18, 1979

A circus without a tent.   5
—CAREY McWILLIAMS, *Southern California Country*, 1946

If you tilt the whole country sideways, Los Angeles is the place where every-   6
thing will fall.   —FRANK LLOYD WRIGHT, attributed

Strip the phoney tinsel off Hollywood and you'll find the real tinsel under-   7
neath.   —OSCAR LEVANT, in Leslie Halliwell,
The Filmgoer's Book of Quotes [1973]
[Levant—pianist, composer, actor, media celebrity, and mordant wit—went to
Hollywood in the 1920s. He became a close friend of George Gershwin and a
major interpreter of his music. Levant began self-destructing in the 1950s, taking pills of various sorts, which was a common path to addiction in that
period.]

Hollywood is a place where there is no definition of your worth earlier than   8
your last picture.   —MURRAY KEMPTON, *The Day of the Locust*,
in *Part of Our Time*, 1955

It's redundant to die in L.A.   —TRUMAN CAPOTE, 1975, quoted   9
in Jay Presson Allen's play *Tru* [1989]
[More at CALIFORNIA.]

In Hollywood, if you don't have happiness, you send out for it.   10
—REX REED, quoted in J. R. Colombo,
Colombo's Hollywood, 1979

Hollywood ceased to be Hollywood when television moved into the American   11
home . . . Hollywood today is unimpressive, seems outmoded, a pale memory
of itself.   —ALFRED KAZIN, Introduction, 1983,
to Nathanael West's *The Day of the Locust*

Memphis, Tenn.

The great height of the trees, the quantity of pendant vine branches that hang   12
amongst them; and the variety of gay plumaged birds, particularly the small
green parrot, made us feel we were in a new world.
—FRANCES TROLLOPE, *Domestic Manners
of the Americans*, 1832

1   A dreary, dingy, muddy, melancholy town.
                        —CHARLES MACKAY, *Down the Mississippi,*
                            in *Life and Liberty in America, or, Sketches of a Tour*
                            in the United States and Canada in 1857–1858, 1859
[This is the same Mackay who wrote the classic sociological study *Popular
Delusions and the Madness of Crowds.*]

Miami, Fla.

2   Miami is . . . of unimaginable awfulness—much like other American seaside
resorts but on an unprecedented scale: acres of cheap white shops, mountain
ranges of white hotels.   —EDMUND WILSON, letter to Elena Wilson,
                                    Nov. 26, 1949

3   Miami Beach is where neon goes to die.
                        —LENNY BRUCE, quoted by Barbara Gordon,
                            Saturday Review, May 20, 1972

4   In Miami Beach the air conditioning is pushed to that icy point where women
may wear fur coats over their diamonds in the tropics.
                        —NORMAN MAILER, *Miami and the Siege of Chicago,* 1968

5   Miami is more American than America.
                        —GARRY WILLS, *Nixon Agonistes,* 1970

Milwaukee, Wisc.

6   Milwaukee and its environs provided a gray landscape, drawn with hard lines
and great attention to detail.
                        —CECIL BEATON, *It Gives Me Great Pleasure,* 1955

Mobile, Ala.

7   Mobile stays in the heart, the loveliest of cities.
                        —CARL CARMER, *Stars Fell on Alabama,* 1934

8   I have never once thought of work in connection with Mobile. *Not anybody
working.*   —HENRY MILLER, *The Air-Conditioned Nightmare,* 1945

Muncie, Ind.

9   This sober, hopeful, well-meaning city.
                        —Robert S. Lynd & Helen Merrell Lynd,
                            Middletown in Transition, 1937
[This was a follow-up by the Lynds to *Middletown* (1929), in which they applied the methods of cultural anthropology to a typical American community.
Their findings at first shocked the natives, many of whom regarded the Lynds
as muckrakers or Marxists. But their studies eventually were accepted as classics of American sociology.]

10   Middletown is *against* the reverse of the things it is for.   —*Ibid.*

11   Middletown is a marrying city.   —*Ibid.*

Nashville, Tenn.

12   The Athens of Dixie.   —ANONYMOUS, motto, quoted in John Gunther,
                            Inside U.S.A., 1947

Newark, N.J.

A city of strivers pushing forward from immigrant enclaves.   1
—GRACE MIRABELLA, with Judith Warner,
In and Out of Vogue, 1995

New Orleans

A city of sin and gayety unique on the North American continent.   2
—HERBERT ASBURY, *The French Quarter:*
An Informal History of the New Orleans Underworld, 1936

There is no architecture in New Orleans except in the cemeteries.   3
—MARK TWAIN, *Life on the Mississippi,* 1883

[Old New Orleans was built upon a cypress swamp, and it is impossible to dig conventional six-foot-deep graves except in some of the newer, higher parts of town. The water table is too close to the surface. As a result, above-ground tombs of varying degrees of ornateness have proliferated.]

New Orleans is the unique American place.   4
—CHARLES KURALT, *Charles Kuralt's America,* 1995

Newport, R.I.

[*See also* EPITAPHS & GRAVESTONES (Longfellow)]

[Newport,] where idleness ranks among the virtues.   5
—OSCAR WILDE, letter to Charles Eliot Norton,
c. July 15, 1882

Newport, Rhode Island, that breeding place—that stud farm, so to speak—of   6
aristocracy; aristocracy of the American type; that auction mart where English nobilities come to trade hereditary titles for American girls and cash.
—MARK TWAIN, Feb. 4, 1907, in *The Autobiography*
of Mark Twain, ed. by Charles Neider [1959]

Newport was charming, but it asked for no education and gave none.   7
—HENRY ADAMS, *The Education of Henry Adams,* 1907

One hundred years after the declaration that "all men are created equal," there   8
began to gather in Newport a colony of the rich, determined to show that some Americans were conspicuously more equal than others.
—ALISTAIR COOKE, *America,* 1973

New York City

[For a view of New York Harbor in 1609, see under NEW YORK.]

They [New Yorkers] talk very loud, very fast, and all together.   9
—JOHN ADAMS, July 23, 1774, *The Diary* [1850]

The renowned and ancient city of Gotham.   10
—WASHINGTON IRVING, *Salmagundi,* 1807–1808

[Irving's allusion was to the folktales about the village of Gotham in Nottinghamshire, England. The so-called wise men of Gotham actually were fools. Thus, twelve Gothamites on a fishing expedition worried that one of their party had drowned because each man forgot to count himself. The sense of "gothamite" gradually improved over the years, however, from "fool" to "wise

fool" to "wiseacre" or "know-it-all," which is how Irving used it when referring to New Yorkers.]

1   Situated on an island, which I think it will one day cover, it rises like Venice,
from the sea, and like the fairest of cities in the days of her glory, receives into
its lap tribute of all the riches of the earth.
          —FRANCES TROLLOPE, *Domestic Manners of the Americans*, 1832
[For a comment on New York society, see Ward McAllister at THE ELITE.]

2   New York is a sucked orange.   —RALPH WALDO EMERSON, *Culture*,
                                                  in *The Conduct of Life*, 1860

3   My own Manhattan, with spires and the sparkling and hurrying tides, and the
ships.   —WALT WHITMAN, *When Lilacs Last
                                               in the Dooryard Bloom'd*, 1865–66
[For more of this poem, see SORROW & GRIEF.]

4   City of hurried and sparkling waters! city of spires and masts!
City nested in bays! my city!   —WALT WHITMAN, *Mannahatta*, 1881

5   East Side, West Side, all around the town,
The tots sang "Ring-a-rosie," "London Bridge is falling down";
Boys and girls together, me and Mamie O'Rourke,
Tripped the light fantastic on the sidewalks of New York.
          —JAMES W. BLAKE, *The Sidewalks of New York*, 1894

6   The Great White Way.
                          —ALBERT BIGELOW PAINE, play title, 1901
[Broadway, of course.]

7   Give my regards to Broadway,
Remember me to Herald Square,
Tell all the gang at Forty-second Street
That I will soon be there.
          —GEORGE M. COHAN, *Give My Regards to Broadway*,
          from *Little Johnny Jones*, 1904

8   When you are away from old Broadway, you are only camping out.
          —GEORGE M. COHAN, quoted in Fred R. Ringel, ed.,
                          America as Americans See It [1932]
[Or as Fred Allen put it, "Everywhere outside New York City is Bridgeport,
Connecticut," quoted in Alistair Cooke, *America*, 1973. See also the saying on
Paul Volcker's ashtray under Anonymous below, p. 101.]

9   *Mammon, n.* The god of the world's leading religion. His chief temple is in the
holy city of New York.
          —AMBROSE BIERCE, *The Devil's Dictionary*, 1906
[*Mammon* means "riches," or "money," in Aramaic. At *Matthew* 6:24, we are
warned, "Ye cannot serve God and mammon." New Yorkers, however, may
cite in their defense *Luke* 16:9, "Make to yourself friends of the mammon of
unrighteousness."]

10   Little old Bagdad-on-the-Subway.
          —O. HENRY, *A Madison Square Arabian Night*,
                          in *The Trimmed Lamp*, 1907
[Henry used the "Bagdad-on-the-Subway" phrase again in *Roads of Destiny, A*

Night in New Arabia, and *What You Want.* Turning to another "on-the-Subway" epithet for New York, Henry wrote, "Well, little old Noisy-ville-on-the-Subway is good enough for me," *The Duel,* in *Strictly Business,* 1910.]

New York is the great stone desert.   1
                                    —ISRAEL ZANGWILL, *The Melting Pot,* 1908

To Europe she was America, to America she was the gateway of the earth. But   2
to tell the story of New York would be to write a social history of the world.
                            —H. G. WELLS, *The War in the Air,* 1908
[Wells foresaw in this novel, written five years after the Wright brothers flew
the first airplane, the development not only of air warfare but of the atomic
bomb.]

It couldn't have happened anywhere but in little old New York.   3
                                    —O. HENRY, *A Little Local Color,*
                                    in *Whirligigs,* 1910

New York is the most fatally fascinating thing in America.   4
                                    —JAMES WELDON JOHNSON,
                                    O, Black and Unknown Bards, 1917

Harlem is the precious fruit in the Garden of Eden, the big apple.   5
                                    —ALAIN LOCKE, c. 1919
[An early example of the "big apple" metaphor, cited in Deirdre Mullane, ed.,
Words to Make My Children Live: A Book of African American Quotations,
1995. Locke who earned a B.A. and Ph.D. from Harvard University, was the
first black Rhodes Scholar, and taught philosophy at Howard University. He
edited *The New Negro,* 1925, an anthology that introduced the writers of the
Harlem Renaissance to a wide audience.]

O Babylon! O Carthage! O New York!   6
                                    —SIEGFRIED SASSOON, *Storm on Fifth Avenue,*
                                    in the *London Mercury* magazine, April 1921

The great big city's a wondrous toy   7
Just made for a girl and boy.
We'll turn Manhattan
Into an isle of joy.   —LORENZ HART, *Manhattan,* 1925

More than any other city in the world, it is the fullest expression of our mod-   8
ern age.   —LEON TROTSKY, *My Life,* 1930

The Bronx?   9
No thonx!
                                    —OGDEN NASH, *Geographical Reflection,* in *Hard-Lines,* 1931
[Bronxites were understandably outraged by this catchy couplet. In 1964, for
the Bronx's golden jubilee, Nash delivered an apology, which read in part: "I
wrote those lines 'The Bronx? No thonx!' / I shudder to confess them. Now I'm
an older, wiser man / I cry, 'The Bronx, God bless them!'"]

Hardly a day goes by, you know, that some innocent bystander ain't shot to   10
death in New York City.   —WILL ROGERS, Nov. 20, 1931, *More Letters*
                                    of a Self-Made Diplomat [1982]
[Rogers's point was that it took a pretty good marksman to hit an innocent person in New York. "One day they shot four," he noted. "That's the best shoot-

ing ever done in this town. Any time you can find four innocent people in New York in one day you are doing well even if you don't shoot them."]

1   New York is so situated that anything you want, you can get in the very block you live in. If you want to be robbed, there is one living in your block; if you want to be murdered, you don't have to leave your apartment house; if you want pastrami or gefilte fish, there is a delicatessen every other door; if it's female excitement you crave, your neighbor's wife will accommodate you.
　　　　　　　　　　　　　　　　　　　　　　—WILL ROGERS, *Ibid.*

2   Only the Dead Know Brooklyn.
　　　　　　—THOMAS WOLFE, story title, in *From Death to Morning*, 1935

3   New York had all the iridescence of the beginning of the world.
　　　　　　　　　　—F. SCOTT FITZGERALD, *The Crack-up*, 1936

4   O sweep of stars over Harlem streets,
　　O little breath of oblivion that is night.
　　A city building to a mother's song,
　　A city dreaming to a lullaby.
　　　　　　—LANGSTON HUGHES, *Stars*, in *From My People*
　　[In a 1963 essay, *In Love with Harlem*, Hughes wrote: "Melting pot Harlem—Harlem of honey and chocolate and caramel and rum and vinegar and lemon and lime and gall. Dusky dream Harlem rumbling into a nightmare tunnel where the subway from the Bronx keeps right on downtown."]

5   Suddenly New York blazes like a magnificent jewel in its fit setting of sea, and earth, and stars.　　　　—THOMAS WOLFE, *The Web and the Rock*, 1939

6   It was a cruel city, but it was a lovely one.　　　　　　　　　—*Ibid.*

7   New York, New York—a helluva town,
　　The Bronx is up but the Battery's down.　　—BETTY COMDEN & ADOLPH GREEN,
　　　　　　　　　　　　　　　　　　　New York, New York, 1945
　　[The authors reworked the lyric slightly for the 1949 film of *On the Town*, bowdlerizing "helluva town" as "wonderful town."]

8   A hundred times have I thought New York is a catastrophe and fifty times: It is a beautiful catastrophe.　　　　—LE CORBUSIER, *The Fairy Catastrophe*,
　　　　　　　　　　　　　　　　in *When Cathedrals Were White*, 1947

9   New York City isn't a melting pot, it's a boiling pot.
　　　　　　　　　　—THOMAS E. DEWEY, remark to John Gunther,
　　　　　　　　　　　　　　　　Inside U.S.A., 1947
　　[For the original melting pot metaphor, see under Israel Zangwill at AMERICA & AMERICANS. The concept was still pertinent forty years later, according to *US News & World Report*, April 14, 1986, which recorded that a sign in Times Square read, "If the United States is a melting pot, then New York makes it bubble."]

10   New York is to the nation what the white church spire is to the village—the visible symbol of aspiration and faith, the white plume saying the way is up!
　　　　　　—E. B. WHITE, *Here Is New York*, in *Holiday* magazine,
　　　　　　April 1949

11   On any person who desires such queer prizes, New York will bestow the gift of loneliness and the gift of privacy.　　　　　　　　　　—*Ibid.*

The only credential the city asked was the boldness to dream. For those who 1
did, it unlocked its gates and its treasures, not caring who they were or where
they came from.   —MOSS HART,
Act One, 1959

Terrible things happen to young girls in New York City.   2
                              —MARY MARGARET MCBRIDE,
                                A Long Way from Missouri, 1959

There is no greenery. It is enough to make a stone sad.   3
                              —NIKITA KHRUSHCHEV, quoted by Bruce Weber,
                                New York Times [June 21, 1992]
[Khrushchev, the premier of the USSR, toured the U.S. in 1959.]

This is Harlem, where anything can happen.   4
                              —CHESTER HIMES, *The Crazy Kill*, 1959
[The speaker is police detective Grave Digger Jones.]

If you should happen after dark   5
To find yourself in Central Park
Ignore the paths that beckon you
And hurry, hurry to the zoo
And creep into the tiger's lair.
Frankly you'll be safer there.
                              —OGDEN NASH, in *Everyone but Thee and Me*, 1964

New York was heaven to me. And Harlem was Seventh Heaven.   6
                              —MALCOLM X,
                                The Autobiography of Malcolm X, 1965

Ford to City: Drop Dead.   7
                              —NEW YORK DAILY NEWS, headline, Oct. 30, 1975
[Columnist Jimmy Breslin has said reporters William Brink and Michael
O'Neill should be credited with this headline. At the time, Pres. Gerald Ford
has just promised to veto any bill to provide bailout funds to the nearly bank-
rupt city. For another great headline, see Abel Green at MEDIA.]

When you've left New York, you ain't going nowhere.   8
                              —ANONYMOUS, legend on ashtray, spotted in 1980, on desk
                                of Federal Reserve Board chairman Paul Volcker,
                                according to Martin Mayer, *The Money Bazaars*, 1985

New York is the true City of Light in any season.   9
                              —CHARLES KURALT, *Charles Kuralt's America*, 1995

Niagara, N.Y.

[*See* **Buffalo, N.Y.,** above, *and* NEW YORK (Vachel Lindsay)]

Nome, Alaska

You'll find a magic city   10
On the shore of Bering Strait.
Which shall be for you a station
To unload your arctic freight.
                              —SAM DUNHAM, c. 1900, in Peter Yapp,
                                A Travellers' Dictionary of Quotations, 1983

Oakland, Calif.

1   What was the use of my having come from Oakland. . . . there is no there there.
—GERTRUDE STEIN, *Everybody's Autobiography*, 1937

Paterson, N.J.

2   Paterson lies in the valley under the Passaic Falls
its spent waters forming the outline of his back. He
lies on his right side, head near the thunder
of the waters filling his dreams.
—WILLIAM CARLOS WILLIAMS, *Six Poems from Paterson*

Peoria, Ill.

3   Will it play in Peoria?
—ANONYMOUS

[The origin of this query is obscure. Gorton Carruth and Eugene Ehrlich in *American Quotations*, 1988, cite it as a traditional phrase in America politics, and it may derive from vaudeville. Political lexicographer William Safire gives considerable credit to Pres. Richard Nixon's aide John Ehrlichman, who used the phrase, "It'll play in Peoria" to mean that a policy or plan was politically viable. Mr. Ehrlichman told William Safire that he first used the expression while running a course for political campaign workers in New York City in 1968. "Onomatopoeia was the only reason for Peoria, I suppose. And it personified—exemplified—a place, removed from media centers on the coasts, where the national verdict is cast, according to the Nixon doctrine," *Safire's New Political Dictionary*. Earlier, around the turn of the century, Ambrose Bierce similarly recognized the symbolic status of Peoria. In his *Devil's Dictionary* (1906), he wrote, "According to the most trustworthy statistics the number of adult dullards in the United States is but little short of thirty millions. The intellectual center of the race is somewhere about Peoria, Illinois." Charles Dudley Warner used "Peoria" in the same generic, somewhat disparaging sense in an 1875 essay, *The Whims of Travel*: "Foreign peoples, life, manners, religion, cities, are to be studied in the soft glow of ancientness, and not in the sudden flare of a pitch-pine knot that you have brought from Peoria."]

Philadelphia

4   Three Philadelphia lawyers are a match for the very devil himself.
—ANONYMOUS, c. 1800

[More at LAWYERS.]

5   Spitting and swearing are nearly out of fashion in Philadelphia . . . at this moment we cannot recall more than two or three gentlemen who would think of such a thing as spitting on the carpet of a lady's drawing room.
—*A Pleasant Peregrination in Pennsylvania*, 1836,
cited in Samuel Eliot Morison, *The Oxford History
of the American People* [1965], without author

6   Philadelphia: Corrupt and Contented.
—LINCOLN STEFFENS, title of three-part series of articles
on Philadelphia, in *The Shame of the Cities*, 1904

7   I liked poor dear queer flat comfortable Philadelphia almost ridiculously (for what it is—extraordinarily *cossu* and materially civilized).
—HENRY JAMES, letter to Edmund Gosse, Feb. 16, 1905
[Gentlemen are not supposed to discuss money, which explains James's lapse

into the French *cossu,* meaning "rich." The city's comfortable charms were of some years standing. As Benjamin Franklin said, when told that the British under Sir William Howe had taken Philadelphia in 1777, "I beg your pardon, Sir, Philadelphia has taken Howe."]

I went to Philadelphia one Sunday. The place was closed.   1
—W. C. FIELDS, attributed
[One of Fields's many jokes at the expense of his native city. See also EPITAPHS & GRAVESTONES.]

Philadelphia, a metropolis sometimes known as the City of Brotherly Love,   2
but more accurately as the City of Bleak Afternoons.
—S. J. PERELMAN, *Westward Ha!,* 1948

Philadelphia, the home of respectability, and the city of respectable homes.   3
—ANONYMOUS, saying, quoted in Nathaniel Burt,
The Perennial Philadelphians, 1963

In Philadelphia, Philadelphians feel, the Right Thing is more natural and more   4
firmly bred into [them] than anywhere else.
—STEPHEN BIRMINGHAM, *The Golden Dream,* 1978

Pittsburgh, Pa.

The land at the point is 20 or 25 feet above the common surface of of the wa-   5
ter; and a considerable bottom of flat, well-timbered land all around it, very convenient for building.
—GEORGE WASHINGTON, *Journal,* 1754
[This was Washington's view on a scouting mission of the future site of Fort Duquesne where the Allegheny and Monongahela rivers meet to form the Ohio. Washington lost his journal when he surrendered Fort Necessity, southeast of present-day Uniontown, Pa., to the French on July 4, 1754, and it was first published in Paris in 1756 by the French government as a propaganda document to justify their own activities in North America.]

Pittsburgh is like Birmingham in England; at least its townspeople say so. . . .   6
It certainly has a great quantity of black smoke hanging about it.
—CHARLES DICKENS,
American Notes, 1842

Hell with the lid taken off.   7
—JAMES PARTON, in *The Atlantic Monthly,* 1868

Plymouth, Mass.

Plymouth is a somewhat flourishing town even at this day, but its principal   8
pride is its historical recollections.
—CHARLES FRANCIS ADAMS, *Diary,* Sept. 14, 1835

Pocatello, Idaho

You can't go back to Pocatello.   9
—RICHARD L. NEUBERGER, remark c. 1943–1944,
quoted in Jonathan Daniels, *Frontier on the Potomac* [1946]
[Pocatello, Idaho, said to be a fine small city, here stands for any provincial community to which a Washington politician would not want to return. According to *Safire's New Political Dictionary,* the adage was coined during a

lunch conversation between Daniels and Neuberger, later a senator from Oregon. They were discussing the tendency of politicians to settle in Washington after they have left office. Neuberger probably had in mind the Thomas Wolfe quote on going home; see HOME.]

Portland, Maine

1 Often I think of the beautiful town
That is seated by the sea;
Often in thought go up and down
The pleasant streets of that dear old town,
And my youth comes back to me.
—HENRY WADSWORTH LONGFELLOW, *My Lost Youth*,
in *Putnam's Magazine*, 1855
[Longfellow was born and raised in Portland.]

2 Oh happy Portlanders, if they only knew their own good fortune! They get up early, and go to bed early. The women are comely and sturdy, able to take care of themselves without any fal-lal of chivalry; and the men are sedate, obliging, and industrious.   —ANTHONY TROLLOPE, *North America*, 1862

Portland, Ore.

3 Portland produces lumber and jig-saw fittings for houses, and beer and buggies, and bricks and biscuit; and, in case you should miss the fact, there are glorified views of the town hung up in public places with the value of the products set down in dollars. All this is excellent and exactly suitable to the opening of a new country; but when a man tells you it is civilization, you object.
—RUDYARD KIPLING, *American Notes*, 1891
[Kipling didn't like Portland much. There was a sewage problem when he was there.]

Providence, R.I.

4 Where bay and tranquil river blend,
And leafy hillsides rise,
The spires of Providence ascend
Against the ancient skies.   —H. P. LOVECRAFT, *Providence*

Reno, Nev.

5 The biggest little city in the world.
—ANONYMOUS, saying, pre-1960
[Reno was Nevada's most populous city until surpassed by Las Vegas in the 1950s. It also was for many years the divorce capital of the United States, thanks to a 1931 law that allowed people to end their marriages there after just six weeks of legal residence—and to Reno's location on the western edge of Nevada, close to Californians desiring to shed their spouses.]

Rochester, N.Y.

6 The very streets seemed to be starting up of their own accord, ready-made, and looking as fresh and new, as if they had been turned out of the workmen's hands but an hour before—or that a great boxfull of new houses had been sent by steam from New York, and tumbled out onto the half-cleared land.
—BASIL HALL, *Travels in North America*, 1829
[Capt. Hall retired from the British navy in 1842 and took up traveling and book writing.]

St. Louis, Mo.

The city of St. Louis is, in the solidity of its buildings, the extent of its   1
commerce, and the reputed wealth of its capitalists, the third in importance
in the States. I have seen no place in the interior which gives the same impression of solid wealth and extensive commerce.
—RICHARD COBDEN, diary entry, 1859

It is the capital city of the great west, the frontier town between the prairie and   2
the settled country.
—EDWARD DICEY, *Six Months in the Federal States*, 1863
[Although he called St. Louis a "frontier town," Dicey noted, "There is no look
left . . . of a newly settled city. The hotels are as handsome and as luxurious as
in any of the elder States. The shop windows are filled with all the evidences
of an old civilization." And he went on to praise the sophisticated reading
habits of the residents.]

Meet me in St. Louis, Louis,   3
Meet me at the fair.
—ANDREW B. STERLING, *Meet Me in St. Louis*, 1904
[The fair was the Louisiana Purchase Exposition, celebrating the centennial of
the giant land acquisition in 1803.]

Salt Lake City, Utah

I packt up my duds & left Salt Lake, which is a 2nd Soddum & Gemorrer, in-   4
habitid by as theavin & onprincipled a set of retchis as ever drew breth in eny
spot on the globe.   —ARTEMUS WARD, *A Visit to Brigham Young*,
in *Artemus Ward, His Book*, 1862

One must thank the genius of Brigham Young for the creation of Salt Lake   5
City,—an inestimable hospitality to the Overland Emigrants, and an efficient
example to all men in the vast desert, teaching how to subdue and turn it to a
habitable garden.
—RALPH WALDO EMERSON, *Journals*, Oct. 1863
[See also UTAH.]

Salt Lake City was healthy—an extremely healthy city. They declared that   6
there was only one physician in the place and he was arrested every week regularly and held to answer under the vagrant act for having "no visible means of
support."   —MARK TWAIN, *Roughing It*, 1872

San Francisco

The miners came in forty-nine,   7
The whores in fifty-one;
And when they got together
They produced the native son.

—ANONYMOUS, song, 1852 (or later)
[Virtuous women were in such short supply in San Francisco during the early
years of the gold rush that some prominent pioneers married professional ones,
especially favoring those who had accumulated substantial "doweries." Herbert Asbury reported in *The Barbary Coast* (1933) that this bawdy song was
"still sung by San Franciscans who do not take their municipal glories too
seriously."]

I have seen purer liquors, better segars, truer guns and pistols, larger dirks and   8
bowie knives, and prettier courtezans, here in San Francisco, than in any other

place I have ever visited; and it is my unbiased opinion that California can and does furnish the best bad things that are obtainable in America.
—HINTON R. HELPER, *Land of Gold:*
Reality versus Fiction, 1855

1   San Francisco is a mad city—inhabited for the most part by perfectly insane people whose women are of a remarkable beauty.
—RUDYARD KIPLING, *American Notes,* 1891

2   San Francisco has only one drawback. 'Tis hard to leave.   —*Ibid.*

3   If, as some say, God spanked the town
For being over frisky,
Why did he burn the churches down
And save Hotaling's Whiskey?
—ANONYMOUS, 1906 comment on the San Francisco fire
[Eve Golden in a letter to *The New York Times,* July 25, 1993, quoted this ditty from memory. She was addressing the question of whether fires, floods, and other natural catastrophes are God's response to people's sinful ways.]

4   San Francisco is perhaps the most European of all American cities.
—CECIL BEATON,
It Gives Me Great Pleasure, 1955

5   When you get tired of walking around San Francisco, you can always lean against it.   —TRANSWORLD GETAWAY GUIDE,
San Francisco, 1975–76

Santa Fe

6   Santa Fe, New Mexico, is the strangest place for fashion in America. They dress in what goes well with a highly polished aura. I imagine people there dress for their past lives.
—ANDREI CODRESCU, in *The New York Times,* Oct. 24, 1993

Savannah, Ga.

7   I pitched upon this place, not only for the pleasantness of the situation, but because . . . I thought it healthy; for it is sheltered from the western and southern winds by vast woods of pine-trees.
—JAMES EDWARD OGLETHORPE, letter, Feb. 20, 1733
[Gen. Oglethorpe, a British philanthropist as well as a military man, established the colony of Georgia as a refuge for debtors—and also to protect neighboring colonies from Spanish forays to the north. Savannah was Oglethorpe's first settlement, this letter being written just eight days after his arrival on the spot.]

8   Savannah is a living tomb about which there still clings a sensuous aura as in old Corinth.   —HENRY MILLER,
The Air-Conditioned Nightmare, 1945

Seattle, Wash.

9   Seattle is a comparatively new-looking city that covers an old frontier like frosting on a cake.   —WINTHROP SARGENT,
in *The New Yorker,*
June 26, 1978

Springfield, Ill.

[*See also* PARTING (Lincoln)]

In this, the City of my Discontent,   1
Sometimes there comes a whisper from the grass.
"Romance, Romance—is here. No Hindu town
Is quite so strange. No Citadel of Brass
By Sindbad found, held half such love and hate;
No picture-palace in a picture-book
Such webs of Friendship, Beauty, Greed, and Fate!"
In this, the City of my Discontent,
Down from the sky, up from the smoking deep
Wild legends new and old burn round my bed
While trees and grass and men are wrapped in sleep.
Angels come down, with Christmas in their hearts,
Gentle, whimsical, laughing, heaven-sent;
And, for a day, fair Peace have given me
In this the City of my Discontent.   —VACHEL LINDSAY, in *The Sangamon*
                              County Peace Advocate, Dec. 1909

Tulsa, Okla.

Tulsa, "oil capital of the world," as it calls itself, is a tough, get-rich-quick,   2
heady town about as sensitive as corduroy.   —EDNA FERBER, *Cimarron*, 1930

Tulsa is a residential suburb of Claremore [Rogers's hometown], where we park   3
our millionaires to keep them from getting under our feet.
                              —WILL ROGERS, in Alex Ayres, ed.,
                              The Wit and Wisdom of Will Rogers [1993]

Van Horn, Tex.

Come to Van Horn to live. The climate is so healthy we had to shoot a man to   4
start our graveyard.
                    —ANONYMOUS, placard, Jackson House Hotel, pre–World War I,
                    cited in Mody C. Boatright,
                    Folk Laughter on the American Frontier [1949]

Washington, D.C.

[*See also* CONGRESS; GOVERNMENT]

To Washington, central star of the constellation, may it enlighten the whole   5
world.   —[MARQUIS DE] LAFAYETTE, toast, 1824

Look to the city of Washington, and let the virtuous patriots of the country   6
weep at the spectacle. There corruption is springing into existence, and fast
flourishing.   —ANONYMOUS, *Letters of Wyoming* . . .
                              in Favour of Andrew Jackson, 1824
[Most of the letters, originally published in the Philadelphia *Columbian Observer* in June and July of 1823, were written by John H. Eaton, who became
Jackson's secretary of war after he was elected president in 1828. Eaton is remembered in history mainly for marrying a beautiful but forward young
woman, the daughter of a Washington innkeeper, who was rumored to have
been his mistress—and, horrors, also mistress to others. This caused such an
uproar, socially and politically, that Eaton had to resign his office in 1831.]

1   It is sometimes called the City of Magnificent Distances, but it might with greater propriety be termed the City of Magnificent Intentions.
—CHARLES DICKENS, *American Notes*, 1842

2   Washington is full of famous men and the women they married when they were young.   —FANNY DIXWELL HOLMES, to Pres. Theodore Roosevelt, at a gathering in honor of her husband, Supreme Court Justice Oliver Wendell Holmes, Jan. 8, 1903

3   Things get very lonely in Washington sometimes. The real voice of the great people of America sometimes sounds faint and distant in that strange city. You hear politics until you wish that both parties were smothered in their own gas.
—WOODROW WILSON, speech, St. Louis, Sept. 5, 1919

4   If I wanted to go crazy, I would do it in Washington because it would not be noticed.   —IRWIN S. COBB, attributed

5   The heart of America is felt less here [Washington] than at any place I have ever been.   —HUEY LONG, speech in the U.S. Senate, May 17, 1932

6   The fundamental fact about Washington is that it was created for a definite purpose and has been developed, with many modifications, according to a definite plan. Therein lies its unique distinction among American cities.
—FEDERAL WRITERS' PROJECT, *Washington, D.C.: A Guide to the Nation's Capital*, 1942

7   There are a number of things wrong with Washington. One of them is that everyone has been too long away from home.
—DWIGHT D. EISENHOWER, attributed, press conference, May 11, 1955
[The remark somehow did not make it into the official transcript.]

8   Washington isn't a city, it's an abstraction.
—DYLAN THOMAS, interview, in John Malcolm Brinnin, *Dylan Thomas in America*, 1956

9   The more I observed Washington, the more frequently I visited it, and the more people I interviewed there, the more I understood how prophetic L'Enfant was when he laid it out as a city that goes around in circles.
—JOHN MASON BROWN, *Through These Men*, 1956

10   Somebody once said that Washington is a city of Southern efficiency and Northern charm.   —JOHN F. KENNEDY, comment to trustees and advisory committee of the national cultural center, Nov. 14, 1961

11   Too small to be a state but too large to be an asylum for the mentally deranged.
—ANNE GORSUCH BURFORD, speech, Vail, Colo., July 27, 1984
[Burford, a Reagan administration appointee, headed the Environmental Protection Agency. Her tenure was distinguished by an apparent determination not to enforce environmental laws. She left after being cited for contempt of Congress. Her assistant administrator, Rita Lavelle, a protégé of Attorney General Edwin Meese, was convicted of perjury and served three months in prison. Burford, by the way, borrowed this comment from James Petigru; see SOUTH CAROLINA.]

If you want a friend in Washington, go buy a dog.   1
>   —ANONYMOUS, saying, quoted in *The New York Times*,
>   March 3, 1994

Weehawken, N.J.

The domes of the Church of   2
the Paulist Fathers in Weehawken
against a smoky dawn—the heart stirred—
are beautiful as St. Peter's
approached after years of anticipation.
>   —WILLIAM CARLOS WILLIAMS,
>   *January Morning*, "Suite,"
>   in *Al Que Quiere!*, 1917

[This is a continuation of Williams's thoughts on travel; see TRAVEL.]

CITIES ABROAD

Florence

Everything about Florence seems to be colored with a mild violet, like diluted   3
wine.   —HENRY JAMES, letter, to Henry James, Sr., Oct. 26, 1869

This is the fairest picture on our planet, the most enchanting to look upon, the   4
most satisfying to the eye and the spirit. To see the sun sink down, drowned in
his pink and purple and golden floods, and overwhelm Florence with tides of
color that make all the sharp lines dim and faint and turn the solid city to a
city of dreams, is a sight to stir the coldest nature, and make a sympathetic one
drunk with ecstasy.   —MARK TWAIN, entry 1892,
>   *Mark Twain's Autobiography* [1924]

London

London is the epitome of our times and the Rome of today.   5
>   —RALPH WALDO EMERSON, *English Traits*, 1856

The muddy tide of the Thames, reflecting nothing, and hiding a million un-   6
clean secrets within its breast . . . is just the dismal stream to glide by such a
city.   —NATHANIEL HAWTHORNE, *Our Old Home*, 1863

When it's three o'clock in New York, it's still 1938 in London.   7
>   —BETTE MIDLER, quoted in the London *Times*, Sept. 21, 1978

Moscow

It did look like the other side of the moon should look—gray, flat, and spooky.   8
>   —HARPO MARX, *Harpo Speaks*, 1961

The Russians have a saying . . . "Moscow is downhill from all the Russias,"   9
meaning that the best of everything flows down into Moscow.
>   —HEDRICK SMITH, *The Russians*, 1977

Paris

A loud modern New York of a place.   —RALPH WALDO EMERSON, *Journal*,   10
>   July 1833

1   Good Americans when they die go to Paris.
                              —THOMAS GOLD APPLETON, saying, c. 1850
[Appleton, a Bostonian, is credited with this bon mot in Oliver Wendell
Holmes's *The Autocrat of the Breakfast-Table*, 1858. Referring to this epigram,
Oscar Wilde posed the question, "And when bad Americans die, where do they
go to?" The answer: "Oh, they go to America," *A Woman of No Importance*,
1893.]

2   How you gonna keep 'em down on the farm after they've seen Paree?
                              —SAM M. LEWIS & JOE YOUNG, refrain and song title, 1919
["They" are American soldiers coming home from France.]

3   America is my country and Paris is my home town.
                              —GERTRUDE STEIN, *An American and France*, 1936

4   The last time I saw Paris, her heart was warm and gay,
     I heard the laughter of her heart in every street cafe.
                              —OSCAR HAMMERSTEIN II, *The Last Time I Saw Paris*, 1940
[Music by Jerome Kern. France, beloved of many Americans, fell to Germany
in 1940. See also Elliot Paul below.]

5   The last time I see Paris will be on the day that I die. The city is inexhaustible
     and so is its memory.
                              —ELLIOT PAUL, *The Last Time I Saw Paris*, 1942
[Paul fought in World War I and stayed on in Europe, forging a successful career
as journalist and book writer.]

6   Paris seems to be full of American girls who are hiding from their mothers.
                              —JAMES THURBER, *Credits and Curios*, 1962

7   Paris is a moveable feast.   —ERNEST HEMINGWAY, epigraph,
                                                     A Moveable Feast, 1964
[The sentence reads in full: "If you are lucky enough to have lived in Paris as a
young man, then wherever you go for the rest of your life, it stays with you, for
Paris is a moveable feast."]

Rome

8   More imagination wanted at Rome than at home to appreciate the place.
                              —HERMAN MELVILLE, *Journal of a Visit to Europe
                              and the Levant*, 1857

9   I've seen Rome, and I shall go to bed a wiser man than I last rose—yesterday
     morning.   —HENRY JAMES, letter to William James, Oct. 30, 1869

10   Rome was a poem pressed into service as a city.
                              —ANATOLE BROYARD, *New York Times*, March 24, 1974

St. Petersburg

11   A silent, lonely beauty.
                              —LILLIAN HELLMAN, referring to what was then Leningrad
                              (1944), in *An Unfinished Woman*, 1969

Venice

12   A city for beavers.   —RALPH WALDO EMERSON, *Journal*, June 1833

White swan of cities slumbering in thy nest . . . 1
White phantom city, whose untrodden streets
Are rivers, and whose pavements are the shifting
Shadows of the palaces and strips of sky.
> —HENRY WADSWORTH LONGFELLOW, *Venice,* 1876

Venice is like eating an entire box of chocolate liqueurs at one go. 2
> —TRUMAN CAPOTE, "Sayings of the Week,"
> in the London *Observer,* Nov. 26, 1961

A wholly materialistic city is nothing but a dream incarnate. Venice is the 3
world's unconscious. —MARY MCCARTHY, *Venice Observed,* 1961

It is the city of mirrors, the city of mirages, at once solid and liquid, at once air 4
and stone. —ERICA JONG, *A City of Love and Death: Venice,*
> in *The New York Times,* March 23, 1986

CIVIL DISOBEDIENCE

SEE LAW; PACIFISM & NONVIOLENCE;
RESISTANCE

CIVILIZATION

The civilized man has the habits of the house. His house is a prison. 5
> —HENRY DAVID THOREAU, *Journal,* April 26, 1841
[More at RACES & PEOPLES.]

We think our civilization near its meridian, but we are yet only at the cock- 6
crowing and the morning star.
> —RALPH WALDO EMERSON, *Politics,* in *Essays:*
> *Second Series,* 1844

Civilization degrades the many to exalt the few. 7
> —A. BRONSON ALCOTT, *Table Talk,* 1877

Our civilization is still in the middle stage: scarcely beast, in that it is no 8
longer wholly guided by instinct; scarcely human, in that it is not yet wholly
guided by reason. —THEODORE DREISER, *Sister Carrie,* 1900

Civilization is the lamb's skin in which barbarism masquerades. 9
> —THOMAS BAILEY ALDRICH, "Leaves from a Notebook,"
> *Ponkapog Papers,* 1903

Civilization advances by extending the number of important operations which 10
we can perform without thinking about them.
> —ALFRED NORTH WHITEHEAD,
> *An Introduction to Mathematics,* 1911
[See another Whitehead definition, from 1933, below.]

You can't say civilization don't advance, however, for in every war they kill 11
you in a new way. —WILL ROGERS, *New York Times,* Dec. 23, 1929

A general definition of civilization: a civilized society is one exhibiting the five 12
qualities of truth, beauty, adventure, art, peace.
> —ALFRED NORTH WHITEHEAD, *Adventures of Ideas,* 1933

1   what man calls civilization
    always results in deserts.   —DON MARQUIS, *archy does his part*, 1935

2   Civilization is the progress toward a society of privacy.
                                        —AYN RAND, *The Fountainhead*, 1943

3   The test of a civilization is in the way that it cares for its helpless members.
                                        —PEARL S. BUCK, *My Several Worlds*, 1954

CIVIL WAR, THE
1861–65

See also AMERICAN HISTORY: MEMORABLE MOMENTS;
EPITAPHS & GRAVESTONES (U.S. Grant and Henry
Timrod); MILITARY STRATEGY; SLAVERY; UNION, THE; WAR

4   It is an irrepressible conflict between opposing and enduring forces.
                                —WILLIAM HENRY SEWARD, *The Irrepressible Conflict*,
                                speech, Rochester, N.Y., Oct. 25, 1858
    [Seward, an influential senator from New York, and later Secretary of State,
    saw no way to avoid war over the slavery issue.]

5   Say to the seceded states, "Wayward sisters, depart in peace."
                                —WINFIELD SCOTT, letter to William Henry Seward,
                                March 3, 1861
    [Gen. Scott, who hoped to avoid civil war, thus counseled Seward, who was
    about to become Lincoln's Secretary of State. Scott, incidentally, had a long
    and distinguished career, despite his irreverent nickname: Old Fuss and Feath-
    ers. (He insisted that his troops display a sharp, military appearance, and was
    given to carrying a plumed hat on ceremonial occasions.) A day later, Pres.
    Abraham Lincoln urged in his inaugural address, "We must not be enemies"—
    see PEACE for the entire passage.]

6   I had no feeling of self-reproach, for I fully believed the contest was inevitable
    and was not of our seeking. The United States was called upon not only to de-
    fend its sovereignty, but its right to exist as a nation. . . . To me it was simply
    a contest, politically speaking, as to whether virtue or vice should rule.
                                —ABNER DOUBLEDAY, thoughts at Fort Sumter, April 12, 1861,
                                in *Reminiscences of Forts Sumter and Moultrie, 1860–'61*
                                [1876]
    [Capt. Doubleday, who did *not* invent baseball as is often claimed, was second-
    in-command at Sumter and fired the first cannon shot at the Confederates at
    about seven o'clock in the morning. By this time, the Confederates already had
    been pounding away for two-and-one-half hours. At 1:30 P.M., on April 13, after
    thirty-three hours of bombardment, the Union commander, Major Robert An-
    derson, ordered that the fort's flag be taken down. The fort was on fire and he
    had no more ammunition.
    For Ralph Waldo Emerson's reaction to the attack on Sumter, see WAR.]

7   See, there is Jackson, standing like a stone wall.
                                —BARNARD E. BEE, first Battle of Bull Run, July 21, 1861
    [Bee, a Confederate general, who died in the battle, said this referring to the
    First Brigade of the Army of the Shenandoah under the command of Brigadier-
    General Thomas Jonathan Jackson. The resolute stand by Jackson's Virginians
    (who at that moment were actually lying flat on the ground, not standing) was
    the key to reversing what appeared at first to be a certain defeat for the South.
    The nickname "Stonewall" rapidly replaced Jackson's given names.
    For Jackson's military maxims, see MILITARY STRATEGY.]

All quiet along the Potomac.   1
> —GEORGE B. MCCLELLAN, dispatches to Washington, 1861

[All was too quiet for Pres. Lincoln and public opinion in the North. Gen. Mc-
Clellan, commander in chief of the Union armies, was supposed to be advancing on Richmond, capital of the Confederacy. His reluctance to go forward cost
him his job. He regained the command after the second Battle of Bull Run and
lasted through the Battle of Antietam.

The regular appearance of the "all quiet" phrase in headlines, all too frequently accompanied by a subhead such as "A Picket Shot," inspired the
mournful song below.]

"All quiet along the Potomac," they say,   2
Except now and then a stray picket
Is shot as he walks on his beat to and fro,
By a rifleman hid in the thicket.

'Tis nothing—a private or two now and then
Will not count in the news of the battle;
Not an officer lost—only one of the men,
Moaning out, all alone, the death-rattle.
> —ETHEL LYNN BEERS, *The Picket Guard*,
> in *Harper's Weekly*, Sept. 30, 1861

[The music was by James Hewitt. The fifth and last verse follows below.]

All quiet along the Potomac to-night;   3
No sound save the rush of the river;
While soft falls the dew on the face of the dead—
The picket's off duty forever   —*Ibid.*

We must cut our way out as we cut our way in.   4
> —ULYSSES S. GRANT, when told that he was surrounded,
> Belmont, Mo., Nov. 7, 1861, cited in Eugene Lawrence,
> *Grant on the Battle-Field*, in *Harper's New Monthly
> Magazine*, XXXIX, 1869

If McClellan is not using the army, I should like to borrow it for a while.   5
> —ABRAHAM LINCOLN, comment,
> April 9, 1862

Mine eyes have seen the glory of the coming of the Lord.   6
> —JULIA WARD HOWE, *Battle Hymn of the Republic*, 1862

[This is the first line of the song that became the anthem of the Union cause.
More at GOD.]

No terms except an unconditional and immediate surrender can be accepted. I   7
propose to move immediately upon your works.
> —ULYSSES S. GRANT, message to Confederate Major General
> Simon Bolivar Buckner at Fort Donelson, Tenn.,
> Feb. 16, 1862

[Grant's message popularized the phrase "unconditional surrender," thanks
partly to the coincidence of the initial letters with the first two initials of his
own name. Buckner, commander of this Confederate fort on the Cumberland
River, had asked to negotiate terms of surrender. Upon receiving this reply
from Grant, he gave over the fort. This victory, along with the capture of Fort
Henry across the river ten days earlier, marked a turning point in the war. "Unconditional Surrender" Grant had shown his mettle.]

1   I can't spare this man. He fights.
                    —ABRAHAM LINCOLN,
                              speaking of Gen. Ulysses S. Grant, April 1862
[After the bloody Battle of Shiloh, a costly and scant victory for the Union, Lincoln was repeatedly urged to remove Grant as commander. This was the president's reply to A. K. McClure.]

2   We are coming Father Abraham, three hundred thousand more.
                    —JAMES SLOAN GIBBONS, first line of song, July 1862
[Gibbons, a Philadelphia Quaker who had moved to New York, wrote this popular marching song after Lincoln, hoping to make up Union losses in the Peninsular campaign, appealed to the states on July 2, 1862, to raise "three hundred thousand more" soldiers. The music for the song was composed by Stephen Foster.]

3   No, Captain, the men are right. Kill the brave ones; they lead on the others.
                    —THOMAS JONATHAN "STONEWALL" JACKSON,
                              remark, second battle of Manassas
                              (called Bull Run by the Federals), August 29, 1862
[This was Jackson's rebuke to an officer who told his men that they should have captured a Union major instead of killing him; the officer had gallantly led a cavalry charge.]

4   All persons held as slaves . . . are, and henceforward shall be, free.
                    —ABRAHAM LINCOLN, *Emancipation Proclamation*, Jan. 1, 1863
[See also SLAVERY.]

5   Yes, we'll rally 'round the flag, boys, we'll rally once again,
    Shouting the battle cry of freedom.
                    —GEORGE FREDERICK ROOT, *The Battle Cry of Freedom*, 1863
[The phrase "rally 'round the flag" has been ascribed to Gen. Andrew Jackson at the Battle of New Orleans, and was used in political campaigns before Root picked it up for this popular war song.]

6   A rich man's war and a poor man's fight.
                    —ANONYMOUS, slogan of draft rioters in New York City,
                              July 1863
[A person who had $300 to pay for a substitute could avoid the draft.]

7   The Father of Waters again goes unvexed to the sea.
                    —ABRAHAM LINCOLN, comment on the fall of Vicksburg, Miss.,
                              letter to James C. Conkling, August 26, 1863
[With the conquest of Vicksburg on July 4, the North had gained control of the full length of the Mississippi. On the same day, Gen. Robert E. Lee began the Confederate retreat from Gettysburg, Penn., following three days of battle. So the tide of war turned on two fronts on the Fourth of July, 1863. Thanking Grant in a letter on July 13 for the victory at Vicksburg, Lincoln, who had harbored doubts about the general's tactics, did something that few people—and fewer presidents—ever do, saying, "I now wish to make personal acknowledgment that you were right, and I was wrong."]

8   Fourscore and seven years ago, our fathers brought forth on this continent a new nation, conceived in liberty, and dedicated to the proposition that all men are created equal.
                    —ABRAHAM LINCOLN, Gettysburg Address, Nov. 19, 1863
[More at GETTYSBURG ADDRESS.]

I propose to fight it out on this line if it takes all summer.   1
                              —ULYSSES S. GRANT, dispatch to Washington,
                    May 11, 1864
[Grant had been beaten back by Gen. Robert E. Lee's forces at the Spottsylva-
nia Court House. In this dispatch to Gen. Henry Wager Halleck, Grant announced his intention to persevere. Lincoln echoed Grant's words in a speech
on June 16, saying, "We are going through on this line if it takes three more
years."]

Wherever the enemy goes, let our troops go also.   2
                              —ULYSSES S. GRANT, dispatch from City Point, Va.,
                    to Gen. Henry W. Halleck, August 1, 1864

Damn the torpedoes! Go ahead!   3
                              —DAVID GLASGOW FARRAGUT, battle of Mobile Bay,
                    August 5, 1864
[The order is sometimes quoted as "Full speed ahead." A longer version, also
reliably reported, is "Damn the torpedoes! Captain Drayton, go ahead. Jouett,
full speed!"
   In this bloody battle, Admiral Farragut headed a fleet of fourteen wooden
ships and four monitors, iron-clad vessels first used in 1862. In order to be able
to continue to command even if wounded, Farragut lashed himself to the rig-
ging of his flagship, the *Hartford*. Torpedoes—actually mines—sank the Union's
lead ship, the monitor *Tecumseh*, halting the advance of the fleet until Farragut issued the order to go on. The badly needed victory that followed bolstered Northern spirits and, together with Sherman's march through Georgia,
revived Pres. Lincoln's chances of reelection.]

Breckinridge, what do you think of the Dred Scott decision and the rights of   4
the South in the Territories now?
                              —JUBAL EARLY, Shenandoah Valley,
                    August 1864
[Gen. Early of Virginia, who had not favored secession, to John Breckinridge of
Kentucky, who ran in 1860 as a Southern Democrat against Northern Democrat Stephen Douglas, Republican Abraham Lincoln, and Whig John Bell. On
this occasion, it was the middle of the night; the Confederate army had been
devastated by Maj. Gen. Philip Sheridan, and was in retreat. Breckinridge was
dozing on his horse when Early woke him with this question.
   Humor spiced Early's command style. In May, at the Battle of the Wilderness, Early had accosted a healthy soldier leaving the scene and ordered him
back to the front. When the man protested that he was a chaplain, Early retorted, "Chaplain, chaplain, eh? You have been praying these many years to go
to heaven, and now when you have a chance to get there in fifteen minutes,
you are running away!"
   These accounts are from the memoirs of Major David French Boyd, *Reminiscences of the War in Virginia*, 1994. For the Dred Scott decision, see AMER-
ICAN HISTORY: MEMORABLE MOMENTS.]

Hold out. Relief is coming.   —WILLIAM TECUMSEH SHERMAN, signal   5
                    to Gen. John Murray Corse,
                    battle of Allatoona Pass, Oct. 5, 1864
[Although wounded and with two-thirds of his small force fallen, Corse did
hold out all day and night until Sherman's troops got to him. The popular version of the signal, "Hold the fort! for I am coming," is the wording used in an
1874 gospel song by Philip Paul Bliss.]

1   The terrible grumble, and rumble, and roar,
Telling the battle was on once more,
And Sheridan twenty miles away.
                    —THOMAS B. READ, *Sheridan's Ride*, Oct. 1864
[Generations of schoolchildren (in the North) declaimed this poem, composed
a few days after the battle of Cedar Creek on October 19. The poem tells how
Gen. Philip H. Sheridan, returning from a conference in Washington, encountered panic-stricken troops and galloped on his great black Morgan, Rienzi,
twenty miles to the battlefield, where he rallied his army and converted an apparent defeat into victory. Painter-poet Thomas B. Read was then a major on
the staff of another author of some note: Gen. Lew *(Ben Hur)* Wallace.]

2   "Hurrah! Hurrah! we bring the jubilee!
Hurrah! Hurrah! the flag that makes you free!"
So we sang the chorus from Atlanta to the sea,
While we were marching through Georgia.
                    —HENRY CLAY WORK, *Marching Through Georgia*,
                    Dec. 1864
[This song by the author of *Father, Dear Father, Come Home with Me Now*
(see ALCOHOL & DRINKING) was composed shortly after Sherman occupied Savannah on December 21. On December 22, Sherman telegraphed Lincoln: "I
beg to present you as a Christmas gift the city of Savannah, with 150 heavy
guns and plenty of ammunition, also about 25,000 bales of cotton."
    In a message to Grant on September 9, Sherman had predicted, "I can make
this march and make Georgia howl." He cut a swathe of destruction up to
sixty miles wide in a campaign that was a military triumph but a political
disaster. The march, which Sherman continued from Savannah northward
through the Carolinas, crippled the Confederacy and shortened the conflict, almost certainly saving lives, but it left Southerners permanently embittered.
    The song also lived on. Adopted by other armies, including the British and
Japanese, it was still played and sung in the World War II.]

3   With malice toward none, with charity for all, with firmness in the right, as
God gives us to see the right, let us strive on to finish the work we are in; to
bind up the nation's wounds, to care for him who shall have borne the battle,
and for his widow, and for his orphan—to do all which may achieve and cherish a just and lasting peace among ourselves, and with all nations.
                    —ABRAHAM LINCOLN, Second Inaugural Address, March 4, 1865
[With victory at hand, Lincoln called for charity and equal justice in the Southern states. See also Grant below.]

4   The war is over—the rebels are our countrymen again.
                    —ULYSSES S. GRANT, April 9, 1865
[Grant silencing his cheering troops after Robert E. Lee surrendered at Appo-
mattox. See also Grant's call for peace in 1868 at AMERICAN HISTORY: MEMO-
RABLE MOMENTS.]

5   The real war will never get in the books. And so goodbye to the war.
                    —WALT WHITMAN, *The Real War Will Never Get in the Books*,
                    1882
[Whitman served as a nurse to wounded soldiers in the Civil War. Robert E. Lee
made a similar comment in 1868; see HISTORY.]

6   In the South, the war is what A.D. is elsewhere; they date from it.
                    —MARK TWAIN, *Life on the Mississippi*, 1883

There will never be anything in America more interesting than the Civil War 1
never.   —GERTRUDE STEIN, *Everybody's Autobiography*, 1937

CLOTHES   SEE FASHION & CLOTHES

COLORADO   *See also* CITIES (Denver)

Pike's Peak or bust.   2
                                        —ANONYMOUS, 1858
[The rallying cry of immigrants to Denver, after gold was found in Pike's Peak
in 1858. Some wagons displayed the sign, "Busted, by gosh."]

Colorado men are we,   3
From the peaks gigantic, from the great sierras and the high plateaus,
From the mine and from the gully, from the hunting trail we come,
Pioneers! O pioneers!   —WALT WHITMAN, *Pioneers! O Pioneers!*,
                               1865, in *Leaves of Grass* [1881]

This is the real Switzerland of America.   —THEODORE ROOSEVELT, remark 4
                                             during visit to Colorado, 1905

We found God lavish there in Colorado.   —HART CRANE, "Indiana," in 5
                                             To the Brooklyn Bridge, 1930
[The poet adds, "But passing sly"; the passage concerns disappointment in the
promise of fortunes to be made in Colorado following the discovery of gold
there in 1858.]

Colorado is a grand seat to see the world from.   6
            —WILL ROGERS, Jan. 1, 1933, in *Weekly Articles, Vol. V* [1982]

Colorado, the most spectacular of the mountain states.   7
                              —JOHN GUNTHER, *Inside U.S.A.*, 1947

Motto

Nil sine numine.   8
Nothing without Providence.

COMMITMENT   *See also* DETERMINATION, EFFORT,
                                PERSISTENCE, & PERSEVERANCE; LOYALTY

Hew to the line, let the chips fall where they may.   9
                    —ROSCOE CONKLING, nomination speech,
                    Republican National Convention, June 5, 1880
[Sen. Conkling of New York nominated Gen. Ulysses S. Grant for an unprece-
dented third term. The convention, however, went for James A. Garfield of
Ohio.]

COMMON SENSE   *See also* KNOWLEDGE & INFORMATION
                                      (Gertrude Stein); WISDOM

Where sense is wanting, everything is wanting.   10
                    —BENJAMIN FRANKLIN, *Poor Richard's Almanack*, 1754

1   Nothing astonished men so much as common sense and plain dealing.
            —RALPH WALDO EMERSON, *Art*, in *Essays: First Series*, 1841

2   Common sense always takes a hasty and superficial view.
            —HENRY DAVID THOREAU, *A Week on the Concord
            and Merrimack Rivers*, 1849

3   Common sense is compelled to make its way without the enthusiasm of any-
    one; all admit it grudgingly.   —EDGAR WATSON HOWE,
                                      The Indignations of E. W. Howe, 1933

4   Common sense is the collection of prejudices acquired by age eighteen.
            —ALBERT EINSTEIN, in *Scientific American* magazine, Feb. 1976

5   I just want to take common sense to high places.
            —JESSE JACKSON, speech, Democratic National Convention,
            July 20, 1988

COMMUNICATION

See also MANAGEMENT TECHNIQUES;
MEDIA; SCIENCE: TECHNOLOGY

6   We are in great haste to construct a magnetic telegraph from Maine to Texas,
    but Maine and Texas, it may be, have nothing important to communicate.
            —HENRY DAVID THOREAU, 1849
    [Cited by Bill Henderson in an op-ed piece in *The New York Times*, March 16,
    1994. Henderson, who is a director of the Lead Pencil Club, a subsidiary of the
    Pushcart Press, observed that Thoreau wrote this with a lead pencil that he
    made himself. Thoreau's father, John Thoreau, was a leading pencil manufac-
    turer. Thoreau was not impressed by most inventions and improvements. See
    also SCIENCE: TECHNOLOGY.]

7   What we've got here is failure to communicate.
            —FRANK R. PIERSON, *Cool Hand Luke*, 1967
    [An ironic comment directed at prisoner Paul Newman by a nasty chain-gang
    boss, played by Strother Martin. This quickly became a byword in an era full of
    communication failures—between generations, races, sexes, computers, and
    so on.]

COMMUNISM

See also SOCIALISM

8   Communism is twentieth-century Americanism.
            —EARL BROWDER, slogan of the U.S. Communist Party,
            1930–1945
    [Browder was ousted as head of the party in 1945 for advocating international
    harmony. He explained in an interview in *American Heritage*, December 1971,
    that this statement "meant that America's revolutionary heritage had been
    inherited by the Communists, and America's role in the world was a revolu-
    tionary one."]

9   The economy of communism is an economy which grows in an atmosphere of
    misery and want.
            —ELEANOR ROOSEVELT, *My Day*, Feb. 12, 1947
    [For the Cold War; see under Bernard Baruch at AMERICAN HISTORY: MEMORABLE
    MOMENTS.]

From what I hear, I don't like it [Communism] because it isn't on the level. 1
      —GARY COOPER, testifying as a friendly witness,
          House Committee on Un-American Activities, 1947
[The committee, usually known as HUAC, was conducting a probe of alleged
Communism in the movie business. Chaired by Rep. J. Parnell Thomas, a New
Jersey Republican, the committee broke the ground for McCarthyism and
made infamous the question: "Are you now or have you ever been a member
of the Communist Party?" Committee member Richard M. Nixon gained a na-
tionwide reputation for anti-Communist zeal in his questioning of former
State Department official Alger Hiss. For the first major strike by Sen. Mc-
Carthy, see AMERICAN HISTORY: MEMORABLE MOMENTS, his Wheeling, W. Va.,
speech.]

Communism is a corruption of a dream of justice. 2
      —ADLAI STEVENSON, speech, Urbana, Ill., 1951

Capitalism, it is said, is a system wherein man exploits man. And communism 3
is—vice versa.   —DANIEL BELL, *The End of Ideology*, 1960

Better Red than dead.   —ANONYMOUS, slogan of the nuclear 4
          disarmament movement, c. 1960
[Opponents of nuclear weapons in the U.S. picked up this slogan from the
British. It was based on a passage from the philosopher Bertrand Russell. Also
popular was the rejoinder, "Better dead than Red," used as a book title in 1964
by British author Stanley Reynolds.]

[Communism] has never come to power in a country that was not disrupted by 5
war or internal corruption or both.   —JOHN F. KENNEDY, speech, July 3, 1963

COMPLAINTS

I hate to be a kicker, I always long for peace, 6
But the wheel that does the squeaking is the one that gets the grease.
      —JOSH BILLINGS, *The Kicker* [Complainer], c. 1870

Never complain, never explain. 7
      —HENRY FORD II, saying
[More at EXCUSES & EXPLANATIONS.]

CONFLICT   *See also* ARGUMENTS; DIFFERENCES; RACES & PEOPLES (Tocqueville)

So strong is the propensity of mankind to fall into mutual animosities, that 8
where no substantial occasion presents itself, the most frivolous and fanciful
distinctions have been sufficient to kindle their unfriendly passions and excite
their most violent conflicts. But the most common and durable source of factions has been the various and unequal distribution of property.
      —JAMES MADISON, *The Federalist, No. 10*, 1787

A house divided against itself cannot stand. 9
      —ABRAHAM LINCOLN, speech, Republican State Convention,
        Springfield, Ill., June 16, 1858
[More at THE UNION.]

1 There is nothing I love so much as a good fight.
—FRANKLIN D. ROOSEVELT, quoted in *The New York Times*,
Jan. 22, 1911

CONGRESS   *See also* CITIES (Pocatello; Washington, D.C.);
POLITICS & POLITICIANS

2 We pour legislation into the senatorial saucer to cool it.
—GEORGE WASHINGTON, quoted in Moncure D. Conway,
*Omitted Chapters of History Disclosed in the Life
and Papers of Edmund Randolph* [1888]
[Probably an apocryphal remark, but the "senatorial saucer" was frequently in
the news in 1995, when conservative Georgia Republican Newt Gingrich
pushed through a record-breaking volume of legislation in the first one hundred days of his tenure as Speaker of the House. As recounted by Conway, the
senatorial saucer appears in a conversation between Washington and Thomas
Jefferson. The passage runs: "There is a tradition that, on his return from
France, Jefferson called Washington to account at the breakfast-table for having agreed to a second chamber [in Congress]. 'Why,' asked Washington, 'did
you pour that coffee into your saucer?' 'To cool it,' quoth Jefferson. 'Even so,'
said Washington, 'We pour legislation into the senatorial saucer to cool it.'"]

3 That 150 lawyers should do business together ought not to be expected.
—THOMAS JEFFERSON, *Autobiography*, Jan. 6, 1821

4 I have been told I was on the road to Hell, but I had no idea it was just a mile
down the road with a dome on it.
—ABRAHAM LINCOLN, quoted in Rep. Morris K. Udall,
Too Funny to Be President [1988]

5 Whiskey is taken into the committee rooms in demijohns and carried out in
demagogues.   —MARK TWAIN, *Notebooks*, 1868,
quoted in Albert Bigelow Paine,
Mark Twain, A Biography [1912]

6 To my mind, Judas Iscariot was nothing but a low, mean, premature Congressman.   —MARK TWAIN, letter to the editor,
New York Daily Tribune, printed March 10, 1873

7 The finest Congress money can buy.

—MARK TWAIN, attributed
[The closest citation in Twain's writings, according to the Library of Congress's
Respectfully Quoted, is: "I think I can say, and say with pride, that we have
some legislatures that bring higher prices than any in the world." This is from
a speech written for a Fourth of July celebration in London in 1875, but the
American ambassador, General Schenck, canceled all speakers after himself.
See also note to Will Rogers, below.]

8 It could probably be shown by facts and figures that there is no distinctly native American criminal class except Congress.
—MARK TWAIN, *Pudd'nhead Wilson's New Calendar*,
in *Following the Equator*, 1897

9 The new Congressman always spends the first week wondering how he got
there and the rest of the time wondering how the other members got there.
—ANONYMOUS, *The Saturday Evening Post*, Nov. 4, 1899

[Question to the chaplain of the U.S. Senate:] Dr. Hale, do you pray for the senate?   1
[Answer:] No, I look at the senators and pray for the people.
—EDWARD EVERETT HALE, quoted in Van Wyck Brooks,
New England: Indian Summer, 1865–1915 [1940]
[Hale, best known as the author of *The Man Without a Country*, was a Unitarian minister and served as Senate chaplain from 1903 to his death in 1909. He probably did not mean the remark to be quite as sharp as it reads.]

No man, however strong, can serve ten years as a schoolmaster, priest, or sen-   2
ator, and remain fit for anything else.   —HENRY ADAMS, *The Education of*
Henry Adams, 1907

You can't use tact with a Congressman! A Congressman is a hog! You must   3
take a stick and hit him on the snout!
—ANONYMOUS, remark by cabinet member, quoted
in Henry Adams, *The Education of Henry Adams,* 1907
[*Bartlett's* names Jacob Dolson Cox, Secretary of the Interior, as the suspected perpetrator of this unkind comment.]

A little group of willful men.   4
—WOODROW WILSON, March 1917
[The president was referring to about a dozen Republican senators who blocked passage of a bill to permit arming of U.S. merchant ships, which were under attack by German submarines.]

Now and then an innocent man is sent to the legislature.   5
—FRANK MCKINNEY "KIN" HUBBARD,
Abe Martin's Broadcast, 1930
[Folksy, savvy Abe Martin was Hubbard's alter ego.]

The thing about my jokes is they don't hurt anybody. . . . But with Congress—   6
every time they make a joke it's a law. And every time they make a law it's a
joke.   —WILL ROGERS, in P. J. O'Brien, *Will Rogers,*
Ambassador of Good Will, Prince of Wit and Wisdom [1935]
[Rogers had a lot of fun at the expense of Congress. "There are only a few original jokes," he said, "and most of them are in Congress," also called by Rogers "the national joke factory." Despite this, he believed the American Congress to be the best in the world—in fact, "the best Congress money can buy." See also Mark Twain, above.]

People ask me where I get my jokes. Why, I just watch Congress and report the   7
facts.   —WILL ROGERS, in Alex Ayres, ed.,
The Wit and Wisdom of Will Rogers [1962]

A congressman's first obligation is to get elected; his second is to get reelected.   8
—RUSSELL LONG, saying
[Sen. Long of Louisiana was the son of demagogue-dictator Huey Long, who served as governor and senator.]

Don't try to go too fast. Learn your job. Don't ever talk until you know what   9
you're talking about. . . . If you want to get along, go along.
—SAM RAYBURN, traditional advice, quoted in Neil MacNeil,
Forge of Democracy, the House of Representatives [1963]
[U.S. Rep. Sam Rayburn of Texas came to Congress in 1913, and served as Speaker of the House under presidents Roosevelt, Truman, Eisenhower, and Kennedy. He was "Mr. Democrat."]

1   Congress is so strange. A man gets up to speak and says nothing. Nobody listens—and then everybody disagrees.
—BORIS MARSHALOV, quoted by Sen. Alexander Wiley,
Laughing with Congress, 1947
[Marshalov was a Russian-born actor.]

2   If you give Congress a chance to vote on both sides of an issue, it will always do it.
—LES ASPIN, interview, *New York Times*, Dec. 9, 1982
[Rep. Aspin, a Democrat from Wisconsin, was an influential member of the House Armed Services Committee, and later briefly served as Secretary of Defense.]

CONNECTICUT

3   The land of steady habits.
—ANONYMOUS
[Traditional epithet for Connecticut since the 18th century, perhaps because Connecticut voters so often supported political incumbents. And see Thomas Jefferson's interpretation below.]

4   No one that can and will be diligent in this place need fear poverty nor the want of food and raiment.
—SARAH KEMBLE KNIGHT, *Journal*, Dec. 24, 1704
[*The Journal of Madam Knight* is one of the best-known colonial American travel diaries. It details the author's trip by horseback from Boston to New York and back during five months in 1704–1705.]

5   "Farewell Connecticut," said I, as I passed along the bridge. "I have had a surfeit of your ragged money, rough roads, and enthusiastic people."
—ALEXANDER HAMILTON, *Itinerarium*, August 30, 1744
[This is not the famous Hamilton who was shot by Burr, but an Annapolis physician; see Boston under CITIES for more on him.]

6   Connecticut in her blue-laws, laying it down as a principle, that the laws of God should be the laws of man.   —THOMAS JEFFERSON,
letter to John Adams, Jan. 24, 1814

7   The last [state] expected to yield its steady habits (which were essentially bigoted in politics as well as religion).
—THOMAS JEFFERSON, letter to Marquis de Lafayette,
May 14, 1817

8   'Tis a rough land of earth and stone and tree,
Where breathes no castled lord or cabined slave;
Where thought, and tongues, and hands are bold and free,
And friends will find a welcome, foes a grave;
And where none kneel, save when to Heaven they pray,
Nor even then, unless in their own way.
—FITZ-GREENE HALLECK, *Connecticut*, c. 1820

9   I was born and reared in Hartford, in the State of Connecticut—anyway, just over the river in the country. So I am a Yankee of the Yankees—and practical; yes, and nearly barren of sentiment, I suppose—or poetry in other words.
—MARK TWAIN, *A Connecticut Yankee
in King Arthur's Court*, 1889

The warm, the very warm heart of "New England at its best," such a vast 1
abounding Arcadia of mountains and broad vales and great rivers and large
lakes and white villages embowered in prodigious elms and maples. It is extraordinarily beautiful and graceful and idyllic—for America.
—HENRY JAMES, letter to Sir T. H. Warren,
May 29, 1911

Little Connecticut, with but 4,800 square miles of area, lies just outside New 2
York City, and is made up, in almost equal parts, of golf links and squalid factory towns. —H. L. MENCKEN, *Americana*, 1925

Aggressive, pervasive, with a foot in every American door, they [Connecticut 3
peddlers] gave the country at large its first clear notions of the New England
character. . . . The word *Yankee* came to mean *Connecticut Yankee*, and
throughout the Old South, long before Abolition Days, it came to be pronounced "Damyank." —ODELL SHEPARD,
Connecticut Past and Present, 1939
[Southerners may have picked up the expression from Dutch inhabitants of
New York, who referred to Connecticut people as "damn Yankees" as early as
1798. They also used *Yankee* as a verb meaning "to cheat." The word apparently is of Dutch extraction, coming either from the *Jan Kees*, i.e., John Cheese,
or *Janke*, Little John. The Yankees themselves did not adopt the term for themselves until 1776; see the song *Yankee Doodle* at AMERICAN REVOLUTION.]

Motto

Qui transtulit sustinet. 4
He who transplanted still sustains.

CONSCIENCE
See also RELIGION

Conscience is the inner voice which warns us somebody may be looking. 5
—H. L. MENCKEN, *A Mencken Chrestomathy*, 1949

I cannot and will not cut my conscience to suit this year's fashions. 6
—LILLIAN HELLMAN, letter to the chairman
of the House Committee on Un-American Activities,
May 19, 1952
[Singer Paul Robeson, also in trouble for leftist views, put it: "I saw no reason
my convictions should change with the weather," *Here I Stand*, 1958.]

The one thing that doesn't abide by majority rule is a person's conscience. 7
—HARPER LEE, *To Kill a Mockingbird*, 1960

CONSERVATIVES
See POLITICS & POLITICIANS

CONSISTENCY

A foolish consistency is the hobgoblin of little minds, adored by little states- 8
men and philosophers and divines. With consistency a great soul simply has
nothing to do. —RALPH WALDO EMERSON, *Self-Reliance*,
in *Essays: First Series*, 1841
[See also Emerson at MEDIOCRITY and F. Scott Fitzgerald at MIND, THOUGHT, &
UNDERSTANDING.]

1   Do I contradict myself?
    Very well then I contradict myself,
    (I am large, I contain multitudes.)   —WALT WHITMAN, *Song of Myself,*
                                                  in *Leaves of Grass,* 1855

2   Consistency requires you to be as ignorant today as you were a year ago.
                                    —BERNARD BERENSON, *Notebook,* 1892

3   Let it be said that I am right rather than consistent.
                    —JOHN MARSHALL HARLAN, quoted in Tinsley E. Yarbrough,
                        Judicial Enigma: The First Justice Harlan [1995]
    [Harlan, a Kentuckian, was referring to his conversion from a supporter of slav-
    ery to an advocate of civil rights. See Harlan at THE CONSTITUTION.]

CONSTITUTION, THE   *See also* FREEDOM; FREE SPEECH;
                                               PRESS, THE; RIGHTS; SUPREME COURT

4   I have the happiness to know that it is a rising, and not a setting sun.
                        —BENJAMIN FRANKLIN, Sept. 17, 1787, as members of the
                    Constitutional Convention signed the engrossed document
    [Franklin referred to a sun that was painted on the back of the chair occu-
    pied by George Washington, president of the convention. Noting to delegates
    sitting nearby that painters often had trouble distinguishing a rising sun
    from a setting one, Franklin said that he had "often and often, in the course of
    the session, looked at that behind the president, without being able to tell
    whether it was rising or setting." Only now, as the last members signed the
    document, did he have the happy answer. The observation was recorded by
    James Madison, whose notes provide the principal record of the convention's
    debates.
       Franklin's support of the Constitution had surprised some delegates, because
    he was known to favor a unicameral legislature. But he urged support for the
    document, noting that at his age, 81, he had grown to have more respect for the
    judgment of others. The speech was read for him by James Wilson, because
    Franklin's voice was too weak to be heard; but his message was eloquent. He
    explained that he consented to the Constitution, "because I expect no better,
    and because I am not sure that it is not the best." Franklin expressed the wish
    that other delegates "who may still have objections to it, would with me,
    doubt a little of their own infallibility."]

5   We, the people of the United States, in order to form a more perfect union, es-
    tablish justice, insure domestic tranquillity, provide for the common defense,
    promote the general welfare, and secure the blessings of liberty to ourselves
    and our posterity, do ordain and establish this Constitution for the United
    States of America.   —CONSTITUTION OF THE UNITED STATES, Preamble,
                                  Sept. 17, 1787
    [Delegates to the Federal Constitutional Convention signed the great docu-
    ment on this date; it became effective on June 21, 1788, when ratified by the re-
    quired number of states, nine. The all-important Bill of Rights usually is said
    to include the first ten amendments, although strictly it is the first nine
    amendments; all ten amendments were adopted December 15, 1791. James
    Madison, more than any other delegate, was responsible for the shape of the
    Constitution as well as the Bill of Rights.]

6   A bill of rights is what the people are entitled to against every government on
    earth.   —THOMAS JEFFERSON, letter to James Madison, Dec. 1787

Our new Constitution is now established, and has an appearance that promises 1
permanency; but in this world nothing can be said to be certain, except death
and taxes.   —BENJAMIN FRANKLIN, letter to Jean-Baptiste Leroy,
Nov. 13, 1789

THE BILL OF RIGHTS   2

Amendment 1

Congress shall make no law respecting an establishment of religion, or prohibiting the free exercise thereof; or abridging the freedom of speech, or of the
press; or the right of the people peaceably to assemble, and to petition the Government for a redress of grievances.

Amendment 2

A well regulated militia, being necessary to the security of a free state, the
right of the people to keep and bear arms, shall not be infringed.

Amendment 3

No soldier shall, in time of peace be quartered in any house, without the consent of the owner, nor in time of war, but in a manner to be prescribed by law.

Amendment 4

The right of the people to be secure in their persons, houses, papers, and effects
against unreasonable searches and seizures, shall not be violated, and no war-
rants shall issue, but upon probable cause, supported by oath or affirmation,
and particularly describing the place to be searched, and the persons or things
to be seized.

Amendment 5

No person shall be held to answer for a capital, or otherwise infamous crime,
unless on a presentment or indictment of a grand jury, except in cases arising
in the land or naval forces, or in the militia, when in actual service in time of
war or public danger; nor shall any person be subject for the same offence to be
twice put in jeopardy of life or limb; nor shall be compelled in any criminal
case to be a witness against himself, nor be deprived of life, liberty, or property,
without due process of law; nor shall private property be taken for public use,
without just compensation.

Amendment 6

In all criminal prosecutions, the accused shall enjoy the right to a speedy and
public trial, by an impartial jury of the state and district wherein the crime
shall have been committed, which district shall have been previously ascer-
tained by law, and to be informed of the nature and cause of the accusation; to
be confronted with the witnesses against him; to have compulsory process for
obtaining witnesses in his favor, and to have the assistance of counsel for his
defence.

Amendment 7

In suits at common law, where the value in controversy shall exceed twenty
dollars, the right of a trial by jury shall be preserved, and no fact tried by a jury,
shall be otherwise re-examined in any court of the United States, than according to the rules of the common law.

Amendment 8

Excessive bail shall not be required, nor excessive fines imposed, nor cruel and
unusual punishments inflicted.

Amendment 9

The enumeration in the Constitution, of certain rights, shall not be construed to deny or disparage others retained by the people.

Amendment 10

The powers not delegated to the United States by the Constitution, nor prohibited by it to the states, are reserved to the states respectively, or to the people.

———

1   The basis of our political system is the right of the people to make and to alter their constitutions of government. But the constitution which at any time exists, till changed by an explicit and authentic act of the whole people, is sacredly obligatory upon all.
—GEORGE WASHINGTON, Farewell Address, Sept. 17, 1796

2   A constitution is framed for ages to come, and is designed to approach immortality as nearly as human institutions can approach it.
—JOHN MARSHALL, *Cohens v. Virginia*, 1821
[But Chief Justice Marshall also noted that "in a constitution intended to endure for ages to come" there is provision for it "to be adapted to the various *crises* of human affairs," *McCulloch v. Maryland*, 1819.]

3   The people made the Constitution, and the people can unmake it.   —*Ibid.*

4   It is, Sir, the people's Constitution.
—DANIEL WEBSTER, speech, U.S. Senate, Jan. 26, 1830
[More at GOVERNMENT.]

5   Let us then stand by the Constitution as it is, and by our country as it is, one, united, and entire. . . . We have one country, one Constitution, and one destiny.   —DANIEL WEBSTER, speech at Whig party meeting,
Niblo's Saloon, New York City, March 15, 1837

6   A convenant with death and an agreement with hell.
—WILLIAM LLOYD GARRISON, resolutions of the Massachusetts
Anti-Slavery Society, Jan. 27, 1843
[Garrison, a fierce abolitionist, thus condemned the Constitution, which did not outlaw slavery. He publicly burned a copy of the Constitution on July 4, 1854. See also William Henry Seward below.]

7   The Constitution of the United States was made not merely for the generation that then existed, but for posterity—unlimited, undefined, endless, perpetual posterity.   —HENRY CLAY, speech, U.S. Senate, Feb. 6, 1850

8   There is a higher law than the Constitution.
—WILLIAM HENRY SEWARD, speech, U.S. Senate, March 11, 1850
[Seward, an influential New York abolitionist, and later Secretary of State, in this speech was protesting the Compromise of 1850, a set of bills that included tolerance of slavery in some parts of the U.S.]

9   The [U.S. Constitution] is the most wonderful work ever struck off at a given time by the brain and purpose of man.
—WILLIAM GLADSTONE, *Kin Beyond the Sea*,
in *North American Review*, Sept.–Oct. 1878
[Gladstone was prime minister of Great Britain four times between 1868 and 1894.]

What's the Constitution between friends?   1
                    —TIMOTHY J. CAMPBELL, attributed c. 1885
[The anecdote underlying this story was recounted by Grover Cleveland in
Presidential Problems, 1904. The story involves a legislator trying to persuade
a friend and colleague to vote for a particular measure. When the friend remarked that the bill was unconstitutional, the legislator exclaimed, according
to Pres. Cleveland, "What does the Constitution amount to between friends?"
The remark is usually attributed to Campbell in the form given above.]

Our Constitution is color-blind, and neither knows nor tolerates classes   2
among citizens. In respect of civil rights, all citizens are equal before the law.
The humblest is the peer of the most powerful.
                    —JOHN MARSHALL HARLAN, dissent in *Plessy v. Ferguson*, 1896
[*Plessy* established, over Harlan's sole dissent, the principle that segregation, or
"separate but equal" facilities for blacks and whites, was acceptable under the
U.S. Constitution. This was reversed in 1954 in *Brown v. the Board of Education*; see below, and AMERICAN HISTORY: MEMORABLE MOMENTS and RACES &
PEOPLES.
    Harlan's dissent in *Plessy* popularized the phrase "separate but equal." The
Louisiana statute that was challenged in this case used the wording "equal but
separate," but the terms were commonly reversed. Harlan summarized the
statute: "By the Louisiana statute, the validity of which is here involved, all
railway companies . . . carrying passengers in that state are required to have
separate but equal accommodations for white and colored persons," *Ibid.*]

The Constitution follows the flag.   3
                    —ANONYMOUS, dictum of the Democratic party, c. 1900
[The Democrats took an anti-imperialist stand in the Spanish-American War,
and opposed the acquisition of the Philippines. At the least, they argued, Constitutional rights should be extended to the newly subject people. The Democrats, however, were out of power, and as Mr. Dooley remarked, the Supreme
Court could read the election results; see SUPREME COURT.]

It is a fortunate thing for society that the courts do not get the same chance at 4
the Ten Commandments that they do at the Constitution of the United States.
                    —PHILANDER C. JOHNSON, *Senator Sorghum's
                    Primer of Politics*, 1906

The Constitution is what the judges say it is.   5
                    —CHARLES EVANS HUGHES, speech, Elmira, N.Y.,
                    May 3, 1907
[Hughes later had to protest the use of the quotable comment to suggest that
constitutional law is a matter of caprice. In the 1907 speech he was speaking of
the dignity of the courts: "The judiciary is the safeguard of our liberty and of
our property under the Constitution," he said.]

The American Constitution, one of the few modern political documents   6
drawn up by men who were forced by the sternest circumstances to think out
what they really had to face instead of chopping logic in a university class-
room.   —GEORGE BERNARD SHAW, Preface, *Getting Married*, 1908

The best test of truth is the power of the thought to get itself accepted in the
competition of the market. . . . That at any rate is the theory of our Constitution. It is an experiment, as all life is an experiment.
                    —OLIVER WENDELL HOLMES, JR., *Abrams v. U.S.*, 1919
[More at FREE SPEECH.]

1   The makers of our Constitution . . . conferred, as against the Government, the right to be let alone—the most comprehensive of rights and the right most valued by civilized men.
                    —LOUIS BRANDEIS, *Olmstead v. U.S.*, dissenting opinion, 1928

2   If there is any principle of the Constitution that more imperatively calls for attachment than any other it is the principle of free thought—not free thought for those who agree with us but freedom for the thought that we hate.
                    —OLIVER WENDELL HOLMES, JR.,
                    dissent, *U.S. v. Schwimmer*, 1929
     [The Supreme Court decided 6–3 in this case that Hungarian-born Rosika Schwimmer could not become a U.S. citizen because of her outspoken pacifism. This was Holmes's last great dissent. In 1946, the court reversed itself, deciding in *Girouard v. U.S.* that an applicant for U.S. citizenship did not have to swear to bear arms in the country's defense.]

3   Our Constitution is so simple and practical that it is possible always to meet extraordinary needs by changes in emphasis and arrangement without loss of essential form.   —FRANKLIN D. ROOSEVELT, First Inaugural Address,
                    March 4, 1933

4   Under our constitutional system, courts stand against any winds that blow as havens of refuge for those who might otherwise suffer because they are helpless.   —HUGO L. BLACK, *Chambers v. Florida*, 1938
     [More at SUPREME COURT.]

5   If the Constitution is to be construed to mean what the majority at any given period in history wish the Constitution to mean, why a written Constitution and deliberate processes of amendment?
                    —FRANK J. HOGAN, "Presidential Address,"
                    American Bar Association convention,
                    San Francisco, July 10, 1939
     [Hogan, a legendary Washington attorney and insider, was a first cousin to James F. Byrnes.]

6   If there is any fixed star in our constitutional constellation, it is that no official, high or petty, can prescribe what shall be orthodox politics, nationalism, religion, or other matters of opinion, or force citizens to confess by word or act that faith therein.
                    —ROBERT H. JACKSON, Supreme Court ruling
                    in *West Virginia Department of Education v. Barnette*, 1943
     [The court misspelled the name of the plaintiff, Walter Barnet.]

7   The Constitution does not provide for first and second class citizens.
                    —WENDELL L. WILLKIE, *An American Program*, 1944

8   Separate educational facilities are inherently unequal.
                    —EARL WARREN, *Brown v. Board of Education of Topeka*,
                    May 17, 1954
     [More at AMERICAN HISTORY: MEMORABLE MOMENTS.]

9   The Fifth Amendment is an old friend and a good friend. It is one of the great landmarks in man's struggle to be free of tyranny, to be decent and civilized.
                    —WILLIAM O. DOUGLAS, *An Almanac of Liberty*, 1954
     [The Fifth Amendment gives people the right not to incriminate themselves and thus reduces the usefulness of statements extracted by violence and

threats. Justice Douglas's reminder was timely. In the 1950s, Americans were watching televised Congressional hearings into domestic Communism and gangsterism, and taking the Fifth Amendment had become, in the minds of many, tantamount to pleading guilty. See AMERICAN HISTORY: MEMORABLE MOMENTS for some of the high points of the McCarthy era. See under GOVERNMENT for Douglas on getting government off the backs of people.]

Take such proceedings . . . as are necessary and proper to admit to public schools on a rational nondiscriminatory basis with all deliberate speed the parties to these cases.   —EARL WARREN, *Brown v. Board of Education,* follow-up ruling, 1955 [1]

[The phrase "with all deliberate speed" was apparently suggested by Justice Felix Frankfurter, who had used this wording in a dissenting opinion in 1942 in *Chrysler Corp. v. United States.* Frankfurter was drawing on Justice Oliver Wendell Holmes, Jr., whose decision in *Virginia v. West Virginia,* 1911, included the sentence: "A state cannot be expected to move with the celerity of a private business man; it is enough if it proceeds with all deliberate speed." In a letter written in 1909, Holmes ascribed what he called this "delightful phrase" to the English Chancery. Fred Shapiro, however, editor of *The Oxford Dictionary of American Legal Quotations,* reports that scholars have been unable to verify this attribution. The phrase does appear in Sir Walter Scott's *Rob Roy* (1817) in a legal context and in a 1819 letter from Lord Byron to John Murray. In *The Hound of Heaven,* 1893, Francis Thompson wrote, "And with unperturbèd pace, / Deliberate speed, majestic instancy, / They beat . . ."]

If the First Amendment means anything, it means that a state has no business telling a man, sitting alone in his own house, what books he may read or what films he may watch. Our whole constitutional heritage rebels at the thought of giving government the power to control men's minds.

—THURGOOD MARSHALL, *Stanley v. Georgia,* 1969 [2]

Most of the other provisions in the Bill of Rights protect specific liberties or specific rights of individuals. . . . In contrast, the free-press clause extends protection to an institution. The publishing business is, in short, the only organized private business that is given explicit constitutional protection.

—POTTER STEWART, speech, Yale Law School, 1974 [3]

CONVERSATION   *See also* ARGUMENTS; TALK

The music that can deepest reach, And cure all ill, is cordial speech. [4]
—RALPH WALDO EMERSON, *Merlin's Song,* in *May-Day and Other Pieces,* 1867

[A character in A. R. Gurney's play *The Cocktail Hour* (1988) recalls this couplet, and must be deterred from interrupting the conversation to go look it up in *Bartlett's.* The quote, alas, fell from grace and was deleted from the 1992 edition of *Bartlett's.* The moral: never throw out a reference book.]

Many can argue, not many converse. [5]
—A. BRONSON ALCOTT, *Concord Days,* 1872

In America, people talk either to say or to listen to *memorable* things—but there is no atmosphere.   —JOHN BUTLER YEATS, letter to Ruth Hart, July 3, 1912 [6]

1 In the room the women come and go
   Talking of Michelangelo.
                        —T. S. ELIOT, *The Love Song of J. Alfred Prufrock*, 1917

2 Most conversations are simply monologues delivered in the presence of a witness.   —MARGARET MILLAR, *The Weak-Eyed Bat*, 1942

3 If you can't say anything good about someone—sit right here by me.
                        —ALICE ROOSEVELT LONGWORTH, saying, *New York Times*,
                                obituary [1979]
   [According to *Bartlett's*, she had this embroidered on a pillow in her sitting room.]

4 We do not talk—we bludgeon one another with facts and theories gleaned from cursory readings of newspapers, magazines, and digests.
                        —HENRY MILLER, *The Shadows*,
                                in *The Air-Conditioned Nightmare*, 1945

COSMOLOGY   *SEE* SCIENCE: PHYSICS & COSMOLOGY

COUNTRY LIFE & PEOPLE   *See also* FARMS & FARMERS

5 We do not believe any more in the superior innocence and virtue of a rural population.   —JAMES FENIMORE COOPER, *New York*

6 They [wood stumps] warmed me twice—once while I was splitting them, and again when they were on the fire.
                        —HENRY DAVID THOREAU, "Housewarming,"
                                Walden, 1854
   [From the proverbial, "Who splits his own wood warms himself twice."]

7 Beneath her torn hat glowed the wealth
   Of simple beauty and rustic health.
                                —JOHN GREELEAF WHITTIER,
                                Maud Muller, 1854

8 I saw the spiders marching through air,
   Swimming from tree to tree that mildewed day
   In latter August when the hay
   Came creaking into the barn.
                        —ROBERT LOWELL, *Mr. Edwards and the Spider*, 1946
   [Mr. Edwards is the 18th-century Calvinist theologian Jonathan Edwards. At about age 12, he wrote his observations of spiders; see NATURE: ANIMALS. For Edwards on moral behavior, see under VIRTUE.]

COURAGE   *See also* FEAR; HEROES; MILITARY, THE

9 The battle, sir, is not to be to the strong alone; it is to the vigilant, the active, the brave.   —PATRICK HENRY, speech, Virginia
                                Convention, March 23, 1775

10 One man with courage makes a majority.
                        —ANDREW JACKSON, saying
   [See also Henry David Thoreau and Wendell Phillips at MAJORITIES & MINORITIES, and Calvin Coolidge at LAW.]

Courage is resistance to fear, mastery of fear—not absence of fear.   1
> —MARK TWAIN, *Pudd'nhead Wilson's Calendar*
> in *Pudd'nhead Wilson*, 1894

Courage is the price that life exacts for granting peace.   2
The soul that knows it not, knows no release
From little things;
Knows not the livid loneliness of fear,
Nor mountain heights where bitter joy can hear
The sound of wings.
> —AMELIA EARHART, *Courage*

[Her plane went down in 1937. See also Charles Lindbergh at ADVENTURE.]

CRAFTINESS   *See also* WISDOM, WORDS OF

Many foxes grow gray, but few grow good.   3
> —BENJAMIN FRANKLIN, *Poor Richard's Almanack*, 1749

The best place to hide anything is in plain view.   4
> —EDGAR ALLAN POE, *The Purloined Letter*, 1844

A good memory is often a great help; but knowing just when to forget things   5
sometimes counts for more.   —PHILANDER C. JOHNSON, *Senator
> Sorghum's Primer of Politics*, 1906

Never fight fair with a stranger, boy. You'll never get out of the jungle that way.   6
> —ARTHUR MILLER, *Death of a Salesman*, 1949

Never put anything in writing that you can convey by a wink or a nod.   7
> —EARL LONG, saying

[Gov. Earl Long of Louisiana was Huey Long's younger brother. A. J. Liebling's marvelous account of the zany 1959 gubernatorial race in *The Earl of Louisiana* (1962) reveals Earl as in part a shrewd liberal, even on racial issues, in the guise of a semidemented good old boy.]

CRIME, CRIMINALS, & DETECTIVES   *See also* DANGER & DANGEROUS
                                        PEOPLE; EVIDENCE; LAW

Character is always known. Thefts never enrich; alms never impoverish; mur-   8
der will speak out of stone walls.
> —RALPH WALDO EMERSON, commencement address,
> Harvard Divinity School, 1838

[The belief that murder will out, and even stones will bear witness is found in the Bible: "The stone shall cry out of the wall," *Habakkuk* 2:11 and *Luke* 19:14. Chaucer observed, "Mordre wol out, certeyn, it wol nat not faille," in "The Prioress's Tale," from the *Canterbury Tales*. Shakespeare wrote in *Macbeth*, "The very stones prate of my whereabout," II, i; and "Blood will have blood. / Stones have been known to move and trees to speak," III, iv. The thought that murder will out is expressed also in *Hamlet*, II, ii; *The Merchant of Venice*, II, ii; and in *Richard III*, I, iv. Prior to Shakespeare, John Webster, in *The Duchess of Malfi*, focused on the horror of murder: "Other sins only speak; murder shrieks out."]

1 Commit a crime and the world is made of glass.
—RALPH WALDO EMERSON, *Compensation*, in *Essays:*
First Series, 1841

2 The rich rob the poor, and the poor rob one another.
—SOJOURNER TRUTH, saying, c. 1850

3 Frankie and Johnny were lovers, lordee, and how they could love,
Swore to be true to each other, true as the stars above;
He was her man, but he done her wrong.
—ANONYMOUS, ballad, c. 1840–90
[Frankie discovers Johnny's infidelity. She shoots him with a forty-five revolver, and is hanged for the crime; see below. Many versions exist of this folk
ballad, which Carl Sandburg called America's "classical gutter song." Frankie
is a prostitute, and Johnny (or Albert or Allen) is her fancy man, who two-times
her with Alice Fly (or Bly). The ballad has provided the plots for plays (notably
by Mae West and John Huston), several films, and a ballet.]

4 The sheriff took Frankie to the gallows,
Hung her until she died;
They hung her for killing Johnny,
And the undertaker waited outside;
She killed her man, 'cause he done her wrong.   —*Ibid.*

5 We never sleep.   —ALLAN PINKERTON, motto of the
Pinkerton Agency, c. 1855
[Known from its earliest days as "the Eye," the agency is apparently the origin
of the phrase "private eye," meaning detective.]

6 Let no guilty man escape.
—ULYSSES S. GRANT, July 29, 1875
[Pres. Grant issued this order after learning the evidence concerning the
malfeasance of the Whiskey Ring, a conspiracy of federal officials and distillers
that cost the government millions of dollars in revenues.]

7 Oh, the dirty little coward
That shot Mr. Howard,
Has laid poor Jesse in his grave.
—*The Ballad of Jesse James*, 1882
[Robert Ford, in conspiracy with his brother Charles, shot Jesse James in the
back of the head, on April 3, 1882. The Fords were members of the James gang,
but had made a deal with the governor of Missouri to betray Jesse in return for
amnesty and a $10,000 reward. Jesse was living in St. Joseph, Mo., under the
alias of Thomas Howard. He was unarmed, standing on a chair, straightening a
picture at the time of his death. Ford came to be despised for an act that was
seemingly a favor to the body politic. Jesse's brother Frank surrendered, stood
two trials, managed to get off both times, and died in 1915. The words of the
ballad are echoed in the line that Jesse's mother had inscribed on her son's
tombstone: "Murdered by a Traitor and Coward Whose Name Is Not Worthy
to Appear Here."]

8 Where justice is denied, where poverty is enforced, where ignorance prevails,
and where any one class is made to feel that society is in an organized conspiracy to oppress, rob, and degrade them, neither persons nor property will be
safe.   —FREDERICK DOUGLASS, speech, 24th anniversary
of Emancipation, Washington, D.C., April 1886

Early one June morning in 1872, I murdered my father—an act which made a   1
deep impression on me at the time.   —AMBROSE BIERCE,
An Imperfect Conflagration, 1886

Lizzie Borden took an ax   2
And gave her mother forty whacks.
When she saw what she had done,
She gave her father forty-one!

—ANONYMOUS, 1893
[Lizzie Borden was acquitted of the murder of her parents in a jury trial in June
1893 in her hometown of Falls River, Mass. People have been second-guessing
the jury ever since, but at the time it wasn't even a close call. The jury came to
their verdict in a little over an hour, and there was applause in the courtroom
when it was announced. The jury may have been biased; or, if the verdict was
correct, the murderer may have been the family maid.]

Given a child falling into a river, an old person in a burning building, and a   3
woman fainting in the street, a band of convicts would risk their lives to give
aid as quickly at least as a band of millionaires.   —CLARENCE DARROW,
Resist Not Evil, 1903

Lack of respect for law is characteristic of the American people as a whole. Un-   4
til we acquire a vastly increased sense of civic duty we should not complain
that crime is increasing or the law ineffective.
—ARTHUR TRAIN,
Courts and Criminals, 1912
[Train was an assistant district attorney of New York County, and went on to
a long and distinguished career in private practice, writing books and plays on
the side. He helped to found The Authors League of America in 1912.]

While there is a lower class, I am in it. While there is a criminal class, I am of   5
it. While there is a soul in prison, I am not free.
—EUGENE DEBS, statement during trial
on charges of violating the 1917 Espionage Act,
June 16, 1918
[The great Socialist leader was in jail twice, once following the Pullman strike
of 1894 and again when convicted at this trial. He was the sort of man who
made friends with wardens and inmates alike. His fellow-Hoosier and friend,
poet James Whitcomb Riley, wrote of him, "And there's 'Gene Debs—a man 'at
stands / And jes' holds out in his two hands / As warm a heart as ever beat / Be-
twixt here and the Jedgement Seat." And similarly, "God was feeling mighty
good when He created 'Gene Debs, and He didn't have anything else to do all
day."]

It's awful hard to get people interested in corruption unless they can get some   6
of it.   —WILL ROGERS, *Weekly Articles*,
April 22, 1928

Any man might do a girl in   7
Any man has to, needs to want to
Once in a lifetime, do a girl in.   —T. S. ELIOT,
Sweeney Agonistes, 1932

They shoot horses, don't they?   8
—HORACE MCCOY, *They Shoot Horses, Don't They?*, 1935
[Response to a police query: "Why did you kill her?"]

1   Well, as through this world I ramble,
I've seen lots of funny men;
Some will rob you with a six-gun,
And some with a fountain pen.
—WOODY GUTHRIE, *Pretty Boy Floyd*
[Actually, Charles Arthur "Pretty Boy" Floyd favored a machine gun. He held up so many banks in the Southwest that he became something of a folk hero to the many Okies whose mortgages had been foreclosed. He also killed at least a half dozen people before he himself was gunned down by the FBI in 1934.]

2   Knights had no meaning in this game. It wasn't a game for knights.
—RAYMOND CHANDLER, *The Big Sleep*, 1939
[See also Chandler at HEROES.]

3   Round up the usual suspects.
—JULIUS EPSTEIN, PHILIP EPSTEIN, & HOWARD KOCH,
Casablanca, screenplay, 1942

4   Crime does not pay—enough.
—CLAYTON RAWSON, motto of the Mystery Writers
of America, 1945

5   [Q. Why do you rob banks?]
[A.] Because that's where the money is.
—WILLIE SUTTON, attributed
[Sutton, a notorious bank robber, is said to have given this response to a reporter's query. He drew on the quote for the title of his autobiography, *Where the Money Was* (1976), but denied that the words were actually his. "The credit belongs to some enterprising reporter who apparently felt a need to fill out his copy," he said.]

6   Down these mean streets must go a man who is not himself mean; who is neither tarnished nor afraid.
—RAYMOND CHANDLER, *The Simple Act of Murder*, 1950
[More at HEROES.]

7   Crime is only a left-handed form of human endeavor.
—BEN MADDOW & JOHN HUSTON, *The Asphalt Jungle*, 1950
[Classic film noir, from the novel by W. R. Burnett. Huston also directed.]

8   If you can't do the time, don't do the crime.
—ANONYMOUS, saying among criminals, cops, judges, etc.
[Cited in Ed McBain, *Heat*, 1981, among many sources.]

9   I don't know what it says about human nature, but there are few activities more stimulating than planning a crime.
—ROBERT PLUNKET, book review, *New York Times*, Oct. 6, 1991

CRISES   *SEE* BAD TIMES; PROBLEMS; TROUBLE

CRITICISM   *See also* ART: CRITICISM

10   Don't throw stones at your neighbors', if your own windows are glass.
—BENJAMIN FRANKLIN, *Poor Richard's Almanack*, August 1736
[Proverbial.]

I find the pain of a little censure, even when it is unfounded, is more acute than   1
the pleasure of much praise.
> —THOMAS JEFFERSON, letter to Francis Hopkinson,
> March 13, 1789

It is not the critic who counts.   2
> —THEODORE ROOSEVELT, speech, the Sorbonne,
> Paris, France, April 23, 1910

[More at ACTION & DOING.]

A remark generally hurts in proportion to its truth.   3
> —WILL ROGERS, in Alex Ayres, ed., *The Wit and Wisdom*
> *of Will Rogers* [1933]

If any has a stone to throw   4
It is not I, ever or now.
> —ELINOR HOYT WYLIE, *The Pebble*, in *Collected Poems* [1932]

There is so much good in the worst of us,   5
And so much bad in the best of us,
That it ill behooves any of us
To find fault with the rest of us.   —ANONYMOUS

CULTURE   *See* ART; CIVILIZATION; GRACE; MANNERS

CUSTOM   *See* HABIT & CUSTOM

D

DANGER & DANGEROUS PEOPLE

See also ADVENTURE;
CRIME, CRIMINALS, & DETECTIVES; EVIL;
RUTHLESSNESS; SECURITY & SAFETY; VIOLENCE

1 Men who are familiarized to danger, meet it without shrinking, whereas those
who have never seen service often apprehend danger where no danger lies.
—GEORGE WASHINGTON, letter to the president
of the Continental Congress, Feb. 9, 1776

2 I will cut your throat whilst you are sleeping. . . . You know me! Look out!
—JUNIUS BRUTUS BOOTH, letter
to Pres. Andrew Jackson, July 4, 1835
[Booth, a talented but unstable actor—his fencing in the roles of Hamlet and
Richard III sometimes forced other actors to fight for their lives—was the son
of an actor and the father of three actors: Junius Brutus, Edwin, and John
Wilkes Booth, the assassin of Abraham Lincoln.
   Jackson was the first American president to face an assassination attempt. On
January 30, 1835, during a funeral at the Capitol building, Richard Lawrence, an
insane, unemployed house painter, shot twice at the president with two different pistols from close range. It was a damp day and the gunpowder failed to
ignite.]

3 I never quarrel, sir. But sometimes I fight, sir, and whenever I fight, sir, a funeral follows.   —THOMAS HART BENTON,
remark in the U.S. Senate, 1850
[Benton represented Missouri in the Senate 1821–51, and in the House 1853–55.
He was eventually defeated for supporting the Union against the South. The
painter of the same name was his grandnephew.]

4 As soon as there is life, there is danger.
—RALPH WALDO EMERSON, *Public and Private Education*,
speech, Parker Fraternity, Boston, Mass., Nov. 27, 1864

5 When you call me that, *smile*.   —OWEN WISTER, *The Virginian*, 1902
[A line in the all-American tradition that recently brought us Dirty Harry's

"Make my day"; see Joseph Stinson below. The Virginian, too, was a gun-slinger: "Trampas spoke: 'Your bet, you son-of-a- ——.' The Virginian's pistol came out, and his hand lay on the table, holding it unaimed. And with a voice as gentle as ever . . . he issued his orders to the man Trampas:—'When you call me that, *smile.*'" The line was immortalized for later generations by Gary Cooper in the film that was made from the book in 1929.]

A good many things go around in the dark besides Santa Claus.   1
—HERBERT HOOVER,
speech at the John Marshall Republican Club,
St. Louis, Mo., Dec. 16, 1935

Considering how dangerous everything is, nothing is really very frightening.   2
—GERTRUDE STEIN,
Everybody's Autobiography, 1937

I'll get you, my pretty, and your little dog, too.   3
—NOEL LANGLEY, FLORENCE RYERSON,
& EDGAR ALLAN WOLFE,
The Wizard of Oz, screenplay, 1939
[The Wicked Witch of the West, played by Margaret Hamilton, in a memorable threat to Dorothy.]

He can run but he can't hide.   —JOE LOUIS, remark to the press,   4
1946
[Louis was speaking of Billy Conn prior to their rematch fight in June 1946. Conn was the quicker man but not as strong. In their first match, in 1941, Conn was ahead until round thirteen, when Louis knocked him out. Conn lasted eight rounds in 1946. He lost to Louis once more, on a decision in a six-round exhibition match in 1948. In 1991, at the outset of the Gulf War, Pres. George Bush said of Iraq's dictator Saddam Hussein, "He can run but he can't hide." But Saddam did hide.]

God Forgives, Outlaws Don't.   —ANONYMOUS, gravestone for   5
motorcyclist killed in 1977 in Vietnam

There is no more exhilarating feeling than being shot at without result.   6
—RONALD REAGAN, 1981
[Pres. Reagan tended to borrow lines as needed. In this case, after he was wounded by a would-be assassin, he drew on Winston Churchill's "Nothing is more exhilarating as to be shot at without result," *The Story of the Malakan Field Force,* 1898. In a less literary allusion, he told his wife Nancy, when she rushed to his side in the hospital, that he should have ducked—see Jack Dempsey at SPORTS. See also under WAR for George Washington's reaction to bullets whistling.]

Go ahead, make my day.   —JOSEPH C. STINSON, *Sudden Impact,*   7
1983
[Clint Eastwood as tough cop Dirty Harry challenges a bad guy to make a move. Pres. Ronald Reagan used the line to threaten legislators who favored tax increases; see TAXES.
The expression "make my day" dates back a ways. For example, in 1936, P. G. Wodehouse wrote, "That will just make my day," *The Luck of the Bodkins*; and in 1909, Florence Louisa Barclay wrote in *The Rosary,* "I knew her presence made my day, and her absence meant the chill of night."]

1   When you're dancing with a bear, you have to make sure you don't get tired and sit down. You've got to wait till the bear is tired before you get a rest.
—JOYCELYN ELDERS, quoted in *The New York Times*,
Sept. 14, 1993
[Dr. Elders was appointed Surgeon General by Pres. Bill Clinton. An outspoken African-American, she was controversial from the beginning, and was fired for comments on sex education in which she appeared to support teaching masturbation.]

DEATH   *See also* EPITAPHS & GRAVESTONES; LAST WORDS

2   Xerxes the Great did die,
And so must you and I.   —NEW ENGLAND PRIMER, c. 1688

3   Death is but crossing the world, as friends do the seas; they live in one another still.   —WILLIAM PENN, *Some Fruits of Solitude*, 1693

4   Death observes no ceremony.   —JOHN WISE, *A Vindication of the Government
of New England Churches*, 1717
[Rev. Wise knew death and danger well. He served as chaplain on two military expeditions. He was later imprisoned for a tax protest, and took up the cause of the victims in the Salem witch trial.]

5   A man is not completely born until he is dead. Why then should we grieve that a new child is born among the immortals, a new member added to their happy society?   —BENJAMIN FRANKLIN, letter to Miss E. Hubbard,
Feb. 23, 1756
[Hubbard was the stepdaughter of Franklin's late brother John. The letter reveals an aspect of Franklin that he did not often show in public. He went on to console her with another metaphor: "Our friend and we are invited abroad on a party of pleasure, which is to last for ever. His chair was ready first, and he is gone before us. We could not all conveniently start together; and why should you and I be grieved at this, since we are soon to follow, and know where to find him?"]

6   I die hard but I am not afraid to go.   —GEORGE WASHINGTON, on his deathbed,
Dec. 14, 1799
[Washington said these words to Dr. James Craik, his old and friend and neighbor, and also his physician. He died the same day, a little before midnight; see LAST WORDS.]

7   Our machines have now been running seventy or eighty years, and we must expect that, worn as they are, here a pivot, there a wheel, now a pinion, next a spring, will be giving way; and however we may tinker them up for a while, all will at length surcease motion.
—THOMAS JEFFERSON,
letter to John Adams, July 15, 1814
[See also Jefferson at SEASONS & TIMES.]

8   This fever called "living" is conquered at last.
—EDGAR ALLAN POE, *For Annie*, 1849

9   There is no death, only a change of worlds.
—SEATTLE, speech, c. 1854, in W. C. Vanderwerth, ed.,
Famous Speeches by Noted Indian Chieftans [1971]

The long mysterious Exodus of death.   1
                                       —HENRY WADSWORTH LONGFELLOW,
                                            The Jewish Cemetery at Newport, 1858

Because I could not stop for Death—   2
He kindly stopped for me—
The carriage held but just ourselves—
and immortality.   —EMILY DICKINSON, poem no. 712, c. 1863

The report of my death was an exaggeration.   3
                                              —MARK TWAIN, June 1892
[For more see THE PRESS.]

The nearest friends can go   4
With anyone to death, comes so far short
They might as well not try to go at all.   —ROBERT FROST,
                                                      Home Burial, 1914

I have a rendezvous with death   5
At some disputed barricade.   —ALAN SEEGER, *I Have a Rendezvous
                                              with Death*, 1916
[More at WORLD WAR I.]

So here it is at last, the distinguished thing.   6
                                    —HENRY JAMES, on his approaching death, 1916,
                                         in Edith Wharton, *A Backward Glance* [1934]

It costs me never a stab nor squirm   7
To tread by chance upon a worm.
"Aha, my little dear," I say,
"Your clan will pay me back some day."
                                    —DOROTHY PARKER, *Thoughts for a Sunshiny Morning*,
                                         in *Sunset Gun*, 1928

Of all escape mechanisms, death is the most efficient.   8
                                    —H. L. MENCKEN, *A Book of Burlesques*, 1928

Down, down, down into the darkness of the grave   9
Gently they go, the beautiful, the tender, the kind;
Quietly they go, the intelligent, the witty, the brave.
I know. But I do not approve. And I am not resigned.
                                    —EDNA ST. VINCENT MILLAY, *Dirge Without Music*, 1928

Why can't the dead die!   —EUGENE O'NEILL,   10
                                          Mourning Becomes Electra, 1931

Dying   11
Is an art, like everything else.   —SYLVIA PLATH, *Lady Lazarus*,
                                                   1962–63
[More at SUICIDE.]

It's not that I'm afraid to die. I just don't want to be there when it happens.   12
                                    —WOODY ALLEN, *Death (A Play)*,
                                         in *Without Feathers*, 1975
[In *The Early Essays* in the same collection, Allen pointed out, "On the plus
side, death is one of the few things that can be done as easily lying down."]

DECISION   *See also* BOLDNESS & INITIATIVE; INDECISION; REGRET (Robert Frost)

1   The rarest gift that God bestows on man is the capacity for decision.
—DEAN ACHESON, speech,
Freedom House, New York City,
April 13, 1965

DECLARATION OF INDEPENDENCE   *See also* AMERICAN REVOLUTION;
INDEPENDENCE DAY

2   Resolved: That these united colonies are, and of right ought to be, free and independent states.
—RICHARD HENRY LEE, resolution presented at the Continental
Congress, June 7, 1776
[This resolution, introduced by Lee of Virginia and seconded by John Adams of Massachusetts, led to the Declaration of Independence.]

THE DECLARATION OF INDEPENDENCE

3   When in the course of human events, it becomes necessary for one people to dissolve the political bands which have connected them with another, and to assume among the powers of the earth, the separate and equal station to which the Laws of Nature and Nature's God entitle them, a decent respect to the opinions of mankind requires that they should declare the causes which impel them to the separation.

We hold these truths to be self-evident, that all men are created equal, that they are endowed by their Creator with certain unalienable rights, that among these are life, liberty and the pursuit of happiness.—That to secure these rights, governments are instituted among men, deriving their just powers from the consent of the governed,—That whenever any form of government becomes destructive of these ends, it is the right of the people to alter or to abolish it, and to institute new government, laying its foundation on such principles and organizing its powers in such form, as to them shall seem most likely to effect their safety and happiness. Prudence, indeed, will dictate that governments long established should not be changed for light and transient causes; and accordingly all experience hath shown, that mankind are more disposed to suffer, while evils are sufferable, than to right themselves by abolishing the forms to which they are accustomed. But when a long train of abuses and usurpations, pursuing invariably the same object envinces a design to reduce them under absolute despotism, it is their right, it is their duty, to throw off such government, and to provide new guards for their future security.—Such has been the patient sufferance of these Colonies; and such is now the necessity which constrains them to alter their former Systems of Government. The history of the present King of Great Britain is a history of repeated injuries and usurpations, all having in direct object the establishment of an absolute tyranny over these States. To prove this, let facts be submitted to a candid world.

He has refused his assent to laws, the most wholesome and necessary for the public good.

He has forbidden his Governors to pass laws of immediate and pressing importance, unless suspended in their operation till his assent shall be obtained; and when so suspended, he has utterly neglected to attend to them.

He has refused to pass other laws for the accommodation of large districts of people, unless those people would relinquish the right of representation in the Legislature, a right inestimable to them and formidable to tyrants only.

He has called together legislative bodies at places unusual, uncomfortable, and distant from the depository of their public records, for the sole purpose of fatiguing them into compliance with his measures.

He has dissolved representative houses repeatedly, for opposing with manly firmness his invasions on the rights of the people.

He has refused for a long time, after such dissolutions, to cause others to be elected; whereby the legislative powers, incapable of annihilation, have returned to the people at large for their exercise; the State remaining in the mean time exposed to all the dangers of invasion from without, and convulsions within.

He has endeavored to prevent the population of these States; for that purpose obstructing the laws for naturalization of foreigners; refusing to pass others to encourage their migration hither, and raising the conditions of new appropriations of lands.

He has obstructed the administration of justice, by refusing his assent to laws for establishing judiciary powers.

He has made judges dependent on his will alone, for the tenure of their offices, and the amount and payment of their salaries.

He has erected a multitude of new offices, and sent hither swarms of officers to harass our people, and eat out their substance.

He kept among us, in times of peace, standing armies, without the consent of our legislatures.

He has affected to render the military independent of and superior to civil power.

He has combined with others to subject us to a jurisdiction foreign to our constitution, and unacknowledged by our laws; giving his assent to their acts of pretended legislation:

For quartering large bodies of armed troops among us:

For protecting them, by a mock trial, from punishment for any murders which they should commit on the inhabitants of these States.

For cutting off our trade with all parts of the world:

For imposing taxes on us without our consent:

For depriving us in many cases, of benefits of trial by jury:

For transporting us beyond seas to be tried for pretended offences:

For abolishing the free system of English laws in a neighbouring Province, establishing therein an arbitrary government, and enlarging its boundaries so as to render it at once an example and fit instrument for introducing the same absolute rule into these Colonies:

For taking away our Charters, abolishing our most valuable laws, and altering fundamentally the forms of our governments:

For suspending our own Legislatures, and declaring themselves invested with power to legislate for us in all cases whatsoever.

He has abdicated government here, by declaring us out of his protection and waging war against us.

He has plundered our seas, ravaged our coasts, burnt our towns, and destroyed the lives of our people.

He is at this time transporting large armies of foreign mercenaries to complete the works of death, desolation and tyranny, already begun with circumstances of cruelty & perfidy scarcely paralleled in the most barbarous ages, and totally unworthy the head of a civilized nation.

He has constrained our fellow citizens taken captive on the high seas to bear arms against their country, to become the executioners of their friends and brethren, or to fall themselves to their hands.

He has excited domestic insurrections amongst us, and has endeavoured to bring on the inhabitants of our frontiers, the merciless Indian savages, whose known rule of warfare, is an undistinguished destruction of all ages, sexes and conditions.

In every stage of these oppressions we have petitioned for redress in the most humble terms: Our repeated petitions have been answered only by repeated injury. A prince, whose character is thus marked by every act which may define a tyrant, is unfit to be the ruler of a free people.

Nor have we been wanting in attention to our British brethren. We have warned them from time to time of attempts by their legislature to extend an unwarrantable jurisdiction over us. We have reminded them of the circumstances of our emigration and settlement here. We have appealed to their native justice and magnanimity, and we have conjured them by the ties of our common kindred to disavow these usurpations, which, would inevitably interrupt our connections and correspondence. They too have been deaf to the voice of justice and of consanguinity. We must, therefore, acquiesce in the necessity, which denounces our separation, and hold them, as we hold the rest of mankind, enemies in war, in Peace Friends.—

WE, THEREFORE, the REPRESENTATIVES of the UNITED STATES OF AMERICA, in General Congress, assembled, appealing to the Supreme Judge of the world for the rectitude of our intentions, do, in the name, and by authority of the good people of these Colonies, solemnly publish and declare, That these United Colonies are, and of right ought to be FREE AND INDEPENDENT STATES; that they are absolved from all allegiance to the British Crown, and that all political connection between them and the State of Great Britain, is and ought to be totally dissolved; and that as Free and Independent States, they have full power to levy war, conclude peace, contract alliances, establish commerce, and to do all other acts and things which Independent States may of right do.—And for the support of this Declaration, with a firm reliance on the protection of Divine Providence, we mutually pledge to each other our lives, our fortunes and our sacred honor.

—THOMAS JEFFERSON, July 4, 1776

[In the opening section, Jefferson had written, "We hold these truths to be sacred and undeniable." Benjamin Franklin, a good editor, substituted "self-evident." Nearly a century earlier, John Locke, whose writings had been studied by most delegates to the Continental Congress, had declared that all men had rights to life, liberty, and property. The idea that a good government should promote happiness of the governed was not original to Jefferson, but his substitution of "pursuit of happiness" for "property" in the traditional Lockean formulation put a distinctly American imprint on the Declaration—and on the newborn nation itself.]

1   We must indeed all hang together, or most assuredly we shall all hang separately.

—BENJAMIN FRANKLIN, 1776

[Dark humor from Franklin during the signing of the Declaration of Independence. According to tradition, Franklin said this in response to John Hancock's comment, "We must all be unanimous; there must be no pulling different ways; we must all hang together." The attribution, however, is rather late, dating from c. 1840.]

DELAWARE

2   Delaware is like a diamond, diminutive, but having within it inherent value.

—JOHN LOFLAND, 1847, quoted in Federal Writers' Project,
Delaware: A Guide to the First State, 1938

3   A state that has three counties when the tide is out, and two when it is in.

—JOHN J. INGALLS, speech, U.S. Senate, c. 1885

4   This is a small and measly state, owned by a single family, the Du Ponts.

—H. L. MENCKEN, *Americana*, 1925

Delaware has fought and bucked, hated, reviled, admired and fawned upon, ig- 1
nored and courted the Du Ponts, but in the end, it has invariably bowed to Du
Pont's benevolent paternalism.
> —JAMES WARNER BELLAH, *Delaware,* in *American Panorama*
> *East of the Mississippi,* 1960

There are two political parties in Delaware: the Du Ponts and the anti–Du Ponts, 2
with the proviso that many Du Ponts are members of the anti–Du Pont family.
> —JAMES L. PHELAN & ROBERT C. POZEN,
> *The Company State,* 1973

Motto

Liberty and independence.   3

DELAY   *See also* INDECISION

Delay is preferable to error.   4
> —THOMAS JEFFERSON, letter to George Washington, May 16, 1792

Never do today what you can do as well tomorrow.   5
> —AARON BURR, quoted in James Parton,
> *The Life and Times of Aaron Burr* [1857]

Do not delay;   6
Do not delay; the golden moments fly!   —HENRY WADSWORTH LONGFELLOW,
> *The Masque of Pandora,* 1875

procrastination is the art of keeping up with yesterday   7
> —DON MARQUIS, "certain maxims of archy,"
> in *archy and mehitabel,* 1927

DEMOCRACY   *See also* GOVERNMENT; MAJORITIES & MINORITIES;
PEOPLE, THE; POLITICS & POLITICIANS

If the people be the governors, who shall be the governed?   8
> —JOHN COTTON, *The Bloody Tenent Washed and Made Clean*
> *in the Blood of the Lamb,* 1647

[Cotton, a Boston minister, preferred monarchy or aristocracy to democracy.
"They are both clearly approved and directed in the scriptures," he claimed.
Cotton and Gov. John Winthrop were opposed by Roger Williams, who was
eventually exiled and went on to found the Providence Plantation, the core of
the Rhode Island colony.]

Our real disease . . . is democracy.   —ALEXANDER HAMILTON, letter to 9
Theodore Sedgwick

The sober second thought of the people shall be law.   10
> —FISHER AMES, speech, Massachusetts Convention, Jan. 1788

[He was speaking in support of biennial elections.]

Though the will of the majority is in all cases to prevail, that will, to be right- 11
ful, must be reasonable.
> —THOMAS JEFFERSON, First Inaugural Address, March 4, 1801

[More at MAJORITIES & MINORITIES.]

1   Democracy never lasts long. It soon wastes, exhausts, and murders itself. There never was a democracy yet that did not commit suicide.
—JOHN ADAMS, letter to John Taylor, April 15, 1814
[For another perspective on democracy and survival see under AMERICA & AMERICANS for Abraham Lincoln's 1838 speech at the Young Men's Lyceum in Springfield, Ill.]

2   The tendency of democracy is, in all things, to mediocrity.
—JAMES FENIMORE COOPER, *The American Democrat*, 1838

3   Democracy as I understand it, requires me to sacrifice myself *for* the masses, not *to* them. Who knows not that, if you would save the people, you must often oppose them.
—ORESTES A. BROWNSON, *An Oration on the Scholar's Mission*

4   The ballot is stronger than the bullet.   —ABRAHAM LINCOLN, speech,
May 19, 1856

5   Government of the people, by the people, for the people.
—ABRAHAM LINCOLN, Gettysburg Address, Nov. 19, 1863
[More at GETTYSBURG ADDRESS.]

6   I will not gloss over the appalling dangers of universal suffrage.
—WALT WHITMAN, *Democratic Vistas*, 1871

7   The rise of democracy as an effective force in the nation came in with western preponderance under Jackson and William Henry Harrison, and it meant the triumph of the frontier—with all of its good and all of its evil elements.
—FREDERICK J. TURNER, *The Significance of the Frontier in American History*, 1893

8   The democracy born of free land, strong in selfishness and individualism, intolerant of administrative experience and education, and pressing individual liberty beyond its proper bounds, has dangers as well as its benefits.
—*Ibid.*
[See also THE FRONTIER; INDIVIDUALITY & INDIVIDUALISM.]

9   The world must be made safe for democracy.
—WOODROW WILSON,
speech to the U.S. Congress, April 2, 1917
[More at WORLD WAR I. For Franklin D. Roosevelt's call for the U.S. to be the arsenal of democracy, see under AMERICAN HISTORY: MEMORABLE MOMENTS.]

10 The cure for the evils of democracy is more democracy!
—H. L. MENCKEN, *Notes on Democracy*, 1926

11 I swear to the Lord
I still can't see
Why Democracy means
Everybody but me.   —LANGSTON HUGHES, *The Black Man Speaks*,
in *Jim Crow's Last Stand*, 1943
[See also Hughes at AMERICA & AMERICANS.]

12 The blind lead the blind. It's the democratic way.
—HENRY MILLER, *With Edgard Varèse in the Gobi Desert*,
in *The Air-Conditioned Nightmare*, 1945

If our democracy is to flourish, it must have criticism; if our government is to   1
function, it must have dissent.
>   —HENRY STEELE COMMAGER, *Freedom, Loyalty, Dissent,* 1954

Democracy is the recurrent suspicion that more than half of the people are   2
right more than half of the time.   —E. B. WHITE, *The Wild Flag,* 1946

Under democracy, one party always devotes its chief efforts to trying to prove   3
that the other is unfit to rule—and both commonly succeed and are right.
>   —H. L. MENCKEN, *Minority Report:*
>   *H. L. Mencken's Notebooks* [1956]

I never vote—it only encourages them.   4
>   —ANONYMOUS
[According to a column by wordmaster William Safire in *The New York Times,*
January 22, 1995, comedian Steve Allen credited this insight to an anonymous
feisty old woman.]

DEMOCRATS   *See* POLITICS & POLITICIANS

DEPRESSION, THE   *See also* AMERICAN HISTORY:
MEMORABLE MOMENTS; ECONOMICS

Wall St. Lays an Egg.   —SIME SILVERMAN, headline, *Variety,*   5
Oct. 30, 1929
[The economic boom that began in 1922 was running on fumes by 1929. The
overheated, highly speculative Wall St. securities market collapsed in "the
Panic" of October and November. Two devastating crashes occurred in October—on the 24th, with 13 million shares traded, and on the 29th, with 16 million shares traded. By mid-November, $30 billion had been erased from the
value of stocks. Losses more than doubled by 1932.]

Prosperity is just around the corner.   —HERBERT HOOVER,   6
attributed
[This was the popular distillation of various statements of assurance made by
Hoover and others following the 1929 stock market crash. According to Paul F.
Boller, Jr., and John George in *They Never Said It,* the closest Hoover came to
the popular version was in a 1931 speech to the U.S. Chamber of Commerce,
when he declared, "We have now passed the worst and with continued unity of
effort we shall rapidly recover. There is one certainty of the future of a people
with the resources, intelligence, and character of the people of the United
States—that is, prosperity." Eventually, the phrase became an ironic joke, used
mockingly as as a political attack phrase by the Democrats.]

The grass will grow in the streets of a hundred cities.   7
>   —HERBERT HOOVER, speech, Oct. 31, 1932
[The warning became associated with the Depression, although Hoover was
speaking in a different context; see under ECONOMICS.]

Depressions are farm led and farm fed.   8
>   —ANONYMOUS, saying, 1930s, quoted in Studs Terkel,
>   *Hard Times: An Oral History of the Great Depression* [1970]
[The speaker is farmer Emil Lorik, who joined the Minnesota state senate in
1927. In his first session, five hundred farmers marched up Capitol Hill. "It

thrilled me," he said. "I didn't know farmers were smart enough to organize. They stayed there two days. It was a strength I didn't realize we had."

As farmers' purchasing power shrank, farm-equipment manufacturers went out of business, starting a spiral of economic decline.]

1   Once I built a railroad, now it's done.
Brother can you spare a dime?
                              —E. Y. "YIP" HARBURG, *Brother Can You Spare a Dime?*,
                                   song, 1932
[The music was by Jay Gorney. The title repeats a common request by street beggars, and the song, Harburg's first major hit, was a sort of anthem of the Depression. Its blunt recognition of the national crisis probably helped Franklin D. Roosevelt in his campaign for the presidency.]

2   With the slow menace of a glacier, depression came on. No one had any measure of its progress; no one had any plan for stopping it. Everyone tried to get out of its way.   —FRANCES PERKINS,
                                                        People at Work, 1934
[Perkins, the first woman in the U.S. cabinet, was Secretary of Labor 1933–44. In the winter of 1931–32—when there was no unemployment insurance or other safety net—unemployment accounted for twenty percent of the labor force, or some ten million people. Vaudevillians, reacting to reports that business was improving, quipped, "Is Hoover dead?"; see also the joke about Hoover's engineering expertise at INSULTS. The following winter, incredibly, the numbers grew worse: one third of the workforce, sixteen million people, unemployed. Industrial workers were making less than eight cents per hour, with some women getting a penny or two per hour. The first light of hope glimmered in Franklin D. Roosevelt's inaugural speech in March 1933; see AMERICAN HISTORY: MEMORABLE MOMENTS.]

3   I see one-third of a nation ill-housed, ill-clad, ill-nourished.
                              —FRANKLIN D. ROOSEVELT, Second Inaugural Address,
                                   Jan. 20, 1937

DESIRES   *See also* HAPPINESS

4   If you desire many things, many things will seem but a few.
                              —BENJAMIN FRANKLIN,
                                   Poor Richard's Almanack, 1732–1757

5   The fundamental principle of human action—the law that is to political economy what the law of gravitation is to physics—is that men seek to gratify their desires with the least exertion.
                              —HENRY GEORGE, *Progress and Poverty*, 1879
[George, one of the most popular and influential of American economists, regarded land as the key economic commodity from which all values derive. Consequently, he proposed a single tax on land.]

6   Men have a thousand desires to a bushel of choices.
                              —HENRY WARD BEECHER, *Proverbs from Plymouth Pulpit*, 1887

7   Protect me from what I want.
                                                        —JENNY HOLZER, saying
[Holzer, a post-Conceptualist artist, incorporates aphorisms and condensed narratives in her multimedia exhibits.]

DESPAIR
See also FAILURE

We should never despair.   1
> —GEORGE WASHINGTON, letter to Maj. Gen. Philip Schuyler,
> July 15, 1777

[More at DETERMINATION, EFFORT, PERSISTENCE, & PERSEVERANCE.]

And that white sustenance—   2
Despair.   —EMILY DICKINSON, poem no. 640, c. 1862

Safe despair it is that raves—   3
Agony is frugal.
Puts itself severe away
For its own perusal.   —EMILY DICKINSON, poem no. 1243, c. 1873

Lord save us all from old age and broken health and a hope tree that has lost the   4
faculty of putting out blossoms.   —MARK TWAIN,
> letter to Joe. T. Goodman, April 1891

And nothing to look backward to with pride,   5
And nothing to look forward to with hope.
> —ROBERT FROST, *The Death of the Hired Man*, 1914

The damned don't cry.   —EUGENE O'NEILL, "The Haunted,"   6
Mourning Becomes Electra, 1931

In the real dark night of the soul, it is always three o'clock in the morning.   7
> —F. SCOTT FITZGERALD, *The Hours*, in *The Crack-Up*, 1945

[Fitzgerald was referring to the writings of the 16th-century mystic St. John of
the Cross, who entitled a treatise *The Dark Night of the Soul*. In *The Ascent of
Mount Carmel*, St. John spoke of the "the dark night of the soul through which
the soul passes on its way to the Divine Light." A time of despair commonly
precedes an intense mystical experience.]

DESPERATION
See DESPAIR; UNHAPPINESS

DESTINY
See FATE & DESTINY

DETAILS & OTHER SMALL THINGS
See also BIGNESS; SMALLNESS

A little neglect may breed great mischief . . . for want of a nail the shoe was   8
lost; for want of a shoe the horse was lost; for want of a horse the rider was lost.
> —BENJAMIN FRANKLIN, *Poor Richard's Almanack*, June 1758

[The thought is sometimes extended with, "For the want of a rider the battle
was lost." Franklin, himself, after stating the proverb, added that the rider was
"overtaken and slain by the enemy, all for want of care about a horse shoe
nail." It is proverbial, included, for example, in George Herbert's *Jacula Pru-
dentum*, 1651. See also Poor Richard at DETERMINATION, EFFORT, PERSISTENCE, &
PERSEVERANCE.]

Little drops of water,   9
Little grains of sand,
Make the mighty ocean
And the pleasant land.

So the little minutes,
Humble though they be,
Make the mighty ages
Of eternity.   —JULIA CARNEY, *Little Things*, 1845

1   Little deeds of kindness,
Little words of love
Help to make earth happy
Like the heaven above.   —*Ibid.*

2   Our life is frittered away by detail. —HENRY DAVID THOREAU, "Where I Lived
and What I Lived For," *Walden*, 1854
[More at SIMPLICITY.]

3   God is in the details.
—ANONYMOUS
[Probably of European origin, popularized here by architect Ludwig Mies van
der Rohe and others. Sometimes attributed to Gustave Flaubert: "*Le bon Dieu
est dans le détail.*" A variant is "The devil is in the details."]

4   Small is beautiful.   —E. F. SCHUMACHER, *Small Is Beautiful:
Economics As If People Mattered*, 1973

DETECTIVES   *See* CRIME, CRIMINALS, & DETECTIVES

DETERMINATION, EFFORT,   *See also* ACTION & DOING;
PERSISTENCE, & PERSEVERANCE   COMMITMENT; ENTHUSIASM & ZEAL;
                                    ENDURANCE; PATIENCE; RESISTANCE; WILL

5   There are no gains without pains.   —BENJAMIN FRANKLIN,
Poor Richard's Almanack, 1745
[This proverbial wisdom was used also by Adlai Stevenson in accepting the De-
mocratic party's presidential nomination in 1952.]

6   Little strokes
Fell great oaks.   —BENJAMIN FRANKLIN, *Poor Richard's Almanack*,
August 1750
[Proverbial. For example, in the 16th century, John Lyly included in his *Eu-
phues: The Anatomy of Wit*: "Many strokes overthrow the tallest oaks." And
in *Henry VI, Part III*, Shakespeare wrote: "Many strokes, though with a little
axe, / Hew down and fell the hardest timber'd oak."]

7   We should never despair; our situation before has been unpromising and has
changed for the better, so I trust, it will again. If new difficulties arise, we must
only put forth new exertions and proportion our efforts to the exigency of the
times.   —GEORGE WASHINGTON, letter to Maj. Gen. Philip Schuyler
on the fall of Fort Ticonderoga, July 15, 1777

8   I am in earnest—I will not equivocate—I will not excuse—I will not retreat a
single inch—AND I WILL BE HEARD!
—WILLIAM LLOYD GARRISON, *The Liberator*,
first issue, Boston, Jan. 1, 1831
[More at SLAVERY.]

I know of no more encouraging fact than the unquestionable ability of man to   1
elevate his life by a conscious effort.   —HENRY DAVID THOREAU, "Where
I Lived and What I Lived For,"
Walden, 1854

Nothing in the world can take the place of persistence. Talent will not; noth-   2
ing is more common than unsuccessful men with talent. Genius will not; un-
rewarded genius is almost a proverb. Education will not; the world is full of
educated derelicts. Persistence and determination are omnipotent. The slogan
"press on" has solved and always will solve the problems of the human race.
                —CALVIN COOLIDGE, attributed on the cover
of the program for his memorial service, 1933
[A famous but never verified quotation.]

Quitters never win. Winners never quit.   3
                —ANONYMOUS, traditional adage for football locker rooms

Keep on truckin'.   —ROBERT CRUMB, cartoon slogan, poster   4

Perseverance is the hard work you do after you get tired of doing the hard work   5
you already did.   —NEWT GINGRICH, *Quotations from Speaker Newt*, 1995

DEVIL, THE   *See also* EVIL

That there is a Devil is a thing doubted by none but such as are under the in-   6
fluences of the Devil. For any to deny the being of a Devil must be from an ignorance or profaneness worse than diabolical.
                —COTTON MATHER, *The Wonders of the Invisible World*, 1693
[Rev. Mather's concept of the devil and hell was quite scientific—as he understood science: "[The Devil] impregnates the air with such malignant salts, as
meeting with the salt of our microcosm, shall immediately cast us into the
fermentation and putrefaction which will utterly dissolve all the vital ties
within us." The text is contemporaneous with the Salem witch trials, which
Mather did not support but for which his writings nevertheless were an inspiration.]

One of the principal objects of American reverence is the devil. There are mul-   7
titudes who are shocked to hear his name mentioned lightly, and who esteem
such mention profanity.   —J. G. HOLLAND, *Everyday Topics*, 1876

As a rule, the devils have been better friends to man than the gods.   8
                —ROBERT G. INGERSOLL, speech, Boston, April 23, 1880

Demonology is the shadow of theology.   9
                —RALPH WALDO EMERSON, *Demonology*, in
Lectures and Biographical Sketches, 1883

The Devil and me, we don't agree;   10
I hate him, and he hates me.   —ANONYMOUS, Salvation Army Hymn, c. 1890

We may not pay Satan reverence, for that would be indiscreet, but we can at   11
least respect his talents.   —MARK TWAIN, *Concerning the Jews*,
in *Harper's Magazine*, Sept. 1899

A person [Satan] who has during all time maintained the imposing position   12
of spiritual head of four-fifths of the human race, and political head of the

whole of it, must be granted the possession of executive abilities of the loftiest order.   —*Ibid.*

1 The snake stood up for evil in the Garden.
                                              —ROBERT FROST, *The Ax-Helve,* 1923

2 The death of Satan was a tragedy
   For the imagination.   —WALLACE STEVENS, *Esthétique du Mal,* 1947

3 The devil made me do it.
                                                          —FLIP WILSON, saying
   [Wilson, a stand-up comic, was a television star in the 1960s and early 1970s. This line was the favorite excuse of one his stock characters, Geraldine.]

DIFFERENCES   *See also* CONFLICT; INDIVIDUALITY & INDIVIDUALISM;
                              MADNESS & SANITY; MAJORITIES & MINORITIES

4 As long as the reason of man continues fallible, and he is at liberty to exercise it, different opinions will be formed.   —JAMES MADISON, *The Federalist,*
                                                                  No. 10, 1787

5 Every difference of opinion is not a difference of principle.
                              —THOMAS JEFFERSON, First Inaugural Address, March 4, 1801
   [More at THE UNION.]

6 But the great Master said, "I see
   No best in kind, but in degree;
   I gave a various gift to each,
   To charm, to strengthen, and to teach."   —HENRY WADSWORTH LONGFELLOW,
                                                      The Singers, 1849

7 It were not the best that we should all think alike; it is difference of opinion that makes horse races.   —MARK TWAIN, *Pudd'nhead Wilson's Calendar,*
                                                  in *Pudd'nhead Wilson,* 1894

8 I never saw a purple cow,
   I never hope to see one;
   But I can tell you, anyhow,
   I'd rather see than be one.   —GELETT BURGESS, *The Purple Cow,*
                                                  in *The Lark* magazine, 1895
   [This wildly popular bit of silliness eventually embarrassed its author. In 1914, Burgess protested, "Ah, yes, I wrote "The Purple Cow"—I'm sorry, now, I wrote it! / But I can tell you anyhow, / I'll kill you if you quote it."
       Burgess also is remembered for apparently coining one of the essential terms in the language of book publishing, *blurb,* and for originating the use of *bromide* for a trite and soothing thought; see Burgess at ART: CRITICISM.]

9 There is very little difference between one man and another; but what little there is, is very important.
                              —WILLIAM JAMES, quoting an unidentified carpenter,
                                  in *The Will to Believe,* 1897

10 Conformists die, but heretics live forever.   —ELBERT HUBBARD,
                                                              saying
   [Quoted in *The New York Times,* Jan. 25, 1996, in an article on the revival of

the America Arts and Crafts Movement led by Hubbard and Gustav Stickley, approximately one century after its founding. Hubbard's arts-and-crafts center at the Roycroft Inn, near Buffalo, was also enjoying a renaissance.]

To think is to differ.   —CLARENCE DARROW,   1
remark during the Scopes "monkey" trial,
Dayton, Tenn., July 13, 1925

Human diversity makes tolerance more than a virtue; it makes it a require-   2
ment for survival.   —RENÉ DUBOS, *Celebrations of Life*, 1981

Without deviation from the norm, progress is not possible.   3
—FRANK ZAPPA, quoted in *New York* magazine,
June 20, 1994

If you aren't doing something different, you aren't doing anything at all.   4
—NEIL CARGILE, motto,
quoted in John Berendt, *High-heel Neil*,
in *The New Yorker*, Jan. 16, 1995
[Cargile, a prominent figure in Nashville society, is a pilot, independent businessman (heavy dredging operations), polo player, and cross-dresser. An even more prominent cross-dresser in American history was Lord Cornbury, who served as first governor of New York, from 1702 to 1708. He wore gowns on occasion, ostensibly to show his resemblance to his cousin Queen Anne.]

DIPLOMACY   *See also* FOREIGN POLICY

In statesmanship get the formalities right, never mind about the moralities.   5
—MARK TWAIN, *Pudd'nhead Wilson's New Calendar*,
in *Following the Equator*, 1897

Diplomacy, n. The patriotic art of lying for one's country.   6
—AMBROSE BIERCE, *The Devil's Dictionary*, 1906

Diplomacy is utterly useless where there is no force behind it.   7
—THEODORE ROOSEVELT, speech, Naval War College,
Newport, R.I., June 2, 1897
[This statement prefigured his "big stick" adage; see FOREIGN POLICY.]

Diplomacy is to do and say   8
The nastiest thing in the nicest way.   —ISAAC GOLDBERG, *The Reflex*

Diplomacy shall proceed always frankly and in the public view.   9
—WOODROW WILSON, "Fourteen Points" address to Congress,
Jan. 8, 1918
[More at FOREIGN POLICY.]

[An ambassador:] A politician who is given a job abroad in order to get him out   10
of the country.   —ANONYMOUS, cited in H. L. Mencken,
A New Dictionary of Quotations [1942]

Diplomats don't mind starting a war because it's a custom that they are to be   11
brought safely home before the trouble starts.
—WILL ROGERS, in Alex Ayres, ed.,
The Wit and Wisdom of Will Rogers [1993]

1   Diplomacy . . . is not the art of asserting ever more emphatically that attitudes should not be what they clearly are. It is not the repudiation of actuality, but the recognition of actuality, and the use of actuality to advance our national interests.   —ADLAI STEVENSON, 1954, quoted in *American Heritage* [Oct. 1973]

2   Diplomacy has rarely been able to gain at the conference table what cannot be gained or held on the battlefield.   —WALTER BEDELL SMITH, 1954
[Gen. Smith made this remark on returning from the Geneva Conference on Indo-China.]

3   The first requirement of a statesman is that he be dull. This is not always easy to achieve.   —DEAN ACHESON, in *The Observer*, June 21, 1970

DISHONESTY & LIES   *See also* HONESTY; TRUTH

4   He who permits himself to tell a lie once, finds it much easier to do a second and third time, till at length it becomes habitual; he tells lies without attending to it, and truths without the world's believing him. This falsehood of the tongue leads to that of the heart, and in time depraves all its good dispositions.
    —THOMAS JEFFERSON, *Notes on the State of Virginia*, 1781–1785

5   Sin has many tools, but a lie is the handle which fits them all.
    —OLIVER WENDELL HOLMES, SR.,
    The Autocrat of the Breakfast-Table, 1858

6   I never seen anybody but lied, one time or another.
    —MARK TWAIN, *Huckleberry Finn*, 1885
[Huck is speaking. This from the opening paragraph of the book.]

7   A lie is an abomination unto the Lord and an ever present help in time of need.
    —JOHN A. TYLER MORGAN, comment in the U.S. Senate, c. 1890
[The remark is attributed to Sen. Morgan in David McCullough's book on the building of the Panama Canal, *The Path Between the Seas*, 1977. Morgan, who represented Alabama in the Senate for many years, ardently favored a Nicaraguan canal. More recently, Democratic presidential candidate Adlai Stevenson made essentially the same observation on the useful lie in a speech in Springfield, Illinois, January 1951.]

8   One of the most striking differences between a cat and a lie is that a cat has only nine lives.   —MARK TWAIN, *Pudd'nhead Wilson's Calendar*, in *Pudd'nhead Wilson*, 1894

9   Mendacity is the system we live in.   —TENNESSEE WILLIAMS, *Cat on a Hot Tin Roof*, 1955

10   Don't lie if you don't have to.   —LEO SZILARD, *Science*, No. 176, 1972

DIVISIONS & BARRIERS

11   Something there is that doesn't love a wall.
    —ROBERT FROST, *Mending Wall*, 1914
[Apart from the symbolic resonance, Frost was referring literally to the tendency of stone walls to fall apart. He disliked the outdated state requirement that he help his neighbor to rebuild a stone wall. See NEIGHBORS.]

Before I built a wall I'd ask to know   1
What I was walling in or walling out.
                                                           —*Ibid.*
[John F. Kennedy jotted down a variant of this, "Don't ever take a fence down
until you know the reason why it was put up," in a notebook that he kept in
1945–46. He attributed it to G. K. Chesterton, but the line has not been found
in any of Chesterton's many works. Kennedy may have just been misremem-
bering Frost.]

A door is what a dog is perpetually on the wrong side of.   2
                    —OGDEN NASH, *A Dog's Best Friend Is His Illiteracy,*
                    in *The Private Dining Room,* 1953

DOCTORS & MEDICINE   *See also* HEALTH; ILLNESS & REMEDIES; SCIENCE:
                          BIOLOGY & PHYSIOLOGY; SCIENCE: PSYCHOLOGY

God heals and the doctor takes the fee.   —BENJAMIN FRANKLIN,   3
                                           Poor Richard's Almanack, 1736

The inexperienced and presumptuous band of medical tyros let loose upon the   4
world destroys more of human life in one year than all the Robin Hoods, Car-
touches, and Macheaths do in a century.
            —THOMAS JEFFERSON, letter to Dr. Caspar Wistar, June 21, 1807
[Cartouche was an 18th-century French highwayman. Macheath was the London cutthroat whom we know from John Gay's *Beggar's Opera* and Bertolt
Brecht's *The Threepenny Opera.* The famous Robin Hood, obviously, was not
regarded as such a hero in Jefferson's day as he is now.]

Consider the deference which is everywhere paid to a doctor's opinion. Noth-   5
ing more strikingly betrays the credulity of mankind than medicine.
            —HENRY DAVID THOREAU,
            A Week on the Concord and Merrimack Rivers, 1849

Surgeons must be very careful   6
When they take the knife!
Underneath their fine incisions
Stirs the culprit—*life*!   —EMILY DICKINSON, poem no. 108, c. 1859

What I call a good patient is one, who having found a good physician, sticks to   7
him till he dies.   —OLIVER WENDELL HOLMES, SR., lecture, New York City,
            March 2, 1871

When a doctor looks me square in the face and kant see no money in me, then   8
i am happy.   —JOSH BILLINGS, *Josh Billings' Encyclopedia of Wit
            and Wisdom,* 1874

Your doctor bill should be paid like your income tax, according to what you   9
have. There is nothing that keeps poor people poor as much as paying doctor
bills.   —WILL ROGERS, *Weekly Articles,* July 13, 1930

[Re specialists:] Take the throat business. A doctor that doctors on the upper   10
half of your throat doesn't even know where the lower part goes to.
            —WILL ROGERS, in Alex Ayres, ed.,
            The Wit and Wisdom of Will Rogers [1993]

1   I hate doctors! They'll do anything—anything to keep you coming to them. They'll sell their souls! What's worse, they'll sell yours, and you'll never know it until one day you find yourself in hell.
—EUGENE O'NEILL, *A Long Day's Journey into Night*, 1956

2   The kind of doctor I want is one who when he's not examining me is home studying medicine.   —GEORGE S. KAUFMAN, attributed in Howard Teichmann,
George S. Kaufman: An Intimate Portrait, 1972
[Kaufman, the funniest playwright of his generation, rarely joked about his health. He was a notorious hypochondriac.]

3   Half of what you learn in medical school is wrong. The problem is figuring out which half.

—ANONYMOUS
[Dr. Dan A. Oren of the National Institute of Health reported in a letter to *The New York Times* (June 29, 1995) that at Yale University in the 1980s, medical students were taught this aphorism Dr. Oren's records trace the saying to England, possibly originated by Sidney Burwell. See also John Wanamaker at ADVERTISING & ADVERTISING SLOGANS.]

DOING   See ACTION & DOING

DOUBT   See INDECISION; SKEPTICISM

DREAMS & DREAMERS   See also DREAMS & SLEEP; REALITY,
ILLUSIONS, & IMAGES; IDEAS &
IDEALS; VISION & PERCEPTION

4   If one advances confidently in the direction of his dreams, and endeavors to live the life which he has imagined, he will meet with a success unexpected in common hours.   —HENRY DAVID THOREAU, "Conclusion," *Walden*, 1854

5   Don't part with your illusions. When they are gone you may still exist but you have ceased to live.   —MARK TWAIN, *Pudd'nhead Wilson's New Calendar*,
in *Following the Equator*, 1897

6   Make strong old dreams lest this our world lose heart.
—EZRA POUND, Postscript to his first book of poems,
A Lume Spento, 1908

7   There's a long, long trail a-winding
Into the land of my dreams,
Where the nightingales are singing
And a white moon beams;
There's a long, long night of waiting
Until my dreams all come true,
Till the day when I'll be going down that
Long, long trail with you.   —STODDARD KING, *There's a Long, Long Trail*,
1913
[Music by Zo Elliott.]

8   The republic is a dream.
Nothing happens unless first a dream.
—CARL SANDBURG, *Washington Monument by Night*, 1922

What happens to a dream deferred?   1
Does it dry up
Like a raisin in the sun? ...
Or does it explode?   —LANGSTON HUGHES, *Harlem*, 1951

I have a dream today.   —MARTIN LUTHER KING, JR., speech   2
                                 at the Lincoln Memorial, Washington, D.C.,
                                 to the great civil rights march, August 28, 1963
[More at AMERICAN HISTORY: MEMORABLE MOMENTS.]

We all have the same dreams.   —JOAN DIDION, *The Book*   3
                                              of Common Prayer, 1977

DREAMS & SLEEP

A traveler five hours doth crave   4
To sleep, a student seven will have,
And nine sleeps every idle knave.   —JOHN JOSSELYN, *An Account of Two*
                                       Voyages to New England, 1675
[Josselyn included this ditty in his report on the settlements in Maine, annexed
to Massachusetts in 1650. He liked Maine men in the north but didn't think
much of those in the southern part of the territory, who had recently emigrated
from Massachusetts. See also MAINE.]

Up, sluggard, and waste not life; in the grave will be sleeping enough. 5
                              —BENJAMIN FRANKLIN,
                               Poor Richard's Almanack, 1741

Judge of your natural character by what you do in your dreams.   6
                              —RALPH WALDO EMERSON, *Journal*, 1833
[Lewis Mumford, in *American Heritage*, February 1969, also cited a passage
from Emerson written in 1832: "Dreams and beasts are the two keys by which
we are to find out the secrets of our own nature. All mystics use them." Mumford commented, "The theory of Beasts is Darwin and evolution; the theory of
Dreams is Freud and the unconscious."]

Dreaming men are haunted men.   —STEPHEN VINCENT BENÉT, 7
                                               John Brown's Body, 1928

In sleep we lie all naked and alone, in sleep we are united at the heart of night 8
and darkness, and we are strange and beautiful asleep; for we are dying in the
darkness, and we know no death.
                              —THOMAS WOLFE, *Death the Proud Brother*,
                               in *From Death to Morning*, 1935

A dream is a wish your heart makes.   —WALT DISNEY, *Sleeping Beauty*, 1959 9

Dreaming permits each and every one of us to be quietly and safely insane 10
every night of our lives.   —WILLIAM DEMENT,
                                               in *Newsweek*, Nov. 30, 1959
[Dr. Dement was a psychiatrist.]

In our dreams, we are always young.   —SADIE DELANY, *Having Our Say: The* 11
                                         Delany Sisters' First 100 Years, 1993
[The Delany sisters were both over one hundred years old when their memoirs
appeared in 1993.]

DUTY   *See* ACTION & DOING; RESPONSIBILITY; VIRTUE

E

EATING   *See* FOOD, WINE, & EATING

ECONOMICS   *See also* BUSINESS; CAPITALISM & CAPITAL V. LABOR;
                              COMMUNISM; DEPRESSION, THE; MONEY & THE RICH; POVERTY
                              & HUNGER; RICH & POOR, WEALTH & POVERTY; SOCIALISM

1 A national debt, if it is not excessive, will be to us a national blessing.
              —ALEXANDER HAMILTON, letter to Robert Morris, April 30, 1781
   [But see Hamilton below on debt and taxes.]

2 To extinguish a debt which exists and to avoid contracting more are ideas almost always favored by public feeling and opinion; but to pay taxes for the one
   or the other purpose, which are the only means of avoiding the evil, is always
   more or less unpopular.   —ALEXANDER HAMILTON,
                                                             c. 1790–94
   [Professor Thomas McGraw of the Harvard Graduate School of Business Administration drew attention to this comment by Hamilton in *The New York
   Times*, May 2, 1993. He added that Hamilton had observed that one commonly
   sees the very people who declaim against public debt "vehement against every
   plan of taxation which is proposed to discharge old debts, or to avoid new." The
   debt that worried Hamilton and Pres. George Washington as well was the huge
   Revolutionary War bill of $75.4 million, fifteen times annual revenues. U.S.
   debt in 1993 was four times annual revenues. See also Andrew Jackson below.]

3 Not worth a continental.   —ANONYMOUS,
                                                                   c. 1790
   [A popular expression for worthlessness. The "continental currency" was paper money issued by Congress after the Revolution. The nation was deep in
   debt and could not back up the currency. The continental quickly inflated to
   the point that one silver dollar was equal to $40 in continentals.]

4 As a very important source of strength and security, cherish public credit. One
   method of preserving it is to use it as sparingly as possible.
              —GEORGE WASHINGTON, Farewell Address, Sept. 17, 1796

We must not let our rulers load us with perpetual debt.   1
                                   —THOMAS JEFFERSON, letter to Samuel Kercheval, July 12, 1816

If a national debt is considered a national blessing, then we can get on by bor-   2
rowing. But as I believe it is a national curse, my vow shall be to pay the national debt.   —ANDREW JACKSON, veto statement, Bank Renewal Bill,
                                July 10, 1832
[Much of this speech was written by future Supreme Court Justice Roger B.
Taney, then Jackson's Secretary of the Treasury.]

The Forgotten Man.   —WILLIAM GRAHAM SUMNER,   3
                                                        speech title, 1885
[Professor Sumner, speaking at Yale University, said, "The forgotten man
works and votes—generally he prays—but his chief business in life is to
pay. . . . Who and where is the forgotten man in this case, who will have to pay
for it all?" Roosevelt used the symbol of the forgotten man in 1932; see under
POVERTY & HUNGER. See also Richard M. Nixon's "silent majority" under MA-
JORITIES & MINORITIES.]

The problem of our age is the proper administration of wealth, so that the ties   4
of brotherhood may still bind together the rich and poor in harmonious relationship.   —ANDREW CARNEGIE, *Wealth,* 1889

You shall not press down upon the brow of labor this crown of thorns. You   5
shall not crucify mankind upon a cross of gold.
                       —WILLIAM JENNINGS BRYAN, "Cross of Gold" speech,
                       Democratic National Convention, Chicago, July 8, 1896
[This stirring climax to a powerful speech won Bryan the presidential nomination on the fifth ballot. The convention was dominated by Midwestern and
Western populists who opposed the exclusive gold standard for currency and
favored the free coinage of silver. In debate in Congress in 1892, Bryan had
called the post–Civil War law that had eliminated the silver dollar "the crime
of 1873." New laws in 1878 and 1890 had reinstated the government purchase
of silver to the point that the country was flooded with it. In 1893, the government, headed by Democrat Grover Cleveland, backed off support of silver, a retreat that the free-silver forces believed exacerbated the financial panic of
1893. The crisis split the Democratic party. The 1896 platform called for free
silver coinage in a fixed ratio to gold of sixteen to one. Many Democrats, especially Easterners, had difficulty supporting the platform and the candidate; see,
for example, David Bennett Hill at POLITICS & POLITICIANS.]

There are those who believe that if you will only legislate to make the well-to-   6
do prosperous, their prosperity will leak through on those below. The Democratic idea, however, has been that if you make the masses prosperous, their
prosperity will find its way up through every class which rests above them.
                                                            —*Ibid.*
[Prosperity that will "leak through" to the masses is the same as prosperity
that is supposed to "trickle down," an approach to wealth distribution advocated by Republican presidents Ronald Reagan and George Bush. Republicans
commonly used the term "supply side" in place of "trickle down," however.
As budget director David Stockman explained in an indiscreet interview in
The Atlantic (Dec. 1981): "It's kind of hard to sell 'trickle down,' so the supply-
side formula was the only way to get a tax policy that was really 'trickle-
down.'" A supply-side policy is one that uses tax cuts and other means to favor
suppliers, usually corporations. The theory is that as producers have more

money, jobs will increase, and, in the general prosperity, tax revenue will rise. George Bush once called it "voodoo economics"; see below.]

1   If Americans are going to start worrying about whether they can afford a thing or not, you are going to ruin the whole characteristic of our people.
                          —WILL ROGERS, in Alex Ayres, ed.,
                          The Wit and Wisdom of Will Rogers [1993]
["If we want anything, all we have to do is go and buy it on credit," Rogers observed. "So that leaves us without any economic problems whatsoever, except some day to have to pay for them." This was in *Daily Telegrams*, Sept. 6, 1928, about one year before the market crash.]

2   There's no such thing as a free lunch.

                          —ANONYMOUS
[Often phrased, "There ain't no such thing as a free lunch." Word maven William Safire, writing in *The New York Times Magazine*, has dated "free" lunches to the 1840s in the West, where bars offered food to customers who bought drinks. Later, free lunches were served in schools. In 1934, New York City mayor Fiorello La Guardia on his inauguration day announced, "*È finita la cuccagna!*"—meaning, the free meal (graft) is over. The concept that lunch is never free emerged in the late 1930s. A *New York Times* editorial in 1938 included the announcement, "There ain't no such thing as free lunch"; the editorial was reprinted on June 1, 1949. The axiom became associated with conservative economist Milton Friedman, a Nobel Prize winner, who used the no-free-lunch phrase in a book title in 1975. The adage in the form of an acronym—TANSTAAFL—was used by best-selling science-fiction writer Robert Heinlein in *The Moon Is a Harsh Mistress*.]

3   Credit is the lifeblood of business, the lifeblood of prices and jobs.
                          —HERBERT HOOVER, speech at Des Moines, Iowa, Oct. 4, 1932
[Pres. Hoover spoke of perils facing the country, including the "strangulation of credit through the removal of $3 billions of gold and currency by foreign drains and by the hoarding of our own citizens from the channels of our commerce and business." See also Daniel Webster at BUSINESS.]

4   The grass will grow in the streets of a hundred cities.
                          —HERBERT HOOVER, speech, Madison Square Garden,
                          New York City, Oct. 31, 1932
[A traditional image of economic catastrophe. Here, Pres. Hoover was speaking in favor of the Smoot-Hawley protective tariff that he promised to retain. Hoover predicted that if Franklin D. Roosevelt were to be elected and eliminate the tariff, disaster would strike nationwide. "Whole towns, communities, and forms of agriculture . . . have been built up under this system of protection," he said. "The grass will grow in the streets of a hundred cities, a thousand towns; the weeds will overrun millions of farms, if that protection is taken away."
    Henry F. Woods in *American Sayings* (1945) pointed out that earlier politicians had used similar language. At the outbreak of the Civil War, Southerners prophesied that when the North was deprived of Southern raw materials, grass would grow in Northern cities. The *Louisville Courier*, in July 1861, reported that the grass was already sprouting in New York City.
    William Jennings Bryan in his "Cross of Gold" speech (see above) also warned of grass in the streets; see FARMS & FARMERS. Incidentally, when campaigning for reelection in 1936, Roosevelt enjoyed remarking that he was still looking for the grass that was supposed to grow on city streets.]

5   A lot of fellows nowadays have a B.A., M.D., or Ph.D.
    Unfortunately, they don't have a J.O.B.   —"FATS" DOMINO, attributed

A recession is when your neighbor loses his job; a depression is when you lose   1
yours.
                                                                —ANONYMOUS
[Pres. Harry S. Truman used this line, according to Ralph Keyes's *Nice Guys
Finish Seventh*; so did Ronald Reagan in his 1980 presidential campaign.]

I'm always looking for a one-armed economist [one who can't say "On the   2
other hand"]   —HARRY S. TRUMAN, attributed by Howell Raines,
                                editorial page editor of *The New York Times*
[Peter J. Boyer, writing in *The New Yorker*, August 22 & 29, 1994, quoted
Raines as saying that just as Truman looked for one-armed economists, he
himself wanted one-armed editorial writers.]

There is nothing sacred about the pay-as-you-go idea so far as I am concerned,   3
except that it represents the soundest principle of financing that I know.
                    —HARRY S. TRUMAN, quoted in *The New York Times*,
                    article on the proposed balanced-budget amendment
                    to the Constitution [Jan. 26, 1995]

If a free society cannot help the many who are poor, it cannot save the few who   4
are rich.
                            —JOHN F. KENNEDY, Inaugural Address, 1961
[See also Andrew Carnegie at RICH & POOR.]

I stressed to the President the importance of realizing that in economics, the   5
majority is always wrong.
                            —JOHN KENNETH GALBRAITH, c. 1962
[Quoted in *Plain Tales from the Embassy*, excerpts from letters and quotes dating from Mr. Galbraith's tenure as ambassador to India, *American Heritage*,
October 1969.]

Voodoo economics.   —GEORGE BUSH, speech,   6
                                                    April 1980
[In the Republican presidential primary race in Pennsylvania, Bush thus deri-
sively characterized the "supply side" economic theory espoused by his opponent, Ronald Reagan. According to this theory, a tax cut would actually
increase government revenues by stimulating the economy. After Bush became Reagan's running mate, the phrase came back to haunt him. "God I wish
I hadn't said that," he remarked. He had it right, though. Pres. Reagan's budget
chief David Stockman confided to a reporter for the *The Atlantic* magazine,
that supply-side economics was "a Trojan horse," adding, "None of us really
understands what is going on with all these numbers," November 1981. At a
meeting on June 5, 1981, presidential chief of staff James Baker asked jokingly
(sort of), "You mean it really is voodoo economics after all?" By 1988, Pres.
Reagan—assisted by a Democratic Congress—had run up the national debt to
a record $2 trillion. In 1991, the economy was the central theme in Bill Clin-
ton's presidential campaign. See James Carville at POLITICAL SLOGANS.]

EDUCATION   *See also* BOOKS & READING; KNOWLEDGE & INFORMATION

Where the press is free and every man able to read, all is safe.   7
                    —THOMAS JEFFERSON, letter to Charles Yancey, 1816
[See also Jefferson under THE PRESS.]

It is, Sir, as I have said, a small college. And yet *there are those who love it.*   8
                    —DANIEL WEBSTER, argument in the U.S. Supreme Court case
                    Trustees of Dartmouth College v. Woodward, March 10, 1818

1 It is an axiom in political science that unless a people are educated and enlightened it is idle to expect the continuance of civil liberty or the capacity for
self-government.   —TEXAS DECLARATION OF INDEPENDENCE, March 2, 1836

2 Let the children of the rich and poor take their seats together and know of no
distinction save that of industry, good conduct, and intellect.
                                                        —TOWNSEND HARRIS
[Harris, a merchant, served on and headed New York City's board of education,
and was the chief advocate for founding the present College of the City of New
York in 1847. In the 1850s, he served successfully as a diplomat in Japan.]

3 Education . . . is a great equalizer of the conditions of men—the balance wheel
of the social machinery.   —HORACE MANN, report as Secretary of the
                                      Massachusetts Board of Education, 1848

4 What does education often do? It makes a straight-cut ditch of a free meandering brook.   —HENRY DAVID THOREAU, *Journal*, 1850

5 The public school system of the several states is the bulwark of the American
republic.   —REPUBLICAN PARTY, national platform,
                                            1876
[This platform called for a constitutional amendment to forbid using public
funds for any sectarian school.]

6 The free school is the preserver of that intelligence which is to preserve us as
a free nation.   —REPUBLICAN PARTY, national platform, 1888

7 Soap and education are not as sudden as a massacre, but they are more deadly
in the long run.   —MARK TWAIN, *The Facts Concerning the Recent
                          Registration*, in *Sketches New and Old*, 1867

8 Training is everything. The peach was once a bitter almond; cauliflower is
nothing but cabbage with a college education.
                          —MARK TWAIN, *Pudd'nhead Wilson's Calendar*,
                                in *Pudd'nhead Wilson*, 1894
[But see also the note under Skinner below.]

9 In the first place God made idiots. This was for practice. Then he made school
boards.   —MARK TWAIN, *Pudd'nhead Wilson's New Calendar*,
                          in *Following the Equator*, 1897

10 *Education, n.* That which discloses to the wise and disguises from the foolish
their lack of understanding.   —AMBROSE BIERCE, *The Devil's Dictionary*, 1906

11 They know enough who know how to learn.
       —HENRY BROOKS ADAMS, *The Education of Henry Adams*, 1907

12 A teacher affects eternity. He can never tell where his influence stops.
                                                              —*Ibid.*

13 Who dares to teach must never cease to learn.
               —JOHN COTTON DANA, motto of Kean College of New Jersey,
                 1912
[Dana, a librarian in Newark, was asked to find a suitable inscription for a new
building at Newark State College, Union, N.J., which later became Kean College. Apparently lacking a good dictionary of quotations, he wrote this maxim,
which eventually the college adopted as its motto.]

You can lead a horticulture, but you can't make her think.   1
—DOROTHY PARKER, attributed in *The Ten-Year Lunch*,
documentary on the Algonquin Round Table [1987]
[Parker is said to have made this pun during a round of a word game played by
wits who gathered at the Algonquin Hotel in Manhattan. She was challenged
to use the word *horticulture* in a sentence.]

When eras die, their legacies   2
Are left to strange police.
Professors in New England guard
The glory that was Greece.   —CLARENCE DAY, *Thoughts on Deaths*,
in *Thoughts Without Words*, 1928

School days, I believe, are the unhappiest in the whole span of human exis-   3
tence. They are full of dull, unintelligible tasks, new and unpleasant ordi-
nances, brutal violations of common sense and common decency.
—H. L. MENCKEN, "Travail," *Baltimore Evening Sun*,
Oct. 8, 1928

[Princeton University:] A quaint ceremonious village of puny demigods on   4
stilts.   —ALBERT EINSTEIN, letter to the Queen of Belgium,
Nov. 20, 1933

My boyhood saw   5
Greek islands floating over Harvard Square.
—HORACE GREGORY, *Chorus for Survival*, 1935
[The speaker is Ralph Waldo Emerson.]

He who enters a university walks on hallowed ground.   6
—JAMES BRYANT CONANT, *Notes on the Harvard Tercentenary*,
1936

Education is what survives when what has been learnt has been forgotten.   7
—B. F. SKINNER, *Education in 1984*
[Similarly, Mark Twain wrote in his *Notebook*, published posthumously in
1935, "Education consists mainly in what we have unlearned."]

The whole educational system has become one massive quiz program, with   8
the prizes going to the most enterprising, most repulsively well-informed person—the man with his hand up first.   —HAROLD TAYLOR,
conference, 1947
[Dr. Taylor, chosen at age thirty to head Sarah Lawrence College, was the
youngest college president in the United States. In later years, he pursued a distinguished career in education, the arts, and in support of world peace. He also
observed, "What is wrong with a great deal of higher education in America is
that it is simply boring." Both quotes here are from his *New York Times* obituary, February 2, 1993.]

Separate educational facilities are inherently unequal.   9
—EARL WARREN, *Brown v. Board of Education*, May 17, 1954
[More at AMERICAN HISTORY: MEMORABLE MOMENTS and THE CONSTITUTION.]

Like so many aging college people, Pnin had long since ceased to notice the ex-   10
istence of students on campus.   —VLADIMIR NABOKOV,
Pnin, 1957

[Nabokov taught at Cornell.]

1 I find that the three major administrative problems on campus are sex for the students, athletics for the alumni, and parking for the faculty.
    —CLARK KERR, speech at the University of Washington,
        Time magazine, Nov. 17, 1958
[Mr. Kerr headed the University of California.]

2 One by one the solid scholars
   Get the degrees, the jobs, the dollars.   —W. D. SNODGRASS, *April Inventory*,
        1959

3 The founding fathers in their wisdom decided that children were an unnatural strain on parents. So they provided jails called schools, equipped with torture called education.   —JOHN UPDIKE, *The Centaur*, 1963

4 Without education, you are not going anywhere in this world.
    —MALCOLM X, speech, Militant Labor Forum, New York,
        May 29, 1964

5 High school is closer to the core of the American experience than anything else I can think of.   —KURT VONNEGUT, Introduction, *Our Times Is Now:
        Notes from the High School Underground*,
        John Birmingham, ed., 1970

6 An education enables you to earn more than an educator.
    —ANONYMOUS, in Hans Gaffon, *Resistance to Knowledge*, 1970

7 If you think education is expensive, try ignorance.   —DEREK BOK,
        attributed
[The saying was popular in the 1980s and appeared on bumper stickers. It is not known if it is original with Bok, who was then president of Harvard University.]

ELECTIONS   *See* DEMOCRACY; MAJORITIES & MINORITIES; PEOPLE,
        THE; POLITICAL SLOGANS; POLITICS & POLITICIANS

ELITE, THE   *See also* MANNERS; MONEY & THE RICH

8 Adam was never called *Master* Adam; we never read of Noah *Esquire*, Lot *Knight* and *Baronet*, nor the *Right Honorable* Abraham, Viscount Mesopotamia, Baron of Carian; no, no, they were plain men.
    —BENJAMIN FRANKLIN, *Dogood Papers*, 1722
[On the subject of old families, see Andrew Lytle at FAMILY.]

9 I am an aristocrat. I love liberty, I hate equality.
    —JOHN RANDOLPH, quoted in W. C. Bruce,
        John Randolph of Roanoke, 1923

10 I agree with you that there is a natural aristocracy among men. The grounds of this are virtue and talents.   —THOMAS JEFFERSON, letter to John Adams,
        Oct. 28, 1813

11 The social duties of a gentleman are of a high order. The class to which he belongs is the natural repository of the manners, tastes, tone, and, to a certain extent, the principles of a country.   —JAMES FENIMORE COOPER,
        The American Democrat, 1838

He comes of the Brahmin caste of New England. This is the harmless, inoffen-   1
sive, untitled aristocracy.   —OLIVER WENDELL HOLMES, SR.,
The Brahmin Caste of New England, 1860

There is fast forming in this country an aristocracy of wealth, the worst form   2
of aristocracy that can curse the prosperity of any country.
—PETER COOPER, c. 1875, quoted in Peter Lyon,
The Honest Man, in *American Heritage* [Feb. 1959]
[Cooper, a self-made, successful manufacturer, gave away much of his fortune.]

The pedigree of honey   3
Does not concern the bee—
A clover, any time, to him
Is aristocracy.   —EMILY DICKINSON, poem no. 1627, c. 1884

There are only about four hundred people in New York society.   4
—WARD MCALLISTER, quoted in the *New York Tribune*, 1888

The talented tenth.   —W. E. B. DU BOIS,   5
The Souls of Black Folk, 1903
[More at RACES & PEOPLE.]

Society is any band of folks that kinder throw in with each other, and mess   6
around together for each other's discomfort. The ones with the more money
have more to eat and drink at their affairs, and their clothes cost more, and so
that's called high society.   —WILL ROGERS, *Weekly Articles*, August 10, 1930

The D.A.R.lings   7
Chatter like starlings
Telling their ancestors' names,
While grimly aloof
With looks of reproof,
Sit the Colonial Dames.

And The Cincinnati
All merry and chatty
Dangle their badges and pendants,
But haughty and proud
Disdaining the crowd
Brood the Mayflower Descendants.   —ARTHUR GUITERMAN,
in *The New Yorker*, 1936
[The Society of the Cincinnati was found by veterans of the Revolutionary
War. The organization was named for the fifth-century B.C. Roman general Lu-
cius Quinctius Cincinnatus, who, after a great victory, declined civil office and
returned to his farm. In the 1780s, the Cincinnati were suspected of undemoc-
ratic and even tyrannical tendencies, but criticism faded by the turn of the
century.]

What men value in this world is not rights but privileges.   8
—H. L. MENCKEN, *Minority Report:*
H. L. Mencken's Notebooks, 1956

Eggheads, unite! You have nothing to lose but your yolks!   9
—ADLAI STEVENSON, remark, presidential campaign, 1952
[Stevenson, a Democrat, was the last frankly intellectual presidential candi-
date to represent a major party. "Eggheads" had already become objects of

contempt. According to Stanley and Eleanor Hochman in *The Penguin Dictionary of Contemporary American History,* Stevenson was responding to a column by the influential Stewart Alsop. Quoting his brother, John Alsop, a prominent Republican, Stewart Alsop wrote, "Sure, all the eggheads are voting for Stevenson, but how many eggheads are there?" Stevenson not only dared to be an egghead, but in a seriously anti-Communist era, his quip was based on a passage in the Communist Manifesto, popularly rendered as "Workers of the world unite. You have nothing to lose but your chains."

In the presidential campaign of 1972, Gov. George Wallace of Alabama, introduced a replacement for eggheads, the infamous "pointy-headed intellectuals."]

1 I don't want to belong to any club that will accept me as a member.
—GROUCHO MARX, attributed
[Groucho took credit for the line in his autobiography, *Groucho and Me,* 1959, saying he used it in a telegram when withdrawing from a group called the Delaney Club. His son Arthur and brother Zeppo said that the resignation was from the Friars Club. The original piece of paper, if ever found, will be quite a collector's item.]

2 To the man-in-the-street, who, I'm sorry to say
Is a keen observer of life,
The word *intellectual* suggests right away
A man who's untrue to his wife.
—W. H. AUDEN, *Note on Intellectuals,* in
Collected Shorter Poems, 1927–1957 [1966]

3 The Best and the Brightest. —DAVID HALBERSTAM,
book title, 1969
[Halberstam's title refers ironically to the well-educated and intelligent political advisers who justified involvement in the disastrous Vietnam War. The phrase comes from an 1811 hymn by Reginald Heber: "Brightest and best of the sons of the morning,/ Dawn on our darkness, and lend us thine aid!" The phrase must have been in the air, for in 1822, the poet Percy Bysshe Shelley penned the line, "Best and brightest, come away!" *To Jane: An Invitation.* Thomas Carlyle used a similar phrase: "What is aristocracy? A corporation of the best, of the bravest," *Chartism,* 1840.]

4 A spirit of national masochism prevails, encouraged by an effete corps of impudent snobs who characterize themselves as Americans.
—SPIRO AGNEW, speech, Republican fundraiser,
New Orleans, Oct. 19, 1969
[The vice president was eventually eased out of office after being accused of taking bribes when he was governor of Maryland. But in his prime, he was blessed with a couple of talented speech writers, presidential aides William Safire and Pat Buchanan. His attacks on the press and antiwar protesters included the memorable passage: "In the United States today, we have more than our share of nattering nabobs of negativism. They have joined their own 4-H club, the hopeless, hysterical hypochondriacs of history." Safire has denied having crafted the "effete corps" attack, or Agnew's notorious comment on slums; see CITIES.]

EMOTIONS *See* ANGER; DESPAIR; ENVY; HAPPINESS;
HATE; HEART; LAUGHTER & MIRTH; LOVE;
SORROW & GRIEF; PASSION; UNHAPPINESS

ENDINGS

The opera ain't over till the fat lady sings.   1
                                                            —ANONYMOUS
[A folk saying with numerous variations, including "It ain't over until the fat lady sings," and, "Church ain't out until the fat lady sings," *Southern Words and Sayings*, 1976, Fabia R. Smith and Charles R. Smith, eds. It was used with reference to sports by commentator Dan Cook and Chicago Bulls' coach Dick Motta in the 1970s. See also Yogi Berra below.]

It ain't over till it's over.   —YOGI BERRA,   2
                                                          saying, attributed
[*Bartlett's* says that he was referring to the 1973 National League pennant race. The saying has taken a variety of forms; see also SPORTS.]

ENDS & MEANS   *See* EXPEDIENCY; MODERN TIMES (Einstein)

ENDURANCE   *See also* DETERMINATION, EFFORT,
                                 PERSISTENCE, & PERSEVERANCE; RESIGNATION

Endurance is the crowning quality,   3
And patience all the passion of great hearts.
                        —JAMES RUSSELL LOWELL, *Columbus*, 1844

Sorrow and silence are strong, and patient endurance is godlike.   4
                        —HENRY WADSWORTH LONGFELLOW, *Evangeline*, 1847

ENEMIES

There is no little enemy.   —BENJAMIN FRANKLIN,   5
                                            Poor Richard's Almanack, Sept. 1733

If we could read the secret history of our enemies, we should find in each man's   6
life sorrow and suffering enough to disarm all hostility.
                                    —HENRY WADSWORTH LONGFELLOW,
                                          Driftwood, 1857

They love him for the enemies he has made.   7
                        —EDWARD S. BRAGG, presidential nomination speech,
                                    Cleveland, Ohio, July 9, 1884
[Bragg, a war hero, headed the Wisconsin delegation, which backed Grover Cleveland. Cleveland's enemies were machine politicians allied with Tammany Hall. Cleveland won the nomination and the election.]

Your friends sometimes go to sleep; your enemies never do.   8
                        —THOMAS BRACKETT REED, speech, March 6, 1891

If you attend to your work, and let your enemy alone, someone else will come   9
along some day, and do him up for you.
                        —E. W. HOWE, *Country Town Sayings*, 1911
[Similar to a proverb from India: "If you sit on the bank of a river and wait, your enemy's corpse will soon float by."]

1   We have met the enemy and he is us.
—WALT KELLY, comment by Pogo the possum in the "Pogo"
cartoon strip, used as Earth Day poster in 1971
[See also Kelly at HUMANS & HUMAN NATURE. For the Oliver Hazard Perry original, see WAR OF 1812.]

2   Friends come and go, but enemies accumulate.
—ANONYMOUS, saying in government circles
[Former Republican presidential speech writer Peggy Noonan cited this apho-
rism on January 6, 1994, on the Charlie Rose television show.]

ENGLAND & THE ENGLISH   *See* NATIONS

ENTHUSIASM & ZEAL   *See also* DETERMINATION, EFFORT, PERSISTENCE,
& PERSEVERANCE; EXCESS; PASSION

3   Nothing great was ever achieved without enthusiasm.
—RALPH WALDO EMERSON, *Circles,* in *Essays: First Series,* 1841
[Also, "Every great and commanding moment in the annals of the world is the
triumph of some enthusiasm," *The Reformer* lecture, Boston, January 25, 1841.]

4   A fanatic is a man that does what he thinks th' Lord wud do if He knew th'
facts iv th' case.   —FINLEY PETER DUNNE, *Casual Observations,*
in *Mr. Dooley's Opinions,* 1900

5   *Enthusiasm, n.* A distemper of youth, curable by small doses of repentance in
connection with outward applications of experience.
—AMBROSE BIERCE, *The Devil's Dictionary,* 1906

6   Fanaticism consists in redoubling your efforts when you have forgotten your
aim.   —GEORGE SANTAYANA, *The Life of Reason,* 1905–1906

7   The greatest dangers to liberty lurk in insidious encroachment by men of zeal,
well-meaning but without understanding.
—LOUIS D. BRANDEIS, *Olmstead v. the United States,* 1928

8   When fanatics are on top, there is no limit to oppression.
—H. L. MENCKEN, *Minority Report:*
H. L. Mencken's Notebooks, 1956
[More at GOVERNMENT.]

ENVIRONMENT   *See also* MIDWEST, THE; NATURE;
WEST, THE; WILDERNESS

9   The earth is given as a common stock for man to labor and live on.
—THOMAS JEFFERSON, letter to James Madison, 1785

10   Methinks my own soul must be a bright invisible green.
—HENRY DAVID THOREAU, *A Week on the Concord
and Merrimack Rivers,* 1849

11   The whole civilized country is to some extent turned into a city.
—HENRY DAVID THOREAU, *Travel in Concord,*
in *Excursions, Poems, and Familiar Letters*

I'll scrape the mountains clean, my boys,   1
I'll drain the rivers dry,
A pocket full of rocks bring home,
So brothers, don't you cry!   —ANONYMOUS,
                                                                    c. 1850

[This verse, sung to the tune of *Oh! Susanna*, was popular among prospectors
attracted by the discovery of gold in California in 1848.]

Men as a general rule have very little reverence for trees.   2
                                            —ELIZABETH CADY STANTON,
                                                diary entry, 1900

The nation behaves well if it treats its natural resources as assets which it   3
must turn over to the next generation increased, and not impaired, in value.
            —THEODORE ROOSEVELT, speech, Colorado Livestock Association,
                Denver, Colo., August 29, 1910

Here in the United States, we turn our rivers and streams into sewers and   4
dumping grounds, we pollute the air, we destroy forests, and exterminate fishes,
birds, and mammals—not to speak of vulgarizing charming landscapes with
hideous advertisements. But at last it looks as if our people were awakening.
                    —THEODORE ROOSEVELT, *Our Vanishing Wildlife*,
                        in *The Outlook*, Jan. 25, 1913

Not one cent for scenery.   —JOSEPH CANNON, rejecting a request   5
                                                for a conservation appropriation,
                                                U.S. House of Representatives

["Uncle Joe" Cannon served in the House for forty-six years, and was Speaker
1903–11. The Library of Congress's *Respectfully Quoted*, notes that Pres. Lyndon B. Johnson had commented that conservation had been in eclipse since
Theodore Roosevelt's day, and described Cannon's comment as ultimatum.
"Well, today we are repealing Cannon's Law," Johnson said. "We are declaring
a new doctrine of conservation," speech, September 21, 1965, at signing ceremony making Assateague Island a national seashore area.]

But when the birds are gone, and their warm fields   6
Return no more, where, then, is paradise?
                    —WALLACE STEVENS, *Sunday Morning*, 1923

A river is more than an amenity; it is a treasure.   7
                            —OLIVER WENDELL HOLMES, JR.,
                                New Jersey v. New York et al., 1931

[This Supreme Court case concerned New York's diversion of the Delaware
River. In an important argument for equitable sharing of natural resources, Justice Holmes continued, "It [a river] offers a necessity of life that must be ra-
tioned among those that have the power over it." He concluded that while
New York had the power to cut off the downriver flow, "Such a power . . .
could not be tolerated." See also Laura Gilpin at NATURE.]

it wont be long now it wont be long   8
man is making deserts of the earth
it wont be long now
before man will have it used up
so that nothing but ants
and centipedes and scorpions
can find a living on it.   —DON MARQUIS, *archy does his part*, 1935

1   Pity the Meek, for they shall inherit the earth.
                              —DON MARQUIS, quoted in Frederick B. Wilcox,
                        A Little Book of Aphorisms

2   The nation that destroys its soil destroys itself.
                      —FRANKLIN D. ROOSEVELT, letter to state governors, Feb. 26, 1937

3   I must teach my children to know and to love the earth itself. If they can keep
    in contact with the land and the water and the sky, they can obtain all worth-
    while that life holds.   —CHARLES A. LINDBERGH, journal entry, April 1, 1938,
                        The Wartime Journals of Charles A. Lindbergh [1970]

4   When we see land as a community to which we belong, we may begin to use it
    with love and respect.
                              —ALDO LEOPOLD, *A Sand County Almanac,* 1949
    [See also Robert Frost at AMERICA & AMERICANS.]

5   Conservation is a state of harmony between men and the land.   —*Ibid.*

6   A culture is no better than its woods.
                              —W. H. AUDEN, *Bucolics,* in *Shield of Achilles,* 1955
    [The full passage runs: "This society is going smash; / They cannot fool us with
    how fast they go, / How much they cost each other and the gods! / A culture is
    no better than its woods."]

7   The history of life on earth is the history of living things and their environ-
    ment.   —RACHEL CARSON, *Silent Spring,* 1962

8   Over increasingly large areas of the United States, spring now comes unher-
    alded by the return of the birds, and the early mornings are strangely silent
    where once they were filled with the beauty of bird song.   —*Ibid.*

9   As crude a weapon as a cave man's club, the chemical barrage has been hurled
    against the fabric of life.   —*Ibid.*

10 The supreme reality of our time is the vulnerability of our planet.
                              —JOHN F. KENNEDY, speech, June 28, 1963

11 The Quiet Crisis.   —STEWART L. UDALL,
                                                    book title, 1963
    [Then Secretary of the Interior, Udall wrote this book urging Americans to
    develop a "land ethic."]

12 We abuse land because we regard it as a commodity belonging to us. Conser-
    vation is a state of harmony between men and land.   —*Ibid.*

13 We have met the enemy and he is us.
                              —WALT KELLY, comment by Pogo the possum
                        in the "Pogo" cartoon strip, used as Earth Day poster in 1971,
                        The Best of Pogo, ed., Mrs. Walt Kelly & Bill Crouch, Jr.
    [See also Kelly at HUMANS & HUMAN NATURE.]

14 A tree is a tree—how many do you need to look at?
                              —RONALD REAGAN, speech to the Western Wood Products
                        Association, Sept. 12, 1965
    [Former Reagan press representative Lyn Nofziger wrote in his autobiography

(*Nofziger,* 1992) that in 1966, when Reagan was running for governor of California, he successfully denied making this remark. But Nofziger's secretary had it on tape.]

I am a passenger on the spaceship, Earth.　　　　　　　　　　　　　　　1
　　　　　—R. BUCKMINSTER FULLER,
　　　　　　Operating Manual for the Spaceship Earth, 1969

Why should deserts be asked to blossom?　　　　　　　　　　　　　　2
　　　　　—WALLACE STEGNER, Introduction,
　　　　　　Where the Bluebird Sings to the Lemonade Springs, 1992
[The introduction was based on Stegner's lecture *A Geography of Hope,* delivered at the University of Colorado, and published by the university's press in *A Society to Match Our Scenery,* 1991. Stegner reminds us that aridity is the natural condition of the West, and cannot be overcome except at an excessively high price. "You have to get over the color green," he wrote; "you have to quit associating beauty with gardens and lawn; you have to get used to an unhuman scale," *Thoughts in a Dry Land,* 1972. See also Stegner at WILDERNESS, below, p. 513.]

ENVY

Envy is ignorance.　　　　　　　　—RALPH WALDO EMERSON, *Self-Reliance,*　3
　　　　　　　　　　　　　　　　　in *Essays: First Series,* 1841

Pain, n. An uncomfortable frame of mind that may have a physical basis in　4
something that is being done to the body, or may be purely mental, caused by the
good fortune of another.　　　—AMBROSE BIERCE, *The Devil's Dictionary,* 1906

EPITAPHS & GRAVESTONES　　　*See also* LAST WORDS; LINCOLN, ABRAHAM;
　　　　　　　　　　　　　　　　　　　　　SPORTS (Grantland Rice)

Behold and see as you pass by　　　　　　　　　　　　　　　　　　5
As you are now, so once was I;
As I am now, so you will be—
Prepare for death and follow me.　　　　—ANONYMOUS, commonly used
　　　　　　　　　　　　　　　　on gravestones in Colonial times
[The verse dates back at least to 1376, when it was carved on the tomb of Edward, the Black Prince, according to Avon Neal in *American Heritage,* August 1970.]

The body of B. Franklin, Printer (like the cover of an old book, its contents torn　6
out and stripped of its lettering and gilding), lies here, food for worms; but the
work shall not be lost, for it will (as he believed) appear once more in a new and
more elegant edition, revised and corrected by the Author.
　　　　　—BENJAMIN FRANKLIN, *Epitaph on Himself,* 1728
[Franklin died in 1790.]

Here lyes John Purcell;　　　　　　　　　　　　　　　　　　　　7
And whether he be in heaven or in hell
Never a one of us can tell.　　　　　—ANONYMOUS, in Alexander Hamilton,
　　　　　　　　　　　　　　　Itinerarium, July 6, 1744
[A proposed epitaph for a recently deceased New Yorker. See Boston under
CITIES for details on this Hamilton, who is not Hamilton the Founding Father.]

1   Here Skugg
     Lies snug
     As a bug
     In a rug.   —BENJAMIN FRANKLIN, letter to Georgiana Shipley,
                                      Sept. 26, 1772
     [Skugg was Miss Shipley's pet squirrel.]

2   And the fellow died as well as he lived, but it is part of a sailor's life to die well.
     He had no talk, but he inspired all about him with ardor; he always saw the
     best thing to be done; he knew the best way to do it; and he had no more dodge
     in him than the mainmast.
                          —STEPHEN DECATUR, on Captain James Lawrence,
                              after his death in action between the U.S.S. *Chesapeake*
                              and H.M.S. *Shannon* off Boston Harbor on June 1, 1813

3   Here was buried Thomas Jefferson, author of the Declaration of American In-
     dependence, of the statute of Virginia for religious freedom, and father of the
     University of Virginia.   —THOMAS JEFFERSON, epitaph written by himself,
                                       inscribed on his tombstone at Monticello
     [This was found in the top drawer of Jefferson's desk after his death on July 4,
     1826. Notice that he made no mention of the high offices he had attained: gov-
     ernor of Virginia, minister to France, U.S. Secretary of State, Vice President and
     President. As for the Virginia law guaranteeing religious freedom, he and James
     Madison fought nine years to get it passed, and it is one of the sources of the re-
     ligion clauses in the First Amendment, which was written by Madison. See
     also Jefferson at TYRANNY.]

4   He served his country faithfully forty-eight years and was much beloved and
     respected by all who knew him.
                          —ANONYMOUS, gravestone of Ichabod Crane on Staten Island
     [Crane, a hero of the War of 1812, did not resemble the easily afeared "scare-
     crow eloped from a cornfield" that bore his name in Washington Irving's *Leg-
     end of Sleepy Hollow*, 1819.]

5   Quoth the Raven, "Nevermore."   —EDGAR ALLAN POE,
                                            The Raven, 1845,
                                            used on his gravestone in Baltimore
     [More at THE OCCULT.]

6   On fame's eternal camping ground
     Their silent tents are spread
     And glory guards with solemn round
     The bivouac of the dead.   —THEODORE O'HARA,
                                            The Bivouac of the Dead, 1847
     [The poem, written during the Mexican War, commemorates the American
     dead at the battle of Buena Vista, on February 22, 1847. By an act of Congress,
     the verse is displayed at every national cemetery.]

7   He died as he must have wished to die, breathing his last in the Capitol,
     stricken down by the angel of death on the field of his civil glory.
                          —PHILIP HONE, *Diary*,
                              on the death of John Quincy Adams,
                              Feb. 24, 1848
     [After leaving the presidency in 1829, Adams served seventeen years in the
     House, its oldest member at the time of his death, and still an able debater. See
     also Adams at LAST WORDS.]

Gone are the living, but the dead remain, 1
And not neglected; for a hand unseen,
Scattering its bounty like summer rain,
Still keeps their graves and their remembrance green.
                    —HENRY WADSWORTH LONGFELLOW, *The Jewish Cemetery*
                        at Newport, 1852
[The 18th-century Sephardic cemetery at Newport, Rhode Island, had been
abandoned by Longfellow's time. The associated synagogue itself, a notable ex-
ample of colonial Georgian architecture, still stands.]

Unawed by opinion 2
Unseduced by flattery
Undismayed by disaster
He confronted life with antique courage
And death with Christian hope.   —ANONYMOUS, epitaph of James Petigru,
                        Charleston, S.C., 1863
[He confronted life with intelligence, too; see Petigru at SOUTH CAROLINA.]

He was a gallant soldier, and a Christian gentleman. 3
                    —ULYSSES S. GRANT,
                        speaking of Thomas Jonathan "Stonewall" Jackson,
                        1864
[During the Wilderness Campaign, Grant chanced to stay overnight in the
house where Jackson had died. Told of this, Grant uttered this impromptu
epitaph, which would have pleased Jackson greatly. See also Jackson at LAST
WORDS.]

Sleep sweetly in your humble graves, 4
Sleep, martyrs of a fallen cause . . .
Stoop, angels hither from the skies!
There is no holier spot of ground
Than where defeated valor lies,
By mourning beauty crowned!   —HENRY TIMROD, *Ode on the*
                        Confederate Dead, 1867
[The poem was written to be sung as a hymn. Its full title tells the story: *Ode.*
Sung on the occasion of decorating the graves of the Confederate dead, at
Magnolia Cemetery, Charleston, S.C., 1867.]

When fades at length our lingering day, 5
Who cares what pompous tombstones say?
Read on the hearts that love us still,
Hic jacet Joe. *Hic jacet* Bill.   —OLIVER WENDELL HOLMES, SR.,
                        Bill and Joe, 1868
[*Hic jacet* means "here lies."]

Here lies a man who never owned a dollar he could not take up to the Great 6
White Throne.   —ROBERT COLLYER, funeral address for Peter Cooper,
                        April 7, 1883
[Cooper's rare honesty and generosity, highlighted here by the Reverend Dr.
Collyer, prompted a spontaneous popular expression of grief at his death. Flags
in New York City were lowered to half mast, and mourners filed for hours past
his body in All Soul's Church, and followed the coffin for miles through the
city while church bells tolled. See also Cooper at GOD and MONEY & THE RICH.]

Called back.   —EMILY DICKINSON, on her gravestone in West Amherst, Mass., 7
                    from her last letter, May 1886

1   Here lies Champ Clark, who, in the year of our Lord and Master one thousand eight hundred and ninety-four, stood in the American Congress and did battle for the principle that the great body of the American people should have cheaper clothing, cheaper food, cheaper medicine, cheaper necessaries of life, more luxuries, and be better able to educate their children.
—CHAMP CLARK, speech, House of Representatives, Dec. 10, 1894
[Clark, then a lame duck, offered this political epitaph for himself when taunted by a Republican for having lost in the November election. Reports of the Missouri Democrat's political demise were premature, however. Reelected in 1897, he served another twelve terms in the House and was Speaker from 1911 to 1919.]

2   Here lies Frank Pixley—as usual.
—AMBROSE BIERCE
[Pixley, a former California attorney general, founded *The Argonaut* in 1877, and Bierce was one of the magazine's first editors. According to one of Pixley's descendants, English professor Sandra Dutton, Pixley fired Bierce, and after that, the two men found amusement in writing each other's epitaphs.]

3   Warm summer sun, shine kindly here;
Warm southern wind, blow softly here;
Green sod above, lie light, lie light—Good night, dear heart, good
    night, good night.   —MARK TWAIN,
                                                      attributed, 1896
[The verse is on the gravestone in Elmira, New York, of Twain's daughter Susy—"she that had been our wonder and our worship"—who died August 18, 1896. The poem actually was by an Australian, Robert Richardson, written c. 1885, and used with a slight change by Twain. In the original, "southern" read "northern," because the warm wind in Australia is from the north. Twain's friend and biographer, Albert Bigelow Paine, reports that when Twain heard that the lines were being attributed to him, he had Richardson's name cut beneath them on the monument. Still, Twain is often given credit for them.]

4   *Epitaph, n.* An inscription on a tomb showing that virtues acquired by death have a retroactive effect.   —AMBROSE BIERCE, *The Devil's Dictionary*,
                                                      1906
[The dictionary, originally called the *The Cynic's Word Book*—at the publisher's insistence—included definitions used in newspaper columns from as early as 1877. In the entry for *loss*, Bierce countered the retroactive effect of death as best he could in a proposed epitaph for railroad magnate C. P. Huntington: "Here Huntington's ashes long have lain / Whose loss is our own eternal gain, / For while he exercised all his powers, / Whatever he gained, the loss was ours."]

5   Faithful to the cause of Prohibition—
She hath done what she could.   —ANONYMOUS, gravestone of
                                        Carry Nation, Belton, Mo., 1911

6   If, after I depart this vale, you ever remember me and have thought to please my ghost, forgive some sinner and wink your eye at some homely girl.
—H. L. MENCKEN, in *Smart Set* magazine, Dec. 1921

7   God gave him a great vision.
The devil gave him an imperious heart.
The proud heart is still.
The vision lives.   —WILLIAM ALLEN WHITE, editorial on the death of Pres.
                          Woodrow Wilson, *Emporia Gazette*, Feb. 4, 1924
[Wilson suffered a stroke while campaigning to win support for the League of Nations.]

I never met a man I didn't like.   —WILL ROGERS, remark, Tremont Temple   1
Baptist Church, Boston, June 15, 1930
[This was not the first time Rogers expressed this thought. Speculating that he would have enjoyed meeting Trotsky if given the chance, he wrote in *There's Not a Bathing Suit in Russia* (1927), "I have never yet met a man that I dident [*sic*] like." Rogers continued: "When you meet people, no matter what opinion you might have formed of them beforehand, why, after you meet them and see their angle and their personality, why, you can see a lot of good in all of them." The later, more famous statement was made when he was asked by the church minister to address his congregation. Then he said that "When I die, my epitaph or whatever you call those signs on gravestones is going to read: 'I joked about every prominent man of my time, but I never met a man I didn't like.' I am so proud of that I can hardly wait to die so it can be carved. And when you come to my grave you will find me sitting there, proudly reading it." Five years later, Rogers died in a plane crash in Alaska. The abbreviated form of the sentiment is inscribed on his burial stone at the Will Rogers Memorial in Claremore, Oklahoma.]

[Epitaph for a waiter:] By and by   2
God caught his eye.   —DAVID MCCORD, "Remainders,"
Bay Window Ballads, 1935
[Attributed in short form—"God caught his eye"—to playwright George Kaufman, a slightly younger contemporary of McCord's, by critic Howard Teichman in his 1972 biography of Kaufman. Most authoritative sources cite McCord, however.]

Earth, receive an honored guest;   3
William Yeats is laid to rest.
Let the Irish vessel lie
Emptied of its poetry.   —W. H. AUDEN, *In Memory of W. B. Yeats*, 1940

And were an epitaph to be my story,   4
I'd have a short one ready for my own.
I would have written of me on my stone:
I had a lover's quarrel with the world.
—ROBERT FROST, *The Lesson for Today*,
read at Harvard University, June 20, 1941

On the whole, I'd rather be in Philadelphia.   —W. C. FIELDS, attributed,   5
epitaph for himself, 1946
[See also Fields on Philadelphia under CITIES.]

My Jesus mercy.   —ANONYMOUS, gravestone of Al Capone, Chicago, 1947   6

Excuse my dust.   —DOROTHY PARKER, proposed epitaph   7

Over my dead body!   —GEORGE S. KAUFMAN, proposed epitaph, quoted in   8
Robert E. Drennan, *The Algonquin Wits* [1968]

Say that I was a drum major for justice; say that I was a drum major for peace;   9
I was a drum major for righteousness.
—MARTIN LUTHER KING, JR., suggestions for his own funeral,
sermon, Feb. 4, 1968
[The epitaph on his gravestone is from the spiritual with which he ended his "I have a dream" speech at the Lincoln Memorial in the march on Washington in 1963; see AMERICAN HISTORY: MEMORABLE MOMENTS. The words are "Free at last! Free at last! / Thank God Almighty, we are free at last!"]

1   She did it the hard way.   —BETTE DAVIS, headstone inscription,
                                                 Forest Lawn, Hollywood, 1989

EQUALITY   *See also* DEMOCRACY; MANNERS (De Vries); PEOPLE, THE;
                        RACES & PEOPLES; WOMEN; WOMEN & MEN

2   All men are created equal.   —THOMAS JEFFERSON, *Declaration of*
                                                 Independence, July 4, 1776
     [More at DECLARATION OF INDEPENDENCE.]

3   The earth is the mother of all people, and all people should have equal rights
     upon it. You might as well expect the rivers to run backward as that any man who
     was born a free man should be contented when penned up and denied liberty.
                        —JOSEPH THE YOUNGER, *An Indian's View of Indian Affairs*
                        in *The North American Review*, no. 269, vol. 128, 1879
     [Though outranked by several older Nez Percé chiefs, Joseph the Younger, who
     succeeded his father as chief of the Wallowa band in 1871, was regarded by
     whites as the principal leader of the entire tribe. More at TALK.]

4   There is no king who has not had a slave among his ancestors, and no slave who
     has not had a king among his.   —HELEN KELLER, *The Story of My Life*, 1902

ERAS   *See* BAD TIMES; DEPRESSION, THE; GENERATIONS; GOOD TIMES;
                        MODERN TIMES; PAST, THE; POLITICS & POLITICIANS; PRESENT, THE

ERROR   *See* FAULTS & FAILINGS; MISTAKES

ESCAPE

5   The efforts which we make to escape from our destiny only serve to lead us
     into it.   —RALPH WALDO EMERSON, *Fate*, in *The Conduct of Life*, 1860

6   The best way out is always through.   —ROBERT FROST, *A Servant to*
                                             Servants, in *North of Boston*, 1914

7   listen: there's a hell
     of a good universe next door: let's go.   —E. E. CUMMINGS, *pity this busy*
                                                 monster, manunkind, in *One*
                                                 Times One (or *1 x 1*), 1944

ETHICS & MORALITY   *See also* CONSCIENCE; EXPEDIENCY;
                                            RIGHT; VIRTUE

8   My country is the world, and my religion is to do good.
                        —THOMAS PAINE, *The Rights of Man*, 1791
     [In *The Age of Reason*, 1794, Paine elaborated: "The word is my country, all
     mankind are my brethren, and to do good is my religion."]

9   Expedients are for the hour, but principles are for the ages.
                        —HENRY WARD BEECHER, *Proverbs from Plymouth Pulpit*, 1887

10   We can act *as if* there were a God; feel *as if* we were free; consider nature *as if*
     she were full of special designs; lay plans *as if* we were to be immortal; and we
     find then that these words do make a genuine difference in our moral life.
                        —WILLIAM JAMES, *The Varieties of Religious Experience*, 1902

I know only that what is moral is what you feel good after and what is immoral is 1
what you feel bad after. —ERNEST HEMINGWAY,
Death in the Afternoon, 1932

The number of people with any criteria for distinguishing between good and 2
evil is very small. —T. S. ELIOT, Virginia lectures, 1933

The world has achieved brilliance without conscience. Ours is a world of nu- 3
clear giants and ethical infants. —OMAR BRADLEY, speech,
Armistice Day, 1948
[Gen. Bradley commanded U.S. Forces in Normandy in 1944, and became chief
of staff in 1949. He supported Pres. Harry Truman in his confrontation with
Gen. Douglas MacArthur, who at one point advocated use of nuclear weapons
in the Korean conflict. See under MacArthur at AMERICAN HISTORY: MEMORABLE
MOMENTS.]

Puritanism—the haunting fear that someone, somewhere, may be happy. 4
—H. L. MENCKEN, *A Mencken Chrestomathy*, 1949

The needs of society determine its ethics. 5
—MAYA ANGELOU, *I Know Why the Caged Bird Sings*, 1969

EVIDENCE
See also JUSTICE; LAW

Some circumstantial evidence is very strong, as when you find a trout in the 6
milk. —HENRY DAVID THOREAU,
Journal, Nov. 11, 1850
[The reference is to a common consumer fraud of the time—watering of milk.
The line has proven to be a popular one with mystery writers, at least three of
whom have used *A Trout in the Milk* as a book title, according to Jane Horning's *The Mystery Lover's Book of Quotations*.]

Goddamn an eyewitness anyway. He always spoils a good story. 7
—COL. CRISP, c. 1880s
[In David McCullough's *Truman*, this "colonel by agreement" is described as a
perennial Democratic congressional candidate and local orator.]

It is a less evil that some criminals should escape than that the government 8
should play an ignoble part [in gathering evidence].
—OLIVER WENDELL HOLMES, JR., dissent, *Olmstead v. U.S.*, 1928
[One of Holmes's famous dissents. The case, which involved wiretapping of a
bootlegger, was finally completely overturned in 1967 when the Supreme Court
held in *Katz v. U.S.* that government agents had to obtain court orders to place
taps. Justice Louis D. Brandeis also wrote a dissent in *Olmstead*; see PRIVACY.
Holmes led up to his conclusion this way: "It is desirable that criminals
should be detected, and to that end all available evidence should be used. It is
also desirable that the government should not itself foster crimes, when they
are the means by which evidence is to be obtained. . . . We have to choose, and
for my part I think it is a less evil, etc."]

If it walks like a duck, and quacks like a duck, then it just may be a duck. 9
—WALTER REUTHER, attributed
[William Safire, in his *New Political Dictionary*, writes that Mr. Reuther, head
of the United Auto Workers, applied this logic to the question of how to identify a Communist.]

1   The absence of evidence is not evidence of absence.
—MICHAEL PAPAGIANNIS, quoted in C. D. B. Bryan,
Close Encounters of the Fourth Kind: Alien Abductions,
UFOs, and the Conference at M.I.T., 1995
[Papagiannis is an astronomer at Boston University.]

EVIL   *See also* CRIME, CRIMINALS, & DETECTIVES; DANGER &
DANGEROUS PEOPLE; DEVIL, THE; SIN, VICE, & NAUGHTINESS

2   There is a capacity of virtue in us, and there is a capacity of vice to make your
blood creep.   —RALPH WALDO EMERSON, *Journal,* 1831

3   I's wicked, I is.   —HARRIET BEECHER STOWE, *Uncle Tom's Cabin,* 1852

4   There are a thousand hacking at the branches of evil to one who is striking at
the root.   —HENRY DAVID THOREAU, "Economy," *Walden,* 1854

5   No man is justified in doing evil on the grounds of expediency.
—THEODORE ROOSEVELT, *The Strenuous Life,* title essay, 1900

6   Who knows what evil lurks in the hearts of men? The Shadow knows!
—WALTER B. GIBSON (writing as Maxwell Grant), 1930
[Gibson's character The Shadow first appeared, so to speak, on the *Street &*
Smith Detective Hour radio show. The great popularity of the show made this
line famous; it opened each episode.]

7   Between two evils, I always pick the one I never tried before.
—MAE WEST, *Klondike Annie,* 1936

8   Fashions in sin change.   —LILLIAN HELLMAN, *Watch on the Rhine,* 1941

9   Evil is unspectacular and always human
And shares our bed and eats at our own table.
—W. H. AUDEN, *Herman Melville,* "for Lincoln Kirstein,"
in *The Collected Poetry of W. H. Auden,* 1945

10   He who accepts evil without protesting against it is really cooperating with it.
—MARTIN LUTHER KING, JR., *Stride Toward Freedom,* 1958
[King's thought parallels an observation that John F. Kennedy used in speeches:
"The only thing necessary for the triumph of evil is for good men to do nothing." Kennedy attributed the remark to the British statesman and political
philosopher Edmund Burke, but no one has been able to find it in Burke's writings. Perhaps, as Emily Morison Beck suggested in the preface to the 1980 edition of *Bartlett's Familiar Quotations,* the quote is a paraphrase of another
statement by Burke: "When bad men combine, the good must associate; else
they will fall, one by one," *Thoughts on the Cause of the Present Discontents,*
April 23, 1770. Ultimately, one might trace the thought to the Bible: "He who
is not with me is against me," *Matthew* 12:30.]

11   The banality of evil.   —HANNAH ARENDT,
Eichmann in Jerusalem, 1963
[The book was based on professor Arendt's articles in the *The New Yorker* on
the trial of Adolf Eichmann for war crimes. Eichmann, more of a bureaucrat
than a demon, personified to Arendt the institutionalization of evil in a totali-

tarian society. Just before his trial, he remarked, "To sum it all up, I must say I regret nothing." Arendt wrote, "It was as though, in those last minutes, he was summing up the lessons that this long course in human wickedness had taught us—the lesson of the fearsome, word-and-thought-defying *banality of evil.*"

A similar thought was expressed by American poet Stephen Vincent Benét in *John Brown's Body*, 1928. Benét wrote that while "some men wish evil and accomplish it," most "just let it happen." He concluded, "The fault is no decisive villainous knife / But the dull saw that is the routine mind."]

No man is a villain in his own heart.   —JAMES BALDWIN, *Blues for Mr. Charley*,   1
introduction to the play, 1964

EXCELLENCE
See also GRACE; METHOD; VIRTUE

Strive to be the *greatest* man in your country, and you may be disappointed.   2
Strive to be the *best* and you may succeed: he may well win the race that runs by himself.   —BENJAMIN FRANKLIN, *Poor Richard's Almanack*, 1747

If a man can write a better book, preach a better sermon, or make a better   3
mousetrap than his neighbor, though he builds his house in the woods, the world will make a beaten path to his door.
—RALPH WALDO EMERSON, lecture, attributed in Sarah B. Yule
and Mary S. Keene, *Borrowings* [1889]
[Emerson's writings contain only the wordier: "I trust a good deal to common fame, as we all must. If a man has good corn, or wood, or boards, or pigs, to sell, or can make better chairs or knives, crucibles or church organs, than anybody else, you will find a broad hard-beaten road to his house," *Journal*, February 1855. Of course, now that we have advertising instead of common fame, the proposition falters. See also Emerson at ACTION & DOING.]

It is the privilege of any human work which is well done to invest the doer   4
with a certain haughtiness.   —RALPH WALDO EMERSON, *Wealth*, in
The Conduct of Life, 1860

What is our praise or pride   5
But to imagine excellence, and try to make it?
What does it say over the door of Heaven
But *homo fecit?*   —RICHARD WILBUR, *For the New Railway Station in Rome*,
in *Things of This World*, 1956

EXCESS
See also ENTHUSIASM & ZEAL; LUXURY;
PASSION; THINGS & POSSESSIONS

I don't regret a single "excess" of my responsive youth—I only regret, in my   6
chilled age, certain occasions and opportunities I didn't embrace.
—HENRY JAMES, letter to Hugh Walpole, August 21, 1913

Never murder a man who is committing suicide.   7
—WOODROW WILSON, letter to Bernard Baruch, 1916
[This was Pres. Wilson's hands-off strategy for dealing with Charles Evans Hughes, his Republican opponent in the 1916 election. He attributed the precept to "a friend, who says that he has always followed the rule never to murder a man who is committing suicide." Nevertheless, the election was quite close, with Wilson winning by less than 600,000 votes out of almost 18 million cast. The victor wasn't known until three days after the polls closed.]

1   My candle burns at both ends;
    It will not last the night;
    But ah, my foes, and oh my friends—
    It gives a lovely light.   —EDNA ST. VINCENT MILLAY, *First Fig*,
                                                     in *A Few Figs from Thistles*, 1920
    [Legendary Broadway director George Abbott countered, "I do not think burn-
    ing the candle at both ends casts a lovely light; on the contrary, I am of the
    opinion that it is a dandy way to get a nervous breakdown." This was in his au-
    tobiography, written in 1963, when he was seventy-six; he continued to work
    until his death at age 107. Millay, in her later years, settled down to country
    living, but nevertheless died at age fifty-eight. On the other hand, she had won
    a Pulitzer Prize at age twenty-seven.]

2   Too much of a good thing can be wonderful.
                                                —MAE WEST, quoted in Joseph Weintraub, ed.,
                                                     The Wit and Wisdom of Mae West [1967]

EXCUSES & EXPLANATIONS

3   Never explain—your friends do not need it, and your enemies will not believe
    you anyway.   —ELBERT HUBBARD,
                                                                Notebook, 1927

    [See also Henry Ford below.]

4   [On being observed by his wife kissing a chorus girl:] I wasn't kissing her, I was
    whispering into her mouth.   —CHICO MARX, attributed, in Groucho Marx and
                                        Richard J. Anobile, *Marx Brothers Scrapbook*
                                        [1973]

5   Never complain, never explain.   —HENRY FORD II,
                                                                        saying
    [According to the *New York Times* obituary for Ford, he turned to this tradi-
    tional saying after being arrested for drunk driving; the advice is also the title
    of Victor Lasky's biography of Ford. The thought, however, is essentially
    proverbial. Dean Acheson observed, "How vulnerable are those who explain,"
    Time magazine, June 26, 1964. Abroad, Admiral of the Fleet John Arbuthnot
    Baron Fisher noted in a letter to the London *Times*, Sept. 5, 1919: "(It's only
    d——d fools who argue!) Never contradict. Never explain. Never apologize.
    (Those are the secrets of a happy life!)" The earliest attribution is to the En-
    glish Prime Minister Benjamin Disraeli in John Morley's *The Life of William
    Gladstone*, 1903.]

6   The devil made me do it.   —FLIP WILSON,
                                                                        saying
    [A note on Wilson is given at THE DEVIL.]

7   Two wrongs don't make a right, but they make a good excuse.
                    —THOMAS SZASZ, *Social Relations*, in *The Second Sin*, 1973

8   It's not how you win or lose, it's how you place the blame.
                                                                —ANONYMOUS
    [Baseball slugger Ralph Kiner used this quip while broadcasting a Mets game,
    but acknowledged it wasn't original with him. It's a play on the commonplace,
    "It's not how you win or lose, it's how you play the game." See Grantland Rice
    at SPORTS.]

EXERCISE *See* PHYSICAL FITNESS; SPORTS

EXPEDIENCY *See also* DISHONESTY & LIES;
PRESIDENCY, THE (John W. Dean III); RUTHLESSNESS

In times like these in which we live, it will not do to be overscrupulous. 1
    —ALEXANDER HAMILTON, letter to John Jay, May 7, 1800

We do what we must, and call it by the best names. 2
    —RALPH WALDO EMERSON, *Considerations by the Way*,
    in *The Conduct of Life*, 1860

Most of the great results of history are brought about by discreditable means. 3
    —*Ibid.*

Expedients are for the hour, but principles are for the ages. 4
    —HENRY WARD BEECHER,
    Proverbs from Plymouth Pulpit, 1887

No man is justified in doing evil on the grounds of expediency. 5
    —THEODORE ROOSEVELT,
    The Strenuous Life, title essay, 1900

In practice, such trifles as contradictions in principle are easily set aside; the 6
faculty of ignoring them makes the practical man.
    —HENRY BROOKS ADAMS, *The Education of Henry Adams*, 1907

"The true," to put it very briefly, is only the expedient in the way of our think- 7
ing, just as "the right" is only the expedient in our way of behaving.
    —WILLIAM JAMES, *Pragmatism*, 1907
[For a fuller explanation, see James at TRUTH.]

Expediency and justice frequently are not even on speaking terms. 8
    —ARTHUR H. VANDENBERG,
    speech, U.S. Senate, March 8, 1945
[Sen. Vandenberg was referring to the Yalta agreement, in particular to abandoning Poland to Russia.]

EXPERIENCE *See also* LIFE; SUFFERING & PAIN

Experience keeps a dear school, but fools will learn in no other. 9
    —BENJAMIN FRANKLIN,
    Poor Richard's Almanack, Dec. 1743
[*Dear* in the sense of *expensive.*]

One thorn of experience is worth a whole wilderness of warning. 10
    —JAMES RUSSELL LOWELL, *Shakespeare Once More*,
    in *Among My Books*, 1870

We should be careful to get out of an experience only the wisdom that is in it— 11
and stop there; lest we be like the cat that sits down on a hot stove-lid. She will
never sit down on a hot stove-lid again—and that is well; but also she will never
sit down on a cold one anymore.
    —MARK TWAIN, *Pudd'nhead Wilson's New Calendar*,
    in *Following the Equator*, 1897

1   All experience is an arch, to build upon.
—HENRY BROOKS ADAMS, *The Education of Henry Adams*, 1907

2   I've been things and seen places.   —MAE WEST, *I'm No Angel*, 1933

3   We are creatures shaped by our experiences, we like what we know more often than we know what we like.   —WALLACE STEGNER,
Thoughts in a Dry Land, 1972

4   Experience gives us the tests first and the lessons later.
—NAOMI JUDD, public radio interview,
Weekend Edition, Jan. 29, 1994

EXPERTS   *See also* DOCTORS & MEDICINE; LAWYERS

5   An expert is one who knows more and more about less and less.
—NICHOLAS MURRAY BUTLER, attributed,
commencement speech, Columbia University,
New York City

F

FACTS   *See also* KNOWLEDGE & INFORMATION; LIFE (T. S. Eliot)

Facts are stubborn things.   —JOHN ADAMS, speaking as defense attorney   1
for British soldiers accused
in the Boston Massacre trials, Dec. 1770

If a man kick a fact out of the window, when he comes back he finds it again   2
in the chimney corner.   —RALPH WALDO EMERSON,
Journal, 1842
[But see also Emerson at TIME.]

A little fact is worth a whole limbo of dreams.   3
—RALPH WALDO EMERSON, *The Superlative*, 1847

The frontiers are not east or west, north or south, but wherever a man *fronts* a   4
fact.   —HENRY DAVID THOREAU, *A Week on the Concord
and Merrimack Rivers*, 1849
[See also Thoreau under LIFE for going into the woods to front the essential
facts of life.]

Facts are contrary 'z mules.   —JAMES RUSSELL LOWELL,   5
The Biglow Papers, II, 1862

Let us not underrate the value of a fact; it will one day flower into a truth.   6
—HENRY DAVID THOREAU, *Excursions*, 1863

Get your facts straight first, and then you can distort them as much as you   7
please.   —MARK TWAIN, 1889,
quoted in Rudyard Kipling, *From Sea to Sea* [1899]
[Kipling paid a visit to Twain at his brother-in-law's home in Elmira, N.Y., in
the summer of 1889. Kipling was just twenty-four years old and as yet unknown—he was writing travel letters for Indian journals at the time—but he
made quite an impression. In a section of his *Autobiography*, written August
11, 1906, Twain recalled telling his mother-in-law, "He [Kipling] is a stranger
to me, but he is a most remarkable man—and I am the other one. Between us,
we cover all knowledge; he knows all that can be known and I know the rest."

For his part, Kipling, in a letter to India, called the meeting a "golden morning," and wrote: "All my preconceived notions [of Twain's personality] were wrong and beneath the reality. Blessed is the man who finds no disillusion when he is brought face to face with a revered writer." In 1902, Kipling told his American publisher: "I love to think of the great and godlike Clemens. He is the biggest man you have on your side of the water by a damn sight. . . . Cervantes was a relation of his."]

1   The fatal futility of fact.

—HENRY JAMES, *Prefaces*, 1907–1909,
preface to his *The Spoils of Poynton*

2   Let's look at the record.

—AL SMITH, saying,
presidential campaign speeches, 1928

3   You Could Look It Up.

—JAMES THURBER, story title,
The Saturday Evening Post, 1941
[A favorite saying of baseball manager Charles Dillon "Casey" Stengel, probably borrowed from Thurber's story about a manager who sends a midget up to bat in a critical situation. In 1951, flamboyant Bill Veeck—it rhymes with *wreck*—then owner of the St. Louis Browns, actually tried this tactic.]

4   Facts are piffle.

—JOHN DICKSON CARR,
The Crooked Hinge, 1938
[From a great detective with a great name, Dr. Gideon Fell.]

5   Just the facts, ma'am.

—JACK WEBB,
Dragnet, 1950s
[Jack Webb's signature line as Sgt. Joe Friday in the popular television series, which ran from December 16, 1951, to September 6, 1959.]

6   Facts are all accidents. They all might have been different. They all may become different. They all may collapse together.

—GEORGE SANTAYANA, *Persons and Places:
My Host the World*, 1953
[Published the year after Santayana's death.]

7   You can't make the duchess of Windsor into Rebecca of Sunnybrook Farm. The facts of life are very stubborn things.

—CLEVELAND AMORY, news report,
Oct. 6, 1955

FAILINGS

See FAULTS & FAILINGS

FAILURE

See also DESPAIR; SUCCESS & FAME;
WINNING & LOSING, VICTORY & DEFEAT

8   When a man starts down hill everything is greased for the occasion.

—JOSH BILLINGS, saying, quoted in Albert Bigelow Paine,
Mark Twain, A Biography [1912]

9   There is no failure except in no longer trying.

—ELBERT HUBBARD, *The Note Book*, 1927

10   The line between failure and success is so fine that we scarcely know when we pass it: so fine that we are often on the line and do not know it.   —*Ibid.*

No one here [at the End of the Line Cafe] has to worry about where they're   1
going next, because there's no farther they can go. It's a great comfort to them.
                              —EUGENE O'NEILL, *The Iceman Cometh*, 1946
[O'Neill, whose plays are crowded with people at the bottom or heading there,
himself experienced both misery and blazing success. He much preferred the
latter. *New Yorker* magazine theater critic John Lahr wrote in a review of a
1993 revival of *Anna Christie* that in 1922, after collecting his second Pulitzer
Prize in three years, the playwright happily pronounced himself "the Hot Dog
of Drama." See also DESPAIR.]

There is no loneliness greater than the loneliness of a failure. The failure is a   2
stranger in his own house.
                              —ERIC HOFFER, *The Passionate State of Mind*, 1954

Flops are part of life's menu.   3
                              —ROSALIND RUSSELL, *New York Herald Tribune*, April 11, 1957

There can be no real freedom without the freedom to fail.   4
                              —ERIC HOFFER, *The Ordeal of Change*, 1964

FAITH   *See also* IMMORTALITY; RELIGION

The way to see by faith is to shut the eye of reason.   5
                              —BENJAMIN FRANKLIN, *Poor Richard's Almanack*, 1758

What is it that men cannot be made to believe!   6
                              —THOMAS JEFFERSON, letter to Richard Henry Lee, April 22, 1786

Faith is sight and knowledge.   —HENRY DAVID THOREAU, *Journal*,   7
                                              April 10, 1841
[More at VISION & PERCEPTION.]

Faith, like a jackal, feeds among the tombs, and even from these dead doubts   8
she gathers her most vital hope.   —HERMAN MELVILLE, *Moby-Dick*, 1851

While men believe in the infinite, some ponds will be thought to be bottom-   9
less.   —HENRY DAVID THOREAU, "The Pond in Winter," *Walden*, 1854

Doctrine is nothing but the skin of truth set up and stuffed.   10
                              —HENRY WARD BEECHER, *Life Thoughts*, 1858

Faith always implies the disbelief of a lesser fact in favor of a greater.   11
                              —OLIVER WENDELL HOLMES, SR.,
                                  The Professor at the Breakfast-Table, 1860

Faith—is the pierless bridge   12
Supporting what we see
Unto the scene that we do not.   —EMILY DICKINSON, poem no. 915,
                                              c. 1864
[But see, too, Dickinson at SCIENCE.]

I never spoke with God   13
Nor visited in heaven—
Yet certain am I of the spot
As if the checks were given.   —EMILY DICKINSON, poem no. 1052, c. 1865

1   The terrors of truth and dart of death
     To faith alike are vain.   —HERMAN MELVILLE, *The Conflict of*
                                                  Convictions, in *Battle-Pieces,* 1866

2   The essence of belief is the establishment of a habit.
                                   —C. S. PEIRCE, *Illustrations of the Logic of Science, II,*
                                        in *Popular Science Monthly,* Jan. 1878

3   *Faith, n.* Belief without evidence in what is told by one who speaks without
     knowledge of things without parallel.   —AMBROSE BIERCE,
                                                   The Devil's Dictionary, 1906

4   Faith is believing what you know ain't so.
                                   —MARK TWAIN, *Pudd'nhead Wilson's New Calendar,*
                                        in *Following the Equator,* 1897

5   Not Truth, but Faith, it is
     That keeps the word alive.   —EDNA ST. VINCENT MILLAY, *Interim,*
                                                   in *Renascence,* 1917

6   Faith may be defined briefly as an illogical belief in the occurrence of the im-
     probable.   —H. L. MENCKEN, *Prejudices: Third Series,* 1922

7   Faith in a holy cause is to a considerable extent a substitute for the lost faith in
     ourselves.   —ERIC HOFFER, *The True Believer,* 1951

8   Hundreds may believe, but each has to believe by himself.
                       —W. H. AUDEN, *Genius and Apostle,* in *The Dyer's Hand,* 1962

9   If you build it, he will come.   —W. P. KINSELLA,
                                                   Shoeless Joe, 1982
     [Adapted by Phil Alden Robinson for the 1989 movie *Field of Dreams,* the
     story is of an Iowa farmer who believes a voice that tells him that if he builds
     a baseball diamond in a cornfield, he can bring back the great but tarnished
     "Shoeless Joe" Jackson. The line is sometimes misquoted as "If you build it,
     they will come," referring to a promise that tourists will come to the ballfield,
     and thereby save the family farm. In the movie, the relevant line is "People
     will come." For "Say it ain't so, Joe," see under SPORTS.]

FALL   *See* NATURE: SEASONS

FAME   *See* SUCCESS & FAME

FAMILIARITY   *See* INTIMACY & FAMILIARITY

FAMILY   *See also* CHILDREN; GENERATIONS; HOME; MARRIAGE; PARENTS

10   Over the river and through the wood,
     To Grandfather's house we go.   —LYDIA MARIA CHILD, *Thanksgiving Day,*
                                              in *Flowers for Children,* 1844–1846
     [The author did not, in fact, enjoy family life as a child. For more, see THANKS-
     GIVING.]

11   Who shall say I am not
     the happy genius of my household?   —WILLIAM CARLOS WILLIAMS, *Danse*
                                                  Russe, in *Al Que Quiere!,* 1917

One would be in less danger   1
From the wiles of the stranger
If one's own kin and kith
Were more fun to be with.   —OGDEN NASH, *Family Court,*
                                         in *Hard Lines,* 1931

Big sisters are the crab grass in the lawn of life.   2
                           —CHARLES M. SCHULZ, *Peanuts,* 1953

Families break up when people take hints you don't intend and miss hints you   3
do intend.   —ROBERT FROST, interview, *Writers at Work: Second Series,* 1963

No family is older than any other.   —ANDREW LYTLE, interview by   4
                                         Robert Wilson, c. 1978
[Lytle, whose novels are based in the South, wrote in 1975 a history of his own
Tennessee family, spanning two centuries.]

FANATICISM   *See* ENTHUSIASM & ZEAL

FAREWELLS   *See* PARTING

FARMS & FARMERS   *See also* COUNTRY LIFE & PEOPLE; NATURE

Those who labor in the earth are the chosen people of God, if He ever had a cho- 5
sen people.   —THOMAS JEFFERSON, *Notes on the State of Virginia,* 1781–1785

When tillage begins, other arts follow. The farmers, therefore, are the founders 6
of human civilization.   —DANIEL WEBSTER,
                                    Remarks on the Agriculture of England,
                                    speech, Boston State House, Jan. 13, 1840

Blessed be agriculture! If one does not have too much of it.   7
          —CHARLES DUDLEY WARNER, *My Summer in a Garden,* 1870

We have three crops—corn, freight rates, and interest. The farmers farm the   8
land, and the businessmen farm the farmers.
                              —ANONYMOUS, saying attributed to a
                                    Nebraska farm editor, c. 1880
[Hard times in the nation's agricultural heartland extended from the end of the
Civil War almost to the end of the century. In the 1890s, the Populist party,
representing the interests of farmers and laborers, surged to a position of national power. Populist farmers vowed to "raise less corn and more hell," as advised by Mary Lease; see under KANSAS. William Jennings Bryan advocated
Populist principles in his "Cross of Gold" speech; see below.]

Burn down your cities and leave our farms, and your cities will spring up again 9
as if by magic; but destroy our farms and the grass will grow in the streets of
every city in the country.   —WILLIAM JENNINGS BRYAN, "Cross of Gold"
                                    speech, Democratic National Convention,
                                    Chicago, July 8, 1896
[For the meaning of the "cross of gold," see ECONOMICS.]

Depressions are farm led and farm fed.   —ANONYMOUS,   10
                                                      saying, 1930s
[More at THE DEPRESSION.]

1   No one hates his job so heartily as a farmer.
                    —H. L. MENCKEN, *What Is Going On in the World Now?*,
                    in *American Mercury* magazine, Nov. 1933

2   Farming looks mighty easy when your plow is a pencil, and you're a thousand
    miles from the corn field.   —DWIGHT D. EISENHOWER, speech,
                    Peoria, Ill., Sept. 25, 1956

3   The barn is America at its fragrant and warmest best. It stands for the genius
    of a nation built of rich soil and fat cattle.
                    —ROBERT P. TRISTRAM COFFIN, *On the Green Carpet*, 1951
    [Coffin's family owned a farm on Casco Bay in Maine. He won a Pulitzer Prize
    in 1936 for his book of poetry *Strange Holiness*.]

4   It was the best place to be, thought Wilbur, this warm delicious cellar, with the
    garrulous geese, the changing seasons, the heat of the sun, the passage of swal-
    lows, the nearness of rats, the sameness of sheep, the love of spiders, the smell of
    manure, and the glory of everything.   —E. B. WHITE, *Charlotte's Web*, 1952

5   The farmer is the only man in our economy who buys everything he needs at
    retail, sells everything he sells at wholesale, and pays the freight both ways.
                    —JOHN F. KENNEDY, campaign speech, national plowing contest,
                    Sioux Falls, S.D., Sept. 22, 1960

6   The farm is an infinite form.   —WENDELL BERRY, *From the Crest*,
                    in *Clearing*, 1977

FASHION & CLOTHES

7   If thou art clean and warm, it is sufficient, for more doth but rob the poor and
    please the wanton.   —WILLIAM PENN, *Some Fruits of Solitude*, 1693

8   A little of what you call frippery is very necessary towards looking like the rest
    of the world.   —ABIGAIL ADAMS, letter to John Adams, May 1, 1780

9   The fondness for dress among the women [of California] is excessive and is of-
    ten the ruin of many of them.   —RICHARD HENRY DANA, JR.,
                    Two Years Before the Mast, 1840
    [For more comments on these women of the West, see CALIFORNIA.]

10 Beware of all enterprises that require new clothes.
                    —HENRY DAVID THOREAU, "Economy," *Walden*, 1854

11 One wants to be *very* something, *very* great, *very* heroic; or if not that, then at
    least very stylish and very fashionable.
                    —HARRIET BEECHER STOWE, *Dress, or Who Makes the Fashions*,
                    The Atlantic Monthly magazine, 1864

12 All dressed up with nowhere to go.   —WILLIAM ALLEN WHITE,
                    1916
    [White, the influential editor of the *Emporia Gazette* in Kansas, thus described
    the Progressive Party after Theodore Roosevelt, its candidate in 1912, endorsed
    Republican presidential candidate Charles Evans Hughes in 1916. According to
    Henry F. Woods in *American Sayings* (1945), White's actual words were, "all
    dressed up in their fighting clothes, with nowhere to go."]

Where's the man could ease a heart   1
Like a satin gown.   —DOROTHY PARKER, *The Satin Dress*, in *Enough Rope*, 1927

Brevity is the soul of lingerie.   —DOROTHY PARKER, attributed,   2
in Alexander Woollcott,
While Rome Burns [1934]

I tell you men are watching their styles. That's why they all look so funny.   3
—WILL ROGERS, *Weekly Articles*, May 20, 1928

Would you be shocked if I put on something more comfortable?   4
—JAMES WHALE, *Hell's Angels*, 1930
[The line, purred by Jean Harlow, gave the phrase "put on something more
comfortable" an internationally recognized new meaning.]

The bikini is the most important thing since the atom bomb.   5
—DIANA VREELAND, quoted in Grace Mirabella,
with Judith Warner, *In and Out of Vogue*, 1995

Clothes never shut up.   —SUSAN BROWNMILLER, *Femininity*, 1984   6

The neon sign of one's inner thought is the clothes that one puts on one's body.   7
Fashion in many ways defines the self-concept and character of the individual,
and it gives a message to the audience. One has to gear one's message to how
seriously one wants to be taken.   —AL SHARPTON, in *The New York Times*,
Oct. 24, 1993
[Rev. Sharpton's personal style is theatrical. See also JUSTICE.]

FATE & DESTINY   *See also* LIFE; LUCK

Fate is a name for facts not yet passed under the fire of thought, for causes   8
which are unpenetrated.   —RALPH WALDO EMERSON, *Fate*,
in *The Conduct of Life*, 1860

Whatever limits us we call fate.   —*Ibid.*   9

I claim not to have controlled events, but confess plainly that events have con- 10
trolled me.   —ABRAHAM LINCOLN, letter to A. G. Hodges, April 4, 1864

Superiority to fate   11
Is difficult to gain
'Tis not conferred of any
But possible to earn.   —EMILY DICKINSON, poem no. 1081,
c. 1866
[More at IMMORTALITY.]

The current of destiny carries us along. None but a madman would swim   12
against the stream, and none but a fool would exert himself to swim with it.
The best way is to float quietly with the tide.
—WILLIAM CULLEN BRYANT, letter to his mother, June 1821
[Bryant, best remembered as the author of *Thanatopsis*, used this passage in
announcing to his mother that he was getting married. He described himself as
"trapped before I was aware" by the goodness of heart, intelligence, and other
fine qualities of his bride.]

1   We are spinning our own fates, good or evil, and never to be undone.
                    —WILLIAM JAMES, *The Principles of Psychology*, 1890

2   Destiny is not a matter of chance, it is a matter of choice; it is not a thing to be
    waited for, it is a thing to be achieved.   —WILLIAM JENNINGS BRYAN, speech,
                              Washington, D.C., Feb. 22, 1899

3   If fate means you to lose, give him a good fight anyhow.
                    —WILLIAM MCFEE, *Casuals of the Sea*, 1916

4   Any spoke will lead an ant to the hub.   —REX STOUT,
                                                  Fer de Lance, 1934
    [A favorite saying of Stout's detective hero, Nero Wolfe.]

5   In my beginning is my end.   —T. S. ELIOT, *Four Quartets: East Coker*, 1940

FATHERS   *See* PARENTS

FAULTS & FAILINGS   *See also* INSULTS; MISTAKES; TEMPTATION

6   None but the well-bred man knows how to confess a fault or acknowledge
    himself in error. —BENJAMIN FRANKLIN, *Poor Richard's Almanack*, Nov. 1738

7   There is no odor so bad as that which arises from goodness tainted.
                    —HENRY DAVID THOREAU, "Economy," *Walden*, 1854

8   It's not that he "bites off more than he can chaw," . . . but he chaws more than
    he bites off.   —CLOVER ADAMS, letter to her father,
                                                  Dec. 1881
    [Occasionally true of the writer's husband, Henry Adams, but she was aiming
    here at the novelist Henry James. The quote is sometimes attributed to Henry
    James's brother, psychologist William James.
        The omitted material in the quote reads, "as T. G. Appleton said of Nathan."
    Appleton, a minor writer and artist, was a famous conversationalist and is re-
    membered for his epigram on Americans and Paris; see under CITIES. Nathan,
    his father, was a successful businessman and politician.
        Clover Adams committed suicide in 1885 by ingesting potassium cyanide.]

9   He's liked, but he's not well liked.
                    —ARTHUR MILLER, *Death of a Salesman*, 1949

10 Falling short of perfection is a process that just never stops.
                    —WILLIAM SHAWN, quoted in *The New York Times*, obituary
                    [Jan. 9, 1992]
    [Shawn, a notorious perfectionist, was the second editor of *The New Yorker*, suc-
    ceeding the founding editor Harold Ross upon his death in 1951, and remaining
    until 1987, when he was dismissed by the magazine's new owner, S. I. Newhouse.
    When asked how he could afford to spend so much time on details, he answered,
    "It takes as long as it takes," *The New Yorker*, Dec. 28, 1992/Jan. 4, 1993.]

FEAR   *See also* COURAGE

11 Fear is an instructor of great sagacity and the herald of all revolutions. . . . He
    indicates great wrongs which must be revised.
                    —RALPH WALDO EMERSON, *Compensation*,
                    in *Essays: First Series*, 1841

Nothing is to be so much feared as fear.   —HENRY DAVID THOREAU, *Journal,*   1
Sept. 7, 1851
[See also Pres. Franklin D. Roosevelt's first inaugural address at AMERICAN HISTORY: MEMORABLE MOMENTS.]

It occurred to me at once that Harris had been as much afraid of me as I had   2
been of him. This was a new view of the question I had never taken before; but
it was one I never forgot afterwards.   —ULYSSES S. GRANT,
Memoirs, 1885
[Grant's epiphany took place at the end of July 1861, near Florida, Mo., when
he was still a colonel. Leading his unit up a hill toward an encampment of
rebels under General Thomas Harris, he admitted to being so afraid that he
"lacked the moral courage" to call a halt and reconsider plans. Gaining the
crest, however, he saw that the enemy camp was deserted.
    One of the Missourians who fled at Grant's approach was his future publisher and also an author of some note, Mark Twain. In *The Private History of
a Campaign That Failed* (1885), Twain wrote, "In time I came to know that
Union colonel whose coming frightened me out of the war and crippled the
Southern cause to that extent—General Grant. I came within a few hours of
seeing him when he was as unknown as I was myself; at a time when anybody
could have said, 'Grant?—Ulysses S. Grant? I do not remember hearing the
name before.' It seems difficult to realize that there was once a time when such
a remark could be rationally made but there *was,* and I was within a few miles
of the place and the occasion, too, though proceeding in the other direction."]

A fool without fear is sometimes wiser than an angel with fear.   3
—NANCY ASTOR, *My Two Countries,* 1920

The only thing we have to fear is fear itself   4
—FRANKLIN D. ROOSEVELT,
First Inaugural Address, March 4, 1933
[More at AMERICAN HISTORY: MEMORABLE MOMENTS.]

Cowardice, as distinguished from panic, is almost always simply a lack of abil-   5
ity to suspend the functioning of the imagination.
—ERNEST HEMINGWAY, *Men at War,* 1942

Fatigue makes cowards of us all.   —GEORGE S. PATTON, JR.,   6
War As I Knew It, 1947

Our tragedy today is a general and universal physical fear.   7
—WILLIAM FAULKNER, speech accepting
the Nobel Prize for Literature, 1949
[Faulkner was referring to fear of nuclear war.]

We are not descended from fearful men.   8
—EDWARD R. MURROW, *Report on Sen. Joseph R. McCarthy,*
in Murrow's *See It Now* documentary television series,
March 7, 1954
[More at AMERICAN HISTORY: MEMORABLE MOMENTS, p. 34 (Murrow note).]

Fear tastes like a rusty knife and do not let her into your house.   9
—JOHN CHEEVER, *The Wapshot Chronicle,* 1957

FLAG, THE   *see* PATRIOTISM & THE FLAG

FLATTERY

1   Let those flatter who fear: it is not an American art.
—THOMAS JEFFERSON, *The Rights of British America*, 1774

2   We love flattery, even though we are not deceived by it, because it shows that we are of importance enough to be courted.
—RALPH WALDO EMERSON, *Gifts*, in *Essays: Second Series*, 1844

3   Mountains of gold would not seduce some men, yet flattery would break them down.   —HENRY WARD BEECHER, *Proverbs from Plymouth Pulpit*, 1887

4   Flattery is all right—if you don't inhale.
—ADLAI STEVENSON, speech, Feb. 1, 1961
[Democrats don't inhale.]

FLORIDA   *See also* CITIES (Miami)

5   Florida . . . does beguile and gratify me—giving me my first and last (evidently) sense of the tropics, or à peu près, the subtropics, and revealing to me blandness in nature of which I had no idea.   —HENRY JAMES, letter to
Edmund Gosse, Feb. 16, 1905

6   The state with the prettiest name,
the state that floats in brackish water,
held together by mangrove roots.   —ELIZABETH BISHOP, *Florida*, 1939

7   In summer the crackers live off the yams; in winter they live off Yanks.
—ANONYMOUS, Florida saying, in H. L. Mencken,
A New Dictionary of Quotations on Historical Principles, 1942

8   Florida is the world's greatest amusement park.
—BUDD SCHULBERG, *Florida*, in *American Panorama:
East of the Mississippi*, 1960

9   Florida is a golden word . . . the very name Florida carried the message of warmth and ease and comfort. It was irresistible.
—JOHN STEINBECK, *Travels with Charley*, 1962

10   It is a speck of rock in pastel sea. Palms whisper. Songbirds sing. The place has never known a frost.   —CHARLES KURALT, on Key West,
in *Charles Kuralt's America*, 1995

Motto
11   In God we trust.

FLOWERS   *See* NATURE: PLANTS & GARDENS

FOOD, WINE, & EATING   *See also* ALCOHOL & DRINKING; HEALTH

12   Eat to live, and not live to eat.   —BENJAMIN FRANKLIN, *Poor Richard's
Almanack*, May 1733
[The idea dates to classical times, at least, and is ascribed to Socrates. See also Franklin at HEALTH.]

Eat not to dullness; drink not to elevation.   —BENJAMIN FRANKLIN,   1
Autobiography, begun 1771

We never repent having eaten too little.   2
—THOMAS JEFFERSON, "A Decalogue of Canons for observation in
practical life," letter to Thomas Jefferson Smith, Feb. 21, 1825

What moistens the lip and what brightens the eye?   3
What calls back the past, like the rich pumpkin pie?
—JOHN GREENLEAF WHITTIER, *The Pumpkin*, 1844
[More at THANKSGIVING.]

The American does not drink at meals as a sensible man should. Indeed, he has   4
no meals. He stuffs for ten minutes thrice a day.
—RUDYARD KIPLING, *American Notes*, 1891

Perhaps no bread in the world is quite so good as Southern corn bread, and per-   5
haps no bread in the world is quite so bad as the Northern imitation of it.
—MARK TWAIN, *Autobiography* [1924]

I know the taste of watermelon which has been honestly come by, and I know   6
the taste of watermelon which has been acquired by art. Both taste good, but
the experienced know which tastes best.
—Ibid.
[This concludes Twain's paean to the watermelon: "I know how a prize watermelon looks when it is sunning its fat rotundity among pumpkin vines. . . .
I know how inviting it looks when it is cooling itself in a tub of water under
the bed, waiting; I know how it looks when it lies on the table in the sheltered
great floor space between house and kitchen, and the children gathered for the
sacrifice and their mouths watering; I know the crackling sound it makes
when the knife enters its end. . . . I can see its halves fall apart and display the
rich red meat and the black seeds, and the heart standing up, a luxury fit for the
elect; I know how a boy looks behind a yard-long slice of that melon, and I
know how he feels; for I have been there."]

I doubt whether the world holds for anyone a more soul-stirring surprise than   7
the first adventure with ice-cream.   —HEYWOOD BROUN, *Holding a Baby*,
in *Seeing Things at Night*, 1921

I have eaten   8
the plums
that were in the icebox

and which
you were probably
saving
for breakfast

Forgive me
they were delicious
so sweet
and so cold.   —William Carlos Williams,
This Is Just to Say, 1922
[Williams loved plums. In *To a Poor Old Woman* (1935), he described a woman
on the street, carrying a paper bag of plums and eating one: "Comforted / a solace of ripe plums / seeming to fill the air / They taste good to her." See Wallace Stevens below for another poetic plum.]

1   The plum survives its poems.   —WALLACE STEVENS,
                                    The Comedian as the Letter C, 1923
[And ice cream rules. See Stevens at HIGH POSITION: RULERS & LEADERS.]

2   "It's broccoli, dear."
"I say it's spinach, and I say the hell with it."
                            —E. B. WHITE, caption for a Carl Rose cartoon,
                                    The New Yorker, Dec. 8, 1928

3   Beulah, peel me a grape.   —MAE WEST, *I'm No Angel*, 1933

4   No matter how thin you slice it, it's still baloney.
                                    —AL SMITH, saying,
                                    1936 campaign speeches for Alf Landon
[Smith definitely wasn't looking for votes from the processed-meat industry.
Earlier, commenting on Roosevelt's monetary devaluation, he wrote, "I am for
gold dollars as against baloney dollars," *The New Outlook*, December 1933.
And even earlier, when he was governor of New York, he declined to pose with
a trowel at the cornerstone ceremony of the New York State Office Building in
Manhattan. "That's baloney," he said.]

5   It's a naive domestic Burgundy without any breeding, but I think you'll be
amused by its presumption.   —JAMES THURBER, caption for a cartoon
                                    in *The New Yorker*, March 27, 1937

6   You can travel fifty thousand miles in America without once tasting a piece of
good bread.   —HENRY MILLER, *The Staff of Life*,
                                    in *Remember to Remember*, 1947

7   The very discovery of the New World was the by-product of a dietary quest.
                                    —ARTHUR M. SCHLESINGER, JR.,
                                    Paths to the Present, 1949
[The quest was for Eastern spices and seasonings.]

8   Avoid fried meats which angry up the blood.
                            —LEROY "SATCHEL" PAIGE, *How to Stay Young*, 1953
[More at WISDOM, WORDS OF.]

9   Gluttony is an emotional escape—a sign something is eating us.
                            —PETER DE VRIES, *Comfort Me with Apples*, 1956

10 More die in the United States of too much food than of too little.
                    —JOHN KENNETH GALBRAITH, *The Affluent Society*, 1958

11 We prefer our coffee as strong as love, as black as sin, and as hot as Hades.
                                    —T. HALE BOGGS,
                                    tariff bill debate, 1960
[Rep. Boggs, Democrat of Louisiana, spoke in support of the addition of
chicory, a key ingredient of New Orleans coffee, to the list of items that could
be imported without duty.]

12 Food is our common ground, a universal experience.
                                    —JAMES BEARD, *Beard on Food*, 1974

13 Never eat more than you can lift.   —MISS PIGGY (Jim Henson), saying

FOOLS & STUPIDITY

Who knows a fool must know his brother;   1
For one will recommend another.   —BENJAMIN FRANKLIN,
                                                 Poor Richard's Almanack, 1740

It is ill-manners to silence a fool, and cruelty to let him go on.   2
                     —BENJAMIN FRANKLIN, *Poor Richard's Almanack,* 1757

There's nothing we read of in torture's inventions   3
Like a well-meaning dunce with the best of intentions.
                     —JAMES RUSSELL LOWELL, *A Fable for Critics,* 1848

There's a sucker born every minute.   —JOSEPH BESSIMER, 4
                                                              c. 1850
[Con man Joseph "Paper Collar" Bessimer was a friend of P. T. Barnum, to
whom the quote is usually attributed. Robert Pelton, curator of the Barnum
Museum in Bridgeport, Conn., cites Bessimer as the true source.]

Minds so earnest and helpless that it takes them a half-an-hour to get from one 5
idea to its immediately adjacent next neighbor, and then they lie down on
it . . . like a cow on a doormat, so that you can get neither in nor out with
them.   —WILLIAM JAMES, description of audience at a Chautauqua
                   lecture, letter to his wife, July 1896

Let us be thankful for the fools. But for them, the rest of us could not succeed. 6
                     —MARK TWAIN, *Pudd'nhead Wilson's New Calendar,*
                          in *Following the Equator,* 1897
[For Twain on the preponderance of fools, see MAJORITIES & MINORITIES. For
fools on school boards, see EDUCATION.]

Never give a sucker an even break.   7
                                                         —ANONYMOUS
[H. L. Mencken credited speakeasy and nightclub owner Texas Guinan with
popularizing this around 1925—she used to welcome patrons with the greeting, "Hello, sucker." The originator, however, may have been Edward F. Albee,
co-owner of the Keith-Albee vaudeville theaters. W. C. Fields ad-libbed the line
in the 1923 Broadway musical *Poppy,* and used it as a movie title in 1941.]

We are the hollow men   8
We are the stuffed men
Leaning together
Headpiece filled with straw. Alas!   —T. S. ELIOT, *The Hollow Men,* 1925

Ninety-nine percent of the people in the world are fools, and the rest of us are 9
in great danger of contagion.   —THORNTON WILDER, *The Matchmaker,* 1954

There are some people that if they don't know, you can't tell 'em.   10
                     —LOUIS ARMSTRONG, c. 1956, Deirdre Mullane, ed.,
                          *Words to Make My Children Live: A Book of
                          African American Quotations* [1995]

This life's hard, but it's harder if you're stupid.   11
                     —GEORGE V. HIGGINS, *The Friends of Eddie Coyle,* 1972

1   They have a saying in the provinces, "Ignorance is salvageable, but stupid is forever."   —HENRY J. HYDE, speech in the U.S. House of Representatives, April 1995
[Rep. Hyde of Illinois, a conservative in his tenth term in Congress, pulled out this folk saying in the heat of the debate on Congressional term limits favored by zealous younger conservatives. "New is always better?" Mr Hyde asked. "What in the world is conservative about that? Have we nothing to learn from the past? Tradition, history, institutional memory—don't they count anymore?"]

FORCE   *See* POWER; STRENGTH & TOUGHNESS;
                                                        VIOLENCE

FOREIGN POLICY   *See also* AMERICA & AMERICANS (John Quincy
                                       Adams); AMERICAN HISTORY: MEMORABLE
                                       MOMENTS; DIPLOMACY; NATIONS

2   It is our true policy to steer clear of permanent alliances, with any portion of the foreign world.   —GEORGE WASHINGTON, Farewell Address, Sept. 17, 1796
[Washington was deeply suspicious of foreign ways. See also FOREIGNERS.]

3   There can be no greater error than to expect or calculate upon real favors from nation to nation.   —*Ibid.*

4   Observe good faith and justice toward all nations. Cultivate peace and harmony with all.   —*Ibid.*

5   Peace, commerce, and honest friendship with all nations, entangling alliances with none.   —THOMAS JEFFERSON,
                                        First Inaugural Address, March 4, 1801
[A year later, however, when Jefferson learned that Spain had ceded the Louisiana territory to the French, he wrote to the U.S. minister in France, Robert Livingston, "The moment Napoleon takes possession of New Orleans, we must marry ourselves to the British fleet and nation."]

6   We owe it, therefore, to candor and to the amicable relations existing between the United States and those [European] powers to declare that we should consider any attempt on their part to extend their system to any portion of this hemisphere as dangerous to our peace and safety.
                        —JAMES MONROE, message to Congress, Dec. 2, 1823
[The principle that the entire Western Hemisphere is bound up with the national interests of the United States became known as the Monroe Doctrine, and has been widely accepted as a nonnegotiable element in U.S. foreign policy. In 1895, for example, Pres. Grover Cleveland, in ordering England to settle a boundary dispute with Venezuela, pronounced: "Today the United States is practically sovereign on this continent, and its fiat is law upon the subjects to which it confines its interposition."
   In our era, in the midst of the Cold War, Cuba's disregard for the Monroe Doctrine counterpoised to U.S. dedication to that principle led to the embarrassing Bay of Pigs invasion, and subsequently brought the U.S. and Cuba's ally, Russia, to the brink of nuclear conflict. A passage in John F. Kennedy's presidential inauguration speech in 1961 signaled the trouble ahead: "And let every other power know that this hemisphere intends to remain master of its own house."]

The open door.   —John Hay, description of the trade policy the   1
government had negotiated with China, Jan. 2, 1900
[Hay was Secretary of State.]

Speak softly and carry a big stick.   —THEODORE ROOSEVELT, speech,   2
Minnesota State Fair, Sept. 2, 1901
[Roosevelt was vice president at the time, but within two weeks, he succeeded the assassinated William McKinley. In full, his statement was: "There is a homely adage which runs, 'Speak softly and carry a big stick.' If the American nation will speak softly and yet build and keep at a pitch of the highest training a thoroughly efficient navy, the Monroe Doctrine will go far."
The adage was not original with Roosevelt. He described it as a West African proverb. Carl Sandberg thought it was a Spanish proverb. Both may be right as many proverbs appear in widely separated cultures.
An example of the big stick in practice is Roosevelt's famous admission in his memoirs, "I took Panama without consulting the cabinet." At the time of the takeover, in 1903, he had denied having any role in the revolution that separated the Panama territory from Columbia. See also DIPLOMACY.]

Dollar diplomacy.   —ANONYMOUS, characterization of policies of   3
Secretary of State Philander C. Knox, 1909–10
[The phrase was not intended as a compliment, but today there seems nothing exceptional in Knox's efforts to promote American investment abroad and to protect American interests via financial negotiations. Knox served under Pres. William Howard Taft.]

Our policy of watchful waiting.   4
—WOODROW WILSON, State of the Union Address, Dec. 2, 1913
[This was the stance of the U.S. toward Mexico during the turbulent years 1913–20.]

The freedom of the seas is the *sine qua non* of peace, equality, and cooperation.   5
—WOODROW WILSON, speech, U.S. Senate, Jan. 22, 1917
[Freedom of navigation was one of the "Fourteen Points" in Pres. Wilson's famous speech of Jan. 8, 1918, calling for "a general association of nations," which was eventually realized in the League of Nations; see AMERICAN HISTORY: MEMORABLE MOMENTS.
The Fourteen Points were objectives that were later included in the November 1918 armistice. The points, or objectives, were: covenants of peace (see PEACE); freedom of the seas; abolition of trade barriers; general disarmament; adjustment of colonial claims; evacuation of conquered Russian territories; evacuation and restoration of Belgium; return of Alsace-Lorrain to France; adjustment of Italian frontiers; autonomy for subject peoples of Austria and Hungary; guarantees of the integrity of Serbia, Montenegro, and Romania; autonomy for the subject people of the Ottoman Empire (Turkey); an independent Poland; and the association of nations mentioned above.]

There shall be no private understandings of any kind, but diplomacy shall proceed always frankly and in the public view.   6
—WOODROW WILSON, "Fourteen Points" address to Congress, Jan. 8, 1918

Wilson and his Fourteen Points! Bah! Even God Almighty only had ten!   7
—ANONYMOUS, French joke, c. 1919
[This is sometimes attributed to Georges Clemenceau, the French premier. There were jokes in America, too, as Wilson stumbled in the complex peace

negotiations and lost political ground at home. See William Allen White's memorial editorial at EPITAPHS & GRAVESTONES.]

1　I don't know how a lot of these other nations have existed as long as they have till we could get some of our people around and show 'em how to be pure and good like us.　　　　　　　—WILL ROGERS, *More Letters*, Feb. 27, 1932

2　In the field of world policy, I would dedicate this nation to the policy of the good neighbor—the neighbor who resolutely respects himself and, because he does so, respects the rights of others—the neighbor who respects his obligations and who respects the sanctity of his agreements in and with a world of neighbors.　　　　　　　—FRANKLIN D. ROOSEVELT, First Inaugural Address, March 4, 1933

3　He may be a son of a bitch, but he's our son of a bitch.
　　　　　　　—FRANKLIN D. ROOSEVELT, referring to the Nicaraguan dictator Anastasio Somoza, attributed in a number of sources, including William Pfaff in *The New Yorker*, May 27, 1985
[Some forty years later, CIA chief William Casey, discussing the Panamanian dictator Manuel Noriega, said, "He's a bastard, but he's our bastard." This comment, made to U.S. Rep. Lee Hamilton, chair of the House Intelligence Committee, was reported in Haynes Johnson's *Sleepwalking Through History: America in the Reagan Years*, 1991.]

4　Local defense must be reinforced by the further deterrent of massive retaliatory power.　　　　—JOHN FOSTER DULLES, speech to the Council on Foreign Relations, Jan. 12, 1954
[Dulles was secretary of state under Eisenhower from 1953 to 1959, during the Cold War with Russia. His call for "massive retaliatory power"—almost immediately condensed by the media into "massive retaliation"—implied that the United States would respond with overwhelming nuclear strikes to any military threats by Communist nations, even if made only with conventional forces. An attraction of "massive retaliation" was that it was cheaper—in the short run, at least—than maintaining large conventional forces. In the words of then Defense Secretary Charles W. Wilson, it offered "a bigger bang for the buck." It was also a lot scarier since it was coupled with Dulles's predilection for "brinksmanship"; see below. Ernest Gross, who was in the audience for the "massive retaliation" speech, said later, "We all shook our heads and were really worried," *American Heritage*, June 1971.]

5　You have to take chances for peace, just as you must take chances in war. . . . The ability to get to the verge without getting into the war is the necessary art. If you cannot master it, you inevitably get into war. If you try to run away from it, if you are scared to go to the brink, you are lost. . . . We walked to the brink and we looked it in the face.
　　　　　　　—JOHN FOSTER DULLES, interview with James Shepley, *Life* magazine, Jan. 16, 1956
[Dulles's willingness to face down Russian and Chinese communists, even if it meant going to the brink of nuclear war was derided by Adlai Stevenson and other Democrats as "brinksmanship," a term that probably was inspired by the popularity of Stephen Potter's humorous book *Gamesmanship* (1947). In 1953 and 1954, Dulles faced a series of crises in the Far East, centering on the Korean peace talks, the French defeat in Indo-China, and China's desire to recover Taiwan. He reacted with dramatic vigor. As John Kenneth Galbraith observed in a letter to Pres. John F. Kennedy, "The greatest difficulty with Dulles was his yearning for new and exciting variants in policy," October 9, 1961.]

Great nations like great men, should keep their word.   1
      —HUGO BLACK, dissent, *Federal Power Commission and New*
      York Power Authority v. Tuscarora Indian Nation, 1960
[Justice Black sided with the Indians in their losing suit to prevent the Niagara
Power Authority from taking part of their reservation. He continued most elo-
quently: "The record does not leave the impression that the lands of their
reservation are the most fertile, the landscape the most beautiful or their
homes the most splendid specimens of architecture. But this is their home—
their ancestral home. There they, their children, and their forebears were born.
They, too, have their memories and their loves. Some things are worth more
than money and the costs of a new enterprise. I regret that this court is the government agency that breaks faith with this dependent people." Chief Justice
Earl Warren and Justice William O. Douglas joined in this opinion.]

Let us never negotiate out of fear. But let us never fear to negotiate.   2
      —JOHN F. KENNEDY, Inaugural Address, Jan. 20, 1961

A policy that can be accurately, though perhaps not prudently, defined as one   3
of "peaceful coexistence."   —JAMES W. FULBRIGHT, speech
      in the U.S. Senate, March 27, 1964
["Peaceful co-existence" gradually became the desired conclusion to the Cold
War. According to political lexicographer William Safire, the phrase may be of
Russian origin. It surfaced at the Ninth All-Russian Congress of the Soviets in
the form "peaceful and friendly co-existence." An early U.S. citation comes
from a press conference with Pres. Dwight D. Eisenhower on June 30, 1954;
both a reporter and the president used the phrase. The phrase became front-
page news when it was used by the Russian leader Nikita Khrushchev in a
speech on January 6, 1961, just prior to the inauguration of John F. Kennedy.]

The struggle between right and wrong, good and evil.   4
      —RONALD REAGAN, speech to the National Association of
      Evangelicals, March 9, 1983
[Pres. Reagan here was characterizing the conflict between the U.S. and Russia
in the last years of the Cold War. In the same speech, he called Russia "an evil
empire," borrowing the name of the galactic enemy in the 1977 film *Star Wars*
by George W. Lucas, Jr. Naturally, two weeks later, when Reagan proposed con-
structing a space-based missile-defense system—the Strategic Defense Initiative—the system was immediately dubbed "star wars."]

FOREIGNERS   *See also* FOREIGN POLICY; NATIONS;
RACES & PEOPLES; TRAVEL

Against the insidious wiles of foreign influence . . . the jealousy of a free peo-   5
ple ought to be constantly awake; since history and experience prove that foreign influence is one of the most baneful foes of republican government.
      —GEORGE WASHINGTON, Farewell Address, Sept. 17, 1796
[Thomas Jefferson, too, held a baneful view of foreigners, at least those in
cities; see under CITIES.]

They spell it Vinci and pronounce it Vinchy; foreigners always spell better than   6
they pronounce.   —MARK TWAIN, *The Innocents Abroad,* 1869

Give me your tired, your poor,   7
Your huddled masses yearning to breathe free.
      —EMMA LAZARUS, *The New Colossus:*
      Inscription for the Statue of Liberty, 1883
[More at AMERICAN HISTORY: MEMORABLE MOMENTS.]

1   There is no room in this country for hyphenated Americanism.
—THEODORE ROOSEVELT, speech, New York City,
Oct. 12 (Columbus Day), 1915
[With the war in Europe boiling, suspicion of the allegiance of immigrants was at a high, and often took the form of simple prejudice. See also the Roosevelt entry at PATRIOTISM & THE FLAG.]

FORESTS   *See* ENVIRONMENT; WILDERNESS

FORGIVENESS

2   Did man e'er live
Saw priest or woman yet forgive?
—JAMES RUSSELL LOWELL, *Villa France, 1859,*
in *Under the Willows and Other Poems,* 1868

3   Love scarce is love that never knows
The sweetness of forgiving.
—JOHN GREENLEAF WHITTIER, *Among the Hills,* 1869

4   Forgotten is forgiven.   —F. SCOTT FITZGERALD, "Notebooks,"
in *The Crack-Up,* 1945

5   What power has love but forgiveness?
—WILLIAM CARLOS WILLIAMS, *Asphodel, That Greeny Flower,*
in *Journey to Love,* 1955

6   Forgive but never forget.
—JOHN F. KENNEDY, saying, attributed in Theodore Sorensen,
Kennedy [1965]
[Thomas Szasz amplified the thought this way in *The Second Sin* (1973): "The stupid neither forgive nor forget; the naive forgive and forget; the wise forgive but do not forget."]

7   Forgiving presupposes remembering.   —PAUL TILLICH, *The Eternal Now,* 1963

FOURTH OF JULY   *See* INDEPENDENCE DAY

FRANCE   *See* NATIONS

FRANKLIN, BENJAMIN

8   He snatched the lightning from heaven and the sceptre from tyrants.
—A. R. J. TURGOT, inscription
for the Houdon bust of Franklin, 1778
[Turgot, the leading French economist and statesman of his day, referred here to his friend's experiments with lightning and revolution. The actual inscription is in Latin: *"Eripuit fulmen sceptrumque tyrannis."*
When Thomas Jefferson presented his credentials as minister to France in 1785, the French foreign minister asked, "It is you who replace Monsieur Franklin?" To which Jefferson replied, "No one can replace him, Sir. I am only his successor."]

FREEDOM

See also CONSTITUTION, THE;
DEMOCRACY; FREE SPEECH;
INDEPENDENCE DAY; RIGHTS

Without freedom of thought there can be no such thing as wisdom; and no   1
such thing as liberty without freedom of speech.
> —BENJAMIN FRANKLIN,
> *Dogood Papers*, 1722

[An early expression of the revolutionary spirit in the colonies. Franklin was sixteen when he wrote these essays for *The New England Courant* under the pen name Silence Dogood.]

Proclaim liberty throughout the land unto all the inhabitants thereof.   2
> —BIBLE, *Leviticus* 25:10,
> inscribed on the Liberty Bell, 1752

Those who would give up essential liberty to purchase a little temporary safety   3
deserve neither liberty nor safety.
> —BENJAMIN FRANKLIN, speech, Pennsylvania Assembly,
> Nov. 11, 1755

[A variant of this appears on a plaque in the stairwell of the Statue of Liberty on Bedloe's Island in New York Harbor.]

One of the most essential branches of English liberty is the freedom of one's   4
house. A man's house is his castle.
> —JAMES OTIS, argument on the Writs of Assistance,
> Boston, 1761

[More at PRIVACY.]

The God who gave us life, gave us liberty at the same time.   5
> —THOMAS JEFFERSON, *Summary View
> of the Rights of British America*, 1775

Do thou, great liberty, inspire our souls,   6
And make our lives in thy possession happy
Or our deaths glorious in thy just defense.
> —JOSEPH ADDISON, *Cato*, 1713,
> used as the motto of the *Massachusetts Spy*,
> Nov. 22, 1771, to April 6, 1775

[*Cato* may have been the first play published in America, and was very popular. Nathan Hale borrowed from it in his final statement before execution; see AMERICAN REVOLUTION. The *Massachusetts Spy*, a weekly newspaper, was published by Isaiah Thomas, who went on to become the foremost book publisher in the newly independent United States.]

Is life so dear, or peace so sweet, as to be purchased at the price of chains and   7
slavery? Forbid it, Almighty God! I know not what course others may take, but as for me, give me liberty or give me death!
> —PATRICK HENRY, speech,
> Virginia Convention, March 23, 1775

[A ringing declaration, but probably apocryphal. Neither Washington nor Jefferson, who were there, ever mentioned Henry's speech. As in the case of Henry's "if this be treason" challenge, cited in AMERICAN HISTORY: MEMORABLE MOMENTS, this speech was reconstructed many years after the fact by Henry's biographer William Wirt.]

1   Where liberty dwells, there is my country.
                                        —BENJAMIN FRANKLIN, attributed
[Also sometimes attributed to James Otis in the form of the Latin motto: *Ubi libertas, ibi patria.* For Franklin, the root of the attribution may be in a letter to David Hartley, December 4, 1789, in which Franklin wrote: "God grant that not only the love of liberty but a thorough knowledge of the rights of man may pervade all the nations of the earth, so that a philosopher may set his foot anywhere on its surface and say: 'This is my country.'"]

2   Can the liberties of a nation be thought secure when we have removed their only firm basis, a conviction in the minds of the people that these liberties are the gifts of God? That they are not to be violated but with his wrath? Indeed I tremble for my country when I reflect that God is just.
                      —THOMAS JEFFERSON, *Notes on the State of Virginia,* 1781–1785
[Jefferson was warning in particular that slavery violated God's gift of liberty for us all.]

3   The tree of liberty must be refreshed from time to time with the blood of patriots and tyrants. It is its natural manure.
                                        —THOMAS JEFFERSON, letter to
                                        Col. William S. Smith, Nov. 13, 1787

4   Wherever the standard of freedom and independence has been unfurled, there will [America's] heart, her benedictions, and her prayers be.
                                        —JOHN QUINCY ADAMS, July 4, 1821
[More at AMERICA & AMERICANS.]

5   Independence now and forever!   —DANIEL WEBSTER, eulogy,
                                        August 2, 1826
[Webster spoke in memory of Thomas Jefferson and John Adams, who both died on July 4, 1826. Four days earlier, when asked to suggest a toast to be made in his name, Adams had said, "It is my living sentiment, and by the blessing of God, it shall be my dying sentiment, Independence now and Independence forever." See also INDEPENDENCE DAY.]

6   Liberty and independence, forever!
                      —DAVID CROCKETT, Alamo journal, March 5, 1836,
                      in *Colonel Crockett's Exploits and Adventures in Texas* [1837]
[These are the final words of the journal attributed to Crockett, killed later that day, along with all the other defenders of the San Antonio fortress, by Mexicans under General Santa Anna. The entire last paragraph reads: "Pop, pop, pop! Bom, bom, bom! throughout the day. No time for memorandums now. Go ahead! Liberty and independence forever!" For more on the Alamo and Crockett, see William Barrett Travis at AMERICAN HISTORY: MEMORABLE MOMENTS.]

7   We should be men first, and subjects afterward.
                      —HENRY DAVID THOREAU, *Civil Disobedience,* 1849

8   Eternal vigilance is the price of liberty.
                      —WENDELL PHILLIPS, *Public Opinion,* speech,
                      Massachusetts Anti-Slavery Society, Jan. 28, 1852
[Sometimes attributed to Thomas Jefferson or Patrick Henry. The true source seems to be the Irish magistrate and orator John Philpot Curran, who in a speech delivered on July 10, 1790, stated: "The condition upon which God hath given liberty to man is eternal vigilance."]

Those who deny freedom to others deserve it not for themselves. 1
> —ABRAHAM LINCOLN, letter to H. L. Pierce et al., April 6, 1859

When I found I had crossed that line, I looked at my hands to see if I was the 2
same person. There was such a glory over everything.
> —HARRIET TUBMAN, description of her first escape to the North,
> quoted in Sarah H. Bradford, *Harriet, the Moses of Her People,*
> 1869

[She got away for good in 1849, and dedicated herself to freeing others, leading more than 300 slaves out of bondage via the Underground Railroad. In the Civil War, she worked for the Union forces in coastal South Carolina, acting as a nurse, laundress, and spy. She was as eloquent as she was courageous.]

I had reasoned this out in my mind: There was two things I had a right to, lib- 3
erty and death. If I could not have one, I would have the other, for no man
should take me alive. *—Ibid.*

Free at last! Free at last! 4
Thank God Almighty, we are free at last!
> —ANONYMOUS, spiritual

[Quoted by Martin Luther King, Jr., to conclude his speech at the Lincoln Memorial in the march on Washington in 1963; see AMERICAN HISTORY: MEMORABLE MOMENTS. This is his epitaph at South View Cemetery in Atlanta.]

That buoyancy and exuberance which comes with freedom. 5
> —FREDERICK J. TURNER, *The Significance of the Frontier
> in American History,* 1893

[More from this passage at AMERICA & AMERICANS.]

The cost of liberty is less than the price of repression. 6
> —W. E. B. DU BOIS, *The Legacy of John Brown,* 1909

You can only protect your liberties in this world by protecting the other man's 7
freedom. You can only be free if I am free.
> —CLARENCE DARROW, *People v. Lloyd,* 1920

I always say . . . if my fellow citizens want to go to hell, I will help them. It's 8
my job. —OLIVER WENDELL HOLMES, JR.,
> letter to Harold J. Laski, March 4, 1920

The right to be let alone—the most comprehensive of rights. 9
> —LOUIS D. BRANDEIS, *Olmstead v. the United States,* 1928

[More at PRIVACY.]

Freedom is never given; it is won. —A. PHILIP RANDOLPH, keynote speech, 10
> Second National Negro Congress, 1937

[Randolph was the founder of the railway porters' union. He unionized the Pullman company, and was influential in persuading Pres. Harry Truman that the U.S. armed services should be integrated. Rev. Martin Luther King, Jr., made the same point some twenty-five years later; see below.]

In the future days, which we seek to make secure, we look forward to a world 11
founded upon four essential human freedoms.
> —FRANKLIN D. ROOSEVELT, State of the Union message,
> Jan. 6, 1941

[The four freedoms cited by the president were: freedom of speech, freedom of worship, freedom from want, and freedom from fear. The "Four Freedoms" speech is quoted on a plaque in the stairwell of the Statue of Liberty. In 1839, John L. O'Sullivan, who coined the phrase, "manifest destiny," also spoke of the American mission to spread four freedoms; his four were "freedom of conscience, freedom of person, freedom of trade and business pursuits, universality of freedom and equality."]

1   Freedom means the supremacy of human rights everywhere.   —*Ibid.*

2   Liberty is so much latitude as the powerful choose to accord to the weak.
               —LEARNED HAND, speech, University of Pennsylvania Law
               School, May 21, 1944

3   Caged birds accept each other but flight is what they long for.
               —TENNESSEE WILLIAMS, *Camino Real*, 1953

4   Freedom is not a luxury that we can indulge in when at last we have security and prosperity and enlightenment; it is, rather an antecedent to all of these, for without it, we can have neither security nor prosperity nor enlightenment.
               —HENRY STEELE COMMAGER, *Freedom, Loyalty, Dissent*, 1954

5   And this nation, for all its hopes and boasts, will not be fully free until all its citizens are free.   —JOHN F. KENNEDY, civil rights speech to the nation,
               June 11, 1963

6   Freedom is never voluntarily given by the oppressor; it must be demanded by the oppressed.   —MARTIN LUTHER KING, JR.,
                                   letter from Birmingham city jail, 1963
    [See A. Philip Randolph, above.]

FREE SPEECH   *See also* CONSTITUTION, THE;
                                    CENSORSHIP; FREEDOM; PRESS, THE

7   The most stringent protection of free speech would not protect a man in falsely shouting fire in a theater and causing a panic.
               —Oliver Wendell Holmes, Jr., *Schenck v. U.S.*, 1919
    [In the case at hand, the Supreme Court unanimously upheld the conviction of Charles T. Schenck, secretary of the Socialist party, for distributing a circular intended to encourage men to peacefully resist military recruitment. The decision set the precedent that the First Amendment freedoms of press and speech may be abridged when they constitute "a clear and present danger" to the community. Holmes emphasized the imperatives of war, but the doctrine was used in the 1930s and 1940s to sustain convictions of people considered to be politically subversive.]

8   When men have realized that time has upset many fighting faiths, they may come to believe . . . that the ultimate good desired is better reached by the free trade in ideas—that the best test of truth is the power of the thought to get itself accepted in the competition of the market. . . . That at any rate is the theory of our Constitution.
               —OLIVER WENDELL HOLMES, JR., dissent, *Abrams v. U.S.*, 1919
    [George F. Kennan, longtime U.S. ambassador to Russia, pointed out: "The truth is sometimes a poor competitor in the market place of ideas—complicated, unsatisfying, full of dilemmas, always vulnerable to misinterpretation and abuse," *American Diplomacy: 1900–1950* (1951). See also TRUTH.
      Note that Justice Holmes's opinion is a dissent—one of many. He was dubbed "the Great Dissenter."]

FREE WILL   *See* WILL

FRIENDS & FRIENDSHIP

And the song from beginning to end,   1
I found again in the heart of a friend.   —HENRY WADSWORTH LONGFELLOW,
                                          The Arrow and the Song, 1845
[The last two lines of one of Longfellow's most famous if least successful poems, which begins, "I shot an arrow in the air, / It fell to earth, I know not
where." And continues, ". . . I breathed a song into the air, / It fell to earth I
know not where. . . . / Long, long afterward in an oak, / I found the arrow, still
unbroke; / And the song, from beginning to end," etc.]

A friend may well be reckoned the masterpiece of nature.   2
                              —RALPH WALDO EMERSON, *Friendship,*
                                  in *Essays: First Series,* 1841

A friend is person with whom I may be sincere. Before him, I may think aloud.   3
                                                              —*Ibid.*
[See also Emerson below.]

Our friends have no place in the graveyard.   4
                              —HENRY DAVID THOREAU, *A Week on the Concord
                                  and Merrimack Rivers,* 1849
[In our memories they live and inspire us even after death.]

The ornament of a house is the friends who frequent it.
                              —RALPH WALDO EMERSON, *Domestic Life,*   5
                                  in *Society and Solitude,* 1870

The holy passion of friendship is of so sweet and steady and loyal and enduring   6
a nature that it will last through a whole lifetime, if not asked to lend money.
                              —MARK TWAIN, *Pudd'nhead Wilson's Calendar,*
                                  in *Pudd'nhead Wilson,* 1894

Friends are born, not made.   7
                —HENRY ADAMS, *The Education of Henry Adams,* 1907

One friend in a life is much, two are many, three are hardly possible.   8
                                                              —*Ibid.*
[See POWER for Adams on a friend in power.]

There is nothing final between friends.   9
                —WILLIAM JENNINGS BRYAN, May 1914
[Secretary of State Bryan was referring to a strain in relations between Japan
and the U.S. occasioned by a California law forbidding Japanese to own real estate. The Japanese ambassador had not been happy with Bryan's explanation
that there was little that he could do about the situation, and had asked, "I suppose, Mr. Secretary, this decision is final?" In fact, matters were patched up
subsequently.]

Only solitary men know the full joys of friendship. Others have their families;   10
but to a solitary and an exile his friends are everything.
                              —WILLA CATHER,
                                  Shadows on the Rock, 1931

1   Louis, I think this is the beginning of a beautiful friendship.
                            —JULIUS EPSTEIN, PHILIP EPSTEIN, & HOWARD KOCH,
                                    Casablanca, screenplay, 1942
    [Humphrey Bogart to Claude Rains. According to Aljean Harmetz in her 1992
    book on the movie, producer Hal Wallis wrote this great closing line.]

2   It is not often that someone comes along who is a true friend and a good writer.
                                    —E. B. WHITE, *Charlotte's Web,* 1952

FRONTIER, THE   *See also* MIDWEST, THE; WEST, THE

3   It is sometimes said that the abundance of vacant land operates as the safety
    valve of our system.   —GEORGE BANCROFT, *Reform,*
                                        in *New England Magazine,* Jan. 1832.
    [See also the "manifest destiny" quotes from John L. O'Sullivan under AMER-
    ICA & AMERICANS.]

4   So long as cheap land continues to be abundant, so long you cannot drive the
    wages of labor to the starvation point.
                            —ROBERT RANTOUL, JR., 1848, quoted in Luther Hamilton,
                                Memoirs, Speeches, and Writings of Robert Rantoul, Jr.
    [Rantoul was a Democratic congressman from Gloucester, Massachusetts.]

5   Go west, young man, go west.   —JOHN B. L. SOULE, editorial
                                        in the *Terre Haute Express,* 1851
    [The advice was popularized by Horace Greeley in the *New York Tribune.* See
    THE WEST.]

6   Come my tan-faced children
    Follow well in order, get your weapons ready,
    Have you your pistols? have you your sharp-edged axes?
    Pioneers! O pioneers!

    .   .   .
    O you youths, Western youths,
    So impatient, full of action, full of manly pride and friendship,
    Plain I see you Western youths, see you tramping with the foremost,
    Pioneers! O pioneers!

    .   .   .
    All the past we leave behind,
    We debouch upon a newer, mightier world, varied world,
    Fresh and strong the world we seize, world of labor and the march,
    Pioneers! O pioneers!   —WALT WHITMAN, *Pioneers! O Pioneers,* 1865,
                                        in *Leaves of Grass* [1881]

7   The existence of an area of free land, its continuous recession, and the advance
    of American settlement westward, explain American development.
                            —FREDERICK J. TURNER, *The Significance of the Frontier
                                in American History,* 1893
    [For a similar observation by Turner, see THE WEST. Gertrude Stein, too, thought
    that empty space shaped the American character; see AMERICA & AMERICANS.
    For the political and cultural impact of the frontier, see Turner at DEMOCRACY.
        Turner's fine essay was first read to the American Historical Association. In
    the scope of a few pages, Turner defined the role of the frontier in American
    history and announced the frontier's disappearance. See below.]

8   The frontier is productive of individualism.   *—Ibid.*

The frontier has gone, and with its going has closed the first period of American history. 1

—*Ibid.*

[Turner, a young scholar—just thirty-two years old—at the University of Wisconsin, recognized the significance of a little noticed passage in a bulletin from the Superintendent of Census for 1890: "Up to and including 1880, the country had a frontier of settlement, but at present the unsettled area has been so broken into by isolated bodies of settlement that there can hardly be said to be a frontier line. . . . It can not, therefore, any longer have a place in the census reports." But Turner foresaw that the expansionist spirit of Americans would continue: "He would be a rash prophet who should assert that the expansive character of American life has now entirely ceased. Movement has been its dominant fact, and, unless this training has no effect upon people, the American energy will continually demand a wider field for its exercise."]

If there was a road, I could not make it out in the faint starlight. There was 2 nothing but land: not a country at all, but the material out of which countries are made. —WILLA CATHER,
My Antonia, 1918

[This is Nebraska—Black Hawk in the novel, Red Cloud in reality.]

We stand today at the edge of a new frontier. 3

—JOHN F. KENNEDY, presidential nomination acceptance speech, Democratic National Convention, Los Angeles, July 15, 1960

[More at POLITICAL SLOGANS.]

FUTURE, THE   *See also* ENVIRONMENT, THE

I know no way of judging the future but by the past. 4
—PATRICK HENRY, speech, Virginia Convention, March 23, 1775

I like the dreams of the future better than the history of the past. 5
—THOMAS JEFFERSON, letter to John Adams, August 1, 1816

We shall be obliged to gnaw the very crust of the earth for nutriment. 6
—HENRY DAVID THOREAU, *Travel in Concord*,
in *Excursions*, 1863

[Thoreau was reacting to the wholesale cutting of timber and the view that this kind of timbering is a basic right, "as if individual speculators were to be allowed to export the clouds out of the sky, or the stars out of the firmament, one by one."]

The day will come when no badge or uniform or star will be worn. 7
—RALPH WALDO EMERSON, quoted in Lewis Mumford,
Have Courage!, in *American Heritage* magazine, Feb. 1969

The future is no more uncertain than the present. 8
—WALT WHITMAN, *Song of the Broad-Axe*, 1856

I have seen the future and it works. 9
—LINCOLN STEFFENS, letter to Marie Howe,
after visiting Russia, April 3, 1919

[In his *Autobiography*, published in 1931, Steffens states that he made almost the same remark to Bernard Baruch at about the same time: "I have been over into the future and it works." Steffens used the observation repeatedly.]

1   You ain't heard nothin' yet, folks.
                    —AL JOLSON, *The Jazz Singer*, 1927
[This was the first talking motion picture. The line was ad-libbed.]

2   I'll think of it all tomorrow at Tara. . . . After all, tomorrow is another day.
                    —MARGARET MITCHELL, *Gone with the Wind*, 1936

3   In a foreseeable future we shall be smothered by our own numbers. . . . Preoccupation with survival has set the stage for extinction.
                    —JOHN STEINBECK, *Sweet Thursday*, 1954

4   Time and space—time to be alone, space to move about—these may well be the greatest scarcities of tomorrow.
                    —EDWIN WAY TEALE, *Autumn Across America*, 1956

5   The coming century is probably going to be one in which the amount of suffering reaches its maximum.   —LINUS PAULING, quoted in *The New York Times*, obituary, August 21, 1994
[For a place striving to prevent the future, see VERMONT, the quote from Charles Kuralt.]

G

GAMES

See also LAW (Charles Bruce Darrow);
SPORTS

Wrapped in the speculations of this wretched game [chess] you destroy your   1
constitution.   —BENJAMIN FRANKLIN, *Dialogue between Franklin
and the Gout,* 1780
[Franklin, a talented chess buff, regretted the addictive aspects of the game, which
drew him away from "the finest gardens and walks, a pure air, beautiful women,
and the most agreeable and instructive conversation." Occasionally, though, he
managed to combine pleasures—for instance, by playing chess with a friend—
Madame Brillon—while she bathed. (Her tub had a wooden cover.) One evening
they became so absorbed that Franklin did not get home to Passy until eleven
o'clock. Madame Brillon who was less than half Franklin's age, was blessed
with an understanding husband, and she must have been extremely clean.]

[Gambling:] The child of avarice, the brother of iniquity, and the father of mis-   2
chief.   —GEORGE WASHINGTON,
letter, Jan. 15, 1783
[Washington was no prude. Neither was Thomas Jefferson, who wrote: "Gaming corrupts our dispositions, and teaches us a habit of hostility against all
mankind," letter to Martha Jefferson, 1787.]

A stereotyped but unconscious despair is concealed even under what are called   3
the games and amusements of mankind.
—HENRY DAVID THOREAU, "Economy," *Walden,* 1854
[This is part of the passage that begins with the observation that most of us
lead desperate lives; see LIFE.]

The serene confidence which a Christian feels in four aces.   4
—MARK TWAIN, letter to *The Golden Era,*
San Francisco, May 22, 1864

A man's idee in a card game is war—crool, devastatin', an' pitiless. A lady's   5
idee iv it is a combynation iv larceny, embezzlement, an' burglary.
—FINLEY PETER DUNNE, *On the Game of Cards,*
in *Mr. Dooley on Making a Will,* 1919

1 I've seen a game iv cards start among frinds, but I never see frinds in a game iv cards.   —*Ibid.*

2 I like the moment when I break a man's ego.
—BOBBY FISCHER, in *Newsweek,* July 31, 1972
[On the following September 1, Mr. Fischer became the first American to win the world chess championship.]

GARDENS   *See* NATURE: PLANTS & GARDENS

GENERATIONS   *See also* AGES; FAMILY

3 Every man is a quotation from all his ancestors.
—RALPH WALDO EMERSON, *Plato, or The Philosopher,*
in *Representative Men,* 1850

4 You are all a lost generation.   —GERTRUDE STEIN, letter
to Ernest Hemingway, 1926
[The observation is the epigraph of Hemingway's *The Sun Also Rises,* 1926. A *Bartlett's* footnote states that Stein first heard this from a garage owner in the Midi, who called his young mechanics *"une génération perdue."*]

5 Each generation wastes a little more
of the future with greed and lust for riches.
—DON MARQUIS, *archy and mehitabel,* 1927

6 This generation is sowing the seeds of ultimate dissolution.
—HIRAM JOHNSON, letter, 1930
[Johnson was a reformist governor of California, a Republican, and Theodore Roosevelt's running mate on the Progressive Party ticket in 1912. He served in the U.S. Senate from 1917 to his death in 1945.]

7 We are always telling 'em [young people] what we used to not do. We didn't do it because we didn't think of it. We did everything we could think of.
—WILL ROGERS, in Alex Ayres, ed.,
The Wit and Wisdom of Will Rogers [1993]

8 Every generation revolts against its fathers and makes friends with its grandfathers.   —LEWIS MUMFORD, *The Brown Decades,* 1931

9 I have moments of real terror when I think we may be losing this generation.
—ELEANOR ROOSEVELT, May 1934, quoted in Joseph P. Lash,
Eleanor and Franklin [1971]

10 There is a mysterious cycle in human events. To some generations much is given. Of others much is expected. This generation of Americans has a rendezvous with destiny.
—FRANKLIN D. ROOSEVELT, presidential nomination acceptance
speech, Democratic National Convention, June 27, 1936
[*Safire's New Political Dictionary* notes that the president may have had in mind Alan Seeger's "I have a rendezvous with death"; see under WORLD WAR I.]

11 What has posterity ever done for me?   —GROUCHO MARX, attributed

12 I saw the best minds of my generation destroyed by madness.
—ALLEN GINSBERG, *Howl,* 1956
[More at MADNESS.]

Let the word go forth from this time and place, to friend and foe alike, that the   1
torch has been passed to a new generation of Americans.
—JOHN F. KENNEDY, *Inaugural Address*, Jan. 20, 1961

Don't trust anyone over thirty.   2
—ANONYMOUS, c. 1965
[More at YOUTH.]

GENIUS   *See also* MIND, THOUGHT, & UNDERSTANDING

Towering genius disdains a beaten path. It seeks regions hitherto unexplored.   3
—ABRAHAM LINCOLN, speech, Jan. 27, 1838

Great geniuses have the shortest biographies.   4
—RALPH WALDO EMERSON, *Representative Men*, 1850

In every work of genius, we recognize our own rejected thoughts; they come   5
back to us with a certain alienated majesty.
—RALPH WALDO EMERSON, cited in Robert D. Richardson, Jr.,
Emerson: The Mind on Fire [1995]

Genius is one percent inspiration and ninety-nine percent perspiration.   6
—THOMAS ALVA EDISON, c. 1903, quoted by M. A. Rosanoff,
Harper's Monthly Magazine [Sept. 1932]

It takes a lot of time to be a genius, you have to sit around so much doing noth-   7
ing, really doing nothing.
—GERTRUDE STEIN, *Everybody's Autobiography*, 1937

Genius is an African who dreams up snow.   8
—VLADIMIR NABOKOV, *The Gift*, 1937–38
[*The Gift* was Nabokov's last novel written in Russian. The dates are of the
censored serialized versions; it was not published in full until 1952. The author, who came to the U.S. in 1940, collaborated with Michael Scammell on an
English translation in which verse and prose merge, and are printed without
lineation. Leona Toker, writing in *The Reader's Encyclopedia of American Literature*, calls this "one of the greatest feats of translation."]

GEORGIA   *See also* CITIES (Atlanta, Savannah)

My native State! My cherished home!   9
—"R.M.C.," *Georgia*, in *Augusta Mirror*, 1839

In the small towns of the country, however, we found the hospitality of the res-   10
idents all that we could desire, and more than we could enjoy.
—J. S. BUCKINGHAM, *The Slave States of America, 1839*, 1842

A resistless feeling of depression falls slowly upon us, despite the gaudy sun-   11
shine and the green cotton-fields. This, then, is the Cotton Kingdom, the
shadow of a marvelous dream.
—W. E. B. DU BOIS, *The Souls of Black Folk*, 1903
[From a passage on southern Georgia in summer, when the heat is "dull, determined." "The whole land seems forlorn and forsaken," Du Bois observed.]

1   I am determined that at the end of this administration we shall be able to stand up anywhere in the world—in New York, California, or Florida—and say "I'm a Georgian," and be proud of it.
                    —JIMMY CARTER, Inaugural Gubernatorial Address, Atlanta,
                    Jan. 12, 1971

Motto

2   Wisdom, justice, and moderation.

GERMANY   *See* NATIONS

GETTYSBURG ADDRESS   *See also* CIVIL WAR

3   Fourscore and seven years ago, our fathers brought forth on this continent a new nation, conceived in liberty, and dedicated to the proposition that all men are created equal.

Now we are engaged in a great civil war, testing whether that nation or any nation so conceived and so dedicated can long endure. We are met on a great battlefield of that war. We have come to dedicate a portion of that field, as a final resting place for those who here gave their lives that a nation might live. It is altogether fitting and proper that we should do this.

But, in a larger sense, we cannot dedicate—we cannot consecrate—we cannot hallow—this ground. The brave men, living and dead, who struggled here have consecrated it far above our power to add or detract. The world will little note nor long remember what we say here, but it can never forget what they did here. It is for us, the living, rather to be dedicated here to the unfinished work which they who fought here have thus far so nobly advanced. It is rather for us to be here dedicated to the great task remaining before us—that from these honored dead we take increased devotion to that cause for which they gave the last full measure of devotion; that we here highly resolve that these dead shall not have died in vain; that this nation, under God, shall have a new birth of freedom; and that government of the people, by the people, for the people, shall not perish from earth.
                    —ABRAHAM LINCOLN, Gettysburg Address, Nov. 19, 1863
[The battle at Gettysburg, Pennsylvania, was the greatest battle of the war, marking the limit of the Confederacy's advance north. The fighting lasted from July 1 to July 3; on July 4, Gen. Robert E. Lee began to retreat across the Potomac. Lee blundered at Gettysburg by attacking an entrenched army. "All this has been my fault, it is I that have lost this fight," Lee said to Gen. C. M. Wilcox as the remnants of Pickett's division returned from their futile charge. Meanwhile, the Union commander, Gen. George Meade, failed to exploit the victory by pursuing Lee's forces. The Union took 23,000 casualties and the Confederates about 25,000.

Lincoln spoke at the dedication of a permanent cemetery on the Gettysburg battlefield. Edward Everett of Massachusetts was the principal speaker, but the superintendent of the enterprise, David Wills, asked Lincoln to make "a few appropriate remarks."

The greatness of Lincoln's address was not appreciated right away, not even by himself. The president told his friend Ward Lamon as he returned to his seat that the speech was "a flat failure." *The New York Times* called it "dull and commonplace," but Edward Everett wrote Lincoln: "I should be glad if I could flatter myself that I came as near the central idea of the occasion in two hours as you did in two minutes."

The phrase "government of the people, by the people, for the people," in the last sentence of the speech, may have derived from an 1830 speech by Daniel

Webster in the U.S. Senate, which referred to "government, made for the people, made by the people, and answerable to the people"; see under GOVERNMENT. In 1850, in a speech in Boston, Theodore Parker declaimed, "This is what I call the American idea—a government of all the people, by all the people, for all the people.]

GIVING

See CHARITY & PHILANTHROPHY

GOD

See also POLITICS (Sen. George Mitchell); RELIGION

The Lord has more truth and light yet to break forth out of his Holy Word.   1
　　　　　—JOHN ROBINSON, speech as the Pilgrims left for America, 1620
[Robinson, an English nonconformist, was pastor of the Pilgrim community in Holland. He supported emigration to the New World, and would have made the journey himself if the majority of his congregation had decided to go.]

The longer I live, the more convincing proofs I see of this truth, that God governs in the affairs of men. And if a sparrow cannot fall to the ground without his notice, is it probable than an empire can rise without his aid?   2
　　　　　—BENJAMIN FRANKLIN, at the Constitutional Convention, 1787
[A Deist in his youth, Franklin became more religious with age, and at the convention asked that each session begin with a prayer. All but a handful of delegates voted against this motion, but, according to Henry Steele Commager, their main reason was a lack of money to hire a chaplain (*American Heritage*, Dec. 1958).]

In God we trust.   3
　　　　　—U.S. MOTTO
[Francis Scott Key originated the motto in 1814 in the form "In God is our trust" in the fourth verse of *The Star-Spangled Banner*. The more familiar version began appearing on U.S. coins in 1864. This arose from a suggestion made to Secretary of the Treasury Salmon P. Chase by Rev. M. R. Watkinson of Ridleyville, Penn. Rev. Watkinson had been dismayed by Union losses early in the Civil War, and felt that the defeats were linked to "our national shame in disowning God." Therefore, he proposed that God be recognized in some form on coins. The motto was adopted officially by Congress in 1956 and is used now on all coins and paper money.]

God is our name for the last generalization to which we can arrive.   4
　　　　　—RALPH WALDO EMERSON, *Journals*, 1836

Dare to love God without mediator or veil.   5
　　　　　—RALPH WALDO EMERSON, *Divinity School Address*, 1838

God enters by a private door into every individual.   6
　　　　　—RALPH WALDO EMERSON, *Intellect*,
　　　　　in *Essays: First Series*, 1841

One, on God's side, is a majority.   7
　　　　　—WENDELL PHILLIPS, speech on John Brown,
　　　　　Brooklyn, N.Y., Nov. 1, 1859

The only money of God is God. He never pays with any thing less, or any thing   8
else.　　　　　—RALPH WALDO EMERSON, *Worship*,
　　　　　in *The Conduct of Life*, 1860

1   God Himself does not speak prose, but communicates with us by hints, omens, inference, and dark resemblances in objects lying all around us.
—RALPH WALDO EMERSON, *Poetry and Imagination*, in *Letters and Social Aims* [1876]

2   Mine eyes have seen the glory of the coming of the Lord;
He is trampling out the vintage where the grapes of wrath are stored;
He hath loosed the fateful lightning of His terrible, swift sword;
His truth is marching on.
—JULIA WARD HOWE, *Battle Hymn of the Republic*, 1862
[Howe based the *Battle Hymn* on an army marching song that concluded "John Brown's body lies a-moldering in the ground; His soul is marching on." Her song became the anthem of the Union forces. After the war, Howe took up the cause of world peace; see PACIFISM & NONVIOLENCE.]

3   In the beauty of the lilies Christ was born across the sea,
With a glory in His bosom that transfigures you and me;
As he died to make men holy, let us die to make men free.   —*Ibid.*

4   The Almighty has His own purposes.
—ABRAHAM LINCOLN, Second Inaugural Address, 1865
[The conclusion of a passage in which Lincoln comments that in the Civil War both sides prayed to the same God. "The prayers of both could not be answered," Lincoln wrote, "that of neither has been answered fully."]

5   God is and all is well.   —JOHN GREENLEAF WHITTIER, *My Birthday*, 1871

6   God is love, love in action—love universal.
—PETER COOPER, c. 1875, quoted in Peter Lyon, *The Honest Man*, in *American Heritage* [Feb. 1959]
[In the circles of the wealthy, Cooper was an unusually ardent advocate of social responsibility; see under BUSINESS and MONEY & THE RICH.]

7   Our Father-Mother-God, all-harmonies.
—MARY BAKER EDDY, *Science and Health with Key to the Scriptures*, 1875

8   Though the mills of God grind slowly, yet they grind exceedingly small;
Though with patience He stands waiting, with exactness grinds He all.
—HENRY WADSWORTH LONGFELLOW, translation of Friedrich von Logau's *Retribution*, 1654

9   An honest God is the noblest work of man.
—ROBERT G. INGERSOLL, *The Gods, and Other Lectures*, 1876
[Also in the *Notebooks* of the 19th-century English writer Samuel Butler.]

10   I believe that our Heavenly Father invented man because he was disappointed in the monkey.
—MARK TWAIN, dictation for his autobiography, Nov. 24, 1906

11   I myself believe that the evidence for God lies primarily in inner personal experiences.
—WILLIAM JAMES, *Pragmatism*, 1907
[See also Whitehead below.]

God, I can push the grass apart,
And lay my finger on thy heart.   —EDNA ST. VINCENT MILLAY, *Renascence,*
in *Renascence and Other Poems,* 1917

1

God: The John Doe of philosophy and religion.   —ELBERT HUBBARD, *Roycroft Dictionary and Book of Epigrams,* 1923

2

No reason can be given for the nature of God, because that nature is the ground
of rationality.   —ALFRED NORTH WHITEHEAD,
Science and the Modern World, 1925

3

God is in me or else is not at all (does not exist).
   —WALLACE STEVENS, *Adagia,*
in *Opus Posthumous* [1957]

4

God is a mother.   —EUGENE O'NEILL, *Strange Interlude,* 1928

5

It takes a long while for a naturally trusting person to reconcile himself to the
idea that after all God will not help him.
   —H. L. MENCKEN, *Minority Report: H. L. Mencken's
Notebooks* [1956]

6

Sometimes there's a God so quickly.
   —TENNESSEE WILLIAMS, *A Streetcar Named Desire,* 1947

7

Raffiniert is der Herr Gott, aber boshaft is er nicht.
God is subtle, but malicious he is not.
   —ALBERT EINSTEIN, inscription in Fine Hall,
Princeton University
[Einstein's own translation, according to Alan L. Mackay in *The Harvest of a
Quiet Eye,* was "God is slick, but he ain't mean." For Einstein on God and dice,
see SCIENCE: PHYSICS & COSMOLOGY.]

8

It is the final proof of God's omnipotence that he need not exist in order to
save us.   —PETER DE VRIES, *Mackeral Plaza,* 1958

9

Gods do not answer letters.   —JOHN UPDIKE,
Hub Fans Bid Kid Adieu,
in *The New Yorker,* Oct. 22, 1960
[The God in this instance was Theodore Samuel Williams, aka the Kid or the
Splendid Splinter, who concluded a Hall of Fame baseball career on Sept. 26,
1962, by hitting a home run, his 521st, on his final turn at bat in Boston's Fen-
way Park and then, refusing to budge from past practice, declined to acknowledge the cheers of Updike and other fans by coming out of the dugout and tipping
his cap. It says something about New England weather—the day was cold—but
about Boston, too, that only 10,454 people showed up for the occasion.]

10

God is the Celebrity-Author of the World's Best Seller. We have made God into
the biggest celebrity of all, to contain our own emptiness.
   —DANIEL J. BOORSTIN,
The Image, 1962

11

God is a verb.   —R. BUCKMINSTER FULLER,
No More Secondhand God, 1963
[Possibly derived from Ulysses S. Grant; see ACTION & DOING.]

12

1   Like anybody, I would like to live a long life. Longevity has its place. But I'm not concerned about that now. I just want to do God's will. And he's allowed me to go up to the mountain. And I've looked over, and I've seen the promised land. I may not get there with you, but I want you to know tonight that we as a people will get to the promised land. . . . So I'm happy tonight. I'm not worried about anything. I'm not fearing any man. Mine eyes have seen the glory of the coming of the Lord.   —MARTIN LUTHER KING, JR., speech to sanitation
                                    workers, Memphis, Tenn., April 3, 1968
    [Dr. King was shot the next day.]

2   The Buddha, the Godhead, resides as comfortably in the circuits of a digital computer or the gears of a cycle transmission as he does at the top of a mountain or in the petals of a flower.   —ROBERT PIRSIG, *Zen and the Art of*
                                    Motorcycle Maintenance, 1974
    [See Pirsig also at SCIENCE: TECHNOLOGY.]

3   There is no more powerful ally one can claim in a debate than Jesus Christ, or God, or Allah or whatever one calls his Supreme Being. But, like any other powerful weapons, the use of God's name on one's behalf should be used sparingly.
                                    —BARRY GOLDWATER, *Conservatism, Religion,*
                                    and Politics, speech, 1981
    [The Republican senator from Arizona, speaking as one who had spent quite "a number of years carrying the flag of the 'old conservatism,'" here lamented the intrusion of the Moral Majority and other religious groups into politics. For a similar conclusion by a senator from the other end of the political spectrum, see George Mitchell at POLITICS & POLITICIANS.]

4   People see God every day; they just don't recognize him.
                                    —PEARL BAILEY, in Eric V. Copage, *Black Pearls*, 1993

GOOD TIMES

5   The Era of Good Feelings.   —ANONYMOUS
    [A name for the peaceful terms of Republican presidents James Monroe and John Quincy Adams, 1816 to 1828. Jacksonian Democrats had a different name for the period: "The Era of Corruption."]

6   The era of wonderful nonsense.
                                    —WESTBROOK PEGLER, saying
    [Pegler was referring to the 1920s. Henry F. Woods, in *American Sayings* (1945), writes that Pegler originated the phrase in an article later titled *Mr. Gump Himself* and included in his book *'Tain't Right*. Pegler liked the phrase and used it often.]

7   Happy days are here again,
    The skies above are clear again:
    Let us sing a song of cheer again,
    Happy days are here again!   —JACK YELLEN,
                                    Happy Days Are Here Again, 1929
    [The song, with music by Milton Ager, enlivened the 1932 Democratic National Convention, and many thereafter. The incumbent president, Franklin D. Roosevelt used it as a campaign song.]

8   A golden age of poetry and power
    Of which this noonday's the beginning hour.   —ROBERT FROST, inauguration of
                                    John F. Kennedy, Jan. 20, 1961

GOODNESS   *See* ETHICS & MORALITY; KINDNESS; VIRTUE

GOVERNMENT   *See also* BUSINESS; CITIES (Pocatello; Washington, D.C.);
                          CONGRESS; DEMOCRACY; ECONOMICS; INSTITUTIONS;
                          MAJORITIES & MINORITIES; MANAGEMENT TECHNIQUES;
                          POLITICS & POLITICIANS; PRESIDENCY, THE; SUPREME COURT

Society in every state is a blessing, but government, even in its best state, is   1
but a necessary evil; in its worst state, an intolerable one.
                                   —THOMAS PAINE, *Common Sense*, 1776

Government, like dress, is the badge of lost innocence; the palaces of kings are   2
built upon the ruins of the bowers of paradise.   —*Ibid.*

The happiness of society is the end of government.   3
                                   —JOHN ADAMS, *Thoughts on Government*, 1776

The legitimate powers of government extend to such acts only as are injurious   4
to others.   —THOMAS JEFFERSON,
                                        Note on the State of Virginia, 1784
[In coming years, Jefferson came to see a broader role for government; see below. See also Jefferson at THE PEOPLE.]

Why has government been instituted at all? Because the passions of men will   5
not conform to the dictates of reason and justice, without constraint.
                                   —ALEXANDER HAMILTON, *Federalist*, No. 15, 1787–88

What is government itself, but the greatest of all reflections on human nature?   6
If men were angels, no government would be necessary. If angels were to govern men, neither external nor internal controls on government would be necessary. In framing a government which is to be administered by men over men,
the great difficulty lies in this; you must first enable the government to control
the governed; and in the next place oblige it to control itself.
                                   —JAMES MADISON, *Federalist* No. 51, 1788

The natural progress of things is for liberty to yield and government to gain   7
ground.   —THOMAS JEFFERSON,
                                        letter to Col. Edward Carrington, 1788
[This may be the genesis of another quotation commonly but apparently in-
correctly attributed to Jefferson: "Eternal vigilance is the price of liberty." See
Wendell Phillips at FREEDOM.]

The whole art of government consists in being honest.   8
                                   —THOMAS JEFFERSON, *Works*, VI

The very idea of the power and the right of the people to establish government   9
presupposes the duty of every individual to obey established government.
                                   —GEORGE WASHINGTON, Farewell Address, Sept. 17, 1796

What more is necessary to make us wise and happy people? Still one thing   10
more, fellow citizens—a wise and frugal government, which shall restrain men
from injuring one another, which shall leave them otherwise free to regulate
their own pursuits of industry and improvement, and shall not take from the
mouth of labor the bread it has earned. This is the sum of good government,
and this is necessary to close the circle of our felicities.
                                   —THOMAS JEFFERSON, First Inaugural Address, March 4, 1801

1   Sometimes it is said that man cannot be trusted with the government of himself. Can he then be trusted with the government of others?

—*Ibid.*

[Jefferson was optimistic. He answered the question affirmatively, characterizing the new American form of government as "the world's best hope." But at the same time, he accepted resistance to government as natural and sometimes desirable; see RESISTANCE and REVOLUTION.]

2   The care of human life and happiness, and not their destruction, is the first and only legitimate object of good government.

—THOMAS JEFFERSON, message to the citizens of
Washington County, Maryland, March 31, 1809

[A few years later, Jefferson restated this view a little more broadly: "The only orthodox object of the institution of government is to secure the greatest degree of happiness possible to the general mass of those associated under it," letter to F. A. van der Kemp, March 22, 1812.]

3   The world is too much governed.   —FRANCIS P. BLAIR, motto
of the *Washington Globe*, Dec. 1830

[Blair, editor of the *Argus of Western America* in Kentucky, was summoned to Washington in 1830 to found a newspaper that would express the views of Pres. Andrew Jackson and his supporters. See also O'Sullivan below.]

4   It is, Sir, the people's Constitution, the people's government, made for the people, made by the people, and answerable to the people.

—DANIEL WEBSTER, speech,
U.S. Senate, Jan. 26, 1830

[Webster was replying to Sen. Robert Y. Hayne of South Carolina, and indirectly to Vice President John C. Calhoun. They had proposed that states had the right within their boundaries to nullify any federal law. Webster countered that the Constitution belonged not to individual states but to the people. See GETTYSBURG ADDRESS and the note on Lincoln's reference to "government of the people, by the people, for the people."]

5   All government is evil. . . . The best government is that which governs least.

—JOHN L. O'SULLIVAN, *The United States Magazine
and Democratic Review*, 1837

[This view was prevalent in the era—see Emerson below, for example—and prevalent especially among Democrats. See above for the motto Francis Blair chose for the *Washington Globe*. The motto of the *Democratic Review* was: "That government is best which governs least." Among Democrats, mistrust of central government was allied with support for states' rights, and this alliance with Southern views eventually cost the party dearly.

For a response to the least-is-best concept, see Walter Lippman below. For a modern Republican view, see Ronald Reagan under AMERICA & AMERICANS.]

6   The less government we have, the better.

—RALPH WALDO EMERSON, *Politics*, in *Essays:
Second Series*, 1844

[In the same year, Thoreau, in the opening of his essay *Civil Disobedience*, used the quote, "That government is best which governs least"; see John L. O'Sullivan above.]

7   In every society some men are born to rule, and some to advise.

—RALPH WALDO EMERSON, *The Young American*,
in *Addresses and Lectures*, 1849

No man is good enough to govern another man without that other's consent.   1
—ABRAHAM LINCOLN, speech, Peoria, Ill.,
Oct. 16, 1854

Government of the people, by the people, for the people, shall not perish from   2
the earth.   —ABRAHAM LINCOLN, Gettysburg Address,
Nov. 19, 1863
[More at GETTYSBURG ADDRESS.]

A public office is a public trust.   —ANONYMOUS, motto of   3
Pres. Grover Cleveland's administrations
[The thought was phrased many ways over the years. Henry Clay, in a speech
in Ashland, Kentucky, in 1829, said: "Government is a trust, and the officers
of the government are trustees; and both the trust and the trustees are created
for the benefit of the people." John C. Calhoun, speaking on February 13, 1835,
said: "The very essence of a free government consists in considering offices as
public trusts, bestowed for the good of the country, and not for the benefit of
an individual or party." In 1872, Charles Sumner noted, "The phrase 'public office is a public trust' has of late become common property." Grover Cleveland,
among many references to this concept, wrote in accepting the Democratic
presidential nomination in 1892: "Public officers are the trustees of the people." See also Thomas Jefferson on assuming a public trust at POLITICS &
POLITICIANS.]

Government is force.   —JOHN ADAMS INGALLS, article,   4
New York *World*, 1890
[For more see under Ingalls at POLITICS & POLITICIANS.]

It is perfectly true that the government is best which governs least. It is   5
equally true that the government is best which provides most.
—WALTER LIPPMANN, *A Preface to Politics*, 1913
[A response to John L. O'Sullivan; see above.]

Neither snow, nor rain, nor heat, nor gloom of night stays these couriers from   6
the swift completion of their appointed rounds.
—GENERAL POST OFFICE, NEW YORK CITY, inscription, 1913
[Adapted from a passage in Herodotus, *The Histories*, 5th cent. B.C. More at
NATURE: WEATHER.]

Our government is the potent, the omnipresent teacher. For good or ill, it   7
teaches the whole people by its example. Crime is contagious. If the government becomes the lawbreaker, it breeds contempt for law, it invites every man
to become a law unto himself, it invites anarchy.
—LOUIS BRANDEIS, *Olmstead v. U.S.*, dissenting opinion, 1928

I am against government by crony.   —HAROLD L. ICKES, resigning as   8
Secretary of the Interior, Feb. 1946

No man should be in public office who can't make more money in private life.   9
—THOMAS E. DEWEY, maxim, cited in Richard Norton Smith,
Thomas E. Dewey [1982]

The worst government is the most moral. One composed of cynics is often   10
very tolerant and humane. But when fanatics are on top, there is no limit to oppression.   —H. L. MENCKEN, *Minority Report:*
H. L. Mencken's Notebooks [1956]

1   A government that is big enough to give you all you want is big enough to take
it all away.   —BARRY GOLDWATER, speech,
Oct. 21, 1964
[A popular theme in the resurgence of conservative Republicanism. See also
Ronald Reagan below.]

2   Today, government is involved in almost every aspect of our lives.
—BERNARD BARUCH, presenting his papers
to Princeton University, May 11, 1964

3   Government is like a big baby—an alimentary canal with a big appetite at one
end and no responsibility at the other.
—RONALD REAGAN, saying, used in the
gubernatorial campaign, 1966
[Reagan continued to use this simile, for example, in a speech on March 11,
1981, in a joint session of Parliament in Ottawa, Canada.]

4   Yet as I read the Constitution, one of its essential purposes was to take government off the backs of people and keep it off.
—WILLIAM O. DOUGLAS, dissenting opinion,
in *W.E.B. Du Bois Clubs v. Clark*, 1967

5   If it ain't broke, don't fix it.   —BERT LANCE, *Nation's Business*,
May 27, 1977
[A bit of proverbial wisdom popularized by Pres. Jimmy Carter's first budget director. As elucidated in *Nation's Business*: "Bert Lance believes he can save
Uncle Sam billions if he can get the government to adopt a single motto: 'If it
ain't broke, don't fix it.' He explains: 'That's the trouble with government: Fixing things that aren't broken and not fixing things that are broken.'"]

6   We do not get all the government we pay for—thank God.
—MILTON FRIEDMAN, quoted by George Will, *David Brinkley
Show*, American Broadcasting Corp., Oct. 4, 1992

GRACE   *See also* SIMPLICITY

7   'Tis the gift to be simple,
'Tis the gift to be free,
'Tis the gift to come down
Where we ought to be.   —ANONYMOUS, *Simple Gifts*,
Shaker song, c. 1848

8   Grace under pressure.   —ERNEST HEMINGWAY,
c. 1926
[This was Hemingway's definition of *guts* according to Dorothy Parker, *The
Artist's Reward*, in *The New Yorker*, Nov. 20, 1929. He evidently also used the
phrase in 1926 to describe Gerald Murphy's first efforts at downhill skiing, as
recounted in Honoria Murphy Donnelly and Richard N. Billings, *Sara & Gerald*, 1982. The phrase was echoed in Hemingway's articles on bullfighting; see
under SPORTS. And it was quoted memorably by John F. Kennedy in *Profiles in
Courage*.]

9   To learn to dance by practicing dancing or to live by practicing living, the principles are the same. . . . One becomes, in some area, an athlete of God.
—MARTHA GRAHAM, May 15, 1945

GREATNESS

Lives of great men all remind us. 1
We can make our lives sublime.
And, departing, leave behind us
Footprints on the sands of time. —HENRY WADSWORTH LONGFELLOW,
A Psalm of Life, 1839

To be great is to be misunderstood. —RALPH WALDO EMERSON, 2
Self-Reliance,
in *Essays; First Series*, 1841

A great man is always willing to be little. —RALPH WALDO EMERSON, 3
Compensation,
in *Essays: First Series*, 1841
[See Emerson at VIRTUE for "the essence of greatness."]

Great men, great nations, have not been boasters and buffoons, but perceivers 4
of the terror of life, and have manned themselves to face it.
—RALPH WALDO EMERSON,
Fate, in *The Conduct of Life*, 1860

There is no indispensable man. —FRANKLIN D. ROOSEVELT, 5
campaign speech,
New York, Nov. 3, 1932
[He was borrowing from Woodrow Wilson; see under HUMANS & HUMAN
NATURE.]

Great men can't be ruled. —AYN RAND, *The Fountainhead*, 1943 6

GREECE *See* NATIONS

GRIEF *See* DEATH; SORROW & GRIEF

GUESTS *See also* HOSPITALITY

My evening visitors, if they cannot see the clock, should be able to find the 7
time in my face. —RALPH WALDO EMERSON,
Journal, 1842

A dinner invitation, once accepted is a sacred obligation. If you die before the 8
dinner takes place, your executor must attend the dinner.
—WARD MCALLISTER, 1890
[Quoted in *American Heritage*, April 1975. McAllister was the chap who said
that there were only four hundred people in New York society; see THE ELITE.]

Some people can stay longer in an hour than others can in a week. 9
—WILLIAM DEAN HOWELLS, attributed

To be an ideal guest, stay at home. —EDGAR WATSON HOWE, 10
Country Town Sayings, 1911

My father used to say 11
"Superior people never make long visits." —MARIANNE MOORE, *Silence*,
in *Collected Poems*, 1935

GULF WAR, 1991

1   Just two hours ago, allied air forces began an attack on military targets in Iraq and Kuwait. These attacks continue as I speak.

—GEORGE BUSH, Jan. 16, 1991

[The president addressed the nation on television, the medium that was already broadcasting dramatic air attacks on Baghdad. The war was precipitated by Iraq's invasion of Kuwait on August 2, 1990.]

2   Our strategy for going after this army is very, very simple. First, we are going to cut it off, and then, we are going to kill it.

—COLIN POWELL, press conference, Jan. 23, 1991

[Gen. Powell was referring to the Iraqi army, considered at that time to be the fourth-greatest army in the world.]

3   Seven months ago, America and the world drew a line in the sand. We declared that aggression against Kuwait would not stand, and tonight America and the world have kept their word.

—GEORGE BUSH,
Feb. 27, 1991

[Allied forces, led by the U.S., drove Iraqi troops out of Kuwait and back toward Baghdad. When the war ended, however, Iraqi leader Saddam Hussein was still in power, supported by a considerable military presence.]

4   Saddam Hussein still has his job. Do you?   —ANONYMOUS, bumper sticker,
1991–92

[The nation was in a recession, with high unemployment. In the presidential election, Democratic challenger Bill Clinton ousted Pres. George Bush.]

H

HABIT & CUSTOM

Customs represent the experiences of mankind. [1]
>—HENRY WARD BEECHER, *Proverbs from Plymouth Pulpit*, 1887

Habit is . . . the enormous flywheel of society, its most precious conservative [2]
agent. It alone is what keep us all within the bounds of ordinance.
>—WILLIAM JAMES, *The Principles of Psychology*, 1890

Nothing so needs reforming as other people's habits. [3]
>—MARK TWAIN, *Pudd'nhead Wilson's Calendar*,
>in *Pudd'nhead Wilson*, 1894

Most of the things we do, we do for no better reason than that our fathers have [4]
done them or our neighbors do them, and the same is true of a larger part than
what we suspect of what we think. —OLIVER WENDELL HOLMES, JR., speech,
>Boston, Jan. 8, 1897

Habit is stronger than reason. —GEORGE SANTAYANA, *Interpretations of* [5]
>*Poetry and Religion*, 1900

For the ordinary business of life, an ounce of habit is worth a pound of in- [6]
tellect. —THOMAS B. REED, speech at Bowdoin College, Maine,
>July 25, 1902

Laws are sand, customs are rock. Law can be evaded and punishment escaped, [7]
but an openly transgressed custom brings sure punishment.
>—MARK TWAIN, *The Gorky Incident*, 1906
[See also Adlai Stevenson below.]

Habit is far stronger than the lessons of experience. [8]
>—HELEN MCCLOY, *Cue for Murder*, 1942
[The speaker is Dr. Basil Willing, a psychiatrist-detective.]

Laws are never as effective as habits. —ADLAI STEVENSON, speech, [9]
>New York City, August 28, 1952

1   I don't have any bad habits. They might be bad habits for other people, but they're all right for me.   —EUBIE BLAKE, *Eubie*, 1979

HAPPINESS   *See also* DESIRES; PLEASURE & HEDONISM; UTOPIA

2   My heart is like a feather and my spirits are dancing.
—ABIGAIL ADAMS, letter, April 1776
[She was happy because she had just received a packet of letters—"a feast to me"—from her husband, John.]

3   Human felicity is produced not so much by great pieces of good fortune that seldom happen, as by little advantages that occur every day.
—BENJAMIN FRANKLIN, *Autobiography* [1791]

4   It is neither wealth nor splendor, but tranquillity and occupation, which give happiness.   —THOMAS JEFFERSON, letter to Mrs. A. S. Marks, 1788

5   Little deeds of kindness,
Little words of love
Help to make earth happy
Like the heavens above.
—JULIA CARNEY, *Little Things*, 1845
[More at DETAILS & OTHER SMALL THINGS.]

6   Happiness remains the only sanction of life; where happiness fails, existence remains a mad and lamentable experiment.
—GEORGE SANTAYANA, *The Life of Reason*, 1905–1906

7   That is happiness; to be dissolved into something complete and great.
—WILLA CATHER, *My Ántonia*, 1918
[This line is inscribed on the author's gravestone in Jaffrey, N.H.]

8   We were very tired, we were very merry—
We had gone back and forth all night on the ferry.
—EDNA ST. VINCENT MILLAY, *Recuerdo*,
in *A Few Figs from Thistles*, 1920

9   There are two things to aim at in life: first to get what you want; and, after that, to enjoy it. Only the wisest of mankind achieve the second.
—LOGAN PEARSALL SMITH, *Afterthoughts*, 1931

10 Happiness lies not in the mere possession of money; it lies in the joy of achievement, in the thrill of creative effort.
—FRANKLIN D. ROOSEVELT, First Inaugural Address,
March 4, 1933

11 toujours gai, archy, toujours gai.
—DON MARQUIS, *archy's life of mehitabel*, 1933

12 Somewhere over the rainbow
Bluebirds fly.
Birds fly over the rainbow—
Why then, oh why can't I?   —E. Y. "YIP" HARBURG, *Over the Rainbow*,
song for the movie *The Wizard of Oz*, 1939
[Metro-Goldwyn-Mayer studio executives and the movie's director, Victor

Fleming, wanted to drop the rainbow number—the start of the movie was too slow, they thought. Harburg and composer Harold Arlen protested and Louis B. Mayer finally ruled, "Let the boys have the damn song . . . it can't hurt" (quoted in Harold Meyerson and Ernie Harburg, *Who Put the Rainbow in "The Wizard of Oz"?*, 1993).]

Don't let's ask for the moon! We have the stars!   1
                                   —OLIVE HIGGINS PROUTY, *Now, Voyager*, 1941
[A Bette Davis line in the 1942 movie version.]

Happiness Makes Up in Height for What It Lacks in Length.   2
                                   —ROBERT FROST, poem title, 1942

Happiness is an imaginary condition, formerly often attributed by the living to   3
the dead, now usually attributed by adults to children, and by children to
adults.   —THOMAS SZASZ, *Emotions*,
                                   in *The Second Sin*, 1973

Follow your bliss.   —JOSEPH CAMPBELL, motto, *The Power of Myth*   4
                                   [1988]
[Published the year after Campbell's death. His best known book was *The Hero with a Thousand Faces*, 1949. Some of his ideas are reflected in the mega-movie *Star Wars*, 1977.]

HARDING, WARREN G.

I suppose I ought to be thankful for one thing: that you're a boy. If you'd been   5
born a girl, by this time, every boy in town would have had his way with you.
                                   —GEORGE T. HARDING, attributed
[Harding's father is reported to have said this to his son about 1880, when Warren was fifteen; quoted in Mark Sullivan, *Our Times*, 1935.]

A tin-horn politician with the manner of a rural corn doctor and the mien of a   6
ham doctor.   —H. L. MENCKEN, on Warren Harding, "Lodge,"
                                   Baltimore Evening Sun, June 15, 1920

A fitting representative of the common aspirations of his fellow citizens.   7
                                   —CALVIN COOLIDGE, accepting the vice-presidential nomination,
                                   Republican National Convention, July 27, 1920
[This was as far as Coolidge was willing to go in praise of his party's candidate for president. Harding's own campaign manager, Harry M. Daugherty, predicted that his selection would take place in "a smoke-filled room" and be based more on exhaustion than preference; see POLITICS & POLITICIANS. Daugherty was right, and Harding became known as "everybody's second choice."
   Harding's performance as candidate and president inspired a wealth of creative insults, and he still represents the nadir of presidential competence. In 1981, when consumer advocate Ralph Nader told a reporter, "Ronald Reagan is the most ignorant president since Warren Harding," he meant just about as ignorant as a man can be and still find his way to the Oval Office. Nevertheless, Harding was likeable, and Americans responded to his call for a return to "normalcy," despite the infelicity of the term; see AMERICAN HISTORY: MEMORABLE MOMENTS. Contrary to some accounts, he probably did *not* say in 1921, "When a lot of people are out of work, unemployment results." On the other hand, he evidently invented the ever-useful phrase "Founding Fathers." According to Richard Hanser, in *American Heritage* magazine (June 1970), Harding used the phrase in speeches in 1918, 1920, and most prominently in his inaugural ad-

dress on March 4, 1921: "I must utter my belief in the divine inspiration of the founding fathers."

Harding died suddenly in 1923, and thus missed the unraveling of the Teapot Dome scandal, in which the pervasive corruption of his administration became painfully clear.]

1   He writes the worst English I have ever encountered. It reminds me of a string of wet sponges; it reminds me of tattered washing on the line; it reminds me of stale bean soup, of college yells, of dogs barking idiotically through endless nights. It is so bad that a sort of grandeur creeps into it. It drags itself out of the dark abysm (I was about to write abscess!) of pish, and crawls insanely up to the topmost pinnacle of posh. It is rumble and bumble. It is flap and doodle. It is balder and dash.   —H. L. MENCKEN, *Baltimore Evening Sun,*
March 7, 1921

2   His speeches left the impression of an army of pompous phrases moving over the landscape in search of an idea. Sometimes these meandering words would actually capture a straggling thought and bear it triumphantly a prisoner in their midst, until it died of servitude and overwork.
—WILLIAM G. McADOO, quoted in Leon A. Harris,
The Fine Art of Political Wit [1964]
[Sen. McAdoo was a leader of the Democratic opposition.]

3   He has a bungalow mind.   —WOODROW WILSON, quoted in Thomas A. Bailey,
Woodrow Wilson and the Great Betrayal [1945]

4   If ever there was a he-harlot, it was this same Warren G. Harding.
—WILLIAM ALLEN WHITE, attributed, c. 1926

5   the only man, woman, or child who wrote a
simple declarative sentence with seven grammatical errors
"is dead."   —E. E. CUMMINGS, *the first president to be loved by his,*
in *Viva,* 1931

6   Harding was not a bad man. He was just a slob.
—ALICE ROOSEVELT LONGWORTH,
Crowded Hours, 1933

HASTE V. GOING SLOW   *See also* SPEED

7   Nothing is more vulgar than haste.   —RALPH WALDO EMERSON,
The Conduct of Life, 1860
[More at MANNERS.]

8   No man who is in a hurry is quite civilized.
—WILL DURANT, *What Is Civilization?*

9   If a thing is worth doing, it is worth doing slowly . . . very slowly.
—GYPSY ROSE LEE, in *Leo Rosten's Carnival of Wit,* 1994
[Ms. Lee, née Rose Louise Hovick, was a graceful and intelligent ecdysiast—a thinking man's stripper—though she also is said to have said, "Men aren't attracted to me by my mind, but what I don't mind."]

10   Never hurry and never worry!   —E. B. WHITE, *Charlotte's Web,*
1952
[Charlotte's advice to Wilbur—what a friend!]

HATE
See also POLITICS & POLITICIANS (Henry Adams)

To be loved is to be fortunate, but to be hated is to achieve distinction. 1
—MINNA ANTRIM, *Naked Truth and Veiled Allusions*, 1902

I tell you, there is such a thing as creative hate! 2
—WILLA CATHER, *The Song of the Lark*, 1915

I think I know enough of hate 3
To say that for destruction ice
Is also great
And would suffice. —ROBERT FROST, *Fire and Ice*,
1923

[More at THE WORLD.]

I've played the traitor over and over; 4
I'm a good hater but a bad lover. —ELINOR HOYT WYLIE, *Peregrine*,
in *Collected Poems* [1932]

Fear of something is at the root of hate for others, and hate within will even- 5
tually destroy the hater. —GEORGE WASHINGTON CARVER,
George Washington Carver: Man of God, 1954

Hatred paralyzes life; love releases it. —MARTIN LUTHER KING, JR., 6
Strength to Love, 1963

[More at LOVE.]

Hate cannot drive out hate. Only love can do that. 7
—MARTIN LUTHER KING, JR., *Where Do We Go from Here:
Chaos or Community?*, 1967

The price of hating other human beings is loving oneself less. 8
—ELDRIDGE CLEAVER, *On Becoming*, in *Soul on Ice*, 1968

Those who hate you don't win unless you hate them—and then you destroy 9
yourself. —RICHARD M. NIXON, good-bye remarks to his White House
staff the day after resigning as president, August 9, 1974

HAVES & HAVE-NOTS
See CAPITALISM & CAPITAL V. LABOR;
RICH & POOR, WEALTH & POVERTY

HAWAII

That peaceful land, that beautiful land, that far-off home of solitude and soft 10
idleness, and repose, and dreams, where life is one long slumberous Sabbath,
the climate one long summer day, and the good that die experience no change,
for they but fall asleep in one heaven and wake up in another.
—MARK TWAIN, speech, April 1889
[The occasion was a dinner in honor of a baseball team captained by Albert
Spalding that had returned from a worldwide tour via what were then the
Sandwich Islands—"these enchanted islands," as Twain called them at the
time of his visit there in 1866. Similarly, in a letter to H. P. Wood, secretary of
the Hawaii Promotion Committee, Twain identified Hawaii as "the loveliest
fleet of islands that lies anchored in any ocean." See also Twain on baseball at
SPORTS.]

1   Mr. President, we want those islands. We want them because they are the step-
    ping stone across the sea. Necessary to our safety, they are necessary to our
    commerce.   —HENRY M. TELLER, addressing Pres. William McKinley,
                                  1898
    [Sen. Teller was a Republican from Colorado.]

2   We need Hawaii just as much and a good deal more than we did California. It
    is manifest destiny.   —WILLIAM MCKINLEY, remark to his aide
                                  George Cortelyou, 1898
    [In this year, Hawaii was annexed, a move favored by Pres. McKinley.]

3   The Hawaiian people have been from time immemorial lovers of poetry and
    music, and have been apt in improvising historic poems, songs of love, and
    chants of worship.   —LYDIA KAMEKEHA LILIUOKALANI,
                                  Hawaii's Story, 1898
    [For an example of Hawaiian law in poetry, see Kamehameha I at PRAYERS.]

4   In what other land save this one is the commonest form of greeting not "Good
    day," nor "How d'ye do," but "Love"? That greeting is *Aloha*—love, I love you,
    my love to you. . . . It is a positive affirmation of the warmth of one's own
    heart-giving.   —JACK LONDON,
                                  My Hawaiian Aloha, 1916

5   Hawaii is a paradise—and I can never cease proclaiming it; but I must append
    one word of qualification: *Hawaii is a paradise for the well-to-do.*
                                  —*Ibid.*

6   Hawaii is the only place I know where they lay flowers on you while you are
    alive.   —WILL ROGERS, in Alex Ayres, ed.,
                                  The Wit and Wisdom of Will Rogers [1993]

7   The spiritual destiny of Hawaii has been shared by a Calvinist theory of pa-
    ternalism enacted by the descendants of missionaries who carried it there: a
    will to do good for unfortunates regardless of what the unfortunates thought
    about it.   —FRANCINE DU PLESSIX GRAY, *Hawaii:
                                  The Sugar-Coated Fortress,* 1972

Motto

8   *Ua mau ke ea o ka aina i ka pono.*
            The life of the land is perpetuated by righteousness.

HEALTH

See also ALCOHOL & DRINKING; DOCTORS &
MEDICINE; FOOD, WINE, & EATING; ILLNESS &
REMEDIES; PHYSICAL FITNESS; TOBACCO

9   To lengthen thy life lessen thy meals.   —BENJAMIN FRANKLIN, *Poor Richard's
                                  Almanack,* Oct. 1733

10 Early to bed and early to rise, makes a man healthy, wealthy, and wise.
                                  —BENJAMIN FRANKLIN, *Poor Richard's
                                  Almanack,* Oct. 1735
    [James Thurber suggested, "Early to rise and early to bed makes a man healthy,
    wealthy, and dead," *The Shrike and the Chipmunks,* in *Fables for Our Times,*
    1940. Rarely is Thurber bested on his own ground, but George Ade has a lighter

touch with, "Early to bed and early to rise, and you never meet any prominent people," quoted in Carl Sandburg, *The Proverbs of a People,* in *Good Morning, America,* 1928.]

Nine men in ten are suicides.   1
> —BENJAMIN FRANKLIN, *Poor Richard's Almanack,* 1749

Measure your health by your sympathy with morning and spring.   2
> —HENRY DAVID THOREAU, *Journal,* Feb. 25, 1859

The first wealth is health.   —RALPH WALDO EMERSON, *Power,*   3
> in *The Conduct of Life,* 1860

[For another quote on wealth and health, see John Greenleaf Whittier at COUNTRY LIFE & PEOPLE.]

If you mean to keep as well as possible, the less you think about your health   4
the better.   —OLIVER WENDELL HOLMES, SR.,
> *Over the Teacups,* 1891

He had much experience of physicians, and said, "The only way to keep your   5
health is to eat what you don't want, drink what you don't like, and do what
you'd druther not."   —MARK TWAIN, *Pudd'nhead Wilson's New Calendar,*
> in *Following the Equator,* 1897

It's not the men in my life that counts, it's the life in my men.   6
> —MAE WEST, *I'm No Angel,* 1933

Live clean, think clean, and don't go to burlesque shows.   7
> —CHARLES ATLAS, saying

[Atlas was the most famous bodybuilder in the world from about 1925 into the 1950s. For more, see under Charles Roman at ADVERTISING, ADVERTISING SLOGANS, & PUBLICITY.]

Avoid fried meats which angry up the blood. If your stomach disputes you, lie   8
down and pacify it with cool thoughts.
> —LEROY "SATCHEL" PAIGE, *How to Stay Young,* 1953

[More at WISDOM, WORDS OF.]

[The key to longevity:] Keep breathing.   9
> —SOPHIE TUCKER, newspaper reports, Jan. 13, 1964

If I'd known I was going to live this long, I'd have taken better care of myself. 10
> —EUBIE BLAKE, attributed

[A popular saying, widely attributed. Blake, a legendary ragtime pianist and composer, performed into his nineties. Born in 1883, the son of former slaves, he lived to be 100—old enough to see the Broadway musical based on his life, *Eubie!,* produced in 1979.

The saying was also used by the great Yankee slugger Mickey Mantle, who came from a family affected by Hodgkin's disease. Many of the males in the Mantle family died young, including his father, at age thirty-nine; a son, at age thirty-six; his grandfather and two uncles. Mantle was a famous carouser, and decades of heavy drinking and cancer killed him in 1995 at age sixty-three.]

Slender people bury the dead.   —EILEEN FORD, on *The Dick Cavett Show,* 11
> quoted in Michael Gross, *Model* [1995]

[Ford runs a famous agency for models. See also Barbara Paley at MONEY.]

HEART

See also LOVE

1   The heart is like a viper, hissing and spitting poison at God.
—JONATHAN EDWARDS, *The Freedom of the Will*, 1754

2   The heart has its sabbaths and jubilees in which the world appears as a hymeneal feast, and all natural sounds and the circle of the seasons are erotic odes and dances.   —RALPH WALDO EMERSON,
Love, in *Essays: First Series*, 1841
[For Emerson on God's temple in the heart, see RELIGION.]

3   The heart is forever inexperienced.
—HENRY DAVID THOREAU, *A Week on the Concord
and Merrimack Rivers*, 1849

4   It is the heart, and not the brain.
That to the highest doth attain.   —HENRY WADSWORTH LONGFELLOW,
The Building of the Ship, 1849

5   What other dungeon is so dark as one's own heart!
—NATHANIEL HAWTHORNE, *The House of the Seven Gables*, 1851
[More at SELF.]

6   The holiest of holidays are those
Kept by ourselves in silence and apart;
The secret anniversaries of the heart.
—HENRY WADSWORTH LONGFELLOW, *Holidays*

7   The heart hath its own memory, like the mind.
—HENRY WADSWORTH LONGFELLOW, *From My Arm-chair*, 1879
[More at CHARITY & PHILANTHROPY.]

8   Pity me that the heart that is slow to learn
What the swift mind beholds at every turn.
—EDNA ST. VINCENT MILLAY, *Sonnets*, 1941

9   One should have a heart for every fate.
—EMANUEL CELLER, remark to the press, 1972
[Mr. Celler, after fifty years in the U.S. House of Representatives, was defeated in an upset by political newcomer Elizabeth Holtzman.]

HEAVENS, THE

See NATURE: THE HEAVENS, THE SKY

HEDONISM

See PLEASURE & HEDONISM

HELL

10   Easy it is for God, when he pleases, to cast his enemies down to Hell.
—JONATHAN EDWARDS, *Sinners in the Hands
of an Angry God*, sermon, July 8, 1741

11   If there is no Hell, a good many preachers are obtaining money under false pretenses.
—WILLIAM A. "BILLY" SUNDAY
[Billy Sunday, who died in 1936, was a mesmerizing revivalist preacher. Wher-

ever he pitched his tent, the crowds would come. H. L. Mencken included this adage in his dictionary of quotations. He also cites the American proverb just below.]

Cheer up, there ain't no hell.   —ANONYMOUS, American proverb   1

To work hard, to live hard, to die hard, and then to go to hell after all would be   2
too damned hard.   —CARL SANDBURG,
The People, Yes, 1936

Hell is oneself.   3
T. S. ELIOT, *The Cocktail Party*, 1949
[Robert Lowell said almost the same thing; see below. By contrast, Jean-Paul Sartre claimed "Hell is others," *No Exit*, 1944.]

I myself am hell.   4
—ROBERT LOWELL, *Skunk Hour*, 1959
[More at MADNESS.]

HEROES   *See also* VIRTUE

Self-trust is the essence of heroism.   —RALPH WALDO EMERSON, *Heroism*,   5
in *Essays: First Series*, 1841

Every hero becomes a bore at last.   6
—RALPH WALDO EMERSON, *Representative Men*, 1850

A hero cannot be a hero unless in an heroic world.   7
—NATHANIEL HAWTHORNE, *Journals*, May 7, 1850

Like an armed warrior, like a plumed knight.   8
—ROBERT INGERSOLL, nomination speech
for Sen. James G. Blaine, Republican National Convention,
Cincinnati, 1876
[Democrats ridiculed this characterization of Sen. Blaine, an important politician, but possibly corrupt, and certainly not a knight on horseback. When he was nominated again in 1884, mugwump Republicans supported the Democratic candidate, Grover Cleveland; for more on *mugwump*, see LANGUAGE & WORDS. See also "the happy warrior" below.]

The chief business of the nation, as a nation, is the setting up of heroes, mainly   9
bogus.   —H. L. MENCKEN, *Prejudices: Third Series*, 1923

He is the happy warrior of the political battlefield.   10
—FRANKLIN D. ROOSEVELT,
nominating Al Smith for president,
Democratic National Convention, June 26, 1924
[Roosevelt was alluding to Wordsworth's *Character of the Happy Warrior*, 1807: "Who is this happy Warrior? Who is he/ That every man in arms should wish to be?" In a letter to *The New York Times*, which ran on December 22, 1994, John Karol of Orford, N.H., maintained that credit for the "happy warrior" sobriquet should be given to Judge Joseph Proskauer, who managed Smith's New York gubernatorial campaigns in 1920 and 1922. Roosevelt was apparently wary of using literary references. Smith held on for a record 103 ballots at the convention before losing to John W. Davis, who was wiped out by Calvin Coolidge in November.]

1   This thing about being a hero, about the main thing to do is to know when to
die. Prolonged life has ruined more men than it ever made.
—WILL ROGERS, *The Autobiography of Will Rogers* [1949]

2   The hero is a feeling, a man seen
As if the eye was an emotion,
As if in seeing we saw our feeling
In the object seen.   —WALLACE STEVENS, *To a Hero in a Time of Crisis*

3   In the spring of '27, something bright and alien flashed across the sky, a young
Minnesotan who seemed to have nothing to do with his generation did a heroic
thing, and for a moment, people set down their glasses in country clubs and
speakeasies and thought of their old best dreams.
—F. SCOTT FITZGERALD, on Charles Lindbergh,
quoted in *Bartlett's*, 16th edition

4   Show me a hero and I will write you a tragedy.
—F. SCOTT FITZGERALD, *Notebooks* [1978]

5   A fiery horse with the speed of light, a cloud of dust, and a hearty, "Hi-yo,
Silver!"   —FRAN STRYKER, announcer's introduction,
The Lone Ranger radio show, March 11, 1933
[The show first aired on February 2, but it took the writer several weeks to
come up with the signature shout. "Hi-yo, Silver!"]

6   Faster than a speeding bullet! More powerful than a locomotive! Able to leap
tall buildings in a single bound! Look! Up in the sky! It's a bird! It's a plane! It's
Superman!   —GEORGE LOTHER, program introduction,
Superman radio show, first broadcast, Feb. 12, 1940
[Superman was created in 1934 by Jerry Siegel, a graduate of Glenville High
School in Cleveland who had little luck with girls. The fantasy character was
also luckless—but only as Clark Kent. Siegel's partner in a would-be career in
comics was Joe Shuster, who improved the character with tights, a cape, and a
handsome face. After moving to New York, and meeting hard times, they sold
the character in March 1938 to DC Comics for $130. In June, the first Super-
man comic book appeared, and it was immediately obvious that the young
men had made a disastrous mistake. They were never able to gain a share of Superman's earnings. Siegel, a clerk-typist, died in 1996. Shuster, a messenger,
died in 1992.]

7   No hero is mortal till he dies.
—W. H. AUDEN, *A Short Ode to a Philologist*, 1962

8   Down these mean streets must go a man who is not himself mean; who is neither tarnished nor afraid.
—RAYMOND CHANDLER, *The Simple Art of Murder*, 1950
[Chandler also said of his hero-detective: "He must be, to use a rather weathered phrase, a man of honor, by instinct and inevitability, and certainly without saying it. He must be the best man in his world, and a good enough man for
any world."]

9   The dead hero becomes immortal. He becomes more vital with the passage of
time.   —DANIEL J. BOORSTIN,
The Image, 1962
[Distinguishing between the hero and the celebrity, Boorstin wrote, "The hero
created himself; the celebrity is created by the media."]

Every hero mirrors the time and place in which he lives. He must reflect men's 1
innermost hopes and beliefs in a public way.
    —MARSHALL FISHWICK, *The Hero, American Style,* 1969

One must think like a hero to behave like a merely decent human being. 2
    —MAY SARTON, *Journal of a Solitude,* 1973,
        used as the epigraph to John Le Carré's *Russia House*

A hero is a man who would argue with the gods, and so awakens devils to con- 3
test his vision.   —NORMAN MAILER, Special Preface, First Berkely Edition,
        The Presidential Papers, 1976

No man is a hero to his septic tank cleaner. 4
    —DAVID OWEN, *The Walls Around Us,* 1991
[The theme on which this varies is "No man is a hero to his valet," Anne Bigot
de Cornuel, *Lettres de Mme. Aissé,* August 13, 1728.]

Heroes are pretty well all washed up in America these days. 5
    —RUSSELL BAKER, column on Washington, D.C.,
        Mayor Marion S. Barry, Jr., quoted by Marilyn Stasio,
        New York Times Book Review, Oct. 14, 1990.

HIGH POSITION: *See also* GOVERNMENT; CONGRESS;
RULERS & LEADERS   POLITICS & POLITICIANS; POWER;
                              PRESIDENCY, THE; VICE PRESIDENCY, THE

There are men, who by their sympathetic attractions, carry nations with them, 6
and lead the activity of the human race.
    —RALPH WALDO EMERSON, *Power,* in *The Conduct of Life,* 1860

All kings is mostly rapscallions. 7
    —MARK TWAIN, *The Adventures of Huckleberry Finn,* 1885

Every man who has attained to high position is a sincere believer of the sur- 8
vival of the fittest.   —PHILANDER C. JOHNSON,
        Senator Sorghum's Primer of Politics, 1906

The only emperor is the emperor of ice-cream. 9
    —WALLACE STEVENS, *The Emperor of Ice-Cream,* 1923

A king can stand people's fighting, but he can't last long if people start 10
thinking.   —WILL ROGERS, *The Autobiography of Will Rogers* [1949]

My first qualification for this great office is my monumental personal in- 11
gratitude.   —FIORELLO LA GUARDIA,
        comment on importuning office seekers, 1934
[La Guardia, of course, was mayor of New York. The quote is from Ernest Cu-
neo, *Life with Fiorello,* 1995]

The real leader has no need to lead—he is content to point the way. 12
    —HENRY MILLER, *The Wisdom of the Heart,* 1941

The final test of a leader is that he leaves behind him in other men the convic- 13
tion and the will to carry on.   —WALTER LIPPMAN, *Roosevelt Has Gone,*
        in the *New York Herald Tribune,*
        April 14, 1945

1   All very successful commanders are prima donnas and must be so treated.
—GEORGE S. PATTON, JR., *War As I Knew It*, 1947

2   You cannot be a leader, and ask other people to follow you, unless you are willing to follow, too.
—SAM RAYBURN, saying
[This is from *The Leadership of Speaker Sam Rayburn, Collected Tributes of his Congressional Colleagues*, a compilation of tributes paid him on June 12, 1961, when he had served as Speaker of the House for sixteen years and 273 days—twice as long as any predecessor.]

HISTORY   *See also* PAST, THE

3   I consider the true history of the American Revolution, and the establishment of our present Constitution, as lost forever; and nothing but misrepresentations, or partial accounts of it, will ever be recovered.
—JOHN ADAMS, quoted in Lt. Francis Hall, *Travels in Canada and the United States in 1816 and 1817*, 1818
[In particular, Adams referred to the lack of records of speeches in Congress from 1774 to 1776. A century later, Robert E. Lee (see below) and Walt Whitman (see CIVIL WAR) expressed similar skepticism, doubting that the truth about the Civil War would ever be told.]

4   A morsel of genuine history is a thing so rare as to be always valuable.
—THOMAS JEFFERSON, letter to John Adams, Sept. 8, 1817

5   History fades into fable; fact becomes clouded with doubt and controversy; the inscription molders from the tablet; the statue falls from the pedestal. Columns, arches, pyramids, what are they but heaps of sand; and their epitaphs, but characters written in the dust?
—WASHINGTON IRVING, *The Sketch Book*, 1820

6   I am ashamed to see what a shallow village tale our so-called history is.
—RALPH WALDO EMERSON, *History*, in *Essays; First Series*, 1841

7   Fellow citizens, we cannot escape history. We . . . will be remembered in spite of ourselves.   —ABRAHAM LINCOLN,
second annual message to Congress, Dec. 1, 1862

8   It is history that teaches us to hope.
—ROBERT E. LEE, letter to Charles Marshall, c. 1866

9   The time is not come for impartial history. If the truth were told just now, it would not be credited.   —ROBERT E. LEE, c. 1868, quoted in David MaCrae,
The Americans at Home, 1870
[Similar to Walt Whitman's, "The real war will never get in the books"; see CIVIL WAR. See also Philip Graham at THE PRESS.]

10 Bismarck, when asked what was the most important fact in modern history, replied: "The fact that North America speaks English."
—GURNEY BENHAM, *Benham's Book of Quotations* [1948]

11 *History, n.* An account mostly false, of events mostly unimportant, which are brought about by rulers, mostly knaves, and soldiers, mostly fools.
—AMBROSE BIERCE, *The Devil's Dictionary*, 1906

The history of every country begins in the heart of a man or a woman.   1
—WILLA CATHER, *O Pioneers!*, 1913

History is more or less bunk.   2
—HENRY FORD, quoted in the *Chicago Tribune*,
May 25, 1916
[Ford made this comment in an interview with journalist Charles N. Wheeler.
"Records of old wars mean nothing to me," he said. "History is more or less
bunk. It's tradition."]

History has many cunning passages, contrived corridors   3
And issues.   —T. S. ELIOT, *Gerontion*, 1920

The history of the world is the record of a man in quest of his daily bread and   4
butter.   —HENDRIK WILLEM VAN LOON,
The Story of Mankind, 1921

Upon this point, a page of history is worth a volume of logic.   5
—OLIVER WENDELL HOLMES, JR.,
New York Trust Co. v. Eisner, 1921

All history is modern history.   6
—WALLACE STEVENS, *Adagia*, in *Opus Posthumous* [1957]

Men make history and not the other way around.   7
—HARRY S. TRUMAN, quoted in *This Week* magazine,
Feb. 22, 1959
[See Abraham Lincoln under FATE for a different view.]

The only thing new in the world is the history you don't know.   8
—HARRY S. TRUMAN,
quoted by Merle Miller in *Plain Speaking* [1982]

History consists of the inside of the outside.   9
—HOWARD NEMEROV, *The Homecoming Game*, 1957
[Also stated, in the opening scene, as: "The historian examines the outsides of
past events, with a view to discovering what their insides were."]

Man is a history-making creature.   —W. H. AUDEN, *The Dyer's Hand*,   10
1962
[More at THE PAST.]

History is . . . very chancy.   11
—SAMUEL ELIOT MORISON,
The Oxford History of the American People, 1965

History is a guide to navigation in perilous times.   12
—DAVID MCCULLOUGH, quoted in Harold L. Klawans,
Life, Death and In Between, 1992

The main thing history teaches us that history teaches us—nothing.   13
—TRUMAN CAPOTE, 1975, quoted in Jay Presson Allen,
Tru [1989]
[Actor Robert Morse, who re-created Capote in this play, pronounced "noth-
ing" emphatically as "nuttin!"]

HOLIDAYS

See also CHRISTMAS; INDEPENDENCE DAY; NEW YEAR; THANKSGIVING

1   The holiest of holidays are those
    Kept by ourselves in silence and apart.
                    —HENRY WADSWORTH LONGFELLOW, *Holidays*
    [More at THE HEART.]

2   Every holiday ought to be named Labor Day.
                    —WILL ROGERS, in Alex Ayres, ed.,
                        The Wit and Wisdom of Will Rogers [1993]

HOME

See also FAMILY; PARTING (Lincoln)

3   A man's house is his castle.
                    —JAMES OTIS, argument on the Writs of Assistance, Boston, 1761
    [More at PRIVACY.]

4   Abstracted from home, I know no happiness in this world.
                    —THOMAS JEFFERSON, letter to Lt. de Unger, 1780

5   'Mid pleasures and palaces though we may roam,
    Be it ever so humble, there's no place like home.
                    —JOHN HOWARD PAYNE, *Home, Sweet Home,*
                        song for the opera *Clari, or The Maid of Milan,* 1823
    [The song, with music by Henry R. Bishop, was popular for decades and was
    used in concert by the most popular sopranos of the era—Adelina Patti, Jenny
    Lind, Dame Nellie Melba.]

6   Home is the kingdom and love is the king.
                    —WILLIAM RANKIN DURYEA, *A Song for Hearth and Home,*
                        in the *New York Home Journal,* 1866

7   As the homes, so the state.
                    —A. BRONSON ALCOTT, *Tablets,* 1868
    [Alcott, an educator and reformer, was the father of Louisa May Alcott.]

8   The best thing about traveling is going home.
                    —CHARLES DUDLEY WARNER, *The Whims of Travel,*
                        Sept. 12, 1875
    [More at TRAVEL.]

9   Eden is that old-fashioned house
    We dwell in every day
    Without suspecting our abode
    Until we drive away.   —EMILY DICKINSON, poem no. 1657, no date

10 [Husband:] "Home is the place where, when you have to go there,
    They have to take you in."
    [Wife:] "I should have called it
    Something you somehow haven't to deserve."
                    —ROBERT FROST, *The Death of the Hired Man,* 1914

11 Home is where the heart is.   —ANONYMOUS, in Elbert Hubbard,
                        A Thousand and One Epigrams, 1914
    [An old saying, sometimes attributed to the Roman writer Pliny.]

It takes a heap o' livin' in a house t' make it home.   1
                      —EDGAR A. GUEST, *Home,*
              in *The Collected Works of Edgar A. Guest,* 1934
[Ogden Nash pointed out that to make a house a home also "takes a heap o'
payin'," *A Heap o' Livin'.*]

You Can't Go Home Again.   2
                          —THOMAS WOLFE, book title, 1940
[For going home to Pocatello, see CITIES (Pocatello).]

Home is where one starts from.   3
                      —T. S. ELIOT, *Four Quartets: East Coker,* 1940
[Eliot started in St. Louis and eventually attended Harvard University. In 1913,
while he was traveling abroad on a postgraduate fellowship, war erupted. He
could not get back to the U.S., and he became in time thoroughly English.]

HONESTY   *See also* DISHONESTY & LIES; EXPEDIENCY;
                                        HONOR; TRUTH; VIRTUE

Of more worth is one honest man to society, and in the eyes of God, than all   4
the crowned ruffians that ever lived.
                      —THOMAS PAINE, *Common Sense,* 1776

I hope I shall always possess firmness and virtue enough to maintain (what I   5
consider the most enviable of all titles) the character of an "Honest Man."
                      —GEORGE WASHINGTON, letter to Alexander Hamilton,
                      August 28, 1788
[See also below.]

I hold the maxim no less applicable to public than to private affairs, that hon-   6
esty is always the best policy.
                      —GEORGE WASHINGTON, Farewell Address, Sept. 17, 1796
[The maxim is an old one; Cervantes, for example, used it in *Don Quixote.*
Washington stood by this principle, and his reputation for honesty inspired the
fable promulgated by an early biographer, Mason Lock "Parson" Weems, that
as a boy he cut down a cherry tree and confessed his guilt, saying, "I cannot tell
a lie."
    Thanks to his invariable integrity, Washington was asked by friends and
neighbors to serve as executor of their estates—so many that his own estate
suffered as a result.]

One great error is that we suppose mankind more honest than they are.   7
                      —ALEXANDER HAMILTON, speech, Constitutional Convention,
                      Philadelphia, June 22, 1787

Men are disposed to live honestly, if the means of doing so are open to them.   8
                      —THOMAS JEFFERSON, letter to M. Barré de Marbois,
                      June 14, 1817

Nothing astonishes men so much as common sense and plain dealing.   9
                      —RALPH WALDO EMERSON, *Art,* in *Essays: First Series,* 1841

There is no well-defined boundary line between honesty and dishonesty.   10
                      —O. HENRY, *Bexar Scrip No. 2692,* in *Rolling Stones,* 1912

You can't cheat an honest man.   —W. C. FIELDS, saying and film title, 1939   11

HONOR

See also HEROES; HONESTY; VIRTUE

1   I would lay down my life for America, but I cannot trifle with my honor.
—JOHN PAUL JONES, letter to A. Livingston, Sept. 4, 1777

2   When faith is lost, when honor dies,
The man is dead!
—JOHN GREENLEAF WHITTIER, *Ichabod,* 1850
[The poem is a denunciation of Daniel Webster for supporting the Compromise of 1850, which included a more stringent fugitive slave law.]

3   The louder he talked of his honor, the faster we counted our spoons.
—RALPH WALDO EMERSON, *Worship,* in *The Conduct of Life,* 1860

4   Honor knows no statute of limitations.
—SAMUEL E. MOFFETT, in *Mark Twain's Autobiography* [1924]
[Writing in 1909, Twain said that this "happy remark" by his late nephew had "traveled around the globe." Twain introduced the comment in connection with his account of the collapse of his publishing company. Friends urged Twain to declare personal bankruptcy, but he felt morally bound to assume the firm's debts. In sorting out his affairs, he was aided greatly by Henry H. Rogers, a Standard Oil lawyer who belied his cutthroat reputation on Wall Street by telling Twain: "Business has its laws and customs and they are justified; but a literary man's reputation is his life; he can afford to be money poor, but he cannot afford to be character poor; you must earn the cent per cent, and pay it."]

5   The nation's honor is dearer than the nation's comfort; yes, than the nation's life itself.   —WOODROW WILSON, speech, Jan. 26, 1919

6   A man of honor, by instinct and inevitability.
—RAYMOND CHANDLER, *The Simple Art of Murder,* 1950
[More at HEROES.]

HOPE

See also OPTIMISM & PESSIMISM

7   He that lives upon hope will die fasting.
—BENJAMIN FRANKLIN, "Preface: Courteous Reader,"
Poor Richard's Almanack, 1758
[Or, in the adult version: "He that lives upon hope, dies farting," *Poor Richard's Almanack,* 1736.]

8   Hope is the thing with feathers—
That perches in the soul—
And sings the tune without the words—
And never stops—at all.
—EMILY DICKINSON,
poem no. 254, c. 1861

9   Hope is a strange invention—
A patent of the heart—
In unremitting action
Yet never wearing out.   —EMILY DICKINSON, poem no. 1392, c. 1877

10   Hope is the only universal liar who never loses his reputation for veracity.
—ROBERT G. INGERSOLL, speech, Manhattan Liberal Club,
printed in *Truth-Seeker,* weekly periodical, Feb. 28, 1892

There is nothing so well known as that we should not expect something for   1
nothing—but we all do and call it Hope.
—EDGAR WATSON HOWE, Country Town Sayings, 1911
[A Kansas newspaperman, aphorist, and novelist, Howe was known as "The
Sage of Potato Hill."]

When hope is taken away from a people, moral degeneration follows swiftly   2
after.   —PEARL S. BUCK, letter to The New York Times, Nov. 15, 1941

What man is strong enough to reject the possibility of hope?   3
—PAUL AUSTER, The Locked Room, 1986

HOSPITALITY   *See also* GUESTS; MANNERS

Hospitality consists in a little fire, a little food, and an immense quiet.   4
—RALPH WALDO EMERSON, Journal, 1856

When an American says, "Come and see me," he means it.   5
—WILKIE COLLINS
[Collins, one of the originators of the modern mystery novel, was one of the
few 19th-century travelers in the U.S. who had nice things to say about the
young country. This quote is cited in Catherine Peters, The King of Inventors:
A Life of Wilkie Collins, Princeton University Press, 1993.]

Why don't you come up sometime, 'n see me?   6
—MAE WEST, She Done Him Wrong, 1933
[Essentially the same line is in her play Diamond Lil, 1928.]

I hate cocktail parties. They're for people who're not good enough to invite for   7
dinner—then they stay to dinner.
—ELSA MAXWELL, quoted in a letter to The New York Times
from Harvard Hollenberg of New York City, Dec. 22, 1989

HUMANS &   *See also* DIFFERENCES; DREAMS & SLEEP (Emerson);
HUMAN NATURE   INDIVIDUALITY & INDIVIDUALISM;
                                               PEOPLE, THE

Men and melons are hard to know.   8
—BENJAMIN FRANKLIN, Poor Richard's Almanack, 1733
[See also Franklin below and at HYPOCRISY.]

Man: A tool-making animal.   9
—BENJAMIN FRANKLIN, quoted by James Boswell,
entry for April 7, 1778, Life of Johnson [1791]
[Boswell told Samuel Johnson that he thought Dr. Franklin's definition was a
good one, but the great lexicographer disagreed, "But many a man never made a
tool," he objected, "and suppose a man without arms, he could not make a tool."
Nevertheless, Franklin deserves credit for expressing the basic idea long before
the better-known statement by Thomas Carlyle: "Man is a tool-using animal. . . . Without tools he is nothing, with tools he is all," Sartor Resartus,
1833–34. In our own time, humorist Tim Allen has observed, "Man is the only
animal to borrow tools," cited by Robert L. Welsch, Natural History, April 1994.]

In this world, a man must be either anvil or hammer.   10
—HENRY WADSWORTH LONGFELLOW,
The Story of Brother Bernardus, in Hyperion, 1839

1   I am a parcel of vain strivings tied
    By a chance bond together.   —HENRY DAVID THOREAU, *Sic Vita*, 1841

2   Mankind are earthen jugs with spirits in them.
                              —NATHANIEL HAWTHORNE, notebook entry, 1842,
                              in *Passages from the American Notebooks* [1868]

3   The savage in man is never quite eradicated.
                              —HENRY DAVID THOREAU, *Journal*, 1859

4   Man is everywhere a disturbing agent. Whenever he plants his foot, the har-
    monies of nature are turned to discords.
                              —GEORGE PERKINS MARSH, *Man and Nature*, 1864
    [Marsh was a lawyer, scholar, politician, and diplomat—minister to Turkey
    and the first U.S. minister to Italy. He was also a pioneer in conservation,
    whose work took hold and flourished in his native state, Vermont.]

5   Be ashamed to die until you have won some victory for humanity.
                              —HORACE MANN, graduation address,
                              Antioch College, Ohio, 1859

6   Nothing is so hard to understand as that there are human beings in this world
    besides one's self and one's set.
    —WILLIAM DEAN HOWELLS, *Their Wedding Journey*, 1872

7   If you pick up a starving dog and make him prosperous, he will not bite you.
    This is the principal difference between a dog and a man.
                              —MARK TWAIN, *Pudd'nhead Wilson's Calendar*,
                              in *Pudd'nhead Wilson*, 1894

8   The deepest principle of human nature is the craving to be appreciated.
                              —WILLIAM JAMES, letter, April 6, 1896
    [This is from Professor James's thank-you note to Radcliffe students in Philoso-
    phy 2A, who had presented him with an azalea plant. The gift made him realize
    that he had omitted this "deepest principle" from his classic *Principles of Psy-
    chology* because, as he told the students, "I had never had it gratified till now."]

9   Man is the only animal that blushes. Or needs to.
                              —MARK TWAIN, *Pudd'nhead Wilson's New Calendar*,
                              in *Following the Equator*, 1897

10 You tell me whar a man gits his corn-pone, en I'll tell you what his 'pinions is.
                              —MARK TWAIN, *Corn-Pone Opinions*, 1901
    [In this reminiscence, Twain is quoting Jerry, a young slave, whose eloquence
    deeply impressed the even younger Twain, who was about fifteen. Jerry's point
    was that people adopt the views held by the majority of those around them. In
    retrospect, Twain decided that the process was profound and unconscious. "We
    are creatures of outside influences; as a rule we do not think, only imitate,"
    Twain concluded. "Broadly speaking, corn-pone stands for self-approval. Self-
    approval is acquired mainly from the approval of other people. The result is
    conformity." Similarly in his autobiography, Twain wrote: "In the matter of
    slavish imitation, man is the monkey's superior all the time. The average man
    is destitute of independence of opinion."]

11 Herein lies the tragedy of the age: . . . that men know so little of men.
                              —W. E. B. DU BOIS, *The Souls of Black Folk*, 1903

Man, n. An animal so lost in rapturous contemplation of what he thinks he is 1
as to overlook what he indubitably ought to be. His chief occupation is exter-
mination of other animals and his own species, which, however, multiplies
with such insistent rapidity as to infest the whole habitable earth and Canada.
—AMBROSE BIERCE, *The Devil's Dictionary*, 1906

There is no indispensable man. 2
—WOODROW WILSON,
presidential nomination acceptance speech,
Democratic National Convention, August 7, 1912
[Wilson was advocating a campaign on issues. He said, "A presidential campaign may easily degenerate into a mere personal contest and so lose its real
dignity. There is no indispensable man." His opponents were the incumbent
William Howard Taft, a Republican, and former president Theodore Roosevelt,
running as a Progressive.

Franklin Roosevelt also used this aphorism while campaigning in 1932; see
under GREATNESS. The French say, *"Il n'y a point d'homme nécessaire."*]

I never met a man I didn't like. 3
—WILL ROGERS, remark, June 15, 1930
[More at EPITAPHS & GRAVESTONES.]

Pity this busy monster, manunkind, 4
not. —E. E. CUMMINGS, *Pity this busy monster, manunkind*,
in *One Times One* (or *1 x 1*), 1944
[More at PROGRESS.]

I decline to accept the end of man. . . . I believe that man will not merely en- 5
dure: he will prevail. He is immortal, not because he alone among creatures
has an inexhaustible voice, but because he has a soul, a spirit capable of compassion and sacrifice and endurance.
—WILLIAM FAULKNER, speech
accepting the Nobel Prize for Literature,
Dec. 10, 1950

We has met the enemy and it is us. —WALT KELLY, comment 6
by Pogo the possum
in the "Pogo" cartoon strip
[A variation was used as a slogan on an Earth Day poster in 1971; see ENVIRON-
MENT. In *Respectfully Quoted*, published by the Library of Congress, editor
Suzy Platt turned up this earlier version: "Resolve then, that on this very
ground, with small flags waving and tinny blasts on tiny trumpets, we shall
meet the enemy, and not only may he be ours, he may be us," *The Pogo Papers*,
Foreword, 1953. For Oliver Hazard Perry's military dispatch, see WAR OF 1812.]

HUMOR
See also INSULTS & PUT-DOWNS;
LAUGHTER & MIRTH

Wit makes its own welcome and levels all distinctions. 7
—RALPH WALDO EMERSON, *The Comic*,
in *Letters and Social Aims*, 1876

The quality of wit inspires more admiration than confidence. 8
—GEORGE SANTAYANA, *The Sense of Beauty*, 1896

1   The secret source of humor itself is not joy but sorrow. There is no humor in
heaven.   —MARK TWAIN, *Pudd'nhead Wilson's New Calendar,*
in *Following the Equator,* 1897
[For distinctively Western humor, See Twain's biographer Albert Bigelow Paine
at THE WEST.]

2   It's hard to be funny when you have to be clean.
—MAE WEST, from Joseph Weintraub, ed.,
The Wit and Wisdom of Mae West [1967]

3   Everything is funny as long as it is happening to somebody else.
—WILL ROGERS, *Warning to Jokers: Lay Off the Prince,*
in *The Illiterate Digest,* 1924

4   coarse
jocosity
catches the crowd
shakespeare
and I
are often
low browed.   —DON MARQUIS, *archy and mehitabel,* 1927

5   Wit is the only wall
Between us and the dark.   —MARK VAN DOREN,
Wit, in *A Winter Diary and Other Poems,* 1935

6   Everybody likes a kidder, but nobody lends him money.
—ARTHUR MILLER, *Death of a Salesman,* 1949

7   The wit makes fun of other persons; the satirist makes fun of the world; the
humorist makes fun of himself.
—JAMES THURBER, in Edward R. Murrow television interview
[For the difference between vivacity and wit, as defined by Josh Billings, see the
note under Mark Twain on lightning and the lightning bug at LANGUAGE &
WORDS.]

8   Humor . . . is emotional chaos remembered in tranquillity.
—JAMES THURBER, *New York Post,* Feb. 29, 1960
[Thurber refers to William Wordsworth's immortal definition of poetry: "Poetry . . . takes its origin from emotion remembered in tranquillity," Preface to
the 2nd edition of *Lyrical Ballads,* 1800.]

HUNGER   *See* POVERTY & HUNGER

HURRYING   *See* HASTE V. GOING SLOW; SPEED

HYPOCRISY

9   Mankind are very odd creatures: one half censure what they practice, the other
half practice what they censure; the rest always say and do as they ought.
—BENJAMIN FRANKLIN, *Poor Richard's Almanack,* 1752

10   As for conforming outwardly, and living your own life inwardly, I don't think
much of that.   —HENRY DAVID THOREAU, letter to Harrison Blake,
August 9, 1850

We live in an atmosphere of hypocrisy throughout. The men believe not in the   1
women, nor the women in the men.

     —WALT WHITMAN, *Democratic Vistas*, 1871.

A hypocrite is a person who—but who isn't?   2

     —DON MARQUIS, attributed in Frederick B. Wilcox,
     A Little Book of Aphorisms

Hypocrisy is the vice of vices. . . . Integrity can indeed exist under the cover of   3
all other vices except this one. . . . Only the hypocrite is really rotten to the
core.   —HANNAH ARENDT, *On Revolution*, 1963

I

IDAHO

See also CITIES (Pocatello)

1   It is a melancholy strange-looking country, one of fractures and violence and fire.   —JOHN C. FRÉMONT, 1843

2   Idaho is torn, above all, between two other states, between the pull of Washington in the north, that of Utah in the south. Half of Idaho belongs to Spokane, I heard it said, and the other half to the Mormon church.
      —JOHN GUNTHER, *Inside U.S.A.*, 1947

I asked an Idaho patriot why potatoes were so big. Answer: "We fertiliz'em
3   with cornmeal and irrigate them with milk."   —*Ibid.*

Dice 'em, hash 'em, boil 'em, mash 'em!
4   Idaho, Idaho, Idaho!   —ANONYMOUS, football cheer, quoted by
      Charles Kuralt, *Dateline America*, 1979
[The reference is to Idaho's dominant crop, potatoes. By the 1990s, however, Idaho was attracting reverse immigration from California, and farming was receding somewhat in importance while electronic industries were gaining ground.]

Motto

Esto perpetua.
5   May she endure forever. (Also translated: "It is perpetual.")

IDEAS & IDEALS

See also DREAMS & DREAMERS; VIRTUE

There was never an idea started that woke up men out of their stupid indiffer-
6   ence but its originator was spoken of as a crank.
      —OLIVER WENDELL HOLMES, SR.,
      The Autocrat of the Breakfast-Table, 1858
[Mark Twain said the same thing. See NEW THINGS.]

I died for beauty—but was scarce   1
Adjusted in the tomb
When one who died for truth was lain
In an adjoining room   —EMILY DICKINSON, poem no. 449,
                                                            c. 1862
[This is the first stanza. The third reads: "And so, as kinsmen, met at night, /
We talked between the rooms / Until the moss had reached our lips / And cov-
ered up—our names."]

All our scientific and philosophic ideals are altars to unknown gods.   2
                                        —WILLIAM JAMES,
                                        The Dilemma of Determinism, 1884

Loyalty to petrified opinion never yet broke a chain or freed a human soul.   3
                                        —MARK TWAIN, attributed,
                                        inscribed beneath his bust
                                        in the Hall of Fame

There is no force so democratic as the force of an ideal.   4
                                        —CALVIN COOLIDGE, speech,
                                        New York City, Nov. 27, 1920

An idea isn't responsible for the people who believe in it.   5
                                        —DON MARQUIS, *The Sun Dial*
[Marquis wrote columns for the New York *Sun* 1913–22, and then moved on to
the *New York Tribune*.]

To die for an idea: it is unquestionably noble. But how much nobler would it   6
be if men died for ideas that were true.
                                        —H. L. MENCKEN, *Prejudices: Fifth Series*

Men are mortal; but ideas are immortal.   7
                                        —WALTER LIPPMAN, *A Preface to Morals*, 1929

There is nothing wrong with Americans except their ideals.   8
                                        —G. K. CHESTERTON, in *The New York Times*, Feb. 1, 1931
[More at AMERICA & AMERICANS.]

You can't shoot an idea.   9
                                        —THOMAS E. DEWEY, debate with Harold Stassen
                                        on whether to outlaw the Communist Party, 1948

If you believe in an ideal, you don't own it, it owns you.   10
                                        —RAYMOND CHANDLER,
                                        quoted in Frank MacShane,
                                        The Life of Raymond Chandler [1978]

Every man with an idea has at least two or three followers.   11
                                        —BROOKS ATKINSON,
                                        Once Around the Sun, 1951

A man may die, nations may rise and fall, but an idea lives on. Ideas have en-   12
durance without death.
                                        —JOHN F. KENNEDY, speech, Greenville, N.C., Feb. 8, 1963

ILLINOIS

See also CITIES (Cairo, Chicago, Peoria, Springfield)

1   The official language of the State of Illinois shall be known henceforth as the American language, and not as the English language.
—ACTS OF THE LEGISLATURE OF ILLINOIS, ch. 127, sec. 178, 1923, in H. L. Mencken, *New Dictionary of Quotations on Historical Principles,* 1942

2   Its women are lovely and stubborn, its men angry and ingenious. Is there a land anywhere like southern Illinois?
—BAKER BROWNELL, *The Other Illinois,* 1958

3   Illinois is perhaps the most American of all the states. It's the U.S.A. in a capsule. Here our virtues and our faults are most exaggerated and magnified. Here somehow the heroes seem more heroic, the villains more villainous, the buffoons more comic. Here violence is more unrestrained, and the capacity for greatness is as limitless as the sweep of unending cornfields.
—CLYDE BRION DAVIS, *Illinois,* in *American Panorama: East of the Mississippi,* 1960

Motto

4   State sovereignty—national union.

ILLNESS & REMEDIES

See also DOCTORS & MEDICINE; SUFFERING & PAIN

5   We forget ourselves and our destinies in health, and the chief use of temporary sickness is to remind us of these concerns.
—RALPH WALDO EMERSON, *Journal,* 1821

6   There was a little bird,
Its name was Enza,
I opened the window
And in-flu-enza.
—ANONYMOUS, 1918
[The lethal swine flu epidemic of 1918, called at the time Spanish influenza, killed 21 million people, about the same number that died in World War I. More than a half million died in the U.S.]

7   Ivry sick man is a hero, if not to th' wurruld or aven to th' fam'ly, at laste to himsilf.
—FINLEY PETER DUNNE, *Going to See the Doctor,* in *Mr. Dooley on Making a Will,* 1919

8   Illness is the night-side of life, a more onerous citizenship. Everyone who is born holds dual citizenship, in the kingdom of the well and the kingdom of the sick.
—SUSAN SONTAG, *Illness as Metaphor,* 1977
[See also Ralph Waldo Emerson at SUFFERING & PAIN.]

9   There is a healthy way to be ill.
—GEORGE SHEEHAN, *New York Times* obituary, Nov. 2, 1993
[Cardiologist Sheehan became one of the great amateur runners of his day after

taking up the sport at age forty-three. He continued to run after developing cancer seven years before his death.]

Ask not what disease the person has, but rather what person the disease has.   1
—OLIVER SACKS, Epigraph, *An Anthropologist on Mars: Seven Paradoxical Tales*, 1995

ILLUSIONS

See DREAMS & DREAMERS; REALITY, ILLUSIONS, & IMAGES

IMAGES

See REALITY, ILLUSIONS, & IMAGES

IMAGINATION

See DREAMS & DREAMERS; MIND, THOUGHT, & UNDERSTANDING; VISION & PERCEPTION

IMMORTALITY

Superiority to fate   2
Is difficult to gain
'Tis not conferred of any
But possible to earn

A pittance at a time
Until to her surprise
The soul with strict economy
Subsist till Paradise.   —EMILY DICKINSON, poem no. 1081, c. 1866

The only secret people keep   3
Is immortality.   —EMILY DICKINSON, poem no. 1748, undated

The fact of having been born is a bad augury for immortality.   4
—GEORGE SANTAYANA,
The Life of Reason, 1905–1906

Immortality is not a gift,   5
Immortality is an achievement;
And only those who strive mightily
Shall possess it.   —EDGAR LEE MASTERS,
The Village Atheist,
in *The Spoon River Anthology*, 1915

The universe is a stairway leading nowhere unless man is immortal.   6
—EDGAR YOUNG MULLINS, *The Father Almighty*,
quoted in Joseph Fort Newton, *My Idea of God*, 1926

The truth is, no one really believes in immortality. Belief must mean some-   7
thing more than desire or hope.
—CLARENCE DARROW, *The Story of My Life*, 1932

INDECISION

See also DECISION; DELAY

There is no more miserable human being than one in whom nothing is habit-   8
ual but indecision.   —WILLIAM JAMES,
The Principles of Psychology, 1890

1   He who hesitates is sometimes saved.
                           —JAMES THURBER, *The Glass in the Field*,
                           in *Fables for Our Time*, 1940

2   It is human nature to stand in the middle of a thing.
                           —MARIANNE MOORE, *A Grave*, in *Collected Poems*, 1951

3   Some problems are so complex that you have to be highly intelligent and well
    informed just to be undecided about them.
                           —LAURENCE J. PETER, *Peter's Almanac*, 1982
    [In the same book, Peter also condensed a wordy statement by Harvey G. Cox
    in *On Not Leaving It to the Snake*, 1967, into the pithy: "Not to decide is to
    decide."]

4   I've made up my mind both ways.
                           —CHARLES DILLON "CASEY" STENGEL, quoted in
                           the Ken Burns television series *Baseball*, part IV [1994]

INDEPENDENCE DAY   *See also* DECLARATION OF
                                             INDEPENDENCE; FREEDOM

5   It will be celebrated by succeeding generations as the great anniversary festi-
    val. It ought to be commemorated as the day of deliverance, by solemn acts of
    devotion to God almighty. It ought to be solemnized with pomp and parade,
    with shows, games, sports, guns, bells, bonfires, and illuminations from one
    end of this continent to the other, from this time forward forevermore.
                           —JOHN ADAMS, 2d letter to Abigail Adams, July 3, 1776
    [Adams had in mind celebrating July 2, when the independence resolution was
    adopted in committee. Traditionally, we celebrate on July 4, the date the Con-
    tinental Congress approved the Declaration of Independence. Adams, and
    everyone else, soon came to regard July 4 as the memorable occasion.]

6   Is it the Fourth?
                           —THOMAS JEFFERSON, last words, July 3, 1826
    [His doctor assured him that it soon would be; the day would be the fiftieth an-
    niversary of independence. Jefferson became delirious shortly afterward, but
    did live to the fourth. John Adams survived him by about two hours. See also
    Adams at LAST WORDS.]

7   Independence forever!
                           —JOHN ADAMS, July 4, 1826
    [Adams was responding to the sound of canon firing in celebration of the great
    anniversary. See also LAST WORDS and Daniel Webster at FREEDOM.]

INDIANA   *See also* CITIES (Muncie)

8   Blest Indiana! in whose soil
    Men seek the sure rewards of toil,
    And honest poverty and worth
    Find here the best retreat on earth,
    While hosts of preachers, doctors, lawyers,
    All independent as wood-sawyers,
    With men of every hue and fashion,
    Flock to the rising "Hoosier" nation.   —JOHN FINLEY, *The Hoosiers' Nest*,
                                               c. 1830
    [Finley gave the 1830 date for this poem, claiming to have published it origi-

nally in the *Richmond* (Indiana) *Palladium;* no one has been able to verify this. The poem was used as a New Year's greeting by newspaper carrier boys in 1832 (*Indiana Democrat*) and 1833 (*Indianapolis Journal,* which published the work on January 1).

The origin of the term *Hoosier* is unknown, the most colorful guess—by James Whitcomb Riley, "the Hoosier poet"—is that as a result of people biting off each other's ears in drunken brawls, the question sometimes arose, "Whose ear is this?" Other guesses are that it comes from "husher," or "whoosher," or the greeting, "Who's yere?"]

Oh the moonlight's fair tonight along the Wabash.
From the fields there comes the breath of new-mown hay;   1
Thro' the sycamores the candle lights are gleaming,
On the banks of the Wabash far away.   —PAUL DRESSER, *On the Banks
                                               of the Wabash Far Away,* 1897

I come from Indiana, the home of more first-rate second-class men than any
state in the Union.   —THOMAS RILEY MARSHALL,   2
                                               Recollections, 1925
[Marshall was Woodrow Wilson's vice president, most remembered today for his insight into the country's need for a really good five-cent cigar; see TO-BACCO.]

Motto
The crossroads of America.   3

INDIANS   *See* RACES & PEOPLES

INDIVIDUALITY & INDIVIDUALISM   *See also* DIFFERENCES; SELF

He may well win the race that runs by himself.   4
              —BENJAMIN FRANKLIN, *Poor Richard's Almanack,* 1747
[More at EXCELLENCE.]

Individuality is the aim of political liberty.   5
              —JAMES FENIMORE COOPER, *The American Democrat,* 1838

If a man does not keep pace with his companions, perhaps it is because he   6
hears a different drummer. Let him step to the music which he hears, however
measured or far away.   —HENRY DAVID THOREAU,
                                               "Conclusion," *Walden,* 1854

Individualism in America has allowed a laxity in regard to governmental af-   7
fairs which has rendered possible the spoils system and all the manifest evils
that follow from the lack of a highly developed civic spirit.
              —FREDERICK J. TURNER, *The Significance
                 of the Frontier in American History,* 1893
[See also Turner at AMERICA & AMERICANS and THE FRONTIER for more on American individualism. For the spoils system, see William Marcy at POLITICS & POLITICIANS.]

Rugged individualism.   8
              —HERBERT HOOVER, speech, New York City, Oct. 22, 1928
[More at AMERICA & AMERICANS.]

1   One is hip or one is square, one is a rebel or one conforms, one is a frontiers-
man in the Wild West of American night life, or else a square cell, trapped in
the totalitarian tissues of American society, doomed willy-nilly to conform if
one is to succeed.   —NORMAN MAILER, *The White Negro*, 1957

INFORMATION   *See* KNOWLEDGE & INFORMATION

INJUSTICE   *See also* JUSTICE

2   This is an age of the world where nations are trembling and convulsed. A
mighty influence is abroad, surging and heaving the world, as with an earthquake. And is America safe? Every nation that carries in its bosom great and
unredressed injustice has in it the elements of this last convulsion.
—HARRIET BEECHER STOWE,
Uncle Tom's Cabin, 1852
[This is from the last chapter. The book's immense popularity itself contributed to the coming convulsion.]

3   Injustice anywhere is a threat to justice everywhere.
—MARTIN LUTHER KING, JR., letter from Birmingham city jail, 1963

4   There comes a time when . . . men are no longer willing to be plunged into an
abyss of injustice.
—Ibid.
[More at RESISTANCE.]

INSTITUTIONS   *See also* GOVERNMENT

5   An institution is the lengthened shadow of one man.
—RALPH WALDO EMERSON, *Self-Reliance*,
in *Essays: First Series*, 1841
[In his *Journal*, in 1832, Emerson wrote, "We do not make a world of our own,
but fall into institutions already made, and have to accommodate ourselves to
them to be useful at all."]

6   In a changing world, worthy institutions can be conserved only by adjusting
them to the changing time.   —FRANKLIN D. ROOSEVELT, speech,
Syracuse, N.Y., Sept. 29, 1936

INSULTS   *See also* ELITE, THE (Adlai Stevenson and Spiro Agnew);
FAULTS & FAILINGS; FOOLS & STUPIDITY; HARDING, WARREN G.

7   You and I were long friends: you are now my enemy, and I am
Yours,
B. Franklin
—BENJAMIN FRANKLIN, letter to William Strahan,
of London, England, July 5, 1775
[Strahan was a fellow printer (of Samuel Johnson's *Dictionary of the English
Language*, among other works) as well as—the occasion for this letter—a
Member of Parliament. Franklin was thinking of patriot blood shed at Lexing-
ton and Bunker Hill when he wrote this letter, but he did what wise people
generally do with letters that are written in anger: he never mailed it. Thus, the
old friends remained friends despite the war between their nations.]

[He] means well, very well. But he means it feebly.   1
                    —GOUVERNEUR MORRIS, on the French foreign minister,
                        the Comte de Montmorin, 1790
[Morris was America's third minister to France, following Benjamin Franklin
and Thomas Jefferson, and he had the most dangerous tour of duty, staying in
Paris throughout the Reign of Terror. Morris was both shrewd and brave. Of
Lafayette he wrote, "If the sea runs high, he will be unable to hold the helm."
The quotes here were cited by Arnold Whitridge in *A Representative of Amer-
ica*, in *American Heritage*, June 1976.]

He is a man of splendid abilities but utterly corrupt. He shines and stinks like   2
rotten mackerel by moonlight.
                    —JOHN RANDOLPH, speaking of Rep. Edward Livingston
                        of New York, c. 1800, cited in William Cabell Bruce,
                        John Randolph of Roanoke [1922]
[Randolph, commonly called John Randolph of Roanoke, served almost continuously in Congress from 1799 to 1833. He was well educated, highly intelligent, and famed for his venomous wit. For his comment on the appointment
in 1825 of Richard Rush as Secretary of the Treasury, see below. Of Martin Van
Buren's political tactics, he said, "He rowed to his object with muffled oars."
On at least one occasion, however, he was bested. Meeting Henry Clay on a
narrow walkway in a muddy Washington street, he refused to let the other
man pass, declaring, "Sir, I never give way for a scoundrel." To which Clay, gallantly stepping aside, replied, "I always do."]

Never were abilities so much below mediocrity so well rewarded; no, not when   3
Caligula's horse was made Consul.
                    —JOHN RANDOLPH, speaking of Pres. John Quincy Adams's
                        appointment of Richard Rush as Secretary of the Treasury,
                        published as an appendix to a speech in the U.S. House of
                        Representatives, Feb. 1, 1828
[In 1828, Rush was Adams's vice-presidential running mate in a bid for reelection. Adams was beaten by Andrew Jackson, and took up a new, if more modest career as a U.S. Representative.
  Speaking of Caligula, Randolph was an odd bird, himself—distinctly feminine in appearance, which was the cause of much comment and no doubt pain
to Randolph. John Quincy Adams said of him, according to Edward Boykin's
Wit and Wisdom of Congress (1961), "His face is livid, gaunt his whole body,
his breath is green with gall; his tongue drips poison." Congressman Tristram
Burges was even more pointed, implying that Randolph was "impotent of
everything but malevolence of purpose," and concluding, "I rejoice that the father of lies can never become the father of liars," quoted in William Cabell
Bruce, *John Randolph of Roanoke*, 1922.
  Politically, Randolph was an ardent libertarian and protector of states' rights
and the Constitution, as he saw it. He fought a duel with Henry Clay, and became increasingly eccentric in his later years.]

One might as well try to spoil a rotten egg as to damage Dan's character.   4
                    —GEORGE TEMPLETON STRONG, in Allen Nevins, ed.,
                        The Diary of George Templeton Strong, entry c. 1859
[On February 27, 1859, U.S. Congressman Daniel E. Sickles of New York City
shot to death Washington, D.C., district attorney Philip Barton Key—son of
Francis Scott Key, author of *The Star-Spangled Banner*. Sickles, a notorious
ladies' man himself, killed Key for having an affair with Sickles's wife. The
congressman pleaded temporary insanity—an unprecedented plea in American
courts, and was acquitted by a sympathetic jury. Sickles went on to serve as a

general in the Civil War, playing a near disastrous role at Gettysburg (and losing a leg in the process) when he advanced his corps without orders, moving so
far in front of the rest of the Union line that he could be attacked on both
flanks. After the war, Sickles continued to mix public service with private
scandals until his death at age ninety-five.

George Templeton Strong was a New York lawyer and a friend of Abraham
Lincoln. He produced a colorful and historically valuable diary.]

1   You take the lies out of him, and he'll shrink to the size of your hat; you take
the malice out of him, and he'll disappear.
                              —MARK TWAIN, *Life on the Mississippi*, 1833

2   He is useless on top of the ground; he ought to be under it, inspiring the cabbages.   —MARK TWAIN, *Pudd'nhead Wilson's Calendar*,
                              in *Pudd'nhead Wilson*, 1894

3   He saw nearly all things as through a glass eye, darkly.
                              —MARK TWAIN,
                                  Fenimore Cooper's Literary Offenses, 1895

4   No more backbone than a chocolate éclair.
                              —THEODORE ROOSEVELT, characterization
                              of Pres. William McKinley, c. 1897, cited in V. C. Jones,
                                  Last of the Rough Riders, in *American Heritage* [July 1969]
[Roosevelt, then Assistant Secretary of the Navy, may have picked up the image from Thomas B. Reed, Speaker of the House of Representatives. Variants
from the same era include Ulysses S. Grant's opinion that James A. Garfield
was "not possessed of the backbone of an angleworm" and a comment by
Oliver Wendell Holmes, Jr., on a colleague: "I could carve out of a banana a
judge with more backbone than that."]

5   They never open their mouths without subtracting from the sum of human
knowledge.   —THOMAS BRACKETT REED, remark about two colleagues in
                              the House of Representatives, quoted in Samuel W. McCall,
                                  The Life of Thomas Brackett Reed, 1914
["Czar" Reed, a Maine Republican, served as Speaker of the House 1889–91
and 1895–99. He was referring here to two colleagues in that august body. Of
another—William M. Springer of Illinois—he said in 1881, "If I ever 'made
light' of his remarks, it is more than he ever made of them himself."]

6   A scab is a two-legged animal with a corkscrew soul, a waterlogged brain, a
combination backbone of jelly and glue. Where others have hearts, he carries a
tumor of rotten principles.   —JACK LONDON, *A Scab*,
                                  in *C.I.O. News* [Sept. 13, 1946]
[See also London at CAPITALISM & CAPITAL v. LABOR.]

7   The covers of this book are too far apart.
                              —AMBROSE BIERCE, attributed in C. H. Grattan,
                                  Bitter Bierce, 1929

8   There is less in this than meets the eye.
                              —TALLULAH BANKHEAD, remark to Alexander Woollcott
                              at Maurice Maeterlinck's play *Aglavaine and Selysette*,
                              Jan. 3, 1922
[Attribution by *Bartlett's*. For a quote about Tallulah, see Howard Dietz
below.]

And it is the word "hummy," my darlings, that marks the first place in *The*   1
House at Pooh Corner at which Tonstant Weader fwowed up.
> —DOROTHY PARKER, *Constant Reader* column,
> *The New Yorker*, Oct. 20, 1928

[Parker is also said to have coined the terse review: "It is not a novel to be
thrown aside lightly. It should be thrown aside with great force"; quoted in
A. Johnston, *Legend of a Sport*, in *The New Yorker*. See her theater reviews
below.]

[On being told that former Pres. Calvin Coolidge had died:] How do they   2
know?   —WILSON MIZNER, 1933, attributed,
> in *The International Dictionary of 20th Century Biography*,
> Edward Vernoff and Rima Shore, eds. [1987]

[Also attributed to Dorothy Parker and Alice Roosevelt Longworth.]

[Pres. Herbert] Hoover is the world's greatest engineer: he's drained, ditched,   3
and damned the United States.
> —ANONYMOUS joke, c. 1931

[Hoover, a distinguished engineer and a decent, generally competent man, was
overwhelmed by the economic catastrophe that hit the country in 1929. His
tendency to deny the depth of the problem ruined his credibility. People tended
to ascribe to him dumb comments that he probably or certainly did not make;
see "Prosperity is just around the corner," for example, at THE DEPRESSION, or
this attribution: "Many people have left their jobs for the more profitable one
of selling apples," quoted by Robert Dallek in his biography of Lyndon Johnson, *Lone Star Rising*.]

She ran the whole gamut of emotions from A to B.   4
> —DOROTHY PARKER, commenting on Katharine Hepburn
> in the play *The Lake*, 1933, attributed

House Beautiful is play lousy.   5
> —DOROTHY PARKER, theater review, *The New Yorker*, 1933

[Another theatrical effort was dismissed with the advice, "If you don't knit,
bring a book," quoted in *The New Yorker* in an essay on Parker by Joan Acocella, August 16, 1993.]

My dear, I don't give a damn.   6
> —MARGARET MITCHELL, *Gone with the Wind*, 1936

[Rhett Butler's definitive dismissal of Scarlett O'Hara. In the screenplay by Sidney Howard, the line is, "Frankly, my dear, I don't give a damn." Producer
David O. Selznik fought to keep in the "damn," and paid a $5,000 fine for
breaking the Motion Picture Production Code. The code administrators had argued for "Frankly, my dear, I don't care."]

A labor-baiting, poker-playing, whiskey-drinking, evil old man whose name is   7
Garner.   —JOHN L. LEWIS, testimony, Labor Committee,
> U. S. House of Representatives, July 27, 1939

[Lewis headed both the United Mine Workers of America and the Congress of
Industrial Organizations (C.I.O.) at the time. John Nance Garner was vice president of the United States.]

There goes the famous good time that was had by all.   8
> —BETTE DAVIS, speaking of a starlet,
> attributed in Leslie Halliwell,
> *The Filmgoer's Book of Quotes* [1990]

1   She looked as though butter wouldn't melt in her mouth or anywhere else.
                                                —ELSA LANCHESTER, *Ibid.*

2   There but for the grace of God goes God.
                                    —HERMAN J. MANKIEWICZ, c. 1941,
                        quoted by Pauline Kael in *The New Yorker,* 1971
[Mankiewicz and Orson Welles wrote the 1941 movie *Citizen Kane.* Welles
also directed and starred in the classic film, and is the butt of this gentle gibe
from his colleague.]

3   [Dewey is like] the little man on the wedding cake.
                            —popularized by ALICE ROOSEVELT LONGWORTH, 1944
[The bon mot has been credited to a number of people, including Harold Ickes,
Walter Winchell, and Ethel Barrymore. Mrs. Longworth herself told William
Safire that she heard it from a friend, Grace Hodgson Flandrau.
    Dewey—short, mustachioed, and young (42 in 1944) for a presidential candi-
date—proved to be a lightning rod for witticisms. The New York Republican
was "The Boy Orator of the Platitude," according to one anonymous pundit,
and former Interior Secretary Harold Ickes described him as the kind of person
"who, when he had nothing to do, went home and cleaned his bureau drawers." In 1948, when he announced his candidacy for the presidency for a second
time, Ickes said that "Dewey has thrown his diaper into the ring," while Mrs.
Longworth dismissed his chances with the observation, "You can't make a
soufflé rise twice." Upon his loss to Truman that year, wise heads nodded
sagely and agreed that he had "snatched defeat from the jaws of victory."]

4   To err is Truman.

                                                —ANONYMOUS, c. 1946
[Truman, during the first years of his presidency, was often regarded as something of an embarrassment. Another joke compared him unfavorably with
Franklin Delano Roosevelt: "For years, we had the champion of the common
man in the presidency. Now we have the common man." Truman answered tit
for tat. For example, he called Sen. J. William Fulbright of Arkansas "half-
bright"—after Fulbright suggested, following the 1946 congressional elections,
when the Democrats were swamped, that Truman appoint a Republican Secretary of State to succeed him and then resign.
    For Truman's attack on the music critic who didn't like his daughter's
singing, see ART: CRITICISM.]

5   What a dump!

                                    —LENORE COFFEE, *Beyond the Forest,* 1949
[In this movie, Bette Davis had the line and made it famous. But it was used
also in *Night Court,* 1932, with a similar delivery by Anita Page.]

6   A day away from Tallulah is like a month in the country.
                                                —HOWARD DIETZ, ascribed
[In a brief profile on Bankhead, Brendan Gill, in *The New Yorker,* reported that
Tallulah spoke at the rate of almost seventy thousand words per day, "the
equivalent of a short novel." Dietz, by the way, was one of those multital-
ented, competent people that we seem to have fewer of lately. He was a successful lyricist—e.g., *Dancing in the Dark*—librettist—opera as well as
musical comedy—and publicity executive with MGM, credited with creating
the Leo the Lion trademark.]

It is a pity that his wisdom, his judgment, his tact, and his sense of humor lag   1
so far behind his ambition.
> —DWIGHT D. EISENHOWER, note to a friend re
> Senate Majority Leader William Knowland of California, 1953,
> quoted in Stephen E. Ambrose, *Eisenhower: The President*

[The very conservative and notoriously dim Knowland prompted the president to comment in his diary "There seems to be no final answer to the question, 'How stupid can you get?'" The Eisenhower administration itself drew a few barbs. His cabinet was described in *The New Republic*'s anonymous TRB column—written by Richard Strout—as "eight millionaires and a plumber"; the labor secretary had formerly headed the plumbers' union, the rest were a corporate lawyer, John Foster Dulles, and businessmen, three from the auto industry. Defeated Democratic candidate Adlai Stevenson remarked, "The New Dealers have all left Washington to make way for the car dealers."]

[Re William Jennings Bryan:] His mind was like a soup dish, wide and shallow.   2
> —IRVING STONE, *They Also Ran*, 1966

As I used to say about my old Yonkers Raceway boss Al Tananbaum—if I ever   3
need a heart transplant I want his, because it hardly ever has been used.
> —IRVING RUDD, *The Sporting Life*, 1990

[Rudd was a press agent—not a PR person, please. See under ADVERTISING, ADVERTISING SLOGANS, & PUBLICITY.]

He inherited some good instincts from his Quaker forebears, but by diligent   4
hard work, he overcame them.
> —JAMES RESTON, comment on Pres. Richard Nixon,
> *Deadline: Our Times and The New York Times*, 1991

INTIMACY & FAMILIARITY

Familiarity breeds contempt—and children.   5
> —MARK TWAIN, *Notebooks*

[The adage, minus the reference to children, dates to ancient times and is the moral of Aesop's fable *The Fox and the Lion*. For an up-to-date comment on the effects of a certain intimacy, see David Owen at HEROES.]

Familiarity breeds contentment.   6
> —GEORGE ADE, *The Uplift That Moved Sideways*,
> in *Hand-Made Fables*, 1920

IOWA   *See also* CITIES (Des Moines)

Ioway, Ioway, that's where the tall corn grows!   —ANONYMOUS, c. 1840   7

There is no group of two and a half million people in the world who worship   8
God as Iowans do.   —ANONYMOUS (professor at Iowa State College),
> quoted by H. L. Mencken, in *Americana*, 1925

[More at CITIES (Des Moines).]

The gold mines and the diamond mines of the world are cheap and trivial com-   9
pared to the produce that Iowa breeds out of its land every year.
> —PHIL STONG, *Hawkeyes*, 1940

[*Hawkeyes* is a history of Iowa. Stong's novel *State Fair*, 1932, was made into a movie three times, the first version starring Will Rogers. Iowans are called

Hawkeyes after the Indian warrior Chief Black Hawk, who survived the massacre of his band in 1832, and was later set free in Iowa, where he spent his last days.]

1   The character of Iowa is essentially bucolic in the best senses of that word (and, to be quite honest, occasionally in some of the worst).   —*Ibid.*

2   Iowa spells agriculture, and agriculture in this part of the world spells corn. This is the heart of agrarian America.

—JOHN GUNTHER, *Inside U.S.A.,* 1947

3   "Is this heaven?"
"It's Iowa."
"I could have sworn it was heaven."

—W. P. KINSELLA, *Shoeless Joe,* 1982

[Adapted by Phil Alden Robinson for the 1989 movie *Field of Dreams.* See FAITH for the most famous line from this movie.]

Motto

4   Our liberties we prize and our rights we will maintain.

IRELAND & THE IRISH   *See* NATIONS

ITALY & ITALIANS   *See* NATIONS

J

JACKSON, ANDREW

If General Jackson wants to go to Heaven, who's to stop him? 1
                                                    —ANONYMOUS
[Perhaps apocryphal, but this is said to be the response of one of Jackson's
slaves, who, after Jackson's death, was asked whether he thought the great man
had gone to heaven. See also Jackson at LAST WORDS.]

Little advanced in civilization over the Indians with whom he made war. 2
                        —ELIJAH HUNT MILLS, in Marquis James,
                            Andrew Jackson—Portrait of a President [1933]

A natural king 3
With a raven wing,
Cold no more,
Weary no more,
Old, old,
Old, old,
Andrew Jackson.   —VACHEL LINDSAY, *Old, Old, Old, Old Andrew Jackson*,
                        spoken by the author, Jefferson's Birthday Dinner,
                        Spokane, Wash., April 15, 1925

JAPAN   *See* NATIONS

JEFFERSON, THOMAS   *See also* EPITAPHS & GRAVESTONES;
                                   INDEPENDENCE DAY; LAST WORDS; TYRANNY

He lives and will live in memory and gratitude of the wise and good, as a lu- 4
minary of science, as a votary of liberty, as a model of patriotism, and as a benefactor of human kind.
                —JAMES MADISON, in memory of Thomas Jefferson, 1826

[Jefferson was] perhaps the most incapable executive that ever filled the presi- 5
dential chair. . . . It would be difficult to imagine a man less fit to guide a state
with honor and safety through the stormy times that marked the opening of
the present century.   —THEODORE ROOSEVELT,
                                            The Naval War of 1812, 1882

1   I think this is the most extraordinary collection of human talent, of human knowledge, that has ever been gathered at the White House—with the possible exception of when Thomas Jefferson dined alone.
    —JOHN F. KENNEDY, speech, dinner honoring 49 Nobel Prize
    winners, in *The New York Times*, April 30, 1962

JUDGES   *See also* LAW

2   The acme of judicial distinction means the ability to look a lawyer straight in the eye for two hours and not hear a damned word he says.
    —JOHN MARSHALL, quoted in Albert J. Beveridge,
    The Life of John Marshall [1916–1919]

3   The perfect judge fears nothing—he could go front to front before God,
Before the perfect judge all shall stand back—life and death shall stand
  back—heaven and hell shall stand back.
    —WALT WHITMAN, *Great Are the Myths*,
    in *Leaves of Grass*, 1860

4   Even judges sometimes progress.
    —EMMA GOLDMAN, *The Social Aspects of Birth Control*,
    in *Mother Earth* magazine, April 1916

5   I don't want to know what the law is, I want to know who the judge is.
    —ROY M. COHN, saying
[Cohn, a feared New York defense attorney, first gained notoriety as a young counsel to Red-hunting Sen. Joseph McCarthy.]

6   Judges are the weakest link in our system of justice, and they are also the most protected.   —ALAN DERSHOWITZ, *Newsweek*, Feb. 20, 1978

7   Judicial restraint is but another form of judicial activism.
    —LAURENCE H. TRIBE, *American Constitutional Law*, 1978

8   We must never forget that the only real source of power that we as judges can tap is the respect of the people.
    —THURGOOD MARSHALL, in the *Chicago Tribune*,
    August 15, 1981

JULY FOURTH   *See* INDEPENDENCE DAY

JURIES

9   In controversies respecting property, and in suits between man and man, the ancient trial by jury is preferable to any other, and ought to be held sacred.
    —VIRGINIA DECLARATION OF RIGHTS, 1776

10 Juries . . . have the effect . . . of placing the law in the hands of those who would be most apt to abuse it.
    —JAMES FENIMORE COOPER, *The Redskins*, 1846

11 A jury too frequently have at least one member more ready to hang the panel than hang the traitor.
    —ABRAHAM LINCOLN, letter to Erastus Corning et al.,
    June 12, 1863

We have a criminal justice system which is superior to any in the world; and 1
its efficiency is only marred by the difficulty of finding twelve men every day
who don't know anything and can't read.
> —MARK TWAIN, *Americans and the English*,
> speech, July 4, 1872

The jury system puts a ban upon intelligence and honesty, and a premium 2
upon ignorance, stupidity, and perjury.   —MARK TWAIN, *Roughing It*, 1872

Jury, n. A number of persons appointed by a judge to assist the attorneys in pre- 3
venting law from degenerating into justice.
> —AMBROSE BIERCE, *The Devil's Dictionary*, 1906

I never saw twelve men in my life that if you could get them to understand a 4
human case, were not true and right.
> —CLARENCE DARROW, summation in the Sweet case,
> Detroit, 1926

[When not in the process of flattering jurors, Darrow recognized a number of
exceptions; for example, he wrote in *Attorney for the Defense:* "Never take a
wealthy man on a jury. He will convict, unless the defendant is accused of violating the anti-trust law, selling worthless stocks or bonds, or something of
that kind. Next to the Board of Trade, for him, the penitentiary is the most important of all public buildings," *Esquire*, May 1936.]

Trial by jury is a rough scales at best. 5
> —LEARNED HAND, *United States v. Brown*, 1935

[Hand was the most influential and respected U.S. judge not to make it to the
highest court, and was often referred to as the tenth Supreme Court justice.]

A court is only as sound as its jury, and a jury is only as sound as the men who 6
make it up.   —HARPER LEE, *To Kill a Mockingbird*, 1960

Why should anyone think that twelve persons brought in from the street, se- 7
lected in various ways for their lack of general ability, should have any special
capacity for deciding controversies between persons?
> —ERWIN GRISWOLD, quoted in Stephen J. Adler, *The Jury*, 1994

[Griswold was dean of Harvard Law School. In the *Harvard Law Review*, in
1899, Oliver Wendell Holmes acknowledged that jurors show no great insight
or unusual judgment. "They will introduce into their verdict a certain amount—
a very large amount, so far as I have observed—of popular prejudice," he said.
But he also speculated that this is in fact an advantage, for "thus [they] keep
the administration of the law in accord with the wishes and feelings of the
community," *Law in Science and Science in Law*.]

JUSTICE   *See also* INJUSTICE; JUDGES; JURIES; LAW

Without justice, courage is weak. 8
> —BENJAMIN FRANKLIN, *Poor Richard's Almanack*, Jan. 1734

Justice is always in jeopardy.   —WALT WHITMAN, *Democratic Vistas*, 1870 9

The laws of changeless justice bind 10
Oppressor and oppressed;
And close as sin and suffering joined,
We march to fate abreast.
> —JOHN GREENLEAF WHITTIER, *At Port Royal*, 1862

[The occasion of the poem was the capture by Union forces of Port Royal,
South Carolina, on November 7, 1861. This liberated some 10,000 slaves on is-

lands between Charleston and Savannah, who then became part of an abolitionist venture in which the freed people were educated and set up as cotton
farmers.]

1   We are the whirlwinds that winnow the West—
    We scatter the wicked like straw!
    We are the Nemeses, never at rest—
    We are Justice, and Right, and the Law!
                            —MARGARET ASHMUN,
                        The Vigilantes, in *The Pacific Monthly*, 1907

2   It is higher and nobler to be kind. . . . If we should deal out justice only, in this
    world, who would escape?   —MARK TWAIN, *Autobiography* [1924]

3   Injustice is relatively easy to bear; what stings is justice.
                            —H. L. MENCKEN, *Prejudices, Third Series*, 1922

4   Justice is not to be taken by storm. She is to be wooed by slow advances.
                            —BENJAMIN CARDOZO, *The Growth of the Law*, 1924

5   There is no such thing as justice—in or out of court.
                            —CLARENCE DARROW, interview, *New York Times*, April 19, 1936

6   Thou shalt not ration justice.
                            —LEARNED HAND, speech to the Legal Aid Society
                                of New York, Feb. 16, 1951

7   Your justice would freeze beer!   —ARTHUR MILLER, *The Crucible*, 1953

8   Swift justice demands more than just swiftness.
                            —POTTER STEWART, dissenting opinion
                                in *Henderson v. Bannan*, 6th Circuit, 1958

9   No, no, we are not satisfied, and we will not be satisfied until justice rolls
    down like waters and righteousness like a mighty stream.
                            —MARTIN LUTHER KING, JR., speech at the Lincoln Memorial
                                in Washington, D.C., to 200,000 civil rights marchers,
                                August 28, 1963
    [More at AMERICAN HISTORY: MEMORABLE MOMENTS.]

10 Rush to Judgment.

                            —MARK LANE, book title, 1966
    [The title has become a tag for any hurried and biased approach to deciding
    who or what is responsible for a wrong. Lane was writing about the Warren
    Commission report on the assassination of Pres. John F. Kennedy.]

11 You go . . . lookin' for justice, and that's what you find, Just-Us.
                            —RICHARD PRYOR, quoted in Mel Watkins,
                                On the Real Side [1944]

12 No justice. No peace.   —AL SHARPTON, saying,
                                c. 1994
    [Rev. Al Sharpton is an African-American activist and politician, based in
    New York City.]

K

KANSAS

Bleeding Kansas.　　　—ANONYMOUS, popular epithet for the Kansas territory　　1
　　　　　　　　　　　in the 1850s
[After the Kansas-Nebraska Act of 1854, which opened the possibility that
Kansas could become a slave state if its residents so chose, the territory be-
came a battleground between free-soil (antislavery) and pro-Southern forces.
Kansas became a state in 1861.]

The Crime against Kansas.　　　　　　　　　　　　　　　　　　　　　　2
　　　　　　　　　　—CHARLES SUMNER, title of speech in the U.S. Senate,
　　　　　　　　　　　May 19–20, 1856
[An impassioned antislavery speech, larded with rich personal invective: Sumner described supporters of slavery as "hirelings picked from the drunken spew
and vomit of an uneasy civilization." Senators Andrew P. Butler and Stephen A.
Douglas, the authors of the Kansas-Nebraska Act (see above), were portrayed as
the Don Quixote and Sancho Panza of "the harlot, slavery." All this led to the
lowest of low points in congressional history: to avenge family and Southern
honor, Preston S. "Bully" Brooks, a representative from South Carolina and a
distant cousin of Butler, invaded the Senate chamber on May 22, and, catching
Sumner unawares at his desk, nearly beat him to death with a stout cane.]

It takes three log houses to make a city in Kansas, but they begin *calling* it a　　3
city as soon as they have staked out the lots.
　　　　　　　　　　　　　—HORACE GREELEY,
　　　　　　　　　　　　　　　*An Overland Journey from New York
　　　　　　　　　　　　　　　to San Francisco . . . in 1859,* 1860

In God we trusted, in Kansas we busted.　　　　　　　　　　　　　　　4
　　　　　　　　　　　　　　　　　　　　—ANONYMOUS, 1870s
[Sign on wagons of would-be western pioneers who didn't make it. Quoted by
Wallace Stegner in *Thoughts in a Dry Land,* 1972.]

The roosters lay eggs in Kansas.　　　　　　　　　　　　　　　　　5
The roosters lay eggs as big as beer kegs.
And the hair grows on their legs in Kansas.　　　　—ANONYMOUS, song, c. 1880

1   Oh, they chew tobacco in Kansas,
     Oh, they say that drink's a sin in Kansas.
                                    —ANONYMOUS, folk song,
                                       in John Gunther, *Inside U.S.A.* [1947]

2   What you Kansas farmers ought to do is raise less corn and more hell.
                                    —MARY LEASE, attributed, speech, 1890
     [Roger Butterfield in *The American Past* (1957) wrote that this advice may
     have originated with a newspaper reporter.]

3   What's the Matter with Kansas?
                                    —WILLIAM ALLEN WHITE, title of editorial, *Emporia Gazette*,
                                       August 15, 1896
     [The answer, according to this famous editorial, is that the state's top politi-
     cians were a bunch of loonies and failures. White loved Kansas, though. He
     concluded, "Kansas is all right. She has started to raise hell, as Mrs. Lease ad-
     vised, and she seems to have an overproduction."]

4   The only way you could tell a citizen from a bootlegger in Kansas was the boot-
     legger was sober.   —WILL ROGERS, quoted in Alex Ayres, ed.,
                                       The Wit and Wisdom of Will Rogers [1993]

5   Toto, I've a feeling we're not in Kansas any more.
                                    —NOEL LANGLEY, FLORENCE RYERSON, & EDGAR ALLEN WOLFE,
                                       The Wizard of Oz, screenplay, 1939

6   Kansas is the child of Plymouth Rock.
                                    —WILLIAM ALLEN WHITE *Autobiography*, 1946

7   A kind of gravity point for American democracy.
                                    —JOHN GUNTHER, *Inside U.S.A.*, 1947

8   First in freedom, first in wheat.
                                    —ANONYMOUS, Kansas saying,
                                       quoted in Dwight D. Eisenhower, *Eisenhower Speaks*, 1948

9   Kansas, by reason of history and location at the heart of our continental power,
     is a kind of social, political, and cultural barometer for all America.
                                    —ADLAI STEVENSON, Kansas—*A Kind of Prophecy*,
                                       speech, Wichita, Kansas, Oct. 7, 1954

10   Kansas, in sum, is one of our finest states and lives a sane, peaceful, and pros-
     perous life.   —PEARL S. BUCK, *America*, 1971

Motto

11   *Ad astra per aspera.*
                          To the stars through difficulties.

KENTUCKY   *See also* CITIES (Frankfort); MEXICAN
                                         WAR (Zachary Taylor)

12   He's gone to hell or Kentucky.
                                    —ANONYMOUS, c. 1785
     [The saying, which was popular in Virginia, referred to a man who had disap-
     peared, leaving behind debts or indictments.]

Heaven is a Kentuck of a place.   1
>   —TIMOTHY FLINT, *Recollections of the Last Ten Years Passed
>   in Occasional Residences and Journeyings in the Valley
>   of the Mississippi,* 1826

[The comparison of fertile Kentucky to Heaven was made so often by early visitors—as well as by local boosters—that "Kentuck" or "Kentucky" became
synonymous for any ideal place, as in, "(New York) is a real Kentuck of a
place," W. A. Caruthers, *A Kentuckian in New York,* 1834.]

The dark and bloody ground.   2
>   —THEODORE O'HARA, *The Bivouac of the Dead,* 1847

[The name *Kentucky* is sometimes said to be an Indian term meaning "dark
and bloody ground." Not so, according to George R. Stewart, who suggested in
American Place Names that it probably comes from the Iroquois *kentake,*
meadow land. The Harper *Dictionary of Place Names* cites the Wyandot
(Huron) term, *ken-ta-teh,* land of tomorrow. Henry F. Woods noted in *American Sayings,* however, that the Cherokee chief Dragging Canoe did warn in
1775 that the land was a "bloody ground"—evidently from the hunting, battles, and burials there—and that it would be dark and hard to settle. Possibly
he was trying to scare off representatives of the Transylvania Land Company
that acquired the land by treaty that year. The phrase, "Sons of the dark and
bloody ground" was used by poet and soldier Theodore O'Hara in *The Bivouac
of the Dead,* quoted above.]

Great, tall, raw-boned Kentuckians, attired in hunting shirts, and trailing their 3
loose joints over a vast extent of territory with the easy lounge peculiar to the
race.   —HARRIET BEECHER STOWE,
>   *Uncle Tom's Cabin,* 1852

The sun shines bright in the old Kentucky home.   4
>   —STEPHEN FOSTER, *My Old Kentucky Home,* 1853

Weep no more, my lady;   5
Oh, weep no more today!
We will sing one song for the old Kentucky home,
For the old Kentucky home, far away.   —*Ibid.*

Here's a health to old Kentucky,   6
Where the fathers through the years,
Hand down the courtly graces
To the sons of cavaliers;
Where the golden age is regnant,
And each succeeding morn
Finds "the corn is full of kernels,
And the Colonels full of corn."   —WILLIAM J. LAMPTON,
>   *To Old Kentucky*

[The phrase in quotations in the last couplet is a bit of traditional folk wit, author unknown, with the final "corn" being short for "corn whisky." The pun
dates to at least the opening decades of the 19th century. In 1825, Chief Justice
John Marshall penned the ditty: "In the blue grass region, / A paradox was
born: / The corn was full of kernels / and the *colonels* full of corn."]

The songbirds are the sweetest   7
In Kentucky;
The thoroughbreds are fleetest
In Kentucky;

Mountains tower proudest,
Thunder peals the loudest,
The landscape is the grandest—
And politics—the damnedest
In Kentucky.
　　　　　　　　　　　—JAMES H. MULLIGAN, *In Kentucky*

1　Wherever a Kentuckian may be, he is more than willing to boast of the beauties and virtues of the native state. He believes without reservation that Kentucky is the garden spot of the world, and is ready to dispute with anyone who questions the claim.
　　　　　　　　　　　—FEDERAL WRITERS' PROJECT, *Kentucky:
A Guide to the Bluegrass State*, 1939

Motto

2　　　　　　United we stand, divided we fall.

KINDNESS
　　　　　　　　　　　　　　　　　　　　　　　See also VIRTUE

3　I expect to pass through this world but once; any good thing, therefore, that I can do, or any kindness that I can show to any fellow creature, let me do it now; let me not defer or neglect it, for I shall not pass this way again.
　　　　　　　　　　　—ANONYMOUS
[*Bartlett's* points out that this has been attributed to many people, and most often to Stephen Grellet, a French Quaker cleric, who came to the U.S. in 1795. But no attribution has been verified.]

4　By chivalries as tiny,
A blossom, or a book,
The seeds of smiles are planted—
Which blossom in the dark.　　　—EMILY DICKINSON, poem no. 55, c. 1858

5　If I can stop one heart from breaking,
I shall not live in vain
If I can ease one life the aching
Or cool one pain

Or help one fainting robin
Unto his nest again
I shall not live in vain.　　　—EMILY DICKINSON, poem no. 919, c. 1864

6　It is higher and nobler to be kind.
　　　　　　　　　　　—MARK TWAIN, *Autobiography* [1924]
[More at JUSTICE.]

7　I have always depended on the kindness of strangers.
　　　　　　　　　　—TENNESSEE WILLIAMS, *A Streetcar Named Desire*, 1947
[Blanche DuBois's exit line.]

8　Nothing has happened today except kindness.
　　　　　　　　　　—GERTRUDE STEIN, *A Diary*, in *Alphabets and Birthdays*, 1957

9　A kinder, gentler, nation.
　　　　　　　　　　—GEORGE BUSH, presidential nomination acceptance speech,
　　　　　　　　　　Republican National Convention, New Orleans,
　　　　　　　　　　August 18, 1988
[More information at POLITICAL SLOGANS.]

KNOWLEDGE & INFORMATION   *See also* EDUCATION; FACTS

Forewarned, forearmed.   1
>   —BENJAMIN FRANKLIN, *Poor Richard's Almanack*, 1736

[Another proverb recycled by Franklin. Cervantes included it in *Don Quixote*, 1615.]

Knowledge . . . is the great sun in the firmament. Life and power are scattered   2
with all its beams.
>   —DANIEL WEBSTER, speech at the laying of the cornerstone,
>   Bunker Hill Monument, June 17, 1825

Knowledge is the knowing that we cannot know.   3
>   —RALPH WALDO EMERSON, *Representative Men*, 1850

It is better to know nothing than to know what ain't so.   4
>   —JOSH BILLINGS, *Josh Billings' Encyclopedia of Wit
>   and Wisdom*, 1874

[This is essentially a proverb, used in various forms by Benjamin Franklin and others. Abroad, Friedrich Wilhelm Nietzsche wrote in *Thus Spake Zarathustra* (1883–91), "Better know nothing than half know many things." John Maynard Keynes opined, "It is better to be approximately right than precisely wrong." See also Thomas Jefferson at THE PRESS—the note after his comment on there being nothing in newspapers that can be believed.]

Many men are stored full of unused knowledge . . . they are stuffed with use-   5
less ammunition.
>   —HENRY WARD BEECHER, *Proverbs from Plymouth Pulpit*, 1887

Knowledge is the recognition of something absent; it is a salutation, not an   6
embrace.   —GEORGE SANTAYANA, *The Life of Reason:
>   Reason in Common Sense*, 1905–1906

Knowledge is always accompanied with accessories of emotion and purpose.   7
>   —ALFRED NORTH WHITEHEAD, *Adventures of Ideas*, 1933

Die knowing something. You are not here long.   8
>   —WALKER EVANS,
>   unpublished text for his subway photographs, c. 1940,
>   quoted in Belinda Rathbone, *Walker Evans* [1995]

[The full passage runs: "Stare. It is the way to educate your eye, and more. Stare, pry, listen, eavesdrop. Die knowing something . . . (etc.)." Evans was one of America's great photographers, most remembered for his photos of Alabama tenant farmers in the Depression, published in *Let Us Now Praise Famous Men*, 1938, with a text by James Agee.]

Everybody gets so much information all day long that they lose their common   9
sense.   —GERTRUDE STEIN, untitled essay from 1946,
>   in *Reflection on the Atomic Bomb* [1973]

To live effectively is to live with adequate information.   10
>   —NORBERT WIENER, *The Human Use of Human Beings*, 1954

So much has already been written about everything that you can't find out any-   11
thing about it.   —JAMES THURBER, *The New Vocabularianism*,
>   in *Lanterns and Lances*, 1961

1   Information is power.   —ARTHUR SYLVESTER, remarks,
                                        Sigma Delta Chi dinner, New York City, 1962
[A common observation. Assistant Defense Secretary Sylvester made more
waves when he asserted that the "government's right, if necessary, to lie." This
was just after the Cuban missile crisis.]

2   The greater our knowledge increases, the more our ignorance unfolds.
                                        —JOHN F. KENNEDY, speech,
                                        Rice University, Sept. 12, 1962

KOREAN WAR,
1950–53

3   The attack upon Korea makes it plain beyond all doubt that Communism has
passed beyond the use of subversion to conquer independent nations, and will
now use armed invasion and war.
                            —HARRY S. TRUMAN, comment to the press, June 27, 1950
[The division of Korea, along the 38th parallel, into North Korea, dominated by
the Soviet and Chinese Communists, and the South, governed by the United
Nations, persisted after the end of World War II. In 1948, elections in South Korea created a democratic state. On June 24, 1950, the Communist People's
Army invaded South Korea. The U.N. Security Council called for all members
to help repel the invaders. (The Council was being boycotted by the U.S.S.R.,
which otherwise could have vetoed the resolution.) Pres. Truman ordered the
first U.S. military response on June 27.]

4   Retreat, hell! We're only attacking in another direction.
                                        —OLIVER P. SMITH,
                                        vicinity of Chosin Reservoir,
                                        Korea, Dec. 4, 1950
[Maj. Gen. Smith conducted an epic retreat when his 1st Marine Division, surrounded by Chinese troops and outnumbered by more than ten to one, fought
its way back to the coast, bringing their dead with them. The troops were evacuated by ship.]

5   In the simplest of terms, what we are doing in Korea is this: We are trying to
prevent a third world war.
                            —HARRY S. TRUMAN, address to the nation, April 16, 1951
[The occasion of the president's address was his recall of Gen. Douglas
MacArthur for insubordination.]

6   In war there is no substitute for victory.
                                        —DOUGLAS MACARTHUR, speech,
                                        joint session of Congress, April 19, 1951
[From his "old soldiers never die" speech; see AMERICAN HISTORY: MEMORABLE
MOMENTS. A couple of weeks earlier, in a letter to House Speaker Joseph Martin, Jr., Gen. MacArthur had used the same phrase: "There is no substitute for
victory." Martin, a Republican, read the letter aloud in the House on April 5,
despite knowing that it might lead to the general's downfall, for MacArthur
was challenging the authority of his commander in chief, Pres. Harry Truman.
MacArthur in his letter advocated "meeting force with maximum counter-
force." The target was China, which had intervened on the side of North Korea
against South Korea and its American allies. MacArthur advised bombing
China and calling in the Nationalist forces of Gen. Chiang Kai-shek. Truman
relieved MacArthur of command on April 11.]

This strategy would involve us in the wrong war, at the wrong place, at the   1
wrong time, and with the wrong enemy.
—OMAR BRADLEY, testimony, U. S. Senate, May 15, 1951
[The subject was widening the war, as advocated by Gen. Douglas MacArthur.
Gen. Bradley was testifying as chairman of the Joint Chiefs of Staff in combined hearings of the Foreign Relations and Armed Services committees in-
vestigating the dismissal of Gen. MacArthur by Pres. Harry S. Truman. See
also THE MILITARY.]

I shall go to Korea.   —DWIGHT D. EISENHOWER, campaign speech,   2
Detroit, Mich., Oct. 25, 1952
[Eisenhower, who was running for president, promised to restart stalled peace
talks. As president-elect, he did go to Korea at the end of November. The
armistice was signed in July 1953.]

This was a police action, a limited war, whatever you want to call it, to stop ag-   3
gression and to prevent a big war.   —HARRY S. TRUMAN, in Merle Miller,
Plain Speaking [1974]
[This unpopular, costly, and indecisive conflict never involved a U.S. declaration of war. The euphemistic "police action" arose in a roundabout way. On
June 29, 1950, at Truman's first press conference following North Korea's invasion of South Korea, the president said that the United States was "not at
war" but just suppressing a raid by "a bunch of bandits." A reporter then asked
if it would be fair "to call this a police action under the United Nations?" "Yes.
That is exactly what it amounts to," Truman replied, thus justifying such
headlines the next day as "Truman Calls Intervention 'Police Action.'" The
anonymous reporter, in turn, may have picked up the phrase from a Senate
speech by William F. Knowland. Speaking of the air force's mission, the California Republican declared: "The action this government is taking is a police
action against a violator of the law of nations and the Charter of the United
Nations."]

L

LABOR   *See* CAPITALISM & CAPITAL V. LABOR; WORK & WORKERS

LANGUAGE   *See also* AMERICA & AMERICANS (Whitman
& WORDS   on American names); ART: STYLE IN
         WRITING & EXPRESSION; ART: WRITING;
         NORTH CAROLINA (Byrd on Buncombe); TALK

1

Morals and manners will rise or decline with our attention to grammar.
         —JASON CHAMBERLAIN, inaugural speech,
         University of Vermont, 1811

2

I very seldom during my whole stay in the country heard a sentence elegantly
turned and correctly pronounced from the lips of an American. There is always
something either in the expression or the accent that jars the feelings and
shocks the taste.   —FRANCES TROLLOPE, *Domestic Manners*
         of the Americans, 1832
[Like most British visitors of the period (see also Capt. Marryat below), Mrs.
Trollope did not agree with the American view that they spoke a superior English. For example, James Fenimore Cooper asserted in *Notions of the Americans* (1828) that "The people of the United States, with the exception of a few
of German or French descent, speak, as a body, incomparably better English
than the people of the mother country." Cooper reached this conclusion, despite noting serious faults in American English; see below.]

3

The common faults of American language are ambition of effect, a want of
simplicity, and turgid abuse of terms.   —JAMES FENIMORE COOPER,
         The American Democrat, 1838

4

It is remarkable how very debased the language has become in a short period in
America.   —FREDERICK MARRYAT,
         A Diary in America, 1839
[Capt. Marryat—a former British navy officer and author of *Mr. Midshipman
Easy* and other novels—was personally disconcerted by one such "debase-
ment" while accompanying a young woman to view Niagara Falls. After she
slipped from a rock, he asked if she had hurt her "leg." Consternation! She
turned away from him, "evidently much shocked, or much offended." He

begged to know why, and after some hesitation she explained that "the word *leg* was never mentioned before ladies." The proper term turned out to be *limb*. She herself was not nearly as particular as some people, she told the Captain, "for I know those who always say limb of a table, or limb of a piano-forte."]

Every word was once a poem. Every new relation is a new word.   1
           —RALPH WALDO EMERSON, *The Poet*,
           in *Essays: Second Series*, 1844

Language is the archives of history.   *—Ibid.*   2

Each word was at first a stroke of genius.   *—Ibid.*   3

Language is fossil poetry.   *—Ibid.*   4

A word is dead
When it is said,
Some say.

I say it just   5
Begins to live that day.   —EMILY DICKINSON, poem no. 1212, c. 1872

She dealt her pretty words like blades,   6
As glittering they shone,
And every one unbared a nerve
Or wantoned with a bone.   —EMILY DICKINSON, in *Further Poems* [1924]

A *mugwump* is a fellow with his mug on one side of the fence and his wump   7
on the other.
           —ANONYMOUS, possibly c. 1884
[The most famous early mugwumps, or political independents, were Republican liberals, led by Carl Schurz of Missouri, who in 1884 supported Democrat Grover Cleveland rather than the Republican candidate, James G. Blaine. The anonymous definition, which has been tracked in print only to the 1930s, has been credited to Rep. Albert J. Engel, who used it in a 1936 speech, and to Harold Willis Dodds, president of Princeton from 1933 to 1937, but it is almost certainly older. *Mugwump* itself is Algonquin for *chief* and was used by the Rev. John Eliot in 1663 in place of *duke* when translating the Old Testament for Native Americans. For more on Blaine, see Robert Ingersoll at HEROES. See Horace Porter at POLITICAL SLOGANS for additional information on mugwumps.]

The difference between the *almost*-right word and the *right* word is really a   8
large matter—it's the difference between the lightning bug and the lightning.
           —MARK TWAIN, letter to George Bainton, Oct. 15, 1888,
           reprinted as *Reply to the Editor of "The Art of Authorship,"*
           1890
[Twain may have lifted this image from his good friend Josh Billings (Henry Wheeler Shaw), who had died five years before. Billings's immensely popular sayings included the observation that "the difference between vivacity and wit is the same as the difference between the lightning-bug and the lightning." The plagiarism almost certainly was unconscious. Twain, who was about the last writer in need of stealing from others, had done this sort of thing inadvertently before. The dedication of his first book, *Innocents Abroad* (1869), repeated the dedication of a collection of poems by Oliver Wendell Holmes. Twain had read the poems but forgotten the dedication. He was mortified when the unintentional theft was pointed out to him, wrote an abject apology to Holmes, and

was immediately and completely forgiven. See also Twain at ART: STYLE IN WRITING & EXPRESSION.]

1   The only people that should use the word "we" are editors, kings, and persons with tapeworms.   —MARK TWAIN, attributed in *The New Yorker*, Talk of the Town [May 1, 1989]
[Commonly attributed to Twain in several forms, but we editors have not been able to verify it.]

2   Words are slippery.   —HENRY BROOKS ADAMS, *The Education of Henry Adams*, 1907

3   The short words are the best.   —WILLIAM JAY GAYNOR, saying
[Judge Gaynor was Tammany Hall's candidate for New York City mayor in 1909. An erudite and testy man, he proved to be uncontrollably honest—and blunt. One of his unhappy opponents was William Randolph Hearst, who used his paper the New York *Morning Journal* as a base for attacks on Gaynor. The judge and reform prevailed in the election, but in August 1910, a disgruntled city worker, who was a *Journal* reader, shot and seriously wounded Gaynor; the mayor never fully recovered. A photographer from Joseph Pulitzer's *Evening World* by chance caught the shooting in a now-famous photograph. The city editor is said to have reacted with delight: "Blood all over him—and exclusive, too!"
    See the note at the Zelda Fitzgerald quote at ADVERTISING, ADVERTISING SLOGANS, & PUBLICITY for more on Gaynor.]

4   A shorter and more ugly word.   —THEODORE ROOSEVELT, 1907
[Roosevelt apparently hesitated to accuse financier Edward H. Harriman explicitly of lying. But this was his implicit characterization of a published claim by Harriman that in 1904 Roosevelt had agreed in essence to exchange an ambassadorship for much needed campaign funds. Roosevelt did call the claim "a deliberate and willful untruth," adding, "by rights it should be characterized by an even shorter and more ugly word." The word *lie* is one of those terms that almost guarantee that a libel suit will be filed, and one had best be sure of winning it.]

5   One of our defects as a nation is a tendency to use what have been called "weasel words."   —THEODORE ROOSEVELT, speech, St. Louis, May 31, 1916
[Roosevelt heard of weasel words as a young man while visiting Maine. He stayed with the Sewall family, whom he liked very much, excepting perhaps Sam Sewall, a deacon. Roosevelt wrote that Sam was "very adroit in using fair-sounding words which completely nullified the meaning of other fair-sounding words which preceded them." Deacon Sewall's brother, Dave, explained, "His words weasel the meaning of the words in front of them, just like a weasel when he sucks the meat out of an egg and leaves nothing but the shell." Roosevelt commented, "I always remembered 'weasel words' as applicable to certain forms of oratory, especially political oratory," *My Debt to Maine* in the anthology *Maine My State*, 1919.
    In his speech in May 1916, quoted above, Roosevelt was attacking Woodrow Wilson's call for universal voluntary military training. "You can have universal training, or you can have voluntary training," Roosevelt said, "but when you use the word 'voluntary' to qualify the word 'universal,' you are making a 'weasel word'; it has sucked all the meaning out of 'universal.'"]

Omit needless words. —WILLIAM STRUNK, JR., *The Elements* 1
of Style, 1918
[More at ART: STYLE IN WRITING & EXPRESSION.]

Honeyed words like bees, 2
Gilded and sticky, with a little sting. —ELINOR HOYT WYLIE, *Pretty Words*,
in *Collected Poems* [1932]

I love smooth words, like gold-enameled fish 3
Which circle slowly with a silken swish. —*Ibid.*

Words are weapons, and it is dangerous . . . to borrow them from the arsenal of 4
the enemy. —GEORGE SANTAYANA, *Orbiter Scripta*, 1936

Words are chameleons, which reflect the color of their environment. 5
—LEARNED HAND, *Cabell v. Markham*, 1945

You can stroke people with words. —F. SCOTT FITZGERALD, 6
The Crack-Up, 1945

Man does not live by words alone, despite the fact that sometimes he has to eat 7
them. —ADLAI STEVENSON, speech,
Denver, Col., Sept. 5, 1952
[By contrast, Robert Louis Stevenson claimed, "Man does not live by bread
alone, but principally by catchwords," *Virginibus Puerisque*, title essay, 1881.]

Slang is a language that rolls up its sleeves, spits on its hands, and goes to work. 8
—CARL SANDBURG, *New York Times*, Feb. 13, 1959

I can answer you in two words—im possible. —SAMUEL GOLDWYN, 9
attributed
[Fake quotes—malapropisms especially—collected around movie producer
Samuel Goldwyn (born Goldfisch) in much the same way as they did later
around baseball star Yogi Berra. Among other reputed Goldwynisms: "Gentlemen, include me out," "Quick as a flashlight," "You've got to take the bull by
the teeth," and "If nobody wants to see your picture, there's nothing you can
do to stop them." See also Goldwyn on verbal contracts at LAW.]

Words are a great trap. —MARIANNE MOORE, answering a question from 10
the audience, 92nd St. Y, New York City, 1968

Only where there is language is there world. 11
—ADRIENNE RICH, *The Demon Lover*, in *Leaflets*, 1969

The use of language is all we have to pit against death and silence. 12
—JOYCE CAROL OATES, speech, National Book Awards, 1969

Language is a virus from outer space. 13
—WILLIAM S. BURROUGHS, quoted in *Home of the Brave*,
multimedia production by Laurie Anderson, 1985

LAST WORDS

See also DEATH; EPITAPHS & GRAVESTONES;
FREEDOM (David Crockett); LIFE (Crowfoot); SUICIDE

To be like Christ is to be a Christian. —WILLIAM PENN, last words, 1718 14

1   I only regret that I have but one life to lose for my country.
            —NATHAN HALE, at the gallows in Artillery Park, N.Y.,
                    Sept. 22, 1776
[See AMERICAN REVOLUTION for more on Hale, and for his doomed counterpart
in the British army, Maj. John André.]

2   'Tis well.
            —GEORGE WASHINGTON, Dec. 14, 1799
[Washington had already told his doctor that he was dying hard but not afraid;
see DEATH. He was, however, frightened of being buried alive—something that
probably happens more often than we like to think. Just before death, he in-
structed his secretary, Tobias Lear, "I am just going. Have me decently buried,
and do not let my body be put into the vault in less than three days after I am
dead. Do you understand me?" When Lear nodded, Washington then spoke his
last, and died a few hours later, close to midnight.]

3   Is it the Fourth?
            —THOMAS JEFFERSON, last words, July 3, 1826
[Jefferson did live one day more day, reaching the fiftieth anniversary of the
Fourth of July, as he had hoped.]

4   Thomas Jefferson survives.
            —JOHN ADAMS, July 4, 1826
[Jefferson had died about two hours earlier; see also INDEPENDENCE DAY. At the
time of John Adams's death, his son John Quincy Adams was president of the
United States.]

5   This is the last of earth! I am content.   —JOHN QUINCY ADAMS,
                                            Feb. 23, 1848
[Adams, after serving as the sixth president of the U.S., went on to represent
Massachusetts in the U.S. House of Representatives for seventeen years. He
suffered a stroke there on February 21 and died two days later. See also Philip
Hone on Adams at EPITAPHS & GRAVESTONES.]

6   Oh, do not cry—be good children and we will all meet in heaven.
            —ANDREW JACKSON, June 8, 1845
[Jackson, on his deathbed, to his griefstricken household.]

7   The South! The South! God knows what will become of her.
            —JOHN C. CALHOUN, March 31, 1850

8   An American kneels only to his god, and faces his enemy.
            —W. H. CRITTENDON, Havana, August 16, 1851
[On being ordered by a Spanish officer to kneel down before being shot as a fil-
ibusterer—a soldier of fortune—in Cuba.]

9   This *is* beautiful country.   —JOHN BROWN, on his way to
                            the gallows, Dec. 2, 1859
[To the hangman he said, "Do not keep me waiting. I am ready at any time."
For his statement at his trial, see AMERICAN HISTORY: MEMORABLE MOMENTS.]

10   One world at a time.   —HENRY DAVID THOREAU, remark
                        in the last week of his life, 1862
[This is said to have been Thoreau's answer when a visitor, somewhat imper-
tinently, asked how "the opposite shore" appeared to him. Other reports of
last, or nearly last, words from Thoreau include: "I did not know we had

ever quarreled, aunt," in response to his aunt Louisa's inquiry as to whether he had made his peace with God"; and, to his sister Sophie, "Now comes good sailing."]

Texas. Texas.   —SAMUEL HOUSTON, attributed last words, 1863   1

Let us cross over the river and rest under the shade of the trees.   2
                    —THOMAS JONATHAN "STONEWALL" JACKSON, May 10, 1863
[Gen. Jackson, a victim of friendly fire, was shot inadvertently on May 2 by his own troops while returning from a nighttime reconaissance of Union lines during the battle of Chancellorsville. The deeply religious Jackson had written in an 1862 letter: "God has fixed the time for my death. I do not concern myself about that, but to be always ready, no matter when it may overtake me.—That is the way all men should live, and then all would be equally brave." See under CIVIL WAR for Jackson's nickname and under EPITAPHS & GRAVE-STONES for U. S. Grant on Jackson's character.]

Strike the tent.   —ROBERT E. LEE, attributed last words,   3
                    Oct. 12, 1870
[Some accounts say Lee prefaced these words with "Tell Hill he *must* come up," but Emory Thomas concluded in *Robert E. Lee* (1995) that all these "last words" were part of the process of making Lee's life into a legend even as he lay dying. In truth, Lee suffered a massive stroke on September 28 that left him passive and apparently speechless for the last two weeks of his life.]

Now comes the mystery.   —HENRY WARD BEECHER, March 8, 1887   4

[Life] is the little shadow which runs across the grass and loses itself in the sun-   5
set.
                    —CROWFOOT, last words, 1890
[More at LIFE.]

Not our will, but His be done.   —WILLIAM MCKINLEY, on his deathbed,   6
                    Sept. 11, 1901
[President McKinley was shot by an anarchist.]

Put out the light.   —THEODORE ROOSEVELT, last words, Jan. 6, 1919   7

It is very beautiful over there.   —THOMAS EDISON, Oct. 18, 1931   8

I'm glad it was me instead of you, Frank. The country needs you.   9
                    —ANTON CERMAK, deathbed words to Franklin D. Roosevelt,
                    Miami, Feb. 15, 1933
[Cermak, the mayor of Chicago, was talking to president-elect Roosevelt, when someone fired shots in their direction. Cermak was wounded in the abdomen and died.]

Rosebud.   —HERMAN J. MANKIEWICZ & ORSON WELLES,   10
                    Citizen Kane, screenplay, 1941
[Kane's last communication. *Rosebud* was the name of Kane's sled when he was a boy. See also REGRET.]

I have a terrific pain in the back of my head.   11
                    —FRANKLIN D. ROOSEVELT, suffering a cerebral hemorrhage,
                    April 12, 1945
[The ailing president was in the living room of the Little White House in Warm Springs, Ga., working and reading. With him were his cousins Margaret Lynch

(Daisy) Suckley and Laura Delano, Lucy Mercer Rutherfurd, and a portrait painter, Elizabeth Shoumatoff. The last words have also been recorded as, "I have a terrific headache." He collapsed immediately and never recovered consciousness. The news flew round the world. In Germany, Propaganda Minister Goebbels telephoned Hitler, "My Führer! I congratulate you. Roosevelt is dead. . . . It is the turning point!"]

1   What is the answer? [*I was silent.*] In that case, what is the question?
  —GERTRUDE STEIN, last words, 1946, reported in
  Alice B. Toklas, *What Is Remembered* [1963]

2   Seventeen whiskeys. A record, I think.
  —DYLAN THOMAS, after a fatal bout of drinking at the
  White Horse Tavern in Manhattan in 1953
  [Thomas was Welsh, of course, but his spirit is very much alive in this American bar, where he was a regular for a time.]

3   I had rather be a servant in the house of the Lord than sit in the seat of the mighty. —ALBEN BARKLEY,
  April 30, 1956

  [He was vice president under Harry S. Truman, 1949–53.]

4   Like anybody, I would like to live a long life. Longevity has its place. But I'm not concerned about that now. I just want to do God's will. And he's allowed me to go up to the mountain. And I've looked over, and I've seen the promised land. I may not get there with you, but I want you to know tonight that we as a people will get to the promised land. . . .
  So I'm happy tonight. I'm not worried about anything. I'm not fearing any man. Mine eyes have seen the glory of the coming of the Lord.
  —MARTIN LUTHER KING, JR., speech to sanitation workers,
  Memphis, Tenn., April 3, 1968
  [King was shot the next morning. The speech is renowned for its sense of impending death. Seconds before he was hit, King said to his friend Ben Branch, "Ben, make sure you play *Precious Lord, Take My Hand*. Play it real pretty for me."]

LAUGHTER & MIRTH   *See also* HUMOR

5   A human being should beware how he laughs, for then he shows all his faults.
  —RALPH WALDO EMERSON, *Journals*, 1836

6   A laugh's the wisest, easiest answer to all that's queer.
  —HERMAN MELVILLE, *Moby-Dick*, 1851

7   Mirth is the mail of anguish.   —EMILY DICKINSON, poem no. 165,
  c. 1860
  [*Mail* in the sense of armor.]

8   Laughing has always been considered by theologians as a crime.
  —ROBERT G. INGERSOLL, speech, Chicago, Nov. 26, 1882

9   Against the assault of laughter, nothing can stand.
  —MARK TWAIN, *The Mysterious Stranger* [1922]

10 We laugh and laugh. Then cry and cry—Then feebler laugh. Then die.
  —MARK TWAIN, *Notebook* [1935]

Laugh, and the world laughs with you; 1
Weep, and you weep alone;
For the sad old earth must borrow its mirth,
But has trouble enough of its own. —ELLA WHEELER WILCOX, *Solitude*, in
Collected Poems, 1917

One horse-laugh is worth ten thousand syllogisms. 2
—H. L. MENCKEN, *Prejudices: Fourth Series*, 1924

LAW

See also CONSTITUTION, THE; CRIME, CRIMINALS, & DETECTIVES; EVIDENCE; HABIT & CUSTOM (Santayana and Stevenson); JUDGES; JURIES; JUSTICE; LAWYERS; SUPREME COURT; WEST, THE (Anonymous).

Laws like to cobwebs catch small flies; 3
Great ones break through before your eyes.
—BENJAMIN FRANKLIN, *Poor Richard's Almanack*, 1734
[An update from Solon, 7th century B.C.: "Laws are like spiders' webs: If some poor weak creature come up against them, it is caught; but a big one can break through and get away," quoted in Diogenes Laërtius, *Lives of Eminent Philosophers*, 3d century A.D.]

Laws too gentle are seldom obeyed; too severe, seldom executed. 4
—BENJAMIN FRANKLIN, *Poor Richard's Almanack*, 1756

A government of laws, and not of men. —JOHN ADAMS, "Novanglus" papers, 5
Boston Gazette, 1774
[Adams credited the phrase to the English political writer James Harrington, who used the expression in his Utopian work, *The Commonwealth of Oceana*, 1656. Thanks to Adams, the phrase appears in Article 30 of the Declaration of Rights in the Massachusetts Constitution, 1780.]

That it is better one hundred guilty persons should escape than that one inno- 6
cent person should suffer is a maxim that has been long and generally approved.
—BENJAMIN FRANKLIN, letter to Benjamin Vaughan,
March 14, 1785
[The maxim, identified as such, was also cited by Voltaire: "'Tis much more prudence to acquit two persons, though actually guilty, than to pass sentence of condemnation on one that is virtuous and innocent," *Zadig*, 1749. It is enshrined in Sir William Blackstone's *Commentaries on the Laws of England* (1765–69): "It is better that ten guilty persons escape than one innocent suffer."]

The execution of the laws is more important than the making them. 7
—THOMAS JEFFERSON, letter to the Abbé Arnond, 1789

Law is whatever is boldly asserted and plausibly maintained. 8
—AARON BURR, attributed, quoted in James Parton,
The Life and Times of Aaron Burr [1857]

In general, the great can protect themselves, but the poor and humble require 9
the arm and shield of the law. —ANDREW JACKSON, letter to
John Quincy Adams, August 26, 1821

Scarcely any political question arises in the United States that is not resolved, 10
sooner or later, into a judicial question.
—ALEXIS DE TOCQUEVILLE, *Democracy in America*, 1835

1   Good men must not obey the laws too well.
     —RALPH WALDO EMERSON, *Politics*, in *Essays: Second Series*, 1844

2   It is not desirable to cultivate a respect for the law, so much as for the right.
     —HENRY DAVID THOREAU, *Civil Disobedience*, 1849
     [In 1843, Thoreau refused to pay a state tax as a protest against the legality of
     slavery in the U.S. Constitution. He was arrested in 1846 by constable and tax
     collector Samuel Staples, who was trying to get his accounts in order prepara-
     tory to resigning. Thoreau spent only one night in jail; a woman—probably his
     Aunt Maria—paid the tax. Actually, according to Thoreau scholar Walter
     Harding, Thoreau probably should not have been in jail at all: the applicable
     law mandated seizure of property to cover any unpaid tax. But then we would
     not have this essay on civil disobedience, which is the seminal text advocating
     passive resistance as a political tool. See also Thoreau at MEXICAN WAR.]

3   There is more law in the end of a policeman's nightstick than in a decision of
     the Supreme Court.   —ALEXANDER S. WILLIAMS,
                                                              attributed c. 1870
     [Inspector "Clubber" Williams earned his soubriquet while a patrolman in
     Hell's Kitchen, on the west side of Manhattan. Moving across town, he became
     a captain in the Gas House district, where he subdued the notorious Gas House
     Gang with a squad of club-swinging policemen. In 1876, he went on to serve in
     the 29th precinct, in the center of Manhattan, which acquired a new name
     when Williams told a friend, "I've had nothing but chuck steak for a long time,
     and now I'm going to get a little of the tenderloin."]

4   The life of the law has not been logic: it has been experience.
     —OLIVER WENDELL HOLMES, JR., *The Common Law*, 1881

5   The law embodies the story of a nation's development through many cen-
     turies, and it cannot be dealt with as if it contained only the axioms and corol-
     laries of a book of mathematics.   —*Ibid.*

6   Hear ye! Hear ye! This honorable court's now in session; and if any galoot
     wants to snort afore we start, let him step up the bar and name his pizen.
                                                         —ROY BEAN, attributed
     [Numerous sources report—with minor variations in wording—that this is
     how Judge Bean opened court sessions following his appointment in 1882 as
     justice of the peace in Langtry, Texas. Bean's fame stretched so far that train
     passengers often stopped off at Langtry to get a look at the "Law West of the
     Pecos" (in the words of the sign that graced his saloon-cum-court). When he
     died in 1903, newspapers all over the nation ran his obituary. See also Bean at
     TEXAS in the note on the anonymous quote regarding the absence of law west
     of the Pecos.]

7   The law is not the place for the artist or the poet. . . . The law is the calling of
     thinkers.   —OLIVER WENDELL HOLMES, JR., *The Profession of the Law*,
                                              lecture to Harvard undergraduates, Feb. 17, 1886

8   Law is merely the expression of the will of the strongest for the time being, and
     therefore, laws have no fixity, but shift from generation to generation.
     —BROOKS ADAMS, *The Law of Civilization and Decay*, 1896

9   Great cases like hard cases make bad law.
     —OLIVER WENDELL HOLMES, JR., *Northern Securities Co. v. U.S.*, 1904
     [Holmes is alluding to the legal byword: "Hard cases make bad law."]

No man is above the law and no man is below it; nor do we ask any man's per- 1
mission when we require him to obey it.
—THEODORE ROOSEVELT, speech, Jan. 1904

General propositions do not decide concrete cases. 2
—OLIVER WENDELL HOLMES, JR., dissent,
Lochner v. New York, 1905

It is a fortunate thing for society that the courts do not get the same chance at 3
the Ten Commandments as they do at the Constitution of the United States.
—PHILANDER C. JOHNSON, *Senator Sorghum's
Primer of Politics*, 1906

Lawsuit, n. A machine which you go into as a pig and come out as a sausage. 4
—AMBROSE BIERCE, *The Devil's Dictionary*, 1906

If facts are changing, the law cannot be static. 5
—FELIX FRANKFURTER, speech, 1912

It cannot be helped, it is as it should be, that the law is behind the times. 6
—OLIVER WENDELL HOLMES, JR., speech, Harvard Law School
Association of New York, Feb. 15, 1913

No great idea in its beginning can ever be within the law. How can it be within 7
the law? The law is stationary. The law is fixed. The law is a chariot wheel
which binds us all regardless of conditions or place or time.
—EMMA GOLDMAN, *Address to the Jury*, in *Mother Earth*,
July 17, 1917

One with the law is a majority. —CALVIN COOLIDGE, speech, July 27, 1920 8

The law must be stable but it must not stand still. 9
—ROSCOE POUND, *Introduction to the Philosophy of Law*, 1922
[Pound, who became dean of the Harvard School of Law, was one of nation's
foremost legal theorists.]

Go to jail. Go directly to jail. Do not pass Go. Do not collect $200. 10
—CHARLES BRUCE DARROW, Community Chest card
in Monopoly, 1931
[Darrow created the popular board game.]

If we would guide by the light of reason, we must let our minds be bold. 11
—LOUIS D. BRANDEIS, *N. Y. State Ice Co. v. Liebmann*, 1932

Legal concepts are supernatural entities which do not have a verifiable exis- 12
tence except to the eyes of faith. —FELIX S. COHEN, *Transcendental
Nonsense and the Functional
Approach*, 1935

The law [is] a horrible business. —CLARENCE DARROW, interview, 13
New York Times, April 19, 1936

I am the law. —FRANK HAGUE, quoted in *The New York Times*, 14
Nov. 11, 1937
[Hague, the boss of Jersey City and Hudson County, was testifying in a legis-
lative investigation when he made this comment. He had been asked by

what right he had prohibited picketing and the distribution of prolabor literature.]

1   Under our constitutional system, courts stand against any winds that blow as havens of refuge for those who might otherwise suffer because they are helpless, weak, outnumbered, or because they are non-conforming victims of prejudice and public excitement.   —HUGO L. BLACK, *Chambers v. Florida,*
1938.
[More from this decision is given at SUPREME COURT.]

2   A verbal contract isn't worth the paper it's written on.
—SAMUEL GOLDWYN, attributed
[Unlike most other Goldwynisms—see LANGUAGE & WORDS—which were purely fictitious, this quote is a distortion of something the movie producer actually said. Referring to Joseph M. Schenck, a Hollywood executive whose word was considered his bond, Goldwyn declared, according to *They Never Said It* (1989) by Paul F. Boller, Jr., and John George: "His verbal contract is worth more than the paper it's written on." The mangled version made a better story, however, and this is the one that press agents and columnists popularized.]

3   The law is bigger than money, but only if the law works hard enough.
—THOMAS E. DEWEY, quoted in Richard Norton Smith,
Thomas E. Dewey [1982]

4   We don't give a damn about the law. Down here we make our own law.
—EUGENE "BULL" CONNOR, quoted in *The Afro-American,*
Nov. 22, 1958
[Connor, the Public Safety Commissioner of Birmingham, Ala., was responding to a question about the legality of arresting for vagrancy three African-American ministers from Montgomery, who had come to Birmingham to confer with a colleague.]

5   Morality cannot be legislated but behavior can be regulated. Judicial decrees may not change the heart, but they can restrain the heartless.
—MARTIN LUTHER KING, JR., *Strength to Love,* 1963

6   An individual who breaks a law that conscience tells him is unjust, and who willingly accepts the penalty of imprisonment in order to arouse the conscience of the community over its injustice, is in reality expressing the highest respect for the law.   —MARTIN LUTHER KING, JR., *Why We Can't Wait,* 1964

LAWYERS

7   One thing I supplicate your majesty: that you will give orders, under a great penalty, that no bachelors of law should be allowed to come here [the New World]; for not only are they bad themselves, but they also make and contrive a thousand iniquities.   —VASCO NUÑEZ DE BALBOA,
to Ferdinand V of Spain, 1513

8   In no country, perhaps, in the world is the law so general a study. The profession itself is numerous and powerful, and in most provinces [in America] it takes the lead.   —EDMUND BURKE, speech in Parliament moving
his resolution on conciliation with the colonies,
March 22, 1775

Accuracy and diligence are much more necessary to a lawyer than great com- 1
prehension of mind or brilliancy of talent.
—DANIEL WEBSTER, letter to Thomas Merrill, Nov. 11, 1803

The New England folks have a saying that three Philadelphia lawyers are a 2
match for the very devil himself.   —ANONYMOUS, *Salem Observer*,
March 13, 1824
[The reputation of Philadelphia lawyers was already several decades old. Fred
R. Shapiro in *American Legal Quotations* (1993) cites a reference from 1788 in
the *Columbian Magazine:* "They have a proverb here [in London] . . . in speaking of a difficult point, they say, 'It would puzzle a Philadelphia lawyer.'"
Shapiro speculates that the reputation of Philadelphia lawyers may stem from
Andrew Hamilton's defense of publisher John Peter Zenger in New York in
1735. Zenger was charged with libel, and his acquittal helped to establish truth
as a defense in such cases.]

The lawyers of the United States form a party which is but little feared and 3
scarcely perceived. . . . But this party extends over the whole community, and
penetrates into all the classes which compose it; it acts upon the country im-
perceptibly, but finally fashions it to suit its own purposes.
—ALEXIS DE TOCQUEVILLE, *Democracy in America*, 1835

Civil laws are familiarly known only to lawyers, whose direct interest it is to 4
maintain them as they are, whether good or bad, simply because they themselves are conversant with them.   —*Ibid.*

Resolve to be honest at all events: and if in your judgment you cannot be an 5
honest lawyer, resolve to be honest without being a lawyer. Choose some other
occupation.   —ABRAHAM LINCOLN, notes for a lecture, 1850

Weary lawyers with endless tongues.   —JOHN GREENLEAF WHITTIER, 6
Maud Muller, 1854

To succeed in other trades, capacity must be shown; in the law, concealment 7
will do.   —MARK TWAIN,
Pudd'nhead Wilson's New Calendar,
in *Following the Equator*, 1897

Lawyer, n. One skilled in circumvention of the law. 8
—AMBROSE BIERCE, *The Devil's Dictionary*, 1906

Dice, n. Small polka-dotted cubes of ivory, constructed like a lawyer to lie on 9
any side, but commonly on the wrong one.
—AMBROSE BIERCE, *The Enlarged Devil's Dictionary* [1967]

A law, Hennessy, that might look like a wall to you or me would look like a tri- 10
umphal arch to the experienced eye of a lawyer.
—FINLEY PETER DUNNE, *Mr. Dooley on the Power of the Press*,
in *American Magazine*, no. 62, 1906

America is the paradise of lawyers.   —DAVID J. BREWER, 11
attributed
[Justice Brewer was credited with this by Champ Clark, who was Speaker of
the House 1911–19, in his autobiography, *My Quarter Century of American
Politics*, 1920.]

1   Why is there always a secret singing
    When a lawyer cashes in?
    Why does a hearse horse snicker
    Hauling a lawyer away?   —CARL SANDBURG, *The Lawyers Know Too Much*,
                              in *Smoke and Steel*, 1920
    [Sandburg also used a popular joke about lawyers in *The People, Yes*; see below.]

2   Lawyer: The only man in whom ignorance of the law is not punished.
                    —ELBERT HUBBARD, *Roycroft Dictionary and Book of Epigrams*,
                    1923

3   People are getting smarter nowadays; they are letting lawyers instead of their
    conscience be their guide.   —WILL ROGERS, *How to Stop the Bootleggin'*,
                              weekly column, April 8, 1923
    [The joke reappears in the screenplay of *Detective Story*, 1951, by Philip Yordan
    and Robert Wyler: "What do you got in place of a conscience? Don't answer. I
    know—a lawyer." Wyler was the brother of the director, William Wyler. The
    movie was an adaptation of Sidney Kingsley's Broadway play of the same title.]

4   There are two things wrong with almost all legal writing. One is its style. The
    other is its content.   —FRED RODELL, *Goodbye to Law Reviews*,
                              in *Virginia Law Review*, 38, 1936
    [Yale Law Professor Rodell's article raised quite a storm. David Margolick de-
    scribed it in 1980 in the *National Law Journal* as "perhaps the most widely
    read—and most controversial article in all of legal literature." But it did no
    good, at least not in the eyes of Professor Rodell, who dismissed law-review au-
    thors generally as "professional purveyors of pretentious poppycock" in a 1980
    follow-up, *Goodbye to Law Reviews—Revisited.*]

5   "Have you a criminal lawyer in this burg?"
    "We think so, but we haven't been able to prove it on him yet."
                              —CARL SANDBURG, *The People, Yes*, 1936

6   Daniel Webster: You seem to have an excellent acquaintance with the
       law, sir.
    The Devil: Sir, that is no fault of mine. Where I come from, we have always
       gotten the pick of the Bar.   —STEPHEN VINCENT BENÉT,
                                       The Devil and Daniel Webster, 1939

7   There's gotta be a law—even for lawyers.
                    —HARRY RUSKIN & NIVEN BUSCH,
                       The Postman Always Rings Twice, screenplay, 1946
    [Lana Turner to her lawyer, Hume Cronyn.]

8   Courage is the most important attribute of a lawyer. . . . It should pervade the
    heart, the halls of justice, and the chambers of the mind.
                    —ROBERT F. KENNEDY, speech, University of San Francisco
                    Law School, Sept. 29, 1962

9   A lawyer with his briefcase can steal more than a hundred men with guns.
                              —MARIO PUZO, *The Godfather*, 1969

10 Ninety percent of our lawyers serve ten percent of our people. We are over-
    lawyered and under-represented.   —JIMMY CARTER, speech,
                                       100th anniversary of the Los Angeles
                                       County Bar Association, May 4, 1978

I'm not a potted plant. —BRENDAN SULLIVAN, hearing in the U.S. Senate, 1
July 9, 1987
[Attorney Sullivan was justifying his aggressive tactics in defense of his client,
Col. Oliver North.]

LAZINESS

See also DREAMS & SLEEP (first two entries)

Laziness travels so slowly that poverty soon overtakes it. 2
—BENJAMIN FRANKLIN, *The Way to Wealth*, July 7, 1757

The man who does not betake himself at once and desperately to sawing is 3
called a loafer, though he may be knocking at the doors of heaven all the while.
—HENRY DAVID THOREAU,
"The Pond in Winter," *Walden*, 1854

LEADERS

See HIGH POSITION: RULERS & LEADERS

LEISURE

It is a great art to saunter. —HENRY DAVID THOREAU, *Journal*, 4
April 26, 1841
[In *Walking*, 1862, Thoreau suggests that *saunter* comes from the French *la
Sainte Terre*, the Holy Land. In the Middle Ages, wandering beggars would
claim to be going *à la Sainte Terre*, and thus came to be called *Saint-Terrers*.
Professional etymologists reject this charming theory in favor of the view that
saunter comes from the Middle English *santren*, to muse, or the 15th-century
saunteryng, aimless talk. In any case, Thoreau thought that the saunter was
the right gait for travel; see SPEED.]

I loaf and invite my soul; 5
I lean and loaf at my ease, observing a spear of
Summer grass. —WALT WHITMAN, *Song of Myself*, 1855

Turn on, tune in, drop out. —TIMOTHY LEARY, saying, 1960s 6

LIBERALS

See POLITICS & POLITICIANS

LIBERTY

See FREEDOM

LIES

See DISHONESTY & LIES

LIFE

See also FATE & DESTINY; TIME; WORLD

Our days begin with trouble here, 7
Our life is but a span,
And cruel death is always near,
So frail a thing is man. —THE NEW ENGLAND PRIMER, c. 1683

Dost thou love life, then do not squander time, for that's the stuff life is 8
made of. —BENJAMIN FRANKLIN, *Poor Richard's Almanack*,
June 1746
[Franklin, however, had a weakness for that great time-waster, chess; see GAMES.
See also Franklin at TIME.]

Wish not so much to live long as to live well. —*Ibid.* 9

1 We are always getting ready to live but never living.
　　　　　　　　　　　　　　　　　—RALPH WALDO EMERSON,
　　　　　　　　　　　　　　　　　Journal, April 13, 1834
　　[For another Emerson view of life, from 1847, see below.]

2 Tell me not in mournful numbers,
　　Life is but an empty dream!
　　For the soul is dead that slumbers,
　　And things are not what they seem.

　　Life is real! Life is earnest!
　　And the grave is not its goal;
　　Dust thou art, to dust returnest,
　　Was not spoken of the soul.　　　—HENRY WADSWORTH LONGFELLOW,
　　　　　　　　　　　　　　　　　A Psalm of Life, 1839

3 Life is a series of surprises.　　—RALPH WALDO EMERSON, *Circles*,
　　　　　　　　　　　　　　　　　in *Essays: First Series*, 1841

　　[See also Emerson at PATTERNS.]

4 These struggling tides of life that seem
　　In wayward, aimless course to tend,
　　Are eddies of the mighty stream
　　That rolls to its appointed end.　　—WILLIAM CULLEN BRYANT,
　　　　　　　　　　　　　　　　　The Crowded Street, 1843

5 Life consists in what a man is thinking of all day.
　　　　　　　　　　　　　　　　　—RALPH WALDO EMERSON, *Journal*,
　　　　　　　　　　　　　　　　　1847

6 My life has been the poem I would have writ,
　　But I could not both live and utter it.　　—HENRY DAVID THOREAU,
　　　　　　　　　　　　　　　　　*A Week on the Concord
　　　　　　　　　　　　　　　　　and Merrimack Rivers*, 1849

7 The mass of men lead lives of quiet desperation. What is called resignation is
　　confirmed desperation.　　　　　—HENRY DAVID THOREAU,
　　　　　　　　　　　　　　　　　"Economy," *Walden*, 1854

8 I went to the woods because I wished to live deliberately, to front only the es-
　　sential facts of life, and see if I could not learn what it had to teach, and not,
　　when I came to die, discover that I had not lived.
　　　　　　　　　　　　　　　　　—HENRY DAVID THOREAU, "Where I Lived,
　　　　　　　　　　　　　　　　　and What I Lived For," *Walden*, 1854

9 I love a broad margin to my life.　　—HENRY DAVID THOREAU,
　　　　　　　　　　　　　　　　　"Solitude," *Walden*, 1854

10 Ships that pass in the night, and speak each other in passing,
　　Only a signal shown and a distant voice in the darkness;
　　So on the ocean of life we pass and speak one another,
　　Only a look and a voice; then darkness again and a silence.
　　　　　　　　　　　　　　　　　—HENRY WADSWORTH LONGFELLOW,
　　　　　　　　　　　　　　　　　The Theologian's Tale: Elizabeth,
　　　　　　　　　　　　　　　　　in *Tales of a Wayside Inn*, 1863–74

The outward wayward life we see,   1
The hidden springs we may not know—
It is not ours to separate
The tangled skein of will and fate.   —JOHN GREENLEAF WHITTIER,
Snow-Bound, 1866

That it will never come again   2
Is what makes life so sweet.   —EMILY DICKINSON, poem no. 1741

Life is a shadowy, strange, and winding road.   3
    —ROBERT G. INGERSOLL, speech, Chicago, Nov. 26, 1882

What is life? It is the flash of a firefly in the night. It is the breath of a buffalo   4
in the wintertime. It is the little shadow which runs across the grass and loses
itself in the sunset.   —CROWFOOT,
    last words, 1890
[He was a Blackfoot warrior and orator.]

Life is the game that must be played.   —EDWIN ARLINGTON ROBINSON,   5
Ballade by the Fire: Envoy

Believe that life *is* worth living, and your belief will help create the fact.   6
    —WILLIAM JAMES, *The Will to Believe*, 1897

The events of life are mainly small events—they only seem large when we are   7
close to them.
    —MARK TWAIN, *Autobiography* [1924]
[See also Twain at MIND, THOUGHT, & UNDERSTANDING.]

Life is painting a picture, not doing a sum.   8
    —OLIVER WENDELL HOLMES, JR., *The Class of '61*, speech,
    Cambridge, Mass., June 28, 1911

There are only two or three human stories, and they go on repeating them-   9
selves as fiercely as if they had never happened before.
    —WILLA CATHER, *O Pioneers!*, 1913

Life is action and passion. I think it is required of a man that he should share   10
the action and passion of his time at peril of being judged not to have lived.
    —OLIVER WENDELL HOLMES, JR., speech,
    to Harvard Law School alumni, New York City, Feb. 1916

And life is too much like a pathless wood.   —ROBERT FROST, *Birches*, 1916   11

The proper function of man is to live, not to exist. I shall not waste my days in   12
trying to prolong them. I shall use my time.
    —JACK LONDON, to friends, 1916, reported in the *Bulletin*,
    San Francisco, Dec. 2, 1916
[Known as London's credo, this speech began: "I would rather be ashes than dust!
I would rather that my spark burn out in a brilliant blaze than it be stifled by
dry-rot. I would rather be a superb meteor, every atom of me in magnificent
glow, than a sleepy and permanent planet." A life of adventure and extraordinary achievement broke his health and he died two months later, at forty.]

I have measured out my life with coffee spoons.   13
    —T. S. ELIOT, *The Love Song of J. Alfred Prufrock*, 1917

1   I want to love first, and live incidentally.
—ZELDA FITZGERALD, letter to F. Scott Fitzgerald, 1919

2   Life is just one damn thing after another.
—ELBERT HUBBARD, *The Roycroft Dictionary and
Book of Epigrams*, 1923
[The quote also has been attributed to New York *Sun* reporter Ward O'Malley,
according to *Nice Guys Finish Seventh* by Ralph Keyes. For a response, see
Edna St. Vincent Millay, below.]

3   Pray for the dead and fight like hell for the living!
—MOTHER JONES, *Autobiography*, 1925

4   Life is for each man a solitary cell whose walls are mirrors.
—EUGENE O'NEILL, *Lazarus Laughed*, 1927

5   Strange interlude! Yes, our lives are merely strange dark interludes in the elec-
trical display of God the Father!   —EUGENE O'NEILL,
Strange Interlude, 1928

[See also O'Neill at THE PRESENT.]

6   It's not true that life is one damn thing after another—it's one damn thing over
and over.   —EDNA ST. VINCENT MILLAY,
letter to Arthur Davison Ficke,
Oct. 24, 1930

7   Birth, copulation, and death.
That's all the facts when you come to brass tacks.
—T. S. ELIOT, *Sweeney Agonistes*, 1932

8   Life is an offensive, directed against the repetitious mechanism of the universe.   —ALFRED NORTH WHITEHEAD, *Adventures of Ideas*, 1933

9   Do any human beings ever realize life while they live it?—every, every
minute?   —THORNTON WILDER, *Our Town*, 1938

10 Life, as it is called, is for most of us one long postponement.
—HENRY MILLER, *The Enormous Womb*,
in *The Wisdom of the Heart*, 1941

11 The song sparrow, who knows how brief and lovely life is, says, "Sweet, sweet,
sweet interlude; sweet, sweet, sweet interlude."
—E. B. WHITE, *Charlotte's Web*, 1952

12 Our existence is but a brief crack of light between two eternities of darkness.
—VLADIMIR NABOKOV, *Speak, Memory*, 1947
[Or, hardly more cheery: "Human life is but a series of footnotes to a vast ob-
scure unfinished manuscript," *Pale Fire*, 1962.]

13 Let's face it, life is mainly wasted time.   —JOHN BERRYMAN, 1954
[Poet Berryman made this remark to a promising student, Philip Levine, who
included it in his *The Bread of Time: Toward an Autobiography*, 1994.]

14 Life is the process of finding out, too late, everything that should have been
obvious at the time.   —JOHN D. MACDONALD,
The Only Girl in the Game, 1960

We are involved in a life that passes understanding, and our highest business is ¹
our daily life.   —JOHN CAGE, *Where Are We Going?*
And What Are We Doing?, in *Silence*, 1961

There is always inequity in life. Some men are killed in a war, and some men ²
are wounded, and some men never leave the country. . . . Life is unfair.
—JOHN F. KENNEDY, press conference, March 23, 1962

Man's life is not a business.   ³
—SAUL BELLOW, *Herzog*, 1964
[Herzog makes this point in a letter to the president protesting that IRS regu-
lations are turning Americans into a nation of bookkeepers.]

Like sands through the hourglass, so are the days of our lives.   ⁴
—TED CORDAY & ERNA PHILLIPS, signature line,
Days of Our Lives soap opera, 1965
[The line, spoken by star Macdonald Carey and written by the show's creators,
includes a loose reference to the last verse of the 23rd Psalm: "Surely goodness
and mercy shall follow me all the days of my life: and I will dwell in the house
of the Lord for ever."]

There must be more to life than having everything.   ⁵
—MAURICE SENDAK, *Higglety, Pigglety Pop!*, 1967

Dying is no big deal. The least of us can manage that. Living is the trick.   ⁶
—WALTER "RED" SMITH, funeral eulogy for
golf impresario Fred Corcoran, 1977

Life is something to do when you can't get to sleep.   ⁷
—FRAN LEBOWITZ, *Metropolitan Life*, 1978

Our lives carry us along in ways we cannot control, and almost nothing stays   ⁸
with us.   —PAUL AUSTER, *The Locked Room*, 1986

Life is short, and it's up to you to make it sweet.   ⁹
—SADIE DELANY, *Having Our Say: The Delany Sisters' First
100 Years*, 1993, written with her sister, Bessie Delany
[The Delany sisters were both over one hundred years old when this book was
published.]

LINCOLN, ABRAHAM

[*Note to the reader:* Beware of Lincoln quotes that fit contemporary political
debates. Fakes abound. In particular, since 1916, a number of maxims invented
by Rev. William John Henry Boetcker have been misidentified as sayings
of Lincoln and widely promulgated. For example, Ronald Reagan, addressing
the Republican National Convention in 1992, quoted Lincoln thus: "You cannot strengthen the weak by weakening the strong. You cannot help the wage
earner by pulling down the wage payer. You cannot help the poor by destroying
the rich. You cannot help men permanently by doing for them what they
could and should do for themselves." That is Boetcker speaking, not Lincoln,
as *New York Times* writer Herbert Mitgang promptly pointed out. Other
counterfeits include "You cannot keep out of trouble by spending more than
your income" and "You cannot establish sound security on borrowed money."
In 1954, Postmaster General Summerfield used these same all-too-apt
Boetcker-Lincoln quotes, and he, too, was corrected, by scholar Roy Basler and

Democratic National Committee Chairman Stephen A. Mitchell in an Associated Press article. George Seldes, in *The Great Quotations*, claims that Summerfield's most immediate source was a 1942 leaflet from the Committee for Constitutional Government. A convicted German agent, Edward A. Rumely, was one of the leaders of that committee.

The infamous anti-Catholic "Lincoln warning," which alludes to a "dark cloud coming from Rome," is also spurious. And serving the other extreme of political spectrum, lines such as "All that serves labor serves the nation" are not authentic Lincoln.]

1 Fox populi.
—ANONYMOUS,
Vanity Fair, 1863
[A negative evaluation of the president, punning on *vox populi* and Lincoln's respect for ordinary citizens. As Carl Sandberg wrote in *Abraham Lincoln, the War Years*, "To him the great hero was The People. He could not say too often that he was merely their instrument." For more on *vox populi*, see under William Tecumseh Sherman at THE PEOPLE.]

2 He is a barbarian, Scythian, Yahoo, a gorilla in respect of outward polish, but a most sensible, straight-forward old codger.
—GEORGE TEMPLETON STRONG, in Allen Nevins, ed.,
The Diary of George Templeton Strong
[Strong, a wealthy New York lawyer, was a friend of Lincoln.]

3 Now he belongs to the ages.
—EDWIN STANTON, at Lincoln's deathbed, April 15, 1865
[War Secretary Stanton's view of Lincoln had changed over time from contempt to admiration. He wept as he pronounced this eulogy. The moment was recorded in the diary of John Hay, a secretary to Lincoln. He and Stanton "rushed into the little room across from the theater where Lincoln lay . . . a look of unspeakable peace came upon his worn features. It was Stanton who broke the silence by saying, 'Now he belongs to the ages.'"]

4 I mourned and yet shall mourn with ever-returning spring.
—WALT WHITMAN, *When Lilacs Last in the Dooryard Bloom'd*,
1865–66
[From Whitman's lyric elegy for Lincoln; more at SORROW & GRIEF. See also below. In the war, Whitman served as a volunteer helping to care for wounded Union soldiers.]

5 O Captain! my Captain! our fearful trip is done,
The ship has weathered every rack, the prize we sought is won.
—WALT WHITMAN, *O Captain! My Captain!*, 1865–66
[The reference is to the Civil War and the death of Lincoln, and the poem ends " . . . on the deck my Captain lies, / Fallen cold and dead."]

6 His heart was as great as the world, but there was no room in it to hold a memory of a wrong.
—RALPH WALDO EMERSON, *Greatness*,
in *Letters and Social Aims*, 1876

7 And when he fell in whirlwind, he went down
As when a lordly cedar, green with boughs,
Goes down with a great shout against the hills,
And leaves a lonesome place against the sky.
—EDWIN MARKHAM, *Lincoln, the Man of the People*,
in *Lincoln and Other Poems*, 1901

The prairie-lawyer, master of us all.   1
> —VACHEL LINDSAY, *Abraham Lincoln Walks at Midnight*, 1914

In this temple, as in the hearts of the people for whom he saved the Union, the   2
memory of Abraham Lincoln is inscribed forever.
> —ROYAL CORTISSOZ, inscription, Lincoln Memorial,
> Washington, D.C., dedicated Memorial Day, 1922

[The author was art critic at the *New York Herald Tribune.*]

A lonesome train on a lonesome track,   3
Seven coaches painted black . . .
A slow train, a quiet train,
Carrying Lincoln home again.
> —MILLARD LAMPELL,
> *The Lonesome Train*, 1943

LOSERS

See FOOLS & STUPIDITY; SPORTS; WINNING
& LOSING, VICTORY & DEFEAT

LOUISIANA

See also AMERICAN HISTORY:
MEMORABLE MOMENTS (Livingston on
the Louisiana Purchase); CITIES (New Orleans)

The thousands of warblers and thrushes, the richly blossoming magnolias, the   4
holly, beech, tall yellow poplar, red clay earth, and hilly ground delighted my
eye.
> —JOHN JAMES AUDUBON, *Journal*, 1820

[Audubon was visiting at Oakley Farm, near Bayou Sara.]

Smoothly the ploughshare runs through the soil, as a keel through   5
   the water.
All the year round the orange-groves are in blossom; and grass grows
More in a single night than in a whole Canadian summer.
Here, too, numberless herds run wild and unclaimed in the prairies.
> —HENRY WADSWORTH LONGFELLOW,
> *Evangeline*, 1847

[The narrative poem is based on an apparently true story of a young couple separated when England exiled some 6,000 French settlers from Acadia in Nova Scotia. The poem was an immediate success, and is, of course, required reading in Louisiana, where a large group of exiles formed what we now call Cajun communities. Huey Long turned the popular story to political advantage in one of the great political speeches of his era; see below.]

And it is here, under this oak where Evangeline waited for her lover,   6
Gabriel. . . . But Evangeline is not the only one who has waited here in disappointment. Where are the schools that you have waited for your children to have, that have never come? Where are the roads and highways that you send your money to build, that are no nearer now than before? Where are the institutions to care for the sick and disabled? Evangeline wept bitter tears in her disappointment, but it lasted through only one lifetime. Your tears in this country, around this oak, have lasted for generations. Give me the chance to dry the tears of those who still weep here!
> —HUEY P. LONG, speech,
> 1927

[Long was running for governor, and was elected with massive popular support. He combined a yen for absolute power with a compelling vision of social justice. He was assassinated in 1935.]

1   In Louisiana, the live-oak is the king of the forest, and the magnolia is its queen.   —JOSEPH JEFFERSON, *The Autobiography of Joseph Jefferson,* 1917
[Jefferson was an actor.]

2   The poor people of Louisiana have only three friends: Jesus Christ, Sears and Roebuck, and Earl Long.   —RON SHELTON, *Blaze,* screenplay, 1989
[Paul Newman, playing Earl Long, speaks this line in the film about Governor Long's infatuation with stripper Blaze Starr; the movie drew on her book, *Blaze Starr,* written with Huey Perry. According to Ralph Keyes's *Nice Guys Finish Seventh,* however, the line had an earlier incarnation in Georgia, where the reference was to that state's governor Eugene Talmadge.]

Motto

3   Union, justice, and confidence.

LOVE   *See also* HEART; MARRIAGE; SEX; WOMEN & MEN

4   If you would be loved, love and be loveable.   —BENJAMIN FRANKLIN, *Poor Richard's Almanack,* 1755

5   All mankind love a lover.   —RALPH WALDO EMERSON, *Love,* in *Essays: First Series,* 1841

6   Love is omnipresent in nature as motive and reward. Love is our highest word and the synonym of God.   —RALPH WALDO EMERSON, *Ibid.*

7   The passion of love is not felt with the same intensity by either sex in this country as even in France; still less so than in England, and with nothing approaching the ardour with which this passion burns in Portugal, in Spain, in Italy.   —J.S. BUCKINGHAM, *The Slave States of America, 1839,* 1842

8   Love keeps the cold out better than a cloak. It is food and raiment.
    —HENRY WADSWORTH LONGFELLOW, *The Spanish Student,* 1843

9   Give all to love;
    Obey thy heart.   —RALPH WALDO EMERSON, *Give All to Love,* in *Poems,* 1847

10 Better to be wounded, a captive and a slave, than always to walk in armor.
    —MARGARET FULLER, *Summer on the Lakes,* 1844

11 Love is the bright foreigner, the foreign self.
    —RALPH WALDO EMERSON, *Journal,* 1849

12 Oh, the earth was *made* for lovers.   —EMILY DICKINSON, poem no. 1, *Valentine Week,* c. 1850

13 Love is anterior to life—
    Posterior to death—
    Initial of creation, and
    The exponent of earth.   —EMILY DICKINSON, poem no. 917, 1864

Unable are the loved to die,   1
For love is immortality,
Nay, it is deity.   —EMILY DICKINSON, poem no. 1809, c. 1864

Love iz like the meazles; we kant have it bad but onst, and the later in life we   2
have it the tuffer it goes with us.   —JOSH BILLINGS, *Josh Billings:*
His Sayings, 1865

So blind is life, so long at last is sleep,   3
And none but love to bid us laugh or weep.
                —WILLA CATHER, *Evening Song,* in *April Twilights,* 1903

Earth's the right place for love: 4
I don't know where it's likely to go better.   —ROBERT FROST, *Birches,* 1916

I want to love first, and live incidentally.   5
                —ZELDA FITZGERALD, letter to F. Scott Fitzgerald, 1919

What thou lovest well is thy true heritage.   6
                —EZRA POUND, *Hugh Selwyn Mauberley:*
E.P. Ode pour l'élection de son sepulchre, 1920

Love at the lips was touch   7
As sweet as I could bear;
And once that seemed too much;
I lived on air.   —ROBERT FROST, *To Earthward,* 1923

Love is an emotion experienced by the many and enjoyed by the few.   8
                —GEORGE JEAN NATHAN, *Attitude Toward Love and Marriage,*
in *The Autobiography of an Attitude,* 1925
[Nathan, the most distinguished and feared theater critic of his day, also observed, "Love is the emotion that a woman feels always for a poodle dog and
sometimes for a man," *General Conclusions About the Coarse Sex,* in *The
Theater, the Drama, the Girls,* 1921.]

and kisses are a better fate than wisdom.   9
                —E. E. CUMMINGS, *since feeling is first,* in *Is 5,* 1926

By the time you swear you're his,   10
Shivering and sighing,
And he vows his passion is
Infinite, Undying—
Lady, make a note of this:
One of you is lying.   —DOROTHY PARKER, *Unfortunate Coincidence,*
in *Enough Rope,* 1927

Oh, life is a glorious cycle of song,   11
A medley of extemporanea;
And love is a thing that can never go wrong;
And I am Marie of Roumania.   —DOROTHY PARKER, *Comment,* in *Ibid.*

The love we give away is the only love we keep.   12
                —ELBERT HUBBARD, *The Note Book,* 1927

What is love? . . . It is the morning and the evening star.   13
                —SINCLAIR LEWIS, *Elmer Gantry,* 1927

1 As the rain falls
so does
your love

bathe every
open
object of the world —WILLIAM CARLOS WILLIAMS, *Rain*, in *Poems*, 1930

Love is
2 unworldly
and nothing
comes of it but love.

—*Ibid.*

[See also Williams at FORGIVENESS.]

3 love is the whole and more than all. —E. E. CUMMINGS,
*my father moved
through dooms of love*, 1940

4 Love is more serious than philosophy.
—W. H. AUDEN, *For the Time Being: A Christmas Oratorio*,
In Memoriam Constance Rosalie Auden, 1870–1941

5 love is a deeper season
than reason;
my sweet one
(and april's where we're). —E. E. CUMMINGS, *yes is a pleasant country*,
in *One Times One* (or *1 x 1*), 1944

6 I am the least difficult of men. All I want is boundless love.
—FRANK O'HARA, *Meditations in an Emergency*, 1957

7 Love is born of faith, lives on hope, and dies of charity.
—GIAN CARLO MENOTTI, notebook for opera *Maria Golovin*,
1958

8 Make love not war.

—ANONYMOUS, 1960s
[Ubiquitous student slogan protesting the Vietnam War.]

9 Love is that condition in which the happiness of another person is essential to
your own. —ROBERT A. HEINLEIN,
Stranger in a Strange Land, 1961

10 Hatred paralyzes life; love releases it. Hatred confuses life; love harmonizes it.
Hatred darkens life; love illumines it. —MARTIN LUTHER KING, JR.,
Strength to Love, 1963

11 Love means not ever having to say you're sorry.
—ERICH SEGAL, *Love Story*, 1970
[In the movie, the line is, "Love means never having to say you're sorry."]

12 Nobody loves me but my mother,
And she could be jiving, too.
—B.B. KING, blues lyric, quoted by Roy Blount, Jr.,
New York Times Book Review [Dec. 11, 1994]

LOVE, EXPRESSIONS OF

If ever two were one, then surely we.
If ever man were loved by wife, then thee.
If every wife was happy with a man,
Compare with me ye women if you can.   —ANNE BRADSTREET, *To My Dear*
and Loving Husband, 1678

[Anne Bradstreet grew up in Sempringham Castle in England, where her father, Thomas Dudley, was steward to the earl of Lincoln. She married Simon Bradstreet at about age sixteen—the date of her birth is uncertain. She and her husband and parents came to America two years later in the company of Gov. John Winthrop and other Puritans. She was the first important poet in the colonies. She raised eight children; seven survived her, a rare record in that harsh environment. She lived to age fifty-eight.]

Thou wast that all to me, love,
For which my soul did pine—
A green isle in the sea, love,
A fountain and a shrine,
All wreathed with fairy fruits and flowers,
And all the flowers were mine.   —EDGAR ALLAN POE,
To One in Paradise, 1834

Thou art to me a delicious torment.   —RALPH WALDO EMERSON, *Friendship*,
in *Essays: First Series*, 1841

I was a child and she was a child
In this kingdom by the sea,
But we loved with a love that was more than love—
I and my Annabel Lee.   —EDGAR ALLAN POE, *Annabel Lee*, 1849

Why don't you speak for yourself, John?
    —HENRY WADSWORTH LONGFELLOW,
The Courtship of Miles Standish, 1858

[Priscilla Mullens posed this question to John Alden, who had been wooing her in behalf of his friend Miles Standish, the military leader of the Plymouth colony—but an older man. Moreover, the object of his affection is not pleased by this approach to courtship. "If I am not worth the wooing, I surely am not worth the winning," she remarks.

Longfellow was a descendant of John and Priscilla, and the famous question had been handed down in family lore. Alden, incidentally, was one of the signers of the Mayflower Compact, agreed to aboard ship in 1620.]

A woman waits for me, she contains all, nothing is lacking.
    —WALT WHITMAN, *A Woman Waits for Me*,
in *Leaves of Grass*, 1871

Around her neck she wore a yellow ribbon,
She wore it for her lover who was far, far away.
    —ANONYMOUS, folk song, in Oscar Brand,
Bawdy Songs and Back-Room Ballads [1960]

[Union soldiers during the Civil War wore yellow neckerchiefs and tradition has it that their wives and sweethearts remembered them by wearing yellow ribbons, much as medieval women carried the colors of their knightly champions. This may be the source of the folk song, which provided the theme and title for the 1949 John Ford movie about calvalrymen on the plains, *She Wore a Yellow Ribbon*, as well as the 1971 incident, reported by Pete Hamill in the *New York Post*, in which a woman in Brunswick, Georgia, let her husband, returning from four years in prison in New York, know that she still loved him by tying twenty or thirty yellow handkerchiefs around a tree in the middle of the town. Hamill's story formed the basis for the 1973 hit song by Irwin Levine and L. Russell Brown, *Tie a Yellow Ribbon Around the Ole Oak Tree*, and this song, in turn, inspired Penne Laingen, of Bethesda, Maryland, wife of one of the Americans held hostage in Iran for 444 days in 1979–81, to start a campaign to remember the captives in far-off Teheran with yellow ribbons. A decade later, during the Gulf War of 1990–91, the nation again was festooned with yellow ribbons, but this time signifying support for the war itself as well as for the Americans sent to fight it.]

1   Will you love me in December as you do in May?
                              —JAMES J. WALKER,
                                   Will You Love Me in December?, song
[Jimmy Walker borrowed from John Alexander Joyce, who wrote: "I shall love you in December / With the love I gave in May!" Walker's verse was set to music in 1905 by Ernest R. Ball. Walker went on to become mayor of New York City in the 1920s. As an earlier quote master, Bergen Evans, pointed out, Walker's whoopee lifestyle was scandalous, even for the roaring twenties. Evans commented, "The answer of the public to the query in his song was 'No.'"]

2   Music I heard with you was more than music,
    And bread I broke with you was more than bread.
    Now that I am without you, all is desolate;
    And all that once was so beautiful is dead.
                              —CONRAD AIKEN, *Bread and Music*, 1914

3   I wish they were emeralds.   —CHARLES MACARTHUR,
                                   offering peanuts to Helen Hayes, c. 1925
[The line worked. And twenty years later, he gave her emeralds. "I wish they were peanuts," he said.]

4   Why is it no one ever sent me yet
    One perfect limousine, do you suppose?
    Ah no, it's always just my luck to get
    One perfect rose.   —DOROTHY PARKER, *One Perfect Rose*,
                                   in *Enough Rope*, 1927

5   Spices hung about him. He was a glance from God.
                              —ZORA NEALE HURSTON, *Their Eyes Were Watching God*, 1937

6   Here's looking at you, kid.   —JULIUS EPSTEIN, PHILIP EPSTEIN,
                                        & HOWARD KOCH, *Casablanca*,
                                        screenplay, 1942

[Humphrey Bogart to Ingrid Bergman.]

7   He was my North, my South, my East and West,
    My working week and my Sunday rest,
    My noon, my midnight, my talk, my song;
    I thought that love would last forever: I was wrong.
                              —W. H. AUDEN, *Songs and Older Musical Pieces*, III,
                                   in *The Collected Poetry of W. H. Auden* [1945]

Him that I love, I wish to be   1
Free—
Even from me.   —ANNE MORROW LINDBERGH, *Even*,
                          in *The Unicorn and Other Poems, 1935–1955*, 1956

LOYALTY   *See also* CHANGE (Lincoln); UNITY

True to friend and foe.   —WILLIAM F. "BUFFALO BILL" CODY, personal motto,   2
                          in announcer's spiel prior to the star's entrance
                          in his touring Wild West show, from 1883

An ounce of loyalty is worth a pound of discretion.   3
                          —ELBERT HUBBARD, *The Note Book*, 1927

I meant what I said   4
And I said what I meant—
An elephant's faithful
One hundred per cent!   —DR. SEUSS (Theodor Seuss Geisel),
                                    Horton Hatches the Egg, 1940

Keep the faith, baby!   —ADAM CLAYTON POWELL, JR.,   5
                                              motto and book title, 1967
[Based on the Bible, *II Timothy*, 4:7, "I have fought a good fight, I have finished
my course, I have kept the faith." Powell succeeded his father as pastor of the
Abyssinian Baptist Church in Harlem in 1937 and later became the nation's
most famous African-American congressman.]

LUCK   *See also* FATE & DESTINY

Shallow men believe in luck. . . . Strong men believe in cause and effect.   6
                          —RALPH WALDO EMERSON, *Worship*,
                             in *The Conduct of Life*, 1860

The only sure thing about luck is that it will change.   7
                          —BRET HARTE, *The Outcasts of Poker Flat*, 1869

Luck is not chance—   8
It's toil—
Fortune's expensive smile is earned.   —EMILY DICKINSON,
                                                 poem no. 1350, c. 1876

Sometimes a crumb falls   9
From the tables of joy
Sometimes a bone
Is flung
To some people love is given
To others
Only heaven.   —LANGSTON HUGHES, *Luck*, in *Fields of Wonder*, 1947

now and then   10
there is a person born
who is so unlucky
that he runs into accidents
which started out to happen to somebody else.
                          —DON MARQUIS, *archy's life of mehitabel*, 1933

1   If it wasn't for bad luck, I wouldn't have no luck at all.
                              —ALBERT KING, *Born under a Bad Sign*, 1993
    [A folk saying that takes many forms, including this, from King's blues classic.]

2   Luck is not something you can mention in the presence of self-made men.
                              —E. B. WHITE, *Control*, in *One Man's Meat*, 1944

3   Luck Is the Residue of Design.   —BRANCH RICKEY,
                                                      lecture title, 1950
    [At the time, Rickey was running the Brooklyn Dodgers.]

4   Luck is what happens when preparation meets opportunity.
                              —DARRELL ROYAL, quoted in James A. Michener,
                                         Sports in America, 1976
    [Royal had considerable "luck," coaching University of Texas football teams to
    184 victories.]

LUXURY   *See also* EXCESS; THINGS & POSSESSIONS

5   It is for cake that we all run in debt.   —RALPH WALDO EMERSON,
                                                       Journals, 1840

6   Most of the luxuries, and many of the so-called comforts, of life are not only
    not indispensable, but positive hindrances to the elevation of mankind.
                              —HENRY DAVID THOREAU, "Economy," *Walden*, 1854

7   In the affluent society no useful distinction can be made between luxuries and
    necessaries.   —JOHN KENNETH GALBRAITH, *The Affluent Society*, 1958

8   Give me the luxuries in life and I will willingly do without the necessities.
                              —FRANK LLOYD WRIGHT, *New York Times*,
                                        obituary, April 9, 1959

M

MADNESS & SANITY

See also ALIENATION; DIFFERENCES; SCIENCE: PSYCHOLOGY

Sanity is very rare. —RALPH WALDO EMERSON, *Journal*, 1836   1

Here's an object more of dread   2
Than aught the grave contains—
A human form with reason fled,
While wretched life remains.—

—ABRAHAM LINCOLN,
letter to William Johnston,
Sept. 6, 1846

[Lincoln himself suffered from severe depressions, and perhaps for this reason was impressed by the misfortune of a childhood acquaintance who became insane at age nineteen and never recovered. Probably the young man was afflicted with schizophrenia.]

Much madness is divinest sense—   3
To a discerning eye—
Much sense—the starkest madness—
'Tis the majority
In this, as all, prevail—
Assent—and you are sane—
Demur—you're straightway dangerous—
And handled with a chain.   —EMILY DICKINSON, poem no. 435, c. 1862

Our occasional madness is less wonderful than our occasional sanity.   4
—GEORGE SANTAYANA, *The Life of Reason:
Reason in Common Sense*, 1905–1906

When we remember that we are all mad, the mysteries disappear and life   5
stands explained. —MARK TWAIN, *Notebook* [1935]

Sanity is madness put to good uses.   —GEORGE SANTAYANA, *Little Essays*, 1921   6

Insanity runs in my family. It practically *gallops*!   7
—JOSEPH KESSERLING, *Arsenic and Old Lace*, 1941
[Mortimer Brewster's explanation of why he can't get married.]

1   Even paranoids have enemies.   —DELMORE SCHWARTZ, saying

2   I saw the best minds of my generation destroyed by madness,
        starving hysterical naked,
    dragging themselves through the negro streets at dawn looking for an
        angry fix
    angelhead hipsters burning for the ancient heavenly connection to
        the starry dynamo in the machinery of the night.
                                            —ALLEN GINSBERG, *Howl*, 1956

3   The only people for me are the mad ones, the ones who are mad to live, mad to
    talk, mad to be saved, desirous of everything at the same time, the ones who
    never yawn or say a commonplace thing, but burn, burn like fabulous yellow
    roman candles exploding like spiders across the stars and in the middle you see
    the blue centerlight pop and everybody goes "Aww!"
                                        —JACK KEROUAC, *On the Road*, 1957

4   My mind's not right.
    .   .   .
    I myself am hell;
    nobody's here.
                                        —ROBERT LOWELL, *Skunk Hour*, 1959
    [For a similar quote, see T. S. Eliot at HELL. Both poets refer to Milton's *Paradise Lost*, in which Satan declares, "Myself am hell."]

5   I think perhaps all of us go a little crazy at times.
                                            —ROBERT BLOCH, *Psycho*, 1959
    [An observation by Norman Bates.]

6   If you talk to God, you are praying. If God talks to you, you have schizophrenia.
                                            —THOMAS SZASZ, *Emotions*,
                                            in *The Second Sin*, 1973

7   Sanity is like a clearing in the jungle where the humans agree to meet from time
    to time and behave in certain fixed ways that even a baboon could master.
                                —WILFRID SHEED, *In Love with Daylight*, 1995

MAINE   *See also* CITIES (Portland)

8   Land of the Bad People (*Terra Onde di Mala Gente*).
                                        —GIOVANNI DA VERRAZZANO, May 1524
    [This was the name Verrazzano gave the Maine coast near Casco Bay on account of the "crudity and evil manners" of the local Abnaki Indians. But the
    Abnaki were not nearly as "bad" as the Caribs who met Verrazzano as he
    waded ashore in 1528 on an island in the Lesser Antilles, probably Guadeloupe.
    They killed and ate him immediately.]

9   The people of the province of Maine may be divided into magistrates, husbandmen or planters, and fishermen; of the magistrates some be royalists, the
    rest perverse spirits, the like are the planters and fishers, of which some be
    planters and fishers both, others mere fishers.
                            —JOHN JOSSELYN, *An Account of Two Voyages to New England*,
                            1675
    [An early view of the land of lobsters and potatoes. See also Josselyn at DREAMS
    & SLEEP.]

This is what you might call a brand-new country.   1
—HENRY DAVID THOREAU, The Maine Woods, 1850

Maine, perhaps, will soon be where Massachusetts is. A good part of her terri- 2
tory is already as bare and commonplace as much of our neighborhood, and her
villages generally are not so well shaded as ours.
—HENRY DAVID THOREAU, Travel in Concord,
in Excursions, Poems, and Familiar Letters, 1863

As Maine goes, so goes the nation.   —ANONYMOUS, political   3
observation, from c. 1840
[The maxim generally held true for presidential elections in the second half of
the 19th century and until Franklin D. Roosevelt's victory in 1932. Maine, a
Republican stronghold, held its state elections before the national elections. In
a Republican-dominated era, Maine voters seemed in tune with the nation. But
in 1936 Maine was one of only two states to support Alf Landon (the "Kansas
Coolidge"). "As Maine goes, so goes Vermont," quipped Roosevelt's campaign
manager, James A. Farley, after the election. Farley had predicted a sweep except for these two states. The bottom line on Maine and presidential elections:
It has supported more presidential losers than any other state. See also POLITI-
CAL SLOGANS (the note on "Tippecanoe and Tyler, too")].

Here's to the state of Maine, the land of the bluest skies, the greenest earth, the 4
richest air, the strongest, and what is better, the sturdiest men, the fairest, and
what is best of all, the truest women under the sun.
—THOMAS B. REED, speech,
Portland, Maine, August 7, 1900
[Reed, one of Maine's most famous politicians, served twenty-two years in the
House of Representatives, six of them as Speaker. His nickname was "Czar
Reed."]

Maine has as much geology as some states that are twice her size, which is 5
highly creditable to her, of course.
—IRVIN S. COBB, Land of Balsalm Pillows and Filling Stations,
in his American Guyed Book series

Maine was the first state to vote dry and, if I am one to say, will be among the 6
last to become so.   —*Ibid.*

I am lingering in Maine this winter, to fight wolves and foxes. The sun here is 7
less strong than Florida's, but so is the spirit of development.
—E. B. WHITE,
A Report in January, 1958

"Don't ever ask directions of a Maine native," I was told.   8
  "Why ever not?"
  "Somehow we think it is funny to misdirect people and we don't smile when
we do it, but we laugh inwardly. It is our nature."
—JOHN STEINBECK, Travels with Charley, 1962

[Note the state's motto, below.]

Motto

Dirigo.   9
I direct. [Or, "I guide."]

MAJORITIES & MINORITIES

See also DEMOCRACY; DIFFERENCES;
RACES & PEOPLES

1 All, too, will bear in mind this sacred principle, that though the will of the majority is in all cases to prevail, that will to be rightful must be reasonable; that the minority possess their equal rights, which equal law must protect, and to violate which would be oppression. —THOMAS JEFFERSON, First Inaugural Address, March 4, 1801

2 Tyranny of the Majority. —ALEXIS DE TOCQUEVILLE, section title, *Democracy in America*, 1835
[Tocqueville was worried by the "irresistible strength of democratic institutions" in the U.S., and by "the inadequate securities which one finds there against tyranny."]

3 A man more right than his neighbors constitutes a majority of one. —HENRY DAVID THOREAU, *Civil Disobedience*, 1849
[See also Andrew Jackson at COURAGE, Calvin Coolidge at LAW, and Wendell Phillips below.]

4 One, on God's side, is a majority. —WENDELL PHILLIPS, speech on John Brown, Brooklyn, N.Y., Nov. 1, 1859

5 Shall we judge a country by the majority or by the minority? By the minority, surely. —RALPH WALDO EMERSON, *Considerations by the Way*, in *The Conduct of Life*, 1860

6 The history of most countries has been that of majorities—mounted majorities, clad in iron, armed with death, treading down the ten-fold more numerous minorities. —OLIVER WENDELL HOLMES, SR., speech to the Massachusetts Medical Society, May 30, 1860

7 Neither current events nor history show that the majority rules, or ever did rule. —JEFFERSON DAVIS, letter to James Frazier Jacquess & James R. Gilmore, July 17, 1864
[Davis was president of the Confederacy, 1861–65.]

8 Hain't we got all the fools in town on our side? and ain't that a big enough majority in any town? —MARK TWAIN, *Huckleberry Finn*, 1884
[The "king" addresses this question to the "duke."]

9 A majority can do anything. —JOSEPH G. CANNON, saying, quoted in the Baltimore *Sun*, March 4, 1923
[The *Sun*'s article marked the retirement of "Uncle Joe" Cannon, who served in the House for forty-six years, and as Speaker 1903–11.]

10 No democracy can long survive which does not accept as fundamental to its very existence the recognition of the rights of minorities. —FRANKLIN D. ROOSEVELT, letter to the National Association for the Advancement of Colored People, June 25, 1938

11 You, the great silent majority of my fellow Americans. —RICHARD M. NIXON, speech to the nation on the Vietnam War, Nov. 3, 1969
[Nixon appealed directly to Americans who were worried by the antiwar, coun-

terculture protests of the 1960s. "And so tonight," he said, "to you, the great silent majority of my fellow Americans—I ask for your support."

The phrase "silent majority" had been employed previously by Nixon, along with such variants as "silent center" and "quiet majority," but this was the speech that popularized the expression in a political sense. [Back in the 19th century, "silent majority" referred to those who had died and outnumbered the living.] John F. Kennedy employed the same antithesis in 1956 in *Profiles in Courage*, referring to congressmen who "may have been representing the actual sentiments of the silent majority of their constituents in opposition to the screams of a vocal minority." See also William Graham Sumner's "forgotten man" under ECONOMICS.]

MANAGEMENT TECHNIQUES

See also BUSINESS; GOVERNMENT; METHOD; MILITARY STRATEGY

A memorandum is written not to inform the reader but to protect the writer. 1
—DEAN ACHESON,
quoted in the *Wall Street Journal*
[Sept. 8, 1977]

Guidelines for bureaucrats: (1) When in charge, ponder. (2) When in trouble, delegate. (3) When in doubt, mumble. —JAMES H. BOREN, 2
New York Times,
Nov. 8, 1970
[An experienced governmental bureaucrat who had metamorphosed into an independent consultant, Boren was founder and president of NATAPROBU, the National Association of Professional Bureaucrats. He explained that NATA-PROBU had dedicated itself to "optimize the status quo by fostering adjustive adherence to procedural abstractions and rhetorical clearances," *Time* magazine, Nov. 23, 1970.]

MANNERS

See also CONVERSATION; ELITE, THE; GRACE; GUESTS; HOSPITALITY; STYLE

A gentleman makes no noise; a lady is serene. 3
—RALPH WALDO EMERSON, *Manners*,
in *Essays: Second Series*, 1844

Manners are the happy way of doing things. 4
—RALPH WALDO EMERSON, *Behavior*,
in *The Conduct of Life*, 1860

Manners make the fortune of the ambitious youth. —*Ibid.* 5

Manners require time, as nothing is more vulgar than haste. —*Ibid.* 6

Never be haughty to the humble; never be humble to the haughty. 7
—JEFFERSON DAVIS, speech,
Richmond, Va., July 22, 1861
[Davis was unable to master this excellent advice himself. In the words of the editor of the *Southern Literary Messenger*, he was "cold, haughty, peevish, narrow-minded, pig-headed, *malignant*."]

1   To attempt to describe any phase of American manners without frequent reference to the spittoon is impossible. It would be like the play of Hamlet with the part of Hamlet omitted.
                    —G. A. SALA, *My Diary in America in the Midst of War,* 1865
    [Oscar Wilde agreed. "America is one long expectoration," he announced in a newspaper interview during his 1882 tour of the U.S.]

2   Good manners are made up of petty sacrifices.
                                        —RALPH WALDO EMERSON,
                                        Letters and Social Aims, 1876

3   The stately manners of the old school.   —HENRY WADSWORTH LONGFELLOW,
                                        Michael Angelo, 1883

4   Good breeding consists in concealing how much we think of ourselves and how little we think of the other person.   —MARK TWAIN, *Notebook* [1935]

5   To do *exactly as your neighbors* do is the only sensible rule.
                                        —EMILY POST, *Etiquette,* 1922

6   Morals are three-quarters manners.   —FELIX FRANKFURTER,
                                                saying
    [The Supreme Court Justice was quoted in Harlan Phillips, *Felix Frankfurter Reminiscences,* 1960.]

7   You never want to give a man a present when you know he's feeling good. You want to do it when he's down.
                    —LYNDON B. JOHNSON, quoted in Doris Kearns Goodwin,
                    Lyndon Johnson and the American Dream [1976]

8   The trouble with treating people as equals is that the first thing you know they may be doing the same thing to you.   —PETER DE VRIES,
                                        The Prick of Noon, 1985

MARINES   *See* MILITARY, THE

MARRIAGE   *See also* FAMILY; HOME; LOVE; PARENTS; WOMEN & MEN

9   Keep your eyes wide open before marriage, half shut afterwards.
                                        —BENJAMIN FRANKLIN,
                                        Poor Richard's Almanack, June 1738
    [For more on marriage, see *Poor Richard* at SIN, VICE, & NAUGHTINESS.]

10 A single man . . . is an incomplete animal. He resembles the odd half of a pair of scissors.   —BENJAMIN FRANKLIN, letter to a young man,
                                        June 25, 1745
    [A couple of hundred years later, much-married actress Zsa Zsa Gabor agreed— sort of: "A man is incomplete until he has married. Then he is finished," *Newsweek,* March 28, 1960.]

11 I'll be no submissive wife,
    No, not I; no, not I.
    I'll not be slave for life,
    No, not I; no, not I.   —ALEXANDER LEE, *I'll Be No Submissive Wife,*
                                        1835
    [As this song indicates, women's liberation was in the air early in America.]

I have now come to the conclusion never again to think of marrying, and for 1
this reason: I can never be satisfied with anyone who would be blockhead
enough to have me. —ABRAHAM LINCOLN, April 1, 1838,
after being rejected by Mary Owen

Is not marriage an open question, when it is alleged . . . that such as are in the 2
institution wish to get out, and such as are out wish to get in.
—RALPH WALDO EMERSON, *Representative Men*, 1850
[The great French essayist Montaigne made just this allegation when he wrote
in 1580 that marriage "happens as with cages: the birds without despair to get
in, and those within despair of getting out."]

Brigham Young has two hundred wives. He loves not wisely but two hundred 3
well. —ARTEMUS WARD, quoted in *The Windsor Magazine* [1895]

The husband and wife are one, and that one is the husband. 4
—ANONYMOUS, Harvard Law School professor,
c. 1855
[From D. M. Marshman, Jr., *The Four Ages of Joseph Choate* in *American
Heritage* magazine, April 1975. The unnamed professor is said to have promulgated this maxim as the basic principle in marital law. At that time, there
were no entrance or exit requirements at Harvard Law, other than paying tuition and not getting into too much trouble. The more gracious side of 19th-
century marital relationships was illustrated by the eminent lawyer Joseph
Choate, who, when asked at a dinner party who he would most like to be if he
were not Joseph A. Choate, replied, "Why, Mrs. Choate's second husband."]

Marriage, to women as to men, must be a luxury, not a necessity; an incident 5
of life, not all of it. —SUSAN B. ANTHONY, speech, 1875

The men that women marry, 6
And why they marry them, will always be
A marvel and a mystery to the world. —HENRY WADSWORTH LONGFELLOW,
Michael Angelo, 1883

Who was that lady I saw you with last night? 7
She ain't no lady; she's my wife. —JOSEPH WEBER & LEW FIELDS,
vaudeville lines, 1887

Who marries who is a small matter after all. 8
—WILLA CATHER, *The Song of the Lark*, 1915
[The speaker is the novel's heroine, opera singer Thea Kronborg. Joan Acocella,
in *The New Yorker* (Nov. 27, 1995), wrote: "This scene is a kind of turning
point in the history of literature. . . . In the bulk of literature about women,
who marries whom—or, at least, who goes to bed with whom—is not simply
not a small matter; it is the subject."]

Two can live cheaper than one. —RING LARDNER, *Big Town*, 9
1921
[Lardner may not have coined this proverb but his is the earliest example of the
thought in Oxford University Press's *A Dictionary of American Proverbs*,
1992.]

It takes patience to appreciate domestic bliss; volatile spirits prefer unhappiness. 10
—GEORGE SANTAYANA, *The Life of Reason*, 1905–1906

1 *Marriage, n.* a community consisting of a master, a mistress, and two slaves, making in all, two. —AMBROSE BIERCE, *The Devil's Dictionary*, 1906

2 The sanctity of the institution of marriage shall be upheld. Pictures shall not infer [*sic*] that low forms of sex relationship are the accepted or common thing.
—MOTION PICTURE PRODUCERS AND DISTRIBUTORS, INC.,
A Code for the Industry, 1930

3 "That's bigamy."
"Yes, and it's big of me, too. It's big of all of us. I'm sick of these conventional marriages. One woman and one man was good enough for your grandmother. But who wants to marry your grandmother?"
—GROUCHO MARX, in *Animal Crackers*, 1930

4 Married women are kept women, and they are beginning to find it out.
—LOGAN PEARSALL SMITH, *Other People*, in *Afterthoughts*, 1931

5 Most everybody in the world climbs into their graves married.
—THORNTON WILDER, *Our Town*, 1938

6 A husband, a good marriage, is earth.
—ANNE MORROW LINDBERGH, diary entry, 1944,
Diaries and Letters [1972]

7 There's nothing so nice as a new marriage.
—BEN HECHT, *Spellbound*, screenplay, 1945
[The line, spoken by a Viennese psychiatrist, continues "No psychoses yet, no aggressions, no guilt complexes." The movie was adapted from a book, *The House of Dr. Edwardes* by Francis Beeding, and was directed, of course, by Alfred Hitchcock.]

8 I married beneath me—all women do. —NANCY ASTOR, speech,
Oldham, England, 1951
[The American-born Lady Astor was the first woman to sit in the House of Commons, from 1919 to 1945. Her husband, Waldorf Astor, was a politician and publisher.]

9 The best part of married life is the fights. The rest is merely so-so.
—THORNTON WILDER, *The Matchmaker*, 1954

10 Take my wife—please! —HENNY YOUNGMAN,
saying
[An old vaudeville line; see also Albany under CITIES. Another Youngman routine goes: Q: "How's your wife?" A: "Compared to what?"]

11 Love and marriage, love and marriage,
Go together like a horse and carriage. —SAMMY CAHN, song,
Love and Marriage, 1955

12 Every marriage is a battle between two families struggling to reproduce themselves. —CARL A. WHITAKER, obituary,
New York Times [April 25, 1995]
[Dr. Whitaker was a pioneer in psychotherapy with families.]

13 The heart of marriage is memories. —BILL COSBY, *Love and Marriage*, 1989

MARYLAND   *See also* CITIES (Baltimore)

Heaven and earth never agreed to frame a better place for man's habitation. 1
                    —JOHN SMITH, on Chesapeake Bay, 1606
[More at VIRGINIA.]

Our summer in Maryland was delightful. . . . In no part of North America are 2
the natural productions of the soil more various, or more beautiful.
            —FRANCES TROLLOPE, *Domestic Manners of the Americans*, 1832
[She wrote in particular of abundance of delicious strawberries and other fruit.]

Maryland! My Maryland!   —JAMES RYDER RANDALL, song title, 3
                                1861
[Traditionally played—to the tune of *O Tannenbaum*—at the Preakness
Stakes, the second event of racing's triple crown, this is a fiercely anti-Northern
song. Written by a native Baltimorean just after a mob of Southern sympathiz-
ers had attacked the 6th Massachusetts Regiment as it proceeded through
the city en route to Washington, the song begins, "The despot's heel is on thy
shore," and concludes, "Huzza! she spurns the Northern scum! / She breathes!
she burns! she'll come! she'll come! / Maryland! My Maryland!"]

In truth he had never seen a finished landscape; but Maryland was a raggedness 4
of a new kind.   —HENRY ADAMS, *The Education of Henry Adams*, 1907

Motto

Fatti maschii, parole femine.   5
Manly deeds; womanly words.

MASSACHUSETTS   *See also* CITIES (Amherst, Boston,
                                Concord, Plymouth)

The first public love of my heart is the Commonwealth of Massachusetts. 6
            —JOSIAH QUINCY, speech, U.S. House of Representatives,
            Jan. 14, 1811

The State of Massachusetts is made up of the enterprise of its inhabitants. 7
            —CHARLES FRANCIS ADAMS, *Diary*, Sept. 21, 1835

No slave-hunt in our borders—no pirate on our strand! 8
No fetters in the Bay State—no slave upon our land!
            —JOHN GREENLEAF WHITTIER, *Massachusetts to Virginia*, 1843

Nantucket! . . . a mere hillock, and elbow of sand; all beach without a back- 9
ground. Some gamesome wights will tell you that they have to plant weeds
there; they don't grow naturally; that pieces of wood in Nantucket are carried
about like bits of the true cross in Rome; that one blade of grass makes an oa-
sis, three blades in a day's walk a prairie.
            —HERMAN MELVILLE, *Moby-Dick*, 1851

Down to the Plymouth Rock, that had been to their feet as a doorstep 10
Into a world unknown,—the cornerstone of a nation!
            —HENRY WADSWORTH LONGFELLOW,
            The Courtship of Miles Standish, 1858

1   Massachusetts has a good climate, but it needs a little anthracite coal.
—RALPH WALDO EMERSON, *Journal*, 1857–58

2   A man may stand there [Cape Cod] and put all America behind him.
—HENRY DAVID THOREAU, *Cape Cod* [1865]

3   Have faith in Massachusetts!   —CALVIN COOLIDGE, speech,
state legislature, Jan. 7, 1914

4   Flowers through the window
lavender and yellow

changed by white curtains—
smell of cleanliness—

Sunshine of late afternoon—
On the glass tray

a glass pitcher, the tumbler
turned down, by which

a key is lying—And the
immaculate white bed   —WILLIAM CARLOS WILLIAMS, *Nantucket*, 1934

5   Settlers of Massachusetts
Were of two sets:
Those by grace of God elected;
Those rejected.

One way to tell the sainted
From the tainted
Was that those whose prayers were heeded
Had succeeded.

As a rule it therefore followed
That the hallowed
Were the favored upper classes
Not the masses.   —GILMAN M. OSTRANDER, *The Social Structure of Early
Massachusetts*, in *American Heritage*, Feb. 1958

Motto

6   *Ense petit placidam sub libertate quietem.*
By the sword we seek peace, but peace only under liberty.

MATHEMATICS   *See* SCIENCE: MATHEMATICS & STATISTICS

MATURITY   *See* EXPERIENCE; MIDDLE AGE & MIDLIFE CRISIS

MEDIA   *See also* ADVICE (Nathanael West); CITIES (Los Angeles); PRESS, THE

7   Who will underrate the influence of loose popular literature in debauching the
popular mind?   —WALT WHITMAN, article in the *Brooklyn Daily Times*, 1857

8   Spoken speech is one thing, written speech is quite another. Print is the proper
vehicle for the latter, but it isn't for the former. The moment "talk" is put into
print you recognize that it is not what it was when you heard it.
—MARK TWAIN, letter to Edward Bok, c. Dec. 1888
[Twain was commenting on the text of an interview that Bok, editor of *Ladies'*

Home Journal, had conducted with him. Seeing his words in print, said Twain, made him realize that this interview, like most, was "pure twaddle and value-less."]

Publishers are demons, no doubt about it. 1
—WILLIAM JAMES, attributed in John Winokur,
Writers on Writing [1986]

Publicity is justly commended as a remedy for social and industrial diseases. 2
Sunlight is said to be the best of disinfectants; electric light the most efficient
policeman. —LOUIS D. BRANDEIS, *What Publicity Can Do,*
in *Harper's Weekly,* Dec. 20, 1913

The New Yorker will be the magazine that is not edited for the old lady in 3
Dubuque. —HAROLD ROSS, prospectus for the magazine, 1924

One picture is worth a thousand words. —FRED R. BARNARD, 4
in *Printers' Ink,* March 10, 1927
[Barnard called this a Chinese proverb, but actually it is a rewrite of an earlier
Bernard aphorism, "One look is worth a thousand words," *Printers' Ink,* Dec.
8, 1921.]

Sticks Nix Hick Pix. —ABEL GREEN, headline, 5
Variety, July 17, 1935
[*Variety* was famous for its boffo headlines. This one means that movies with
rural subjects don't do well in rural communities. For a famous headline on an
urban theme, from the *Daily News,* see CITIES (New York).]

I believe television is going to be the test of the modern world, and that in this 6
new opportunity to see beyond the range of our vision, we shall discover either
a new and unbearable disturbence of the general peace or a saving radiance in
the sky. We shall stand or fall by television.
—E. B. WHITE, *Removal,* in *Harper's Magazine,* 1938

The problem with television is that people must sit and keep their eyes glued 7
to the screen; the average American family hasn't time for it. Therefore the
showmen are convinced that for this reason, if no other, television will never
be a serious competitor of broadcasting.
—THE NEW YORK TIMES, editorial, March 1939
[Good analysis, wrong conclusion.]

The hand that rules the press, the radio, the screen, and the far-spread maga- 8
zine rules the country. —LEARNED HAND, memorial speech for
Justice Louis Brandeis, Dec. 21, 1942

Joe Gillis: You used to be in pictures. You used to be big. 9
Norma Desmond: I am big. It's the pictures that got small.
—CHARLES BRACKETT, BILLY WILDER,
& D. M. MARSHMAN, JR.,
Sunset Blvd., screenplay, 1950
[Desmond's last line: "All right, Mr. DeMille, I'm ready for my close-up now."]

Some television programs are so much chewing gum for the eyes. 10
—JOHN MASON BROWN,
interview, July 28, 1955
[Brown, a Harvard graduate, joined the U.S. Navy in World War II, and as a battle correspondent took part in the invasions of Sicily and Normandy. He went

on to a somewhat quieter life as drama critic, writer, and lecturer. The quote here also has been attributed to Frank Lloyd Wright and Fred Allen.]

1   [Television:] a medium, so called because it is neither rare nor well done.
                                            —ERNIE KOVACS, quoted in Leslie Halliwell,
                                            The Filmgoer's Book of Quotes [1973]

2   In television we have the greatest instrument for mass persuasion in the history of the world.   —BUDD SCHULBERG, *A Face in the Crowd,*
                                            screenplay, 1957

3   During the peak viewing periods, television in the main insulates us from the realities of the world in which we live. If this state of affairs continues, we may alter an advertising slogan to read: LOOK NOW, PAY LATER.
                                            —EDWARD R. MURROW, speech to radio and television
                                            news directors, Chicago, 1958

4   [If you watch television from morning through night] I can assure you that you will observe a vast wasteland.
                                            —NEWTON MINOW, speech to the National Association
                                            of Broadcasters, May 9, 1961
    [The wasteland charge, which seems mild now, was startling at the time, the equivalent of announcing that the emperor is not wearing clothes. Moreover, the speaker was the head of the Federal Communications Commission, and he had the support of Pres. John F. Kennedy. Minow's specific charges are depressingly familiar: "You will see a procession of game shows, violence, audience participation shows, formula comedies about totally unbelievable families, blood and thunder, mayhem, violence, sadism, murder, western bad men, western good men, private eyes, gangsters, more violence, and cartoons. And endlessly, commercials—many screaming, cajoling, and offending." Minow, by the way, had been a law partner of Adlai Stevenson.]

5   It is not enough to cater to the nation's whims, you must also meet the nation's needs.
                                            —*Ibid.*
    [And he threatened not to renew their licenses if they failed to meet the nation's needs.]

6   It [television] is a medium of entertainment which permits millions of people to listen to the same joke at the same time, and yet remain lonesome.
                                            —T. S. ELIOT, quoted in the *New York Post,* Sept. 22, 1963

7   Because television can make so much money doing its worst, it often cannot afford to do its best.   —FRED W. FRIENDLY, *Due to Circumstances
                                            Beyond Our Control,* 1967

8   Unlike the print media, television writes on the wind.
                                            —LYNDON B. JOHNSON, speech, 1968
    [This "Power of the Media" speech was given shortly after Pres. Johnson announced that he would not seek reelection. More follows.]

9   Where there's great power, there must also be great responsibility. This is true for broadcasters just as it's true for presidents.   —*Ibid.*

10 Television pollutes identity.   —NORMAN MAILER,
                                            St. George and the Godfather, 1972

The publishing business is . . . the only organized private business that is given 1
explicit constitutional protection. —POTTER STEWART, speech,
Yale Law School, 1974

Nothing is real unless it happens on television. 2
—DANIEL BOORSTIN, in *The New York Times*,
Feb. 19, 1978
[Two decades later, writer-director-actor Buck Henry similarly observed,
"You aren't anybody in America if you're not on TV. In short, you don't exist
unless you're on TV," quoted by Bernard Weinraub, *New York Times*, Oct. 10,
1995.]

MEDICINE   *See* DOCTORS & MEDICINE

MEDIOCRITY

I hope in these days we have heard the last of conformity and consistency. . . . 3
Let us affront and reprimand the smooth mediocrity and squalid contentment
of the times. —RALPH WALDO EMERSON, *Self-Reliance*,
in *Essays: First Series*, 1841

[*See also* CONSISTENCY.]

Blessed are those who have no talent! —RALPH WALDO EMERSON, 4
Journal, Feb. 1850

Intolerance of mediocrity has been the main prop of my independence. 5
—ELSA MAXWELL, *R.S.V.P.*, 1954

Women want mediocre men, and men are working hard to be as mediocre as 6
possible. —MARGARET MEAD, in *Quote Magazine*,
May 15, 1958

Some men are born mediocre, some men achieve mediocrity, and some men 7
have mediocrity thrust upon them. With Major Major it had been all three.
—JOSEPH HELLER, *Catch-22*, 1961
[The Shakespeare quote underlying Heller's joke is: "Some are born great, some
achieve greatness, and some have greatness thrust upon 'em," *Twelfth Night*,
II,v.]

Even if he is mediocre, there are lots of mediocre judges, and people, and 8
lawyers. They are entitled to a little representation, too, aren't they.
—ROMAN L. HRUSKA, Senate hearings on the nomination of
G. Harrold Carswell to the Supreme Court, 1970
[Sen. Hruska of Nebraska, a Republican, was trying to defend a nomination made
by Pres. Richard Nixon. It didn't help. The Senate rejected Judge Carswell.]

The only sin is mediocrity. —MARTHA GRAHAM, quoted in 9
The New York Times, March 31, 1985

MEMORY   *See also* CRAFTINESS (Philander C. Johnson); PAST, THE

[Memory is] the thread on which the beads of man are strung, making the per- 10
sonal identity which is necessary to moral action.
—RALPH WALDO EMERSON, *Memory*

1 When I was younger I could remember anything, whether it happened or not, but I am getting old, and soon I shall remember only the latter.
—MARK TWAIN, quoted in prefatory note to
Albert Bigelow Paine, *Mark Twain, A Biography* [1912]
[Twain played with this idea in various forms. On another occasion, according to Paine, he paraphrased a remark by Josh Billings, saying: "It isn't so astonishing the things that I can remember, as the number of things I can remember that aren't so."]

2 Some memories are realities, and are better than anything that can ever happen to one again.   —WILLA CATHER, *My Ántonia*, 1918

3 In memory, everything seems to happen to music.
—TENNESSEE WILLIAMS, *The Glass Menagerie*, 1944
[See also Williams at THE PRESENT.]

4 Americans are impatient with memory.
—JAMAICA KINCAID, *Alien Soil*, in *The New Yorker*, June 21, 1993

5 Nobody belongs to us except in memory.
—JOHN UPDIKE, *Grandparenting*, 1994

MEN   *See also* HUMANS & HUMAN NATURE;
WOMEN & MEN

6 All men would be tyrants if they could.   —ABIGAIL ADAMS, letter to
John Adams, March 31, 1776

[More at WOMEN & MEN.]

7 A man is a god in ruins.   —RALPH WALDO EMERSON, *Nature*, 1836

8 *Male n.* A member of the unconsidered, or negligible sex. The male of the human race is commonly known (to the female) as Mere Man. The genus has two varieties: good providers and bad providers.
—AMBROSE BIERCE, *The Devil's Dictionary*, 1906

9 Men build bridges and throw railroads across deserts, and yet they contend successfully that the job of sewing on a button is beyond them. Accordingly, they don't have to sew buttons.
—HEYWOOD BROUN, *Holding a Baby*,
in *Seeing Things at Night*, 1921

10 A man in the house is worth two in the street.
—MAE WEST, *Belle of the Nineties*, 1934
[For the life in her men, see HEALTH.]

11 What's the use of being a little boy if you are going to grow up to be a man?
—GERTRUDE STEIN, *Everybody's Autobiography*, 1937

12 A man's role is uncertain, undefined, and perhaps unnecessary.
—MARGARET MEAD, *Male and Female*, 1948

13 A man can be destroyed but not defeated.
—ERNEST HEMINGWAY, *The Old Man and the Sea*, 1952

Why can't a woman be more like a man?   1
Men are so honest, so thoroughly square;
Eternally noble, historically fair.   —ALAN JAY LERNER, *My Fair Lady*,
                                                                          1956
[Music by Frederick Loewe. The show was adapted from George Bernard
Shaw's play *Pygmalion* (1913).]

Now me, when I want ready-made trouble, I dig up a handsome man.   2
                        —GLORIA NAYLOR, *The Women of Brewster Place*, 1982

MEN & WOMEN   *See* WOMEN & MEN

MENTAL ILLNESS   *See* MADNESS & SANITY

METHOD   *See also* EXCELLENCE; MANAGEMENT
                                                    TECHNIQUES; MILITARY STRATEGY

Method goes far to prevent trouble in business.   3
                        —WILLIAM PENN, *Some Fruits of Solitude*, 1693
[More at BUSINESS.]

There are some enterprises in which a careful disorderliness is the true method.   4
                        —HERMAN MELVILLE, *Moby-Dick*, 1851

There is a best way of doing everything, if it be to boil an egg.   5
                        —RALPH WALDO EMERSON, *Behavior,* in *The Conduct of Life,* 1860

Chaos often breeds life, when order breeds habit.   6
                        —HENRY ADAMS, *The Education of Henry Adams,* 1907

There's a way to do it better—Find it.   7
                        —THOMAS ALVA EDISON, directive to a research assistant,
                                c. 1919, cited in Robert Debs Heinl,
                                Dictionary of Military and Naval Quotations

Take a method and try it. If it fails, admit it frankly and try another.   8
                        —FRANKLIN D. ROOSEVELT, speech, Oglethorpe University,
                                Atlanta, Ga., May 22, 1932
[More at ACTION & DOING.]

A good plan violently executed *Now* is better than a perfect plan next week.   9
                        —GEORGE S. PATTON, JR., *War As I Knew It,* 1947

Chaos is a friend of mine.   —BOB DYLAN, explaining his music,   10
                                quoted in *Newsweek,* Dec. 9, 1985

MEXICAN WAR, 1846–48   *See also* EPITAPHS & GRAVESTONES (O'Hara)

It is for the interest of mankind that its [the United States'] power and territory   11
should be extended—the farther the better.
                        —WALT WHITMAN, editorial, *Brooklyn Eagle,* Dec. 2, 1847
[Whitman was writing in defense of this war, which was precipitated by the an-
nexation of Texas late in 1845. Whitman essentially accepted John L. O'Sulli-

van's manifest-destiny concept; see AMERICA & AMERICANS. Thoreau, however, viewed the war very differently; see below. For the loss of the Alamo in 1836, one of the events leading to the Mexican War, see AMERICAN HISTORY: MEMORABLE MOMENTS.]

1 Tell him to go to hell.   —ZACHARY TAYLOR, reply to Gen. Santa Anna's
demand for surrender, Buena Vista,
Feb. 22, 1847
[Gen. Taylor's forces were reduced at this time, and the battle was Mexico's best chance at a major victory. But the U.S. troops prevailed, and the Mexicans withdrew.]

2 Hurrah for Old Kentucky! That's the way to do it. Give 'em hell, damn'em.
—ZACHARY TAYLOR, rallying cry, to the 2d Kentucky Brigade,
Battle of Buena Vista, Mexico, Feb. 23, 1847

3 How does it become a man to behave toward this American government to-day? I answer that he cannot without disgrace be associated with it.
—HENRY DAVID THOREAU, *Civil Disobedience,* 1849
[Thoreau saw the war as an illegitimate design to extend slavery. As an abolitionist, he had stopped paying the Massachusetts poll tax (a head tax) in 1843, and as a result was arrested in 1846 and spent one night in prison. His subsequent essay on civil disobedience is a key text in pacifist resistance movements. See also Thoreau under LAW.
In 1914, the U.S. intervened in Mexico again, during the revolution, and Lincoln Steffens commented later in his autobiography, "We Americans can't seem to get it that you can't commit rape a little." Will Rogers added a few years later, "We could never understand why Mexico wasn't crazy about us. We always had their goodwill, oil, coffee, and minerals at heart," in Alex Ayres, ed., *The Wit and Wisdom of Will Rogers* (1993).
It was in the Mexican War, incidentally, that American marines reached the "halls of Montezuma"; see THE MILITARY.]

4 Poor Mexico! So far from God and so close to the United States.
—PORFIRIO DÍAZ, attributed, in John S. D. Eisenhower,
The U.S. War with Mexico, 1846–1848 [1989]
[Gen. Díaz was president of Mexico from 1877 to 1911.]

MEXICO   *See* NATIONS

MICHIGAN   *See also* CITIES (Detroit)

5 Milton must have travelled in Michigan before he wrote the garden parts of
Paradise Lost.   —HARRIET MARTINEAU, *Society in America,* 1837

6 The Michiganders were a people without identity, without community of purpose or past, without tradition. Then Ford.
—LEONARD LANSON CLINE, in Ernest H. Gruening, ed.,
These United States, 1924

7 Michigan . . . is the skyscraper, the mass-production line, and the frantic rush into what the machine will some day make of us, and at the same time, it is golden sand, blue water, green pine trees on empty hills, and a wind that comes down from the cold spaces, scented with the forests that were butchered by

hard-handed men in checked flannel shirts and floppy pants. It is the North Country wedded to the force that destroyed it.
—BRUCE CATTON, *Michigan*, in *American Panorama, East of the Mississippi*, 1960

The earth was generous and outgoing here in the heartland. 1
—JOHN STEINBECK, *Travels with Charley*, 1962

Motto

Si quaeris peninsulam amoenam, circumspice. 2
If you seek a pleasant peninsula, look around you.

MIDDLE AGE & MIDLIFE CRISIS   *See also* AGES

After thirty, a man wakes up sad every morning, excepting perhaps five or six, 3
until the day of his death.   —RALPH WALDO EMERSON, *Journal*, 1834

Men, like peaches and pears, grow sweet a little while before they begin to 4
decay.   —OLIVER WENDELL HOLMES, SR.,
The Autocrat of the Breakfast-Table, 1858

A man reaches the zenith at forty, the top of the hill. From that time forward 5
he begins to descend. If you have any great undertaking ahead, begin it now.
You will never be so capable again.
—JOHN HAY, remark to Mark Twain, quoted in
Alfred Bigelow Paine, *Mark Twain, A Biography* [1912]

Forty is ten years older than thirty-nine. 6
—FRANK IRVING COBB, c. 1912
[Cobb, chief editor on Joseph Pulitzer's New York *World*, wrote this in a note
to Pulitzer. To Pulitzer himself he ascribed the view that "Everybody is a damn
fool until he is forty, and not necessarily very intelligent after that." Quoted in
Louis M. Starr, *Joseph Pulitzer and His Most 'Indegoddampendent' Editor*, in
American Heritage, June 1968.]

By the time a person has achieved years adequate for choosing a direction, the 7
die is cast and the moment has long since passed which determined the future.
—ZELDA FITZGERALD, *Save Me the Waltz*, 1932

Life Begins at Forty.   —WALTER PITKIN, book title, 1932 8

[Middle age] is the time when a man is always thinking that in a week or two 9
he'll feel just as good as ever.   —DON MARQUIS, attributed in B. Wilcox,
A Little Book of Aphorisms

Middle age is when you've met so many people that every new person you 10
meet reminds you of someone else.   —OGDEN NASH, *Versus*, 1949

They call that [44 years] middle age, but I don't know too many 88-year-olds. 11
—BURT REYNOLDS, quoted in *The New York Times*,
July 24, 1980
[The screen star was commenting ruefully on his own advancing years.]

[On turning fifty:] When you're planning to live to one hundred, it's only half- 12
time.   —JOE NAMATH, quoted in *The New York Times*, Jan. 29, 1994

MIDDLE CLASS

1   The whole country seems to have melded into one middle class.
—ALEXIS DE TOCQUEVILLE, *Democracy in America*, 1835

2   The booboisie.   —H. L. MENCKEN, neologism for the bourgeoisie

3   His name was George F. Babbitt [and] he was nimble in the calling of selling houses for more than people could afford to pay.
—SINCLAIR LEWIS, *Babbitt*, 1922
[See also Babbitt at SCIENCE: TECHNOLOGY and UNHAPPINESS.]

4   Us middle class never have to worry about having old furniture to point out to our friends. We buy it on payments, and before it's paid for, it's plenty antique.
—WILL ROGERS, in Alex Ayres, ed.,
The Wit and Wisdom of Will Rogers [1993]

MIDWEST, THE   *See also* FRONTIER, THE; WEST, THE.

5   [The Great Prairies] A vast country, incapable of sustaining a dense population.
—JAMES FENIMORE COOPER, *The Prairie*, 1827

6   There, in the Mississippi Valley, beyond a question, and in a very brief time, will be cities and towns to rival any in the world in population, in commercial enterprise, and in the production of art, in the refinements of cultivated life and manners, and I fear, in *luxury*.
—CALVIN COLTON, *Manual for Emigrants to America*, 1832

7   In the Western settlements we may behold democracy arrived at its utmost limits.   —ALEXIS DE TOCQUEVILLE, *Democracy in America*, 1835

8   The new states of the West are already inhabited, but society has no existence among them.   —*Ibid.*

9   In this country you can look farther and see less than any other place in the world.
—ANONYMOUS, 19th century
[The saying dates from the time when grassland plains extended from Indiana to the foot of the Rockies.]

10   These are the gardens of the desert, these
The unshorn fields, boundless and beautiful,
For which the speech of England has no name—
The prairies.   —WILLIAM CULLEN BRYANT, *The Prairies*, 1833

11   A world of grass and flowers stretched around me, rising and falling to gentle undulations, as if an enchanter had struck the ocean swell, and it was at rest forever.
—ELIZA STEELE, c. 1840
[She traveled from Chicago to Peoria in 1840. Quoted in *The New York Times*, Feb. 15, 1995.]

12   The clean, bright, gardened townships spoke of country fare and pleasant summer evenings on the stoop. It was a sort of paradise.
—ROBERT LOUIS STEVENSON, *Across the Plains*, 1892
[Stevenson's account is of his trip across the United States in 1879.]

The grass was the country, as the water is the sea.   1
                                        —WILLA CATHER, *My Ántonia*, 1918
[The scene is Nebraska. See also Cather at THE FRONTIER.]

July came on with that breathless, brilliant heat which makes the plains of   2
Kansas and Nebraska the best corn country in the world. It seemed as if we
could hear the corn growing in the night; under the stars one caught a faint
crackling in the dewy, heavy odoured cornfields where the feathered stalks
stood so juicy and green.   —*Ibid.*

The Corn Belt is a gift of the gods—the rain god, the sun god, the ice god, and   3
the gods of geology.   —J. RUSSELL SMITH, *North America*, 1925

Nobody can possibly understand the Middle West who has not, for fun or   4
profit, once looked through the catalogue of a great mail order company.
                                        —JOHN GUNTHER, *Inside U.S.A.*, 1947

The Midwest is exactly what one would expect from a marriage between New   5
England puritanism and rich soil.   —*Ibid.*

MILITARY, THE   *See also* EPITAPHS & GRAVESTONES; HIGH
                                        POSITION: RULERS & LEADERS (Patton);
                                        MILITARY STRATEGY; WAR

Discipline is the soul of an army. It makes small numbers formidable; procures   6
success to the weak and esteem to all.
                        —GEORGE WASHINGTON, letter to the captains
                        of the Virginia Regiments, July 1759
[In general orders on July 6, 1777, Washington wrote, "Discipline more than
numbers gives one army superiority over another."]

Without a respectable navy—alas America!   7
                        —JOHN PAUL JONES, letter to Robert Morris, Oct. 17, 1776

To place any dependence upon militia, is assuredly, resting upon a broken staff.   8
                        —GEORGE WASHINGTON, letter to the president of Congress,
                        Sept. 24, 1776
[Washington found local militia units to be useful in harrying the British in
guerrilla-type actions, but in the spring of 1780, after nearly four years of war,
he still cautioned against reliance on them, telling Virginians when Nathanael
Greene assumed command in the South: "We must have a permanent force,
not a force that is constantly fluctuating and sliding from under us as a
pedestal of ice would do from a statue in a summer's day."]

I intend to go *in harm's way*.   9
                        —JOHN PAUL JONES, letter, Nov. 16, 1778
[More at AMERICAN REVOLUTION.]

[United under one government, we] will avoid the necessity of those over-   10
grown military establishments, which, under any form of government, are in-
auspicious to liberty, and which are to be regarded as particularly hostile to
republican liberty.   —GEORGE WASHINGTON,
                                        Farewell Address, Sept. 17, 1796
[Another great general who became president, Dwight D. Eisenhower, made a
similar point; see below.]

1   Bravery is a quality not to be dispensed with in officers—like charity, it covers
a great many defects.   —BENJAMIN STODDERT, letter to James Simons,
Dec. 13, 1798
[Stoddert was the first Secretary of the Navy.]

2   The spirit of this country is totally adverse to a large military force.
—THOMAS JEFFERSON, letter to Chandler Price, Feb. 28, 1807

3   For a people who are free, and who mean to remain so, a well-organized and
armed militia is their best security.   —THOMAS JEFFERSON,
message to Congress, Nov. 8, 1808
[Jefferson was more approving of militias than was Washington—see above—
but he had not the field experience in leading them.]

4   Every citizen [should] be a soldier. This was the case with the Greeks and the
Romans, and must be that of every free state.
—THOMAS JEFFERSON, letter to James Monroe, 1813

5   Long may she ride, our Navy's pride,
And spur to resolution:
And seaman boast, and landsmen toast,
The Frigate Constitution.   —ANONYMOUS, U.S. Navy Song,
The Frigate Constitution, c. 1813
[Also called "Old Ironsides," this forty-four-gun frigate is probably the most fa-
mous American naval vessel. She was launched in 1797, and took part in the
undeclared war with France, the battles against Barbary pirates based in
Tripoli, and the War of 1812. When she was scheduled to be scrapped in 1830,
a patriotic poem by Oliver Wendell Holmes, Sr., aroused a popular protest that
saved the vessel. She is now at the Boston naval yard. See also Holmes at
PATRIOTISM & THE FLAG.]

6   It is part of a sailor's life to die well.
—STEPHEN DECATUR, on Captain James Lawrence,
after his death in action on June 1, 1813
[More at EPITAPHS & GRAVESTONES.]

7   From the halls of Montezuma,
To the shores of Tripoli,
We fight our country's battles,
On the land as on the sea.
—ANONYMOUS, *The Marines' Hymn*, 1847
[Tripoli was the capital of one of the Barbary States, Tripolitania, now part of
Libya. Government-sponsored piracy along the Barbary Coast plagued U.S.
shipping in the early 19th century, especially 1800–15, the period of the so-
called Tripolitan War. The great hero of these hostilities was Stephen Decatur;
see PATRIOTISM & THE FLAG.
Halls of Montezuma refers to the National Palace in Mexico City, seized by
American troops in September 1847, in the battle of Chapultepec in the Mexican War.
For a marine's prayer, see under WORLD WAR II, the anonymous epitaph for a
marine killed at Guadalcanal.]

8   A soldier has a hard life, and but little consideration.
—ROBERT E. LEE, letter to his wife, Nov. 5, 1855

If it moves, salute it. If it doesn't move, pick it up. If you can't pick it up, 1
paint it.   —ANONYMOUS, U.S. Navy saying

A man who is good enough to give his blood for his country is good enough to 2
be given a square deal afterwards.   —THEODORE ROOSEVELT, speech,
                                                          Springfield, Ill., July 4, 1903
[More at POLITICAL SLOGANS.]

Militarism is the great preserver of our ideals of hardihood, and human life 3
with no use for hardihood would be contemptible.
                              —WILLIAM JAMES, *The Moral Equivalent of War*, 1910
[For more of James's thinking on the value of rigorous training, see PACIFISM &
NONVIOLENCE.]

Semper paratus.   4
Always Ready.   —U.S. COAST GUARD, motto, 1915

I have a rendezvous with death   5
At some disputed barricade.
                         —ALAN SEEGER, *I Have a Rendezvous with Death*, 1916
[More at WORLD WAR I.]

First in the fight. Always faithful.   6
                              —U.S. MARINES, recruiting poster, World War I

All a soldier needs to know is how to shoot and salute.   7
                                        —JOHN J. PERSHING, attributed
[After commanding the American Expeditionary Force in Europe in World War
I, Pershing served as army chief of staff from 1921 until his retirement in 1924.]

Military intelligence—a contradiction in terms.   8
                              —OSWALD GARRISON VILLARD, lecture c. 1920,
                                  personal report from a member of the audience,
                                  Lt. Donald Armstrong
[Armstrong later became a brigadier general. Villard published *The Nation*
magazine.]

You can't pick up a paper without seeing where the Marines were landed to   9
keep some nation from shooting each other, and if necessary we shoot them to
keep them from shooting each other.   —WILL ROGERS,
                                                 Weekly Articles, July 5, 1925

Men do not take good iron to make nails nor good men to make soldiers.   10
                              —PEARL S. BUCK, *The Young Revolutionist*, 1932
[Prescient of the fatal flaws in the Nationalist Chinese army.]

Gung ho!   —EVANS FORDYCE CARLSON, motto, Second Raider Battalion,   11
                   U.S. Marines, from Feb. 1942
[The expression, which attained wide popularity as a byword for zealous, en-
thusiastic performance of one's duty, does not come, as battalion commander
Col. Carlson himself thought—and as reported in some dictionaries—from the
Chinese words for "work together," but from the abbreviated name for the
Chinese Industrial Cooperative Societies first formed in 1939. For more de-
tails, see Hugh Rawson's *Devious Derivations*, 1994.]

1   Spartan simplicity must be observed. Nothing will be done merely because it contributes to beauty, convenience, comfort, or prestige.
—U. S. ARMY, message from the
Office of the Chief Signal Officer, May 29, 1945

2   Look at an infantryman's eyes, and you can tell how much war he has seen.
—BILL MAULDIN, *Up Front*, 1945

3   No sane man is unafraid in battle, but discipline produces in him a form of vicarious courage.   —GEORGE S. PATTON, JR., *War As I Knew It*, 1947

4   Any commander who fails to obtain his objective, and who is not dead or severely wounded, has not done his full duty.   —*Ibid.*

5   It is sad to remember that when anyone has fairly mastered the art of command, the necessity for that art usually expires—either through the termination of the war or through the advanced age of the commander.   —*Ibid.*

6   When I joined the Army, even before the turn of the century, it was the fulfillment of all my hopes and dreams. The hopes and dreams have long since vanished. But I still remember the refrain of one of the most popular barracks ballads of that day, which proclaimed most proudly that, "Old soldiers never die. They just fade away."   —DOUGLAS MACARTHUR, speech,
joint session of Congress, April 19, 1951
[More at AMERICAN HISTORY: MEMORABLE MOMENTS. The song is an old one. The Library of Congress's volume of quotations suggests that the song is a parody of a 19th-century gospel hymn, *Kind Words Can Never Die*, which was known to cadets at West Point, where MacArthur was in the class of 1903. The earliest printed version dates from 1917 in England in *Tommy's Tunes*, compiled by Frederick T. Nettleton. There are small differences in the wording in different versions of the song.]

7   If there is one basic element in our Constitution, it is civilian control of the military.   —HARRY S. TRUMAN, *Memoirs*, 1955

8   In the councils of government, we must guard against the acquisition of unwarranted influence, whether sought or unsought, by the military-industrial complex. The potential for the disastrous rise of misplaced power exists and will persist.   —DWIGHT D. EISENHOWER, Farewell Address,
Jan. 17, 1961
[Pres. Eisenhower's original warning, according to physicist Robert L. Park, was against a "military-industrial-scientific complex." Professor Park, writing in *The New York Times* on June 27, 1994, said that science adviser James Killian persuaded the president to drop the reference to science.]

9   There are all sorts of things to be done in this country. . . . I see no reason why the sums which are now going into these sterile, negative mechanisms that we call war munitions shouldn't go into something positive.
—DWIGHT D. EISENHOWER, quoted in Stephen E. Ambrose,
Eisenhower: The President [1983]

10 The deterrence of war is the primary objective of the armed forces.
—MAXWELL D. TAYLOR, *The Uncertain Trumpet*, 1960
[Gen. Taylor was army chief of staff from 1955 to 1959, resigning in protest of the Eisenhower administration's reliance on massive retaliation; see John Foster Dulles at FOREIGN POLICY. Taylor was appointed chairman of the Joint

Chiefs of Staff by Pres. John F. Kennedy in 1962. His statement here is one of many versions of "Washington's maxim," which derives from the Roman writer Vegetius; see George Washington and Theodore Roosevelt at WAR.]

There was only one catch and that was Catch-22, which specified that a con- 1
cern for one's own safety in the face of dangers that were real and immediate was the process of a rational mind. Orr was crazy and could be grounded. All he had to do was ask; and as soon as he did he would no longer be crazy and would have to fly more missions. Orr would be crazy to fly more missions and sane if he didn't, but if he was sane he had to fly them. If he flew them he was crazy and didn't have to; but if he didn't want to he was sane and had to. Yossarian was moved deeply by the absolute simplicity of this clause of Catch-22 and let out a respectful whistle.
                                        —JOSEPH HELLER, *Catch-22*, 1961
[The now-famous paradoxical Catch-22 was originally dubbed Catch-18. But Leon Uris that same year had a great success with *Mila 18*, which led Heller to change the number in his title from 18 to 22 shortly before publication. *Catch-22* garnered mixed, mostly poor reviews, and never made it to the *New York Times* best-seller list. But it went on to become one of the great publishing successes of the century.]

Catch-22 says they [superior officers] have a right to do anything we can't stop 2
them from doing.   —*Ibid.*

You seldom hear of the fleets except when there's trouble, and then you hear a 3
lot.
          —JOHN S. McCAIN, JR., *Norfolk Star Ledger*, August 4, 1964
[McCain oversaw the Vietnam War at its height as Commander-in-Chief of the Pacific Command. During the whole of his tour in charge, 1968–72, his eldest son, John S. McCain III, a naval pilot who later became a Republican senator from Arizona, was a prisoner of war in Hanoi.]

A nation that continues year after year to spend more money on military de- 4
fense than on programs of social uplift is approaching spiritual death.
          —MARTIN LUTHER KING, JR., *Where Do We Go from Here?*
          Chaos or Community?, 1967

When I was in the military, they gave me a medal for killing two men, and a 5
discharge for loving one.   —LEONARD MATLOVICH, the inscription on
                                  Sgt. Matlovich's tombstone, cited by Anna
                                  Quindlen, *New York Times* [June 27, 1993]

I don't care if a soldier is straight as long as he can shoot straight.   6
                          —BARRY GOLDWATER, attributed, c. 1993
[Goldwater, a Republican senator from Arizona who ran for president in 1964, is an old-fashioned libertarian Republican. In the 1990s, he became something of a hero among homosexual Americans for his outspoken conviction that government should not be concerned with people's private lives.]

MILITARY STRATEGY   *See also* GULF WAR (Colin Powell)

Get there first with the most men.   —NATHAN BEDFORD FORREST,   7
                                                saying during the Civil War
[Gen. Forrest, an aggressive, intelligent, and effective commander, plagued the Union armies. Sometimes his advice is phrased, "Git thar fustest with the mostest." But there is no evidence that he spoke nonstandard or silly English.

American humorists of the period leaned heavily on such misspellings, as in this passage from Artemus Ward's *Shakespeare Up-to-Date:* "Twice is he armed that hath his quarrel just, / And three times he who gets his fist in fust."]

1   The art of war is simple enough. Find out where your enemy is. Get at him as soon as you can. Strike at him as hard as you can and as often as you can, and keep moving on.   —ULYSSES S. GRANT, attributed

2   Always mystify, mislead, and surprise the enemy, if possible.
                              —THOMAS JONATHAN "STONEWALL" JACKSON,
                              strategical motto, during Civil War
    [This is the distilled version of Jackson's strategic vision. In the *Battles and Leaders* series published in *Century* magazine and then in book form (1888), one of Stonewall's officers, John D. Imboden, said that long before Jackson became famous he often cited the two following maxims: "Always mystify, mislead, and surprise the enemy, if possible; and when you strike and overcome him, never let up in the pursuit so long as your men have strength to follow; for an army routed, if hotly pursued, becomes panic-stricken, and can then be destroyed by half their number. The other rule is, never fight against heavy odds, if by any possible manoeuvering you can hurl your own force on only a part, and that the weakest part, of your enemy and crush it. Such tactics will win every time, and a small army may thus destroy a large one in detail, and repeated victory will make it invincible."]

3   There is no better way of defending a long line than by moving into the enemy's territory.   —ROBERT E. LEE, letter to Gen. John R. Jones, CSA,
                              March 21,1863
    [The letter presaged Lee's advance into Pennsylvania that summer, which culminated in the Battle of Gettysburg.]

4   Call no council of war. It is proverbial that councils of war never fight.
                              —HENRY W. HALLECK, telegram to Gen. George Gordon Meade,
                              July 13, 1863
    [Halleck, General-in-Chief of the Union Armies, wanted Gen. Meade, who had won at Gettysburg ten days before, to engage Lee's army again. But Meade, whose forces also had suffered terribly at Gettysburg, already had been talked out of an attack by his corps commanders at a council of war on the 12th. After hearing that the Confederates had been allowed to retreat to safety across the Potomac on the night of the 13th, Lincoln cried "Great God! . . . Our Army held the war in the hollow of their hand and they would not close it."]

5   A pint of sweat will save a gallon of blood.
                              —GEORGE S. PATTON, message to troops, Oct. 1942

6   All experience goes to show that wars cannot be won by bombing alone.
                              —WALTER LIPPMANN, *Washington Post*, June 22, 1965
    [The implication, of course, is that the infantry is always needed. As Lippmann also observed in the *Post* earlier that year, on February 18: "Nobody has yet found a way of bombing that can prevent foot soldiers from walking." At the time the U.S. was emphasizing bombing in the Vietnam War.]

7   When you get into a war, you should win as quick as you can, because your losses become a function of the duration of the war. . . . Get everything you need and win it.   —DWIGHT D. EISENHOWER, press conference,
                              March 15, 1968

MIND, THOUGHT, & UNDERSTANDING   *See also* GENIUS; IDEAS & IDEALS; VISION & PERCEPTION; WILL

What is the hardest task in the world? To think.   1
> —RALPH WALDO EMERSON, *Intellect,*
> in *Essays: First Series,* 1841

There is no such thing as being too profound.   2
> —EDGAR ALLAN POE, *The Murders in the Rue Morgue,* 1841

[The speaker is C. Auguste Dupin, the most famous forefather of the modern fictional detective.]

What are the earth and all its interests beside the deep surmise which pierces   3
and scatters them?   —HENRY DAVID THOREAU, *A Week on the*
> *Concord and Merrimack Rivers,* 1849

A moment's insight is sometimes worth a life's experience.   4
> —OLIVER WENDELL HOLMES, SR.,
> *The Professor at the Breakfast-Table,* 1860

The brain—is wider than the sky—   5
For—put them side by side—
The one the other will contain
With ease—and you—beside.   —EMILY DICKINSON, poem no. 632, 1862

The brain is just the weight of God—   6
For—heft them—pound for
Pound—
And they will differ—if they do—
As syllable from sound.   —*Ibid.*

Imagination is the secret and marrow of civilization. It is the very eye of faith.   7
> —HENRY WARD BEECHER, *Proverbs from Plymouth Pulpit,* 1887

As the brain changes are continuous, so do all these consciousnesses melt into   8
each other like dissolving views. Properly they are but one protracted consciousness, one unbroken stream.   —WILLIAM JAMES,
> *The Principles of Psychology,* 1890

[This is from the highly influential chapter "The Stream of Thought," in which the term "stream of consciousness" first appears. This flow of con-sciousness, or what French writer Édouard Dujardin earlier called "the interior monologue," is at the center of many of the great novels of the 20th century, including, most famously, *Ulysses,* by James Joyce.]

Life does not consist mainly—or even largely—of facts and happenings. It con-   9
sists mainly of the storm of thoughts that is forever blowing through one's
head.
> —MARK TWAIN, *Autobiography* [1924]

[Note the similarity between the observations of Twain and William James, above. Awareness of the constant activity of the mind in shaping perceived re-ality was very much in the air in this era. Referring to the "storm of thoughts," Twain continued: "Could you set them down stenographically? No. . . . Fif-teen stenographers hard at work couldn't keep up. Therefore, a full autobiogra-phy has never been written, and it never will be." Twain's own autobiography was never finished. He wrote passages for it over many years, and it was pub-lished posthumously.]

1   If you make people think they're thinking, they'll love you: but if you really make them think, they'll hate you   —DON MARQUIS,
archy and mehitabel, 1927

2   The test of a first-rate intelligence is the ability to hold two opposed ideas in the mind at the same time, and still retain the ability to function. One should, for example, be able to see that things are hopeless and yet be determined to make them otherwise.   —F. SCOTT FITZGERALD, *The Crack-Up*,
originally published in *Esquire* magazine, 1936
[See also Ralph Waldo Emerson at CONSISTENCY.]

3   Understanding is a very dull occupation.
—GERTRUDE STEIN, *Everybody's Autobiography*, 1937

4   Men are not prisoners of fate, but only prisoners of their own minds.
—FRANKLIN D. ROOSEVELT, speech,
Pan American Day, April 15, 1939

5   The mind is an enchanting thing,
is an enchanted thing.   —MARIANNE MOORE,
The Mind Is an Enchanting Thing, 1944

6   The Power of Positive Thinking.   —NORMAN VINCENT PEALE,
book title, 1952
[The very successful Rev. Peale was an all-American cleric. "Pray big! Believe Big! Act Big!" he urged. His politics were conservative, his theology vaguely liberal. He campaigned for Dwight D. Eisenhower, prompting Adlai Stevenson to joke that he found "Paul appealing, and Peale appalling" (*Skeptical Inquirer*, winter 94, Martin Gardner review of *God's Salesman* by Carol V. R. George, 1933).]

7   The mind is the expression of the soul, which belongs to God and must be let alone by government.   —ADLAI STEVENSON, speech,
Salt Lake City, Utah, Oct. 14, 1952

8   Imagination is more important than knowledge.
—ALBERT EINSTEIN, *On Science*

9   A mind is a terrible thing to waste.   —UNITED NEGRO COLLEGE FUND,
advertising slogan, adopted 1983
[Reportedly garbled by Vice President Dan Quayle into "What a waste it is to lose one's mind," quoted in Douglas Brinkley, *The Majic Bus: An American Odyssey*, 1993.]

10   The mind is what the brain does.
—STEPHEN KOSSLYN, quoted in *The New York Times*,
science section, April 22, 1986

MINNESOTA   *See also* CITIES (Duluth); HEROES (F. Scott Fitzgerald)

11   What a glorious new Scandinavia might not Minnesota become! . . . None of [the American states] appear to me to have a greater or more beautiful future before them than Minnesota.   —FREDRIKA BREMER,
Homes of the New World, 1853

Lake Wobegon, where all the women are strong, all the men are good looking,   1
and all the children are above average.
>—GARRISON KEILLOR, *A Prairie Home Companion*,
>signature line, radio show, started 1974

Minnesotans are just different, that's all.   2
>—CHARLES KURALT, *Dateline America*, 1979

[In particular, Kuralt noted that "with the wind-chill factor hovering at fifty-
seven below . . . there were all these Minnesotans running around outdoors,
happy as lambs in the spring." And he took up the "different" theme in his
next book, too; see below.]

Minnesotans are different from the rest of us. . . . Minnesotans don't   3
smoke. . . . Minnesotans recycle. . . . Minnesotans return the grocery cart to
the store. Minnesotans do not consume butterfat. . . . Minnesotans bike with
their helmets on. Minnesotans fasten their seat belts. Minnesotans hold the
door for you. Minnesota men don't leave the toilet seat up. Minnesotans do not
blow their horn behind you when the light turns green; they wait for you to notice. Minnesotans are nicer than other people.
>—CHARLES KURALT, *Charles Kuralt's America*, 1995

Motto

>*L'Étoile du Nord.*   4
>The Star of the North.

MINORITIES   *See* MAJORITIES & MINORITIES; RACES & PEOPLES

MIRACLES

Men talk about Bible miracles because there is no miracle in their lives. Cease   5
to gnaw that crust. There is ripe fruit over your head.
>—RALPH WALDO EMERSON,
>*Journal*, June 1850

To me every hour of the light and dark is a miracle,   6
Every cubic inch of space is a miracle.   —WALT WHITMAN, *Miracles*, 1881

Miracles are laughed at be a nation that r-reads thirty millyon newspapers a   7
day an' supports Wall sthreet.
>—FINLEY PETER DUNNE, *Casual Observations*,
>in *Mr. Dooley's Opinions*, 1900

Miracles are propitious accidents, the natural causes of which are too compli-   8
cated to be readily understood.   —GEORGE SANTAYANA,
>*The Ethics of Spinoza*, 1901

One miracle is just as easy to believe as another.   9
>—WILLIAM JENNINGS BRYAN, at the Scopes "monkey" trial,
>Dayton, Tenn., July 21, 1925

Miracles are to come. With you I leave a remembrance of miracles.   10
>—E. E. CUMMINGS, Introduction,
>*New Poems*, in *Collected Poems*, 1938

1   It's a very mixed blessing to be brought back from the dead.
                    —KURT VONNEGUT, Palm Sunday sermon, St. Clement's
                    Episcopal Church, New York City, quoted by John Leonard,
                    New York Times, April 30, 1980

MISANTHROPY   *See also* ALIENATION

2   Any man who hates dogs and babies can't be all bad.
                    —LEO C. ROSTEN, speaking of W. C. Fields,
                    Masquer's Club, 1939
    [Often attributed to Fields in the form: "Anyone who hates children and dogs
    can't be all bad." One of columnist William Safire's correspondents unearthed
    a 1937 version by Cedric Worth in *Harper's* magazine: "No man who hates
    dogs and children can be all bad." Worth, in turn, was recalling a comment by
    a *New York Times* reporter, Byron Darton, following a party in 1930 at which
    the conversation was dominated by a man who detested dogs.]

MISSISSIPPI

3   Mississippi will drink wet and vote dry—so long as any citizen can stagger to
    the polls.   —WILL ROGERS, attributed, pre–1919 and the start of Prohibition

4   Mississippi begins in the lobby of a Memphis, Tennessee, hotel and extends
    south to the Gulf of Mexico. It is dotted with little towns concentric about the
    ghosts of the horses and mules once tethered to the hitch-rail enclosing the
    county courthouse and it might almost be said to have only two directions,
    north and south, since until a few years ago it was impossible to travel east or
    west in it unless you walked or rode on the horses or mules.
                    —WILLIAM FAULKNER, *Mississippi*, in *American Panorama:
                    East of the Mississippi*, 1960

5   When you're in Mississippi, the rest of America doesn't seem real. And when
    you're in the rest of America, Mississippi doesn't seem real.
                    —BOB PARRIS MOSES, c. 1961, quoted by Jack Newfield,
                    Amite County, in *Bread and Roses Too* [1971]

Motto

6   *Virtute et armis.*
                    By valor and arms.

MISSOURI   *See also* CITIES (Kansas City, St. Louis)

7   As an agricultural region, Missouri is not surpassed by any state in the Union.
    It is indeed the farmers' kingdom.
                    —ANONYMOUS, *The History of Jackson County*, 1881

8   I am from Missouri. You've got to show me.
                    —WILLARD D. VANDIVER, speech, U. S. Navy Yard,
                    Philadelphia, 1899
    [The passage reads in full: "I come from a state that raises corn and cotton and
    cockleburs and Democrats, and frothy eloquence neither convinces or satisfies
    me. I am from Missouri. You've got to show me." Henry F. Woods in *American
    Sayings* (1945) notes that the key comment was not original with Vandiver, but
    he was one of the first to take pride in a characteristic previously linked to an
    alleged inability among Missourians to grasp instructions quickly. Pride pre-

vailed, and Missouri became popularly known as the "show-me state," in honor of Missourians' commonsensical skepticism. Vandiver was a member of the U.S. House of Representatives. Woods differs from other sources in giving a date of 1902 for the speech. It first became widely known in the 1912 presidential race, when Champ Clark of Missouri was a candidate. For more on Clark, see the note with Richard Nixon's "Checkers" speech at AMERICAN HISTORY: MEMORABLE MOMENTS.

Being "from Missouri" eventually dropped its geographical anchor and became a metaphor for being sceptical. In 1923, Elbert Hubbard wrote, "Be from Missouri, of course; but for God's sake forget it occasionally," *The Roycroft Dictionary and Book of Epigrams,* 1923.]

Motto

Salus populi suprema lex esto.   1
The welfare of the people shall be the supreme law.

MISTAKES   *See also* FAULTS & FAILINGS

The only one who makes no mistakes is one who never does anything.   2
    —THEODORE ROOSEVELT, saying, inscribed on the house
    in which he was born, the Theodore Roosevelt
    National Historical Site in New York City

When I make a mistake, it's a beaut!   3
    —FIORELLO H. LA GUARDIA,
    attributed comment on a bad appointment

A reign of error.   4
    —ROBERT K. MERTON, *The Self-Fulfilling Prophecy,* 1948
[The sentence in full reads: "The specious validity of the self-fulfilling prophecy perpetuates a reign of error." More at SCIENCE.]

MODERN TIMES   *See also* BAD TIMES; SCIENCE:
    TECHNOLOGY

All the modern inconveniences.   5
    —MARK TWAIN, *Life on the Mississippi,* 1883

The age demanded an image   6
Of its accelerated grimace,
Something for the modern stage,
Not, at any rate, an Attic grace.
    —EZRA POUND, *Hugh Selwyn Mauberley:*
    E. P. Ode pour l'élection de son sépulchre, 1920

One of the crying needs of the time is for a suitable burial service for the ad-   7
mittedly damned.   —H. L. MENCKEN, *Prejudices*

In the nightmare of the dark   8
All the dogs of Europe bark,
And the living nations wait,
Each sequestered in its hate.

    —W. H. AUDEN, *In Memory of W. B. Yeats,* 1940

1   The century on which we are entering can be and must be the century of the common man.
—HENRY A. WALLACE, speech, May 8, 1942
[Wallace was Pres. Franklin Roosevelt's vice president in 1942. Subsequently, he ran for president on the Progressive Party ticket in 1948.]

2   We have grasped the mystery of the atom and rejected the Sermon on the Mount.
—OMAR BRADLEY, speech, Armistice Day, 1948
[Gen. Bradley led the U.S. forces in the invasion of Normandy, and as commander of the 12th Army group was the key commander in the victory in Europe. See also Martin Luther King, Jr., at SCIENCE: TECHNOLOGY.]

3   At this very moment, we have the necessary techniques, both material and psychological, to create a full and satisfying life for everyone.
—B. F. SKINNER, *Walden Two*, 1948

4   Perfection of means and confusion of goals seem, in my opinion, to characterize our age.   —ALBERT EINSTEIN, *Out of My Later Years*, 1950

5   There are evidently limits to the achievements of science; and there are irresolvable contradictions both between prosperity and virtue, and between happiness and "the good life," which had not been anticipated in our philosophy. The discovery of these contradictions threatens our culture with despair.
—REINHOLD NIEBUHR, *The Irony of American History*, 1952

6   I saw the best minds of my generation destroyed by madness.
—ALLEN GINSBERG, *Howl*, 1956
[More at MADNESS.]

MONEY & THE RICH   *See also* BUSINESS; CAPITAL & CAPITALISM
V. LABOR; ECONOMICS; LUXURY; RICH &
POOR, WEALTH & POVERTY; SUCCESS

7   Nothing but money
Is sweeter than honey.
—BENJAMIN FRANKLIN, *Poor Richard's Almanack*, 1735

8   There are three faithful friends—an old wife, an old dog, and ready money.
—*Ibid.*, Jan. 1738

9   If you would know the value of money, go and try to borrow some.
—*Ibid.*, 1758

10   A penny saved is a penny earned.   —ANONYMOUS, proverb often
attributed to Benjamin Franklin
[For all his advice about money, records of the Bank of North America in Philadelphia show that Franklin was overdrawn at least three times a week.]

11   Hardly anything but money remains to create strongly marked differences between them [Americans] and to raise some of them above the common level.
—ALEXIS DE TOCQUEVILLE, *Democracy in America*, 1835
[Tocqueville introduced this observation with the general comment, "When the reverence that belonged to what is old has vanished, birth, condition, and profession no longer distinguish men." See also Tocqueville at AMERICA & AMERICANS.]

The almighty dollar, that great object of universal veneration throughout our 1
land. —WASHINGTON IRVING, *The Creole Village,*
in *The New Yorker,* Nov. 12, 1836
[The passage recalls Ben Jonson's "That for which all virtue now is sold, / And
almost every vice—almighty gold," *Epistle to Elizabeth, Countess of Rutland,*
in *Epigrams,* 1616.]

Of all the sources of human pride, mere wealth is the basest and most vulgar- 2
minded. Real gentlemen are almost invariably above this low feeling.
—JAMES FENIMORE COOPER,
The American Democrat, 1838

Money, which represents the prose in life, and which is hardly mentioned in 3
parlors without an apology, is, in its effects and laws, as beautiful as roses.
—RALPH WALDO EMERSON, *Nominalist and Realist,*
in *Essays: Second Series,* 1844

A man is rich in proportion to the number of things which he can afford 4
to let alone.
—HENRY DAVID THOREAU, "Where I Lived and What I Lived For,"
Walden, 1854

5

That man is the richest whose pleasures are the cheapest.
—HENRY DAVID THOREAU, *Journal,*
March 3, 1856

6

Moral principle is a looser bond than pecuniary interest.
—ABRAHAM LINCOLN, speech, Oct. 1856

7

The production of wealth is not the work of any one man, and the acquisition
of great fortunes is not possible without the cooperation of multitudes of
men; . . . therefore the individuals to whose lot these fortunes fall . . . should
never lose sight of the fact that as they hold them by the will of society expressed in statute law, so they should administer them as trustees for the benefit of society as inculcated by moral law.
—PETER COOPER, c. 1875, quoted in Peter Lyon,
The Honest Man, in *American Heritage*
[Feb. 1959]
[Cooper practiced what he preached, spending the fortune that he made on
philanthropic ventures, including founding Cooper Union in New York City.
See also Cooper at BUSINESS; THE ELITE; and REVOLUTION; as well as Robert Col-
lyer's eulogy at EPITAPHS & GRAVESTONES.]

8

Conspicuous consumption of valuable goods is a means of reputability to the
gentleman of leisure.
—THORSTEIN VEBLEN, *The Theory of the Leisure Class,* 1899

9

In order to stand well in the eyes of the community, it is necessary to come up
to a certain, somewhat indefinite, conventional standard of wealth.
—*Ibid.*

10

I risked much, but I made much.
—P. T. BARNUM
[A *New York Times* article from August 29, 1993, on the Barnum Museum in
Bridgeport, Conn., stated that while Barnum did not say anything about suck-
ers being born every minute—see FOOLS & STUPIDITY—he did say this.]

1   I believe the power to make money is a gift of God. . . . I believe it is my duty
to make money and still more money and to use the money I make for the good
of my fellow man according to the dictates of my conscience.
                                        —JOHN D. ROCKEFELLER, interview, 1905
[Mr. Dooley explained Rockefeller's divine mandate thus: "He's kind iv a society f'r the previntion of crooly to money. If he finds a man misusing his
money, he takes it away fr'm him an' adopts it," Finley Peter Dunne, *Mr. Dooley Says*, 1910.]

2   *Impunity, n.* Wealth.   —AMBROSE BIERCE, *The Devil's Dictionary*, 1906

3   *Money, n.* A blessing that is of no advantage to us excepting when we part
with it.   —*Ibid.*

4   Malefactors of great wealth.   —THEODORE ROOSEVELT, speech,
                                        Provincetown, Mass., August 20, 1907
[Pres. Roosevelt, who had created legislation to regulate the railroads, was
blamed by financiers for the stock market panic of 1907. In this speech, he suggested that "certain malefactors of great wealth" might have conspired to
bring on the crisis and discredit regulation.]

5   Let me tell you about the very rich. They are different from you and me.
                                        —F. SCOTT FITZGERALD, *The Rich Boy*, 1926
[Peter De Vries noted in the *Washington Post*, July 30, 1989: "The rich aren't
like us—they pay less taxes." See also Ernest Hemingway below and Leona
Helmsley at TAXES.]

6   When a man tells you that he got rich through hard work, ask him: "Whose?"
                                        —DON MARQUIS, quoted in Edward Anthony,
                                        O Rare Don Marquis [1962]

7   What's a thousand dollars? Mere chicken feed. A poultry matter.
                                        —GROUCHO MARX, *The Cocoanuts*, 1929

8   No one can live on one salary any more.
                                        —WILL ROGERS, *Daily Telegrams*, Oct. 19, 1929

9   There are few sorrows, however poignant, in which a good income is of no
avail.   —LOGAN PEARSALL SMITH, *Afterthoughts*, 1931

10 Money is like an arm or a leg—use it or lose it.
                                        —HENRY FORD, interview in *The New York Times*, Nov. 8, 1931

11 Man was lost if he went to a usurer, for the interest ran faster than a tiger upon
him.   —PEARL S. BUCK, *The First Wife*,
                                        in *The First Wife and Other Stories*, 1933

12 The rich were dull and they drank too much.
                                        —ERNEST HEMINGWAY, *The Snows of Kilimanjaro*, 1936
[In the next paragraph of the story, Hemingway refers to the Fitzgerald quote
above about the rich being different from you and me, and includes a retort,
"Yes, they have more money." Hemingway accepted credit for this quip,
but evidently the remark was made by critic Mary Colum at a lunch in 1936
with Hemingway and famed editor Maxwell Perkins. It was directed not at
Fitzgerald but at Hemingway, who had boasted, "I am getting to know the
rich." Colum replied, "The only difference between the rich and other people

is that the rich have more money," Matthew J. Bruccoli, *Scott and Ernest,*
1978.]

Money is power, freedom, a cushion, the root of all evil, the sum of blessings. 1
           —CARL SANDBURG, *The People, Yes,* 1936
[The biblical allusion is to *I Timothy* 6:10: "The love of money is the root of all
evil."]

I do want to get rich but I never want to do what there is to do to get rich. 2
           —GERTRUDE STEIN, *Everybody's Autobiography,* 1937
[She also noted, "There are so many ways of earning a living and most of them
are failures."]

When money talks, few are deaf.   EARL DERR BIGGERS, *Charlie Chan* 3
           in Honolulu, screenplay, 1938

They say money doesn't stink. I sometimes wonder. 4
           —RAYMOND CHANDLER, *Farewell My Lovely, 1940*

A full pocketbook often groans more loudly than an empty stomach. 5
           —FRANKLIN D. ROOSEVELT, speech, Nov. 1, 1940

Not even a collapsing world looks dark to a man who is about to make his for- 6
tune.   —E. B. WHITE, *Intimations,* in *One Man's Meat,* 1944

Money should circulate like rainwater . . . setting up a little business here and 7
furnishing a good time there.
           —THORNTON WILDER, *The Matchmaker,* 1956

Money will not make you happy, and happy will not make you money. 8
           —GROUCHO MARX, saying, attributed
           in *The New York Times* [Jan. 29, 1955]

Money, it turned out, was exactly like sex. You thought of nothing else if you 9
didn't have it and thought of other things if you did.
           —JAMES BALDWIN, *The Black Boy Looks at the White Boy,*
           in *Nobody Knows My Name,* 1961

A billion here and a billion there and pretty soon you're talking real money. 10
           —EVERETT M. DIRKSEN, attributed
[Dirksen of Illinois, a Republican, was Senate minority leader from 1959 to his
death in 1969. This comment is widely attributed to him, but the curator at
the Dirksen Congressional Center was unable to track down the quote for the
Wall Street Journal. That paper reported, however, on January 1, 1985, that the
curator added, "That doesn't mean he didn't say it."]

You can never be too skinny or too rich. 11
           —BARBARA "BABE" PALEY, saying, attributed
[She was the wife of CBS founder and head, Bill Paley. The quote has also been
attributed to Gloria Vanderbilt, Rose Kennedy, Truman Capote, and the
Duchess of Windsor (who had it embroidered on a pillow). See also Eileen Ford
at HEALTH.]

It is better to lose opportunity than capital. 12
           —SUSAN M. BYRNE, on *Wall Street Week in Review,*
           Feb. 15, 1985

1   Greed is healthy.   —IVAN BOESKY, speech, University of California
                                          Business School in Berkeley, 1986
    [Boesky, a high-flying financier, was later charged with fraud and jailed. He was
    the model for the villain, Gordon Gekko, in the 1987 movie *Wall Street*, co-
    authored and directed by Oliver Stone. Gekko tells stockholders, "Greed, for
    lack of a better word, is good. Greed is right. Greed works."]

MONTANA   *See also* CITIES (Butte)

2   Montana's real trouble . . . is that her graveyards aren't big enough.
                          —ARTHUR FISHER, quoted in Ernest Gruening, ed.,
                          These United States, A Symposium, 1923

3   Montana: High, Wide, and Handsome.
                          —JOSEPH KINSEY HOWARD, book title, 1943

4   I am in love with Montana. . . . Montana seems to me to be what a small boy
    would think Texas is like from hearing Texans.
                          —JOHN STEINBECK, *Travels with Charley*, 1962

5   [Montana:] The last best place on earth.
                          —ANONYMOUS, motto, cited in exhibit of art and crafts
                          from Montana at The Silo in New Milford, Conn.

Motto
6   *Oro y plata.*
                          Gold and silver.

MOON   *See* NATURE: THE HEAVENS, THE SKY

MORALITY   *See* ETHICS & MORALITY; VIRTUE

MORNING   *See* NATURE: TIMES OF DAY

MOTHERS   *See* PARENTS

MYSTICISM & MYSTERY

7   Mystery is the antagonist of truth. It is a fog of human invention that obscures
    truth and represents it in distortion.
                          —THOMAS PAINE, *The Age of Reason*, 1794

8   In the deepest heart of all of us there is a corner in which the ultimate mystery
    of things works sadly.   —WILLIAM JAMES, *The Will to Believe*, 1897

9   The mystic can live happily in the droning consciousness of his own heart-
    beats and those of the universe.   —GEORGE SANTAYANA, *Winds of Doctrine*,
                          1913

10 Mystics always hope that science will some day overtake them.
                          —BOOTH TARKINGTON, *Looking forward to the
                          Great Adventure*, 1926

I said to my soul, be still, and let the dark come upon you   1
which shall be the darkness of God.   —T. S. ELIOT, *Four Quartets:*
East Coker, 1940
[The allusion is *Psalms* 46:10: "Be still, and know that I am God."]

The most beautiful thing we can experience is the mysterious. It is the source   2
of all true art and science.   —ALBERT EINSTEIN, *What I Believe*

N

NATIONS

See also CITIES; FOREIGNERS; FOREIGN POLICY; MEXICAN WAR; RACES & PEOPLES; SPANISH-AMERICAN WAR

AFRICA

1 It is still yesterday in Africa. It will take millions of tomorrows to rectify what has been done here.
—LORRAINE HANSBERRY, *Les Blancs*, 1972

ANCIENT WORLD

2 [*See also* GREECE]

The Naiad airs have brought me home
To the glory that was Greece,
And the grandeur that was Rome.
—EDGAR ALLAN POE, *To Helen*, 1831

ARGENTINA

3 A shadow state gripped by psychoses because the world has passed it by.
—JOHN GUNTHER, *Inside South America*, 1967

AUSTRALIA

4 *Australia, n.* A country lying in the South Sea, whose industrial and commercial development has been unspeakably retarded by an unfortunate dispute among geographers as to whether it is a continent or an island.
—AMBROSE BIERCE, *The Devil's Dictionary*, 1906

BRAZIL

5 It's such a useless thing for a man to want to be: the p-p-president of Brazil.
—TRUMAN CAPOTE, *Breakfast at Tiffany's*, 1957

CANADA

Canada is a mighty good neighbor and a mighty good customer. That's a com- 1
bination that is hard to beat.   —WILL ROGERS, in Alex Ayres, ed.,
           The Wit and Wisdom of Will Rogers [1993]

I don't even know what street Canada is on.   2
           —AL CAPONE, remark, 1931, quoted in Roy Greenaway,
           The News Game [1966]

Geography has made us neighbors. History has made us friends. Economics 3
has made us partners, and necessity has made us allies. Those whom God has
so joined together, let no man put asunder.
           —JOHN F. KENNEDY, address, Canadian Parliament,
           May 17, 1961

We tended to imagine Canada as a kind of vast hunting preserve convenient to 4
the United States.   —EDMUND WILSON, *O Canada*, 1965

CHINA

[Re the maxim that the word of a Chinese man is as good as his bond:] That 5
might have been in the old days, but not since the missionaries and businessmen come in. Chinese are just as human as anybody now.
           —WILL ROGERS, in Alex Ayres, ed.,
           The Wit and Wisdom of Will Rogers [1993]

ENGLAND

[*See also* CITIES, Cities Abroad: **London**]

The extremes of opulence and of want are more remarkable, and more con- 6
stantly obvious, in this country than in any other I ever saw.
           —JOHN QUINCY ADAMS, diary, Nov. 8, 1816

An Englishman who has lost his fortune is said to have died of a broken heart. 7
           —RALPH WALDO EMERSON, *English Traits*, 1856

England and the United States are natural allies, and should be the best of 8
friends.   —U. S. GRANT, *Memoirs*, 1885

An Englishman is never so natural as when he's holding his tongue.   9
           —HENRY JAMES, *The Portrait of a Lady*, 1881

England is the paradise of individuality, eccentricity, heresy, anomalies, hob- 10
bies, and humors.
           —GEORGE SANTAYANA, *Soliloquies in England*, 1922

To be an Englishman is to belong to the most exclusive club there is.   11
           —OGDEN NASH, *England Expects*

In England's case, uniquely, God and Mammon *are* one.   12
           —JOHN GUNTHER, *Inside Europe*, 1938

The English never abolish anything. They put it in cold storage.   13
           —ALFRED NORTH WHITEHEAD, *Dialogues of Alfred North
           Whitehead*, Jan. 19, 1945, recorded by Lucien Price [1955]

1 Great Britain has lost an empire and has not yet found a role.
　　　　　　　—DEAN ACHESON, speech, U.S. Military Academy,
　　　　　　　West Point, Dec. 5, 1962

EUROPE

2 Can we never extract the tapeworm of Europe from the brain of our countrymen?　　　　　—RALPH WALDO EMERSON, *Culture,* in *The Conduct of Life,*
　　　　　　　1860

3 Europe's old dynastic slaughterhouse
(Area of murder-plots of thrones, with scent left yet or wars and
　　scaffolds everywhere).
　　　　　　　—WALT WHITMAN, *Song of the Redwood Tree,* 1873

4 America has never quite forgiven Europe for having been discovered somewhat
earlier in history than itself.　　　　—OSCAR WILDE, *The American Man,* in
　　　　　　　Court and Society Review, April 1887

5 Every time Europe looks across the Atlantic to see the American Eagle, it observes only the rear end of an ostrich.　　　　—H. G. WELLS, *America,* 1907

FRANCE

[*See also* CITIES, Cities Abroad: **Paris**]

6 France has neither winter, summer, nor morals—apart from these drawbacks it
is a fine country.　　　　　　　—MARK TWAIN, in *Notebook* [1935]

7 Fifty million Frenchmen can't be wrong.
　　　　　　　—ANONYMOUS, saying of American troops in World War I,
　　　　　　　1917–18

8 In France, every argument becomes a matter of principle; the practical results
are relegated to second place.
　　　　　　　—EDWARD C. BANFIELD, 1961, quoted by Michael Lind,
　　　　　　　New York Times Book Review, July 23, 1995

GERMANY

9 Whenever the literary German dives into a sentence, that is the last you are going to see of him till he emerges on the other side of the Atlantic with his verb
in his mouth.　　　　　　　—MARK TWAIN, *A Connecticut Yankee
　　　　　　　in King Arthur's Court,* 1889

GREECE

[*See also* ANCIENT WORLD]

10 Greece is the home of the Gods.
　　　　　　　—HENRY MILLER, *The Colossus of Maroussi,* 1941

IRELAND

11 The Irish with their glowing hearts and reverent credulity, are needed in this
cold age of intellect and skepticism.　　　—LYDIA MARIA CHILD, *Letters from
　　　　　　　New York,* No. 33, Dec. 8, 1842

I'm troubled, I'm dissatisfied, I'm Irish.   1
>   —MARIANNE MOORE, *Spenser's Ireland*, 1941

[The 16th-century English poet Edmund Spenser wrote one prose work, *A View of the Present State of Ireland*. Moore's poem begins: "Spenser's Ireland / has not altered:— / a place as kind as it is green, / the greenest place I've never seen. / Every name is a tune."]

There's no use being Irish unless you know the world is going to break your   2
heart.   —DANIEL PATRICK MOYNIHAN, attributed,
>   quoted in *The New York Times*, August 12, 1994

ITALY

[*See also* CITIES, Cities Abroad: **Florence, Rome, Venice**]

Italy is well deserving the character it has acquired of being the Garden of Eu- 3
rope—and of being likewise the abode of poverty, villainy—filth and extortion.
>   —WASHINGTON IRVING, *Journal*, April 22, 1805

Italy gives us antiquity with good roads, cheap living, and above all, a sense of   4
freedom from responsibility.   —JAMES RUSSELL LOWELL, *Leaves from My Journal*
>   *in Italy and Elsewhere*, 1854

Say that the Creator made Italy from designs by Michael Angelo!   5
>   —MARK TWAIN, *The Innocents Abroad*, 1869

I am inclined to notice the ruin in things, perhaps because I was born in Italy.   6
>   —ARTHUR MILLER, *A View from the Bridge*, 1955

Italy v. Switzerland

In Italy for thirty years under the Borgias, they had warfare, terror, murder,   7
bloodshed. They produced Michaelangelo, Leonardo da Vinci, and the Renaissance. In Switzerland, they had brotherly love, five hundred years of democracy, and peace, and what did they produce? The cuckoo clock.
>   —ORSON WELLES, *The Third Man*, 1949

[The screenplay was by Graham Greene, but Welles is said to have added this passage himself.]

JAPAN

I think we have thrown Japan morally backward a thousand years; she is going   8
to adopt our vices (which are much too large for her).
>   —LAFCADIO HEARN, letter to Basil Hall Chamberlain,
>   Jan. 14, 1893

[Japan was changing quickly. The last rebellion of the feudal samurai had been crushed in 1877; the army adopted the German general-staff system in 1878; political parties formed in 1881; a constitution was promulgated in 1889. A slogan of the period was *fukoku-kyohei*, rich country—strong army. And see below.]

The development of the mathematical faculty in the race—unchecked by our   9
class of aesthetics and idealisms—ought to prove a serious danger to western
civilization at last.   —LAFCADIO HEARN, letter to Basil Hall Chamberlain,
>   Feb. 1895

[Hearn's reasoning is questionable—Western aesthetics and idealisms proved to be weak moral reeds in the 20th century—but he knew which way the wind was blowing. The Sino-Japanese War, a quick victory on land and sea for

Japan, was winding down as he wrote. The subsequent war with Russia (1904–1905) was another quick victory for Japan, this time over a Western power.]

1 Under all the amazing self-control and patience, there exists an adamantine something very dangerous to reach.
—LAFCADIO HEARN, *Out of the East,* 1895
[Hearn, incidentally, felt at home in Japan; married a Japanese, became a citizen of the country, and taught there.]

2 I saw the native home in Japan as a supreme study in elimination—not only of dirt, but the elimination of the insignificant. . . . I found this ancient Japanese dwelling to be a perfect example of the modern standardizing I had myself been working out. —FRANK LLOYD WRIGHT, c. 1914 in *An Autobiography* [1979]

3 [On the Japanese:] They got everything we got, and if they haven't, you show it to 'em and they will make it. —WILL ROGERS, *Weekly Articles,* Jan. 17, 1932

4 While we spend energy and imagination on new ways of cleaning the floors of our houses, the Japanese solve the problem by not dirtying them in the first place. —BERNARD RUDOFSKY, *The Kimono Mind: An Informed Guide to Japan,* 1965

5 The Japanese have perfected good manners and made them indistinguishable from rudeness. —PAUL THEROUX, *The Great Railway Bazaar,* 1975

MEXICO

[*See also* MEXICAN WAR]

6 Napoleon has no right to Mexico. Mexico may deserve a licking. That is possible enough. Most people do. But nobody has any right to lick Mexico except the United States. We have a right, I flatter myself, to lick the entire continent, including ourselves, any time we want to.
—ARTEMUS WARD, *Artemus Ward (His Travels) Among the Mormons* (1863), 1865

7 Poor Mexico! So far from God and so close to the United States.
—PORFIRIO DÍAZ, attributed in John S. D. Eisenhower, *The U.S. War with Mexico, 1846–1848* [1989]
[Gen. Díaz was president and dictator of Mexico 1876–80 and 1884–1971.]

THE PACIFIC

8 The power that rules the Pacific . . . is the power that rules the world.
—ALBERT J. BEVERIDGE, speech, U.S. Senate, 1900
[A farsighted global view from the American heartland: Sen. Beveridge, a Republican, represented Indiana from 1899 to 1911.]

RUSSIA

[*See also* CITIES, Cities Abroad: **Moscow, St. Petersburg;** FUTURE, THE (Steffens)]

9 Russia seems at present the great bug-bear of the European politicians on the land, as the British Leviathan is on the water.
—JAMES MADISON, letter to Richard Rush, Nov. 20, 1821

You can take the whole of the United States of America, from Maine to Cali-   1
fornia and from Lake Superior to the Gulf of Mexico, and set it down in the
middle of Siberia, without touching anywhere the boundaries of the latter's
territory.   —GEORGE KENNAN,
                                        Siberia and the Exile System, 1891

Russia is omnipotence. . . . who can ever penetrate that polar mystery?   2
                                    —HENRY ADAMS, letter
                                        to Brooks Adams, June 5, 1895

The Russians are devout believers in an eye for an eye, or if possible two.   3
                                    —JOHN GUNTHER,
                                        Inside Russia Today, 1962

In a Russian tragedy, everybody dies. In a Russian comedy, everybody dies, too.   4
But they die happy.   —BARRY FARBER, in his radio talk show, WMCA,
                            New York City, cited in Suzy Platt, ed.,
                            Respectfully Quoted, Library of Congress [1989]

The brain is ill-equipped to comprehend the meaning of a nation that encom-   5
passes eleven time zones.   —HEDRICK SMITH, *The Russians,* 1977

The Russians are connoisseurs of the cold.   —*Ibid.*   6

At the Cabinet meeting this morning Zbig [national security adviser Zbigniew   7
Brzezinski] made an interesting comment that under Lenin the Soviet Union
was like a religious revival, under Stalin like a prison, under Khrushchev like
a circus, and under Brezhnev like the U.S. Post Office.
                                    —JIMMY CARTER, diary, Nov. 7, 1977

When they go to take a bite out of the world, the Soviets are not fussy eaters.   8
                            —RICHARD M. NIXON, *The Real War,* 1980

An evil empire.   —RONALD REAGAN, speech, National Association   9
                                    of Evangelicals, March 9, 1983
[Russia was the evil empire, according to Pres. Reagan. The label was borrowed
from the 1977 film *Star Wars* by George W. Lucas, Jr. See also FOREIGN POLICY.]

SCANDINAVIA

The folk who live in Scandinavia   10
Are famous for their odd behavia.
They have the frigidest of climates
And avoid their bellicose fellow-primates.
Though salesmen cluster at their door,
They don't want anybody's war.
It isn't that they put on airs;
They merely mind their own affairs.
                    —OGDEN NASH, *Fellow Creatures III: The Northerners,*
                        in *I'm a Stranger Here Myself,* 1938

SOUTH AMERICA

Few South Americans have ulcers.   11
                    —JOHN GUNTHER, *Inside South America,* 1967

1   "You must not judge people by their country," a lady advised me. "In South America, it is always wise to judge people by their altitude."
            —PAUL THEROUX, *The Old Patagonian Express*, 1979

SPAIN

2   If the people of Spain have one common trait it is pride, and, if they have another, it is common sense, and if they have a third, it is impracticality.
            —ERNEST HEMINGWAY, *Death in the Afternoon*, 1932

SWEDEN

3   If ever there was a Yankeer than Yankee, he's a Swede.
            —HENRY ADAMS, letter to Elizabeth Cameron, Sept. 10, 1901

SWITZERLAND

[*See also* **Italy v. Switzerland**]

4   Continually since I have been in Switzerland have I been struck with the similarity in sentiment and manners between the Swiss and the Americans—It is impossible this nation can always be kept under, the love of liberty burns too strongly in their bosoms.   —WASHINGTON IRVING, *Journal*, May 8, 1805

5   Switzerland is a small, steep country, much more up and down than sideways, and is all stuck over with brown hotels built on the cuckoo clock style of architecture.   —ERNEST HEMINGWAY, in the *Toronto Star Weekly*, March 4, 1922

6   The Swiss who are not a people so much as a neat clean small quite solvent business.   —WILLIAM FAULKNER, *Intruder in the Dust*, 1948

TURKEY

7   A humorless soldierly people whose arts are courage, honor, and bloodletting.
            —NELSON ALGREN, *Who Lost an American?*, 1963

8   Before World War I, Turkey was known as the "Sick Man of Europe"; now it is almost a terminal case.   —RICHARD M. NIXON, *The Real War*, 1980

VENEZUELA

9   This pioneer democracy, built on foundations, not of rock, but blood hard as rock.   —ROBERT LOWELL, *Caracas I*, in *Notebook*, 1970

NATIVE AMERICANS   *See* RACES & PEOPLES

NATURE   *See also* COUNTRY LIFE & PEOPLE; ENVIRONMENT;
                        FARMS & FARMERS; MIDWEST, THE; SCIENCE;
                        UNIVERSE, THE; WEST, THE; WILDERNESS

10 It were happy if we studied nature more in natural things, and acted according to nature, whose rules are few, plain, and most reasonable.
            —WILLIAM PENN, *Some Fruits of Solitude*, 1693

With beauty before me, I walk   1
With beauty behind me, I walk
With beauty above and about me, I walk,
It is finished in beauty,
It is finished in beauty.
> —ANONYMOUS, Navaho night chant, in Frank Bergon
> & Zeese Papaniklas, *Looking Far West* [1978]

Everything in nature contains all the powers of nature. Everything is made of   2
one hidden stuff.   —RALPH WALDO EMERSON, *Compensation*,
> in *Essays: First Series*, 1841

[For Emerson on nature's secrets, see SCIENCE.]

Nature, as we know her, is no saint.   3
> —RALPH WALDO EMERSON, *History*, in *Essays: First Series*, 1841

Nature provides exceptions to every rule.   4
> —MARGARET FULLER, *The Great Lawsuit: Man versus Men,*
> *Woman versus Women*, in *The Dial*, July 1843

Nature is one and continuous everywhere.   5
> —HENRY DAVID THOREAU, *A Week on the*
> *Concord and Merrimack Rivers*, 1849

Heaven is under our feet as well as over our heads.   6
> —HENRY DAVID THOREAU, "The Pond in Winter," *Walden*, 1854

Nature is full of genius, full of the divinity; so that not a snowflake escapes its   7
fashioning hand.   —HENRY DAVID THOREAU, *Journal*, Jan. 5, 1856

I believe in the forest, and in the meadow, and in the night in which the corn   8
grows.   —HENRY DAVID THOREAU, *Walking*, 1862

Mountains are earth's undecaying monuments.   9
> —NATHANIEL HAWTHORNE, *The Notch of the White Mountains* [1868]

There are no short cuts in evolution.   10
> —LOUIS D. BRANDEIS, speech, Boston, April 22, 1904

[For William Jennings Bryan on evolution, see SCIENCE: BIOLOGY.]

There are no sermons in stones. It is easier to get a spark out of a stone than a   11
moral.   —JOHN BURROUGHS, *Time and Change*, 1912

Nature, n. The Unseen Intelligence which loved us into being, and is disposing   12
of us by the same token.   —ELBERT HUBBARD, *The Roycroft Dictionary*
> *and Book of Epigrams*, 1923

Nothing is so cruel, so wanton, so unfeeling as nature; she moves with the   13
weight of a glacier carrying everything before her.
> —CLARENCE DARROW, *The Story of My Life*, 1932

Only to the white man was nature a wilderness, and only to him was the land   14
"infested" with "wild" animals and "savage" people. To us it was tame. Earth
was bountiful, and we were surrounded with the blessings of the Great Mystery.
> —LUTHER STANDING BEAR, *Land of the Spotted Eagle*, 1933

[He was chief of the Oglala Sioux.]

1 Perhaps nature is our best assurance of immortality.
    —ELEANOR ROOSEVELT, *My Day*, newspaper column,
    April 24, 1945

2 A river seems a magic thing. A magic, moving, living part of the very earth it-
    self.   —LAURA GILPIN, *The Rio Grande*, 1949

3 In nature, there is less death and destruction than death and transmutation.
    —EDWIN WAY TEALE,
    Circle of the Seasons, 1953

4 The "control of nature" is a phrase conceived in arrogance.
    —RACHEL CARSON, *Silent Spring*, 1962
    [More at SCIENCE: TECHNOLOGY.]

5 Nature uses only the longest threads to weave her patterns, so each small piece
    of her fabric reveals the organization of the entire tapestry.
    —RICHARD FEYNMAN, personal papers, quoted in James Gleick,
    Genius: The Life and Science of Richard Feynman, 1992

NATURE: ANIMALS

6 Everything belonging to the spider is admirable.
    —JONATHAN EDWARDS, *The Spider*, c. 1714
    [Edwards was about age twelve when he wrote about spiders. See Robert Low-
    ell at COUNTRY LIFE & PEOPLE for a poem about Edwards and his observation of
    spiders.]

7 I wish the bald eagle had not been chosen as the representative of our country;
    he is a bird of bad moral character . . . like those among men who live by sharp-
    ing and robbing, he is generally poor, and often very lousy. . . .
    The turkey . . . is a much more respectable bird, and withal a true original
    native of America.   —BENJAMIN FRANKLIN, letter to Sarah Bache,
    Jan. 26, 1784

8 The air was literally filled with Pigeons, and the noon-day light was obscured
    as by an eclipse.   —JOHN JAMES AUDUBON, *Passenger Pigeon*,
    in *Ornithological Biography*, 1831–39
    [Audubon was describing the flight of Passenger Pigeons over the Kentucky
    barrens in 1813. He also wrote that the sound of approaching pigeons—some-
    times in flocks of more than a billion—was like that of a hard gale at sea. The
    mass of pigeons was so thick that they could be knocked down with poles.
    When they alit, the weight of their numbers caused branches to break. The up-
    roar continued all night. These birds were easy to kill, and Audubon described
    the men in his company taking large numbers that night, and setting hogs on
    the pigeons remaining.
    The species became extinct when the last passenger pigeon, named Martha
    Washington, died in the Cincinnati Zoo, at age twenty-nine, on September 1,
    1914.]

9 There is something in the unselfish and self-sacrificing love of a brute, which
    goes directly to the heart of him who has had frequent occasion to test the pal-
    try friendship and gossamer fidelity of mere man.
    —EDGAR ALLAN POE, *The Black Cat*, 1843

The country before us thronged with buffalo. They were crowded so densely 1
together that in the distance their rounded backs presented a surface of uniform blackness.
—FRANCIS PARKMAN, *The Oregon Trail,* 1847
[At that time some sixty million bison roamed the plains along the Oregon
Trail. White settlers and hunters then killed almost all of them within a few
years.]

The bluebird carries the sky on its back. 2
—HENRY DAVID THOREAU, *Journal,* April 3, 1852

I think I could turn and live with animals, they are so placid and 3
    self-contained
I stand and look at them long and long.
—WALT WHITMAN, *Song of Myself,* 1855

Split the lark—and you'll find the music— 4
Bulb after bulb, in silver rolled—
Scantily dealt to the summer morning
Saved for your ear when lutes be old.
—EMILY DICKINSON, poem no. 861, c. 1864

Bees are black, with gilt surcingles— 5
Buccaneers of buzz.   —EMILY DICKINSON,
                                                      poem no. 1404, c. 1877

[A surcingle is a belt or girth.]

MAJOR 6
Born a Dog
Died a Gentleman.

—ANONYMOUS
[Identified in *American Heritage,* Feb. 1973, as a line on an old Maryland
gravestone for a dog.]

Cats and monkeys, monkeys and cats—all human life is there. 7
—HENRY JAMES,
The Madonna of the Future, 1879

A jay hasn't got any more principle than a Congressman. A jay will lie, a jay 8
will steal, a jay will deceive, a jay will betray; and four times out of five, a jay
will go back on his solemnest promise.   —MARK TWAIN,
                                                Jim Baker's Blue Jay Yarn,
                                                in *A Tramp Abroad,* 1880

A noiseless patient spider.   —WALT WHITMAN, 9
                                                A Noiseless Patient Spider, 1881

The dog was created especially for children. He is the god of frolic. 10
—HENRY WARD BEECHER,
Proverbs from Plymouth Pulpit, 1887

Of all God's creatures there is only one that cannot be made the slave of 11
the lash. That one is the cat. If man could be crossed with the cat, it would
improve man, but it would deteriorate the cat.
—MARK TWAIN, *Notebook* [1935]

1   Oh, a wondrous bird is the pelican!
His beak holds more than his belican.
He takes in his beak
Enough food for a week.
But I'll be darned if I know how the helican.
—Dixon Lanier Merritt, in the *Nashville Banner,* April 22, 1913

2   The bull is godlike.   —William Carlos Williams, *The Bull,* 1922

3   At evening, casual flocks of pigeons make
Ambiguous undulations as they sink.
Downward to darkness, on extended wings.
—Wallace Stevens, *Sunday Morning,* 1923

4   Pigeons on the grass alas.
—Gertrude Stein, *Four Saints in Three Acts,* 1927

5   The turtle lives 'twixt plated decks
Which practically conceal its sex.
I think its clever of the turtle.
In such a fix to be so fertile.   —Ogden Nash, *Autres Bêtes, Autres Moeurs,*
in *Hard Lines* 1931

6   As the cat
climbed over
the top of

the jamcloset
first the right
forefoot

carefully then the hind
stepped down

into the pit of
the empty
flowerpot.   —William Carlos Williams, *Poem,* c. 1930–31

7   An elephant's faithful
One hundred per cent!   —Dr. Seuss (Theodor Seuss Geisel),
Horton Hatches the Egg, 1940

[More at Loyalty.]

8   The trouble with a kitten is
THAT
Eventually it becomes a
CAT.   —Ogden Nash, *The Kitten,* in *The Face Is Familiar,* 1941

9   The song of canaries
Never varies,
And when they're moulting
They're pretty revolting.
—Ogden Nash, *The Canary,* in *Ibid.*
[Canaries were popular pets in this era, and people put a lot of effort into their
care and encouraging them to sing. Dorothy Parker called her canary Onan, be-
cause he spilled his seed upon the ground.]

Dogs display reluctance and wrath   1
If you try to give them a bath.
They bury bones in hideaways,
And half the time they run sideaways.
> —OGDEN NASH, *An Introduction to Dogs*, in *Ibid.*

If a dog jumps in your lap, it is because he is fond of you. If a cat does the same   2
thing, it is because your lap is warmer.
> —ALFRED NORTH WHITEHEAD, *Dialogues of Alfred North
> Whitehead*, recorded by Lucien Price [1955]

The best thing about animals is that they don't talk much.   3
> —THORNTON WILDER, *The Skin of Our Teeth*, 1942

I saw the spiders marching through air.   4
> —ROBERT LOWELL, *Mr. Edwards and the Spider*, 1946

[More at COUNTRY LIFE & PEOPLE.]

Booming and booming of the new-come bee.   5
> —WALLACE STEVENS,
> *Notes Toward a Supreme Fiction*, 1947

Our ability to perceive quality in nature begins, as in art, with the pretty. It ex-   6
pands through successive stages of the beautiful to values as yet uncaptured by
language. The quality of cranes lies, I think, in this higher gamut, as yet beyond the reach of words.   —ALDO LEOPOLD, *A Sand County Almanac*, 1949

People on horses look better than they are.   7
> —MARYA MANNES, *More in Anger*, 1958

[The next line is "People in cars look worse than they are."]

If we had better hearing, and could discern the descants of sea birds, the rhyth-   8
mic tympani of schools of mollusks, or even the distant harmonics of midges
hanging over meadows in the sun, the combined sound might lift us off our
feet.   —LEWIS THOMAS, *The Lives of a Cell*, 1974

It's not easy being green.   —JIM HENSON, saying of Kermit the Frog on   9
> *Sesame Street*, television show

NATURE: THE HEAVENS, THE SKY

The man who has seen the rising moon break out of the clouds at midnight has   10
been present like an archangel at the creation of light and of the world.
> —RALPH WALDO EMERSON, *History*, in *Essays: First Series*, 1841

The sky is the daily bread of the eyes.   11
> —RALPH WALDO EMERSON, *Journal*, May 25, 1843

Silently, one by one, in the infinite meadows of heaven,   12
Blossomed the lovely stars, the forget-me-nots of the angels.
> —HENRY WADSWORTH LONGFELLOW, *Evangeline*, 1847

Give me the splendid silent sun with all his beams full-dazzling.   13
> —WALT WHITMAN, *Give Me the Splendid Silent Sun*, 1865

1 Lo, the moon ascending,
Up from the east, the silvery round moon,
Beautiful over the house-tops, ghastly, phantom moon,
Immense and silent moon.   —WALT WHITMAN,
Song of the Universal, 1881

2 The moon? It is a griffin's egg
Hatching tomorrow night . . .
Yet gentle will the griffin be,
Most decorous and fat,
And walk up to the Milky Way
And lap it like a cat.   —VACHEL LINDSAY, *Yet Gentle Will the Griffin Be
(What Grandpa Told the Children)*, 1912

3 The book of moonlight is not written yet.
    —WALLACE STEVENS, *The Comedian as the Letter C,*
in *Harmonium*, 1923
[See below for another Stevens line on the moon.]

4 Blessed moon
noon
of night

that through the dark
bids Love
stay.   —WILLIAM CARLOS WILLIAMS, *Full Moon*, first version, 1924

5 who knows if the moon's
a balloon, coming out of a keen city
in the sky—filled with pretty people?
    —E. E. CUMMINGS, *who knows if the moon's a balloon,*
in *&* [*And*], 1925

6 The moon is the mother of pathos and pity.
    —WALLACE STEVENS,
Lunar Paraphrase, in *Harmonium*, 1931

7 The moon is a friend for the lonesome to talk to.
    —CARL SANDBURG, *Moonlight and Maggots,*
in *Complete Poems*, 1950

8 Comets are the nearest thing to nothing that anything can be and still be something.   —NATIONAL GEOGRAPHIC,
press release, March 31, 1955

9 The moon is a different thing to each one of us.
    —FRANK BORMAN, from Apollo VIII, Dec. 24, 1968
[For the moon landing, see SCIENCE: TECHNOLOGY.]

10 Space changes nobody. You bring back from space what you bring into space.
    —STUART A. ROOSA, comment to Andrew Chaiken,
quoted in Chaiken's *Man on the Moon*, 1994
[Roosa flew on the Apollo 14 moon mission in 1971, remaining in orbit and doing scientific experiments while Alan Shepard and Edgar Mitchell were on the
moon. He died in 1994.]

NATURE: PLANTS & GARDENS

See also ENVIRONMENT (Reagan); WILDERNESS (for forests)

But though I am an old man, I am but a young gardener.   1
> —THOMAS JEFFERSON, letter to Charles Wilson Peale, August 20, 1811

The groves were God's first temples.   2
> —WILLIAM CULLEN BRYANT, *A Forest Hymn*, 1825

The rose that lives its little hour   3
Is prized beyond the sculptured flower.
> —WILLIAM CULLEN BRYANT, *A Scene on the Banks of the Hudson*, 1828

Woodman, spare that tree!   4
Touch not a single bough!
In youth it sheltered me,
And I'll protect it now.
> —GEORGE POPE MORRIS, *Woodman, Spare That Tree!*, 1830

The birch, most shy and ladylike of trees.   5
> —JAMES RUSSELL LOWELL, *An Indian Summer Reverie*, 1846

The pine is the mother of legends.   6
> —JAMES RUSSELL LOWELL, *The Growth of a Legend*, 1847

Earth laughs in flowers.   7
> —RALPH WALDO EMERSON, *Hamatreya*, in *Poems*, 1847

A weed is no more than a flower in disguise.   8
> —JAMES RUSSELL LOWELL, *A Fable for Critics*, 1848

[See also Emerson below.]

One of the attractive things about the flowers is their beautiful reserve.   9
> —HENRY DAVID THOREAU, *Journal*, June 17, 1853

I have great faith in a seed. Convince me that you have a seed there, and I am   10
prepared to expect wonders.
> —HENRY DAVID THOREAU, "The Dispersion of Seeds," from his journal, published in Bradley P. Dear, ed., *Faith in a Seed* [1993]

I was determined to know beans.   11
> —HENRY DAVID THOREAU, "The Beanfield," *Walden*, 1854

Flowers are the sweetest things God ever made and forgot to put a soul into.   12
> —HENRY WARD BEECHER, *Life Thoughts*, 1858

The Amen! of nature is always a flower.   13
> —OLIVER WENDELL HOLMES, SR., *The Autocrat of the Breakfast-Table*, 1858

When lilacs last in the dooryard bloom'd.   14
> —WALT WHITMAN, *When Lilacs Last in the Dooryard Bloom'd*, 1865–66

[More at SORROW & GRIEF.]

1　To own a bit of ground, to scratch it with a hoe, to plant seeds and watch their renewal of life—this is the commonest delight of the race, the most satisfactory thing a man can do. —CHARLES DUDLEY WARNER,
My Summer in a Garden, 1870
[But see also Warner at FARMS & FARMERS.]

2　What is a weed? A plant whose virtues have not yet been discovered.
—RALPH WALDO EMERSON, *Fortune of the Republic*, 1878
[See also James Russell Lowell above.]

3　The dandelion's pallid tube
Astonishes the grass,
And winter instantly becomes
An infinite alas. —EMILY DICKINSON, poem no. 1519, c. 1881

4　I like trees because they seem more resigned to the way they have to live than other things do. —WILLA CATHER, *O Pioneers!*, 1913

5　I think that I shall never see
A poem lovely as a tree.

—JOYCE KILMER, *Trees*, 1913
[See also Ogden Nash at ADVERTISING.]

6　Poems are made by fools like me,
But only God can make a tree. —*Ibid.*

7　Rose is a rose is a rose. —GERTRUDE STEIN, *Sacred Emily*, 1913

8　[On picking blueberries:] It's a nice way to live,
Just taking what Nature is willing to give,
Not forcing her hand with harrow and plow. —ROBERT FROST, *Blueberries*,
in *North of Boston*, 1914

9　One could do worse than be a swinger of birches.
—ROBERT FROST, *Birches*, 1916

10　There's a tree that grows in Brooklyn. Some people call it the Tree of Heaven. No matter where its seed falls, it makes a tree which struggles to reach the sky.
—BETTY SMITH, *A Tree Grows in Brooklyn*, 1943
[The ailanthus tree is an inner city survivor. It has many negative features: seeds that scatter in excessive profusion, weak limbs, and unpleasantly odiferous homely greenish flowers. But it will grow just about anywhere—although as this book was going to press, New York City's ailanthus trees were reported to be dying.]

NATURE: SEAS & OCEANS　　　　*See also* SHIPS & SAILING

11　The sea is feline. It licks your feet.
—OLIVER WENDELL HOLMES, SR.,
The Professor at the Breakfast-Table, 1860

12　Implacable I, the implacable sea;
Implacable most when most I smile serene—
Pleased not appeased by myriad wrecks in me.
—HERMAN MELVILLE, *Pebbles*, in *John Marr and Other Sailors*, 1888

The sea is woman, the sea is wonder—
Her other name is fate.   —EDWIN MARKHAM, *Virgilia*, 1905   1

The seas are the heart's blood of the earth.   2
                    —HENRY BESTON, *The Headlong Wave*,
                        in *The Outermost House*, 1928

The sea hates a coward.   3
                    —EUGENE O'NEILL, *Mourning Becomes Electra*, 1931

The sea has many voices,   4
Many gods and many voices.
                    —T. S. ELIOT, *Four Quartets: The Dry Salvages*, 1941

For all at last returns to the sea—to Oceanus, the ocean river, like the ever-   5
flowing stream of time, the beginning and the end.
                    —RACHEL CARSON, last sentence, *The Sea Around Us*, 1950

it's always ourselves we find in the sea.   6
                    —E. E. CUMMINGS, *maggie and millie
                        and molly and may*, in *95 Poems*, 1958

NATURE: SEASONS   *See also* SEASONS & TIMES

The melancholy days are come, the saddest of the year, of wailing winds, and   7
naked woods, and meadows brown and sere.
                    —WILLIAM CULLEN BRYANT, *The Death of the Flowers*, 1825

In . . . the fall, the whole country goes to glory.   8
                    —FRANCES TROLLOPE, *Domestic Manners of the Americans*,
                        1832

[On the beginning of summer:] The season of hope and promise is passed, and   9
already the season of small fruits has arrived. We are a little saddened because
we begin to see the interval between our hopes and their fulfillment.
                    —HENRY DAVID THOREAU, "The Dispersion of Seeds,"
                        from his journal, in *Faith in a Seed*, 1993

Spring in the world!   10
And all things are made new!
                    —HENRY WADSWORTH LONGFELLOW, *Hyperion*, 1839

And what is so rare as a day in June?   11
Then, if ever, come perfect days.
                    —JAMES RUSSELL LOWELL, *The Vision of Sir Launfal*, 1846
[In the prelude, Lowell wrote, "No price is set on the lavish summer; / June
may be had by the poorest comer."]

These are the days when birds come back—   12
A very few—a bird or two—
To take a backward look.

These are the days when the skies resume
The old—old sophistries of June—
A blue and gold mistake.   —EMILY DICKINSON,
                                                         poem no. 130, c. 1859

1   There's a certain slant of light,
   Winter afternoons—
   That oppresses, like the heft
   Of cathedral tunes.   —EMILY DICKINSON, poem no. 258, c. 1861

2   The word May is a perfumed word. It is an illuminated initial. It means youth,
love, song, and all that is beautiful in life.
     —HENRY WADSWORTH LONGFELLOW, journal entry, May 1, 1861

3   Then came the lovely spring with a rush of blossoms and music,
Flooding the earth with flowers, and the air with melodies vernal.
     —HENRY WADSWORTH LONGFELLOW,
     The Theologian's Tale, Tales of a Wayside Inn, 1863–74

4   November always seemed to be the Norway of the year.
     —EMILY DICKINSON, letter to Dr. and Mrs. J. G. Holland, 1864

5   Our summer made her light escape
   Into the beautiful.   —EMILY DICKINSON, no. 1540, c. 1865

6   The sun that brief December day
Rose cheerless over hills of gray,
And, darkly circled, gave at noon
A sadder light than waning moon.   —JOHN GREENLEAF WHITTIER,
     Snow-Bound; A Winter Idyl, 1866

7   November is the most disagreeable month in the whole year.
     —LOUISA MAY ALCOTT, *Little Women*, 1868

8   A little madness in the Spring
Is wholesome even for the king.
     —EMILY DICKINSON, poem no. 1333, c. 1875
[The correct dates for Dickinson's poems do not always match the traditional
numerical order.]

9   O, it sets my heart a-clickin' like the tickin' of a clock,
When the frost is on the punkin and the fodder's in the shock.
     —JAMES WHITCOMB RILEY,
     When the Frost Is on the Punkin, 1883

10   The scarlet of the maples can shake me like a cry
Of bugles going by.
And my lonely spirit thrills
To see the frosty asters like a smoke upon the hills.
     —BLISS CARMAN, *A Vagabond Song*,
     in *Songs in Vagabondia*, 1894

11   In the Good Old Summer Time.
     —REN SHIELDS, song title, 1902
[Music by George Evans.]

12   Summer afternoon—summer afternoon; to me those have always been the two
most beautiful words in the English language.
     —HENRY JAMES, quoted in Edith Wharton,
     A Backward Glance [1934]

Spring came on forever,   1
Spring came on forever,
Said the Chinese nightingale.
                    —VACHEL LINDSAY, *The Chinese Nightingale*, 1917

Winter is icumen in,   2
Lhude sing Goddamm,
Raineth drop and staineth slop,
And how the wind doth ramm!
Sing: Goddamm.
                          —EZRA POUND, *Ancient Music*, 1917
[A play on the anonymous *Cuckoo Song* from about 1250: "Sumer is icumen
in, / Lhude sing cuccu! / Groweth sed, and bloweth med, / And springth the
wude nu— / Sing cuccu!"]

The leaves fall early this autumn, in wind.   3
The paired butterflies are already yellow with August
Over the grass in the West garden;
They hurt me. I grow older.   —EZRA POUND, *The River Merchant's Wife:
                                  A Letter (After Rihaku)*

Blaze the mountains in the windless autumn,   4
Frost-clear, blue-nooned, apple-ripening days.
                          —SARAH N. CLEGHORN, *Vermont*,
                              in *Portraits and Protests*, 1917

Winter lies too long in country towns; hangs on until it is stale and shabby, old 5
and sullen.
                          —WILLA CATHER, *My Ántonia*, 1918
[The town in the novel is Black Hawk, Nebraska. The author grew up in Red
Cloud, Nebraska.]

April is the cruellest month, breeding   6
Lilacs out of the dead land, mixing
Memory and desire, stirring
Dull roots with spring rain.   —T. S. ELIOT, *The Waste Land*, 1922

The way a crow   7
Shook down on me
The dust of snow
From a hemlock tree

Has given my heart a change of mood
And saved some part
Of a day I had rued.   —ROBERT FROST, *Dust of Snow*, 1923

When the world is puddle-wonderful.   8
                          —E. E. CUMMINGS, *Chansons Innocentes*, 1923
[The season is "Just- / spring when the world is mud- / luscious."]

A wind has blown the rain away and blown   9
the sky away and all the leaves away,
and the trees stand. I think I too have known
autumn too long.
              —E. E. CUMMINGS, *Realities*, V, in *Tulips and Chimneys*, 1923

1   April
Comes like an idiot, babbling and strewing flowers.
—EDNA ST. VINCENT MILLAY, *Spring*

2   In summer the song
sings itself.   —WILLIAM CARLOS WILLIAMS, *The Botticellian Trees*, 1930

3   Summertime
And the livin' is easy,
Fish are jumpin', and the cotton is high.
—IRA GERSHWIN, *Porgy and Bess*, 1935
[Music by George Gershwin.]

4   These are the desolate, dark weeks.
—WILLIAM CARLOS WILLIAMS, *These*, 1938

5   The year plunges into night
and the heart plunges
lower than night.   —*Ibid.*

6   O sweet spontaneous
earth how often
has the naughty thumb of science prodded
thy
beauty
thou answereth them only with
spring.   —E. E. CUMMINGS, *Tulips and Chimneys*, 1924

7   Spring, the cruelest and fairest of the seasons, will come again. And the strange
and buried men will come again, in flower and leaf the strange and buried men
will come again, and death and the dust will never come again, for death and
the dust will die.   —THOMAS WOLFE, *Look Homeward Angel*, 1929

8   All things on earth point home in old October: sailors to sea, travelers to walls
and fences, hunters to field and hollow and the long voice of the hounds, the
lover to the love he has forsaken.
—THOMAS WOLFE, *Of Time and the River*, 1935

9   When the short day is brightest, with forest and fire,
The brief sun flames the ice, on pond and ditches,
In windless cold that is the heart's beat,
Reflecting in a watery mirror
A glare that is blindness in the early afternoon.
—T. S. ELIOT, *Four Quartets: Little Gidding*, 1942

10   The house was quiet and the world was calm.
The reader became the book; and the summer night
Was like the conscious being of the book.
The house was quiet and the world was calm.
—WALLACE STEVENS, *The House Was Quiet
and the World Was Calm*, in *Transport to Summer*, 1947

11   August creates as she slumbers, replete and satisfied.
—JOSEPH WOOD KRUTCH, *August*, in *Twelve Seasons*, 1949

One swallow does not make a summer, but one skein of geese, cleaving the   1
murk of a March thaw, is the spring.   —ALDO LEOPOLD,
                                                A Sand County Almanac, 1949
[And, Leopold added, "A March morning is only as drab as he who walks in it
without a glance skyward, ear cocked for geese."]

All things seem possible in May.   2
                              —EDWIN WAY TEALE, *North with the Spring,* 1951

For man, autumn is a time of harvest, of gathering together. For nature, it is a   3
time of sowing, of scattering abroad.
                      —EDWIN WAY TEALE, *Autumn Across America,* 1956

Over increasingly large areas of the United States, spring now comes unher-   4
alded by the return of birds.
                              —RACHEL CARSON, *The Silent Spring,* 1962

[More at ENVIRONMENT.]

NATURE: TIMES OF DAY

Blue evening falls,   5
Blue evening falls;
Near by in every direction,
It sets the corn tassels trembling.
                      —ANONYMOUS, song of the Papago Indians
                        of Southern Arizona and northern Sonora, Mexico

The lark is up to meet the sun,   6
The bee is on the wing,
The ant his labor has begun,
The woods with music ring.

Shall bird and bee and ant be wise
While I my moments waste?
Oh, let me with the morning rise
And to my duties haste.
                              —WILLIAM MCGUFFEY, *Third Reader,* 1837
[McGuffey's *Readers* educated millions of American schoolchildren, from the
1830s into the 1920s, teaching them not so incidentally the author's socially
correct and politically conservative views.]

The day is done, and the darkness   7
Falls from the wings of night,
As a feather is wafted downward
From an eagle in his flight.   —HENRY WADSWORTH LONGFELLOW,
                                            The Day Is Done, 1845

And the night shall be filled with music,   8
And the cares, that infest the day,
Shall fold their tents, like the Arabs,
And as silently steal away.   —*Ibid.*

You've gut to git up airly   9
Ef you want to take in God.
                              —JAMES RUSSELL LOWELL,
                                The Biglow Papers, 1848

1   I'll tell you how the sun rose—
    A ribbon at a time.   —EMILY DICKINSON, poem no. 318, 1862

2   In the long, sleepless watches of the night.
                    —HENRY WADSWORTH LONGFELLOW, *The Cross of Snow*, 1879

3   I have been one acquainted with the night.
                    —ROBERT FROST, *Acquainted with the Night*, 1928

4   Night falls fast.
    Today is in the past.   —EDNA ST. VINCENT MILLAY, *Not So Far as the Forest*,
                               in *Huntsman, What Quarry?*, 1939

5   Outside the open window
    The morning air is all awash with angels.
                        —RICHARD WILBUR,
                        Love Calls Us to the Things of This World, 1956

NATURE: WEATHER

6   Thunder is the voice of God, and, therefore, to be dreaded.
                    —INCREASE MATHER, *Remarkable Providences*, 1684

7   I expand and live in the warm day like corn and melons.
                    —RALPH WALDO EMERSON, *Nature*, 1836

8   Through woods and mountain passes
    The winds, like anthems, roll.   —HENRY WADSWORTH LONGFELLOW,
                                        Midnight Mass for the Dying Year, 1839

9   How beautiful is the rain!
    After the dust and heat,
    In the broad and fiery street,
    In the narrow lane,
    How beautiful is the rain!   —HENRY WADSWORTH LONGFELLOW,
                                                  Rain in Summer, 1846

10 Everybody talks about the weather, but nobody does anything about it.
                    —MARK TWAIN, editorial, Hartford *Courant*, August 24, 1897
    [Twain is the probable author of this observation. He was living in Hartford at
    the time, and *Bartlett's* points out that Robert Underwood Johnson, in his
    memoirs, quotes Twain as saying, "We all grumble about the weather, but noth-
    ing is *done* about it." On the other hand, Charles Dudley Warner, associate ed-
    itor of the *Courant*, was a witty man in his own right and may have coined the
    joke himself. Or the line could just have been going around the town.
        Twain, though, was very weather conscious. For example, in a speech to the
    New England Society in New York City, on December 22, 1876, he advised, "If
    you don't like the weather in New England, just wait a few minutes." See also
    Twain at NEW ENGLAND.]

11 Neither snow, nor rain, nor heat, nor gloom of night stays these couriers from
    the swift completion of their appointed rounds.
                        —GENERAL POST OFFICE, NEW YORK CITY,
                        inscription, 1913
    [Adapted from a passage in Herodotus, *The Histories*, 5th cent. B.C. Herodotus
    was describing the couriers used by the Persian king Xerxes to carry news

across his empire: "Nothing mortal travels so fast as these Persian messengers," the historian wrote, describing a relay method similar to the American pony express. "These men will not be hindered from accomplishing . . . the distance which they have to go, either by snow, or rain, or heat, or by the darkness of night."]

The fog comes 1
on little cat feet.
It sits looking
over the harbor and city
on silent haunches
and then moves on. —CARL SANDBURG, *Fog,* 1916

Thank heavens, the sun has gone in, and I don't have to go out and enjoy it. 2
—LOGAN PEARSALL SMITH, *Afterthoughts,* 1931

It ain't a fit night out for man or beast. —W. C. FIELDS, 3
The Fatal Glass of Beer, 1933
[Fields originally used the line in a sketch in Earl Carroll's Broadway show *Vanities,* and then as a title for a Mack Sennett movie. In a letter of February 8, 1944, he spoke of making the phrase a byword, and added that he was not the originator. He suspected that it came from an old melodrama.]

what if a much of which of a wind 4
gives the truth to summer's lie;
bloodies with dizzying leaves the sun
and yanks immortal stars awry.
—E. E. CUMMINGS, *what if a much of a which of a wind,*
in *One Times One* (or *1 x 1*), 1944

[To his cat, who disliked rain:] I know what's wrong, my dear, but I really do 5
not know how to turn it off.
—ALBERT EINSTEIN, quoted in Banesch Hoffmann,
Albert Einstein: Creator and Rebel [1972]

NAVY *See* MILITARY, THE

NEBRASKA

In regard to this extensive section of the country, I do not hesitate in giving the 6
opinion that it is almost wholly unfit for cultivation, and, of course, uninhabitable by a people depending on agriculture for their subsistence.
—STEPHEN H. LONG, c. 1820
[Major Long, an explorer, is quoted in James C. Olson, *History of Nebraska,* 1966. Long was wrong. Nebraska is the Corn Husker State.]

Hurrah for Greer county! The land of the free, 7
The land of the bedbug, grasshopper, and flea;
I'll sing of its praises, I'll tell of its fame,
While starving to death on my government claim.
—ANONYMOUS, song, c. 1870
[Fleas were a serious problem in pioneer sod homes; they lived in the walls. Another verse, apparently from the same song, warns of even more critters: "How happy am I when I crawl into bed; / A rattlesnake hisses a tune at my head! / A gay little centipede, all without fear, / Crawls over my pillow and into my ear," quoted in *American Heritage,* August 1973.]

1   We were at sea—there is no other adequate expression—on the plains of Nebraska.   —ROBERT LOUIS STEVENSON, *Across the Plains*
with Other Memories and Essays, 1892

2   The green plain ran till it touched the skirts of heaven.   *—Ibid.*

3   What livelihood can repay a human creature for a life spent in this huge sameness? . . . A sky full of stars is the most varied spectacle that he can hope for.
—Ibid.

4   It is almost unheard of to find a town in Nebraska that has a past; it is sometimes rather difficult to find one that has a present, though all of them have, or
think they have, a future.
—WILLA CATHER, article on the fortieth anniversary
of the founding of Brownville, Nebr., 1894,
reprinted in *American Heritage* [Oct. 1970]
[In 1996, the population of Brownville was 148. It was about 5,000 in 1880.]

5   Here the Middle West merges with the West.
—FEDERAL WRITERS' PROJECT, *Nebraska:*
A Guide to the Cornhusker State, 1939

6   A mile wide, an inch deep, stand it on end and it will reach to heaven, so
muddy that the catfish have to come up to sneeze.
—ANONYMOUS, characterization of the South Platte River,
Life, August 30, 1943

Motto

7   Equality before the law.

NECESSITY

8   Necessity never made a good bargain.
—BENJAMIN FRANKLIN, *Poor Richard's Almanack*, April 1735

9   Great necessities call out great virtues.
—ABIGAIL ADAMS, letter to John Quincy Adams, Jan. 19, 1780
[For an example of great necessity from the era, see George Washington at
AMERICAN REVOLUTION, entry for Dec. 25, 1776.]

10   I know this—a man got to do what he got to do.
—JOHN STEINBECK, *The Grapes of Wrath*, 1939

NEGOTIATION   *See* DIPLOMACY; FOREIGN POLICY
(John F. Kennedy)

NEIGHBORS   *See also* MANNERS (Emily Post)

11   I am as desirous of being a good neighbor as I am of being a bad subject.
—HENRY DAVID THOREAU, *Civil Disobedience*, 1849

12   Good fences make good neighbors.
—ROBERT FROST, *Mending Wall*, 1914
[This proverbial saying is spoken in the poem by a farmer, a neighbor of Frost's,
who urges the reluctant poet to help in rebuilding a fence, some of which, at

least, was on the farmer's property. Such mutual fence maintenance was a duty mandated by a 1790 Vermont law. The idea behind the law was that fences, which control wandering livestock, are in the common good and therefore the responsibility of repairing them should be shared. Frost, in this poem, takes a different view: "My apple trees will never get across [the fence line] / And eat the cones under his pines, I tell him." This cuts no ice with the farmer. In 1989, the Vermont Supreme Court, citing changing land-use patterns, found the law unconstitutional. See also DIVISIONS & BARRIERS.]

I do not love my neighbor as myself, and apologize to no one. [1]
      —EDGAR WATSON HOWE, *Success Easier Than Failure*, 1917

This is the grave of Mike O'Day, [2]
Who died defending his right of way.
His right was clear, his will was strong,
But he's just as dead as if he'd been wrong.   —ANONYMOUS, 20th century

NEVADA
See also CITIES (Aurora, Carson City, Las Vegas, Reno)

The country looks something like a singed cat, owing to the scarcity of shrub- [3]
bery, and also resembles that animal in the respect that it has more merits than its personal appearance would seem to indicate.
      —MARK TWAIN, *Washoe.—'Information Wanted,'*
      c. May 1, 1864, in Tom Quirk, ed., *Tales, Speeches,*
      Essays, and Sketches/Mark Twain [1994]

Nevada—it's freedom's last stand in America. [4]
      —WILL ROGERS, in Alex Ayres, ed.,
      The Wit and Wisdom of Will Rogers [1993]

Anyone who is under the impression that the world is becoming too crowded [5]
should move to Nevada.   —J. B. PRIESTLEY, *Midnight on the Desert*, 1937

The desolation of Nevada is awesome.   —NEIL MORGAN, *Westward Tilt—* [6]
      The American West Today, 1963

Neon looks good in Nevada.   —JOHN McPHEE, *Basin and Range*, 1980 [7]

Motto

All for our country. [8]

NEW ENGLAND
See also CITIES (Boston)]

I have lived in a country seven years, and all that time I never heard one pro- [9]
fane oath, and all that time I never did see a man drunk in that land. Where was that country? It was New England.
      —GILES FIRMIN, sermon to the Lords and Commons, c. 1675
[On this subject, H. L. Mencken, in his quotations dictionary, cites J. G. Holland, who wrote that in the early colonial records of New England "rigidity of doctrine . . . and definitive laws against every form of social vice, go hand in hand with every form of vice. There was adultery in high places and adultery in low," *Everyday Topics*, 1876.]

1   The New Englanders are a people of God, settled in those which were once the Devil's territories. —COTTON MATHER,
Wonders of the Invisible World, 1693

2   The sway of the clergy in New England is indeed formidable. No mind beyond mediocrity dares there to develop itself.
—THOMAS JEFFERSON, letter to Horatio Gates Spafford, 1816

3   The great vice of this New England people is their adoration of Mammon.
—CHARLES FRANCIS ADAMS, *Diary,* Oct. 6, 1833
[Adams was himself a New Englander to the bone, the son of one president and the grandson of another. For another comment on New Englanders and Mammon, see John Updike, below.]

4   The Brahmin Caste of New England.
—OLIVER WENDELL HOLMES, SR., book title, 1860
[See also THE ELITE.]

5   I saw but one drunken man through all New England, and he was very respectable.
—ANTHONY TROLLOPE, *North America,* 1862
[Trollope continued: "He was, however, so uncommonly drunk that he might be allowed to count for two or three.]

6   You can always tell the Irish,
You can always tell the Dutch,
You can always tell a Yankee,
But you cannot tell him much.
—ANONYMOUS, folk saying, probably 19th century
["Dutch" here may refer to German immigrants, the *Deutsch* as they called themselves, but which native Americans misheard as the more familiar term.]

7   There is a sumptuous variety about the New England weather that compels the stranger's admiration—and regret. . . . In the spring, I have counted one hundred and thirty-six different kinds of weather inside of twenty-four hours.
—MARK TWAIN, speech to the New England Society,
New York City, Dec. 22, 1876
[This was the society's seventy-first dinner. See also Twain at NATURE: WEATHER.]

8   The one great poem of New England is her Sunday.
—HENRY WARD BEECHER, *Proverbs from Plymouth Pulpit,* 1887

9   Here where the wind is always north-northeast,
And children learn to walk on frozen toes.
—EDWIN ARLINGTON ROBINSON, *New England*

10 The most serious charge which can be brought against New England is not Puritanism but February. —JOSEPH WOOD KRUTCH,
The Twelve Seasons, 1949

11 [In New England:] The ghosts of Hawthorne and Melville still sit on those green hills. The worship of Mammon is also somewhat lessened there by the spirit of irony.
—JOHN UPDIKE, quoted in the London *Observer,* Mar. 25, 1979

NEW HAMPSHIRE

In the mountains of New Hampshire, God Almighty has hung out a sign to   1
show that there He makes men.
                    —DANIEL WEBSTER, *On the Old Man of the Mountain*,
                    attributed
[The reference is to the rock outcrop in the White Mountains that is the focus
of Nathaniel Hawthorne's story *The Great Stone Face*. The outcrop, which resembles a face in profile, is familiarly called "The Old Man of the Mountain."]

The god who made New Hampshire   2
Taunted the lofty land with little men.
                    —RALPH WALDO EMERSON,
                    Ode Inscribed to W. H. Channing, 1846
[This is Emerson's response to Webster's claim.]

She's one of the two best states in the Union.   3
Vermont's the other.
                    —ROBERT FROST, *New Hampshire*, 1923
[Frost came from Vermont. See also Maxfield Parrish at VERMONT.]

Politically, New Hampshire is as unproductive as an abandoned farm.   4
                    —RALPH D. PAINE, in Ernest Gruening, ed.,
                    These United States, 1924
[Perhaps unproductive, but hardly uninfluential—its presidential primary is
now a major early indicator of candidates' relative strength.]

If two New Hampshire men aren't a match for the devil, we might as well give   5
the country back to the Indians.   —STEPHEN VINCENT BENÉT, *The Devil
                    and Daniel Webster*, 1936

I like your nickname, "The Granite State." It shows the strength of character,   6
firmness of principle, and restraint that have long characterized New Hampshire.   —GERALD FORD, speech, Concord, N.H.,
                    April 17, 1975

Motto

Live free or die.   7

NEW JERSEY   *See also* CITIES (Hoboken, Newark,
                    Paterson, Weehawken)

The new proprietors [of New Jersey] inveigled many over by this tempting ac-   8
count of the country: that it was a place free from those three great scourges of
mankind—priests, lawyers, and physicians. Nor did they tell a word of a lie, for
the people were as yet too poor to maintain these learned gentlemen.
                    —WILLIAM BYRD, 1728,
                    cited in *American Heritage*, June 1976

[New Jersey is like] a beer barrel, tapped at both ends, with all the live beer run-   9
ning into Philadelphia and New York.
                    —BENJAMIN FRANKLIN, attributed by Abram Browning,
                    speech, Centennial Exposition in Philadelphia [1876]

1   On our left, the bold features of nature [the Palisades] rise as in the days of yore, unimpaired, unchangeable; grey cliffs, like aged battlements, tower perpendicularly from the water to their height of several hundred feet.
                              —FRANCIS HALL, *Travels in Canada*
                              and the United States in 1816 and 1817, 1818
    [Lt. Hall, an English visitor, traveled up the Hudson.]

2   Like China, New Jersey absorbs the invader.
                              —FEDERAL WRITERS' PROJECT, *New Jersey:*
                              A Guide to Its Present and Past, 1939

3   I'm empty and aching and I don't know why.
    Counting the cars on the New Jersey Turnpike.
    They've all come to look for America.   —PAUL SIMON, *America*, 1967

Motto

4   Liberty and prosperity.

NEW MEXICO   *See also* CITIES (Santa Fe)

5   In New Mexico he always awoke a young man. . . . His first consciousness was a sense of the light dry wind blowing in through the windows, with the fragrance of hot sun and sagebrush and sweet clover; a wind that made one's body feel light and one's heart cry, "Today, today," like a child's.
                              —WILLA CATHER, *Death Comes for the Archbishop*, 1927

6   The mesa plain had an appearance of great antiquity, and of incompleteness; . . . The country was still waiting to be made into a landscape.   —*Ibid.*

7   Space is the keynote of the land—vast, limitless stretches of plain, desert, and lofty mountains, with buttes and mesas and purple distances to rest the eye.
                              —FEDERAL WRITERS' PROJECT, *New Mexico:*
                              A Guide to the Colorful State, 1940

8   Stone, stone
    layered and beaten
    under the confessed brilliance
    of this desert noon.   —WILLIAM CARLOS WILLIAMS, *New Mexico*, 1949

9   New Mexico is old, stupendously old and dry and brown, and wind-worn by the ages.   —CHARLES KURALT, *Charles Kuralt's America*, 1995

Motto

10   It grows as it goes.

NEW THINGS   *See also* EXCELLENCE (Emerson's
                                            mousetrap); SCIENCE: TECHNOLOGY

11 The man with a new idea is a crank until the idea succeeds.
                              —MARK TWAIN, *Pudd'nhead Wilson's New Calendar*,
                              in *Following the Equator*, 1897
    [See also Oliver Wendell Holmes, Sr., at IDEAS & IDEALS for a similar quote.]

Even in slight things, the experience of the new is rarely without some stirring   1
of foreboding.   —ERIC HOFFER, *The Ordeal of Change*, 1964

NEW YEAR

Across East River in the night   2
Manhattan is ablaze with light.
No shadow dares to criticize
The popular festivities.
Hard liquor causes everywhere
A general *détente*, and Care
For this state function of Good Will
Is diplomatically ill;
The Old Year dies a noisy death.   —W. H. AUDEN, *New Year Letter*,
                                                      Jan. 1, 1940

NEW YORK   *See also* CITIES (Albany, Avon, Buffalo,
                                                 New York City, Rochester)

The lands were pleasant, with grass and flowers and goodly trees . . . and very   3
sweet smells came from them.
                        —ROBERT JUET, *Juet's Journal of Hudson's Voyage*
[Juet was an officer on the *Half Moon*. He is describing here New York Harbor
in late summer, 1609.]

A bleak, blackguard, beggarly climate, of which I can say no good, except that   4
it suits me and some others of the same or similar persuasion whom (by all
rights) it ought to kill.
                        —ROBERT LOUIS STEVENSON, letter to Miss Ferrier, April 1888
[Stevenson wrote this from Trudeau sanitarium at Saranac, to which he had
come in a vain attempt to cure his "persuasion," i.e., tuberculosis. Sufferers
rarely named their disease, much as a later generation avoided "cancer."]

A deathless glory is at play: 5
Niagara, Niagara . . .
                                        —VACHEL LINDSAY, *Niagara*, 1917
[More at CITIES (Buffalo). The great falls do not impress all equally. Oscar Wilde
observed: "I was disappointed with Niagara—most people must be disappointed with Niagara. Every American bride is taken there, and the sight of the
stupendous waterfall must be one of the earliest, if not the keenest disap-
pointments in American married life," *Impressions of America*, 1883.]

Fresh green breast of the New World.   6
                        —F. SCOTT FITZGERALD, *The Great Gatsby*, 1925
[Long Island as described in the closing passage of the novel.]

Motto

Excelsior.   7
Ever upward.

NEWSPAPERS   *See* MEDIA; PRESS, THE

NONVIOLENCE   *See* PACIFISM & NONVIOLENCE

NORTH CAROLINA

1   Surely there is no place in the world where the inhabitants live with less labor than in North Carolina.
                              —WILLIAM BYRD, *A Journey to the Land of Eden in 1733* [1866]
[Byrd's observation was not intended as a compliment. A cultivated Virginia squire (his plantation at Westover featured a billiard table, upon which, according to his diary, he once gave his wife a "flourish"), Byrd looked down on uncouth backwoodsmen, who worked only as hard as they had to—not a great strain by Byrd's lights, given the felicity of the climate and the ease of raising crops. He dismissed North Carolina as "Lubberland." See also Timothy Dwight at VERMONT.]

2   I'm talking to Buncombe.   —FELIX WALKER, debate,
                              U.S. House of Representatives, 1820
[This is the source of our word *bunk.* The story is that Rep. Walker, whose district included Buncombe County, N.C., interrupted debate on the Missouri Compromise with a long, tedious, and irrelevant speech. When told that it was no use to go on because other members were leaving the House, Walker replied, "Never mind; I'm talking to Buncombe." Afterward, whenever any congressman made a speech only for the sake of getting his name in the newspapers back home, he was said to be "talking to (or for) Buncombe." The term subsequently acquired the broader sense of nonsense or humbug and was converted first to *bunkum* and then, by 1900, to the modern *bunk.*]

3   First at Bethel, furthest at Gettysburg, and last at Appomattox.
                              —ANONYMOUS, characterization
                              of the state's military prowess
[The slogan was popularized by the 1st North Carolina Volunteers, who became known as the Bethel Regiment, after participating in the first clash between Federal and Confederate troops at Bethel Church, Virginia, on June 10, 1861.]

4   The Land of the Sky.   —CHRISTIAN REID, novel title, 1876

5   North Carolina is a valley of humility between two mountains of conceit.
                              —ANONYMOUS
[The Library of Congress, in *Respectfully Quoted*, selected this version rather than Mencken's, "valley of humiliation." The mountains of conceit are Virginia and South Carolina. A similar comment, which Mencken attributes to a journalist named Stewart from Charleston, South Carolina, is: "A strip of land lying between two states," c. 1861.]

6   I'm a Tar Heel born,
    I'm a Tar Heel bred,
    And when I die,
    I'll be a Tar Heel dead.   —ANONYMOUS, University of North Carolina
                              fight song
[*Tar Heel* was originally an insult, referring to a Civil War Battle in which a North Carolinian brigade failed to hold its position. Mississippians said that they had forgotten to tar their heels that morning. Also, the soil in some parts of North Carolina contains tar pitch, turpentine from the pine forests.]

In my honest and unbiased judgment, the good Lord will place the Garden of   1
Eden in North Carolina when he restores it to earth. He will do this because he
will have so few changes to make in order to achieve perfection.
                              —SAM J. ERVIN, JR., *Humor of a Country Lawyer,* 1983
[Senator Ervin of North Carolina won international acclaim as chairman of the
Senate committee that investigated the Watergate scandal; see WATERGATE. His
skillful performance belied his repeated assertions that he was just a country
lawyer. Actually, he graduated from Harvard Law School.]

Motto

Esse quam videri.   2
To be rather than to seem.

NIGHT   *See* NATURE: TIMES OF DAY

NORTH DAKOTA

North Dakota is a doomed state. In twenty years, it will revert to the Indian   3
and the buffalo. We must be moving on.
                    —ANONYMOUS, early settler, quoted in Frank P. Stockbridge,
                         The North Dakota Man Crop, World's Work magazine,
                         Nov. 1912

I would never have been president if it had not been for my experiences in   4
North Dakota.   —THEODORE ROOSEVELT, quoted in Elwyn B. Robinson,
                         History of North Dakota [1966]

A state of unbounded plains and hills and badlands.   5
                              —FEDERAL WRITERS' PROJECT, *North Dakota:*
                                   A Guide to the Northern Prairie State, 1938

Freely admitted is the rural character of the state, and there is seldom an at- 6
tempt to cover native crudities with a veneer of Eastern culture.   —*Ibid.*

Motto

Liberty and union, now and forever, one and inseparable.   7

[This is drawn from a toast by Daniel Webster; see THE UNION.]

O

Occult, the

1 Once upon a midnight dreary, while I pondered, weak and weary,
Over many a quaint and curious volume of forgotten lore—
While I nodded, nearly napping, suddenly there came a tapping,
As of someone gently rapping, rapping at my chamber door.
　　　　　　　　　　　　　—Edgar Allan Poe, *The Raven*, 1845
[What the cryptic Raven utters was used on Poe's gravestone; see Epitaphs &
Gravestones.]

2 Us ignorant people laugh at spiritualists, but when they die, they go mighty
peaceful and happy.　　　　—Will Rogers, *Daily Telegrams*, July 7, 1930

2a Belief in magic is older than writing.
　　　　　　　　　　　　　—Zora Neale Hurston, *Mules and Men*, 1935

3 I have gone out, a possessed witch,
haunting the black air, braver at night;
dreaming evil, I have done my hitch
over the plain houses, light by light.
　　　　　　　　　　　　　—Anne Sexton, *Her Kind*, in *To Bedlam
　　　　　　　　　　　　　and Partway Back*, 1960

4 May the Force be with you.　　　　—George Lucas, *Star Wars*, 1977

Oceans　　　　　　　　　　　　　*See* nature: seas & oceans

Ohio　　　　　　*See also* cities (Cincinnati, Cleveland, Columbus)

5 Ohio is the farthest west of the east and the farthest north of the south.
　　　　　　　　　　　—Louis Bromfield, attributed, in Peter Yapp,
　　　　　　　　　　　　　The Traveller's Dictionary of Quotations [1983]

6 [Ohio:] A giant carpet of agriculture studded by great cities.
　　　　　　　　　　　　　—John Gunther, *Inside U.S.A.*, 1947

Why, O why, O why-o   1
Why did I ever leave Ohio,
Why did I wander
To see what lies yonder
When life was so happy at home?   —BETTY COMDEN & ADOLPH GREEN,
                                                 Wonderful Town, 1953
[This terrific musical, composed by Leonard Bernstein, was based on the 1941
play *My Sister Eileen* by Joseph Fields and Jerome Chodorov, which was derived from Ruth McKenney's 1938 best-seller, *My Sister Eileen*. Eileen and her
husband, novelist Nathanael West, died in an automobile crash three days before the Broadway opening of *My Sister Eileen*. The Wests were on their way to
the funeral of F. Scott Fitzgerald.]

Motto

With God, all things are possible.   2

OKLAHOMA   *See also* CITIES (Tulsa)

You just throw anything out in Oklahoma, and all you have to do is come back   3
and harvest it.
                        —WILL ROGERS, *How to Be Funny*, May 29, 1926
[Rogers was a native of Oklahoma, "the Garden of Eden of the West."]

They swarmed on Oklahoma from every state in the Union.   4
                                     —EDNA FERBER, *Cimarron*, 1930
[They swarmed twice. In 1889, Indian territory was opened for settlement at
noon on April 22. Speculators and would-be settlers lined up at the boundary;
those who crossed early were called "sooners," which is how Oklahoma came
to be known as the Sooner state. Ferber wrote in this popular novel that the in-
flow was much more dramatic a few years later, when people came from all
corners of the nation hoping to get rich from Oklahoma oil.]

Okie use' ta mean you was from Oklahoma. Now it means you're a dirty son-   5
of-a-bitch. Okie means you're scum. Don't mean nothing itself, it's the way
they say it.
                        —JOHN STEINBECK, *The Grapes of Wrath*, 1939
[You don't hear "Okie" much anymore, but it was still a term of derision almost twenty years after the migrations out of Oklahoma and other midwestern prairie states in the 1930s. Drought and erosion turned twenty-five
thousand square miles to dust.]

Oklahoma,   6
Where the wind comes sweepin' down the plain,
And the wavin' wheat
Can sure smell sweet
When the wind comes right behind the rain.
                              —OSCAR HAMMERSTEIN II, *Oklahoma!*,
                                 title song of the musical *Oklahoma!*, 1943
[This great show, with music by Richard Rodgers, was dismissed at its New
Haven tryout by producer Mike Todd, who specialized in extravaganzas, and
who in middle age became Elizabeth Taylor's third husband. "No legs, no
jokes, no chance," he pronounced—as recalled in a *New York Times* editorial,
Feb. 7, 1993.]

Motto

1　　*Labor omnia vincit.*
　　Works conquers all things.

OLD AGE   *See also* AGES; MIDDLE AGE & MIDLIFE CRISIS

2　The older I grow, the more apt I am to doubt my own judgment, and to pay
　more respect to the judgment of others.
　　　　　　　　　—BENJAMIN FRANKLIN, speech, Constitutional Convention,
　　　　　　　Sept. 17, 1787
　[Franklin, with this gentle, self-deprecating remark, made on the last day of the
　convention, urged delegates to put aside whatever objections they might have
　and adopt the Constitution. More at THE CONSTITUTION.]

3　By my rambling digressions I perceive myself to be growing older.
　　　　　　　　　　　—BENJAMIN FRANKLIN, *Autobiography* [1798]
　[Franklin, the old man among our young founding fathers, wrote his autobiog-
　raphy off and on from 1771 to shortly before his death in 1790; the book covers
　the first part of his life.
　　Despite the disclaimer in this quotation, Franklin remained sharp to the end.
　William Pierce, a fellow delegate to the Constitutional Convention said of him
　in 1787: "He is 82 years old, and possesses an activity of mind equal to a youth
　of 25 years of age."]

4　Tranquility is the old man's milk. I go to enjoy it in a few days, and to exchange
　the roar and tumult of bulls and bears for the prattle of my grandchildren and
　senile rest.　　　　　　　　—THOMAS JEFFERSON, letter to Edward Rutledge,
　　　　　　　June 24, 1797
　[Jefferson was vice president at the time and evidently bored. His desire for se-
　nile rest did not last, and he served as president 1801–1809. In 1820, approach-
　ing his seventy-seventh birthday, he returned to this theme: "Tranquility is
　the *summum bonum* of old age," he wrote to Mark L. Hill, on April 5. Jeffer-
　son and John Adams both died on July 4, 1826; see INDEPENDENCE DAY.]

5　My one fear is that I may live too long. This would be a subject of dread to me.
　　　　　　　　　—THOMAS JEFFERSON, letter to Philip Mazzai, March 1801

6　Whenever a man's friends begin to compliment him about looking young, he
　may be sure that they think he is growing old.
　　　　　　　　　—WASHINGTON IRVING, *Bachelors*, in *Bracebridge Hall*, 1822

7　It is time to be old,
　To take in sail.　　　　　—RALPH WALDO EMERSON, *Terminus*, in *Poems*, 1847

8　A person is always startled when he hears himself seriously called an old man
　for the first time.　　　　　　　　—OLIVER WENDELL HOLMES, SR.,
　　　　　　　The Autocrat of the Breakfast-Table, 1858
　[Or as Leon Trotsky observed in his *Diary in Exile, 1935:* "Old age is the most
　unexpected of all the things that can happen to a man."]

9　For age is opportunity no less
　Than youth itself, though in another dress,
　And as the evening twilight fades away,
　The sky is filled with stars invisible by day.
　　　　　　　　　—HENRY WADSWORTH LONGFELLOW, *Morituri Salutamus*, 1875

To be seventy years young is sometimes far more cheerful and hopeful than to   1
be forty years old.

> —OLIVER WENDELL HOLMES, SR., letter to Julia Ward Howe
> on her 70th birthday, May 27, 1889

Old age is like an opium-dream. Nothing seems real except what is unreal.   2

> —OLIVER WENDELL HOLMES, SR.,
> *Over the Teacups*, 1891

I grow old . . . I grow old . . .   3
I shall wear the bottoms of my trousers rolled.

> —T. S. ELIOT,
> *The Love Song of J. Alfred Prufrock*, 1917

[He will roll his trousers as his stature shrinks with age.]

Here I am, an old man in a dry month,   4
Being read to by a boy, waiting for rain.   —T. S. ELIOT, *Gerontion*, 1920

The older I grow the more I distrust the familiar doctrine that age brings   5
wisdom.   —H. L. MENCKEN,

> *Prejudices, Third Series*, 1922

One aged man—one man—can't fill a house.   6

> —ROBERT FROST, *An Old Man's Winter Night*,
> in *Mountain Interval*, 1923

dance mehitabel dance   7
caper and shake a leg
what little blood is left
will fizz like wine in a keg.   —DON MARQUIS, *mehitabel dances with boreas*,

> in *archy and mehitabel*, 1927

Between the years of ninety-two and a hundred and two, however, we shall   8
be ribald, useless, drunken, outcast person we have always wished to be. . . .
We look forward to a disreputable, vigorous, unhonored, and disorderly old
age.

> —DON MARQUIS, *The Almost Perfect State*, 1927

[Some of the outrageous details of this state: "We shall not walk at all, but re-
cline in a wheel chair and bellow for alcoholic beverages . . . write ribald songs
against organized society" . . . shoot out the lights at night with a .45 caliber
revolver, and address public meetings "(to which we have been invited because
of our wisdom) in a vein of jocund malice."]

The riders in a race do not stop short when they reach the goal. There is a lit-   9
tle finishing canter before coming to a standstill. There is time to hear the kind
voice of friends and to say to one's self, "The work is done."

> —OLIVER WENDELL HOLMES, JR., radio broadcast honoring
> his ninetieth birthday, March 8, 1931

Oh, to be seventy again! [At age ninety-two, upon seeing a pretty, young   10
woman.]

> —OLIVER WENDELL HOLMES, JR., attributed, 1933

[The remark is also attributed to French Premier Georges Clemenceau, who
lived to be eighty-eight. Holmes, who was born in 1841, served on the Supreme
Court 1902–32, that is, into his nineties. He died in 1935. See also Mark Twain
on still appreciating young women at age seventy, at WOMEN.]

1   The last years of life are the best, if you are a philosopher.
                    —GEORGE SANTAYANA, quoted by F. Champion Ward,
                        former chancellor of the New School for Social Research,
                        Op-Ed page, *New York Times*, Sept. 24, 1993

2   There is no such thing as old age, there is only sorrow.
                    —EDITH WHARTON, *A Backward Glance*, 1934

3   No memory of having starred
    Atones for later disregard,
    Or keeps the end from being hard.   —ROBERT FROST,
                                                    Provide, Provide, 1936
    [For Frost's unsentimental solution to this problem, see CHARITY & PHILAN-
    THROPY, where the Frost quote is the next verse from this poem.]

4   As de old folks always say, Ah'm born but Ah ain't dead. No tellin' what Ah'm
    liable tuh do yet.   —ZORA NEALE HURSTON,
                                                Their Eyes Were Watching God, 1937

5   Oh, it's a long, long while
    From May to December,
    But the days grow short,
    When you reach September.
                    —MAXWELL ANDERSON, *September Song*,
                        music by Kurt Weill, *Knickerbocker Holiday*, 1938

6   Oh, the days dwindle down
    To a precious few . . .
    And these few precious days
    I'll spend with you.   —*Ibid.*

7   [Old age:] It's the only disease you don't look forward to being cured of.
                    —HERMAN J. MANKIEWICZ & ORSON WELLES,
                        Citizen Kane, screenplay, 1941

8   A man is not old until regrets take the place of dreams.
                    —JOHN BARRYMORE, quoted in Gene Fowler,
                        Good Night, Sweet Prince, 1943

9   It is a terrible thing for an old woman to outlive her dogs.
                    —TENNESSEE WILLIAMS, Prologue, *Camino Real*, 1953

10 To me, old age is always fifteen years older than I am.
                    —BERNARD BARUCH, quoted in the press
                        on his eighty-fifth birthday, August 20, 1955

11 I'll never make the mistake of being seventy again.
                    —CHARLES DILLON "CASEY" STENGEL, remark to the press,
                        on being fired as manager of the New York Yankees, 1960
    [Stengel, whose teams had won ten American League pennants and seven
    World Series in a dozen years, was dismissed five days after the Yankees lost
    the 1960 Series to the Pittsburgh Pirates. The quote is from Robert W.
    Creamer's *Stengel: His Life and Times*, 1984. See also Stengel below.]

12 When everything else physical and mental seems to diminish, the appreciation
    of beauty is on the increase.
                    —BERNARD BERENSON, *Sunset and Twilight*, 1963

Most people my age are dead at the present time.   1
>   —CHARLES DILLON "CASEY" STENGEL,
>   quoted in the Ken Burns television series *Baseball*,
>   part IV, 1994

Being seventy is not a sin.   —GOLDA MEIR, quoted by David Reed,   2
>   *Reader's Digest*, July 1971

How old would you be if you didn't know how old you was?   3
>   —LEROY "SATCHEL" PAIGE, attributed

What's wrong with me? I'm old. I'm getting old and coming apart.   4
>   —THURGOOD MARSHALL, response to a reporter's question,
>   press conference on his retirement
>   from the Supreme Court, 1992

Getting old ain't for sissies.   —BETTE DAVIS, quoted by Paul Newman, 5
>   on *60 Minutes* television show
>   [Sept. 3, 1995]

OPPORTUNITY

Only that day dawns to which we are awake.   6
>   —HENRY DAVID THOREAU, "Conclusion,"
>   *Walden*, 1854

America has been another name for opportunity.   7
>   —FREDERICK J. TURNER,
>   *The Significance of the Frontier in American History*, 1893

There is no security on this earth; there is only opportunity.   8
>   —DOUGLAS MACARTHUR, quoted in, Courtney Whitney,
>   *MacArthur: His Rendezvous with History* [1955]

It ain't enough to get the breaks. You gotta know how to use 'em.   9
>   —HUEY P. LONG, saying

Know Your Opportunity—Seize It.   —TENNESSEE WILLIAMS, family motto 10

It is better to lose opportunity than capital.   11
>   —SUSAN M. BYRNE, *Wall Street Week in Review*
>   television show, Feb. 15, 1985

OPPRESSION   *See* TYRANNY

OPTIMISM & PESSIMISM   *See also* DESPAIR; HOPE

'Tis always morning somewhere.   12
>   —HENRY WADSWORTH LONGFELLOW, *The Birds of Killingsworth*,
>   in *Tales of a Wayside Inn*, 1863–74

The nearer the dawn, the darker the night.   13
>   —HENRY WADSWORTH LONGFELLOW,
>   *The Baron of St. Castine*, in *Ibid.*

1   The man who is a pessimist before forty-eight knows too much; the man who
    is an optimist after he is forty-eight knows too little.
                                        —MARK TWAIN, *Notebook*, 1883
    [Twain composed the aphorism upon the occasion of his own forty-eighth
    birthday.]

2   Cheer up, the worst is yet to come.
                                —PHILANDER CHASE JOHNSON, *Shooting Stars*,
                                    in *Everybody's Magazine*, May 1920

3   The optimist proclaims that we live in the best of all possible worlds; and the
    pessimist fears this is true.
                            —JAMES BRANCH CABELL, *The Silver Stallion*, 1926
    [The same thought was expressed later and more forcefully by J. Robert Op-
    penheimer: "The optimist thinks this is the best of all possible worlds, and the
    pessimist knows it," *The Bulletin of Atomic Scientists*, Feb. 1951.]

4   an optimist is a guy
    that has never had
    much experience.   —DON MARQUIS, *archy and mehitabel*, 1927

5   A pessimist is a man who has been compelled to live with an optimist.
                                    —ELBERT HUBBARD, *The Note Book*, 1927
    [Or, from the same era, Don Marquis: "A pessimist is a person who has had to
    listen to too many optimists," quoted in Frederick B. Wilcox, *A Little Book of
    Aphorisms*.]

6   Optimism is the content of small men in high places.
                    —F. SCOTT FITZGERALD, "Note-Books," in *The Crack-Up* [1945]

7   O, merry is the optimist,
    With the troops of courage leaguing.
    But a dour trend
    In any friend
    Is somehow less fatiguing.   —PHYLLIS MCGINLEY, *A Pocketful of Rye*, 1940

8   An optimist . . . is a person who thinks the future is uncertain.
                                —RUSSELL CROUSE & HOWARD LINDSAY,
                                        State of the Union, 1948

9   Every day, in every way, things are getting worse and worse.
                        —WILLIAM F. BUCKLEY, in *The National Review*, July 2, 1963

10 Perpetual optimism is a force multiplier.
                                —COLIN POWELL, *My American Journey*, 1995
    [Gen. Powell, who was chairman of the Joint Chiefs of Staff in the Gulf War,
    included a set of maxims in his autobiography. This was number thirteen. For
    another, see ACTION & DOING.]

OREGON   *See also* CITIES (Portland)

11 Or lose thyself in the continuous woods
    Where rolls the Oregon, and hears no sound
    Saving his own dashings.   —WILLIAM CULLEN BRYANT, *Thanatopsis*, 1817

I must walk toward Oregon and not toward Europe.   1
—HENRY DAVID THOREAU, *Walking*, 1862
[More at THE WEST.]

Oregon is seldom heard of. Its people believe in the Bible, and hold that all rad-   2
icals should be lynched. It has no poets and no statesmen.
—H. L. MENCKEN, in *The American Mercury*, 1925.

Motto

She flies with her own wings.   3

[Formerly, "The Union."]

P

PACIFIC, THE   *See* NATIONS; WORLD WAR

PACIFISM & NONVIOLENCE   *See also* LAW (Martin Luther King, Jr.,
                                                 2nd quote); PEACE; VIOLENCE

1 Disarm, disarm. The sword of murder is not the balance of justice. Blood does
not wipe out dishonor, nor violence indicate possession.
          —JULIA WARD HOWE, peace proclamation, London, 1870
[Howe, author of *The Battle Hymn of the Republic*—see under GOD—was re-
pelled by the bloodshed of the Civil War and the Franco-Prussian War. In 1872,
she established June 2 as Mothers' Peace Day, dedicated to world peace. She organized the annual holiday in Boston, and in 1915, Pres. Woodrow Wilson authorized a national Mother's Day holiday.]

2 So long as antimilitarists propose no substitute for war's disciplinary function,
no *moral equivalent of war*, . . . so long they fail to realize the full inwardness
of the situation.   —WILLIAM JAMES, *The Moral Equivalent of War*,
          in *Memories and Studies*, 1911
[James proposed a national martial training program to prepare young men for
responsible citizenship. See also James at THE MILITARY.]

3 There is such a thing as a man being too proud to fight.
          —WOODROW WILSON, speech to foreign-born citizens,
          Philadelphia, May 10, 1915
[See also Wilson at PEACE. Note, Oswald Garrison Villard claimed in *Fighting
Years*, 1939, that he originated this saying.]

4 Nonviolence is a powerful and just weapon. . . . It is a sword that heals.
          —MARTIN LUTHER KING, JR., *Why We Can't Wait*, 1963

5 We must rise to the majestic heights of meeting physical force with soul force.
          —MARTIN LUTHER KING, JR., speech at the Lincoln Memorial
          in Washington, D.C., to 200,000 civil rights marchers,
          August 28, 1963
[More at AMERICAN HISTORY: MEMORABLE MOMENTS.]

PAIN *See* SUFFERING & PAIN

PAINTING *See* ART: VISUAL

PARENTS *See also* CHILDREN; FAMILY

Men are what their mothers made them.   1
—RALPH WALDO EMERSON, *Fate*, in *The Conduct of Life*, 1860

What is home without a mother?   2
—THOMAS ALVA EDISON, diary, July 12, 1885
[Edison was musing on the home life of chickens in the technological future.
William Holzer, the brother of his deceased wife, was developing an electric in-
cubator. "Just think," Edison wrote, "electricity employed to cheat a poor hen
out of the pleasures of maternity. Machine-born chickens. What is home without a mother?"]

There is no slave out of heaven like a loving woman; and, of all loving women,   3
there is no such slave as a mother.
—HENRY WARD BEECHER, *Proverbs from Plymouth Pulpit*, 1887

What the mother sings to the cradle goes all the way down to the coffin.   4
—*Ibid.*
[For the importance of "the hand that rocks the cradle," see W. R. Wallace at
WOMEN.]

A mother's advice is safest for a boy to follow.   5
—HENRY THOMAS BURN, speech,
Tennessee House of Representatives, August 1920
[At the urging of his mother, Burn cast a tie-breaking vote in favor of the 19th
Amendment, granting suffrage to American women; see AMERICAN HISTORY:
MEMORABLE MOMENTS.]

wot in hell   6
have I done to deserve
all these kittens.   —DON MARQUIS, *archy and mehitabel*, 1927

Mother Knows Best.   —EDNA FERBER, story title, 1927   7

Mothers are the only race of people that speak the same tongue. A mother in   8
Manchuria could converse with a mother in Nebraska and never miss a word.
—WILL ROGERS, radio broadcast, May 11, 1930

I doubt if a charging elephant, or a rhino, is as determined or as hard to check   9
as a socially ambitious mother.   —WILL ROGERS, *Daily Telegrams* column,
May 10, 1932

my father moved through dooms of love.   10
—E. E. CUMMINGS, poem title, 1940

Trust yourself. You know more than you think you do.   11
—BENJAMIN SPOCK, *Baby and Child Care*, 1946
[Dr. Spock's advice to new parents, the opening line of his classic text.]

1   I have found the best way to give advice to your children is to find out what
they want and then advise them to do it.
—HARRY S. TRUMAN, television interview, May 27, 1955

2   The thing that impresses me most about America is the way parents obey their
children.   —DUKE OF WINDSOR (Edward VIII),
in *Look* magazine, March 5, 1957

3   A boy's best friend is his mother.   —JOSEPH STEFANO,
screenplay of *Psycho*, 1960
[The speaker is Norman Bates, played by Tony Perkins. The movie was based
on Robert Bloch's novel of the same name.]

4   A Jewish man with parents alive is a fifteen-year-old boy, and will remain a
fifteen-year-old boy till they die.   —PHILIP ROTH, *Portnoy's Complaint*,
1969

5   Most American children suffer too much mother and too little father.
—GLORIA STEINEM, in *The New York Times*, August 26, 1971

6   Loving someone as a parent can produce a cloud that conceals from vision
what correct behavior is.   —JOHN IRVING, *The Cider-House Rules*, 1985

7   I may be dead, but I'm still your mother.
—NICKY SILVER, *Raised in Captivity*, 1995

PARTING

8   With a heart full of love and gratitude, I now take my leave of you.
—GEORGE WASHINGTON, farewell to his officers,
Fraunces Tavern, New York City, Dec. 4, 1783
[More at AMERICAN HISTORY: MEMORABLE MOMENTS.]

9   No one, not in my situation, can appreciate my feeling of sadness at this parting. To this place, and the kindness of these people, I owe everything. Here I
have lived a quarter of a century, and have passed from a young to an old man.
Here my children have been born, and one is buried. I now leave not knowing
when or whether ever I may return, with a task before me greater than that
which rested upon Washington.
—ABRAHAM LINCOLN, farewell remarks on leaving Springfield,
Ill., for Washington, D.C., Feb. 11, 1861

10 Parting is all we know of heaven,
And all we need of hell.   —EMILY DICKINSON, poem no. 1732,
in *Poems*, V [1891]

11 If that plane leaves the ground and you're not with him, you'll regret it. Maybe
not today, maybe not tomorrow, but soon and for the rest of your life.
—JULIUS EPSTEIN, PHILIP EPSTEIN, & HOWARD KOCH,
Casablanca, screenplay, 1942
[See also LOVE, EXPRESSIONS OF.]

12 There is a time for departure, even when there is no certain place to go.
—TENNESSEE WILLIAMS, *Camino Real*, 1953

PASSION

See also ENTHUSIASM & ZEAL; EXCESS; LOVE

Passion is a sort of fever in the mind, which ever leaves us weaker than it found us. 1
—WILLIAM PENN, *Some Fruits of Solitude*, 1693

A man in a passion rides a wild horse. 2
—BENJAMIN FRANKLIN, *Poor Richard's Almanack*, 1749

The end of passion is the beginning of repentance. —*Ibid.* 3

Men are often false to their country and their honor, false to duty and even to 4
their interest, but multitudes of men are never long false or deaf to their passions. —FISHER AMES, speech, Boston, Feb. 8, 1800

Passion, though a bad regulator, is a powerful spring. 5
—RALPH WALDO EMERSON, *Considerations by the Way*, in *The Conduct of Life*, 1860

Through our great good fortune, in our youth our hearts were touched with 6
fire. —OLIVER WENDELL HOLMES, JR., Memorial Day speech, Keene, N.H., 1884

The way to avoid evil is not by maiming our passions, but by compelling them 7
to yield their vigor to our moral nature.
—HENRY WARD BEECHER, *Proverbs from Plymouth Pulpit*, 1887

Life is action and passion. 8
—OLIVER WENDELL HOLMES, JR., speech,
to Harvard Law School alumni, New York City, Feb. 1916
[More at LIFE.]

Violent physical passions do not in themselves differentiate men from each 9
other, but rather tend to reduce them to the same state.
—T. S. ELIOT, *After Strange Gods*, 1934

PAST, THE

See also HISTORY; MEMORY; PRESENT, THE

We are not free to use today, or to promise tomorrow, because we are already 10
mortgaged to yesterday. —RALPH WALDO EMERSON, *Journal*, 1858

The dogmas of the quiet past are inadequate to the stormy present. 11
—ABRAHAM LINCOLN, annual message to Congress,
Dec. 1, 1862

We have to do with the past only as we can make it useful to the present and 12
the future. —FREDERICK DOUGLASS, *The Life and Writings
of Frederick Douglass*, Philip S. Foner, ed., Vol. II [1950]

There is no time like the old time, when you and I were young. 13
—OLIVER WENDELL HOLMES, SR.,
No Times Like the Old Time, 1865

Those who cannot remember the past are condemned to repeat it. 14
—GEORGE SANTAYANA, *The Life of Reason*, 1905–1906

1   I tell you the past is a bucket of ashes.
                              —CARL SANDBURG, *The Prairie*, 1918
[H. L. Mencken, in his dictionary of quotations, includes this Sandburg statement but as an anonymous saying.]

2   The precious, incommunicable past.
                              —WILLA CATHER, *My Ántonia*, 1918
[From the last line of the book: "Whatever we had missed, we possessed together the precious, incommunicable past."]

3   Yesterday,
    A night-gone thing
    A sun-down name.   —LANGSTON HUGHES, *Youth*, in *From My People*

4   The past is the present, isn't it? It's the future, too.
                              —EUGENE O'NEILL, *Long Day's Journey into Night*, 1956

5   Only the past when you were happy is real.   —*Ibid.*

6   Man is a history-making creature who can neither repeat his past nor leave it
    behind.   —W. H. AUDEN, *D. H. Lawrence*, in *The Dyer's Hand*, 1962

7   Don't look back. Something may be gaining on you.
                         —LEROY "SATCHEL" PAIGE, from his autobiography,
                              How to Stay Young, 1953
[Not original with Paige, but identified with him. More at WISDOM, WORDS OF.]

8   Which of us has overcome his past?
                         —JAMES BALDWIN, *Alas, Poor Richard*, 1961
[But the past can point the way to a better future, Baldwin advised: "Know
whence you came. If you know whence you came, there is really no limit to
where you can go," *The Fire Next Time*, 1962.]

PATIENCE   *See also* DETERMINATION, EFFORT,
                                    PERSISTENCE, & PERSEVERANCE

9   Learn to labor and to wait.
                         —HENRY WADSWORTH LONGFELLOW, *A Psalm of Life*, 1839
[More at ACTION & DOING.]

10 Patience all the passion of great hearts.
                         —JAMES RUSSELL LOWELL, *Columbus*, 1844
[More at ENDURANCE.]

11 Sorrow and silence are strong, and patient endurance is godlike.
                         —HENRY WADSWORTH LONGFELLOW, *Evangeline*, 1847

PATRIOTISM & THE FLAG   *See also* AMERICA & AMERICANS;
                              AMERICAN HISTORY: MEMORABLE MOMENTS;
                                    SERVING ONE'S COUNTRY

12 I am not a Virginian, but an American.
                         —PATRICK HENRY, speech in the First Continental Congress,
                              Philadelphia, Oct. 14, 1774

The summer soldier and the sunshine patriot. 1
　　　　　—THOMAS PAINE, *The American Crisis*, Dec., 1776
[More at AMERICAN REVOLUTION.]

I would go to hell for my country. 2
　　　　　—THOMAS JEFFERSON, upon being appointed commissioner
　　　　　to France, 1785

Guard against the postures of pretended patriotism. 3
　　　　　—GEORGE WASHINGTON, Farewell Address,
　　　　　Sept. 17, 1796

Oh, say, can you see by the dawn's early light, 4
What so proudly we hailed at the twilight's last gleaming?
Whose broad stripes and bright stars, through the perilous fight,
O'er the ramparts we watched were so gallantly streaming?
And the rockets' red glare, the bombs bursting in air,
Gave proof through the night that our flag was still there.
Oh, say, does that star-spangled banner yet wave
O'er land of the free and the home of the brave.
　　　　　—FRANCIS SCOTT KEY, *The Star-Spangled Banner*,
　　　　　Sept. 14, 1814
[Key watched the nighttime attack on Fort McHenry, one of the harbor de-
fenses of Baltimore, and wrote *The Star-Spangled Banner* the next day. He had
been detained by the British Commander Admiral Cockburn after successfully
negotiating the release of a Washington physician taken along as a hostage by
the British when they evacuated that city. The poem quickly became famous
and was set to the music of *Anacreon in Heaven*, an English song that had been
adapted to American sentiments under the title *Adams and Liberty*. The *Star-
Spangled Banner* became the official U.S. anthem in 1931. Lines from its
fourth verse gave us our national motto; see under GOD.]

Our country! In her intercourse with foreign nations, may she always be in the 5
right; but our country, right or wrong.
　　　　　—STEPHEN DECATUR, toast at dinner in his honor,
　　　　　Norfolk, Va., April 1816
[Commodore Decatur was feted nationwide for his 1815 campaign against the
pirates of the Barbary Coast of North Africa; see *The Marine Hymn* under THE
MILITARY. This version of his patriotic toast is from the 1848 biography by
Alexander Slidell Mackenzie. According to *Bartlett's*, an account in the *Niles'
Weekly Register* of Baltimore, April 20, 1816, quoted Decatur as saying, "Our
Country—In her intercourse with foreign nations, may she always be in the
right, and always successful, right or wrong."
　On August 1, 1816, John Quincy Adams wrote to his father John Adams,
"My toast would be, may our country be always successful, but whether suc-
cessful or otherwise, always right." Near the end of the century, Carl Schurz
offered, "Our country, right or wrong. When right, to be kept right. When
wrong, to be put right," in a speech at the Anti-Imperialistic Conference, in
Chicago, Ill., October 17, 1899; see also Adams below. The English writer G. K.
Chesterton, in an essay on patriotism, likened Decatur's toast to "My mother,
drunk or sober."]

When a whole nation is roaring Patriotism at the top of its voice, I am fain to 6
explore the cleanliness of its hands and the purity of its heart.
　　　　　—RALPH WALDO EMERSON, *Journal*, 1824

1 Let our object be, Our Country, our whole Country, and nothing but our
Country.   —DANIEL WEBSTER, speech, setting of the cornerstone,
Bunker Hill monument, June 17, 1825

2 Ay, tear her tattered ensign down!
Long has it waved on high.
And many an eye has danced to see
That banner in the sky.   —OLIVER WENDELL HOLMES, SR.,
                                       Old Ironsides, 1830
[The poem was written to protest the proposed scrapping of the frigate U.S.S.
Constitution. See THE MILITARY for more on this famous ship.]

3 I name thee Old Glory!
                                       —WILLIAM DRIVER, 1831
[Capt. Driver, the originator of "Old Glory" as a name for the U.S. flag, first
used the phrase in saluting a new flag flown on his brig, the *Charles Dogget*,
which was setting sail from Salem, Mass., to the South Pacific. Three decades
later, in 1862, Driver's "Old Glory" was flown from the dome of the state capitol in Nashville, Tenn., after Union forces had recaptured the city. Driver, a
bold supporter of the Union, had hidden the flag in the coverlet of his bed to
save it from Confederate partisans.]

4 My country, 'tis of thee,
Sweet land of liberty,
Of thee I sing;
Land where my fathers died,
Land of the pilgrims' pride,
From every mountain side
Let freedom ring.   —SAMUEL FRANCIS SMITH, *America*,
                                 Fourth of July program,
                                 Boston Sabbath School Union, 1831

5 Nothing is more embarrassing in the ordinary intercourse of life than this irritable patriotism of Americans.   —ALEXIS DE TOCQUEVILLE,
                                         Democracy in America, 1835

6 Say not thou, "My country right or wrong,"
Nor shed thy blood for an unhallowed cause.
                            —JOHN QUINCY ADAMS,
                              Congress, Slavery, and an Unjust War, c. 1847

7 Rally 'round the flag, boys.
                    —GEORGE FREDERICK ROOT, *The Battle Cry of Freedom*, 1863
[More at CIVIL WAR.]

8 "Shoot, if you must, this old gray head,
But spare your country's flag," she said.
                      —JOHN GREENLEAF WHITTIER, *Barbara Frietchie*,
                        in *The Atlantic*, Oct. 1863
[The poem refers to an alleged incident in the Civil War, when troops under
Stonewall Jackson had occupied Frederick, Maryland, in September 1862. Barbara Frietchie, then over ninety-five years old, is said to have waved the American flag in front of the Confederate troops. Gen. Jackson cut short the
confrontation. "'Who touches a hair of yon gray head/ Dies like a dog! March
on!' he said."]

Gold is good in its place, but living, brave, patriotic men are better than gold.   1
       —ABRAHAM LINCOLN, remarks,
       at the White House, Nov. 10, 1864

There is the national flag. He must be cold, indeed, who can look upon its folds   2
rippling in the breeze without pride of country.
       —CHARLES SUMNER, *Are We a Nation?*, Nov. 19, 1867
[Sen. Sumner was an ardent abolitionist and a harsh enemy of the South during
Reconstruction. See also SLAVERY.]

[The American flag:] Beautiful as a flower to those who love it, terrible as a me-   3
teor to those who hate it, it is the symbol of the power and glory, and the
honor, of . . . Americans.
       —GEORGE FRISBIE HOAR, 1878
[Sen. Hoar, a Massachusetts Republican, opposed the expansionist program of
Pres. William McKinley, his party's leader. He also vigorously opposed government corruption.]

I think patriotism is like charity—it begins at home.   4
       —HENRY JAMES, *The Portrait of a Lady*, 1881

The virtue of patriotism is subordinate in most souls to individual and family   5
aggrandizement.   —ELIZABETH CADY STANTON & SUSAN B. ANTHONY,
       History of Woman Suffrage,
       written with Mathilda Joslyn Gage, 1881

I pledge allegiance to my flag and the republic for which it stands: one nation,   6
indivisible, with liberty and justice for all.
       —FRANCIS BELLAMY, in *Youth's Companion*, Sept. 8, 1892
[Allegiance to the flag was first pledged at the dedication of the World's Fair
Grounds in Chicago, on October 21, 1892; this was also the first celebration of
Columbus Day; Bellamy was chairman of the executive committee listed in
the program for the celebration. *Respectfully Quoted,* published by the Library
of Congress in 1989, gives dates for the various changes leading to our present
version, including most significantly, and controversially, the phrase "under
God," added by law in 1945. The pledge today reads: "I pledge allegiance to the
flag of the United States of America, and to the republic for which it stands,
one nation under God, indivisible, with liberty and justice for all."]

Don't haul down the flag.   7

       —ANONYMOUS, slogan c. 1898
[While some Americans deplored the era's imperialism—see SPANISH-AMERICAN
WAR—others welcomed the sight of Old Glory flying on foreign shores.]

In the beginning of a change, the patriot is a scarce man, and brave, and hated   8
and scorned. When his cause succeeds, the timid join him, for then it costs
nothing to be a patriot.   —MARK TWAIN, *Notebook* [1935]

I'm a Yankee Doodle Dandy.   9
A Yankee Doodle do or die;
A real live nephew of my Uncle Sam's,
Born on the Fourth of July.   —GEORGE M. COHAN, *Yankee Doodle Dandy*,
       from *Little Johnny Jones*, 1904
[For the original *Yankee Doodle,* dating to 1755, see Anonymous at this date
under AMERICA & AMERICANS.]

1   *Patriot, n.* One to whom the interests of a part seem superior to those of the
whole. The dupe of statesmen and the tool of conquerers.
                                    —AMBROSE BIERCE, *The Devil's Dictionary*, 1906

2   Oh, it's home again and home again, America for me!
I want a ship that's westward bound to plough the rolling sea
To the blessed land of Room Enough beyond the ocean bars,
Where the air is full of sunlight and the flag is full of stars.
                                    —HENRY VAN DYKE, *America for Me*, June 1909

3   The flag is the embodiment, not of sentiment, but of history.
                                    —WOODROW WILSON, speech, June 14, 1915
[This was a Flag Day speech, the anniversary of the official adoption of the flag
on June 14, 1777.]

4   The hyphenated American always hoists the American flag undermost.
                                    —THEODORE ROOSEVELT,
                                    Fear God and Take Your Own Part, 1916
[A rather nasty slur on immigrants. Similarly, Pres. Woodrow Wilson com-
plained in a speech on May 16, 1914, "Some Americans need hyphens in their
names, because only part of them has come over." He stated that he was not
putting all immigrants into this category. But he maintained that, with World
War I in progress, there was too much partisanship based on national origins.
See also Roosevelt's 1918 pronouncement against fifty-fifty Americans under
AMERICA & AMERICANS, and against hyphenated Americanism at FOREIGNERS.]

5   Patriotism is not a short and frenzied outburst of emotion, but the tranquil and
steady dedication of a lifetime.
                                    —ADLAI STEVENSON, speech, New York City, August 27, 1952

6   You're not supposed to be so blind with patriotism that you can't face reality.
Wrong is wrong, no matter who does it or who says it.
                                    —MALCOLM X, *Malcolm X Speaks*, 1965

7   U.S.A.—Love It or Leave It.   —ANONYMOUS, bumper sticker, c. 1970

PATTERNS

8   The life of man is a self-evolving circle.
                                    —RALPH WALDO EMERSON, *Circles*, in *Essays: First Series*, 1841

9   Christ! What are patterns for?
                                    —AMY LOWELL, *Patterns*, in *Men, Women, and Ghosts*, 1916
[More at WAR.]

PEACE   *See also* PACIFISM & NONVIOLENCE;
                                                      RESISTANCE

10   There never was a good war or a bad peace.
                                    —BENJAMIN FRANKLIN, letter to Josiah Quincy,
                                    Sept. 11. 1783
[Franklin was one of the negotiators who in Paris, on September 3, 1783, signed
the peace treaty with Great Britain ending the Revolutionary War.]

11   Peace hath higher tests of manhood
Than battle ever knew.   —JOHN GREENLEAF WHITTIER, *The Hero*, 1853

We must not be enemies. Though passion may have strained, it must not break   1
our bonds of affection. The mystic chords of memory, stretching from every
battlefield and patriot grave, to every heart and hearthstone, all over this broad
land, will yet swell the chorus of the Union, when again touched, as surely
they will be, by the better angels of our nature.
    —ABRAHAM LINCOLN, First Inaugural Address, March 4, 1861

A just and lasting peace.   2
    —ABRAHAM LINCOLN, Second Inaugural Address, March 4, 1865
[More at CIVIL WAR.]

Let us have peace.   —ULYSSES S. GRANT, presidential nomination   3
           acceptance speech, May 29, 1868

Better to live in peace than begin a war and lie dead.   4
    —JOSEPH THE YOUNGER,
      cited in Time-Life Books, *The Indians* [1973]
[The Nez Percé leader's Indian name was Hinmaton-Yalaktit, or Thunder
Rolling the Mountains. He surrendered in Montana after the battle of Bear Paw
Mountains in 1877. See also RESIGNATION.]

There is a price which is too great to pay for peace, and that price can be put in   5
one word. One cannot pay the price of self-respect.
    —WOODROW WILSON, speech, Des Moines, Iowa, Feb. 1, 1916
[See also Wilson at RIGHT; and for a different Wilson view, see him at PACIFISM
& NONVIOLENCE. For his call for peace near the end of World War I, see AMERI-
CAN HISTORY: MEMORABLE MOMENTS.]

Open covenants of peace, openly arrived at.   6
    —WOODROW WILSON, "Fourteen Points" address to Congress,
      Jan. 8, 1918
[This speech, which prefigured the proposal to create a League of Nations, featured a program of peace as its first point: "The program of the world's peace,
therefore, is our program; and that program, the only possible program, as we
see it, is this: Open covenants of peace, openly arrived at, after which there
shall be no private understandings of any kind but diplomacy shall proceed always frankly and in the public view." For more on the speech, see FOREIGN POL-
ICY and AMERICAN HISTORY: MEMORABLE MOMENTS.]

You and me, we've made a separate peace.   7
    —ERNEST HEMINGWAY, *In Our Time*, 1924

Peace, like charity, begins at home.   8
    —FRANKLIN D. ROOSEVELT, speech, August 14, 1936

Let us not deceive ourselves: we must elect world peace or world destruction.   9
    —BERNARD BARUCH, speech,
      United Nations Atomic Energy Commission,
      June 14, 1946
[See also Baruch at SCIENCE: TECHNOLOGY.]

God and the politicians willing, the United States can declare peace upon the   10
world and win it.
    —ELY CULBERTSON, *Must We Fight Russia?*, 1946
[Culbertson, a bridge expert, was the inventor of the first successful bidding
system. Born in Rumania, he was captain of the U.S. team in 1933, 1934, and

1937, and founded and edited *Bridge World*. From 1940, he devoted much time and effort to promoting world peace.]

1   It isn't enough to talk about peace. One must believe in it. And it isn't enough to believe in it. One must work at it.
—ELEANOR ROOSEVELT, *Voice of America* radio broadcast, Nov. 11, 1951

2   Peace cannot be kept by force. It can only be achieved by understanding.
—ALBERT EINSTEIN, *Notes on Pacifism*

3   Arms alone are not enough to keep the peace. It must be kept by men.
—JOHN F. KENNEDY, State of the Union message, 1963

4   Peace is a process—a way of solving problems.
—JOHN F. KENNEDY, speech, American University, 1963

PENNSYLVANIA   *See also* CITIES (Philadelphia; Pittsburgh)

5   Pennsylvania is the Keystone of the Democratic arch.
—PENNSYLVANIA DEMOCRATIC COMMITTEE, address, 1803, in H. M. Jenkins, *Pennsylvania* [1903]
[This is the earliest example in *The Oxford English Dictionary* of "keystone" in the sense of "Keystone State," Pennsylvania's most common nickname today.]

6   The cradle of toleration and freedom of religion.
—THOMAS JEFFERSON, letter to Thomas Cooper, Nov. 2, 1822

7   The Pennsylvania mind, as minds go, was not complex; it reasoned little and never talked; but in practical matters it was the steadiest of all American types; perhaps the most efficient; certainly the safest.
—HENRY ADAMS, *The Education of Henry Adams*, 1907

8   Still the pine-woods scent the noon; still the catbird sings his tune;
Still the autumn sets the maple-forest blazing;
Still the grape-vine through the dusk flings her soul-compelling musk;
Still the fire-flies in the corn make night amazing!
. . .
The things that truly last when men and times have passed,
They are all in Pennsylvania this morning!
—RUDYARD KIPLING, *Philadelphia*, in *Rewards and Fairies*, 1910

Motto

9   Virtue, liberty, and independence.

PEOPLE, THE   *See also* DEMOCRACY; HUMANS & HUMAN NATURE; PUBLIC OPINION & THE PUBLIC

10   The people are the only sure reliance for the preservation of our liberty.
—THOMAS JEFFERSON, letter to James Madison, 1787

The will of the people is the only legitimate foundation of government, and to 1
protect its free expression should be our first object.
—THOMAS JEFFERSON, letter to Benjamin Waring, March 1801

There is but little virtue in the action of masses of men. 2
—HENRY DAVID THOREAU, *Civil Disobedience*, 1849

The measure of the progress of civilization is the progress of the people. 3
—GEORGE BANCROFT, speech, New York Historical Society, 1854

Why should there not be a patient confidence in the ultimate justice of the peo- 4
ple? Is there any better or equal hope in the world?
—ABRAHAM LINCOLN, First Inaugural Address, 1861

You may fool all the people some of the time; you can even fool some of the 5
people all of the time; but you can't fool all of the people all the time.
—ABRAHAM LINCOLN, attributed
[Possibly apocryphal. *Barlett's* cites Alexander K. McClure, who in *Lincoln's
Yarns and Stories*, 1904, recounts that the president made this remark to a
caller at the White House. There are numerous updates to the thought. The
newspaper columnist F.P.A. (Franklin Pierce Adams) declared in *Nods and
Becks*, 1924, that "The trouble with this country is that there are too many
politicians who believe, with a conviction based on experience, that you can
fool all of the people all of the time." James Thurber noted, "You can fool too
many of the people too much of the time," *The Owl Who Was God*, in *The
New Yorker*, April 25, 1949. Movie producer Joseph Levine quipped, "You can
fool all the people if the advertising is right and the budget is big enough," *New
York Times*, obituary, August 1, 1987.]

Vox populi, vox humbug. —WILLIAM TECUMSEH SHERMAN, 6
letter to his wife, June 2, 1863
[Sherman was referring to the historic "*Vox populi, vox Dei*—The voice of the
people is the voice of God," attributed to Alcuin, c. A.D. 800. He may also have
known Alexander Pope's "The people's voice is odd; It is, and it is not, the
voice of God," *Imitations of Horace* (1733–38). Alexander Hamilton, too,
found the voice of the people suspect: "The voice of the people has been said to
be the voice of God; . . . it is not true in fact. The people are turbulent and
changing; they seldom judge or determine right." See also Hamilton at RICH &
POOR, WEALTH & POVERTY. And for a punning variation, see the anonymous
Vanity Fair quote under ABRAHAM LINCOLN.]

Government of the people, by the people, for the people. 7
—ABRAHAM LINCOLN, Gettysburg Address, Nov. 19, 1863
[More at GETTYSBURG ADDRESS.]

The pitifulest thing out is a mob. —MARK TWAIN, *Huckleberry Finn*, 1885 8

If all the good people were clever, 9
And all the clever people were good,
The world would be nicer than ever
We thought that it possibly could.
—ELIZABETH WORDSWORTH, *The Good and the Clever*,
in *St. Christopher and Other Poems*, 1890
[Elizabeth Wordsworth was the great-niece of the English poet William Words-
worth.]

1 I am the people—the mob—the crowd—the mass.
Do you know that all the great work of the world is done through
  me?   —CARL SANDBURG, *I Am the People, the Mob,* 1916

2 The apparition of these faces in the crowd;
Petals on a wet, black bough.
        —EZRA POUND, *In a Station of a Metro,* 1916
[Pound studied Oriental poetry, as is evident in this famous couplet. For other
faces in the crowd, see W. H. Auden below.]

3 No one . . . has ever lost money by underestimating the intelligence of the
great masses of the plain people. —H. L. MENCKEN, *Notes on Journalism,*
        Chicago Tribune, Sept. 19, 1926
[Popularized as: "No one ever went broke underestimating the intelligence of
the American people."]

4 Private faces in public places
Are wiser and nicer
Than public faces in private places.   —W. H. AUDEN,
        Orators, 1932

[From the dedication, which is to Stephen Spender.]

5 The people will live on.
The learning and blundering people will live on.
They will be tricked and sold and again sold
And go back to the nourishing earth for rootholds.
    —CARL SANDBURG, *The People, Yes,* 1936

6 About one-fifth of the people are against everything all the time.
    —ROBERT F. KENNEDY, speech,
    University of Pennsylvania, May 6, 1964

7 The silent majority.
    —RICHARD M. NIXON, speech, Nov. 3, 1969
[More at MAJORITIES & MINORITIES. The "silent majority" recalls William Graham Sumner's "forgotten man"; see under ECONOMICS.]

8 The American people have the Constitutional right to be wrong.
    —WARREN RUDMAN, comment in the Senate Select Committee
    hearing on the Iran-Contra affair, July 1987

PERCEPTION   *See* VISION & PERCEPTION

PERSEVERANCE   *See* COMMITMENT; DETERMINATION, EFFORT,
      PERSISTENCE, & PERSEVERANCE; ENDURANCE;
      PATIENCE; WINNING & LOSING, VICTORY & DEFEAT

PESSIMISM   *See* OPTIMISM & PESSIMISM

PHILANTHROPY   *See* CHARITY & PHILANTHROPY

PHILOSOPHY   *See also* REALITY, ILLUSIONS, & IMAGES

9 The test of a religion or philosophy is the number of things it can explain.
    —RALPH WALDO EMERSON, *Journal,* 1836

To be a philosopher is . . . so to love wisdom as to live according to its dictates, 1
a life of simplicity, independence, magnaminity, and trust.
—HENRY DAVID THOREAU, "Economy," *Walden,* 1854

Let us not pretend to doubt in philosophy what we do not doubt in our hearts. 2
—C. S. PEIRCE, *Collected Papers,* Vol. V, para. 265
[See also Peirce at SKEPTICISM and in the note on the William James quote at
TRUTH.]

The philosophy which is so important in each of us is not a technical matter; 3
it is our more or less dumb sense of what life honestly and deeply means.
—WILLIAM JAMES, *Pragmatism,* 1907
[See also James at EXPEDIENCY and TRUTH.]

Every philosophy is tinged with the coloring of some secret imaginative, 4
which never emerges explicitly into its trains of reasoning.
—ALFRED NORTH WHITEHEAD,
Science and the Modern World, 1925

The safest general characterization of the European philosophical tradition is 5
that it consists of a series of footnotes to Plato.
—ALFRED NORTH WHITEHEAD, *Process and Reality,* 1929

Philosophy begins in wonder. And at the end, when philosophic thought has 6
done its best, the wonder remains.
—ALFRED NORTH WHITEHEAD, *Modes of Thought,* 1938

Metaphysics is almost always an attempt to prove the incredible by an appeal 7
to the unintelligible.   —H. L. MENCKEN, *Minority Report:*
H. L. Mencken's Notebooks [1956]

PHOTOGRAPHY   *See* ART: VISUAL

PHYSICAL FITNESS   *See also* HEALTH; SPORTS

The sovereign invigorator of the body is exercise, and of all the exercises, walk- 8
ing is best.   —THOMAS JEFFERSON, letter to Thomas Mann Randolph, Jr.,
August 27, 1786
[Randolph later married Jefferson's daughter Martha.]

I wish to preach, not the doctrine of ignoble ease, but the doctrine of the stren- 9
uous life.   —THEODORE ROOSEVELT, speech at the Hamilton Club,
Chicago, April 10, 1899
[See William James at POVERTY & HUNGER for the strenuous life lived by the
poor.]

I have never taken any exercise, except sleeping and resting, and I never intend 10
to take any. Exercise is loathsome.
—MARK TWAIN, speech, on his 70th birthday,
Delmonico's, New York City, Dec. 5, 1905

Whenever the urge to exercise comes upon me, I lie down for a while and it 11
passes.   —ROBERT MAYNARD HUTCHINS, quoted in Harry S. Ashmore,
The Life of Robert Maynard Hutchins
[Hutchins headed the University of Chicago from 1929 to 1951. He enjoyed
good health and died at age seventy-eight.]

1 Avoid running at all times.   —LEROY "SATCHEL" PAIGE,
                                                      How to Stay Young, 1953
   [More at WISDOM, WORDS OF.]

2 We are underexercised as a nation. We look instead of play. We ride instead of
   walk. Our existence deprives us of the minimum physical activity essential for
   healthy living.   —JOHN F. KENNEDY, speech,
                                National Football Foundation, Dec. 5, 1961

PHYSICS   *See* SCIENCE: PHYSICS & COSMOLOGY

PHYSIOLOGY   *See* SCIENCE: BIOLOGY & PHYSIOLOGY

PLANTS   *see* NATURE: PLANTS & GARDENS

PLEASURE & HEDONISM

3 Pain wastes the body, pleasure the understanding.
                              —BENJAMIN FRANKLIN, *Poor Richard's Almanack,* 1735

4 I do not agree that an age of pleasure is no compensation for a moment of pain.
                              —THOMAS JEFFERSON, letter to John Adams, August 1, 1816

5 That man is richest whose pleasures are the cheapest.
                              —HENRY DAVID THOREAU, *Journal,* March 11, 1856

6 Drink and dance and laugh and lie,
   Love, the reeling midnight through,
   For tomorrow we shall die!
   (But, alas, we never do.)   —DOROTHY PARKER, *The Flaw in Paganism,*
                                         in *Death and Taxes,* 1931

POETRY   *See* ART: POETRY

POLITICAL PARTIES   *See* POLITICS & POLITICIANS

POLITICAL SLOGANS

7 Stand with Washington.
                              —ANONYMOUS, slogan of the Federalist party, 1790s
   [The Federalists, the party of Alexander Hamilton, favored a strong central authority and republican, rather than purely democratic, government. By contrast, Thomas Jefferson's Republican Democrats (later simply Democrats)
   favored states' rights and power vested directly with the people. Pres. Washington, who belonged to no party, eventually appeared to favor the Federalists,
   and thus this slogan arose.]

8 A corrupt bargain.   —ANONYMOUS, rallying cry of Jacksonian Democrats,
                                 1827–28
   [The phrase refers to the appointment of Henry Clay as secretary of state by
   Pres. John Quincy Adams. Clay, the Speaker of the House, was a loser in the
   presidential campaign of 1824, in which four candidates split the vote. Jackson
   received a plurality of the popular vote but fell well short of the required majority in the electoral college. The decision, therefore, went to the House of

Representatives, where Clay, having no chance for the presidency himself, and heartily detesting Jackson, assembled the necessary majority of thirteen states for Adams. He persuaded his own state, Kentucky, to vote for Adams, contrary to the instructions of the state legislature to support Jackson. Naturally, Clay's subsequent appointment was seen as a quid pro quo. Jackson went on to win in 1828.]

Root, hog, or die. [1]

—ANONYMOUS, political saying, c. 1830s

[A pithy summation of the political spoils system, popularized in the Jacksonian period. An 1836 publication, *Calumet and War Club*, put it this way: "Root, hog, or die—work for your office, or leave it—support the party, right or wrong—are the terms of our agreement." The expression probably arose among farmers, who turned hogs loose in the woods and prairies to fend for themselves. Davy Crockett used the admonition in his 1834 attributed autobiography, referring to it there as an "old saying." He used it to mean: work hard or suffer undesirable consequences. See also William Marcy at POLITICS & POLITICIANS.]

Two dollars a day and roast beef. [2]

—ANONYMOUS, slogan of the Whig party, 1840

[See also the quotes directly below, as well as "the full dinner pail" and "a chicken in every pot" slogans also below. In the presidential campaign of 1840, Democratic incumbent Martin Van Buren was handicapped by a national financial crisis. The full slogan of the Whigs, who were running William Henry Harrison, was: "Van's policy, fifty cents a day and French soup. Our policy, two dollars a day and roast beef." The "French soup" was a reference to Van Buren's allegedly elegant lifestyle.]

Tippecanoe and Tyler too. [3]

—ANONYMOUS, Whig campaign slogan, 1840

[The Whig candidates in 1840 were William Henry Harrison, "the Hero of Tippecanoe," and, for the vice-presidency, John Tyler. They bested Democratic incumbent Martin Van Buren. Harrison was famous for defeating (more or less) the Shawnee Indians in battle at the Tippecanoe River in Indiana in 1811. The slogan was incorporated in a popular campaign song: "And have you heard the news from Maine, / And what old Maine can do? / She went hell-bent for Governor Kent, / And Tippecanoe and Tyler too, / And Tippecanoe and Tyler too." Gov. Kent was Edward Kent, whose victory in that summer's Maine election—until 1958 Maine voted in advance of the national election in November—was the first sign of a Whig sweep nationally. This also seems to be the source of the saying, "As Maine goes, so goes the nation"; see MAINE.]

Farewell, dear Van, [4]
You're not our man;
To guide the ship,
We'll try old Tip.

—ANONYMOUS, Whig campaign song, 1840

[Van is Martin Van Buren; Tip is William Henry Harrison; see note above. Sharp-witted Martin Van Buren, a loyal Jacksonian Democrat, gained a reputation as an overly elegant elitist, while the rather dim Harrison, who came from a wealthy family, was portrayed as a simple man of the people, raised in a log cabin.

This election also popularized the expression "O.K." A humorous abbreviation of "Oll [or "Orl"] Korrect," it became associated with Van Buren because of the coincidence of the initials with those of his nickname, "Old Kinderhook," referring to his hometown in New York. Van Buren's supporters in New York, for example, formed a Democratic O.K. Club. After the election, victorious Whigs claimed that O.K. actually stood for an Arabic phrase which, when read backward, translated as "Kicked Out."]

1   Fifty-four forty or fight.   —WILLIAM ALLEN, attributed,
Democratic presidential campaign slogan, 1844
[Sen. William Allen ("Earthquake Allen") of Ohio, a supporter of James K. Polk for president, is said to have invented this catchy slogan. The reference is to a latitude in the Oregon territory; the territory was controlled by Great Britain, but jointly occupied by Americans and British. Sen. Allen spoke in favor of a U.S. acquisition as far north as Alaska. Polk won, but in 1846, the U.S. and Britain settled their differences amicably. The U.S. took over Oregon territory up to the forty-ninth parallel, dividing the Oregon tract approximately in half. Included in the U.S. portion was land that is now divided into the states of Washington, Oregon, and Idaho.]

2   Vote early and vote often.

—ANONYMOUS
[In *The Age of Jackson*, Arthur M. Schlesinger, Jr., associates this with New York City political strongman and iconoclast Mike Walsh. A bold friend of the underprivileged, Walsh headed the Spartan Band, a group of rowdies who participated actively in local elections. On March 31, 1858, in a speech in the U.S. Congress, Rep. William Porcher Miles referred to the "vote early and often" adage as "advice openly displayed on the election banners in one of our northern cities."]

3   I think I hear his cheerful voice,
"On column! Steady! Steady!"
So handy and so prompt was he,
We called him Rough and Ready.   —ANONYMOUS,
Whig presidential campaign song, 1848
[Old Rough and Ready, Zachary Taylor, gained his appealing nickname in a marginally successful assault on outnumbered Seminole Indians in Florida in 1837. He was popularly regarded as a hero for his exploits in the Mexican War, and became the presidential candidate of the Whig party in 1848. He died after a year in office and was succeeded by Millard Fillmore.]

4   We Polked you in '44, we shall Pierce you in '52.
—ANONYMOUS,
Democratic campaign slogan, 1852
[Franklin Pierce became the nation's fourteenth president, defeating his commander in the Mexican War, Whig candidate Gen. Winfield Scott. His failure to implement his party's expansionist foreign policy and his pro-Southern domestic policy ruined his standing in his own party, and he was not renominated.]

5   Free soil, free men, Frémont.
—ANONYMOUS, Republican campaign slogan, 1856
[Abolitionist William C. Frémont was the first presidential nominee of the Republican party. "Free-soil" meant no slavery, and the free-soil battleground was Kansas. The Republican slogan was inspired by the Free Soil Party's 1848 rallying cry: "Free Soil, Free Speech, Free Labor, and Free Men." Despite a stirring campaign, Frémont lost to Democrat James Buchanan.]

I know nothing but my Country, my whole Country, and nothing but Country.   1
—ANONYMOUS, American (Know-Nothing)
Party slogan, 1856
[The Know-Nothing movement, dating to the 1840s, was so-called because its leading members belonged to secret organizations and would profess to know nothing when questioned as to their aims and their leaders. The movement was anti-immigrant and nationalistic. The Know-Nothings emerged from the semisecret Order of the Star-Spangled Banner, formed in New York in 1849. As the numbers of Catholic immigrants swelled, and their political influence increased, the Know-Nothings became more respectable, re-forming as the American party in 1854. Despite considerable success in congressional elections, the party was politically inept, and almost immediately divided on the slavery issue. The Know-Nothing candidate in 1856 was former president Millard Fillmore; he hoped to unite North and South, but of course failed. In 1855, Abraham Lincoln made the following observation: "As a nation we began by declaring that *'all men are created equal.'* We now practically read it, 'all men are created equal, *except negroes.* When the Know-Nothings get control, it will read 'all men are created equal, except negroes, *and foreigners, and Catholics,'*" letter to Joshua Speed.]

Don't swap horses.   2
—ANONYMOUS, Republican presidential campaign slogan, 1864
[This derived from a comment by Pres. Lincoln on the inadvisiblity of changing horses in midstream; see CHANGE. Democrats recycled this bit of folk wisdom in FDR's reelection campaigns of 1940 and 1944. They also used an ironic twist in 1932 when, with the nation's economy in shambles and Herbert Hoover running for reelection, the Dems maintained that the Republican motto must be "Don't swap barrels while going over Niagara."]

Turn the rascals out.   3
—CHARLES A. DANA, slogan, presidential election of 1872
[Dana, the editor of the New York *Sun*, made this phrase famous while urging the defeat of Pres. Ulysses S. Grant. Horace Greeley, editor of the *New York Tribune*, was running against Grant as a candidate of both the Democratic party and the Liberal Republican party—not a label likely to be revived these days. Grant won.]

Rum, Romanism, and rebellion.   —SAMUEL DICKINSON BURCHARD, remark,   4
New York City, Oct. 9, 1884
[Rev. Dr. Burchard, at a reception for Republican presidential candidate James G. Blaine, commented, "We are Republicans, and don't propose to identify ourselves with the party whose antecedents have been rum, Romanism, and rebellion." Blaine lost to Grover Cleveland, in part because he failed to distance himself, as we now say, from this inflammatory insult. The remark became a rallying cry for the Democrats.]

A mugwump is a person educated beyond his intellect.   5
—HORACE PORTER, slogan, presidential election of 1884
[In 1884, Republican mugwumps, or, more politely, political independents, deserted presidential candidate James G. Blaine in favor of Democrat Grover Cleveland. Another reason that Blaine lost was a supporter's indiscreet reference to Democrats as belonging to the party of "rum, Romanism, and rebellion"; see Samuel Dickinson Burchard above. Maine's Thomas Reed described mugwumps as "longtailed birds of Paradise." See also LANGUAGE & WORDS.
Horace Porter served under Ulysses S. Grant both in the Army and the White

House. In 1897, he became ambassador to France, and at the end of his tour, in 1905, he brought back the body of John Paul Jones.]

1   Blaine, Blaine, James G. Blaine,
The Continental liar from the state of Maine.
—ANONYMOUS, heckling slogan, 1884
[A piece of simpleminded doggerel aimed at the Republican presidential candidate. For the Republican rejoinder, see below.]

2   Ma, Ma, where's my Pa?
—ANONYMOUS, heckling slogan, 1884
[The question was popularly directed at Democratic presidential candidate Grover Cleveland, who admitted having fathered, or possibly fathered, an illegitimate child; at any rate he supported the child. The popular Democratic rejoinder was, "Gone to the White House, ha, ha, ha," and Cleveland did indeed go there.]

3   Sixteen to one.
—ANONYMOUS, Democratic party slogan, 1896
[The Democratic platform called for the free coinage of silver in a ratio of sixteen to one to gold. See also William Jennings Bryan's "Cross of Gold" speech at ECONOMICS.]

4   Four more years of the full dinner pail.
—ANONYMOUS, Republican party slogan, 1900
[The Republicans promised continuing prosperity with the reelection of William McKinley over William Jennings Bryan.]

5   No crown of thorns, no cross of gold.
—ANONYMOUS, Democratic party slogan, 1900
[The reference is to candidate Bryan's "Cross of Gold" speech; see ECONOMICS.]

6   McKinley drinks soda water; Bryan drinks rum; McKinley is a gentleman, Bryan is a bum.   —ANONYMOUS, heckling verse, presidential campaign, 1900

7   We'll stand pat.   —MARK HANNA, remark to reporter
on campaign strategy, 1900
[Sen. Hanna of Ohio—"the kingmaker"—was referring to his strategy for reelecting William McKinley. The stand-pat notion was included four years later in an unmemorable Republican slogan in support of Theodore Roosevelt, who had succeeded the assassinated McKinley, "Same old flag and victory—stand pat." Sixty years later, candidate Richard M. Nixon, running against John F. Kennedy, asserted repeatedly, "America cannot stand pat." He dropped the slogan after it was pointed out that his wife's name was Pat. Instead he used, "America cannot stand still."]

8   We demand that big business give people a square deal.
—THEODORE ROOSEVELT, 1901
[Roosevelt was referring to setting limits on U.S. Steel. The term "square deal" was his favorite metaphor for fairness. In his autobiography, Roosevelt added to his original thought, "In turn, we must insist that when anyone engaged in big business honestly endeavors to do right, he shall himself be given a square deal."
In a famous speech at Springfield, Ill., on July 4, 1903, Roosevelt said, "A man who is good enough to give his blood for his country is good enough to be

given a square deal afterwards. More than that no man is entitled to, less than that no man shall have."

On the campaign trail, his pledge to the American people was "I stand for the square deal." In 1910, in *The New Nationalism,* he explained, "When I say I am for the square deal, I mean not merely that I stand for fair play under the present rules of the game, but that I stand for having those rules changed so as to work for a more substantial equality of opportunity and of reward for equally good service."

A square deal in card games is a fair, equitable deal, as in, for example, "Thought I had better give him a square deal," Mark Twain, *Life on the Mississippi,* 1883.

According to William Safire in his *New Political Dictionary,* Lincoln Steffens claimed to have suggested the square-deal metaphor to Roosevelt. Use of card-playing metaphors in politics is traditional, witness the "New Deal" and the "Fair Deal"; see below. The redoubtable Colonel David (Davy) Crockett noted in his *Life of Martin Van Buren,* 1835, that "Statesmen are gamesters, and the people are the cards they play with . . . the way they cut and shuffle is a surprise to all beginners."]

Get on the raft with Taft.   1
—ANONYMOUS, Republican campaign slogan, 1908
[Taft had been Pres. Theodore Roosevelt's Secretary of War—now called Secretary of Defense. He defeated William Jennings Bryan.]

A New Nationalism.   —THEODORE ROOSEVELT, campaign motto, 1912   2

A New Freedom.   3
—WOODROW WILSON, campaign motto, 1912
[The voters preferred the New Freedom.]

He kept us out of war.   —MARTIN H. GLYN, keynote address,   4
Democratic National Convention, 1916
[The convention selected incumbent Woodrow Wilson for president. Glyn's statement became a campaign slogan.]

Harding, you're the man for us.   5
We think the country's ready
for another man like Teddy.
We need another Lincoln
To do the country's thinkin.
Mister Harding,
You're the man for us.   —AL JOLSON, campaign song, 1920

Return to normalcy.   6
—WARREN G. HARDING, campaign slogan, 1920
[See Harding at AMERICAN HISTORY: MEMORABLE MOMENTS, and also WARREN G. HARDING.]

Law and Order.   —ANONYMOUS, motto on banners waved by supporters   7
of Calvin Coolidge for the vice-presidential nomination
at the 1920 Republican National Convention
[Coolidge became the "law and order" candidate because as governor of Massachusetts he reacted with force to a strike by police; see CAPITALISM & CAPITAL v. LABOR. The call for "law and order" has arisen frequently in American politics, usually in a conservative context. Thus, in 1842, the Law and Order Party

in Rhode Island opposed extending the right to vote to males who didn't own property, and in 1857 the proslavery party in Kansas changed its name to the Law and Order Party. In the 1960s, "law and order" was a rallying cry for Republicans who hoped to turn back the liberal tide of that era.]

1   Cox and cocktails.
> —ANONYMOUS, Democratic presidential campaign slogan, 1920

[Presidential candidate James Middleton Cox of Ohio favored the League of Nations and the repeal of Prohibition. He lost badly in a three-way race against Warren Harding and Eugene Debs. Cox's running mate was Franklin D. Roosevelt.]

2   Convict No. 9653 for President.
> —ANONYMOUS, Socialist presidential
> campaign slogan
> for Eugene Debs, 1920

[Debs, the great socialist leader, who was regarded with affection even by many of his political enemies, was serving a ten-year prison term in 1920. His crime was publicly denouncing the federal prosecution of persons charged with sedition under the 1917 Espionage Act. Nevertheless, he got nearly 920,000 votes. Pres. Harding ordered his release in 1920. But Debs, age sixty-five, was finished as a major political figure.]

3   Keep cool with Coolidge.
> —ANONYMOUS, campaign slogan for
> Republican presidential candidate
> Calvin Coolidge, 1924

4   Coolidge or chaos.
> —*Ibid.*

[In 1924, Coolidge, who had inherited the presidency from Warren Harding, ran against two major candidates, Democrat John W. Davis and the Progressive Party's Robert M. La Follette. There were also six minor parties in the race, including the Prohibition Party, the Socialist Labor Party, and the Communist Party.]

5   A chicken in every pot, a car in every garage.
> —ANONYMOUS, Republican presidential campaign slogan, 1928

[Incumbent Republican president Herbert Hoover, in his nomination acceptance speech, prophesied an end to poverty in the U.S.; see AMERICAN HISTORY: MEMORABLE MOMENTS. The "chicken in every pot" slogan was taken from Henry IV of France, who reputedly said, "I want there to be no peasant in my realm so poor that he will not have a chicken in his pot every Sunday."]

6   Every man a king!
> —HUEY LONG, slogan in the 1928 Louisiana
> gubernatorial campaign and title of Long's
> autobiography, 1933

[Populist to some, demagogue to others, Long won in this campaign, and, in 1932, was elected to the U.S. Senate. He declared for the presidency in 1934. Will Rogers commented, "He found me and pinned a button on me, called EVERY MAN A KING, and it said everybody was to divide up their wealth. I am working with him on a percentage." Will Rogers died in a plane crash in 1935. A month later Long was assassinated.]

7   Share our wealth.
> —HUEY LONG, political slogan, carved on his tomb
> in the Capitol in Baton Rouge, La.

[In February 1934, Long announced the creation of the Share Our Wealth Society, calling for a more equal distribution of wealth among rich and poor. Share

Our Wealth clubs sprang up nationally, but especially in the impoverished South.]

A new deal for the American people.   1
> —FRANKLIN D. ROOSEVELT, presidential nomination acceptance
> speech, Democratic National Convention, Chicago,
> July 2, 1932
[See also AMERICAN HISTORY: MEMORABLE MOMENTS.]

Happy days are here again.   —JACK YELLEN,   2
                                        Happy Days Are Here Again, 1929
[More at GOOD TIMES.]

Life, liberty, and Landon.   3
> —ANONYMOUS, Republican presidential campaign slogan
> for Alf Landon, 1936
[Landon won only Maine and Vermont.]

Roosevelt for ex-President.   4
> —ANONYMOUS, Republican presidential campaign slogan, 1940
[The Republican candidate Wendell Willkie, an industrialist, had been a Democrat until 1940. He did better than any other contender against Roosevelt, tallying more than 22 million votes.]

Let's re- re- re-elect Roosevelt.   5
> —ANONYMOUS, Democratic presidential campaign slogan, 1944

Had enough?   6
> —ANONYMOUS, Republican presidential campaign slogan, 1944
[The Republican candidate was Thomas Dewey, and the voters answered no.]

Give 'em hell, Harry!   7
> —ANONYMOUS, Democratic rallying cry, 1948
[Pres. Harry S. Truman, apparently running behind the Republican challenger Thomas Dewey, was cheered on by this popular slogan. He first heard the cry in Seattle, and it followed him to victory. Going into the home stretch, he told Vice President Alben Barkley "I'm going to fight hard. I'm going to give them hell," Sept. 27, 1948. See also Truman at TRUTH.]

I like Ike.   —ANONYMOUS, Republican campaign slogan   8
                                          for Dwight D. "Ike" Eisenhower, 1952
[A great slogan—almost everybody did like Ike—recycled in 1956 as "I still like Ike."]

You never had it so good.   —ANONYMOUS, Democratic campaign slogan   9
                                          for candidate Adlai Stevenson, 1952
[A good effort, much better than the weak 1956 slogans "We need Adlai badly" and "We're madly for Adlai." Stevenson also pledged that his administration would be in tune with "a new America." This was picked up by John F. Kennedy and reappeared as the New Frontier.]

A New Frontier.   10
> —JOHN F. KENNEDY, presidential campaign slogan, 1960
[The tag line came from his nomination acceptance speech at the Democratic convention in Los Angeles on July 15, 1960: "We stand today at the edge of a new frontier—the frontier of the 1960s, a frontier of unknown opportunities

and paths, a frontier of unfulfilled hopes and threats." He explained, "The new frontier of which I speak is not a set of promises, it is a set of challenges. It sums up not what I intend to *offer* the American people but what I intend to *ask* of them." In his inaugural speech, he returned to the concept of citizen service; see SERVING ONE'S COUNTRY.

The "new frontier" phrase had been used before. In 1934, Henry Wallace published a book entitled *New Frontiers*, and in 1936, Alf Landon, the Republican candidate for president also spoke of "a new frontier . . . a frontier of invention and new wants." Kennedy, though, made the phrase his own, his equivalent of FDR's New Deal and Truman's Fair Deal. The programs that typified Kennedy's New Frontier were in space exploration, civil rights, education, medical care for the aged, and farm policy. In 1979, Pres. Jimmy Carter and speechwriter Rick Herzberg introduced A New Foundation, but it did not catch on.]

1   All the way with LBJ.   —ANONYMOUS, Democratic presidential campaign slogan for Lyndon Baines Johnson, 1964

2   The Great Society.

—LYNDON B. JOHNSON, political slogan, 1964
[In *The Penguin Dictionary of Contemporary American History*, Stanley and Eleanor Hochman point out that President Johnson first tried the tag line "a better deal" to describe the type of government he hoped to bring to the American people. When that flopped, he recalled the phrase "a great society" in a speech written for him by Richard Goodwin, March 4, 1964. He successfully launched the slogan on April 23 at a Democratic fundraiser in Chicago: "We have been called upon—are you listening?—to build a great society of the highest order, a society not just for today or tomorrow, but for three or four generations to come." The best publicized occasion of its use was in May at the University of Michigan; see AMERICAN HISTORY: MEMORABLE MOMENTS.

Great Society programs were introduced in a flood of legislation designed to end poverty and promote civil rights. Republicans noted that a 1914 book by Graham Wallace titled *The Great Society* was a socialist text. The Vietnam War, however, ended Johnson's social initiatives.]

3   In your heart you know he's right.   —ANONYMOUS, Republican campaign slogan for presidential candidate Barry Goldwater, 1964
[Republicans also advertised that Goldwater offered "a choice not an echo." Ironically, thirty years later, Goldwater, the old warrior of the right, came to be considered too libertarian, too free-thinking, and too liberal for contemporary Republicans.]

4   Nixon's the one.   —ANONYMOUS, Republican campaign slogan aimed at winning the presidential nomination for Richard Nixon, 1968
[Nixon's supporters prevailed and the phrase entered the language, but was easily turned against Nixon. For example, after the 1972 campaign, when the official party slogan was "Nixon now more than ever," skeptics resurrected "Nixon's the one" with reference to the national Watergate whodunit.]

5   Are you better off today than you were four years ago?
—PAUL SIMMONS, slogan for Illinois Gov. Jim Thompson, late 1970s
[It was picked up and used to great effect by Republican presidential candidate Ronald Reagan in 1980. His target was Pres. Jimmy Carter.]

A kinder, gentler nation.   —GEORGE BUSH, presidential nomination   1
speech, Republican National Convention,
New Orleans, August 18, 1988
[This instantly famous phrase was selected by speechwriter Peggy Noonan to distinguish Vice President Bush from Pres. Ronald Reagan, who was often accused of a bland heartlessness. Nancy Reagan caught on fast. When Bush announced, "I want a kinder, gentler nation," she is said to have asked immediately, "Kinder and gentler than who?"
This speech also included the reference to "a thousand points of light"; see AMERICA & AMERICANS.]

It's the economy, stupid.   2
—JAMES CARVILLE, saying, 1992
[Carville, campaign manage for Bill Clinton, put up a sign with this message in his campaign-headquarters office, meaning that attention to the faltering economy was the key to victory. Woodrow Wilson made the same point more politely; see POLITICS & POLITICIANS.]

POLITICS & POLITICIANS   *See also* COMMUNISM; CONGRESS;
DEMOCRACY; GOVERNMENT; MAJORITIES &
MINORITIES; POLITICAL SLOGANS;
PRESIDENCY, THE; SOCIALISM

I agree with you that in politics the middle way is none at all.   3
—JOHN ADAMS, letter to Horatio Gates, March 23, 1776

The meekness of Quakerism will do in religion, but not in politics.   4
—DE WITT CLINTON, c. 1803
[Clinton dominated New York politics in the first quarter of the 19th century as assemblyman, state senator, U.S. senator, mayor of New York City, and three-term governor of the state. Among other good works, he promoted public schools, public sanitation, relief for the poor, the abolition of slavery, and—his crowning achievement—construction of the Erie Canal.]

When a man assumes a public trust, he should consider himself as public   5
property.   —THOMAS JEFFERSON, remark to Baron von Humboldt,
attributed in Rayner, *Life of Jefferson* [1834]
[See also Grover Cleveland's motto—"A public office is a public trust"—at GOVERNMENT, author anonymous.]

[The Democrats] see nothing wrong in the rule that to the victors belong the   6
spoils of the enemy.
—WILLIAM MARCY, speech, U.S. Senate, Jan. 25, 1832
[Sen. Marcy of New York was defending Pres. Andrew Jackson's policy of appointing his own supporters to government positions. In particular, he was defending the appointment of Martin Van Buren—another New Yorker and a future president—as ambassador to Great Britain. This "spoils system," which Jackson called "rotation in office," is taken for granted today. Jackson himself replaced less than ten percent of office holders in his first eighteen months. See also Richard Croker and Huey Long below, pp. 391 and 393, respectively.]

We are reformers in spring and summer; in autumn and winter, we stand by   7
the old; reformers in the morning, conservers at night. Reform is affirmative, conservatism negative; conservatism goes for comfort, reform for truth.
—RALPH WALDO EMERSON, *The Conservative*,
lecture, Boston, May 9, 1841

1   Conservatism makes no poetry, breathes no prayer, has no invention; it is all memory. Reform has no gratitude, no prudence, no husbandry.   —*Ibid.*

2   A party is perpetually corrupted by personality.
                    —RALPH WALDO EMERSON, *Politics,* in *Essays: Second Series,* 1844

3   It is the fashion of a certain set to assume to despise "politics." . . . But to our view, the spectacle is always a grand one—full of the most august and sublime attributes.   —WALT WHITMAN, *American Democracy,*
                    in the *Brooklyn Eagle,* April 20, 1847

4   An honest politician is one who when he's bought stays bought.
                    —SIMON CAMERON, attributed, c. 1850
    [Cameron was the Republican boss of Pennsylvania, widely accused of doing a lot of political buying and selling. George Seldes, in *The Great Quotations,* wrote that fellow politician Thomas B. Reed attributed this line to Cameron. See also Cameron below.]

5   I never said all Democrats were saloon-keepers. What I said was that all saloon-keepers are Democrats.   —HORACE GREELEY, attributed, c. 1860

6   What is conservatism? Is it not adherence to the old and tried against the new and untried?   —ABRAHAM LINCOLN, speech, Feb. 27, 1860

7   You scratch my back, I'll scratch yours.
                    —SIMON CAMERON, attributed
    [Cameron did so much scratching as Lincoln's Secretary of War that it became a national scandal, and he had to be eased from office. Lincoln named him ambassador to Russia.]

8   The Democratic party is like a mule. It has neither pride of ancestry nor hope of posterity.   —IGNATIUS DONNELLY, speech,
                    Minnesota legislature, 1860
    [Donnelly, who enjoyed a long political career, including three terms as a Republican representative in Congress, was a genuine American crackpot, holding forth in best-selling books that Bacon wrote Shakespeare, that a close call with a comet had caused the ice ages, and that the biblical Eden was in the lost continent of Atlantis.]

9   There are always two parties, the party of the past and the party of the future: the establishment and the movement.
                    —RALPH WALDO EMERSON,
                    Historic Notes of Life and Letters in New England, 1867

10 Politics makes strange bedfellows.   —CHARLES DUDLEY WARNER,
                    My Summer in a Garden, 1870
    [Warner, editor of the *Hartford Courant* and *Harper's Magazine,* probably had in mind Shakespeare's, "Misery acquaints a man with strange bedfellows," *The Tempest,* II,ii.]

11 Waving the bloody shirt.
                    —OLIVER PERRY MORTON, saying, c. 1876
    [Sen. Morton of Indiana made this phrase popular as a description of the tendency of post–Civil War Republicans to appeal to sectionalism and anti-Confederate sentiment to get votes. The "bloody shirt," sometimes euphemized by Victorians as "the ensanguined garment," has a pre–Civil War history.]

The idea is to inflame emotions by displaying bloodstained clothes of someone who's been killed. The oldest example of "bloody shirt" in this sense in *The Oxford English Dictionary* is from Sir Philip Sidney's *Arcadia* (pre-1586).]

Politics are impossible without spoils. . . . You have to deal with men as they   1
are . . . you must bribe the masses with spoils.
                    —RICHARD CROKER, quoted in Richard Norton Smith,
                        Thomas E. Dewey [1982]
["Boss" Croker of New York City flourished in the late 1880s. He was the political descendant of William Marcy, see above.]

The purification of politics is an iridescent dream.   2
                    —JOHN JAMES INGALLS, article, *New York World*, 1890
[Sen. Ingalls of Kansas was a nationally popular orator. In this cynical assessment of the political arena, he continued, "Government is force. . . . The Decalogue and the Golden Rule have no place in a political campaign. The commander who lost the battle through the activity of his moral nature would be the derision and jest of history.]

I am a Democrat still—very still.   3
                    —DAVID BENNETT HILL, comment to reporter following
                        the nomination of William Jennings Bryan in 1900
[Hill, a former governor of New York and presidential candidate, had difficulty supporting the convention's free-silver policies and its candidate, William Jennings Bryan. See also ECONOMICS. Four years earlier, when Bryan won the first of his three nominations for the presidency, Hill had commented, "I am a Democrat, but not a revolutionist."]

I am as strong as a bull moose and you can use me to the limit.   4
                    —THEODORE ROOSEVELT, letter to Sen. Mark Hanna,
                        June 27, 1900
[Roosevelt's references to himself as a bull moose gave the Progressive Party, founded in 1912, its nickname.]

Reformers Only Morning Glories.   5
                    —GEORGE WASHINGTON PLUNKITT, title of speech, c. 1900
[Plunkitt, a Tammany Hall state senator, observed: "The fact is that a reformer can't last in politics. He can make a show of it for a while, but he always comes down like a rocket."]

Th' dimmycratic party ain't on speakin' terms with itsilf.   6
                    —FINLEY PETER DUNNE, *Mr. Dooley Discusses Party Politics*,
                        in *Mr. Dooley's Opinions*, 1900

A statesman is a successful politician who is dead.   7
                    —THOMAS BRACKETT REED, attributed
["Czar" Reed represented Maine from 1877 to 1899, and was Speaker in 1889–91 and 1895–99. He made this observation to Rep. Henry Cabot Lodge, according to Edward Boykin's *The Wit and Wisdom of Congress*, 1961. Harry Truman, another politician who waited long to be called a statesman, used the same thought: "A statesman is a politician who's been dead ten or fifteen years," *New York World-Telegram & Sun*, April 12, 1958.]

Politics is the art of turning influence into affluence.   8
                    —PHILANDER C. JOHNSON,
                        Senator Sorghum's Primer of Politics, 1906
[And vice versa.]

1   Somehow a party platform always reminds me a lot of New Year's resolutions.
                                                                        —*Ibid.*

2   The man who goes into politics because he needs the money isn't likely to do
    as much harm as the man who goes into it merely because he has money to
    burn.   —*Ibid.*

3   A true politician never forgets a favor; that is to say, if by chance he does some-
    one else a favor, he never forgets it.   —*Ibid.*

4   Politics, as a practice, whatever its professions, has always been the systematic
    organization of hatreds.   —HENRY ADAMS,
                                    The Education of Henry Adams, 1907

5   Knowledge of human nature is the beginning and end of political education.
                                                                        —*Ibid.*

6   Modern politics is, at bottom, a struggle not of men but of forces.   —*Ibid.*

7   Prosperity is necessarily the first theme of a political campaign.
                                    —WOODROW WILSON, speech, Sept. 4, 1912
    [See also James Carville at POLITICAL SLOGANS.]

8   Men who form the lunatic fringe in all reform movements.
                                    —THEODORE ROOSEVELT, *Autobiography*, 1913
    [The passage runs: "Among the wise and high-minded people who in self-
    respecting and genuine fashion strive earnestly for peace, there are the foolish
    fanatics always to be found in such a movement and always discrediting it—
    the men who form the lunatic fringe in all reform movements."]

9   In a smoke-filled room in some hotel.   —HARRY M. DAUGHERTY, quoted in
                                    The New York Times, Feb. 21, 1920
    [Daugherty was Warren G. Harding's campaign manager, and the *Times* quoted
    his prediction that at the Republican Convention in June, his candidate would
    be selected for the presidential nomination. "The convention will be dead-
    locked," he predicted, "and after the other candidates have gone their limit,
    some twelve or fifteen men, worn out and bleary-eyed for lack of sleep, will sit
    down around a table in a smoke-filled room in some hotel and decide the nom-
    ination. When that time comes, Harding will be selected." Daugherty later de-
    nied using the phrase "smoke-filled room," but he had the scenario right, and
    the smoke-filled room came to symbolize professional party politics.]

10 I never took a quarter from anyone who couldn't afford it.
                                    —JAMES CURLEY, quoted in Jack Beatty, *The Rascal King* [1993]
    [Mayor Curley of Boston was the model for Edwin O'Connor's Irish city boss,
    Frank Skeffington, in *The Last Hurrah*, 1956.]

11 I tell you folks, all politics is applesauce.
                                    —WILL ROGERS, *The Illiterate Digest*, 1924

12 Any party which takes credit for the rain must not be surprised if its opponents
    blame it for the drought.
                                    —DWIGHT W. MORROW, remark, quoted in William Safire,
                                    Safire's New Political Dictionary [1993]
    [A lawyer, banker, and diplomat, Morrow also was father of Anne Morrow
    Lindbergh.]

Politics has got so expensive that it takes a lot of money to even get beat with 1
nowadays.   —WILL ROGERS, *Daily Telegrams,* June 28, 1931

Politicians, after all, are not over a year behind public opinion.   2
        —WILL ROGERS, *The Autobiography of Will Rogers* [1949]
[And in another bit of faint praise: "Politicians are doing the best they can according to the dictates of no conscience"; quoted in Alex Ayres, ed., *The Wit and Wisdom of Will Rogers,* 1993.]

Politics is the best show in America.   —WILL ROGERS, *Weekly Articles,* 3
        Dec. 18, 1932

You can't adopt politics as a profession and remain honest.   4
        —LOUIS MCHENRY HOWE, speech, Jan. 17, 1933
[Howe was a trusted, invaluable aide to Franklin D. Roosevelt.]

The man who pulls the plow gets the plunder in politics.   5
        —HUEY P. LONG, speech, U.S. Senate, Jan. 30, 1934

A conservative is a man who has plenty of money and doesn't see any reason 6
why he shouldn't always have plenty of money. . . . A Democrat is a fellow
who never had any money but doesn't see why he shouldn't have some money.
        —WILL ROGERS, quoted in Alex Ayres, ed.,
        The Wit and Wisdom of Will Rogers [1993]

I am not a member of any organized political party—I am a Democrat.   7
        —WILL ROGERS, quoted in P. J. O'Brien, *Will Rogers,*
        Ambassador of Good Will, Prince of Wit and Wisdom, 1935
[Rogers also remarked, "You've got to be [an] optimist to be a Democrat, and
you've got be a humorist to stay one," *Gold Gulf* radio show, June 24, 1934.]

All politics is local.   8
        —THOMAS P. "TIP" O'NEILL, saying
[In his autobiography, *Man of the House,* O'Neill credited his father with this.
Tip O'Neill, Speaker of the House from 1977 to 1987, was the last of Boston's
larger-than-life Irish politicians.]

A liberal is a man who is willing to spend someone else's money.   9
        —CARTER GLASS, quoted in an Associated Press interview,
        Sept. 24, 1938
[This may not have been original with Sen. Glass, but as a newspaper publisher
he knew how to exploit a good line. Glass, a conservative Virginia Democrat,
staunchly opposed Pres. Franklin D. Roosevelt's New Deal, and fought for
states' rights and segregation.]

A radical is a man with both feet firmly planted in the air.   10
        —FRANKLIN D. ROOSEVELT, radio speech, Oct. 26, 1939

A conservative is a man with two perfectly good legs who, however, has never 11
learned how to walk forward.   —*Ibid.*

A reactionary is a somnambulist walking backward.   —*Ibid.* 12

a politician is an arse upon 13
which everyone has sat except a man.   —E. E. CUMMINGS, *a politician,* in
        One Times One (or *1 x 1*), 1944

1   The object of liberalism has never been to destroy capitalism . . . only to keep the capitalists from destroying it.
—ARTHUR M. SCHLESINGER, JR., *The Age of Jackson*, 1945

2   We mean by "politics" the people's business—the most important business there is.   —ADLAI STEVENSON, speech, Chicago, Nov. 19, 1955

3   An independent is a guy who wants to take the politics out of politics.
—ADLAI STEVENSON, *The Art of Politics*

4   Money is the mother's milk of politics.
—JESSE UNRUH, saying, quoted in *The New York Times*,
obituary, Aug. 6, 1987
[Unruh, speaker of the California assembly, was a dominant Democrat.]

5   Politics is not the art of the possible. It consists in choosing between the disastrous and the unpalatable.   —JOHN KENNETH GALBRAITH,
Ambassador's Journal, 1969
[Galbraith is referring to Otto von Bismarck's "Politics is the art of the possible, the attainable . . . the next best," conversation with Meyer von Waldeck, August 11, 1867.]

6   Sometimes party loyalty asks too much.
—JOHN F. KENNEDY, quoted in Arthur M. Schlesinger, Jr.,
A Thousand Days: John F. Kennedy in the White House [1965]

7   Political action is the highest responsibility of a citizen.
—JOHN F. KENNEDY, speech, Oct. 20, 1960

8   All politics are based on the indifference of the majority.
—JAMES RESTON, *New York Times*, June 12, 1968

9   The liberals can understand everything but people who don't understand them.
—LENNY BRUCE, in John Cohen, *Essential Lenny Bruce*, 1970

10   We campaign in poetry, but when we're elected, we're forced to govern in prose.   —MARIO CUOMO, speech, Yale University, 1985

11   A conservative is a liberal who's been mugged.
—ANONYMOUS, saying, 1980s
[The converse is: "A liberal is a conservative who's been arrested," quoted in Tom Wolfe, *The Bonfire of the Vanities*, 1987.]

12   Although he is regularly asked to do so, God does not take sides in American politics.   —GEORGE MITCHELL,
comment in Senate Select Committee
hearing on the Iran-Contra affair, July 1987
[Sen. Mitchell of Maine was reprimanding Col. Oliver North for implying that he and God were of the same mind on covert political activities. See also Lincoln at PRAYER and Barry Goldwater at GOD.]

13   Politics is knowing when to pull the trigger.
—MARIO PUZO, *Godfather III*, screenplay, 1990

POSSESSIONS   *See* LUXURY; THINGS & POSSESSIONS

POVERTY & HUNGER   *See also* ECONOMICS; MONEY & THE RICH; RICH & POOR, WEALTH & POVERTY

Light purse, heavy heart.   —BENJAMIN FRANKLIN, *Poor Richard's Almanack*, 1749   1

They are slaves who fear to speak   2
For the fallen and the weak.   —JAMES RUSSELL LOWELL, *Stanzas on Freedom*, 1843

Poverty demoralizes.   —RALPH WALDO EMERSON,   3
Wealth, in *The Conduct of Life*, 1860

Over the hill to the poor-house, I'm trudging my weary way.   4
—WILL CARLETON, *Over the Hill to the Poor-house*, in *Farm Ballads*, 1873

The awful phantom of the hungry poor.   —HARRIET PRESCOTT SPOFFORD,   5
A Winter's Night, c. 1875

Poverty indeed *is* the strenuous life—without brass bands, or uniforms, or hys-   6
teric popular applause, or lies, or circumlocutions.
—WILLIAM JAMES, *The Varieties of Religious Experience*, 1902
[James was referring to Theodore Roosevelt's call to all to take up the strenuous life; see PHYSICAL FITNESS.]

It's no disgrace t'be poor, but it might as well be.   7
—FRANK MCKINNEY "KIN" HUBBARD, *Short Furrows*, 1911

No man can worship God or love his neighbor on an empty stomach.   8
—WOODROW WILSON, speech, New York City, May 23, 1912

The forgotten man at the bottom of the economic pyramid.   9
—FRANKLIN D. ROOSEVELT, radio speech, April 7, 1932
[Roosevelt, then governor of New York, was speaking from Albany. In an eco-
nomic crisis that he compared to the war crises of 1917, he said that the nation
must regain faith in the forgotten man, and "build from the bottom up not the
top down." Roosevelt took the phrase from a famous 1885 speech by William
Graham Sumner; see under ECONOMICS. See also Roosevelt's Second Inaugural
Address, AMERICAN HISTORY: MEMORABLE MOMENTS.]

It's the anarchy of poverty   10
delights me.   —WILLIAM CARLOS WILLIAMS, *The Poor*

There is something about poverty that smells like death. Dead dreams drop-   11
ping off the heart like leaves in a dry season and rotting around the feet.
—ZORA NEALE HURSTON,
Dust Tracks on a Road, 1942

A hungry man is not a free man.   12
—ADLAI STEVENSON, speech, Sept. 6, 1952

If a free society cannot help the many who are poor, it cannot save the few who   13
are rich.   —JOHN F. KENNEDY, Inaugural Address, 1961

1   People who are much too sensitive to demand of cripples that they run races ask of the poor that they get up and act just like everyone else in socicty.
—MICHAEL HARRINGTON, *The Other America*, 1962

2   There is a monotony about the injustices suffered by the poor that perhaps accounts for the lack of interest the rest of society shows in them. Everything seems to go wrong with them. They never win. It's just boring.
—DWIGHT MACDONALD, review of Michael Harrington's
The Other America, in *The New Yorker*, 1963
[Macdonald's review helped to catalyze Lyndon B. Johnson's War on Poverty.]

3   This administration . . . declares unconditional war on poverty in America.
—LYNDON B. JOHNSON, State of the Union speech, Jan. 8, 1964
[More at AMERICAN HISTORY: MEMORABLE MOMENTS.]

4   We been down so long we got no way to go but up.
—FANNIE LOU HAMER, saying c. 1964,
quoted in *In This Affluent Society*,
television documentary, WNET [Jan. 16, 1995]
[Hamer was an influential African-American leader, one of the founders of the Mississippi Freedom Democratic Party, which, in 1972, unseated the regular delegation at the Democratic National Convention. Another saying associated with Hamer is "I'm sick and tired of being sick and tired."]

5   We could use less foreign aid and more home aid.
—PEARL BAILEY, *Pearl's Kitchen*, 1973

POWER   *See also* STRENGTH & TOUGHNESS; VIOLENCE; TYRANNY

6   I am more and more convinced that man is a dangerous creature and that power, whether vested in many or a few, is ever grasping, and like the grave, cries, "Give, Give."   —ABIGAIL ADAMS,
letter to John Adams, Nov. 27, 1775

7   In the general course of human nature, a power over a man's subsistence amounts to a power over his will.
—ALEXANDER HAMILTON, *The Federalist*, 1787–1788

8   An honest man can feel no pleasure in the exercise of power over his fellow citizens.   —THOMAS JEFFERSON, letter to John Melish, Jan. 13, 1813

9   Power always thinks it has a great soul and vast views beyond the comprehension of the weak, and that it is doing God's service, when it is violating all His laws.   —JOHN ADAMS, letter to Thomas Jefferson, Feb. 2, 1816

10 Where the people possess no authority, their rights obtain no respect.
—GEORGE BANCROFT, *To the Workingmen of Northampton*,
in the *Boston Courier*, Oct. 22, 1834

11 Power ceases in the instant of repose.
—RALPH WALDO EMERSON, *Self-Reliance*,
in *Essays: First Series*, 1841

12 You shall have joy, or you shall have power, said God; you shall not have both.
—RALPH WALDO EMERSON, *Journal*, Oct. 1842

Life is a search after power.

—RALPH WALDO EMERSON, *Power,*
in *The Conduct of Life,* 1860 1

Power is the first good.

—RALPH WALDO EMERSON, *Inspiration,* 2
in *Letters and Social Aims,* 1876

A friend in power is a friend lost. 3

—HENRY BROOKS ADAMS, *The Education of Henry Adams,* 1907

Power intoxicates men. It is never voluntarily surrendered. It must be taken 4
from them.

—JAMES F. BYRNES, quoted in *The New York Times,*
May 15, 1956

Power never takes a back step—only in the face of more power. 5

—MALCOLM X, *Malcolm X Speaks Out,* 1965

We have, I fear, confused power with greatness. 6

—STEWART UDALL, commencement speech,
Dartmouth College, 1965

Power is the great aphrodisiac. 7

—HENRY KISSINGER, in *The New York Times,* Jan. 19, 1971

PRAIRIES

See MIDWEST, THE

PRAYER

See also GOD; PRAYERS; RELIGION

In his prayers he says, thy will be done: but means his own, at least acts so. 8

—WILLIAM PENN, *Some Fruits of Solitude,* 1693

Prayer is the contemplation of the facts of life from the highest point of view. 9

—RALPH WALDO EMERSON, *Self-Reliance,*
in *Essays: First Series,* 1841

Prayer as a means to effect a private end is theft and meanness. *—Ibid.* 10

Of course—I prayed— 11
And did God care?
He cared as much as on the air
A bird—had stamped her foot
And cried, "Give me."

—EMILY DICKINSON, poem no. 376, c. 1862

Prayer is the little implement 12
Through which men reach
Where presence—is denied them.

—EMILY DICKINSON, poem no. 437, c. 1862

Both [North and South] read the same Bible, and pray to the same God; and 13
each invokes His aid against the other. It may seem strange that any men
should dare to ask a just God's assistance in wringing their bread from the
sweat of other men's faces; but let us judge not, that we be not judged.

—ABRAHAM LINCOLN, Second Inaugural Address, 1865

Prayer is not to be used as a confessional, to cancel sin. 14

—MARY BAKER EDDY, *Science and Health,*
with Key to the Scriptures, 1875

1   You can't pray a lie.   —MARK TWAIN, *Huckleberry Finn*, 1885

2   *Pray, v.* To ask that the rules of the universe be annulled in behalf of a single petitioner, confessedly unworthy.
                                    —AMBROSE BIERCE, *The Devil's Dictionary*, 1906

3   Prayer, among sane people, has never superseded practical efforts to secure the desired end.   —GEORGE SANTAYANA, *The Life of Reason: Reason in Religion*, 1905–1906.

4   The prayers of all good people are good.   —WILLA CATHER, *My Ántonia*, 1918

5   The trouble with our praying is, we just do it as a means of last resort.
                                    —WILL ROGERS,
                                    Weekly Articles, May 11, 1930

6   One of the greatest of all efficiency methods is prayer power.
                                    —NORMAN VINCENT PEALE,
                                    The Power of Positive Thinking, 1952
    [See also Rev. Peale at MIND, THOUGHT, & UNDERSTANDING.]

7   The only decent activity in the world [is] to pray for everyone, in solitude.
                                    —JACK KEROUAC, quoted in *The New York Times Book Review*
                                    [April 9, 1995]

8   Do not pray for easy lives. Pray to be stronger men.
                                    —JOHN F. KENNEDY, at a prayer breakfast,
                                    Washington, D.C., Feb. 7, 1963

PRAYERS & BLESSINGS

9   O my people,
    Honor thy god;
    Respect alike men great and humble;
    See to it that our aged, our women, and our children
    Lie down to sleep by the roadside
    Without fear of harm.
    Disobey, and die.   —KAMEHAMEHA I,
                                    Law of the Splintered Paddle
    [Kamehameha of Hawaii became king of his people in 1810.]

10 Lord, grant that I may always be right, for Thou knowest I am hard to turn.
                                    —ANONYMOUS
    [An anonymous Scotch-Irish prayer, quoted in *Truman* by David McCullough
    (1992).]

11 May you be in heaven for twenty minutes before the Devil discovers that you're dead.   —ANONYMOUS, Saint Patrick's Day greeting

12 God, give us grace to accept with serenity the things that cannot be changed, courage to change the things which should be changed, and the wisdom to distinguish the one from the other.
                                    —REINHOLD NIEBUHR, *The Serenity Prayer*, 1934

Give strength to their arms, stoutness to their hearts, steadfastness in their 1
faith.
     —FRANKLIN D. ROOSEVELT, D day prayer, June 6, 1944
[More at WORLD WAR II.]

I thank You God for most this amazing   2
day: for the leaping greenly spirits of trees
and a blue true dream of sky; and for everything
which is natural which is infinite which is yes.
    —E. E. CUMMINGS, *I Thank You God for Most This Amazing,*
     in *Xiape,* 1950

PREJUDICE   *See also* RACES & PEOPLES

No man is prejudiced in favor of a thing knowing it to be wrong. He is attached 3
to it on the belief of it being right.
     —THOMAS PAINE, *The Rights of Man,* 1791

It is never too late to give up our prejudices.   4
    —HENRY DAVID THOREAU, "Economy," *Walden,* 1854

We are chameleons, and our partialities and prejudices change places with an 5
easy and blessed facility. —MARK TWAIN, *When in Doubt, Tell the Truth,*
     in A. B. Paine, ed., *Speeches* [1923]

Prejudice, n. A vagrant opinion without visible means of support. 6
    —AMBROSE BIERCE, *The Devil's Dictionary,* 1906

Everyone is a prisoner of his own prejudices. No one can eliminate preju- 7
dices—just recognize them.   —EDWARD R. MURROW, Dec. 31, 1955

PRESENT, THE   *See also* MODERN TIMES; PAST, THE; TIME

The vanishing volatile froth of the present, which any shadow will alter, any 8
thought blow away, any event annihilate, is every moment converted into the
adamantine record of the past. —RALPH WALDO EMERSON, *Journal,* 1832

With the past, as past, I have nothing to do; nor with the future as future. I live 9
now, and will verify all past history in my own moments.   —*Ibid.*

We can see well into the past; we can guess shrewdly into the future; but that 10
which is rolled up and muffled in impenetrable folds is today.   —*Ibid.*

The dogmas of the quiet past are inadequate to the stormy present. 11
    —ABRAHAM LINCOLN, annual message to Congress, Dec. 1, 1862

Each day the world is born anew   12
For him who takes it rightly.
    —JAMES RUSSELL LOWELL, *Gold Egg: A Dream Fantasy,*
     in *Under the Willows and Other Poems,* 1868

Let anyone try . . . to notice or attend to the *present* moment of time. One of 13
the most baffling experiences occurs. Where is it, this present? It has melted in
our grasp, fled ere we could touch it, gone in the instant of becoming.
    —WILLIAM JAMES, *The Principles of Psychology,* 1890

1   We want to live in the present, and the only history that is worth a tinker's damn is the history we make today.
                                    —HENRY FORD, in the *Chicago Tribune*, May 25, 1916

2   The only living life is in the past and future—the present is an interlude—strange interlude in which we call on past and future to bear witness we are living.
                                    —EUGENE O'NEILL, *Strange Interlude*, 1928
    [See also the O'Neill quote from this play at LIFE.]

3   Exhaust the little moment. Soon it dies.
    And be it gash or gold it will not come
    Again in this identical guise.
                                    —GWENDOLYN BROOKS, *Exhaust the Little Moment*,
                                        in *Annie Allen*, 1949

4   Life is all memory, except for the one present moment that goes by you so quick you hardly catch it going.
                                    —TENNESSEE WILLIAMS,
                                    The Milk Train Doesn't Stop Here Any More, 1963

5   The word "now" is like a bomb through the window, and it ticks.
                                    —ARTHUR MILLER, *After the Fall*, 1964

6   Today is the first day of the rest of your life.
                                    —ANONYMOUS, saying, c. 1970s
    [This upbeat adage is sometime attributed to Charles Dederich, who founded Synanon in 1958. The reputation of this self-help community for substance abusers faded in the 1970s as Dederich and other members of the organization were charged with civil and criminal wrongdoing.]

7   Every day you wake up is a beautiful day.
                                    —JOHN WAYNE, quoted in Lauren Bacall, *Now* [1994]
    [The actor, dying of cancer, spoke in response to a movie crew member who said to him, "Boy, it's a beautiful day!"]

PRESIDENCY, THE

8   Every vital question of state will be merged in the question, "Who will be the next president?"   —ALEXANDER, HAMILTON, *The Federalist*, 1787–88

9   My movements to the chair of government will be accompanied by feelings not unlike those of a culprit who is going to the place of his execution.
                                    —GEORGE WASHINGTON, letter to Henry Knox, April 1, 1789

10   [The presidency] is but a splendid misery.
                                    —THOMAS JEFFERSON, letter to Elbridge Gerry, May 13, 1797
    [More at THE VICE PRESIDENCY.]

11   I have learned to expect that it will rarely fall to the lot of imperfect man to retire from this station with the reputation and the favor which bring him into it.
                                    —THOMAS JEFFERSON,
                                    First Inaugural Address, 1801

No man who ever held the office of president would congratulate a friend on   1
obtaining it. He will make one man ungrateful, and a hundred men his enemies, for every office he can bestow.
> —JOHN ADAMS, to his son John Quincy Adams,
> elected president in 1824

[Presidents were required to make hundreds of government appointments personally, a burden that was somewhat lightened with the establishment of the
Civil Service system in the 1880s. See James. A Garfield below.]

I can with truth say mine is a situation of dignified slavery.   2
> —ANDREW JACKSON, letter to Robert J. Chester, Nov. 30, 1829

The president is the direct representative of the American people . . . responsi-   3
ble to them.   —ANDREW JACKSON, message protesting his censure
> by the Senate, April 15, 1834

[This concept, a commonplace today, was daring in its time. Robert Remini, in
his biography of Jackson, describes the outrage among those who held that the
president was directly responsible to Congress. Daniel Webster immediately
counterattacked, referring to presidential accountability to the people as an
"airy and unreal responsibility." As for the president being the representative
of the people, Webster boomed, "This is not the language of the Constitution.
The Constitution no where calls him the representative of the American people; still less their direct representative. . . . I hold this, Sir, to be a mere assumption, and dangerous assumption."

The protest message was co-authored by Secretary of the Treasury Roger
Taney and Attorney General Benjamin Butler. The issue that led to censure
was the government's withdrawal of funds from the Bank of the United States.]

The farmer imagines power and place are fine things. But the president has   4
paid for his White House. It has commonly cost him all his peace and the best
of his manly attributes. To preserve for a short time so conspicuous an appearance before the world, he is content to eat dust before the real masters who
stand behind the throne.   —RALPH WALDO EMERSON, *Compensation,*
> in *Essays: First Series,* 1841

No president who performs his duties faithfully and conscientiously can have   5
any leisure.
> —JAMES K. POLK, diary, Sept. 1, 1847

[Polk also complained, "Though I occupy a very high position, I am the hardest working man in the country." Hard work took its toll, and he died three
months after leaving office. Polk, a Tennessee Democrat, had not sought the
office. He emerged as a compromise candidate when ex-president Martin Van
Buren of New York and Lewis Cass of Michigan deadlocked at the 1844 convention.]

I had rather be right than be president.   6
> —HENRY CLAY, speech, U. S. Senate, 1850

[Clay made this remark when taunted in the Senate for once again setting on a
course away from the White House. Clay had five times sought the presidency
without success. On this occasion, he was speaking in defense of the series of
resolutions originated by him in 1848 to avoid civil war over issues of slavery
and states' rights. The package of compromises collectively is now called the
Compromise of 1850.

In 1890, Rep. William McK. Springer, speaking in the House, resurrected
Clay's "I would rather be right than be president," and the Speaker, Thomas

Brackett Reed, known as "Czar Reed," retorted, "Well, the gentleman need not be disturbed. He will never be either." And referring to William Jennings Bryan, the Speaker said that he had "rather be wrong than president."]

1   If forced to choose between the penitentiary and the White House for four years, I would say the penitentiary, thank you.
—WILLIAM TECUMSEH SHERMAN, letter
to Gen. Henry W. Halleck, Sept. 1864
[Sherman's attitude stiffened further after observing the unhappy experience of his fellow warrior Ulysses S. Grant as president; see Sherman below.]

2   My God, what is there in this place that a man should ever want to get in it?
—JAMES A. GARFIELD, 1881
[Pres. Garfield suffered particularly from the importuning of job seekers. He wrote, "Once or twice I felt like crying out in the agony of my soul against the greed for office and its consumption of my time," quoted in *American Heritage* magazine, April 1974. A few weeks later, he was shot by a disgruntled office seeker; when he rallied, more office seekers rushed to his bedside; he died two months later.]

3   I will not accept if nominated, and will not serve if elected.
—WILLIAM TECUMSEH SHERMAN,
telegram to the Republican National Convention, 1884
[Commonly rendered as, "If nominated, I will not accept. If elected, I will not serve." But the simpler wording is as quoted by Sherman's son, Thomas. The convention nominated James G. Blaine, who lost to Grover Cleveland; see POLITICAL SLOGANS.]

4   Great men are not chosen president, firstly, because great men are rare in politics; secondly, because the method of choice does not bring them to the top; thirdly, because they are not, in quiet times, absolutely needed.
—JAMES BRYCE, *The American Commonwealth,* 1888

5   *Presidency, n.* The greased pig in the field game of American politics.
—AMBROSE BIERCE, *The Devil's Dictionary,* 1906

6   I'll be damned if I am not getting tired of this. It seems to be the profession of a president simply to hear other people talk.
—WILLIAM HOWARD TAFT, comment to an aide, 1910
[Quoted in *American Heritage* magazine, April 1974.]

7   My hat is in the ring.
—THEODORE ROOSEVELT, remark, Feb. 21, 1912
[Roosevelt, speaking during a railroad stop in Ohio, added, "The fight is on and I am stripped to the buff." On February 24, he wrote seven state governors: "I will accept the nomination for the presidency if it is tendered to me." Roosevelt ran as a third-party candidate against his former friend and fellow Republican, the incumbent president, William Howard Taft. His Progressive party was popularly called the Bull Moose party. It split the Republican vote, leading to the election of Woodrow Wilson.]

8   The White House is a bully pulpit.   —THEODORE ROOSEVELT,
remark to George Haven Putnam
[Putnam quoted this remark at his eulogy for Roosevelt at the Century Club in New York City, 1919; also cited in Hamilton Basso, *Mainstream.* In Putnam's introductory essay to *The Works of Theodore Roosevelt,* vol. 9, he explains

that he had accused the president of a tendency to preach, and Roosevelt had replied, "Yes, Haven, most of us enjoy preaching, and I've got such a bully pulpit."]

The president cannot be disturbed.   1
        —CHARLES E. HUGHES, JR., Nov. 1916
[Charles Evans Hughes, the Republican candidate for president, retired on election night in the belief that he had won. A New York reporter called after midnight to say tell him that, unexpectedly, the California vote looked close. Someone, evidently Hughes's son, put off the reporter as quoted above. "Well, when he wakes up," the reporter advised, "just tell him he isn't president." That was a guess, but a good one. Hughes did indeed lose to incumbent Woodrow Wilson.]

"Afther lookin' the candydates over," said Mr. Dooley, "an' studyin' their   2
qualifications carefully, I can't truthfully say that I see a prisidintial possibility
in sight."   —FINLEY PETER DUNNE, *Mr. Dooley on Baseball*,
        in *Mr. Dooley on Making a Will
        and Other Necessary Evils*, 1919

I do not choose to run for president in 1928.   3
       —CALVIN COOLIDGE, statement to reporters,
       at the White House, August 2, 1928

Every man has a few mental hair shirts and . . . presidents differ only by their   4
larger wardrobe.   —HERBERT HOOVER, letter to President Thompson
       of Ohio State University, 1930

[The presidency:] It is preeminently a place of moral leadership.   5
     —FRANKLIN D. ROOSEVELT, quoted in *The New York Times*,
     Sept. 11, 1932

The first twelve years are the hardest.   6
      —FRANKLIN D. ROOSEVELT, remark on the presidency,
      press conference, Jan. 19, 1945

You must not ask the president of the United States to get down in the gutter   7
with a guttersnipe.
          —HARRY S. TRUMAN, 1951
[This was Truman's response to a suggestion that he could destroy Sen. Joseph McCarthy by leaking a dossier on McCarthy's sex life. The remark was recorded by writer John Hersey, who was there, gathering material for a *New Yorker* profile of the president, and who included it in his *Aspects of the Presidency*, 1980. HST continued in this vein: "Nobody, not even the president of the United States, can approach too close to a skunk, in skunk territory, and expect to get anything out of it except a bad smell. If you think somebody is telling a big lie about you, the only way to answer is with the whole truth."]

They pick a president and then for four years they pick on him.   8
        —ADLAI STEVENSON, speech,
        August 28, 1952

He'll sit right here and he'll say do this, do that! And nothing will happen. Poor   9
Ike—it won't be a bit like the Army.
         —HARRY S. TRUMAN, Nov. 1952
[Truman made this remark after meeting with Gen. Dwight D. Eisenhower,

the president-elect. The quote is from Margaret Truman's biography of her father.]

1   The president is the representative of the whole nation, and he's the only lobbyist that all the 160 million people in this country have.
—HARRY S. TRUMAN, speech, Columbia University,
April 27, 1959
[For Truman's reaction when he first inherited the presidency, see AMERICAN HISTORY: MEMORABLE MOMENTS. And for some negative reactions to his performance in office, see INSULTS.]

2   No *easy* problems ever come to the president of the United States. If they are easy to solve, someone else has solved them.
—DWIGHT D. EISENHOWER, quoted by John F. Kennedy
in *Parade* magazine, April 8, 1962

3   The function and responsibility of the president is to set before the American people the unfinished business, the things we must do if we are going to succeed as a nation.   —JOHN F. KENNEDY, comment,
Crestwood, Mo., Oct. 22, 1960

4   In the White House, the future rapidly becomes the past; and delay is itself a decision.   —THEODORE SORENSEN, *Nation's Business*, June 1963

5   The office of the presidency is the only office in this land of all the people.
—LYNDON B. JOHNSON, speech, 1964

6   A president's hardest task is not do what is right but to know what is right.
—LYNDON B. JOHNSON, State of the Union speech, 1965

7   The White House is another world. Expediency is everything.
—JOHN W. DEAN III,
quoted by Mary McGrory,
New York Post, June 18, 1973
[See also WATERGATE.]

8   He must summon his people to be with him—yet stand above, not squat beside them. He must question his own wisdom and judgment but not too severely. He must hear the opinion and heed the powers of others—but not too abjectly. He must be aggressive without being contentious, decisive without being arrogant, and compassionate without being confused.
—EMMET JOHN HUGHES,
The Living Presidency, 1973

9   When the president does it, that means that it is not illegal.
—RICHARD M. NIXON, television interview
with David Frost, May 4, 1977
[Pres. Nixon was speaking of his approval of a domestic surveillance plan that involved burglaries and opening mail.]

10   Remembering him [Truman] reminds people what a man in that office ought to be like. It's character, just character. He stands like a rock in memory now.
—ERIC SEVAREID, interview
[News analyst Sevareid was interviewed by David McCullough for *Truman*, 1992.]

PRESS, THE *See also* ADVERTISING, ADVERTISING SLOGANS, & PUBLICITY; CENSORSHIP; CONSTITUTION, THE (Potter Stewart); FREE SPEECH; MEDIA

The freedom of the press is one of the great bulwarks of liberty, and can never be restrained but by despotic governments. 1
  —GEORGE MASON, *Virginia Bill of Rights*, June 12, 1776

The liberty of the press is essential to the security of the state. 2
  —JOHN ADAMS, Free-Press Clause, Massachusetts Constitution, 1780

Our liberty depends on the freedom of the press, and that cannot be limited without being lost. 3
  —THOMAS JEFFERSON, letter to Dr. J. Currie, 1786
[Jefferson was keenly aware of the faults of the press. Just before the quote above, he wrote, "I deplore . . . the putrid state into which the newspapers have passed," but added, "It is, however, an evil for which there is no remedy."]

Were it left to me to decide whether we should have a government without newspapers, or newspapers without a government, I should not hesitate a moment to prefer the latter. 4
  —THOMAS JEFFERSON, letter to Col. Edward Carrington, Jan. 16, 1787

No government ought to be without censors; and where the press is free, no one ever will. 5
  —THOMAS JEFFERSON, letter to George Washington, 1792

It is better to leave a few of its [the press's] noxious branches to their luxuriant growth, than by pruning them away, to injure the vigor of those yielding the proper fruits. 6
  —JAMES MADISON, *Report on the Virginia Resolutions, 1799–1800*, in Jonathan Elliot, *Debates on the Adoption of the Federal Constitution* [1876]

Nothing can now be believed which is seen in a newspaper. 7
  —THOMAS JEFFERSON, letter to J. Norville, 1807
[Newspapers, incidentally, were more vicious in Jefferson's day than now, with less regard for the truth. Later in this letter, Pres. Jefferson suggested: "Perhaps an editor might begin a reformation in some way such as this. Divide his paper into four chapters, heading the 1st, Truths. 2nd, Probabilities. 3d, Possibilities. 4th, Lies. the first chapter would be very short."
  He also claimed, "The man who never looks into a newspaper is better informed than he who reads them, inasmuch as he who knows nothing is nearer to the truth than he whose mind is filled with falsehoods and errors."]

The only security of all is in a free press. 8
  —THOMAS JEFFERSON, letter to Marquis de Lafayette, 1823
[See also Jefferson's letter to Charles Yancey under EDUCATION.]

We live under a government of men and morning newspapers. 9
  —WENDELL PHILLIPS, speech, Jan. 28, 1852

I will never again command an army in America if we must carry along paid spies. I will banish myself to some foreign country first. 10
  —WILLIAM TECUMSEH SHERMAN, letter to his wife, Feb. 1863
[Sherman hated the press not only because of news reports critical of him, but

also because he thought that reporters provided intelligence to the Confederates either privately or in the course of reporting news. He is said to have complained, "Napoleon himself would have been defeated with a free press." He
came close to executing one journalist as a spy; Pres. Lincoln intervened.]

1   It is a newspaper's duty to print the news and raise hell.
                                        —THE CHICAGO TIMES, 1861

2   The average consumption of newspapers by an American must amount to
     about three a day.   —ANTHONY TROLLOPE, *North America*, 1862

3   When a dog bites a man that is not news. But when a man bites a dog, that is
     news.
                    —CHARLES A. DANA, "What Is News?" New York *Sun*, 1882
     [Dana was the owner and publisher of the *Sun*, the top newspaper of its era. Its
     motto was "If you see it in the *Sun* it's so." The quote is sometimes attributed
     to *Sun* editor John B. Bogart, as in Frank M. O'Brien's *The Story of the Sun*,
     where the statement runs: "When a dog bites a man that is not news, because
     it happens so often. But if a man bites a dog, that is news."]

4   Newspapers are read at the breakfast and dinner tables. God's great gift to man
     is appetite. Put nothing in the paper that will destroy it.
                            —W. R. NELSON, quoted by H. L. Mencken,
                                A New Dictionary of Quotations [1942]
     [Nelson was the publisher of the *Kansas City Star.*]

5   All the news that's fit to print.   —ADOLPH SIMON OCHS,
                                    motto of *The New York Times*, 1896
     [Ochs made the point in full in a speech upon assuming ownership of the paper
     on August 18, 1896. "It will be my earnest aim that the *New York Times* give
     the news, all the news, in concise and attractive form, in language that is per-
     missible in good society." He also pledged that the paper would give the news
     early, and "impartially, without fear or favor, regardless of party, sect, or inter-
     est involved," and that the paper would provide a forum for "intelligent dis-
     cussion from all shades of opinion."
          Similar idealistic statements from the same period include: "We shall tell no
     lies about persons or policies for love, malice, or money," E. W. Scripps,
     founder of the Scripps-Howard chain; C. L. Knight, founder of the present
     Knight-Ridder chain, told his son, John, "Better you should set fire to your
     plant, and leave town by the light of it, than to remain a human cash-register
     editor." According to Joan Konner, who cited these comments in a paper,
     Is Journalism Losing Its Standards?, excerpted in the *Columbia Journalism
     Review*, Nov./Dec. 1995, owners today no longer lead the way on standards.]

6   The report of my death has been grossly exaggerated.
                            —MARK TWAIN, quoted in a cable from London,
                                            Associated Press, 1897
     [The *New York Journal* ran the story on June 2, with the quote as, "The re-
     port of my death was an exaggeration." The press had confused Twain with
     his cousin Dr. James Ross Clemens, who had been ill in London when
     Twain, too, was there. Reports circulated that Twain himself was near death
     or indeed dead. A young Associated Press reporter, sent to check on the
     writer's health, showed Twain his cabled instructions: "If Mark Twain very
     ill, five hundred words. If dead, send one thousand." Twain handed back the ca-
     ble, saying, "You don't need as much as that. Just say the report of my death

has been grossly exaggerated." The young man took this seriously and was almost back at his office before he saw the joke, which he then relayed to the world.]

Most people don't think for themselves. They lean on newspapers.   1
       —THOMAS J. PENDERGAST, saying quoted in David McCullough,
       Truman [1992]
[Pendergast, the "Big Boss" of Kansas City, sponsored the young Harry Truman. See also Pendergast at WISDOM, WORDS OF.]

Th' newspaper does ivrything f'r us. It . . . comforts th' afflicted, afflicts th'   2
comfortable, buries th' dead an' roasts thim aftherward.
       —FINLEY PETER DUNNE, *Observations by Mr. Dooley,* 1902
[In the omitted section of the quote, Mr. Dooley observes that newspapers also run the police, and banks, and the military, and the legislature, as well as baptizing the young and marrying the foolish. The reference to affliction is based on the adage, "The duty of a newspaper is to comfort the afflicted and afflict the comfortable."]

The first duty of an editor is to gauge the sentiment of his readers, and then tell   3
them what they like to believe. . . . His second duty is to see that nothing is said in the news items or editorials which may discountenance any claims made by his advertisers, discredit their standing or good faith, or expose any weakness or deception in any business venture that is or may become a valuable advertiser.
       —THORSTEIN VEBLEN, *The Theory of Business Enterprise,* 1904

I don't care what the papers say about me as long as they spell my name right.   4
       —"BIG TIM" SULLIVAN, saying
[The thought also has been attributed to P. T. Barnum, George M. Cohan, Samuel Goldwyn, and others. Sullivan, by the way, was a Tammany Hall luminary around the turn of the century—the 19th to 20th century. One of his political colleagues was "Little Tim" Sullivan. Big Tim is remembered as one of the first large-scale political bosses. Later in life, he experienced a decline, possibly due to Alzheimer's. He was found dead on train tracks in Eastchester, N.Y., and was not immediately identified. He is responsible for making Columbus Day a legal holiday in New York and for making it a felony to carry a concealed weapon.]

The men with the muckrakes are often indispensable to the wellbeing of soci-   5
ety, but only if they know when to stop raking the muck, and to look upward to the celestial crown above them. . . . If they gradually grow to feel that the whole world is nothing but muck, their power of usefulness is gone.
       —THEODORE ROOSEVELT, speech for the laying of the
       cornerstone of the House Office Building, April 14, 1906
[Roosevelt popularized the term "muckraker" for those who expose society's ills. His patience with muckrackers wore thin with the publication of David Graham Phillips's series of articles titled *The Treason of the Senate.* The term *muckraker* comes from John Bunyan's *The Pilgrim's Progress* (1678): "A man that could look no way but downwards with a muckrake in his hand."]

Sunlight is said to be the best of disinfectants.   6
       —LOUIS D. BRANDEIS, *What Publicity Can Do,*
       in *Harper's Weekly,* Dec. 20, 1913
[More at MEDIA.]

1   [Editor:] A person employed on a newspaper, whose business it is to separate the wheat from the chaff and see to it that the chaff is printed.
—ELBERT HUBBARD, *Roycroft Dictionary and Book of Epigrams*, 1923

2   All I know is just what I read in the newspapers.
—WILL ROGERS, saying, used as a lead-in for his comedy and commentary routines

3   The funnies occupy four pages of the paper and editorials two columns. That proves that merit will tell.
—WILL ROGERS, *Weekly Articles*, August 2, 1925

4   [Strategy for dealing with the press during World War II:] Don't tell them a thing. After it's over, tell them who won.
—ERNEST J. KING, cited by Christopher Buckley, *New York Times Book Review* [March 12, 1995]
[Admiral King was Chief of Naval Operations.]

5   The difference between burlesque and the newspapers is that the former never pretended to be performing a public service by exposure.
—I. F. STONE, *I. F. Stone's Weekly*, Sept. 7, 1952

6   People everywhere confuse
What they read in the newspapers with news.
—A. J. LIEBLING, *A Talkative Something or Other*, in *The New Yorker*, April 7, 1956

7   Freedom of the press is guaranteed only to those who own one.
—A. J. LIEBLING, *Do You Belong in Journalism?* in *The New Yorker*, May 14, 1960

8   If the myth gets bigger than the man, print the myth.
—DOROTHY JOHNSON, *The Man Who Shot Liberty Valance*
[John Ford directed the 1962 movie based on this book, adapted by Warner Bellan and Willis Goldbeck.]

9   Once a newspaper touches a story, the facts are lost forever, even to the protagonists.
—NORMAN MAILER, in *Esquire*, June 1960

10 A good newspaper . . . is a nation talking to itself.
—ARTHUR MILLER, in *The Observer*, Nov. 26, 1961

11 [Journalism:] The first rough draft of history.
—PHILIP GRAHAM, April 29, 1963
[A popular shortening of remarks by the *Washington Post*'s publisher to *Newsweek* correspondents in London. The full sentence is: "So let us today drudge on about our inescapably impossible task of providing every week a first rough draft of a history that will never be completed about a world we can never really understand."]

12 The press is the enemy.
—RICHARD M. NIXON, remark to aides, 1969
[The same year, he also observed, "If we treat the press with a little more contempt, we'll probably get better treatment."]

Only a fool expects the authorities to tell him what the news is.   1
                —RUSSELL BAKER, *The Good Times*, 1989

PRIDE & VANITY

Pride is said to be the last vice the good man gets clear of.   2
       —BENJAMIN FRANKLIN, *Poor Richard's Almanack*, 1732–57

Pride breakfasted with Plenty, dined with Poverty, and supped with Infamy.   3
                         —*Ibid.*

Pride costs us more than hunger, thirst, and cold.   4
             —THOMAS JEFFERSON, "A Decalogue of Canons
              for observation in practical life,"
              letter to Thomas Jefferson Smith, Feb. 21, 1825

Pride ruined the angels.   5
        —RALPH WALDO EMERSON, *The Sphinx*, in *The Dial*, Jan. 1841

There was one who thought he was above me, and he was above me until he   6
had that thought.   —ELBERT HUBBARD,
             Roycroft Dictionary and Book of Epigrams, 1923

I never wanted to be a crumb. If I had to be a crumb, I'd rather be dead.   7
         —SALVATORE "LUCKY" LUCIANO, quoted in
         Richard Norton Smith, *Thomas E. Dewey* [1982]

Half of the harm that is done in this world   8
Is due to people who want to feel important.
            —T. S. ELIOT, *The Cocktail Party*, 1950

When you've got it, flaunt it.   9
           —MEL BROOKS, *The Producers*, screenplay, 1968

I'm the straw that stirs the drink.   10
         —REGGIE JACKSON, remark in spring training
           with the Yankees, May 1977
[In the 1977 World Series, on October 18, Jackson hit three consecutive home
runs, on the first pitches from three different pitchers.]

PRIVACY   *See also* SECRETS; SECURITY & SAFETY;
                      SOLITUDE & LONELINESS

One of the most essential branches of English liberty is the freedom of one's   11
house. A man's house is his castle; and whilst he is quiet, he is as well guarded
as a prince in his castle.
         —JAMES OTIS, argument on the Writs of Assistance,
         Boston, 1761
[The Writs of Assistance allowed customs officers to break into ships, shops,
houses, or any place in search of smuggled goods. In opposition, Otis referred
to an axiom of common law, also stated by the great English jurist Sir Edward
Coke: "For a man's house is his castle, *et domus sua cuique tutissimum
refugium*," *Third Institute*, 1644. The Latin translates, "One's home is the
safest refuge to everyone." This comes from the ancient world, *The Pandects*,
or *Digest of Justinian*.]

1   The saint and poet seek privacy.   —RALPH WALDO EMERSON, *Culture,*
                                                         in *The Conduct of Life,* 1860
[The full sentence is: "The saint and poet seek privacy to ends the most public and universal."]

2   The right to be let alone—the most comprehensive of rights and the right most valued by civilized men.
                                       —LOUIS D. BRANDEIS, *Olmstead v. the U.S.,* 1928
[Justice Brandeis wrote that the framers of the Constitution conferred this right upon individuals as against the government. See also Justice Holmes's dissent at EVIDENCE.]

3   Civilization is the progress toward a society of privacy.
                                       —AYN RAND, *The Fountainhead,* 1943

4   Gentlemen do not read each other's mail.
                             —HENRY L. STIMSON, *On Active Service in Peace and War,*
                                       with McGeorge Bundy, 1948
[The former Secretary of State gave this as his reason for closing down American codebreaking operations in 1929 by withdrawing department support from the Military Information Department's Cipher Bureau, informally known as the American Black Chamber. Such high-minded considerations now seem quaint. As longtime CIA Director Alan Dulles said in *The Craft of Intelligence* (1963): "When the fate of a nation and the lives of its soldiers are at stake, gentlemen do read each other's mail—if they can get their hands on it." In any case, after 1929, the Army and Navy continued to work on codes and code breaking, with the result that the U.S. learned to read Japanese and German coded messages during World War II.]

5   We are rapidly entering the age of no privacy, where everyone is open to surveillance at all times; where there are no secrets from government.
                                       —WILLIAM O. DOUGLAS, dissenting opinion,
                                       Osborn v. the United States, 1966

6   If the right of privacy means anything, it is the right of the *individual,* married or single, to be free from unwarranted governmental intrusion into matters so fundamentally affecting a person as the decision whether to bear or beget a child.
                                       —WILLIAM J. BRENNAN, JR., *Eisenstadt v. Baird,* 1972
[This ruling, which applied to contraception, carried forward the Supreme Court's precedent in another contraception case, *Griswold v. Connecticut,* 1965, in which Justice William O. Douglas wrote, "Would we allow the police to search the sacred precincts of marital bedrooms for telltale signs of contraceptives?" Justice Brennan's decision prefigured the court's landmark decision in *Roe v. Wade* the following year; see AMERICAN HISTORY: MEMORABLE MOMENTS.
    The court's support of a person's right to choice in reproduction ran counter to a 1927 decision, in *Buck v. Bell,* which upheld compulsory sterilization of a reputedly retarded woman whose family allegedly had a history of retardation. "Three generations of imbeciles are enough," concluded Justice Oliver Wendell Holmes, Jr. Recent research has suggested that the woman targeted here, Carrie Buck, and her daughter, who died young, actually may have been of normal intelligence, and certainly were not imbeciles. The *Buck* decision is an embarrassment; Holmes's belief in eugenics evidently clouded his judgment.]

The right of privacy . . . is broad enough to encompass a woman's decision   1
whether or not to terminate her pregnancy.

—HARRY A. BLACKMUN, *Roe v. Wade,* 1973

[The Court's conclusion is given at AMERICAN HISTORY: MEMORABLE MOMENTS.]

PROBLEMS

See also TROUBLE

Problems are only opportunities in work clothes.   —HENRY J. KAISER, saying   2

Our problems are man-made. Therefore, they can be solved by man.   3

—JOHN F. KENNEDY, speech, The American University,
June 10, 1963

All progress is precarious, and the solution of one problem brings us face to   4
face with another problem.

—MARTIN LUTHER KING, JR., *Strength to Love,* 1963

You're either part of the solution or part of the problem.   5

—ELDRIDGE CLEAVER, saying, attributed, c. 1968

[*Bartlett's* cites a 1968 speech in San Francisco, not further identified. Making
a point somewhat similar to Cleaver's, Buell Gallagher, president of the City
College of New York, told the graduating class of 1964, "Be part of the answer,
not part of the problem, as the American revolution proceeds."]

PROCRASTINATION

See DELAY; INDECISION

PROFESSIONS

See DOCTORS & MEDICINE; LAWYERS;
NEW JERSEY (William Byrd)

PROGRESS

See also CIVILIZATION

And step by step, since time began,   6
I see the steady gain of man.   —JOHN GREENLEAF WHITTIER,
The Chapel of the Hermits, 1851

Every step of progress the world has made has been from scaffold to scaffold,   7
and from stake to stake.   —WENDELL PHILLIPS, speech, Oct, 15, 1851

Human progress is furthered, not by conformity, but by aberration.   8

—H. L. MENCKEN,
Prejudices: Third Series, 1922

Life means progress, and progress means suffering.   9

—HENDRIK WILLEM VAN LOON, *Tolerance,* 1925

Progress might have been all right once, but it has gone on too long.   10

—OGDEN NASH, attributed

Pity this busy monster, manunkind,   11
not. Progress is a comfortable disease.

—E. E. CUMMINGS, *Pity this busy monster, manunkind,*
in *One Times One* (or *1 x 1*), 1944

1   All progress has resulted from people who took unpopular positions.
                    —ADLAI E. STEVENSON, speech at Princeton University,
                    March 22, 1954
    [Robert Ingersoll put it: "The history of progress is written in the lives of infi-
    dels," in a speech in New York City, May 1, 1881.]

2   Progress imposes not only new possibilities for the future but new restrictions.
                    —NORBERT WIENER, *The Human Use of Human Beings*, 1954
    [Wiener, a leading mathematician and pioneer in the mathematics of computer
    theory, originated the term *cybernetics*, from the Greek word for "helmsman."]

3   All progress is precarious.
                    —MARTIN LUTHER KING, JR., *Strength to Love*, 1963
    [More at PROBLEMS.]

4   There can be no progress if people have no faith in tomorrow.
                    —JOHN F. KENNEDY, *Berlin East and West*,
                    in *The Pursuit of Justice*, 1964

5   Progress robs us of past delights.   —SAM ERVIN, JR.,
                                            Humor of a Country Lawyer, 1983
    [Sen. Ervin, a Democrat from North Carolina, was the chairman of the Senate
    committee that investigated the Watergate scandal in 1973. He was given to
    prefacing needle-sharp observations with the comment, "I'm just a country
    lawyer." See also WATERGATE.]

6   We have made progress in everything, yet nothing has changed.
                    —DERRICK BELL, *And We Are Not Saved*, 1987
    [Bell, a professor at Harvard University Law School, took a leave of absence, de-
    manding that a minority woman be appointed to the faculty. He was dis-
    missed.]

PROVERBS   *See* QUOTATIONS & PROVERBS

PRUDENCE & PRACTICAL WISDOM   *See* WISDOM, WORDS OF

PSYCHOLOGY   *See* SCIENCE: PSYCHOLOGY

PUBLICITY   *See* ADVERTISING, ADVERTISING SLOGANS,
                                    & PUBLICITY; MEDIA; PRESS, THE

PUBLIC OPINION & THE PUBLIC   *See also* PEOPLE, THE

7   The public must and will be served.
                    —WILLIAM PENN, *Some Fruits of Solitude*, 1693

8   I have learned to hold popular opinion of no value.
                    —ALEXANDER HAMILTON, letter to George Washington, 1794

9   Public opinion in this country is everything.
                    —ABRAHAM LINCOLN, speech, Columbus, Ohio, Sept. 16, 1859
    [Lincoln gave public opinion considerable weight in his deliberations. Prior to
    this statement, he observed, "A universal feeling, whether well or ill founded,
    cannot be safely disregarded," speech, Peoria, Ill., October 16, 1854. Similarly,

"With public sentiment, nothing can fail; without it, nothing can succeed," speech, Ottawa, Ill., July 31, 1858.]

The public be damned.   —WILLIAM H. VANDERBILT,   1
                                comment to a news reporter, Oct. 2, 1882
[More at BUSINESS.]

There is nothing that makes more cowardly and feeble men than public opin- 2
ion.   —HENRY WARD BEECHER, *Proverbs from Plymouth Pulpit*, 1887

The most dangerous thing for a bad cause is to expose it to the opinion of the 3
world. The most certain way that you can prove that a man is mistaken is by
letting all his neighbors know what he thinks, by letting all his neighbors discuss what he thinks, and if he is in the wrong you will notice that he will stay
at home, he will not walk on the street. He will be afraid of their judgment of
his character.
                                —WOODROW WILSON, speech, Pueblo, Colo., 1919
[For another favorable comment on public opinion, see Mark Twain at ART:
CRITICISM.]

We are ruled by public opinion, not by statute law.   4
                                —ELBERT HUBBARD, *The Note Book*, 1927

There is no group in America that can withstand the force of an aroused pub- 5
lic opinion.   —FRANKLIN D. ROOSEVELT, remark on signing the National
                       Industrial Recovery Act, June 16, 1933

QUESTIONS & ANSWERS

1   *Who* are we? *Where* are we?
                                    —HENRY DAVID THOREAU, *Ktaadn*, written 1848,
                                        in *The Maine Woods* [1864]
[The whole passage reads: Talk of mysteries! Think of our life in nature—daily
to be shown matter, to come in contact with it—rocks, trees, wind on our
cheeks! the *solid* earth! the *actual* world! the *common sense! Contact! Contact! Who* are we? *Where* are we?"]

2   And so I leave it to all of you:
Which came out of the opened door,—the lady, or the tiger?
                                    —FRANK R. STOCKTON, *The Lady or the Tiger,*
                                        in *Century Magazine,* Nov. 1882
[Originally called *The King's Arena,* this enormously popular tale has become
an American classic. The story involves a young hero who dares to fall in love
with a king's daughter, and she responds in kind. The cruel king, after discovering the romance, condemns the youth to enter a great arena and open one of
two doors. Behind one is a beautiful maiden whom he may marry; behind the
other is a tiger. The princess learns which door conceals what. She directs her
beloved to open the door on the right. And then the fable ends with the famous
query.]

3   The outcome of any serious research can only be to make two questions grow
where only one grew before.
                                    —THORSTEIN VEBLEN, *The Place of Science
                                        in Modern Civilization and Other Essays,* 1919

4   Who he?
                                    —HAROLD ROSS, editorial query
[Ross, the first editor of *The New Yorker,* was famous for irreverent questions,
this being one of his favorites. In a birthday tribute to Ross, Roger Angell
asked, "Who we?," *The New Yorker,* Nov. 9, 1992.]

5   To ask the hard question is simple.   —W. H. AUDEN, poem no. 27, *Poems,*
                                        1933

It is better to ask some of the questions than to know all of the answers.   1
—James Thurber, The Scottie Who Knew Too Much,
in The Thurber Carnival, 1945

What is the answer? [*I was silent.*] In that case, what is the question?   2
—Gertrude Stein, last words, 1946,
reported in Alice B. Toklas, What Is Remembered [1963]

Does she or doesn't she?—   3
—Shirley Polykoff, advertisement for Miss Clairol, 1955

[The men who ran *Life* magazine were so troubled by this provocative line that they rejected the ad for the hair tint when it was originally submitted by Foote, Cone & Belding. Polykoff got them to accept it by suggesting that they poll women staffers, who proved to be less offended than their male bosses had expected. See also the Anonymous entry at Reputation.]

The questions which one asks oneself begin, at last, to illuminate the world,   4
and become one's key to the experience of others.
—James Baldwin, Nobody Knows My Name, 1961

The answer, my friend, is blowin' in the wind.   5
—Bob Dylan, Blowin' in the Wind, 1962

There aren't any embarrassing questions—just embarrassing answers.   6
—Carl Rowan, The New Yorker, Dec. 7, 1963

[Journalists find this a useful defense when criticized for asking impertinent questions. Sydney Harris, in the *Chicago Daily News,* March 27, 1958, wrote "More trouble is caused in the world by indiscreet answers than by indiscreet questions."]

Some questions don't have answers, which is a terribly difficult lesson to learn.   7
—Katharine Graham, quoted by Jane Howard,
Ms. Magazine, Oct. 1974

Quotations & Proverbs   *See also* Wisdom, Words of

Nothing gives an author so much pleasure as to find his works respectfully   8
quoted by other learned authors.
—Benjamin Franklin, Poor Richard's Almanack, 1758

I hate quotation. Tell me what you know.   9
—Ralph Waldo Emerson, Journal, May 1849

Proverbs are the sanctuary of the intuitions.   10
—Ralph Waldo Emerson, Compensation,
in Essays: First Series, 1841

Though old the thought and oft expressed,   11
'Tis his at last who says it best.
—James Russell Lowell, For an Autograph, 1868

The use of proverbs is characteristic of an unlettered people. They are invalu-   12
able treasures to dunces with good memories.
—John Hay, Castilian Days, 1871

[Hay was a private secretary to Lincoln, and later was posted to Spain. He served as Secretary of State under presidents William McKinley and

Theodore Roosevelt and framed the Open Door policy; see under FOREIGN
POLICY.]

1   Next to the originator of a good sentence is the first quoter of it.
                              —RALPH WALDO EMERSON, *Quotation and Originality,*
                                  in *Letters and Social Aims,* 1876
     [For a different type of quotation, see Emerson at GENERATIONS.]

2   By necessity, by proclivity, and by delight, we all quote.
                              —RALPH WALDO EMERSON, *Ibid.*

3   [Proverbs:] the ready money of human experience.
                              —JAMES RUSSELL LOWELL, *My Study Windows,* 1871

4   Famous remarks are very seldom quoted correctly.
                              —SIMEON STRUNSKY, *No Mean City,* 1944

R

RACES & PEOPLES   *See also* CITIES (New York City, quotes on Harlem);
INJUSTICE; MAJORITIES & MINORITIES; NATIONS;
RESISTANCE; SLAVERY

I believe the Indian to be in body and mind equal to the white man.   1
                    —THOMAS JEFFERSON, letter to François Jean de Beauvoir,
                        Chevalier de Chastellux, June 7, 1785

These lands are ours. No one has a right to remove us, because we were the   2
first owners. The Great Spirit above has appointed this place for us, on which
to light our fires, and here we will remain.
                                        —TECUMSEH, 1810
[The Shawnee chief sent this message to Pres. James Madison via Joseph Bar-
ron. See also Tecumseh at RESISTANCE.]

When the white man had warmed himself before the Indians' fire and filled   3
himself with their hominy, he became very large. With a step he bestrode the
mountains, and his feet covered the plains and the valleys. His hand grasped
the eastern and western sea, and his head rested on the moon.
                                        —SPECKLED SNAKE, speech, 1829
[The Creek leader was reacting to Pres. Andrew Jackson's plan to move the
Cherokees, Chickasaws, Chocktaws, Creeks, and Seminoles west of the Mississippi River; see Jackson at SUPREME COURT.]

Brothers, I have listened to a great many talks from our great father, but they   4
always began and ended in this: "Get a little further; you are too near me."
                                        —*Ibid.*

We first crush people to the earth, and then claim the right of trampling on   5
them forever, because they are prostrate.
                    —LYDIA MARIA CHILD, *An Appeal on Behalf of That Class
                        of Americans Called Africans*, 1833

We told them [the white men] to let us alone, and keep away from us; but they   6
followed on, and beset our paths, and they coiled themselves among us like the
snake.   —BLACK HAWK, speech, Prairie du Chien, Wisc., August 1835

1   The danger of a conflict between the white and the black inhabitants perpetually haunts the imagination of the Americans like a bad dream.

—ALEXIS DE TOCQUEVILLE,
Democracy in America, 1835

2   The Indian . . . stands free and unconstrained in nature, is her inhabitant and
not her guest, and wears her easily and gracefully. But the civilized man has the
habits of the house. His house is a prison.

—HENRY DAVID THOREAU, *Journal*, April 26, 1841

3   Their name is on your water—
Ye may not wash it out.

—LYDIA HUNTLEY SIGOURNEY,
Indian Names, 1841

4   If the Negro be a soul, if the woman be a soul, apparelled in flesh, to one master only are they accountable.

—MARGARET FULLER, *The Great Lawsuit: Man versus Men,
Woman versus Women*, in *The Dial*, July 1843

5   They [the Irish] are looked upon with contempt for their want of aptitude in
learning new things; their ready and ingenious lying; their eye-service. These
are the faults of an oppressed race, which must require the aid of better circumstances through two or three generations to eradicate.

—MARGARET FULLER, untitled essay, in Alice Rossi, ed.,
The Feminist Papers [1973]

6   The doom of extinction is over this wretched nation [the Indians in the Oregon
Territory]. The hand of Providence is removing them to give place to a people
more worthy of so beautiful and fertile a country.

—GUSTAVUS HINES, 1850
[Hines was a Methodist minister. With the influx of white people along the
Oregon Trail, the Indians in their path died in huge numbers of smallpox,
cholera, measles, and other diseases to which they had no immunity. This
quote was cited in *The New York Times*, June 1, 1993.]

7   When the last red man shall have vanished from this earth, and his memory is
only a story among the whites, these shores will still swarm with the invisible
dead of my people. And when your children's children think they are alone in
the fields, the forests, the shops, the highways, or the quiet of the woods, they
will not be alone. . . . Your lands will throng with the returning hosts that once
filled them and still love this beautiful land. The white man will never be
alone.

—SEATTLE, speech, c. 1854
[The speech was probably given in the Salish dialect to the governor of the
Washington Territory. A translation by Dr. Henry Smith was published in
1887. Since then, Seattle's words have been richly embellished. In the 1971
film *Home*, the speech was transformed into an ecological manifesto.]

8   By the shores of Gitche Gumee,
By the shining Big-Sea-Water,
Stood the wigwam of Nokomis,
Daughter of the Moon, Nokomis

—HENRY WADSWORTH LONGFELLOW,
The Song of Hiawatha, 1855
[For generations of school children, Hiawatha was one of a mere handful of ad-
mirable Indians to appear in their lessons. Longfellow, of course, was flexible

in his history, but his hero, a man of peace, was evidently modeled on the Ojibway leader of that name who founded the Iroquois Confederacy.

The poem has inspired a number of parodies, including *The Song of Milkanwatha* by George A. Strong, included in Franklin P. Adams, *Innocent Merriment*, 1942: "When he killed the Mudjokivis, / Of the skin he made him mittens, / Made them with the fur side inside, / Made them with the skin side outside; / He, to get the warm side inside, / Put the inside skin side outside; / He, to get the cold side outside, / Put the warm side fur side inside. / That's why he put the fur side inside, / Why he put the skin side outside, / Why he turned them inside outside."]

All I ask for the Negro is that if you do not like him, let him alone. If God gave   1
him but little, that little let him enjoy.
—ABRAHAM LINCOLN, speech, July 17, 1858

The destiny of the colored American . . . is the destiny of America.   2
—FREDERICK DOUGLASS, speech, Emancipation League,
Boston, Mass., Feb. 12, 1862

The relation subsisting between the white and colored people of this country   3
is the great, paramount, imperative and all-commanding question for this age
and nation to solve.
—FREDERICK DOUGLASS, speech, Church of the Puritans,
New York City, May 1863
[See also W. E. B. Du Bois, below.]

The earth is the mother of all people, and all people should have equal rights   4
upon it.   —JOSEPH THE YOUNGER, *An Indian's View
of Indian Affairs*, in *The North American Review*,
no. 269, vol. 128, 1879
[More at EQUALITY and TALK.]

There are surely bad races and good races . . . and the Irish belong to the cate-   5
gory of the impossible.   —HENRY JAMES, letter to Mrs. Henry James, Sr.,
Feb. 7, 1881
[More quotes on the Irish are at NATIONS.]

In all the relations of life and death, we are met by the color line.   6
—FREDERICK DOUGLASS, speech, Convention of Colored Men,
Louisville, Ky., Sept. 24, 1883

The only good Indians I ever saw were dead.   7
—PHILIP H. SHERIDAN,
remark to the Comanche chief Toch-a-way, Jan. 1869
[According to various accounts of the time, Gen. Sheridan uttered this retort to the chief at Fort Cobb in Indian Territory after Toch-a-way identified himself as a "good Indian." The remark was widely reported and popularly condensed to: "The only good Indian is a dead Indian." Sheridan denied that he had ever made the comment, and it is possible that the quote became attached to him because of his reputation as an Indian fighter. Or, some believe, the culprit may have been a subordinate, possibly Capt. Charles Nordstrum. Certainly, the sentiment was not original to Sheridan. Ralph Keyes reports in *Nice Guys Finish Seventh* that Rep. J. M. Cavanaugh of Montana told the House on May 28 of the previous year, "I have never in my life seen a good Indian (and I have seen thousands) except when I have seen a dead Indian."]

1   When you first came, we were very many, and you were few; now, you are
many, and we are getting very few, and we are poor.
                                    —RED CLOUD, speech, Cooper Union, New York City,
                    July 16, 1870
[For Justice Hugo Black's comments on the relations between the U.S. and the
Indian nations, see FOREIGN POLICY.]

2   I will fight no more forever.   —JOSEPH THE YOUNGER, speech at the end
                    of the Nez Percé War, 1877
[More at RESIGNATION. See also Chief Joseph at PEACE.]

3   A Century of Dishonor.   —HELEN FISKE HUNT JACKSON, title of her history
                    of the government's treatment of Indians, c. 1881

4   Do you know who I am?
                                    —SITTING BULL, question directed to a delegation
                    of U.S. senators, Standing Rock Sioux reservation, 1883

5   The life of white men is slavery. They are prisoners in towns or farms.
                        —SITTING BULL, quoted in Robert M. Utely, *The Lance
                    and the Shield: The Life and Times of Sitting Bull* [1993]

6   Once I moved about like the wind. Now I surrender to you, and that is all.
                                    —GERONIMO,
                    March 27, 1886
[The great Apache warrior escaped from military custody the next day, but on
September 3 gave himself up for good—the last Native American to surrender
formally to the U.S. To catch him and his band of about fifty men, the U.S. and
Mexico had combined forces, the Americans deploying forty-two companies of
infantry and cavalry, while Mexico contributed another four thousand troops.
Exiled to Florida for a time, Geronimo spent his last years in Oklahoma, dying
at Fort Sill in 1909.]

7   The sure guarantee of the peace and security of each race is the clear, distinct,
unconditional recognition by our governments, national and state, of every
right that inheres in civil freedom, and of the equality before the law of all citizens of the United States, without regard to race.
                                    —JOHN MARSHALL HARLAN,
                    dissent in *Plessy v. Ferguson*, 1896
[For more from this great dissent, see THE CONSTITUTION. It was in *Plessy* that
the Supreme Court accepted the argument that so-called separate but equal accommodations for black and white were Constitutional. Harlan saw clearly
that the claim that segregated accommodations would be equal was a "thin
disguise." *Plessy v. Ferguson* was reversed in 1954 in *Brown v. the Board of Education*; see below and under AMERICAN HISTORY: MEMORABLE MOMENTS.]

8   We have ground the manhood out of them, and the shame is ours and not
theirs, and we should pay for it.   —MARK TWAIN, letter to Francis Wayland,
                    Dean of the Yale Law School
[In this letter, Twain offered to pay the tuition of a black student at law school.
In addition to supporting this student, he also paid the costs at a Southern
school of a black student who went on to become a minister.]

9   The difference between the brain of the average Christian and that of the average Jew—certainly in Europe—is about the difference between a tadpole's and

an archbishop's. It's a marvelous race, by long odds the most marvelous race the world has produced, I suppose.

—MARK TWAIN, letter to Rev. Joseph Twitchell, Oct. 23, 1897

The little brown brother.   1

—WILLIAM HOWARD TAFT, 1900

[More at SPANISH-AMERICAN WAR.]

The problem of the twentieth century is the problem of the color line.   2

—W. E. B. DU BOIS, *To The Nations of the World*,
speech, Pan-African conference, London, 1900

One ever feels his twoness—an American, a Negro; two souls, two thoughts,   3
two unreconciled strivings; two warring ideals in one dark body, whose dogged
strength alone keeps it from being torn asunder.

The history of the American Negro is the history of this strife—this longing
to attain self-conscious manhood, to merge his double self into a better and
truer self.

—W. E. B. DU BOIS, *The Souls of Black Folk*, 1903
[In 1993, referring to this passage, Charles Johnson wrote in *The New York
Times Book Review*, "Four generations of black artists, scholars, and community leaders have accepted these powerful words as their point of departure
when deliberating on the complex phenomenon of race."]

The talented tenth.   4

—*Ibid.*
[Du Bois introduced the concept of a talented elite in this book and in his essay *The Talented Tenth*, 1903. The tenth, according to Du Bois, were those
black leaders who by talent, education, and fortune could immediately begin
to lead the way out of "contamination and death." He wrote, "The Negro race,
like all races, is going to be saved by its exceptional men." He referred mainly
to Northern, urban, college-educated men and women.]

America is God's crucible, the great melting pot.   5

—ISRAEL ZANGWILL, *The Melting Pot*, 1908
[More at AMERICA & AMERICANS.]

The Pilgrim Fathers landed on the shores of America and fell upon their knees. 6
Then they fell upon the aborigines.

—ANONYMOUS
[The date of this witticism is not known, but early 20th century may be about
right. It has been attributed to William Maxwell Evarts, who printed a version
of it in the *Louisville Courier-Journal* on July 4, 1913, and also to Oliver Wendell Holmes, Sr., Bill Nye, and George Frisbie Hoar. Incidentally, the original
families, who arrived in 1620, lived for a time at peace with the native people
of New England. But that era ended catastrophically fifty-four years later
with the outbreak of King Philip's War. For a description of the Pilgrims falling to their knees, see William Bradford at AMERICAN HISTORY: MEMORABLE
MOMENTS.]

If George [King George V] comes to Chicago, I'll crack him in the snoot.   7

—WILLIAM HALE THOMPSON, 1927
[An alleged Anglo menace figured prominently in the 1927 Chicago mayoralty
campaign. Thompson, running for a third term, promised to weed out nefari-
ous British tendencies in the public schools. According to Henry F. Woods in

American Sayings (1945), Thompson's prime targets were the king of England
and the superintendent of schools.]

1 My forefathers didn't come over on the *Mayflower,* but they met the boat.
—WILL ROGERS, saying
[Rogers was referring to his Cherokee ancestors.]

2 Bury my heart at Wounded Knee.
—STEPHEN VINCENT BENÉT, *American Names,* 1927
[On December 29, 1890, U.S. troops massacred two hundred Sioux warriors,
women, and children at Wounded Knee Creek in South Dakota. This was the
last important "battle" in the Indian Wars.]

3 One of the things that makes a Negro unpleasant to white folk is the fact that
he suffers from their injustice. He is thus a standing rebuke to them.
—H. L. MENCKEN, *Notebooks,* 1930, in *Minority Report:*
H. L. Mencken's Notebooks [1956]

4 To be a Jew is destiny.   —VICKI BAUM, *And Life Goes On,* 1932

5 Only to the white man was nature a wilderness, and only to him was the land
"infested" with "wild" animals and "savage" people.
—LUTHER STANDING BEAR, *Land of the Spotted Eagle,* 1933
[More at NATURE.]

6 Among the thousand white persons, I am a dark rock surged upon, and over-
swept.   —ZORA NEALE HURSTON, *Mules and Men,* 1935

7 No democracy can long survive which does not accept as fundamental to its
very existence the recognition of the rights of minorities.
—FRANKLIN D. ROOSEVELT, letter to the National Association
for the Advancement of Colored People, June 25, 1938

8 We live here and they live here. We black and they white. They got things and
we ain't. They do things and we can't. It's just like living in jail.
—RICHARD WRIGHT, *Native Son,* 1940

9 It is not healthy when a nation lives within a nation, as colored Americans are
living inside America. A nation cannot live confident of its tomorrow if its
refugees are among its own citizens.
—PEARL S. BUCK, *What America Means to Me,* 1942

10 I swear to the Lord
I still can't see
Why Democracy means
Everybody but me.
—LANGSTON HUGHES, *The Black Man Speaks,*
in *Jim Crow's Last Stand,* 1943

11 The Eskimos are a gentle people. I like gentle people, because there are so
many in the world who are not gentle. Sometimes in a big city, I just sit all day
in my room, with my head down, afraid to go out and talk to tough people. I expect Eskimos have spells like that too.
—ERNIE PYLE, *Home Country* [1947]
[The most beloved correspondent of World War II because he wrote about people rather than battles, Pyle was killed by Japanese machine gun fire on an island near Okinawa in 1945.]

As long as the Negroes are held down by deprivation and lack of opportunity, the other poor people will be held down alongside them.   1
>   —JAMES "BIG JIM" FOLSOM, Christmas speech, 1949

I am an invisible man.   2
>   —RALPH ELLISON, *Invisible Man*, 1952

[The opening line of Ellison's instantly successful and still influential novel. A few lines later, the speaker explains, "I am invisible, understand, simply because people refuse to see me." The book, at the end, suggests that we may all be to a degree invisible. The last line reads: "Who knows but that, on the lower frequencies, I speak for you?"]

We conclude that in the field of public education "separate but equal" has no place.   3
>   —EARL WARREN, *Brown v. Board of Education*, May 17, 1954

[More at AMERICAN HISTORY: MEMORABLE MOMENTS. See also THE CONSTITUTION, and John Marshall Harlan, above, whose dissenting view in 1896 became the law of the land in 1954 when the Supreme Court, headed by Earl Warren, handed down its unanimous decision in *Brown*.]

The history of an oppressed people is hidden in the lies and the agreed-upon myths of its conquerors.   —MERIDEL LE SUEUR, *Crusaders*, 1955   4

Being a star has made it possible for me to get insulted in places where the average Negro could never hope to get insulted.   5
>   —SAMMY DAVIS, JR., *Yes I Can*, 1965

We shall overcome, we shall overcome,   6
We shall overcome some day,
Oh, deep in my heart, I do believe
We shall overcome some day.
>   —ANONYMOUS, civil rights song of the 1960s

[According to *Bartlett's*, the song dates from the mid-19th century and was made into a Baptist hymn, titled *I'll Overcome Some Day*, by C. Albert Tindley about 1900. It became well known as a labor protest song when used by black workers on strike in Charleston, S.C., in 1946.]

If we do not now dare everything, the fulfillment of that prophecy, recreated   7
from the Bible in a song by a slave, is upon us:

>   God gave Noah the rainbow sign,
>   No more water, the fire next time!

>   —JAMES BALDWIN, *The Fire Next Time*, 1963

[This work was first published in *The New Yorker* in 1962, and caused an uproar. White readers were unaccustomed to being criticized in one of their own magazines. See, for example, below.]

The American Negro has the great advantage of having never believed that col-   8
lection of myths to which white Americans cling: that their ancestors were all freedom-loving heroes, that they were born in the greatest country the world has ever seen, or that Americans are invincible in battle and wise in peace, that Americans have always dealt honorably with Mexicans and Indians and all other neighbors or inferiors, that American men are the world's most direct and virile, that American women are pure.   —*Ibid.*

If you're born in America with a black skin, you're born in prison.   9
>   —MALCOLM X, interview, June 1963

1   Segregation now. Segregation tomorrow. Segregation forever.
                                                —GEORGE WALLACE,
                              inauguration speech as governor of Alabama, 1963
    [These notorious lines reportedly were written by Asa Earl Carter, a right-wing
    extremist with a somewhat flexible persona. Under the pseudonym Forrest
    Carter, he wrote the well-received, politically correct memoirs of an Indian
    named Little Tree.]

2   I have a dream that one day on the red hills of Georgia, the sons of former
    slaves and the sons of former slaveowners will be able to sit down together at
    the table of brotherhood.
                         —MARTIN LUTHER KING, JR., speech at the Lincoln Memorial
                              in Washington, D.C., August 28, 1963
    [More at AMERICAN HISTORY: MEMORABLE MOMENTS. See also King and Richard
    Pryor at JUSTICE.]

3   I have a dream that my four little children will one day live in a nation where
    they will not be judged by the color of their skin but by the content of their
    character.   —*Ibid.*

4   We didn't land on Plymouth Rock, my brothers and sisters—Plymouth Rock
    landed on *us*.   —MALCOLM X, *The Autobiography of Malcolm X*, 1965

5   I firmly believe that Negroes have the right to fight against these racists by any
    means that are necessary.
                                                                      —*Ibid.*
    ["By any means necessary" emerged as a rallying call for militant action. It is
    now associated mostly with African-American radical action, but in the 1960s
    it had a general appeal. Thus, Abbie Hoffman, one of the founders of the Youth
    International Party, whose members were called Yippies, pledged in 1968,
    "We'll build our society in the vacant lots of the old, and we'll do it by any
    means necessary."]

6   You do not wipe away the scars of centuries by saying, "Now, you are free to
    go where you want, do what you desire, and choose the leaders you please."
    You do not take a man who, for years, has been hobbled by chains, liberate
    him, bring him to the starting line of the race, saying, "You are free to compete
    with the others."   —LYNDON B. JOHNSON, speech, Howard University, 1965

7   Black is beautiful.
                                                —ANONYMOUS, slogan, c. 1966
    [The phrase was linked with the Black Power movement (see below), but the
    idea was expressed decades earlier by Langston Hughes, who wrote in *The Ne-
    gro Artist and the Racial Mountain*, "Why should I want to be white? I am a
    Negro—and beautiful!" (*The Nation*, June 23, 1926). Similarly, in his poem *Ne-
    gro*, from the same year, Hughes wrote, "I am a Negro: / Black as the night is
    black, / Black like the depths of my Africa." Finally, of course, going back to
    the Bible, the Douay version of *The Song of Solomon*, 1:5, has the sentence, "I
    am black but beautiful."]

8   Black power . . . is a call for black people in this country to unite, to recognize
    their heritage, to build a sense of community. . . . It is a call to reject the racist
    institutions and values of this society.
                              —STOKELY CARMICHAEL & CHARLES VERNON HAMILTON,
                                   Black Power!, 1967
    [Carmichael, who later took the name Kwame Toure, is usually credited with

inventing the phrase "black power"; he certainly popularized it, beginning in the summer of 1966, when he led a continuation of a civil rights walk by James Meredith, who was shot and wounded on June 6, 1966. But the phrase and the concept were in the air that year. For example, the more moderate Adam Clayton Powell, Jr., in a speech at Howard University on May 29, 1966, said, "Our life must be purposed to implement human rights. . . . To demand these God-given rights is to seek black power—the power to build black institutions of splendid achievement."]

Death is a slave's freedom.   —NIKKI GIOVANNI, speech at the funeral   1
                                      of Martin Luther King, Jr., 1968

Our nation is moving toward two societies, one black, one white—separate   2
and unequal.   —OTTO KERNER, JR.,
                                      *Report of the National Advisory Commission
                                      on Civil Disorders*, 1968

My only concern was to get home after a hard day's work.   3
                                      —ROSA PARKS, *Time* magazine,
                                      Dec. 15, 1975
[Parks, an African-American seamstress from Montgomery, Ala., was speaking of December 1, 1955, when she refused to give up her seat at the front of a bus to a white man. For this defiance of the rule that blacks had to sit in the back of a bus, she was arrested; and this led to a black boycott of buses in the city. The successful protest was led by a young minister, Martin Luther King, Jr. Elsewhere, Parks acknowledged that she had felt for some time that she would never again give up her seat on demand; she was not simply too tired to move. "The only tired I was, was tired of giving in," she said in *Rosa Parks: My Story*, written with Jim Haskins, 1992. She won the Nobel Peace Prize in 1980.]

Say It Loud: I'm Black and Proud.   —JAMES BROWN, song title, 1979   4

Our nation is a rainbow—red, yellow, brown, black, and white—and we're all   5
precious in God's sight.
                                      —JESSE JACKSON, Democratic National Convention,
                                      San Francisco, July 17, 1984
[More at AMERICA & AMERICANS.]

We don't have to be what you want us to be.   6
                                      —BILL RUSSELL, quoted by George Vecsey,
                                      New York Times, 1985
[Bill Russell played center for the Boston Celtics when they ran up one of the finest records of any team in sports, winning eleven championships in thirteen years, 1956–69. As player-coach for the last two years of that stretch, he was the first black leader of a major U.S. professional sports team.]

I am somebody.   —JESSE JACKSON, motto   7

My Daddy told me it doesn't matter if it's a white snake or a black snake, it can   8
still bite you.
                                      —THURGOOD MARSHALL, saying
[Carl Rowan, author of a biography of Justice Marshall, said that he applied this specifically to Clarence Thomas, a conservative Republican, nominated to the Supreme Court by Pres. George Bush after Marshall's retirement in 1991.]

1   Racism is not an excuse to not do the best you can.
                         —ARTHUR ASHE, *Sports Illustrated*, July 1991

2   A white man with a million dollars is a millionaire, and a black man with a million dollars is a nigger with a million dollars.
                         —ANONYMOUS, saying used by New York city mayor
                         David Dinkins, 1980s
    [This bitter comment had been around for several decades at least. Mayor Dinkins was quoted by Ellis Cose in *The Rage of the Privileged Class*, 1993.]

REALTY, ILLUSIONS, & IMAGES   *See also* APPEARANCES; ART: AESTHETICS;
                                           DREAMS & DREAMERS

3   All that we see or seem
    Is but a dream within a dream.
                         —EDGAR ALLAN POE, *A Dream Within a Dream*, 1827

4   Things are not what they seem.
                         —HENRY WADSWORTH LONGFELLOW, *A Psalm of Life*, 1839
    [More at LIFE.]

5   A true account of the actual is the rarest poetry, for common sense always takes a hasty and superficial view.
                         —HENRY DAVID THOREAU, *A Week on the Concord
                         and Merrimack Rivers*, 1849

6   Be it life or death, we crave only reality.
                         —HENRY DAVID THOREAU,
                         "Where I Lived and What I Lived For," *Walden*, 1854

7   We wake from one dream into another dream.
                         —RALPH WALDO EMERSON,
                         Illusions, in *The Conduct of Life*, 1860

8   Certainty generally is an illusion, and repose is not the destiny of man.
                         —OLIVER WENDELL HOLMES, JR., *The Path of the Law*, 1897

9   Between the idea and the reality
    Between the motion
    And the act
    Falls the Shadow.   —T. S. ELIOT, *The Hollow Men*, 1925

10 Humankind
    Cannot bear very much reality.
                         —T. S. ELIOT, *Murder in the Cathedral*, 1935
    [The same sentence is in Eliot's *Burnt Norton* in *Four Quartets*, 1943. See also Eliot at SCIENCE: PHYSICS & COSMOLOGY.]

11 In the American metaphysic, reality is always material reality, hard, resistant, unformed, impenetrable, and unpleasant.
                         —LIONEL TRILLING, *Reality in America*,
                         in *The Liberal Imagination*, 1950

12 It helps to see the actual world to visualize a fantastic world.
                         —WALLACE STEVENS, Milton J. Bates, ed.,
                         expanded *Opus Posthumous*

Life is washed in the speechless real.   1
> —JACQUES BARZUN, *The House of Intellect*, 1959

We suffer primarily not from our vices or our weaknesses, but from our illu-   2
sions. We are haunted, not by reality, but by those images we have put in place
of reality.   —DANIEL J. BOORSTIN,
> Introduction, *The Image*, 1962

Obsessed by a fairy tale, we spend our lives searching for a magic door and a   3
lost kingdom of peace.   —EUGENE O'NEILL, *More Stately Mansions*, 1964

First baseball umpire: "Balls and strikes, I call them as I sees them."   4
Second umpire: "Balls and strikes, I call them as they are."
Third umpire: "Balls and strikes, they ain't nothing until I call them."
> —ANONYMOUS, in Alan L. Mackay, ed.,
> *The Harvest of a Quiet Eye*, 1977

Each person paints their picture of reality with a brush dipped in the pigments   5
of the past.   —JERRY ANDRUS, conference,
> Center for the Scientific Investigation of Claims
> of the Paranormal, Seattle, Wash., June 1994
[Andrus, a magician, delighted the audience with demonstrations of how ex-
pectations based on past experience mislead us in perceiving present events.
See also magician Dai Vernon at ART: THEATER, DRAMA, & MAGIC.]

REASONS & REASONABLE PEOPLE

So convenient a thing it is to be a *reasonable creature*, since it enables one to   6
find or make a reason for everything one has a mind to do.
> —BENJAMIN FRANKLIN, *Autobiography*, started 1771
> [published in full, 1868]

Every man's own reason must be his oracle.   7
> —THOMAS JEFFERSON, letter to Dr. Benjamin Rush,
> March 6, 1813

Nature hates calculators.   —RALPH WALDO EMERSON, *Nature*,   8
> in *Essays: Second Series*, 1844

There are few things more exciting to me . . . than a psychological reason.   9
> —HENRY JAMES, *The Art of Fiction*, 1888

A man always has two reasons for what he does—a good one and the real one.   10
> —JOHN PIERPONT MORGAN, quoted in Owen Wister,
> *Roosevelt: The Story of a Friendship* [1930]

Come now, let us reason together.   11
> —LYNDON B. JOHNSON, saying
[From *Isaiah* 1:18: "Come now, and let us reason together."]

A study of the art of motorcycle maintenance is really a miniature study of the   12
art of rationality itself.
> —ROBERT PIRSIG,
> *Zen and the Art of Motorcycle Maintenance*, 1974
[More at SCIENCE: TECHNOLOGY.]

REGRET

1   To regret deeply is live afresh.
—HENRY DAVID THOREAU, *Journal*, Nov. 13, 1839

2   Why should I mourn at the untimely fate of my people? Tribe follows tribe, and nation follows nation, and regret is useless.
—SEATTLE, speech, c. 1854
[For more from and about this speech, see Seattle under RACES & PEOPLES.]

3   For of all sad words of tongue or pen,
The saddest are these: "It might have been!"
—JOHN GREENLEAF WHITTIER, *Maud Muller*, 1856

4   I shall be telling this with a sigh
Somewhere ages and ages hence:
Two roads diverged in a wood, and I—
I took the one less traveled by,
And that has made all the difference.
—ROBERT FROST, *The Road Not Taken*, 1916

5   Footfalls echo in the memory
Down the passage which we did not take
Towards the door we never opened
Into the rosegarden.   —T. S. ELIOT,
Four Quartets: Burnt Norton, 1935

6   I could have had class. I could've been a contender. I could've been somebody. Instead of a bum, which is what I am. Instead of a bum, which is what I am.
—BUDD SCHULBERG,
Waterfront, 1955
[The novel appeared a year after the film, *On the Waterfront*, written by Schulberg and starring Marlon Brando as Terry Malloy, who "could've been a contender."]

7   Maybe Rosebud was something he couldn't get or something he lost. Anyway, it wouldn't explain a man's life. No, I guess Rosebud is just a piece in a jigsaw puzzle, a missing piece.   —HERMAN J. MANKIEWICZ & ORSON WELLES,
Citizen Kane, screenplay, 1941
[Kane's deathbed whisper was "Rosebud," and the movie turns on the search for why he said this. See also LAST WORDS.]

RELIGION   *See also* ATHEISM; FAITH; GOD; MIRACLES;
PRAYER; PRAYERS

8   Job feels the rod,
Yet blesses God.   —THE NEW ENGLAND PRIMER, c. 1688

9   To be like Christ is to be a Christian.   —WILLIAM PENN, last words, 1718

10 It does me no injury for my neighbor to say there are twenty gods, or no God.
—THOMAS JEFFERSON,
Notes on the State of Virginia, 1782
[The observation is part of an argument for freedom of religion. In full, Jefferson wrote, "The legitimate powers of government extend to such acts only as are injurious to others. But it does me no injury for my neighbor to say there

are twenty gods, or no God. It neither picks my pocket nor breaks my leg." See also Jefferson at TYRANNY (letter to Benjamin Rush) and EPITAPHS & GRAVE-STONES.]

Every man, conducting himself as a good citizen, and being accountable to God   1
alone for his religious opinions, ought to be protected in worshipping the Deity according to the dictates of his own conscience.
　　　　　　　　—GEORGE WASHINGTON,
　　　　　　　　　　letter to the United Baptist Churches in Virginia,
　　　　　　　　　　May 1789

I believe in one God and no more, and I hope for happiness beyond this life.   2
I believe in the equality of man; and I believe that religious duties consist in doing justice, loving mercy, and endeavoring to make our fellow creatures happy.　　　　　　　　　　　　　—THOMAS PAINE,
　　　　　　　　　　　　　　The Age of Reason, 1794
[See also Paine at ETHICS & MORALITY.]

Priests and conjurors are of the same trade.　　　　　　　　　—*Ibid.*   3

Any system of religion that has anything in it that shocks the mind of a child   4
cannot be a true system.　　　　　　　　　　　　　　　—*Ibid.*

Democracy has given to conscience absolute liberty.   5
　　　　　　　　—GEORGE BANCROFT, address to the Democratic Elector
　　　　　　　　　　of Massachusetts, *Boston Post*, Oct. 16, 1835
[For a comment on the variety of churches associated with that liberty, see Frances Trollope at AMERICA & AMERICANS.]

If a man entertain heretical sentiments, who shall be his judge? Our creator   6
has not delegated this power to man. He is himself the only competent judge; and it concerns him much more than it does us to define the crime and inflict the penalty.　　　　—RICHARD M. JOHNSON, address to Barnabas Bates et al.,
　　　　　　　　　　New York Evening Post, April 1, 1840
[Col. Johnson of Kentucky, hero of the Battle of the Thames in the War of 1812, was a popular congressman, a great defender of the common people, and served as vice president for one term under Andrew Jackson. A tendency to venality in the management of his financial affairs, and an interracial liaison, undermined his political career.]

I like the silent church before the service begins, better than any preaching.   7
　　　　　　　　—RALPH WALDO EMERSON, *Self-Reliance*,
　　　　　　　　　　in *Essays: First Series*, 1841

For every Stoic was a Stoic; but in Christendom where is the Christian?   8
　　　　　　　　　　　　　　　　　　　　　—*Ibid.*

God builds his temple in the heart on the ruins of churches and religions.   9
　　　　　　　　—RALPH WALDO EMERSON, *Worship*,
　　　　　　　　　　in *The Conduct of Life*, 1860

Some keep the Sabbath going to church—   10
I keep it, staying at home—
With a bobolink for a chorister—
And an orchard for a dome.
　　　　　　　　　　　　—EMILY DICKINSON,
　　　　　　　　　　　　　poem no. 324, 1862

1   Once we had wooden chalices and golden priests, now we have golden chalices
    and wooden priests.   —RALPH WALDO EMERSON, *The Preacher,* 1867

2   Leave the matter of religion to the family altar, the church and the private
    school, supported entirely by private contributions. Keep the church and state
    forever separate.   —ULYSSES S. GRANT, speech, Des Moines, Iowa, 1875

3   The country that has got the least religion is the most prosperous, and the
    country that has got the most religion is the least prosperous.
                        —ROBERT G. INGERSOLL, speech, Boston, April 23, 1880

4   Religion . . . is a man's total reaction upon life.
                    —WILLIAM JAMES, *The Varieties of Religious Experience,* 1902

5   Religion is a monumental chapter in the history of human egotism.   —*Ibid.*

6   *Heathen, n.* A benighted creature who has the folly to worship something that
    he can see and feel.   —AMBROSE BIERCE, *The Devil's Dictionary,* 1906

7   The Bible is literature, not dogma.   —GEORGE SANTAYANA,
                                                The Ethics of Spinoza, 1910
    [See also Mark Twain at ATHEISM.]

8   Religion is the love of life in the consciousness of impotence.
                        —GEORGE SANTAYANA, *Winds of Doctrine,* 1913

9   Give me that old-time religion,
    It's good enough for me.   —ANONYMOUS, hymn

10 As society is now constituted, a literal adherence to the moral precepts scat-
    tered throughout the gospels would mean sudden death.
                    —ALFRED NORTH WHITEHEAD, *Adventures of Ideas,* 1933

11 It ain't necessarily so—
    The things that you're liable
    To read in the Bible—
    It ain't necessarily so.
                            —IRA GERSHWIN, *Porgy and Bess,* 1935
    [Music by George Gershwin.]

12 Caesar and Christ had met in the arena, and Christ had won.
                —WILLIAM DURANT, *The Story of Civilization,* Vol. 3, 1944

13 We must respect the other fellow's religion, but only in the sense and to the ex-
    tent that we accept his theory that his wife is beautiful and his children smart.
                            —H. L. MENCKEN, *Minority Report:*
                            H. L. Mencken's Notebooks [1956]

14 Fear of death and fear of life both become piety.   —*Ibid.*

15 If you really want to make a million, the quickest way is to start your own
    religion.   —L. RON HUBBARD, lecture,
                    Eastern Science Fiction Association, Newark, N.J., 1947
    [Hubbard was the founding spirit of Scientology, which was incorporated as a
    church in 1965. The quote comes courtesy of Sam Moscowitz, attributed in B.

Corydon and L. Ron Hubbard, Jr., *L. Ron Hubbard,* 1987. Moscowitz said that Hubbard observed that writing science fiction for about a penny a word was no way to make a living, especially as compared to founding a religion.]

The cosmic religious experience is the strongest and noblest driving force be-   1
hind scientific research.   —ALBERT EINSTEIN, attributed, *New York Times,*
obituary, April 19, 1956

Every day, people are straying away from the church and going back to God.   2
—LENNY BRUCE, quoted in *The Essential Lenny Bruce,*
compiled and edited by John Cohen [1970]

The church must be reminded that it is not the master or the servant of the   3
state, but rather the conscience of the state.
—MARTIN LUTHER KING, JR., *Strength to Love,* 1963

I read about an Eskimo hunter who asked the local missionary priest, "If I did   4
not know about God and sin, would I go to hell?" "No," said the priest, "not if
you did not know." "Then why," asked the Eskimo earnestly, "did you tell
me?"   —ANNIE DILLARD, *Pilgrim at Tinker Creek,* 1974

People don't come to church for preachments, of course, but to daydream   5
about God.   —KURT VONNEGUT, Palm Sunday sermon,
St. Clement's Episcopal Church, New York City, quoted by
John Leonard in *The New York Times,* April 30, 1980

REPUBLICANS   *See* POLITICS & POLITICIANS

REPUTATION   *See also* HONOR; VIRTUE (Lincoln)

What people say behind your back is your standing in the community in which   6
you live.   —E. W. HOWE, *Sinner Sermons,* 1926

Reputation, like a face, is the symbol of its possessor and creator, and another   7
can use it only as a mask.
—LEARNED HAND, *Yale Electric Company v. Robertson,* 1928
[This was a trademark case.]

If we disregard what the world says of someone, we live to repent it.   8
—LOGAN PEARSALL SMITH, *All Trivia,* 1935

Some say she do and some say she don't.   9
—ANONYMOUS, African-American folksaying

All a man has got to show for his time here on earth is what kind of name he   10
had.   —MUHAMMAD ALI, on refusing induction
into the U.S. Army, 1967
[See also Ali at VIETNAM WAR.]

RESIGNATION   *See also* ENDURANCE; PATIENCE

What is called resignation is confirmed desperation.   11
—HENRY DAVID THOREAU, "Economy," *Walden,* 1854
[More at LIFE.]

1   Hear me, my chiefs, I am tired; my heart is sick and sad. From where the sun now stands, I will fight no more forever.
                —JOSEPH THE YOUNGER, speech at the end of the Nez Percé War,
                October 1877

2   Teach us to care and not to care.
    Teach us to sit still.   —T. S. ELIOT, *Ash Wednesday*, 1930

RESISTANCE   *See also* AMERICAN HISTORY: MEMORABLE MOMENTS
                        (quotes on the Alamo); DETERMINATION, EFFORT,
                        PERSISTENCE, & PERSEVERANCE; LAW (Henry David Thoreau,
                        Martin Luther King, Jr.); REVOLUTION; TYRANNY

3   The spirit of resistance to government is so valuable on certain occasions that I wish it to be always kept alive. It will often be exercised when wrong, but better so than not to be exercised at all.
                —THOMAS JEFFERSON, to Abigail Adams, Feb. 22, 1787
    [See also Jefferson on resistance to tyrants at TYRANNY.]

4   Our lives are in the hands of the Great Spirit. He gave to our ancestors the lands which we possess. We are determined to defend our lands, and if it is His will, our bones shall whiten upon them, but we will never give them up.
                —TECUMSEH, speech to Maj. Gen. Henry Procter
                of the British army, Sept. 1813
    [The Shawnee chief had allied his people with the British, and he covered Procter's retreat into Canada. Tecumseh was killed on October 5 in the battle of the Thames River.]

5   He is whipped oftenest, who is whipped easiest, and that slave who has the courage to stand up for himself against the overseer, although he may have many hard stripes at the first, becomes, in the end, a freeman even though he sustain the formal relation of a slave.
                —FREDERICK DOUGLASS, *My Bondage and My Freedom*, 1855
    [Douglass escaped from slavery on his second try, in 1838, and found work in New Bedford, Mass., where he became a spokesman and leader of the abolitionist cause, with a national following. See also Douglass at SLAVERY.]

6   We beg no longer; we entreat no more; we petition no more. We defy them.
                —WILLIAM JENNINGS BRYAN, "Cross of Gold" speech,
                Democratic National Convention, Chicago, July 7, 1896
    [See ECONOMICS for more on this speech. "Them" in this passage refers to Eastern financiers.]

7   There comes a time when the cup of endurance runs over, and men are no longer willing to be plunged into an abyss of injustice where they experience the blackness of corroding despair.
                —MARTIN LUTHER KING, JR., letter from Birmingham
                city jail, April 16, 1963
    [King was addressing fellow ministers in the South, white men who recognized the injustice of segregation but had deplored the confrontations and civil disobedience used in opposing it.]

RESPONSIBILITY

8   Only aim to do your duty, and mankind will give you credit where you fail.
                —THOMAS JEFFERSON, *The Rights of British America*, 1774

They are slaves who fear to speak
For the fallen and the weak.

1

—JAMES RUSSELL LOWELL,
Stanzas on Freedom, 1843

Duty, oh duty,
Why are thou not a
Sweetie or a cutie?

2

—OGDEN NASH, 1935

[This version of Nash's ditty is cited, without a title, in Robert Debs Heinl, *Dictionary of Military and Naval Quotation*, 1966. A longer version is included in Nash's *The Face Is Familiar*, 1941. It is titled *Kind of an Ode to Duty*, and reads: "Oh duty, / Why hast thou not the visage of a sweetie or a cutie?"]

I believe that every right implies a responsibility; every opportunity, an obligation; every possession, a duty.   —JOHN D. ROCKEFELLER, speech, July 8, 1941

3

A burden in the bush is worth two on your hands.

4

—JAMES THURBER, *The Hunter and the Elephant*,
in *Fables for Our Times*, 1943

The buck stops here.

5

—HARRY S. TRUMAN, motto

[In *Truman* (1992), David McCullough relates that Truman's faithful friend Fred Canfil saw a sign with this motto on the warden's desk at the federal reformatory in El Reno, Oklahoma, and had a copy made for Truman, who briefly kept it on his desk in the White House. Word maven William Safire has explained that the buck was a marker, often a silver dollar, used in poker games to indicate the upcoming dealer. The buck could be passed on if a player did not want the responsibility of dealing. Sen. Daniel Patrick Moynihan, however, told Mr. Safire that, in the Navy, the buck is a small dining-table marker that shows which officer is to be served first. It is moved from place to place daily. If the buck stops at one place, that officer always is served first—not the image we associate with the Truman saying.]

Our privileges can be no greater than our obligations. The protection of our rights can endure no longer than the performance of our responsibilities.

6

—JOHN F. KENNEDY, speech, May 18, 1963

REVENGE

Living well is the best revenge.   —GERALD MURPHY & SARA MURPHY,
personal motto

7

[The quote usually is associated with the Murphys, expatriate friends of Scott and Zelda Fitgerald, and the models for Dick and Nicole Diver in *Tender Is the Night* (1934). The thought is proverbial, however. George Herbert recorded it in this exact form in his 1640 collection of *Outlandish Proverbs*.]

Don't get mad, get even.   —JOSEPH PATRICK KENNEDY, attributed

8

REVOLUTION

See also AMERICAN REVOLUTION;
FUTURE, THE (Lincoln Steffens); RESISTANCE;
RUTHLESSNESS; TYRANNY; VIOLENCE

A little rebellion now and then is a good thing, and as necessary in the political world as storms in the physical.

9

—THOMAS JEFFERSON, letter to James Madison, Jan. 30, 1787

[Jefferson was referring to Shays' Rebellion, an antitax revolt in Massachusetts.]

1   The tree of liberty must be refreshed from time to time with the blood of patriots and tyrants. It is its natural manure.
                    —THOMAS JEFFERSON, letter to Col. William S. Smith, Nov. 13, 1787

2   A share in two revolutions is living to some purpose.
                                        —THOMAS PAINE, quoted in Eric Foner,
                                        Tom Paine and Revolutionary America

3   An oppressed people are authorized, whenever they can, to rise and break their
fetters.   —HENRY CLAY, speech in the Congress, March 24, 1818

4   The great wheel of political revolution began to move in America.
                    —DANIEL WEBSTER, speech for the the laying of the cornerstone
                    for the Bunker Hill Monument, June 17, 1825

5   Every revolution was at first a thought in one man's mind.
                                        —RALPH WALDO EMERSON, *History*,
                                        in *Essays: First Series*, 1841
[Similarly, Wendell Phillips said of John Brown: "Insurrection of thought always precedes insurrection of arms," speech, Harpers Ferry, November 1, 1859.]

6   God gave Noah the rainbow sign, No more water, the fire next time!
                            —ANONYMOUS, slave song, cited by James Baldwin in
                            The Fire Next Time [1963]
[See Baldwin at RACES & PEOPLES.]

7   All men recognize the right of revolution.
                            —HENRY DAVID THOREAU, *Civil Disobedience*, 1849

8   A mighty influence is abroad, surging and heaving the world, as with an earthquake.
                    —HARRIET BEECHER STOWE, *Uncle Tom's Cabin*, 1852
[More at INJUSTICE.]

9   Be not deceived. Revolutions do not go backward.
                            —ABRAHAM LINCOLN, speech, May 19, 1856
[The same thought was expressed by the abolitionist William Henry Seward in
his speech *The Irrepressible Conflict*: "Revolutions never go backward,"
Rochester, N.Y., October 25, 1858. And abolitionist Wendell Phillips made the
same remark in a speech on February 17, 1861. We do not immediately think
of the Civil War as a revolution, but to abolitionists it was indeed.]

10 Revolutions are not made by men in spectacles.
                            —OLIVER WENDELL HOLMES, SR., *The Young Practitioner*,
                            speech, New York City, March 2, 1871

11 There may at some future day be a whirlwind precipitated upon the moneyed
men of this country.   —PETER COOPER, c. 1875, quoted in Peter Lyon,
                            The Honest Man, in *American Heritage* [Feb. 1959]
[Cooper was a wealthy, self-made manufacturer and philanthropist.]

12 What happens to a dream deferred?
    Does it dry up
    Like a raisin in the sun? . . .
    Or does it explode?   —LANGSTON HUGHES, *Harlem*, 1951

Those who make peaceful revolution impossible will make violent revolution   1
inevitable.   —JOHN F. KENNEDY, remarks to Latin American diplomats
at the White House, March 13, 1962

Revolution is bloody, revolution is hostile, revolution knows no compromise,   2
revolution overturns and destroys everything that gets in its way.
—MALCOLM X,
Message to the Grass Roots, Nov. 1963

A revolution is like a forest fire. It burns everything in its path.   3
—MALCOLM X, interview with A. B. Spellman,
Monthly Review, May 1964

Our own revolution has ended the need for revolution forever.   4
—WILLIAM C. WESTMORELAND,
speech to Daughters of the American Revolution,
quoted in Daniel Berrigan, *America Is Hard to Find* [1972]
[Gen. Westmoreland was commander of the U.S. forces in Vietnam from 1964
to 1968.]

REVOLUTIONARY WAR   *See* AMERICAN REVOLUTION

RHODE ISLAND   *See also* CITIES (Newport, Providence)

Aquethneck shall henceforth be called the Ile of Rhods or Rhod-Island.   5
—RHODE ISLAND COLONIAL ASSEMBLY,
March 13, 1694
[Roger Williams, founder of the colony, apparently had read a translation of
Giovanni da Verrazzano's account of his voyage along the New England coast
in 1524 in which he reported discovering "an island in the form of a triangle,
distant from the mainland 10 leagues, about the bigness of the Island of
Rhodes."
Williams erred in supposing that Verrazzano meant Aquidneck, or Aquethneck, future site of Newport, according to Samuel Eliot Morison's *The European Discovery of America: The Northern Voyages.* Nevertheless, the name
stuck and was transferred to the colony as a whole. Variations in the spelling
of the name, by the way, are of no significance.]

The country people in the island, in general, are very unpolished and rude.   6
—ALEXANDER HAMILTON,
Itinerarium, August 18, 1744
[For background on Dr. Hamilton, see Boston under CITIES.]

Rhode Island was settled and is made up of people who found it unbearable to   7
live anywhere else in New England.
—WOODROW WILSON, speech, New York City, Jan. 29, 1911

Texas could wear Rhode Island as a watch fob.   8
—PAT NEFF,
quoted in John Gunther, *Inside U.S.A.* [1947]
[Neff was governor of Texas, 1921–25.]

Motto

Hope.   9

RICH & POOR, WEALTH & POVERTY

See also CAPITALISM & CAPITAL V. LABOR; ECONOMICS; ELITE, THE; MONEY & THE RICH; POVERTY & HUNGER; WORK & WORKERS

1   It is a reproach to religion and government to suffer so much poverty and excess.
　　　　　　　　　　　　　　　　　　　　　　　—WILLIAM PENN,
　　　　　　　　　　　　　　　　　　　　　Some Fruits of Solitude, 1693

2   The most common and durable source of factions has been the various and unequal distribution of property.
　　　　　　　　　—JAMES MADISON, *The Federalist, No. 10,* 1787
[More at CONFLICT.]

3   All communities divide themselves into the few and the many. The first are the rich and well-born, the other the mass of the people.
　　　　　　　　　　　　　　　　　—ALEXANDER HAMILTON, speech,
　　　　　　　　　　　　　　　　　Constitutional Convention, 1787
[Hamilton described the second group, the people, as "turbulent and changing." He advocated giving the first group a permanent share in government, and predicted that it would be in their own self-interest to maintain good government. See also Hamilton at THE PEOPLE, in the note under William T. Sherman.]

4   The problem of our age is the proper administration of wealth, so that the ties of brotherhood may still bind together the rich and poor in harmonious relationship.
　　　　　　　　　　　　　　—ANDREW CARNEGIE, *Wealth,* 1889
[See also John F. Kennedy at ECONOMICS.]

5   How the Other Half Lives.
　　　　　　　　　　　　　　—JACOB A. RIIS, book title, 1890
[Riis's book described the horrific conditions of life in New York City tenements. The photographs are still shocking.]

6   To be a poor man is hard, but to be a poor race in a land of dollars is the very bottom of hardships.
　　　　　　　　　—W. E. B. DU BOIS, *The Souls of Black Folk,* 1903
[See also Du Bois at RACES & PEOPLES and Frederick Douglass at CRIME, CRIMINALS, & DETECTIVES.]

7   The golf links lie so near the mill
　　That almost every day
　　The laboring children can look out
　　And see the men at play.
　　　　　　—SARAH N. CLEGHORN, *The Golf Links Lie So Near the Mill,*
　　　　　　　Franklin P. Adams's column, *The Conning Tower,*
　　　　　　　in the *New York Tribune,* 1919

8   I've been rich and I've been poor. Rich is better.
　　　　　　　　　　　　　　　　　—SOPHIE TUCKER, attributed
[Some think Joe E. Lewis said it first but, as Ralph Keyes points out in *Nice Guys Finish Seventh* (1992), Lewis and Tucker often performed together and either might have borrowed it from the other.]

The only incurable troubles of the rich are troubles that money can't   1
    cure,
Which is a kind of trouble that is even more troublesome if you are
    poor.   —OGDEN NASH, *The Terrible People*,
                                         in *Verses from 1929 On*, 1959

The meek shall inherit the earth but not the mineral rights.   2
                                        —J. PAUL GETTY, attributed

RIGHT   *See also* ETHICS & MORALITY; VIRTUE

Be always sure you're right—then go ahead.   3
                     —DAVID CROCKETT, his motto from the War of 1812,
                     cited in *Narrative of the Life of David Crockett*, 1834

They are slaves who dare not be   4
In the right with two or three.
                          —JAMES RUSSELL LOWELL, *Stanza on Freedom*, 1843

It is not desirable to cultivate a respect for the law, so much as for the right.   5
                          —HENRY DAVID THOREAU, *Civil Disobedience*, 1849
[More at LAW. See also Thoreau at MAJORITIES & MINORITIES for "a man more
right than his neighbors."]

Let us have faith that right makes might.   6
                          —ABRAHAM LINCOLN, speech at Cooper Union,
                          New York City, Feb. 27, 1860
[More at VIRTUE.]

The humblest citizen of all the land, when clad in the armor of a righteous   7
cause, is stronger than all the hosts of error.
                          —WILLIAM JENNINGS BRYAN, speech,
                          Democratic National Convention,
                          Chicago, July 8, 1896

Always do right. This will gratify some people and astonish the rest.   8
                          —MARK TWAIN, speech, Greenpoint Presbyterian Church,
                          Brooklyn, N.Y., 1901
[See also Twain at VIRTUE.]

"The right" is only the expedient in our way of behaving.   9
                          —WILLIAM JAMES, *Pragmatism*, 1907
[More at EXPEDIENCY.]

The world is divided into people who think they are right.   —ANONYMOUS 10

The right is more precious than peace.   11
                          —WOODROW WILSON, speech to Congress, April 2, 1917
[This is from the speech in which he asked Congress to enter the war to make
the world safe for democracy; see WORLD WAR I.]

The time is always ripe to do right.   12
                          —MARTIN LUTHER KING, JR.,
                          letter from Birmingham city jail, April 16, 1963

1   May God prevent us from becoming "right-thinking men"—that is to say, men who agree perfectly with their own police.
                    —THOMAS MERTON,
                    New York Times, obituary, Dec. 11, 1968
[Merton, a Trappist monk and priest, and an excellent writer, was one of the most effective advocates of his day for Catholicism, mysticism, and the life of the spirit.]

2   Rise above principle and do what's right.
                    —WALTER HELLER, speech to Congress, May 7, 1985

RIGHTS   *See also* CONSTITUTION, THE; DEMOCRACY;
                                        FREEDOM; FREE SPEECH; PRESS, THE;
                                        PRIVACY; SUPREME COURT

3   [All men] are endowed by their Creator with certain inalienable rights.
                    —THOMAS JEFFERSON, *The Declaration of Independence*,
                    July 4, 1776
[More at DECLARATION OF INDEPENDENCE.]

4   A bill of rights is what the people are entitled to against every government on earth.
                    —THOMAS JEFFERSON, letter to James Madison, Dec. 1787
[See also THE CONSTITUTION.]

5   They have rights who dare maintain them.
                    —JAMES RUSSELL LOWELL, *The Present Crisis*, 1884

6   I am the inferior of any man whose rights I trample under foot.
                    —ROBERT G. INGERSOLL,
                    Prose Poems and Selections, 1884

7   There is no such thing as rights anyhow. It is a question of whether you can put it over. In any legal sense or practical sense, whatever is, is "a right."
                    —CLARENCE DARROW, debate on Prohibition,
                    quoted in Kevin Tierney, *Darrow* [1979]

8   It is fair to judge peoples by the rights they will sacrifice the most for.
                    —CLARENCE DAY,
                    This Simian World, 1920

ROOSEVELT, ELEANOR   *See* VIRTUE (Adlai Stevenson)

ROOSEVELT, FRANKLIN DELANO

9   Two-thirds mush and one-third Eleanor.
                    —ALICE ROOSEVELT LONGWORTH, on her cousin FDR, quoted
                    in George Wolfskill and John A. Hudson, *All but the People:
                    Franklin D. Roosevelt and his Critics, 1933–39* [1969]

10   Meeting Roosevelt was like uncorking your first bottle of champagne.
                    —WINSTON CHURCHILL, quoted on *The American Experience*
                    television show, Public Broadcasting System [March 17, 1995]

ROOSEVELT, THEODORE

I don't think my name will mean much to the bear business, but you're wel- 1
come to use it.
> —THEODORE ROOSEVELT, letter to Morris Michtom of Brooklyn,
> New York, who asked permission to use the president's
> nickname for a line of toy stuffed bears, c. 1903

[In November 1902, Roosevelt had refused to shoot a bear that had been run
down by dogs and lassoed. A cartoon by Clifford Berryman made the incident
instantly famous, and Roosevelt was dubbed Teddy Bear.]

I am as strong as a bull moose. 2
> —THEODORE ROOSEVELT, letter to Sen. Mark Hanna,
> June 27, 1900

[More at POLITICS & POLITICIANS.]

Now look, that damned cowboy is president of the United States. 3
> —MARK HANNA, remark to Hermann H. Kohlsaat,
> Sept. 16, 1901, quoted in Kohlsaat,
> *From McKinley to Harding* [1923]

[This conversation took place in a Pullman railroad car shortly after the train
pulled out of Buffalo, N.Y., where President McKinley, shot on September 6,
had died two days before. Hanna—Marcus Alonzo Hanna, in full—an Ohio industrialist, Republican Party power broker, U.S. Senator, and manager of
McKinley's successful 1896 presidential campaign, had agreed only grudgingly
to TR's nomination for the vice presidency in 1900—mainly, it was said, to get
rid of "that wild man." With Kohlsaat's discreet intercession, Hanna and the
president reached a working accommodation that lasted until Hanna's death in
1904.]

An interesting combination of St. Vitus and St. Paul. 4
> —JOHN MORLEY, description of Roosevelt

[Morley, British statesman and author, also remarked when Roosevelt was
president, "The two outstanding natural phenomena of America are Niagara
Falls and Theodore Roosevelt," quoted in Mark Sullivan, *Our Times,* Vol. II,
1927.]

He was pure act. 5
> —HENRY ADAMS, *The Education of Henry Adams,* 1907

[Adams wrote in full, "Roosevelt, more than any other man living within the
range of notoriety, showed the singular primitive quality . . . that medieval
theology assigned to God—he was pure act."]

A charlatan of the very highest skill. 6
> —H. L. MENCKEN, *Prejudices: Second Series,* 1920

He was a walking day of judgment. 7
> —JOHN BURROUGHS, in *Forest and Stream,* Jan. 1928

[The comment was made with affection.]

He wanted to be the bride at every wedding and the corpse at every funeral. 8
> —NICHOLAS ROOSEVELT, *A Front Row Seat,* 1953

RULERS

See HIGH POSITION: RULERS & LEADERS

RUMOR

1   Rumor travels faster, but it don't stay put as long as truth.
—WILL ROGERS, *Politics Getting Ready to Jell*,
in *The Illiterate Digest*, 1924

2   So the rumors are true?
Rumors are always true. You know that.
—MICHAEL TOLKIN, *The Player*, screenplay, 1992
[Especially in Hollywood. Tolkin also wrote the novel on which the movie was based. Robert Altman directed.]

RUSSIA   *See* NATIONS

RUTHLESSNESS   *See also* DANGER & DANGEROUS PEOPLE;
EXPEDIENCY; REVOLUTION; STRENGTH &
TOUGHNESS; VIOLENCE;

3   The cat in gloves catches no mice.
—BENJAMIN FRANKLIN, *Poor Richard's Almanack*, Feb. 1754

4   When you strike at a king you must kill him.
—RALPH WALDO EMERSON, attributed
[According to *Bartlett's*, this was recalled by Oliver Wendell Holmes, Jr., and quoted in Max Lerner, *The Mind and Faith of Justice Holmes*, 1943. Emerson penned a slightly longer version of the same thought as a *Journal* entry in September 1843: "Never strike a king unless you are sure you shall kill him."]

5   When you see a rattlesnake poised to strike, you do not wait until he has struck before you crush him.
—FRANKLIN D. ROOSEVELT, fireside radio talk, Sept. 11, 1941
[A justification for so-called preventive war. The strategy was, in fact, not used by the U.S., and three months later, Japan attacked Pearl Harbor. See WORLD WAR II.]

S

SAFETY *See* SECURITY & SAFETY

SAILING & SAILORS *See* MILITARY, THE; SHIPS & SAILING

SCANDINAVIA *See* NATIONS

SCEPTICISM *See* SKEPTICISM

SCIENCE

Every science has for its basis a system of principles as fixed and unalterable as   1
those by which the universe is regulated and governed. Man cannot make principles; he can only discover them.
> —THOMAS PAINE, *The Age of Reason,* 1794

Nature tells every secret once.   —RALPH WALDO EMERSON, *Behavior,*   2
> in *The Conduct of Life,* 1860

Men love to wonder, and that is the seed of our science.   3
> —RALPH WALDO EMERSON, *Works and Days,*
> in *Society and Solitude,* 1870

Science is a first-rate piece of furniture for a man's upper chamber, if he has   4
common sense on the ground-floor.
> —OLIVER WENDELL HOLMES, SR.,
> *The Poet at the Breakfast-Table,* 1872

Faith is a fine invention   5
When gentlemen can see.
But microscopes are prudent
In an emergency.
> —EMILY DICKINSON, poem c. 1880,
> in *Poems, Second Series* [1891]

1   There's always wan encouragin' thing about th' sad scientific facts that come out ivry week in th' pa-apers. They're usually not thrue.
                              —FINLEY PETER DUNNE, *On the Descent of Man*,
                              in *Mr. Dooley on Making a Will*, 1919

2   Familiar things happen, and mankind does not bother about them. It requires a very unusual mind to undertake the analysis of the obvious.
                              —ALFRED NORTH WHITEHEAD,
                              Science and the Modern World, 1925

3   Every science begins as philosophy and ends as art.
                              —WILL DURANT, *The Story of Philosophy*, 1926

4   Every great advance in science has issued from a new audacity of imagination.
                              —JOHN DEWEY, *The Quest for Certainty*, 1929

5   Theory like mist on eyeglasses. Obscure facts.
                              —EARL DERR BIGGERS, *Charlie Chan in Egypt*, 1935
    [Biggers wrote the books; the movie came out in 1935.]

6   Most of the fundamental ideas of science are essentially simple, and may, as a rule, be expressed in a language comprehensible to anyone.
                              —ALBERT EINSTEIN, with Leopold Infeld,
                              The Evolution of Physics, 1938
    [See also Einstein below.]

7   I am become Death, the shatterer of worlds.
                              —J. ROBERT OPPENHEIMER, quoting from the *Bhagavad Gita*
                              at the test of the first atom bomb,
                              July 16, 1945, cited in N. P. Davis,
                              Lawrence and Oppenheimer
    [See also Martin Luther King, Jr., at SCIENCE: TECHNOLOGY.]

8   The self-fulfilling prophecy is, in the beginning, a *false* definition of the situation evoking a new behavior which makes the originally false conception come *true.* The specious validity of the self-fulfilling prophecy perpetuates a reign of error.
                              —ROBERT K. MERTON, *The Self-Fulfilling Prophecy*, 1948
    [Merton is one of the founders of the sociology of science, and has the unusual distinction in his field of being admired both by academics and a much wider audience. An example of a self-fulfilling prophecy would be a case in which a teacher is told *falsely* that a group of students is exceptionally talented (or dull); experiments show that the teacher is likely then to treat the students in such a way that they actually display exceptional talent (or lack of it).]

9   The degradation of the position of the scientist as independent worker and thinker to that of a morally irresponsible stooge in a science-factory has proceeded even more rapidly and devastatingly than I had expected.
                              —NORBERT WIENER, in *Bulletin of the Atomic Scientists*,
                              Nov. 4, 1948

10 You imagine that I look back on my life's work with calm satisfaction, but from nearby it looks quite different. There is not a single concept of which I am convinced it will stand firm, and I feel uncertain whether I am in general on the right track.   —ALBERT EINSTEIN, letter to Maurice Solovine,
                              March 28, 1949

The whole of science is nothing more than a refinement of everyday thinking.   1
—ALBERT EINSTEIN, *Out of My Later Years*, 1950

Science is the attempt to make the chaotic diversity of our sense-experience   2
correspond to a logically uniform system of thought.   —*Ibid.*

Science is the search for truth.   —LINUS PAULING, *No More War!*, 1958   3

I am sorry to say that there is too much point to the wisecrack that life is ex-   4
tinct on other planets because their scientists were more advanced than ours.
—JOHN F. KENNEDY,
speech, Dec. 11, 1959

In science, the excellent is not just better than the ordinary; it is almost all that   5
matters.   —U.S. PRESIDENT'S SCIENCE ADVISORY COMMITTEE,
*Scientific Progress, the Universities
and the Federal Government*, 1960

SCIENCE: BIOLOGY & PHYSIOLOGY   *See also* DOCTORS & MEDICINE;
HEALTH; NATURE (Brandeis)

Of physiology from top to toe I sing.   6
—WALT WHITMAN, *I Sing the Body Electric*, c. 1870

There is no more reason to believe that man descended from some inferior an-   7
imal than there is to believe that a stately mansion has descended from a small
cottage.   —WILLIAM JENNINGS BRYAN,
in the Scopes "monkey" trial,
Dayton, Tenn., July 28, 1925
[High school teacher John Scopes was tried for teaching Darwin's theory of
evolution. Bryan aided the prosecution and Clarence Darrow participated in
the defense. The law under which Scopes was tried—and convicted—remained
on the books in Tennessee until 1967.]

Science is taking on a new aspect that is neither purely physical nor purely bi-   8
ological. It is becoming the study of organisms. Biology is the study of the
larger organisms; whereas physics is the study of the smaller organisms.
—ALFRED NORTH WHITEHEAD,
Science and the Modern World, 1926

Amoebas at the start   9
Were not complex;
They tore themselves apart and started Sex.   —ARTHUR GUITERMAN, *Sex*

SCIENCE: MATHEMATICS & STATISTICS

The union of the mathematician with the poet, fervor with measure, passion   10
with correctness, this surely is the ideal.
—WILLIAM JAMES, *Clifford's Lectures and Essays*, 1879

Figures won't lie, but liars will figure.   11
—CHARLES H. GROSVENOR, saying
[Gen. Grosvenor, a Republican member of the U.S. House of Representatives
from Ohio, was referring to the process of predicting election outcomes. He
may have had in mind Thomas Carlyle's comment, "A witty statesman said,
you might prove anything by figures." At any rate, Grosvenor himself was a

famous forecaster of presidential elections, which earned him the nickname "Old Figgers." He served in the House 1885–91 and 1893–1907.

Another whiz with figures was New York governor and Democratic presidential candidate Al Smith. "He could make statistics sit up, beg, roll over, and bark," said Robert Moses.]

1   There are three kinds of lies: lies, damned lies, and statistics.
                                           —MARK TWAIN, *Autobiography*, 1924
[Twain said that he was quoting British statesman Benjamin Disraeli. The actual author is not known for certain.]

2   The science of pure mathematics . . . may claim to be the most original creation of the human spirit.   —ALFRED NORTH WHITEHEAD,
                                      Science and the Modern World, 1925

3   Prayers for the condemned man will be offered on an adding machine. Numbers constitute the only universal language.
                                  —NATHANAEL WEST, *Miss Lonelyhearts*, 1933

SCIENCE: PHYSICS & COSMOLOGY   *See also* UNIVERSE, THE

4   The world we live in is but thickened light.
                                  —RALPH WALDO EMERSON, *The Scholar*, 1883

5   What is actual is actual only for one time
    And only for one place.   —T. S. ELIOT, *Ash Wednesday*, 1930

6   Physical concepts are free creations of the human mind, and are not, however it may seem, uniquely determined by the external world.
      —ALBERT EINSTEIN, with Leopold Infeld, *The Evolution of Physics*, 1938

7   God does not play dice with the universe.
                                      —ALBERT EINSTEIN, saying, attributed
[In Philipp Frank, *Einstein, His Life and Times*, 1947, the wording is given as, "I shall never believe that God plays dice with the world." Einstein here was objecting to the randomness at the heart of the theory of quantum mechanics, in which probabilities replace precise measurements and predictions. Werner Heisenberg's uncertainty principle states that one cannot determine both the momentum and position of a particle at any given time—which allows for all sorts of bizarre events, at least in theory. John Wheeler of Princeton University likes to tell students, "If you aren't confused by quantum physics, then you haven't really understood it." He ascribes this insight to Niels Bohr, the father of quantum physics. Bohr, however, was not moved by complaints about his theory. He responded to Einstein, "Nor is it our business to prescribe to God how he should run the world." See also Einstein at GOD, and Wheeler and Daniel Greenberger below.]

8   There is nothing in the world except empty curved space. Matter, charge, electromagnetism, and other fields are only manifestations of the curvature of space.   —JOHN A. WHEELER, 1957,
                            quoted in *New Scientist* [Sept. 26, 1974]

9   There is no democracy in physics. We can't say that some second-rate guy has as much right to opinion as Fermi.   —LUIS ALVAREZ, in D. S. Greenberg,
                                  The Politics of Pure Science, 1967
[Alvarez won the Nobel Prize in physics in 1968.]

Neutrinos, they are very small.   1
They have no charge and have no mass
And do not interact at all.
The earth is just a silly ball
To them, through which they simply pass,
Like dustmaids down a drafty hall
Or photons through a sheet of glass.

> —JOHN UPDIKE, *Cosmic Gall*

[Physicists have since rethought the no-mass proposition.]

A black hole has no hair.   —JOHN A. WHEELER, *Gravitation*,   2
> with Charles W. Misner & Kip S. Thorne, 1973

There is in space a small black hole   3
Through which, say our astronomers,
The whole damn thing, the universe,
Must one day fall. That will be all.

> —HOWARD NEMEROV, *Cosmic Comics*, 1975

Laws of thermodynamics: 1) You cannot win. 2) You cannot break even. 3) You   4
cannot get out of the game.   —ANONYMOUS, in Alan L. Mackay, ed.,
> *The Harvest of a Quiet Eye*, 1977

Einstein said that if quantum mechanics is right, then the world is crazy. Well,   5
Einstein was right. The world is crazy.

> —DANIEL GREENBERGER, quoted in John Horgan, *Quantum
> Philosophy*, in *Scientific American* magazine, July 1992

[Greenberger teaches at City College, New York.]

SCIENCE: PSYCHOLOGY   *See also* DREAMS & SLEEP (Emerson); MADNESS & SANITY; MIND, THOUGHT, & UNDERSTANDING

I wished by treating psychology *like* a natural science, to help her become one.   6
> —WILLIAM JAMES,
> *A Plea for Psychology as a Natural Science*, 1892

Psychology which explains everything   7
explains nothing,
and we are still in doubt.
> —MARIANNE MOORE, *Marriage*, in *Collected Poems*, 1951

Of course, behaviorism "works." So does torture.   8
> —W. H. AUDEN, *A Certain World*, 1970

If you talk to God, you are praying. If God talks to you, you have schizophrenia.   9
> —THOMAS SZASZ, *Emotions*, in *The Second Sin*, 1973

SCIENCE: TECHNOLOGY   *See also* MEDIA; MODERN TIMES; PROGRESS

Railroad iron is a magician's rod, in its power to evoke the sleeping energies of   10
land and water.   —RALPH WALDO EMERSON, *The American Scholar*,
> first delivered at the Phi Beta Kappa Society,
> Harvard University, August 31, 1837,
> in *Essays: First Series*, 1841

1   What hath God wrought!   —SAMUEL F. B. MORSE,
                                        electric telegraph message, May 24, 1844
[This biblical quotation, from *Numbers* 23:23, was suggested to Morse by Annie Ellsworth, daughter of the U.S. Commissioner of Patents. The occasion
was the formal opening of the first telegraph line, between Washington and
Baltimore. Other messages had been sent earlier. On May 1, when the line
from Washington extended only to Annapolis Junction, a colleague of Morse
telegraphed to Washington the surprising news that the Whig national convention in Baltimore had picked an unknown, Theodore Frelinghuysen, to run
for vice president with Henry Clay in the national election that fall. When
Morse read the message in the Capitol, "The ticket is Clay and Frelinghuysen," many people refused to believe it. Even after the news was confirmed by
convention delegates returning to Washington by train, some who doubted
that the new invention really worked suggested that Morse had just made a
lucky guess.]

2   Is it fact, or have I dreamt it—that, by means of electricity, the world of matter
has become a great nerve, vibrating thousands of miles in a breathless point of
time.   —NATHANIEL HAWTHORNE,
                                        The House of the Seven Gables, 1851

3   Our inventions are wont to be pretty toys, which distract our attention from
serious things. They are but improved means to an unimproved end.
                                        —HENRY DAVID THOREAU, *Walden*, 1854
[Thoreau also wrote in *Walden*, "We do not ride on the railroad; it rides upon
us." And see Thoreau at COMMUNICATION and in the next quote below.]

4   Men have become tools of their tools.   —*Ibid.*

5   Have you heard of the wonderful one-hoss shay,
That was built in such a logical way
It ran a hundred years to the day?
                                —OLIVER WENDELL HOLMES, SR., *The Deacon's Masterpiece*,
                                in *The Autocrat of the Breakfast-Table*, 1858

6   Mr. Watson, come here, I want to see you.
                                —ALEXANDER GRAHAM BELL, to his assistant,
                                        Thomas A. Watson, March 10, 1876
[These were the first words communicated by telephone. The message was
sent in Bell's laboratory-lodgings in Boston. Bell was in the bedroom and Watson, his assistant, in the laboratory down the hall, with two closed doors between them. See also Edison below.]

7   Hello!
                                —THOMAS ALVA EDISON, letter to T.B.A. David, August 15, 1877
[The first telephone lines were constantly open, necessitating a signal or greeting of some sort to get the attention of the other party. Alexander Graham Bell
(see above) favored the nautical "Ahoy," but Edison's suggestion quickly won
out. The 1877 letter in which Edison proposed "hello," which "can be heard
ten to twenty feet away," to Mr. David, president of the Central District and
Printing Co. in Pittsburgh, was discovered in AT&T archives in 1993 by Allen
Koenigsburg, a professor at Brooklyn College in New York.]

8   Success. Four flights Thursday morning all against twenty-one mile wind.
Started from level with engine power alone. Average speed through air thirty-

one miles. Longest fifty-seven seconds. Inform press. Home Christmas. Oreville [*sic*] Wright.

> —WILBUR WRIGHT & ORVILLE WRIGHT, telegram to their father,
> Bishop Milton Wright of Dayton, Ohio,
> from Kitty Hawk, N.C., Dec. 17, 1903

[The automobile] is a picture of the arrogance of wealth. . . . Nothing has   1
spread socialist feeling more than the use of the automobile.

> —WOODROW WILSON, 1906

[Wilson was president of Princeton at this time. This remark was cited in *Goggles & Side Curtains* by Gerald Carson, *American Heritage*, April 1967.]

To George F. Babbitt . . . his motor-car was poetry and tragedy, love and hero-   2
ism.   —SINCLAIR LEWIS, *Babbitt*, 1922

In the past human life was lived in a bullock cart; in the future it will be lived   3
in an aeroplane; and the change of speed amounts to a difference in quality.

> —ALFRED NORTH WHITEHEAD,
> *Science and the Modern World*, 1925

Bridges are America's cathedrals.   4

> —ANONYMOUS, in *Respectfully Quoted: A Dictionary
> of Quotations Requested from the Congressional Research
> Service*, Suzy Platt, ed., Library of Congress [1989]

[American bridges have inspired awe and affection. In *American Heritage* (Dec. 1973) an unnamed staff writer described bridges as "those gaunt and wistful structures on whose weathered surfaces can be read so much of our history." See also Hart Crane and Langston Hughes below.]

O sleepless as the river under thee,   5
Vaulting the sea, the prairies' dreaming sod,
Unto us lowliest sometime sweep, descend
And of the curveship lend a myth to God.

> —HART CRANE, "To Brooklyn Bridge," in *The Bridge*, 1930

De railroad bridges's   6
A sad song in the air.   —LANGSTON HUGHES, *Homesick Blues*

The clock, not the steam engine, is the key-machine of the modern industrial   7
age.   —LEWIS MUMFORD, *Technics and Civilization*, 1934

The machine yes the machine   8
never wastes anybody's time
never watches the foreman
never talks back.   —CARL SANDBURG, *The People, Yes*, 1936

The Italian Navigator has reached the New World.   9

> —ARTHUR HOLLY COMPTON,
> telephone message to James B. Conant, Dec. 2, 1942

[With this coded message on an unsecure phone, Dr. Compton announced the dawning of the Atomic Age. The "navigator" was Enrico Fermi, leader of a team of physicists that had just produced the first self-sustaining atomic chain reaction. The test was conducted in a reactor assembled in a squash court beneath the football stadium of the University of Chicago. Continuing the coded conversation, Dr. Conant, headed of the National Defense Research Committee, asked, "And how did he find the Natives?" "Very friendly," Compton replied. The conversation was reported by Laura Fermi in a memoir, *Atoms in the Family*.]

1   Everything in life is somewhere else, and you get there in a car.
                                   —E. B. WHITE, *Fro-Joy*, in *One Man's Meat*, 1944

2   We are here to make a choice between the quick and the dead.
                                   —BERNARD BARUCH, introducing plan for international
                                       control of atomic energy, United Nations Atomic Energy
                                       Commission, June 14, 1946
[See also PEACE.]

3   Do not fold, spindle, or mutilate.
                                   —ANONYMOUS, instructions on punched cards used
                                       with early computers, from the 1950s
[The punched cards—flexible and hence called software—were devised by a statistician, Dr. Herman Hollerith, for tabulating the 1890 census, which otherwise would not have been finished before the next one was conducted in 1900. Sensing that his automated accounting system might have commercial applications, he set up the Computing-Tabulating-Recording Co. Through mergers, this firm evolved into International Business Machines, while the cards, using "Hollerith Coding," became known generically as "IBM cards." Without Hollerith's cards, it would not have been possible for Frederick Jackson Turner to discern in 1893 the end of a significant epoch in American history; see Turner at THE FRONTIER.]

4   Garbage in, garbage out.
                                                          —ANONYMOUS, 1950s
[A succinct explanation of why computer findings may be errant, sometimes summarized in the acronymn GIGO. A related aphorism from the same period is: "To err is human, but to really foul things up requires a computer."]

5   The automobile changed our dress, manners, social customs, vacation habits, the shape of our cities, consumer purchasing patterns, common tastes, and positions in intercourse.   —JOHN KEATS, *The Insolent Chariots*, 1958

6   The "control of nature" is a phrase conceived in arrogance, born of the Neanderthal age of biology and the convenience of man.
                                   —RACHEL CARSON, *Silent Spring*, 1962

7   Our scientific power has outrun our spiritual power. We have guided missiles and misguided men.
                                   —MARTIN LUTHER KING, JR., *Strength to Love*, 1963
[See also Gen. Omar Bradley and Albert Einstein at MODERN TIMES, and J. Robert Openheimer at SCIENCE above.]

8   That's one small step for [a] man, one giant leap for mankind.
                                   —NEIL A. ARMSTRONG, disembarking
                                       from the Eagle moon lander, July 20, 1969
["A man" is the wording in the official version of the Apollo 11 mission. But according to recordings of this moment—the first step on the moon—the "a" was lost in transmission.
    This first moon landing bordered on the miraculous, but some observers, for various reasons, stood apart from the general enthusiasm. W. H. Auden wrote, "The moon is a desert. I have seen deserts."]

Here men from the planet Earth first set foot on the moon, July 1969 A.D. We 1
came in peace for all mankind.
> —NASA (National Aeronautic and Space Administration),
> plaque on the moon

[For a moon flight that went wrong, see James A. Lovell, Jr., at AMERICAN HISTORY: MEMORABLE MOMENTS.]

The real problem is not whether machines think but whether men do. 2
> —B. F. SKINNER,
> *Contingencies of Reinforcement,* 1969

Old elephants limp off to the hills to die; old Americans go out to the highway 3
and drive themselves to death with huge cars.
> —HUNTER S. THOMPSON, *Fear and Loathing in Las Vegas,* 1972

A motorcycle functions entirely in accordance with the laws of reason, and a 4
study of the art of motorcycle maintenance is really a miniature study of the
art of rationality itself.
> —ROBERT PIRSIG,
> *Zen and the Art of Motorcycle Maintenance,* 1974

[Pirsig objected to the "barriers of dualistic thought that prevent a real understanding of what technology is—not an exploitation of nature, but a fusion of nature and the human spirit into a new kind of creation that transcends both," *ibid.* See also GOD.]

If true computer music were ever written, it would be listened to only by other 5
computers. —MICHAEL CRICHTON,
> *Electronic Life: How to Think About Computers,* 1983

For a successful technology, reality must take precedence over public relations, 6
for Nature cannot be fooled.
> —RICHARD P. FEYNMAN, appendix to presidential commission
> report on the explosion of the space shuttle *Challenger*
> following a cold-weather liftoff, Jan. 28, 1986

[Feynman, a Nobel Prize winner and one of the most imaginative and charming of modern physicists, served on the presidential panel that investigated the *Challenger* disaster, in which all seven crew members were killed. Cutting through the ponderous, defensive, televised proceedings, Feynman dropped into a glass of ice water a sample of the rubber used for the O-ring seals that connected segments of the booster rockets. This demonstrated on the spot that cold destroyed the material's resiliency. Not for another month, however, did NASA concede that joint failure was the most likely cause of the explosion.]

Thanks to modern technology . . . history now comes equipped with a fast- 7
forward button. —GORE VIDAL,
> *Screening History,* 1992

Beware the technological juggernaut, reckon the terrible costs, understand the 8
worlds being lost in the world being gained, reflect on the price of the machine
and its systems in your life, pay attention to the natural world and its increasing destruction, resist the seductive catastrophe of industrialism.
> —KIRKPATRICK SALE, *Rebels Against the Future:*
> *Lessons for the Computer Age,* 1995

SEAS *See* NATURE: SEAS & OCEANS

SEASONS & TIMES

See also MODERN TIMES; NATURE: SEASONS

1   There is a fullness of time when men should go, and not occupy too long the ground to which others have a right to advance.
—THOMAS JEFFERSON, letter to Dr. Benjamin Rush, 1811

2   Death and taxes and childbirth! There's never any convenient time for any of them!   —MARGARET MITCHELL, *Gone with the Wind*, 1936

3   There's a time in every man's life, and I've had plenty of them.
—CHARLES DILLON "CASEY" STENGEL, quoted in the Ken Burns television series *Baseball*, part IV, 1994

4   The time to repair the roof is when the sun is shining.
—JOHN F. KENNEDY, State of the Union address, 1962

SECRETS

See also SECURITY & SAFETY

5   Three may keep a secret, if two of them are dead.
—BENJAMIN FRANKLIN, *Poor Richard's Almanack*, July 1735

6   Everyone is a moon, and has a dark side which he never shows to anybody.
—MARK TWAIN, *Pudd'nhead Wilson's New Calendar*, in *Following the Equator*, 1897

7   We dance round in a ring and suppose,
But the Secret sits in the middle and knows.
—ROBERT FROST, *The Secret Sits*, in *Time Out*, 1943

8   Absolute secrecy corrupts absolutely.
—FRED HITZ, interview, *New York Times*, July 30, 1995
[Hitz, the Inspector General of the C.I.A., adapted Lord Acton's classic, "Power tends to corrupt, and absolute power corrupts absolutely," letter to Bishop Mandell Creighton, April 5, 1887.]

SECURITY & SAFETY

See also PRIVACY; SECRETS; TALK
(Anonymous)

9   He that's secure is not safe.
—BENJAMIN FRANKLIN, *Poor Richard's Almanack*, August 1748

10   There is no safety in numbers, or in anything else.
—JAMES THURBER, *The Fairly Intelligent Fly*, in *The New Yorker*, Feb. 4, 1939

11   There is no home here. There is no security in your mansions or your fortresses, your family vaults or your banks or your double beds. Understand this fact, and you will be free. Accept it, and you will be happy.
—CHRISTOPHER ISHERWOOD, *Los Angeles*, 1947, in *Exhumations* [1966]
[Isherwood is speaking of California, "this untamed, undomesticated, aloof, prehistoric landscape which relentlessly reminds the traveler of his human condition and the circumstances of his tenure upon the earth."]

Security is like liberty in that many are the crimes that are committed in its 1
name.   —ROBERT H. JACKSON,
                              dissenting opinion in *U.S. v. Shaughnessy*, 1950

Safety has really killed all our business.   2
                              —LEE IACOCCA, complaint to Pres. Richard Nixon, 1971
[Iacocca and Henry Ford II were lobbying privately against safety rules. They
were caught on the now famous White House tape recorder. Nixon responded
by delaying all new federal safety regulations.]

SELF

Trust thyself: every heart vibrates to that iron string.   3
                              —RALPH WALDO EMERSON, *Self-Reliance*,
                              in *Essays: First Series*, 1841

Nothing can bring you peace but yourself. Nothing can bring you peace but the 4
triumph of principles.
                                                                      —*Ibid.*
[The last sentences of this classic essay.]

What other dungeon is so dark as one's own heart! What jailer so inexorable as 5
one's self.   —NATHANIEL HAWTHORNE,
                              The House of the Seven Gables, 1851

I should not talk so much about myself if there were anybody else whom I   6
knew as well.   —HENRY DAVID THOREAU, "Economy," *Walden*, 1854

I celebrate myself, and sing myself.   7
                              —WALT WHITMAN, *Song of Myself*,
                              in *Leaves of Grass*, 1855
[In celebrating himself, Whitman, did not exclude others. Thus the opening
lines of this poem read: "I celebrate myself, / And what I assume you shall assume, / For every atom belonging to me as good belongs to you." For Whitman
on contradicting himself, see CONSISTENCY.]

I dote on myself, there is that lot of me and all so luscious.   —*Ibid.* 8

Not in the clamor of the crowded street,   9
Not in the shouts and plaudits of the throng,
But in ourselves, are triumph and defeat.
                              —HENRY WADSWORTH LONGFELLOW, *The Poets*, 1876

To understand oneself is the classic form of consolation; to elude oneself is the 10
romantic.   —GEORGE SANTAYANA, *The Genteel Tradition
                              in American Philosophy*, in *Winds of Doctrine*, 1913

Men can starve from a lack of self-realization as much as they can from a lack 11
of bread.   —RICHARD WRIGHT, *Native Son*, 1940

I myself am hell.   12
                              —ROBERT LOWELL, *Skunk Hour*, 1959
[More at MADNESS.]

I, I, I!—a burden to be surrendered.   —TENNESSEE WILLIAMS, *Cahiers Noirs* 13

1 Self-knowledge is always bad news.
>> —JOHN BARTH, quoted by David Bouchier, *Morning Edition*
>> radio show, Public Broadcasting System, Dec. 12, 1994

SELF-RELIANCE   *See also* SELF

2 God helps them that help themselves.
>> —BENJAMIN FRANKLIN, *Poor Richard's Almanack*, June 1736
>> [An old saying. Aesop, in *Hercules and the Waggoner*, expressed the same idea:
>> "The gods help them that help themselves."]

3 Discontent is the want of self-reliance.
>> —RALPH WALDO EMERSON, *Self-Reliance*,
>> in *Essays: First Series*, 1841

[More at UNHAPPINESS.]

4 Voyager upon life's sea, to yourself be true,
And whate'er your lot may be, paddle your own canoe.
>> —ANONYMOUS, *Harper's Monthly*, May 1854

5 He was a self-made man who owed his lack of success to nobody.
>> —JOSEPH HELLER, *Catch-22*, 1961

SERVING ONE'S COUNTRY   *See also* PATRIOTISM & THE FLAG

6 The Moral Equivalent of War.
>> —WILLIAM JAMES, book title, 1910
>> [James, a pacifist, believed in drafting young men into national service as the
>> moral equivalent of war. See also James at PACIFISM & NONVIOLENCE and THE
>> MILITARY.]

7 And so my fellow Americans: ask not what your country can do for you—ask
what you can do for your country.
>> —JOHN F. KENNEDY, Inaugural Address, Jan. 20, 1961
>> [This call to serve the nation was not entirely original with Pres. Kennedy.
>> *Bartlett's* cites a number of predecessors, including a Memorial Day address by
>> Oliver Wendell Holmes, Jr., in 1884: "We pause . . . to recall what our country
>> has done for each of us, and to ask ourselves what we can do for our country in
>> return." *The Oxford Dictionary of Quotations* found a similar exhortation in
>> the funeral oration for John Greenleaf Whittier in 1892.
>>
>> In his presidential nomination acceptance, Kennedy had said that he would
>> be calling upon Americans to take action to help their country. See POLITICAL
>> SLOGANS, note under Kennedy's New Frontier.]

8 I challenge a new generation of young Americans to a season of service.
>> —BILL CLINTON, Inaugural Address, Jan. 20, 1993

SEX   *See also* LOVE; SCIENCE: PHYSIOLOGY &
>> BIOLOGY (Guiterman);
>> SIN, VICE, & NAUGHTINESS

9 Eighth and lastly. They are so grateful!!
>> —BENJAMIN FRANKLIN, letter to a young friend (sometimes
>> identified as *Reasons for Preferring an Elderly Mistress*),
>> June 25, 1745

Sex contains all, bodies, souls,   1
Meanings, proofs, purities, delicacies, results, promulgations,
Songs, commands, health, pride, the maternal mystery, the seminal
    milk,
All hopes, benefactions, bestowals, all the passions, loves, beauties,
    delights of the earth.
                            —WALT WHITMAN, *A Woman Waits for Me*, 1856

I have an inalienable constitutional and natural right to love whom I may, to   2
love as long or as short a period as I can, to change that love every day if I
please!   —VICTORIA CLAFLIN WOODHULL, in *Woodhull
                            and Claflin's Weekly*, Nov. 20, 1871

Higgamus hoggamus, woman's monogamous;   3
Hoggamus higgamus, men are polygamous.

                                                        —ANONYMOUS
[Apparently from the last part of the 19th century. On the issue of polygamy, in
about 1925, Pres. Calvin Coolidge and his wife are said to have visited a poultry farm, separately and with different guides. Mrs. Coolidge asked how often
the rooster performed his duty, and was told "several times a day." She replied,
"Tell that to Mr. Coolidge." Upon receiving the news, the president asked
whether the rooster always performed with the same hen, and was told, "No,
each time with a different hen." The president responded, "Tell that to Mrs.
Coolidge." This version of the story is courtesy of Kenneth Maxwell, *The Sex
Imperative.*]

Men seldom make passes   4
At girls who wear glasses.
                            —DOROTHY PARKER, *News Item*, in *Enough Rope*, 1927

Is Sex Necessary?   —JAMES THURBER & E. B. WHITE, book title, 1929   5

It's better to be looked over than overlooked.   6
                            —MAE WEST, *Belle of the Nineties*, 1934

A laugh at sex is a laugh at destiny.   7
                            —THORNTON WILDER, *The Journals of Thornton Wilder*

My big trouble is that I always think whoever I'm necking with is a pretty in- 8
telligent person.
                            —J. D. SALINGER, *The Catcher in the Rye*, 1951
[The great novelist and poet Thomas Hardy suffered from a similar flaw according to biographer Martin Seymour-Smith: "The least sign of passion or
sexual interest from a woman was enough to set him off into the belief that she
must be capable of good writing," *Hardy*, 1994.]

Years from now—when you talk about this—and you will!—be kind.   9
                            —ROBERT ANDERSON,
                            Tea and Sympathy, 1953
[This, the last line of the play was spoken, originally, by Deborah Kerr, who is
married, not happily, to a gung-ho football coach at an all-male prep school.
She befriends a troubled student accused of being a homosexual (Tony Perkins
followed John Kerr—no relation to Deborah Kerr—in the role). The play is now
dated in that the possibility of being prosecuted for child abuse is not one of the
woman's foremost worries.]

1   You mustn't force sex to do the work of love or love to do the work of sex.
                                                —MARY MCCARTHY, *The Group*, 1963

2   I've looked on a lot of women with lust. I've committed adultery in my heart
    many times. This is something that God recognizes that I will do—and I have
    done it—and God forgives me for it.
                                                —JIMMY CARTER, interview in *Playboy*, Oct. 1976

3   I hear America swinging,
    The carpenter with his wife or the mason's wife, or even the mason,
    The mason's daughter in love with the boy next door, who is in love
            with the boy next door to him,
    Everyone free, comrades in arms together, freely swinging.
                                                —PETER DE VRIES,
                                                  I Hear America Swinging, 1976
4   [A takeoff, of course, on the Whitman poem; see AMERICA & AMERICANS.]

    Sex Is Never an Emergency.
                                                —ELAINE PIERSON, title of guide for college students

SHIPS & SAILING   *See also* BUSINESS (quote from John Woolman);
                          MILITARY, THE (for the U.S.S. *Constitution*);
                          NATURE: SEAS & OCEANS

5   I wish to have no connection with any ship that does not sail *fast*.
                                                —JOHN PAUL JONES, letter, Nov. 16, 1778
    [More at AMERICAN REVOLUTION.]

6   There is not so helpless and pitiable an object in the world as a landsman be-
    ginning a sailor's life.
                                                —RICHARD HENRY DANA, JR., *Two Years Before the Mast*, 1840

7   He was a true sailor, every finger a fishhook.
                                                —RICHARD HENRY DANA, JR., *Ibid.*

8   Christ save us all from a death like this.
    On the reef of Norman's Woe!   —HENRY WADSWORTH LONGFELLOW,
                                                  The Wreck of the Hesperus, 1841
    [This extremely popular poem was based on the 1839 shipwreck of the
    schooner *Hesperus* off Norman's Reef near Gloucester, Massachusetts. More
    than twenty bodies washed ashore.]

9   You are freedom's swift-winged angels, that fly around the world.
                                                —FREDERICK DOUGLASS, *Narrative of the Life
                                                  of Frederick Douglass, An American Slave,
                                                  Written by Himself*, 1845

10 Build me straight, O worthy Master!
    Staunch and strong, a goodly vessel.   —HENRY WADSWORTH LONGFELLOW,
                                                  The Building of the Ship, 1849
    [The reference is to the "ship of state." See AMERICA & AMERICANS.]

11 A whale ship was my Yale College and my Harvard.
                                                —HERMAN MELVILLE, *Moby-Dick*, 1851

I love to sail forbidden seas.   1
                                                                —*Ibid.*
[More at TRAVEL.]

I remember the black wharves and the slips,   2
And the sea-tides tossing free;
And the Spanish sailors with bearded lips,
And the beauty and majesty of the ships,
And the magic of the sea.
                        —HENRY WADSWORTH LONGFELLOW, *My Lost Youth*,
                              in *Putnam's Magazine*, August 1855

The wonder is always new that any sane man can be a sailor.   3
                        —RALPH WALDO EMERSON, *English Traits*, 1856

O Captain! my Captain! our fearful trip is done.   4
                        —WALT WHITMAN, *O Captain! My Captain!*, 1865–66
[More at ABRAHAM LINCOLN.]

We said there warn't no home like a raft, after all. Other places do seem so 5
cramped up and smothery, but a raft don't. You feel mighty free and easy and
comfortable on a raft.   —MARK TWAIN, *Huckleberry Finn*, 1885

Any man who has to ask about the annual upkeep of a yacht can't afford one. 6
                        —JOHN PIERPONT MORGAN, attributed

Ships at a distance have every man's wish on board.   7
                        —ZORA NEALE HURSTON, *Their Eyes Were Watching God*, 1937

SICKNESS   *See* ILLNESS & REMEDIES

SILENCE   *See also* TALK

Three silences there are: the first of speech,   8
The second of desire, the third of thought.
                        —HENRY WADSWORTH LONGFELLOW, *The Three Silences
                              of Molinos*, for John Greenleaf Whittier's 70th birthday,
                              Dec. 18, 1877

We shall walk in velvet shoes: 9
Wherever we go
Silence will fall like dews
On white silence below.   —ELINOR HOYT WYLIE, *Velvet Shoes*, 1921

It is a good practice to leave a few things unsaid.   10
                        —ELBERT HUBBARD, *The Roycroft Dictionary
                              and Book of Epigrams*, 1923

Drawing on my fine command of language, I said nothing.   11
                        —ROBERT BENCHLEY, *Chips off the Old Benchley*, 1949

Try as we may to make a silence, we cannot.   —JOHN CAGE, *Silence*, 1961 12

Nobody ever got in trouble keeping his mouth shut.   13
                        —ELMORE LEONARD, *52 Pick-up*, 1974

SIMPLICITY

See also ART: AESTHETICS; ART: STYLE IN WRITING & EXPRESSION; COUNTRY LIFE & PEOPLE; GRACE

1   A refined simplicity is the characteristic of all high bred deportment, in every country.   —JAMES FENIMORE COOPER, *The American Democrat*, 1838

2   Our life is frittered away by detail. . . . Simplify, simplify.
—HENRY DAVID THOREAU, "Where I Lived and What I Lived For," *Walden*, 1854
[Making the point at greater length in the same passage, Thoreau wrote: "Simplicity, simplicity, simplicity! I say, let your affairs be as two or three, and not a hundred or a thousand; instead of a million, count half a dozen, and keep your accounts on your thumb-nail."]

3   I had three chairs in my house: one for solitude, two for friendship, three for society.   —HENRY DAVID THOREAU, "Visitors," *Walden*, 1854

4   The art of art, the glory of expression, and the sunshine of the light of letters, is simplicity.   —WALT WHITMAN, Preface, *Leaves of Grass*, 1855–92

5   Less is more.
—LUDWIG MIES VAN DER ROHE, motto
[For more information, see the note on Mies under ART: AESTHETICS.]

6   The ability to simplify means to eliminate the unnecessary so that the necessary may speak.   —HANS HOFMANN, *Search for the Real*, 1930

7   Everything should be made as simple as possible, but not simpler.
—ALBERT EINSTEIN, quoted in *The Reader's Digest*, Oct. 1977

SIN, VICE, & NAUGHTINESS

See also ALCOHOL & DRINKING; EVIL; HEDONISM; SEX; TEMPTATION

8   Where there's marriage without love, there will be love without marriage.
—BENJAMIN FRANKLIN, *Poor Richard's Almanack*, May 1734

9   Sin travels faster than they that ride in chariots.
—CHARLES DUDLEY WARNER, *My Summer in a Garden*, 1871

10   [In colonial New England] there was adultery in high places and adultery in low.
—J. G. HOLLAND, *Everyday Topics*, 1876
[More at NEW ENGLAND, in the note under Giles Firmin quote.]

11   We're poor little lambs who've lost our way.
Baa! Baa! Baa!
We're little black sheep who've gone astray,
Baa—aa—aa!
Gentleman rankers out on the spree,
Damned from here to eternity,
God ha' mercy on such as we,
Baa! Yah! Baa!
—RUDYARD KIPLING, *Gentlemen Rankers*, c. 1890
[The Ballad is probably better known in America than in England. It is called here "The Whiffenpoof Song," after the Yale University singing group.]

There is a charm about the forbidden that makes it unspeakably desirable.   1
—MARK TWAIN, *Notebook* [1935]

The probable fact is that we are descended not only from monkeys but from   2
monks.   —ELBERT HUBBARD,
*The Roycroft Dictionary
and Book of Epigrams*, 1923

We are punished by our sins, not for them.   3
—ELBERT HUBBARD, *The Note Book* [1927]

"Goodness, what beautiful diamonds!"   4
"Goodness had nothing to do with it, dearie."
—MAE WEST, *Diamond Lil*, 1928
[The same joke is in West's 1932 debut movie *Night After Night*. The line was
one of her favorites, and she titled her autobiography, *Goodness Had Nothing
to Do with It*, 1959.]

When I'm good, I'm very, very good, but when I'm bad, I'm better.   5
—MAE WEST, *I'm No Angel*, 1933

I used to be Snow White—but I drifted.   6
—MAE WEST,
quoted in Joseph Weintraub,
The Wit and Wisdom of Mae West [1967]

Enjoyed it! One more drink and I'd have been under the host.   7
—DOROTHY PARKER, on being asked if she'd enjoyed
a cocktail party, quoted in Howard Teichmann,
George S. Kaufman [1972]
[See also Parker at PLEASURE & HEDONISM.]

If all the girls attending it [the Yale prom] were laid end to end—I wouldn't be   8
surprised.   —DOROTHY PARKER,
quoted in Alexander Woollcott,
While Rome Burns, 1934

All the things I really like to do are either immoral, illegal, or fattening.   9
—ALEXANDER WOOLLCOTT,
quoted in Howard Teichmann,
George S. Kaufman [1972]
["Woolly," as he was called, grew larger than life, so large that someone
quipped that "he was all Woollcott and a yard wide." He was the model for
the outrageously egocentric Sheridan Whiteside in *The Man Who Came to
Dinner* by Moss Hart and George Kaufman, and he took over the role on the
road.]

Home is heaven and orgies are vile,   10
But you need an orgy once in a while.
—OGDEN NASH, *Home 99 44/100% Sweet Home*,
in *The Primrose Path*, 1935

The only people who should really sin   11
Are the people who can sin with a grin.
—OGDEN NASH, *Inter-Office Memorandum*,
in *I'm a Stranger to Myself*, 1938

1   Maybe just whistle. You know how to whistle, don't you, Steve? You just put
your lips together and blow.   —JULES FURTHMAN & WILLIAM FAULKNER,
To Have and Have Not,
screenplay, 1944
[In this scene, a young Lauren Bacall tells Humphrey Bogart that if he needs
her, he should whistle. In real life, the two later married, and she gave him a
silver whistle to call her.
   Whistling for one's beloved has a long literary history. A Beaumont and
Fletcher play, *Wit Without Money,* written in 1639, includes the line, "Whistle and she'll come to you." And in the 18th century, a charming if headstrong
young lady in a Robert Burns poem promises, "O whistle, and I'll come to you,
my lad: / Tho' father and mother and a' should gae mad." In this connection,
note that the proverb, "A whistling girl and a crowing hen always come to the
same bad end," also has been traced back to 18th-century Scotland.]

2   Never practice two vices at once.   —TALLULAH BANKHEAD,
Tallulah, 1952

3   I'm pure as the driven slush.

—TALLULAH BANKHEAD, attributed
[Tallulah, in her 1952 autobiography said that she had three phobias: "I hate to
go to bed, I hate to get up, and I hate to be alone." Tallulah was terrific but tir-
ing. See Howard Dietz at INSULTS.]

4   Go very light on the vices, such as carrying on in society.
—LEROY "SATCHEL" PAIGE, *How to Stay Young,* 1953
[More at WISDOM, WORDS OF.]

5   The more underdeveloped the country, the more overdeveloped the women.
—JOHN KENNETH GALBRAITH,
letter to Pres. John F. Kennedy,
April 27, 1961
[Galbraith, one of the century's leading economists, served as ambassador to
India and at times found his mind wandering from the tedious routines of
diplomacy. This trend that he claimed to have discovered he described as the
"one redeeming feature" in the obligatory visits to other embassies. For additional Galbraithian generalizations, see under CITIES and ECONOMICS.]

6   For travelers going sidereal
The danger they say is bacterial.
I don't know the pattern
On Mars or Saturn
But on Venus it must be venereal.
—ROBERT FROST, *For Travelers Going Sidereal,* c. 1962
[The final adjective is technically correct, but American newspapers have al-
ways steered away from it when reporting interplanetary probes, preferring
"Venerean," "Venerial," or, most often, "Venusian," instead of "Venereal," for
obvious reasons.]

7   [Re baseball players who break curfew:] It ain't getting it that hurts them, it's
staying up all night looking for it. They got to learn that if you don't get it by
midnight, you ain't gonna get it, and if you do, it ain't worth it.
—CHARLES DILLON "CASEY" STENGEL,
quoted in Robert Creamer, *Stengel* [1984]

SKEPTICISM

Ignorance is preferable to error; and he is less remote from the truth who be- 1
lieves nothing, than he who believes what is wrong.
                                    —THOMAS JEFFERSON,
                                        Notes on the State of Virginia, 1781–85

The pragmatist knows that doubt is an art which has to be acquired with 2
difficulty.
                            —C. S. PEIRCE, *Collected Papers* [1931–58]
[See also Peirce at PHILOSOPHY.]

Skepticism is the chastity of the intellect. 3
                    —GEORGE SANTAYANA, *Skepticism and Animals Faith,* 1923

One never know, do one?   —THOMAS "FATS" WALLER, saying, 4
                                used in the movie *Stormy Weather,* 1943

SKY, THE   *See* NATURE: THE HEAVENS, THE SKY

SLAVERY   *See also* AMERICAN HISTORY: MEMORABLE MOMENTS
                        (John Brown); CIVIL WAR, THE; INJUSTICE;
                        RACES & PEOPLES; RESISTANCE; SOUTH, THE

I tremble for my country when I reflect that God is just. 5
                                    —THOMAS JEFFERSON,
                                        Notes on the State of Virginia, 1781–85
[Jefferson was warning that liberties come from God and that enslaving fellow
human beings would call down His wrath. More at FREEDOM.]

We raise de wheat, 6
Dey gib us de corn,
We bake de bread,
Dey gib us de cruss,
We sif de meal
Dey gib us de huss [husks].   —ANONYMOUS, slave verse, date not certain,
                    cited in Mel Watkins, *On the Real Side* [1994]

On this subject, I do not wish to think, or speak, or write with moderation. . . . 7
I am in earnest—I will not equivocate—I will not excuse—I will not retreat a
single inch—AND I WILL BE HEARD!
                            —WILLIAM LLOYD GARRISON, in *The Liberator,*
                                Boston, Jan. 1, 1831
[Garrison, who had already been jailed in Baltimore for his ardent abolitionist
writings, promised here, in the first issue of *The Liberator,* not to give quarter
to his enemies, although he was in danger in Boston, too. The final sentence
above is inscribed on his monument in Boston. See also Garrison and William
Henry Seward at THE CONSTITUTION.]

When Israel was in Egypt's land, 8
Let my people go;
Oppressed so hard they could not stand,
Let my people go.   —ANONYMOUS, *Go Down, Moses,*
                                early 19th century

1   We need not always weep and moan,
Let my people, go;
And wear these slavery chains forlorn,
Let my people go.

What a beautiful morning that will be,
Let my people go;

When time breaks up in eternity,
Let my people go.   —*Ibid.*

2   Wide through the landscape of his dreams
The lordly Niger followed;
Beneath the palm trees on the plain,
Once more a king he strode.
                    —HENRY WADSWORTH LONGFELLOW, *The Slave's Dream,*
                         in *Poems on Slavery,* 1842

3   Every nation that carries in its bosom great and unredressed injustice has in it
the elements of this last convulsion.
                    —HARRIET BEECHER STOWE, *Uncle Tom's Cabin,* 1852
[More at INJUSTICE. *Uncle Tom's Cabin* sold 300,000 copies its first year in
print, and was an extraordinarily effective political document. It did as much
to arouse Americans against slavery as the Communist Manifesto did to
arouse workers against capitalism. When Pres. Abraham Lincoln first met Mrs.
Stowe, in 1862, during the Civil War, he is reported to have said, "So you're the
little woman who wrote the book that started this great war!"
    Harriet Beecher Stowe, incidentally, stood less than five feet.]

4   Slavery is founded in the selfishness of man's nature—opposition to it, in his
love of justice.   —ABRAHAM LINCOLN, speech, Peoria, Ill.,
                                          Oct. 16, 1854
[Lincoln had served a term in Congress, 1847–49, but was not widely known
until he made this speech. Continuing the thought, he foresaw the terrible
struggle to come, saying, "These principles are in eternal antagonism; and
when brought into collision so fiercely, as slavery extension brings them,
shocks, and throes, and convulsions must ceaselessly follow."]

5   A peculiar institution.
                    —NEW YORK TRIBUNE, article, Oct. 19, 1854
[The phrase had been around for a while, in the sense that slavery was regarded
as an institution peculiar to the South. The earliest example of it in writing
comes in the plural form in James S. Buckingham's *The Slave States of America,* 1842. "Slavery is usually called here 'our peculiar institutions.'"]

6   You have seen how a man was made a slave; you shall see how a slave was
made a man.   —FREDERICK DOUGLASS, *The Narrative of the Life
                                   of Frederick Douglass,* 1845
[Thus Douglass begins his account of how he fought back when his master of
the moment, Edward Covey, a so-called "nigger-breaker," tried to punish him.
His resistance so intimidated Covey that he never attempted to lay a finger on
Douglass again. This was "the turning-point" for Douglass in his life as a slave:
"My long-crushed spirit rose, cowardice departed, bold defiance took its place;
and I now resolved that, however long I might remain a slave in form, the day
had passed forever when I could be a slave in fact. I did not hesitate to let it be
known of me that the white man who succeeded in whipping me must also

succeed in killing me." The *Narrative* was a best-seller for its period, selling some thirty thousand copies in its first five years and influencing many people, Harriet Beecher Stowe among them. See also Douglass at RESISTANCE.]

This government cannot endure permanently half slave and half free.   1
—ABRAHAM LINCOLN, speech, Republican State Convention,
Springfield, Ill., June 16, 1858
[More at THE UNION; see also Dred Scott at AMERICAN HISTORY: MEMORABLE MOMENTS.]

As I would not be a *slave,* so I would not be a *master.*   2
—ABRAHAM LINCOLN, handwritten note, c. August 1, 1858

My paramount object in this struggle *is* to save the Union, and is *not* either to   3
save or destroy slavery. If I could save the Union without freeing *any* slave, I would do it; if I could save it by freeing *all* the slaves, I would do it; and if I could do it by freeing some and leaving others alone, I would also do that.
—ABRAHAM LINCOLN, reply to Horace Greeley, August 19, 1862
[Greeley had asked Lincoln to make emancipation a government goal. Lincoln resented Abolitionist pressure, but was at the point of espousing their goal. See below.]

Thenceforward, and forever free.   —ABRAHAM LINCOLN,   4
Preliminary Emancipation
Proclamation, Nov. 22, 1862
[Lincoln issued the so-called Preliminary Emancipation Proclamation following the narrow victory at Antietam. The document ordered: "On the first day of January in the year of our Lord, one thousand eight hundred and sixty-three, all persons held as slaves within any state, or designated part of a state, the people whereof shall then be in rebellion against the United States shall be then, thenceforward, and forever free." The formal Proclamation was issued Jan. 1, 1863. The Thirteenth Amendment to the Constitution, which abolished slavery, was passed in 1865. See also CIVIL WAR.]

In giving freedom to the slave, we assure freedom to the free—honorable alike   5
in what we give and what we preserve. We shall nobly save or meanly lose the last, best hope of earth.   —ABRAHAM LINCOLN, second annual
message to Congress, Dec. 1, 1862
[Here Lincoln ties emancipation to his most beloved cause, saving the Union, "The last, best hope of earth." Lincoln may have had in mind Thomas Jefferson's First Inaugural Address, March 4, 1801, in which the president referred to the government of the United States as "the world's best hope."]

Where slavery is, there liberty cannot be; and where liberty is, there slavery   6
cannot be.   —CHARLES SUMNER, *Slavery and the Rebellion,* speech,
Cooper Institute, New York, Nov. 5, 1864
[The senator from Massachusetts was a staunch abolitionist and one of the early organizers of the Republican party. He is perhaps best remembered for suffering a near fatal beating on the Senate floor from Preston S. Brooks, nephew of Sen. Andrew Pickens Butler of South Carolina.]

Now the war begun.   —SOJOURNER TRUTH, on being sold to a harsh master,   7
Narrative of Sojourner Truth, 1878
[She took her name, she reported, after she left "the house of bondage." "I wa'n't goin' to keep nothin' of Egypt on me," she explains. "And the Lord gave

me Sojourner because I was to travel up an' down the land showin' the people their sins, an' being a sign unto them." After a time, she asked for a second name, "and the Lord gave me Truth, because I was to declare the truth to the people."]

1 I know why the caged bird sings, ah me,
When his wing is bruised and his bosom sore,
When he beats his bars and he would be free;
It is not a carol of joy or glee,
But a prayer that he sends from his heart's deep core.
—PAUL LAURENCE DUNBAR, *Sympathy*
[Born the son of former slaves, Dunbar became a nationally known poet. The first line here was used by Maya Angelou in her celebrated autobiography, *I Know Why the Caged Bird Sings*, 1969.]

2 The slave system on our place, in large measure, took the spirit of self-reliance and self-help out of the white people.
—BOOKER T. WASHINGTON, *Up from Slavery*, 1901

SLEEP
See DREAMS & SLEEP

SLOWNESS
See HASTE V. GOING SLOW

SMALLNESS
See also BIGNESS; DETAILS & OTHER SMALL THINGS

3 Nothing little counts.
—A. PHILIP RANDOLPH, speech, policy conference, March on Washington Movement, Detroit, Sept. 26, 1942
[More at BIGNESS.]

4 Small Is Beautiful.
—ERNST FRIEDRICH SCHUMACHER, book title, 1973
[The subtitle is "Economics as If People Mattered."]

SOCIALISM
See also COMMUNISM

5 I am for socialism because I am for humanity.
—EUGENE DEBS, speech, Jan. 1, 1897

6 Any man who is not something of a socialist before he is forty has no heart. Any man who is still a socialist after he is forty has no head.
—WENDELL L. WILLKIE, quoted in Richard Norton Smith, *Thomas E. Dewey* [1982]

SOLDIERS
See EPITAPHS & GRAVESTONES; MILITARY, THE

SOLITUDE & LONELINESS
See also ALIENATION; PRIVACY

7 No man should live where he can hear his neighbor's dog bark.
—NATHANIEL MACON, saying

8 I went to the woods because I wished to live deliberately.
—HENRY DAVID THOREAU, "Where I Lived and What I Lived for," *Walden*, 1854
[More at LIFE.]

I never found the companion that was so companionable as solitude.   1
　　　　　　—HENRY DAVID THOREAU, "Solitude," *Walden*, 1854

The holiest of holidays are those   2
Kept by ourselves in silence and apart.
　　　　　　—HENRY WADSWORTH LONGFELLOW, *Holidays*
[More at THE HEART.]

I am lonely, lonely   3
I was born to be lonely,
I am best so!   —WILLIAM CARLOS WILLIAMS, *Danse Russe*,
　　　　　　in *Al Que Quiere!*, 1917

Avoid the reeking herd,   4
Shun the polluted flock,
Live like that stoic bird
The eagle of the rock.
　　　　　　—ELINOR HOYT WYLIE, *The Eagle and the Mole*, 1921

I want to be alone.   —GRETA GARBO, saying and also one of her lines   5
　　　　　　in the movie *Grand Hotel*, 1932
[Garbo's *New York Times* obituary in 1990 stated that she actually said, "I
want to be let alone." The screenplay for *Grand Hotel* was written by William
A. Drake, from the novel by Vicki Baum.]

Solitude is the playfield of Satan.   —VLADIMIR NABOKOV, *Pale Fire*, 1962   6

Solitude is un-American.   —ERICA JONG, *Fear of Flying*, 1973

Solitude is the salt of personhood. It brings out the authentic flavor of every   7
experience.   —MAY SARTON, *Rewards of a Solitary Life*,
　　　　　　in *The New York Times*, 1990

SORROW & GRIEF   *See also* REGRET; SUFFERING & PAIN;
　　　　　　UNHAPPINESS

Grief drives men into habits of serious reflection, sharpens the understanding,   8
and softens the heart.
　　　　　　—JOHN ADAMS, letter to Thomas Jefferson, May 6, 1816

Every man has his secret sorrows which the world knows not; and oftentimes   9
we call a man cold, when he is only sad.
　　　　　　—HENRY WADSWORTH LONGFELLOW,
　　　　　　Hyperion, 1839

Sorrow makes us all children again.   —RALPH WALDO EMERSON, *Journal*, 1842   10

When lilacs last in the dooryard bloom'd,   11
And the great star early droop'd in the western sky in the night,
I mourn'd, and yet shall mourn with ever-returning spring.
　　　　　　—WALT WHITMAN,
　　　　　　When Lilacs Last in the Dooryard Bloom'd,
　　　　　　1865–66
[An elegy for Lincoln; see also *O Captain! My Captain!* at ABRAHAM LINCOLN.]

1 Sorrow is my own yard
   where the new grass
   flames as it has flamed
   often before but not
   with the cold fire
   that closes round me this year.
                    —WILLIAM CARLOS WILLIAMS,
                       The Widow's Lament in Springtime, in *Sour Grapes*, 1921

2 Between grief and nothing, I will take grief.
                    —WILLIAM FAULKNER, *The Wild Palms*, 1939

SOUL, THE   *See also* IMMORTALITY; MYSTICISM (Eliot)

3 Dust thou art, to dust returnest,
   Was not spoken of the soul.
                    —HENRY WADSWORTH LONGFELLOW, *A Psalm of Life*, 1839
   [More at LIFE.]

4 With all your science, can you tell me how it is, and whence it is that light
   comes into the soul?   —HENRY DAVID THOREAU, *Travel in Concord*,
                                  in *Excursions* [1863]

5 My soul an't yours Mas'r! You haven't bought it,—ye can't buy it! It's been
   bought and paid for, by one that is able to keep it.
                    —HARRIET BEECHER STOWE, *Uncle Tom's Cabin*, 1852

6 The windows of my soul I throw
   Wide open to the sun.   —JOHN GREENLEAF WHITTIER, *My Psalm*, 1859

7 The soul can split the sky in two,
   And let the face of God shine through.
                             —EDNA ST. VINCENT MILLAY, *Renascence*,
                                in *Renascence and Other Poems*, 1917

8 My soul has grown deep like the rivers.
                    —LANGSTON HUGHES, *The Negro Speaks of Rivers*, 1926

9 He [man] is immortal, not because he alone among creatures has an inexhaustible voice, but because he has a soul, a spirit capable of compassion and
   sacrifice and endurance.
                             —WILLIAM FAULKNER, speech accepting the Nobel Prize
                                for Literature, 1949
   [More at HUMANS & HUMAN NATURE.]

10 Teach me, like you, to drink creation whole
   And casting out my self, become a soul.
                             —RICHARD WILBUR, *The Aspen and the Stream*,
                                in *Advice to a Prophet and Other Poems*, 1961

SOUTH, THE   *See also* SLAVERY

11 The South! The South! God knows what will become of her!
                    —JOHN C. CALHOUN, deathbed words, March 31, 1850

Way down upon the Swanee ribber, 1
Far, far away,
Dere's where my heart is turning ebber,
Dere's where de old folks stay.
—STEPHEN FOSTER, *Old Folks at Home*, 1851
[The Suwannee River runs from Georgia through north Florida to the Gulf of Mexico.]

Cotton Is King; or, the Economical Relations of Slavery. 2
—DAVID CHRISTY, book title, 1855
[Christy opposed slavery, but was not a typical abolitionist. He favored colonization of American slaves.

Cotton, the dominant crop in the South in the 19th century, declined in importance slowly but steadily after the Civil War, almost disappearing by the 1970s. Twenty years later, however, it showed signs of resurgence. In 1995, the price of cotton topped $1 per pound for the first time since the Civil War, and Southern farmers rushed to plant cotton again. See also W. E. B. Du Bois at GEORGIA for a quote on the kingdom of cotton.]

I wish I was in de land ob cotton, 3
Old times dar am not forgotten.
Look away, look away,
Look away, Dixie Land.
—DANIEL DECATUR EMMET,
I Wish I Was in Dixie's Land, 1859
[Written by a famous minstrel, an Ohioan as it happens, this song was first sung by Bryant's Minstrels at Mechanics' Hall on Broadway in New York City on April 4, 1859. It quickly became popular in the North as well as the South, but the Confederates made it their own, playing it at Jefferson Davis's inauguration as provisional president in Montgomery, Ala., on February 18, 1861, and treating it as their national anthem. Lincoln reclaimed *Dixie* for the reformed Union after Lee's surrender on April 9, 1865, requesting a military band to play the tune, which, he said, "is federal property" now. The next day, when a crowd gathered at the White House to celebrate the war's end, Lincoln elaborated. "I have always thought 'Dixie' one of the best tunes I ever heard," he stated. "I have heard that our adversaries over the way have attempted to appropriate it as a national air. I insisted yesterday that we had fairly captured it. I presented the question to the Attorney General, and he gave his opinion that it is our lawful prize. I ask the band to give us a good turn on it."

The song is now usually sung minus the original dialect and "Dixie's," as in "In Dixie's land, I'll take my stan'! / To lib an' die in Dixie," is almost always rendered "Dixie." The origin of the term *Dixie* has been much debated. It probably derives from the French *dix*, ten, printed on ten-dollar notes issued prior to the Civil War by the Citizens Bank of Louisiana, the term being applied first to New Orleans where the bills circulated and then to the entire South. Despite Lincoln's efforts, the song still belongs to the South.]

Forty acres and a mule. —ANONYMOUS, catch phrase describing 4
the Freedman's Bureau Act of 1865
[The number of acres refers to the stipulation in the 1865 law that abandoned and confiscated land in the South was to be divided into forty-acre lots for rental and sale to former slaves and white refugees loyal to the Union. According to Professor Eric Foner, in a letter to *The New York Times* (Oct. 25, 1994), the mention of mules refers to an order by Gen. William Sherman, issued prior to the new law, setting aside tens of thousands of acres in South Carolina and Georgia for the former slaves and authorizing the Army to lend mules to the

settlers. Under Pres. Andrew Johnson, this law, signed by Pres. Abraham Lincoln, was abrogated; the land was returned to former owners; the black settlers were required to sign labor contracts, and if they refused, they were evicted.]

1   Oh, I'm a good old rebel, that's what I am

. . .

I won't be reconstructed, and I don't give a damn.
                              —INNES RANDOLPH, *A Good Old Rebel*, c. 1870
[An early appearance of the good old boy, historically not necessarily good, not a boy, and not usually old either.]

2   The wrecks of slavery are fast growing a fungus crop of sentiment.
                              —WILLIAM DEAN HOWELLS,
                                  Their Wedding Journey, 1872

3   The solid South.
                              —JOHN S. MOSBY, letter, 1876
[Mosby, who had been an exceptionally bold Confederate general, used this phrase in a letter announcing that he would abandon sectional loyalty and support the Republican candidate for president, Rutherford B. Hayes. The South was solidly, ardently Democratic for some seventy years, from the end of the Civil War to the rise of the Dixiecrat movement in 1948. At that time, states' rights Democrats opposed to their party's strong civil rights platform, named Gov. Strom Thurmond of South Carolina and Gov. Fielding L. Wright of Mississippi to head a presidential ticket. Gradually, white Southerners simply joined the Republicans, leading to a dramatic reversal of fortune for the Democratic party in the South. See also Fannie Lou Hamer at POVERTY.]

4   A southerner talks music.   —MARK TWAIN, *Life on the Mississippi*, 1883

5   Tortured with history.
                              —HART CRANE, "The River (Mississippi)," in *The Bridge*, 1930

6   Southern trees bear strange fruit,
    Blood on the leaves and blood at the root.
    Black bodies swinging
    In the southern breeze
    Strange fruit hanging
    From the poplar trees.

                              —LEWIS ALLAN, *Strange Fruit*, 1939

[Popularized by Billie Holiday.]

7   The old South was plowed under. But the ashes are still warm.
                              —HENRY MILLER,
                                  The Air-Conditioned Nightmare, 1945

8   There's nothing I treasure more as a writer than being a Southerner.
                              —ALEX HALEY, remark, c. 1990,
                                  quoted in *The New York Times* [July 31, 1994]

9   You can't be Southern without being black, and you can't be a black Southerner without being white.   —RALPH ELLISON, comment, 1994,
                                  quoted in *The New York Times*
                                  [July 31, 1994]
[At Harvard University in 1973, Ellison said, "All of us are part white, and all of y'all are part colored."]

SOUTH AMERICA   *See* NATIONS

SOUTH CAROLINA   *See also* CITIES (Charleston, Columbia)

In South Carolina, the spirit and the links of social life are aristocratic to a de-   1
gree which I cannot approve of, however much I may like certain people there.
And aristocracy there has this in common with aristocracies of the present
time; that, while the aristocratic virtues and greatness have vanished, merely
the pretension remains.
> —FREDERIKA BREMER, *The Homes of the New World:*
> *Impressions of America,* 1853

South Carolina is too small for a republic and too large for an insane asylum.   2
> —JAMES L. PETIGRU, remark to Robert Barnwell Rhett,
> Christmas week, Charleston, S.C., 1860

[The remark was a response to a question from Rhett, a leader of the secessionist movement. Rhett wanted to know if Petigru supported the secessionist
cause. He did not, and unfortunately for the South, his realistic assessment
was largely ignored. South Carolina, in particular, paid a heavy price in 1865
when Sherman's men assaulted the state that had started the war. "The whole
army is burning with insatiable desire to wreck vengeance on South Carolina,"
Sherman wrote Gen. Henry Halleck. "I almost tremble at her fate but feel that
she deserves all that seems to be in store for her." The destruction was much
greater than in Sherman's more famous march through Georgia. One of Sherman's generals, John A. Logan, is credited with the ditty, sung by his corps as
they marched: "Hail Columbia, happy land; / If I don't burn you, I'll be
damned!" Another officer wrote home, "In Georgia, few houses were burned;
here few escaped."
    For more on Petigru, see EPITAPHS & GRAVESTONES. For a recycled version of
the quote here, see Anne Gorsuch Burford at CITIES (Washington, D.C.).]

South Carolinians are among the rare folk in the South who have no secret   3
envy of the Virginians.   —FEDERAL WRITERS' PROJECT, *South Carolina:*
> *A Guide to the Palmetto State,* 1941

The South Carolinian has fire in his head, comfort in his middle, and a little   4
lead in his feet. Proud of his past, often scornful of innovations, he is not willing to adapt unless thoroughly convinced that it is a good thing.   *—Ibid.*

Mottoes

Animis opibusque parati.   5
Prepared in mind and resources.

Dum spiro spero.   6
While I breathe, I hope.

SOUTH DAKOTA

A part of hell with the fires burnt out.   7
> —GEORGE ARMSTRONG CUSTER, speaking of the Bad Lands
> in southwestern South Dakota, c. 1874, attributed,
> in John Gunther, *Inside U.S.A.* [1947]

I was not prepared for the Bad Lands. They deserve this name. They are like the   8
work of an evil child.   —JOHN STEINBECK, *Travels with Charley,* 1962

1   I guess it is the physical and cultural remoteness of South Dakota that compels everyone to memorialize almost every South Dakotan who has ever left the state and achieved some recognition. As a child I would pore over newspapers and magazines, looking for some sign that the rest of the world knew we existed.   —TOM BROKAW, in John Milton,
South Dakota: A Bicentennial History, 1977

Motto

2   Under God, the people rule.

SPAIN   *See* NATIONS

SPANISH-AMERICAN WAR, 1898

3   I should welcome any war. The country needs one.
—THEODORE ROOSEVELT, 1897
[Roosevelt was Assistant Secretary of the Navy. He got his wish a year later. The quote is from V. C. Jones, *Last of the Rough Riders,* in *American Heritage,* July 1969.]

4   Remember the Maine.
—ANONYMOUS, war slogan, 1898
[The slogan was popularized in Hearst and Pulitzer newspapers after the U.S. battleship *Maine,* anchored in Havana harbor, was destroyed by an explosion of unknown origin on Feb. 15, 1898. Two hundred and sixty Americans died; ninety survived. A U.S. government report in March suggested that Spain was either directly or indirectly responsible. A popular children's rhyme sprang up: "Remember the Maine! / To hell with Spain!" The U.S. declared war against Spain in April; the war ended in December. Cuba was liberated from Spain but put under the tutelage of the U.S. See also Elbert Hubbard's "message to Garcia" at ACTION & DOING.]

5   You furnish the pictures and I'll furnish the war.
—WILLIAM RANDOLPH HEARST, telegram allegedly sent
to artist Frederic Remington in Havana, Cuba, March 1898
[Reporter James Creelman related the story of this perhaps apocryphal cable. Hearst denied sending such a message but did not object to the content: His *New York Journal* called the brief war "the *Journal*'s war." U.S. business interests and popular opinion supported insurgents against the Spanish government in Cuba and the Philippines. Historian Brooks Adams, bicycling with Oliver Wendell Holmes, remarked, "This war is the first gun in the battle for the ownership of the world."]

6   You may fire when you are ready, Gridley.
—GEORGE DEWEY, order at Manila Bay, May 1, 1898
[With these words, Commodore Dewey began the Battle of Manila Bay, destroying the Spanish fleet of ten vessels, with no American casualties. Dewey's friend Capt. Charles Vernon Gridley was captain of the flagship *Olympia.* He was ill and died a few months later. Under the December peace treaty, the U.S. acquired the Philippines for $20 million. It was a troubled acquisition; see William Howard Taft below.]

7   Rough-tough, we're the stuff! We want to fight and we can't get enough!
—ROUGH RIDERS (1st U.S. Volunteer Cavalry), attributed,
rallying cry while en route to Cuba, June 1898

Don't cheer, men; the poor devils are dying.   1
    —JOHN WOODWARD PHILIP, the battle of Santiago, July 3, 1898
[The dying men were from the Spanish flagship *Viscaya*, a cruiser that exploded under American fire. Capt. Jack Philip commanded the U.S.S. *Texas*, part of the North Atlantic squadron blockading Santiago harbor. Admiral Cervera's fleet of four cruisers and three destroyers attempted to escape the blockade and were all sunk in the U.S. attack. There was later a dispute as to who should be honored for the victory: Commodore Winfield S. Schley, who directed the actual battle, or his superior, Commodore William T. Sampson, who was a little distance away. "There's glory enough for all," said Schley.]

It has been a splendid little war, begun with the highest motives, carried on   2
with magnificent intelligence and spirit, favored by that fortune which loves the brave.
    —JOHN HAY, letter to Theodore Roosevelt, July 27, 1898
[Hay was Secretary of State. The mugwumps, who opposed imperialist power politics, saw it differently. They quipped, "Dewey took Manila with the loss of one man—and all our institutions." At the end of this four-month war, America had suddenly acquired a colonial empire.]

Take up the White Man's burden—   3
Send forth the best ye breed—
Go bind your sons to exile
To serve your captives' need   —RUDYARD KIPLING,
    The White Man's Burden, 1899
[A few lines from Kipling's sardonic warning to Americans that imperialism is a hard undertaking.]

The little brown brother.   4
    —WILLIAM HOWARD TAFT, 1900
[Taft, Commissioner of the Philippines, was enlightened for his time and intended the unfortunate "little brown brother" designation to inspire decent treatment of the Philippine people. Meanwhile, the conquered Filipinos resisted American domination with stinging guerilla attacks. The Americans were not happy. "He may be a brother of big Bill Taft, / But he ain't no brother of mine," wrote Robert F. Morrison in the *Manila Sunday Times*. As for the pejorative *little*, it may be somewhat forgivable in the case of Taft, who weighed more than 300 pounds—they had to make special chairs for him when he taught at his alma mater, Yale. Even rather large persons looked little to him.]

SPEED   *See also* BOLDNESS & INITIATIVE; HASTE
        V. GOING SLOW; SCIENCE: TECHNOLOGY

In skating over thin ice, our safety is in our speed.   5
    —RALPH WALDO EMERSON, *Prudence*, in *Essays: First Series*, 1841

The swiftest traveler is he that goes afoot.   —HENRY DAVID THOREAU,   6
    "Economy," *Walden*, 1854
[See also Thoreau at LEISURE.]

Black care rarely sits behind the rider whose pace is fast enough.   7
    —THEODORE ROOSEVELT,
    quoted in David McCullough, *Truman* [1992]

1   Speed and curves—what more do you want?
—ANONYMOUS, quoted in Carl Sandburg,
The Proverbs of a People, in *Good Morning, America*, 1928

2   With all deliberate speed.   —EARL WARREN, *Brown v. Board of Education*,
follow-up ruling, 1955
[More at THE CONSTITUTION.]

SPORTS   *See also* ART: WRITING ("Red" Smith);
WINNING & LOSING, VICTORY & DEFEAT

3   Offense is the best defense.
—ANONYMOUS
[Traced to the 1700s in Bartlett Jere Whiting, ed., *Early American Proverbs and Proverbial Phrases*, 1977.]

4   Base ball [*sic*] has been known in the Northern States as far back as the memory of the oldest inhabitant reacheth, and must be regarded as the national pastime, the same as cricket is by the British.
—ANONYMOUS, *Porter's Spirit of the Times*, Jan. 31, 1857
[Fans began referring proudly to baseball as the "national pastime" or "national game" as early as 1856, but it became truly national during the Civil War, when what had been a city game was introduced to soldiers from all areas.]

5   Oh, somewhere in this favored land the sun is shining bright;
The band is playing somewhere, and somewhere hearts are light,
And somewhere men are laughing, and somewhere children shout;
But there is no joy in Mudville—mighty Casey has struck out.
—ERNEST LAWRENCE THAYER, *Casey at the Bat: A Ballad of the Republic, Sung in the Year 1888*, June 3, 1888
[At Harvard, Thayer was *Lampoon* editor and William Randolph Hearst was business manager. Thayer graduated magna cum laude and wrote *Casey*; Hearst, who had been expelled, printed it in the San Francisco *Examiner*.]

6   Baseball is the very symbol of the outward and visible expression of the drive and push and rush and struggle of the raging, tearing, booming nineteenth century.
—MARK TWAIN, speech, April 1889
[Twain spoke at a dinner honoring a team captained by Albert Spalding. Twain also used the occasion to praise a place that they had visited; see HAWAII.]

7   Slide, Kelly, Slide.
—J. W. KELLY, song title, 1889
[The song came from the chant that arose whenever Michael "King" Kelly, catcher for the old Boston Nationals, got on base. A fine all-around player, and later Hall of Famer, Kelly generally is credited with turning base stealing into an art. He once stole six bases in a single game.]

8   [Golf:] A good walk spoiled.
—MARK TWAIN, attributed
[The attribution is commonly accepted, but Britt Gustafson at the Mark Twain House in Hartford cannot find the source in Twain's writings.]

9   Hit 'em where they ain't.
—WILLIAM "WEE WILLIE" KEELER, personal motto, from 1897
[In 1897, Keeler, the diminutive (five-foot-four, 140-pound) right fielder for the

Boston Orioles, was on a tear—he wound up the year hitting .432. When Abe Yager of the Brooklyn *Eagle* asked how he did it, Keeler answered, "Simple. I keep my eyes clear and hit 'em where they ain't."]

The bigger they come, the harder they fall.   1
                              —JOHN L. SULLIVAN, saying, c. 1900
[An old adage, but often associated with this fearless boxer and with the slightly younger Robert "Ruby Bob" Fitzsimmons, an Australian-English fighter, who is said to have used the line before his 1899 bout with the much heavier Jim Jeffries. "Gentleman Jim" Corbett may have directed the remark to Sullivan himself before beating him in a heavyweight championship bout in New Orleans in 1897. Another provocative Sullivan saying was, "I can lick any man in the house!"]

He too serves a purpose who only stands and cheers.   2
            —HENRY BROOKS ADAMS, *The Education of Henry Adams*, 1907

Take me out to the ballgame,   3
Take me out with the crowd,
Buy me some peanuts and Cracker Jack,
I don't care if I never get back;
Let me root, root, root for the home team.
If they don't win, it's a shame;
For it's one, two, three strikes,
You're out, at the old ballgame.
                    —JACK NORWORTH, *Take Me Out to the Ballgame*, 1908
[The music is by Albert Von Tilzer. This is the chorus, by the way. The verse is about a female fan who went to every home game, knew all the players by their first names, corrected the umpires loudly, and cheered for the home team. "Katie Casey was baseball mad, / Had the fever and had it bad." When her young beau called on a Saturday and asked if she'd like to go to a show, "Miss Kate said, 'No, / I'll tell you what you can do.'" Chorus.]

These are the saddest of possible words,   4
"Tinker-to-Evers-to-Chance."
                    —FRANKLIN PIERCE ADAMS, *Baseball's Sad Lexicon*
                          in the *New York Mail*, July 1910
[The Chicago Cubs trio of shortstop Joe Tinker, second baseman Johnny Evers, and first baseman Frank Chance made it into baseball's Hall of Fame as a unit in 1946 partly on the strength of this poem. Despite FPA's lament (he was a New York Giant fan), they did not make very many double plays by modern standards. As Chicago sportswriter Warren Brown reported in *Don't Believe Everything You Read* (*The Second Fireside Book of Baseball*, 1958), during their glory years, 1906–1909, the Tinker-to-Evers-to-Chance combination accounted for a grand total of—hold your breath—just 29 double plays!]

Under the wide and starry sky   5
Dig the grave and let me lie;
Gladly I've lived and gladly die
Away from the world of strife;
These be the lines you grave for me;
Here he lies where he wants to be;
Lies at rest by the nineteenth tee,
Where he lied all through his life."
            —GRANTLAND RICE, *The Duffer's Requiem (with Apologies to
            R.L.S.)*, in *The Winning Shot*, with Jerome D. Traverse, 1915

1   Say it ain't so, Joe.
                                          —ANONYMOUS, Sept. 1920
[Plea allegedly made by a tearful boy to Chicago Black Sox great "Shoeless" Joe
Jackson as he emerged from a hearing on charges that he and seven other players had been bribed to throw the 1919 World Series to the Cincinnati Reds. All
were banned from baseball for life.]

2   Win this one for the Gipper.
                          —KNUTE ROCKNE, exhortation to the Notre Dame
                                      football team, from 1921
[Legend has it that as George Gipp, Notre Dame's first All-American, lay dying
of a strep infection on December 14, 1920, he asked coach Rockne to use his
name to inspire the team someday when it was down. Such sentiment doesn't
sound true for Gipp, a wild-living, hard-drinking, big-gambling man, but it was
in character for Rockne to employ it, and he apparently did so more than once,
most famously to motivate the Irish to upset Army in 1928. Rockne also has
been credited with "When the going gets tough, the tough get going"; see under STRENGTH & TOUGHNESS.
   In the movie, *Knute Rockne, All American*, 1940, writer Robert Buckner
cleaned up Gipp's character. Ronald Reagan as Gipp brought tears to millions
of eyes with a plaintive but manly deathbed request: "Someday when things
are tough, maybe you can ask the boys to go in there and win just one for the
Gipper."]

3   Quitters never win. Winners never quit.
                                          —ANONYMOUS,
                          traditional adage for football locker rooms

4   Gentlemen, you are now going out to play football against Harvard. Never
    again in your whole life will you do anything so important.
                                          —T. A. D. JONES,
                          Yale University locker room, Nov. 24, 1923
[Inspired by coach Jones, the Bulldogs beat Harvard 13–0, breaking a string of
four Crimson victories.]

5   Outlined against a blue-gray October sky, the Four Horsemen rode again. In
    dramatic lore they are known as Famine, Pestilence, Destruction, and Death.
    These are only aliases. Their real names are Stuhldreher, Miller, Crowley, and
    Layden.   —GRANTLAND RICE,
                          article on a Notre Dame–Army football game,
                                      New York Tribune, Oct. 19, 1924
[The game was played at the Polo Grounds in New York. Notre Dame won
13–7, thanks in large part to the Four Horsemen in the backfield: Harry
Stuhldreher, quarterback; and Don Miller, Jim Crowley, and Elmer Layden,
running backs. Led by these four fearsome players, Notre Dame went on
to enjoy an undefeated season including victory in the Rose Bowl over
Stanford.]

6   A streak of fire, a breath of flame,
    Eluding all who reach the clutch;
    A gray ghost thrown into the game
    That rival hands may never touch.
                          —GRANTLAND RICE, description of Harold "Red" Grange
[Grange became a professional in 1925 and for two years thrilled crowds as an
open-field runner for the Chicago Bears. A knee injury in 1927 forced him to

develop other skills. Defense became the strongest part of his game and he was team captain as well. As an undergraduate he led Illinois to an extraordinary victory over the University of Michigan, which had been undefeated for three years. He returned the opening kick for a touchdown; scored three more td's in ten minutes, and in the second half, ran for a fifth touchdown, and passed for a sixth. It was a home game, October 18, 1924, the day that the Illini dedicated Memorial Stadium at Champaign. Illinois won 39–14 before a crowd of 65,000. Grange became known as "the galloping ghost."

　　Robert Gallagher quoted this verse by Rice in an *American Heritage* interview with Grange, December 1974. Gallagher did not date the verse, but presumably Rice was not at the Illinois–Michigan game, since he was in New York City one day later writing up the Notre Dame–Army game with the Four Horsemen; see above. So the "gray ghost" verse probably came some time later.]

Tennis anyone?　1
　　　　　　　　　　　　　　　　　　　　　　　　—ANONYMOUS
[The line is a proverbial theatrical device for getting characters off the stage in a scene change. Humphrey Bogart was said to have actually spoken such a line in a play in the 1920s, but he denied it, and no one has found a citation.]

Honey, I just forgot to duck.　2
　　　　　　—JACK DEMPSEY, telephone call to his wife, Sept. 23, 1926
[Dempsey had lost the heavyweight title to Gene Tunney, and called his wife from the dressing room. In 1981, Pres. Ronald Reagan re-used the rueful remark in conversation with his wife, Nancy, after being shot and wounded by a would-be assassin, John Hinckley.]

For when the One Great Scorer comes to mark against your name,　3
He writes—not that you won or lost—but how you played the game.
　　　　　　　　　　　　—GRANTLAND RICE, *Alumnus Football*,
　　　　　　　　　　　　　　　last two lines, 1930
[Pres. Richard M. Nixon, in his memoirs, wrote with affection of his football coach at Whittier College, Wallace Newman: "He had no tolerance for the view that how you play the game counts more than whether you win or lose. He used to say, 'Show me a good loser and I'll show you a loser.'" Newman was following the footsteps of Knute Rockne; see WINNING & LOSING, VICTORY & DEFEAT. See also football coach Alonzo Gaither below.

　　Baseball coach Billy Martin also had no respect for good losers. "If there is such a thing as a good loser, then the game is crooked," he said, according to sportswriter Douglas Martin, *New York Times*, June 27, 1993.]

We wuz robbed!　4
　　　　　—JOE JACOBS, remark after the Max Schmeling–Jack Sharkey
　　　　　　　　　heavyweight title fight, June 21, 1932
[Jacobs was Schmeling's manager, and the fight ended in a controversial split decision for Sharkey. In a fight two years earlier, Sharkey had kayoed Schmeling, but because the winning punch was a low blow, Schmeling was awarded the title. Sharkey failed in his single defense of his title, in 1933. The giant Prima Carnera, whom he had beaten in 1931, got revenge with a right-hand uppercut knockout. Sharkey's last fight was against the young Joe Louis in 1936.]

Always Alert / Be Better / Concentrate Constantly / Don't Dally / Ever Earnest　5
/ Fair Feeling / Get Going / Hit Hard / Imitate Instructor / Just Jump / Keep Keen / Less Loafing / Move Meaningly / Never New / Only Over / Praise Part-

ner / Quash Qualms / Relax Rightly / Stand Straight / Take Time / Umpire Usually / Vary Volleys / Work Wiles / Xceed Xpectations / Yell Yours / Zip Zip.
—HAZEL HOTCHKISS WIGHTMAN, "Letters of Advice: Mrs. Wightman's Tennis Alphabet" in her book *Better Tennis*, 1933
[Mrs. Wightman was America's first great woman tennis champion, winning national titles in singles and doubles from 1909 to 1943.]

1   The race is not always to the swift nor the battle to the strong—but that's the way to bet it.
—DAMON RUNYON, *More Than Somewhat*
[The allusion is to *Ecclesiastes* 9:11: "The race is not to the swift, nor the battle to the strong, neither yet bread to the wise, nor yet riches to men of understanding, nor yet favor to men of skill; but time and chance happeneth to them all."]

2   I should've stood in bed.   —JOE JACOBS, remark after the opening game of the 1935 World Series, in Detroit
[This was the first major league ball game that Jacobs, who was more familiar with boxing (see above), had attended. It was a frigid day, Jacobs was ill, and he had bet on the Cubs, who lost.]

3   I zigged when I should have zagged.
—JACK ROPER, attributed, explanation of how heavyweight champion Joe Louis knocked him out, April 17, 1939

4   I'll moider der bum.   —TONY GALENTO, threat prior to heavyweight championship bout, June 28, 1939
["Two-ton" Tony was fighting Joe Louis, and he didn't murder him—he lost.]

5   Our tools for the pursuit of wildlife improve faster than we do, and sportsmanship is a voluntary limitation in the use of these armaments. It is aimed to augment the role of skill and shrink the role of gadgets in the pursuit of wild things.   —ALDO LEOPOLD, *A Sand County Almanac*, 1949

6   I can teach a lot more character winning than I can losing.
—ALONZO GAITHER, saying, *New York Times*, obituary [Feb. 10, 1994]
[This legendary football coach at historically black Florida A&M held a win-loss-tie record from 1945 to 1969 of 203–36–4.]

7   He had the three great requisites of a matador: courage, skill in his profession, and grace in the presence of the danger of death.
—ERNEST HEMINGWAY, *The Dangerous Summer*, 1958
[Hemingway was referring to Antonio Ordóñez. *The Dangerous Summer* is based on Hemingway's articles on bullfighting in *Life* magazine. See also Hemingway at GRACE.]

8   Whoever wants to know the heart and mind of America had better learn baseball, the rules and realities of the game—and do it by watching first some high school or small-town teams.
—JACQUES BARZUN, *God's Country and Mine*, 1954

Zest, they've zest.
"Hope springs eternal in the Brooklyn breast."
—MARIANNE MOORE, *Hometown Piece*
for Messrs. Alston and Reese, 1956
[A lifelong Brooklyn resident, Moore wrote this paean at World Series time. The Dodgers had beaten the Yankees 4–3 in the 1955 series, their first World Series victory. In 1956 they lost by the same margin.]

It was hard to say, about football as about games in general, which was more impressive, the violence or the rationality.
—HOWARD NEMEROV, *The Homecoming Game,* 1957

Football isn't a contact sport, it's a collision sport. Dancing is a contact sport.
—VINCE LOMBARDI, quoted in James A. Michener,
Sports in America [1976]
[See also Lombardi at WINNING & LOSING, VICTORY & DEFEAT.]

Float like a butterfly,
Sting like a bee!
Rumble young man! Rumble!
Waa!
—MUHAMMAD ALI & DREW "BUNDINI" BROWN,
their "war cry," *The Greatest: My Own Story*
[For another fighter's line that has passed into general usage, see Joe Louis on Billy Conn—"He can run, but he can't hide"—under DANGER.]

My business is hurting people.
—SUGAR RAY ROBINSON, testimony,
New York State Boxing Commission,
May 23, 1962

Can't *anybody* play this here game?
—CHARLES DILLON "CASEY" STENGEL, remark, 1962
[Casey was talking about the New York Mets, who lost 120 games in this, their first season—the most defeats by a major league team since 1899. With the words slightly transposed to "Can't anybody here play this game," Casey's saying was publicized widely as the Met's badge of ineptitude, according to Robert W. Creamer's *Stengel: His Life and Times,* 1984.]

Pitching is a large subject.
—MARIANNE MOORE, *Baseball and Writing,*
in *Tell Me, Tell Me,* 1966

In America, it is sport that is the opiate of the masses.
—RUSSELL BAKER, *New York Times,* Oct. 3, 1967

The game isn't over till it's over.
—YOGI BERRA, saying, attributed
[A variation on the traditional remark, "The game isn't over until the last man is out." See also ENDINGS.
Berra made this observation in 1973 while the New York Mets, then managed by him, were embroiled in a tight pennant race, which they eventually won. This is one of many quotations popularly attributed to Berra, but usually without much evidence. Many of them are malapropisms, perhaps reflecting the complex thought patterns of Casey Stengel, who managed the New York Yankees when Berra played catcher. Among the better-known Berra-isms:
"You can observe a lot by watching." (An actual remark, made Oct. 24, 1963,

at the press conference at which he was introduced as the new manager of the New York Yankees.)

"It's like *déjà vu* all over again" (but unlike Berra to lapse into French).

"The future ain't what it used to be." (A kind of corollary to the above.)

"Nobody ever goes there anymore. It's too crowded." (Said by his wife and friends to be a real quote but, as Ralph Keyes pointed out in *Nice Guys Finish Seventh*, the same line also appears in a 1943 *New Yorker* short story by John McNulty.)

"When you arrive at a fork in the road, take it."

"Anybody who is popular is bound to be disliked."

"You have got to be very careful if you don't know where you are going, because you might not get there."

"You can't win all the time. There are guys out there who are better than you." (But in Berra's case, not many, and he has ten World Series rings to prove it.)]

1   The point of the game is not how well the individual does but whether the team wins. That is the beautiful heart of the game, the blending of personalities, the mutual sacrifices for group success.
—BILL BRADLEY, *Life on the Run*, 1976

2   [Baseball:] It breaks your heart. It is designed to break your heart.
—A. BARTLETT GIAMATTI, *The Green Fields of the Mind*, 1977

3   Thank you, God, for giving me strength and making me a ballplayer.
—JIM "CATFISH" HUNTER, on Catfish Hunter Day
at Yankee Stadium, Sept. 16, 1979

4   Merit will win, it was promised by baseball.
—A. BARTLETT GIAMATTI, *Take Time for Paradise*, 1989

5   Football combines the two worst features of modern American life: it's violence punctuated by committee meetings.
—GEORGE WILL, in *Baseball*, produced by Ken Burns,
Public Broadcasting System, 1994

SPRING   *See* NATURE: SEASONS

STATISTICS   *See* SCIENCE: MATHEMATICS & STATISTICS

STRENGTH & TOUGHNESS   *See also* BIGNESS; RUTHLESSNESS;
VIOLENCE

6   Concentration is the secret of strength in politics, in war, in trade, in short in all management of human affairs.
—RALPH WALDO EMERSON, *The Conduct of Life*, 1860

7   There is a homely adage which runs: "Speak softly and carry a big stick; you will go far."
—THEODORE ROOSEVELT, speech, Sept. 2, 1901
[Stephen Jay Gould traced this adage to an African proverb (*Natural History* magazine, May 1985). Carl Sandburg in *The Proverbs of a People*, published in *Good Morning, America*, 1928, said that it is a Spanish proverb.]

A nation does not have to be cruel to be tough.   1
                    —FRANKLIN D. ROOSEVELT, radio speech, Oct. 13, 1940

Physical strength can never permanently withstand the impact of spiritual   2
force.   —FRANKLIN D. ROOSEVELT, speech, May 4, 1941

If you can't stand the heat, get out of the kitchen.   3
                                            —HARRY S. TRUMAN, saying
[David McCullough in *Truman*, 1992, said this is an old Missouri saying that
Truman first heard in the 1930s.]

When the going gets tough, the tough get going.   4
                                                      —ANONYMOUS
[This maxim was popularized by John N. Mitchell, attorney general (1969–72)
in the first Nixon administration, but used earlier by John F. Kennedy's father,
Joseph P. Kennedy, according to J. H. Cutler's *Honey Fitz* (1962). It also has
been attributed to football coach Knute Rockne.]

STUPIDITY   *See* FOOLS & STUPIDITY

STYLE   *See also* ART: STYLE IN WRITING & EXPRESSION;
                                          FASHION & CLOTHES; GRACE

Style is character.   —JOAN DIDION, *Georgia O'Keeffe*,   5
                                       1976, in *The White Album* [1979]
[Reminiscent of the most famous dictum on style: *"Le style est l'homme
même"*—"The style is the man himself"—by Georges Louis Leclerc de Buffon,
Discours sur le style, 1753.]

People are much too concerned about having good taste. . . . It's not a character   6
flaw if you don't have good taste.
                    —PAIGE RENSE, editor of *Architectural Digest*,
                    quoted in *The New York Times*, Oct. 25, 1993

SUCCESS & FAME   *See also* WINNING & LOSING, VICTORY & DEFEAT

Success has ruined many a man.   7
                    —BENJAMIN FRANKLIN, *Poor Richard's Almanack*, 1752

There is always room at the top.   —DANIEL WEBSTER, attributed   8

How dreary to be somebody,   9
How public—like a frog—
To tell your name the livelong June
To an admiring bog.   —EMILY DICKINSON, poem no. 288, 1861

Fame is a bee,   10
It has a song—
It has a sting—
Ah, too, it has a wing.   —EMILY DICKINSON,
                                       poem no. 1763, date not known

Success is counted sweetest   11
By those who ne'er succeed.   —EMILY DICKINSON, *Success*, in *Poems*, V [1890]

1   All you need in this life is ignorance and confidence, and then success is sure.
—MARK TWAIN, letter to Mrs. Foote, Dec. 2, 1887

2   Fame is a vapor, popularity an accident; the only earthly certainty is oblivion.
—MARK TWAIN, *Notebook*, c. 1868–1869

3   Success is to be measured not so much by the position that one has reached in life as by the obstacles which he has overcome while trying to succeed.
—BOOKER T. WASHINGTON, *Up from Slavery*, 1901

4   The highest form of vanity is love of fame.
—GEORGE SANTAYANA, *The Life of Reason: Reason in Society*, 1905–1906

5   The moral flabbiness born of the exclusive worship of the bitch-goddess SUCCESS. That—with the squalid cash interpretation put on the word success—is our national disease.
—WILLIAM JAMES, letter to H. G. Wells, Sept. 11, 1906

6   Success, like charity, covers a multitude of sins.
—ALFRED THAYER MAHAN, *Naval Strategy*, 1911
[More at WINNING & LOSING, VICTORY & DEFEAT.]

7   Success consists in the climb.   —ELBERT HUBBARD, *The Roycroft Dictionary and Book of Epigrams*, 1923

8   Pray that success will not come any faster than you are able to endure it.
—*Ibid.*

9   Some men succeed by what they know; some by what they do; and a few by what they are.   —*Ibid.*

10   Success has killed more men than bullets.
—TEXAS GUINAN, saying used in nightclub act

11   Be nice to people on your way up because you'll need them on your way down.
—WILSON MIZNER, quoted in Alva Johnson, *The Incredible Mizners*, from *New Yorker* profiles [1942, 1950]
[Also attributed to Jimmy Durante.]

12   Success is relative.   —T. S. ELIOT, *The Family Reunion*, 1939

13   Success is always dangerous, and early success is deadly.
—CALDER WILLINGHAM, *New York Times* obituary [Feb. 21, 1995], quoting interview, 1953
[In 1947, Willingham, age twenty-four, became an overnight success with his novel *End as a Man*, about bad times at a military school similar to the Citadel in South Carolina. He never equaled this achievement as a novelist but had a good career in the movies, most famously as the writer, with Buck Henry, of the screenplay for *The Graduate* (1967). See BUSINESS for advice to the graduate re "plastics."]

14   Once we find the fruits of success, the taste is nothing like what we had anticipated.   —WILLIAM INGE, introduction to collection of his major plays [1990]
[Inge in the 1950s was one of America's most successful playwrights; his hits

included *Come Back, Little Sheba* and *Picnic.* In the 1960s his reputation declined, and in 1973 he committed suicide.]

The celebrity is a person who is known for his well-knownness.   1
—DANIEL J. BOORSTEIN, *The Image,* 1962

A sign of a celebrity is often that his name is worth more than his services.   2
—*Ibid.*

In the future, everyone will be world-famous for fifteen minutes.   3
—ANDY WARHOL, *Andy Warhol's Exposures,* catalogue of his photographs, exhibition in Stockholm, Sweden, 1968

Whenever a friend succeeds, a little something in me dies.   4
—GORE VIDAL, *Sunday Times Magazine,* Sept. 16, 1973

Eighty percent of success is showing up.   5
—WOODY ALLEN, saying
[Politicians of different persuasions popularized variations of this remark. Pres. George Bush several times remarked that "Ninety percent of life is showing up," while New York governor Mario Cuomo fudged with, "Most of life is just a matter of showing up." Word columnist William Safire queried Allen on the matter, and Allen confirmed that he had used the eighty-percent figure in an interview and that he had been talking about success, not life generally (*New York Times Magazine,* August 13, 1989). See also Theodore Roosevelt at WISDOM.]

Success breeds arrogance and complacency.   6
—ROSS PEROT, *Frontline* television documentary on General Motors, Oct. 12, 1993

SUFFERING & PAIN

See also ILLNESS & REMEDIES; SORROW; TROUBLE; UNHAPPINESS

No pain, no palm; no thorns, no throne; no gall, no glory; no cross, no crown.   7
—WILLIAM PENN,
No Cross, No Crown, 1669

He has seen but half the universe who has not been shown the house of pain.   8
—RALPH WALDO EMERSON,
letter to his aunt Mary Moody Emerson

Know how sublime a thing it is   9
To suffer and be strong.
—HENRY WADSWORTH LONGFELLOW, *The Light of the Stars,*
in *Voices of the Night,* 1839

A *wounded* deer—leaps highest.   —EMILY DICKINSON, poem no. 165, c. 1860   10

After great pain, a formal feeling comes.   —EMILY DICKINSON,   11
poem no. 341 c. 1862

Pain—has an element of blank—   12
It cannot recollect
When it begun—or if there were
A time when it was not.   —EMILY DICKINSON, poem no. 650, c. 1862

1   If pain could have cured us, we should long ago have been saved.
>   —GEORGE SANTAYANA, *The Life of Reason:*
>   *Reason in Common Sense*, 1905–1906

2   God will not look you over for medals, degrees, or diplomas, but for scars!
>   —ELBERT HUBBARD, *The Note Book*, 1927

3   About suffering they were never wrong,
The Old Masters: how well they understood
Its human position; how it takes place
While someone else is eating or opening a window or just walking
>   dully along.
>   —W. H. AUDEN, *Musée des Beaux Arts*, in *Another Time*, 1940

4   Child, the key is to love your wounds.
>   —SADIE DELANY, quoted in *The New York Times*, April 18, 1995
[The memoirs of sister Sadie and Bessie Delany, spanning one hundred years,
appeared in 1991.]

SUICIDE

5   The question is whether [suicide] is the way *out*, or the way *in*.
>   —RALPH WALDO EMERSON,
>   *Journal*, 1839

6   Razors pain you;
Rivers are damp;
Acid stains you;
And drugs cause cramp;
Guns aren't lawful;
Nooses give;
Gas smells awful;
You might as well live.
>   —DOROTHY PARKER, *Résumé*,
>   in *Enough Rope*, 1927

7   To my friends: My work is done. Why wait?
>   —GEORGE EASTMAN, suicide note, March 14, 1932
[Eastman, the great inventor, manufacturer, and philanthropist, was plagued by
illness in his final years.]

8   Dying
Is an art, like everything else.
I do it exceptionally well.
>   —SYLVIA PLATH, *Lady Lazarus*, 1962–63
[*Lady Lazarus* is one of the *Ariel* poems, which Plath wrote during the half
year before her suicide in 1963.]

9   A suicide kills two people . . . that's what it's for.
>   —ARTHUR MILLER, *After the Fall*, 1964
[Miller was married for five years to film star Marilyn Monroe, who committed suicide in 1962.]

SUMMER

See NATURE: SEASONS

SUPREME COURT   *See also* CONSTITUTION, THE; PRIVACY (Brennan)

John Marshall has made his decision, now let him enforce it.   1
                                                —ANDREW JACKSON, 1832
[Pres. Jackson was making the point that the Supreme Court must depend on the executive branch of government to enforce its decisions. The decision that riled Jackson came in a case involving Indian rights. Chief Justice Marshall and the court had ruled on March 3, 1832, against the state of Georgia, which sought to annex territories belonging to the Creeks and Cherokees. (Gold had been discovered in Cherokee country in 1828.) The remark, reported by Horace Greeley, has a decidedly Jacksonian ring and many historians accept it. Jackson's sympathies were all with the state. Robert Remini demurs, however, concluding in his 1988 *Life of Andrew Jackson* that Old Hickory never said it, there being no reason for him to do so: The court had not issued any orders that required enforcement by the executive branch. Whatever the case, Jackson did ignore the court's ruling. The Creeks and then the Cherokees were pressured into relinquishing their lands by treaty and in 1838 were exiled west of the Mississippi. For the Cherokees, this forcible removal along what came to be called "The Trail of Tears" cost them nearly a quarter of their population of 18,000. See also Speckled Snake at RACES & PEOPLES.]

Th' supreme coort follows th' iliction returns.   2
           —FINLEY PETER DUNNE, *The Supreme Court's Decision,*
            in *Mr. Dooley's Opinions,* 1900
[This was the era of the Spanish-American War and American empire building, which was largely a Republican venture. The Democrats, taking a liberal view of the rights of people conquered by Americans, contended that "the Constitution follows the flag." In particular, they argued that the Constitution should apply to the people of the newly acquired Philippine Islands. The Democrats, however, failed to wrest the presidency from William McKinley, and the Supreme Court failed to find that the Constitution applied in the Philippines. As Mr. Dooley noted, in full: "No matther whether th' constitution follows th' flag or not, th' supreme coort follows th' iliction returns."]

The Nine Old Men.   3
           —DREW PEARSON & ROBERT S. ALLEN, book title, 1936
[This was not meant as a compliment.]

Under our constitutional system, courts stand against any winds that blow   4
as havens of refuge for those who might otherwise suffer because they are helpless, weak, outnumbered, or because they are non-conforming victims of prejudice and public excitement. . . . No higher duty, or more solemn responsibility, rests upon this Court than that of translating into living law and maintaining this Constitutional shield deliberately planned and inscribed for the benefit of every human being subject to our Constitution—of whatever race, creed, or persuasion.
           —HUGO L. BLACK, *Chambers v. Florida,* 1938.
[Black, a former senator from Alabama, had once been a member of the Ku Klux Klan; the membership was confirmed after Black joined the Supreme Court in 1937. H. L. Mencken joked, "Hugo won't have to buy any new robes. All he'll have to do is dye his old ones black" (quoted by Johnny Greene, in *The Dixie Smile,* in *Harper's,* Sept. 2, 1946).
    Black, however, was not a racist at heart, and when Chief Justice Charles Evan Hughes gave him a chance to redeem his reputation in the *Chambers* case, he rose to the occasion with a magnificent decision. In this case, four

black murder suspects had confessed following an all-night police "interrogation." Their confessions led to convictions, and they had been sentenced to die.]

SWEDEN   *See* NATIONS

SWITZERLAND   *See* NATIONS

T

TALK

See also CONVERSATION; LANGUAGE & WORDS; SILENCE

Great talkers, little doers.

—BENJAMIN FRANKLIN,
Poor Richard's Almanack, 1733

[*Poor Richard* was based on skillful honing of proverbs and aphorisms. For example an earlier, wordier version of this saying goes, "The greatest talkers are the least doers," James Howell, *Lexicon Tetraglotten*, London, 1660.]

1

Here comes the orator! with his flood of words, and his drop of reason.

—*Ibid.*, Oct. 1735

2

A word to the wise is enough, and many words won't fill a bushel.

—BENJAMIN FRANKLIN, "Preface: Courteous Reader,"
Poor Richard's Almanack, 1758

3

No, never say nothin' without you're compelled tu,
An' then don't say nothin' thet you can be held tu.

—JAMES RUSSELL LOWELL, *The Biglow Papers*,
"The Courtin'" in Series II, 1866

4

I have heard talk and talk, but nothing is done. Good words do not last long unless they amount to something.

—JOSEPH THE YOUNGER, in *An Indian's View of Indian Affairs*,
in *The North American Review*, no. 269, vol. 128, 1879

[Chief Joseph of the Nez Percé, was referring to the broken promises of white men. He continued: "Words do not pay for my dead people. They do not pay for my country, now overrun by white men. They do not protect my father's grave. They do not pay for all my horses and cattle. Good words will not give me back my children." More at EQUALITY.]

5

The only bird that can talk is the parrot, and he doesn't fly very well.

—WILBUR WRIGHT, saying

[This was attributed to aviation pioneer Wright by astronaut Neil Armstrong in a speech at the White House on July 20, 1994, the twenty-fifth anniversary of the first moon landing. From the same era as the Wright brothers, John D.

6

Rockefeller, in his later years, liked to recite another bit of wisdom based on a bird: "A wise old owl lived in an oak / The more he saw, the less he spoke / The less he spoke, the more he heard / Why aren't we all like that old bird?" A close variant of this verse appeared in the English humor magazine *Punch* in 1875.]

1   If you don't say anything, you won't be called on to repeat it.
                                    —CALVIN COOLIDGE, attributed
[The notoriously silent Coolidge was pure Vermont Yankee. Alice Roosevelt Longworth, in *Crowded Hours*, 1933, passed along a Coolidge joke, a comment that her doctor attributed to one of his patients: "Though I yield to no one in my admiration for Mr. Coolidge, I do wish he did not look as if he had been weaned on a pickle." Coolidge had a light side, however. See his comment on the virility of the rooster, in the note on the anonymous "Higgamus, hoggamus" verse at SEX.]

2   Talking's something you can't do judiciously unless you keep in practice.
                                    —DASHIELL HAMMETT, *The Maltese Falcon*, 1930

3   Loose lips sink ships.   —ANONYMOUS, World War II slogan

4   When you're leading, don't talk.
                                    —THOMAS E. DEWEY, remark during the 1948 presidential
                                    campaign, Richard Norton Smith, *Thomas E. Dewey* [1982]

TAXES

5   Taxation without representation is tyranny.
                                    —JAMES OTIS, attributed by John Adams and others, 1763
[The aphorism circulated in many forms in reaction to the taxes imposed on the colonies in the 1760s by Great Britain. Otis's exact words are not known. In 1764, he wrote in *Rights of the Colonies*, "No parts of His Majesty's dominions can be taxed without their consent." See also AMERICAN HISTORY: MEMORABLE MOMENTS, the anonymous slogan from 1765, above, p. 25.]

6   In this world nothing can be said to be certain, except death and taxes.
                                    —BENJAMIN FRANKLIN, letter to Jean-Baptiste Leroy,
                                    Nov. 13, 1789
[More at THE CONSTITUTION.]

7   The power to tax involves the power to destroy.
                                    JOHN MARSHALL, *McCulloch v. Maryland*, March 6, 1819
[Chief Justice Marshall here rejected the claim of the state of Maryland that it had a right to tax the Bank of the United States. In so doing, he expanded and bolstered the power of the federal government. Daniel Webster, one of the attorneys for the bank, had argued: "An *unlimited* right to tax implies a right to destroy." See also the second quote from Oliver Wendell Holmes, Jr., below for more on the power to destroy.]

8   The wisdom of man never yet contrived a system of taxation that would operate with perfect equality.
                                    —ANDREW JACKSON, *Proclamation to the People of
                                    South Carolina*, Dec. 10, 1832

Of all debts, men are least willing to pay taxes. What a satire is this on gov-   1
ernment!   —RALPH WALDO EMERSON, *Politics*, in *Essays: First Series*, 1844

The beggar is taxed for a corner to die in.   —JAMES RUSSELL LOWELL,   2
The Vision of Sir Launfal, 1848

The thing generally raised on city land is taxes.   3
—CHARLES DUDLEY WARNER, *My Summer in a Garden*, 1870

The tax-gatherer is viewed as a representative of oppression.   4
—FREDERICK J. TURNER, *The Significance of the Frontier in
American History*, 1893
[Life on the frontier promotes individualism, Turner wrote, adding: "The ten-
dency is anti-social. It produces antipathy to control"—including imposition
of taxes. See also Turner at AMERICA & AMERICANS.]

I am in favor of an income tax. When I find a man who is not willing to bear his   5
share of the burdens of the government which protects him, I find a man who
is unworthy to enjoy the blessings of a government like ours.
—WILLIAM JENNINGS BRYAN, speech, Democratic National
Convention, July 8, 1896

What is the difference between a taxidermist and a tax collector? The taxider-   6
mist takes only your skin.
—MARK TWAIN, notebook entry, Dec. 30, 1902, in
Albert B. Paine, ed., *Mark Twain's Notebook* [1935]

Taxes are what we pay for civilized society.   7
—OLIVER WENDELL HOLMES, JR., *Compañía General de Tabacos
de Filipinas v. Collector of Internal Revenue*, 1904

The income tax has made more liars out of the American people than golf has.   8
—WILL ROGERS, *The Illiterate Digest*, 1924
[This first appeared as one of his weekly articles, April 8, 1923, entitled "Help-
ing the Girls with their Income Taxes."]

The power to tax is not the power to destroy while this court sits.   9
—OLIVER WENDELL HOLMES, JR., *Panhandle Oil Co., v.
Mississippi ex rel. Knox*, 1930

Taxes are paid in the sweat of every man who labors.   10
—FRANKLIN D. ROOSEVELT, speech, Pittsburgh, Oct. 19, 1932

Anyone may arrange his affairs so that his taxes may be as low as possible; he   11
is not bound to choose the pattern which will best pay the Treasury; there is
not even a patriotic duty to increase one's taxes.
—LEARNED HAND, *Helvering v. Gregory*, 1934
[One keeps taxes low through the use of legal tax umbrellas. As explained in an
anonymous verse, probably from this era, "The rain, it raineth all around, /
Upon the just and unjust fellas, / But more upon the just because / The unjust
have the just's umbrellas," *American Heritage*, Dec. 1973.]

Taxes, after all, are the dues that we pay for the privileges of membership in an   12
organized society.   —FRANKLIN D. ROOSEVELT, campaign speech,
Worcester, Mass., Oct. 21, 1936

1   Why shouldn't the American people take half my money from me? I took all of
it from them.   —EDWARD FILENE, quoted in Arthur M. Schlesinger, Jr.,
The Coming of the New Deal, 1959
[Filene founded the famous Filene's department store in Boston.]

2   Don't tax you,
Don't tax me,
Tax that man behind the tree.
—ANONYMOUS, political saying
[Sen. Russell B. Long described this as the basic principle of tax reform, *Forbes*
magazine, Dec. 15, 1976.]

3   [We should] have a tax structure which looks like someone designed it on
purpose.   —WILLIAM E. SIMON, quoted in *Blueprints for Tax Reform*, 1977

4   I have only one thing to say to the tax increasers: Go ahead, make my day.
—RONALD REAGAN, speech, American Business Conference,
Washington, D.C., March 13, 1985
[The president was threatening to veto legislation increasing taxes. He borrowed
a line from the Dirty Harry movie *Sudden Impact*; see under Stinson at DANGER
& DANGEROUS PEOPLE.]

5   We don't pay taxes. Only the little people pay taxes.
—LEONA HELMSLEY, quoted in *The New York Times*, July 12, 1989
[A witness in the trial of Helmsley on charges of tax evasion alleged that the
"hotel queen" made this imprudent remark. As provocative as "Let them eat
cake"—words that Marie-Antoinette probably never uttered, incidentally—the
quote helped to convict the elderly Helmsley and send her to jail.]

6   The Congress will push me to raise taxes, and I'll say, no, and they'll push, and
I'll say no, and they'll push again. And all I can say to them is, read my lips: No
new taxes.   —GEORGE BUSH, presidential nomination acceptance speech,
Republican National Convention, August 18, 1988
[This rousing and wildly applauded pledge was the emotional high point of the
convention. But it was perhaps too memorable, for Congress did push, and in
1990, Pres. Bush did raise taxes, which ignited a political firestorm from which
he never recovered. Bush was trying to adopt the Hollywood-style menace popularized by his predecessor Ronald Reagan, who posed as "Dirty Harry" when
threatening to veto tax increases; see above. Bush's "read my lips" was borrowed from the 1973 screenplay for *Magnum Force*, by John Milius and
Michael Cimino. The phrase has roots in rock music and is the title of a 1957
song by Joe Greene and a 1978 album by Tim Curry. Mr. Curry told William
Safire of *The New York Times* that he picked up the phrase from an Italian-
American recording engineer. More from this speech at AMERICA & AMERICANS
and AMERICAN HISTORY: MEMORABLE MOMENTS.]

TECHNOLOGY

See SCIENCE: TECHNOLOGY

TELEVISION

See MEDIA

TEMPTATION

See also SIN, VICE, & NAUGHTINESS

7   It is not the great temptations that ruin us; it is the little ones.
—JOHN W. DE FOREST, *Seacliff, or The Mystery of
the Westervelts*, 1859

There are several good protections against temptation, but the surest is cowardice. —MARK TWAIN, *Pudd'nhead Wilson's New Calendar*, in *Following the Equator*, 1897

1

We should be judged, not by our acts, but by our temptations. —ELBERT HUBBARD, *The Roycroft Dictionary and Book of Epigrams*, 1923

2

The last temptation is the greatest treason:
To do the right deed for the wrong reason.
—T. S. ELIOT, *Murder in the Cathedral*, 1935

3

I generally avoid temptation unless I can't resist it.
—MAE WEST, *My Little Chickadee*, 1940
[Similar to Oscar Wilde's "I can resist everything except temptation," *Lady Windemere's Fan*, 1892.]

4

TENNESSEE
See also CITIES (Memphis, Nashville)

The Bostonian looks down upon the Virginian—the Virginian on the Tennessean. —*Southern Literary Messenger*, XIX, 1853

5

The Perfect Thirty-six. —ANONYMOUS, designation for Tennessee, the 36th state to ratify the 19th Amendment, giving women the right to vote, August 18, 1920
[The amendment required ratification by two-thirds of the states, or thirty-six states. Tennessee put the amendment over the top. The deciding vote was cast by Henry Thomas Burn (see AMERICAN HISTORY: MEMORABLE MOMENTS) acting on the advice of his mother (see WOMEN). The phrase "perfect thirty-six" was used in newspapers to refer not only to the number of states but also to supposedly perfect female dimensions: 36–24–36.]

6

Tennessean's lives are unhurried. Though they may complain about weather, poor crops, bad business and politics, beneath all is a certain feeling of security. The farmer will leave his plowing, the attorney his lawsuit, the business man his accounts, for a moment's or an hour's conversation with stranger or friend.
—FEDERAL WRITERS' PROJECT,
Tennessee: A Guide to the State, 1939

7

What you need for breakfast, they say in East Tennessee, is a jug of good corn liquor, a thick beefsteak, and a hound dog. Then you feed the beefsteak to the hound dog. —CHARLES KURALT, *Dateline America*, 1979

8

Motto
Tennessee—America at its best. Agriculture and Commerce.

9

TEXAS
See also CITIES (Amarillo, Austin, Dallas, El Paso, Laredo, Van Horn)

The province of Techas will be the richest state of our Union without any exception. —THOMAS JEFFERSON, letter to James Monroe, May 15, 1820

10

Remember the Alamo! —SIDNEY SHERMAN, battle cry, April 21, 1836
[More at AMERICAN HISTORY: MEMORABLE MOMENTS.]

11

1   If I owned Texas and Hell, I would rent out Texas and live in Hell.
                                    —PHILIP H. SHERIDAN, remark, Officers' Mess,
                                    Fort Clark, Texas, 1855

2   The rattlesnake bites and the scorpion stings,
    The mosquito delights with its buzzing wings;
    The sand burs prevail and so do the ants,
    And those who sit down need soles on their pants.

3   The summer heat is a hundred and ten—
    Too hot for the Devil, too hot for men;
    The wild boar roams thru the black chaparral—
    'Tis a Hell of a place is this Texas Hell.
                                    —E. U. COOK, last two verses, *Hell in Texas*, 1886
    [Cook, manager of Keystone Land and Cattle Co., wrote this poem following
    the drought of 1885–86. It was very popular among all those Texans not dead of
    heat stroke. In the poem, the Lord gives a decidedly poor piece of property
    along the Rio Grande to the Devil, who furnishes it with thorns, fleas, taran-
    tulas, and similar amenities.]

4   Texas. Texas.   —SAMUEL HOUSTON, last words, 1863

5   There is no law west of the Pecos.   —ANONYMOUS,
                                                                saying 1880s
    [Justice of the Peace Roy Bean was an exception, of sorts, to this general obser-
    vation. In his saloon-courtroom, The Jersey Lily, in Langtry, Texas, Bean ad-
    vertised himself as "Judge Roy Bean, Notary Public" and "The Law West of the
    Pecos." Both the saloon and town were named by Bean in honor of the actress
    Lillie Langtry.
        Among Bean's many colorful legal pronouncements was a cause-of-death
    ruling: "The gent met his death at the hands of an unknown party who was a
    damned good pistol shot," attributed, c. 1895. It is said that Bean once fined a
    dead man forty dollars for carrying a concealed weapon, but when a friend of
    Bean's was charged with the same offense, he ruled that the man was not guilty
    because he was standing still when arrested and so could not be said to be "car-
    rying" a weapon. On another occasion, he supposedly freed the murderer of a
    Chinese railroad worker because he could find no law on the books that made
    it a crime "to kill a Chinaman."]

6   Here was a society dominated entirely by the masculine principle.
                                    —J. B. PRIESTLEY, *Journey Down a Rainbow*, 1955

7   Texas, in the eyes of its inhabitants and in maps supplied to visitors, occupies
    all of the North American continent but a fraction set aside for the United
    States, Canada, and Mexico.   —LORD KINROSS,
                                                The Innocents at Home, 1959

8   Texas is a state of mind. Texas is an obsession. Above all, Texas is a nation in
    every sense of the word.   —JOHN STEINBECK, *Travels with Charley*, 1962

9   Once you are in Texas it seems to take forever to get out, and some people
    never make it.   —*Ibid.*

Motto

10   Friendship.

THANKSGIVING

Ah! on Thanksgiving day, when from east and from west, 1
From North and from South come the pilgrim and guest.
                    —JOHN GREENLEAF WHITTIER,
                    The Pumpkin, 1844

What moistens the lip and what brightens the eye? 2
What calls back the past, like the rich pumpkin pie?   —*Ibid.*

Over the river and through the wood, 3
To grandfather's house we go.
The horse knows the way
To carry the sleigh
Through the white and drifted snow.
Trot fast my dapple gray!
Spring over the ground
Like a hunting-hound!
For this is Thanksgiving Day!
Over the river and through the wood—
Now grandmother's cap I spy!
Hurrah for the fun!
Is the pudding done?
Hurrah for the pumpkin pie!   —LYDIA MARIA CHILD,
                    Thanksgiving Day,
                    in *Flowers for Children*, 1844–46
[Note, it is "grandfather's" house in the original, not "grandmother's." The au-
thor's paternal grandfather, Benjamin Francis, had a house in Medford, Massa-
chusetts. He was a veteran of the Revolutionary War, and both of his wives had
died before the author was born. Lydia Maria Child, a prominent reformer and
author, did not in fact have happy memories of family life. "Cold, shaded, and
uncongenial was my childhood and youth," she reported in an interview in
1877. "Whenever reminiscences rise before me, I turn my back on them as
quickly as possible."]

The year which is drawing toward its close has been filled with the blessings 4
of fruitful fields and healthful skies. . . . I do, therefore, invite my fellow citizens . . . to set apart and observe the last Thursday of November next as a day
of thanksgiving and praise to our beneficent Father who dwelleth in the
heavens.
                    —ABRAHAM LINCOLN, Oct. 3, 1863
[This proclamation was the fruit of a thirty-year campaign by Sarah Hale,
the editor of *Godey's Lady's Book*, to establish Thanksgiving as a national
holiday.]

And therefore I, William Bradford 5
(By the grace of God today,
And the franchise of this good people),
Governor of Plymouth, say—
Through virtue of vested power—ye
Shall gather with one accord,
And hold it the month of November,
Thanksgiving unto the Lord.   —MARGARET JUNKIN PRESTON,
                    The First Thanksgiving,
                    c. 1875

1 Dear the people coming home,
Dear glad faces long away,
Dear the merry cries, and dear
All the glad and happy play.
Dear the thanks, too, that we give
For all of this Thanksgiving Day. —HARRIET PRESCOTT SPOFFORD, *Every Day*
Thanksgiving Day, in *Poems*, 1881

2 Heap high the board with plenteous cheer and gather to the feast,
And toast that sturdy Pilgrim band whose courage never ceased.
—ALICE WILLIAMS BROTHERTON, *The First Thanksgiving Day*

3 'Twas founded be th' Puritans to give thanks f'r bein' presarved fr'm th' Indians, an' . . . we keep it to give thanks we are presarved fr'm th' Puritans.
—FINLEY PETER DUNNE, *Thanksgiving*, in *Mr. Dooley's Opinions*, 1900

THEATER

See ART: THEATER, DRAMA, & MAGIC

THINGS & POSSESSIONS

See also LUXURY

4 Things have their laws as well as men; things refuse to be trifled with.
—RALPH WALDO EMERSON, *Politics*, in *Essays: Second Series*, 1844

5 Things are of the snake. —RALPH WALDO EMERSON, *Ode Inscribed to*
W. H. Channing, in *Poems*, 1847
[The Satanic snake.]

6 Things are in the saddle,
And ride mankind. —*Ibid.*

7 A coin, sleeve button, or collar button dropped in a bedroom will hide itself
and be hard to find. A handkerchief in bed *can't* be found.
—MARK TWAIN, Albert B. Paine, ed., *Mark Twain's Notebook* [1935]

8 The mortality of all inanimate things is terrible to me, but that of books most
of all. —WILLIAM DEAN HOWELLS, letter to Charles Eliot Norton,
April 6, 1903

9 The goal of all inanimate objects is to resist man and ultimately to defeat him.
—RUSSELL BAKER, in *The New York Times*, June 18, 1968

10 Inanimate objects are classified scientifically into three major categories—
those that don't work, those that break down, and those that get lost.
—*Ibid.*

THOUGHT

See MIND, THOUGHT, & UNDERSTANDING

TIME

See also FUTURE, THE; LIFE; PAST,
THE; PRESENT, THE; SEASONS & TIMES

11 Lost time is never found again. —BENJAMIN FRANKLIN,
Poor Richard's Almanack, Jan. 1748
[See also Poor Richard on time and life, at LIFE.]

Remember that time is money. —BENJAMIN FRANKLIN,   1
Advice to a Young Tradesman, 1748.
[See also Franklin at MONEY.]

Time makes more converts than reason.   —THOMAS PAINE, Introduction,   2
Common Sense, 1776

Look not mournfully into the past. It comes not back again. Wisely improve   3
the present. It is thine. Go forth to meet the shadowy future, without fear, and
with a manly heart.   —HENRY WADSWORTH LONGFELLOW, *Hyperion*, 1839

Time dissipates to shining ether the solid angularity of facts.   4
    —RALPH WALDO EMERSON, *History*, in *Essays: First Series*, 1841
[See also Emerson at FACTS.]

So the little minutes,   5
Humble though they be,
Make the mighty ages
Of eternity.
    —JULIA CARNEY, *Little Things*, 1845
[More at DETAILS & OTHER SMALL THINGS.]

As if you could kill time without injuring eternity.   6
    —HENRY DAVID THOREAU, "Economy," *Walden*, 1854

Time is but the stream I go a-fishing in.   —HENRY DAVID THOREAU, "Where I   7
Lived and What I Lived For,"
Walden, 1854
[Thoreau continued the metaphor of the stream this way: "I drink at it; but
while I drink I see the sandy bottom and detect how shallow it is. Its thin cur-
rent slides away, but eternity remains."]

Backward, turn backward, O Time, in your flight,   8
Make me a child again just for tonight!   —ELIZABETH AKERS ALLEN,
Rock Me to Sleep, 1860
[Along with *Casey at the Bat* (see SPORTS) and *The Night Before Christmas* (see
CHRISTMAS), *Rock Me to Sleep* was one of the great 19th-century recitation
pieces.]

Time flies over us, but leaves its shadow behind.   9
    —NATHANIEL HAWTHORNE, *The Marble Faun*, 1860

The surest poison is time.   —RALPH WALDO EMERSON, *Old Age*,   10
in *Society and Solitude*, 1870

Time has laid his hand   11
Upon my heart, gently, not smiting it,
But as a harper lays his open palm
Upon his harp to deaden its vibrations.   —HENRY WADSWORTH LONGFELLOW,
The Cloisters, in *The Golden
Legend*, 1872

Ah, the clock is always slow.   12
It is later than you think.   —ROBERT W. SERVICE, *Songs of a Sourdough*, 1907,
retitled *The Spell of the Yukon*, 1915

1   The small intolerable drums
Of time are like slow drops descending.
—EDWIN ARLINGTON ROBINSON, *The Poor Relation,*
in *Man Against the Sky,* 1816

2   Time is a great legalizer, even in the field of morals.
—H. L. MENCKEN, *Prejudices: First Series,* 1919

3   Our life is spent trying to find something to do with the time we have rushed
through life trying to save.   —WILL ROGERS,
The Autobiography of Will Rogers [1949]

4   Time present and time past
Are both perhaps present in time future,
And time future contained in time past.   —T. S. ELIOT, *Four Quartets:*
Burnt Norton, 1935

5   Time is the school in which we learn,
Time is the fire in which we burn.   —DELMORE SCHWARTZ, *For Rhoda,* 1938

6   Time the destroyer is time the preserver.
—T. S. ELIOT, *Four Quartets: The Dry Salvages,* 1941

7   Time is the longest distance between two places.
—TENNESSEE WILLIAMS, *The Glass Menagerie,* 1945

8   For us believing physicists, the distinction between past, present, and future is
only an illusion, even if a stubborn one.
—ALBERT EINSTEIN, letter to Michele Angelo Besso's son
after his father's death, March 21, 1955

9   I must govern the clock, not be governed by it.
—GOLDA MEIR, quoted by Oriana Fallaci, in *L'Europeo,* 1976.

10   People spend so much time fretting about what they did yesterday and dread-
ing what might happen tomorrow, they miss out on all their todays.
—JOHN D. MACDONALD, *One Fearful Yellow Eye,* 1960

TIMES   *See* GOOD TIMES; BAD TIMES; SEASONS & TIMES

TIMES OF DAY   *See* NATURE: TIMES OF DAY

TOBACCO

11   I remember with shame how formerly, when I had taken two or three pipes, I
was presently ready for another, such a bewitching thing it is; but I thank God
he has now given me power over it; sure there are many who may be better employed than sucking a stinking tobacco-pipe.
—MARY ROWLANDSON, *A True History of the Captivity*
and Restoration of Mrs. Mary Rowlandson, 1682
[Mary Rowlandson was among those abducted by Indians who attacked Lan-
caster, Massachusetts, on February 10, 1676. The captives became pawns in a
larger game—King Philip's War—but she was ransomed after eleven weeks and
five days. During her captivity, she overcame many hardships—and also gave
up smoking. Her account became a 17th-century best-seller.]

The believing we do something when we do nothing is the first illusion of tobacco. —RALPH WALDO EMERSON, *Journal*, 1859

1

Some things are better eschewed than chewed; tobacco is one of them. —GEORGE DENNISON PRENTICE, *Prenticeana*, 1860

2

A man of no conversation should smoke. —RALPH WALDO EMERSON, *Journal*, 1866

3

The roots of tobacco plants must go clear through to hell. —THOMAS ALVA EDISON, diary, July 12, 1885
[Edison had a tobacco habit; he chewed tobacco, smoked heavy cigars and knew they were making him sick. Still, he lived to be eighty-four. This day's diary entry was cited in *American Heritage*, Dec. 1970.]

4

I have made it a rule never to smoke more than one cigar at a time. I have no other restrictions as regards smoking. —MARK TWAIN, speech, on his seventieth birthday, Delmonico's, New York City, Dec. 5, 1905
[Twain confided that (like Edison) he didn't exercise either; see PHYSICAL FITNESS.]

5

Tobacco is as indispensable as the daily ration. We must have thousands of tons of it without delay. —JOHN JOSEPH PERSHING, cable to Washington, 1917
[Gen. Pershing was commander in chief of the American Expeditionary Force in World War I.]

6

What this country needs is a really good five-cent cigar. —THOMAS RILEY MARSHALL, remark in the U.S. Senate, reported in the *New York Tribune*, Jan. 4, 1920
[Vice President Marshall, a former governor of Indiana, reportedly made this remark to John Crockett, chief clerk of the Senate, during a tedious Senate debate on the needs of the nation. See under VICE PRESIDENCY for another astute Marshall observation.]

7

TOLERANCE

The highest result of education is tolerance. —HELEN KELLER, *Optimism*, 1903

8

Shallow understanding from people of goodwill is more frustrating than absolute misunderstanding. Lukewarm acceptance is much more bewildering than outright rejection. —MARTIN LUTHER KING, JR., letter from Birmingham city jail, 1963

9

TRAVEL

[Traveling] makes men wiser but less happy. —THOMAS JEFFERSON, letter to Peter Carr, August 10, 1787

10

No man should travel until he has learned the language of the country he visits. Otherwise he voluntarily makes himself a great baby—so helpless and so ridiculous. —RALPH WALDO EMERSON, *Journal*, 1833

11

1 Traveling is a fool's paradise.   —RALPH WALDO EMERSON, *Self-Reliance*,
                                        in *Essays: First Series*, 1841
[Emerson wrote that it is "for want of self culture" that educated Americans
had created "the idol of traveling." After calling travel "a fool's paradise," he
noted, "We owe to our first journeys the discovery that place is nothing."]

2 I love to sail forbidden seas, and land on barbarous coasts.
                                        —HERMAN MELVILLE, *Moby-Dick*, 1851

3 I have traveled a good deal in Concord.
                        —HENRY DAVID THOREAU, "Economy," *Walden*, 1854
[Thoreau preferred to travel by foot; see LEISURE and SPEED.]

4 We go to Europe to be Americanized.   —RALPH WALDO EMERSON, *Culture*,
                                        in *The Conduct of Life*, 1860

5 I can wish the traveller no better fortune than to stroll forth in the early
evening with as large a reserve of ignorance as my own.
                        —HENRY JAMES, *Collected Travel Writings* [1993]

6 In order to travel one must have a home, and one that is loved and pulling a little at the heart-strings all the while; for the best thing about traveling is going
home.   —CHARLES DUDLEY WARNER, *The Whims of Travel*, Sept. 12, 1875

7 To forget pain is to be painless; to forget care is to be rid of it; to go abroad is to
accomplish both.   —MARK TWAIN, letter to Dr. John Brown, June 22, 1876

8 Afoot and light-hearted I take to the open road,
Healthy, free, the world before me
The long brown path before me leading wherever I choose.
                        —WALT WHITMAN, *Song of the Open Road*, 1881
[In our time, poet Louis Simpson asked, "Where are you, Walt? / The Open
Road goes to the used-car lot."]

9 Why do people so love to wander? I think the civilized parts of the world will
suffice for me in the future.   —MARY CASSATT, letter
                        to Louisine Havemeyer, Feb. 11, 1911

10 I have discovered that most of
the beauties of travel are due to
the strange hours we keep to see them.
                        —WILLIAM CARLOS WILLIAMS, *January Morning*, "Suite,"
                        in *Al Que Quiere!*, 1917
[See also CITIES (Weehawken).]

11 My heart is warm with the friends I make,
And better friends I'll not be knowing;
Yet there isn't a train I wouldn't take,
No matter where it's going.
                        —EDNA ST. VINCENT MILLAY, *Travel*,
                        in *Second April*, 1921

12 The woods are lovely, dark and deep.
But I have promises to keep,
And miles to go before I sleep,
And miles to go before I sleep.
                        —ROBERT FROST, *Stopping by Woods
                        on a Snowy Evening*, 1923

Men travel faster now, but I do not know if they go to better things.   1
　　　　　　　　—WILLA CATHER, *Death Comes for the Archbishop*, 1927

Winter is coming and tourists will soon be looking for a place to mate.   2
　　　　　　　　　　　　　—WILL ROGERS,
　　　　　　　　　　　　　　Daily Telegram, Oct. 27, 1932
[Tourists bothered Rogers. He wrote to Pres. Calvin Coolidge from Europe in
1926, "We, unfortunately, don't make a good impression collectively. . . .
There ought to be a law prohibiting over three Americans going anywhere
abroad together."]

Come with me to the Casbah.   3
　　　　　　　　　　　　　　—ANONYMOUS, from c. 1938
[The quote often is attributed to Charles Boyer, who is supposed to have said
it, with a heavy dose of Gallic innuendo, in the 1938 movie *Algiers*. But as Tom
Burnham pointed out in *More Misinformation*, Boyer never uttered the line in
any film or stage appearance. He said that his press agent of the time invented
the invitation.]

We shall not cease from exploration   4
And the end of all our exploring
Will be to arrive where we started
And know the place for the first time.　　—T. S. ELIOT, *Four Quartets:
　　　　　　　　　　　　　　　　　　　Little Gidding*, 1940

I rather expect that from now on I shall be travelling north until the end of my   5
days.　　　　　　　　　　　—E. B. WHITE, *Stuart Little*, 1945

Thanks to the interstate highway system, it is now possible to travel from   6
coast to coast without seeing anything.
　　　　　　　　　　—CHARLES KURALT, *On the Road*, 1980

TREES　　　　　　　*See* NATURE: PLANTS & GARDENS; WILDERNESS

TROUBLE　　　　　　*See also* ANXIETY & WORRY; BAD TIMES; DANGER &
　　　　　　　DANGEROUS PEOPLE; DEPRESSION, THE; ILLNESS & REMEDIES;
　　　　　　　　PROBLEMS; SORROW; SUFFERING & PAIN; UNHAPPINESS

Into each life some rain must fall,   7
Some days must be dark and dreary.　　—HENRY WADSWORTH LONGFELLOW,
　　　　　　　　　　　　　　　　　The Rainy Day, 1842

And the cares that infest the day,   8
Shall fold their tents like the Arabs,
And as silently steal away.　　　　　—HENRY WADSWORTH LONGFELLOW,
　　　　　　　　　　　　　　　　　The Day Is Done, 1844
[More at ART: MUSIC.]

If you see ten troubles coming down the road, you can be sure that nine will   9
run into the ditch before they reach you, and you will have to battle with only
one of them.
　　　　　　　　　　　　　—CALVIN COOLIDGE, saying
[Herbert Hoover, who inherited the results of Pres. Coolidge's laissez-faire approach to national affairs, had a comment on this Yankee saying: "The trouble
with this philosophy was that when the tenth trouble reached him, he was
wholly unprepared. . . . The outstanding instance was the rising boom and orgy

of mad speculation which began in 1927," quoted by John Kenneth Galbraith, *The Days of Boom or Bust,* in *American Heritage,* August 1958.]

1   The kiss of death.
—AL SMITH, remark, 1926
[Smith, the Democratic governor of New York, was referring to his old enemy William Randolph Hearst, who had come out in support of Republican Ogden Mills in the 1926 gubernatorial election. When Smith got the news, he commented happily, "It's the kiss of death!" He was right and went on to a fourth term.]

2   "Difficulties" is the name given to things which it is our business to overcome.
—ERNEST J. KING, graduation address,
U. S. Naval Academy,
Annapolis, Md., June 19, 1942
[Admiral King had been named Chief of Naval Operations the preceding March.]

3   If anything can go wrong, it will.
—EDWARD A. MURPHY, JR., c. 1949
[The search for Murphy, the originator of "Murphy's law," rivaled the hunt for Kilroy, but seems to have been more successful. Various authorities (e.g., Robert L. Forward in *Science 83,* Jan.–Feb 1983, and George E. Nichols in the *Listener,* Feb. 16, 1984) have assigned credit for the law to Capt. Edward A. Murphy, a development engineer from the Wright Field Aircraft Laboratory, in Ohio, then working on crash research tests at Edwards Air Force Base in California. After tracing a malfunction in a strain gauge he had designed to the botched wiring of a particular technician, he is said to have observed, "If there's a way to do it wrong, he will." The law has inspired many variations. Thus, Murphy's First Law of Biology is "Under any given set of environmental conditions an experimental animal behaves as it damn well pleases." Murphy's Law of Thermodynamics reads: "Things get worse under pressure." The law's corollaries include "Nothing is as easy as it looks" and "Everything takes longer than you think."]

4   Everybody fasten your seat belts. It's going to be a bumpy night.
—JOSEPH L. MANKIEWICZ, *All About Eve,* 1950
[Bette Davis speaking.]

5   Great crises produce great men and great deeds of courage.
—JOHN F. KENNEDY,
Profiles in Courage, 1956

6   If you can keep your head when all about you are losing theirs, it's just possible you haven't grasped the situation.   —JEAN KERR, *Please Don't Eat the Daisies,* 1957
[The reference, of course, is to Rudyard Kipling's poem *If,* from 1910, which contains the lines "If you can keep your head when all about you / Are losing theirs, and blaming it on you,"—and if you can do a lot of other mature and heroic things—then "Yours is the earth and everything that's in it, / And— which is more—you'll be a man, my son!"]

7   When written in Chinese, the word *crisis* is composed of two characters. One represents danger and the other represents opportunity.
—JOHN F. KENNEDY, speech,
United Negro College Fund,
Indianapolis, Ind., April 12, 1959

TRUST

Trust men and they will be true to you.   1
　　　　　—RALPH WALDO EMERSON, *Prudence*, in *Essays: First Series*, 1841

Thrust [trust] ivrybody—but cut th' ca-ards.   2
　　　　　　　　　—FINLEY PETER DUNNE, *Casual Observations*,
　　　　　　　　　in *Mr. Dooley's Opinions*, 1900

TRUTH   *See also* CENSORSHIP; DISHONESTY & LIES; SKEPTICISM

Truth often suffers more by the heat of its defenders than from the arguments   3
of its opposers.   —WILLIAM PENN, *Some Fruits of Solitude*, 1693

Such is the irresistible nature of truth that all it asks, and all it wants, is the   4
liberty of appearing.   —THOMAS PAINE, *The Rights of Man*, 1791–92

There is not a truth existing which I fear, or would wish unknown to the   5
world.   —THOMAS JEFFERSON, letter to Henry Lee, 1826

There is nothing so powerful as truth—and often nothing so strange.   6
　　　　　—DANIEL WEBSTER, argument in the case of the
　　　　　murder of Captain White, April 26, 1830

The ability to discriminate between that which is true and that which is false   7
is one of the last attainments of the human mind.
　　　　　—JAMES FENIMORE COOPER, *The American Democrat*, 1838

Truth crushed to earth shall rise again.   8
　　　　　—WILLIAM CULLEN BRYANT, *The Battlefield*, 1839
[See also Bryant at THE WORLD.]

God offers to every mind its choice between truth and repose. Take which you   9
please—you can never have both.   —RALPH WALDO EMERSON, *Intellect*,
　　　　　in *Essays: First Series*, 1841
[See Emerson on a similar choice between power and joy at POWER.]

Truth forever on the scaffold.   10
　　　　　—JAMES RUSSELL LOWELL, *The Present Crisis*, 1844
[More at TYRANNY.]

It takes two to speak the truth—one to speak, and another to hear.   11
　　　　　—HENRY DAVID THOREAU,
　　　　　A Week on the Concord and Merrimack Rivers, 1849

Truth is the silliest thing under the sun. Try to get a living by the truth—and   12
go to the soup societies. Heavens! Let any clergyman try to preach the truth
from its very stronghold, the pulpit, and they would ride him out of his church
on his own pulpit banister.   —HERMAN MELVILLE, letter to
　　　　　Nathaniel Hawthorne, June 1851

Rather than love, than money, than fame, give me truth.   13
　　　　　—HENRY DAVID THOREAU, "Conclusion," *Walden*, 1854

1   Truth is tough.   —OLIVER WENDELL HOLMES, SR.,
                                          The Autocrat at the Breakfast-Table, 1860

2   As scarce as truth is, the supply has always been in excess of the demand.
                                       —JOSH BILLINGS, *Josh Billings: His Sayings,* 1865

3   Who dares
    To say that he alone has found the truth?
                                       —HENRY WADSWORTH LONGFELLOW,
                                          The New England Tragedies, 1868

4   Tell all the truth, but tell it slant— . . .
    The truth must dazzle gradually—
    Or every man be blind.   —EMILY DICKINSON, poem no. 1129, c. 1868

5   Truth is such a rare thing, it is delightful to tell it.
                                       —EMILY DICKINSON, letter to
                                          Col. Thomas Wentworth Higginson, August, 1870
    [He was one of the few men in her life. They corresponded for twenty-four
    years, from the time she was thirty-two until her death in 1886.]

6   Truth is the only safe ground to stand upon.
                                       —ELIZABETH CADY STANTON, *The Woman's Bible,* 1895

7   The man who finds a truth lights a torch.
                                       —ROBERT G. INGERSOLL, *The Truth,* 1897

8   When in doubt, tell the truth.   —MARK TWAIN,
                                          Pudd'nhead Wilson's New Calendar,
                                          in *Following the Equator,* 1897

9   Truth is stranger than Fiction, but it is because Fiction is obliged to stick to
    possibilities; Truth isn't.   —*Ibid.*

10 Truth is the most valuable thing we have. Let us economize it.   —*Ibid.*

11 Truth is mighty and will prevail. There is nothing the matter with this, except
    that it ain't so.   —MARK TWAIN, Albert B. Paine, ed.,
                                          Mark Twain's Notebook [1935]

12 Truth *happens* to an idea. It *becomes* true, is *made* true by events. Its verity *is*
    in fact an event, a process.
                                       —WILLIAM JAMES, *Pragmatism,* 1907
    [James, a pragmatist philosopher, took up the central question of what it
    means to say that a statement or theory is true. He argued that it means that
    we can specify "what definite difference" the statement will make at "definite
    instants" of our life. The meaning and truth of ideas depend upon their "prac-
    tical consequences," "usefulness," and "workability." This contrasted with
    traditional notions that one can deduce absolute truths, as well as with the
    equally traditional suspicion that there may not be any such thing as truth. On
    the latter question, C. S. Peirce, who invented the term *pragmatism,* wrote:
    "Every man is fully satisfied that there is such a thing as truth or he would not
    ask any questions," *Collected Papers,* vol. V, para. 211. See also Albert Ein-
    stein below.]

"The true," to put it very briefly, is only the expedient in the way of our thinking.   1
                                                                        —*Ibid.*
[More at EXPEDIENCY.]

There are no whole truths; all truths are half-truths.   2
                —ALFRED NORTH WHITEHEAD, prologue, *Dialogues of
                Alfred North Whithead* [1955], recorded by Lucien Price

Most of the change we think we see in life   3
Is due to truths being in and out of favor.
                —ROBERT FROST, *The Black Cottage*, 1914

The best test of truth is the power of the thought to get itself accepted in the   4
competition of the market.   —OLIVER WENDELL HOLMES, JR.,
                                          Abrams v. U.S., 1919

[More at FREE SPEECH.]

The truth is always modern, and there never comes a time when it is safe to   5
give it voice.   —CLARENCE DARROW, writing on Voltaire,
                cited in George Seldes, ed., *The Great Quotations* [1960]
[One of Mr. Seldes's own books was titled *Tell the Truth and Run.*]

For truth there is no deadline.   —HEYWOOD BROUN, *The Nation* magazine,   6
                                     Dec. 30, 1939

I never give them hell. I just tell the truth and they think it's hell.   7
                                     —HARRY S. TRUMAN, saying
[Truman started giving the Republicans hell in 1948 during his railroad trip
across the U.S.; see also AMERICAN HISTORY: MEMORABLE MOMENTS; POLITICAL
SLOGANS.]

Truth is what stands the test of experience.   8
                —ALBERT EINSTEIN, *Out of My Later Years*, 1950

The most casual student of history knows that, as a matter of fact, truth does   9
not necessarily vanquish. . . . The cause of truth must be championed, and it
must be championed dynamically.   —WILLIAM F. BUCKLEY, JR.,
                                     God and Man at Yale, 1951

There's a saying: Only children and old folks tell the truth.   10
                —BESSIE DELANY, *Having Our Say: The Delany Sisters'
                First 100 Years*, written with her sister, Sadie, 1993

TURKEY   *See* NATIONS

TYRANNY   *See also* JUSTICE (Whittier); REVOLUTION

Rebellion to tyrants is obedience to God.   11
                —THOMAS JEFFERSON, personal motto, written on his seal
[Jefferson was insired to adopt this motto after hearing Patrick Henry's "If this
be treason" speech, according to Saul Padover's biography of the third president; for details on Henry, see AMERICAN HISTORY: MEMORABLE MOMENTS.
Decades later, on February 24, 1823, Jefferson wrote Edward Everett that he believed that the maxim originated with one of the regicides of Charles I of England. *Bartlett's* notes that he probably was referring to John Bradshaw

(1602–1659). See also Jefferson at REVOLUTION for his observation that the tree of liberty must be refreshed with the blood of patriots and tyrants.]

1   All men would be tyrants if they could.
                          —ABIGAIL ADAMS, letter to John Adams, March 31, 1776
    [More at WOMEN & MEN.]

2   Tyranny, like hell, is not easily conquered.
                          —THOMAS PAINE, *The American Crisis*, Dec. 23, 1776

3   I have sworn upon the altar of God, eternal hostility against every form of tyranny over the mind of men.   —THOMAS JEFFERSON, letter to
                          Benjamin Rush, Sept. 23, 1800
    [The tyranny to which Jefferson referred included assaults on his character and presidential candidacy by the Christian clergy, particularly in Philadelphia. Rush, a Philadelphia physician, had written his friend Jefferson to report an apparently coordinated series of anti-Jefferson sermons. Jefferson responded to his accusers in this letter, with sentiments that are now inscribed on the rotunda of the Jefferson Memorial in Washington—without identification of Jefferson's target, of course. See also Jefferson at EPITAPHS & GRAVESTONES; RELIGION; RESISTANCE; as well as at THE UNION, below.]

4   Truth forever on the scaffold, Wrong forever on the throne.
                          —JAMES RUSSELL LOWELL, *The Present Crisis*, 1844

5   Repression is the seed of revolution.   —DANIEL WEBSTER, speech, 1845

6   Mounted majorities, clad in iron, armed with death.
                          —OLIVER WENDELL HOLMES, SR., speech,
                          Massachusetts Medical Society, May 30, 1860
    [More at MAJORITIES & MINORITIES.]

7   The more complete the despotism, the more smoothly all things move on the surface.   —ELIZABETH CADY STANTON, *History of Woman Suffrage*,
                          written with Susan B. Anthony and Mathilda Gage, 1881

8   How hard the tyrants die!   —ELBERT HUBBARD, *The Roycroft Dictionary
                          and Book of Epigrams*, 1923

9   Fascism is capitalism plus murder.   —UPTON SINCLAIR, *Singing Jailbirds*, 1924

10 As nightfall does not come at once, neither does oppression. In both instances, there is a twilight when everything remains seemingly unchanged. And it is in such twilight that we all must be most aware of change in the air—however slight—lest we become unwitting victims of the darkness.
                          —WILLIAM O. DOUGLAS, quoted by Professor Gary T. Marx,
                          Massachusetts Institute of Technology, letter to
                          The New York Times, August 15, 1989

U

UNHAPPINESS

See also ALIENATION; SORROW; SUFFERING & PAIN; TROUBLE

Discontent is the want of self-reliance: it is infirmity of will. 1
  —RALPH WALDO EMERSON, *Self-Reliance,*
    in *Essays: First Series,* 1841

If misery loves company, misery has company enough. 2
  —HENRY DAVID THOREAU, *Journal,* Sept. 1, 1851

The mass of men lead lives of quiet desperation. 3
  —HENRY DAVID THOREAU, "Economy," *Walden,* 1854
[More at LIFE.]

I've never done a single thing I've wanted to in my whole life! I don't know's 4
I've accomplished anything except just get along.
  —SINCLAIR LEWIS, *Babbitt,* 1922

Nobody loves me, 5
Everybody hates me,
Going into the garden
To eat worms.   —ANONYMOUS, nursery verse, probably of English derivation,
      included in Iona and Peter Opie, *I Saw Esau,* rev. ed. [1992]

UNION, THE

See also UNITY

Every difference of opinion is not a difference of principle. We have been called 6
by different names brethren of the same principle. We are all Republicans—we
are all Federalists. If there be any among us who would wish to dissolve this
Union or to change its republican form, let them stand undisturbed as monuments to the safety with which error of opinion may be tolerated where reason
is left free to combat it.   —THOMAS JEFFERSON, First Inaugural Address, 1801

Liberty and Union, now and forever, one and inseparable! 7
  —DANIEL WEBSTER, speech in Congress, Jan. 1830
[This line marks the high point of the Hayne-Webster debate, in which Web-
ster opposed the claim of Robert Hayne of South Carolina that a state had the

right to nullify a federal law as unconstitutional. The Southern position, Webster phrased as "Liberty first and Union afterwards."]

1　Our Federal Union! It must and shall be preserved.
—ANDREW JACKSON, April 30, 1830
[At a formal birthday dinner, Pres. Jackson offered this toast to John Calhoun of South Carolina. Calhoun's counter toast was: "The Union, next to our liberty most dear. May we all remember that it can be preserved only by respecting the rights of states."

Robert Remini, in his biography *The Life of Andrew Jackson*, observes that Jackson's personal slogan was "Our Federal Union, It Must Be Preserved."]

2　Sail on, O Union, strong and great!
—HENRY WADSWORTH LONGFELLOW,
The Building of the Ship, 1849

[More at AMERICA & AMERICANS.]

3　All your strength is in your union.
All your danger is in discord.
—HENRY WADSWORTH LONGFELLOW,
The Song of Hiawatha, 1855

[More at UNITY.]

4　A house divided against itself cannot stand. I believe this government cannot endure permanently half slave and half free. I do not expect the Union to be dissolved. I do not expect the house to fall, but I do expect it will cease to be divided.
—ABRAHAM LINCOLN, speech,
Republican State Convention,
Springfield, Ill., June 16, 1858
[In accepting the Republican nomination for the U.S. Senate, before he confronted the incumbent Democrat, Stephen A. Douglas, in a series of instantly famous debates, Lincoln succinctly described the crisis facing the nation. The reference to "a house divided" has two biblical sources. *Mark* 3:25 reads: "If a house be divided against itself, that house cannot stand." *Matthew* 12:25 is more colorful and prophetic in terms of American history: "Every kingdom divided against itself is brought to desolation; and every city or house divided against itself, shall not stand."

Lincoln had been warned that a speech this blunt might cost him the election. He responded, "The time has come when those sentiments should be uttered, and if it is decreed that I should go down because of this speech, then let me go down linked with the truth—let me die in the advocacy of what is just and right."]

5　A Union that can only be maintained by swords and bayonets, and in which strife and civil war are to take the place of brotherly love and kindness, has no charm for me.
—ROBERT E. LEE, letter to his son, Jan. 1861
[Lee was still a colonel. The Union was coming apart as he wrote. South Carolina had seceded the previous month. Mississippi, Alabama, Georgia, and Louisiana did so in January. On April 18, the day after Virginia, Lee's own state, seceded, Gen. Winfield Scott offered to make him field commander of the Union army, but Lee declined, saying, "Save in defense of my native state, I never desire again to draw my sword." Scott, Lee's friend and also a Virginian, replied, "You have made the greatest mistake of your life, but I feared it would be so."]

My paramount object in this struggle *is* to save the Union, and is *not* either to   1
save or destroy slavery.   —ABRAHAM LINCOLN, reply to Horace Greeley,
August 19, 1862
[More at SLAVERY.]

We shall nobly save or meanly lose the last, best hope of earth.   2
—ABRAHAM LINCOLN, second annual message to Congress,
Dec. 1, 1862
[More at SLAVERY.]

UNITED STATES MOTTO   *See* under GOD.

UNITY   *See also* AMERICA & AMERICANS (*E pluribus unum*);
DECLARATION OF INDEPENDENCE (Benjamin Franklin);
LOYALTY; UNION, THE

Then join hand in hand, brave Americans all!   3
By uniting we stand, by dividing we fall.
—JOHN DICKINSON, *The Liberty Song*, 1768

All your strength is in your union.   4
All your danger is in discord;
Therefore be at peace henceforward,
And as brothers live together.   —HENRY WADSWORTH LONGFELLOW,
The Song of Hiawatha, 1855

A house divided against itself cannot stand.   5
—ABRAHAM LINCOLN, Republican State Convention,
Springfield, Ill., June 16, 1858
[More at THE UNION.]

UNIVERSE, THE   *See also* NATURE; SCIENCE: PHYSICS &
COSMOLOGY; WORLD, THE

The universe is all chemistry, with a certain hint of a magnificent *Whence* or   6
Whereto.   —RALPH WALDO EMERSON, letter to Caroline Sturgis Tappan,
in Stephen E. Whicher, ed.,
Selections from Ralph Waldo Emerson, 1960

I accept the universe.   7
—MARGARET FULLER, attributed
[We have been unable to find good authority for this common attribution.
Some reliable reference works, such as *Bartlett's*, list no source; others do not
list the quote. Nevertheless, the alleged remark comes complete with an alleged reaction: "By gad, she'd better," by Thomas Carlyle—and he did meet
Fuller in London in 1846. William James, in *The Varieties of Religious Experience* (1902), not only passed along the Fuller remark, he added that it "is reported to have been a favorite utterance."]

Law rules throughout existence, a law which is not intelligent, but Intelli-   8
gence.   —RALPH WALDO EMERSON, *Fate*,
in *The Conduct of Life*, 1860

1   O amazement of things—even the least particle!
                    —WALT WHITMAN, *Song at Sunset*, 1860

2   A man said to the universe:
    "Sir, I exist."
    "However," replied the universe,
    "The fact has not created in me
    A sense of obligation."   —STEPHEN CRANE,
                            War Is Kind and Other Lines, 1899

3   Whenever we try to pick out anything by itself, we find it hitched to every-
    thing else in the universe.   —JOHN MUIR, quoted by John T. Nichols,
                            Natural History magazine [Nov. 1992]

4   The universe is not hostile, nor yet is it friendly. It is simply indifferent.
                    —JOHN HAYNES HOLMES,
                        The Sensible Man's View of Religion, 1933

5   The more the universe seems comprehensible, the more it also seems point-
    less.   —STEVEN WEINBERG, *The First Three Minutes*, 1972

6   The universe is a spiraling Big Band in a polka-dotted speakeasy, effusively gen-
    erating new light every one-night stand.
                    —ISHMAEL REED, quoted in Jim (James A.) Haskins,
                        The Cotton Club, 1977
    [For a similar thought, see Philip Roth at ART: THEATER, DRAMA, & MAGIC.]

USEFULNESS

7   What good is a newborn baby?
                    —BENJAMIN FRANKLIN, remark at first balloon ascension,
                        Champs de Mars, France, August 27, 1783
    [Franklin, fascinated by the invention, was responding to someone in the huge
    crowd who asked, "What good is it?" This balloon was an unmanned hydrogen
    balloon that traveled fifteen miles. As it came down, it was attacked and de-
    stroyed by terrified peasants. Franklin also had a good view of the first free
    flight of a manned balloon, which was launched near his Paris house about
    three months later. This was a hot-air balloon invented by the Montgolfier
    brothers.]

8   Democratic nations . . . will habitually prefer the useful to the beautiful, and
    they will require that the beautiful be useful.
                    —ALEXIS DE TOCQUEVILLE, *Democracy in America*, 1835

9   Nothing useless is, or low.   —HENRY WADSWORTH LONGFELLOW,
                                    The Builders, 1849

10 Aim above morality. Be not simply good; be good for something.
                    —HENRY DAVID THOREAU, *Walden*, 1854

UTAH   *See also* CITIES (Salt Lake City)

11 This is the place!   —BRIGHAM YOUNG, at first sight of the
                            Great Salt Lake valley, July 24, 1847
    [Young recognized it as the place he had seen in a vision—possibly, though he
    didn't say this, inspired by a long conversation the preceding month with Jim

Bridger, the famous mountain man and guide, who knew the territory like the back of his hand.]

Let the Mormons have the territory to themselves—it is worth very little to   1
others.   —HORACE GREELEY, *An Overland Journey from New York to San Francisco . . . in 1859,* 1860

Utah has always had a way of doing things different.   2
          —FEDERAL WRITERS' PROJECT, *Utah: A Guide to the State,* 1941

Water in Utah is precious, savored as champagne might be in another land. Life   3
does not come easy. . . . Utah's loveliness is a desert loveliness, unyielding and frequently sterile.   —*Ibid.*

Utah is the only place in the world where Jews are Gentiles.   4
          —ANONYMOUS, quoted in John Gunther, *Inside U.S.A.,* 1947
[Non-Mormons are classified as Gentiles.]

Motto

Industry.   5

UTOPIA

In my Kosmos there will be no feeva of discord . . . all my emotions will func-   6
tion in hominy and kind feelings.   —GEORGE JOSEPH HERRIMAN,
Krazy Kat
[The cartoon strip was first published in 1913. Many connoisseurs of this art form regard it as the best strip ever.]

In the Big Rock Candy Mountains   7
There's a land that's fair and bright
Where the hand-outs grow on bushes
And you sleep out every night;
Where the box cars all are empty,
And the sun shines every day
On the birds and the bees
And the cigarette trees,
And the lemonade springs
Where the blue bird sings—
In the Big Rock Candy Mountains.
                                              —ANONYMOUS, c. 1920
[Folk song experts John and Alan Lomax called this a favorite hobo chantey. Wallace Stegner used the verse as a symbol of the popular perception that the riches of the American West are inexhaustible. He noted that the ballad was supposedly written by Harry "Haywire Mac" McClintock in 1928. But Stegner heard his own father sing it long before then. In *Thoughts in a Dry Land* (1972), Stegner wrote that some people call Utah's Sigurd, or Pahvant, Mountain the Big Rock Candy Mountain. It is as colorful as a peppermint stick, he said.]

V

VALUE

1 When the well's dry, we know the worth of water.
—BENJAMIN FRANKLIN, *Poor Richard's Almanack*, Jan. 1746

2 What we obtain too cheap, we esteem too lightly; it is dearness [high cost] only that gives everything its value. —THOMAS PAINE, *The American Crisis*, 1776–1783

3 In short, I conceive that a great part of the miseries of mankind are brought upon them by the false estimates they have made of the value of things, and by their giving too much for their whistles. —BENJAMIN FRANKLIN, letter to Madame Brillon, Nov. 10, 1779

4 There is no such thing as absolute value in this world. You can only estimate what a thing is worth to *you*. —CHARLES DUDLEY WARNER, *My Summer in a Garden*, 1871

5 What is false in the science of facts may be true in the science of values.
—GEORGE SANTAYANA, *Interpretations of Poetry and Religion*, 1900

6 Diamonds Are a Girl's Best Friend. —LEO ROBIN, song title, *Gentlemen Prefer Blondes*, 1949
[The successful musical, starring Carol Channing, was adapted from Anita Loos's 1925 novel of the same title.]

7 *Nothing* is intrinsically valuable; the value of everything is attributed to it, assigned to it from outside the thing itself, by people.
—JOHN BARTH, *The Floating Opera*, 1956

VARIETY
See DIFFERENCES

VENEZUELA
See NATIONS

VERMONT

I lift up my eyes to the hills.   1
From whence does my help come?
My help comes from the Lord, who made heaven and earth.
                                                —BIBLE, *Psalms* 121:1–2
[In Vermont, Psalm 121 is known as "the Vermont Psalm."]

A Sunday-school teacher asked a child . . . "In what state were mankind left af- 2
ter the fall?"—"In the state of Vermont."   —HARRIET MARTINEAU,
                                                Society in America, 1837

Vermont, O maiden of the hills,   3
My heart is there with thee!   —WENDELL PHILLIPS STAFFORD,
                                                "Song of Vermont,"
                                                The Land We Love, 1916
[For the hills in autumn, see Sarah Cleghorn at NATURE: SEASONS.]

These men cannot live in regular society. They are too idle, too talktative, too   4
passionate, too prodigal, too shiftless, to acquire either property or character.
They are impatient of the restraints of law, religion, morality; grumble about
taxes by which rulers, ministers, and schoolmasters, are supported; and complain incessantly, as well as bitterly, of the extortions of mechanics, farmers,
merchants, and physicians, to whom they are always indebted.
                                —TIMOTHY DWIGHT,
                                Travels in New England and New York, 1821
[A not uncommon view of frontiersmen by those who lived along the more civilized seaboard. Compare the assessment of Dwight, a president of Yale, with
William Byrd's earlier opinion of backwoodsmen in NORTH CAROLINA.]

Statistics prove that no Vermonter ever left the state unless transportation was   5
furnished in advance. She is what you call a "hard-boiled state." The principal
ingredients are granite, rock salt, and Republicans. The last being the hardest
of the three.   —WILL ROGERS, March 29, 1925, quoted in Donald Day,
                                The Autobiography of Will Rogers [1949]
[But Vermonters have elected Democratic governors in recent years.]

I love Vermont because of her hills and valleys, her scenery and invigorating   6
climate, but most of all, because of her indomitable people. They are a race of
pioneers who have almost beggared themselves to serve others. If the spirit of
liberty should vanish in other parts of the union, and support of our institutions should languish, it could all be replenished from the generous store held
by the people of this brave little state of Vermont.
                                —CALVIN COOLIDGE, speech,
                                Bennington, Vt., Sept. 21, 1928

This state bows to nothing: the first legislative measure it ever passed was "to   7
adopt the laws of God . . . until there is time to frame better."
                                —JOHN GUNTHER, *Inside U.S.A.*, 1947

I live in New Hampshire so I can get a better view of Vermont.   8
                                —MAXFIELD PARRISH,
                                Vermont Life, 1952
[Parrish was an extremely successful book illustrator and muralist. See also
Robert Frost at NEW HAMPSHIRE.]

1   Vermont's a place where barns come painted
    Red as a strong man's heart,
    Where stout carts and stout boys in freckles
    Are highest forms of art.   —ROBERT TRISTRAM COFFIN,
                                             Vermont Looks Like a Man, 1955
    [According to *Simpson's Contemporary Quotations,* by James B. Simpson, this
    is the last poem that Coffin contributed to the *New York Herald Tribune*'s ed-
    itorial page prior to his death on January 20, 1955.]

2   All in all, Vermont is a jewel state, small but precious.
                                      —PEARL S. BUCK, *Pearl Buck's America,* 1971

3   They deliberately chose Vermont, and a hard-working, old-fashioned life. I
    hear this attitude of Vermonters described as "preventing the future."
                                 —CHARLES KURALT, *Charles Kuralt's America,* 1995

Motto

4   Freedom and unity.

VICE PRESIDENCY, THE

5   My country has in its wisdom contrived for me the most insignificant office
    that ever the invention of man contrived or his imagination conceived.
                             —JOHN ADAMS, letter to Abigail Adams, Dec. 19, 1793
    [Adams was the first vice president, and most politicians since have agreed
    with his assessment of the job. In 1993, Vice President Al Gore, while visiting
    the former Soviet republic of Kyrgyzstan, was asked at a town meeting
    whether he dreamed of being president. Embarrassed, he replied, "Would you
    believe me if I told you that since I was a young child I dreamed of becoming
    Vice President of the United States?" Even in Kyrgyzstan that got a big laugh.
    Thomas Jefferson, though, professed to think that the vice presidency was a
    pretty good post; see below.]

6   The second office of the land is honorable and easy, the first is but a splendid
    misery.   —THOMAS JEFFERSON, letter to Elbridge Gerry,
                                             May 13, 1797
    [Jefferson was vice president when he wrote this; Adams was president. Jeffer-
    son himself became president in 1801.]

7   I do not propose to be buried until I am really dead.
                             —DANIEL WEBSTER, attributed response when offered the
                                vice-presidential position on the Whig ticket, 1848

8   The vice president of the United States is like a man in a cateleptic state: he
    cannot speak; he cannot move; he suffers no pain; and yet he is perfectly con-
    scious of everything that is going on around him.
                             —THOMAS RILEY MARSHALL, statement to the press, c. 1920
    [From H. L. Mencken's dictionary of quotations. The citation is vague, but the
    attribution is probably okay. Marshall was vice president under Woodrow Wil-
    son, 1913–21.]

9   The vice presidency isn't worth a pitcher of warm spit.
                                      —JOHN NANCE GARNER, attributed, c. 1934
    ["Spit," it generally is agreed, is a euphemism for "piss," a word that was rarely

put in print at that time. A former Texas congressman and Speaker of the House, "Cactus Jack" served as vice president during Franklin D. Roosevelt's first two terms (1933–41). See also Garner below.]

A spare tire on the automobile of government.   1
                    —JOHN NANCE GARNER, speaking of the vice presidency,
                    to the press, June 19, 1934

[Re the vice presidency:] Here is one instance in which it is the man who   2
makes the office, not the office the man.
                    —HARRY S. TRUMAN, *Years of Decision*, 1955

I think the vice president should do anything the president wants him to do. 3
                    —RICHARD M. NIXON, quoted in Earl Mazo, *Richard Nixon:*
                    A Political and Personal Portrait, 1959

VIETNAM WAR, 1961–75   *See also* ELITE, THE (Halberstam)

You have the broader considerations that might follow what you would call   4
the "falling domino" principle. You have a row of dominos set up, you knock
over the first one, and what will happen to the last one is the certainty that it
will go over very quickly.   —DWIGHT D. EISENHOWER, press conference,
                                   April 7, 1954
[As the president spoke, Vietnam, a French colony, was fighting for independence. French forces in Vietnam were besieged by the Viet Minh at Dien Bien
Phu. Despite the prospect of falling dominos, the U.S. declined to aid France.
A month later, Dien Bien Phu fell, ending the war and freeing Vietnam.]

We are not going to send American boys nine or ten thousand miles away from 5
home to do what Asian boys ought to be doing for themselves.
                    —LYNDON B. JOHNSON, speech, Akron University, Akron, Ohio,
                    Oct. 21, 1964
[At this time, Johnson was trying to draw a clear political line between himself
and Republican presidential candidate Barry Goldwater, who was calling for an
American air strike against North Vietnam. For example, in a speech on September 25, Johnson said, "There are those who say, you ought to go north and
drop bombs. . . . We don't want our American boys to do the fighting for Asian
boys. We don't want to get involved in a nation with 700 million people and get
tied down in a land war in Asia." But as revealed in the Pentagon Papers, the
administration had already determined that air attacks against North Vietnam
would be used—once the election was over. As for the efficacy of bombing, see
Walter Lippman at MILITARY STRATEGY.]

Hey, hey, LBJ, how many kids did you kill today?   6
                    —ANONYMOUS, heckling slogan of the 1960s
                    anti–Vietnam War movement

You don't need a weatherman to know which way the wind blows.   7
                    —BOB DYLAN, *Subterranean Homesick Blues*, 1965
[This line from Dylan's song became an antiwar slogan with overtones of menace in 1969, when a group from Students for a Democratic Society adopted the
line as a title of a program calling on white liberals to support liberation movements worldwide. The most militant and violent of this group formed a splinter organization, Revolutionary Youth Movement I, which called itself the
Weathermen and went in for bombings and robberies.]

1   Keep asking me, no matter how long
On the war in Viet Nam, I sing this song
I ain't got no quarrel with the Viet Cong.
                    —MUHAMMAD ALI, press conference, Miami, Fla., Feb. 1966
[Ali, then world heavyweight boxing champion, read the poem after his local
draft board had promoted him from I-Y, deferred status, to I-A, making him el-
igible for the draft. A year later, when he received his army induction notice,
he declined on religious grounds to serve. Neither the courts nor boxing authorities accepted this reason. He was sentenced to five years in prison and
stripped of his title. On appeal, however, his conviction was reversed and his
boxing license restored. He returned to the ring in 1970 and regained the
heavyweight crown in 1974. See REPUTATION for his explanation of his reason
for sticking by his beliefs.]

2   I believe there is a light at the end of what has been a long and lonely tunnel.
                    —LYNDON B. JOHNSON, speech, Sept. 21, 1966
["Light at the end of the tunnel" had been used earlier in this context—by John
F. Kennedy in a press conference in 1962 and by Joseph Alsop in a 1965 column, among others, and it was to be repeated so many times that it became an
ironic catchphrase summing up the futility of the Vietnam War. In *Day by Day*
(1977), Robert Lowell wrote that "If we see light at the end of the tunnel, / It's
the light of the oncoming train."]

3   Declare the United States the winner and begin de-escalation.
                    —GEORGE AIKEN, speech, U.S. Senate, Oct. 19, 1966
[Wise advice from Vermont's canny senior senator.]

4   It became necessary to destroy the town to save it.
                    —ANONYMOUS, U.S. Army Major on the bombing
                    of the town of Ben Tre, quoted by the Associated Press,
                    Feb. 8, 1968

5   If when the chips are down, the world's most powerful nation, the United
States of America, acts like a pitiful, helpless giant, the forces of totalitarian-
ism and anarchy will threaten free nations and institutions throughout the
world.   —RICHARD M. NIXON, speech,
                                              April 30, 1970
[The frightening image of a helpless United States was used by the president in
this televised address to the nation to explain the necessity for a major offensive into Cambodia. Nixon went all out here, stating "I would rather be a one-
term president and do what I believe is right than to be a two-term president at
the cost of seeing America becoming a second-rate power and to see this nation
accept its first defeat in its proud 190-year history."
    Despite the powerful rhetoric, the reaction of the war-weary public was
largely negative. The U.S. had not won the "hearts and minds" of the Vietnamese—a basic goal of the struggle—nor even of its own people. For an early
use of "hearts and minds," see John Adams at AMERICAN REVOLUTION, letter to
Hezekiah Niles, 1818.]

6   The war the soldiers tried to stop.   —JOHN F. KERRY, speech at antiwar rally,
                                              Washington D.C., April 26, 1971
[Kerry, a former Navy lieutenant and spokesman for the Vietnam Veterans
Against the War, was characterizing the Vietnam War as he predicted it would
be remembered. He later became a U.S. senator from Massachusetts.]

I love the smell of napalm in the morning. It smells like victory.   1
                              —FRANCIS FORD COPPOLA,
                              Apocalypse Now, screenplay, 1979
[For another reaction to the smell of war, see Ralph Waldo Emerson at WAR.]

Vietnam was the first war ever fought without censorship. Without censor-   2
ship, things can get terribly confused in the public mind.
                    —WILLIAM C. WESTMORELAND, 1982, quoted in Stanley
                       Hochman & Eleanor Hochman, eds., *The Penguin*
                          Dictionary of Contemporary American History [1997]
[Gen. Westmoreland commanded American forces in Vietnam 1964–68. He
urged a major commitment of troops, which did not lead to victory but did fire
up war protests back home.]

In the end, we simply cut and ran. The American national will had collapsed.   3
                    —GRAHAM A. MARTIN, on the tenth anniversary of the fall of
                       Saigon, *New York Times*, April 30, 1985
[Martin was the last American ambassador to South Vietnam.]

VIOLENCE   *See also* CRIME, CRIMINALS, & DETECTIVES; DANGER &
                    DANGEROUS PEOPLE; PACIFISM & NONVIOLENCE; REVOLUTION;
                              RUTHLESSNESS; STRENGTH & TOUGHNESS

Force cannot give right.   —THOMAS JEFFERSON, *Summary View of the*   4
                              Rights of British America, 1774

The sword of murder is not the balance of justice. Blood does not wipe out dis-   5
honor, nor violence indicate possession.   —JULIA WARD HOWE, peace
                                          proclamation, London, 1870
[More at PACIFISM & NONVIOLENCE.]

In violence, we forget who we are.   —MARY MCCARTHY, *On the Contrary*, 1961   6

Be peaceful, be courteous, obey the law, respect everyone; but if someone puts   7
his hand on you, send him to the cemetery.   —MALCOLM X,
                                          Malcom X Speaks [1965]

I say violence is necessary. It is as American as apple pie.   8
                    —H. "RAP" BROWN press conference at the Student Nonviolent
                       Co-ordinating Committee headquarters, Washington, D.C.,
                       July 27, 1967
[Brown was defending the use of violence in the pursuit of civil rights. This
kind of talk challenged the leadership of Martin Luther King, Jr., and signaled
a sea change in the civil rights movement. It obviously represented a radical
transformation of the Student Nonviolent Co-ordinating Committee.]

Returning violence for violence multiples violence, adding deeper darkness to   9
a night already devoid of stars.   —MARTIN LUTHER KING, JR.,
                                          Where Do We Go from Here:
                                          Chaos or Community?, 1967

VIRGINIA   *See also* SOUTH CAROLINA (Federal Writers' Project)

We found shoal water, where we smelt so sweet and so strong a smell, as if   10
we had been in the midst of some delicate garden abounding with all kinds of

odoriferous flowers, by which we were assured that the land could not be far distant.
—ARTHUR BARLOW, quoted in *The First Voyage Made to
North America,* July 2, 1584, in Richard Hakluyt, *Principall
Navigations . . . of the English Nation* [1598–1600]

1 [Barlow was a ship captain.]

If Virginia had but horses and kine in some reasonable proportion, I dare assure myself, being inhabited with English, no realm in Christendom were comparable to it.
—RALPH LANE, 1585, in Richard Hakluyt, *Ibid.*

2 Virginia,
Earth's onely paradise.

Where nature hath in store
Fowle, venison and fish
And the fruitfull'st soyle
Without your toyle
Three harvests more,
All greater than you wish.
—MICHAEL DRAYTON,
To the Virginian Voyage, 1606
[Drayton composed the ballad for the departure from London on December 20, 1606, of the 120 colonists who founded Jamestown. The early colonists spent more time looking for gold than farming, however, with the result that most died of starvation and disease. The survivors were preparing to abandon the colony in 1610 when reinforcements arrived with ample supplies.]

3 Heaven and earth never agreed to frame a better place for man's habitation.
—JOHN SMITH, on Chesapeake Bay, 1607
[Capt. Smith added the proviso, "were it fully manured and inhabited by industrious people." He continued, "Here are mountains, hills, plains, valleys, rivers, and brooks, all running most pleasantly into a fair bay, compassed but for the mouth with fruitful and delightsome land," *The General History of Virginia, New England, and the Summer Isles,* 1624.]

4 The country is not mountainous nor yet low, but such pleasant plain hills and fertile valleys, one prettily crossing another, and watered so conveniently with their sweet brooks and crystal springs, as if art itself had devised them.
—JOHN SMITH, *The Description of Virginia,* 1607
[Nevertheless, the first wave of settlers probably would have perished had it not been for the effective leadership of Capt. Smith. He established some sense of order in Jamestown and made friends with the local chieftan, Powhatan—thanks apparently to the intercession of Powhatan's daughter Pocahontas.]

5 The Virginians have little money and great pride, contempt of Northern men, and great fondness for a dissipated life. They do not understand grammar.
—NOAH WEBSTER, *Letter from Williamsburg, Va.,* c. 1785

6 On the whole, I find nothing anywhere else, in point of climate, which Virginia need envy to any part of the world.
—THOMAS JEFFERSON, letter to
Martha Jefferson Randolph,
May 31, 1791

7 The higher Virginians seem to venerate themselves as men.
—JOHN DAVIS, *Travels of Four Years and a Half in
the United States of America,* 1803

Our society is neither scientific nor splendid, but independent, hospitable, correct, and neighborly.   —THOMAS JEFFERSON, letter to Nathaniel Bowditch, Oct. 26, 1818

1

The good Old Dominion, the blessed mother of us all.
        —THOMAS JEFFERSON, *Thoughts on Lotteries*, Feb. 1826
[Jefferson's thoughts were occasioned by terrible debts. Fearful of being thrown out of Monticello, he proposed to pay off his most pressing obligations by selling properties around it through a lottery. News of his plight led citizens in New York, Boston, Philadelphia, Richmond, and other cities to hold public meetings at which funds quickly were raised for the old and ailing patriot. Thus, when he died five months later, it was peacefully in his own home.]

2

You can work for Virginia, to build her up again, to make her great again. You can teach your children to love and cherish her.
        —ROBERT E. LEE, to the daughter of Dr. Prosser Tabb, at White Marsh, Gloucester County, Va., May 1870

3

Carry me back to old Virginny,
That's where the cotton and the corn and taters grow.
        —JAMES A. BLAND, *Carry Me Back to Old Virginny*, 1875

4

Red river, red river,
Slow flow heat is silence
No will is as still as a river
Still.   —T. S. ELIOT, *Virginia*, 1934

5

Never ask people where they are from. If they are from Virginia, they will tell you so; if not, it will embarrass them to have to confess that they aren't.
        —ANONYMOUS, quoted in H. L. Mencken, *A New Dictionary of Quotations* [1942]

6

That, without any fear of succeeding, the intrepid native Virginian will dauntlessly attempt to conceal his superiority to everybody else, remains a tribal virtue which has not escaped the comment of anthropologists.
        —JAMES BRANCH CABELL, *Let Me Live*, 1947

7

His [the Virginian's] dream was to found an aristocratic republic, in which superior individuals would emerge to rule the many.
        —CLIFFORD DOWDEY, *Virginia*, in *American Panorama: East of the Mississippi*, 1960

8

Motto

Sic semper tyrannis.
Thus ever to tyrants.

9

[John Wilkes Booth uttered this after shooting Pres. Lincoln; see AMERICAN HISTORY: MEMORABLE MOMENTS.]

VIRTUE   *See also* ETHICS & MORALITY; HEROES; HONESTY; HONOR; IDEAS & IDEALS; KINDNESS; REPUTATION; RESPONSIBILITY; RIGHT

Resolved, never to do anything which I should be afraid to do if it were the last hour of my life.   —JONATHAN EDWARDS, *Seventy Resolutions*

10

1 The happiness of man as well as his dignity consists in virtue.
                              —JOHN ADAMS, *Thoughts on Government*, 1776
   [See below for a second thought three years later.]

2 Virtue is not always amiable.   —JOHN ADAMS, diary entry, Feb. 9, 1779

3 Hands to work; hearts to God.
                                                      —SHAKER motto
   [The first Shaker community was founded in 1774 in Mount Lebanon, New
   York, by Mother Ann Lee. She and eight others had come to America from England to escape religious persecution. Membership in Shaker communities
   reached six thousand by 1860, but had died out some one hundred years later.
   The Shakers believed in communal ownership of property, equality of the
   sexes, and celibacy (four of Mother Lee's children had died young).]

4 Virtue is the governor, the creator, the reality.
                              —RALPH WALDO EMERSON, *Self-Reliance*,
                                 in *Essays: First Series*, 1841

5 The essence of greatness is the perception that virtue is enough.
                              —RALPH WALDO EMERSON, *Heroism*, in *Ibid.*
   [See also Emerson at COMMON SENSE.]

6 The only reward of virtue is virtue.   —RALPH WALDO EMERSON,
                                                 Friendship, in *Ibid.*

7 Are the honorable, the just, the high-minded and compassionate, the majority
   anywhere in the world?   —HARRIET BEECHER STOWE, final chapter,
                              or afterword, to *Uncle Tom's Cabin*, 1852
   [See also Thoreau, who writing in defense of John Brown's raid on Harper's
   Ferry said, "I hear many condemn these men because they were so few"—the
   rest follows two quotes below.]

8 As for doing good, that is one of the professions which are full.
                              —HENRY DAVID THOREAU, "Economy,"
                                 Walden, 1854

9 When were the good and the brave ever in a majority?
                              —HENRY DAVID THOREAU, *A Plea for Captain John Brown*, 1859

10 Let us have faith that right makes might, and in that faith, let us, to the end,
   dare to do our duty as we understand it.
                              —ABRAHAM LINCOLN, speech at Cooper Union, New York City,
                                 Feb. 27, 1860

11 Character is like a tree and reputation like its shadow. The shadow is what we
   think of it; the tree is the real thing.   —ABRAHAM LINCOLN,
                                                 in Anthony Gross,
                                                 Lincoln's Own Stories, 1912

12 Dearest says that is the best kind of goodness: not to think about yourself, but
   to think about other people.   —FRANCES HODGSON BURNETT,
                                         Little Lord Fauntleroy, 1885
   ["Dearest" is what little Fauntleroy calls his mother. He was modeled on the
   author's son Vivian, who grew up to be a successful editor and enthusiastic

sportsman. He died of a heart attack in 1937 on Long Island Sound, a few minutes after rescuing four people whose boat had capsized. While many passages in his mother's famous book are now cloying, the story is pretty good, and she herself was no prude.]

Be noble! and the nobleness that lies 1
In other men, sleeping, but never dead,
Will rise in majesty to meet thine own.
>—JAMES RUSSELL LOWELL, Sonnet IV,
>*The Complete Poetical Works of James Russell Lowell* [1900]

[Inscribed at Union Station, Washington, D.C. A similar thought from Lowell was selected by Harvard University president Charles W. Eliot for inscription in the main reading room of the Library of Congress: "As one lamp lights another, nor grows less, / So nobleness enkindleth nobleness," *Yussouf,* in *Ibid.*]

Few things are harder to put up with than the annoyance of a good example. 2
>—MARK TWAIN, *Pudd'nhead Wilson's Calendar,*
>in *Pudd'nhead Wilson,* 1894

[See also Twain at RIGHT.]

Character, not circumstances, makes the man. 3
>—BOOKER T. WASHINGTON, Jan. 31, 1896

[Cited in Deirdre Mullane, ed., *Words to Make My Children Live: A Book of African American Quotations,* 1995.]

Be good and you will be lonesome. 4
>—MARK TWAIN, *Pudd'nhead Wilson's New Calendar,*
>in *Following the Equator,* 1897, motto for frontispiece

Saint, n. a dead sinner revised and edited.
>—AMBROSE BIERCE, *The Devil's Dictionary,* 1906 5

No one can build his security upon the nobleness of another person.
>—WILLA CATHER, *Alexander's Bridge,* 1912 6

Some persons are likeable in spite of their unswerving integrity.
>—DON MARQUIS, quoted in Edward Anthony, 7
>*O Rare Don Marquis* [1962]

He profits most who serves best.
>—A. F. SHELDON, motto for Rotary International, 1922 8

No good deed goes unpunished. —CLARE BOOTHE LUCE, attributed, 9
William Safire, *New York Times Magazine,* Jan. 9, 1994

[One of numerous attributions for this thought, which exists in several variations, as Safire pointed out in this article.]

It is often easier to fight for principles than to live up to them. 10
>—ADLAI STEVENSON, speech, New York City, August 27, 1952

She would rather light candles than curse the darkness, and her glow has 11
warmed the world. —ADLAI STEVENSON, eulogy for Eleanor Roosevelt,
United Nations, Nov. 9, 1962

[See also the Christopher Society motto under ACTION & DOING.]

1   Just say no.

—NANCY REAGAN, motto, campaign against drug abuse
[The First Lady gave this advice initially to schoolchildren in Oakland, Cal., in 1984. It became the motto of the Nancy Reagan Drug Abuse Fund, founded in 1985. In *The Penguin Dictionary of Contemporary American History* (1997), Stanley and Eleanor Hochman remind readers that this venture had a limited impact. At the 1988 Democratic National Convention, Rev. Jesse Jackson stated, "We need a real war on drugs. We can't just say no. It's deeper than that."]

VISION & PERCEPTION

See also DREAMS & DREAMERS; MIND, THOUGHT, & UNDERSTANDING

2   We are as much as we see. Faith is sight and knowledge. The hands only serve the eyes.   —HENRY DAVID THOREAU, *Journal*, April 10, 1841

3   People see only what they are prepared to see.
—RALPH WALDO EMERSON, *Journal*, 1863

4   Try to be one of the people on whom nothing is lost.
—HENRY JAMES, *The Art of Fiction*, 1888

5   *Cynic, n.* a blackguard whose faulty vision sees things as they are, not as they ought to be.   —AMBROSE BIERCE, *The Devil's Dictionary*, 1906

6   The fellow that can only see a week ahead is always the popular fellow, for he is looking with the crowd. But the one that can see years ahead, he has a telescope, but he can't make anybody believe he has it.
—WILL ROGERS, *The Autobiography of Will Rogers* [1949]

7   Stare. It is the way to educate your eye, and more.
—WALKER EVANS, unpublished text for his subway photographs,
c. 1940
[More at KNOWLEDGE.]

8   We should not be surprised that the Founding Fathers didn't foresee everything, when we see that the current Fathers hardly ever foresee anything.
—HENRY STEELE COMMAGER, interview in *American Heritage*,
Feb. 1970

9   If I didn't believe it with my own mind, I never would have seen it.
—ANONYMOUS, graffito, Bard College,
Annandale-on-Hudson, N.Y., c. 1971, book review,
New York Times, Feb. 12, 1996

10   The vision thing.

—GEORGE BUSH, phrase, 1987
[Unfortunately for Vice President Bush, his use of this phrase was picked up by the popular press as emblematic of a decline in political rhetoric and, of course, vision. Thus Marci McDonald, writing in *MacLean's* (Dec. 9, 1991), commented that Bush's supposed "inability to come to grips with what he used to repeatedly refer to as 'the vision thing' . . . haunted him, however undeservedly, through early 1988." Nevertheless, he was elected president, and served one term.]

The important thing is not the camera but the eye.   1
—ALFRED EISENSTAEDT, interview, *New York Times*,
Sept. 26, 1994

[Eisenstaedt was on the staff of the first *Life* magazine in 1936. In 1994, at age ninety-five, he was still coming in to the office every day. He died the following year.]

W

WAR

See also AMERICAN REVOLUTION; CIVIL WAR, THE;
GULF WAR; KOREAN WAR; MEXICAN WAR; MILITARY, THE;
MILITARY STRATEGY; PEACE; SPANISH-AMERICAN WAR;
VIETNAM WAR; WAR OF 1812; WORLD WAR I; WORLD WAR II

1 I heard the bullets whistle; and believe me, there is something charming in the sound. —GEORGE WASHINGTON, letter to his mother, May 3, 1754
[This was after the battle of Great Meadows in the French and Indian War. Others have reacted similarly; for example, see Ralph Waldo Emerson below and Ronald Reagan at DANGER & DANGEROUS PEOPLE.]

2 He who is the author of a war lets loose the whole contagion of hell and opens a vein that bleeds a nation to death.
—THOMAS PAINE, *The American Crisis,* no. V, March 21, 1778

3 It is the object only of war that makes it honorable. —*Ibid.*

4 There never was a good war or a bad peace.
—BENJAMIN FRANKLIN,
letter to Josiah Quincy, Sept. 11, 1783

5 To be prepared for war is one of the most effectual means of preserving peace.
—GEORGE WASHINGTON, first annual address to Congress,
Jan. 8, 1790
[The president spoke to both houses of Congress—what has since come to be known as the annual State of the Union speech. Here Washington paraphrased part of a passage he admired from *De rei militari,* written in the fourth-century by Vegetius: "He, therefore, who desires peace should prepare for war. He who aspires to victory should spare no pains to form his soldiers. And he who hopes for success should fight on principle, not chance." In 1990, Pres. George Bush, as he prepared the nation for the Gulf War, also drew on the maxims of Vegetius and Washington. See also Theodore Roosevelt below, p. 520.]

Sometimes gunpowder smells good. 1
     —RALPH WALDO EMERSON, April 1861, cited in Samuel Eliot
    Morison, *The Oxford History of the American People* [1965]
[Emerson was referring to the attack on Fort Sumter. Like many other North-
erners, he was glad that the issue of slavery would at last be settled, "Now we
have a country again," he wrote.
For the smell of napalm see Francis Ford Coppola at VIETNAM WAR.]

War is an organized bore. —OLIVER WENDELL HOLMES, JR., remark to a visitor 2
     after being wounded at Antietam, 1862
[Holmes enlisted in the Union army before completing his senior year at Harvard and was wounded three times in three years, twice severely.]

It is well that war is so terrible, or we should grow too fond of it. 3
     —ROBERT E. LEE, remark to Gen. James Longstreet,
     Battle of Fredericksburg, Dec. 13, 1862
[Lee had just seen an attack by Union forces repulsed. Not everyone is so sus-
ceptible to war's attractions. Lee, himself, was much amused by a black cook
who explained that he had managed to avoid being wounded because, "I stays
back wid de ginerals."]

War is cruelty, and you cannot refine it. —WILLIAM TECUMSEH SHERMAN, 4
     letter to James M. Calhoun,
     mayor of Atlanta, Sept. 12, 1864

The legitimate object of war is a more perfect peace. 5
    —WILLIAM TECUMSEH SHERMAN, speech, St. Louis, July 20, 1865
[The epigram is inscribed upon his statue in Washington, D.C.]

All wars are boyish and are fought by boys. 6
     —HERMAN MELVILLE, *The March into Virginia,*
    in *Battle-Pieces,* 1866

War is hell. —WILLIAM TECUMSEH SHERMAN, attributed, graduation speech, 7
    Michigan Military Academy, June 19, 1879
[The passage, for which there is no contemporary verification, reportedly ran
thus: "I am sick and tired of war. Its glory is all moonshine. It is only those who
have never fired a shot nor heard the shrieks and groans of the wounded who
cry aloud for blood, more vengeance, more desolations. War is hell."
 Similarly, in a speech in Columbus, Ohio, on August 11, 1880, Sherman was
reported in a local paper to have said, "There is many a boy here today who
looks on war as all glory, but, boys, it is all hell."]

War educates the senses, calls into action the will, perfects the physical consti- 8
tution, brings men into such swift and close collision in critical moments that
man measures man. —RALPH WALDO EMERSON, *War,* in *Miscellanies* [1884]

War loses a great deal of its romance after a soldier has seen his first battle. 9
    —JOHN SINGLETON MOSBY, *War Reminiscences,* 1887

It is not merely cruelty that leads men to love war, it is excitement. 10
    —HENRY WARD BEECHER, *Proverbs from Plymouth Pulpit,* 1887

They were going to look at war, the red animal—war, the blood-swollen god. 11
    —STEPHEN CRANE, *The Red Badge of Courage,* 1895

1   Preparation for war is the surest guaranty for peace.
                                        —THEODORE ROOSEVELT, *Washington's Forgotten Maxim*,
                                        speech, Naval War College, 1897
[Here Assistant Secretary of the Navy Roosevelt referred to Washington's advice that military preparedness helps to prevent wars; see above. Roosevelt's
speech called for "a great navy . . . an armament fit for the nation's needs, not
primarily to fight, but to avert fighting." The president, however, was less than
sincere here. He was an enthusiastic warrior, some would say warmonger.
Washington, on the other hand, while advocating preparedness, was suspicious
of military establishments; see THE MILITARY.]

2   It has been a splendid little war.   —JOHN HAY, letter to
                                                Theodore Roosevelt, July 27, 1898
    [More at SPANISH-AMERICAN WAR.]

3   A pattern called a war.
    Christ! What are patterns for?   —AMY LOWELL, *Patterns*,
                                               in *Men, Women, and Ghosts*, 1916

4   War is the only place where a man really lives.
                        —GEORGE S. PATTON, letter to Gen. John J. "Black Jack" Pershing,
                        quoted in Carlo D'Este, *A Genius for War* [1995]
    [Patton's first battle experience was in Mexico in Gen. Pershing's 1916–17 ex-
    pedition against the rebel leader Pancho Villa.]

5   The first casualty when war comes is truth.
                                        —HIRAM JOHNSON, remark in the U. S. Senate, 1918
    [This has long been attributed to Sen. Johnson. Suzy Platt, editor of *Respect-
    fully Quoted*, published by the Library of Congress, could not verify the attri-
    bution, but does give an earlier and similar source for the same idea: Samuel
    Johnson, "Among the calamities of war, may be justly numbered the diminu-
    tion of the love of truth, by the falsehoods which interest dictates, and
    credulity encourages," *The Idler*, Nov. 11, 1758.]

6   What Price Glory?   —MAXWELL ANDERSON & LAURENCE STALLINGS,
                                   title of antiwar play about World War I, 1924

7   You can't say civilization don't advance, however, for in every war they kill
    you in a new way.   —WILL ROGERS, *New York Times*, Dec. 23, 1929

8   All wars are planned by old men
    In council rooms apart.
                                        —GRANTLAND RICE, *Two Sides of War*, 1930
    [See also Herbert Hoover below.]

9   Wars may be fought with weapons, but they are won by men.
                                        —GEORGE S. PATTON, in the *Cavalry Journal*, Sept. 1933

10 Take the profits out of war, and you won't have any war.
                                        —WILL ROGERS, *Daily Telegrams*, Dec. 14, 1934

11 Sometime they'll give a war and nobody will come.
                                        —CARL SANDBURG, *The People, Yes*, 1936

12 I have seen war. . . . I hate war!   —FRANKLIN D. ROOSEVELT, speech
                                            at Chautauqua, N.Y., August 14, 1936

War is a contagion. —FRANKLIN D. ROOSEVELT, "Quarantine the 1
Aggressors" speech, Chicago, Oct. 5, 1937

Although war is evil, it is occasionally the lesser of two evils. 2
—McGEORGE BUNDY,
essay, Yale College, 1940
[Bundy graduated first in his class at Yale and, as special assistant to national
security affairs for Presidents Kennedy and Johnson from 1961 to 1966, was
one of "the best and the brightest" who presided over the war in Vietnam.]

As a woman I can't go to war, and I refuse to send anyone else. 3
—JEANETTE RANKIN, c. 1941, quoted in Hannah Josephson,
Jeanette Rankin: First Lady in Congress [1974]

You can no more win a war than you can win an earthquake. 4
—*Ibid.*
[Rep. Rankin of Montana, the first woman elected to Congress, cast the only
vote against declaring war on Japan in 1941. This was consistent with her
position on April 6, 1917, when she was in her first term. "I want to stand by my
country, but I cannot vote for war," she said then, concluding, "I vote no."]

Help me to remember somewhere out there a man died for me today. As long 5
as there be war, I must ask and answer, "Am I worth dying for?"
—ANONYMOUS, prayer kept by Eleanor Roosevelt
at her bedside during World War II

God help me, I love it. —GEORGE S. PATTON, after a tank battle, 6
attributed

Older men declare war. But it is youth that must fight and die. And it is youth 7
who must inherit the tribulation, the sorrow, and the triumphs that are the af-
termath of war. —HERBERT HOOVER, speech,
Republican National Convention,
June 27, 1944

War may make a fool of man, but it by no means degrades him; on the contrary 8
it tends to exalt him. —H. L. MENCKEN, *Minority Report:
H. L. Mencken's Notebooks* [1956]

No one won the last war, and no one will win the next. 9
—ELEANOR ROOSEVELT, letter to Harry S. Truman, Nov. 5, 1948

In war there is no substitute for victory. 10
—DOUGLAS MACARTHUR, speech, joint session of Congress,
April 19, 1951
[From his "old soldiers never die" speech; see AMERICAN HISTORY: MEMORABLE
MOMENTS, and KOREAN WAR.]

In war there is no second prize for the runner-up. 11
—OMAR BRADLEY, *USA: In Military Review,* Feb. 1950

The wrong war, at the wrong place, at the wrong time, and with the wrong enemy. 12
—OMAR BRADLEY, testimony to committees
on Armed Services and Foreign Affairs,
U.S. Senate, May 15, 1951
[More at KOREAN WAR.]

1   It is fatal to enter any war without the will to win it.
—DOUGLAS MACARTHUR, speech,
Republican National Convention, 1952

2   War will never cease until babies begin to come into the world with larger cerebrums and smaller adrenal glands.   —*Ibid.*

3   War is the unfolding of miscalculations.   —BARBARA TUCHMAN,
The Guns of August, 1962

4   That's the way it is in war. You win or lose, live or die—and the difference is just an eyelash.   —DOUGLAS MACARTHUR, *Reminiscences*, 1964

5   All the gods are dead except the god of war.
—ELDRIDGE CLEAVER, *Soul on Ice*, 1968

6   War is a bore interrupted only by moments of sheer terror when men die.
—NBC NEWS,
voice of correspondent, Vietnam, May 1969

7   Either man is obsolete or war is.   —BUCKMINSTER FULLER,
I Seem to Be a Verb, 1970

8   There will be no veterans of World War III.
—WALTER MONDALE, speech, Sept. 5, 1984
[Sen. Mondale, a Democrat, ran for president against Republican Ronald Reagan. Mondale's lack of martial spirit and, worse, his commitment to raise taxes, doomed his candidacy.]

WAR OF 1812, 1812–14 (Treaty of Ghent) or 1812–15 (Battle of New Orleans)

9   If you wish to avoid foreign collision, you had better abandon the ocean—surrender your commerce, give up all your prosperity.
—HENRY CLAY, speech, U.S. House of Representatives,
Jan. 22, 1812
[The U.S. and Great Britain had been battling at sea for years. War was declared on June 18.]

10   For the hotter the war, boys, the quicker the peace.
—ANONYMOUS, Republican broadside, Boston,
just after declaration of the War of 1812

11   Don't give up the ship.
—JAMES LAWRENCE, June 1, 1813
[Reports vary on the exact words of Lawrence, who was mortally wounded this day, but he gave this order in essence as his frigate, the U.S.S. *Chesapeake*, was being boarded by British sailors from H.M.S. *Shannon*. Lawrence, by some accounts, said, "Tell the men to fire faster and not to give up the ship. Fight her till she sinks." He lingered in a delirium until June 4, repeating many times, "Don't give up the ship." The captain of the *Shannon*, too, died from wounds suffered in the battle.
    Some prefer to credit the famous order to Oliver Hazard Perry, who conveyed this signal by a flag during the Battle of Lake Erie, see below. For more on Lawrence see Stephen Decatur at EPITAPHS & GRAVESTONES.]

We have met the enemy and they are ours—two ships, two brigs, one schooner,   1
and one sloop.   —OLIVER HAZARD PERRY,
                              message to Gen. William Henry Harrison,
                              Battle of Lake Erie, Sept. 10, 1813
[For Pogo's version, see Walt Kelly under HUMANS & HUMAN NATURE.]

Oh, say, can you see by the dawn's early light,   2
What so proudly we hailed at the twilight's last gleaming?
              —FRANCIS SCOTT KEY, *The Star-Spangled Banner*, Sept. 14, 1814
[More at PATRIOTISM & THE FLAG.]

By the Eternal, they shall not sleep on our soil!   3
                              —ANDREW JACKSON, Dec. 23, 1814
[The reaction of Gen. Jackson upon learning that twelve thousand British
troops were disembarking in New Orleans. He orchestrated their defeat at the
battle of New Orleans on January 8, without knowing that the Treaty of
Ghent, formally ending the war, had been signed two weeks earlier.]

The last American war was to us only something to talk or read about; but to   4
the Americans, it was the cause of misery in their own homes.
              —SAMUEL TAYLOR COLERIDGE, *Table-Talk*, May 3, 1830

WAR WITH MEXICO   *See* MEXICAN WAR

WASHINGTON   *See also* CITIES (Seattle)

Rainier, from Puget Sound, is a sight for the gods, and when one looks upon   5
him he feels that he is in the presence of the gods.
              —PAUL FOUNTAIN, *The Eleven Eaglets of the West*, 1905

Washington is a puzzling state. We think of it as cool, pristine and evergreen.   6
Yet the civilization around Puget Sound is industrial, cosmopolitan, intense,
wracked by economic boom and bust.
              —NEAL R. PIERCE, *The Pacific States of America*, 1972

Motto

Alki.   7
By and by.
[*Alki* is a Chinook term.]

WASHINGTON, D.C.   *See* CITIES

WASHINGTON, GEORGE   *See also* DEATH (Washington);
                              LAST WORDS (Washington); PRESIDENCY, THE

George Washington, Commander of the American armies, who, like Joshua of   8
old, commanded the sun and the moon to stand still, and they obeyed him.
                              —BENJAMIN FRANKLIN, attributed,
                              toast at a state dinner in France, c. 1784
[Franklin's biographer James Parton relates that Franklin is said to have made
this toast after the British ambassador had announced, "England—the sun—
whose bright beams enlighten and fructify the remotest corners of the earth,"
and the French ambassador had proposed, "France—the moon—whose mild,
steady and cheering rays are the delight of all nations, consoling them in dark-

ness." Parton did not, however, find the story particularly credible: "If such toasts were given, it must have been late in the third bottle or at the opening of the fourth," *The Life and Times of Benjamin Franklin*, 1864.

Franklin served as ambassador to France during and after the Revolution. On March 5, 1780, he wrote back to Washington, "Here [in France] you would know and enjoy what posterity will say of Washington. For a thousand leagues have nearly the same effect with a thousand years." (*Note:* We would say "as a thousand years.") Franklin genuinely admired Washington, which is reflected in a codicil that he added to his will on June 23, 1789: "My fine crab-tree walking-stick, with a gold head curiously wrought in the form of the cap of liberty, I give to my friend and the friend of mankind, General Washington. If it were a scepter, he has merited it and would become it."]

1

O, Washington! thou hero, patriot sage,
Friend of all climes, and pride of every age!   THOMAS PAINE, attributed

2

He has not the imposing pomp of a *Maréchal de France* who gives *the order*. A hero in a republic, he excites another sort of respect which seems to spring from the sole idea that the safety of each individual is attached to his person. . . . The goodness and benevolence which characterize him are evident in all that surrounds him, but the confidence that he calls forth never occasions improper familiarity.   —FRANÇOIS JEAN DE CHASTELLUX,
                                              Travels in North America, 1786
[The Marquis de Chastellux—author, philosopher, and soldier—met Washington after coming to America as a major general in Rochambeau's army in 1780. They became friends, and in 1787, Washington wrote de Chastellux a bantering letter of congratulations upon his marriage at age fifty-four to a pretty Irish woman of about twenty-eight. The following year de Chastellux died.]

3

The character and services of this gentlemen are sufficient to put all those men called kings to shame. . . . He accepted no pay as commander-in-chief; he accepts none as President of the United States.
                          —THOMAS PAINE, *The Rights of Man*, 1791–92
[But in a letter to Washington, written July 30, 1796, Paine called him "treacherous in private friendship . . . and a hypocrite in public life, the world will be puzzled to decide whether you are an apostate or an imposter; whether you have abandoned good principles, or whether you ever had any." Paine had been imprisoned in France in 1793–94 and felt that Washington could have intervened to save him.]

4

[Washington] errs as other men do, but errs with integrity.
                          —THOMAS JEFFERSON, letter to William B. Giles, Dec. 31, 1795

5   The father of his country.
                          —FRANCIS BAILEY, caption for portrait of Washington,
                              Nordamericanische Kalendar, 1799

6   First in war, first in peace, first in the hearts of his countrymen.
                          —HENRY LEE, eulogy, passed as a resolution in the
                              U.S. Congress, Dec. 26, 1799
[Lee, nicknamed "Light Horse Harry," was a devoted friend to Washington. In the 20th century, the eulogy was parodied to characterize the old Washington Senators baseball team: "Washington—first in war, first in peace, and last in the American League."]

I can't tell a lie, Pa; you know I can't tell a lie. I did cut it with my hatchet.   1
—Mason Locke "Parson" Weems, *The Life and Memorable Actions of George Washington*, 5th edition
[Washington was honored for his honesty, but there is no basis for the story that as a boy he confessed to chopping down a cherry tree.]

He was, indeed, in every sense of the words, a wise, a good, and a great man.   2
—Thomas Jefferson, letter to Walter Jones, Jan. 2, 1814

The character of Washington . . . is a fixed star in the firmament of great   3
names, shining without twinkling or obscuration, with a clear, steady, beneficent light.   —Daniel Webster, letter to the New York Committee for the Celebration of the Birthday of Washington, Feb. 20, 1851

G. Washington was about the best man this country ever sot eyes on. He was   4
a clear-heded, warm-hearted, and stiddy goin man. He never slopt over! The prevailin' weakness of most public men is to slop over! . . . Washington never slopt over. That wasn't George's stile. He luved his country dearly. He wasn't after the spiles [spoils]. He was a human angil in a 3 kornered hat and knee britches.   —Artemus Ward, "Fourth of July Oration," 1859

WATERGATE

A third-rate burglary attempt.   —Ronald L. Ziegler, press conference,   5
Key Biscayne, Florida, June 19, 1972
[Presidential press secretary Ziegler was characterizing the break-in on June 17 at the offices of the Democratic National Committee in Washington's Watergate complex. Presciently, one of the Watergate burglars, E. Howard Hunt, an ex-CIA man who wrote mystery stories on the side, had noted in *Angel Eyes*, 1961: "Don't think I can't smell a cover-up."]

Katie Graham's gonna get her tit caught in a big fat wringer if that's published.   6
—John N. Mitchell, telephone interview, Sept. 29, 1972, quoted in Carl Bernstein and Bob Woodward, *All the President's Men* [1974]
[Attorney General Mitchell, chairman of the Committee to Re-elect the President (CREEP), was referring here to *Washington Post* publisher Katharine Graham. The story that reporter Bernstein was checking in this phone call accused Mitchell of controlling a secret fund that financed the Watergate break-in and other espionage operations against the Democrats. The next day, after the story appeared, minus the anatomical reference, deleted at the order of editor Ben Bradlee, publisher Graham, who had been told of it, disconcerted Bernstein by asking if he had any more messages for her. Incidentally, Mitchell's quaint "wringer" metaphor was already archaic thanks to the development of automatic clothes dryers.]

Well, I think we ought to let him hang there. Let him twist slowly, slowly in   7
the wind.   —John D. Ehrlichman, telephone conversation with presidential counsel John W. Dean III, March 6, 1973
[Presidential adviser Ehrlichman's proposed victim here was L. Patrick Gray III, whose nomination as director of the FBI was stalled in the Senate because Gray did not have answers for the questions senators were asking about Watergate.]

1   We have a cancer within, close to the presidency, that is growing. It is growing
daily.   —JOHN W. DEAN III, to Pres. Richard M. Nixon,
                                    White House tape, March 21, 1973

2   It's a limited hang-out. It's not an absolute hang-out.
                                            —*Ibid.*, March 22, 1973
[Presidential counsel Dean was recommending that the White House cooperate
minimally with the Senate Watergate Committee in order to get the president
himself "up above and away from" the breaking Watergate scandal. Presidential
adviser John Ehrlichman termed it a "modified limited hang-out."]

3   I don't give a shit what happens. I want you all to stonewall it.
                        —RICHARD M. NIXON, White House tape, March 22, 1973
[Pres. Nixon's use of "stonewall" probably derives from the resolute defense by
Confederate General Thomas Jonathan "Stonewall" Jackson at the first Battle
of Bull Run in 1861. The term also has been used to describe parliamentary
proceedings in Australia and New Zealand that involve long-winded speeches
and other delaying actions, but there the allusion is to a batter in cricket who
is said "to stonewall" when playing purely defensively.]

4   This is the operative statement. The others are inoperative.
                        —RONALD L. ZIEGLER, press conference, April 17, 1973
[Ziegler was retracting almost a year's worth of denials that the White House
had been involved in covering up the Watergate break-in.]

5   I asked him what he meant by "deep six." He leaned back in his chair and said:
"You cross the [Potomac] river at night, don't you? Well, when you cross over
the river on your way home, just toss the briefcase into the river."
                        —JOHN W. DEAN III, Senate Watergate Committee hearings,
                        June 25, 1973
[Dean was reporting John Ehrlichman's advice about what to do with a brief-
case found in the White House office safe of Watergate burglar E. Howard
Hunt, Jr. "Deep six" is old naval slang for jettisoning cargo or other gear.]

6   There was also maintained what was called an "enemies list," which was
rather extensive and continually being updated.   —*Ibid.*

7   The central question is simply put: What did the president know and when did
he know it?   —HOWARD H. BAKER, JR.,
                        Senate Watergate Committee hearings, June 25, 1973
[Sen. Baker, a Republican and the minority leader of the Senate Watergate
Committee, learned the answer to this oft-repeated question on August 5,
1974, when Pres. Nixon acceded to a unanimous Supreme Court decision and
released transcripts of conversations with his chief of staff, H. R. Haldeman,
that were, as Mr. Nixon described it, "at variance with" his previous denials
that he had known about the Watergate coverup prior to John Dean's "cancer
on the presidency" speech; see above. The incriminating conversations, dating
from June 23, 1972, just six days after the Watergate break-in, represented the
"smoking pistol," or undeniable direct evidence, that Mr. Nixon had been part
of the Watergate cover-up conspiracy. Facing impeachment, Mr. Nixon resigned on August 9, 1974. See below.]

8   I'm not a crook.   —RICHARD M. NIXON, press conference,
                                    Disney World, Nov. 11, 1973
[The president's remarks in full were: "I made my mistakes, but in all my years
of public life, I have never, *never* profited from public service. . . . I welcome

this kind of examination because people have got to know whether or not their president is a crook. Well, I'm not a crook."]

I have never been a quitter. To leave office before my term is completed is abhorrent to every instinct in my body.   1
> —RICHARD M. NIXON, announcing his resignation as president, national radio address, August 8, 1974

[See also, under HATE, his comments to his staff the next morning.]

Our long national nightmare is over. Our Constitution works.   2
> —GERALD FORD, Inaugural statement upon succeeding Richard M. Nixon as president, August 9, 1974

I screwed up terribly in what was a little thing and it became a big thing.   3
> —RICHARD M. NIXON, television interview with David Frost, May 4, 1977

I brought myself down. I gave them a sword. And they stuck it in, and they   4
twisted it with relish. And I guess if I had been in their position, I'd have done the same thing.   *—Ibid.*

WEALTH

See MONEY & THE RICH; POVERTY & HUNGER; RICH & POOR, WEALTH & POVERTY

WEATHER

See NATURE: WEATHER

WEST, THE

See also CITIES and entries for states; FRONTIER, THE; MIDWEST, THE; WISDOM, WORDS OF (Anonymous cowboy sayings)

Few people even know the true definition of the term "West"; and where is its   5
location?—phantom-like it flies before us as we travel.
> —GEORGE CATLIN, *Letters and Notes on the Manners, Customs, and Conditions of the North American Indians,* 1841

Eastward I go only by force; but westward I go free. . . . I must walk toward   6
Oregon and not toward Europe.
> —HENRY DAVID THOREAU, *Walking,* 1862

[Speaking of his inclination to leave behind cities and walk west into the wilderness, Thoreau wrote, "Something like this is the prevailing tendency of my countrymen."]

Ain't no law west of St. Louis, ain't no God west of Fort Smith.   7
> —ANONYMOUS, saying, 19th century

[Fort Smith is in Arkansas. See a similar anonymous comment at TEXAS.]

Go west, young man, and grow up with the country.   8
> —HORACE GREELEY, editorial, *New York Tribune*

[Greeley, editor of the *Tribune,* had reprinted John B. L. Soule's 1851 editorial advice: "Go west, young man, go west"; see under THE FRONTIER. Later, in an editorial of his own, he added to Soule's thought as shown here. Greeley was a dominant voice in his era, and for many years the original saying was popularly attributed to him.

For quotes on America as the westernmost and youngest civilization, see under Bishop Berkeley at AMERICA & AMERICANS.]

1   Home, home on the range,
Where the deer and the antelope play;
Where seldom is heard a discouraging word,
And the skies are not cloudy all day.
                            —ANONYMOUS, cowboy song, 1860s or earlier
[Folk music expert John A. Lomax first recorded this song in San Antonio,
Texas, in 1908, from a "Negro singer who ran a beer saloon out beyond the
Southern Pacific depot, in a scrubby mesquite grove" (*Folk Song U.S.A.*). Not
sung so often nowadays is the third verse: "The red man was pressed from this
part of the West, / He's likely no more to return / To the banks of the Red River
where seldom if ever / Their flickering campfires burn."]

2   Oh, bury me not on the lone prairie,
Where the wild coyote will howl over me,
In a narrow grave just six by three,
Oh, bury me not on the lone prairie!
                                            —ANONYMOUS, cowboy song
[In *Folk Song U.S.A.*, John A. and Alan Lomax say that this song derives from
an English sailors' song.]

3   Come along, boys, and listen to my tale
I'll tell you of my troubles on the old Chisholm trail.
                                —ANONYMOUS, *The Old Chisholm Trail*
[The Chisholm Trail was the major route for cattle drives from Texas to Kansas
just after the Civil War, and this song, according to John A. and Alan Lomax in
Folk Song U.S.A., was sung by most cowboys. New verses were made up con-
stantly, furnishing in aggregate a vivid record of cowboy life.]

4   In this country you can look farther and see less than any other place in the
world.
                                        —ANONYMOUS, 19th century
[The saying dates from the time when grassland plains extended from Indiana
to the foot of the Rockies. See also NEBRASKA.]

5   To the West, to the West, to the land of the free,
Where the mighty Missouri rolls down to the sea,
Where a man is a man, even though he must toil
And the poorest may gather the fruits of the soil.
                    —ANONYMOUS, ballad recalled by Andrew Carnegie (d. 1919)
                            toward the end of his life, in Samuel Gompers,
                            Seventy Years of Life and Labor [1925]

6   O you youths, Western youths,
So impatient, full of action, full of manly pride and friendship,
Plain I see you Western youths, see you tramping with the foremost,
Pioneers! O pioneers!   —WALT WHITMAN, *Pioneers! O Pioneers*, 1865,
                                            in *Leaves of Grass* [1881]
[More at THE FRONTIER.]

7   [Out West] change has grown to metamorphosis. The sons of civilization,
drawn by the fascinations of a fresher and bolder life, thronged to the western
wilds in multitudes which blighted the charm that had lured them.
                    —FRANCIS PARKMAN, preface, 1892 edition of *The Oregon Trail*
[See under NATURE: ANIMALS for his description of buffalo along the Oregon
Trail.]

American history has been in a large degree the history of the colonization of   1
the Great West.   —FREDERICK J. TURNER, *The Significance*
                                 of the Frontier in American History, 1893
[See also Turner at THE FRONTIER.]

Out where the handclasp's a little stronger,   2
Out where the smile dwells a little longer,
That's where the West begins.   —ARTHUR CHAPMAN, *Out Where*
                                        the West Begins, 1917

Western humor . . . grew out of a distinct condition—the battle with the fron-   3
tier. . . . It is the freshest, wildest humor in the world, but there is tragedy behind it.   —ALBERT BIGELOW PAINE,
                                    Mark Twain, A Biography, 1924

Everything in the West is on a grander scale, more intense, vital, dramatic.   4
                          —EDWARD WESTON, diary entry, c. 1937,
                              quoted in Nancy Newhall, ed., *From the Daybooks*
                              of Edward Weston: California [1966]

Nobody watches TV westerns more avidly than cowboys.   5
                    —LARRY MCMURTRY, *Cowboys, Movies, Myths and Cadillacs:*
                        Realism in the Western, in W. R. Robinson, ed.,
                        with George Garrett, *Man and the Movies,* 1967

I've always acted alone. Americans admire that enormously. Americans ad-   6
mire the cowboy leading the caravan alone astride his horse, the cowboy entering a village or city alone on his horse.
                          —HENRY A. KISSINGER,
                              interview with Oriana Fallaci,
                              The New Republic, Dec. 16, 1972
[This was Secretary of State Kissinger's response to Ms. Fallaci's question
about how he had attained "incredible superstar status," becoming "almost
more famous and popular than the president," i.e., Richard M. Nixon.]

The West at large is hope's native home.   7
                    —WALLACE STEGNER,
                        Where the Bluebird Sings to the Lemonade Springs,
                        Introduction, 1992
[This introduction was based on Stegner's *A Geography of Hope,* a lecture delivered at the University of Colorado, and published by the university's press
in *A Society to Match Our Scenery,* 1991.]

Ghost towns and dust bowls, like motels, are western inventions.   —*Ibid.*   8

WEST VIRGINIA

The state is one of the most mountainous in the country; sometimes it is   9
called the "little Switzerland" of America, and I once heard an irreverent local
citizen call it the "Afghanistan of the United States."
                              —JOHN GUNTHER, *Inside U.S.A.,* 1947

We West Virginians are very tired of being considered inhabitants of just a do-   10
minion of the Old Dominion; we would like to make it clear that our state has

been independent for ninety years. Some residents take a very strong line about this and always refer to it in conversation as "*West*—By God—*Virginia!*"
—JOHN KNOWLES, *West Virginia,*
in *American Panorama: East of the Mississippi,* 1960

1 Here is hard-core unemployment, widespread and chronic; here is a region of shacks and hovels for housing; here are cliffs and ravines without standing room for a cow or chickens. In this region of steep mountains, a person is exceptionally fortunate if he is able to hack out two or three ten-foot rows of land for potatoes or beans. —ERSKINE CALDWELL, *Around America,* 1964

2 Country roads, take me home
To the place I belong,
West Virginia, mountain momma
Take me home, country roads.
—JOHN DENVER,
with Bill Danoff & Taffy Nivert,
Take Me Home, Country Roads, 1971

3 Almost Heaven.
—ANONYMOUS, bumper stickers, c. 1976,
reported in Gorton Carruth & Eugene Ehrlich,
American Quotations, 1988

Motto

4 *Montani semper liberi.*
Mountaineers are always free.

WILDERNESS *See also* ENVIRONMENT; FRONTIER, THE; NATURE; WEST, THE

5 There is something in the proximity of the woods which is very singular. It is with men as it is with plants and animals that grow and live in the forests; they are entirely different from those that live in the plains.
—MICHEL GUILLAUME JEAN DE CRÈVECOEUR,
Letters from an American Farmer, 1782

6 This is the forest primeval. The murmuring pines and the hemlocks,
Bearded with moss, and in garments green, indistinct in the twilight,
Stand like Druids of old, with voices sad and prophetic.
—HENRY WADSWORTH LONGFELLOW,
Evangeline, A Tale of Acadie, 1847

7 I went to the woods because I wished to live deliberately, to front only the essential facts of life. —HENRY DAVID THOREAU, *Walden,* "Where I Lived,
and What I Lived For," 1854
[More at LIFE.]

8 In wildness is the preservation of the world.
—HENRY DAVID THOREAU, *Walking,* 1862
[The motto of the Wilderness Society.]

9 It is a wild rank place, and there is no flattery in it.
—HENRY DAVID THOREAU, *Cape Cod,* 1865
[See also Thoreau under MASSACHUSETTS re Cape Cod.]

10 In God's wildness lies the hope of the world—the great fresh, unblighted, unredeemed wilderness. —JOHN MUIR, note from Alaska, 1890

The clearest way into the universe is through a forest wilderness. [1]
—JOHN MUIR, *John of the Mountains*, 1938

Wilderness is the raw material out of which man has hammered the artifact [2]
called civilization. —ALDO LEOPOLD, *A Sand County Almanac*, 1949

Something will have gone out of us as a people if we ever let the remaining [3]
wilderness be destroyed. —WALLACE STEGNER, "the wilderness letter,"
to David Pesonen, University of California
Wildlands Research Center, 1960
[Stegner, whose novels were set in the American West, was a lifelong advocate
of conservation of natural resources.]

God made the wilderness for man and all other creatures to use, to adore, but [4]
not to destroy. —WILLIAM O. DOUGLAS,
My Wilderness: The Pacific West, 1962

A Wilderness Bill of Rights. [5]
—WILLIAM O. DOUGLAS, book title, 1965
[Douglas, a leader of liberal causes on the Supreme Court, was also a promi-
nent environmentalist.]

The remaining western wilderness is the geography of hope. [6]
—WALLACE STEGNER, Introduction,
Where the Bluebird Sings to the Lemonade Springs, 1992
[This was a saying of Stegner's, also used in *A Geography of Hope*, a lecture de-
livered at the University of Colorado, and published by the university's press
in *A Society to Match Our Scenery*, 1991. See also THE WEST.]

WHITES
See RACES & PEOPLES

WILL
See also DETERMINATION, EFFORT, PERSISTENCE, & PERSEVERANCE

A fat kitchen, a lean will. [7]
—BENJAMIN FRANKLIN, *Poor Richard's Almanack*, 1732–57

Will springs from the two elements of moral sense and self-interest. [8]
—ABRAHAM LINCOLN, speech, Springfield, Ill., June 26, 1857

"There's no free will," says the philosopher; [9]
"To hang is most unjust."
"There is no free will," assents the officer;
"We hang because we must."
—AMBROSE BIERCE, *Collected Works*, VIII, 1911

Will and wisdom are both mighty leaders. Our times worship will. [10]
—CLARENCE DAY, *Humpty-Dumpty and Adam*,
in *The Crow's Nest*, 1921

We have to believe in free will. We've got no other choice. [11]
—ISAAC BASHEVIS SINGER, London, *Times*, June 21, 1982

WINE
See FOOD, WINE, & EATING

WINNING & LOSING, VICTORY & DEFEAT

See also FAILURE; SPORTS; SUCCESS & FAME

1   To the victors belong the spoils.
—WILLIAM MARCY, speech,
U.S. Senate, Jan. 25, 1832
[More at POLITICS & POLITICIANS.]

2   [I feel] somewhat like the boy in Kentucky who stubbed his toe while running to see his sweetheart. The boy said he was too big to cry, and far too badly hurt to laugh.   —ABRAHAM LINCOLN, reply when asked to comment
on the Democrats winning state elections in New York,
quoted in *Leslie's Illustrated Weekly,* Nov. 22, 1862
[Adlai Stevenson, after losing in the 1952 presidential election, used this same anecdote, crediting Lincoln. "I'm too old to cry, but it hurts too much to laugh," he said.]

3   Too much success is not wholly desirable; an occasional beating is good for men—and nations.   —ALFRED THAYER MAHAN, *Life of Nelson,* 1897

4   Errors and defeats are more obviously illustrative of principles than successes are. . . . Defeat cries aloud for explanation; whereas success, like charity, covers a multitude of sins.   —ALFRED THAYER MAHAN, *Naval Strategy,* 1911

5   Winners never give up.
—ANONYMOUS, "work-incentive" poster, 1920s
[This slogan accompanied a picture of George Washington, and was preceded by "When others lost heart and quit, Washington fought on—and won." See also the perennial locker room advice at SPORTS. And for another uplifting workplace slogan, AMBITION & ASPIRATION.]

6   Show me a good and gracious loser, and I'll show you a failure.
—KNUTE ROCKNE, comment to Wisconsin
basketball coach Walter Meanwell, 1920s
[See also SPORTS, the note to the Grantland *Alumnus Football* Rice quote, and the Vince Lombardi quote, below.]

7   Winning isn't worthwhile unless one has something finer and nobler behind it.
—AMOS ALONZA STAGG, *Touchdown!,* 1927
[Stagg's football teams won 315 games during his 71-year career, spent mainly at the University of Chicago. He is credited with introducing the huddle, the snap from center, the man in motion, the line shift, and cross blocking.]

8   Lose as if you like it; win as if you were used to it.
—TOMMY HITCHCOCK, saying c. 1935
[Hitchcock was a famous and dashing polo player.]

9   There can only be one winner, folks, but isn't that the American way?
—HORACE McCOY, *They Shoot Horses, Don't They?,* 1935

10   Nice guys finish last.
—LEO DUROCHER, July 5, 1946
[Popular version of comment by Brooklyn Dodgers' manager Durocher on the New York Giants baseball team, spotlighted by sportswriter Jimmy Cannon to explain Durocher to the world, and used as a book title by Durocher in 1975. The comment in full ran: "I called off his [Giant manager Mel Ott's] players'

names as they came marching up the steps behind him, 'Walker Cooper [who had a brother named Morton Cooper], Mize, Marshall, Kerr, Gordon, Thomson. Take a look at them. All nice guys. They'll finish last. Nice guys. Finish last.'"

The Giants did finish last—thirty-six games out—but on the last day of the season, they beat the Dodgers, forcing them into a playoff with St. Louis, which the Dodgers lost 2–0.]

You know what makes a good loser? Practice.   1
—ERNEST HEMINGWAY,
speaking to his son Gregory "Gig" H. Hemingway,
quoted in *Papa, a Personal Memoir* [1976]

Never have so few lost so much so stupidly and so fast.   2
—DEAN ACHESON, 1951, quoted in Daniel Yergin, *The Prize*, 1991
[Secretary of State Acheson was referring to the huge British losses when Iran nationalized the oil industry. The comment plays on Winston Churchill's, "Never in the field of conflict was so much owed by so many to so few," August 1940. Churchill was expressing gratitude to the Royal Air Force for battling German bombers and fighters.]

You can't win them all.   3
—RAYMOND CHANDLER, *The Long Goodbye*, 1954
[Eric Partridge dated this expression to c. 1940 in *A Dictionary of Catch Phrases*, but Chandler's use is the earliest given in *The Concise Oxford Dictionary of Proverbs*. It did not become common until the 1960s.]

Sometimes it's worse to win a fight than to lose.   4
—BILLIE HOLIDAY, *Lady Sings the Blues*, 1956

Winning isn't everything, it's the only thing.   5
—VINCENT LOMBARDI, attributed
[Lombardi coached the formidable Green Bay Packers 1959–69, and this quote was widely associated with him. It may have originated, however, with coach Henry "Red" Sanders of Vanderbilt University. *Respectfully Quoted*, published by The Library of Congress, credits Sanders with this c. 1948. Sanders was later quoted in *Sports Illustrated* as quipping, "Sure winning isn't everything. It's the only thing," December 26, 1955. Lombardi tried to persuade people that what he himself said was something gentlemanly on the lines of "Winning isn't everything, but wanting (or making the effort) to win is." Others recollect him taking the harder position. Later he told writer James A. Michener that he wished he had never said "the damn thing," that he had meant that it was important to make an effort and to have a goal: "I sure as hell didn't mean for people to crush human values and morality," *Sports in America*, 1976.]

There's an old saying that victory has a hundred fathers and defeat is an or-   6
phan.   —JOHN F. KENNEDY, press conference, State Department,
Washington, D.C., April 21, 1961
[Kennedy made the "old saying" famous on this occasion by taking on his own shoulders as "the responsible officer of the government" full blame for the aborted invasion of Cuba at the Bay of Pigs four days before. The saying—Kennedy himself couldn't remember at the time where he had picked it up—apparently comes from *The Ciano Diaries: 1939–43*, in which Mussolini's foreign minister, Count Galeazzo Ciano, noted on September 9, 1942: "As always, victory finds a hundred fathers, but defeat is an orphan."]

1   A man's not finished when he's defeated; he's finished when he quits.
                              —RICHARD M. NIXON, letter to Sen. Edward Kennedy
                                 after the accident at Chappaquiddick, July 18, 1969
[Quoted by William Safire after former Pres. Nixon's death in 1994. See also
Nixon at HATE.]

2   It's easy to do anything in victory. It's in defeat that a man reveals himself.
                              —FLOYD PATTERSON, in Henry Mullan,
                                 The Book of Boxing Quotations [1988]
[Patterson, a soft-spoken boxer, won the heavyweight championship in 1956 at
age twenty-one. He lost to Swedish fighter Ingemar Johansson in 1959, but regained the crown by beating Johansson in 1960—becoming the first heavyweight champ to win back that title. In 1962, he fell to a glowering Sonny
Liston in a first-round k.o., lost to Liston again the next year, and despite a long
effort never again reached the first rank.]

3   Losing is the only American sin.   —JOHN R. TUNIS, quoted by Mark Shields,
                                 The MacNeil/Lehrer NewsHour
                                 [March 19, 1992]
[Shields called Tunis "the greatest American sports writer."]

WINNER   *See* NATURE: SEASONS

WISCONSIN   *See also* CITIES (Milwaukee)

4   Wisconsin is the soul of a great people. She manifests the spirit of the con-
queror, whose strength has subdued the forest, quickened the soil, harvested
the forces of nature and multiplied production. From her abundance she serves
food to the world.   —FRED L. HOLMES, *Old World Wisconsin*, 1944

5   Wisconsin's politics have traditionally been uproar politics—full of the yam-
mer, the squawk, the accusing finger, the injured howl. Every voter is an amateur detective, full of zeal to get out and nip a little political inequity in the
bud.   —GEORGE SESSIONS PERRY, *Cities of America*, 1947

Motto

6   Forward.

WISDOM   *See also* ADVICE; COMMON SENSE

7   It is a characteristic of wisdom not to do desperate things.
                              —HENRY DAVID THOREAU, "Economy," *Walden*, 1854

8   Wisdom is of the soul.   —WALT WHITMAN, *Song of the Open Road*,
                                 in *Leaves of Grass*, 3d ed., 1860

9   It is the province of knowledge to speak, and it is the privilege of wisdom to
listen.   —OLIVER WENDELL HOLMES, SR.,
                                 The Poet at the Breakfast-Table, 1872

10 Wisdom is wealth.   —JOSEPH WHEELER, speech, U.S. House of
                                 Representatives, Feb. 1883

[More at BOOKS & READING.]

The art of being wise is the art of knowing what to overlook.   1
                              —WILLIAM JAMES,
                                   The Principles of Psychology, 1890

Wisdom comes by disillusionment.   2
                              —GEORGE SANTAYANA, *The Life of Reason,* 1905–1906

Nine-tenths of wisdom consists in being wise in time.   3
                              —THEODORE ROOSEVELT, speech, June 14, 1917

Wise Man: One who sees the storm coming before the clouds appear.   4
                              —ELBERT HUBBARD, *The Roycroft Dictionary
                                   and Book of Epigrams,* 1923

To know when to be generous and when firm—this is wisdom.   —*Ibid.* 5

WISDOM, WORDS OF   *See also* ADVICE; CRAFTINESS; HEALTH;
                                              QUOTATIONS & PROVERBS;
                                              SEASONS & TIMES (Kennedy)

You have the world before you. Stoop as you go through it, and you will miss   6
many hard bumps.   —COTTON MATHER, advice to
                                          Benjamin Franklin, 1724
[Franklin, in a letter to his son, May 12, 1784, revealed that Mather had given
him this advice some sixty years earlier.]

Work as if you were to live a hundred years,   7
Pray as if you were to die tomorrow.
                              —BENJAMIN FRANKLIN, *Poor Richard's Almanack,*
                                   May 1757

The bigger the mouth, the better it looks when shut.   8
Only a fool argues with a skunk, a mule, or a cook.
Kickin' never gets you nowhere, 'les'n you're a mule.
There ain't no hoss that can't be rode.
It's sometimes safer to pull your freight than pull your gun.
Faint heart never filled a flush.
Never call a man a liar because he knows mor'n you do.
                              —ANONYMOUS, cowboy sayings,
                                   in Ramon F. Adams, *Western Words:
                                   A Dictionary of the American West* [1968]

Put all your eggs in one basket—and watch that basket!   9
                              —MARK TWAIN, *Pudd'nhead Wilson's Calendar,*
                                   in *Pudd'nhead Wilson,* 1894
[By rights this should be credited to Andrew Carnegie, but so many authorities,
including *Bartlett's,* cite Twain that we stay with the attribution to avoid confusion. As early as 1912, however, Twain's biographer Albert Bigelow Paine revealed that the canny comment was delivered by Andrew Carnegie at a dinner
with Twain and others on April 6, 1893. Twain was trying to persuade Carnegie
to join him in investing in an automatic typesetting machine. "Carnegie regarded him through half-closed eyes as was his custom," wrote Paine, "and answered, 'That's a mistake. Put all your eggs in one basket ... etc.'" The
investment, incidentally, was a major factor in Twain's subsequent bankruptcy;
see also Moffett at HONOR above, p. 236.]

1   Be prepared.

—Boy Scouts, motto

[The founder of the Scouts, Sir Robert Baden-Powell, explained, "The scouts' motto is founded on my initials, it is: BE PREPARED, which means you are always to be in a state of readiness in mind and body to do your DUTY," *Scouting for Boys*, 1908.]

2   Work hard, keep your mouth shut, and answer your mail.

—Thomas J. Pendergast, advice to Harry S. Truman, 1934

[Pendergast, the political boss of Kansas City, gave this advice to Harry Truman upon his departure for his first term in the U.S. Senate.]

3   To get along, go along.

—Sam Rayburn, saying

[More at Congress.]

4   Never trust a man who combs his hair straight from the left armpit.

—Alice Roosevelt Longworth, quoted in Michael Teague,
Mrs. L.: Conversations with Alice Roosevelt [1991]

[Mrs. L., daughter of Teddy Roosevelt, was speaking specifically of Gen. Douglas MacArthur, who wore his hair in strands over the top of his head.]

5   Avoid fried meats which angry up the blood. If your stomach disputes you, lie down and pacify it with cool thoughts. Keep the juices flowing by jangling around gently as you move. Go very light on the vices, such as carrying on in society. The social ramble ain't restful. Avoid running at all times. Don't look back. Something may be gaining on you.   —Leroy "Satchel" Paige,
from his autobiography,
How to Stay Young, 1953

[Some of the credit for this appealing advice—maybe most of it—should go to *Collier's* magazine writer Richard Donovan, who wrote a profile of Paige, a legendary star of the Negro leagues, and one of the greatest and most enduring of baseball pitchers. According to *Good Advice* (1982) by brothers William Safire and Leonard Safir, when Donovan's editor asked for some "typical Paige quotes" to use in a box, Donovan "cooked up" these words of wisdom. Paige later appropriated them. What isn't clear is how close Donovan came to comments actually made by Paige.]

6   Never eat at a place called Mom's. Never play cards with a man named Doc. And never lie down with a woman who's got more troubles than you.

—Nelson Algren, *What Every Young Man Should Know*

[Algren said that he learned this from "a Negro lady." He and others sometimes used slightly different formulations. For example, mystery writer Ross Macdonald advises in *Black Money* (1966), "Never sleep with anyone whose troubles are worse than your own."]

7   Keep your eyes open and your mouth shut.

—John Steinbeck, *Sweet Thursday*, 1954

8   If it ain't broke, don't fix it.

—Anonymous, folk adage

[Given widespread currency in 1977 by Bert Lance, director of the Office of Management and Budget under Pres. Jimmy Carter. Lance could not fix his own problems with investigations into personal banking irregularities, and he resigned the same year.]

Have fun. And go home when you're tired.   1
> —GEORGE ABBOTT, saying, *New York Times*,
> obituary, Feb. 2, 1995

WOMEN   *See also* WOMEN & MEN

Men of sense of all ages abhor those customs which treat us only as the vassals   2
of your sex.   —ABIGAIL ADAMS, letter to John Adams, March 31, 1776

A woman's whole life is a history of the affections.   3
> —WASHINGTON IRVING, *The Broken Heart*,
> in *The Sketch Book of Geoffrey Crayon, Gent.*, 1819–20

There is in every true woman's heart a spark of heavenly fire which lies dor-   4
mant in the broad daylight of prosperity; but which kindles up, and beams and
blazes in the dark hour of adversity.   —WASHINGTON IRVING, *The Wife*,
> in *Ibid.*

If I were asked . . . to what the singular prosperity and growing strength of that   5
people [Americans] ought mainly to be attributed, I should reply: to the superiority of their women.   —ALEXIS DE TOCQUEVILLE,
> *Democracy in America*, 1835

A woman should always challenge our respect, and never move our compassion.   6
> —RALPH WALDO EMERSON, *Journal*, 1836

As men become aware that few have had a fair chance, they are inclined to say   7
that no woman has had a fair chance.   —MARGARET FULLER, *Woman in
> the Nineteenth Century*, 1845

[That little man in black says] woman can't have as much rights as man be-   8
cause Christ wasn't a woman. Where did your Christ come from? . . . From
God and a woman. Man has nothing to do with him.
> —SOJOURNER TRUTH, Women's Rights Convention, Akron, Ohio
[The man in black was a clergyman in the audience. In another personal take
on Christian dogma, Truth commented, "If the first woman God ever made
was strong enough to turn the world upside down all alone, these women together ought to be able to turn it back and get it right side up again." *Ibid.*]

America is now wholly given over to a damned mob of scribbling women.   9
> —NATHANIEL HAWTHORNE, letter, 1855, quoted in
> Caroline Ticknor, *Hawthorne and His Publisher* [1913]

A Lady with a Lamp shall stand   10
In the great history of the land,
A noble type of good,
Heroic womanhood.   —HENRY WADSWORTH LONGFELLOW,
> *Santa Filomena*, 1858

A beautiful woman is a practical poet.   —RALPH WALDO EMERSON, *Beauty*,   11
> in *The Conduct of Life*, 1860

All native American women are intelligent. It seems to be their birthright.   12
> —ANTHONY TROLLOPE, *North America*, 1862
[Trollope especially admired women in the eastern cities, whom he thought
were graceful, beautiful, charming companions, lacking "nothing that a lover
can desire in his love." About western women he had reservations: "They are

as sharp as nails, but then they are also as hard. They know, doubtless, all that they ought to know, but then they know so much more than they ought to know. They are tyrants to their parents, and never practice the virtue of obedience till they have half-grown-up daughters of their own."]

1 The hand that rocks the cradle
Is the hand that rules the world.   —W. R. WALLACE,
The Hand That Rules the World, c. 1865

2 Join the union, girls, and together say, "Equal Pay for Equal Work!"
—SUSAN B. ANTHONY, in *The Revolution*, March 18, 1869

3 A sufficient measure of civilization is the influence of good women.
—RALPH WALDO EMERSON, *Civilization*,
in *Society and Solitude*, 1870

4 Woman must not depend upon the protection of man, but must be taught to protect herself.   —SUSAN B. ANTHONY, speech, July 1871

5 I promulgate new races of teachers, and of perfect women, indispensable to endow the birth-stock of a new world.   —WALT WHITMAN, *Democratic Vistas*, 1871

6 The queens in history compare favorably with the kings.
—ELIZABETH CADY STANTON & SUSAN B. ANTHONY, *History of
Woman Suffrage*, written with Mathilda Joslyn Gage, 1881

7 The prolonged slavery of women is the darkest page in human history.
—*Ibid.*

8 Our young women are haunted by the idea that they ought . . . to "improve" their minds. They are utterly unconscious of the pathetic impossibility of improving those poor little hard, thin, wiry, one-stringed instruments which they call their minds, and which haven't range enough to master one big emotion much less to express it in words or figures.
—HENRY ADAMS, letter to the
American Historical Association, 1885
[This letter was written in the same year that his wife, Marian, usually called Clover, committed suicide. They had been married for thirteen years.]

9 Girls are charming creatures. I shall have to be twice seventy years before I change my mind as to that.   —MARK TWAIN, March 7, 1906,
in *Autobiography* [1924]
[The thought was occasioned by fond memories of a visit to Vassar twenty-one years before—and by anticipation of a talk that he planned to give at Barnard College that afternoon.]

10 A thoroughly beautiful woman and a thoroughly homely woman are creations which I love to gaze upon, and which I cannot tire of gazing upon, for each is perfect in her own line.   —MARK TWAIN, *Autobiography* [1924]

11 What a woman wants is what you're out of. She wants more of a thing when it's scarce.   —O. HENRY, *Cupid à la Carte*, in *Heart of the West*, 1907

12 Hurray and vote for suffrage.   —FEBB ENSMINGER BURN, letter to her son,
August 1920
["Be a good boy," she urged. And Henry Thomas Burn, age twenty-three, was.

He broke a tie in the Tennessee legislature, tipping the balance to ratification of the Nineteenth Amendment, giving women the right to vote; see AMERICAN HISTORY: MEMORABLE MOMENTS.]

I was, being human, born alone;
I am, being woman, hard beset;   1
I live by squeezing from a stone
The little nourishment I get.   —ELINOR HOYT WYLIE,
                                                  Let No Charitable Hope,
                                                  in *Collected Poems* [1932]

At first a woman doesn't want anything but a husband, but as soon as she gets   2
one, she wants everything else in the world.
                    —EDGAR WATSON HOWE, *Country Town Sayings,* 1911

A free race cannot be born of slave mothers.   3
                    —MARGARET SANGER, *Women and the New Race,* 1920

No lady is ever a gentleman.   —JAMES BRANCH CABELL,   4
                                                  Something About Eve, 1927

It won't be no time till some woman will become so desperate politically and   5
just lose all prospectus of right and wrong and maybe go from bad to worse
and finally wind up in the Senate.   —WILL ROGERS, *Weekly Articles,*
                                              March 31, 1929

Can we today measure devotion to husband and children by our indifference to   6
everything else?   —GOLDA MEIR, *The Plough Woman,* 1930

The true worth of a race must be measured by the character of its womanhood.   7
                    —MARY MCLEOD BETHUNE, speech, A *Century of Progress*
                    of Negro Women, Chicago Women's Federation,
                    June 3, 1933

A Woman Is a Sometime Thing.   8
                    —IRA GERSHWIN, song title, *Porgy and Bess,* 1935
[Music by George Gershwin.]

All elegant women have acquired a technique of weeping which has no . . .   9
fatal effect on the makeup.   —ANAÏS NIN, *Winter of Artifice,* 1939

It was a blonde. A blonde to make a bishop kick a hole in a stained glass window. 10
                    —RAYMOND CHANDLER, *Farewell, My Lovely,* 1940

A woman's work is seldom done.   —THORNTON WILDER,   11
                                                  The Skin of Our Teeth, 1942
[A play on the old saying, "Man may work from sun to sun, / But woman's
work is never done."]

Women have simple tastes. They can get pleasure out of the conversation of   12
children in arms and men in love.   —H. L. MENCKEN, *Sententiae,*
                                            in *A Mencken Crestomathy,* 1949

When women kiss it always reminds one of prize-fighters shaking hands.   13
                                                  —*Ibid.*

1 A woman's best protection is a little money of her own.
—CLARE BOOTHE LUCE, attributed

2 A liberated woman is one who has sex before marriage and a job after.
—GLORIA STEINEM,
quoted in *Newsweek* magazine,
March 28, 1960

3 Women would rather be right than reasonable.
—OGDEN NASH, *Frailty, Thy Name Is a Misnomer*,
in *Marriage Lines*, 1964

4 Many women do not recognize themselves as discriminated against; no better
proof could be found of the totality of their conditioning.
—KATE MILLETT, *Sexual Politics*, 1969

5 Raging hormonal tides.   —EDGAR BERMAN, characterization of a causative
factor in women's behavior, 1970
[Dr. Berman, an adviser to Vice President Hubert Humphrey, was forced to resign from the Democratic National Committee's planning council after announcing that hormonal tides interfered with women's competence.]

6 If I have to, I can do anything.
I am strong, I am invincible, I am woman.
—HELEN REDDY, *I Am Woman*, 1972

7 So few grown women like their lives.   —KATHARINE GRAHAM,
quoted by Jane Howard,
Ms. Magazine, Oct. 1974

8 A strong woman is a woman determined
To do something that others are determined not to be done.
—MARGE PIERCY, *For a Strong Woman*

9 Some of us are becoming the men we wanted to marry.
—GLORIA STEINEM, speech, Yale University, Sept. 1981

WOMEN & MEN   *See also* MEN; WOMEN

10 Do not put such unlimited power into the hands of husbands. Remember all
men would be tyrants if they could. [We women] will not hold ourselves bound
by any laws in which we have no voice or representation.
—ABIGAIL ADAMS, letter to John Adams,
March 31, 1776

11 I cannot say that I think you are very generous to the ladies; for, whilst you are
proclaiming peace and good will to men, emancipating all nations, you insist
upon retaining an absolute power over wives.
—ABIGAIL ADAMS, letter to John Adams,
May 7, 1776

12 I will never consent to have our sex considered an inferior point of light. Let
each planet shine in their own orbit. God and nature designed it so—if man is
Lord, woman is *Lordess*—that is what I contend for.
—ABIGAIL ADAMS, letter to Eliza Peabody, her sister, July 19, 1779

There exists, in the world of men, a tone of feeling towards women as towards 1
slaves, such as is expressed in the common phrase, "Tell that to women and
children." —MARGARET FULLER, *The Great Lawsuit: Man versus Men,*
Woman versus Women, in *The Dial,* July 1843

We hold these truths to be self-evident; that all men and women are created 2
equal. —ELIZABETH CADY STANTON, *Declaration of Sentiment,*
First Woman's Rights Convention, Seneca Falls, N.Y.,
July 19, 1848

As unto the bow, the cord is, 3
So unto the man is woman,
Though she bends him, she obeys him,
Though she draws him, yet she follows,
Useless each without the other. —HENRY WADSWORTH LONGFELLOW,
The Song of Hiawatha, 1855

Man has his will—but woman has her way. —OLIVER WENDELL HOLMES, SR., 4
The Autocrat of the
Breakfast-Table, 1858

Men, their rights and nothing more; women, their rights and nothing less. 5
—SUSAN B. ANTHONY, 1868
[The motto of *The Revolution,* a newspaper founded by Anthony in 1868, was
"The True Republic—men, their rights and nothing more," etc.]

The men believe not in the women, nor the women in the men. 6
—WALT WHITMAN, *Democratic Vistas,* 1871
[More at HYPOCRISY.]

A woman never forgets her sex. She would rather talk with a man than an an- 7
gel, any day. —OLIVER WENDELL HOLMES, SR.,
The Poet at the Breakfast-Table, 1872

The masculine tone is passing out of the world. It's a feminine, a nervous, hys- 8
terical, chattering, canting age. —HENRY JAMES, *The Bostonians,* 1886

Hogamus higamus, 9
Men are polygamous,
Higamous hogamous
Women monogamous.
—ANONYMOUS, c. 1895
[The verse has several variations.]

You are not permitted to kill a woman who has wronged you, but nothing for- 10
bids you to reflect that she is growing older every minute. You are avenged
1,440 times a day. —AMBROSE BIERCE, *Epigrams*

Scratch a lover, and find a foe. —DOROTHY PARKER, *Ballads of a Great* 11
Weariness, in *Enough Rope,* 1927

Where women cease from troubling and the wicked are at rest. 12
—ANONYMOUS, slogan on the barroom floor
of the Princeton Club in New York
[The floor was demolished and the slogan not carried forward into the nineties—
1990s.]

1   A woman will always have to be better than a man in any job she undertakes.
                    —ELEANOR ROOSEVELT, *My Day,* Nov. 29, 1945

2   There is no spectacle on earth more appealing than a beautiful woman in the
act of cooking dinner for someone she loves.
                    —THOMAS WOLFE, quoted in
                    The American Heritage Cookbook [1964]

3   Maleness in America is not absolutely defined; it has to be kept and re-earned
every day, and one essential element in the definition is beating women in
every game that both sexes play.   —MARGARET MEAD,
                                              Male and Female, 1948
    [See also Mead at MEDIOCRITY.]

4   Men have a much better time of it than women. For one thing, they marry
later. For another thing, they die earlier.
                    —H. L. MENCKEN, *A Mencken Chrestomathy,* 1949

5   If men could get pregnant, abortion would be a sacrament.
                    —FLORYNCE KENNEDY, quoted in *Ms. Magazine,* March 1973
    [Kennedy, a lawyer and civil rights activist, was speaking in the year of *Roe v.
    Wade;* see AMERICAN HISTORY: MEMORABLE MOMENTS.]

6   Men and women belong to different species, and communication between
them is a science still in its infancy.   —BILL COSBY, *Love and Marriage,* 1989

7   It takes a smart woman to fall in love with a good man.
                    —SADIE & BESSIE DELANY,
                    Having Our Say: The Delany Sisters' First 100 Years, 1993

WOODS   *See* WILDERNESS

WORDS   *See* LANGUAGE & WORDS

WORK & WORKERS   See also CAPITALISM & CAPITAL V. LABOR;
                                ACTION & DOING; EXCELLENCE; FARMS & FARMERS

8   Love labor: . . . It is wholesome for thy body and good for thy mind.
                    —WILLIAM PENN, *Some Fruits of Solitude,* 1693

9   The used key is always bright.   —BENJAMIN FRANKLIN,
                                             Poor Richard's Almanack, July 1744

10 I shall never ask, never refuse, nor ever resign an office.
                    —BENJAMIN FRANKLIN, *Autobiography,*
                    begun 1771 [published in full, 1868]

11 When men are employed they are best contented.   —*Ibid.*

12 O sing me a song of the Factory Girl
    So merry and glad and free—
    The bloom on her cheeks, of health it speaks!—
    O a happy creature is she.   —JOHN H. WARLAND,
                                            Song of the Manchester Factory Girl
    [Arthur M. Schlesinger, Jr., in *The Age of Jackson,* notes that Warland, a de-
    fender of the privileged classes, wrote many Whig campaign songs.]

We put our love where we have put our labor. 1
　　　　　　　　　　—RALPH WALDO EMERSON, *Journal*, 1836
[See also Emerson at EXCELLENCE.]

The life of labor does not make men, but drudges. 　　　　　—*Ibid.* 2

Under the spreading chestnut tree 3
The village smithy stands;
The smith a mighty man is he
With large and sinewy hands.
And the muscles of his brawny arms
Are strong as iron bands.

His brow is wet with honest sweat,
He earns whate'er he can,
And looks the whole world in the face,
For he owes not any man.
　　　　—HENRY WADSWORTH LONGFELLOW, *The Village Blacksmith*, 1842

And blessed are the horny hands of toil! 4
　　　　　　　　—JAMES RUSSELL LOWELL, *A Glance Behind the Curtain*,
　　　　　　　　　　in *The Democratic Review*, Sept. 1843
[One of those lines that school children tend to remember for the wrong
reasons.]

Men for the sake of getting a living forget to live. 5
　　　　　　　　　　—MARGARET FULLER, *Summer on the Lakes*, 1844

It is not necessary that a man should earn his living from the sweat of his brow 6
unless he sweats easier than I do. 　　　　　　　　—HENRY DAVID THOREAU,
　　　　　　　　　　　　　　　　　　　　Walden, 1854

Every man's task is his life-preserver. 　　—RALPH WALDO EMERSON, *Worship*, 7
　　　　　　　　　　in *The Conduct of Life*, 1860

Labor is the superior of capital, and deserves much the higher consideration. 8
　　　　　　　　　　—ABRAHAM LINCOLN,
　　　　　　　　　　　first annual message to Congress,
　　　　　　　　　　　Dec. 3, 1861
[More at CAPITALISM & CAPITAL V. LABOR.]

Join the union, girls. 　　—SUSAN B. ANTHONY, in *The Revolution* newspaper, 9
　　　　　　　　　　March 18, 1869
[More at CAPITALISM & CAPITAL V. LABOR.]

John Henry told his captain, 10
"A man ain't nothin' but a man,
And before I'd let that steam-drill beat me down,
I'd die with this hammer in my hand."
　　　　　　　　　　—ANONYMOUS, folk song, 1870s
[John Henry, an African-American steel driver for the C. & O. railroad com-
pany, died about 1873 during the construction of the Big Bend Tunnel in West
Virginia. He evidently bested a steam drill in a steel-driving contest, and in leg-
end, that contest killed him. Actually, according to John and Alan Lomax in
Folksong U.S.A., he died in a rock fall a few years later, one of many, perhaps
hundreds of men killed while building that tunnel.]

1   Labor disgraces no man.   —ULYSSES S. GRANT, speech,
                                          Midland International Arbitration Union,
                                          Birmingham, England, 1877
[More at CAPITALISM & CAPITAL V. LABOR.]

2   Work is not the curse, but drudgery is.   —HENRY WARD BEECHER, *Proverbs*
                                                       from Plymouth Pulpit, 1887

3   Raise less corn and more hell.   —MARY LEASE, attributed,
                                                 speech to Kansas farmers, 1890
[More at KANSAS.]

4   No race can prosper till it learns there is as much dignity in tilling a field as in
    writing a poem.   —BOOKER T. WASHINGTON, speech,
                                               Atlanta Exposition, Sept. 18, 1895

5   Every child should be taught that useful work is worship and that intelligent
    labor is the highest form of prayer.   —ROBERT G. INGERSOLL,
                                                    How to Reform Mankind, 1896

6   Far and away the best prize that life offers is the chance to work hard at work
    worth doing.   —THEODORE ROOSEVELT, Labor Day speech,
                                              Syracuse, N.Y., 1903

7   Come all you rounders for I want you to hear
    The story of a brave engineer.
    Casey Jones was the rounder's name,
    On a big eight-wheeler of a mighty fame.

                                          —ANONYMOUS, c. 1907
[There are many versions of this popular ballad. Most readers know Carl Sandburg's verses in *The American Songbook,* 1927. He drew on the rendition of
the vaudevellian Tallifero Laurence Sibert (or Siebert) dating from 1909. And
Sibert's work was based on an earlier song by Wallace Saunders, who apparently deserves credit for the original ballad. In *Folksong U.S.A.,* John and Alan
Lomax say that Saunders, "a Negro engine wiper," cleaned the blood of his
friend Casey Jones from the cab of engine No. 638. Another railroad worker,
Cornelius Steen, heard a railroad ballad in Kansas City that Saunders adapted
in memory of Jones. See also below.]

8   Casey Jones! Orders in his hand.
    Casey Jones! Mounted to his cabin,
    Took his farewell trip to the promised land.

                                          —*Ibid.*
[Engineer John Luther Jones, from Cayce, Kentucky, was famous for his skill in
getting the most out of the engine of the Illinois Central's Cannonball Express,
which ran from Memphis, Tennessee, to Canton, Mississippi. Jones also made
the most of a train's whistle, producing a memorable, mournful sound. He died
in April 1906, after filling in as engineer on the 10:00 P.M. run out of Memphis.
The inscription on Jones's monument in Calvary Cemetery in Jackson, Tennessee, are the lines from the ballad describing his mission: "For I'm going to
run till she leaves the rail / Or make it on time with the southbound mail."
Racing through the night, Jones sighted boxcars ahead, and told his fireman to
jump. Jones died at his post, braking and sounding the whistle.
    Jones had a pretty good safety record up to then, other than a few derail-
ments, and derailments were common, as witness this perhaps apocryphal en-

gineer's communication from the same period: "Off again, on again, gone again. Finnegan."]

You may tempt the upper classes
With your villainous demitasses,
But Heaven will protect the working girl.   —EDGAR SMITH, *Heaven Will
                                                Protect the Working Girl*
[Sung by Marie Dressler in *Tillie's Nightmare*, c. 1914.]

1

No work with interest is ever hard. I am always certain of results. They always
come if you work hard enough.   —HENRY FORD, *My Life and Work*, 1922

2

Working people have a lot of bad habits, but the worst of them is work.
          —CLARENCE DARROW,
              quoted in Lincoln Steffens, *Autobiography*, 1931

3

There is no substitute for hard work.   —THOMAS ALVA EDISON, *Life*, 1932

4

Figure it out. Work a lifetime to pay off a house. You finally own it, and there's
no one to live in it.   —ARTHUR MILLER, *Death of a Salesman*, 1949

5

The average male gets his living by such depressing devices that boredom becomes a sort of natural state to him.
              —H. L. MENCKEN, *In Defense of Women*

6

The bitter and sweet come from the outside, the hard from within, from one's
own efforts.   —ALBERT EINSTEIN, *Out of My Later Years*, 1950

7

When you cease to make a contribution, you begin to die.
          —ELEANOR ROOSEVELT, letter to Mr. Horne, Feb. 19, 1960

8

Here on earth God's work must truly be our own.
          —JOHN F. KENNEDY, Inaugural Address, Jan. 20, 1961

9

If work was a good thing the rich would have it all and not let you do it.
          —ELMORE LEONARD, *Split Images*, 1961

10

Work is a four-letter word.   —ANONYMOUS, bumper sticker, from a comment
              by Yippie founder Abbie Hoffman, 1960s
[Cf. Tennessee Williams below.]

11

I am the cry of the poor
Who work in the fields
Who water the earth
With our sweat . . .

Long have we suffered
Being sold like slaves
Now we can all see
Our triumph is coming.
          —EPIFIANO CAMACHO, *Strike of the Roses*, 1965,
              in Stan Steiner, *La Raza: The Mexican Americans* [1969]
[Camacho, a rose grafter, led a strike that began on May 3, 1965, at Mount Ar-
bor Nurseries, in McFarland, California. This led eventually to the organization
of Cesar Chavez's National Farm Workers Association.]

12

1   The working class is loyal to friends, not ideas.
—NORMAN MAILER, *The Armies of the Night*, 1968

2   In a hierarchy, every employee tends to rise to his level of incompetence.
—LAURENCE J. PETER,
The Peter Principle, 1969

3   There is no prestige whatsoever attached to actually working. Workers are invisible.   —MARGE PIERCY, *The Grand Coolie Damn*,
in Robin Morgan ed., *Sisterhood Is Powerful*, 1970

4   The loveliest of all four-letter words—Work!
—TENNESSEE WILLIAMS, *Memoirs*, 1975

WORLD, THE   *See also* LIFE; NATURE; UNIVERSE, THE

5   Abstract yourself with a holy violence from the dung heap of this world.
—ROGER WILLIAMS, to John Winthrop, governor
of the Massachusetts Bay Colony, c. 1635
[Williams, who challenged the authority of the colony's government, was banished in 1635, and abstracted himself to the Rhode Island region, where he founded Providence.]

6   The world is a severe schoolmaster, for its frowns are less dangerous than its smiles and flatteries, and it is a difficult task to keep in the path of wisdom.
—PHYLLIS WHEATLEY,
letter to John Thornton, Oct. 30, 1774
[Wheatley was kidnapped from Africa at about age eight, and arrived in Boston in 1761. She began to write poetry at age fourteen, and finding no publisher in America, traveled to England. Her *Poems on Various Subjects, Religious and Moral*, published in 1773 in England, is the first book by an African-American. She was freed in the mid-1770s, and died in poverty some ten years later.]

7   Look on this beautiful world, and read the truth
In her fair pages.   —WILLIAM CULLEN BRYANT,
The Ages, 1821

8   To different minds, the same world is a hell, and a heaven.
—RALPH WALDO EMERSON,
Journal, Dec. 20, 1822

9   Good-bye proud world! I'm going home.
Thou art not my friend and I'm not thine.
—RALPH WALDO EMERSON, *Good-bye*, in *Poems*, 1847

10   I came into this world, not chiefly to make this a good place to live in, but to live in it, be it good or bad.   —HENRY DAVID THOREAU,
Civil Disobedience, 1849

11   The world is so big, and I am so small,
I do not like it at all at all.   —WOODROW WILSON, quoted by
Adlai Stevenson, in Leon Harris,
The Fine Art of Political Wit [1965]

12   O world, I cannot hold thee close enough!   —EDNA ST. VINCENT MILLAY,
God's World, 1917

Some say the world will end in fire,   1
Some say in ice.
From what I've tasted of desire
I hold with those who favor fire.
But if it had to perish twice,
I think I know enough of hate
To say that for destruction ice
Is also great
And would suffice.   —ROBERT FROST, *Fire and Ice*, 1923

This is the way the world ends   2
Not with a bang but a whimper.   —T. S. ELIOT, *The Hollow Men*, 1925

No. I do not weep at the world—I am too busy sharpening my oyster knife.   3
    —ZORE NEALE HURSTON, *Colored Me*, in *World Tomorrow*, 1928

The world is a fine place and worth fighting for.   4
    —ERNEST HEMINGWAY, *For Whom the Bell Tolls*, 1940

I had a lover's quarrel with the world.   5
    —ROBERT FROST, *The Lesson for Today*,
    read at Harvard University, June 20, 1941
[More at EPITAPHS & GRAVESTONES.]

The world only exists in your eyes—your conception of it. You can make it as   6
big or as small as you want to.   —F. SCOTT FITZGERALD, *The Crack-Up*, 1945

The most incomprehensible thing about the world is that it is comprehensible.   7
    —ALBERT EINSTEIN, obituary, *New York Times*, April 19, 1955

The world is a force, not a presence.   —WALLACE STEVENS, *Adagia*, in   8
    Opus Posthumous [1957]

WORLD WAR I, 1914–18 (U.S. entered in 1917)

We're going to try to get the boys out of the trenches by Christmas.   9
    —HENRY FORD, statement to the press, Nov. 1915
[Ford's promise has been reported in several versions. This is from Allan Nevins
and Frank Ernest Hill, *Ford: Expansion and Challenge, 1915–1933* (1957).
Christmas is a traditional target date for ending conflicts, and some question
whether the Christmas reference here was an embellishment of Ford's actual
words. Gen. John J. Pershing was also credited, later, with aiming to get troops
home by Christmas; see the note to the anonymous quote below on Hoboken.
In 1951, people hoped that the Korean conflict would be decided by Christmas,
after Gen. Douglas MacArthur launched a major U.S.–U.N. offensive in Korea
on November 24, the day after Thanksgiving. He hoped to reach the Yalu River
before December 25, but ran into several hundred thousand Chinese troops
who had come to the aid of North Korea, and barely escaped total disaster.
    In 1915, two years before America entered the European war, Ford, who was
a pacifist, chartered a ship and sailed for the Continent with a peace delegation. The venture was ridiculed by the press, but Ford never regretted the effort: "I wanted to see peace," he commented later. "I at least tried to bring it
about. Most men did not even try."]

Wake up America.   —AUGUSTUS P. GARDNER, speech, Oct. 16, 1916   10

1   I have a rendezvous with death
    At some disputed barricade,
When spring comes round with rustling shade
    And apple blossoms fill the air.
    .   .   .

But I've a rendezvous with death
    At midnight in some flaming town,
When spring trips north again this year,
    And I to my pledged word am true.
I shall not fail that rendezvous.
                      —ALAN SEEGER,
                   I Have a Rendezvous
                    with Death, 1916
[Seeger was killed in 1916, while fighting with the French army. The poem may have been the inspiration for Franklin D. Roosevelt's "This generation of Americans has a rendezvous with destiny." The poem was a favorite of John F. Kennedy.]

2   It must be a peace without victory.   —WOODROW WILSON, speech,
                      U.S. Senate, Jan. 22, 1917
[The president was describing the kind of peace that he believed was needed to end war in Europe. More at AMERICAN HISTORY: MEMORABLE MOMENTS.]

3   The world must be made safe for democracy.
               —WOODROW WILSON, speech to the U.S. Congress
                asking for a declaration of war, April 2, 1917
[In this speech, the president recommended declaring war on Germany. "The right is more precious than peace," he said, "and we shall fight for the things which we have always carried nearest our hearts." Those things were democracy, the rights and liberties of small nations, and the freedom of all peoples.
    Wilson is sometimes associated with the argument that the war would be "the war that will end war." H. G. Wells, however, is the apparent author of the phrase, and used it as a book title in 1914. The British statesman Lloyd George is said to have remarked, "This war, like the next war, is a war to end war."]

4   It is a war against all nations.   —*Ibid.*

5   If it be not treason, it grazes the edge of treason.
                      —JOHN SHARP WILLIAMS,
                debate, U.S. Senate, April 4, 1917
[Sen. Williams, Democrat of Mississippi, thus characterized comments by George W. Norris, an isolationist Republican from Nebraska, who opposed the decision to declare war.]

6   Food will win the war.
                      —ANONYMOUS slogan, 1917
[The slogan was associated with the voluntary—later mandated—food programs run by Herbert Hoover.]

7   It's heaven, hell, or Hoboken.
                        —ANONYMOUS, 1917
[U.S. troops left for and returned from the war at the port of Hoboken, New Jersey. Thus soldiers on their way overseas realized that they would end up at one of these three places. The phrase was published in verses by Albert Jay Cook in

Stars and Stripes. In 1918, Gen. John J. Pershing is said to have pledged, "Hell, heaven, or Hoboken by Christmas."]

You're in the Army now,
You're not behind a plow.
You'll never get rich,
You son of a bitch.
You're in the Army now.   —ANONYMOUS, soldier's song, c. 1917

1

And we won't come back till it's over over there.
                —GEORGE M. COHAN, *Over There,* 1917

2

Lafayette, we are here.   —CHARLES E. STANTON, at the tomb of
                                    the Marquis de Lafayette, Paris, July 4, 1917
[Probably the best-remembered statement by an American in World War I. The comment has been attributed to both Gen. John Pershing and Col. Stanton, a nephew of Lincoln's Secretary of War, Edwin M. Stanton. People who were there remember different speakers, but Pershing himself credited Stanton. Henry F. Woods in *American Sayings* (1945) writes that the famous line was the closing sentence in a short speech by Stanton: "America has joined forces with the Allied Powers, and what we have of blood and treasure are yours. Therefore it it that with loving pride we drape the colors in tribute of respect to this citizen of your great republic. And here and now, in the presence of the illustrious dead, we pledge our hearts and our honor in carrying this war to a successful issue. Lafayette, we are here."]

3

There lie many fighting men,
Dead in their youthful prime.
Never to laugh nor love again
Nor taste the summertime.   —JOYCE KILMER, *Rouge Bouquet,*
                                          March 7, 1918
[*Rouge Bouquet* was a woods and battleground.]

4

The first hundred years are the hardest.
                —ANONYMOUS, saying among members of the
                American Expeditionary Force, c. 1918

5

Come on you sons of bitches! Do you want to live forever?
                                    —DANIEL DALY,
                                    battle cry, June 4, 1918
[Marine Sergeant Daly used this rallying call in the Battle of Belleau Wood. The late word expert Stuart Flexner reported that in World War I, U.S. soldiers used the phrase "son of a bitch" so often that the French called them "les sommo-biches."
    As with "don't fire until you see the whites of their eyes"—see AMERICAN REVOLUTION—this battle cry has a precedent. On June 18, 1757, at Kolin, Frederick the Great is said to have shouted at his Guards, "Rascals, would you live forever?"]

6

There died a myriad,
And of the best, among them,
For an old bitch gone in the teeth,
For a botched civilization.   —EZRA POUND, *Hugh Selwyn Mauberley:*
                                        E.P. Ode pour l'élection de son sépulchre,
                                        1920

7

WORLD WAR II, 1939–45 (U.S. entered in 1941)

1   This is—London.   —EDWARD R. MURROW, opening line for his radio
                                              broadcasts from London, 1939–45
[Murrow's reports brought the war into American living rooms, eroding isolationist sentiment and inspiring affection for the beleaguered British.]

2   On this tenth day of June 1940, the hand that held the dagger has struck it into
    the back of its neighbor.   —FRANKLIN D. ROOSEVELT, speech,
                                            University of Virginia, June 10, 1940
[The "stab in the back," as it was popularly known, was struck by Italy, when
it declared war on France, already conquered and occupied by German troops.]

3   I shall say it again and again and again. Your boys are not going to be sent into
    any foreign wars.   —FRANKLIN D. ROOSEVELT, campaign speech,
                                            Boston, Oct. 30, 1940
[But the president did believe that the country should help the nations that
were fighting fascism and tyranny. Two months later, he made his "arsenal of
democracy" speech; see AMERICAN HISTORY: MEMORABLE MOMENTS. After the
attack on Pearl Harbor and the German declaration of war on the U.S., American boys were in the war.]

4   It is significant that despite the claims of air enthusiasts no battleship has yet
    been sunk by bombs.
                    —ANONYMOUS, caption for photograph of the U.S.S. *Arizona,*
                        Army–Navy Game program, Nov. 29, 1941, cited in Walter Lord,
                        Day of Infamy [1957]
[The Arizona was bombed and sunk in Pearl Harbor, December 7, 1941.]

5   Praise the Lord and pass the ammunition.
                    —HOWELL M. FORGY, Pearl Harbor, Dec. 7, 1941
[With these words, Forgy, a navy chaplain on the cruiser *New Orleans,* encouraged sailors hoisting shells to the guns firing on Japanese warplanes. They
were widely repeated and later used in a popular song by Frank Loesser. The
rallying cry has also been attributed to another Pearl Harbor navy chaplain,
William A. Maguire (1890–1953); according to *They Never Said It,* by Paul F.
Boller, Jr., and John George, it was used as far back as the Civil War.]

6   Yesterday, December 7, 1941—a date which will live in infamy—the United
    States of America was suddenly and deliberately attacked by naval and air
    forces of the empire of Japan.
                    —FRANKLIN D. ROOSEVELT, message to Congress requesting that
                        it declare a state of war existing between the U.S. and Japan,
                        Dec. 8, 1941

7   We are now in this war. We are all in it, all the way.
                    —FRANKLIN D. ROOSEVELT, message to the nation, Dec. 9, 1941

8   We are going to win the war, and we are going to win the peace that follows.
                                            —*Ibid.*

9   Sighted sub. Sank same.   —DONALD F. MASON, radio dispatch,
                                            Jan. 28, 1942
[Mason, a chief aviation machinist mate in the U.S. Navy, was flying a patrol
plane over the Atlantic, when he spotted an enemy submarine, sank it with
depth charges, and radioed this message to his base.]

This war is a new kind of war. It is warfare in terms of every continent, every   1
island, every sea, every air lane in the world.
              —FRANKLIN D. ROOSEVELT, fireside radio talk, Feb. 23, 1942

We're the battling bastards of Bataan;   2
No momma, no papa, no Uncle Sam;
No aunts, no uncles, no nephews, no nieces,
No rifles, no planes or artillery pieces,
And nobody gives a damn.   —ANONYMOUS, military song,
                                                Bataan peninsula, Philippines,
                                                winter 1941–42
[Following the attack on Pearl Harbor, the eighty thousand American and Fil-
ipino troops on Bataan were doomed to defeat. Despite pleas from their com-
mander, Gen. Douglas MacArthur, no reinforcements were sent, and
MacArthur was reassigned in March. In April, the overwhelmed defenders, under Gen. Jonathan Wainwright, surrendered. Ten thousand had died in battle;
fourteen thousand died in the Death March that followed. See also William
Thomas Cummings at ATHEISM and MacArthur quotes below.]

I shall return.   —DOUGLAS MACARTHUR, remark,   3
                                                March 11, 1942
[Gen. MacArthur first made this pledge to his fellow officers and friends as he
left the Philippines, according to Henry F. Woods in *American Sayings* (1945).
Upon landing in Melbourne, Australia, on March 20, he again announced, "I
came through and I shall return." See also MacArthur below.]

No army has ever done so much with so little.   4
              —DOUGLAS MACARTHUR, comment on the fall of Bataan,
                  quoted in *The New York Times*, April 11, 1942

And when he goes to heaven   5
To Saint Peter he will tell:
Another Marine reporting, sir;
I've served my time in hell.   —ANONYMOUS, epitaph, grave of Marine
                                             Pfc. Cameron, Guadalcanal, 1942
[The battle for the island of Guadalcanal in the Solomon Sea lasted from Au-
gust 7, 1942, to February 9, 1943. The costly American victory led to the first
Japanese retreat in the Pacific islands. Nine marines were awarded the Medal
of Honor for their part in the struggle.]

Oversexed, overfed, over here.   6
                                             —ANONYMOUS, British saying
[From 1942 to 1944, American troops were stationed in Britain in great numbers. They were both admired and resented, as reflected in this quip, which is
sometimes attributed to entertainer Tommy Trinder.]

I seen my duty and I done it.   7
                                          —JAMES H. HOWARD, Jan. 1944
[Flying a P-51 Mustang fighter, Howard became separated from his squadron
but spotted a group of B-17 bombers returning from a raid in Germany. The
Flying Fortresses were under attack by German fighters. For more than a half
hour, he fought off some thirty German planes, downing at least four. He was
awarded the Medal of Honor, and retired from the U.S. Air Force with the rank
of brigadier general. Earlier in the war, he had been a member of Col. Claire L.
Chennault's volunteer Flying Tigers, who fought the Japanese in Burma and
China.]

1   The eyes of the world are upon you. The hopes and prayers of liberty-loving people everywhere march with you.   —DWIGHT D. EISENHOWER, order
                                                                to troops preparing to invade
                                                                Normandy, June 6, 1944

2   Gentlemen, we are being killed on the beaches. Let's go inland and be killed.
                                        —NORMAN D. COTA, Omaha Beach, France,
                                                                June 6, 1944
    [Brig. Gen. "Dutch" Cota was assistant division commander of the 29th Division. His comment may have been improved in recollection. Stephen Ambrose in his 1994 book on D day gives the quote as: "Don't die on the beaches. Die up on the bluff, if you have to die. But get off the beaches or you're sure to die."
        The same day, Cota also gave the U.S. Army Rangers their motto, "Rangers lead the way," when he told the Ranger commander, "I'm expecting the Rangers to lead the way."]

3   Almighty God: Our sons, pride of our nation, this day have set upon a mighty endeavor, a struggle to preserve our republic, our religion, and our civilization, and to set free a suffering humanity. Lead them straight and true: Give strength to their arms, stoutness to their hearts, steadfastness in their faith.
                                        —FRANKLIN D. ROOSEVELT, D day prayer, June 6, 1944
    [This is from a long prayer read by Pres. Roosevelt over the radio at 10:00 P.M. on D day.]

4   We sure liberated the hell out of this place.
                                        —ANONYMOUS, U.S. soldier in a French village, 1944,
                                            quoted in Max Miller, *The Far Shore* [1945]

5   The Third Fleet's sunken and damaged ships have been salvaged and are retiring at high speed toward the enemy.   —WILLIAM F. HALSEY, radio dispatch,
                                                                Oct. 15, 1944
    [Admiral Halsey's response to Japanese reports that the American fleet had been destroyed. The message was addressed to Admiral Chester Nimitz.]

6   Follow me!   —AUBREY S. NEWMAN, battle cry,
                                                                Oct. 20, 1944
    [In the return of American troops to the Philippines, Col. Newman's infantry regiment was pinned down by Japanese fire on the beach at Leyte island. He shouted this order, leading a charge that was credited with saving his men. Col. Newman won a Distinguished Service Cross, and the 24th Infantry Division adopted his cry as a motto. Later, the Army put out recruiting posters that urged, "Get up and get moving! Follow me!"]

7   I have returned. By the grace of almighty God, our forces stand again on Philippine soil.   —DOUGLAS MACARTHUR, landing at Leyte,
                                                                Oct. 20, 1944

8   I'll run away again if I have to go out there.
                                        —EDDIE D. SLOVIK, confession, introduced at his court-martial,
                                                                Nov. 11, 1944
    [Pvt. Slovik, never soldier material, landed at Omaha Beach in 1944, but quickly lost heart and hid in his foxhole. He reported for duty six weeks later, but acknowledged he could not face the fighting. He was killed by a firing squad in January 1945, the last U.S. soldier to be executed for desertion. See also Joseph Heller at THE MILITARY.]

Nuts!   —ANTHONY MCAULIFFE, reply to German query   1
                                   as to whether he was ready to surrender Bastogne,
                                   Battle of the Bulge, Dec. 22, 1944
[Brig. Gen. McAuliffe, known affectionately as "Old Crock," most probably
used a stronger term. Kurt Vonnegut, Jr., an infantry scout, remarked later,
"Can you imagine the commanding general of the 101st Airborne saying anything but 'shit'?"
  McAuliffe's defiant rejoinder recalled Maj. Charles W. Whittlesey's "They
can go to hell," given in World War I in reply to a similar query from the Germans. Maj. Whittlesey's "Lost Battalion" was isolated in a ravine in the
Meuse-Argonne battle in Oct. 1918. He won the Congressional Medal of Honor
for valor in this battle.]

Uncommon valor was a common virtue.   2
                                                —CHESTER NIMITZ, 1945
[Admiral Nimitz was referring to the Marines' conquest of Iwo Jima, February–May 1945. More than 5,000 Marines were killed; an additional 17,400
were wounded. Of the Japanese force of 23,000, only 216 were taken alive.]

From my mother's sleep I fell into the State,   3
And hunched in its belly till my wet fur froze.
Six miles from earth, loosed from its dream of life,
I woke to black flak and the nightmare fighters.
When I died they washed me out of the turret with a hose.
         —RANDALL JARRELL, *The Death of the Ball Turret Gunner*, 1945
[Jarrell served in the Air Force. This is probably the most famous World War II
combat poem by an American.]

I am become Death, the shatterer of worlds.   4
                    —J. ROBERT OPPENHEIMER, quoting from the *Bhagavad-Gita*
                    at the test of the first atom bomb, July 16, 1945,
                    cited in N. P. Davis, *Lawrence and Oppenheimer*
[See also Martin Luther King, Jr., at SCIENCE: TECHNOLOGY.]

Kilroy was here.   —ANONYMOUS, U.S. military graffito slogan, 5
                                   World War II
[No one knows for sure the origin of this slogan, which was emblazoned all
over the world on walls, ships, tanks, and anything else that could be written
upon. Wherever one went, Kilroy seemed to have been there first. Troops hitting beaches in the second wave of an invasion often were greeted with signs
announcing "Kilroy was here." Leading candidates as the source of the phrase
include an inspector of military equipment, James J. Kilroy, who chalked his
name on items that he checked, and Francis J. Kilroy, Jr., a sergeant in the
Army Air Transport Command, who had a friend or friends who made a game
of writing his name wherever they went.]

The flags of freedom fly all over Europe.   6
                       —HARRY S. TRUMAN, VE[Victory in Europe]-Day, May 8, 1945
[The president, speaking on radio at nine in the morning, told the nation that
Germany had surrendered.]

The war's over. One or two of those things, and Japan will be finished.   7
                        —LESLIE R. GROVES, remark to deputy
                        after first atomic bomb test, July 16, 1945
[Gen. Groves was in charge of the Manhattan Project that developed the bomb.]

1   Sixteen hours ago an American plane dropped one bomb on Hiroshima. . . . It is an atomic bomb. It is a harnessing of the basic power of the universe. The force from which the sun draws its power has been loosed against those who brought war to the Far East.   —HARRY S. TRUMAN, message to the nation, August 6, 1945

2   * * * Official Truman Announces Japanese Surrender * * *
                    —THE NEW YORK TIMES, message on electric "zipper" sign, August 14, 1945
[At 7:03 P.M., this message ran on the illuminated moving headlines sign that ran around the Times Tower on Times Square in New York. Thousands of people below were waiting for this official confirmation of Japan's surrender.
   The zipper sign, incidentally, ran and conveyed news continuously from 1928 to 1963, and was operated off and on after that.]

3   To save your world you asked this man to die:
Would this man, could he see you now, ask why?
                    —W. H. AUDEN, *Epitaph for an Unknown Soldier*, 1945

WRITERS & WRITING   *See* ART: STYLE IN WRITING & EXPRESSION; BOOKS & READING

WYOMING

4   Whoopee ti yi yo, git along, little dogies,
It's your misfortune and none of my own;
Whoopee ti yi yo, git along, little dogies,
For you know Wyoming will be your new home.
                    —ANONYMOUS, cowboy song, c. 1870
[A series of relatively mild winters encouraged cattlemen to make greater use of open ranges in Wyoming in the 1870s and early 1880s.]

5   I looked into a gulf seventeen hundred feet deep with eagles and fish hawks circling far below. And the sides of that gulf were one wild welter of color—crimson, emerald, cobalt, ochre, amber, honey splashed with port wine, snow white, vermilion, lemon, and silver gray, in wide washes. . . . So far below that no sound of its strife could reach us, the Yellowstone River ran—a finger-wide strip of jade green.   —RUDYARD KIPLING,
                    American Notes, 1891
[Kipling reported riding in a buggy through Yellowstone with "an adventurous old lady from Chicago and her husband, who disapproved of (the) scenery as being 'ongodly.' I fancy it scared them." Robert Louis Stevenson, who visited the state at about the same time, found the scenery depressing: "Sagebrush, eternal sagebrush; over all, the same weariful and gloomy coloring, grays warming into brown, grays darkening toward black; and for sole sign of life, here and there a few fleeing antelopes," *Across the Plains*, 1892.]

6   Wyoming is a land of great open spaces with plenty of elbow room, . . . There are sections of the state where it is said you can look farther and see less than any other place in the world.   —FEDERAL WRITERS' PROJECT, *Wyoming: A Guide to Its History, Highways, and People*, 1941

7   About the only thing that will make a Wyoming cattleman reach for his gun nowadays is to call him a "farmer." A "rancher," he wants it clearly under-

stood, drinks only canned milk, never eats vegetables, and grows nothing but
hay and whiskers.   —JOHN GUNTHER, *Inside U.S.A.*, 1947

[Wyoming:] One of my favorite states—of existence.   1
                —VLADIMIR NABOKOV, introducing his poem
                The Ballad of Longwood Glen,
                at the 92nd St. Y, New York City, 1964

Motto

Equal rights.   2

XYZ

YOUTH

See also AGES; CHILDREN

1   In our youth is our strength; in our inexperience, our wisdom.
                                        —HERMAN MELVILLE, *White-Jacket*, 1850
    [More at AMERICA & AMERICANS.]

2   A boy's will is the wind's will,
    And the thoughts of youth are long, long thoughts.
                            —HENRY WADSWORTH LONGFELLOW, *My Lost Youth*, 1858

3   So nigh is grandeur to our dust,
    So near is God to man,
    When Duty whispers low, *Thou must,*
    The youth replies, *I can.*   —RALPH WALDO EMERSON,
                                                      Voluntaries, 1867

4   In America, the young are always ready to give to those who are older than
    themselves the full benefits of their inexperience.
                                —OSCAR WILDE, *The American Invasion,*
                                  in *Court and Society Review,* March 1887

5   One may return to the place of his birth.
    He cannot go back to his youth.   —JOHN BURROUGHS, *The Return,*
                                                  in *Bird and Bough,* 1906

6   One could do worse than be a swinger of birches.
                                        —ROBERT FROST, *Birches,* 1916

7   All lovely things will have an ending,
    All lovely things will fade and die,
    And youth that's now so bravely spending,
    Will beg a penny by and by.   —CONRAD AIKEN, *All Lovely Things,*
                                            in *Twins and Moves,* 1916
    [Aiken's own youth was blighted at age ten, when he heard gun shots and found
    the bodies of his father and mother—killed by his father in a murder-suicide.]

No time to marry, no time to settle down;
I'm a young woman, and I ain't done runnin' around.
     —BESSIE SMITH, *Young Woman's Blues*, 1927

1

Little brown boy,
Slim, dark, big-eyed,
Crooning love songs to your banjo
Down at the Lafayette—Gee, boy, I love the way you hold your head,
High sort of and a bit to one side,
Like a prince, a jazz prince.   —HELENE JOHNSON, *Poem*,
         in Countee Cullen, ed.,
         Caroling Dusk: An Anthology
         of Verse by Negro Poets, 1927

2

Youth is the pollen
That blows through the sky
And does not ask why. —STEPHEN VINCENT BENÉT, *John Brown's Body*, 1928

3

The American ideal is youth—handsome, empty youth.
    —HENRY MILLER, *The Wisdom of the Heart*, 1941

4

The secret of eternal youth is arrested development.
    —ALICE ROOSEVELT LONGWORTH, quoted in *American Heritage*,
    Feb. 1969

5

We have a saying in the movement that we don't trust anybody over thirty.
    —JACK WEINBERG, interview, *San Francisco Chronicle*, c. 1965,
    cited in the *Washington Post*, March 23, 1970
[The saying was associated with the free speech movement at the University of
California, which started in the early 1960s, and with the Youth International
Party, which was founded in 1968 and whose members were called Yippies.
The originator may indeed be Weinberg, then a twenty-four-year-old student at
the Berkeley campus of the University of California. Years later, he told Ralph
Keyes, author of *They Never Said It*, that he had called it a saying in order to
give the words more zing. Actually, he had made them up on the spot, he said,
and believed that they were original to him.]

6

ZEAL   *See* ENTHUSIASM & ZEAL

Author Index

Abbott, George
(1887–1995)
burning the candle at both ends (note), 178:1
have fun, 537:1
motivation & your job, 55:10
Acheson, Dean
(1893–1971)
decision, 140:1
explain, those who (note), 178:5
Great Britain, 330:1
a memorandum, 297:1
never have so few lost so much, 533:2
a statesman, 152:3
Acton, [Lord]
(1834–1902)
power (note), 450:8
Adams, Abigail
(1744–1818)
customs which treat us only as vassals, 537:2
frippery, 186:8
Lord & Lordess, 540:12
men would be tyrants, 540:10
my heart is like a feather, 222:2
necessities, great, 350:9
power, 396:6
wives, absolute power over, 540:11
Adams, Brooks
(1848–1927)
law, 274:8
this war is the first gun (note), 468:5
Adams, Charles Francis
(1807–1886)
action, 1:5
Massachusetts, 301:7
New England & worship of Mammon, 352:3
Plymouth, 103:8
Adams, Clover *(d. 1885)*
chaws more than he bites off, 188:8
Adams, Franklin Pierce
(wrote under ini-

tials F.P.A.)
(1881–1960)
Boston (note), 87:10
Tinker-to-Evers-to-Chance, 471:4
you can fool all of the people (note), 377:5
Adams, Henry [Brooks]
(1838–1918)
the America mind, 21:2
chaos v. order, 307:6
cheers, who stands and, 471:2
contradictions in principle, 179:6
experience, 180:1
friend, one, 203:8
friends are born, 203:7
learn, know how to, 160:11
Maryland, 301:4
Newport, 97:7
the Pennsylvania mind, 376:7
political education, 392:5
politics, 392:4, 6
power, a friend in, 397:3
[Roosevelt, T.:] pure act, 439:5
Russia, 333:2
schoolmaster, priest, or senator, 121:2
a teacher, 160:12
women, our young, 538:8
words, 268:2
Yankee & a Swede, 334:3
Adams, [Pres.] John
(1735–1826)
[Baltimore:] dirtiest place, 87:1
day of deliverance, 246:5
democracy, 144:1
facts, 181:1
government & happiness, 215:3
government of laws & not of men, 273:5
grief, 463:8
history of the American Revolution, 232:3

independence forever (note), 200:5
Jefferson still survives, 270:4
[New Yorkers] talk loud, 97:9
office, most insignificant, 508:5
a poet in your pocket, 52:7
politics & the middle way, 389:3
power, 396:9
president, the office of, 401:1
press, liberty of, 405:2
revolution was in the hearts and minds of the people, 41:2
virtue, 514:1,2
Adams, [Pres.] John Quincy *(1767–1848)*
abroad in search of monsters, 17:4
his face is livid (note), 249:3
I am content, 270:5
opulence & want, 329:6
our country always right (note), 371:5
say not "My country right or wrong", 372:6
Adams, Samuel
(1722–1803)
country shall be independent, 26:2
glorious morning for America, 38:3
Addams, Jane
(1860–1935)
private beneficence, 80:9
Addison, Joseph
(1672–1719)
liberty, 199:6
we can die but once (note), 39:2
Ade, George
(1866–1944)
the cocktail, 12:3
early to bed (note), 266:10–267
familiarity breeds, 253:6

Adler, Stella
(1902–1992)
actors, 57:1
Agnew, Spiro T[heodore] *(1918–1996)*
effete corps of impudent snobs, 164:4
nabobs of negativism (note), 164:4
slum, if you've seen one, 85:5
Aiken, Conrad
(1899–1973)
music I heard with you, 290:2
youth, 556:7
Aiken, [Sen.] George
(1892–1984)
declare the U.S. the winner, 510:3
Albee, Edward F[rancis]
(1857–1930)
never give a sucker an even break (note), 193:7
Alcott, A[mos] Bronson
(1799–1888)
civilization, 111:7
homes, 234:7
not many converse, 129:5
Alcott, Louisa May
(1832–1888)
books, 65:10
Christmas, 83:6
November, 344:7
Alcuin *(735–804)*
voice of the people (note), 377:6
Aldrich, Thomas Bailey
(1836–1907)
civilization, 111:9
Algren, Nelson (given name, Nelson Algren Abraham)
(1909–1981)
a humorless soldierly people, 334:7
never eat at a place called Mom's, 536:6
Ali, Muhammad [given name, Cassius Marcellus Clay, Jr.]
(b. 1942)
float like a butterfly, 475:4

Ali, Muhammad (*cont.*)
  no quarrel with the
    Viet Cong, 510:1
  what kind of name he
    had, 431:10
Allan, Lewis
  Southern trees bear
    strange fruit, 466:6
Allen, Elizabeth Akers
  (*1832–1911*)
  turn backward, O
    Time, 491:8
Allen, Ethan
  (*1738–1789*)
  great Jehovah and the
    Continental Con-
    gress, 37:8
Allen, Fred (*1894–1956*)
  Boston, 88:5
  California, 74:1
  New York City (note),
    98:8
Allen, William
  (*1803–1879*)
  fifty-four forty or
    fight, 382:1
Allen, Woody [born,
    Allen Stuart Konigs-
    berg] (*b. 1935*)
  death, 139:12 & note
  success & showing
    up, 479:5
Alvarez, Luis [Walter]
  (*b. 1911*)
  physics, 444:9
American ("Know-
    Nothing") Party
  I know nothing but
    my country, 383:1
Ames, Fisher
  (*1758–1808*)
  sober second thought
    of the people, 143:10
  passions, 369:4
Amory, Cleveland
  (*b. 1917*)
  facts, 182:7
Anderson, Maxwell
  (*1888–1959*)
  days dwindle down,
    362:6
  September, when you
    reach, 362:5
  What Price Glory?,
    520:6
Anderson, Robert
  [Woodruff] (*b. 1917*)
  be kind, 453:9
  theater, & a living,
    56:3
André, [Maj.] John
  (*1751–1780*)
  I met my fate like a
    brave man, 40:4
Andrus, Jerry
  reality, 427:5
Angelou, Maya
  (*b. 1928*)
  ethics, 175:5
Anonymous
  ad astra per ardua
    (note), 14:3
  ad astra per aspera,
    260:11
  Adlai (note), 387:9
  aim high, 14:5
  Albany, 85:7
  all the way with LBJ,
    388:1
  Arizona, come to,
    44:6
  Arkansas, 45:4,5,6
  Army now, you're in
    549:1

ars longa, vita brevis
  (note), 46:4
the Athens of Dixie,
  96:12
balls and strikes,
  427:4
base ball [sic], 470:4
Bataan, 551:2
beauty, with, 335:1
better dead than Red,
  119:4
Big Rock Candy
  Mountains, 505:7
black is beautiful,
  424:7
Blaine, Blaine, 384:1
blame, how you place
  the, 178:8
the blues, 51:7
Boston (note), 87:6,
  88:4
Boy Orator of the
  Platitude (note),
  252:3
bridges, 447:4 & note
broke, if it ain't, 536:8
Buffalo gals, 88:7
bury me not on the
  lone prairie, 528:2
by and by, 523:7
California annexes
  the U.S., 92:6
canoe, paddle your
  own, 452:4
the Casbah, 495:3
Casey Jones 544:7,
  544:8
[Chicago:] city that
  works, 91:1
a chicken in every
  pot, 386:5
Chisolm trail, 528:3
common man [as
  president], 252:4
a computer (note),
  448:4
Congressman, 120:9,
  121:3
a conservative is,
  394:11
the Constitution fol-
  lows the flag, 127:3
Continental, not
  worth a, 156:3
convict no. 9653 for
  president, 386:2
Coolidge, 386:4
corporations, 68:1
a corrupt bargain,
  380:8
country, in this, 528:4
coward, dirty little,
  132:7
[cowboy sayings],
  535:8
Cox and cocktails,
  386:1
crops, three—corn,
  freight rates, & in-
  terest, 185:8
crossroads of Amer-
  ica, 247:3
death, prepare for,
  169:5
depressions are farm
  led, 145:8
Des Moines, 92:8
dirigo, 295:9
details, God [or, the
  devil] is in the, 148:3
Detroit, 93:2
the devil & me, 149:10
dinner pail, the full,
  384:4

dog, born a, 337:6
dogies, git along,
  554:4
dollar diplomacy,
  195:3
do not fold, spindle,
  mutilate, 448:3
don't swap horses,
  383:2
don't tax, 486:2
don't tread on me,
  16:1
duty, let every man
  do his, 26:1
an education, 162:6
endure forever, may
  she, 242:5
enemies accumulate,
  166:2
enemy's corpse (note),
  165:9
E Pluribus Unum,
  16:3
equality before the
  law, 350:7
Era of Good Feelings,
  214:5
Eureka, 74:5
evening falls, blue,
  347:5
ever upward, 355:7
faithful to the cause
  of Prohibition,
  172:5
farewell, dear Van,
  381:4
fat lady sings, ain't
  over till the, 165:1
fault, to find, 135:5
Finnegan (note),
  544:8–545
the fire next time,
  434:6
first in freedom &
  wheat, 260:8
the first 100 years are
  the hardest, 549:5
flag, don't haul down
  the, 373:7
flies with her own
  wings, 365:3
fold, spindle or muti-
  late, 448:3
food & war, 548:6
form & function
  (note), 48:5
forty acres & a mule,
  465:4
forward, 534:6
fox populi, 284:1
Frankie and Johnny,
  132:3,4
free at last!, 201:4
free lunch, 158:2
freedom and unity,
  508:4
free soil—Frémont,
  382:5
Frenchmen, 50 mil-
  lion, 330:7
*The Frigate Constitu-
  tion*, 312:5
garbage in/out, 448:4
give 'em hell, Harry,
  387:7
give me that old time
  religion, 430:9
go down Moses, 459:8
God enriches, 44:11
God gave Noah, 434:6
God spanked the
  town, 106:3
gold and silver, 326:6

Greer county, 349:7
had enough?, 387:6
heaven, may you be
  in, 398:11
he kept us out of the
  war, 385:4
hell, there ain't no,
  229:1
here lies John Purcell,
  169:7
he served his country
  faithfully, 170:4
he who transplanted,
  123:4
hey, hey LBJ, 509:6
higgamus hoggamus,
  woman's monoga-
  mous, 453:2
Hoboken, 548:7
hog, the still (note),
  74:8
hogamus higamus,
  541:9
home & heart, 234:11
home on the range,
  528:1
Hoover, 146:2 (note),
  251:3
hope, 435:9
husband and wife are
  one, 299:4
Idaho!, 242:4
if it ain't broke, 536:8
if it moves, salute it,
  313:1
if you can't do the
  time, 134:8
I like Ike, 387:8
I'll scrape the moun-
  tains, 167:1
I'm a two-gun man,
  63:3
I'm the corpsemaker,
  63:2
I'm wild and wooly,
  64:1
I never would have
  seen it, 516:9
It grows as it goes,
  354:10
influenza, 244:6
industry, 505:5
in your heart you
  know he's right,
  388:3
Ioway, Ioway, 253:7
I stays back wid de
  ginerals (note),
  519:3
I still like Ike (note),
  387:8
I've never been seen
  nothin', 45:8
I want what I want
  (note), 12:4
Jackson & heaven,
  255:1
John Henry, 543:10
Kansas,
  259:1,4,5–260:1
Kentucky, 260:12
Kilroy was here,
  553:5
know nothing but my
  country, 383:1
land of steady habits,
  122:3
land of the bedbug,
  349:7
Laredo, streets of, 94:4
Las Vegas, 94:5
law and order, 385:7
let my people go,
  460:1

a liberal, 393:9,
394:11 (note)
liberated the hell out
of this place, 552:4
liberties, 254:4
liberty and indepen-
dence, 143:3
liberty and prosperity,
354:4
liberty and union,
357:7
life, liberty, and Lan-
don, 387:3
life of the land, 226:8
lips, loose, 484:3
live free or die, 353:7
Lizzie Borden, 133:2
Lord, grant that I may
always be right,
398:10
lost is old simplicity,
60:1
love it or leave it,
374:7
love, make, 288:8
Ma, Ma, where's my
Pa?, 384:2
Maine, remember the,
468:4
Maine goes, as, 295:3
a man died for me to-
day, 521:5
many deeds, 301:5
McKinley drinks soda
water, 384:6
medical school, 154:3
a mile wide, an inch
deep, 350:6
the miners &
whores, 105:7
Missouri—farmers'
kingdom, 320:7
[Montana:] last best
place on earth,
326:5
Montezuma, halls of,
312:7
mountaineers are al-
ways free, 530:4
mugwump, 267:7
my Jesus mercy, 173:6
New York, 100:9
(note), 101:8
Nixon's the one,
388:4
no battleship yet
sunk by bombs,
550:4
no cross of gold, 384:5
North Carolina,
356:3,5
North Dakota, 357:3
north to the future,
10:11
offense is the best de-
fense, 64:10
O.K. (note), 381:4
oro y plata, 326:6
outlaws, 137:5
overcome, we shall,
423:6
oversexed, overfed,
551:6
parrot—can talk but
not fly, 483:6
pass through this
world but once,
262:3
a penny saved, 322:10
people, welfare of the,
321:1
the people rule, 46:3,
468:2
Peoria, 102:3 & note

perfect 36, 487:6
Philadelphia, 102:5,
103:3
Philadelphia lawyers,
277:2
Pike's Peak or bust,
117:2
the Pilgrim Fathers,
421:6
pleasant peninsula,
309:2
politician given a job
abroad, 151:10
Polked you & shall
Pierce you, 382:4
prepared in mind,
467:5
Providence, nothing
without; 117:8
public office—public
trust, 217:3
quitters & winners,
149:3
a rattlesnake hisses
(note), 349:7
rebellion to tyrants,
38:7
recession & depres-
sion, 159:1
Red, better dead than,
119:4
regnat populus, 46:3
religion, that old
time, 430:9
remember the Maine,
468:4
[Reno:] biggest little
city, 104:5
right, people who
think they are,
437:10
right of way, 351:2
rights, equal, 555:2
rights, we dare defend
our, 9:7
Roosevelt, let's re-
elect, 387:5
Roosevelt for ex-Pres-
ident, 387:4
root or die, 381:1
Rough and Ready, we
called him, 382:3
Saddam Hussein,
6:6–7 (note), 220:4
St. James Infirmary
(note), 95:4
say it ain't so, Joe,
472:1
Seward's folly, 9:8
shadow, secure the, 4:8
she flies with her own
wings, 365:3
sixteen to one, 384:3
some say she do,
431:9
Southie is my home
town, 88:1
speed and curves,
470:1
stand with Washing-
ton, 380:7
star of the North,
319:4
stars, to the (note),
14:3, 260:11
state sovereignty,
244:4
strokes, many, 148:6
a sucker, 193:7
sword & peace, 302:6
Taft, get on the raft
with, 385:1
taxation, no, 25:6
Tar Heel, I'm a, 356:6

Tennessee, 487:9
tennis anyone?, 473:1
thermodynamics,
laws of, 445:4
thirty, anyone over,
557:6
Tippecanoe and Tyler
too, 381:3
'tis the gift to be sim-
ple, 218:7
to be rather than to
seem, 357:2
today is the first day,
400:6
the tough get going,
477:4
town, necessary to de-
stroy the, 510:4
Truman, to err is,
252:4
two dollars a day and
roast beef, 381:2
umbrellas [taxes]
(note), 485:11
unawed by opinion [J.
Petigru], 171:2
union, justice, and
confidence, 286:3
united we stand, 37:7
Utah, 505:4
[Van Horn:] climate,
107:4
Virginia, if they are
from, 513:6
virtue, liberty, inde-
pendence, 376:9
vote, I never, 145:4
vote early & often,
382:2
[Wall Street:] begins
in a graveyard, 70:6
war, a rich man's,
114:6
war, the hotter the,
522:10
Washington, the city
of, 107:6
Washington, a friend
in, 109:1
Washington, stand
with, 380:7
Washington fought on
(note), 532:5
we raise de wheat,
459:6
we shall overcome,
423:6
West, to the, 528:5
west of St. Louis,
527:7
west of the Pecos,
488:5
[West Virginia] almost
heaven, 530:3
where women cease
from troubling,
541:12
while I breathe I
hope, 467:6
White House, ha, ha,
ha (note), 384:2
white man with a
million dollars,
462:2
Wilson and his 14
Points, 195:7
winners never give
up, 532:5
winners never quit,
472:3
win them all, you
can't (note), 533:3
with God all things
are possible, 359:2

wisdom, justice &
moderation, 210:2
work, 360:1, 545:11
world turned upside
down, 40:6
worms, to eat, 501:5
Wyoming will be
your new home,
554:4
yams & Yanks, 190:7
Yankee, you can al-
ways tell a, 352:6
Yankee Doodle, 15:3
yellow ribbon, she
wore a, 289:7
you never had it so
good, 387:9
Anonymous Announcer
It's Superman!, 230:6
**Anthony, Susan
B[rownell]**
(1820–1906)
equal pay for equal
work, 75:7
join the union, girls,
75:7
marriage, 299:5
men, women, &
rights, 541:5
patriotism, 373:5
queens & kings, 538:6
rights and nothing
more, 541:5
woman must not de-
pend upon, 538
women, prolonged
slavery of, 538:7
**Antrim, Minna
[Thomas]**
(fl. c. 1900)
hated, to be, 225:1
Appleton, Thomas Gold
(1812–1884)
bites off more than he
can chaw (note),
188:8
Paris, 110:1
Arbus, Diane [born, Ne-
merov] *(1923–1971)*
photograph them, 57:5
Arendt, Hannah
(1906–1975)
banality of evil, 176:11
hypocrisy, 241:3
Armstrong, Louis
(1901–1971)
you can't tell 'em,
193:10
you'll never know
(note), 51:12
Armstrong, Neil
(b. 1930)
one giant leap for
mankind, 448:8
Arnold, Matthew
(1822–1888)
[Chicago:] a great un-
interesting place,
90:1
Arthur, Timothy Shay
(1809–1885)
demon rum, 11:4
Asbury, Herbert
(1891–1963)
city of sin and gayety,
97:2
Ashe, Arthur
(1943–1993)
racism, 426:1
Ashmun, Margaret
(c. 1880–1940)
justice, and right,
and the law,
258:1

Aspin, Les *(1938–1995)*
Congress, 122:2
Astaire, Fred [given
name, Frederick
Austerlitz] *(b. 1899)*
I just put my feet in
the air, 50:8
Astor, [Lady] Nancy
[Witcher Lang-
horne] *(1879–1964)*
fear, 189:3
marriage, 300:8
Atkinson, Brooks
(1894–1984)
sweet water from foul
well?, 48:2
an idea, 243:11
Atlas, Charles (born,
Angelo Siciliano)
(1893–1972)
live clean, 227:7
Auden, W[ystan] H[ugh]
(1907–1973)
all the dogs of Europe
bark, 321:8
Americans, 24:4
behaviorism, 445:8
books, 66:12
believe, hundreds
may, 184:8
evil, 176:9
he was my North, my
South, 290:7
hero, the dead, 230:7
a history-making
creature, 370:6
intellectual, the
word, 164:2
love, 288:4
love—I thought
would last forever,
290:7
man is a history-
making creature,
370:6
the moon is a desert
(note), 448:8
the Old Year dies,
355:2
pleasure [as] a guide,
49:9
private faces in public
places, 378:4
question, the hard,
414:5
review a bad book,
49:10
suffering, 480:3
USA, God bless the,
23:3
woods, 168:6
Yeats, William, 173:3
you asked this man to
die, 554:3
Audubon, John James
(1785–1851)
Louisiana, 285:4
passenger pigeons,
336:8
Auster, Paul *(b. 1947)*
hope, 237:3
our lives carry us
along, 283:8

**Baden-Powell, Robert
Stephenson Smyth**
(Baden Powell of
Gilwell, 1st Baron)
(1857–1941)
be prepared, 536:1
Bailey, Francis
(1735–1815)
father of his country,
524:5

Bailey, Pearl
(1918–1990)
God, 214:4
more home aid, 396:5
Baker, [Sen.] Howard
(b. 1925)
what did the presi-
dent know?, 526:7
Baker, James *(b. 1930)*
voodoo economics
(note), 159:6
Baker, Russell *(b. 1925)*
heroes, 231:5
news, 409:1
sport, 475:8
objects, inanimate (2),
490:9,10
Balboa, Vasco Nuñez de
(c. 1475–1519)
bachelors of law,
276:7
Baldwin, James
(1924–1987)
the American Negro,
423:8
the fire next time,
423:7
know whence you
came (note), 370:8
money, 325:9
no man a villain in
his own heart, 177:1
past, 370:8
the questions which
one asks oneself,
415:4
Bancroft, George
(1800–1891)
abundance of vacant
land, 204:3
capitalist & laborer,
75:1
civilization & the
people, 377:3
democracy, conscience
& liberty, 429:5
the manifest purpose
of Providence
(note), 18:3
the people, authority,
& rights, 396:10
Banfield, Edward C.
(b. 1916)
in France, every argu-
ment becomes a
matter of principle,
330:8
Bangs, Edward *(fl. 1776)*
Yankee Doodle (note),
15:3
**Bankhead, Tallulah
[Brockman]**
(1903–1968)
less than meets the
eye, 250:8
pure as the driven
slush, 458:3
two vices at once,
458:2
Barclay, Florence Louisa
(1862–1921)
made my day (note),
137:7
**Barkley, Alben W[il-
liam]** *(1877–1956)*
a servant in the house
of the Lord, 272:3
Barlow, Arthur, *(16th
cent.)*
we found shoal water,
511:10
Barnard, Fred[erick] R.
picture worth 1,000
words, 303:4

**Barnum P[hineas] T[ay-
lor]** *(1810–1891)*
I risked much, 323:10
a sucker born every
minute (note), 193:4
Barrymore, John
(1882–1942)
a man is not old,
362:8
Barrymore, Lionel
(1878–1954)
the Great Actor, 55:5
Barth, John [Simmons]
(b. 1930)
self-knowledge, 452:1
value, 506:7
Baruch, Bernard
(1870–1965)
a choice between the
quick and the dead,
448:2
cold war, 32:6
government, 218:2
old age, 362:10
peace, world, 375:9
Barzun, Jacques
(b. 1907)
baseball, 474:8
real, the speechless,
427:1
Bates, Katherine Lee
(1859–1929)
America the Beauti-
ful, 20:1
thine alabaster cities,
84:7
Baum, Vicki
(1888–1960)
to be a Jew, 422:4
Bean, [Judge] Roy
(c. 1825–1903)
a damned good pistol
shot (note), 488:5
the Law West of the
Pecos (note), 488:5
hear ye! hear ye!,
274:6
Beard, James
(1903–1985)
food, 192:12
Beaton, [Sir] Cecil [Wal-
ter Hardy]
(1904–1980)
Milwaukee, 96:6
San Francisco, 106:4
Beaumont, Francis
(c. 1584–1616) **&
Fletcher, John**
(1579–1625)
whistle and she'll
come to you (note),
458:1
Bee, [Gen.] Bernard E.
(1824–1861)
Jackson like a
stonewall, 112:7
Beecher, Henry Ward
(1813–1887)
advertisements, 5:2
customs, 221:1
desires & choices,
146:6
doctrine, 183:10
the dog, 337:10
expedients v. princi-
ples, 174:9
flattery, 190:3
flowers, 341:12
giving & cackling,
80:8
imagination, 317:7
knowledge, unused,
263:5
a mother, 367:3

mother sings, what
the, 367:4
the mystery, 271:4
passions, our, 369:7
public opinion, 413:2
sells himself for the
value of an ounce,
69:3
war, 519:10
work, 544:2
Beers, Ethel Lynn [Eliot]
(1827–1879)
all quiet along the Po-
tomac, 113:2,3
Bell, Alexander Graham
(1847–1922)
Mr. Watson, come
here, 446:8
Bell, Daniel *(b. 1919)*
capitalism & commu-
nism, 119:3
Bell, Derrick *(b. 1930)*
progress, 412:6
Bellah, James Warner
(1899–1976)
Delaware, 143:1
Bellamy, Francis
(1856–1931)
I pledge allegiance,
373:6
Bellow, Saul *(b. 1915)*
life is not a business,
283:3
Bellows, George [Wes-
ley] *(1882–1925)*
art, 48:1
Benchley, Robert
(1889–1945)
drawing on my fine
command of lan-
guage, 455:11
martini, a dry (note),
12:3
Benét, Stephen Vincent
(1898–1943)
Daniel Webster & the
devil, 278:6
dreaming men, 155:7
New Hampshire men
& the devil, 353:5
the routine mind
(note), 176:11–177
Wounded Knee, 422:2
youth, 557:3
**Benham [William] Gur-
ney** *(1849–1944)*
English, 232:10
**Benton, [Sen.] Thomas
Hart** *(1782–1858)*
sometimes I fight,
136:3
Berenson, Bernard
(1865–1959)
beauty, appreciation
of, 362:12
consistency, 124:2
**Berkeley, [Bishop]
George** *(1685–1753)*
westward the course
of empire, 15:2
Berlin, Irving
(1888–1989)
Christmas, a white,
84:2
a pretty girl, 61:11
show business, 55:9
Berman, Edgar, M.D.
(1919–1987)
raging hormonal
tides, 540:5
Berra, ("Yogi")
Lawrence Peter
(b. 1925)
it ain't over, 165:2

déjà vu all over again (note), 475:9
a fork in the road (note), 475:9
the future (note), 475:9
the game isn't over, 475:9
if you don't know where you are going (note), 475:9
nobody ever goes there anymore (note), 475:9
popular, anybody who is (note), 475:9
you can observe a lot (note), 475:9
you can't win all the time (note), 475:9
Berry, Wendell *(b. 1932)*
the farm, 186:6
Berryman, John *(1914–1972)*
life & wasted time, 282:13
ways to ruin a poem, 54:1
writing, one's own, 58:6
Bessimer, Joseph ("Paper Collar")
a sucker born every minute, 193:4
Beston, Henry [Shea-han] *(1888–1968)*
the seas, 343:2
Bethune, Mary McLeod *(1875–1955)*
womanhood, 539:7
Beveridge, [Sen.] Albert D. *(1862–1927)*
the Pacific, 332:8
Bible
alms & a trumpet (note), 80:8
black but beautiful (note), 424:7
a city that is set on a hill (note), 14:9–15
the days of my life (note), 283:4
he who is not with me (note), 176:10
hills, I lift up my eyes to the, 507:1
house divided (note), 502:4
I am God (note), 327:1
let judgment run down as waters (note), 36:1
liberty, proclaim, 199:2
mammon (note), 98:9
money, love of (note), 325:1
the race is not to the swift (note), 474:1
reason together, let us (note), 427:11
the stone shall cry out (note), 131:8
vision, where there is no (note), 31:5
Bierce, Ambrose [Gwin-nett] *(1842–1913?)*
advice, 8:5
angry, speak when you are, 42:6
Australia, 328:4
book, the covers of this, 250:7

bore, 67:1
cynic, 516:5
dice, 277:9
diplomacy, 151:6
education, 160:10
enthusiasm, 166:5
epitaph, 172:4
faith, 184:3
free will, 531:9
heathen, 430:6
here lies Frank Pixley, 172:2
history, 232:11
[C. P.] Huntington's ashes (note), 172:4
I murdered my father, 133:1
jury, 257:3
labor, 76:2
lawsuit, 275:4
lawyer, 277:8
male, 306:8
mammon & New York, 98:9
man, 238:1
marriage, 300:1
money, 324:3
pain, 169:4
patriot, 374:1
Peoria (note), 102:3
pray, 398:2
prejudice, 399:6
presidency, 402:5
[realism:] nature as seen by toads (note), 57:9
saint, 515:5
wealth & impunity, 324:2
woman growing older, 541:10
Biggers, Earl Derr *(1884–1933)*
money, 325:4
theory, 442:5
Billings, Josh [born, Henry Wheeler Shaw] *(1818–1885)*
better to know nothing, 263:4
a doctor, 153:8
down hill, when a man starts, 182:8
love, 287:2
opera, wimmin in (note), 51:2
squeaking [wheel], 119:6
truth, 498:1
vivacity & wit (note), 267:8
Bill of Rights, 125–126
Bing, Rudolf *(b. 1902)*
opera, 52:5
Bird, Isabella
[Cincinnati] bathed in mellow light, 91:5
Birmingham, Stephen *(b. 1931)*
Philadelphians, 103:4
Bishop, Elizabeth *(1911–1979)*
Florida, 190:6
Bismarck [Prince] Otto von *(1815–1898)*
North America & English, 232:10
politics (note), 394:5
Black, Hugo L[a Fayette] *(1886–1971)*
courts as havens, 481:4
great nations, 197:1

Black Hawk *(1767–1838)*
let us alone, 417:6
Blackmun, [Justice] Harry A. *(b. 1908)*
the right of privacy, 411:1
a woman's decision, 37:3
Blackstone [Sir] William *(1723–1780)*
better that ten guilty persons escape (note), 273:6
Blair, Francis P[reston] *(1791–1876)*
world too much governed, 216:3
Blake, Eubie [given names, James Hubert] *(1882–1983)*
habits, bad, 222:1
to live this long, 227:10
Blake, James W. *(1862–1935)*
sidewalks of New York, 98:5
Bland, James A. *(1854–1911)*
carry me back to old Virginny, 513:4
Bliss, Philip Paul *(1838–1876)*
hold the fort (note), 115:5
Bloch, Robert *(1917–1994)*
a little crazy, 294:5
Boesky, Ivan *(b. 1937)*
greed, 326:1
Bogart, Humphrey
an actor's job is to act, 56:8
Bogart, John B. *(1845–1921)*
when a dog bites a man (note), 406:3
Boggs, T. Hale *(1914–1972)*
coffee, 192:11
Bohr, Niels *(1885–1962)*
God, to prescribe to (note), 444:7
quantum physics (note), 444:7
Bok, Derek *(b. 1930)*
if you think education is expensive, 162:7
Boorstin, Daniel J. *(b. 1914)*
advertising, 7:5
a celebrity, 479:2
the celebrity, 479:1
God, 213:11
the hero, 230:9
a pseudo-event, 7:6
reality & images, 427:2
television, 305:2
Booth, John Wilkes *(1838–1865)*
the South is avenged!, 29:1
Booth, Junius Brutus *(1796–1852)*
I will cut your throat, 136:2
Boren, James H. *(b. 1925)*
guidelines for bureaucrats, 297:2
Borman, Frank *(b. 1928)*
the moon, 340:9

Bossidy, John Collins *(1860–1928)*
Boston [toast to], 87:10
Brackett, Charles *(1892–1969)*, **Wilder, Billy** *(b. 1906)*, **& Marshman, D. M., Jr.**
the pictures got small, 303:9
I'm ready for my close-up (note), 303:9
Bradford, William *(1590–1657)*
actions, great and honorable, 1:1
pilgrims, 14:8
they fell upon their knees, 25:5
Bradley, [Sen.] Bill *(b. 1943)*
the point of the game, 476:1
Bradley [Gen.] Omar *(1893–1981)*
the atom v. Sermon on the Mount, 322:2
ethical infants, 175:3
wrong war/wrong place, 264:7
war, 521:11
Bradstreet, Anne [Dudley] *(c. 1612–1672)*
if ever two were one, 289:1
youth & middle age & old age, 8:8
Bragg, Edward S[tuyvesant] *(1827–1912)*
enemies he has made, 165:7
Brandeis, Louis D[embitz] *(1856–1941)*
if we would guide by the light of reason, 275:11
evolution, 335:10
government, 217:7
the right to be let alone, 410:2
sunlight, 303:2
zeal, men of, 166:7
Bremer, Frederika *(1801–1865)*
Minnesota, 318:11
South Carolina, 467:1
Brennan, [Justice] William J., Jr. *(b. 1906)*
damn obscenity thing (note), 78:4
privacy, the right of, 410:6
Brewer, [Justice] David J. *(1837–1910)*
America is the paradise of lawyers, 277:11
Brisbane, Albert *(1809–1890)*
society as it is now, 60:4
Britt, Steuart Henderson *(b. 1907)*
doing business without advertising, 7:3
Brokaw, Tom *(b. 1940)*
South Dakota, 468:1
Bromfield, Louis *(1896–1956)*
Ohio, 358:5

Brooks, Gwendolyn
(b. 1917)
the little moment,
400:3
Brooks, Mel *(b. 1926)*
flaunt it, 409:9
Brooks, Peter C.
(fl. 1845)
corporations, 68:6
Brooks, Phillips
(1835–1893)
O little town of Beth-
lehem, 83:7
Brotherton, Alice
Williams
(fl. 1880s–1930)
heap high the board,
490:2
Broun, [Matthew] Hey-
wood [Campbell]
(1888–1939)
ice cream, 191:7
men, 306:9
truth, 499:6
Browder, Earl Russell
(1891–1973)
communism, 118:8
Brown, Drew ("Bun-
dini")
float like a butterfly,
475:4
Brown, H[ubert Gerold]
"Rap" *(b. 1943)*
violence, 511:8
Brown, James *(b. 1933)*
I'm black and proud,
425:4
Brown, John
(1800–1859)
forfeit my life (note),
28:2
not wrong but right,
28:2
this *is* a beautiful
country, 270:9
Brown, John Mason
(1900–1969)
t.v. programs & chew-
ing gum, 303:10
Washington [D.C.],
108:9
Brownell, Baker
(1887–1965)
southern Illinois,
244:2
Browning, Robert
(1812–1889)
Chicago (note), 90:1
less is more (note),
48:3
Brownmiller, Susan
(b. 1935)
clothes, 187:6
Brownson, Orestes
A[ugustus]
(1803–1876)
democracy, 144:3
Broyard, Anatole
(1920–1990)
Rome, 110:10
Bruce, Lenny [born,
Leonar Alfred
Schneider]
(1925–1966)
church & God, 431:2
liberals, 394:9
Miami Beach, 96:3
Bryan, William Jen-
nings *(1860–1925)*
burn down your cities
& leave our farms,
185:9
cross of gold, 157:5
destiny, 188:2

friends, nothing final
between, 203:9
income tax, 485:5
man & some inferior
animal, 443:7
miracle, one, 319:9
prosperity [that] will
leak through, 157:6
a righteous cause,
437:7
we defy them, 432:6
Bryant, William Cullen
(1794–1878)
destiny, 187:12
the groves, 341:2
life, tides of, 280;4
the melancholy days,
343:7
the Oregon, 364:11
the prairies, 310:10
the rose, 341:3
truth, 497:8
world, this beautiful,
546:7
Bryce, James
(1838–1922)
cities, the govern-
ment of, 84:6
most typically Ameri-
can place, 90:2
president, great men
not chosen, 402:4
Buck, Pearl S[yden-
stricker]
(1892–1973)
civilization & its help-
less members, 112:3
colored Americans,
422:9
Kansas, 260:10
soldiers, 313:10
a usurer & interest,
324:11
Vermont, 508:2
Buckingham, J[ames]
S[ilk] *(1786–1855)*
Alabama, 9:2
hospitality [in Geor-
gia], 209:10
love in this country,
286:7
Buckley, William F., Jr.
(b. 1925)
truth, 499:9
worse and worse,
364:9
Buckner, Robert
(b. 1906)
win just one for the
Gipper (note), 472:2
Buffon, Georges Louis
Leclerc de
(1707–1788)
style (note), 477:5
Bundy, McGeorge
(1919–1996)
war, 521:2
Bunyan, John
(1628–1688)
a muckrake in his
hand (note), 407:5
Burchard, Samuel
Dickinson
(1812–1891)
rum, Romanism and
rebellion, 383:4
Burford, Anne M. Gor-
such *(b. 1942)*
Washington [D.C.],
108:11
Burges, Tristram
(1770–1853)
the father of lies
(note), 249:3

Burgess, [Frank] Gelett
(1866–1951)
I know what I like,
49:5
purple cow, 150:8
Burke, Edmund
(1729–1797)
America, 15:4
the profession [the
law] is numerous
and powerful, 276:8
when bad men com-
bine (note), 176:10
Burn, Febb Ensminger
vote for suffrage,
538:12–539
Burn, Henry Thomas
(1897–1977)
a mother's advice,
367:5
to free 17 million
from political slav-
ery, 30:6
Burnett, Frances [Eliza]
Hodgson
(1849–1924)
goodness, the best
kind of, 514:12
Burns, Robert
(1759–1796)
O whistle, and I'll
come to you (note),
458:1
Burr, Aaron
(1756–1836)
law, 273:8
never do today what
you can do tomor-
row, 143:5
Burroughs, John
(1837–1921)
stones, no sermons
in, 335:11
[T. Roosevelt] was a
walking day of judg-
ment, 439:7
youth, 556:5
Burroughs, William
S[eward] *(b. 1914)*
language, 269:13
Burton, [Capt. Sir]
Richard [Francis]
(1821–1890)
a dead man for break-
fast, 89:3
Burton, Robert
(1577–1640)
Columbus & America
& God, 14:7
Busch, Niven
(1903–1991) &
Ruskin, Harry
(d. 1969)
there's gotta be a law,
278:7
Bush, George [Herbert
Walker] *(b. 1924)*
allied air forces began
an attack, 220:1
a classic bully (note),
6:6–7
cold war, 37:5
light, a thousand
points of, 24:9
a line in the sand,
220:3
nation, a kinder, gen-
tler, 389:1
read my lips, 486:6
taxes, no new, 486:6
the vision thing,
516:10
voodoo economics,
159:6

Butler, Nicholas Mur-
ray *(1862–1947)*
an expert, 180:5
Byrd, William, II
(1674–1744)
North Carolina,
356:1
priests, lawyers, and
physicians, 353:8
Byrne, Susan M.
(b. 1946)
capital v. opportunity,
71:6
Byrnes, James F[rancis]
(1879–1972)
power intoxicates,
397:4

Cabell, James Branch
(1879–1958)
no lady is a gentle-
man, 539:4
the optimist & pes-
simist, 364:3
Virginian, the intrepid
native, 513:7
Cage, John *(b. 1912)*
life, 281:1
silence, 455:12
Cahn, Sammy [born,
Samuel Cohen]
(b. 1913)
love and marriage,
300:11
Caldwell, Erskine
(1903–1987)
here is hard-core
unemployment,
530:1
Calhoun, John C[ald-
well] *(1782–1850)*
the cohesive power of
banks, 68:5
offices as public
trusts (note),
217:3
the South! the South!,
270:7
the Union & the
rights of states
(note), 502:1
Calonne, Charles-
Alexandre de
(1734–1802)
difficult & impossible
(note), 4:1
Camacho, Epifiano
I am the cry of the
poor, 545:12
Cameron, Simon
(1799–1889)
honest politician
stays bought, 390:4
back, scratch my,
390:7
Campbell, Joseph
(1904–1987)
bliss, follow your,
223:4
Campbell, Timothy J.
(1840–1904)
the Constitution be-
tween friends, 127:1
Cannon, [Rep.] Joseph
G[urney]
(1836–1926)
a majority, 296:9
not one cent for
scenery, 167:5
Caples, John R.
(b. 1900)
all laughed when I sat
down at the piano,
5:6

Capone, Al[fonso]
(1899–1947)
Canada, 329:2
Capote, Truman
(1924–1984)
California, 74:3
Brazil, to want to be
president of, 328:5
history, 233:13
Venice, 111:2
**Cardozo, Benjamin
Nathan** *(1870–1938)*
justice, 258:4
Carey, Macdonald
(1913–1994). See
Corday, Ted
Cargile, Neil
doing something dif-
ferent, 151:4
Carleton, Will
(1845–1912)
over the hill to the
poor-house, 395:4
**Carlson, [Col.] Evans
Fordyce** *(1896–1947)*
gung ho, 313:11
Carlyle, Thomas
(1795–1881)
best & bravest (note),
164:3
man is a tool-using
animal (note), 237:9
Carman, [William] Bliss
(1861–1929)
maples, the scarlet of,
344:10
Carmer, Carl [Lamson]
(1893–1976)
Alabama, 9:5
Birmingham, 87:4
Mobile, 96:7
Carmichael, Stokely
[adopted name,
Kwame Toure] *(b.
1941)* & Hamilton,
Charles Vernon
black power, 424:8
Carnegie, Andrew
(1838–1919)
administration of
wealth, 157:4
put all your eggs in
one basket (note),
535:9
Carney, Julia
(1823–1908)
little drops of water,
147:9
little deeds of kind-
ness, 148:1
little minutes,
147:9–148
Carr, John Dickson
(1906–1977)
facts, 182:4
Carson, Rachel [Louise]
(1907–1964)
all returns to the sea,
343:5
the chemical barrage,
168:9
life on earth, 168:7
nature, control of,
448:6
spring [is] strangely
silent, 168:8
Carter, Jimmy *(b. 1924)*
adultery in my heart,
454:2
California, 74:4
I'm a Georgian, 210:1
over-lawyered, 278:10
the Soviet Union,
333:7

**Carver, George Wash-
ington** *(1864?–1943)*
fear & hate, 225:5
Carville, James *(b. 1944)*
the economy, stupid,
389:2
Casey, William
(1913–1987)
our bastard (note),
196:3
Cassatt, Mary
(1845–1926)
the civilized parts of
the world, 494:9
Cather, Willa [Sibert]
(1873–1947)
corn country, 311:2
friendship & solitary
men, 203:10
the grass was the
country, 311:1
happiness, 222:7
hate, creative, 225:2
history begins in the
heart, 223:1
human stories, 281:9
land, there was noth-
ing but, 205:2
love, 287:3
memories, 306:2
the mesa plain, 354:6
Nebraska, 350:4
New Mexico, 354:5
nobleness, 515:6
past, the precious,
370:2
prayers, 398:4
the thing not named,
47:9
travel faster now,
495:1
trees, 342:4
who marries who,
299:8
winter, 345:5
Catlin, George
(1796–1872)
"West," the term,
527:5
Catton, Bruce
(1899–1978)
Michigan, 308:7–309
Cavanaugh, [Rep.] J. M.
I have never seen a
good Indian, 419:7
Celler, Emmanuel
(1888–1981)
a heart for every fate,
228:9
Cermak, Anton
(1873–1933)
glad it was me instead
of you, Frank, 271:9
**Chamberlain, [Rev.] Ja-
son** *(fl. 1811)*
morals & manners &
grammar, 266:1
Chandler, Raymond
(1888–1959)
art & redemption, 47:1
a blonde, 539:10
an ideal, 243:10
knights, 134:2
down these mean
streets a man must
go, 230:8
a man of honor (note),
230:8
money, 325:4
win them all, you
can't, 533:3
Chaplin, Ralph
solidarity forever,
76:3

Chapman, Arthur
(1873–1935)
where the West be-
gins, 529:2
**Charles of Prussia,
[Prince]** *(fl. c. 1745)*
whites of their eyes
(note), 38:4
Chase, Alexander
(b. 1926)
the movie actor, 56:7
**Chastellux, Francois
Jean [Marquis de]**
(1734–1788)
goodness and benevo-
lence [of George
Washington[,
524:2
Chaucer, Geoffrey
(c. 1343–1400)
mordre wol out
(note), 131:8
your own thing (note),
2:2
Chayevsky, Paddy
(1923–1981)
I'm mad as hell, 42:10
Cheever, John
(1912–1982)
fear, 189:9
**Chesterton, G[ilbert]
K[eith]** *(1874–1936)*
Americans & their
ideals, 22:8
my country right
or wrong (note),
371:5
Chiat/Day
it keeps going and go-
ing, 8:2
Chicago Times
print news & raise
hell, 406:1
Chicago Tribune
Dewey Defeats Tru-
man, 33:1
Child, Lydia Maria
(1802–1880)
grandfather's house,
489:3
the Irish, 330:11
the United States is a
warning, 19:2
we first crush people
to the earth, 417:5
Choate, Joseph H[odges]
(1832–1914)
Mrs. Choate's second
husband (note),
299:4
Christopher Society
better to light one
candle, 3:2
Christy, David
(1802–c.1868)
cotton is king, 465:2
**Church, Francis
Pharcellus**
(1839–1906)
yes, Virginia, 83:8
Churchill, Winston
(1874–1965)
being shot at (note),
137:6
Roosevelt, 438:10
**Ciano, [Count]
Galeazzo**
(1903–1944)
victory & defeat
(note), 533:6
Clark, Champ [given
forenames, James
Beauchamp]
(1850–1921)

the boys keep kickin'
my dawg aroun'
(note), 34:1
here lies Champ
Clark, 172:1
Clay, Henry *(1777–1852)*
the Constitution,
126:7
government is a trust
(note), 217:3
I always do (note),
249:2
an oppressed people,
434:3
to avoid foreign colli-
sion, 522:9
rather be right than
president, 401:6
**Cleaver, [Leroy]
Eldridge** *(b. 1935)*
hating, price of, 225:8
solution & problem,
411:5
war, the god of, 522:5
**Cleghorn, Sara N[or-
cliffe]** *(1876–1959)*
autumn, 345:4
the golf links & the
mill, 436:7
Cleveland, Grover
(1837–1908)
a public office/trust,
217:3
public offenders are
trustees (note), 217:3
sovereign on this con-
tinent (note), 194:6
Cline, Leonard Lanson
(1893–1923)
Michiganers, 308:6
Clinton, De Witt
(1769–1828)
Quakerism & poli-
tics, 389:4
Clinton, [Pres.] Bill
[born, William
Jefferson Blythe]
(b. 1946)
America, 25:1
a season of service,
452:8
Clough, Arthur Hugh
(1819–1861)
westward the land is
bright (note), 15:2
Cobb, Frank Irving
(1869–1923)
being 39, 309:6
**Cobb, Irwin S[hrews-
bury]** *(1876–1944)*
Maine, 295:5,6
Washington [D.C.],
108:4
Cobden, Richard
[Cincinnati:] along
the Ohio River, 91:6
St. Louis, 105:1
Codrescu, Andrei
(b. 1946)
Santa Fe, 106:6
**Cody, William F. ("Buf-
falo Bill")**
(1846–1917)
true to friend and foe,
291:2
Coffee, Lenore
(1900–1984)
what a dump!, 252:5
**Coffin, Robert P.
Tristram**
(1892–1955)
the barn & America,
186:3
Vermont, 508:1

Cohan, George M[ichael] *(1878–1942)*
Broadway, 98:7,8
Yankee Doodle Dandy, 373:9
over there, 549:2

Cohen, Felix S. *(1907–1953)*
legal concepts, 275:12

Cohn, Roy *(1927–1986)*
the law & the judge, 256:5

Coke, [Sir] Edward *(1552–1634)*
corporations (note), 68:1
home is his castle (note), 409:11

Coleridge, Samuel Taylor *(1772–1834)*
the last American war, 523:4

Collins, [William F.] Wilkie *(1824–1889)*
American [hospitality], 237:5

Collyer, [Rev. Dr.] Robert
a dollar to the Great White Throne, 171:6

Colton, Calvin *(1789–1857)*
in the Mississippi Valley, 310:6

Comden, Betty *(b. 1919)* **& Green, Adolph** *(b. 1915)*
New York, 100:7
why did I ever leave Ohio?, 359:1

Commager, Henry Steele *(b. 1902)*
criticism & dissent, 145:1
Founding Fathers & current Fathers, 516:8
freedom, 202:4

Compton, Arthur Holly *(1892–1962)*
the Italian Navigator, 447:9

Conant, James Bryant *(1893–1978)*
a university [is] hallowed ground, 161:6

Conkling, Roscoe *(1829–1888)*
hew to the line, 117:9

Connor, Eugene (Bull) *(d. 1973)*
we make our own law, 276:4

Conrad, Joseph *(1857–1924)*
the discovery of America, 22:4

Constitution of the United States, 124:5–126

Cook, E. U. *(fl. c. 1885)*
Texas, 488:2,3

Cooke, [Alfred] Alistair *(b. 1908)*
Newport, 97:8

Coolidge, Calvin *(1872–1933)*
business & the American people, 22:5
[Harding:] a fitting representative, 223:7

ideal, force of an, 243:4
if you don't say anything, 484:1
the law & a majority, 275:8
Massachusetts, 302:3
persistence, 149:2
president, not choose to run for, 403:3
strike, no right to, 76:7
tell that to Mrs. Coolidge (note), 453:3
troubles, 495:9
Vermont, 507:6

Cooper, Gary *(1901–1961)*
[Communism:] I don't like it, 119:1

Cooper, James Fenimore *(1789–1851)*
democracy & mediocrity, 144:2
a gentleman, 162:11
individuality & freedom, 247:5
juries, 256:10
language, American, 266:3
Prairies, the Great, 310:5
a rural population, 130:5
simplicity, 456:1
true, that which is, 497:7
wealth, mere, 323:2

Cooper, Peter *(1791–1883)*
an aristocracy of wealth, 163:2
dealers in money, 69:1
God, 212:6
moneyed men, 434:11
wealth, the production of, 323:7

Coppola, Francis Ford *(b. 1939)*
napalm in the morning, 511:1

Corbusier, Le. See Le Corbusier

Corday, Ted & Phillips, Erna
days of our lives (spoken by Macdonald Carey), 283:4

Cornfeld, Bernard *(1927–1995)*
rich? sincerely want to be, 7:4

Cortissoz, Royal *(1869–1948)*
Abraham Lincoln, 285:2

Cosby, Bill *(b. 1937)*
marriage, 300:13
men and women, 542:6

Cota, [Brig. Gen.] Norman D. ("Dutch") *(1893–1971)*
let's go inland and be killed, 552:2
Rangers lead the way (note), 552:2

Cotton, John *(1585–1652)*
if the people be governors, 143:8

Cowley, Malcolm *(1898–1990)*
criticism & writing books, 49:8

Crane, Hart *(1899–1937)*
Colorado, 117:5
tortured with history, 466:5
vaulting the sea, 447:5

Crane, Stephen *(1871–1900)*
the universe, 504:2
war, 519:11

Crèvecoeur, Michel Guillaume Jean de (pen name, J. Hector St. John) *(1735–1813)*
forests, 530:5
melted into a new race, 16:8
what then is the American?, 16:7

Crichton, Michael D. *(b. 1942)*
computer music, 449:5

Crisp, Col. *(fl. late 19th century)*
an eye witness, 175:7

Crittendon, W. H. *(d. 1851)*
an American kneels only to God, 270:8

Crockett, David ("Davy") *(1786–1836)*
Arkansaw, 45:2
[be] right—then go ahead, 1:3
half-horse, half-alligator, 62:6
liberty and independence, 200:6
men who will never lay down their arms (note), 27:3
statesmen are gamesters (note), 384:8–385

Croker, ["Boss"] Richard *(1841–1922)*
politics & spoils, 391:1

Crouse, Russell *(1893–1966)*
an optimist, 364:8

Crowfoot *(1821–1890)*
what is life?, 281:4

Crumb, Robert *(b. 1943)*
keep on truckin', 149:2
not everything's for children, 79:1

Culbertson, Ely *(1891–1955)*
the United States & peace, 375:10

Cummings, E[dward] E[stlin] *(1894–1962)*
Cambridge ladies, 88:3
the dull are the damned, 67:2
father, my, 367:10
God, i thank You, 399:2
[Harding] & a sentence with 7 errors, 224:5
kisses, 287:9
love, 288:3,5
a politician, 393:13
manunkind, 411:11
miracles, 319:10
the moon, 340:5
progress, 411:11
puddle-wonderful, 345:8

science & spring, 346:6
the sea, 343:6
universe next door, 174:7
wind, a which of a, 349:4
a wind has blown the rain away, 345:9

Cummings, William Thomas *(1933–1944)*
no atheists in the foxholes, 59:5

Cuomo, Mario *(b. 1932)*
we campaign in poetry, 394:10

Curley, James Michael *(1874–1958)*
never took from anyone who couldn't afford it, 392:10

Curran, John Philot *(1750–1857)*
liberty & vigilance (note), 200:8

Custer, George Armstrong *(1839–1876)*
a part of hell, 467:7

Daily News
Ford to city: drop dead, 101:7

Daly, Daniel *(1873–1937)*
come on you sons of bitches, 549:6

Dana, Charles A[nderson] *(1819–1897)*
turn the rascals out, 383:3
when a dog bites a man, 406:3

Dana, John Cotton *(1856–1929)*
to teach & to learn, 160:13

Dana, Richard Henry, Jr. *(1815–1882)*
[California's] men & women, 72:2
fondness for dress, 186:9
a sailor's life, 454:6
a true sailor, 454:7

Darrow, Charles Bruce *(1889–1967)*
go to jail, 275:10

Darrow, Clarence *(1857–1938)*
belief in God, 59:4
convicts & millionaires, 133:3
immortality, 245:7
justice, there is no such thing as, 258:5
law, 275:13
liberties, 201:7
nature, 335:13
rights, 438:7
to think is to differ, 151:1
trade-unions, 76:4
truth, 499:5
twelve men, 257:4
wealthy man on a jury (note), 257:4
work, 545:3

Daugherty, Harry M[icajah] *(1860–1941)*
a smoke-filled room, 392:9

Davis, Bette
(1908–1989)
getting old, 363:5
good time had by all,
251:8
the hard way, 174:1
See also 223:1 (we
have the stars!),
252:5 (what a
dump!), & 496:4
(fasten your seat
belts)
Davis, Clyde Brion
(1894–1962)
Illinois, 244:3
Davis, Jefferson
(1808–1889)
haughty & humble,
297:7
majority rules, 296:7
Davis, John *(1775–1854)*
Virginians, 512:7
Davis, Sammy, Jr.,
(1925–1990)
being a star, 423:5
Day, Clarence [Shep-
ard], Jr. *(1874–1935)*
rights, 438:8
professors in New
England, 161:2
will, our times wor-
ship, 531:10
Dean, Jay Hanna
("Dizzy")
(1911–1974)
braggin, 64:2
Dean, John W., III
(b. 1938)
cancer on the presi-
dency, 526:1
deep six, 526:5
enemies list, 526:6
hang-out, a limited,
526:2
the White House &
expedience, 404:7
Debs, Eugene V[ictor]
(1855–1926)
Chicago, 90:7
lower class & crimi-
nal class, 133:5
socialism, 462:5
Decatur, Stephen
(1779–1820)
died as well as he
lived, 170:2
our country right or
wrong, 371:5
Declaration of Indepen-
dence, 140:3
De Forest, John W[il-
liam] *(1826–1906)*
temptations, 486:7
Delany, Bessie (given
names A. Elizabeth)
(b. 1891–1995)
a smart woman & a
good man, 542:7
truth, 499:10
Delany, Sadie (given
names Sarah
Louise) *(b. 1889)*
dreams, in our,
155:11
life, 283:9
your wounds, 480:4
Dement, William
(b. 1928)
dreaming, 155:10
Democratic Party
all the way with LBJ,
388:1
Cox and cocktails,
386:1

a corrupt bargain,
380:8
fifty-four forty or
fight, 382:1
he [Woodrow Wilson]
kept us out of the
war, 385:4
no crown of thorns,
no cross of gold,
384:5
Polked you & shall
Pierce you, 382:4
Roosevelt, let's re-
elect, 387:5
sixteen to one, 384:3
Adlai (note), 387:9
you never had it so
good, 387:9
Dempsey, Jack (given
first names,
William Harrison)
(1895–1983)
I just forgot to duck,
473:2
Denver, John *(b. 1943)*
West Virginia, 530:2
De Pradt. See Pradt
Dershowitz, Alan
(b. 1938)
judges, 256:6
De Sylvia, Buddy [given
names, George
Gard] *(1895–1950)*
California, here I
come, 73:10
De Tocqueville. See
Tocqueville
De Vries, Peter
(1910–1993)
America swinging,
454:3
equals, treating peo-
ple as, 298:8
gluttony, 192:9
God, 213:9
Dewey, George
(1837–1917)
fire when you are
ready, Gridley,
468:6
Dewey, John
(1859–1952)
science & imagina-
tion, 442:4
Dewey, Thomas E.
(1902–1971)
idea, you can't shoot
an, 243:9
law & money, 276:3
New York City,
100:9
public office, 217:9
talk, don't, 484:4
Díaz, Porfirio
(1830–1915)
poor Mexico, 308:4
Dicey, Edward *(b. 1832)*
[St. Louis:] capital
city of the great
west, 105:2
all the evidences of an
old civilization
(note), 105:2
Dickens, Charles
(1812–1870)
Cairo [Ill.], 89:2
Cincinnati, 91:3 &
note
City of Magnificent
Intentions, 108:1
Pittsburgh, 103:6
Dickinson, Emily
(1830–1886)
Amherst, 86:1

beauty, I died for,
243:1
bees, 337:5
book, there is no
frigate like a, 65:11
the brain, 317:5,6
called back, 171:7
chivalries, 262:4
dandelion's pallid
tube, 342:3
death, 139:2
deer, wounded,
479:10
despair, 147:2,3
Eden, 234:9
faith, 183:12
faith & microscopes,
441:5
fame, 477:10
fate, superiority to,
245:2
God, I never spoke
with, 183:13
hope, 236:8,9
if I can stop one heart
from breaking,
262:5
immortality, 245:3
June, old sophistries
of, 343:12
the lark, 337:4
life so sweet, 281:2
love, 286:13, 287:1
lovers, 286:12
luck, 291:8
madness, 293:3
mirth, 272:7
November, 344:7
pain, 479:12
pain, after great,
479:11
parting, 368:10
pedigree of honey,
163:3
prayer, 397:11,12
the Sabbath, 429:10
somebody, to be,
477:9
spring, a little mad-
ness in the, 344:8
success, 477:11
summer, 344:6
sun rose, how the,
348:1
surgeons & life, 153:6
truth, 498:4,5
winter afternoons,
344:1
a word, 267:5
words, she dealt her
pretty, 267:6
Dickinson, John
(1732–1794)
by uniting we stand,
503:3
Didion, Joan *(b. 1935)*
dreams, 155:3
stories, 58:12
style is character,
477:5
Dietz, Howard
(1896–1983)
composers, 52:4
Tallulah, 252:6
Diller, Phyllis *(b. 1917)*
stay up and fight, 42:8
Dirksen, [Sen.] Everett
McKinley
(1896–1969)
a billion here, a bil-
lion there, 325:10
Disney, Walt
(1901–1966)
a dream, 155:9

Dillard, Annie *(b. 1945)*
God & sin & hell,
431:4
Diller, Phyllis *(b. 1917)*
never go to bed mad,
42:8
Dodge, Mabel
(1879–1962)
soul & flesh, 64:7
Domino, Antoine D.,
Jr., ("Fats") *(b. 1928)*
a J.O.B., 158:5
Donne, John
(1572–1631)
my America (note),
15:2
Donnelly, Ignatius
(1831–1901)
the Democratic party
is like a mule, 390:8
Dooley, Mr. See Dunne,
Peter Finley
Doubleday, [Capt.]
Abner *(1819–1893)*
the contest was in-
evitable, 112:6
Douglas, [Justice]
William O[rville]
(1898–1980)
Fifth Amendment,
128:9
government off the
backs of the people,
218:4
marital bedrooms
(note), 410:6
oppression, 500:10
privacy, the age of no,
410:5
wilderness, 531:4,5
Douglass, Frederick
(1818–1895)
the color line, 419:6
the destiny of the col-
ored American,
419:2
how a slave was made
a man, 460:6
the past, 369:12
relation between
white and colored
people, 419:3
where justice is de-
nied, 131:8
whipped oftenest,
432:5
you are freedom's
angels, 454:9
Dowdey, Clifford S., Jr.
(b. 1904)
[the Virginian's]
dream, 513:8
Drayton, Michael
(fl. ca. 1606)
Virginia, 512:2
Dreiser, Theodore
(1871–1945)
art, 46:11
civilization, our,
111:8
Dresser, Paul
(1857–1906)
on the banks of the
Wabash, 247:1
Drew, Daniel
(1797–1879)
hog, the still, 74:8
Driver, William
(1803–1886)
Old Glory, 372:3
Du Bois, W[illiam]
E[dward] B[urghardt]
(1868–1963)
the color line, 421:2

Du Bois, W[illiam] E[dward] B[urghardt] (cont.)
the Cotton Kingdom, 209:11
forlorn, land (note) 209:11
his twoness, American, a Negro, 421:3
liberty, the cost of, 201:6
men know so little of men, 238:11
poor, to be, 436:6
talented tenth, 421:4
Dubos, René (1901–1982)
diversity & tolerance, 151:2
Duke of Windsor. See Windsor, Duke of
Dulles, John Foster (1888–1959)
brink, go to the, 196:5
gentlemen & each other's mail (note), 410:4
massive retaliatory power, 196:4
Dunbar, Paul Laurence (1872–1906)
I know why the caged bird sings, 462:1
Dunham, Sam [Nome:] a magic city, 101:10
Dunne, Finley Peter (1867–1936)
cards, 207:5, 208:1
cards, cut the, 497:2
th' dimmycratic party, 391:6
a fanatic, 166:4
lawyer, the experienced eye of a, 277:10
miracles, 319:7
money, prevention of cruelty to (note), 324:1
newspaper comforts th'afflicted, afflicts th' comfortable, 407:2
a prisidintial possibility, 403:2
scientific facts, 442:1
sick man, 244:7
Supreme Coort, 481:2
[Thanksgiving] founded by the Puritans, 490:3
Durant, Will[iam James] (1885–1981)
Caesar and Christ, 430:12
hurry, in a, 224:8
science, 442:3
Durocher, Leo (b. 1906)
nice guys finish last, 532:10
Duryea [or Duryee], [Rev.] William Rankin (b. 1838?)
home & love, 234:6
Dwight, Timothy (1752–1817)
these men cannot live in regular society, 507:4

Dylan, Bob [born, Robert Zimmerman] (b. 1941)
the answer is blowin' in the wind, 415:5
chaos, 307:10
times they are a-changin', 80:1
weatherman, 509:7

Eakins, Thomas (1844–1916)
in a big picture, 57:3
Earhart, Amelia [Putnam] 1898–1937)
courage, 131:2
Early, [Gen.] Jubal [Anderson] (1816–1894)
Dred Scott, 115:4
praying to go to heaven (note), 115:4
Eastman, George (1854–1932)
why wait?, 480:7
you press the button, 5:3
Eddy, Mary [Morse] Baker [Glover Patterson] (1821–1910)
Father-Mother-God, 212:7
prayer, 397:14
Edison, Thomas Alva (1847–1931)
beautiful over there, 271:8
genius, 209:6
hello!, 446:7
a mother, 367:2
tobacco, 493:4
way, a better, 307:7
work, hard, 545:4
Edward VIII. See Windsor, Duke of
Edwards, Jonathan (1703–1758)
the heart is like a viper, 228:1
hell, 228:10
last hour of my life, 513:10
the spider, 336:6
Ehrlichman, John (b. 1925)
hang out, a limited (note), 526:2
Peoria (note), 102:3
twist slowly, slowly in the wind, 525:7
Einstein, Albert (1879–1955)
common sense, 118:4
goals, confusion of, 322:4
efforts, one's own, 545:7
God does not play dice, 444:7
God is not malicious, 213:8
I feel uncertain, 442:10
I know what's wrong, 349:5
imagination, 318:8
the mysterious, 327:2
past, present & future, 492:8
peace, 376:2
physical concepts, 444:6
[Princeton:] a village, 161:4
religious experience, the cosmic, 431:1

science, 443:1,2, 442:6
simple as possible, as, 456:7
truth, 499:8
whether I am on the right track, 442:10
world, incomprehensible thing about the, 547:7
Eisenhower, Dwight D[avid] (1890–1969)
bridge to Asia, 10:8
dominos, a row of, 509:4
the eyes of the world are upon you, 552:1
farming, 186:2
Knowland, William, 253:1 & note
Korea, I shall go to, 265:1
military-industrial establishment, 314:8
problems, no easy, 404:2
war munitions, 314:9
Washington [D.C.], 108:7
win as quick as you can, 316:7
Eisenstaedt, Alfred (1898–1995)
the eye, 517:1
Elders, [Dr.] Jocycelyn (b. 1933)
dancing with a bear, 138:1
Eliot, T[homas] S[tearns] (1888–1965)
actual, what is, 444:5
April, 345:6
beginning, in my, 188:5
birth, copulation, & death, 282:7
a cold coming we had of it, 84:1
do a girl in, 133:7
exploration, we shall not cease from, 495:4
God, the darkness of, 327
good & evil, 175:2
hell is oneself, 229:3
history, 233:3
here I am an old man, 361:3
hollow men, 193:8
home, 235:3
I have measured out my life in coffee spoons, 281:13
a medium of entertainment, 304:6
music, 52:2
objective correlative, 47:8
old, I grow, 361:3
talking of Michaelangelo, 130:1
the passage which we did not take, 428:5
people who want to feel important, 409:8
passions, violent physical, 369:9
poetry, genuine, 53:7
poets, 53:3,7
reality, 426:10
red river, 513:5

the sea, 343:4
Shadow, falls the, 426:9
success, 478:12
temptation, 487:3
time, 492:4,6
to care & not to care, 432:2
world ends, this is the way, 547:2
when the short day is brightest, 346:9
Ellington, Duke [given names, Edward Kennedy] (1899–1974)
swing, that, 51:11
Ellison, Ralph [Waldo] (1914–1994)
invisible man, 423:2
I may speak for you (note), 423:2
Southern, be, 466:9
white, part (note), 466:9
Elvas, Knight [or Gentleman] of (fl. 1540)
trees & woods [in Arkansas], 45:1
Emerson, Mary Moody (1774–1863)
do what you are afraid to do, 1:4
Emerson, Ralph Waldo (1803–1882)
America is a country of young men, 19:4
America means opportunity, 19:4
Americanism, shallow, 19:7
ancestors, 208:3
art is a jealous mistress, 46:7
a beautiful woman, 61:8
better book, sermon, mousetrap, 177:3
boil at different degrees, 42:4
book that is not a year old, 65:9
books, 65:3
born to rule, 216:7
Boston, 87:7
cake & debt, 292:5
calculators, 427:8
California days, 73:1
calmness, 74:6
chalices & priests, 430:1
a child, 81:4
children, 81:5,10
Christian, where is the, 429:8
church, I like the silent, 429:7
cities degrade us, 84:4
a city for beavers, 110:12
civilization, our, 111:6
civilization & a good woman, 538:3
common sense and plain dealing, 118:1
conformity & consistency & mediocrity, 305:3
concentration, 476:6
conservatism & reform, 389:7, 390:1
consistency, a foolish, 123:8

cool, keep, 74:7
crime, commit a, 132:1
the day will come when no badge or uniform, 205:7
demonology, 149:9
destiny, our, 174:5
discontent, 501:1
do your thing, 2:2
dream, we wake from one, 426:7
Dreams & Beasts (note), 155:6
dreams & natural character, 155:6
duty whispers, when, 556:3
an Englishman who has lost his fortune, 329:7
enthusiasm, 166:3 & note
envy, 169:3
Europe, the tapeworm of, 330:2
fact, 181:2,3
fate, 187:8,9
fear, 188:11
flattery, 190:2
flowers, 341:7
a friend, 203:2,3
friends, 203:5
genius, work of, 209:5
a gentleman & a lady, 297:3
a giver, 80:3
God, 211:4,5,6,8, 212:1
God builds his temple in the heart, 429:9
God who made New Hampshire, 353:2
government, less, 216:6
great, to be, 219:2
a great man, 219:3
great men, 219:4
gunpowder smells good, 519:1
haste, 224:6
health, 227:3, 244:5
heart, 228:2
heart great as the world, 284:6
hero, every, 229:6
heroism, 229:5
history, our so-called, 232:6
hitch your wagon to a star, 14:3
honor, the louder he talked of his, 236:3
hospitality, 237:4
an institution, 248:5
I live now, 399:9
institutions (note), 248:5
identity, personal, 305:10
it will be all the same 100 years hence, 74:7
king, strike at, 440:4
knowledge, 263:3
labor, 543:2, 543:1
language, 267:2,4
laughs, beware how he, 272:5
law rules through out existence, 503:8
laws, obey, 274:1
life & danger, 136:4
life & thinking, 280:5

life is a series of surprises, 280:3
life—a self-evolving circle, 374:8
living, never, 280:1
London, 109:5
love, 286:6,9,11
lover, all mankind love a, 286:5
luck, 291:6
the majority or the minority, 296:5
manners, 297:4,5,6, 298:2
marriage, 299:2
Massachusetts, 302:1
means, discreditable, 179:3
mediocrity & squalid contentment, 305:3
men & mothers, 367:1
men who lead, 231:6
miracles, 319:5
money, 323:3
moon; the rising, 339:10
mousetrap, better, 177:3
murder will speak out, 131:8
nature, 335:2,3
nature & calculators, 427:8
nature & every secret, 441:2
New York—a sucked orange, 98:2
now, I live, 399:9
old, time to be, 360:1
pain, the house of, 479:8
[Paris:] a loud modern place, 109:10
a party corrupted by personality, 390;2
the party of the past and the party of future: the establishment and the movement, 390:9
passion, 369:5
past, adamantine record of, 399:8
patriotism, 371:6
peace & yourself, 451:4
place is nothing (note), 494:1
poet, world waiting for its, 52:10
poetry, 52:11
poverty, 395:3
power, 396:11,12, 397:1,2
prayer, 397:9,10
present, the, 399:8, 399:9, 399:10
the president has paid dear for his White House, 401:4
pride, 409:5
proverbs, 415:10
quotation, I hate, 415:9
quote, we all, 416:2
quoter, the first, 416:1
railroad iron is a magician's rod, 445:10
reading, 65:5
revolution & a thought, 434:5
a sailor, 455:3

the saint & poet & poetry, 410:1
Salt Lake City, 105:5
sanity, 293:1
see only what they are prepared to see, 516:3
shot hear round the world, 41:3
size, no virtue goes with, 62:3
the sky, 339:11
smoke, man of no conversation should, 493:3
sorrow, 463:10
speech, cordial, 129:4
speech, short and positive, 54:7
spoons, the faster we counted, 263:3
suicide, 480:5
talent, those who have no, 305:4
task, ever man's, 543:7
taxes, willing to pay, 485:1
the test of a religion or philosophy, 378:9
thin ice & speed, 469:5
things, 490:4–6
think, to, 317:1
thirty, after, 309:3
time, 491:10
time & facts, 491:4
times hard/money scarce, 61:1
thyself, trust, 451:3
tobacco, 493:1
today, 399:10
torment, delicious, 289:3
toys, strewn (note), 81:5
travel & language, 493:11
traveling, 491:1 & note
trust men, 497:1
truth v. repose, 497:9
universe, the, 503:6
virtue, 514:4–6
virtue in us & vice, 176:2
visitors, 219:7
war, 519:8
the warm day, 348:7
way, a best, 307:5
we are the builders of our fortunes, 2:7
we do what we must, 179:2
weed? what is a, 342:2
we have a country again (note), 519:1
wit, 239:7
a woman, 537:6
woman, a beautiful, 61:8
wonder & science, 441:3
word, 267:1,3
word, expunged, 77:8
work done well, 177:4
world, the same, 546:8
world, proud, 546:9
the world & its poet, 52:10
world is but thickened light, 444:4
writing & God, 57:7
yesterday, mortgaged to, 369:10

yourself & principles, 451:4
the youth replies I can, 556:3
Emmet, Daniel Decatur *(1815–1904)*
Dixie's Land, 465:3
Epstein, Julius J. *(b. 1909)* **and Philip G.** *(1909–1952),* **& Koch, Howard** *(1902–1995)*
friendship, a beautiful, 204:1
here's looking at you, 290:6
play it, Sam, 52:3
the usual suspects, 134:3
regret it, you'll, 368:11
Ervin [Sen.] Sam[uel James], Jr. *(1896–1985)*
I'm just a country lawyer (note), 412:5
North Carolina, 357:1
progress, 412:5
Evans, Walker *(1903–1975)*
stare . . . die knowing something, 263:8

Farber, Barry
Russian tragedy/comedy, 333:4
Farley, James A[loysius] *(1888–1976)*
Maine & Vermont (note), 295:3
Farragut, [Adm.] David Glasgow *(1801–1870)*
damn the torpedoes, 115:3
Faulkner, William *(1879–1962)*
fear, 189:7
grief, 464:2
if a writer has to rob his mother, 58:9
man will prevail, 239:5
Mississippi, 320:4
a soul, a spirit, 464:9
the Swiss, 334:6
writer's only responsibility, 58:8
you know how to whistle, don't you?, 458:1
Federalist Party
stand with Washington, 380:7
Federal Writers' Project
[Arizona:] land of extremes, 44:8
a Kentuckian, 262:1
[Nebraska:] Middle West merges with the West, 350:5
New Jersey, 354:2
[New Mexico:] keynote of the land, 354:7
[North Dakota:] rural character, 357:6
[North Dakota:] boundless plains and hills, 357:5
South Carolinians, 467:3,4
Tennessean's lives, 487:7

Federal Writers' Project
(*cont.*)
Utah, 505:2,3
Washington [D.C.],
108:6
Wyoming, 554:6
Ferber, Edna
(*1887–1968*)
mother knows best,
367:7
Oklahoma, 359:4
Tulsa, 107:2
**Feynman, [Dr.] Richard
P.** (*1918–1988*)
nature, 336:5, 449:6
technology, 449:6
Fields, Lew (*1867–1941*)
wife, she's my, 299:7
Fields, W. C. [born
William Claude
Dukenfeld]
(*1879–1946*)
ain't a fit night out,
349:3
hates children and
dogs (note), 320:2
honest man, 235:11
Philadelphia, 103:1,
173:5
Filene, Edward
[tax] money, 486:1
Fink, Mike
(*1770?–1823*)
I'm a Salt River
roarer!, 63:1
Finley, John
(*1797–1866*)
Hoosier nation,
246:8
Firmin, Giles
(*fl. c. 1675*)
New England, 351:9
Fischer, Bobby [given
names, Robert
James] (*b. 1943*)
break a man's ego,
208:2
**Fisher, John Arbuthnot
Baron** (*1841–1920*)
never explain (note),
178:5
Fisher, Arthur (*b. 1931*)
Montana's graveyards,
326:2
Fishwick, Marshall
(*b. 1923*)
hero, every, 231:1
**Fitzgerald, F[rancis]
Scott** (*1896–1940*)
American lives, no
second acts in,
22:11
breast of the new
world, 355:6
dark night of the soul,
147:7
forgotten is forgiven,
198:4
a hero, 230:4
a heroic thing, 230:3
intelligence, a first
rate, 318:2
New York, 100:3
optimism, 364:6
rich, the very, 324:5
words, you can stroke
people with, 269:6
the world, 547:6
young Minnesotan
did a heroic thing,
230:3
Fitzgerald Zelda
(*1900–1948*)
advertising, 6:3

I still believe [in ad-
vertisements]
(note), 5:6–6
love first, and live in-
cidentally, 287:5
the moment which
determined the fu-
ture, 309:7
Fitzsimmons, Robert
(*1862–1917*)
the bigger they come
(note), 471:1
Flaubert, Gustave
(*1812–1880*)
le détail (note), 148:3
Flint, Timothy
heaven & Kentuck,
261:1
Folsom, James ("Big
Jim") (*1908–1987*)
as long as the Negroes
are held down,
423:1
Ford, Eileen (*b. 1922*)
slender people,
227:11
**Ford, [Pres.] Gerald
R[udolph]** (*b. 1913*)
the Granite State,
353:6
nightmare, long na-
tional, 527:2
Ford, Henry
(*1863–1947*)
history is bunk, 233:2
money, 324:10
out of the trenches by
Christmas, 547:9
peace, I wanted to see
(note), 547:9
present, we want to
live in the, 400:1
work, 545:2
Ford, Henry II
(*1917–1987*)
never complain [or]
explain, 178:5
Forgy, Howell M.
(*b. 1908*)
pass the ammunition,
550:5
Forrest, Nathan Bedford
(*1821–1877*)
first with the most,
315:7
**Foster, Stephen
[Collins]**
(*1826–1864*)
I came from Alabama,
9:3
Kentucky Home, the
old, 261:4,5
Swanee River, 465:1
Foster, Vincent W., Jr.
(*d. 1993*)
deathbed & office
(note), 71:7
**Fountain, Paul
[Mount] Ranier,**
523:5
F. P. A. See under
Adams, Franklin
Pierce
Frankenthaler, Helen
(*b. 1928*)
light & scale, 57:4
Frankfurter, Felix
(*1882–1965*)
all deliberate speed
(note), 129:1
if facts are changing,
275:5
morals & manners,
298:6

Franklin, Benjamin
(*1706–1790*)
Adam was never
called *Master*
Adam, 162:8
anger, 42:3
baby, what good is a
newborn, 504:7
best, strive to be,
177:2
better guilty persons
should escape,
273:6
body of B. Franklin,
169:6
cat in gloves, 440:3
cause, our, 39:5
[chess:] wretched
game, 207:1
Christ's birthday, 82:7
Constitution, our
new, 125:1
creditors, 67:7
death and taxes, 125:1
desire many things,
146:4
digressions & growing
older, 360:3
the doctor takes the
fee, 153:3
early to bed, early to
rise, 226:10
eat, 109:12, 110:1
employed, when men
are, 542:11
enemy, no little, 165:5
enemy, you are now
my, 248:7
experience, 179:9
faith, 183:5
fat kitchen & lean
will, 531:7
fault, to confess a,
188:6
felicity, 222:3
a fool, 193:1,2
forewarned, fore-
armed, 263:1
foxes grow gray, 131:3
freedom of thought &
speech, 199:1
gains & pains, 148:5
God governs, 211:2
God helps them that
help themselves,
452:2
hope, 236:7 & note
laws, 273:3,4,6
laziness, 279:2
liberty, 199:3, 200:1 &
note
life & time, 279:8
a little neglect, 147:8
live well, 279:9
loved, if you would
be, 286:4
man: a tool-making
animal, 237:9
mankind are very
odd, 240:9
marriage, 298:9
marriage without love
& love without
marriage, 456:8
meals, lessen thy,
226:9
men & melons, 237:8
money, 322:7–9
necessity, 350:8
a new child among
the immortals,
138:5
[New Jersey]—a beer
barrel, 353:9

an office, 542:10
the older I grow,
360:2
the orator, 483:2
pain & pleasure,
380:3
passion, 369:2,3
peace, never was a
bad, 374:10
a penny saved, 322:10
Philadelphia has
taken Howe (note),
102:7–103
pride, 409:2,3
purse, light, 395:1
quoted by other
learned authors,
415:8
a reason for every-
thing one has a
mind to do, 427:6
a republic if you can
keep it, 17:1
secure is not safe,
450:9
secret, three may
keep, 450:5
sense, 117:10
single man, 298:10
Skugg, here lies, 170:1
sluggard, up, 155:5
stones, don't throw,
134:10
strokes, little, 148:6
success, 477:7
suicides, nine of ten
men are, 227:1
sun, a rising, 124:4
talkers & doers, 483:1
they are so grateful,
452:9
time, 490:11, 491:1
time & life, 279:8
trade, 67:8
the turkey, 336:7
the used key, 542:9
the value of water,
506:1
the value of things,
506:3
war, never was a
good, 518:4
Washington, General
(note), 523:8
we are soon to follow
(note), 138:5
we must all hang to-
gether, 142:1
word to the wise,
483:3
work/pray, 535:7
Frederick the Great
(*1712–1786*)
the whites of their
eyes (note), 38:4
would you live for-
ever (note), 549:6
Freeman, Cliff (*b. 1941*)
where's the beef, 7:8
Free Soil Party
free soil, free speech
(note), 382:5
Frémont, John C[harles]
(*1813–1890*)
a melancholy coun-
try, 242:1
Friedman, Milton
(*b. 1912*)
free lunch (note),
158:2
government, 218:6
Friendly, Fred W.
(*b. 1915*)
television, 304:7

Frost, Robert
(1874–1963)
age, a golden, 214:8
aged man, one, 361:6
the best way out is
through, 174:6
birches, 556:6
California, 73:9
disregard, later, 362:3
families & hints,
185:3
figure a poem makes,
53:14
free verse, 53:9
friends & death, 139:4
happiness, 223:3
home, 234:10
life, 281:11
love, 287:4,7
the land was ours,
23:2
miles to go before I
sleep, 494:12
night, acquainted
with the, 348:3
nothing to look for-
ward to, 147:5
poem & love, 53:14
poetry, 53:15
provide, provide, 80:10
the Secret, 450:7
the snake stood up for
evil, 150:1
snow, the dust of,
345:7
travelers going side-
real, 458:6
truths in and out of
favor, 499:3
two roads diverged,
528:4
Vermont & New
Hampshire, 353:3
a wall, 152:11, 153:1
what nature is willing
to give, 342:8
world, a lover's quar-
rel with, 173:4
world will end in fire,
546:1
writer, no tears in
the, 58:4
**Fulbright, [Sen.] J[ames]
William** *(b. 1905)*
peaceful coexistence,
197:3
**Fuller, R[ichard] Buck-
minster** *(1895–1983)*
God is a verb, 213:2
spaceship Earth, 169:1
war, 522:7
**Fuller, [Sarah] Margaret
[Marchese] Ossoli**
(1810–1850)
child, to come home
to a, 81:6
[the Irish] are looked
upon with con-
tempt, 418:5
live, forget to, 543:5
men & women, 541:1
nature, 335:4
the Negro & the
woman, 418:4
no woman has had a
fair chance, 537:7
universe, the, 503:7
wounded, better to
be, 286:10
Furthman, Jules
(1888–1960)
you know how to
whistle, don't you?,
458:1

Gabor, Zsa Zsa *(b. 1919)*
a man is incomplete
until married (note),
298:10
**Gage, [Lt. Gen.]
Thomas**
(1721–1787)
this cursed place, 38:5
Gaither, Alonzo
(d. 1994)
teaching character by
winning, 474:6
**Galbraith, John Ken-
neth** *(b. 1908)*
city government, 85:1
Dulles (note), 196:5
in economics the ma-
jority is always
wrong, 159:5
food, too much,
192:10
luxuries, 292:7
politics, 394:5
underdeveloped
countries & over-
developed women,
458:5
**Galento, ("Two-Ton")
Tony** *(1910–1979)*
I'll moider der bum,
474:4
Gallagher, Buell
(1904–1979)
be part of the answer,
not the problem
(note), 411:5
Garbo, Greta
(1905–1990)
I want to be alone,
463:5
Gardner, Augustus P.
wake up America,
547:10
Garfield, James A[bram]
(1831–1881)
God & the govern-
ment, 29:2
the greed for office
(note), 402:2
what is there in this
place, 402:2
Garner, John Nance
(1868–1967)
vice presidency,
508:9, 509:1
**Garrison, William
Lloyd** *(1805–1879)*
a covenant with
death, 126:6
I will be heard, 459:7
Gaynor, William Jay
(1849–1913)
words, short, 268:3
Geisel, Theodor (Ted) S.
See Seuss, Dr.
Gelbart, Larry *(b. 1928)*
Hitler out of town
with a musical,
56:5
**General Post Office,
New York City**
neither snow, nor
rain, nor heat,
348:11
George, Henry
(1839–1897)
capital & labor, 76:1
desires, 146:5
George, W. L.
Boston, 88:2
Geronimo *(1829?–1909)*
I surrender, 420:6
my land [Arizona],
44:5

Gershwin, Ira
(1896–1983)
it ain't necessarily so,
430:11
summertime, 346:3
a woman, 539:8
Getty, John Paul
(1892–1976)
the meek, 437:2
Giamatti, A. Bartlett
(1938–1989)
it [baseball] breaks
your heart, 476:2
merit & baseball,
476:4
Gibbons, James Sloan
(1810–1892)
we are coming Father
Abraham, 114:2
Gibson, Walter B.
(1897–1985)
who knows what evil
lurks, 176:6
**Gilbert, [Sir] W[illiam]
S[chwenck]**
(1836–1911)
the Kodaks do their
best (note), 5:3
Gilpin, Laura
(1891–1979)
a river, 336:2
**Gingrich, [Rep.]
Newt[on Leroy]**
(b. 1943)
America is a ro-
mance, 25:3
perseverance, 149:5
Ginsberg, Allen
(b. 1926)
best minds of my gen-
eration destroyed
by madness,
294:2
poetry, 54:4
Giovanni, Nikki
(b. 1943)
death is a slave's free-
dom, 67:1
**Gladstone, William
[Ewart]** *(1809–
1898)*
[the Constitution:]
most wonderful
work, 126:9
**Glasgow, Ellen [Ander-
son Gholson]**
(1874–1945)
appearances, 43:7
Glass, Carter
(1858–1946)
a liberal, definition of,
393:9
Glyn, Martin H.
(1871–1924)
he [Woodrow Wilson]
kept us out of war,
385:4
Goldberg, Isaac
(1887–1938)
diplomacy, 151:8
Goldman, Emma
(1869–1940)
judges progress,
256:4
the law, 275:7
Goldwater, Barry
(b. 1909)
God, 214:3
a government that is
big, 218:1
extremism & modera-
tion, 36:7
I don't care if a soldier
is straight, 315:6

Goldwyn, Samuel (born,
Samuel Goldfish)
(1882–1974)
if nobody wants to
see your picture
(note), 269:9
im possible, 269:9
include me out (note),
269:9
quick as a flashlight
(note), 269:9
take the bull by the
teeth (note), 269:9
verbal contract, 276:2
Goodwin, Richard
(b. 1931)
a great society (note),
388:2
Gore, Al *(b. 1948)*
dreamed of becoming
Vice President
(note), 508:5
Gorsuch, Anne. See
Burford
Gouge, William M.
directors of a com-
pany, 68:3
Graham, Katharine
(b. 1917)
questions and an-
swers, 415:7
women & their lives,
540:7
Graham, Martha
(1894–1991)
an athlete of God,
218:9
the body, 64:9
dancing is discovery,
50:9
dance is the hidden
language, 50:10
mediocrity, 305:9
movement, 50:11
theater, 56:10
Graham, Philip
(1919–1963)
the first rough drafts
of history, 408:11
**Grant, Ulysses S[imp-
son]** *(1822–1885)*
afraid, Harris had
been, 189:2
backbone of an angle-
worm (note), 250:4
church & state, 430:2
England, 329:8
a gallant soldier, 171:3
I am a verb, 2:9
I shall fight it out on
this line, 115:1
labor disgraces no
man, 75:8
let no guilty man es-
cape, 132:6
let us have peace, 29:3
unconditional surren-
der, 113:7
war, the art of, 316:1
the war is over, 116:4
we must cut our way
out, 113:4
wherever the enemy
goes, 115:2
**Gray, Francine Du
Plessix Gray**
(b. 1941)
Hawaii, 226:7
Greeley, Horace
(1811–1872)
Democrats & saloon-
keepers, 390:5
[Denver:] this log city,
92:5

Greeley, Horace (*cont.*)
  go west, 527:8
  Kansas, 259:3
  the territory [Utah] is
    worth very little,
    505:1
Green, Abel
  (*1900–1973*)
  stix nix hicks pix,
    303:5
Green, Adolph. See un-
  der Comden, Betty
Green, Thomas Jeffer-
  son (*1801–1863*)
  the Alamo, 27:4
Greenberg, [Meyer]
  Michael
  (*1928–1995*)
  the joy of giving, 80:1
Greenberger, Daniel
  (*b. 1933*)
  quantum mechanics,
    445:4
Greene, Nathanael
  (*1742–1786*)
  we fight, get beat,
    fight again, 40:5
  we were like a crab
    (note), 40:5
Gregory, Horace
  (*1898–1981*)
  Greek islands over
    Harvard Square,
    161:5
Grellet, Stephen
  [Étienne de Grellet
  du Mabillier]
  (*1773–1855*)
  pass through this
    world but once
    (note), 262:3
Griffin, Eleanore
  (*d. 1995*) & Schary,
  Dore (*b. 1905*)
  no such thing as a bad
    boy, 82:6
Griswold, Erwin
  (*1904–1994*)
  12 persons, 257:7
Gropius, Walter
  (*1883–1969*)
  architecture, 48:7
Grosvenor, Charles H.
  (*1833–1917*)
  figures & liars, 443:11
Groves, Leslie R.
  (*1898–1970*)
  Japan will be finished,
    553:7
Guess, William Francis
  an old Charlestonian,
    89:8
Guest, Edgar A[lbert]
  (*1881–1959*)
  done, thing that
    couldn't be, 4:2
  home & a heap o'
    livin', 235:1
Guinan, Texas (given
  names, Mary Louise
  Cecilia) (*1884–
  1933*)
  hello, sucker (note),
    193:7
  success, 478:10
Guiterman, Arthur
  (*1871–1943*)
  D. A. R.lings, 163:7
  sex, 443:9
Gunther, John
  (*1901–1970*)
  Argentina, 328:3
  Atlanta, 86:3
  Butte, 89:1 & note

[Cleveland:] metropo-
  lis with good citi-
  zenship, 91:7
  Colorado, 117:7
  Dallas & Fort Worth,
    92:4
  [El Paso] city of the
    four C's, 93:5
  England, 329:12
  Houston, 94:2
  Idaho, 242:2,3
  Iowa, 254:2
  [Kansas] a gravity
    point, 260:7
  the Middle West,
    311:4
  the Midwest, 311:5
  Ohio, 358:6
  Russians, 333:3
  South Americans,
    333:11
  this state [Vermont]
    bows to nothing,
    507:7
  West Virginia, 529:9
  a Wyoming cattle-
    man, 554:7
Gurney, A. R.
  cocktail hour, 13:5
Guthrie, Woody [given
  names, Woodrow
  Wilson]
  (*1912–1967*)
  some will rob you,
    134:1
  this land is your land,
    23:10

Hague, Frank
  (*1876–1956*)
  I am the law, 275:14
Hakluyt, Richard
  (*1553–1616*)
  likelihood of gold or
    silver, 72:1
Halberstam, David
  (*b. 1934*)
  best and the brightest,
    164:3
Hale, Edward Everett
  (*1822–1909*)
  senators & the peo-
    ple, 121:1
  the something that I
    can do, 2:8
  lend a hand, 80:5
Hale, Nathan
  (*1755–1776*)
  one life to lose for my
    country, 39:2
Haley, Alex
  (*1921–1992*)
  being a Southerner,
    466:8
Hall, [Capt.] Basil
  (*1788–1844*)
  streets starting up of
    their own accord,
    104:6
Hall, [Lt.] Francis
  Charleston, 89:6
  cliffs [Palisades], 354:1
Halleck, Fitz-Greene
  (*1790–1867*)
  [Connecticut:] a
    rough land, 122:8
Halleck, [Gen.] Henry
  Wager (*1815–1872*)
  call no council of war,
    316:4
Halsey, William F.
  (*1882–1959*)
  ships have been sal-
    vaged, 552:5

Hamburger, Philip
  [Paul] (*b. 1914*)
  Des Moines, 92:9
Hamer, Fannie Lou
  (*1917–1977*)
  down so long, 396:4
  sick and tired (note),
    396:4
Hamilton, Alexander
  (*1712–1756*)
  Boston, 87:5
  Connecticut, 122:5
  the country people in
    this island, 435:9
  here lies John Purcell,
    169:7
Hamilton, Alexander
  (*1755–1804*)
  debt,national, 156:1
  debt & taxes, 156:2
  democracy, 143:9
  the few and the many,
    436:3
  overscrupulous, to be,
    179:1
  people, the voice of
    (note), 377:6
  popular opinion, 412:8
  power over a man's
    subsistence, 396:7
  president, who will be
    the next, 400:8
  we suppose mankind
    more honest than
    they are, 235:7
  why government?,
    215:5
Hamilton, Charles Ver-
  non. See under
  Carmichael,
  Stokely
Hammerstein, Oscar I
  (*1846–1919*)
  man in the theater
    business, 55:4
  opera, 51:5
Hammerstein, Oscar II
  (*1895–1960*)
  Kansas City, 94:3
  Oklahoma, 359:6
  Paris, the last time I
    saw, 110:4
Hammett, [Samuel]
  Dashiell
  (*1894–1961*)
  talking, 484:2
Hand, Learned
  (*1872–1961*)
  jury, trial by, 257:5
  justice, thou shalt not
    ration, 258:6
  liberty, 202:2
  press, the hand that
    rules the, 303:8
  publicity, the art of,
    7:1
  reputation, 431:7
  taxes, 485:11
  words, 269:5
Hanna, Mark [given
  first names, Marcus
  Alonzo]
  (*1837–1904*)
  [T. Roosevelt] damned
    cowboy is presi-
    dent, 439:3
  we'll stand pat, 384:7
Hansberry, Lorraine
  (*1930–1965*)
  Africa, 328:1
Harburg, Edgar Y. (Kip)
  (*1898–1981*)
  brother, can you spare
    a dime, 146:1

over the rainbow,
    222:12
Harding, George T.
  thankful you're a boy,
    223:5
Harding, Warren
  Gamaliel
  (*1865–1923*)
  Founding Fathers
    (note), 223:7–224
  normalcy, 30:5, 385:6
Harfield, Henry
  bankers, 71:2
Harlan, John Marshall
  (*1833–1911*)
  civil freedom &
    equality, 420:7
  Constitution is color-
    blind, 127:2
  right rather than con-
    sistent, 124:3
  separate but equal
    (note), 127:2
Harper, Robert Goodloe
  (*1765–1825*)
  not one cent for trib-
    ute, 26:5
Harrell, Tom (*b. 1946*)
  form & rhythm,
    52:6
Harrington, Michael
  (*1928–1989*)
  the poor, 396:1
Harris, Sydney J[ustin]
  (*b. 1917*)
  indiscreet answers &
    questions (note),
    415:6
Harris, Townsend
  (*1804–1878*)
  children of the rich
    and poor, 160:2
Hart, Lorenz [Milton]
  (*1895–1943*)
  Manhattan, 99:7
Hart, Moss (*1904–1961*)
  [New York] & the
    boldness to dream,
    101:1
Harte, [Francis] Bret
  (*1836–1902*)
  the curtain's mystic
    fold, 55:3
  luck, 291:7
Hawthorne, Nathaniel
  (*1804–1864*)
  electricity, 446:2
  a hero, 229:7
  mankind, 238:2
  mountains, 335:9
  one's own heart &
    self, 451:5
  the Thames, 109:6
  time, 491:9
  women, a damned
    mob of scribbling,
    537:9
Hay, John [Milton]
  (*1838–1905*)
  door, the open, 195:1
  forty, zenith at, 309:5
  a look of unspeakable
    peace (note), 284:3
  Perdicaris alive, 29:8
  proverbs, 415:12
  war, a splendid little,
    469:2
Hayes, Alfred
  (*1911–1985*)
  Joe Hill, 77:1
Hayes, [Archbishop]
  Patrick (*1867–1938*)
  children troop down
    from heaven, 82:4

Hearn, Lafcadio
(1850–1904)
Japan, 331:8,9, 332:1
Hearst, William Randolph *(1863–1951)*
you furnish the pictures, 468:5
Heber, Reginald
(1783–1826)
brightest and best
(note), 164:3
Hecht, Ben *(1894–1964)*
marriage, a new,
300:7
Heinlein, Robert A.
(1907–1988)
free lunch (note),
158:2
love, 288:9
Heller, Joseph *(b. 1923)*
Catch-22, 315:1,2
mediocrity, 305:7
a self-made man,
452:5
Heller, Walter [Wolfgang] *(1915–1987)*
principle v. what's
right, 438:2
Hellman, Lillian
(1905–1984)
conscience, 123:6
[St. Petersburg:] a
silent, lonely
beauty, 110:11
sin, fashions in,
176:8
Helmsley, Leona
(b. c.1920)
little people pay,
486:5
Helper, Hinton R[owan]
(1829–1909)
San Francisco, 105:8
Hemingway, Ernest
(1899–1961)
books, good, 66:6
cowardice, 189:5
grace under pressure,
218:8
grace & death, 474:7
Huckleberry Finn,
66:7
loser, what makes a
good, 533:1
a man, 306:13
moral, what is, 175:1
Paris, 110:7
peace, a separate,
375:7
the rich, 324:12
shit detector, 58:10
Spain, people of,
334:2
Switzerland, 334:5
the world is a fine
place, 547:4
writer, for a true, 58:7
Henry, Buck *(b. 1930)*
TV (note), 305:2
Henry, Buck & Willingham, Calder
(1922–1995)
plastics, 70:10
Henry, O. [pen name of
William Sydney
Porter] *(1862–1910)*
Bagdad-on-the-Subway, 98:10
Californians, 73:6
City, in the Big, 84:10
honesty & dishonesty, 235:10
little old New York,
99:3

Noisy-ville-on-the-
Subway (note),
98:10
what a woman wants,
538:11
Henry, Patrick
(1736–1799)
the battle & the
brave, 130:9
future & past, 205:4
give me liberty or
death, 199:7
I am an American,
370:12
treason, if this be,
25:7
**Henry IV (Henry of
Navarre)**
(1533–1610)
a chicken in his pot
every Sunday (note),
386:5
Henson, Jim
(1936–1990)
never eat more than,
192:13
not easy being green,
339:9
Herodotus *(c. 485–425
B.C.)*
either by snow, or rain
(note), 348:11–349
**Herriman, George
Joseph** *(1880–1944)*
in my Kosmos,
505:6
**Herzen, Alexander
Ivanovich**
(1812–1870)
America, 191:1 &
note
Higgins, George F.
(b. 1939)
stupid, if you're,
193:11
Hill, David Bennett
(1843–1910)
a Democrat still,
391:3
Hill, Joe [born, Joel Hagglund, changed to
Joseph Hillstrom,
then shortened]
(1879–1915)
organize!, 76:6
pie in the sky (note),
76:6
Himes, Chester
(1909–1984)
Harlem, 101:4
Hines, [Rev.] Gustavus
(fl. c. 1850)
this wretched nation,
418:6
Hippocrates *(c. 460–
c. 370 B.C.)*
life & art (note), 46:4
Hitchcock, Alfred
(1899–1980)
nobody can like an
actor, 56:2
Hitchcock, Tommy
(1900–1944)
lose/win, 532:8
Hitz, Fred
secrecy, absolute,
450:8
Hoar, George Frisbie
(1826–1904)
[the flag:] beautiful as
a flower, 373:3
Hoffer, Eric *(1902–1983)*
fail, freedom to, 183:4
failure, the, 183:2

faith in a holy cause,
184:7
new,the, 355:1
Hoffman, Abbie
(1936–1989)
by any means necessary (note), 424:5
Hoffman, Hans
(1880–1966)
simplify, to, 456:6
Hogan, Frank
(1877–1944)
the Constitution,
128:5
Holiday, Billie (born,
Eleanora Fagan)
(1915–1959)
sometimes it's worse
to win a fight, 533:4
strange fruit (see under Allan, Lewis)
Holland, J[osiah] G[ilbert] *(1819–1881)*
adultery (note), 351:9
American[s] & the
devil, 149:7
**Holmes, Fanny
Bowditch Dixwell**
(1840–1929)
Washington [D.C.],
108:2
Holmes, Fred L.
(1883–1946)
Wisconsin, 534:4
**Holmes, [Rev.] John
Haynes** *(1879–1964)*
the universe, 504:4
Holmes, Oliver Wendell, Sr. *(1809–1894)*
Boston State-house,
87:6
Brahmin caste of
New England,
163:1
certainty & repose,
426:8
ensign, her tattered,
372:2
faith, 183:11
a flower, 341:13
health, 227:4
hic jacet Joe, 171:5
an idea, 242:6
insight, 317:4
knowledge & wisdom, 534:9
old age, 361:2
old man, when called
an, 360:8
the old time, 369:13
majorities, mounted,
296:6
man has his will,
541:4
men grow a little
sweet, 309:4
a good patient, 153:7
revolutions, 434:10
science, 441:4
the sea, 342:11
seventy years young,
361:1
shay, the wonderful
one-hoss, 446:5
sin & a lie, 152:5
truth, 498:1
we must sail, 2:6
woman has her way,
541:4
a woman would
rather talk with a
man, 541:7
verdict, their (note),
257:7

**Holmes, [Justice] Oliver
Wendell, Jr.**
(1841–1935)
advice, 8:3
all deliberate speed
(note), 129:1
backbone, banana, &
a judge (note), 250:4
cases, great, 274:9
certainty is generally
an illusion, 426:8
the Constitution &
free thought, 128:2
country, what we can
for our (note), 452:7
fire, our hearts were
touched with, 369:6
free speech & shouting fire, 202:7
free trade in ideas,
202:8
general propositions
& concrete cases,
275:2
history, a page of,
233:5
if my fellow citizens
want to go to hell,
201:8
imbeciles, three generations of (note),
410:6
the law, 274:4,5,7,8,
275:6
a less evil that some
criminals escape,
175:8
life, 281:9,10
riders in a race, 361:9
a river, 167:7
seventy again, O to
be, 361:10
taxes & power to tax,
485:7,9
truth accepted in
competition,
202:8
war, 519:2
what we do and
think, 221:4
Holzer, Jenny *(b. 1950)*
a relaxed man, 74:9
protect me from what
I want, 146:7
Hone, Philip
(1780–1851)
[J. Q. Adams] breathing his last, 170:7
Hoover, Herbert Clark
(1874–1964)
apples, selling (note),
251:3
credit, 158:3
grass will grow in the
streets, 158:4
hair shirts, mental,
403:4
a noble experiment,
12:7
poverty, triumph
over, 31:1
prosperity around the
corner, 145:6
rugged individualism,
22:7
things that go around
in the dark, 137:1
war & youth, 521:7
**House Un-American
Activities
Committee**
member of the Communist party?
(note), 119:1

Houston, Samuel
(1793–1863)
Texas, 271:1
Houston Press
the 49th star twin-
kles, 10:7
**Howard, [Brig. Gen.]
James H.** *(d. 1995)*
I seen my duty,
551:7
Howard, Joseph Kinsey
(1906–1951)
Montana, 326:3
Howard, Sidney
(1891–1939)
frankly I don't give a
damn (note), 251:6
Howe, Edgar Watson
(1853–1937)
advice, 8:6
common sense, 118:3
credit v. money, 70:3
enemy, your, 165:9
guest, an ideal, 219:10
hope, 237:1
music, good, 51:6
neighbor, my, 351:1
scare, a good, 8:6
what people say be-
hind your back,
431:6
a woman, 539:2
Howe, Irving
(1920–1994)
critics, 50:4
Howe, Julia Ward
(1819–1910)
disarm, disarm, 366:1
glory of the coming of
the Lord (Battle
Hymn of the Re-
public), 212:2
in the beauty of the
lilies, 212:3
the sword, 511:5
Howe, Louis McHenry
(1871–1936)
politics, 393:4
Howells, William Dean
(1837–1920)
books, mortality of,
490:8
human beings, 238:6
the novel, 57:9
prose, simple, 54:10
slavery, the wrecks of,
466:2
stay longer in an
hour, 219:9
Howland, Bob *(fl. 1860)*
all quiet in Aurora,
86:6
Hruska, Roman L.
(b. 1904)
even if he is
mediocre, 305:8
Hubbard, Elbert [Green]
(1859–1915)
Albany, 85:8
conformists &
heretics, 150:10
[editor sees] that the
chaff is printed,
408:1
explain, never, 178:3
failure, 182:9, 10
Garcia, a message to,
3:3
God, 213:2
lawyer, 278:2
life is one damn thing
after another, 282:2
love, 287:12
loyalty, 291:3

Missouri but, be from
(note), 320:8–321
monkeys & monks,
457:2
nature, 335:12
one who thought he
was above me, 409:6
a pessimist & opti-
mist, 364:5
public opinion, 413:4
scars & God, 480:2
sins, 457:3
success, 478:7,8,9
temptations, 487:2
tyrants, 500:8
unsaid, leave a few
things, 455:10
wisdom, 535:5
wise man, 535:4
**Hubbard, Frank McKin-
ney ("Kin")**
(1868–1930)
classic music, 51:9
legislature, 121:5
poor, to be, 397:5
**Hubbard L[afayette]
Ron[ald]**
(1913–1986)
start your own reli-
gion, 430:15
**Hughes, [Chief Justice]
Charles Evans**
(1862–1948)
the Constitution, 127:5
the judiciary (note),
127:5
Hughes, Charles E., Jr.
(1889–1950)
president, cannot be
disturbed, 403:1
Hughes, Emmet John
(1920–1982)
he [the President]
must summon his
people to be with
him, 404:8
Hughes, Langston
(1902–1967)
Alabama, daybreak
in, 9:6
America, 23:6,7
a crumb from the ta-
bles of joy, 291:9
democracy, 144:11,
422:10
a dream deferred, 155:1
Harlem, 100:4 & note
I am a Negro (note),
424:7
railroad bridges, 447:6
a raisin in the sun,
434:12
soul, my, 464:8
yesterday, 370:3
Hunter,Jim ("Catfish")
(b. 1946)
thank you, God, 476:3
Hurston, Zora Neale
(1901–1960)
Ah ain't dead, 362:4
he was a glance from
God, 290:5
I am a dark rock
surged upon, 422:6
magic, 358:2a
poverty, 395:11
ships at a distance,
455:7
world, the, 547:3
Huston, John
(1906–1987) &
Maddow, Ben
(1909–1992)
crime, 134:7

**Hutchins, Robert May-
nard** *(1899–1977)*
exercise, the urge to,
379:11
Huxley, Aldous
(1894–1963)
City of Dreadful Joy,
95:1
nineteen suburbs,
94:7
Hyde, Henry J. *(b. 1924)*
new is always better?
(note), 194:1
stupid is forever,
194:1

Iacocca, Lee *(b. 1924)*
safety & business,
451:2
Ickes, Harold L[eClair]
(1874–1952)
government by crony,
217:8
cleaned his bureau
drawers (note),
252:3
thrown his diaper
into the ring (note),
252:3
Illinois Legislature
official language
of Illinois,
244:1
Ingalls, John James
(1833–1900)
[Delaware] has 3
counties, 142:3
government is force
(note), 391:2
the purification of
politics, 391:2
Inge, William
(1913–1973)
success, 478:14
**Ingersoll, Robert
G[reen]** *(1833–1899)*
devils v. gods,
149:8
god, an honest,
212:9
hope, 236:10
laughing, 272:8
life, 281:3
a plumed knight,
229:8
progress & infidels
(note), 412:1
religion, 430:3
rights, 438:6
a truth, 498:7
useful work, 544:5
Irving, John *(b. 1942)*
loving as a parent,
368:6
Irving, Washington
(1783–1859)
compliment[s] about
looking young,
360:6
dollar, the almighty,
323:1
Gotham, 97:10
history, 232:5
Italy, 331:3
Switzerland, 334:4
woman's heart,
537:4
woman's life, 573:3
Isherwood, Christopher
(1904–1986)
California, 73:11
landscape, prehistoric
(note), 450:11
security, 450:11

Jackson, Andrew
(1767–1845)
debt, national, 157:2
John Marshall, 481:1
law, arm & shield of
the, 273:9
monopoly & privi-
leges, 68:2
one man with
courage, 130:10
the president, 402:3
a situation of digni-
fied slavery, 401:2
surprise the enemy if
possible, 316:2
taxation, 484:8
they shall not sleep
on our soil, 523:3
Union, our Federal,
502:1 & note
we will all meet in
heaven, 270:6
Jackson, Jesse *(b. 1941)*
America, the genius
of, 24:8
America is like a
quilt (note), 24:7
common sense, 118:8
I am somebody, 425:7
rainbow, our nation is
a, 24:7
we can't just say no
(note), 516:1
Jackson, Joseph Henry
(1894–1955)
that work had better
be banned? 78:3
**Jackson, Helen [Maria]
Fiske Hunt**
(1830–1885)
A Century of Dis-
honor, 420:3
Jackson, Reggie (given
names, Reginald
Martinez) *(b. 1946)*
straw that stirs the
drink, 409:10
Jackson, Robert H.
(1892–1954)
fixed star in our con-
stitutional constel-
lation, 128:6
security, 451:1
**Jackson, Thomas
Jonathan
("Stonewall")**
(1824–1863)
death, my (note),
271:2
kill the brave ones,
114:3
let us cross over the
river, 271:2
surprise the enemy,
316:2
Jacobs, Jane *(b. 1916)*
cities, 84:11, 85:4
Jacobs, Joe *(1896–1940)*
should have stood in
bed, 474:2
wuz robbed, 473:4
James, Henry
(1843–1916)
art & economy, 47:7
art & life, 46:8,9
Baltimore, 87:2
cats and monkeys,
337:7
[Concord] the biggest
little place, 92:3
[Connecticut] heart of
New England, 123:1
criticize, to (note),
49:4

distinguished thing, 139:6
an Englishman, 329:9
excess, do not regret a single, 177:6
fact, futility of a, 182:1
a feminine age, 541:8
Florence, 109:3
Florida, 190:5
human nature, 238:8
Irish, the, 419:5
patriotism begins at home, 373:4
people on whom nothing is lost, 516:4
Philadelphia, 102:7
psychological, continuously (note), 57:9
reason, a psychological, 427:9
reviewing v. criticism, 49:4
Rome, 110:9
summer afternoon, 344:12
the traveller, 494:5

James, William
(1842–1910)
act as if there were a God, 174:10
bitch-goddess success, 478:5
consciousness—one unbroken stream, 317:8
difference between one man and another, 150:9
fates, our own, 188:1
God, evidence for, 212:11
habit, 221:2
ideals, 243:2
indecision, 245:8
life is worth living, 281:6
the mathematician & the poet, 443:10
militarism, 313:3
minds & reality (note), 57:9
minds so helpless, 193:5
moral equivalent of war, 452:6
mystery of things, the ultimate, 326:8
philosophy, 379:3
poverty, 395:6
the present moment, 399:13
psychology, 445:6
publishers are demons, 303:1
religion, 430:4,5
success, the bitch-goddess, 478:5
the true & the right, 179:7
truth, 498:12
war, moral equivalent of, 366:2
wise, the art of being, 535:1

Janis, Sidney
(1896–1989)
don't read the review, 50:3

Jarrell, Randall
(1914–1965)
washed me out of the turret, 553:3

Jefferson, Joseph
(1829–1905)
Louisiana, 286:1

Jefferson, Thomas
(1743–1826)
all men are created equal, 140:3
alliances, entangling, 194:5
angry, when (note), 42:5
aristocracy, natural, 162:10
banking establishments, 67:11
believe, to, 183:6
a bill of rights, 124:6
blood of patriots & tyrants, 200:3
books, 65:2
censure, pain of, 135:1
the clergy & New England, 352:2
coercion, [of] opinion, 77:6
Connecticut, 122:6,7
country, would go to hell for my, 371:2
debt, perpetual, 157:1
Declaration of Independence, 140:3
delay, 143:4
difference of opinion, 501:6
doing, always, 1:2
Dominion, the good Old, 513:2
duty, aim to do your, 432:8
the earth is given as a common stock, 166:9
eaten too little, we never repent of having, 191:2
an editor & his paper (note), 405:7
error & truth, 77:7
errs with integrity, 524:4
eternal vigilance & liberty (note), 200:8
evils which have never happened, 43:1
flatter, let those who, 190:1
force, 511:4
Fourth? is it the, 246:6, 270:3
freedom of the press, 405:3
a free press, 405:8
future, dreams of the, 205:5
gardener, I am but a young, 341:1
gaming (note), 207:2
gods, twenty, 428:10
government, good, 216:2
government, the institution of (note), 216:2
government, legitimate powers of, 215:4
government, resistance to, 432:3
government, wise and frugal, 215:10
government & being honest, 215:8

government & the press, 405:5
government of others, 216:1
government v. liberty, 215:7
happiness, 222:4
here was buried Thomas Jefferson, 170:3
he who believes nothing, 459:1
history, a morsel of, 232:4
home, 234:4
the Indian equal to the white man, 417:1
I tremble for my country, 459:5
labor in the earth, those who, 185:5
laws, execution of, 273:7
lawyers [in Congress], 120:3
liberties, 200:2
liberty, 199:5, 200:3
lie once, to tell a, 152:4
live honestly, 235:8
live too long, 360:5
machines, our, 138:7
majority, the will of, 296:1
medical tyros, 153:4
merchants love nobody, 67:10
militia, 312:3
military force, a large, 312:2
Napoleon (note), 194:5
a newspaper, 405:7 & note
newspapers & government, 405:4
no one can replace him (note), 198:8
[Pennsylvania:] cradle of toleration, 376:6
the people & liberty, 376:10
people, will of the, 377:1
pleasure & pain, 380:4
power, the exercise of, 396:8
[presidency:] to retire from, 400:11
press, free, 405:5,8
press, freedom of the, 405:3
pride, cost of, 409:4
a public trust, 389:5
read, ever man able to, 159:7
reason, every man's own, 427:7
rebellion, a little, 433:9
resistance to government, 432:3
rights, a bill of, 438:4
rights, inalienable, 140:3
second office of the land, 508:6
society, our, 513:1
soldier, every citizen [should] be a, 312:4
speeches measured by the hour, 66:14

spirit of '76, 41:1
a splendid misery, 400:10
steady habits, 122:7
Techas [Texas], the province of, 487:10
those who labor in the earth, 185:5
time, a fullness of, 450:1
tranquility & old age, 360:4 & note
[traveling] makes men wiser but, 493:10
a truth, 497:5
tyranny over the mind of man, 500:3
tyrants, resistance to, 499:11
Union, this, 501:6
Virginia, 512:6
walking, 379:8
Washington, George, 525:2
we are all Republicans & Federalists, 501:6
the world's best hope (note), 216:1

John of the Cross, [Saint] *(1542–1591)*
dark night of the soul (note), 147:7

Johnson, Diane
(b. 1934)
the enraged, 42:9

Johnson, Dorothy
(1905–1984)
myth bigger than the man, 408:8

Johnson, Helene
(1906–1995)
little brown boy, 557:2

Johnson, James Weldon
(1871–1938)
Lift Evr'y Voice, 51:4
New York, 99:3

Johnson, Hiram
(1866–1945)
this generation, 208:6
war & truth, 520:5

Johnson, Lyndon B[aines]
(1908–1973)
American boys & Asian boys, 509:5 & note
broadcasters, 304:9
conservation (note), 167:5
great society, 36:6
light at the end of tunnel, 510:2
poverty, war on, 36:5
a present, give a man, 298:7
a president's hardest task, 404:6
the presidency, 404:5
reason together, let us, 427:11
the scars of centuries, 424:4
television writes on the wind, 304:8

Johnson, Philander Chase *(1866–1939)*
courts & the Constitution, 127:4
high position, 231:8

Johnson, Philander
Chase (*cont.*)
a party platform, 392:1
politician, a true,
392:3
politics, 391:8, 392:2
when to forget things,
131:5
the worst is yet to
come, 364:2
Johnson, Richard
M[entor]
(1780–1850)
heretical sentiments,
429:6
Johnson, Samuel
(1709–1784)
American, love all
mankind except an,
16:6
war & truth (note),
520:5
Jolson, Al *(1886–1950)*
Harding, 385:5
you ain't heard
nothin' yet, 206:1
Jones, John Paul
(1747–1792)
any ship that does not
sail *fast*, 454:5
honor, my, 236:1
I have not yet begun
to fight, 40:3
navy, a respectable,
311:7
Jones, Mother [given
forenames, Mary
Harris] *(1830–1930)*
living, fight like hell
for the, 282:4
Jones, T.A.D. [Thomas
Albert Dwight]
(1887–1957)
play football against
Harvard, 472:4
Jong, Erica *(b. 1942)*
city of mirrors
[Venice], 111:4
solitude is un-Ameri-
can, 24:5
Jonson, Ben
(c. 1573–1637)
almighty gold (note),
323:1
Joseph the Younger
[Chief] *(1840–1904)*
equal rights, 174:3
I will fight no more,
432:1
peace v. war, 375:4
talk and talk, 483:5
words (note), 483:5
Josselyn, John
(1638–1675)
Maine, people of,
294:9
sleep, 155:4
Jowett, Benjamin
(1873–1893)
the way to get things
done (note), 71:4
Judd, Naomi *(b. 1946)*
experience, 180:4
Juet, Robert *(fl. 1609)*
[New York:] the lands
were pleasant, 355:3

Kaiser, Henry J.
(1882–1967)
problems, 411:2
Kamehameha I
(c. 1738–1819)
honor they God,
398:9

Kaufman, George S.
(1889–1961)
doctor I want, 154:2
epitaph for a waiter
(note), 173:2
over my dead body!
173:8
satire, 55:7
Kazin, Alfred *(b. 1915)*
Hollywood, 95:11
Keats, John *(b. 1920)*
the automobile, 448:5
Keeler, William ("Wee
Willie") *(1872–1925)*
hit 'em where they
ain't, 470:9
Keillor, Garrison
(b. 1942)
Lake Wobegon, 319:1
Keller, Helen [Adams]
(1880–1968)
education & toler-
ance, 493:8
literature, 66:2
king & slave, 174:4
Kelly, J. W.
slide, Kelly, 470:7
Kelly, Walt *(1913–1973)*
enemy is us, 168:13,
239:6
Kempton, Murray
(b. 1918)
Hollywood, 95:8
Kendall, Amos
(1789–1869)
those who produce all
wealth, 75:2
Kennan, George
(1845–1924)
Siberia, 333:1
Kennan, George F.
(b. 1904)
Siberia, 333:1
the truth—a poor
competitor (note),
202:8
Kennedy, Florynce
(b. 1916)
if men could get preg-
nant, 542:5
Kennedy, John Fitzger-
ald *(1917–1963)*
ask not what your
country can do for
you, 452:7
Berliner, Ich bin ein,
35:5
change is the law of
life, 80:2
communism, 119:5
crises, great, 496:5
crisis, the word, 496:7
evil, the triumph of
(note), 176:10
the farmer, 186:5
a fence (note), 153:1
forgive, but, 198:6
free, nation will not
be fully, 202:5
Frontier, A New,
387:10
geography has made
us neighbors, 329:3
God's work, 545:9
hemisphere, this
(note), 194:6
an idea lives on,
243:12
Jefferson, 256:1
knowledge, 264:2
life is unfair, 283:2
the many who are
poor, the few who
are rich, 159:4

materially rich &
spiritually poor,
47:4
negotiate, never fear
to, 197:2
a new frontier,
387:10–388
party loyalty, 394:6
peace, to keep the,
376:3
peace is a process,
376:4
planet, vulnerability
of our, 168:10
poetry, 54:3
political action, 394:7
poor, the many who
are, 159:4
pray to be stronger
men, 398:8
president, function
and responsibility,
404:3
privileges & obliga-
tions, 433:6
problems, our, 411:3
progress, 412:4
revolution, peaceful,
435:1
scientists, 443:4
silent majority (note),
296:11–297
the time to repair the
roof, 450:4
torch passed to a new
generation, 209:1
under-exercised as a
nation, 380:2
victory & defeat,
533:6
Washington [D.C.],
108:10
work, God's, 545:9
Kennedy, Joseph Patrick
(1888–1969)
don't get mad, get
even, 42:7
Kennedy, Robert F.
(1925–1968)
courage & a lawyer,
278:8
one fifth of the people
are against every-
thing, 378:6
Kent, Corita
a painting, 57:6
Kerner, Otto, Jr.
(1908–1976)
two societies, one
black, one white,
425:2
Kerouac, Jack
(1922–1969)
the end of a conti-
nent, 74:2
the mad ones, 294:3
to pray for everyone,
398:7
Kerr, Clark *(b. 1911)*
problems on campus,
162:1
Kerr, Jean *(b. 1923)*
beauty, 62:2
if you can keep your
head, 496:6
Kerry, [Sen.] John F.
(b. 1943)
the war the soldiers
tried to stop,
511:6
Kesselring, Joseph
(1902–1967)
insanity runs in my
family, 293:7

Key, Francis Scott
(1779–1843)
in God is our trust
(note under U.S.
Motto)
oh, say, can you see?,
371:4
Keynes, John Maynard
(1883–1946)
better to be approxi-
mately right (note),
263:4
Khrushchev, Nikita
Sergeyevich
(1894–1971)
no greenery [in New
York], 101:3
Kilmer, Joyce
(1886–1918)
a tree, 342:5,6
dead in their youthful
prime, 549:4
Kincaid, Jamaica
(b. 1945)
Americans & mem-
ory, 25:2
Kiner, Ralph *(b. 1922)*
how you place the
blame, 178:8
King, Albert
(1923–1992)
bad luck, 292:1
King, B.B. *(b. 1923)*
nobody loves me,
288:12
King, Clarence
(1842–1901)
Californian
scoundrels, 73:2
King, [Adm.] Ernest J.
(1878–1956)
difficulties, 496:2
don't tell them a
thing, 408:4
King, Martin Luther, Jr.
(1929–1968)
bitterness & hatred,
35:7
character, the content
of their, 424:3
church, 431:3
democracy, make real
the promises of,
35:6
dream, I have a,
424:2,3
evil, 176:10
free at last, 36:4
freedom, 202:6
freedom ring, let, 36:4
God's will, I just want
to do, 214:1
hate, 225:7
hatred & love, 288:10
I have a dream, 36:2,3
I've seen the
promised land,
272:4
injustice, 248:3
I was a drum major
for justice, 173:9
judicial decrees, 276:5
justice rolls down like
waters, 36:1
military defense, 315:4
nonviolence, 366:4
now is the time, 35:6
philanthropy, 81:1
play it real pretty for
me (note), 272:4
progress, 411:4
respect for the law,
276:6
right, to do, 437:12

scientific power &
spiritual power,
448:7
shallow understand-
ing, 493:9
soul force, 35:7
violence, 511:9
we are not satisfied,
258:9
when the cup of en-
durance runs over,
432:7
King, Stoddard
(1889–1933)
a long, long trail,
154:7
**Kinross, Lord (John
Patrick Douglas
Balfour)** *(1904–1976)*
Texas, 488:7
Kinsella, W. P. *(b. 1935)*
if you build it, he will
come, 184:9
Iowa, 254:3
Kipling, Rudyard
(1865–1936)
American meals, 191:4
a Bostonian, 87:9
Chicago, 90:3
Clemens, the great
(note), 181:7–182
a gulf [in Wyoming],
554:5
if you can keep your
head (note), 496:6
Pennsylvania, 376:8
Portland, 104:3
San Francisco,
106:1,2
scenery—"ongodly"
(note), 554:5
we're poor little
lambs who've lost
our way, 456:11
the White Man's bur-
den, 469:3
Kirstein, Lincoln
(1907–1995)
true originality, 48:4
Kissinger, Henry
(b. 1923)
Americans admire the
cowboy, 529:6
power, 397:7
Knight, C. L. *(d. 1933)*
a human cash-register
editor (note), 406:5
Knight, Sarah Kemble
(1666–1727)
diligent in this place
[Connecticut],
122:4
**Knott, [Rep.] J[ames]
Proctor** *(1830–1911)*
Duluth, 93:3,4
Knowles, John
(1926–1979)
we West Virginians,
529:10
Koch, Howard See un-
der Epstein, Julius J.
Kosslyn, Stephen
the mind, 318:10
Kovacs, Ernie
(1919–1962)
[television] neither
rare nor well done,
304:1
Kronenberger, Louis
(b. 1904)
advertising copy, 7:2
Krutch, Joseph Wood
(1893–1970)
August, 346:11

New England & Feb-
ruary, 352:10
Kuralt, Charles *(b. 1934)*
Alaska's forests,
10:10
[Arizona:] a tough
country, 44:10
breakfast in East Ten-
nessee, 487:8
[Key West:] a speck of
rock, 190:10
the interstate high-
way system, 495:6
Minnesotans, 319:2,3
New Mexico, 354:9
New Orleans, 97:4
New York, 101:9
Vermont, 508:3

**Lafayette, Marie Joseph
Paul Yves Roch
Gilbert du Mooiter,
Marquis de**
(1757–1834)
Washington [D.C.],
107:5
**La Guardia, Fiorello
Henry** *(1882–1947)*
free lunch (note),
158:2
this great office,
231:11
when I make a mis-
take, 321:3
Lampell, Millard
(b. 1919)
a lonesome train,
285:3
Lampton, William J.
Kentucky, 261:6
Lance, Bert *(b. 1931)*
if it ain't broke, 218:5
Lanchester, Elsa
(1902–1986)
butter wouldn't melt,
252:1
Land, Edwin Herbert
(1909–1991)
the bottom line, 71:3
Lane, Mark *(b. 1927)*
rush to judgment,
285:10
Lane, [Sir] Ralph
(1530–1603)
Virginia, 512:1
Langer, Suzanne K.
(1895–1985)
art, 47:5
Langley, Noel *(b. 1911),*
with Ryerson, Flo-
rence, and Wolfe,
Edgar Allan
I'll get you, my pretty,
137:3
not in Kansas any-
more, 260:5
**Lardner, Ring[old
Wilmer]**
(1885–1933)
two can live cheaper
then one, 299:9
Lauder, Leonard
(b. 1933)
experience & money,
71:5
**Lawrence, D[avid] H[er-
bert]** *(1885–1930)*
America, 22:2
the essential Ameri-
can soul, 22:1
Lawrence, James
(1781–1813)
don't give up the ship
1812, 522:11

Lazarus, Emma
(1849–1887)
give me your tired,
your poor, 29:5
Leary, Timothy
(1920–1996)
tune in, turn on, drop
out, 279:6
Lease, Mary [Elizabeth]
(1853–1933) not
Mary Ellen
less corn, more hell,
260:2
Le Corbusier [given
name, Charles
Edouard Jeanneret-
Gris] *(1887–1965)*
New York, 100:8
Lee, Alexander *(c. 1835)*
ballad writer
I'll be no submissive
wife, 298:11
Lee, Gypsy Rose [born,
Rose Louise Hov-
ick] *(1914–1970)*
my mind (note),
224:9
worth doing slowly,
224:9
Lee, [Nellie] Harper
(b. 1926)
conscience, 123:7
a court & its jury,
257:6
Lee, Richard Henry
(1732–1794)
colonies ought to be
free, 140:2
Lee, Robert E[dward]
(1807–1870)
defending a long line,
316:3
a union that can only
be maintained by
swords, 502:5
history, 232:8,9
a soldier has a hard
life, 312:8
strike the tent, 271:3
Virginia, you can
work for, 513:3
war, 519:3
Lebowitz, Fran *(b. 1950)*
life, 283:7
**Lee, Henry ("Light
Horse Harry")**
(1756–1818)
first in the hearts of
his countrymen,
524:6
Leland, Lilian
a tree in California,
73:5
Leonard, Elmore
(b. 1925)
keeping his mouth
shut, 455:13
work, 545:10
Leopold, Aldo
(1886–1948)
conservation, 168:5
cranes, 339:6
land, 168:4
March & geese, 347:1
& note
sportsmanship,
474:5
wilderness & civiliza-
tion, 531:2
Lerner, Alan Jay
(1918–1986)
why can't a woman
be more like a man,
307:1

**Leslie, (John Randolph)
Shane (Sir) Baronet**
(1885–1971)
[Denver:] you can live
without much
lungs, 92:7
Le Sueur, Meridel
(b. 1900)
the history of an op-
pressed people,
423:4
Levant, Oscar
(1906–1972)
Hollywood, 95:7
Levine, Joseph E.
(1905–1987)
advertising (note),
377:5
Lewis, Alfred Henry
(c. 1858–1914)
the people and their
beer, 12:4
Lewis, C[live] S[taples]
(1898–1963)
a thousand points of
light (note), 24:9
Lewis, John
a nonviolent revolu-
tion (note), 34:3
Lewis, John L[lewellyn]
(1880–1969)
evil old man named
Garner, 251:7
Lewis, Sam[uel M.]
(1883–1959) &
Young, Joe
(1889–1939)
Paree, 110:2
Lewis, Sinclair
(1885–1951)
Babbitt, George F.,
310:3
Babbitt & his motor
car, 447:2
just get along, 501:4
love, 287:13
professors & litera-
ture, 47:10
**Liberace, [Wladziu
Valentino]**
(1919–1987)
cried all the way to
the bank, 50:2
Liberty Bell
proclaim liberty
throughout the
land, 199:2
**Liebling, A[bbot]
J[oseph]** *(1904–1963)*
freedom the press,
408:7
newspapers & news,
408:6
**Liliuokalani, Lydia
Kamekeha**
(1838–1917)
the Hawaiian people,
226:3
Lincoln, Abraham
(1809–1865)
the Almighty, 212:4
ballot v. bullet, 144:4
blockhead enough to
have me, 299:1
capital & labor, 75:6
character is like a
tree, 514:11
common-looking peo-
ple, 64:4
conservatism,
390:6
country belongs to
the people, 19:3
drinkers (note), 11:5

Lincoln, Abraham
   (cont.)
duty, do our, 514:10
earth, last best hope
   of, 503:2
events have con-
   trolled me, 187:10
the Father of Waters,
   114:7
fool all the people
fourscore and seven
   years ago, 210:3
free, forever, 461:4
free, shall be, 114:4
freedom, those who
   deny, 201:1
freedom to the slave,
   461:5
genius, towering,
   209:3
Gettysburg Address,
   210:3
God, [North & South]
   pray to the same,
   397:13
govern another man,
   to, 217:1
government of the
   people, 210:3
Grant & whiskey,
   11:5
he fights, 114:1
Hell with a dome,
   120:4
history, we cannot es-
   cape, 232:7
honest, resolve to be,
   277:5
horses in midstream,
   79:4
a house divided, 502:4
if destruction be our
   lot, 18:1
if McClellan is not
   using the army,
   113:5
juries, 256:11
I shall try to correct
   errors, 79:3
Know-Nothings
   (note), 383:1
labor & capital, 75:6
laborers can strike,
   75:5
the last best hope of
   earth, 461:5
let me go down
   linked with the
   truth (note), 502:4
little woman who
   started this great
   war (note), 460:3
malice toward none,
   116:3
marrying, never again
   to think of, 299:1
memory, mystic
   chords of, 375:1
military giant, some
   trans-Atlantic
   (note), 18:1
moral principle v. pe-
   cuniary interest,
   323:6
Negro, all I ask for
   the, 419:1
patriotic men, 373:1
people, fool all the,
   377:5
parting, this, 368:9
past & present,
   399:11
people, justice of the,
   377:4

prayers of both could
   not be answered,
   397:13 & 212:4
   (note)
public opinion, 412:9
public sentiment
   (note), 412:9–413
reason fled, 293:2
revolutions do not go
   backward, 434:9
right makes might,
   514:10
slave, as I would not
   be a, 461:2
slavery, 460:4
thanksgiving, a day
   of, 489:4
too big to cry, 532:2
Union, the, 375:1
the Union & slavery,
   461:3
a universal feeling
   (note), 412:9
will, 531:8
Lindbergh, Anne Mor-
   row (b. 1906)
him that I love, 291:1
husband & marriage,
   300:6
Lindbergh, Charles
   A[ugustus]
   (1902–1974)
earth, 168:3
pioneers (note), 4:6
strange unmortal
   space, 4:6
Lindsay, Howard
   (1889–1968)
an optimist, 364:8
Lindsay, Vachel
   (1879–1931)
Andrew Jackson,
   255:3
Buffalo & Niagara,
   88:9
California, 73:8
the moon, 340:2
the prairie lawyer,
   285:1
the spring, 345:1
[Springfield:] city of
   my discontent,
   107:1
Lippmann, Walter
   (1889–1974)
government, 217:5
ideas are immortal,
   243:7
leader, a great, 231:13
wars & bombing,
   316:6
Livingston, Robert R.
   (1746–1813)
the noblest work of
   our lives, 27:1
Lloyd, Henry Demarest
   (1847–1903)
corporations, 69:5
monopoly, 69:4
Locke, Alain [Leroy]
   (1886–1954)
Harlem, 99:5
Locke, John
   (1632–1704)
all the world was
   America, 15:1
Loeb, Frances Lehman
   (1906–1996)
never going to be
   richest person in
   the cemetery, 81:2
Lofland, John
   (1798–1849)
Delaware, 142:2

Logan, [Gen.] John A.
if I don't burn you, I'll
   be damned (note),
   467:2
Logau, Friedrich von
   (1604–1655)
God, the mills of,
   212:8
Lombardi, Vince[nt T.]
   (1913–1970)
football, 475:3
winning, 533:5
London, Jack [given
   names, John Grif-
   fith] (1876–1916)
Alaska, 10:5
Aloha, 226:4
Hawaii, 226:5
a scab, 76:5, 250:6
to live, not to exist,
   281:12
Long, Earl Kemp
   (1895–1960)
a wink and a nod,
   131:7
Long, Huey Pierce
   (1893–1935)
the breaks, 363:9
every man a king,
   386:6
plunder & politics,
   393:5
share our wealth,
   386:7
Washington [D.C.],
   108:5
your tears have lasted
   for generations,
   285:6
Long, [Maj.] Stephen H.
   (1784–1864)
[Nebraska:] unfit for
   cultivation, 349:6
Long, [Sen.] Russell
   (b. 1918)
congressman's first
   obligation, 121:8
Longfellow, Henry
   Wadsworth
   (1807–1882)
age is opportunity,
   360:9
anvil or hammer,
   237:10
Arabs, fold their tents
   like the, 50:13
arrow in the air
   (note), 203:1
art, 46:4–6
books, 65:12
Boston, a solid man
   of, 87:8
a boy's will, 556:2
the cares that infest
   the day, 347:8
children's hour, 81:11
Christmas day, 83:5
[Cincinnati:] Queen
   of the West, 91:4
dawn, 363:13
day is done & dark-
   ness falls, 347:7
the dead remain, 171:1
death, exodus of,
   139:1
death on reef of Nor-
   man's woe, 454:8
delay, do not, 143:6
fate of a nation was
   riding, 42:2
footprints in the
   sands of time, 219:1
the forest primeval,
   530:6

friend, in the heart of
   a, 203:1
gift to each, 150:6
Gitche Gumee, 418:8
God, the mills of,
   212:8
girl who had a little
   curl, 82:2
hard words & a child,
   81:9
the heart, 80:6, 228:4,
   6
holidays, the holiest
   of, 228:6
John Brown (note),
   28:2
king, once more a,
   460:2
learn to labor, 2:1
a lady with a lamp,
   537:10
life, real and earnest,
   280:2
life—some rain must
   fall, 495:7
love, 268:8
manners, stately, 298:3
May, 344:2
men that women
   marry, 299:6
midnight ride of Paul
   Revere, 41:4
morning, 363:12
music, night shall be
   filled with, 50:13
music & poetry, 50:12
night, sleepless
   watches of, 348:2
one if by land, 42:1
ourselves, 451:9
past & present & fu-
   ture, 491:3
patient endurance,
   370:11
patter of little feet,
   82:1
Paul Revere, 41:4
Plymouth Rock,
   301:10
[Portland, Me.:] the
   beautiful town,
   104:1
Queen of the West
   [Cincinnati], 91:4
rain, how beautiful is
   the, 348:9
sail on, O ship of
   state, 18:4
ships & the sea, 455:2
ships that pass in the
   night, 280:10
silences, three, 455:8
singers, God sent his,
   51:1
smithy, the village,
   543:3
smoothly the
   ploughshare runs,
   285:5
something attempted
   & done, 2:3
sorrow & silence,
   165:4
sorrow & suffering,
   165:6
sorrows, secret, 463:9
the soul, 280:2
so unto the man is
   woman, 541:3
spring, 343:10, 344:3
stars, the lovely,
   339:12
suffer and be strong,
   479:9

things are not what
they seem, 426:4
time, 491:11
truth, 428:3
Union, O, 502:2
union, 503:4
up and doing, 2:1
useless is, nothing,
504:9
[Venice:] white swan
of cities, 111:11
vessel, a goodly,
454:10
why don't you speak
for yourself?, 289:5
the winds, 348:8
womanhood, heroic,
537:10
worth the wooing
(note), 289:5
youth, the thoughts
of, 556:2
**Longworth, Alice Roose-
velt** *(1884–1979)*
Harding, 224:6
you can't make a
soufflé rise twice
(note), 252:3
if you can't say any-
thing good, 130:3
man on the wedding
cake, 252:3
never trust a man
who, 536:4
two-thirds mush,
438:9
weaned on a pickle
(note), 484:1
youth, eternal, 557:5
Louis, Joe [given name,
Joseph Louis Bor-
row] *(1914–1981)*
can run/can't hide,
137:4
Lother, George
faster than a speeding
bullet, 230:6
**Lovecraft, H[oward]
P[hillips]**
(1890–1937)
Providence [R. I.],
104:4
Lovell, James A., Jr.
(b. 1928)
we've had a problem,
37:2
Lowell, Amy
(1874–1925)
war & patterns, 520:3
youth & maturity,
8:11
Lowell, James Russell
(1819–1891)
airly [early], git up,
347:9
the birch, 341:5
charity, 80:7
dunce, well-meaning,
193:2
each day the world is
born anew, 399:12
endurance & pa-
tience, 165:3
experience, 179:10,
416:3
facts, 181:5
fallen and the weak,
speak for the,
433:1
forgive, yet, 198:2
Italy, 331:4
June, a day in, 343:11
nobleness, 515:1 &
note

the pine, 341:6
princerple & interest,
68:10
review, can surely,
49:1
right, in the, 437:4
rights, 438:5
say nothin', 483:4
summer, lavish (note),
343:11
taxed for a corner,
485:2
toil, horny hands of,
543:4
truth forever on the
scaffold, 500:4
a weed & a flower,
341:8
who says it best,
415:11
**Lowell, Robert [Trail
Spence]**
(1917–1977)
hell, I myself am,
451:12
light at the end of the
tunnel (note),
510:12
my mind's not right,
294:4
spiders marching
through air, 130:8
this pioneer democ-
racy [Venezuela],
334:9
Lucas, George *(b. 1945)*
may the force be with
you, 358:4
Luce, Clare Boothe
(1903–1987)
a woman's best pro-
tection, 540:1
**Luciano, Salvatore
"Lucky"**
(1896–1962)
to be a crumb, 409:7
Lumet, Sidney *(b. 1924)*
style, 55:2
Lynd, Robert S.
(1892–1970) &
Helen Merrell
(1896–1982)
Middletown, 96:9–11
Lytle, Andrew [Nelson]
(1902–1995)
family, 185:4

MacArthur, Charles
(1895–1956)
emeralds, 290:3
**MacArthur, [Gen.] Dou-
glas** *(1880–1964)*
I have returned, 552:7
I shall return, 551:3
old soldiers, 33:3
opportunity, 363:8
so much with so lit-
tle, 551:4
victory, no substitute
for, 264:6
war, 522:1,2,4
MacDonald, Dwight
(1906–1982)
the poor, 396:2
MacDonald, John D.
(1916–1986)
life, 282:14
yesterday & tomor-
row & todays,
492:10
MacDonald, [John] Ross
[born Kenneth Mil-
lar] *(1915–1983)*
California, 73:13

whose troubles are
worse than your
own (note), 536:6
MacKay, Charles
(1814–1889)
[Columbia, S.C.] an
air of neatness, 92:1
[Memphis:] a dreary
town, 96:1
MacLeish, Archibald
(1892–1982)
a poem, 53:6
Macon, Nathaniel
(1758–1837)
where he can hear his
neighbor's dog bark,
462:7
Maddow, Ben. See un-
der Huston, John
Madison, James
(1751–1836)
a benefactor of hu-
man kind, 255:4
Constitution & Bill of
Rights (note), 124:5
different opinions,
150:4
government, 215:6
noxious branches [of
the press], 406:6
property, 119:8
Russia, 332:9
states, union of these,
17:5
Mad Magazine
me worry? 43:4
**Mahan, [Capt.] Alfred
T[hayer]**
(1840–1914)
Americans must be-
gin to look out-
ward, 20:2
beating, a good, 532:3
defeat & success,
532:4
Mailer, Norman
(b. 1923)
Chicago, 90:11,12
Chicago [& other
cities], 85:3
a hero, 231:3
hip or square, 248:1
Miami Beach, 96:4
a newspaper & a
story, 408:9
television, 304:10
the working class,
546:1
Malcolm X [given
name, Malcolm Lit-
tle] *(1925–1965)*
be peaceful, 511:7
born in America with
a black skin, 423:9
by any means neces-
sary, 424:5
change & violence
(note), 424:5
education, 162:4
New York & Harlem,
101:6
patriotism, 374:6
power, 397:5
Plymouth Rock, 424:4
revolution, 435:2,3
send him to the
cemetery, 511:7
**Mankiewicz, Herman
J[acob]** *(1897–1953)*
disease you don't look
forward to being
cured of, 362:7
millions to be made
out here, 95:2

Rosebud, 271:10,
428:7
there but for the grace
of God goes God,
251:2
**Mankiewicz, Joseph
L[eo]** *(b. 1909)*
ants to a picnic, 49:7
fasten your seat belts,
496:4
Mann, Horace
(1796–1859)
education, 160:3
some victory for hu-
manity, 238:5
Mannes, Marya
(1904–1990)
people on horses,
339:7
Mansfield, Katherine
(1888–1923)
act for yourself, 3:7
**Mantle, Mickey
[Charles]**
(1931–1995)
if I knew I was going
to live this long
(note), 227:10
Marcy, William Learned
(1786–1857)
victors & spoils,
389:6
Marion, Frances
(1886–1973)
San Juan Capistrano,
73:12
Markham, Edwin
(1852–1940)
the sea, 343:1
when he [Lincoln]
fell, 284:7
**Marquis, Don[ald
Robert Perry]**
(1878–1937)
civilization, 112:1
dance mehitabel
dance, 361:7
each generation
wastes more of the
future, 208:5
the earth, 167:8,
168:1
the hypocrite, 241:2
an idea, 243:5
integrity, 515:7
jocosity, coarse,
240:4
kittens, all these,
367:6
old age, disorderly,
361:8
an optimist, 364:4
a pessimist (note),
364:5
poetry, publishing a
volume of, 53:2
procrastination, 143:7
rich through hard
work, 324:6
time when a man is,
309:9
think, really make
them, 318:1
toujours gai, archy,
222:11
unlucky, so, 291:10
**Marryat, [Capt.] Freder-
ick** *(1792–1848)*
Americans & drink,
11:1
language in America,
266:4
"leg" & "limb"
(note), 266:4

Marsh, George Perkins
(1801–1882)
man & nature, 238:4
Marshall, John
(1755–1835)
constitution, 126:2,3
corn & colonels
   (note), 261:6
judicial distinction,
   the acme of, 256:2
tax, the power to,
   484:7
Marshall, Thomas Riley
(1854–1925)
a good five-cent cigar,
   493:7
Indiana, 247:2
the Vice President,
   508:8
Marshall, Thurgood
(1908–1993)
First Amendment,
   129:2
I'm getting old, 363:4
judges & the people,
   256:8
a white snake or a
   black snake, 425:8
Marshalov, Boris
(1902–1967)
Congress, 122:1
Marshman, D. M., Jr.
See under Brackett,
   Charles
Martin, Abe. See Hub-
   bard, Frank McKin-
   ney
Martin, Billy
(1928–1989)
a good loser (note),
   473:3
Martin, Graham A.
(1912–1990)
we simply cut and
   ran, 511:3
Martineau, Harriet
(1802–1876)
Albany, 85:6
Michigan, 308:5
Vermont, 507:2
Marx, Chico (given first
   name, Leonard)
(1886–1961)
whispering in her
   mouth, 178:4
Marx, Groucho [Julius
   Henry] *(1895–1977)*
bigamy, 300:3
club that would ac-
   cept me, 164:1
money, 325:8
posterity, 208:11
a poultry matter,
   324:7
Marx, Harpo [Adolph]
(1888–1964)
like the other side of
   the moon, 109:8
Marx, Karl *(1818–1883)*
classes, struggle be-
   tween (note), 75:2
Mason, Donald F.
(b. 1913)
sighted sub, 550:9
Mason, George
(1725–1792)
press, freedom of the,
   405:1
Masters, Edgar Lee
(1869–1950)
immortality, 245:5
Mather, Cotton
(1663–1728)
the devil, 149:6

New Englanders, 352:1
quarrels & prayers,
   43:8
stoop, 535:6
Mather, Increase
(1639–1723)
thunder, 348:6
Matlovich, Leonard
the military, 315:5
Mauldin, Bill [given
   names, William
   Henry] *(b. 1921)*
an infantryman,
   314:2
Maxwell, Elsa
(1883–1963)
cocktail parties, 237:7
mediocrity, 305:5
Maxwell, William
(b. 1908)
your reader is bright,
   59:1
**McAdoo, [Sen.] William
   G[ibbs]** *(1863–1941)*
[Harding's] speeches,
   224:2
**McAuliffe, [Gen.] An-
   thony** *(1898–1975)*
Nuts!, 553:1
**McBride, Mary Mar-
   garet** *(1899–1976)*
young girls in New
   York, 101:2
**McCain, [Commander]
   John S., Jr.**
(1911–1981)
fleets, 315:3
**McCallister, [Samuel]
   Ward** *(1827–1895)*
a dinner invitation,
   219:8
400 people in New
   York society, 163:4
**McCarthy, [Sen.] Joseph
   [Raymond]**
(1908–1957)
list of 205 members
   of the Communist
   Party, 33:2
**McCarthy, Mary
   [Therese]**
(1912–1989)
sex & love, 454:1
Venice, 111:3
violence, 511:6
**McClellan, [Gen.]
   George B[rinton]**
(1826–1885)
all quiet, 113:1
McCloy, Helen *(b. 1904)*
habit, 221:8
McCord, David *(b. 1897)*
God caught his eye,
   173:2
McCoy, Horace
(1897–1955)
they shoot horses,
   133:8
winner, only one,
   532:9
McCullough, David
(b. 1933)
history, 233:12
McDaniel, Hattie
(1895–1952)
rather play a maid
   than be one, 55:8
McFee, William (given
   name, Morley Pun-
   shon) *(1881–1966)*
fate, 188:3
McGinley, Phyllis
(1905–1977)
the optimist, 364:7

**McGuffey, William
   [Holmes]**
(1800–1873)
with the morning
   rise, 347:6
McKinley, William
(1843–1901)
His [will] be done,
   271:6
we need Hawaii,
   226:2
McMurtry, Larry
(b. 1936)
westerns & cowboys,
   529:5
McPhee, John *(b. 1931)*
clinging to a subcon-
   tinent, 10:9
neon & Nevada, 351:7
McWilliams, Carey
(1905–1980)
[Los Angeles:] a cir-
   cus, 95:5
Mead, Margaret
(1901–1978)
maleness in America,
   542:3
man's role, 306:2
mediocre men,
   305:6
Meir, Golda
(1898–1978)
the clock, 492:9
devotion to husband
   and children, 539:6
seventy, being, 363:2
Mellon, Richard Beatty
(1858–1933)
coal & machine guns,
   70:7
Melville, Herman
(1819–1891)
Americans, 18:5
books & events, 77:9
disorderliness, care-
   ful, 307:4
drunken Christian,
   11:3
faith, 183:8, 184:1
Ishmael, call me, 13:7
I would prefer not to,
   13:8
a laugh, 272:6
Nantucket, 301:9
Rome, 110:8
sail forbidden seas,
   494:2
sea, the implacable,
   342:12
truth, 497:12
visible objects, 43:6
wars are boyish, 519:6
we are the pioneers,
   18:6
a whale ship was my
   Yale, 454:11
youth is our strength,
   18:6
**Mencken, H[enry]
   L[ewis]** *(1880–1956)*
[Baltimore's] old
   charm, 87:3
bibliobibuli, 66:9
booboisie, 67:4
bore one another, to,
   67:4
a burial service for
   the damned, 321:7
a charlatan [T. Roo-
   sevelt], 439:6
Connecticut, 123:2
[Delaware:] a small
   and measly state,
   142:4

conscience, 123:5
death, 139:8
democracy, 144:10,
   145:3
faith, 184:6
farmer—hates his job,
   186:1
forgive some sinner,
   172:6
God will not help,
   213:6
government, the
   worst, 217:10
[Harding] writes the
   worst English,
   224:1
heroes, 229:9
horse-laugh, one,
   273:2
Hugo & new robes
   (note), 481:4
idea, to die for an,
   243:6
justice, 258:3
male, the average,
   545:6
men, 542:4
men the American
   people admire,
   22:6
metaphysics, 379:7
a Negro & white folk,
   422:3
Oregon, 365:2
piety, 430:14
the plain people, in-
   telligence of, 378:3
privileges, 163:8
progress, 411:8
Puritanism, 175:4
religion, the other fel-
   low's, 430:13
school days, 161:3
time, 492:2
a tin horn politician,
   223:6
war, 521:8
when women kiss,
   539:13
wisdom, age brings,
   361:5
women have simple
   tastes, 539:12
Menotti, Gian Carlo
(b. 1911)
love, 288:7
Merritt, Dixon Lanier
(1879–1972)
the pelican, 338:1
Merton, Robert K[ing]
(b. 1910)
error, a reign of, 442:8
self-fulfilling
   prophecy, 442:8
Merton, Thomas
(1915–1969)
music and art and po-
   etry, 47:2
"right-thinking men",
   438:1
Midler, Bette *(b. 1945)*
London, 109:7
**Mies Van Der Rohe,
   Ludwig** *(1886–1969)*
less is more, 48:3
Millar, Margaret
(b. 1915)
conversations, 130:2
**Millay, Edna St. Vin-
   cent** *(1892–1950)*
April, 346:1
candle burns at both
   ends, 178:1
childhood, 82:5

down into the grave,
139:9
faith, 184:5
ferry, all night on the,
222:8
God, 213:1
heart is slow to learn,
228:8
life, 282:6
night, 348:4
the soul, 464:7
a train, 494:11
world, O, 546:12
Miller, Arthur *(b. 1915)*
justice, your, 258:7
a kidder, 240:6
liked but not well
liked, 188:9
never fight fair with a
stranger, 131:6
newspaper, a good,
408:10
"now," the word,
400:5
the ruin in things,
331:6
a suicide, 480:9
work a lifetime to pay
off a house, 545:5
Miller, Henry
(1891–1980)
[America is] prema-
turely old (note),
23:4
bread, good, 192:6
the democratic way,
144:12
Detroit, 92:10
do business [in
Charleston], 89:7
Greece, 330:10
leader, the real,
231:12
life, 282:10
Mobile, 96:8
national vice is waste,
23:5
Savannah, 106:8
South, the old, 466:7
sterilized and
wrapped in cello-
phane, 23:4
we do not talk, 130:4
youth, American
ideal is, 557:4
Millett, Kate *(b. 1934)*
women, 540:4
Mills, Elijah Hunt
(1776–1829)
[A. Jackson] & the In-
dians, 255:2
Milton, John
(1608–1674)
myself am hell (note),
294:4
**Minow, Newton [Nor-
man]** *(b. 1926)*
a vast wasteland,
304:4 & note
nation's whims &
needs, 304:5
Mirabella, Grace
(b. 1930)
[Newark:] city of
strivers, 97:1
Miss Piggy. See under
Henson, Jim
Mitchell, George
(b. 1933)
God & American pol-
itics, 394:12
Mitchell, John N.
(1913–1988)
Katie Graham, 525:6

the tough get going
(note), 477:4
watch what we do, 4:4
Mitchell, Margaret
(1900–1949)
I don't give a damn,
251:6
time, never conve-
nient, 450:2
tomorrow is another
day, 206:2
Mizner, Wilson
(1876–1933)
be nice to people on
your way up, 478:11
[Los Angeles:] a
sewer, 95:3
on the death of
Coolidge, 251:2
research & plagia-
rism, 57:10
Moffett, Samuel E.
(d. 1908)
honor, 236:4
**Mondale, Walter
[Frederick]** *(b. 1928)*
World War III, 522:8
Monroe, James
(1758–1831)
hemisphere, this,
194:6
**Montaigne, Michel
Eyquem de**
(1533–1592)
[marriage] happens as
with cages (note),
299:2
**Moore, Clement
C[larke]**
(1779–1863)
night before Christ-
mas, 82:8, 83:1,2,3
Moore, Marianne
(1897–1972)
beauty, 62:1
human nature to
stand in the middle
of things, 246:2
Ireland, Spenser's
(note), 331:1
Irish, I'm, 331:1
the mind, 318:5
pitching, 475:7
psychology, 445:7
superior people & vis-
its, 219:11
verbal felicity, 55:1
words, 269:10
zest, they've zest,
475:1
Morehead, John Motley
(1796–1866)
a long time between
drinks, 11:2
**Morgan, [Sen.] John A.
Tyler** *(1824–1907)*
a lie, 152:7
Morgan, John Pierpont
(1837–1913)
don't sell America
short, 21:1
reasons, 427:10
yacht, upkeep of a,
455:6
Morgan, Neil *(b. 1924)*
Nevada, 351:6
Morison, Samuel Eliot
(1887–1976)
history, 233:11
**Morley, Christopher
[Darlington]**
(1890–1957)
poet, courage of the,
53:4

**Morley, John,
Viscount Morley
of Blackburn**
(1838–1923)
St. Vitus & St. Paul
[T. Roosevelt],
439:4
Niagara & Roosevelt
(note), 439:4
Morris, George Pope
(1802–1864)
woodman, spare that
tree, 341:4
Morris, Gouverneur
(1752–1816)
he means well, 249:1
[Lafayette] unable to
hold the helm
(note), 249:1
Morrison, Robert F.
(fl. 1900)
he ain't no brother
of mine (note),
469:4
Morrison, Toni *(b. 1931)*
book you really want
to read, 58:15
Morrow, Dwight W.
(1873–1931)
any party which takes
credit for the rain,
392:12
**Morse, Samuel F[inley]
B[reese]**
(1791–1872)
what hath God
wrought!, 446:1
Morton, Oliver Perry
(1823–1877)
waving the blood
shirt, 390:11
Mosby, John S[ingleton]
(1833–1916)
the solid South,
466:3
Moses, Robert
(1888–1981)
statistics (note),
443:11
Moses, Bob Parris
Mississippi, 320:5
**Motion Pictures Pro-
ducers and Distrib-
utors of America,
Inc.**
marriage, 300:2
scenes of passion,
78:1
sex perversion,
78:2
Moulter, Lawrence C.
politics, sports, and
revenge, 88:6
**Moynihan, [Sen.] Daniel
Patrick** *(b. 1927)*
Irish, being, 331:2
Muir, John *(1838–1914)*
hitched to everything
else in the universe,
504:3
in God's wildness,
530:10
the universe & a for-
est wilderness,
531:1
**Mulligan, James
H[ilary] ("Jim")**
(1844–1916)
Kentucky, 261:7–262
Mullins, Edgar Young
(1860–1928)
unless man is immor-
tal, 245:6

Mumford, Lewis
(1895–1990)
the clock, 447:7
the concrete clover-
leaf, 24:2
generation, every,
208:8
Murphy, Edward A., Jr.
(fl. 1949)
if anything can go
wrong, 496:3
Murphy, Gerald *(1888–
1964)* **and Sara**
living well is the best
revenge, 433:7
**Murrow, Edward R[os-
coe]** *(1908–1965)*
London, this is, 550:1
must not confuse dis-
sent with disloy-
alty, 34:2
prejudices, 399:7
television, 304:3
we are not descended
from fearful men
(note), 34:2
Nabokov, Vladimir
(1899–1977)
college people, aging,
161:10
genius, 209:8
life, 282:12 & note
one of my favorite
states [Wyoming],
555:1
solitude, 463:6
Nader, Ralph *(b. 1934)*
indentured to corpo-
rations, 71:1
**Namath, Joseph
William "Joe
Willie"** *(b. 1943)*
halftime, 309:12
**NASA (National Aero-
nautic and Space
Administration)**
first set foot on the
moon [the moon
plaque], 449:1
Nash, Ogden
(1902–1971)
billboard lovely as a
tree, 6:6
the Bronx, 99:9
canaries, 338:9
candy is dandy, 12:1
Central Park, 101:5
dogs, 339:1
a door & a dog, 153:2
duty, 433:2
Englishman, to be an,
329:11
a heap o' payin'
(note), 235:1
kin and kith, 185:1
a kitten, 338:8
liquor is quicker, 13:1
a Martini, 13:2
middle age, 309:10
orgies, 457:10
progress, 411:10
Scandinavia, 333:10
sin & a grin, 457:11
troubles of the rich,
437:1
the turtle, 338:5
women would rather
be right, 540:3
National Geographic
comets, 340:8
Naylor, Gloria *(b. 1950)*
man, a handsome,
307:2

Nathan, George Jean
(1882–1958)
love, 287:8 & note
no such thing as a
dirty theme (note),
48:2
songs, 51:10
NBC News
war, 522:6
Neff, Pat *(1871–1952)*
Texas & Rhode Is-
land, 435:8
Nelson, W. R.
(1841–1915)
newspaper, 406:4
Nemerov, Howard
(1920–1991)
black hole, a small,
445:3
football, 475:2
history, 233:9 & note
**Neuberger, [Sen.]
Richard L.**
(1912–1960)
Pocatello, 103:9
**The New England
Primer**
Job blesses God, 428:8
life is but a span,
279:7
Xerxes the Great did
die, 138:2
**Newman, [Col.] Aubrey
S.** *(1904–1994)*
follow me!, 552:6
Newman, Wallace
a good loser (note),
473:3
New York Daily News.
See Daily News
The New York Times
Japanese surrender,
554:2
television, 303:7
New York Tribune
[slavery] a peculiar in-
stitution, 460:5
Niebuhr, Reinhold
(1892–1971)
God give us grace to
accept with seren-
ity [the Serenity
Prayer], 398:12
limits & despair,
322:5
**Nietzsche, Friedrich
Wilhelm**
(1844–1900)
better know nothing
(note), 263:4
Nikolais, Alwin
(1910–1993)
dance, 50:7
Niles, Hezekiah
(1777–1839)
Society seems un-
hinged, 60:3
Nimitz, Chester
(1885–1966)
uncommon valor,
553:2
Nin, Anaïs *(1903–1977)*
women, all elegant,
539:9
**Nixon, Richard M[il-
house]** *(1913–1994)*
Checkers, 34:1
defeated, when he's,
534:1
game, how you play
the (note), 473:3
hate, 225:9
I brought myself
down, 527:4

I have never been a
quitter, 527:1
I'm not a crook, 526:8
I screwed up terribly,
527:3
majority, the great
silent, 296:11
pitiful, helpless giant,
510:5
president, rather be a
one-term (note),
510:5
the press, 408:12 &
note
a respectable Republi-
can cloth coat, 33:4
the Soviets, 333:8
stonewall it, 526:3
Turkey, 334:8
the Vice President,
509:3
we can't stand Pat
(note), 384:7
when the president
does it, 404:9
you won't have Nixon
to kick around any
more, 35:4
Noonan, Peggy
a thousand points of
light (note), 24:9
a kinder & gentler na-
tion (note), 389:1
Norworth, Jack
(1879–1959)
take me out to the
ballgame, 471:3

Oates, Joyce Carol
(b. 1938)
language, 269:12
O'Brien, Tim *(b. 1943)*
stories, 66:13
Ochs, Adolph S[imon]
(1858–1935)
all the news that's fit
to print, 406:5
give the news, all the
news (note), 406:5
Odell, Allan G.
(1904–1994)
Burma-Shave, 6:5
**Oglethorpe, James Ed-
ward** *(1696–1785)*
[Savannah:] sheltered
from winds, 106:7
O'Hara, Frank
(1926–1966)
boundless love, 288:6
O'Hara, Theodore
(1820–1867)
bivouac of the dead,
170:6
dark and bloody
ground, 261:2
Olmsted, Frederick Law
(1822–1903)
[Austin:] Washington
en petit, 86:7
O'Neill, Eugene
(1888–1953)
the damned, 147:6
the dead, 139:10
doctors, 154:1
fairy tale, obsessed by
a, 427:3
God, 213:5
life, 282:4
no farther [down] they
can go, 183:1
the past, 370:4,5
the present—strange
interlude, 400:2
the sea, 343:3

strange interlude,
282:5
whiskey, gimme a,
12:6
O'Neill, Thomas P.
(1912–1994)
all politics is local,
393:8
Oppenheimer, J. Robert
(1905–1967)
I am become Death,
553:4
the optimist & pes-
simist (note),
364:3
Ostrander, Gilman M.
(b. 1923)
Massachusetts, set-
tlers of, 302:5
O'Sullivan, John L[ouis]
(1813–1895)
freedom of conscience
etc. (note),
201:11–202
government is evil,
216:5
manifest destiny, 18:3
& note
nation of human
progress, 18:2
Otis, James *(1725–1783)*
libertas (note), 200:1
man's house is his
castle, 409:11
taxation without rep-
resentation, 484:5
Owen, David *(b. 1955)*
no man is a hero to,
231:4

Page, William Tyler
(1868–1924)
government of the
people, 21:6
Paige, Satchel [Leroy]
(c. 1906–1982)
avoid fried meats,
536:5
don't look back, 536:5
how old would you
be?, 363:3
vices, go light on,
536:5
Paine, Albert Bigelow
(1861–1937)
Great White Way,
98:6
Western humor, 529:3
Paine, Ralph
(1906–1991)
New Hampshire,
353:4
Paine, Thomas
(1737–1809)
America, the cause of,
16:3
arms must decide the
contest, 38:6
God, I believe in one,
429:2
government, 215:1,2
honest man, 235:4
moderation (note),
36:7
my country & reli-
gion, 174:8 & note
mystery, 326:7
prejudiced, 399:3
priests and conjurors,
429:3
religion, any system
of, 429:4
revolutions, a share in
two, 434:2

science, 441:1
society & govern-
ment, 215:1
summer soldier & the
sunshine patriot,
39:3
these are the times
that try men's
souls, 39:3
time, 491:2
truth, 497:4
tyranny, 500:2
war, 518:2,3
Washington, George,
524:1,3
what we obtain too
cheap, 506:2
Paley, Barbara ("Babe")
(1915–1978)
too skinny or too
rich, 325:11
Papagiannis, Michael
(b. 1932)
absence of evidence,
176:1
Parker, Dorothy
(1893–1967)
authors and actors
and artists, 46:12
drink, one more,
457:7
dust, excuse my,
173:7
for tomorrow we shall
die, 380:6
gamut of emotions,
251:4
the girls attending
[the Yale prom],
457:8
glasses, girls who
wear, 453:4
highballs, 12:9
horticulture, 161:1
House Beautiful,
251:5
how do they know?
(note), 251:2
knit, if you don't
(note), 251:5
life & love, 287:11
lingerie & brevity,
187:2
a lover a foe, 541:11
not a novel to be
thrown aside lightly
(note), 251:1
passion undying,
287:10
rose, one perfect,
290:4
a satin gown, 187:1
seventy-two suburbs
(note), 94:7
Tonstant Weader
fwowed up, 251:1
worm, to tread upon
a, 139:7
you might as well
live, 480:6
Parker, John
(1729–1775)
if they mean to have a
war, 38:2
Parker, Theodore
(1810–1860)
government of all the
people (note),
210:3–211
Parkman, Francis
(1823–1893)
buffalo, 337:1
change [out West],
528:7

Parks, Rosa *(b. 1913)*
my only concern was
to get home, 425:3
tired of giving in
(note), 425:3
Parrish, Maxfield
(1870–1966)
New Hampshire &
Vermont, 507:8
Parton, James
(1822–1891)
Pittsburgh, 103:7
Paterson, Floyd *(b. 1935)*
defeat, 534:2
**Patton, [Gen.] George
S., Jr.** *(1885–1945)*
command, the art of,
314:5
commander who fails
to obtain his objec-
tive, 314:4
commanders are
prima donnas, 232:1
discipline, 314:3
fatigue, 189:6
I love it, 521:6
plan, a good, 307:9
risks, calculated, 65:1
sweat v. blood, 316:5
war, 520:4
wars are won by men,
520:9
Paul, Elliot [Harold]
(1891–1958)
Paris, last time I see,
110:5
Pauling, Linus Carl
(1901–1994)
century, the coming,
206:5
science, 443:3
Payne, John Howard
(1791–1852)
home, 234:5
**Peale, [Rev.] Norman
Vincent**
(b.1898–1993)
power of positive
thinking, 318:6
pray big (note), 318:6
prayer power, 398:6
Pearson, Drew (given
first names, An-
drew Russell)
(1897–1969)
Nine Old Men, 481:3
Peattie, Donald Culross
(1898–1964)
the Grand Canyon,
44:7
**Pegler, [James] West-
brook** *(1894–1969)*
era of wonderful non-
sense, 214:6
**Peirce, C[harles] S[an-
ders]** *(1839–1914)*
belief, 184:2
doubt, 459:2
philosophy, 379:2
truth (note), 498:12
**Pendergast, Thomas
J[oseph]**
(1872–1945)
newspapers, 407:1
work hard, keep your
mouth shut, 536:2
Penn, William
(1644–1718)
Christ, to be like,
269:14
clean and warm, 186:7
death, 138:3
dispute upon every-
thing, to, 44:1

labor, 542:8
method & business,
67:6
nature, 334:10
no pain, no crown,
479:7
passion, 369:1
poverty & excess,
436:1
prayers, in his, 397:8
the public must be
served, 412:7
truth, 497:3
**Pennsylvania Democra-
tic Committee**
Pennsylvania, 376:5
Perkins, Frances
(1882–1965)
America & public
opinion, 22:9
depression, the,
146:2
Perelman, S. J.
(1904–1979)
a dreary industrial
town, 95:4
Philadelphia, 103:2
Perot, Ross *(b. 1930)*
success, 479:6
Perry, George Sessions
(1910–1956)
Detroit, 93:1
Wisconsin's politics,
534:5
Perry, Oliver Hazard
(1758–1819)
don't give up the ship
(note), 522:11
we have met the en-
emy, 523:1
**Pershing, [Gen.] John
Joseph** *(1860–1948)*
all a soldier needs to
know, 313:7
hell, heaven, or
Hoboken (note),
548:7
tobacco, 493:6
**Peter, Laurence J[ohn-
ston]** *(1919–1990)*
decide, not to (note),
246:3
incompetence, rise to
his level of, 546:2
undecided, to be,
246:3
Petigru, James Louis
(1789–1863)
South Carolina, 467:2
Phelan, James L.
(b. 1912) & Pozen,
Robert C.
Delaware, 143:2
Phelps, Austin
(1820–1890)
book, buy the new,
65:13
**Philip, [Rear Adm.]
John Woodward**
(1840–1900)
don't cheer, men,
469:1
Phillips, Erna. See under Corday, Ted
Phillips, Wendell
(1811–1884)
eternal vigilance &
liberty, 200:8
a government of men
and morning news-
papers, 405:9
insurrection of
thought (note),
434:5

one on God's side,
211:7
progress, 411:7
the Puritans & action,
2:5
revolutions (note),
434:9
Pierce, Neal R.
Washington is a puz-
zling state, 523:6
Piercy, Marge *(b. 1936)*
a strong woman, 540:8
workers are invisible,
77:5
Pierson, [Dr.] Elaine
sex, 454:4
Pierson, Frank R.
(b. 1925)
failure to communi-
cate, 118:7
Piggy, Miss. See under
Henson, Jim
Pinkerton, Allan
(1819–1884)
we never sleep, 132:5
Pinkham, Lydia E.
(1819–1883)
only a woman can un-
derstand, 5:1
Pirsig, Robert [Maynard]
(b. 1928)
Buddha/Godhead,
214:2
motorcycle mainte-
nance, 449:4
Pitkin, Walter B.
(1878–1953)
life begins at 40,
309:8
**Pitt, William [Earl of
Chatham]**
(1708–1778)
America, you cannot
conquer, 40:1
Plath, Sylvia
(1932–1963)
dying is an art, 480:8
Plunket, Robert
planning a crime,
134:9
**Plunkitt, George Wash-
ington** *(1842–1924)*
reformers, 391:5
Poe, Edgar Allan
(1809–1849)
Annabel Lee, 289:4
brute, love of a, 336:9
childhood, 81:3
a dream within a
dream, 426:3
fever called "living,"
138:8
Greece, the glory that
was, 328:2
hide anything, best
place to, 131:4
I have not been as
others were, 13:6
"nevermore," quoth
the Raven, 170:5
once upon a midnight
dreary, 358:1
the poetry of words,
52:9
profound, being too,
317:2
thou wast that all to
me, 289:2
**Polk, [Pres.] James
K[nox]** *(1795–1849)*
I am the hardest
working man in the
country (note),
401:5

no president can have
leisure, 401:5
Polykoff, Shirley
does she or doesn't
she?, 415:3
Pope, Alexander
(1688–1744)
the people's voice
(note), 377:6
Porter, Horace
(1837–1921)
a mugwump, 383:5
Porter, William Sydney.
See Henry, O.
Post, Emily [Price]
(1873–1960)
do as your neighbors
do, 298:5
Post Office Motto
neither snow nor rain
stays these couriers,
217:6
Pound, Ezra [Loomis]
(1885–1972)
autumn, 345:3
dreams, old, 154:6
faces in the crowd,
378:2
grimace, accelerated,
321:6
literature, 58:1
lovest well, what
thou, 287:6
poetry, 53:8
there died a myriad,
549:7
winter is icumen in,
345:2
Pound, Roscoe
(1870–1964)
the law, 275:9
**Powell, Adam Clayton,
Jr.** *(1908–1972)*
black power (note),
424:8–429
keep the faith, 291:5
Powell, Colin [Luther]
(b. 1937)
first we are going to
cut it off, 220:2
it can be done! 4:5
optimism, perpetual,
364:10
Pozen, Robert. See under Phelan, James
**Pradt, [Abbé] Do-
minique Dufour**
nation destined to
exert its influence,
17:2
**Prentice, George Denni-
son** *(1802–1870)*
tobacco, 493:2
Prescott, William
(1726–1795)
until you see the
whites of their eyes,
38:4
**Preston, Margaret
Junkin** *(1820–1897)*
doing, 'tis the, 3:2
Thanksgiving, 489:5
Preuss, Charles
(1803–1854)
a paradise, 72:3
**Priestley, J[ohn] B[oyn-
ton]** *(1894–1984)*
Nevada, 351:5
a society dominated
by the masculine
principle, 488:6
Procter, Harley
99 44/100 per cent
pure, 5:5

Prouty, Olive Higgins
(1882–1974)
don't let's ask for the
moon, 222:1
Pryor, Richard *(b. 1940)*
Just-Us, 258:11
Puzo, Mario *(b. 1920)*
a lawyer, 278:9
offer he can't refuse,
70:11
politics, 394:13
Pyle, Ernie *(1900–1945)*
Eskimos, 422:11

Quayle, Dan *(b. 1947)*
waste to lose one's
mind (note), 318:9
Quincy, Josiah
(1744–1775)
Massachusetts,
301:6

Rand, Ayn *(1905–1982)*
civilization & pri-
vacy, 112:2
great men, 219:6
Randall, James Ryder
(1839–1908)
Maryland, 301:3
Randolph, A[sa] Philip
(1889–1979)
freedom, 201:10
millions and billions,
62:5
Randolph, Innes
(1837–1887)
a good old rebel,
466:1
won't be recon-
structed, 466:1
Randolph, John
(1773–1883)
abilities so much be-
low mediocrity,
249:3
he shines and stinks
like rotten mack-
erel, 249:2
I am an aristocrat,
162:9
muffled oars (note),
249:2
Rankin, Jeanette
(1880–1973)
war, 521:3,4
Rantoul, Robert, Jr.
(1805–1852)
cheap land, 204:3
Rawson, Clayton
(1906–1971)
crime does not pay,
134:4
**Rayburn, [Rep.] Sam
[Taliaferro]**
(1882–1961)
a leader, 232:2
to get along, go along,
121:9
**Read, Thomas
B[uchanan]**
(1822–1872)
Sheridan, 116:1
Reagan, Nancy *(b. 1923)*
kinder and gentler
than who? (note),
389:1
just say no, 516:1
Reagan, Ronald *(b. 1911)*
being shot at, 137:6
evil empire, 333:9
Gipper, win just for
the (note), 472:2
government is like a
baby, 218:3

a nation that has a
government, 24:6
struggle between good
and evil, 197:4
tax increasers, 486:4
a tree is a tree,
168:14
Red Cloud *(1822–1909)*
we were very many,
and you were few,
420:1
Reddy, Helen *(b. 1941)*
woman, I am, 540:6
Reed, Ishmael *(b. 1938)*
the universe, 504:6
Reed, Rex *(b. 1938)*
Hollywood, 95:10
**Reed, Thomas B[rack-
ett]** *(1839–1902)*
a billion-dollar coun-
try, 20:3
friends & enemies,
165:8
habit, 221:6
he will never be ei-
ther (note),
401:6–402
made light of his re-
marks (note), 250:5
Maine, 295:4
rather be wrong than
president (note),
401:6–402
a statesman, 391:7
subtracting from the
sum of human
knowledge, 250:5
Reid, Christian
(1846–1920)
the land of the sky,
356:4
Rense, Paige *(b. 1929)*
good taste, 477:6
Republican Party
a chicken in every
pot, 386:5
a choice not an echo
(note), 388:3
Coolidge, 386:3,4
dinner pail, the full,
384:4
don't swap horses,
381:2
had enough?, 387:6
I like Ike, 387:8
in your heart you
know he's right,
388:3
I still like Ike (note),
387:8
life, liberty, and Lan-
don, 387:3
Nixon's the one,
388:4
public school system,
160:5
Roosevelt for ex-Pres-
ident, 387:4
school, the free, 160:6
stand pat (note), 384:7
Taft, get on the raft
with, 385:1
Reston, James [Barrett]
(1909–1995)
instincts, [Nixon's],
253:4
politics, 394:8
Reuther, Walter
(1907–1970)
if it walks like a
duck, 175:9
Revere, Paul
(1735–1818)
a signal, 38:1

Reynolds, Burt *(b. 1936)*
middle age, 309:11
**Rhode Island Colonial
Assembly**
Ile of Rhods, 435:5
Rice, Grantland
(1880–1954)
the Four Horsemen,
472:5
game, how you played
the, 473:3
a gray ghost [Red
Grange], 473:6
lies at rest by the
nineteenth tee,
471:5
wars are planned by
old men, 520:8
Rich, Adrienne *(b. 1929)*
language, 269:11
Richardson, Robert
good night, dear heart
(note), 172:3
Rickey, [Wesley] Branch
(1881–1965)
luck, 292:3
Riesner, Dean. See under Fink
Riis, Jacob [August]
(1849–1914)
how the other half
lives, 436:5
Riley, James Whitcomb
(1849–1916)
Gene Debs (note),
133:5
peach, the ripest, 14:4
when the frost is on
the punkin, 344:9
R.M.C. *(fl. 1839)*
my native state!,
209:9
Robeson, Paul
(1898–1976)
convictions (note),
123:6
Robin, Leo *(1900–1984)*
diamonds are a girl's
best friend, 506:6
Robinson, Earl
(1910–1991)
America, 23:8
**Robinson, Edwin Ar-
lington** *(1869–1935)*
life, 281:5
Miniver Cheevy,
13:9
New England, 352:9
time, small intolera-
ble drums of, 492:1
Robinson, John
(1576?–1625)
Lord has more yet,
211:1
Robinson, Sugar Ray
[given names,
Walker Smith]
(b. 1920)
my business is hurt-
ing people, 475:5
**Rockefeller, John D[avi-
son]** *(1839–1937)*
every right implies a
responsibility,
433:3
money, the power to
make, 324:1
owl, wise (note),
483:6–484
**Rockne, Knute [Ken-
neth]** *(1888–1931)*
the Gipper, 472:2
loser, a good and gra-
cious, 532:6

Roddenberry, Gene
[given names,
Eugene Wesley]
(1921–1991)
to go boldly where no
man has gone be-
fore, 4:7
Rodell, Fred
(1907–1980)
legal writing, 278:4
Rogers, Henry H.
(1840–1909)
reputation (note),
236:4
**Rogers, Will[iam Penn
Adair]** *(1879–1935)*
an actor, 55:6
afford a thing, 158:1
Alaska, 10:6
America & moral
leadership (note),
17:4
Americans, 158:1
Americans abroad to-
gether (note), 495:2
an Arkansaw hillbilly,
46:2
Canada, 329:1
Chinese, 329:5
civilization, 111:11
Colorado, 117:6
Congress, 121:6 &
note, 121:7
a Conservative & a
Democrat, 393:6
corruption, 133:6
a Democrat, 393:6, 7
& note
diplomats, 151:11
a doctor, 153:10
doctor bill, 153:9
economic problems
(note), 158:1
forefathers, my, 422:1
funnies & editorials,
408:3
funny, everything is,
240:3
Hawaii, 226:6
hero, being a, 230:1
holiday, every, 234:2
if it [a stock] don't go
up, 70:5
income tax, 485:8
Kansas, 260:4
king, every man a
(note), 386:6
lawyers, 278:3
Marines, 313:9
men are watching
their styles, 187:3
Mexico (note), 308:3
middle class, us,
310:4
Mississippi will vote
dry, 320:3
mother, a socially
ambitious, 367:9
mothers speak the
same tongue, 367:8
nations, others, 196:1
Nevada, 351:4
never met a man I
didn't like, 173:1
newspapers, what I
read in the, 408:2
New York, 99:10,
100:1
Oklahoma, 359:3
On Tu Long, 67:3
people thinking,
231:10
politicians, 392:11,
393:2 & note

politics, 393:1,3,7
praying, 398:5
publicity, 6:2
public office (note),
  55:6
rumor, 440:1
salary, one, 324:8
see years ahead, 516:6
society, 163:6
spiritualists, 358:2
strong characters
  [in Arkansas],
  46:1
they [the Japanese]
  got everything we
  got, 332:2
time, 492:3
tourists, 495:2
truth hurts, 135:3
Tulsa, 107:3
Vermont, 507:5
war, 520:10
wine & Noah, 12:8
we did everything,
  208:7
woman desperate po-
  litically, 539:5
Roman, Charles
quit kicking sand in
  my face, 6:6
Roosa, Stuart A[llen]
  (1933–1994)
space, 340:10
Roosevelt [Anna]
  Eleanor *(1884–1962)*
change, 24:3
communism, 118:9
contribution, to make
  a, 545:8
the culture of a na-
  tion, 47:3
generation, losing
  this, 208:9
nature, 336:1
peace, 376:1
war, no one won the,
  521:9
a woman, 542:1
Roosevelt, Franklin De-
  lano *(1882–1945)*
arsenal of democracy,
  32:3
bold experimentation,
  3:8
books never die, 66:8
boys, your, 550:3
a conservative, 393:11
Constitution, our,
  128:3
date which will live
  in infamy, 550:6
Fala, dog my, 34:1
fear, the only thing
  we have to, 31:5
the first 12 years,
  403:6
fight, a good, 120:1
freedom & human
  rights, 202:1
freedoms, four essen-
  tial, 201:11
generation of Ameri-
  cans, this, 208.10
good neighbor policy,
  196:2
hand that held the
  dagger, 550:2
happiness, 222:10
happy warrior, 31:2,
  229:10
ill-housed, ill-clad, ill-
  nourished, 146:3
indispensable man,
  no, 219:5

institutions & chang-
  ing times, 248:6
lawlessness, world,
  61:4
lead them straight,
  552:3
man, the forgotten,
  395:9
method, take a,
  307:8
minds, prisoners of
  their own, 318:4
minorities, rights of,
  422:7
neighbor, policy of
  the good, 196:2
new deal, 31:4
pain in my head,
  271:11
peace & charity, 375:8
physical strength &
  spiritual force,
  477:2
place of moral leader-
  ship, 403:5
pocketbook, a full,
  325:5
public opinion,
  arouses, 413:5
a radical, 393:10
a rattlesnake, 440:5
a reactionary, 393:12
rendezvous with des-
  tiny, 208:10
soil, the nation that
  destroys its, 168:2
son of a bitch, our,
  196:3
taxes, 485:10, 12
tough, to be, 477:1
war, 520:12, 521:1
war, a new kind of,
  551:1
war, we are going to
  win the, 550:8
war, we are now in
  this, 550:7
Roosevelt, Nicholas
[T. Roosevelt] bride at
  every wedding,
  439:8
Roosevelt, Theodore
  (1858–1919)
action, get, 3:4
Americanism, 50–50,
  21:7
American, hyphen-
  ated, 374:4
arena, man who is in
  the, 3:5
Armageddon, we
  stand at, 30:1
the bear business,
  439:1
big business & a
  square deal, 384:8
black care & a fast
  pace, 469:7
bull moose, I am as
  strong as a, 391:4
bully pulpit,
  402:8–403
a chocolate eclair &
  McKinley's back-
  bone, 250:4
[Colorado:] Switzer-
  land of America,
  117:4
the critic, 3:5
democracy, triumph
  of, 21:4
diplomacy, 151:7
evil & expediency,
  179:5

the fight is on (note),
  402:7
heart & minds (note),
  41:2
[Jefferson:] incapable
  executive, 255:5
law, no man is above
  the, 275:1
the lunatic fringe,
  392:8
mistakes, 321:2
muckrakes, men with
  the, 407:5
my hat is in the ring,
  402:7
Nationalism, A New,
  385:2
natural resources,
  167:3
navy, a great (note),
  520:1
North Dakota, 357:4
opportunity, 21:4
put out the light,
  271:7
speak softly and
  carry a big stick,
  476:7
a square deal, 384:8
the strenuous life,
  379:9
war—country needs
  one, 468:3
war, preparation for,
  520:1
wealth, malefactors of
  great, 324:4
we turn our rivers
  into sewers, 167:4
wisdom, 535:3
word, shorter and
  more ugly, 268:4
words, weasel, 268:5
work, 544:6
Root, George Frederick
  (1820–1895)
rally 'round the flag,
  114:5
Roper, Jack
I zigged, 474:3
Ross, Harold
  (1892–1951)
The New Yorker,
  303:3
who he?, 414:4
Rosten, Leo C[alvin]
  (b. 1908)
hates babies & dogs,
  320:2
Rostropovich, Mstislav
  Leopoldovich
  (b. 1927)
more is more (note),
  48:3
world [as a] show,
  56:6
Rotary. See Sheldon,
  A. F.
Roth, Philip *(b. 1933)*
a Jewish man with
  parents alive,
  368:4
Rough Riders
rough-tough, we're
  the stuff, 468:7
Rowan, Carl *(b. 1925)*
questions & answers,
  415:6
Rowlandson, Mary
  (ca. 1636–1711)
a stinking tobacco-
  pipe, 492:11
Royal, Darrell *(b. 1924)*
luck, 292:4

Rudd, Irving
a press agent, 8:1
PR people (note), 8:1
heart hardly ever
  used, 253:3
Rudman, [Sen.] Warren
  (b. 1930)
the American people
  have the right to be
  wrong, 378:8
Rudofsky, Bernard
  (b. 1905)
the Japanese, 332:4
Runyon, [Alfred] Da-
  mon *(1884–1946)*
the race . . . to the
  swift, 474:1
Rusk, Dean *(1909–1994)*
eyeball to eyeball,
  35:3
Ruskin, Harry. See under Busch, Niven
Ruskin, John
  (1819–1900)
a country [with] no
  castles, 19:9
Russell, Bill [given first
  names, William Fel-
  ton] *(b. 1934)*
we don't have to be
  what you want us
  to be, 425:6
Russell, Rosalind
  (1911–1976)
flops, 183:3

Sacks, Oliver *(b. 1933)*
disease, 245:1
Safire, William *(b. 1929)*
nattering nabobs of
  negativism (note),
  164:4
Sala, G[eorge] A[ugustus
  Henry] *(1828–1895)*
American manners &
  the spitoon, 298:1
California, the cli-
  mate of, 73:4
cows in [Augusta],
  86:5
Sale, [John] Kirkpatrick
  (b. 1937)
the technological jug-
  gernaut, 449:8
Salinger, J[erome]
  D[avid] *(b. 1919)*
a book & author,
  66:10
how do you know
  what you're going
  to do?, 4:3
a pretty intelligent
  person, 453:8
Sandburg, Carl
  (1878–1967)
[Buffalo] street cars,
  88:8
Casey Jones (note),
  544:7
[Chicago:] hog
  butcher & city of
  the big shoulders,
  90:8
customer is always
  right, 70:4
a dream, 154:8
the fog, 349:1
hell, 229:2
jazzmen, O, 51:8
lawyer, a criminal,
  278:5
the machine, 447:8
money, 325:1
the moon, 340:7

Sandburg, Carl (*cont.*)
the past, 370:1
the people, mob,
crowd, 378:1
people will live on,
378:5
poetry, 53:5
slang, 269:8
smoke, blood, steel,
70:1
war, sometime they'll
give a, 520:11
why does a hearse
horse snicker?,
278:1
Sanders, Henry R.
("Red") (*1905–1958*)
winning (note), 533:5
Sanger, Margaret
(*1883–1966*)
slave mothers, 539:3
Santayana, George
(*1863–1952*)
atheism, 59:3
beauty, 61:9
the Bible, 430:7
domestic bliss, 299:10
fame, love of, 478:4
England, 329:10
facts, 182:6
fanaticism, 166:6
habit, 221:5
happiness, 222:6
immortality, 245:4
knowledge, 263:6
last years of life, 362:1
madness & sanity,
293:4,6
miracles, 318:8
the mystic, 326:9
oneself, 451:10
pain, 480:1
the past, condemned
to repeat, 369:14
prayer, 398:3
religion, 430:8
skepticism, 459:3
values, 506:5
wisdom, 535:2
wit, 239:8
words are weapons,
269:4
the young man & the
old man, 8:12
Sargeant, Winthrop
(*1903–86*)
Seattle, 106:9
Sarton, May
(*1914–1995*)
a hero, 231:2
solitude, 463:7
Sartre, Jean-Paul
(*1905–1980*)
hell (note), 229:3
Sassoon, Siegfried
(*1886–1967*)
New York!, 99:6
Schary, Dore. See Grif-
fin, Eleanore
Schlesinger, Arthur
M[eier], Jr. (*b. 1917*)
a dietary quest, 192:7
liberalism & capital-
ism, 394:1
Schoepf, Johann David
(*late 18th c.?*)
[Charleston has] a
finer manner of life,
89:5
Schulberg, Budd
(*b. 1914*)
Florida, 190:8
I could've been a con-
tender, 428:6

television, 304:2
What Makes Sammy
Run?, 14:6
Schulz, Charles M[on-
roe] (*b. 1922*)
big sisters, 185:2
Schumacher, E[rnst]
F[riedrich]
(*1911–1977*)
small is beautiful,
148:4
Schurz, Carl
(*1829–1906*)
country right or
wrong (note), 371:5
Schwartz, Delmore
(*1913–1966*)
paranoids, 294:1
time, 492:5
Scott, Dred (*1795–1858*)
your petitioner, 27:6
Scott, [Gen.] Winfield
the greatest mistake
of your life (note),
502:5
wayward sisters, de-
part in peace, 112:5
Scripps, E[dward]
W[yllis] (*1854–1926*)
we shall tell no lies
(note), 406:5
Sears, Edmund Hamil-
ton (*1810–1876*)
it came upon the mid-
night clear, 83:4
Seattle (*1786–1866*)
death, 138:9
regret is useless,
428:1
white man will never
be alone, 418:7
Seeger, Alan
(*1888–1916*)
a rendezvous with
death, 548:1
Segal, Erich (*b. 1937*)
love, 288:11
Seldes, George
(*1890–1996*)
tell the truth and run
(note), 499:5
Selznik, David O.
(*1902–1965*)
El Paso and Amarillo,
85:9
Sendak, Maurice
[Bernard] (*b. 1928*)
having everything,
283:5
Service, Robert William
(*1874–1958*)
later than you think,
491:12
God was tired when
he made it [Alaska],
10:4
Yukon, the law of,
10:3
Seuss, Dr. [Theodor
Seuss Geisel]
(*1904–1991*)
an elephant's faithful,
291:4
quick, Henry the Flit,
6:1
Sevareid, Eric
(*1912–1992*)
Truman, 404:10
Seward, William Henry
(*1801–1872*)
conflict, an irrepress-
ible, 112:4
the Constitution,
126:8

revolutions (note),
434:9
Sexton, Anne
(*1928–1974*)
a possessed witch,
358:3
Shakers
hands to work, 514:3
Shakespeare, William
(*1564–1616*)
blood will have blood
(note), 131:8
greatness (note),
305:7
many strokes (note),
148:6
misery & bedfellows
(note), 390:10
what a goodly outside
falsehood hath
(note), 6:3
Sharpton, [Rev.] Al
(*b. 1955*)
clothes, 187:7
justice, 258:12
Shaw, Artie (*b. 1910*)
more would have
been less (note),
48:3
Shaw, George Bernard
(*1856–1950*)
American Constitu-
tion, 127:6
Shaw, Henry Wheeler.
See Billings, Josh
Shawn, Ted [given
name, Edwin Myers
Shawn] (*1891–1972*)
twirl, 50:6
Shawn, William
(*1907–1992*)
it takes as long as it
takes (note), 188:10
falling short of perfec-
tion, 188:10
Sheed, Wilfrid (*b. 1930*)
sanity, 294:7
Sheehan, George, M.D.
(*1919–1993*)
healthy way to be ill,
244:9
Sheen, [Bishop] Fulton
J[ohn] (*1895–1979*)
an atheist, 59:6
Shields, Ren (*1868–1913*)
Good Old Summer-
time, 344:11
Sheldon, A. F.
(*1868–1935*)
who serves best (Ro-
tary motto), 515:8
Shelly, Percy Bysshe
(*1792–1822*)
best and brightest
(note), 164:3
Shelton, Ron
Louisiana, 286:2
Shepard, Odell
(*1884–1967*)
Connecticut Yankee,
123:3
Sheridan, Philip H.
(*1831–1888*)
Indians, the only
good, 419:7
Texas, 488:1
Sherman, Sidney
(*1805–1873*)
remember the
Alamo!, 27:5
Sherman, [Gen.]
William Tecumseh
(*1820–1891*)
hold out, 115:5

I will not accept if
nominated, 402:3
paid spies, 405:10
the penitentiary v. the
White House, 402:1
press, a free (note),
405:10–406
Savannah (note), 116:2
South Carolina,
vengeance on
(note), 467:2
vox populi, 377:6
war, 519:4,5,7
Sibert or Siebert, Talli-
fero Lawrence
(*1877–1917*)
Casey Jones (note),
544:7
Sigourney, Lydia Hunt-
ley (*1791–1865*)
their name is on your
waters, 418:3
Silver, Nicky
I'm still your mother,
368:7
Simmons, Paul (*d. 1994*)
are you better off to-
day?, 388:5
Simon, Paul (*b. 1942*)
New Jersey Turnpike,
354:3
Simon, William
(*b. 1927*)
tax structure, 486:3
Simpson, Louis
(*b. 1923*)
where are you, Walt?
(note), 494:8
Sinclair, Upton [Beall]
(*1878–1968*)
fascism & capitalism,
500:9
a vision of power, 90:6
Singer, Isaac Bashevis
(*b. 1904*)
free will, 531:11
Sitting Bull
(*c.1831–1890*)
do you know who I
am?, 420:4
white men, 420:5
Skinner, B[urrhus]
F[rederic]
(*1904–1990*)
education, 161:7
life, satisfying, 322:3
reading, love of, 66:11
whether machines
think & whether
men do, 449:2
Slosson, Edwin
American crowd, 21:8
Slovik, [Pvt.] Eddie D.
(*1920–1945*)
I'll run away again,
552:8
Smith, Al[fred Emanuel]
(*1873–1944*)
baloney, 192:4
kiss of death, 496:1
record, look at the,
182:2
Smith, Bessie
(*1898–1937*)
I'm a young woman,
557:1
Smith, Betty [Wehner]
(*1904–1972*)
tree that grows in
Brooklyn, 342:10
Smith, Edgar
(*1857–1938*)
the working girl,
545:1

Smith, Hedrick *(b. 1933)*
Moscow, 109:9
nation [with] 11 time
zones, 333:5
Russians, 333:6
Smith, J. Russell
(1874–1966)
the Corn Belt, 311:3
Smith, [Capt.] John
(1580–1631)
a fair bay (note), 512:3
a place for man's
habitation, 512:3
pleasant hills and fer-
tile valleys, 512:4
Smith, Logan Pearsall
(1865–1946)
author, a good, 58:2
enjoy, to, 222:9
income, a good, 324:9
married women,
300:4
reading, 66:5
the sun has gone in,
349:2
what the world says
of someone, 431:8
**Smith, [Maj. Gen.]
Oliver**
retreat, hell, 264:4
Smith, Samuel Francis
(1808–1895)
my country, 'tis of
thee, 372:4
Smith, [Rev.] Sydney
(1771–1845)
who reads an Ameri-
can book?, 17:3
Smith, ("Red") Walter
(1905–1982)
art of fiction is dead,
58:5
living is the trick,
283:6
writing, 58:13
**Smith, [Gen.] Walter
Bedell** *(1895–1961)*
diplomacy, 152:2
**Snodgrass, W[illiam]
D[eWitt]** *(b. 1926)*
solid scholars, 162:2
Socialist Party
convict no. 9653 for
president, 386:2
Sontag, Susan *(b. 1933)*
interpretation, 50:1
literary genius, 58:11
sick, kingdom of the,
244:8
**Southern Literary Mes-
senger**
Bostonian, Virginian,
Tennessean, 487:5
Sorensen, Theodore
(b. 1928)
White House, in the,
404:4
**Soule, John B[absone]
L[ane]** *(1815–1891)*
go west, 204:5
Speckled Snake
(c. 1729–1829)
the white man, 417:3
you are too near me,
417:4
Spock, [Dr.] Benjamin
(b. 1903)
trust yourself, 367:11
**Spofford, Harriet [Eliza-
beth] Prescott**
(1835–1922)
the hungry poor,
395:5
Thanksgiving, 490:1

**Stafford, Wendell
Phillips**
Vermont, 507:3
Stagg, Amos Alonzo
(1862–1925)
winning, 532:7
Stallings, Laurence
(1894–1968)
What Price Glory?,
520:6
Standing Bear, Luther
(1868–1939)
nature & the white
man, 335:14
**Stanley, [Sir] Henry
Morton** (born, John
Rowlands)
(1841–1904)
Dr. Livingstone, 29:4
Stanton, Charles E.
(1859–1933)
Lafayette, we are
here, 549:3
**Stanton, Edwin McMas-
ters** *(1814–1869)*
he belongs to the
ages, 284:3
Stanton, Elizabeth Cady
(1815–1902)
despotism, 500:7
men and women are
equal, 541:2
patriotism, 373:5
the queens in history,
538:6
trees, reverence for,
167:2
truth, 498:6
women, the prolonged
slavery of, 538:7
Stark, [Col.] John
(1728–1822)
or Molly Stark's a
widow, 39:7
Steele, Eliza *(fl. c. 1840)*
a prairie, 310:11
Stefano, Joseph
(b. 1922)
a boy's best friend,
368:3
Steffens, Lincoln
(1866–1936)
Chicago, 90:5
Cities, the Shame of
the, 84:9
cities, the "tough"
among, 90:10
future, I have seen
the, 205:9
Philadelphia, 102:6
Stegner, Wallace
(1909–1993)
deserts asked to blos-
som, 169:2
experiences, shaped
by our, 180:3
ghost towns & dust
bowls, 529:8
green, the color
(note), 169:2
relationship between
people and earth
(note), 23:2
western wilderness is
the geography of
hope, 531:6
the West—hope's na-
tive home, 529:7
wilderness, remain-
ing, 531:3
Stein, Gertrude
(1874–1946)
America & Paris,
110:3

boy & man, 306:11
the Civil War, 117:1
dangerous everything
is, how, 137:2
genius, to be a, 209:7
information & com-
mon sense, 263:9
kindness, 262:9
lost generation,
208:4
[Oakland:] no there
there, 102:1
pigeons on the grass,
338:4
rich, to get, 325:2
rose is a rose, 342:7
understanding,
318:3
U.S., in the, 22:10
ways to earn a living
(note), 325:2
what is the answer?,
415:2
Steinbeck, John [Ernst]
(1902–1968)
Arizona, ramparts of,
44:9
the Badlands, 467:8
a city on hills, 85:2
Florida, 109:9
heartland, here in the,
309:1
keep your eyes open,
536:7
Maine, 295:8
a man's got to do,
350:10
Okie, 359:5
Texas, 488:8,9
we shall be smoth-
ered, 206:3
Steinem, Gloria
(b. 1935)
becoming the men,
540:9
mother & father,
368:5
woman, a liberated,
540:2
**Stengel, ("Casey")
Charles Dillon**
(1890–1975)
can't anyone here
play this game?,
475:6
if you don't get it by
midnight, 458:7
made up my mind
both ways, 246:4
mistake of being 70,
362:11
most people my age
are dead, 363:1
a time in every man's
life, 450:3
Sterling, Andrew B.
*(1874–death date
not known)*
meet me in St. Louis,
105:3
Stevens, Wallace
(1879–1955)
actual world & fan-
tastic world, 426:12
beauty, 61:12
become an ignorant
man again (note),
53:10
bee, booming of the
new-come, 339:5
birds are gone, when
the, 167:6
emperor of ice-cream,
231:9

God, 213:4
the hero, 230:2
history, 233:6
the house was quiet,
346:10
insures all people
against all happen-
ings, 70:8
the moon, 340:6
moonlight, book of,
340:3
pigeons, casual flocks
of, 338:3
the plum, 192:1
a poem, 53:11
the poet, 53:13
poetry, 53:10, 10
(note), & 12
Satan, death of, 150:2
the world, 547:8
**Stevenson, Adlai
E[wing]** *(1900–1965)*
a new America (note),
387:7
Americans are suck-
ers for good news,
24:1
candles, [E. Roosevelt]
would rather light,
515:11
communism, 119:2
diplomacy, 152:1
eggheads unite, 163:9
flattery, 190:4
gains & pains (note),
148:5
a hungry man, 395:12
an independent,
394:3
Kansas, 260:9
laws & habits, 221:9
a lie (note), 152:7
the mind, 318:7
New Dealers & car
dealers (note), 253:1
patriotism, 374:5
Paul v. Peale, 318:6
politics [definition of],
394:2
president, pick a &
pick on, 403:8
principles, 515:10
progress & unpopular
positions, 412:1
words, 269:7
Stevenson, Robert Louis
(1850–1894)
a bleak climate [in
Saranac], 355:4
catchwords (note),
269:7
Nebraska, the plains
of, 350:1
paradise, it was a sort
of, 310:12
plain, the green, 350:2
sagebrush (note),
554:5
sameness, this huge,
350:3
Stewart *(fl. c. 1861)*
a strip of land (note),
356:5
Stewart, [Justice] Potter
(1915–1985)
I know it when I see
it, 78:4
publishing business,
129:3
swift justice, 258:8
Stimson, Henry L[ewis]
(1867–1950)
gentlemen & others'
mail, 410:4

Stinson, Joseph C.
(b. 1947)
bravery, 312:1
make my day, 137:7
Stockman, David
(b. 1946)
all these numbers
(note), 159:6
trickle down (note),
157:6
**Stockton, Frank R.
(Francis Richard)**
(1834–1902)
the lady or the tiger?,
414:2
Stoddert, Benjamin
(1751–1813)
bravery in officers,
312:1
Stone, Irving
(1903–1989)
[Bryan's] mind was
like a soup dish,
253:2
**Stone, I[sidor] F[ein-
stein]** *(1907–1989)*
burlesque & newspa-
pers, 408:5
Stone, Oliver *(b. 1930)*
greed (note), 326:1
Stong, Phil[ip Duffield]
(1899–1957)
Iowa, 253:9, 254:1
Stout, Rex *(1886–1975)*
any spoke will lead an
ant, 188:4
Stowe, Harriet Beecher
(1811–1896)
age where nations
are convulsed,
248:2
conscience & busi-
ness, 68:7
the honorable, the
just, 514:7
injustice, great and
unredressed, 460:3
I 'spect I growed, 81:7
I's wicked, 176:3
is America safe?,
248:2
Kentuckians, 261:3
a mighty influence is
abroad, 248:2
soul, my, 464:5
very stylish, 186:11
**Stravinsky, Igor [Fyo-
dorvich]**
(1882–1971)
music, 52:1
**Strong, George A[ugus-
tus]** *(1832–1912)*
the Mudjokivis (note),
418:8–419
**Strong, George Temple-
ton** *(1820–1875)*
a barbarian, 284:2
Dan Sickles' charac-
ter, 249:4
Strout, Richard
(1898–1992)
eight millionaires & a
plumber (note),
253:1
Strunk, William, Jr.
(1869–1946)
writing, 54:11
Strunsky, Simeon
remark seldom
quoted correctly,
416:4
Stryker, Fran
Hi-yo, Silver! 230:5

Sullivan, Brendan
(b. 1942)
not a potted plant,
279:1
Sullivan, John L.
(1858–1918)
the bigger they come,
471:1
I can lick any man in
the house (note),
471:1
Sullivan, Louis Henri
(1856–1924)
form & function, 48:5
**Sullivan, Timothy ("Big
Tim") D.**
(1853–1913)
as long as they spell
my name right,
407:4
Sumner, [Sen.] Charles
(1811–1874)
the flag, 373:2
hirelings (note), 259:2
Kansas, crime against,
259:2
navigators, intrepid,
10:2
public office (note),
217:3
slavery & liberty,
461:6
**Sumner, William Gra-
ham** *(1840–1910)*
Forgotten Man, 157:3
**Sunday, William A.
(Billy)** *(1863–1936)*
hell, 228:11
Superman Radio Show
faster than a speeding
bullet, 230:6
Sutton, Willie
(1901–1980)
where the money is,
134:5
Swope, Herbert Bayard
(1882–1958)
cold war (note), 32:7
Sylvester, Arthur
(1901–1979)
information is power,
264:1
government is right
to lie (note), 264:1
Szasz, Thomas Stephen
(b. 1920)
forgive but never for-
get (note), 198:6
God, if you talk to,
445:9
happiness, 223:3
two wrongs, 178:7
Szilard, Leo *(1898–1964)*
don't lie, 152:10

Taft, William Howard
(1857–1930)
little brown brother,
469:4
president, profession
of, 402:6
Tandy, Jessica
(1909–1994)
the theater, 56:9
Taney, [Justice] Roger B.
(1777–1864)
the word "citizens"
(note), 27:6–28
**Tarkington, [Newton]
Booth** *(1869–1946)*
drinks he has taken
to, 12:5
mystics, 326:10

Taylor, Harold
(1914–1993)
education, 161:8 &
note
Taylor, Maxwell
(1901–1987)
deterrence of war,
314:10
Taylor, [Pres.] Zachary
(1784–1850)
go to hell, 308:1
hurrah for old Ken-
tucky, 308:2
Teale, Edwin Way
(1899–1980)
autumn, 347:3
May, 347:2
nature, 336:3
time & space—scarci-
ties, 206:4
Tecumseh *(1768–1813)*
lands, we are deter-
mined to defend
our, 432:4
these lands are ours,
417:2
**Teller, [Sen.] Henry
M[oore]**
(1830–1914)
we want those is-
lands, 226:1
Tennyson, Alfred [Lord]
(1809–1892)
old order changeth
(note), 79:5
**Texas Declaration of
Independence**
a people educated,
160:1
**Thackeray, William
Makepeace**
(1811–1863)
Augusta, 86:4
**Thayer, Ernest
Lawrence**
(1863–1940)
mighty Casey, 470:5
Theroux, Paul *(b. 1941)*
the Japanese & man-
ners, 332:5
South America, 334:1
Thomas, Dylan
(1914–1953)
seventeen whiskeys,
272:2
Washington [D.C.],
108:8
Thomas, Lewis, M.D.
(1913–1993)
sound of birds, mol-
lusks, & midges,
339:8
we are the worrying
animal, 43:5
Thompson, Francis
(1859–1907)
deliberate speed
(note), 129:1
Thompson, Hunter S.
(b. 1937)
huge cars, 449:3
**Thompson, William
Hale**
I'll crack him [King
George] in the
snoot, 421:7
Thoreau, Henry David
(1817–1862)
actual, a true account
of the, 426:5
aim, 14:2
American govern-
ment today, 308:3

be good for some-
thing, 504:10
be men first, 200:7
beans, 341:11
beauty, 61:6
bluebird carries the
sky, 337:2
book, reading of a,
65:6
books, 65:5, 7, & 8
brand-new country,
295:1
buying & selling, 68:9
California, 72:4
Cape Cod, 302:2
chairs, three, 456:3
change, 79:2
city, turned into a,
166:11
civilized man, 418:2
clothes, new, 186:10
common sense, 426:5
Concord, 494:3
conforming out-
wardly, 240:10
country turned to a
city, 166:11
day dawns, 363:6
desperation, quiet,
280:7
detail, frittered away
by, 456:2
a different drummer,
247:6
a doctor's opinion,
153:5
dreams, 154:4
eastward, westward,
527:6
education, 160:4
effort, 149:1
enterprises that re-
quire new clothes,
186:10
evil, 176:4
a fact, 181:4,6
facts, the essential,
280:8
faith, 516:2
fear, 189:1
flowers, 341:9
the forest, the
meadow, the night,
335:8
friends, 203:4
games & amuse-
ments, 207:3
good, doing, 514:8
the good & the brave,
514:9
goodness tainted,
188:7
the hands serve the
eyes, 516:2
health, 227:2
the heart, 228:3
heaven is under our
feet, 335:8
I am a parcel of vain
strivings, 238:1
I have traveled a good
deal in Concord,
494:3
I wished to live delib-
erately, 280:8
Indian, the, 418:2
individual speculators
(note), 205:6
the infinite, 183:9
inventions, 446:3
law v. right, 274:2
life, a broad margin to
my, 280:9

life, my, 280:6
lives of quiet despera-
tion, 280:7
loafer knocking at the
doors of heaven,
279:3
luxuries & comforts,
292:6
Maine, 295:1,2
a majority of one,
296:3
man, the savage in,
238:3
masses of men, 377:2
misery, has company
enough, 501:2
myself, talk so much
about, 451:6
nature, 335:5,7
neighbor, a good,
350:11
nutriment, gnaw the
crust of the earth
for, 205:6
one world at a time,
270:10
Oregon, toward,
365:1
philanthropy, 80:4
philosopher, to be a,
379:1
prejudices, 399:4
quarreled, I didn't
know we had ever
(note), 270:10–271
the railroad (note),
446:3
reality, 426:6
regret deeply, to, 428:1
resignation, 280:7
revolution, the right,
434:7
rich, a man is, 323:4
richest whose plea-
sures are cheapest,
323:5
sailing, good (note),
270:10–272
saunter, a great art to,
279:4
season of small fruits,
343:9
see, we are as much
as we, 516:2
seed, faith in a,
341:10
simplify, simplify,
456:2
solitude, 463:1
soul, light comes into
the, 464:4
soul must be green,
166:10
splitting [wood
stumps], 130:6
surmise, the deep,
317:3
sweat of his brow,
543:6
a telegraph, 118:6
time, 491:6,7
tools of their tools,
men have become,
446:4
trade, 68:8
traveler, swiftest,
469:6
trout in the milk,
175:6
truth, 497:11,13
we shall be obliged to
gnaw the earth,
205:6

went to the woods to
live deliberately,
280:8
westward I go free,
527:6
who are we?, 414:1
wildness, 530:8
a wild rank place,
530:9
wisdom, 534:7
woods, I went to the,
280:8
world—to live in it,
546:10
world—one at a time,
270:10
writing, 57:8
Thorpe, Thomas B[angs]
(1815–1878)
its airs will make you
snort, 45:3
Thurber, James
(1894–1961)
a burden in the bush,
433:4
Burgundy, a naive do-
mestic, 192:5
Columbus [Ohio],
92:2
early to rise (note),
226:10
hesitates, he who,
246:1
humor, 240:8
Paris, 110:6
people, you can fool
too many of the
(note), 377:5
questions & answers,
415:1
safety in numbers,
there is no, 450:10
seal bark, you heard a,
44:4
sex necessary?, 453:5
so much has already
been written, 263:11
the wit, the satirist,
the humorist, 240:7
you could look it up,
182:3
Tillich, Paul
(1886–1965)
forgiving, 198:7
Timrod, Henry
(1828–1867)
sleep sweetly in your
humble graves,
171:4
Tindley, C. Albert
(fl. 1900)
I'll overcome some
day (note), 423:6
**Tocqueville, [Count]
Alexis de**
(1805–1859)
America is a land of
wonders, 17:8
a conflict between the
white and the black
inhabitants, 418:1
laws, civil, 277:4
the lawyers of the
United States, 277:3
majority, 296:2
middle class, one,
310:1
money, 17:7, 322:11
patriotism of Ameri-
cans, 372:5
question, political &
judicial, 273:10
the useful, 504:8

the West, 310:8
Western settlements,
310:7
women, the superior-
ity of their, 537:5
Todd, Michael ("Mike")
(born Avram Gold-
enbogen)
(1907–1958)
no legs, no jokes
(note), 359:6
Tolkin, Michael
rumors, 440:2
Toynbee, Arnold
(1889–1975)
America, 23:9
Train, Arthur
(1875–1945)
law, lack of respect
for, 133:4
**Transworld Getaway
Guide**
San Francisco, 106:5
**Travis, [Lt. Col.]
William Barrett**
(1809–1836)
I shall never surren-
der, 27:3
Tribe, Laurence H.
(b. 1941)
judicial restraint,
256:7
Tribune. See New York
Tribune
Trilling, Lionel
(1905–1975)
reality, 426:11
Trollope, Anthony
(1815–1882)
the difficult & the im-
possible (note), 4:1
Frankfort, 93:6
New England, 352:5
newspapers [con-
sumed] by an Amer-
ican, 406:2
Portlanders, 104:2
women, American,
537:12 & note
Trollope, Frances
(1780–1863)
American, from the
lips of an, 266:2
Avon, 86:8
Cincinnati, 91:2
fall glory, 343:8
Maryland, 301:2
[Memphis:] a new
world, 95:12
[New York:] like
Venice, 98:1
religious factions,
17:6
Trotsky, Leon [Lev
Davidovich Bron-
stein] *(1879–1940)*
[New York] & the
modern age, 99:8
old age (note), 360:8
Truman, Harry S.
(1884–1972)
an atomic bomb,
554:1
buck stops here, 433:5
children, to give ad-
vice to your, 368:1
economist, one-
armed, 159:2
flags of freedom,
553:6
guttersnipe, 403:7
half-bright (note),
252:4

heat, if you can't
stand the, 477:3
hell & the truth,
499:7
history, 233:7,8
I'm going to fight
hard/ give them
hell (note), 387:7
Korea, 264:3,5
military, civilian con-
trol of the, 314:7
the moon had fallen
on me (note), 32:6
pay-as-you-go, 159:3
a police action,
265:2
pray for me now, 32:6
[presidency:] not like
the army, 403:9
president [represents]
the whole nation,
404:1
recession & depres-
sion (note), 159:1
review, your lousy,
49:6
skunk territory (note),
403:7
a statesman (note),
391:7
Tsongas, [Sen.] Paul E.
(b. 1941)
cold war, 37:6
deathbed & business,
71:7
Tubman, Harriet
(1815–1913)
a glory over every-
thing, 201:2
liberty & death, 201:3
Tuchman, Barbara
(1912–1989)
war, 522:3
Tucker, Sophie
(c.1884–1966)
a girl needs, 9:1
keep breathing,
227:9
rich & poor, 436:8
Tunis, John R.
(1889–1975)
losing, 534:3
**Turgot, Anne Robert
Jacques, Baron a
l'Aulne** *(1727–1781)*
the hope of this
world, 16:5
lightning and
scepters, 198:8
**Turner, Frederick J[ack-
son]** *(1861–1932)*
America & opportu-
nity, 20:5
democracy, 144:7,8
freedom, 20:4
free land, 204:7
the frontier & Ameri-
can intellect, 20:4
the frontier & indi-
vidualism, 204:8
the frontier has gone,
205:1
the Great West, 529:1
individualism, 247:7
the tax gatherer,
485:4
Twain, Mark [given
name, Samuel Lang-
horne Clemens]
(1835–1910)
abroad, to go, 494:7
aces, four, 207:4
the adjective, 54:8

Twain, Mark (cont.)
advice, 8:4
America, wonderful
to find, 20:7
angry, when, 42:5
approval of other peo-
ple (note), 238:10
Arkansaw, 45:7 &
note
Arkansas City, 86:2
a baby, 82:3
banging and slam-
ming, 50:2
baseball, 470:6
Bible, 59:2, 77:11
book, a successful,
54:9
Boston, New York,
Philadelphia, 84:8
breeding, good, 298:4
California, scenery in,
73:3
the cat, 337:11
a classic [definition
of], 66:1
a coin, button, hand-
kerchief, 490:7
Congress, 120:7,8
a Congressman & Ju-
das Iscariot, 120:6
corn bread, 191:5
corn pone, 238:10
country looks like a
singed cat, 351:3
courage, 131:1
customs, 221:7
a dark side, 450:6
death, the report of
my, 406:6
difference of opinion,
150:7
a dog & a man, 238:7
education, 160:7,
(note) 161:7
eggs in one basket,
535:9
exercise is loathsome,
379:10
an experience, 179:11
facts, get your, 181:7
fame is a vapor, 478:2
familiarity, 253:5
faith, 184:4
first half of life & the
last half, 8:10
Florence, 109:4
fools, 193:6, 296:8
forbidden, the, 457:1
foreigners, 197:6
forty-eight, before &
after, 364:1
France, 330:6
freedom of speech,
freedom of con-
science, 20:8
friendship, 203:6
German, the literary,
330:9
girls, 538:9
golf, 470:8
good, be, 515:4
a good example, 515:2
good night, dear
heart, 172:3
habits, other people's,
221:3
[Hawaiian] islands
(note), 225:10
[Hawaii:] that peace-
ful land, 225:10
health, your, 227:5
Heavenly Father in-
vented man, 212:10
he is useless, 250:2

he telegraphed back
for his blankets
(note), 44:6
humor, 240:1
idea, new, 354:11
illusions, 154:5
Italy, 331:5
a jay & a Congress-
man, 337:8
June bug, a young, 8:9
jury system, 254:2
justice, 258:2
justice system, 257:1
kings is mostly rap-
scallions, 231:7
[Kipling:] a remark-
able man,
181:7–182
laugh and laugh, we,
272:10
laughter, 272:9
law, in the, 277:8
legislatures (note),
120:7
life, 8:10, 281:7, 317:9
lie, a cat and a, 152:8
lies [in the Bible], 59:2
lies & statistics,
444:1
mad, we are all, 293:5
man is the only ani-
mal that blushes,
238:9
a mob, 377:8
modern inconven-
iences, 321:5
modify before we
print, we, 77:10
New England
weather, 352:7
New Orleans, 97:3
Newport, 97:6
old age & broken
health, 147:4
partialities and preju-
dices, our, 399:5
patriot & change,
373:8
persons attempting to
find a motive in
this narrative, 49:3
a pessimist & an opti-
mist, 364:1
pray a lie, you can't,
398:1
profanity (note), 42:5
opinion, petrified,
243:3
the public [as] critic,
49:2
race, the most mar-
velous, 420:9
a raft, 455:5
remember anything, I
could, 306:1
remember, things I
can (note), 306:1
right, always do,
437:8
Salt Lake City, 105:6
Satan, 149:11,12
school boards, 160:9
smoking, 493:5
a southerner talks
music, 466:4
speculate, he should
not, 69:6
speculate in stocks
(note), 69:6
speech, 302:8
statesmanship, 151:5
success, 478:1
take the lies out of
him, 250:1

tax collector & taxi-
dermist, 485:6
temptation & cow-
ardice, 487:1
thoughts, the storm
of, 317:9
through a glass eye
darkly, 250:3
training is everything,
160:8
truth, 498:8,9,10,11
the war [Civil War],
116:6
watermelon, 191:6
"we," the word, 268:1
weather, talks about
the, 348:10
we have ground the
manhood out of
them, 420:8
whiskey into the
committee rooms,
120:5
woman, a thoroughly
beautiful, 538:10
word, the right, 267:8
Yankee, I am a,
122:9
young June bug & old
bird of paradise,
8:9

Udall, Stewart L[ee]
(b. 1920)
conservation, 168:12
The Quiet Crisis,
168:11
we have confused
power with great-
ness, 397:6
United Negro College
Fund
a mind, 318:9
United States. See un-
der U.S.
Unruh, Jesse M.
(1922–1989)
money & politics,
394:4
Updike, John (b. 1932)
bore, healthy male
adult, 67:5
gods & letters, 213:10
ghosts of Hawthorne
and Melville,
352:11
memory, 306:5
neutrinos, 445:1
schools, 162:3
writing great, 58:14
U.S. Army, Office of the
Chief Signal Officer
Spartan simplicity
must be observed,
314:1
U.S. Army Service
Forces
the difficult & the
impossible, 4:1
U.S. Census, Superin-
tendent of
a frontier line (note),
205:1
U.S. Coast Guard
always ready, 313:4
U.S. Marines
first in the fight,
313:6
U.S. Motto
in God we trust, 211:3
U.S. Postal Service.
See General Post
Office, New York
City

U.S. President's Science
Advisory Commit-
tee
science & the excel-
lent, 443:5

Vandenberg, Arthur
Hendrick
(1884–1951)
expediency & justice,
179:8
Vanderbilt, William H.
(1821–1885)
public be damned,
69:2
Vandiver, Willard Dun-
can (1854–1932)
I am from Missouri,
320:8
Van Doren, Mark
(1894–1972)
wit, 240:5
Van Dyke, Henry
(1852–1933)
America for me!,
374:2
Van Loon, Hendrik
Willem (1882–1944)
history, 233:4
life & progress,
411:9
Veblen, Thorstein
[Bunde] (1857–1929)
conspicuous con-
sumption, 323:8
beautiful products,
61:10
editor, first duty of
an, 407:3
research & questions,
414:3
wealth, standard of,
323:9
Vegetius (Flavius Veg-
etius Renatus)
(fl. c. 375)
war, prepare for
(note), 518:5
Vernon, Dai (1894–1992)
the mind is led on
step by step, 57:2
Verrazzano, Giovanni
da (ca. 1485–1528)
an island in the form
of a triangle (note),
435:5
Land of the Bad Peo-
ple, 294:8
Vidal, Gore (b. 1925)
technology & history,
449:7
whenever a friend
succeeds, 479:4
Villard, Oswald Garri-
son (1857–1949)
military intelligence,
313:8
Virginia Declaration of
Rights
trial by jury, 256:9
Voltaire, (given name,
François Marie
Arouet) (1694–1778)
more prudence to ac-
quit two [guilty]
persons (note),
273:6
Vonnegut, Kurt (b. 1922)
brought back from
the dead—a mixed
blessing, 320:1
God, to daydream
about, 431:5
high school, 162:5

Vreeland, Diana
the bikini, 187:5

Walker, Alice *(b. 1944)*
poetry, 54:5
Walker, Felix
(1753–1828)
talking to Buncombe,
356:2
Walker, James John
("Jimmy")
(1881–1946)
book, ruined by a, 66:4
will you love me in
December?, 290:1
Wallace, George
(b. 1919)
pointy-headed intel-
lectuals (note),
163:9–164
segregation now,
424:1
Wallace, Henry A[gard]
(1888–1965)
century of the com-
mon man, 322:1
Wallace, W[illiam]
R[oss] *(1819–1881)*
the hand that rocks
the cradle, 538:1
Waller, Thomas ("Fats")
(1904–1933)
if you got to ask,
51:12
one never know, 459:4
Walpole, Horace
(1717–1797)
America & next Au-
gustan age, 15:5
Wanamaker, John
(1838–1922)
advertising, 5:4
Ward, Artemus (born,
Charles Farrar
Browne)
(1834–1867)
Brigham Young & 200
wives, 299:3
gets his fist in fust
(note), 315:7–316
Mexico, 332:6
Salt Lake [City], 105:4
they shoot folks here
[Carson City], 89:4
Washington, George,
525:4
Warhol, Andy [born,
Andrew Warhola]
(1927–1987)
famous for fifteen
minutes, 479:3
Warland, John H.
the Factory Girl,
542:12

Warner, Charles Dudley
(1829–1900)
agriculture, 185:7
city land & taxes,
84:5
Peoria (note), 102:3
politics & bedfellows,
390:10
seeds, to plant, 342:1
sin, 456:9
travel & home, 494:6
value, 506:4
weather (note), 348:10
Warren, Earl
(1891–1974)
all deliberate speed,
129:1
separate educational
facilities, 34:3 &
423:3

Washburn, [Rep.] Cad-
wallader C.
(1818–1882)
[Alaska] where none
but malefactors will
live, 10:1
Washington, Booker
T[aliaferro]
(1856–1915)
character, 515:3
dignity in tilling a
field, 544:4
the slave system,
462:2
success, 478:3
Washington, George
(1732–1799)
alliances, permanent,
194:2
bullets whistle, I
heard, 518:1
chair of government,
400:9
conquer or die, 39:1
the constitution,
126:1
credit, public, 156:4
danger, 136:1
despair, we should
never, 148:7
discipline, 311:6 &
note
favors from nation to
nation, 194:3
force, a permanent
(note), 311:8
foreign influence,
197:5
[gambling:] child of
avarice, 207:2
good faith and justice,
194:4
government, estab-
lished, 215:9
honest man, 235:5
honesty, 235:6
I die hard, 138:6
I now take my leave
of you, 26:4
a lie (note), 235:6
military establish-
ments, 311:10
militia, 311:8
necessity, dire, 39:4
patriotism, pretended,
371:3
peace and harmony,
194:4
[Pittsburgh site:] con-
venient for build-
ing, 103:5
religious opinions,
429:1
the senatorial saucer,
120:2
'tis well, 270:2
war, to be prepared
for, 518:5
Wayne, John (given
name, Marion
Morrison)
(1907–1979)
a beautiful day,
400:7
speak slow & low,
56:1
Webb, Charles *(b. 1939)*
plastics (note), 70:10
Webb, Jack *(1920–1982)*
just the facts, 182:5
Weber, Joseph
(1867–1942)
wife, she's my,
299:7

Webster, Daniel
(1782–1852)
accuracy & diligence
necessary to a
lawyer, 277:1
the Constitution,
216:4
Country, Our, 372:1
credit & commerce,
68:4
farmers & civiliza-
tion, 185:6
government, people's,
216:4
I do not propose to be
buried, 508:7
independence now,
200:5
knowledge, 263:2
liberty & union, 501:7
& note
repression & revolu-
tion, 500:5
revolution, political,
434:4
room at the top, 477:8
a sign to show that
there he makes
men, 353:1
a small college [Dart-
mouth], 159:8
truth, 497:6
Washington, George,
525:3
Webster, John
(c.1580–c.1625)
murder shrieks out
(note), 131:8
Webster, Noah
(1758–1843)
Virginians, 512:5
Weinberg, Jack *(b. 1940)*
don't trust anybody
over 30, 557:6
Weinberg, Steven
(b. 1933)
universe, the, 504:5
Welles, Orson
(1915–1985)
disease you don't look
forward to being
cured of, 362:7
Italy v. Switzerland,
331:7
Rosebud, 271:10,
428:7
Wellington, Arthur
Wellesley, Duke of
(1769–1852)
fear (note), 31:5
Wells, H[erbert]
G[eorge]
(1866–1946)
Europe & the Ameri-
can Eagle, 330:5
New York, 99:2
Welsh, Joseph N[ye]
(1890–1960)
have you no sense of
decency?, 35:1
Wesley, John
(1703–1791)
deluded rebels in
America, 39:6
West, Mae *(1892–1980)*
come up 'n see me,
237:6
diamonds, what beau-
tiful, 457:4
diary, keep a, 58:3
evils, between two,
176:7
funny, hard to be,
240:2

grape, peel me a, 192:3
I've been things, 180:2
looked over, better to
be, 453:6
man in the house,
306:10
martini, dry, 13:3
the men in my life,
227:6
Snow White, I used to
be, 457:6
temptation, 487:4
too much of a good
thing, 178:2
when I'm good/when
I'm bad, 457:5
West, Nathanael (born,
Nathan Wallenstein
Weinstein)
(1904–1940)
Miss Lonelyhearts,
8:7
numbers, 444:3
Westmoreland, [Gen.]
William C.
(b. 1914)
revolution, our own,
435:4
Vietnam War & cen-
sorship, 511:2
Weston, Edward
(1886–1958)
the West, 529:4
Whale, James
(1896–1957)
something more com-
fortable, 187:4
Wharton, Edith
(1862–1937)
Mrs. Ballinger & Cul-
ture, 46:10
old age & sorrow,
362:2
Wheatley, Phyllis
(c.1753–1784)
the world, 546:6
Wheeler, John
A[rchibald] *(b. 1911)*
black holes, 445:2
quantum physics
(note), 444:7
space, curved, 444:8
Wheeler, [Rep.] Joseph
(1836–1906)
book, every good,
65:14
wisdom, 65:14
Whig Party
farewell, dear Van,
381:4
free soil—Fré-mont,
382:5
Rough and Ready, we
called him, 382:3
Tippecanoe and Tyler
too, 381:3
two dollars a day and
roast beef, 381:2
Whistler, James Abbott
McNeill
(1834–1903)
I am not arguing with
you, 44:3
Whitaker, [Dr.] Carl A.
(1912–1995)
marriage, 300:12
White, E[lwyn] B[rooks]
(1899–1955)
the best place to be,
186:4
broccoli, 192:2
democracy, 145:2
fortune, a man about
to make his, 325:6

White, E[lwyn] B[rooks]
  (*cont.*)
friend & a good
    writer, 204:2
life & a car, 448:1
luck, 292:2
Maine, 295:7
never hurry [or]
    worry, 43:3
New York, 100:10,11
profit system, 77:3
sex necessary?, 453:5
sweet interlude,
    282:11
television, 303:6
tired of living, 14:1
travelling north, 495:5
White, William Allen
  (*1868–1944*)
all dressed up &
    nowhere to go,
    182:12
he-harlot Harding,
    224:4
Kansas, 260:3 & note
the vision lives, 172:7
Whitehead, Alfred
  North (*1861–1947*)
analysis of the obvi-
    ous, 442:2
body, the human, 64:8
civilization, 111:10,12
a dog v. a cat, 339:2
the English, 329:13
God, the nature of,
    213:3
knowledge, 263:7
life, 282:8
life & speed, 447:3
mathematics, 444:2
moral precepts [in]
    the Gospels, 430:10
philosophy, 379:4–6
science, 443:8
truths, 499:2
Whitman, Walt
  (*1819–1892*)
Alabama, as I have
    walked in, 9:4
amazement of things,
    504:1
America and democ-
    racy, 19:8
[American] slang
    names, 19:10
America singing, 19:5
animals, 337:3
body is sacred, 64:3
book, this is no, 65:15
Captain, O, 284:5
city of sparkling wa-
    ters, 98:4
Colorado men are we,
    117:3
[Denver:] cash!, 92:6
do I contradict my-
    self? 124:1
Europe's old dynastic
    slaughterhouse,
    330:3
future & present,
    205:8
hollowness of heart,
    61:2
hypocrisy, 241:1
I contain multitudes,
    124:1
I hear America
    singing, 19:5
I loaf, 279:5
judge, the perfect,
    256:3
justice, 257:9

lilacs last in the door-
    yard bloom'd, 463:11
literature, popular,
    302:7
Manhattan, 98:4
men & women, 541:6
a miracle, 319:6
the moon, 340:1
myself, 451:7,8
physiology, 443:6
pioneers!, 204:6
poets & audiences,
    53:1
politics, 390:3
power & territory,
    307:11
road, the open, 494:8
sex, 453:1
simplicity, 456:4
spider, a noiseless pa-
    tient, 337:9
suffrage, universal,
    144:6
sun, the splendid
    silent, 339:13
United States [are]
    greatest poem, 18:7
war, the real, 116:5
wisdom, 534:8
a woman waits for
    me, 289:6
women, perfect, 538:5
Whittier, John Green-
  leaf (*1807–1892*)
the age is dull and
    mean, 60:6
barefoot boy, 81:8
Bay State, 301:8
December day, 344:6
faith & honor, 236:2
God, 212:5
"it might have
    been!", 428:3
justice, changeless,
    257:10
lawyers, 277:6
life & fate & will,
    281:1
love & forgiving, 198:3
man, the steady gain
    of, 411:6
peace & manhood,
    374:11
of all sad words of
    tongue or pen, 428:3
pumpkin pie, 489:2
shoot if you must this
    old gray head, 372:8
simple beauty & rus-
    tic health, 130:7
soul, the windows of
    my, 464:6
Thanksgiving, 489:1
Wiener, Norbert
  (*1894–1964*)
information, 263:10
progress, 412:2
scientist, degradation
    of the, 442:9
Wightman, Hazel
  Hotchkiss
  (*1886–1974*)
tennis alphabet, 473:5
Wilbur, Richard [Purdy]
  (*b. 1921*)
excellence, 177:5
the morning air, 348:5
soul, become a, 464:10
Wilcox, Ella Wheeler
  (*1855–1919*)
laugh & the world
    laughs with you,
    273:1

Wilde, Oscar
  (*1854–1900*)
America youth of,
    20:6
America & Europe,
    330:4
America & expectora-
    tion (note), 298:1
do not shoot the pi-
    anist, 51:3
Hoboken, 93:7
idleness [in Newport],
    97:5
my genius (note), 93:7
Niagara (note), 355:5
temptation (note),
    487:4
when bad Americans
    die (note), 110:1
whiskey, the first
    course was, 12:2
the young, in Amer-
    ica, 556:4
Wilder, Billy. See under
  Brackett, Charles
Wilder, Thornton
  [Niven] (*1897–1975*)
animals, 339:3
fools, 193:9
into their graves mar-
    ried, 300:5
life—every, every
    minute, 282:9
married life & fights,
    300:9
money, 325:7
sex, a laugh at, 453:7
woman's work,
    539:11
Will, George [Frederick]
  (*b. 1941*)
advertising blather, 7:7
football, 476:5
Williams, Alexander S.
  [Clubber]
  (*1839–1917*)
law & a policeman's
    nightstick, 274:3
tenderloin (note),
    274:3
Williams, [Sen.] John
  Sharp (*1854–1932*)
treason, grazes the
    edge of, 548:5
Williams, Roger
  (*ca. 1603–1683*)
the dung heap of this
    earth, 546:5
Williams, Tennessee
  [Thomas Lanier]
  (*1911–1983*)
caged birds, 202:3
departure, a time for,
    368:12
dogs, to outlive her,
    362:9
a God so quickly,
    213:7
I, I, I, 451:13
kindness of strangers,
    262:7
memory, in, 306:3
mendacity, 152:9
opportunity, 363:10
present moment,
    400:4
snare for the truth,
    56:4
time, 492:7
work, 546:4
Williams, William Car-
  los (*1883–1963*)
alcohol, 13:4

America, the pure
    products of, 22:3
the bull is godlike,
    338:2
the cat climbed, 338:6
flowers through the
    window, 302:4
happy genius of my
    household, 184:11
I am lonely, 463:3
love, 281:1,2
love & forgiveness,
    198:5
moon, blessed, 340:4
Paterson, 102:2
plums, 191:8 & note
poems, to get the
    news from, 54:2
poverty, the anarchy
    of, 395:10
sorrow, 464:1
stone, stone, 354:8
summer, 346:2
travel, the beauties of,
    494:10
Weehawken, 109:2
weeks, the desolate,
    346:4
year plunges into
    night, 346:5
Willingham, Calder. See
    also under Henry,
    Buck &
success, 478:13
Willkie, Wendell
  L[ewis] (*1890–1944*)
a socialist, 462:6
the constitution &
    citizenship, 128:7
Wills, Garry (*b. 1934*)
Miami, 96:5
Wilson, Charles
  (*1890–1961*)
our country & Gen-
    eral Motors, 70:9
Wilson, Edmund
  (*1895–1972*)
Canada, 329:4
Miami, 96:2
Wilson, Flip (given
    name, Clerow)
  (*b. 1933*)
the devil, 150:3
Wilson, Woodrow
  (*1856–1924*)
America first, 21:5
the automobile,
    447:1
a bungalow mind,
    224:3
corporations, 69:8
democracy, the world
    must be made safe
    for, 548:3
diplomacy, 195:6
face, my, 64:5
fight, too proud to,
    366:3
the flag, 374:3
honor, the naton's,
    236:5
man, no indispens-
    able, 239:2
man committing sui-
    cide, 177:7
monopolies, 69:9
nations, a general as-
    sociation of, 30:4
A New Freedom,
    385:3
nothing is done as it
    was, 79:5
open covenants, 375:6

opinion of the world, 413:3

peace, a price too great to pay for, 375:5

peace without victory, 30:2

prosperity & a political campaign, 392:7

Rhode Island, 435:7

the right, 437:11

seas, freedom of the, 195:5

stomach, an empty, 395:8

war against all nations, 548:4

Washington [D.C.], 108:3

watchful waiting, 195:4

willful men, little group of, 121:4

the world is so big and I am so small, 546:11

world made safe for democracy, 548:3

Windsor, Duke of (Edward VIII) *(1894–1972)*

[American] parents & children, 368:2

Winthrop, John *(1588–1649)*

city upon a hill, 14:9

Wise, John *(1652–1725)*

death, 138:4

Wister, Owen *(1869–1938)*

smile, 136:5

Wodehouse, P[elham] G[renville] *(1881–1975)*

make my day (note), 137:7

Wolfe, Thomas [Clayton] *(1900–1938)*

America, we are lost here in, 23:1

beautiful woman cooking dinner, 542:2

Brooklyn, only the dead know, 100;2

home, 235:2

a liberal is (note), 394:11

light, a thousand points of friendly (note), 24:9

New York, 100:5,6

October, 346:8

sleep, in, 155:8

spring, 346:7

a stranger and alone, 13:10

Woodhull, Victoria Claflin *(1838–1927)*

right to love, 453:2

Woollcott, Alexander [Humphreys] *(1887–1943)*

immoral, illegal, or fattening, 457:9

seventy-two suburbs (note), 94:7

Wordsworth, Elizabeth *(1840–1932)*

good people & clever people, 377:9

Wordsworth, William *(1770–1850)*

poetry (note), 240:8

Work, Henry Clay *(1832–1884)*

father, dear father, 12:2

marching through Georgia, 116:2

Worth, Cedric *(fl. c. 1937)*

hates dogs and children (note), 320:2

Wright, Frank Lloyd *(1869–1959)*

architecture, 48:8

home in Japan, 332:2

luxuries, 292:8

plant vines, 48:6

Wright, Richard *(1908–1960)*

jail, it's just like livin in, 422:8

self-realization, 451:11

Wright, Wilbur *(1867–1912)*

talk, the only bird that can, 483:6

Wright, Orville *(1871–1948)*

success, 446:8

Wylie, Elinor [Morton] *(1885–1928)*

avoid the reeking herd, 463:4

hater, a good, 225:4

silence, 455:9

stone to throw, 135:4

woman, being, 539:1

words, 269:2,3

X, Malcolm. See Malcolm X

Yeats, John Butler *(1865–1939)*

talk in America, 129:6

Yellen, Jack *(1892–1991)*

happy days are here again, 214:7

Last of the Red Hot Mamas (note), 9:1

Yordan, Philip *(b. 1913),* and Wyler, Robert

a lawyer (note), 278:3

Young, Brigham *(1801–1877)*

this is the place, 504:11

Young, Joe. See under Lewis, Sam M.

Youngman, Henny *(b. 1906)*

how's your wife (note), 300:10

take my wife, 300:10

Yzquierdo, Pedro *(fl. c.1492)*

light! land!, 25:4

Zangwill, Israel *(1864–1926)*

America is God's . . . melting pot, 21:3

New York, 99:1

Zappa, Frank *(1940–1993)*

deviation from the norm, 151:3

Ziegler, Ron[ald L.] *(b. 1939)*

third-rate burglary, 525:5

the operative statement, 526:4

Keyword Index

Abortion, 37:3
Above
one who thought he
was a. me, 409:6
Abraham
we are coming Father
A., 114:2
Abroad
in search of monsters
to destroy, 17:4
to go a., 494:7
Aces
four a., 207:4
Acres
forty a. and a mule,
465:4
Act
he was pure a., 439:5
Action
& the Puritans, 2:5
get a., 3:4
life is a. and passion,
281:10
men seem to live for
a., 1:5
ACTION & DOING, 1
Actions
great and honorable
a., 1:1
Actor
Great A. must always
act, 55:5
if an a. has a message,
56:8
if you have ever been
an a., 55:6
movie a. is a god in
captivity, 56:7
nobody can like an a.,
56:2
Actors
must not be boring,
57:1
Actual
true account of the a.,
426:5
what is a. is a. only
for one time, 444:5
Ad
astra per aspera,
260:11
astra per ardua (note),
14:3
Adam
was never called Mas-
ter A., 162:8

Adamantine
something very dan-
gerous to reach,
332:2
Adjective
when in doubt, strike
it out, 54:8
Adlai (note), 387:9
Adultery
I've committed a. in
my heart, 454:2
in high places and in
low (note), 456:10
ADVENTURE, 4
Advertisements
in a newspaper, 5:2
ADVERTISING, ADVERTIS-
ING SLOGANS, &
PUBLICITY, 4
Advertising
doing business with-
out a., 7:3
half the money I
spend on a., 5:4
if the a. is right (note),
377:5
infinite promise of
American a., 6:3
problems connected
with a., 7:5
Advertising blather, 7:7
Advertising copy, 7:2
ADVICE, 8
Advice
a. to your children,
368:1
[is the] smallest cur-
rent coin, 8:5
good scare v. good a.,
8:6
he thought he could
give a. better, 8:14
of the elders, 8:3
Advocacy
of what is just and
right (note), 502:4
AESTHETICS. See ART:
AESTHETICS, 47
Affluent society, 292:7
Afford
whether they can a. a
thing, 158:1
Afraid
as much a. of me as I
had been of him,
189:2

Africa
still yesterday in A.,
328:1
Age
demanded an image,
321:6
golden a. of poetry
and power, 214:8
is dull and mean, 60:6
is opportunity, 360:9
most people my a. are
dead, 363:1
AGE, OLD. See OLD AGE,
360
Aged
one a. man 361:6
AGES, 8
Ages
he belongs to the a.,
284:3
Agriculture
blessed be a.!,
185:7
giant carpet of a.,
358:6
Aim
High, 14:5
men hit only what
they a. at, 14:2
Air
is so refined, 92:7
Airs
its a. will make you
snort, 45:3
ALABAMA, 9
Alabama
as I have walked in
A., 9:4
daybreak in A., 9:6
seems to have a bad
name, 9:2
stars fell on A., 9:5
with my banjo on my
knee, 9:3
Alabaster cities, 84:7
Alamo 27:4
remember the A.,
27:5
ALASKA, 9
Alaska
A.'s forests, 10:10
handful of people
clinging to a sub-
continent, 10:9
how A. happened to
be, 10:5

is a great country, 10:6
Albany
those who are in A.,
85:8
you take A., 85:7
ALCOHOL & DRINKING,
11
Alcohol
God created a., 13:4
Alcoholic
bellow for a. bever-
ages (note), 361:8
Alert
Always A., 473:5
ALIENATION, 13
Alki, 523:7
All
dressed up with
nowhere to go,
186:12
for our country, 351:8
men are created
equal, 140:3
quiet along the Po-
tomac, 113:2
Alliances
entangling a. with
none, 194:5
steer clear of perma-
nent a., 194:2
Almighty
dollar, 323:1
has His own pur-
poses, 212:4
Alms (note), 80:8
Aloha, 226:4
Alone
I want to be a., 463:5
Always
Ready, 313:4
Amarillo, 85:9
Amazement
of things, 504:1
Ambassador
politician who is
given a job abroad,
151:10
AMBITION & ASPIRATION,
14
America
& scribbling women,
537:9
A. first, 21:5
A.'s revolutionary
heritage (note),
118:8

America (*cont.*)
  all races and religions,
    that's A. to me, 23:8
  all the world was A.,
    15:1
  and democracy, 19:8
  another name for op-
    portunity, 20:5
  becoming a second-
    rate power (note),
    510:5
  cause of A. is cause of
    all mankind, 16:2
  died of the delusion
    that she had moral
    leadership (note),
    17:4
  discovery of A., 22:4
  don't be a bear on A.
    (note), 21:1
  don't sell A. short,
    21:1
  for me!, 374:2
  genius of A., 24:8
  has not yet settled
    down, 19:1
  heart of A. is felt less
    here, 108:5
  I hear A. singing, 19:4
  in A. there is no at-
    mosphere, 129:6
  is a country of young
    men, 19:6
  is a land of wonders,
    17:8
  is a large, friendly
    dog, 23:9
  is a romance, 25:3
  is God's crucible, 21:3
  is more like a quilt
    (note), 24:7
  is more wild and ab-
    surd, 15:4
  is the paradise of
    lawyers, 277:11
  it was wonderful to
    find A., 20:5
  land for forgetting
    one's own, 19:1
  language [debased] in
    A., 266:4
  let A. be A. again, 23:6
  means opportunity,
    19:4
  [the] melting pot, 21:3
  my new-found land!
    (note), 15:2
  never was A. to me,
    23:7
  a new A. (note), 387:9
  nothing wrong with
    A., 25:1
  Oh, A., the sun sets
    in you, 22:2
  poor deluded rebels in
    A., 39:6
  pure products of A. go
    crazy, 22:3
  so miserable as to
    possess no castles,
    19:9
  the Beautiful, 20:1
  we are lost here in A.,
    23:1
  what a glorious morn-
    ing for A., 38:3
  you cannot conquer,
    40:2
  youth of A., the 20:6
AMERICA & AMERICANS,
  14
American
  [the] A. had no mind,
    21:2

common faults of A.
    language, 266:3
  don't want our A.
    boys to do the fight-
    ing (note), 509:5
  essential A. soul, 22:1
  expansive character of
    A. life (note), 205:1
  hyphenated A., 374:4
  ideal is youth, 557:4
  kneels only to his
    god, 270:8
  love all mankind ex-
    cept an A., 16:6
  manners & the spit-
    toon, 298:1
  most typically A.
    place, 90:2
  national will had col-
    lapsed, 511:3
  no second acts in A.
    lives, 22:11
  not a Virginian but an
    A., 370:12
  ordinary A. crowd,
    21:8
  people admire daring
    liars, 22:6
  people['s chief
    business] is busi-
    ness, 70:2
  professors, 47:10
  sentence from the lips
    of an A., 266:2
  system of rugged indi-
    vidualism, 22:7
  what then is the A.,
    this new man?,
    16:7
  when an A. says,
    "Come and see
    me", 237:5
  who reads an A.
    book?, 17:3
  women are intelli-
    gent, 537:12
AMERICAN CITIES, 85
AMERICAN HISTORY:
  MEMORABLE MO-
  MENTS, 25
AMERICAN REVOLUTION,
  37
Americanism
  fifty-fifty, 21:7
  hyphenated, 198:1
  shallow, 19:7
Americans
  [are] like omelettes,
    24:4
  are chosen people,
    18:5
  are impatient with
    memory, 25:2
  are suckers for good
    news, 24:1
  can fix nothing with-
    out a drink, 11:1
  must begin to look
    outward, 20:2
  we A. can't seem to
    get it (note), 308:3
  when bad A. die
    (note), 110:1
  whether A. are to be
    freemen or slaves,
    39:1
Amherst
  heart is plain, 86:1
Ammunition
  pass the a., 550:5
Amoebas
  started Sex, 443:9
Ancestors,
  among his a., 174:4

Ancestors
  quotation from all his
    a., 208:3
Angels
  come down, 107:1
  to hear the a. sing,
    83:4
ANGER, 42
Anger
  is never without a
    reason, 42:3
Angry
  speak when you are
    a., 42:6
  when a., count ten
    (note), 42:5
  when a. count four,
    42:5
Animal
  experimental a. be-
    haves as it damn
    well pleases (note),
    496:3
Animals
  don't talk much,
    339:3
  I could live with a.,
    337:3
ANIMALS. See NATURE.
  ANIMALS, 336
Animis
  opibusque parati,
    467:5
Annabel Lee
  I and my A. L., 289:4
Anniversary
  great a. festival, 246:5
Answer
  is blowin' in the
    wind, 415:5
  what is the a.?, 283,
    415:2
Answers
  indiscreet a., 415:6
ANSWERS. See QUESTIONS
  & ANSWERS, 414
Ants
  & theater critics,
    49:7
ANXIETY & WORRY, 43
Apologize
  never a. (note), 178:5
APPEARANCES, 43
Appearances
  to judge by a., 43:7
Apple
  Big, the, 99:5
Apples
  selling a. (note), 251:3
Appreciated
  craving to be a., 238:8
April
  comes like an idiot,
    346:1
  is the cruellest
    month, 345:6
Arabs
  shall fold their tents
    like the A., 50:13
Architect
  can only advise client
    to plant vines, 48:6
Architecture
  begins where engi-
    neering ends, 48:7
  is life taking form,
    48:8
ARCHITECTURE. See ART:
  ARCHITECTURE, 48
Are
  you better off today?,
    388:5
Argentina
  a shadow state, 328:3

Arguing
  not a., telling, 44:3
ARGUMENTS, 43
Aristocracy
  natural a. among
    men, 162:10
  of wealth, 163:2
  what is a.? (note),
    164:3
Aristocrat
  I am an a., 162:9
Aristocratic
  an a. republic, 513:8
ARIZONA, 44
Arizona
  jagged ramparts of,
    44:9
  where summer spends
    the winter, 44:6
ARKANSAS, 45
Arkansas
  fool from the state of
    A., 45:6
  if I die in A., 45:6
  mis'ry & A., 45:4
Arkansas City, 86:2
Arkansaw [*sic*]
  an A. hillbilly, 46:2
  change the name of
    A.? (note), 45:2
  if that line don't fetch
    them, I don't know
    A.! (note), 45:7
  these A. lunkheads,
    45:7
  where the men are
    half-alligator, 45:2
Armageddon
  we stand at A., 30:1
Armies
  of Europe, Asia, and
    Africa, 18:1
Arms
  must decide the con-
    test, 38:6
Army
  discipline is the soul
    of an a., 311:6
  no a. has ever done so
    much with so little,
    551:4
  our A. held the war in
    their hand (note),
    316:4
  our strategy for going
    after this a., 220:2
  was the fulfillment of
    all my hopes, 33:3
  you're in the A. now,
    549:1
Arrow
  I shot an a. in the air
    (note), 203:1
Ars longa
  vita brevis (note),
    46:4
Arsenal of democracy,
  32:3
ART, 46
Art
  in a. there is a quality
    of redemption, 47:1
  in a. economy is
    beautiful, 47:7
  is a jealous mistress,
    46:7
  is long, 46:4
  is power, 46:5
  is the gift of God, 46:6
  is the objectification
    of feeling, 47:5
  is the stored honey of
    the human soul,
    46:11

makes life, makes interest, 46:9
of depicting nature as seen by toads (note), 57:9
strives for form, 48:1
without life, 46:8
ART: AESTHETICS, 47
ART: ARCHITECTURE, 48
ART: CRITICISM, 49
ART: DANCE, 50
ART: DRAMA. See ART: THEATER, MAGIC, & DRAMA, 55
ART: MUSIC, 50
ART: PAINTING. See ART: VISUAL, 57
ART POETRY, 52
ART: STYLE IN WRITING AND EXPRESSION, 54
ART: THEATER, DRAMA, & MAGIC, 55
ART: VISUAL, 57
ART: WRITING, 57
Asia
a land war in A. (note), 509:5
Ask
if you got to a., 51:12
not what your country can do for you, 452:7
ASPIRATION. See AMBITION & ASPIRATION, 14
Astra,
ad a. per ardua (note), 14:3
ad a. per aspera, 260:11
Asylum
for the mentally deranged, 108:11
ATHEISM, 59
Atheism
my a. is true piety, 59:3
Atheist
has no invisible means of support, 59:6
Atheists
no a. in the foxholes, 59:5
Athens
of Dixie, 96:12
Athlete
of God, 218:9
Atlanta
the architecture of A., 86:3
Atom
& the Sermon on the Mount, 322:2
Atomic bomb, 554:1
Attacking
in another direction, 264:4
August
creates as she slumbers, 346:11
Augusta, 86:4
Augustan
the next A. age, 15:5
Aurora
all quiet in A., 86:6
Austin, 86:7
Australia, 328:4
Author
what he [the a.] whispers, 58:2
wish that the a. was a friend, 66:10

Authors
and actors and artists, 46:12
Automobile
& socialist feeling, 447:1
changed our dress, manners, 448:5
Autumn
and decay could never come, 91:5
frost-clear, 345:4
I have known a. too long, 345:9
is a time of harvest, 347:3
leaves fall early this a., 345:3
Avarice
child of a., 207:2
Avon
this A. flows sweetly, 86:8
Awake
day dawns to which we are a., 363:6
"Awww!", 294:3

Baa!
Baa! Baa!, 456:11
Babbitt
his motor-car was poetry, 447:2
his name was B., 310:3
Baby
inestimable blessing and bother, 82:3
what good is a b.?, 504:7
Back
don't look b., 536:5
what people say behind your b., 431:6
Backbone, 250:4 & note
Bad
best b. things, 105:8–106
if it wasn't for b. luck, 292:1
when b. men combine (note), 176:10
when I'm b., I'm better, 457:5
Bad Lands
deserve this name, 467:8
badlands, 357:5
Badge
no b. or uniform or star, 205:7
BAD TIMES, 60
Bagdad-on-the-Subway, 98:10
Ballgame
take me out to the b., 471:3
Ballot
is stronger than the bullet, 144:4
Ballplayer
thank you, God, for making me a b., 476:3
Balls
and strikes ain't nothing until I call them, 427:4
Baloney, 192:4 & note
Baltimore
wonderful little B., 87:2
Banality
of evil, 176:11

Bang
not with a b. but a whimper, 547;2
Banging
and slamming, 51:1
Bankers
if b. were as smart as you are, 71:2
Banking
establishments are dangerous, 67:11
Banks
cohesive power of the surplus in b., 68:5
why do you rob b.?, 134:5
Banned
that work had better be b., 78:3
Bar
the pick of the B., 278:6
Barbarian
he is a b., 284:2
Barefoot
boy, 81:8
Bargain
corrupt b., 380:8
Barn
is America at its best, 186:3
Barrels
don't swap b. (note), 79:4
BARRIERS. See DIVISIONS & BARRIERS, 152
Baseball
& heart and mind of America, 474:8
& merit, 476:4
breaks your heart, 476:2
is the symbol of the 19th century, 470:6
national pastime, 470:4
Bastard
he's our b. (note), 196:3
Bataan, 551:2
Battle
cry of freedom, 114:5
is to the vigilant, the active, the brave, 139:9
Battlefield
we are met on a great b., 210:3
Battleship
no b. has been sunk by bombs, 550:4
Bay
a fair b. (note), 512:3
Bay State
—no slave upon our land!, 301:8
Be
to b. rather than seem, 357:2
Beaches
we are being killed on the b., 552:2
Beans
I was determined to know b., 341:11
Bear
my name & the b. business, 439:1
when you're dancing with a b., 138:1
Beautiful
b. woman is a practical poet, 61:8
it's b. over there, 271:8

BEAUTY, 61
Beauty
appreciation of b., 362:12
body's beauty lives, 61:12
I died for b., 243:1
is everlasting, 62:1
is monetary in the mind, 61:12
is something indescribable, 61:9
only skin-deep, 62:2
perception of b. is a moral test, 61:6
silent, lonely b., a, 110:11
with b. before me I walk, 61:7
Bed
I should've stood in b., 474:2
Bedfellows
strange b., 390:10 & note
Bedrooms
sacred precincts of marital b. (note), 410:6
Bee
the new-come b., 339:5
Beef
where's the b.?, 7:8
Beer
barrel, tapped at both cnds, 353:9
they just get between the people and its b., 12:4
Bees
are buccaneers of buzz, 337:5
Beginning
in my. b. is my end, 188:5
Behaviorism
of course b. "works", 445:8
Beings
of an inferior order (note), 27:6–28
Belief
& a habit, 184:2
must mean something more than desire, 245:7
Believe
each has to b. by himself, 184:8
I b. in the forest and the meadow, 335:8
if I didn't b. it with my own mind, 516:9
what is it that men cannot be made to b.!, 183:6
Belly
little round b., 83:4
Beloved
and respected, 170:4
Benefactor
of human kind, 255:4
Beneficence
private b., 80:9
Berliner
Ich bin ein B., 31:5
Best
and the Brightest, 164:3
strive to be the b., 177:2
way of doing everything, 307:5

Bethlehem
  O little town of B.,
    83:7
Better
  are you b. off today?,
    388:5
  dead than Red (note),
    119:4
  Red than dead, 119:4
Bible
  [has] upwards of a
    thousand lies, 59:2
  an unexpurgated b.,
    77:11–78
  is literature, 430:7
  things that you're li-
    able to read in the
    B., 430:11
Bibliobibuli, 66:9
Big
  pray b.!, believe b.!
    act b.! (note), 318:6
  Rock Candy Moun-
    tains, 505:7
Bigamy, 300:3
Bigger
  they come, the harder
    they fall, 471:1
Biggest
  little place in Amer-
    ica, 92:3
BIGNESS, 62
Bikini, 187:5
Bill
  a b. of rights, 124:6
Bill of Rights, 125
Billboard
  lovely as a tree, 6:4
Billion
  here and a b. there,
    325:10
Billion-dollar country,
  20:3
BIOLOGY. See SCIENCE:
  BIOLOGY & PHYSIOL-
  OGY, 443
Birch
  most shy and ladylike
    of trees, 341:5
Birches
  swinger of b., 556:6
Bird
  why the caged b.
    sings, 462:1
Birds
  caged b., 202:3
  days when the b.
    come back, 343:12
  when the b. are gone,
    167:6
Birmingham, 87:4
Birth
  copulation, and death,
    282:7
Bitch-goddess
  success, 478:5
Bivouac
  of the dead, 170:6
Black
  born in America with
    b. skin, 423
  but beautiful (note),
    424:7
  I'm B. and Proud,
    425:4
  is beautiful, 424:7
  like the depths of my
    Africa (note),
    424:7
  man with a million
    dollars, 426:2
  power, 424:8
  two societies, one b.,
    one white, 425:2

  we b. and they white,
    422:8
Black hole
  has no hair, 445:2
  small b. h., 445:3
Blaine, James G., 384:1
Blame
  how you place the b.,
    178:8
Bleeding Kansas, 259:1
BLESSINGS. See PRAYERS
  & BLESSINGS, 398
Blind
  lead the blind, 144:12
Blinked
  the other fellow just
    b., 35:3
Bliss
  follow your b., 223:4
Blonde
  to make a bishop
    kick, 539:10
Blood
  all over him (note),
    268:3
  of patriots and
    tyrants, 434:1
  will have blood (note),
    131:8
Bloody
  dark and b. ground,
    261:2
  waving the b. shirt,
    390:11
Blowin'
  in the wind, 415:5
Bludgeon
  we b. one another
    with facts, 130:4
Bluebird
  carries the sky, 337:2
Blues, the, 51
BOASTING, 62
Body
  human b. & art, 64:8
  human b. is sacred,
    64:3
  says what words can-
    not, 64:9
BODY & LOOKS, 64
Boil
  we b. at different de-
    grees, 42:4
BOLDNESS & INITIATIVE,
  64
Bombing, 316:6 & note
Bombs, 550:4
Booboisie, 310:2
Book
  buy the new b., 65:13
  Camerado, this is no
    b., 65:15
  covers of this b. are
    too far apart, 250:7
  may live forever,
    65:14
  new era & the reading
    of a b., 65:6
  no frigate like a b.,
    65:11
  no girl was ever ru-
    ined by a b., 66:4
  should be a new be-
    ginning, 58:7
  successful b. & what
    is left out, 54:9
  that is not a year old,
    65:9
  what really knocks
    me out is a b., 66:10
  you really want to
    read, 58:15
Books
  are to inspire, 65:1

  are the treasured
    wealth of the world,
    65:8
  events, not b., should
    be forbid, 77:9
  good b. are truer than
    if they really hap-
    pened, 66:6
  I cannot live without
    b., 65:2
  the mortality of b.,
    66:3
  must be read deliber-
    ately, 65:7
  never die, 66:8
  none are unde-
    servedly remem-
    bered, 66:12
  read the best b. first,
    65:5
  some b. are so famil-
    iar, 65:10
  sweet serenity of b.,
    65:12
BOOKS & READING, 65
Borden, Lizzie B., 133:2
Bore
  a person who talks
    when, 67:1
  capacity of human be-
    ings to b., 67:4
  healthy male adult b.,
    67:5
BORES & DULLNESS, 66
Boston
  born and educated in
    B., 88:5
  cows laid out B., 87:7
  home of the bean and
    the cod, 87:10
  I have just returned
    from B., 88:5
  in B. they ask, 84:8
  men in B. equal to
    Shakespeare (note),
    87:6
  not age which killed
    B., 88:2
  solid man of B., 87:8
  State-house, 87:6
Bostonian
  never argue with a B.,
    87:9
Bottom line
  is in heaven, 71:3
Boy
  barefoot b., 81:8
  b.'s best friend is his
    mother, 368:3
  b.'s will is the wind's
    will, 556:2
  no such thing as a bad
    b., 82:6
  what's the use of be-
    ing a little b.?, 324
Boys
  are not going to for-
    eign wars, 550:3
  get the b. out of the
    trenches, 547:9
  we are not going to
    send American b.,
    509:5
Braggin'
  ain't b. if you can do
    it, 64:2
Brahmin
  caste of New England,
    163:1
Brain
  changes are continu-
    ous, 317:8
  is just the weight of
    God, 317:6

  is wider than the sky,
    317:5
Branches
  noxious b., 405:6
Brave
  kill the b. ones, 114:3
  met my fate like a b.
    man, 40:5
Bravery
  is a quality not to be
    dispensed with in
    officers, 312:1
Brazil
  the p-p-president of
    B., 328:5
Bread
  piece of good b., 192:6
Break
  when I b. a man's ego,
    208:2
Breakdown
  way to get a nervous
    b. (note), 178:1
Breaks
  ain't enough to get
    the b., 363:9
Breast
  fresh green b. of the
    New World, 355:6
Breathing
  keep b., 227:9
Breeding
  good b., 298:4
Brevity
  is the soul of lingerie,
    187:2
Bride
  the b. at every wed-
    ding, 439:8
Bridge
  to the continent of
    Asia, 10:8
Bridges
  are America's cathe-
    drals, 447:4
  railroad bridges, 447:6
Brightest
  and best (note), 164:3
Brink
  we walked to the b.,
    196:5
Brinksmanship (note),
  196:5
Broadcasters, 304:9
Broadway
  give my regards to B.,
    98:7
  old B., 98:8
Broccoli
  it's b., dear, 192:2
Broke
  if it ain't b., 218:5
Bronx
  the B., God bless
    them! (note), 99:9
  the B.? no thonx!,
    99:9
Brooklyn
  hope springs eternal
    in the B. breast, 512
  Only the Dead Know
    B., 100:2
  tree that grows in B.,
    342:10
Brooklyn Bridge, 447:5
Brother
  can you spare a
    dime?, 146:1
  little brown b., 469:4
  of big Bill Taft (note),
    469:4
Brown
  John B.'s body lies
    amoldering, 221

leading old John B. to execution (note), 28:2

Brute
self-sacrificing love of a b., 336:9

Bryan
drinks rum, 384:6

Buck
stops here, 433:5

Buddha
the Godhead, 214:2

Buffalo
country before us thronged with b., 337:1
gals, 88:7
within the town of B., 88:9

Build
if you b. it, 184:9

Bull
as strong as a b. moose, 391:4
is godlike, 338:2
take the b. by the teeth (note), 269:9

Bullets
I heard the b. whistle, 518:1

Bully
a classic b. (note), 6:6–7
pulpit, 402:8

Buncombe
I'm talking to B., 356:2

Bungalow Mind, 224:3

Burden
in the bush, 433:4

Bureaucrats
guidelines for b., 297:2

Burglary
third-rate b., 525:5

Burgundy
without any breeding, 192:5

Burial
service for the admittedly damned, 321:7

Buried
do not propose to be b., 508:7

Burma-Shave, 6:5

Burn
if I don't burn you (note), 467:2

Bury
me not on the lone prairie, 528:2

BUSINESS, 67

Business
the chief b. of the American people is b., 70:2
do b. [in Charleston], 89:7
was meant for the big fellows, 69:9
wish I had spent more time on my b., 71:7

Businessmen
farm the farmers, 185:8

Busted
by gosh (note), 117:2

Butte
"a mile high, a mile deep", 89:1

Butter
wouldn't melt, 252:1

Button
collar b., 490:7
you press the b., 5:3

Buy
if it don't go up, don't b. it, 70:5

Buying
and selling, 68:9

By and by
God caught his eye, 173:2
[Washington state motto], 523:7

Cabbages
inspiring the c., 250:2

Caesars
Pity all the mighty C. (note), 6:5

Caged
birds, 202:3
why the c. bird sings, 462:1

Cages
[marriage] happens as with c. (note), 299:2

Cairo
dismal Cairo [Ill.], 89:2

Cake
for c. we all run in debt, 292:5

Calculators
nature hates c., 427:8

CALIFORNIA, 72

California
annexes the United States, 72:6
climate of C., 73:4, 9
for every year you live in C., 74:3
furnish[es] the best bad things, 105:8–106
has better days, 73:1
Here I come, 73:10
I have walked in C., 73:8
is a tragic country, 73:11
[is] a wonderful place to live, 74:1
kingdom of C., 72:4
scenery in C., 73:3
southern C., 73:13
state so blessed, 74
tree in C., 73:5
whatever starts in C., 74:4

Californian
scoundrels, 73:2

Californians, 73:6

Caligula
C.'s horse, 249:3

Call
me Ishmael, 13:7

Called
back, 171:7

CALMNESS
is always godlike, 74:6

Cambridge ladies, 88:3

Camerado
this is no book, 65:15

Campaign
in poetry, govern in prose, 394:10

Campus
problems on c., 162:1

Canada
as a hunting preserve, 329:4
don't know what street C. is on, 329:2
mighty good neighbor, 392:1

Canaries
song of c. never varies, 338:9

Cancer
close to the presidency, 526:1

Candle
burns at both ends, 178:1
to light one c., 3:2

Candles
rather light c., 515:11

Candy
is dandy, 13:1

Canoe
paddle your own c., 452:4

Capital
better to lose opportunity than c., 71:6
has its rights, 75:6
is a result of labor, 76:1

Capitalism
& communism, 119:3

CAPITALISM & CAPITAL V. LABOR, 75

Capitalist
feud between the c. and laborer, 75:1

Capitalists
fleece the people, 75:3

Captain
O C.!, my C.!, 284:5

Car
you get there in a c., 448:1

Card
game is war, 207:5

Cards
cut the c., 497:2

Care
to c. and not to c., 432:2

Cares
that infest the day, 50:13

Cars
drive themselves to death in huge c., 449:3
people in c. (note), 339:7

Carson City, 89:3,4

Casbah, 459:3

Cases
concrete c., 275:2
great c., like hard c., 274:9
hard c. make bad law (note), 274:9

Casey
at the Bat, 470:5

Casey Jones, 544:8

Cash
why they create it here!, 92:6

Castle
man's house is his c., 409:11

Cat
as the c. climbed, 388:6
if man could be crossed with the c., 337:11
in gloves catches no mice, 440:3

Catch-22, 315:1, 2

Catchwords (note), 269:7

Cater
not enough to c. to the nation's whims, 304:5

Cats
and monkeys, 337:7

Cause
our c. is the c. of all mankind, 39:5

Celebrity, 517:1, 2

CENSORSHIP, 77

Censorship
without c., things can get terribly confused, 511:2

Censure
pain of a little c., 135:1

Central Park, 101:5

Century
of Dishonor, 420:3
the coming c., 206:5

Certain
nothing c. except death and taxes, 125:1

Certainty
is an illusion, 426:8

Chairs
three c. in my house, 456:3

Chameleons
we are c., 399:5

CHANGE, 79

Change
don't c. horses (note), 79:4
is the law of life, 80:2
things do not c., 79:2
why are we now afraid to c.?, 24:3

Changeth
old order c. (note), 79:5

Changin'
the times they are a- c., 80:1

Chaos
is a friend of mine, 307:10
often breeds life, 307:6

Character
is always known, 131:8
is like a tree, 514:11
it's c., just c., 404:10
judged by the content of their c., 36:3
makes the man, 515:3

Characters
down there [in Arkansas], 46:1

Charity, 80:7

CHARITY & PHILANTHROPY, 80

Charlatan
of the highest skill, 439:6

Charleston, 89:6

Charlestonian, 89:6

Charm
old c. [in Baltimore], 87:3

Chaws
more than he bites off, 188:8

Checkers
our little girl named it C., 34:1

Cheer
don't c., men, 469:1

Cheers
he who only stands and c., 471:2

Chemical
barrage, 168:9

Chewing gum
for the eyes, 303:10
Chicago
is the great American
city, 85:3
is the product of mod-
ern capitalism, 90:7
real city—C., 90:3
where nobody could
forget how the
money was made,
90:12
will give you a
chance, 90:10
you C. people, 90:4
Chicken
in every pot, 386:5 &
note
Child
as soon a c. has left
the room (note),
81:4
hard words bruise a
c., 81:9
make me a c. again
just for tonight,
491:8
to come home to a c.!,
81:6
was never a c. so
lovely, 81:4
Childhood
cold was my c. (note),
489:3
is the Kingdom
Where Nobody
Dies, 82:5
knows the human
heart, 81:3
CHILDREN, 81
Children
advice to your c.,
368:1
are all foreigners, 81:5
beauty and happiness
of c., 81:10
c.'s hour, 81:11
hates c. and dogs
(note), 320:2
not everything's for
c., 79:1
of the rich and poor,
160:2
troop down from
heaven, 82:4
Chinese
are just as human as
anybody now, 329:5
sage, On Tu Long, 67:3
Chips
let the c. fall, 117:9
Chisolm Trail, 528:3
Chivalries, 262:4
Choate
Mrs. C.'s second hus-
band (note), 299:4
Choice
between the quick
and the dead, 448:2
not an echo (note),
388:3
Christ
Caesar and C. had
met, 430:12
how many observe
C.'s birthday, 82:7
in the beauty of the
lilies C. was born,
212:3
to be like C., 428:9
Christian
where in Christen-
dom is the C.?,
429:8

CHRISTMAS, 82
Christmas
happy C. to all, 83:3
I heard the bells on C.
Day, 83:5
out of the trenches by
C., 587
'twas the night before
C., 82:8
White C., 84:2
won't be C. without
any presents, 83:6
Church
I like the silent c.,
429:7
is not the master or
the servant of the
state, 431:3
keep c. and state sepa-
rate forever, 430:2
straying away from
the c., 431:2
Cigar
good five-cent c.,
493:7
Cincinnati
& hogs, 91:2
is a beautiful city,
91:3
Circumstantial
evidence, 175:6
Circus
without a tent, 95:5
CITIES, 84
Cities
alabaster c., 84:7
bureaucratized, sim-
plified c., 85:4
degrade us, 84:4
government of c., 84:6
piled upon one an-
other in large c.,
84:3
Shame of the C., 84:9
this is the sacking of
c., 84:11
we neglect our c.,
84:12
CITIES ABROAD, 109
Citizen
every c. [should] be a
soldier, 312:4
City
a c. upon a hill, 14:9
& note
asked the boldness to
dream, 101:1
biggest little c., 104:5
country is turned into
a c., 166:11
a cruel c., 100:6
dreaming to a lullaby,
100:4
for beavers, 110:12
great big c.'s a won-
drous toy, 99:7
in the Big C., 84:10
land & taxes, 84:5
large c. like an
anthill, 85:6
log c., 92:5
magic c. on Bering
Strait, 101:10
of Dreadful Joy, 95:1
of hurried and
sparkling waters!,
98:4
of Magnificent Inten-
tions, 108:1
of mirrors, 111:4
of my Discontent,
107:1
of sin and gayety, 97:2
of strivers, 97:1

of the big shoulders,
90:8
of the four C's, 93:5
on hills, 85:2
people of a c., 85:1
that works, 91:1
well-meaning c., 96:9
white phantom c.,
111:1
Zenith C. of the Un-
salted Seas, 93:4
CIVIL WAR, THE, 112
Civil War
we are engaged in a
great c. w., 210:3
never be anything
more interesting
than the C.W.,
117:1
Civilian
control of the mili-
tary, 314:7
CIVILIZATION, 111
Civilization
& good women, 538:3
& important opera-
tions, 111:10
& privacy, 112:2
& progress of the peo-
ple, 377:3
always results in
deserts, 112:1
definition of c., 111:12
degrades the many,
111:7
is still in the middle
stage, 111:8
is the lamb's skin,
111:9
[Jackson:] little ad-
vanced in c., 255:1
test of a c., 112:3
yet only at the cock-
crowing, 111:6
you can't say c. don't
advance, 111:11
Civilized
man has the habits of
the house, 418:2
Clark
here lies Champ C.,
172:1
Class
while there is a lower
c., 133:5
Classes
division of society
into two c., 75:4
struggle between the
c. (note), 75:4
Classic
book which people
don't read, 61
Clean
and warm, it is suffi-
cient, 186:7
Cleaning
new ways of c. the
floors, 332:4
Clemens
godlike C. (note),
181:7–182
Cleveland, 91
Cliffs
gray c. like aged bat-
tlements, 354:1
Climate
bleak, beggarly c.,
355:4
Clock
I must govern the c.,
492:7
is the key-machine,
447:7

Clothes
enterprises that re-
quire new c., 186:10
never shut up, 187:6
CLOTHES. See FASHION &
CLOTHES, 186
Clouds
export the c. out of
the sky (note), 205:6
Club
any c. that will accept
me as a member,
164:1
Coal
can't mine c. without
machine guns,
70:7
Coat
a Republican cloth c.,
33:4
Cocktail
the c. is a pleasant
drink, 12:3
Cocktail hour, 13:5
Cocktail parties, 237:7
Coexistence
peaceful, 197:3
Coffee
as strong as love,
192:11
Coffee spoons
measured out my life
with c. s., 281:13
Cohesive
power of public plun-
der (note), 68:5
Cold
coming we had of it,
84:1
Cold war
America won the
c. w., 37:5
we are today in the
midst of a c. w.,
32:7
College
small c. yet there are
those who love it,
159:8
Colonels
full of corn, 261:6
Color
of their skin, 36:3
Color line,
problem of the c. l.,
421:2
we are met by the
c. l., 419:6
COLORADO, 117
Colorado
God [was] lavish in
C., 117:5
is a grand seat, 117:6
men are we, 117:3
most spectacular of
the mountain
states, 117:7
Colored
all of y'all are part c.
(note), 466:9
c. Americans, 422:9
destiny of the c.
American, 419:2
white and c. people,
419:3
Columbia [S.C.], 92:1
Columbus, 14:7
Columbus [Ohio], 92:2
Combine
when bad men c.
(note), 176:10
Come
up sometime, 'n see
me, 237:6

Comets
are the nearest thing
to nothing, 340:8
Comfortable
put on something
more c., 187:4
Command
art of c., 314:5
Commander
who fails to obtain
his objective,
314:4
Commanders
are prima donnas,
232:1
COMMITMENT, 117
Common
century of the c. man,
322:1
man in the presidency
(note), 252:4
COMMON SENSE, 117
Common sense
all admit it grudg-
ingly, 118:3
always takes a hasty
view, 118:2
and plain dealing,
118:1
is the collection of
prejudices, 118:4
to take c. s. to high
places, 118:5
Communicate
failure to c., 118:7
COMMUNICATION, 118
COMMUNISM, 118
Communism
has never come to
power, 119:5
is a corruption of a
dream, 119:2
is an economy which
grows in misery,
118:9
is 20th–century
Americanism,
118:8
Communist
member of the C.
Party? (note), 119:1
members of the C.
Party, 33:2
Company
directors of a c., 68:3
Competition
of the market, 202:7
Complain
never c., 178:5
COMPLAINTS, 119
Composers
shouldn't think too
much, 52:4
Computer
music, 449:5
to really foul things
up requires a c.
(note), 478:4
Concentration
is the secret of
strength, 476:6
Concepts
physical c., 444:6
Concise
vigorous writing is c.,
54:11
Concord, 92
Concord
I have traveled a good
deal in C., 494:3
CONFLICT, 119
Conflict
an irrepressible c.,
112:4

between the white
and the black in-
habitants, 418:1
Conforming
outwardly, 240:10
Conformity, 305:3
CONGRESS, 120
Congress
& both sides of an is-
sue, 122:2
& native American
criminal class,
120:8
I just watch C., 121:7
is so strange, 122:1
jokes are in C. (note),
121:6
the finest C. money
can buy, 120:7
Congressman
c.'s first obligation
is to get elected,
121:8
is a hog!, 121:3
new C., the, 120:9
CONNECTICUT, 122
Connecticut
farewell C., 122:5
in her blue-laws,
122:6
little C., 123:2
Yankee, 123:3
Conquer
resolve to c. or die,
39:1
CONSCIENCE, 123
Conscience
as much c. as any
man in business
can afford, 68:7
cut my c. to suit this
year's fashions,
123:6
democracy has given
[liberty] to c., 429:5
doesn't abide by ma-
jority rule, 123:7
warns us somebody
may be looking,
123:5
what do you got in
place of a c.? (note),
278:3
Consciousness
stream of c. (note),
317:8
Consciousnesses
melt into each other,
317:8
Conservation
is a state of harmony,
168:5
new doctrine of c.
(note), 167:5
Conservatism
goes for comfort,
389:7
makes no poetry,
390:1
what is c.?, 390:6
Conservative
is a liberal who's been
mugged, 394:11
is a man who, 393:6
CONSISTENCY, 123
Consistency
a foolish c., 123:8
requires you to be as
ignorant, 124:2
Conspicuous
consumption, 323:8
Constitution
adapted to crises
(note), 126:2

American C., 127:6
does not provide for
first and second
class citizens, 128:7
establish this C.,
124:5
follows the flag, 127:3
Frigate C., 312:5
if the C. is to be con-
strued, 128:5
is color-blind, 127:2
is framed for ages to
come, 126:2
is sacredly obligatory,
126:1
is what the judges say
it is, 127:5
it is, Sir, the people's
C., 216:4
not included in the C.
(note), 27:6–28
one country, one C.,
one destiny, 126:5
our C. is so simple
and practical, 128:3
people made the c.,
the, 126:2
there is a higher law
than the C., 126:8
was made for poster-
ity, 126:7
what's the C. between
friends?, 127:1
CONSTITUTION, THE, 124
Constitutional
fixed star in our c.
constellation, 128:6
right to be wrong,
378:8
this C. shield, 481:4
Consumption
conspicuous c., 323:8
Contender
I could have been a c.,
428:6
Content
I am c., 270:5
Contentment
squalid c., 305:3
Contest
was inevitable, 112:6
Continent
the end of a c., 74:2
Continental
not worth a c., 156:3
Continental Congress
Great Jehovah and the
C.C., 37:8
Contract
verbal, 276:2
Contradict
do I c. myself?, 124:1
Contribution
when you cease to
make a c., 545:8
CONVERSATION, 129
Conversations, 130:2
Converse
not many c., 129:5
Convict
No. 9653 for Presi-
dent, 386:2
Convictions
[that] change with
the weather (note),
123:6
Convicts
a band of, 133:3
Cool
keep c., 74:7
Coolidge
keep cool with C.,
386:3
or chaos, 386:4

weaned on a pickle
(note), 484:1
Corn
Colonels full of c.,
261:6
raise less c. and more
hell, 260:2
Corn Belt
is a gift of the gods,
311:3
Corn bread, 191:5
Corn-pone
whar a man gits his
c., 238:10
Corporations
can love each other,
69:5
have neither bodies
nor souls, 68:1
indentured to c., 71:1
most men are ser-
vants of c., 69:8
will do what individ-
uals would not
dare, 68:6
Correlative
objective c., 47:8
Corrupt
bargain, 380:8
Corruption
Era of C. (note),
214:5
hard to get people
interested in c.,
133:6
COSMOLOGY. See SCI-
ENCE: PHYSICS &
COSMOLOGY, 444
Cotton
Is King, 465:2
Kingdom, 209:11
Councils
of war never fight,
316:4
Country
all for our c., 351:8
ask not what your c.
can do for you,
452:7
billion-dollar c., 20:3
brand-new c., 295:1
I tremble for my c.,
459:5
I would go to hell for
my c., 371:2
in this c. you can look
farther and see less,
310:9, 528:4
is not mountainous
nor yet low, 512:4
it's a tough c., 44:10
looks something like
a singed cat, 351:3
melancholy strange-
looking c., 242:1
my c., 'tis of thee,
372:4
my c. is the world,
174:8
my whole c. and
nothing but my c.,
383:1
not a c. at all, 205:2
Our C., our whole C,
372:1
our c. & democracy,
21:4
our c. right or wrong,
371:5
roads, take me home,
530:2
say not thou, "My c.
right or wrong",
372:6

Country (*cont.*)
shame to take this c.
away from the rat-
tlesnakes, 73:7
this is a beautiful c.,
270:9
this is my c. (note),
200:1
vast c., 310:5
what we can do for
our c. (note), 452:7
where none but male-
factors will ever
live, 10:1
COUNTRY LIFE & PEOPLE,
130
COURAGE, 130
Courage
is resistance to fear,
131:1
is the price that life
exacts, 131:2
one man with c.
makes a majority,
130:10
Couriers
these c. & their ap-
pointed rounds,
348:11
Court
this honorable c.'s
now in session,
274:6
Courts
& the 10 Command-
ments & the Con-
stitution, 127:4
stand against any
winds that blow,
481:3
Convenant
with death, 126:6
Cover-up (note), 525:5
Cow
purple c., 150:8
Coward
dirty little c. that
shot Mr. Howard,
132:7
Cowardice
[is] lack of ability to
suspend imagina-
tion, 189:5
Cowboy
Americans admire the
c., 529:6
that damned c. is
president, 439:3
wrapped up in white
linen, 94:4
Cows
I never saw so many
c., 86:5
Cox
and cocktails, 386:1
Crab
we were like a c. that
could run either
way (note), 40:5
Crackers
live off the yams,
190:7
Cradle
hand that rocks the
c., 538:1
of toleration and free-
dom, 376:6
what the mother
sings to the c.,
367:4
CRAFTINESS, 131
Cranes
beyond the reach of
words, 339:6

Crazy
all of us go a little c.
at times, 249:5
Credit
buy it on c. (note),
158:1
cherish public c.,
156:4
if he doesn't mind
who gets the c.,
71:4
is [not] as good as his
money, 70:3
is the lifeblood of
business, 158:3
is the vital air of . . .
commerce, 68:4
strangulation of c.
(note), 158:3
Creditors
are a superstitious
sect, 67:7
Crime
commit a c., 132:1
does not pay, 134:4
is a form of endeavor,
134:7
of 1873 (note), 157:5
planning a c., 134:9
CRIME, CRIMINALS & DE-
TECTIVES, 131
Crimes
world teems with c.,
60:1
Criminals
less evil that some
c. . . . escape, 175:7
Crises
great c. produce great
men, 496:5
Crisis
in Chinese the word
c. is composed of
two characters,
496:7
Quiet C., The, 168:11
Critic
not the c. who
counts, 3:5
CRITICISM, 134
Criticism
be kind with your c.,
49:8
CRITICISM. See ART:
CRITICISM, 49
Criticize
to c. is to appreciate
(note), 49:4
Critics
ought to hesitate,
50:4
Crook
I'm not a c., 526:8
Cross
let us c. over the
river, 271:2
No C., No Crown,
479:7
cross of gold, 157:5
Crossroads
of America, 247:3
Crow
shook down on me the
dust of snow, 345:7
Crowded
it's too c. (note),
475:9–476
Cruel
nation does not have
to be c. to be tough,
477:1
Crumb
I never wanted to be a
c., 409:7

Cry
too big to c., 532:2
Culture
ladies who pursue C.,
46:10
of a nation, 47:3
Curtain
behind the [stage] c.'s
mystic fold, 55:3
Custom
lest one good c.
should corrupt
(note), 79:5
CUSTOM. See HABIT &
CUSTOM, 221
Customer
is always right, 70:4
Customs
are rock, 221:7
represent the experi-
ence of mankind,
221:1
Cut
we must c. our way
out, 113:4
Cynic
n. a blackguard whose
faulty vision, 516:5

Dallas, 92:4
Damn
I don't give a d., 251:6
Damned
don't cry, 147:6
Dance
is motion, 50:7
is the hidden lan-
guage of the soul,
50:10
mehitabel dance,
361:7
DANCE. See ART:
DANCE, 50
Dancing
is discovery, 50:9
Dandelion
d.'s pallid tube aston-
ishes the grass,
342:3
Danger
familiarized with d.,
136:1
DANGER & DANGEROUS
PEOPLE, 136
Dangerous
how d. everything is,
137:2
Dark
and bloody ground,
261:2
everyone has a d. side,
450:6
many things go
around in the d.,
137:1
night of the soul,
147:7
Darkness
falls from the wings
of night, 347:7
D.A.R.lings, 163:7
Dasher
Now, D!, now
Dancer!, 83:1
Date
which will live in in-
famy, 550:6
Dawg
the boys keep kickin'
my d. aroun (note),
34:1
Dawn
by the d.'s early light,
371:4

nearer the d., darker
the night, 363:13
Day
every d. is a beautiful
d., 400:7
first d. of the rest of
your life, 400:6
I expand in the warm
d., 348:7
is done, 347:7
make my d., 137:7 &
note 486:4
thank You, God, for
this most amazing
d., 399:2
Days
dwindle down, 362:6
happy d. are here
again, 214:7
melancholy d. are
come, 343:7
of my life (note),
283:4
of our lives, 283:4
when birds come
back, 343:12
Dead
Ah ain't d., 362:4
bivouac of the d.,
170:6
but the d. remain,
171:1
not completely born
until he is d.,
138:5
over my d. body!,
173:8
these d. shall not
have died in vain,
210:3
to be brought back
from the d., 320:1
why can't the d. die!,
139:10
Deal
a new d. for the
American people,
31:4
square, 384:8
DEATH, 144
Death
& escape mecha-
nisms, 139:8
and taxes, 125:1
and taxes and child-
birth!, 450:2
can be done lying
down (note), 139:12
go with anyone to d.,
139:4
God has fixed the
time for my d.
(note), 271:2
I am become D.,
442:7
I could not stop for
D., 139:2
I have a rendezvous
with d., 548:1
is a slave's freedom,
425:1
is but crossing the
world, 138:3
mysterious Exodus of
d., 139:1
no d., only a change
of worlds, 138:9
observes no cere-
mony, 138:4
prepare for d., 169:5
report of my death,
406:6
Debs, 'Gene (note),
133:5

Debt
  national d., 156:1
  pay the national d., 157:2
  perpetual d., 157:1
December
  will you love me in D.?, 290:1
Decency
  have you no sense of d.?, 35:1
Decide
  not to d. is to d. (note), 246:3
DECISION, 140
Decision
  the capacity for d., 140:1
DECLARATION OF INDE-PENDENCE, 140
Dedicated
  to the great task re-maining before us, 210:3
Deed
  no good d. goes un-punished, 515:9
Deeds
  little d. of kindness, 148:1
Deep six, 526:5
DEFEAT. See WINNING & LOSING, VICTORY, & DEFEAT, 532
Defeat
  in d. a man reveals himself, 534:2
  is an orphan, 533:6
  snatched d. from the jaws of victory (note), 252:3
Defending
  a long line, 316:3
Defense
  money [for] military d., 315:4
Defiance
  bold d. took its place (note), 460:6
Defy
  we d. them, 432:6
Déjà vu
  all over again (note), 475:9–476
DELAWARE, 142
Delaware
  & the Du Ponts, 143:1
  is like a diamond, 142:2
DELAY, 143
Delay
  do not d., 143:6
  is preferable to error, 143:4
Deliberate speed, 129:1 & note
DeMille
  Mr. D., I'm ready (note), 303:9
DEMOCRACY, 143
Democracy
  arsenal of d., 32:3
  born of free land, 144:8
  can't see why D. means everybody but me, 144:11
  cure for d. is more d., 144:10
  has given to con-science absolute liberty, 429:5
  is the recurrent suspi-cion, 145:2

never lasts long, 144:1
our real disease is d., 143:9
tendency of d. is to mediocrity, 144:2
this pioneer d., 334:9
world must be made safe for d., 30:3, 548:3
Democrat
  I am a D., 393:7
  I am a D. still, 391:3
  I am D. but not a rev-olutionist (note), 391:3
  is a fellow who never had any money, 393:6
  you've got to be an optimist to be a D. (note), 393:7
Democratic
  party is like a mule, 390:8
  strength of d. institu-tions (note), 296:2
Democrats
  I never said all D. were saloon-keep-ers, 390:5
Demon rum, 11:4
Demonology
  is the shadow of the-ology, 149:9
Denver, 92:5,6,7
Departure
  there is a time for d., 368:12
Depression
  came on, 146:2
DEPRESSION, THE, 145
Depressions
  are farm led, 145:8
Des Moines
  & corn, 92:9
  & ice cream con-sumption, 92:8
Descants
  of sea birds, 339:8
Descended
  not only from mon-keys but from monks, 457:2
Deserts
  asked to blossom, 169:2
Desire
  if you d. many things, 146:4
  men have a thousand d., 146:6
DESIRES, 146
Desires
  to gratify their d., 146:5
Desolate
  dark weeks, 346:4
DESPAIR, 147
Despair
  safe d., 147:3
  stereotypes but un-conscious d., 207:3
  that white sustenance d., 147:2
  we should never d., 147:1
Desperation
  lives of quiet d., 280:7
Despotism, 500:7
Destiny
  a rendezvous with d., 208:10
  carries us along, 187:12

efforts to escape from our d., 174:5
is not a matter of chance, 188:2
manifest d., 18:3
DESTINY. See FATE & DESTINY, 187
Destroy
  necessary to d. the town to save it, 510:4
Destruction
  if d. be our lot, 18:1
Detail
  life is frittered away by d., 456:2
Details
  God is in the d., 148:3
DETAILS & OTHER SMALL THINGS, 147
DETECTIVES. See CRIME, CRIMINALS, & DE-TECTIVES, 131
DETERMINATION, EFFORT, PERSISTENCE, & PER-SEVERANCE, 148
Detroit
  capital of the new planet [is] D., 92:10
  say nice things about D.!, 93:2
  still hell on wheels, 93:1
Deus
  Ditat D., 44:11
Deviation
  from the norm, 151:3
DEVIL, THE, 149
Devil
  and me, we don't agree, 149:10
  before the D. discov-ers that you're dead, 398:11
  is in the details (note), 148:3
  made me do it, 150:3
  object of American reverence is the d., 149:2
  there is a D., 149:6
Devils
  have been better friends, 149:8
  poor d. are dying, 469:1
Dewey
  Defeats Truman, 33:1
  took Manila (note), 469:2
Diamonds
  Are Girl's Best Friend, 506:6
  goodness, what beau-tiful d.!, 457:4
Diary
  keep a d., 58:3
Dice
  constructed like a lawyer, 277:9
  God does not play d., 444:7
Dictatress
  of the world (note), 17:4
Die
  I d. hard, 138:6
  not that I'm afraid to d., 139:12
  to know when to d., 230:1
  tomorrow, we shall d.!, 380:6

we can d. but once to serve our country (note), 39:2
Xerxes the Great did d., 138:2
you asked this man to d., 554:3
Died
  a man d. for me today, 521:5
  he d. as he must have wished to die, 170:7
  there d. a myriad, 549:7
Differ
  to think is to d., 151:1
DIFFERENCES, 150
Difference
  between one man and another, 150:9
  of opinion, 150:7, 501:6
Different
  drummer, 247:6
  if you aren't doing something d., 151:4
Difficult
  the d. is done at once (note), 4:1
Difficulties
  & great and honorable actions, 1:1
  things which [we should] overcome, 496:2
Digressions
  by my rambling d., 360:3
Diligent
  in this place, 122:4
Dime
  can you spare a d.?, 146:1
  every d. we've got (note), 33:4
Dimmycratic [sic]
  party, 391:6
Dinner
  invitation is a sacred obligation, 219:8
DIPLOMACY, 151:5
Diplomacy
  at the conference table, 152:2
  dollar d., 195:3
  is to do and say, 151:8
  is utterly useless [without] force, 151:7
  patriotic art of lying, 151:6
  recognition of actual-ity, 152:1
  shall proceed always frankly, 195:6
Diplomats
  don't mind starting a war, 151:11
Dirtiest
  place in the world [Baltimore], 87:1
Dirty
  no such thing as a d. theme (note), 48:2
Disarm, 366:1
Discipline
  & army superiority (note), 311:6
  & courage, 314:3
  is the soul of an army, 311:6
Discontent
  is the want of self-re-liance, 501:1

Disease
  only d. you don't
    [want] to be cured
    of, 362:7
  what person the d.
    has, 245:1
DISHONESTY & LIES,
  152
Disorderliness
  careful d., 307:4
Dispute
  to d. everything that
    is disputable, 44:1
Dissent
  must not confuse d.
    with disloyalty, 34:2
  our government must
    have d., 145:1
Distinguished
  thing, 139:6
Disputants
  convincing the other
    by argument, 44:2
Divided
  every kingdom d.
    against itself (note),
    502:4
DIVISIONS & BARRIERS,
  152
Dixie
  Land, 465:3
Do
  exactly as your neigh-
    bors, 298:5
  how d. you know
    what you're going
    to d.?, 4:3
  I can d. something,
    2:8
  some say she d., 431:9
  the hardest thing in
    the world for you,
    3:7
  watch what we d.,
    4:4
  your own work (note),
    2:2
  your thing, 2:2
Doctor
  d. bills, 153:9
  deference paid to a
    d.'s opinion, 153:5
  kind of d. I want,
    154:2
  takes the fee, 153:3
  that doctors on the
    upper half of your
    throat, 153:10
  when a d. kant see no
    money in me, 153:8
Doctors
  I hate d.!, 154:1
DOCTORS & MEDICINE,
  153
Doctrine
  the skin of truth
    stuffed, 183:10
Does
  she or doesn't she?,
    415:3
Dog (see also Dawg)
  bites a man is not
    news, 406:3
  born a d., died a gen-
    tleman, 337:6
  if a d. jumps in your
    lap, 339:2
  perpetually on the
    wrong side, 153:2
  was created especially
    for children, 337:10
Dogies
  git along, little d.,
    554:4

Dogmas
  of the quiet past,
    369:11
Dogs
  display reluctance
    and wrath, 339:1
  hates d. and babies,
    320:2
  terrible thing to out-
    live her d., 362:9
Doing
  'tis the d., 3:1
  be up and d., 2:1
  if we are always d., 1:2
DOING. See ACTION &
  DOING, 1
Dollar
  almighty d., 323:1
  diplomacy, 195:3
  never owned a d. he
    could not take up to
    [heaven], 171:6
Dollars
  two d. a day and roast
    beef, 381:2
  what's a thousand d.?,
    324:7
Domestic
  bliss, 299:10
Dominion
  good Old D., 513:2
Domino
  principle, 509:4
Don't
  give up the ship,
    522:11
Done
  a thing well d., 2:4
  it can be, 4:5
  nothing is d. as it was
    d. 20 years ago, 79:5
  something d. has
    earned a night's re-
    pose, 2:3
Door
  open, 195:1
  we never opened,
    428:5
Dooth
  with youre owene
    thyng (note), 2:2
Doubt
  in philosophy & in
    our hearts, 379:2
  is an art, 459:2
Down
  d., d. into the grave,
    139:9
  we been d. so long,
    396:4
  when a man starts d.
    hill, 182:8
Draft
  first rough d. of his-
    tory, 408:11
DRAMA. See ART: THE-
  ATER, DRAMA, &
  MAGIC, 55
Dream
  deferred, 155:1
  first a d., 154:8
  I have a d., 36:2ff.
  is a wish your heart
    makes, 155:9
  republic is a d., 154:8
  we wake from one d.
    into another, 426:7
  within a d., 426:3
Dreaming
  men are haunted
    men, 155:7
  permits [us] to be
    quietly insane,
    155:10

Dreams
  and beasts (note),
    155:6
  in our d. we are al-
    ways young, 155:11
  in the direction of his
    d., 154:4
  make strong old d.,
    154:6
  we all have the same
    d., 155:3
  what you do in your
    d., 155:6
DREAMS & DREAMERS,
  154
DREAMS & SLEEP, 155
Dress
  fondness for d., 186:9
Dressed
  up with nowhere to
    go, 186:12
Drink
  he has taken to d.,
    12:5
  not to elevation,
    191:1
  one more d. and I'd
    have been under the
    host, 457:7
Drinkers
  as a class (note), 11:5
DRINKING. See ALCOHOL
  & DRINKING, 11
Drinks
  a long time between
    d., 11:2
Drum
  major for justice, 173:9
Drummer
  hears a different d.,
    247:6
Drunk
  never did see a man d.
    in that land, 351:9
Drunken
  Christian v. sober
    cannibal, 11:3
Du Ponts, 142:4
Dubuque
  old lady in D., 303:3
Duck
  I just forgot to d.,
    473:2
  if it walks like a d.,
    175:9
Dull
  are the damned, 67:2
Dulles
  difficulty with D.
    (note), 196:5
DULLNESS. See BORES &
  DULLNESS, 66
Duluth
  the word fell upon my
    ear, 93:3
Dump
  what a d.!, 252:5
Dunce
  with the best of in-
    tentions, 193:3
Dust
  excuse my d., 173:7
Duty
  dare to do our d. as
    we understand it,
    514:10
  I seen my d. and I
    done it, 551:7
  let every man do his
    d., 26:1
  oh d., why art thou
    not a cutie?, 433:2
  only aim to do your
    d., 432:8

Dying
  is an art, 480:8
  is no big deal, 298
Eagle
  bird of bad moral
    character, 336:7
  stoic bird, the e. of
    the rock, 463:4
Early
  to bed and e. to rise,
    238 & note
Earth
  e.'s the right place for
    love, 287:4
  is given as a common
    stock, 166:9
  love the e. itself,
    168:3
  making deserts of the
    e., 167:8
  receive an honored
    guest, 173:3
  spaceship E., 169:1
  sweet spontaneous e.,
    346:6
  they shall inherit the
    e., 168:1
  this is the last of e.!,
    270:5
  those who labor in
    the e., 185:5
  was made for lovers,
    286:12
East Side
  West Side, 98:5
Easy
  nothing is as e. as it
    looks (note), 496:3
Eat
  never e. more than
    you can lift, 192:13
  not to dullness, 191:1
  to live, 190:12
Eaten
  never repent having e.
    too little, 191:2
EATING. See FOOD, WINE,
  & EATING, 190
ECONOMICS, 156
Economics
  as If People Mattered
    (note), 462:4
  in e. the majority is
    always wrong,
    159:5
  voodoo e., 159:6 &
    note
Economist
  one-armed e., 159:2
Economy
  it's the e., stupid,
    389:2
Eden
  is that old-fashioned
    house, 234:9
Editor
  first duty of an e.,
    407:3
  human cash-register
    e. (note), 406:5
  might begin a refor-
    mation (note), 405:7
Educated
  an enlightened, 160:1
EDUCATION, 159
Education
  & lack of understand-
    ing, 160:10
  & soap, 160:7
  & tolerance, 493:8
  & what we have
    unlearned (note),
    161:7

enables you to earn,
162:6
higher e. [is] boring
(note), 161:8
if you think e. is expensive, 162:7
is a great equalizer,
160:3
is what survives,
161:7
makes a straight-cut
ditch, 160:4
without e., 162:4
Educational
system—a quiz program, 161:8
Effete
corps of impudent
snobs, 164:4
Effort
conscious e., 149:1
EFFORT. See DETERMINATION, EFFORT, PERSISTENCE, &
PERSEVERANCE, 148
Efforts
one's own e., 545:7
Egg
try to spoil a rotten e.,
249:4
Eggheads
unite!, 163:9
Eggs
put all your e. in one
basket, 535:9
Egypt
wa'n't goin' to keep
nothin' of Egypt
(note), 461:7
El Paso, 85:9, 93:5
Eleanor
two-thirds mush and
one-third E., 438:9
Electricity
by means of e. the
world of matter has
become, 446:2
Elephant
an e.'s faithful 100 per
cent, 291:4
ELITE, THE, 162
Embattled
farmers stood, 41:3
Emeralds
I wish they were e.,
290:3
Emotion
remembered in tranquillity (note),
240:8
Emperor
of ice-cream, 231:9
Empire
evil e., 333:9
Employed
when men are e.,
542:11
Employee
every e. [rises] to his
level of incompetence, 546:2
End
keeps the e. from being hard, 362:3
Endeavor
set upon a mighty e.,
552:3
ENDINGS, 165
ENDURANCE, 165
Endurance
is the crowning quality, 165:3
patient e. is godlike,
165:4

Endure
may she e. forever,
242:5
ENEMIES, 165
Enemies
accumulate, 166:2
list, 526:6
love him for the e. he
has made, 165:7
secret history of our
e., 165:6
we must not be e.,
375:1
your e. never [sleeps],
165:8
Enemy
let your e. alone,
165:9
surprise the e., 316:2
there is no little e.,
165:5
we has met the e. and
it is us, 239:6
we have met the e.
and they are ours,
523:1
wherever the e. goes,
115:2
you are now my e.,
248:7
your e.'s corpse (note),
165:9
England
and the U.S. are natural allies, 329:8
in E. God and Mammon are one, 329:12
the paradise of individuality, 329:10
—the sun (note),
523:8
English
never abolish anything, 329:13
North America
speaks E., 232:10
U.S. & better E.
(note), 266:2
writes the worst E.,
224:1
Englishman
holding his tongue,
329:9
to be an E., 329:11
who has lost his fortune, 329:7
Enough
had e.?, 387:6
Enraged
we are surrounded by
the e., 42:9
Ensign
aye, tear her tattered
e. down!, 372:2
Enterprise
private e., 77:2
the starship E. (note),
4:7
Enterprises
that require new
clothes, 186:10
Entertainment
suppose e. is the purpose of life, 56:6
ENTHUSIASM & ZEAL,
166
Enthusiasm
a distemper of youth,
166:5
nothing great was
ever achieved without e., 166:3
triumph of some e.
(note), 166:3

ENVIRONMENT, 166
ENVY, 169
Envy
is ignorance, 169:3
EPITAPHS & GRAVESTONES, 169
Equal
all men are created e.,
140:3
all should have e.
rights, 174:3
pay for equal work,
75:7
EQUALITY, 174
Equality
before the law, 350:6,
420:7
Equals
trouble with treating
people as e., 298:8
Era
of Corruption (note),
214:5
of Good Feelings,
214:5
of wonderful nonsense, 214:6
Eripuit
*fulmen sceptrumque
tyrannis* (note),
198:8
Error
ignorance is preferable to e., 459:1
reign of e., 442:8
Errors
and defeats, 532:4
I shall try to correct
e., 79:3
Errs
but with integrity,
524:4
ESCAPE, 174
Eskimos
are a gentle people,
422:11
Esse
quam videri, 357:2
Establishment
and the movement,
390:9
Esto perpetua, 242:5
Eternity
& time, 491:6
damned from here to
e., 456:11
remains (note), 491:7
ETHICS & MORALITY,
174
Ethics
& society, 175:5
Étoile du Nord, 319:4
Eureka, 74:5
Europe
all the dogs of E. bark,
321:8
E.'s old dynastic
slaughterhouse,
330:3
every time E. looks
across the Atlantic,
330:5
extract the tapeworm
of E., 330:2
go to E. to be Americanized, 494:4
never quite forgiven
E., 330:4
Evangeline
is not the only one
who has waited
here, 285:6
Evening
blue e. falls, 347:5

Events
have controlled me,
187:10
Ever Upward, 355:7
Every
man a king!, 386:6
EVIDENCE, 175
Evidence
absence of e., 176:1
circumstantial e.,
175:6
EVIL, 176
Evil
banality of e., 176:11
doing e. on the
grounds of expediency, 176:5
empire, 333:9
hacking at the
branches of e., 176:4
he who accepts e.,
176:10
is unspectacular,
176:9
only thing necessary
for the triumph of
e. (note), 176:10
some men wish e.
(note), 176:11–177
what e. lurks in the
hearts, 176:6
Evils
between two e., 176:7
which have never
happened, 43:1
Evolution
no short cuts in e.,
335:10
Example
annoyance of a good
e., 515:2
EXCELLENCE, 177
Excellence, 177:5
Excelsior, 355:7
EXCESS, 177
Excess
I don't regret a single
e., 177:6
EXCUSES & EXPLANATIONS, 178
Executive
abilities of the loftiest
order, 149:12
most incapable e. [to
be president], 255:5
Exercise
is loathsome, 379:10
urge to e., 379:11
Exercises
walking is best, 379:8
Existence
is but a brief crack of
light, 282:12
Expectoration
America is one long e.
(note), 298:1
EXPEDIENCY, 179
Expediency
and justice, 179:8
doing evil on the
grounds of e., 176:5
is everything, 404:7
Expedients
are for the hour, 174:9
EXPERIENCE, 179
Experience
get out of an e. only
the wisdom that is
in it, 179:11
gives us the tests
first, 180:4
is an arch, 180:1
keeps a dear school,
179:9

life of the law has
  been e., 274:4
one thorn of e.,
  179:10
when a person with e.
  meets a person with
  money, 71:5
Experiences
  shaped by our e., 180:3
Experiment
  a noble e., 12:7
Experimentation
  bold, persistent e., 3:8
Expert
  knows more and more
  about less, 180:5
EXPERTS, 180
Explain
  never e., 178:3, 5 &
  note
EXPLANATIONS. See EX-
  CUSES & EXPLANA-
  TIONS, 178
Exploration
  we shall not cease
  from e., 495:4
Extinction
  set the stage for e.,
  206:3
  the doom of e. is over
  this wretched na-
  tion, 418:6
Extremes
  of opulence and of
  want, 329:6
Extremism
  in the defense of lib-
  erty, 36:7
Eye
  important thing is the
  e., 517:1
  less in this than
  meets the e., 250:8
Eyes
  keep your e. open,
  536:7
  of the world are upon
  you, 552:1
Eyewitness
  Goddamn an e., 175:7

Face
  my f., I don't mind it,
  64:5
Faces
  apparition of these f.,
  378:2
  private f. in public
  places, 378:4
Fact
  a little f., 181.3
  becomes clouded
  with doubt, 232:5
  fatal futility of f.,
  182:1
  if a man kick a f. out
  the window, 181:2
  wherever a man
  fronts a f., 181:4
  will one day flower
  into a truth, 181:6
Factory Girl, 542:12
FACTS, 181
Facts
  all the f. when you
  come to brass tacks,
  282:7
  are all accidents,
  182:6
  are contrary 'z mules,
  181:5
  are piffle, 182:4
  are stubborn, 181:1,
  182:7

get your f. straight,
  181:7
just the f., ma'am,
  182:5
of life are very stub-
  born, 182:7
to front only the es-
  sential f., 280:8
Fail
  freedom to f., 183:4
FAILINGS. See FAULTS &
  FAILINGS, 183
FAILURE, 182
Failure
  line between f. and
  success, 182:10
  no f. except in [not]
  trying, 182:9
  the f. is a
  stranger,183:2
  to communicate,
  118:7
Faint
  heart never filled a
  flush, 535:8
Fair
  meet me at the f.,
  105:3
Fairy tale
  obsessed by a f. t.,
  427:3
FAITH, 183
Faith
  —belief without evi-
  dence, 184:3
  feeds among the
  tombs, 183:8
  —illogical belief in
  the improbable,
  184:6
  implies disbelief of a
  lesser fact, 183:11
  in a holy cause,
  184:7
  is a fine invention,
  441:5
  is believing what you
  know ain't so, 184:4
  is sight and knowl-
  edge, 516:2
  is the pierless bridge,
  183:12
  it is that keeps the
  world alive, 184:5
  keep the f., 291:5 &
  note
  truth and dart of
  death to f. are vain,
  184:1
  way to see by f.,
  183:5
Fala (note), 34:1
Fall
  in f., the country goes
  to glory, 343:8
Falsehood
  what a goodly outside
  f. hath! (note), 6:3
FAME. See SUCCESS &
  FAME, 477
Fame
  common f. (note),
  177:3
  is a bee, 477:10
  is a vapor, 478:2
  love of f., 478:4
FAMILIARITY. See INTI-
  MACY &
  FAMILIARITY, 253
Familiarity
  breeds contempt and
  children, 253:5
  breeds contentment,
  253:6

Families
  & hints, 185:3
FAMILY, 184
Family
  no f. is older, 185:4
Famous
  everyone will be
  world-f. for 15 min-
  utes, 479:3
Fanatic
  does what he thinks
  th' Lord wud do,
  166:4
Fanaticism
  consists in redoubling
  your efforts, 166:6
Fanatics, 217:10
FARMS & FARMERS, 192
Farm
  is an infinite form,
  186:6
Farmer
  buys at retail & sells
  at wholesale, 186:5
  no one hates his job
  so heartily as a f.,
  186:1
Farmers
  are the founders of
  human civilization,
  185:6
  embattled f. stood,
  41:3
  smart enough to orga-
  nize (note),
  145:8–146
Farming
  looks mighty easy,
  186:2
Farms
  but destroy our f.,
  185:9
Farther
  there's no f. they can
  go, 183:1
Fascism
  is capitalism plus
  murder, 500:9
FASHION & CLOTHES,
  186
Fashion
  defines the self-con-
  cept, 187:7
Fashionable
  very f., 186:11
Fast
  rider whose pace is f.
  enough, 469:7
Fasten
  your seat belts,
  496:4
Fat
  the f. lady sings, 165:1
  & note
FATE & DESTINY, 187
Fate
  if f. means you to
  lose, 188:3
  is a name for facts,
  187:2
  of a nation was riding
  that night, 42:2
  superiority to f.,
  187:11
  tangled skein of will
  and f., 281:1
  whatever limits us we
  call f., 187:9
Fates
  we are spinning our
  own f., 188:1
Father
  dear father, come
  home, 12:1

my f. moved through
  dooms of love,
  367:10
of his country, 524:5
of Waters again goes
  unvexed, 114:7
talks from our great
  f., 417:4
too little f., 368:5
Fatigue
  makes cowards, 189:6
Fattening
  immoral, illegal, or f.,
  457:9
FAULTS & FAILINGS, 188
Fault
  to confess a f., 188:6
  to find f., 135:5
FEAR, 180
Fear
  fool without f., 189:3
  is an instructor, 188:11
  nothing is to be so
  much feared as f.,
  189:1
  of death and f. of life,
  430:14
  only thing I am afraid
  of is f. (note), 31:5
  only thing we have to
  f. is f. itself, 31:5
  tastes like a rusty
  knife, 189:9
  to speak for the fallen
  and the weak, 433:1
  universal physical f.,
  189:7
  without f. or favor
  (note), 406:5
Fearful
  we are not descended
  from f. men (note),
  34:2
February
  & New England,
  352:10
Feel
  just as good as ever,
  309:9
Feeling
  universal f. cannot be
  safely disregarded
  (note), 412:9
Feet
  I just put my f. in the
  air, 50:8
  patter of little f., 82:1
Felicity, 222:3
Feminine
  nervous, hysterical
  age, 541:8
Fence
  don't take a f. down
  (note), 153:1
Fences
  good f. make good
  neighbors, 350:12
Ferry
  all night on the f.,
  222:8
Few
  they were so f. (note),
  514:7
Fiction
  is dead, 58:5
Fifth Amendment,
  128:9
Fifty-four
  forty or fight, 382:1
Fight
  I f., Sir, 136:3
  I have not yet begun
  to f., 40:3
  I love a good f., 120:1

I propose to f. it out on this line, 115:1
I will f. no more forever, 432:1
it is I that have lost this f. (note), 210:3
like hell for the living!, 282:3
never f. against heavy odds (note), 316:2
never f. fair with a stranger, 131:6
rise and f. again, 40:5
too proud to f., 366:3
Fights
he f., 114:1
Figures
prove anything by f. (note), 443:11
won't lie, but, 443:11
Finnegan (note), 544:8–545
Fire
don't f. unless fired upon, 38:2
don't fire until you see whites of their eyes, 38:4
next time!, 423:7
shouting f., 202:7
when you are ready, Gridley, 468:6
First
at Bethel, furthest at Gettysburg, 356:3
get there f. with the most, 315:7
in freedom, f. in wheat, 260:8
in the fight, 313:6
in war, f. in peace, 524:6
First Amendment
if the F. A. means anything, 129:2
Fist
gets his f. in fust (note), 335:7–336
FITNESS. See PHYSICAL FITNESS, 379
Fix
if it ain't broke, don't f. it, 218:5
FLAG, THE. See PATRIOTISM & THE FLAG, 370
Flag
"spare your country's f.," she said, 372:8
don't haul down the f., 373:7
I pledge allegiance to my f., 373:6
is the embodiment of history, 374:3
our f. was still there, 371:4
rally 'round the f., 122
there is the national f., 373:2
Flags
of freedom fly all over Europe, 553:6
Flashlight
quick as a f. (note), 269:9
Flatter
let those who f. fear, 190:1
FLATTERY, 190
Flattery
is all right, 190:4
we love f., 190:2

would break them down, 190:3
Flaunt it, 409:9
Fleets, 315:3
Flights
success—four f. Thursday morning, 446:4
Flit
the F.!, 6:1
Float
like a butterfly, 475:4
Flops, 183:3
Florence [Italy], 109:3, 4
FLORIDA, 190
Florida
does beguile, 190:5
is a golden word, 190:9
is the world's greatest amusement park, 190:8
Flower
Amen! of nature is a f., 341:13
Flowers
& their beautiful reserve, 341:9
are the sweetest things, 341:12
earth laughs in f., 341:7
through the window, 302:4
Fog
comes on little cat feet, 349:1
Fold
do not f., spindle or mutilate, 448:3
Follow
me!, 552:6
your bliss, 223:4
FOOD, WINE, & EATING, 190
Food
is our common ground, 192:12
too much f., 192:10
will win the war, 548:6
Fool
all of the people all of the time (note), 377:5
all of the people some of the time, 377:5
damn f. until he is 40 (note), 327
to silence a f., 193:2
who knows a f., 193:1
FOOLS & STUPIDITY, 193
Fools
a big enough majority in any town, 296:8
be thankful for the f., 193:6
99 percent of the people are f., 193:9
Football
combines two worst features of American life, 476:5
isn't a contact sport, 475:3
—violence & rationality, 475:2
Footfalls
echo in the memory, 428:5
Footprints
on the sands of time, 219:1

Forbidden
charm about the f., 457:1
Force
cannot give right, 511:4
may the F. be with you, 358:4
meeting physical f. with soul f., 366:5
we must have a permanent f. (note), 311:8
Ford
to City: Drop Dead, 101:7
Foreign
if you wish to avoid f. collision, 522:9
influence, 197:5
less f. aid and more home aid, 396:5
peoples, life, manners (note), 102:3
FOREIGN POLICY, 194
FOREIGNERS, 197
Foreigners
spell better than they pronounce, 197:6
Foresee
Founding Fathers didn't f. everything, 516:8
Forest
I believe in the f. and the meadow, 335:8
primeval, 530:6
wilderness, 531:1
Forests
plants and animals [of] the f., 530:5
Forewarned
forearmed, 263:1
Forget
knowing just when to f. things, 131:5
Forgive
but never forget, 198:6
Forgiven
forgotten is f., 198:4
FORGIVENESS, 198
Forgiving
presupposes remembering, 198:7
Forgotten
Man, 157:3
man at the bottom 395:9
Fork
in the road (note), 475:9–476
Form
ever follows function, 48:5
Fort
hold the f.! (note), 115:5
Fort Worth
is a cattle annex, 92:4
Fortune
f.'s expensive smile, 291:8
man who is about to make his f., 325:6
Fortunes
we are the builders of our, 2:7
Forty
is ten years older than 39, 309:6
Life Begins at F., 309:8
man reaches the zenith at f., 309:5

Forty-ninth
star twinkles, 10:7
Forward, 534:6
Founding Fathers (note), 223:7
Four
more years of the full dinner pail, 384:4
freedoms, 201:11
Horsemen rode again, 472:5
hundred people in New York society, 163:4
Fourscore
and seven years ago, 210:3
Fourth
is it the F.?, 246:6
Fox
populi, 284:1
Foxes
—few grow good, 131:3
France
has neither winter, summer, nor morals, 330:6
in F. every argument becomes a matter of principle, 330:8
—the moon (note), 523:8
Frank
glad it was me instead of you, F., 271:9
Frankfort
is the capital of Kentucky, 93:6
Frankie
and Johnny were lovers, 132:3
FRANKLIN, BENJAMIN, 198
Franklin
the body of B. F., Printer, 169:6
Free
at last!, 36:4
let us die to make men f., 212:3
live f. or die, 353:7
lunch, 158:2
press, 405:8
press (note), 405:10–406
soil, f. men, Frémont, 382:5
thenceforward and forever f., 28:4, 461:4
this nation will not be fully f., 202:5
thought, 125:2
will, 531:11
you can only be f. if I am f., 201:7
FREE SPEECH, 202
Free verse, 53:9
Free-press
Clause, 129:3
FREEDOM, 199
Freedom
and unity, 508:4
battle cry of f., 114:5
exuberance which comes with f., 20:4
f.'s swift-winged angels, 454:9
his [Dred Scott's] right to f., 27:6
is never given, 201:10
is never voluntarily given, 202:6

Freedom (*cont.*)
is not a luxury, 202:4
means the supremacy of human rights, 202:1
New F., 385:3
of one's house, 409:11
of speech, 199:1
of speech or the press, 125 (Amendment 1)
of the press, 408:7
of thought, 199:1
standard of f. unfurled, 17:4
those who deny f. to others, 201:1
when we let f. ring, 36:4

Freedoms
four essential human f., 201:11

Frémont, 382:5

Frenchmen
fifty million F. can't be wrong, 330:7

Fried
avoid f. meats, 536:5

FRIENDS & FRIENDSHIP, 203

Friend
[is] masterpiece of nature, 203:2
a true f. and a good writer, 204:2
in power is a f. lost, 397:3
is person with whom I may be sincere, 203:3
one f. in a life is much, 203:8

Friends
are born, not made, 203:7
have no place in the graveyard, 203:4
nothing final between f., 203:9
ornament of a house is the f., 203:5
three faithful f., 322:8

Friendship
[motto of Texas], 488:10
beginning of a beautiful f., 204:1
boughten f., 80:10
holy passion of f., 203:6
joys of f., 203:10

Frigate
no f. like a book, 65:11

Fringe
lunatic f., 392:8

Frippery, 186:8

FRONTIER, THE, 204

Frontier
& the American intellect, 20:4
has gone, 205:1 & note
is productive of individualism, 204:8
New F., 387:10
triumph of the f., 144:7

Frost
is on the punkin, 344:9

Fruit
strange f., 503
which rotted (note), 23:4

Full
dinner pail, 384:4

Funnies
& editorials, 408:3

Funny
as long as it is happening to somebody else, 240:3
hard to be f., 240:2

FUTURE, THE, 205

Future
ain't what it used to be (note), 475:9–476
dreams of the f., 205:5
I have seen the f., 205:9
is no more uncertain than the present, 205:8
judging the f. by the past, 205:4
meet the shadowy f., 491:3
preventing the f., 508:3
time f. contained in time past, 492:4

Gai
toujours g., archy, 222:11

Gain
steady g. of man, 411:6

Gains
no g. without pains, 148:5

Galloping
ghost (note), 472:6–473

Game
can't anybody play this here g.?, 475:6
how you played the g., 473:3
isn't over till it's over, 475:9
isn't over until the last man is out (note), 475:9
iv cards, 208:1
this wretched g., 207:1

GAMES, 207

Games
and amusements, 207:3

Gaming
corrupts (note), 207:2

Gamut
of emotions from A to B, 251:4

Garbage
in, g. out, 448:4

Garbo Talks! (note), 12:6

Garcia
a message to G., 3:3

Garden of Eden
of the West (note), 359:3

Gardener
I am but a young g., 341:1

GARDENS. See NATURE: PLANTS & GARDENS, 341

Garner
evil old man whose name is G., 251:7

Geese
& spring, 347:1

General Motors
good for our country & G.M., 70:9

GENERATIONS, 208
Generation
best minds of my g. destroyed, 294:2
each g. wastes a little more, 208:5
every g. revolts against its fathers, 208:8
lost g., 208:4
new g. of Americans, 209:1
this g. has a rendezvous with destiny, 208:10
this g. is sowing seeds of dissolution, 208:6
we may be losing this g., 208:9

GENIUS, 209
Genius
disdains a beaten path, 209:3
happy g. of my household, 184:11
in every work of g., 209:5
is an African who dreams up snow, 209:8
is one percent inspiration, 209:6
nothing to declare except my g. (note), 93:7
takes a lot of time to be a g., 209:7

Geniuses, 209:4

Gentleman
makes no noise, 297:3
social duties of a g., 162:11

Gentlemen
do not read each other's mail, 410:4

Geography
has made us neighbors, 329:3

George
if [King] G. comes to Chicago, 421:7

GEORGIA, 209
Georgia
make G. howl (note), 116:2
marching through G., 116:2

Georgian
I'm a G., 210:1

German
whenever the literary G. dives into a sentence, 330:9

Get
there first with the most, 315:7
to g. along, go along, 121:9

GETTYSBURG ADDRESS, 210:3

Ghost
galloping (note), 472:6–473
gray g. thrown into the game, 472:6
to please my g., 172:6
towns and dust bowls, 529:8

Ghosts
of Hawthorne and Melville, 352:11

Giant
pitiful, helpless g., 510:5

Gift
I gave a various g. to each, 150:6

Gipper
win this one for the G., 472:2

Girl
a g. needs good parents, 9:1
if you'd been born a g., 223:5
Pretty G. Is Like a Melody, 61:11
was a little g., who had a little curl, 82:2

Girls
are charming creatures, 538:9

Gitche Gumee
by the shores of G. G., 418:8

Give
do not g. as many rich men do, 80:8
me liberty or give me death!, 199:7
me your tired, your poor, 29:5

Giver
g.'s loving thought, 80:6

Giving
joy of g., 80:11

Glass
through a g. eye darkly, 250:3

Glasses
men seldom make passes at girls who wear g., 453:4

Glory
enough for all (note), 469:1
of everything, 186:4
of the coming of the Lord, 212:2
Old G.!, 372:3
such a g. over everything, 201:2
What Price G.?, 520:6

Gluttony, 192:9

Go
to jail, 275:10
west, young man, 204:5, 527:8
where no man has gone before, 4:7

GOD, 211
God
& generalization, 211:4
act as if there were a G., 174:10
belief in G., 59:4
both [North & South] pray to the same G., 397:13
builds his temple in the heart, 429:9
caught his eye, 173:2
does not play dice with the universe, 444:7
does not speak prose, 212:1
does not take sides in American politics, 394:12
enriches, 44:11
enters by a private door, 211:6
evidence for G., 212:11

final proof of G.'s omnipotence, 213:9
fulfills himself in many ways (note), 79:5
gave him a great vision, 172:7
gave us liberty, 199:5
git up airly ef you want to take in G., 347:9
give us grace to accept with serenity, 398:12
G.'s work must be our own, 545:9
governs in the affairs of men, 211:2
help me, I love it, 521:6
helps them that help themselves, 452:2
honest G. is the noblest work of man, 212:9
honor thy g., 398:9
I can lay my finger on thy heart, 213:1
I believe in one G., 429:2
I never spoke with G., 183:13
if G. talks to you, 294:6
if you talk to G., 294:6
in G. we trust, 211:3
is a mother, 213:5
is a verb, 213:12
is and all is well, 212:5
is in me, 213:4
is in the details, 148:3
is love, 212:6
is subtle but [not] malicious, 213:8
is the Celebrity-Author, 213:11
—the John Doe of philosophy, 213:2
know that I am G. (note), 327:1
love G. without a mediator, 211:5
mills of G. grind slowly, 212:8
nature of G., 213:3
of frolic, 337:10
of war, 522:5
one on G.'s side, 211:7
only G. can make a tree, 342:6
only money of G. is G., 211:8
our Father-Mother-G., 212:7
people see G. every day, 214:4
so quickly, 213:7
spanked the town, 106:3
there but for the grace of G. goes G., 252:2
to daydream about G., 431:5
to prescribe to G., 444:7
use of G.'s name on one's behalf, 214:3
what hath G. wrought?, 446:1
will not help, 213:6
with G. all things are possible, 359:2

God-fearing men and women (note), 22:7
Godless are the dull, 67:1
Gods do not answer letters, 213:10
to say there are 20 g. or no God, 428:10
Going if you don't know where you are g. (note), 475:9–476
it keeps g., and g., 8:2
Gold almighty g., (note), 323:1
cross of g., 157:5
or silver [in California], 72:1
Golden age of poetry and power, 214:8
Golf links lie so near the mill, 436:7
Good and the brave ever in a majority?, 514:9
annoyance of a g. example, 515:2
any g. thing that I can do, 262:3
be g. and be lonesome, 515:4
be g. for something, 504:10
breeding consists in, 298:4
distinguishing between g. and evil, 175:2
doing g., 514:8
Era of G. Feelings, 214:5
famous g. time had by all, 251:8
if all the g. people were clever, 377:9
no g. deed goes unpunished, 515:9
you never had it so good, 387:9
Good night dear heart, 172:3
GOOD TIMES, 214
Goodness best kind of g., 514:12
had nothing to do with it, 457:4
tainted, 188:7
Gospels adherence to the g., 430:10
Gotham ancient city of, 97:10
Gott Herr G., 213:8
Govern to g. another, 217:1
Governed world is too much g., 216:3
GOVERNMENT, 215
Government & happiness, 215:3, 216:2 (note)
all g. is evil, 216:5
art of g. consists in being honest, 215:8
at Washington still lives, 29:2

best g. governs least, 216:5
big enough to give you all you want, 218:1
by crony, 217:8
can [man] be trusted with the g. of others?, 216:1
duty to obey established g., 215:9
how to behave toward this American g.?, 308:3
if the g. becomes the lawbreaker, 217:7
is a trust (note), 217:3
is best which governs least (note), 216:5
is best which provides most, 217:5
is but a necessary evil, 215:1
is force, 217:4
is involved in almost every aspect of our lives, 218:2
is like a big baby, 218:3
is right to lie (note), 264:1
is the badge of lost innocence, 215:2
legitimate object of good g., 216:2
legitimate powers of g., 215:4
less g. we have, the better, 216:6
my movements to the chair of g., 400:9
natural progress [is for] g. to gain ground, 215:7
no g. ought to be without censors, 405:5
of all the people (note), 210:3–211
of laws, 273:5
of the people, by the people, 210:3
should not foster crimes (note), 175:8
take g. off the backs of the people, 218:4
we do not get all the g. we pay for, 218:6
what is g. itself?, 215:6
why has g. been instituted?, 215:5
wise and frugal g., 215:10
Governors if the people be the g., 143:8
Gown a satin g., 187:1
GRACE, 218
Grace in the presence of the danger of death, 474:7
under pressure, 218:8
Graham, Katie, 525:6
Grammar & morals and manners, 266:1
Grammatical sentence with seven g. errors, 224:5

Grand Canyon, 44:7
Grand jury, 125 (Amendment 5)
Grandfather to G.'s house we go, 489:3
Granite State, 353:6
Grant Ulysses S. G.? (note), 189:2
Grape peel me a g., 192:3
Grapes of wrath, 212:2
Grass was the country, 311:1
will grow in the streets, 158:4, 185:9
world of g. and flowers, 310:11
Grateful they are so g.!, 452:9
Grave down into the g., 139:9
GRAVESTONES. See EPITAPHS & GRAVESTONES, 169
Gravity point for American democracy, 260:7
Gray flat, and spooky, 109:8
yon g. head (note), 372:8
Great g. men, g. nations, 219:4
good and a g. man, 525:2
man is always willing to be little, 219:3
men can't be ruled, 219:6
some men are born g. (note), 305:7
to be g. is to be misunderstood, 219:2
White Way, 98:6
Great Britain has lost an empire, 330:1
Great Society, 36:6, 388:2
GREATNESS, 219
Greatness & virtue, 514:5
Greece glory that was G., 328:2
is the home of the Gods, 330:10
Greed and lust for riches, 208:5
for office (note), 402:3
is good (note), 326:1
is healthy, 326:1
Greek islands floating over Harvard Square, 161:5
Green it's not easy being g., 339:9
my own soul must be g., 166:10
Greenery no g. [in New York], 101:3
Greer county, 349:7

Gridley
  fire when ready, G.,
    468:6
GRIEF. See SORROW &
    GRIEF, 463
Grief
  drives men into re-
    flection, 463:8
  I will take g., 464:2
Grieved
  why be g.? (note),
    138:5
Ground
  dark and bloody g.,
    261:2
  to own a bit of g., 342:1
Groves
  were God's first tem-
    ples, 341:2
Grows
  as it goes, 354:10
GUESTS, 219
Guest
  to be an ideal g.,
    219:10
Guilty
  better 100 g. persons
    should escape, 273:6
  let no g. man escape,
    132:6
GULF WAR, 220
Gung ho!, 313:11
Gunpowder
  sometimes g. smells
    good, 519:1

HABIT & CUSTOM, 221
Habit
  —flywheel of society,
    221:2
  is stronger than
    lessons of experi-
    ence, 221:8
  is stronger than rea-
    son, 221:5
  ounce of h., 221:6
Habits
  I don't have any bad
    h., 222:1
  land of steady h.,
    122:3
  laws never as effec-
    tive as h., 221:9
  other people's h., 221:3
Hair
  combs his h. straight
    from his left
    armpit, 536:4
Half
  How the Other H.
    Lives, 436:5
  slave and h. free, 502:4
Halftime
  it's only h., 309:12
Halleluja
  I'm a Bum (note), 76:3
Hand
  that feeds us, 80:3
  that held the dagger,
    550:2
  that rocks the cradle,
    538:1
  that rules the press,
    320:8
Hang
  we must all h. to-
    gether, 142:1
Hang-out
  limited h.-o., 526:2
HAPPINESS, 222
Happiness
  [is] to be dissolved
    into something
    great, 222:7

consists in virtue,
    514:1
  is an imaginary condi-
    tion, 223:3
  lies in creative effort,
    222:10
  of society is the end
    of government,
    215:3
  Makes Up in Height,
    223:2
  pursuit of, 140:3
  tranquillity and occu-
    pation give h., 222:4
  where h. fails, 222:6
Happy
  days are here again,
    214:7
  warrior, 31:2, 229:10
Hard
  cases make bad law
    (note), 274:9
  she did it the h. way,
    174:1
Hardihood
  our ideals of h., 313:3
HARDING, WARREN G.,
    223
Harding
  was just a slob, 224:6
  you're the man for us,
    385:5
Harlem
  of honey (note), 100:4
  precious fruit, the big
    apple, 99:5
  stars over H. streets,
    100:4
  was Seventh Heaven!,
    101:6
  where anything can
    happen, 101:4
Harm
  I intend to go in h.'s
    way, 40:3
Harry
  given em hell, H.!,
    410:7
Harvard
  going out to play foot-
    ball against H.,
    472:4
Harvests
  all greater than you
    wish, 512:2
Haste
  nothing is more vul-
    gar than h., 297:6
HASTE v. GOING SLOW,
    224
Hat
  my h. is in the ring,
    402:7
HATE, 225
Hate
  cannot drive out h.,
    225:7
  creative h., 225:2
  for others, 225:5
  those who h. you
    don't win unless,
    225:9
  to go to bed (note),
    458:3
Hated
  to be h. is to achieve
    distinction, 225:1
Hater
  I'm a good h., 225:4
Hates
  dogs and babies, 320:2
Hating
  price of h. other hu-
    man beings, 225:8

Hatred
  paralyzes life, 288:10
Hatreds
  systematic organiza-
    tion of h., 392:4
Haughty
  never be h. to the
    humble, 297:7
Having
  must be more to life
    than h. everything,
    283:5
HAWAII, 225
Hawaii
  is a paradise, 226:5
  spiritual destiny of
    H., 226:7
  we need H., 226:6
  where they lay flow-
    ers on you, 226:6
Hawaiian
  people [are] lovers of
    poetry and music,
    226:3
He
  done her wrong, 132:3
  must summon his
    people to be with
    him, 404:8
  now h. belongs to the
    ages, 284:3
  was a glance from
    God, 290:5
  was my North, my
    South, my East and
    West, 290:7
  when h. fell in whirl-
    wind, 284:7
  who is not with me
    (note), 176:10
He-harlot, 224:4
Head
  if you can keep your
    h., 496:6
Headache
  I have a terrific h.
    (note), 271:11–272
HEALTH, 226
Health
  first wealth is h.,
    227:3
  less you think about
    your h. the better,
    227:4
Heard
  ain't h. nothin' yet,
    206:1
HEART, 228
Heart
  dungeon so dark as
    one's own h., 451:5
  faint h. never filled a
    flush, 535:8
  has its sabbaths and
    jubilees, 228:2
  hath its own memory,
    80:6
  have a h. for every
    fate, 228:9
  his h. was as great as
    the world, 284:6
  if I ever need a h.
    transplant, 253:3
  is forever inexperi-
    enced, 228:3
  is like a viper, 228:1
  it breaks your h.,
    476:2
  my h. is like a feather,
    222:2
  of America is felt less
    here, 108:5
  secret anniversaries of
    the h., 228:3

that is slow to learn,
    228:8
  to the highest doth at-
    tain, 228:4
Heartland
  here in the h., 309:1
Hearts
  and minds (note),
    510:5
  and minds of the peo-
    ple, 41:2
Heat
  if you can't stand the
    h., 477:3
Heathen
  benighted creature,
    430:6
Heaven
  Almost H., 530:3
  is under our feet,
    335:6
  we will all meet in h.,
    270:6
HEAVEN. See NATURE:
    THE HEAVENS, THE
    SKY, 339
HEDONISM. See PLEASURE
    & HEDONISM, 380
HELL, 228
Hell
  & preachers, 228:11
  down the road with a
    dome on it, 120:4
  give 'em hell, H.!,
    387:7
  I myself am h., 294:4
  I'm going to give
    them h., 32:8, 387:7
    (note)
  if my fellow citizens
    want to go to h.,
    201:8
  is oneself, 229:3
  is others (note),
    229:3
  myself am h. (note),
    294:4
  raise less corn and
    more h., 260:2
  spends the summer
    (note), 44:6
  tell him to go to h.,
    308:1
  there ain't no h., 229:1
  to cast his enemies
    down to H., 228:10
  to work hard and then
    to go to h., 229:2
  with the fires burnt
    out, 467:7
  with the lid taken off,
    103:7
  would I go to h.?,
    431:4
Hello!, 446:7
Helps
  God h. them that
    help themselves,
    452:2
Hemisphere
  this h. & our peace
    and safety, 194:6
  this h. intends to re-
    main master (note),
    194:6
Henry, John, 543:10
Henry the Eighth
  sure had trouble
    (note), 6:5
Here's
  looking at you, kid,
    290:6
Heretical
  sentiments, 429:6

Heretics
live forever, 150:10
Hero
& his septic tank
cleaner, 231:4
& his valet (note),
231:4
becomes a bore, 229:6
created himself (note),
230:9
dead h. becomes im-
mortal, 230:9
h. cannot be a h. un-
less in an heroic
world, 229:7
in a republic, 524:2
is a feeling, 230:2
mirrors the time and
place, 231:1
no h. is mortal until,
230:7
one must think like a
h., 231:2
show me a h., and I
will write you a
tragedy, 230:4
would argue with the
gods, 231:3
HEROES, 229
Heroes
are pretty well all
washed up, 231:5
mainly bogus, 229:9
Heroism
& self-trust, 229:5
Hesitates
he who h. is saved,
246:1
Hesperus
Wreck of the Hespe-
rus, 454:8
Hew
to the line, 117:9
Hic
jacet Joe, 171:5
Hide
best place to h. any-
thing, 131:4
he can't h., 137:4
Higgamus
hoggamus, woman's
monogamous, 453:3
HIGH POSITION: RULERS
& LEADERS, 231
High school, 162:5
Highballs
three h., 12:9
Hill, Joe, 77:1
Hills
I life up my eyes to
the h., 507:1
Hip
one is h. or square,
248:1
Hiroshima, 554:1
HISTORY, 232
History
all h. is modern h.,
233:6
an account mostly
false, 232:11
is bunk, 233:2
is very chancy, 233:11
& daily bread and
butter, 233:4
consists of the inside
of the outside,
233:9
fades into fable,
232:5
first rough draft of h.,
408:11
is a guide to naviga-
tion, 233:12

has many cunning
passages, 233:3
impartial h., 232:9
man is a h.-making
creature, 370:6
men make h., 233:7
morsel of genuine h.,
232:4
now with a fast-for-
ward button, 449:7
of the American Rev-
olution, 232:3
of every country be-
gins in the heart,
233:1
of life on earth, 168:7
page of h. is worth,
233:5
[is] a shallow village
tale, 232:6
teaches us nothing,
233:13
teaches us to hope,
232:8
tortured with h., 466:5
true h. lost forever,
232:3
we cannot escape h.,
232:7
we make today, 400:1
you don't know, 233:8
Hit
'em where they ain't,
471:1
Hitch
your wagon to a star,
14:3
Hitched
to everything else in
the universe, 504:3
Hitler
if H.'s alive, 56:5
Hobgoblin
of little minds, 123:8
Hoboken
beauty [in] H.?, 93:7
heaven, hell, or H.,
548:7
Hog
butcher for the world,
90:8
quiet h. and stillest h.
(note), 74:8
still h., 74:8
Hold
out. Relief is coming,
115:5
the fort! (note), 115:5
Hole
black h., 445:2, 3
Holiday
named Labor Day,
234:2
HOLIDAYS, 234
Holidays
holiest of h., 228:6
Hollow men, 193:8
Hollywood
& happiness, 95:10
& tinsel, 95:7
& your last picture,
95:8
ceased to be H., 95:11
HOME, 234
Home
abstracted from h.,
234:4
concern was to get h.
after a hard day's
work, 425:3
going h., 234:8
heap o' livin' in a
house t' make it h.,
235:1

is the kingdom, 234:6
is the place where,
234:10
is the safest refuge
(note), 409:11
is where one starts
from, 235:3
is where the heart is,
234:11
on the range, 528:1
their ancestral h.
(note), 197:1
there is no h. here,
450:11
there's no place like
h., 234:5
traveling & going
home, 494:6
You Can't Go H.
Again, 235:2
Homes
as the h., so the state,
234:7
Homme
nécessaire (note),
239:2
Honest
can't cheat an h. man,
235:11
character of an "H.
Man", 235:5
one h. man, 235:4
we suppose mankind
more h. than they
are, 235:7
Honestly
men are disposed to
live h., 235:8
HONESTY, 235
Honesty
is always the best pol-
icy, 235:6
line between h. and
dishonesty, 235:10
HONOR, 236
Honor
I cannot trifle with
my h., 236:1
knows no statute of
limitations, 236:4
louder he talked of
his h., 236:3
man of h. (note),
230:8
nation's h. is dearer,
236:5
when h. dies, 236:2
Honorable
are the h. the major-
ity anywhere?,
514:7
Hoosier
nation, 246:8
Hoover
is H. dead? (note),
146:2
the world's greatest
engineer, 251:3
HOPE, 236
Hope
he that lives upon h.,
236:7
is a strange invention,
236:9
is the only universal
liar who, 236:10
is the thing with
feathers, 236:8
last best h. of earth,
461:5
possibility of h., 237:3
they are the h. of this
world, 16:5
we call it H., 237:1

when h. is taken
away from a people,
237:2
while I breathe I h.,
467:6
world's best h. (note),
461:5
Hopeless
hysterical hypochon-
driacs of history
(note), 164:4
Hormonal
raging h. tides, 540:5
Horse
for the want of a h.
(note), 147:8
roughest racking h.
(note), 62:6
Horse-laugh
is worth ten thousand
syllogisms, 273:2
Horses
not best to swap h.,
79:4
people on h., 339:7
they shoot h., 133:8
Horticulture
you can lead a h.,
161:1
HOSPITALITY, 237
Hospitality
consists in a little
fire, 237:4
House
a man's h. is his cas-
tle, 409:11
H. Beautiful is play
lousy, 251:5
divided against itself,
502:4
his h. is a prison,
418:2
livin' in a h. to make
it home, 235:1
was quiet and the
world was calm,
346:10
Houston
in H. the air was
warm and rich,
94:2
we've had a problem
here, 37:2
Huckleberry Finn
& American litera-
ture, 66:7
Huddled masses
yearning to breathe
free, 29:6
Hugo
won't have to buy any
new robes (note),
481:4
Human
knowledge of h. na-
ture, 392:5
only two or three h.
stories, 281:9
Human beings
in this world besides
one's self, 238:6
Humanity
until you have won
some victory for h.,
238:5
HUMANS & HUMAN NA-
TURE, 237
Hummy
the word "h.", 251:1
HUMOR, 239
Humor
is emotional chaos re-
membered in tran-
quillity, 240:8

Humor (*cont.*)
  secret source of h. is
    sorrow, 240:1
  Western h., 529:3
Hundred
  first h. years are the
    hardest, 549:5
HUNGER. See POVERTY &
  HUNGER, 395
Hungry
  man is not a free
    man, 395:12
Huntington's
  ashes (note), 172:4
Hurry
  never h. and never
    worry, 43:3
  no man in a h. is quite
    civilized, 224:8
Hurting
  my business is h. peo-
    ple, 475:5
Hurts
  too much to laugh
    (note), 532:2
Husband
  & a good marriage, is
    earth, 300:6
  and wife are one,
    299:4
  devotion to h. and
    children, 539:6
Husbands
  power into the hands
    of h., 540:10
Hussein
  Saddam H. still has
    his job, 220:4
Hyphenated
  American, 374:4
Hyphens
  in their names (note),
    374:4
HYPOCRISY, 240
Hypocrisy
  atmosphere of h.
    throughout, 241:1
  is the vice of vices,
    241:3
Hypocrite
  in public life (note),
    524:3
  is a person who,
    241:2
  is really rotten to the
    core, 241:3
Hypocrites
  as the h. do (note),
    80:8

I come to this country
  riding a lion, 63:3
I do you know who I
  am?, 420:4
I 'spect I growed, 81:7
I accept the universe,
  503:7
I am a dark rock surged
  upon, 422:6
I am a parcel of vain
  strivings, 238:1
I am become Death,
  442:7
I am but a young gar-
  dener, 341:1
I am content, 270:5
I am from Missouri,
  320:8
I am invincible I am
  woman, 540:6
I am invisible (note),
  423:2
I am just going (note),
  270:2

I am large I contain
  multitudes, 123:6
I am somebody, 425:7
I am the cry of the poor,
  546:10
I am the hardest work-
  ing man (note),
  401:5
I am the law, 275:14
I am the people—the
  mob, 378:1
I am tired; my heart is
  sick and sad, 432:1
I brought myself down,
  527:4
I can lick any man in the
  house! (note), 471:1
I celebrate myself, 451:7
I cried all the way to
  the bank, 50:2
I die hard, 138:6
I died for beauty, 243:1
I don't give a damn,
  251:6
I don't like it [Commu-
  nism], 119:1
I expect no better (note),
  124:4
I expect to pass through
  this world but once,
  262:3
I fell into the State,
  553:3
I grow old—I grow old,
  361:3
I guide, 295:9
I have a dream, 36:2
I have a rendezvous
  with death, 548:1
I have found it, 74:5
I have kept the faith
  (note), 291:5
I have never been a
  quitter, 527:1
I have not been as oth-
  ers were, 13:6
I have not yet begun to
  fight, 40:3
I have returned, 552:7
I, I, I!, 451:13
I intend to go in harm's
  way, 40:2
I know what I like, 49:5
I like Ike, 387:8
I married beneath me,
  300:8
I myself am hell, 294:4
I now take my leave of
  you, 26:4
I only regret that I have
  but one life, 270:1
I pledge allegiance to
  my flag, 373:6
I saw the best minds of
  my generation de-
  stroyed, 294:2
I screwed up terribly,
  527:3
I seen my duty, 551:7
I shall go to Korea,
  265:2
I shall return, 551:3
I stays back wid de gin-
  erals, 519:3
I took Panama (note),
  195:2
I want to be alone,
  463:5
I Want What I Want
  When I Want It!
  (note), 12:4
I was wrong (note),
  114:7
I will be heard!, 459:7

I will not accept if nom-
  inated, 402:3
I would prefer not to,
  13:8
I would rather be ashes
  than dust! (note),
  281:12
I'll get you my pretty,
  137:3
I'll scrape the moun-
  tains clean, 167:1
I'm a Salt River roarer!,
  63:1
I'm that same David
  Crockett, 62:6
I'm the man they call
  Sudden Death, 63:2
I'm Irish, 331:1
I'm mad as hell, 42:10
I'm not a crook, 526:8
I'm sick and tired
  (note), 396:4
I'm the straw
  that stirs the drink,
    409:10
I'm wild and woolly, 61
I's wicked, 176:3
I've
  been things and seen
    places, 180:2
I've never seen nothin,
  45:8
I've seen the promised
  land, 272:4
Ice-cream
  emperor of i., 231:9
  first adventure with
    i., 191:7
IDAHO, 242
Idaho
  & potatoes, 242:3, 4
  is torn, 242:2
IDEAS & IDEALS, 242
Idea
  & its originator, 242:6
  & people who believe
    in it, 243:5
  lives on, 243:12
  man with a new i.,
    354:11
  man with an i., 243:11
  to die for an i., 243:6
  you can't shoot an i.,
    243:9
Ideal
  force of an i., 243:4
  if you believe in an i.,
    243:10
Ideals
  Americans & their i.,
    22:8
  are altars to unknown
    gods, 243:2
Ideas
  are immortal, 243:7
  free trade in i., 202:8
Identity, 305:10
Idleness [in Newport],
  97:5
If
  anything can go
    wrong, 496:3
  ever two were one,
    289:1
  I can stop one heart
    from breaking,
    262:2
  it moves, salute it,
    313:1
  you can keep your
    head, 496:6 & note
Ignorance
  confidence, and suc-
    cess, 478:1

Ignorant
  become an i. man
    again (note), 53:10
Ike
  I like I., 387:8
  poor I., 403:9
Ill
  healthy way to be i.,
    244:9
ILLINOIS, 244
Illinois
  most American of
    all the states,
    244:3
  official language of I.,
    244:1
  southern I., 244:2
ILLNESS & REMEDIES,
  244
ILLUSIONS. See REALITY,
  ILLUSIONS, &
  IMAGES, 426
Illusions
  don't part with your
    i., 154:5
  we suffer from our i.,
    427:2
IMAGES. See REALITY, IL-
  LUSIONS, & IMAGES,
  426
Imagination
  is more important
    than knowledge,
    318:8
  is the secret and mar-
    row of civilization,
    317:7
Imbeciles
  three generations of i.
    (note), 410:6
Imitate
  we only i. (note),
    238:10
Immoral
  illegal, or fattening,
    457:9
Immortal
  unless man is i.,
    245:6
IMMORTALITY, 245
Immortality
  bad augury for i.,
    245:4
  is an achievement,
    245:5
  no one believes in i.,
    245:7
  only secret people
    keep is i., 245:3
Important
  people who want to
    feel i., 409:8
Impossible
  the i. takes a little
    longer, 4:1
Impotent
  of everything but
    malevolence (note),
    249:3
Inanimate
  objects, 490:9, 10
  things, 490:8
Include
  me out (note), 269:9
Income
  a good i., 324:9
Income tax
  has made more liars,
    485:8
  I am in favor of an
    i. t., 485:5
Incompetence
  rise to his level of i.,
    546:2

INDECISION, 245
Indecision, 245:8
Independence
  forever!, 246:7
  now and forever!,
    200:5
  of opinion (note),
    238:10
INDEPENDENCE DAY, 246
Independent
  free and i. states, 142
    (3rd paragraph)
  an i. is a guy who,
    394:3
  the country shall be
    i., 26:2
Indian
  in body and mind
    equal to the white
    man, 417:1
  stands free and un-
    constrained, 418:2
INDIANA, 246
Indiana
  blest I.!, 246:8
  home of more first-
    rate second-class
    men, 247:2
Indians
  only good I. I ever
    saw were dead,
    419:7
Indispensable
  there is no i. man,
    239:2
Individualism
  frontier is productive
    of i., 204:8
  in America, 247:7
  rugged i., 22:7
Individuality
  is the aim of political
    liberty, 247:5
INDIVIDUALITY & INDI-
  VIDUALISM, 247
Industry, 505:5
Infallibility
  doubt their own i.
    (note), 124:4
Infamy
  a date which will live
    in i., 32:5
Infantryman
  look at an i.'s eyes,
    314:2
Infinite
  while men believe in
    the i., 183:9
Influenza, 244:6
Information
  is power, 264:1
  so much i. all day
    long, 263:9
  to live with adequate
    i., 263:10
INFORMATION. See
  KNOWLEDGE & IN-
  FORMATION, 263
Ingratitude
  my monumental per-
    sonal i., 231:11
INITIATIVE. See BOLDNESS
  & INITIATIVE, 64
INJUSTICE, 248
Injustice
  abyss of i., 432:7
  anywhere is a threat,
    248:3
  great and unredressed
    i., 248:2
Innocent
  bystander, 99:10
  one that is i. (note),
    273:6

Inquisitors
  whom will you make
    your i.?, 77:6
Insanity
  runs in my family,
    293:7
Insight
  moment's i., 317:4
Institution
  is the lengthened
    shadow of one man,
    248:5
  peculiar, 460:5
INSTITUTIONS, 248
Institutions
  adjusting them to the
    changing time,
    248:6
  fall into i. already
    made (note), 248:5
INSULTS, 248
Insures
  all people against all
    happenings, 70:8
Integrity
  unswerving i., 515
Intellectual
  the word i. suggests,
    164:2
Intellectuals
  pointy-headed i.
    (note), 163:9–164
Intelligence
  test of a first-rate i.,
    318:2
Interlude
  strange i., 282:5,
    400:2
  sweet i., 282:11
Interpretation, 50:1
INTIMACY & FAMILIARITY,
  253
Inventions
  are wont to be pretty
    toys, 446:3
Invisible
  I am an i. man, 423:2
Invitation
  dinner i.—sacred
    obligation, 219:8
IOWA, 253
Iowa
  character of I., 254:1
  is this heaven? It's I.,
    254:3
  produce that I. breeds,
    253:9
  spells agriculture,
    254:2
Iowans
  & God, 92:8
Ioway
  where the tall corn
    grows!, 253:7
Iraq
  attack on I. and
    Kuwait, 220:1
Ireland
  Spenser's I. (note),
    331:1
Irish
  being I., 331:2
  belong to the category
    of the impossible,
    419:5
  I'm I., 331:1
  with their glowing
    hearts, 330:11
Iron curtain (note),
  32:7
Ironsides
  Old I. (note), 312:5
Ishmael
  call me I., 13:7

Islands
  enchanted i. (note),
    225:10
  loveliest fleet of i.
    (note), 225:10
  we want those i.,
    226:1
It
  ain't necessarily so,
    430:11
  might have been!,
    428:3
  takes as long as it
    takes (note), 188:10
Italian Navigator
  has reached the New
    World, 447:9
Italy
  & Switzerland, 331:7
  Creator made I. with
    Michael Angelo,
    331:5
  Garden of Europe,
    331:3
  gives us antiquity
    with good roads,
    331:4
  I was born in I., 331:6
J.O.B., 158:5
JACKSON, ANDREW, 255
Jackson
  if General J. wants to
    go to Heaven, 255:1
  old, old Andrew J.,
    255:3
  standing like a stone
    wall, 112:7
Jail
  go directly to jail,
    275:10
Japan
  attacked by J., 550:6
  I saw the native home
    in J., 332:2
  we have thrown J.
    morally backward,
    331:8
  will be finished, 553:7
  won, 37:6
Japanese
  have perfected good
    manners, 332:5
  solve the problem,
    332:4
  Surrender, 554:2
Jay
  hasn't got any more
    principle than a
    Congressman, 337:8
Jazzmen
  go to it, O j., 51:8
JEFFERSON, THOMAS, 255
Jefferson
  here was buried
    Thomas J., 170:3
  Thomas J. survives,
    270:4
  when Thomas J.
    dined alone, 256:1
Jesus
  my J. mercy, 173:6
Jew
  brain of the average J.,
    420:9
  to be a J. is destiny,
    422:4
Jewish
  man with parents
    alive, 368:4
Job, 428:8
Joe
  hic jacet J., 171:5
  Hill, 77:1

say it ain't so, J., 472:1
John
  why don't you speak
    for yourself, J.?,
    289:5
John Henry, 543:10
Join
  the union, girls,
    538:2
Joke
  national j. factory
    (note), 121:6
Jones, Casey, 544:8
Judas
  Iscariot—premature
    Congressman, 120:6
JUDGES, 256
Judge
  I want to know who
    the j. is, 256:5
  perfect j. fears noth-
    ing, 256:3
Judges
  & the respect of the
    people, 256:8
  are the weakest link,
    256:6
  sometimes progress,
    256:4
Judgment
  he was a walking day
    of j., 439:7
  let j. run down as wa-
    ters (note), 36:1
  Rush to J., 258:10
Judicial
  acme of j. distinction,
    256:2
  decrees, 276:5
  political question, j.
    question, 273:10
  restraint, 256:7
Judiciary
  is the safeguard
    (note), 127:5
June
  old sophistries of J.,
    343:12
  what is so rare as a
    day in J.?, 343:11
June bug
  a young J. b., 8:9
JURIES, 256
Juries, 256:10
Jury
  member more ready
    to hang the panel,
    256:11
  is only as sound as
    the men who make
    it up, 257:6
  persons appointed by
    a judge, 257:2
  system puts a ban
    upon intelligence,
    257:2
  trial by j. 125
    (Amendment 7),
    256:9, 257:5
Just
  say no, 516:1
JUSTICE, 257
Justice
  & Just-Us, 258:11
  and Right, and the
    Law!, 258:1
  expediency and j.,
    179:8
  if we should deal out
    j. only, 258:2
  is always in jeopardy,
    257:9
  is not to be taken by
    storm, 258:4

Justice (*cont.*)
  laws of changeless j. bind, 257:10
  no j., no peace, 258:12
  no such thing as j., 258:5
  swift j., 258:8
  thou shalt not ration j., 258:6
  until j. rolls down like waters, 36:1
  what stings is j., 258:3
  where j. is denied, 141
  without j. courage is weak, 257:8
  your j. would freeze beer!, 258:7

KANSAS, 259
Kansas
  Bleeding K., 259:1
  citizen & bootlegger in K., 260:4
  Crime against K., 259:2
  farmers ought to raise more hell, 260:2
  feeling we're not in K. any more, 260:5
  in K. we busted, 259:4
  is a kind of barometer, 260:9
  is one of our finest states, 260:10
  is the child of Plymouth Rock, 260:6
  roosters lay eggs in K., 259:5
  they chew tobacco in K., 260:1
  three log houses make a city in K., 259:3
  What's the Matter with K.?, 260:3
Kansas City
  Ev'rythin's up to date in K. C., 94:3
Keep
  the faith, baby!, 291:5
Kelly
  Slide, K., Slide, 470:7
Kentuck
  heaven is a K. of a place, 261:1
Kentuckians
  raw-boned K., 261:3
KENTUCKY, 260
Kentucky, 260
  hurrah for old K.!, 308:2
  is the garden spot of the world, 262:1
  old K. home, 261:5
  politics the damndest in K., 261:7–262
  to hell or K., 260:12
Kickin'
  never gets you nowhere, 535:8
Kid
  here's looking at you, k., 290:6
Kidder
  everybody likes a k., 240:6
Kill
  then we are going to k. it, 220:2
Killed
  being k. on the beaches, 552:2
Kilroy, 553:5

Kin
  and kith, 185:1
Kind
  be, 453:9
  nobler to be k., 258:2
Kinder
  gentler nation, 389:1
KINDNESS, 262
Kindness
  little deeds of k., 148:1
  nothing has happened except k., 262:8
  of strangers, 262:7
King
  can stand people's fighting, 231:10
  every man a k.!, 386:6
  once more a k., 460:2
  when you strike at a k., 440:4
Kings
  is mostly rapscallions, 231:7
Kiss of death, 496:1
Kisses, 287:9
Kitchen
  get out of the k., 477:3
Kitten
  trouble with a k. is THAT, 338:8
Kittens
  wot have I done to deserve these k.?, 367:6
Knees
  they fell upon their k., 25:5
Knight
  like a plumed k., 229:8
Knights
  had no meaning in this game, 134:2
Knit
  if you don't k. (note), 251:5
Know
  better to k. nothing, 263:4
  how did they k.?, 251:2
  nothing but my Country, 383:1
  one never k., do one?, 459:4
  whence you came (note), 370:8
Know-Nothings (note), 383:1
Knowing
  die k. something, 263:8
KNOWLEDGE & INFORMATION, 263
Knowledge
  & emotion and purpose, 263:7
  & ignorance, 264:2
  between us we cover all k. (note), 181:1
  is the great sun, 263:2
  is the knowing that we cannot know, 263:3
  is the recognition of something absent, 263:6
  stored full of unused k., 263:5
Kodaks (note), 5:3
Korea
  attack upon K., 264:3
  I shall go to K., 265:2

what we are doing in K., 264:5
KOREAN WAR, 264
Kosmos
  in my K. no feeva of discord, 505:6
Kuwait, 220:3

L.A.
  redundant to die in L.A., 74:3
LABOR. See CAPITALISM & CAPITAL v. LABOR, 75
Labor
  & capital, 75:6, 76:1
  & love, 543:1
  all that serves l. (note to reader), 283–284
  disgraces no man, 75:8
  in New England, 75:5
  learn to l. and to wait, 2:1
  life of l., 543:2
  love l., 542:8
  omnia vincit, 360:1
  [process] by which A acquires property from B, 78
Lady
  ain't no l.; she's my wife, 299:7
  is serene, 297:3
  no l. is ever a gentleman, 539:4
  or the tiger?, 414:2
  with a Lamp shall stand, 537:10
Lafayette
  we are here, 549:3
Laid
  end to end, 457:8
Lake Wobegon, 319:1
Lambs
  we are poor little l., 456:11
Land
  abundance of vacant l., 204:3
  as a community, 168:4
  cheap l. & wages of labor, could not be far distant, 511:10–512
  existence of free l., 204:7
  fine l. to shun, 10:4
  it is my l., my home, 44:5
  life of the l. is perpetuated by righteousness, 226:8
  nothing but l., 205:2
  of extremes, l. of contrasts, 44:8
  of steady habits, 122:3
  of the Bad People, 294:8
  of the Sky, 356:4
  promised l., 272:4
  a rough land, 122:8
  seems forlorn (note), 209:11
  that peaceful l., 225:10
  this l. is your l., 23:10
  very convenient for building, 103:5
  was ours before we were the land's, 23:2
  we abuse l., 168:12

where my fathers died, 372:4
Landon
  life, liberty, and L., 387:3
Lands
  determined to defend our l., 432:4
  pleasant, with grass and flowers, 355:3
  these l. are ours, 417:2
Landscape
  this prehistoric l. (note), 450:11
LANGUAGE & WORDS, 266
Language
  & world, 269:11
  common faults of American l., 266:3
  drawing on my fine command of l., 455:11
  has become [debased] in America, 266:4
  is a virus from outer space, 269:13
  is fossil poetry, 267:4
  is the archives of history, 267:2
  of the country he visits, 493:11
  v. death and silence, 269:12
Lanterns
  in the North Church steeple, 38:1
Laredo
  the streets of L., 94:4
Lark
  & music, 337:4
Las Vegas, 94:5
Last
  years of life are the best, 362:1
LAST WORDS, 269
Later
  than you think, 491:12
Laugh
  and the world laughs with you, 273:1
  horse-l., 273:2
  l.'s the wisest, easiest answer, 272:6
  we l. and l., 272:10
Laughed,
  when I sat down at the piano, 5:6
Laughing
  & theologians, 272:8
Laughs
  human being should beware how he l., 272:5
LAUGHTER & MIRTH, 272
Laughter, 272:9
LAW, 273
Law
  and Order, 385:7
  arm and shield of the l., 273:9
  bachelors of l., 276:7
  breaks a l. that is unjust, 276:6
  cannot be static, 275:5
  embodies the story of a nation, 274:5
  every time they make a joke it's a l., 121:6
  is a horrible business, 275:13

I am the l., 275:14
in a policeman's
nightstick, 274:3
is expression of the
will of the
strongest, 274:8
is behind the times,
275:6
is bigger than money,
276:3
is stationary, 275:7
is the calling of
thinkers, 274:7
is whatever is boldly
asserted, 273:8
lack of respect for l.,
133:4
life of the l. has been
experience, 274:4
must not stand still,
275:9
no l. west of the
Pecos, 526
no man is above the
l., 275:1
one with the l. is a
majority, 275:8
profession is numer-
ous and powerful,
276:8
respect for the l. v.
the right, 274:2
rules throughout exis-
tence, 503:8
that might look like a
wall, 277:10
there's gotta be a l.,
278:7
to succeed in the l.,
277:7
we make our own
law, 276:4
West of the Pecos
(note), 274:6
Lawlessness
world l., 61:4
Lawns (note), 169:2
Laws
are like spiders' webs
(note), 273:3
are never as effective
as habits, 221:9
civil l., 277:7
execution of the l.,
273:7
government of l., and
not of men, 273:5
have no fixity, 274:8
like to cobwebs, 273:3
obey the l. too well,
274:1
of thermodynamics,
445:4
too gentle, 273:4
Lawsuit, 275:4
LAWYERS, 276
Lawyer
& accuracy and dili-
gence, 277:1
& ignorance of the
law, 278:2
be an honest l., 277:5
can steal more, 278:9
courage & a l., 278:8
have you a criminal l.
[here]?, 278:5
I'm just a country l.
(note), 412:5
skilled in circumven-
tion, 277:8
when a l. cashes in,
278:1
Lawyered
we are over-l., 278:10

Lawyers
America is the par-
adise of l., 277:11
letting l. be their
guide, 278:3
of the United States,
277:3
150 l., 120:3
Philadelphia l., 277:2
priests, l., and physi-
cians, 353:8
weary l. with endless
tongues, 277:6
LAZINESS, 279
Laziness
& poverty, 279:2
LBJ
all the way with LBJ,
388:1
how many kids did
you kill today?,
509:6
LEADERS. See HIGH POSI-
TION: RULERS &
LEADERS, 231
Leader
[must be] willing to
follow, 232:2
final test of a l.,
231:13
real l. has no need to
lead, 231:12
Learn
know how to l., 160:11
Leave
I now take my l. of
you, 26:4
Leg
word "l." was never
mentioned (note),
266:4–267
Legal
concepts, 275:12
writing, 278:4
Legislature
innocent man is sent
to the l., 121:5
Legislatures
that bring higher
prices (note), 120:7
Legs
no l., no jokes (note),
359:6
LEISURE, 279
Lend
a hand, 80:5
Less
in this than meets the
eye, 250:8
is more, 48:3
Let
my people go, 459:8
us alone, 417:6
Liars
will figure, 443:11
Liberal
is a conservative who,
394:11 (note)
is a man who, 393:9
Liberalism
& capitalism, 394:1
Liberals
can understand every-
thing but, 394:9
Liberated
the hell out of this
place, 552:4
Libertas
ubi l., ibi patria
(note), 200:1
Liberties
are the gifts of God,
200:2
our l. we prize, 254:4

Liberty
& eternal vigilance
(note), 200:8
& the powerful, 202:2
and independence,
143:3
and independence,
forever!, 200:6
and prosperity,
354:4
depends on the free-
dom of the press,
405:3
give me l. or give me
death!, 199:7
God gave us l., 199:5
had a right to l. and
death, 201:3
inspire our souls,
199:9
life, l. and the pursuit
of happiness, 140:3
(paragraph 2)
proclaim l., 199:2
tree of l. must be re-
freshed with blood,
200:3
v. repression, 201:6
v. safety, 199:3
where l. dwells, 200:1
Lick
I can l. any man in
the house (note),
471:1
Lie
differences between a
cat and a l., 152:8
don't l. if you don't
have to, 152:10
government's right to
l. (note), 264:1
I can't tell a l., Pa
525:1 & note
is an abomination
unto the Lord,
152:7
sin and a l., 152:5
to tell a l. once, 152:4
Lied
never seen anybody
but l., 152:6
Lies
take the l. out of him,
250:1
we shall tell no l.
(note), 406:5 (note)
LIES. See DISHONESTY &
LIES, 152
LIFE, 279
Life
& danger, 136:4
& storm of thoughts,
317:9
& time, 279:8
a finer manner of l.,
89:5
all the days of my l.
(note), 283:4
Begins at Forty, 309:8
believe that l. is
worth living, 281:6
consists in what a
man is thinking,
280:5
events of l., 281:7
first half of l., 8:10
human l. is but a se-
ries of footnotes
(note), 282:12
if it were the last
hour of my l.,
513:10
is a search after
power, 397:1

is a self-evolving cir-
cle, 374:8
is a series of surprises,
280:3
is a shadowy, strange
road, 281:3
is a solitary cell,
282:4
is action and passion,
281:10
is all memory, 400:4
is an offensive, 282:8
is but a span, 279:7
is just one damn
thing after another,
282:2
is mainly wasted
time, 282:13
is one damn thing
over and over, 282:6
is one long postpone-
ment, 282:10
is painting a picture,
281:8
is real!, 280:2
is short, 283:9
is short, art long
(note), 46:4
is something to do,
283:7
is the game that must
be played, 281:5
is the process of find-
ing out, too late,
282:14
is too much like a
pathless wood,
281:11
is unfair, 283:2
is washed in the
speechless real,
427:1
liberty, and the pur-
suit of happiness,
140:3 (paragraph 2)
love a broad margin
to my l., 280:9
man's l. is not a busi-
ness, 283:3
means progress, 411:9
measured out my l. in
coffee spoons,
281:13
more to l. than having
everything, 283:5
my l. has been the
poem, 280:6
necessary that I
should forfeit my l.
(note), 28:2
one l. to lose for my
country, 39:2
our highest business
is our daily l., 283:1
outward, wayward l.
we see, 281:1
realize l. while they
live it?, 282:9
tides of l., 280:4
what is l.?, 281:4
what makes l. so
sweet, 281:2
Light
a thousand points of,
24:9
at the end of the tun-
nel, 510:2
if I ever made l. of his
remarks (note),
250:5
put out the l., 271:7
rather l. candles than
curse the darkness,
515:11

Light (cont.)
world is but thick-
ened l., 444:4
Light! Land!, 25:4
Lightning
difference between
the l. bug and the l.,
267:8
he snatched the l.
from heaven, 198:8
Like
I know what I l., 49:5
Liked
he's l. but he's not
well l., 188:9
Lilacs
when l. last in the
dooryard bloomed,
463:11
Limousine
one perfect l., 290:4
LINCOLN, ABRAHAM,
283
Lincoln
carrying L. home
again, 285:3
memory of Abraham
L. is inscribed, 285:2
Line
in the sand, 220:3
on this l. if it takes all
summer, 115:1
when I had crossed
that l., 201:2
Lips
loose l. sink ships,
484:3
read my l., 486:6
Liquor
is quicker, 13:1
Listen
my children, 41:4
Literary
genius, 58:11
man's reputation
(note), 236:4
Literature
is my utopia, 66:2
is news that stays
news, 58:1
loose popular l., 302:7
Little
drops of water, 147:9
nothing l. counts,
62:5
strokes fell great
oaks, 148:6
Live
always getting ready
to l., 280:1
clean, think clean,
227:7
free or die, 353:7
I wished to l. deliber-
ately, 280:8
if I'd known I was go-
ing to l. this long,
227:10
one fear is that I may
l. too long, 360:5
proper function of
man is to l., 281:12
well, 279:9
you might as well l.,
480:6
Lives
days of our l., 283:4
of quiet desperation,
280:7
our l. carry us along,
283:8
Livin'
it takes a heap o' l.,
235:1

Living
from the sweat of his
brow, 543:6
gets his l. by such de-
pressing devices,
545:6
getting a l., 543:5
is the trick, 283:6
less than two months
old and tired of l.,
14:1
many ways of earning
a l. (note), 325:2
this fever called "l.",
138:8
well is the best re-
venge, 433:7
Livingstone
Dr. L., I presume, 29:4
Loaf
I l. and invite my
soul, 279:5
Loafer, 279:3
London
is the epitome of our
times, 109:5
it's still 1938 in L.,
109:7
this is L., 550:1
LONELINESS. See SOLI-
TUDE & LONELINESS,
462
Lonely
I was born to be l.,
499
Lonelyhearts
the Miss L. are the
priests, 8:7
Long
it takes as l. as it t.
(note), 188:10
long trail a-winding,
154:7
Longer
everything takes l.
than you think
(note), 496:3
Look
farther and see less
than any other
place, 310:9
you could l. it up,
182:3
Looked
better to be l. over
than overl., 453:6
LOOKS. See BODY &
LOOKS, 64
Loose
lips sink ships, 484:3
Lord
grant that I may al-
ways be right,
398:10
has more truth and
light, 211:1
I'll make a L. of him
(note), 40:3
servant in the house
of the L., 272:3
Los Angeles
a constellation of
plastic, 85:3
the place where
everything will fall,
95:6
Lose
as if you like it, 532:8
Loser,
good, 473:3 (note),
532:6, 533:1
Losing
is the only American
sin, 534:3

LOSING. See WINNING &
LOSING, VICTORY &
DEFEAT, 532
Lost
generation, 208:4
never have so few l.
so much, 533:2
LOUISIANA, 285
Louisiana
in L. the live-oak is
the king, 286:1
poor people of L. have
only three friends,
286:2
LOVE, 286
Love
& forgiving, 198:3
& happiness of an-
other person, 288:9
& a poodle dog (note),
287:8
all I want is bound-
less l., 288:6
and marriage, 300:11
as the rain falls so
does your l., 288:1
at the lips was touch
as sweet, 287:7
earth's the right place
for l., 287:4
give all to l., 286:9
God help me, I l. it,
521:6
him that I l. I wish to
be free, 291:1
I thought that l.
would last forever,
290:7
I want to l. first, 287:5
inalienable right to l.,
453:2
is a deeper season,
288:5
is a thing that can
never go wrong,
287:11
is an emotion experi-
enced by the many,
287:8
is anterior to life,
286:13
is born of faith, 288:7
is immortality, 287:1
is more serious than
philosophy, 288:4
is omnipresent, 286:6
is the bright foreigner,
286:11
is the synonym of
God, 286:6
is the whole and more
than all, 288:3
is unworldly, 288:2
It or Leave It, 399
iz like the meazles,
287:2
keeps the cold out,
286:6
make l. not war,
288:8
means not ever hav-
ing to say you're
sorry, 288:11
none but l. to bid us
laugh or weep,
287:3
releases it [life],
288:10
the passion of l. in
this country, 286:7
to some people l. is
given, 291:9
we give away, 287:12
what is l.?, 287:13

what power has l.
but forgiveness?,
198:5
will you l. me in De-
cember?, 290:1
without marriage,
456:8
LOVE EXPRESSIONS OF,
289
Loved
if you would be l.,
286:4
Lovely
all l. things will have
and ending, 556:7
Lover
all mankind love a l.,
286:5
scratch a l. and find a
foe, 541:11
Lovers
earth was made for l.,
286:12
Loves
nobody l. me, 501:5
nobody l. me but my
mother, 288:12
Lovest
what thou l. well,
287:6
Low browed
Shakespeare and I are
l. b., 240:4
Lowells
talk to the Cabots,
87:10
won't speak to the
Cohns (note), 87:10
LOYALTY, 291
Loyalty, 291:3
LUCK, 291
Luck
& self-made men,
292:2
if it wasn't for bad l.,
292:1
is not chance, it's toil,
291:8
is the Residue of De-
sign, 292:3
is what happens when
preparation meets
opportunity, 292:4
shallow men believe
in l., 291:6
the only sure thing
about l., 291:7
Lumbre! Tierra!, 25:4
Lunatic
fringe, 392:8
Lunch
free l., 158:2
Luxuries
and so-called com-
forts, 292:6
give me the l. in life,
292:8
LUXURY, 292
Lying
one of you is l.,
287:10

Ma
M., where's my Pa?,
384:2
Machine
yes the m., 447:8
Machines
our m., 138:7
whether m. think,
449:2
Mackerel
like a rotten m. by
moonlight, 249:2

Mad
don't get m., get even, 42:7
I'm m. as hell, 42:10
the m. ones, 294:3
never go to bed m., 42:8
only people for me are the m. ones, 294:3
we are all m., 293:5
MADNESS & SANITY, 293

Madness
best minds of my generation destroyed by m., 294:2
door that leads to m., 53:4
much m. is divinest sense, 293:3
occasional m. & occasional sanity, 293:4

Magic
belief in m., 358:2a
MAGIC. See ART: THEATER, DRAMA, & MAGIC, 55

Maid
I'd rather play a m. than be one, 55:8
MAINE, 294

Maine
& geology, 295:5
as M. goes, so goes the nation, 295:3
as M. goes so goes Vermont (note), 295:3
don't ask directions of a M. native, 295:8
here's to the state of M., 295:4
I am lingering in M. 295:7
people of the province of M., 204:9
remember the *M.*, 468:4
was the first state to vote dry, 295:6
what old M. can do (note), 381:3
will soon be where Massachusetts is, 295:2

Majorities
mounted m., clad in iron, 296:6
MAJORITIES & MINORITIES, 296

Majority
'tis the m. prevail, 308
can do anything, 296:9
[nothing shows] that the m. rules, 296:7
of one, 296:3
one man with courage makes a m.,130:10
one on God's side is a m., 296:4
silent m., 296:11
Tyranny of the M., 296:2
will of the m. is to prevail, 296:1

Make
love not war, 288:8
my day, 137:7 & note, 486:4

Male
a member of the negligible sex, 306:8

Malefactors
of great wealth, 324:4

Maleness
in America, 542:3

Malice
with m. toward none, 116:3
Mammon, 98:9 & note

Man
any m. might do a girl in, 133:7
bites a dog—news, 406:3
can be destroyed but not defeated, 306:13
can't cheat an honest m., 235:11
cannot be trusted with the government of himself, 216:1
century of the common m., 322:1
died for me today, 559
difference between a dog and a m., 238:7
down these mean streets a m. must go, 230:8
Forgotten M., 157:3
forgotten m. at the bottom, 395:9
got to do what he got to do, 350:10
an "Honest M.", 235:5
I can't spare this m., 114:1
in the house, 306:10
is a dangerous creature, 396:6
is a god in ruins, 306:7
is a history-making creature, 370:6
is everywhere a disturbing agent, 238:4
is incomplete until married (note), 298:10
is the only animal who blushes, 238:9
little m. on the wedding cake, 252:3
m.'s role is uncertain, 306:12
must be either anvil or hammer, 237:10
an animal so lost in rapturous contemplation, 239:1
never met a m. I didn't like, 173:1
to believe that m. descended from some animal, 443:7
no indispensable m., 239:1
of a few thousand well-chosen words, 8:1
of honor (note), 230:8
one honest m., 235:4
one m. can't fill a house, 385
the savage in m. 238:3
a tool-making/using animal, 237:9
who hates dogs and babies can't be all bad, 320:2

who is in the arena, 3:5
will prevail., 239:5
you asked this m. to die, 591
young m. who has not wept, 8:12
MANAGEMENT TECHNIQUES, 297

Manhattan
is ablaze with light, 355:2
my own M., 98:3
we'll turn M. into an isle of joy, 99:7

Manhood
we have ground the m. out of them, 420:8
Manifest destiny, 18:3
Manifest purpose (note), 18:3

Mankind
all m. are my brethren (note), 174:8
are earthen jugs, 238:2
are very odd creatures, 240:9
we suppose m. more honest than they are, 235:7
Manly deeds, 301:5
MANNERS, 297

Manners
are the happy way of doing things, 297:4
make the fortune, 297:5
—petty sacrifices, 298:2
require time, 297:6
stately m. of the old school, 298:3
Manunkind, 411:11
Maples, 344:10

March
a M. morning (note), 347:1

Marching
through Georgia, 116:2

Margaret
your lousy review of M.'s concert, 49:6
Marie of Roumania
I am M. of R., 287:11

Marine
another M. reporting, sir, 551:5
Marines, 313:9
MARRIAGE, 298

Marriage
a community consisting of, 300:1
every m. is a battle, 300:12
heart of m. is memories, 300:13
is not m. an open question?, 299:2
keep your eyes wide before m., 298:9
love and m., 300:11
must be a luxury, 299:5
a new m., 300:7
sanctity of the institution of m., 300:2
without love, 456:8

Married
best part of m. life is the fights, 300:9

climbs into their graves m., 300:5
I m. beneath me, 300:8
women are kept women, 300:4

Marries
who m. who is a small matter, 299:8

Marrying
never again to think of m., 299:1

Marshall
John M. has made his decision, 481:1

Martini
dry m., 13:3 & note
there is something about a M., 13:2
MARYLAND, 301

Maryland
My Maryland!, 301:3
our summer in M., 301:2
was a raggedness of a new kind, 301:4

Masculine
society dominated entirely by the m. principle, 488:6
tone is passing out of the world, 541:8

Mask
strike through the m.!, 43:6
MASSACHUSETTS, 301

Massachusetts
& the enterprise of its inhabitants, 301:7
has a good climate but, 302:1
have faith in M.!, 302:3
love of my heart is M., 301:6
settlers of M., 302:5

Masses
action of m. of men, 377:2
huddled m., yearning to breathe free, 29:5
sacrifice for the m., 144:3

Massive
retaliatory power, 196:4

Master
I would not be a m., 461:2

Mathematical
development of the m. faculty in the race, 331:9

Mathematician
union of the m. with poet, 443:10
MATHEMATICS. See SCIENCE: MATHEMATICS, & STATISTICS, 443
Mathematics, 444:2

Maturity
condones, 8:11

May
all things seem possible in M., 347:2
the word M., 344:2
Mayflower
my forefathers met the boat, 422:1

McClellan
if M. is not using the army, 113:5

McKinley
  drinks soda water,
    384:6
Me
  & you (note), 451:7
Meals
  [the American] has no
    m., 191:4
  lessen thy m., 226:9
Mean
  streets, 230:8
Means
  [he] m. well, 249:1
  by any m. that are
    necessary, 424:5 &
    note
  discreditable m. &
    great results, 179:3
  perfection of m. and
    confusion of goals,
    322:4
MEDIA, 302
Medical
  tyros, 153:4
  what you learn in m.
    school, 154:3
MEDICINE. See DOCTORS
    & MEDICINE, 153
Mediocre
  even if he is m.,
    305:8
  women want m. men,
    305:6
MEDIOCRITY, 305
Mediocrity
  intolerance of m.,
    305:5
  only sin is m., 305:9
  smooth m., 305:3
  some men have m.
    thrust upon them,
    305:7
Medium
  so called because,
    304:1
  which permits mil-
    lions to listen to
    the same joke,
    304:6
Meek
  shall inherit the earth
    but, 437:2
Meet
  me in St. Louis,
    105:3
Melancholy
  days are come, 343:7
Melting pot, 21:3, 100:9
    (note)
Memorandum, 297:1
Memories
  some m. are realities,
    306:2
MEMORY, 305
Memory
  Americans are impa-
    tient with m., 306:4
  in m. everything
    seems to happen to
    music, 306:3
  life is all m., 400:4
  nobody belongs to us
    except in m., 306:5
MEN, 306
  See also WOMEN &
    MEN, 540
Men
  all m. would be
    tyrants, 540:10
  and melons are hard
    to know, 237:8
  and women belong to
    different species,
    542:6

are what their moth-
    ers made them,
    367:1
becoming the m. we
    wanted to marry,
    540:9
believe not in the
    women, 241:1
build bridges, 306:9
first, and subjects af-
    terward, 200:7
grow sweet a little
    while before they
    begin to decay,
    309:4
have a much better
    time of it than
    women, 542:4
if m. could get preg-
    nant, 542:5
lead lives of quiet des-
    peration, 280:7
little group of willful
    m., 121:4
m. know so little of
    m., 238:11
a new race of m., 16:8
not the m. in my life
    that counts, 227:6
taunted the lofty land
    with little m., 353:2
that women marry,
    299:6
there lie many fight-
    ing m., 549:4
these m. cannot live
    in regular society,
    507:4
we are the hollow m.,
    193:8
who carry nations
    with them, 231:6
who will never lay
    down their arms
    (note), 27:3
Mendacity, 152:9
Merchants
  love nobody, 67:10
Merit
  & baseball, 476:4
Mesa
  plain of great antiq-
    uity, 354:6
Message to Garcia, 3:3
Metaphysics, 379:7
METHOD, 307
Method
  in business, 67:6
  take a m. and try it,
    3:8
MEXICAN WAR, 307
Mexico
  Napoleon has no right
    to M., 3332:6
  poor M.!, 308:4
  why M. wasn't crazy
    about us (note),
    308:3
Miami
  is of unimaginable
    awfulness, 96:2
  is more American
    than America,
    96:5
Miami Beach
  & air conditioning,
    96:4
  is where neon goes to
    die, 96:3
MICHIGAN, 308
Michigan
  & the machine & the
    North Country,
    308:7–309

Milton must have
    traveled in M.,
    308:5
Michiganders
  & Ford, 308:6
Microscopes
  are prudent in an
    emergency, 441:5
Middle
  human nature to
    stand in the m.,
    246:2
  way is none at all,
    389:3
MIDDLE AGE & MIDLIFE
    CRISIS, 309
Middle age
  is when you've met
    so many people,
    309:10
  they call that m. a.,
    but, 309:11
MIDDLE CLASS, 310
Middle class
  melded into one m.c.,
    310:1
  us m. c. never have to
    worry, 310:4
Middle West
  & a great mail order
    company, 311:4
  here the M. W.
    merges with the
    West, 350:5
Middletown
  is a marrying city,
    96:11
  is against the reverse
    of the things it is
    for, 96:10
Midnight
  it came upon the m.
    clear, 83:4
MIDWEST, THE, 310
Midwest
  marriage between pu-
    ritanism and rich
    soil, 311:5
Mile
  wide, an inch deep,
    350:6
Miles
  to go before I sleep,
    494:12
Militarism
  & ideals of hardihood,
    313:3
MILITARY, THE, 311
Military
  civilian control of the
    m., 314:7
  -industrial complex,
    314:8
  intelligence—contra-
    diction in terms,
    313:8
  overgrown m. estab-
    lishments, 311:10
  totally adverse to a
    large m. force, 312:2
  when I was in the m.,
    315:5
MILITARY STRATEGY, 315
Militia
  dependence upon m.,
    311:8
  well-organized and
    armed m., 312:3
  well-regulated, 125
    (Amendment 2)
Millionaires
  eight m. and a
    plumber (note),
    253:1

Millions
  for defense, 26:5
  to be grabbed out
    here, 95:2
Mills
  of God grind slowly,
    212:8
Milwaukee, 96:6
MIND, THOUGHT, &
    UNDERSTANDING,
    317
Mind
  is a terrible thing to
    waste, 318:9
  is an enchanting
    thing, 318:5
  is led on, step by step,
    57:2
  is the expression of
    the soul, 318:7
  is what the brain
    does, 318:10
  made up my m. both
    ways, 246:4
  men aren't attracted
    to me by my m.
    (note), 224:9
  my m.'s not right,
    294:4
  tyranny over the m.
    of man, 500:3
  what a waste to lose
    one's m. (note),
    318:9
Minds
  best m. of my genera-
    tion, 294:2
  men are prisoners of
    their own m., 318:4
  our m. are not here
    simply to copy a re-
    ality (note), 57:9
  so earnest and help-
    less, 193:5
Miners
  came in forty-nine,
    105:7
Miniver Cheevy, 13:9
MINNESOTA, 318
Minnesota, 318:11
Minnesotan
  young M. did a heroic
    thing, 230:3
Minnesotans, 319:2 &
    note, 319:3
MINORITIES. See MAJORI-
    TIES & MINORITIES,
    296
Minorities
  rights of m., 296:10
Minority
  judge a country by the
    m., 296:5
  possess their equal
    rights, 296:1
Minutes
  little m. & eternity,
    147:9–148
MIRACLES, 319
Miracle
  every hour is a m.,
    319:6
  no m. in their lives,
    319:5
  one m. is just as easy
    to believe as an-
    other, 319:9
Miracles
  are laughed at, 319:7
  are propitious acci-
    dents, 319:8
  are to come, 319:10
  a remembrance of m.,
    319:10

MIRTH. See LAUGHTER & MIRTH, 272
Mirth
  is the mail of anguish, 272:7
MISANTHROPY, 320
Misery
  loves company, 501:2
  splendid m. [the Vice Presidency], 508:6
MISSISSIPPI, 320
Mississippi
  begins in the lobby of a Memphis hotel, 320:4
  when you're in M., 320:5
  will drink wet and vote dry, 320:3
  Mississippi Valley, 310:6
MISSOURI, 320
Missouri
  I am from M.—show me, 320:8
  is the farmers' kingdom, 320:7
Mistake
  when I make a m., it's a beaut!, 321:3
MISTAKES, 321
Mistakes
  only one who makes no m., 321:2
Mittens
  of the skin he made him m. (note), 418:8–419
Mob
  pitifulest thing out is a m., 377:8
Mobile
  stays in the heart, 96:7
  work M., 96:8
Moderation
  in principle is always a vice (note), 36:7
Modern
  Inconveniences, 321:5
  our m. age & [New York], 99:8
MODERN TIMES, 321
Modify
  we "m." before we print, 77:10
Moider (sic)
  I'll m. der bum, 474:4
Mom
  never eat at a place called M.'s, 536:6
Moment
  exhaust the little m., 400:3
  I live only in the m., 4:6
MONEY & THE RICH, 322
Money
  & differences, 322:11
  a blessing [only] when we part with it, 324:3
  as beautiful as roses, 323:3
  borrowed m. (note to reader), 283
  dealers in m., 69:1
  if you would know the value of m., 322:9
  is power, freedom, 325:1
  is sweeter than honey, 322:7

is the mother's milk of politics, 394:4
is the root of all evil (note), 325:1
love of m., 17:7
power to make m., 324:1
pretty soon you're talking about real m., 325:10
previntion of crooly to m. (note), 324:1
ready m., 322:8
ready m. of human experience, 416:3
should circulate like rainwater, 325:7
take half my m. from me, 486:1
that's where the m. is, 134:5
they say m. doesn't stink, 325:4
use it or lose it, 324:10
was like sex, 325:9
when m. talks, 325:3
will not make you happy, 325:8
Monkey
  disappointed in the m., 212:10
Monogamous
  higgamus, hoggamus, woman's m., 453:3
Monopoly
  every m., 68:2
  is business at the end of its journey, 69:4
Monroe Doctrine, 194:6
MONTANA, 326
Montana
  —her graveyards aren't big enough, 326:2
  High, Wide, and Handsome, 326:3
  I am in love with M., 326:4
Montani
  semper liberi, 530:4
Montezuma
  from the halls of M., 312:7
Moon
  blessed m., 340:4
  don't let's ask for the m., 223:1
  here men first set foot on the m., 449:1
  I felt like the m. had fallen on me (note), 32:6
  if the m.'s a balloon, 340:5
  is a desert (note), 448:8
  is a different thing to each one of us, 340:9
  is a friend, 340:7
  is the mother of pathos and pity, 340:6
  it is a griffin's egg, 340:2
  lo, the m. ascending, 340:1
  rising m., 339:10
Moonlight
  book of m. is not written, 340:3
Moose
  as strong as a bull m., 391:4

Moral
  equivalent of war, 366:2
  is what you feel good after, 175:1
MORALITY. See ETHICS & MORALITY, 174
Morality
  cannot be legislated, 276:5
  their m. is none of the best, 72:2
Morals
  three-quarters manners, 298:6
Mordre
  wol out (note), 131:8
More
  is more (note), 48:3
  would have been less (note), 48:3
Mormons
  let the M. have the territory to themselves, 505:1
Morning
  air is all awash with angels, 348:5
  always m. somewhere, 363:12
  let me with the m. rise, 347:6
  sympathy with m. and spring, 227:2
  what a glorious m. for America, 38:3
Moscow
  is downhill from all the Russias, 109:9
Mother
  a boy's best friend is his m., 368:3
  I'm still your m., 368:7
  Knows Best, 367:7
  m.'s advice is safest, 367:5
  my m., drunk or sober (note), 371:5
  no such slave as a m., 367:3
  socially ambitious m., 367:9
  too much m., 368:5
  what is home without a m.?, 367:2
  what the m. sings to the cradle, 367:4
Mothers
  free race cannot be born of slave m., 539:3
  men are what their m. made them, 367:1
  speak the same tongue, 367:8
Motion
  all will at length surcease m., 138:7
Motivation
  what's my m.?, 55:10
Motorcycle
  are of m. maintenance, 449:4
Mountaineers
  are always free, 530:4
Mountains
  are earth's undecaying monuments, 335:9
Mourned
  I m. and yet shall mourn, 463:11
Mousetrap
  better m., 177:3

Mouth
  the bigger the m., 535:8
  shut, 455:13
Movement
  never lies, 50:11
Moves
  if it m., salute it, 313:1
Moving
  in what direction we are m., 2:6
Much
  too much of a good thing, 178:2
Muckrake
  with a m. in his hand (note), 407:5
Muckrakes
  men with the m., 407:5
Mugwump, 267:7, 383:5
Munitions, 314:9
Murder
  never m. a man who is committing suicide, 177:7
  shrieks out (note), 131:8
  will speak out of stone walls, 131:8
Murdered
  by a Traitor (note), 132:7
  I m. my father, 133:1
Murderers
  first-class m., 89:4
MUSIC. See ART: MUSIC, 50
Music
  and art and poetry, 47:2
  classic m., 51:9
  heard so deeply, 52:2
  I heard with you was more than m., 290:2
  if m. appears to express something, 52:1
  is the universal language, 50:12
  night shall be filled with m., 50:13
  when people hear good m., 51:6
My
  country, 'tis of thee, 372:4
Myself
  am hell (note), 294:4
  I sing m., 451:7
  I dote on m., 451:8
  I should not talk so much about m., 451:6
Mysteries
  talk of m.! (note), 414:1
Mysterious
  [is the] most beautiful thing, 327:2
MYSTERY. See MYSTICISM & MYSTERY, 326
Mystery
  is the antagonist of truth, 326:7
  ultimate m. of things, 326:8
Mystic
  can live happily, 326:9
MYSTICISM & MYSTERY, 326

Mystics
  hope that science will
    overtake them,
    326:10
Myth
  if the m. gets bigger
    than the m., 408:8

Nail
  for want of a n., 147:8
Name
  as long as they spell
    my n. right, 407:4
  their n. is on your wa-
    ter, 418:3
  what kind of n. he
    had, 431:10
Nantucket, 301
Napalm
  love the smell of n.
    in the morning,
    511:1
Napoleon
  & New Orleans
    (note), 194:5
Nation
  favors from n. to n.,
    194:3
  kinder, gentler n.,
    389:1
  march of a n. destined
    to dominate, 17:2
  n.'s honor, 236:5
  no n. was ever ruined
    by trade, 67:8
  of human progress,
    18:2
  that encompasses 11
    time zones, 333:5
  that has a govern-
    ment—not the other
    way around, 24:6
National
  flower is the concrete
    cloverleaf, 24:2
Nationalism
  New N., 385:2
NATIONS, 328
Nations
  don't know how a lot
    of these other n.
    have existed, 196:1
  a general association
    of, 30:4
  great n. should keep
    their word, 197:1
  justice toward all n.,
    194:4
Nattering
  nabobs of negativism
    (note), 164:4
NATURE, 334
Nature
  & transmutation,
    336:3
  "control of n.", 336:4
  everything in n. con-
    tains all the powers
    of n., 335:2
  is full of genius, 335:7
  is no saint, 335:3
  is one and continu-
    ous, 335:5
  is our best assurance
    of immortality,
    336:1
  just taking what n. is
    willing to give,
    342:8
  nothing is so cruel as
    n., 335:13
  only to the white
    man was n. a
    wilderness, 335:14

provides exceptions
  to every rule,
  335:4
tells every secret
  once, 441:2
Unseen Intelligence,
  335:12
uses only the longest
  threads, 336:5
whose rules are few &
  plain, 334:10
NATURE: ANIMALS, 336
NATURE: THE HEAVENS,
  THE SKY, 339
NATURE: PLANTS & GAR-
  DENS, 341
NATURE: SEAS &
  OCEANS, 342
NATURE: SEASONS, 343
NATURE: TIMES OF DAY,
  347
NATURE: WEATHER, 348
NAUGHTINESS. See SIN,
  VICE, & NAUGHTI-
  NESS, 456
Navigators
  intrepid n., 10:2
Navy
  a respectable n., alas,
    311:7
NEBRASKA, 349
Nebraska
  plains of N., 350:1
  town in N. that has a
    past, 350:4
Necessities
  great n. call out great
    virtues, 350:8
NECESSITY, 350
Necessity
  dire n. must justify
    my attack, 39:4
  never made a good
    bargain, 350:8
Necking
  whoever I'm n. with,
    453:8
Negotiate
  let us never fear to n.,
    197:2
Negro
  all I ask for the N.,
    419:1
  has never believed
    [the] myths, 423:8
  history of the Ameri-
    can N. is the his-
    tory of this strife,
    421:3
  I am a N. and beauti-
    ful (note), 424:7
  if the N. be a soul,
    418:4
  is a standing rebuke,
    422:3
Negroes
  as long as the N. are
    held down, 423:1
  have the right to fight
    against these
    racists, 424:5
NEIGHBORS, 350
Neighbor
  being a good n.,
    350:11
  hear his n.'s dog bark,
    462:7
  policy of the good n.,
    196:2
Neighbors
  do exactly as your n.
    do, 298:5
Neither
  snow, nor rain, 348:11

Neutrinos
  they are very small,
    445:1
NEVADA, 351
Nevada
  desolation of N., 351:6
  it's freedom's last
    stand, 351:4
  move to N., 351:5
  neon looks good in
    N., 351:7
New
  America (note), 387:9
  deal, 31:4
  experience of the n.,
    355:1
  Freedom, 385:3
  Frontier, 387:10
  is always better?
    (note), 194:1
  man with a n. idea,
    354:11
  Nationalism, 385:2
New Dealers
  & car dealers (note),
    253:1
NEW ENGLAND, 351
New England
  & adoration of Mam-
    mon, 352:3
  & February, 352:10
  Brahmin Caste of
    N. E., 352:4
  but one drunken man
    through all N. E.,
    352:5
  heart of N. E. at its
    best, 123:1
  poem of N. E. is her
    Sunday, 352:8
  sway of the clergy in
    N. E., 352:2
  weather, 352:7
New Englanders
  are a people of God,
    352:1
NEW HAMPSHIRE, 353
New Hampshire
  if two N. H. men
    aren't a match for
    the devil, 353:5
  politically N. H. is
    unproductive,
    353:4
  there He makes men,
    353:1
NEW JERSEY, 353
New Jersey
  absorbs the invader,
    354:2
  Turnpike, 354:3
NEW MEXICO, 354
New Mexico
  in N. M. he always
    awoke a young
    man, 354:5
  is old, 354:9
New Orleans
  is the unique Ameri-
    can place, 97:4
  no architecture in
    N. O., 97:3
Newport, 97:6–7
News
  all the n. that's fit to
    print, 406:5
  authorities & what
    the n. is, 409:1
Newspaper
  comforts th' afflicted,
    afflicts th' comfort-
    able, 407:2
  does ivrything f'r us,
    407:2

good n. is a nation
  talking to itself,
  408:10
man who never looks
  into a n. (note),
  405:7
a n. [editor separates]
  the wheat from the
  chaff, 408:1
n.'s duty to print the
  news and raise hell,
  406:1
nothing can now be
  believed which is
  seen in a n., 405:7
once a n. touches a
  story, 408:9
putrid state into
  which the n. have
  passed (note), 405:3
Newspapers
  all I know is just
    what I read in the
    n., 408:2
  are read at breakfast
    and dinner tables,
    406:4
  average consumption
    of n., 406:2
  confuse what they
    read in the n. with
    news, 408:6
  difference between
    burlesque and the
    n., 408:5
  government of morn-
    ing n., 405:9
  government without
    n. or n. without a
    government, 405:4
  they lean on n., 407:1
NEW THINGS, 354
New World
  & a dietary quest,
    192:7
NEW YEAR, 355
NEW YORK, 355
New York
  & anything you want,
    100:1
  & mammon, 98:9
  & the beginning of
    the world, 100:3
  bystander shot to
    death in N. Y. City,
    99:10
  400 people in N. Y.
    society, 163:4
  blazes like a magnifi-
    cent jewel, 100:5
  City isn't a melting
    pot, 100:9
  everywhere outside
    N. Y. City (note),
    98:8
  —a helluva town,
    100:7
  in little old N. Y.,
    99:3
  innocent people in
    N. Y. (note), 99:10
  is a beautiful catastro-
    phe, 100:8
  is a sucked orange,
    98:2
  is the great stone
    desert, 99:1
  is the most fatally fas-
    cinating, 99:4
  is the true City of
    Light, 101:9
  loud, modern, N. Y. of
    a place, 109:10
  O N. Y.!, 99:6

on the sidewalks of
N. Y., 98:5
to tell the story of
N. Y., 99:2
was heaven to me,
101:6
when you've left
N. Y., 101:8
white plume saying
the way is up!,
100:10
will bestow the gift of
loneliness, 100:11
young girls in N. Y.
City, 101:2
New Yorker [magazine],
The, 303:3
Niagara
glory is at play, N.,
N., 355:5
I was disappointed
with N. (note),
355:5
Nice
guys finish last,
532:10
Night
acquainted with the
n., 348:3
ain't a fit n. out, 349:3
dark n. of the soul,
147:7
falls fast, 348:4
long sleepless
watches of the n.,
348:2
shall be filled with
music, 347:8
Nightmare
national n. is over,
527:2
Nil sine numine, 117:8
Nine Old Men, 481:3
Ninety-seven
pound weakling
(note), 6:6
Ninety-nine
& 44/100 percent,
5:5
Ninety-two
between the years of
n.-t. and 102,
361:8
Nixon
N.'s the one, 388:4
you won't have N. to
kick around, 35:4
No
just say n., 516:1
Noble
be n.!, 515:1
Nobleness
enkindleth nobleness
(note), 515:1
of another, 515:6
Noblest
work of our lives,
27:1
Noisy-ville (note),
98:10–99
Nominated
I will not accept if n.,
402:3
Nonviolence
is a powerful and just
weapon, 366:4
NONVIOLENCE. See PACI-
FISM & NONVIO-
LENCE, 366
Normalcy, 30:5 & note
Norman's Woe, 454:8
North
to the future, 10:11
traveling n., 495:5

NORTH CAROLINA, 356
North Carolina
Garden of Eden in
N. C., 357:1
is a valley of humil-
ity, 356:5
less labor [needed] in
N. C., 356:1
NORTH DAKOTA, 357
North Dakota
experiences in N. D.,
357:4
is a doomed state,
357:3
Not a penny! (note),
26:5
Nothing
people on whom n. is
lost, 516:4
to look forward to,
147:5
Novel
the business of the n.,
57:9
November, 344:4,
344:7
Now
I live n., 399:9
is the time to make
real the promises of
democracy, 35:6
word "n." is like a
bomb, 400:5
Numbers
all these n. (note),
159:6
constitute the only
universal language,
444:3
no safety in n., 450:10
Nutriment
gnaw the crust of the
earth for n., 205:6
Nuts!, 553:1

O.K. (note), 381:4–382
Oakland
no there there, 102:1
Oars
with muffled o.
(note), 249:2
Objective correlative,
47:8
Objects
inanimate o., 470:9,
10
Obligations
& privileges, 433:6
Obvious
analysis of the o.,
442:2
OCCULT, THE, 358
OCEANS. See NATURE:
SEAS & OCEANS, 342
Oceanus
the ocean river, 343:5
October
point home in old O.,
346:8
Offense
is the best defense,
470:3
Offer
he can't refuse, 70:11
Office
more time at the o.
(note), 71:7
most insignificant o.
that ever man con-
trived, 508:5
never ask, never
refuse an o., 542:10
second o. of the land,
508:6

wants to hold a public
o. (note), 55:6
See also under Public
office
Offices
as public trusts (note),
217:3
Oh
say, can you see, 371:4
OHIO, 358
Ohio
is the farthest west of
the east, 358:5
why did I ever leave
O.?, 359:1
Ohio River
lying along the right
bank of the O. R.,
91:6
Okie
use' ta mean you was
from Oklahoma,
359:5
OKLAHOMA, 359
Oklahoma
they swarmed on O.,
359:4
throw out anything in
O., 359:3
where the wind
comes sweepin'
down the plain,
359:6
OLD AGE, 360
Old
age and broken
health, 147:4
age is always 15 years
older than I am,
362:10
age is like an opium-
dream, 361:2
age is the most unex-
pected thing (note),
360:8
called an o. man,
360:8
disorderly o. age,
361:8
Folks at Home, 465:1
getting o. ain't for
sissies, 363:5
Glory!, 372:3
growing o., 360:6
how o. would you be
if, 363:3
I grow o., I grow o.,
361:3
I'm o. I'm getting o.
and coming apart,
363:4
it is time to be o.,
360:7
man in a dry month,
361:4
man who will not
laugh, 8:12
man is not o. until,
362:8
no such thing as o.
age, 362:2
no time like the o.
time, 369:13
reverence to what is
o. (note), 322:11
soldiers never die,
33:3
tranquillity is the o.
man's milk, 360:4
Old Dominion, 513:2
Older
I grow, the more apt
to doubt my own
judgment, 360:2

I grow, the more I dis-
trust the familiar
doctrine, 361:5
reflect that she is
growing o. every
day, 541:10
Old Glory!, 372:3
Once
upon a midnight
dreary, 358:1
One
as a signal, 38:1
if by land and two if
by sea, 42:1
man with courage
makes a majority,
130:10
on God's side is a ma-
jority, 296:4
out of many o.,
16:3
Oneself
to understand o.,
451:10
Open
covenants of peace,
375:6
door, 195:1
Opera
ain't over till the fat
lady sings, 165:1
—no business, a dis-
ease, 51:5
the 8 o'clock curtain
at the o., 52:5
wimmin in o. (note)
51:2
Operative statement,
526:4
Opinion
difference of o. that
makes horse races,
150:7
every difference of o.,
501:6
hold popular o. of no
value, 412:8
loyalty to petrified o.,
243:3
of the world, 413:3
See also Public opin-
ion
Opinions
different o., 150:4
OPPORTUNITY, 363
Opportunity
America has been an-
other name for o.,
20:5
America means o.,
19:4
better to lose o. than
capital, 71:6
Know Your O.,
363:10
no security only o.,
363:8
Oppressed
history of an o. peo-
ple, 423:4
people [may] break
their fetters, 434:3
Oppression
does not come at
once, 500:10
Oppressor
and oppressed, 257:10
Optimism
is a force multiplier,
364:10
is the content of
small men, 364:6
OPTIMISM & PESSIMISM,
363

Optimist
& best of all possible
worlds, 364:3
is a guy that has
never had much ex-
perience, 364:4
merry is the o., 364:7
thinks the future is
uncertain, 364:8
Orator
Boy O. of the Plati-
tude (note), 252:3
with his flood of
words, 483:2
Order
breeds habit, 307:6
old o. changeth (note),
79:5
OREGON, 364
Oregon
I must walk toward
O., 527:6
is seldom heard of,
365:2
where rolls the O.,
364:11
Organize!, 76:6
Orgies
are vile, 491
Originality
refocuses the eye,
48:4
Other Half, 436:5
Ourselves
in o. are triumph and
defeat, 451:9
Out
best way o., 174:6
Outlaws
God Forgives, O.
Don't, 137:5
Over
it ain't o. till it's o.,
165:2
the river and through
the wood, 489:3
there, 549:2
Overcome
we shall o., 423:6
Overscrupulous
it will not do to be o.,
179:1
Oversexed
Overfed, over here,
551:6
Owl
wise old o. (note),
483:6–484

Pacific
power that rules the
P., 332:8
PACIFISM & NONVIO-
LENCE, 366
PAIN. See SUFFERING &
PAIN, 479
Pain
after great p., 479:11
has an element of
blank, 479:12
house of p., 479:8
if p. could have cured
us, 480:1
no p., no palm, 479:7
terrific p. in the back
of my head, 271:11
an uncomfortable
frame of mind,
169:4
Painting
a p. [is] a symbol for
the universe, 57:6
Panama
I took P. (note), 195:2

Paradise
a sort of p., 310:12
Paranoids
even p. have enemies,
294:1
Paree
after they've seen P.,
110:2
PARENTS, 367
Parent
loving someone as a
p., 368:6
Parents
obey children, 368:2
Paris
good Americans when
they die go to P.,
110:1
is a moveable feast,
110:7
is my home town,
110:3
last time I saw P.,
110:4
last time I see P.,
110:5
seems to be full of
American girls,
110:6
Parrot, 483:6
PARTING, 368
Parting
is all we know of
heaven, 368:10
sadness at this p.,
368:9
Party
Democratic p. is like
a mule, 390:8
is perpetually cor-
rupted by personal-
ity, 390:2
of the past and the p.
of the future, 390:9
sometimes p. loyalty
asks too much,
394:6
trying to prove that
the other is unfit,
145:3
which takes credit for
the rain, 392:12
PASSION, 369
Passion
end of p. & beginning
of repentance, 369:3
a fever in the mind,
369:1
a powerful spring,
369:5
life is action and p.,
281:10
man in a p. rides a
wild horse, 369:2
scenes of p., 78:1
Passions
never deaf to their p.,
369:4
our p. & our moral
nature, 369:7
violent physical p.,
369:9
PAST, THE, 369
Past
can neither repeat his
p. nor leave it,
370:6
comes not back again,
491:3
dogmas of the quiet
p., 369:11
is a bucket of ashes,
370:1
is the present, 370:4

only the p. is real,
370:5
precious, incommuni-
cable p., 370:2
those who cannot re-
member the p.,
369:14
we have to do with
the p., 369:12
which of us has over-
come his p.?, 370:8
Pastimes
three p.: politics,
sports, and revenge,
88:6
Pat
cannot stand p. (note),
384:7
we'll stand p., 384:7
Paternalism
and state socialism
(note), 22:7
Paterson, 102:2
PATIENCE, 370
Patience
all the passion of
great hearts, 165:3
Patient
endurance is godlike,
370:11
what I call a good p.,
153:7
Patriot
—dupe of statesmen,
374:1
is a scarce man, 373:8
sunshine p., 39:3
Patriotic
brave, p. men, 373:1
PATRIOTISM & THE FLAG,
370
Patriotism
blind with p., 374:6
irritable p. of Ameri-
cans, 372:5
is like charity, 373:4
nation roaring P.,
371:6
postures of pretended
p., 371:3
spirit of p. and sacri-
fice (note), 32:3
steady dedication of a
lifetime, 374:5
virtue of p., 373:5
Patter
of little feet, 82:1
PATTERNS, 374
Patterns
what are p. for?, 520:3
Pay-as-you-go, 159:3
PEACE, 374
Peace
and harmony with all,
194:4
better to live in p.,
375:4
cannot be kept by
force, 376:2
declare p.. upon the
world, 375:10
hath higher tests of
manhood than bat-
tle, 374:11
is a process, 376:4
it isn't enough to talk
about p., 376:1
it must be a p. with-
out victory, 30:2
just and lasting p.,
116:3
let us have p., 375:3
like charity, begins at
home, 375:8

must be kept by men,
376:3
never was a bad p.,
374:10
on earth, 83:4, 5
open covenants of p.,
375:6
price too great to pay
for p., 375:5
a separate p., 375:7
who desires p. should
prepare for war
(note), 518:5
world p. or world de-
struction, 375:9
Peaceful
be p., be courteous,
511:7
coexistence, 197:3
Peace
ripest p. is highest,
14:4
Peale
Paul appealing and P.
appalling, 318:6
Pecos
Law West of the P.
(note), 274:6
no law west of the P.,
488:5
Peculiar
institution, 460:5
Pecuniary
interest, 323:6
Pedigree
of honey, 163:3
Pelican
his beak holds more
than his belican,
338:1
Peninsula
if you seek a pleasant
p., 309:2
PENNSYLVANIA, 376
Pennsylvania
in P. this morning!,
376:8
is the Keystone,
376:5
the P. mind was not
complex, 376:7
Penny
saved is a penny
earned, 322:10
PEOPLE, THE, 376
People
& preservation of our
liberty, 376:10
about 1/5 of the p. are
against everything,
378:6
are turbulent (note),
377:6
civilization &
progress of the p.,
377:3
common-looking p.,
64:4
good p., clever p.,
377:9
government of the p.,
by the p., 210:3
humorless soldierly
p., 334:7
I am the p., 378:1
if the p. be the gover-
nors, 143:8
in the island are un-
polished, 435:6
let my p. go, 459:8
never went broke un-
derestimating the
intelligence of the
p. (note), 378:3

the p.'s government, made by the p., 216:4

the p. rule, 46:3, 468:2

slender p., 227:11

sober second thought of the p., 143:10

some p. can stay longer in an hour, 219:9

superior p. & long visits, 219:11

to him the great hero was The P. (note), 284:1

ultimate justice of the p., 377:6

voice of the p. (note), 377:6

we first crush p. to the earth, 417:5

we the p., 124:5

when you meet p. (note), 173:1

where the p. possess no authority, 396:10

who want to feel important, 409:8

will live on, 378:5

will of the p. & foundation of government, 377:1

you can fool too many of the p. (note), 377:5

you may fool all the p. some of the time, 377:5

PEOPLES. See RACES & PEOPLES, 417

Peoria
dullards in [P.] (note), 102:3

will it play in P.?, 102:3

PERCEPTION. See VISION & PERCEPTION, 516

Perdicaris
alive, or Raisuli dead, 29:8

Perdition
hottest corner of p. (note), 44:6

Perfect
Thirty-six, 487:6

Perfection
falling short of p., 188:10

PERSEVERANCE. See DETERMINATION, EFFORT, PERSISTENCE, & PERSEVERANCE, 148

Perseverance, 149:5

Persian messengers (note), 348:11–349

PERSISTENCE. See DETERMINATION, EFFORT, PERSISTENCE, & PERSEVERANCE, 148

Persistence
nothing can take the place of p., 149:2

Personality
party is perpetually corrupted by p., 390:2

Persons
attempting to find a motive in this narrative, 49:3

Perspiration
99 percent p., 209:6

PESSIMISM. See OPTIMISM & PESSIMISM, 363

Pessimist
& best of all possible worlds (note), 364:3

& optimist & age 48, 364:1

& too many optimists (note), 364:5

has been compelled to live with an optimist, 364:5

Philadelphia
& the Right Thing, 103:4

City of Bleak Afternoons, 103:2

comfortable P., 102:7

Corrupt and Contented, 102:6

has taken Howe (note), 102:8–103

I'd rather be in P., 173:5

lawyers, 277:2

place was closed, 103:1

spitting and swearing in P., 102:5

the home of respectability, 103:3

PHILANTHROPY. See CHARITY & PHILANTHROPY, 80

Philanthropy
appreciated by mankind, 80:4

is commendable, 81:1

Philippine
our forces stand again on P. soil, 552:7

Philosopher
last years are the best if you are a p., 362:1

to be a p. is so to love wisdom, 379:1

Philosophical
tradition is footnotes to Plato, 379:5

PHILOSOPHY, 378

Philosophy
begins in wonder, 379:6

—sense of what life means, 379:3

test of a p., 378:9

tinged with some secret imaginative, 379:4

Photograph
if I didn't p. them, 57:5

Physical
strength v. spiritual force, 477:2

PHYSICAL FITNESS, 379

Physicians
much experience of p., 227:5

priests, lawyers, & physicians, 353:8

Physicists
& past, present and future, 492:8

Physics
no democracy in p., 444:9

PHYSICS. See SCIENCE: PHYSICS & COSMOLOGY, 444

PHYSIOLOGY. See SCIENCE: BIOLOGY & PHYSIOLOGY, 443

Physiology
of p. I sing, 443:6

Pianist
please do not shoot the p., 51:3

Piano
laughed when I sat down at the p., 5:6

learn to play the p. by mail (note), 5:6–6

Picket
p.'s off duty forever, 113:3

stray p. is shot, 113:2

Picture
if nobody wants to see your p. (note), 269:9

in a big p., 57:3

is worth a thousand words, 303:4

Pictures
you furnish the p., 468:5

you used to be in p., 303:9

Pie
in the sky (note), 76:6

Pierce
you in '52, 382:4

Pigeons
air was literally filled with p., 336:8

casual flocks of p., 338:3

on the grass alas, 338:4

Pigs' tails (note), 91:2

Pike's Peak
or bust, 117:2

Pilgrim
Fathers fell upon their knees & aborigines, 421:6

toast that sturdy P. band, 490:2

Pilgrims
they knew they were p., 14:8

Pine
the p. is the mother of legends, 341:6

Pioneers
P.! O P!, 204:6

there must be p. (note), 4:6

we are the p. of the world, 18:6

Pistol
damned good p. shot (note), 488:5

smoking p. (note), 526:7

Pitching
is a large subject, 475:7

Pittsburgh
is like Birmingham, 103:6

Pixley
here lies Frank P., 172:2

Place
discovery that p. is nothing (note), 494:1

a hell of a p., 86:2

for man's habitation, 512:3

great, uninteresting p., 90:1

I pitched upon this p., 106:7

it was the best p. to be, 186:4

last best p. on earth, 326:5

most typically American p., 90:2

my God, what is there in this p.?, 402:2

of moral leadership, 403:5

this cursed, p.!, 38:5

this is the p.!, 504:11

Plagiarism
it's p., 57:10

Plain
ran till it touched heaven, 350:2

Plains
of Kansas and Nebraska, 311:2

of Nebraska, 350:1

Plan
good p. executed Now, 307:9

Plane
if that p. leaves and you're not with him, 368:11

Planet
vulnerability of our p., 168:10

Plant
I'm not a potted p., 279:1

PLANTS. See NATURE: PLANTS & GARDENS, 341

Plastics
just one word—p., 70:10

Platform
party p., 392:1

Plato
series of footnotes to P., 379:5

Play
"As Time Goes By", 52:3

it, Sam, 52:3

"Precious Lord" (note), 272:4

PLEASURE & HEDONISM, 380

Pleasure
& understanding, 380:3

an age of p., 380:4

is by no means an infallible guide, 49:9

Pleasures
man is richest whose p. are the cheapest, 380:5

Ploughshare
smoothly the p. runs, 285:5

Plum
survives its poems, 191:1

Plums, 191:8 & note

Pluribus
E P. Unum, 16:3

Plymouth: 103:8

Plymouth Rock
—cornerstone of a nation, 301:10

landed on us, 424:4

Pnin, 161

Pocatello
you can't go back to P., 103:9

Pocketbook
full p. often groans, 325:5

Poem
  figure a p. makes,
    53:14
  is a meteor, 53:11
  is a nature created by
    the poet (note),
    53:10
  lovely as a tree,
    342:5
  should not mean but
    be, 53:6
  so many ways to ruin
    a p., 54:1
Poems
  difficult to get the
    news from p.,
    54:2
Poet
  the courage of the p.,
    53:4
  is the priest of the in-
    visible, 53:13
  with a p. in your
    pocket, 52:7
  world seems always
    waiting for its p.,
    52:10
POETRY. See ART: PO-
  ETRY, 52
Poetry
  atrophies when it gets
    too far from music,
    53:8
  can communicate be-
    fore it is under-
    stood, 53:7
  cleanses, 54:3
  [is] emotion remem-
    bered in tranquillity
    (note), 240:8
  is a search for the in-
    explicable, 53:12
  is a way of taking life
    by the throat, 53:15
  is always unexpected,
    54:5
  is the opening and
    closing of a door,
    53:5
  [is] the rhythmical
    creation of beauty,
    52:9
  is the subject of the
    poem, 53:10
  must be as new as
    foam, 52:11
  publishing a volume
    of p., 53:2
  serves great ends
    (note), 53:10
  their universal pas-
    time and delight,
    50:12
  what p. does 54:4
Poets
  great p. & great audi-
    ences, 53:1
  immature p. imitate,
    53:3
Pointy-headed
  intellectuals (note),
    163:9–164
Police action
  —a limited war, 265:3
Political
  action is the highest
    responsibility, 394:7
  campaign & prosper-
    ity, 392:7
  education & knowl-
    edge of human na-
    ture, 392:5
  to free 17 million
    from p. slavery, 30:6

POLITICAL SLOGANS, 380
POLITICS & POLITICIANS,
  389
Politicians
  are doing the best
    they can (note),
    393:2
Politician
  honest p. stays
    bought, 390:4
  is an arse, 393:13
  never forgets a favor,
    392:3
  tin-horn p., 223:6
Politicians
  not over a year behind
    public opinion,
    393:1
Politics
  all p. is applesauce,
    392:11
  all p. is local, 393:8
  are based on the indif-
    ference of the ma-
    jority, 394:8
  are impossible with-
    out spoils, 391:1
  as a profession, 393:4
  consists in choosing
    between, 394:5
  fashion to despise
    "p.", 390:3
  God & American p.,
    394:12
  has got so expensive,
    393:1
  in p. the middle way
    is none, 389:3
  is knowing when to
    pull the trigger,
    394:13
  is the art of, 391:8
  is the art of the possi-
    ble (note), 394:5
  is the best show in
    America, 393:3
  makes strange bedfel-
    lows, 390:10
  man who goes into p.
    because he needs
    the money, 392:2
  meekness [will not
    do] in p., 389:4
  money is the
    mother's milk of p.,
    394:4
  plow & plunder in p.,
    393:5
  purification of p.,
    391:2
  struggle not of men
    but of forces, 392:6
  systematic organiza-
    tion of hatreds,
    392:4
  we mean by "p." the
    people's business,
    394:12
Polked
  you in '44, 392:4
Pompous
  an army of p. phrases,
    224:2
POOR, THE. See also
  RICH & POOR,
  WEALTH & POVERTY,
  436
Poor
  ask of the poor that
    they get up, 396:1
  awful phantom of the
    hungry p., 395:5
  I am the cry of the p.,
    545:12

if society cannot help
  the many who are
  p., 159:4
monotony about the
  injustices suffered
  by the p., 396:2
no disgrace to be p.,
  495:7
to be a p. race in a
  land of dollars,
  436:6
you cannot help the
  p. by destroying the
  rich (note to reader),
  283
Poor-house
  over the hill to the
  p.-h., 395:4
Poppycock
  pretentious p. (note),
  278:4
Popular
  anyone who is p.
  (note), 475:9–476
Populi
  salus p. suprema lex
  esto, 321:1
Populus
  regnat p., 46:3
Portland
  produces lumber,
  104:3
Portlanders
  O happy P., 104:2
Positive
  Power of P. Thinking,
  318:6
POSSESSIONS. See THINGS
  & POSSESSIONS, 490
Posterity
  what has p. ever done
  for me?, 208:11
Potomac
  all quiet along the P.,
  113:1
POVERTY & HUNGER, 395
POVERTY. See also RICH
  & POOR, WEALTH &
  POVERTY, 436
Poverty
  anarchy of p., 395:10
  and excess, 436:1
  demoralizes, 395:13
  final triumph over p.,
  31:1
  indeed is the strenu-
  ous life, 495:6
  smells like death,
  395:11
  war on p., 36:5
POWER, 396
Power
  absolute p. corrupts
  (note), 450:8
  always thinks it has a
  great soul, 396:9
  and territory [of the
  U.S.] should be ex-
  tended, 307:11
  ceases in the instant
  of repose, 396:11
  cohesive power of
  public plunder
  (note), 396:1
  friend in p. is a friend
  lost, 397:3
  intoxicates men,
  397:4
  is ever grasping, 396:6
  is the first good, 397:2
  is the great aphro-
  disiac, 397:7
  it was a vision of p.,
  90:6

joy or p., 396:12
life is a search after
  p., 397:1
never takes a back
  step, 397:5
no pleasure in the ex-
  ercise of p., 396:8
of Positive Thinking,
  318:6
over a man's subsis-
  tence, 396:7
we have confused p.
  with greatness,
  397:6
Prairie-lawyer
  master of us all, 285:1
Prairies, 310:10
Praise
  the Lord and pass the
  ammunition, 550:5
Pray
  as if you were to die
  tomorrow, 535:7
  big! (note), 318:6
  do not p. for easy
  lives, 398:8
  for everyone, in soli-
  tude, 398:7
  for me now, 32:6
  to ask that the rules
  of the universe be
  annulled, 398:2
  you can't p. a lie,
  398:1
Prayed
  I p., and did God
  care?, 397:11
PRAYER, 397
Prayer
  among sane people,
  398:3
  as a means, 397:10
  is not a confessional,
  397:14
  is the contemplation
  of, 397:9
  is the little imple-
  ment, 397:12
  power, 398:6
Prayers
  in his p. he says,
  397:8
  of all good people,
  398:4
  of both could not be
  answered (note),
  212:4
PRAYERS & BLESSINGS,
  398
Praying
  these many years to
  go to heaven (note),
  115:4
  trouble with our p.,
  398:5
Precious
  three unspeakably p.
  things, 20:8
PREJUDICE, 399
Prejudice
  a vagrant opinion,
  399:6
PREJUDICED
  in favor of a thing,
  399:3
Prejudices
  everyone is a prisoner
  of his own p., 399:7
  never too late to give
  up our p., 399:4
Prepared
  be p., 536:1
  in mind and re-
  sources, 467:5

PRESENT, THE, 399
Present
 is an interlude, 400:2
 it is thine, 491:3
 moment that goes by
   you so quick, 400:4
 stormy p., 399:11
 to give a man a p.,
   298:7
 volatile froth of the
   p., 399:8
 we want to live in the
   p., 400:1
 where is it, this p.?,
   399:13
PRESIDENCY, THE, 400
Presidency
 cancer close to the p.,
   526:1
 greased pig of Ameri-
   can politics, 402:5
 is the only office of
   all the people, 404:5
President
 & the unfinished
   business [of the] na-
   tion, 404:3
 cannot be disturbed,
   403:1
 great men are not
   chosen p., 402:4
 has paid dear for his
   White House, 401:4
 he accepts [no pay] as
   p., 524:3
 I do not choose to run
   for p., 403:3
 I had rather be right
   than be p., 401:6
 is the direct represen-
   tative of the Ameri-
   can people, 401:3
 is the representative
   of the whole nation,
   404:1
 must not ask the p. to
   get down in the gut-
   ter, 403:7
 no easy problems ever
   come to the p.,
   404:2
 no p. can have any
   leisure, 401:5
 office of a p., 401:
 pick a p. and then
   pick on him,
   403:8
 p.'s hardest task,
   404:6
 profession of a p.,
   402:6
 that damned cowboy
   is p., 439:3
 what did the p. know,
   and when, 526:7
 when the p. does it, it
   is not illegal, 404:9
 who will be the next
   p.?, 400:8
Presidents,
 & hair shirts, 403:4
PRESS, THE, 234
Press
 free (note),
   405:10–406
 free p., 405:8
 freedom of the p.,
   408:7
 hand that rules the p.
   rules the country,
   303:8
 if we treat the p. with
   more contempt
   (note), 408:12

 is the enemy, 408:12
 liberty of the p., 405:2
 where the p. is free,
   405:5
Press agent
 or a publicity man
   (note), 8:1
Pressure
 things get worse un-
   der p. (note), 496:3
Pretty
 Girl Is Like a Melody,
   61:11
PRIDE & VANITY, 409
Pride
 breakfasted with
   Plenty, 409:3
 costs us more than
   hunger, 409:4
 last vice, 409:2
 ruined the angels,
   409:5
Priest
 saw p. or woman yet
   forgive?, 198:2
Priests
 and conjurors, 429:3
 golden chalices and
   wooden p., 430:1
 lawyers, and physi-
   cians, 353:8
Prince
 a jazz p., 557:2
Princerple [*sic*]
 I don't believe in p.,
   68:10
Principle
 contradictions in p.,
   179:6
 rise above p. and do
   what's right,
   438:2
Principles
 are for the ages,
   179:4
 easier to fight for p.
   than to live up to
   them, 515:10
 man cannot make p.,
   441:1
 triumph of p., 451:4
Prisidintial [*sic*]
 can't see a p. possibil-
   ity, 403:2
PRIVACY, 409
Privacy
 civilization & a soci-
   ety of p., 112:2
 entering the age of no
   p., 410:5
 if the right of p.
   means anything,
   410:6
 saint and poet seek p.,
   410:1
Private
 enterprise, 77:1
 no p. understandings,
   195:6
Privileges
 & obligations, 433:6
 men value p., 163:8
PROBLEMS, 411
Problem
 be part of the answer,
   not part of the p.
   (note), 411:5
 part of the solution
   or part of the p.,
   411:5
 solution of one p.
   brings us another,
   411:4
 we've had a p., 37:2

Problems
 are opportunities
   in work clothes,
   411:2
 our p. are man-made,
   411:3
 some p. are so com-
   plex, 246:3
Procrastination, 143:7
Products
 costly and supposedly
   beautiful p., 61:10
Profanity
 v. prayer (note), 42:5
Professors
 in New England, 161:2
 our American p.,
   47:10
Profit system, 77:3
Profound
 no such thing as be-
   ing too p., 317:2
PROGRESS, 411
Progress
 & people who took
   unpopular posi-
   tions, 412:1
 has been from scaf-
   fold to scaffold,
   411:7
 imposes new possibil-
   ities, 412:2
 has gone on too long,
   411:10
 is a comfortable dis-
   ease, 411:11
 is furthered not by
   conformity, 411:8
 is precarious, 412:3
 is written in the lives
   of infidels (note),
   412:1
 means suffering,
   411:9
 no p. if no faith in to-
   morrow, 412:4
 robs us of past de-
   lights, 412:5
 yet nothing has
   changed, 412:6
Prohibition
 faithful to the cause
   of P., 172:5
Promised
 I've seen the p. land,
   272:4
Property
 unequal distribution
   of p., 436:2
Prophecy
 self-fulfilling, 442:8
Prose
 simple p., 54:10
Prosperity
 & a political cam-
   paign, 392:7
 is just around the cor-
   ner, 145:6
 will leak through,
   157:6
PROVERBS. See QUOTA-
   TIONS & PROVERBS,
   415
Proverbs
 are the sanctuary of
   the intuitions,
   415:10
 use of p., 415:12
Provide
 p., p.!, 80:10
Providence
 spires of P., 104:4
Prude
 I saw not one p., 87:5

Pseudo event, 7:6
Psychological
 few things more ex-
   citing than a p. rea-
   son, 427:9
 richly and continu-
   ously p. (note), 57:9
PSYCHOLOGY. See SCI-
   ENCE: PSYCHOLOGY,
   445
Psychology
 treating p. like a
   natural science,
   445:6
 which explains every-
   thing, 445:7
Public
 be damned!, 69:2
 is the only [worth-
   while] critic, 49:2
 must and will be
   served, 412:7
 school system, 160:5
 when a man assumes
   a p. trust, 389:5
 with p. sentiment
   nothing can fail
   (note), 412:9–413
Public office
 is a public trust,
   217:3
 no man should be in
   p. o. who, 217:9
 wants to hold a p. o.
   (note), 55:6
Public officers
 are the trustees of the
   people (note), 217:3
PUBLIC OPINION & THE
   PUBLIC, 412
Public opinion
 force of an aroused
   p. o., 413:5
 in this country is
   everything, 412:9
 is the leader, 22:9
 nothing that makes
   more cowardly men
   than p. o., 413:2
 we are ruled by p.o.,
   413:4
PUBLICITY. See under
   ADVERTISING, AD-
   VERTISING SLOGANS,
   & PUBLICITY, 4
Publicity
 an age of p., 6:2
 —a remedy, 303:2
 is a black art, 7:1
Publishers
 are demons, 303:1
Publishing
 business, 305:1
Puddle-wonderful,
   345:8
Pulpit
 bully p., 402:8
Pumpkin pie
 hurrah for the p. p.!,
   489:3
 rich p. p., 489:2
Punishments
 cruel and unusual p.,
   125 (Amendment 8)
Purcell
 here lyes John P.,
   169:7
Pure
 as the driven slush,
   458:3
Puritanism
 fear that someone
   may be happy,
   175:4

Puritans
'twas founded be th'
  P. to give thanks,
  490:3
gave the world action,
  2:5
Purple cow, 150:8
Purse
  light p., heavy heart,
  395:1

Quaker
  instincts from his Q.
  forebears, 253:4
Quakerism
  meekness of Q., 389:4
Quantum
  if q. mechanics is
  right, 445:5
  if you aren't confused
  by q. physics (note),
  444:7
Quarreled
  did not know we had
  ever q. (note),
  270:10–271
Quarrels
  by our q. we spoil our
  prayers, 43:8
Quarter
  I never took a q.,
  392:10
Queen of the West, 91:4
Queens
  in history compare fa-
  vorably, 538:6
Question
  to ask the hard q.,
  414:5
  what is the q.?, 415:2
QUESTIONS & ANSWERS,
  414
Questions
  & research, 414:3
  better to ask some of
  the q., 415:1
  some q. don't have
  answers, 415:7
  there aren't any em-
  barrassing q., 415:6
  which one asks one-
  self, 415:4
Qui
  transtulit sustinet,
  123:4
Quiet
  hog drinks the most
  swill (note), 74:8
Quits
  man [is] finished
  when he q., 534:1
Quitter
  I have never been a q.,
  527:1
Quitters
  never win, 472:3
Quotation
  I hate q., 415:9
QUOTATIONS &
  PROVERBS, 415
Quote
  we all q., 416:2
Quoted
  by other learned au-
  thors, 415:8
Quoter
  first q., 416:1

Race
  is not always to the
  swift, 474:1
  these are the faults of
  an oppressed r.,
  418:5

RACES & PEOPLES, 417
Racism
  is not an excuse,
  426:1
Radical
  is a man with, 393:10
Raft
  no home like a r.,
  455:5
Railroad
  iron is a magician's
  rod, 445:10
  rides upon us (note),
  446:3
Rain
  how beautiful is the
  r.!, 348:9
  into each life some r.
  must fall, 495:7
  it raineth all around
  (note), 485:11
  takes credit for the r.,
  392:12
Rainbow
  our nation is a r., 24:7
  sign, 434:6
  somewhere over the
  r., 222:12
Rainier, [Mt.], 523:5
Raisin
  in the sun, 155:1
Rally
  'round the flag, 114:5
Range
  home on the r., 528:1
Rangers
  lead the way (note),
  552:2
Rascals
  turn the r. out, 383:3
  would you live for-
  ever? (note), 549:6
Rat
  come out you damned
  old r. (note), 37:8
Rattlesnake
  hisses a tune at my
  head (note), 349:7
  poised to strike,
  440:5
Rattlesnakes
  shame to take this
  country away from
  the r., 73:7
Razors
  pain you, 480:6
Reactionary
  is a somnambulist,
  393:12
Read
  every man able to r.,
  159:7
  my lips, 486:6
Reader
  your r. is at least as
  bright as you, 59:1
READING. See BOOKS &
  READING, 65
Reading
  a love of r., 66:11
  creative r., 65:4
  I prefer, 66:5
Ready
  always R., 313:4
Real
  washed in the speech-
  less r., 427:1
REALITY, ILLUSIONS, &
  IMAGES, 426
Reality
  & pigments of the
  past, 427:5
  has strangled inven-
  tion, 58:5

humankind cannot
  bear very much r.,
  426:10
  in [America] r. is al-
  ways material r.,
  426:11
  minds are not here
  simply to copy a r.
  (note), 57:9
  must take precedence
  over public rela-
  tions, 449:6
  we crave only r.,
  426:6
REASONS & REASONABLE
  PEOPLE, 427
Reason
  every man's own r.
  his oracle, 427:7
  human form with r.
  fled, 293:2
  if we would guide by
  the light of r.,
  275:11
  let us r. together,
  427:11 & note
Reasonable
  convenience to be a r.
  creature, 427:6
Reasons
  man always has two
  r. for what he does,
  427:10
Rebel
  I'm a good old r., 466:1
Rebellion
  little r. now and then,
  433:9
  to tyrants, 499:11
Recession, 159:1
Reconstructed
  I won't be r., 466:1
Record
  let's look at the r.,
  182:2
Red
  better dead than R.
  (note) 119:4
  better R. than dead,
  119:4
  river, 513:5
  when the last r. man
  shall have vanished,
  418:7
Reform
  has no gratitude,
  390:1
  is affirmative, 389:7
Reformer
  can't last in politics
  (note), 391:5
Reformers
  Only Morning Glo-
  ries, 391:5
Region
  of shacks and hovels,
  530:1
REGRET, 428
Regret
  is useless, 428:2
  to r. deeply, 428:1
Reign
  of error, 442:8
Relaxed
  man is not necessar-
  ily a better man,
  74:9
RELIGION, 428
Religion
  & egotism, 430:5
  country that has got
  the least r., 430:3
  free exercise thereof,
  125 (Amendment 1)

is a man's total reac-
  tion, 430:4
  is the love of life,
  430:8
  my r. is to do good,
  174:8
  respect the other fel-
  low's r., 430:13
  start your own r.,
  430:15
  test of a r. or philosophy, 378:9
  that shocks the mind
  of a child, 429:4
  that old-time r.,
  430:9
Religious
  cosmic r. experience,
  431:1
  duties, 429:2
  factions, 17:6
Remark
  [that] hurts, 135:3
Remarks
  famous r., 416:4
REMEDIES. See ILLNESS &
  REMEDIES, 244
Remember
  the Alamo!, 27:5
  the Maine, 468:4
  things I can r. that
  aren't so (note)
  306:1
  those who cannot r.
  the past, 369:14
  when I was young I
  could r. anything,
  306:1
Remembered
  we will be r., 232:7
Remembrance
  of miracles, 319:10
Rendezvous
  with death, 548:1
  with destiny, 208:10
Replace
  no one can r. him
  (note), 198:8
Report
  of my death has been
  grossly exaggerated,
  406:6
Repose
  is not the destiny of
  man, 426:8
Representative
  fitting r. of the com-
  mon aspirations,
  223:7
Repression
  is the seed of revolu-
  tion, 500:5
Republic
  a r. if you can keep it,
  17:11
REPUTATION, 431
Reputation
  is the symbol of its
  possessor, 431:7
  literary man's r.
  (note), 236:4
RESIGNATION, 431
Resignation
  is confirmed despera-
  tion, 431:11
RESISTANCE, 432
Resistance
  to government, 432:3
Resources
  natural r., 167:3
RESPONSIBILITY, 432
Responsibility
  every right implies a
  r., 433:3

Retaliation
massive r. (note),
196:4
Retreat
hell!, 264:4
Return
I shall r., 551:3
Returned
I have r., 552:7
REVENGE, 433
Revenge
living well is the best
r., 433:7
Revere
midnight ride of Paul
R., 41:4
Review
a bad book, 49:10
don't read the r., 50:3
who can't write can
surely r., 49:1
your lousy r. of Mar-
garet's concert, 49:6
Reviewing
& criticism, 49:4
REVOLUTION, 433
REVOLUTION, AMERICAN.
See AMERICAN REV-
OLUTION, 37
Revolution
every r. was at first a
thought, 434:5
great wheel of politi-
cal r., 434:7
have witnessed a non-
violent r. (note),
34:3
is bloody, 435:2
is like a forest fire,
435:3
our own r. ended the
need for r., 435:4
right of r., 434:7
those who make
peaceful r. impossi-
ble, 435:1
was in the hearts and
minds of the peo-
ple, 41:2
Revolutionary
their r. right to dis-
member [the gov-
ernment], 19:3
Revolutions
are not made by men
in spectacles,
434:10
do not go backward,
434:9
share in two r., 434:2
RHODE ISLAND, 435
Rhode Island, 435:7, 8
Rhods, Ile of [sic], 435:5
Rhythm
form is r. on a larger
scale, 52:6
Ribbon
she wore a yellow r.,
289:7
RICH, THE. See also
MONEY & THE RICH,
322
RICH & POOR, WEALTH
& POVERTY, 436
Rich
& other people (note),
324:12
and well-born, &
mass of the people,
436:3
do you sincerely want
to be r.?, 7:6
I want to get rich but,
325:2

in proportion to
things he can let
alone, 323:4
is better, 436:8
materially r. and
spiritually poor,
47:4
pay less taxes (note),
324:5
tells you that he got r.
through hard work,
324:6
troubles of the r.,
437:1
very r. are different,
324:5
were dull, 342:12
Richest
never going to be the
r. person in the
cemetery, 81:2
whose pleasures are
the cheapest, 323:5
Riders
in a race do not stop
short, 361:9
RIGHT, 437
Right
& responsibility,
433:3
always do r., 437:8
be sure you're r., 1:3
better to be approxi-
mately r. (note),
263:4
God prevent us from
becoming "r.-think-
ing men", 438:1
in the r., 437:4
in your heart you
know he's r., 388:3
is more precious than
peace (note), 548:3
is only the expedient,
437:9
makes might, 514:10
man more r. than his
neighbors, 296:3
not wrong but r., 28:2
of privacy, 410:6
or privacy & preg-
nancy, 411:1
people who think
they are r., 437:10
rather be r. than be
president, 401:6
rather than consis-
tent, 124:3
respect for the r.,
437:5
rise above principle
and do r., 438:2
time is always ripe to
do r., 437:12
to be let alone, 128:1,
410:2
Right of way
died defending his
r. o. w., 351:2
Righteous
armor of a r. cause,
437:7
RIGHTS, 438
Rights
bill of, 124:6
equal r., 555:2
no such thing as r.,
438:7
of minorities, 296:10
they have r. who dare
maintain them,
438:5
they will sacrifice the
most for, 438:8

unalienable r., 140:3
(2nd paragraph)
we dare defend our r.,
9:7
whose r. I trample un-
der foot, 438:6
Risked
much, but I made
much, 323:10
Risks
take calculated r.,
65:1
River
is more than an
amenity, 167:7
let us cross over the
r., 271:2
red r., red r., 513:5
seems a magic thing,
336:2
Rivers
we turn our r. into
sewers, 167:4
Road
I take to the open r.,
494:8
Roads
country r., take me
home, 530:2
two r. diverged in a
wood, 428:4
Rob
rich r. the poor, 132:2
some will r. you with
a six-gun, 134:1
why do you r. banks?,
134:5
Robbed
we wuz r.!, 473:4
Rock
a speck of r., 190:10
Rock Candy Moun-
tains, 505:7
Rome
dark cloud coming
from R. (note to
reader), 284–285
(last paragraph)
grandeur that was R.,
328:2
I've seen R., 110:9
more imagination
wanted at R.,
110:8
was a poem, 110:10
Room
at the top, 477:8
in a smoke-filled r.,
392:9
ROOSEVELT, FRANKLIN
DELANO, 438
ROOSEVELT, THEODORE,
439
Roosevelt
for ex-President,
387:4
let's re-re-re-elect R.,
387:5
Niagara Falls and
Theodore R. (note),
439:4
was like your first
bottle of cham-
pagne, 438:10
was pure act, 439:5 &
note
Root
hog, or die, 381:1
Rose
is a r. is a r., 342:7
one perfect r., 290:4
that lives its little
hour, 341:3
Rosebud, 271:10, 428:7

Rough and Ready, 382:3
Rough-tough
we're the stuff!, 468:7
Round
up the usual suspects,
134:3
Rugged
individualism, 22:7
Ruin
notice the r. in things,
331:6
Rule
some men are born to
r., 216:7
RULERS. See HIGH POSI-
TION: RULERS &
LEADERS, 231
Rum
demon r., 11:4
Romanism, and rebel-
lion, 383:4
RUMOR, 440
Rumor
travels faster, 440:1
Rumors
are always true, 440:2
Run
he can r., 137:4
I'll r. away again,
552:8
Running
avoid r. at all times,
380:1
Rural
character of the state,
357:6
virtue of a r. popula-
tion, 130:5
Rush
to Judgment, 258:10
Russia
great bug-bear, 332:9
is omnipotence, 333:2
Russian
in a R. tragedy, 333:4
Russians
are connoisseurs of
the cold, 333:6
are devout believers
in an eye for an eye,
333:3
Rustic
simple beauty and r.
health, 130:7
RUTHLESSNESS, 440

Sabbath
some keep the S. go-
ing to church,
429:10
SAFETY. See SECURITY &
SAFETY, 450
Safety
has really killed all
our business, 451:2
no s. in numbers or
anything, 450:10
Sagebrush
eternal s. (note),
554:5
Sail
I love to s. forbidden
seas, 494:2
SAILING. See SHIPS &
SAILING, 454
Sailing
now comes good s.
(note), 270:10–271
Sailor
he was a true s., 454:7
landsman beginning a
s.'s life, 454:6
part of a s.'s life to die
well, 170:2

Sailor (cont.)
wonder that any sane
man can be a s.,
455:3
Saint
dead sinner revised,
515:5
Salary
no one can live on
one s., 324:8
Salt Lake
City was healthy,
105:6
the creation of S. L.
City, 105:5
which is 2nd Soddum
& Gemorrer, 105:4
Salute
if it moves, s. it, 313:1
Sameness
this huge s., 350:3
Sammy
What Makes S. Run?,
14:6
San Francisco
is European, 106:4
is a lady, 85:3
is a mad city, 106:1
purer liquors in s. F.,
105:8–106
'tis hard to leave,
106:2
walking around S. F.,
106:5
San Juan Capistrano,
73:12
Sand
quit kicking s. in my
face, 6:6
Sands
like s. through the
hourglass, 283:4
SANITY. See MADNESS &
SANITY, 293
Sanity
is like a clearing in
the jungle, 294:7
is madness put to
good uses, 293:6
is very rare, 293:1
Santa Claus
yes, Virginia, there is
a S. C., 83:8
Santa Fe, 106:6
Satan
death of S., 150:2
respect his talents,
149:11
Satire
is what closes on Sat-
urday night, 55:7
Satisfied
no, we are not s., 36:1
Saunter
great art to s., 279:4
Savage
in man, 238:1
Savannah
Christmas gift of the
city of S. (note),
116:2
is a living tomb, 106:8
Say
if you can't s. any-
thing good, 130:3
if you don't s. any-
thing, 484:1
it ain't so, Joe, 472:1
never say nothin,
483:4
Says
who s. it best, 415:11
Scab
God made a scab, 76:5

is a two-legged ani-
mal, 250:6
Scale
supreme gift is s., 57:4
Scandinavia
folk who live in S.,
333:10
Scarecrow
eloped from a corn-
field (note), 170:4
Scars
God will look you
over for s., 480:2
of centuries, 424:6
Scenery
not one cent for s.,
167:5
Scholars
solid s., 162:2
School
boards, 160:9
days, 161:3
free s., 160:6
high s., 162:5
public s. system,
160:5
Schools
jails called s., 162:3
SCIENCE, 441
Science
& a logically uniform
system of thought,
443:2
& a system of princi-
ples, 441:1
& audacity of imagi-
nation, 442:4
& common sense,
441:4
begins as philosophy
and ends as art,
442:3
ideas of s. are essen-
tially simple, 442:6
in s. the excellent is
not just better,
443:5
is a refinement of
everyday thinking,
443:1
is taking on a new as-
pect, 443:8
is the search for truth,
443:3
limits to the achieve-
ments of s., 322:5
wonder—the seed of
our s., 441:3
SCIENCE: BIOLOGY &
PHYSIOLOGY, 443
SCIENCE: MATHEMATICS
& STATISTICS, 443
SCIENCE: PHYSICS & COS-
MOLOGY, 444
SCIENCE: PSYCHOLOGY,
445
SCIENCE: TECHNOLOGY,
445
Scientific
facts, 442:1
power has outrun our
spiritual power,
448:7
Scientist
degradation of the po-
sition of the s.,
442:9
Scientists
their s. were more ad-
vanced than ours,
443:4
Scott
Dred S. decision,
115:4

Scoundrel
I never give way to a
s., 249:2
Scratch
you s. my back, 390:7
Sea
all at last returns to
the s., 343:5
has many voices,
343:4
hates a coward, 343:3
implacable s., 342:12
is feline, 342:11
is woman, 343:1
magic of the s., 455:2
ourselves we find in
the s., 343:6
Seal
you heard a s. bark!,
44:4
Searches
unreasonable s. and
seizures, 125
(Amendment 4)
SEAS. See NATURE: SEAS
& OCEANS, 342
Seas
are the heart's blood
of the earth, 343:2
freedom of the s.,
195:5
Season
of small fruits has ar-
rived, 343:9
SEASONS & TIMES, 450
SEASONS. See NATURE:
SEASONS, 343
Seat belts
fasten your s. b.,
496:4
Seattle
covers an old frontier,
106:9
Second
everybody's s. choice
(note), 223:7
no s. acts in Ameri-
can lives, 22:11
office of the land,
508:6
Secrecy
absolute s. corrupts
absolutely, 450:8
SECRETS, 450
Secret
sits in the middle and
knows, 450:7
three may keep a s. if,
450:5
Secure
he that is s. is not
safe, 450:9
SECURITY & SAFETY, 481
Security
many are the crimes
[done] in its name,
451:1
no s. in your man-
sions, 450:11
no s. on this earth,
363:8
See
fellow that can s.
years ahead, 516:6
I know it when I see
it, 78:4
people s. what they
are prepared to s.,
516:3
we are as much as we
s., 516:2
Seed
I have great faith in a
s., 341:10

Sees
things as they are,
516:5
Segregation
forever, 424:1
SELF, 451
Self
what jailer so inex-
orable as one's s.,
451:5
Self-fulfilling prophecy,
442:8
Self-knowledge
is always bad news,
452:1
Self-made
he was a s.-m. man,
452:5
Self-realization, 451:11
SELF-RELIANCE, 452
Self-reliance
discontent is the
want of s.-r., 452:3
Self-respect
price of s.-r., 375:5
Self-trust
is the essence of hero-
ism, 229:5
Sells
when a man s. 11
ounces for 12, 69:3
Semper
paratus, 313:4
Senator
schoolmaster, priest,
or s., 121:2
Senatorial
saucer, 120:2
Senators
I look a the s. and
pray, 121:1
Sense
where s. is wanting,
117:10
Separate
and unequal, 451
but equal, 34:3
but equal (note), 127:2
educational facilities,
34:3
peace, 375:7
September
the days grow short
when you reach S.,
362:5
Serenity
grace to accept with
s., 398:12
Servant
rather be a s. in the
house of the Lord,
272:3
Serves
he profits most who s.
best, 515:8
Service
necessary to the pub-
lic good (note), 39:2
season of s., 452:8
SERVING ONE'S COUN-
TRY, 452
Seventy
being s. is not a sin,
363:1
never made the mis-
take of being s.
again, 362:11
oh, to be s. again!,
361:10
to be s. years young,
361:1
Seward's
folly/ice box, 9:8 &
note

Sewer
  a trip through a s.,
    95:3
SEX, 452
Sex
  contains all, 453:1
  Is Never an Emer-
    gency, 454:4
  Is S. Necessary?,
    453:5
  a laugh at s., 453:7
  low forms of s. rela-
    tionship, 300:2
  mustn't force s. to do
    the work of love,
    454:1
  perversion, 78:2
Sexual
  interest & good writ-
    ing (note), 453:8
Shadow
  falls the S., 426:9
  secure the s., 4:8
  the S. knows!, 176:6
Share
  our wealth, 386:7
Shay
  wonderful one-hoss
    shay, 446:5
Sheridan
  twenty miles away,
    116:1
SHIPS & SAILING, 454
Ship
  don't give up the s.,
    522:11
  sail on, O S. of State,
    18:4
  that does not sail fast,
    40:2
  whale s. was my Yale
    college, 454:11
Ships
  at a distance have
    every man's wish,
    455:7
  beauty and majesty of
    s., 455:2
  that pass in the night,
    280:10
Shoot
  if you must, this old
    gray head, 372:8
Shooting
  is only a sideline,
    90:9
Shorter
  and more ugly word,
    268:4
Shot
  being s. at without re-
    sult, 137:6
  heard round the
    world, 41:3
Show
  me, 320:8
  what if the world is
    some kind of s.!,
    56:6
Show Business
  No Business Like
    S. B., 55:9
Showing up
  ninety percent of life
    is s. u. (note), 479:5
Siberia, 354
  sic semper tyrannis!,
    29:1
Sick
  citizenship in the
    kingdom of the s.,
    244:8
  ivry s. man is a hero,
    244:7

Sickness
  chief use of tempo-
    rary s., 244:5
Sighted
  sub, 550:9
SILENCE, 455
Silence
  sorrow and s. are
    strong, 370:11
  try as we may to
    make a s., 455:12
  will fall like dews,
    455:9
Silences
  three s. there are, 455:8
Silent
  majority, 296:11
Silver
  Hi-yo, S.!, 230:5
Simple
  'tis the gift to be s.,
    218:7
  as s. as possible but
    not simpler, 456:7
  prose, 54:10
SIMPLICITY, 456
Simplicity
  the art of art is s.,
    54:6
  art of art is s., 456:4
  lost is our old s., 60:1
  refined s., 456:1
  s., simplicity! (note),
    456:2
  Spartan s. must be ob-
    served, 314·1
Simplify
  simplify, 456:2
  to s. means 456:6
SIN, VICE, & NAUGHTI-
  NESS, 456
Sin
  fashions in s. change,
    176:8
  only people who
    should really s.,
    457:11
  travels faster than s.,
    456:9
Sing
  Lift Ev'ry Voice and
    S., 51:4
Singers
  God sent his singers,
    51:1
Single
  man—odd half of a
    pair of scissors,
    298:10
Sins
  punished by our s.,
    457:3
Sisters
  big s., 185:2
  wayward s., 112:5
Sixteen
  to one, 384:3
Size
  no virtue goes with s.,
    62:3
SKEPTICISM, 459
Skepticism
  is the chastity of the
    intellect, 459:3
Skies
  spacious, 20:1
Skinny
  can never be too s. or
    too rich, 325:11
Skugg
  here S. lies snug, 170:1
skunk
  approach too close to
    a s. (note), 403:7

SKY. See NATURE: THE
  HEAVENS, THE SKY,
  339
Sky
  is the daily bread of
    the eyes, 339:11
  the Land of the S.,
    356:4
Slang
  is a language that
    rolls up its sleeves,
    269:8
Slave
  as I would not be a s.,
    461:3
  death is a s.'s free-
    dom, 425:1
  half s. and half free,
    461:1
  in giving freedom to
    the s., 461:5
  see how a s. was
    made a man, 460:6
  system on our place,
    462:2
SLAVERY, 459
Slavery
  & selfishness, 460:4
  & shocks & convul-
    sions (note), 460:4
  badge of s. (note), 34:3
  mine is a situation of
    dignified s., 401:2
  object is not either to
    save or destroy s.,
    461:3
  —our peculiar institu-
    tions (note), 460:5
  political s., 30:6
  where s. is, there lib-
    erty cannot be,
    461:6
  wrecks of s., 466:2
Slaves
  all persons held as s.
    shall be free (note),
    461:4
  all persons held as s.
    shall be free, 114:4
  who fear to speak for
    the fallen and the
    weak, 395:2
SLEEP. See DREAMS &
  SLEEP, 155
Sleep
  in s. we all like
    naked, 155:8
  sweetly in your hum-
    ble graves, 171:4
  they shall not s. on
    our soil, 523:3
  we never s., 132:5
Sleeps
  nine s. every idle
    knave, 155:4
Slender
  people bury the dead,
    227:11
Slide
  Kelly, S., 470:7
SLOGANS, POLITICAL. See
  POLITICAL SLOGANS,
  380
Slowly
  worth doing s., 224:9
SLOWNESS. See HASTE V.
  GOING SLOW, 224
Sluggard
  up s., 155:5
Slum
  if you've seen one s.,
    85:5
Small
  is beautiful, 462:4

SMALL THINGS. See DE-
  TAILS & OTHER
  SMALL THINGS, 147
Smallness, 462
Smile
  when you call me
    that, s., 136:5
Smith
  the happy warrior Al-
    fred S., 31:2
Smithy
  village s., 543:3
Smoke
  -filled room, 392:9
  man of no conversa-
    tion should s., 493:3
  never to s. more than
    one cigar at a time,
    493:5
Smoking
  pistol (note), 526:7
Snake
  stood up for evil,
    150:1
  white s. or black s.,
    425:8
Snare
  [a play is] a s. for the
    truth, 56:4
Snobs
  effete corps of impu-
    dent s., 164:4
Snow
  I used to be S. White,
    457:6
  neither s., nor rain,
    348:11
So
  much owed by s.
    many to s. few
    (note), 533:2
Soap
  and education, 160:7
SOCIALISM, 462
Socialism
  I am for s., 462:5
Socialist
  before he is forty,
    462:6
Society
  Great S., 36:6, 388:2
  high s., 163:6
  in the affluent s.,
    307
  is spiritually a desert,
    60:4
  our s. is neither scien-
    tific nor splendid,
    513:1
  seems everywhere un-
    hinged, 60:3
  this s. is going smash
    (note), 168:6
Soil
  nation that destroys
    its soil, 168:2
Sojourner
  Lord gave me S.
    (note), 461:7–462
Soldier
  all a s. needs to know,
    313:7
  every citizen [should]
    be a s., 312:4
  has a hard life, 312:8
  he was a gallant s.,
    171:3
  I don't care if a s. is
    straight, 315:6
  summer s., 39:3
Soldiers
  men to make s.,
    313:10
  old s. never die, 33:3

Solidarity
forever, 76:3
Solitary
men know joys of
friendship, 203:10
SOLITUDE & LONELINESS,
462
Solitude
companion [never] so
companionable as
s., 463:1
is the playfield of Sa-
tan, 463:6
is the salt of person-
hood, 463:7
is un-American, 24:5
Solution
either part of the s. or
of the problem,
411:5
Somebody
how dreary to be s.!,
477:9
I am s., 425:7
Something
attempted, s. done,
2:3
may be gaining on
you, 536:5
Somewhere
over the rainbow,
222:12
Son of a bitch
he's our s. o. b.,
196:3
Song
found in the heart of a
friend, 203:1
Songs
listen to its [a coun-
try's] s., 51:10
of sadness and of
mirth, 51:1
Sons of bitches
come on you s. o. b.,
549:6
Sooners (note), 359:4
SORROW & GRIEF, 463
Sorrow
and silence are strong,
370:11
in each man's life s.
and suffering, 165:6
is my own yard, 464:1
makes us all children,
463:10
Sorrows
secret s., 463:9
SOUL, THE, 464
Soul
can split the sky in
two, 464:7
dark night of the s.
(note) 147:7
I said to my s., be
still, 327:1
immortal because he
has a s., 239:5
meeting physical
force with s. force,
35:7
must be let alone by
government, 318:7
my s. an't yours,
464:5
my s. has grown deep,
464:8
teach me to become a
s., 464:10
was not spoken of the
s., 280:2
way to the s. is
through the flesh,
64:7

whence it is that light
comes into the s.,
464:4
windows of my s.,
464:6
Souls
they [corporations]
have no s., 68:1
Soup dish
mind like a s. d.,
253:2
SOUTH, THE, 464
South
in the S. the war is
what A.D. is else-
where, 116:6
old S. was plowed un-
der, 466:7
the solid S., 466:3
the S.!, the S.!, 464:11
South America
& altitude, 334:1
South Americans,
333:11
SOUTH CAROLINA, 467
South Carolina
& aristocracy, 467:1
is too small for a re-
public, 467:2
wreck vengeance on
S. C. (note), 467:2
South Carolinian, 467:4
South Carolinians,
467:3
SOUTH DAKOTA, 467
South Dakota
remoteness of S. D.,
468:1
Southern
& being black & be-
ing white, 466:9
trees bear strange
fruit, 466:6
Southerner
I treasure being a S.,
466:8
talks music, 466:4
Southie
is my home town,
88:1
Soviet Union
was like a religious
revival, 333:7
Soviets
are not fussy eaters,
333:8
Space
changes nobody,
340:10
curvature of s., 444:8
is the keynote of the
land, 354:7
Spaceship Earth, 169:1
Spain
people of S. & pride,
334:2
SPANISH-AMERICAN WAR,
468
Spare
tire on the automo-
bile of government,
509:1
Spartan
simplicity must be
observed, 314:1
Speak
for yourself, John,
289:5
low and s. slow,
56:1
softly, 195:2
Speculate
to s. in stocks (note),
69:6

when he should not
s., 69:6
Speech
best s. you will ever
regret, 42:6
cordial s., 129:4
freedom of s., 199:1.
See also FREE
SPEECH, 202
freedom of s. or the
press, 125 (Amend-
ment 1)
short and positive s.,
54:7
spoken s. & written
s., 302:8
Speeches
measured by the
hour, 66:14
SPEED, 469
Speed
all deliberate s., 129:1
& note
and curves, 470:1
change of s. difference
in quality, 447:3
our safety is in our s.,
469:5
Spell
my name right,
407:4
Spending
more than your in-
come (note to
reader), 283
Spero
dum spiro s., 467:6
Spider
is admirable, 336:6
noiseless patient s.,
337:9
Spiders
marching through air,
130:8
spies
paid s., 405:10
Spinach
I say it's s., 192:2
Spirit
of '76, 41:1
Spiritualists, 358:2
Spittoon
& American manners,
298:1
Splendid
misery, 508:6
Spoils
politics are impossi-
ble without s.,
391:1
to the victors belong
the s., 389:6
Spoke
any s. will lead to the
hub, 188:4
Spoons
faster we counted our
s., 236:3
SPORTS, 470
Sport
is the opiate of the
masses, 475:8
Sportsmanship, 474:5
Spring
came on forever,
345:1
cruelest and fairest
of the seasons,
346:7
in the world!, 343:10
little madness in the
S., 344:8
—mud-luscious
(note), 345:8

now comes unher-
alded by birds,
168:8
then came the lovely
s., 344:3
Square deal, 384:8
St. James Hospital
(note), 94:4
St. Louis
the city of St. Louis,
105:1
Meet Me in S. L.,
105:3
St. Petersburg, 110
St. Vitus
combination of St. Vi-
tus and St. Paul,
439:4
Stab
in the back (note),
550:2
Stand
there and put all
America behind,
302:2
with Washington,
380:7
Star
being a s., 423:5
hitch your wagon to a
s., 14:3
of the North, 319:4
Star-spangled banner,
371:4
Stark
or Molly S.'s a widow,
39:7
Stars
—forget-me-nots
of the angels,
339:13
to the s. (note) 14:3
to the s. through diffi-
culties, 260:11
we have the s.!,
223:1
State
my native S.!, 209:9
of unbounded plains
and hills and bad-
lands, 357:5
Ship of S., 18:4
small and measly s.,
142:4
sovereignty—national
union, 244:4
that has three coun-
ties, 142:3
the s. is one of the
most mountainous,
529:9
this s. bows to noth-
ing, 507:7
too small to be a s.,
108:11
with the prettiest
name, 190:6
States
free and independent
s., 140:2
happy union of these
s., 17:5
one of my favorite s.,
555:1
one of the two best s.,
353:3
powers reserved to
the S., 126 (Amend-
ment 10)
rights of the s. (note),
502:1
seceded s., 112:5
slang names [of s.],
19:10

Statesman
  [must] be dull, 152:3
  is a politician who is
    dead, 391:7
Statesmanship, 151
Statesmen
  are gamesters (note),
    384:8–385
Station
  to retire from this s.,
    400:11
STATISTICS. See SCIENCE:
  MATHEMATICS &
  STATISTICS, 473
Statistics
  he could make s. sit
    up (note), 443:11
  lies, damned lies, and
    s., 444:1
Staying up
  all night looking for it
    (note), 458:7
Steady
  habits, 122:7
Steal
  silently s. away, 50:13
Steel
  smoke and blood is
    the mix of s., 70:1
Step
  one small s. for [a]
    man, 448:8
Sterilized
  everything is s., 23:4
Stick
  carry a big s., 195:2
Sticks
  Nix Hick Pix, 303:5
Stomach
  no man can worship
    God on an empty s.,
    395:8
Stone
  layered and beaten,
    354:8
  shall cry out of the
    wall (note), 131:8
  to throw, 135:4
Stones
  don't throw s., 134:10
  no sermons in s.,
    335:11
  prate of my where-
    about (note), 131:8
Stonewall
  it, 526:3
  standing like a s.,
    112:7
Stoop
  as you go, 535:6
Stories
  only two or three hu-
    man s., 281:9
  we tell ourselves s.,
    58:12
  what s. can do,
    66:13
Strange
  fruit, 466:6
  interlude, 282:5,
    400:2
Stranger
  forever a s. and alone,
    13:10
Strangers
  kindness of s., 262:7
STRATEGY. See MILITARY
  STRATEGY, 315
Straw
  that stirs the drink,
    409:10
Stream
  unbroken s. [of con-
    sciousness], 317:8

Street cars, 88:8
Streets
  down these mean s.,
    230:8
  seemed to be starting
    up of their own ac-
    cord, 104:6
STRENGTH & TOUGH-
  NESS, 476
Strenuous
  doctrine of the s. life,
    379:9
Strike
  laborers can s., 75:5
  no right to s. against
    the public safety,
    76:7
  the tent, 271:3
Stripes
  whose broad s. and
    bright stars, 371:4
Strokes
  many s. overthrow
    oaks (note), 148:6
Struggle
  between right and
    wrong, 197:4
STUPIDITY. See FOOLS &
  STUPIDITY, 193
Stupid
  how s. can you get?
    (note), 253:1
  is forever, 194:1
  life is harder if you're
    s., 193:11
STYLE, 477
See also ART: STYLE IN
  WRITING AND EX-
  PRESSION, 54
Style
  good s. is unseen s.,
    55:2
  is character, 477:5
  is the man himself
    (note), 477:5
Styles
  men are watching
    their s., 187:3
Sub
  sighted s., sank same,
    550:9
Subcontinent
  clinging to a s., 10:9
Subtracting
  from the sum of hu-
    man knowledge,
    250:5
Suburbs
  in search of a metrop-
    olis, 94:7
Succeed
  some men s. by what
    they are, 478:9
Succeeds
  whenever a friend s.,
    479:4
SUCCESS & FAME, 477
Success
  & obstacles, 478:3
  bitch-goddess s.,
    478:5
  breeds arrogance and
    complacency, 479:6
  consists in the climb,
    478:7
  80 percent of s. is
    showing up, 479:5
  faster than you are
    able to endure it,
    478:8
  fruits of s., 478:14
  has killed more men
    than bullets,
    478:10

has ruined many a
  man, 477:7
ignorance & confi-
  dence & s., 478:1
is always dangerous,
  478:13
is counted sweetest,
  477:11
is relative, 478:12
too much s., 532:3
Sucker
  born every minute,
    193:4
  never give a s. an
    even break, 193:7
Suffer
  to s. and be strong,
    479:9
SUFFERING & PAIN, 479
Suffering
  & Old Masters, 480:3
Suffrage
  dangers of universal
    s., 144:6
  vote for s., 538:12
SUICIDE, 480
Suicide
  kills two people, 480:9
Suicides
  nine men in 10 are s.,
    227:1
Sumer
  is icumen in (note),
    345:2
Summer
  afternoon, 344:12
  in s. the song sings it-
    self, 346:2
  In the Good Old S.
    Time, 344:11
  lavish s. (note)
    made her light escape,
    344:5
  night, 346:10
  soldier, 39:3
Summertime
  and the livin' is easy,
    346:3
Sun
  the brief s. flames the
    ice, 346:9
  a rising not a setting
    s., 124:4
  if you see it in the S.,
    it's so, 406:3
  rose a ribbon at a
    time, 348:1
  splendid silent s.,
    339:13
  thank heavens the s.
    has gone in, 349:2
  that brief December
    day, 344:6
Sunday
  poem of New England
    is her S., 352:8
Sunlight
  is the best of disinfec-
    tants, 303:2
Sunshine patriot, 39:3
Superior
  class of people, 92:1
  people never make
    long visits, 219:11
Superman!, 230:6
Supply-side
  formula (note), 157:6
Supreme coort [sic]
  follows th' iliction re-
    turns, 481:2
SUPREME COURT, 481
Surgeons
  must be very careful,
    153:6

Surmise
  deep s., 317:3
Surprise
  the enemy, 316:2
Surrender
  I s. to you, and that is
    all, 420:6
  I shall never s., 27:3
  unconditional and
    immediate s.,
    113:7
Survival
  of the fittest, 231:8
Suspects
  the usual s., 134:3
Sustainable relationship
  between people and
  earth (note), 23:2
Sustains
  he who transplanted
    still s., 123:4
Swallow
  one s. does not make
    a summer, 347:1
Swanee River, 465:1
Swap,
  don't s. horses, 383:2
Sweat
  pint of s., 316:5
Swede
  [is] Yankeer than Yan-
    kee, 334:3
Sweet
  interlude, 282:11
  water from a foul
    well?, 48:2
Swiftest
  traveler goes afoot,
    469:6
Swing
  If It Ain't Got That S.,
    51:11
Swinging
  I hear America s.,
    454:3
Swiss
  and the Americans,
    334:4
  are a neat clean busi-
    ness, 334:6
Switzerland
  & Italy & the cuckoo
    clock, 331:7
  is a small, steep coun-
    try, 334:5
  little S. of America,
    334:4
  real S. of America,
    117:4
Sword
  by the s. we seek
    peace, 302:6
  His terrible swift s.,
    212:2
  is not the balance of
    justice, 366:1
Symbol
  of power and glory,
    373:3

Taft
  get on the raft with
    T., 385:1
Talent
  blessed are those who
    have no t.!, 305:4
Talented
  tenth, 421:4
TALK, 483
Talk
  [New Yorkers] talk
    very loud, 97:9
  I have heard t. and t.,
    483:5

Talk (*cont.*)
only bird that can t., 483:6
when you're leading, don't t., 484:4
Talkers
great t., little doers, 483:1
Talking
[needs] practice, 484:2
of Michelangelo, 130:1
Tallulah, 252:6
Tar Heel
I'm a T. H. born, 356:5
Tara
tomorrow at T., 206:2
Tarquin and Caesar
each had his Brutus (note), 25:7
Task
every man's t., 543:7
Taste
good t., 477:6
TAXES, 484
Tax
-gatherer—a representative of oppression, 485:4
collector & taxidermist, 485:6
don't t. you, don't t. me. 486:2
I am in favor of an income t., 485:5
income t. has made more liars, 485:8
increasers—make my day, 486:4
power to t. involves the power to destroy, 484:7
power to t. is not the power to destroy, 485:9
structure which looks designed, 486:3
unlimited right to t. (note), 484:7
Taxation
no t. without representation, 25:6
system of t. & equality, 484:8
vehement against t. (note), 156:2
without representation, 484:5
Taxed
beggar is t. for a corner to die in, 485:2
without their consent (note), 484:5
Taxes
City land & t., 485:3
are paid in sweat, 485:10
are the dues that we pay for society, 485:12
are what we pay for civilized society, 485:7
death and t., 125:1
men are least willing to pay t., 485:1
not a patriotic duty to increase one's t., 485:11
nothing certain except death and t., 484:6
only the little people pay t., 486:5

read my lips—no new t., 486:6
to pay t., 156:2
Teach
who dares to t., 160:13
Teacher
affects eternity, 160:12
Team
point [is] whether the t. wins, 476:1
Techas [Texas], 487:10
Techniques
to create a full and satisfying life, 322:3
Technological juggernaut, 449:8
Technology, 449:4, (note), 449:6
TECHNOLOGY. See SCIENCE: TECHNOLOGY, 445:10
Tee
lies at rest by the 19th t., 471:5
Telegraph
magnetic t., 118:6
Television
can make so much money doing its worst, 304:3
chewing-gum for the eyes, 303:10
instrument for mass persuasion, 304:2
insulates us from the realities of the world, 304:3
nothing is real unless on t., 305:2
pollutes identity, 304:10
the test of the modern world, 303:6
will never be a serious competitor, 303:7
writes on the wind, 304:8
Tell
don't t. them a thing, 408:4
you can't tell 'em, 193:10
Telling
always t. 'em what we used to not do, 208:7
TEMPTATION, 486
Temptation
can resist everything except t. (note), 487:4
I generally avoid t. unless, 487:4
last t. is the greatest treason, 487:3
protections against t., 487:1
Temptations
—little ones [ruin us], 486:7
should be judged by our t., 487:2
Tenderloin, 274:3
TENNESSEE, 487
Tennessean
Virginian looks down on the T., 487:5
Tennesseans
lives unhurried, 487:7

Tennessee
—America at its best, 487:9
breakfast in East T., 487:8
Tennis
anyone?, 473:1
Tent
strike the t., 271:3
Tenth
talented t., 421:4
Tents
shall fold their t., 50:13
TEXAS, 526
Texas
if I owned T. and Hell, 488:1
is a state of mind, 488:8
—it seems to take forever to get out, 488:9
occupies all of the North American continent, 488:7
T. T., 271:1
this T. hell, 488:3
Thames
muddy tide of the T., 109:4
THANKSGIVING, 489
Thanksgiving
day of t., 489:4
on T. come the pilgrim and guest, 489:1
thanks for all of this T. Day, 490:1
this is T. Day!, 489:3
unto the Lord, 489:5
THEATER. See ART: THEATER, DRAMA, & MAGIC, 55
Theater
can make a killing in the t., 56:3
the trouble with the t., 56:9
was a verb, 56:10
Theatrical
man in the t. business, 55:4
Theory
like a mist on eyeglasses, 442:5
There
t. is no t. t., 102:1
Thermodynamics
laws of t., 445:4
They
are as sharp as nails (note), 537:12–538
got everything we got, 332:3
Thing
distinguished t., 139:6
inexplicable presence of the t. not named, 47:9
the t. that couldn't be done, 4:2
THINGS & POSSESSIONS, 490
Things
are getting worse and worse, 364:9
are in the saddle, 490:6
are not what they seem, 280:2
are of the snake, 490:5
have their laws, 490:4

mortality of all inanimate t., 490
most of the t. we do, 221:4
O amazement of t., 504:1
three unspeakably precious t., 20:8
which he can afford to let alone, 323:4
Think
hardest task [is] to t., 317:1
if you make people t., 318:1
whether machines t. & whether men do, 449:2
Thinking
Power of Positive T., 318:6
Third
one-t. of a nation ill-housed, ill-clad, 32:2
Third Fleet
retiring at high speed toward the enemy, 552:5
Third-rate
burglary, 525:1
Thirty
after t., a man wakes up sad, 309:3
don't trust anybody over t., 557:6
Thirty-six
Perfect T.-s., 487:6
Thou
art to me a delicious torment, 289:3
wast that all to me, love, 289:2
THOUGHT. See MIND, THOUGHT, & UNDERSTANDING, 317
Thought
free t., 128:2
freedom of t., 199:1
insurrection of t. (note), 434:5
Thoughts
the storm of t., 317:9
Thousand
points of light, 24:9 & note
Throat
I will cut your t., 136:2
Thrown
not a novel to be t. aside (note), 251:1
Thunder
is the voice of God, 348:6
Thyself
trust t., 451:3
Tillage
when t. begins, 185:6
Tilling
dignity in t. a field, 544:4
TIME, 490
Time
and space, 206:4
as if you could kill t., 491:6
the destroyer and preserver, 492:6
dissipates facts, 491:4
do not squander t., 279:8

famous good t. that
  was had by all,
  251:8
fullness of t. when
  men should go,
  450:1
has laid his hand
  upon my heart,
  491:11
if you can't do the t.,
  134:8
is a great legalizer,
  492:2
is but the stream I
  go a-fishing in,
  491:7
is money, 491:1
is the longest distance
  between two places,
  492:7
is the school, 492:5
leaves its shadow be-
  hind, 491:9
lost t. is never found,
  490:11
makes more converts
  than reason, 491:2
no t. like the old t.,
  369:13
present and time past,
  492:4
small intolerable
  drums of t., 492:1
surest poison is t.,
  491:10
there's a t. in every
  man's life, 450:3
to repair the roof is,
  450:4
turn backward, O, T.,
  491:8
we have rushed
  through, 492:3
Times
  hard and money
  scarce, 61:1
  these are the t. that
  try men's souls, 39:3
  they are a-changin,
  80:1
TIMES. See SEASONS &
  TIMES, 450
TIMES OF DAY. See NA-
  TURE: TIMES OF DAY,
  347
Tinker
  to-Evers-to-Chance,
  471:4
Tip
  we'll try old T., 381:4
Tippecanoe
  and Tyler too., 381:3
Tire
  spare t. on the auto-
  mobile of govern-
  ment, 509:1
Tired
  go home when you're
  tired, 537:1
  of giving in (note),
  425:3
  your t. and your poor,
  29:5
TOBACCO, 492
Tobacco
  better eschewed than
  chewed, 493:2
  first illusion of t.,
  493:1
  is as indispensable as
  the daily ration,
  493:6
  roots of t. must go to
  hell, 493:4

a stinking t.-pipe,
  492:11
Today
  is in the past, 348:4
  is the first day of the
  rest of your life,
  400:6
  muffled in
  impenetrable folds
  is t., 399:10
  never do t., 143:5
Todays
  they miss out on all
  their todays, 492:10
Toil
  horny hands of t.,
  543:4
TOLERANCE & UNDER-
  STANDING, 493
Tolerance
  & education, 493:8
  requirement for sur-
  vival, 151:2
Tomorrow
  At Tara, 206:2
  is another day, 206:2
  we shall die!, 380:6
Tongue
  his t. drips poison
  (note), 249:3
Too
  much of a good thing,
  178:2
Tool
  man [is] a t.-making
  animal, 237:9
Tools
  men have become t.
  of their t., 446:4
  only children to bor-
  row t. (note), 237:9
Top
  room at the t., 477:8
Torpedoes
  damn the t.!, 115:3
Toto
  I've a feeling we're
  not in Kansas, 260:5
Tough
  does not have to be
  cruel to be t., 477:1
  when the going gets
  t., 477:4
TOUGHNESS. See
  STRENGTH &
  TOUGHNESS, 476
Toujours
  gai, archy, 222:11
Tourists
  looking for a place to
  mate, 495:2
Town
  beautiful t. seated by
  the sea, 104:1
  dreary industrial
  town, 95:4
  muddy, melancholy
  t., 96:1
Towns
  in the small t., 209:10
Townships
  clean, bright, gar-
  dened t., 310:12
Trade
  curses everything it
  handles, 68:8
  impure are the chan-
  nels [of] t., 67:9
  no nation was ever
  ruined by t., 67:8
Trade-unions, 76:4
Trail
  long t. a-winding,
  154:7

Train
  lonesome t. on a lone-
  some track, 285:3
  there isn't a t. I
  wouldn't take,
  494:11
Training
  is everything, 160:8
Tranquility, 222:4,
  360:4 & note
TRAVEL, 493
Travel
  & strange hours,
  494:10
  from coast to coast,
  495:6
  men t. faster now,
  495:1
Traveled
  a good deal in Con-
  cord, 494:3
Traveler, 494:5
Traveling
  best thing about t. is
  going home, 494:6
  idol of t. (note), 494:1
  is a fool's paradise,
  494:1
  makes men wiser but,
  493:10
  north, 495:5
Tread
  don't t. on me, 16:1
Treason
  if this be t., 25:7
  it grazes the edge of t,
  548:5
Tree
  is a tree, 168:14
  never see a poem so
  lovely as a t.,
  342:5
  of liberty must be re-
  freshed, 434:1
  that grows in Brook-
  lyn, 342:10
  woodman, spare that
  t.!, 341:4
Trees
  all the t. the year
  round were green,
  45:1
  little reverence for t.,
  167:2
  seem more resigned,
  342:4
Tremble
  I t. for my country,
  200:2
Trial
  by jury, 125 (Amend-
  ment 7)
  speedy and public t.,
  125 (Amendment 6)
Tribute
  not one cent for t.,
  26:5
Trickle-down (note),
  157:6
TROUBLE, 495
Trouble
  & a handsome man,
  307:2
Troubles
  ten t. coming down
  the road, 495:9
Trousers
  wear the bottoms of
  my t. rolled, 361:3
Trout
  in the milk, 175:6
Truckin, 149:4
True
  & false, 497:7

"the t.", 179:7
  to friend and foe,
  291:2
  the t. & the expedi-
  ent, 499:1
Truman
  to err is T., 252:4
TRUST, 497
Trust
  don't t. anybody over
  30, 557:6
  men and they will be
  true, 497:1
  thyself, 451:3
  when a man assumes
  a public t., 389:5
  yourself, 367:11
TRUTH, 497
Truth
  & its defenders,
  497:3
  best test of t., 499:4
  can stand by itself,
  77:7
  choice between t. and
  repose, 497:9
  does not necessarily
  vanquish, 499:9
  forever on the scaf-
  fold, 500:7
  for t. there is no deadline, 499:6
  give me t., 497:13
  happens to an idea,
  498:12
  he alone has found
  the t.?, 498:3
  His t. is marching on,
  212:2
  I just tell the t. and
  they think it's hell,
  499:7
  irresistible nature of
  t., 497:4
  is always modern,
  499:5
  is mighty, 498:11
  is sometimes a poor
  competitor (note),
  202:8
  is stranger than Fic-
  tion, 498:9
  is such a rare thing,
  498:5
  is the most valuable
  thing we have,
  498:10
  is the only safe
  ground, 498:6
  is the silliest thing,
  497:12
  is tough, 498:1
  is what stands the
  test of experience,
  499:8
  it takes two to speak
  the t., 497:11
  lights a torch, 498:7
  must dazzle gradu-
  ally, 498:4
  not a t. existing
  which I fear, 497:5
  nothing so powerful
  as t., 497:6
  only children and old
  folks tell the t.,
  499:10
  shall rise again, 497:8
  —supply [is] in excess
  of demand, 498:2
  Tell the T. and Run
  (note), 499:5
  when in doubt, tell
  the t., 498:8

Truths
being in and out of favor, 499:3
there are no whole t., 499:2
to be self-evident, 140:3 (paragraph 2)
Tulsa, 107:2, 3
Turkey
is a much more respectable bird, 336:7
"Sick Man of Europe", 334:8
Turn
on, tune in, 279:6
Turtle
lives 'twixt plated decks, 338:5
TV
you don't exist unless you're on TV (note), 305:2
Twain
if Mark T. very ill, 500 words (note), 406:6
'Twas
the night before Christmas, 82:8
Twelve
first t. years are the hardest, 403:6
men true and right, 257:4
men who don't know anything, 257:1
persons brought in from the street, 257:7
Twirl
when in doubt, t., 50:6
Twist
slowly, slowly in the wind, 525:7
Two
can live cheaper than one, 299:9
dollars a day and roast beef, 381:2
societies, one black, one white, 425:2
Twoness
one ever feels his t., 421:3
Tyrannis
sic semper t., 29:1
TYRANNY, 499
Tyranny
is not easily conquered, 500:2
of the Majority, 296:2
over the mind of man, 500:3
securities against t. (note), 296:2
Tyrants
all men would be t. if they could, 540:10
how hard the t. die!, 500:8
rebellion to t. is obedience to God, 499:11
thus always to t. (note), 29:1

U.S.A.
Love It or Leave It, 374:7
Unawed
by opinion, 171:2
Uncertain
I feel u., 442:10

Underdeveloped
& overdeveloped, 458:5
Underexercised, 380:2
UNDERSTANDING. See MIND, THOUGHT, & UNDERSTANDING, 317; TOLERANCE & UNDERSTANDING, 493
Understanding
is a very dull occupation, 318:3
shallow u. from people of goodwill, 493:9
UNHAPPINESS, 501:2
Uninhabitable
by a people depending on agriculture, 349:6
UNION, THE, 501
Union
all your strength is in your u., 503:4
join the union, girls, 538:2
justice, and confidence, 286:3
Liberty and U., now and forever, 501:7
maintained by swords, 502:5
my object in this struggle is to save the U., 461:3
our Federal U.!, 502:1
Sail on, O U., 502:2
to form a more perfect u., 124:5
the u. makes us strong, 76:3
wish to dissolve this U., 501:6
Unions
trade-u., 76:4
United
we stand, 37:7
United States
declare the U.S. the winner, 510:3
hollowness at heart in the U.S., 61:2
in the U.S. there is more space where nobody is, 22:10
is a warning, 19:2
of America—a government of the people, 21:6
sovereign on this continent (note), 194:6
themselves are the greatest poem, 18:7
Uniting
by u. we stand, 503:3
UNITY, 503
UNIVERSE, THE, 503
Universe
hell of a good u. next door, 174:7
I accept the u., 503:7
is a spiraling Big Band, 504:6
is all chemistry, 503:6
is not hostile, 504:4
man said to the u., "Sir, I exist,", 504:2
seems comprehensible, seems pointless, 504:5
University
—hallowed ground, 161:6

Unlucky
person who is so u. that, 291:10
Unsaid
leave a few things u., 455:10
Up
be nice to people on your way u., 478:11
Upward
Ever U., 355:7
USA
God bless the U., 23:3
Used
key is always bright, 542:9
Useful
prefer the u. to the beautiful, 504:8
Useless
nothing u. is, 504:9
Usurer
& interest faster than a tiger, 324:11
UTAH, 504
Utah
has a way of doing things different, 505:2
water in U. is precious, 505:3
where Jews are Gentiles, 505:4
UTOPIA, 505

Valley
this v. is a paradise, 72:3
Valor
by v. and arms, 320:6
uncommon v., 553:2
Valuable
nothing is intrinsically v., 506:7
VALUE, 506
Value
dearness gives everything its v., 506:2
false estimates of the v. of things, 506:3
no such thing as absolute v., 506:4
Values
science of v., 506:5
Van
farewell, dear V., 381:4
Van Horn, 107:4
VANITY. See PRIDE & VANITY, 409
Vanity
& love of fame, 478:4
Vassals
of your sex, 537:2
Vegas
—most extreme of American settlements, 94:6
Venezuela, 334:9
Venice
is like chocolate liqueurs, 111:2
is the world's unconscious, 111:3
it rises like V., 98:1
Venus
on V. it must be venereal, 458:6
Verb
God is a v., 213:12
I am a v., 2:9
Verbal
contract, 276:2
felicity, 55:1

Verdict
& popular prejudice (note), 257:7
VERMONT, 507
Vermont
& New Hampshire, 507:8
& preventing the future, 508:3
I love V. because, 507:6
is a jewel state, 508:2
mankind after the fall [left in] V., 507:2
O maiden of the hills, 507:3
—a place where barns come painted red, 508:1
Vermonter
no V. ever left the state unless, 507:5
Verse
writing free v., 53:9
Vessel
a goodly v., 454:10
VICE. See SIN, VICE, & NAUGHTINESS, 456
Vice
capacity of v. to make your blood creep, 176:2
VICE PRESIDENCY, THE, 508
Vice Presidency
isn't worth a pitcher of warm spit, 508:9
Vice president
dreamed of becoming v. p.? (note), 508:5
is like a man in a cataleptic state, 508:8
should do anything the president wants, 509:3
Vices
go very light on the v., 536:5
never practice two v. at once, 458:2
Victors
to the v. belong the spoils, 389:6
Victory
has a hundred fathers, 533:6
in war there is no substitute for v., 264:6
or Die (note), 39:4
VICTORY. See WINNING & LOSING, VICTORY & DEFEAT, 532
Viet Cong, 510:1
VIETNAM WAR, 509
Vietnam
—first war without censorship, 511:2
Vigilance
eternal v. is the price of liberty, 200:8
Village
a quaint ceremonious v., 161:4
Villain
no man is a v. in his own heart, 177:1
Vintage
where the grapes of wrath are stored, 212:2

VIOLENCE, 511
Violence
 first in v. [Chicago],
  90:5
 in v. we forget who
  we are, 511:6
 is as American as ap-
  ple pie, 511:8
 returning v. for v.,
  511:9
VIRGINIA, 511
Virginia
 & climate, 512:6
 earth's only paradise,
  512:2
 if they are from V.,
  they will tell you,
  513:6
 if V. had but horses
  and kine, 512:1
 yes, V., there is a
  Santa Claus, 83:8
 you can work for V.,
  513:3
Virginian
 intrepid native V.,
  513:7
 not a V. but an Ameri-
  can, 370:12
Virginians
 have little money and
  great pride, 512:5
 seem to venerate
  themselves, 512:7
Virginny [sic]
 carry me back to old
  V., 513:4
VIRTUE, 513
Virtue
 & greatness, 514:5
 is not always amiable,
  514:2
 is the governor, 514:4
 liberty, and indepen-
  dence, 376:9
 reward of v. is v., 514:6
Virtues
 acquired by death,
  172:4
Virtute
 et armis, 320:6
VISION & PERCEPTION,
 516
Vision
 thing, 516:10
 where there is no v.
  (note), 31:5
Visitors
 & the clock, 219:7
Visits
 superior people never
  make long v., 219:11
VISUAL ART. See ART: VI-
 SUAL, 57
Voice
 of the people (note),
  377:6
 people's v. is odd
  (note) 377:6
Voodoo
 economics, 169:6
Vote
 early and v. often,
  382:2
 I never v., 145:4
Vox
 populi, vox humbug,
  377:6
 populi, vox Dei (note),
  377:6

Wabash
 moonlight's fair along
  the W., 247:1

Wait
 why w.?, 480:7
Waiting
 do not keep me w.
  (note), 270:9
 watchful, 195:4
Wake
 up America, 547:10
Walk
 good w. spoiled, 470:8
Walking, 379:8
Wall
 before I built a w.,
  153:1
 doesn't love a w.,
  152:11
Wall St.
 begins in a graveyard,
  70:6
 Lays an Egg, 145:5
Wander
 why do people so love
  to w.?, 494:9
Want
 for the w. of a rider
  (note), 147:8
 protect me from what
  I w., 146:7
 to get what you w.,
  222:9
Wanted
 I've never done a sin-
  gle thing I've w. to,
  501:4
WAR, 518
War
 & a more perfect
  peace, 519:5
 & excitement, 519:10
 against all nations,
  548:4
 art of w. is simple,
  316:1
 as a woman I can't go
  to w., 521:3
 be prepared for war
  [to preserve] peace,
  518:5
 by no means degrades
  [man], 521:8
 can no more win a w.,
  521:4
 cold w., 32:7, 37:5
 councils of w. never
  fight, 316:4
 deterrence of w.,
  314:10
 educates the senses,
  519:8
 either man is obsolete
  or w. is, 522:7
 fatal to enter w. with-
  out will to win,
  522:1
 first casualty when w.
  comes is truth,
  520:5
 he kept us out of w.,
  385:4
 hotter the w. quicker
  the peace, 522:10
 I cannot vote for w.
  (note), 521:4
 I hate w.!, 520:12
 I should welcome any
  w., 468:3
 I'll furnish the w.,
  468:5
 if they mean to have a
  w., let is begin here,
  38:2
 in every w. they kill
  you in a new way,
  520:7

in w. there is no 2nd
  prize, 521:11
in w. there is no sub-
  stitute for victory,
  264:6
is a bore interrupted
  only by terror,
  522:6
is a contagion, 521:1
is an organized bore,
  519:2
is cruelty, 519:4
is hell, 519:7 & note
is the only place
  where there a man really
  lives, 520:4
is the unfolding of
  miscalculations,
  522:3
it is well that w. is so
  terrible, 519:3
last American w.—
  the cause of misery,
  523:4
lets loose the conta-
  gion of hell, 518:2
loses its romance,
  519:9
make love not w.,
  288:8
more equivalent of
  w., 366:2
never was a good w.,
  374:10
no one won the last
  w., 421:9
no substitute for w.'s
  disciplinary func-
  tion, 366:2
now the w. begun,
  461:7
object only of w.
  makes it honorable,
  518:3
—occasionally the
  lesser of two evils,
  521:2
older men declare w.
  but it is youth that,
  521:7
on poverty, 36:5
pattern called a w.,
  520:3
preparation for w. is
  guaranty of peace,
  520:1
real war will never
  get in the books,
  116:5
rich man's w., 114:6
so goodbye to the w.,
  116:5
splendid little w.,
  469:2
take the profits out of
  w., 520:10
that will end w.
  (note), 548:3
that's the way it is in
  w., 522:4
—the red animal,
  519:11
they'll give a w. and
  nobody will come,
  520:11
this w. & the owner-
  ship of the world
  (note), 468:5
this w. is a new kind
  of w., 551:1
the w. is over, 116:4
the w. the soldiers
  tried to stop,
  510:6

we are going to win
  the w. & the peace,
  550:8
we are now in this w.,
  550:7
when you get into a
  w., 316:7
will never cease until,
  522:2
wrong w., at the
  wrong place,
  265:1
WAR OF 1812, 522
Warblers
 thousands of w. and
  thrushes, 285:4
Warm
 I expand in the w.
  day, 348:7
Warmed
 they w. me twice,
  130:6
Warrior
 happy w., 31:2 &
  note, 229:10 & note
Wars
 are boyish, 519:6
 are planned by old
  men, 520:8
 are won by men,
  520:9
 cannot be won by
  bombing alone,
  316:6
 not going to be sent
  into any foreign w.,
  550:3
WASHINGTON, 523
Washington, D.C., 107
WASHINGTON, GEORGE,
 523
Washington
 central star of the
  constellation,
  107:5
 character of W. is a
  fixed star, 525:3
 commanded the sun
  and the moon to
  stand still, 523:8
 crazy in W., 108:4
 fought on—and won
  (note), 532:5
 friend of mankind
  (note), 523:8–524
 goes around in circles,
  108:9
 if you want a friend in
  W., 109:1
 is a city of Southern
  efficiency, 108:10
 is a puzzling state,
  523:6
 is a full of famous
  men, 108:2
 isn't a city, 108:8
 look to the city of W.,
  107:6
 never slopt over!,
  525:4
 stand with W., 380:7
 things get lonely in
  W., 108:3
 things wrong with W.,
  108:7
 thou hero, patriot
  sage, 524:1
 W. *en petit*, 86:7
 was created for a defi-
  nite purpose,
  108:6
 what posterity will
  say of W. (note),
  523:8–524

Waste
national vice is w.,
23:5
Wasteland
vast w., 304:4
Watch
what we do, 4:4
Watches
of the night, 348:2
Watchful waiting,
195:4
Watching
observe a lot by w.
(note), 475:9
Water
sweet w. from a foul
well?, 48:2
WATERGATE, 564
Watermelon, 191 &
note
Watson
Mr. W., come here,
446:6
Way
best w. of doing
everything, 307:5
out or way in?, 480:5
to do it better, 307:7
We
are all Republicans/all
Federalists, 26:6
are coming Father
Abraham, 114:2
do what we must,
179:2
don't have to be what
you want us to be,
425:6
hold these truths to
be self-evident,
140:3 (paragraph 2)
never sleep, 132:5
raise de wheat, 459:6
shall meet the enemy
(note), 239:6
shall overcome, 423:6
talked between the
rooms (note), 243:1
the people, 124:5
w.'ll stand pat, 384:7
wuz robbed!, 473:4
were very many, and
you were few,
420:11
Wealth
conventional standard
of w., 323:9
Impunity—W., 324:2
malefactors of great
w., 324:4
mere w., 323:2
production of w.,
323:7
proper administration
of w., 436:4
share our w., 386:7
those who produce all
w., 75:2
WEALTH. See RICH &
POOR, WEALTH &
POVERTY, 436
Wealthy
never take a w. man
on a jury (note),
257:4
Weasel words, 268:5 &
note
WEATHER. See NATURE:
WEATHER, 348
Weather
everybody talks about
the w. but, 348:10
in New England
(note) 348:10, 352:7

Weatherman
don't need a w. to
know, 509:7
Weed
is a flower in disguise,
341:8
what is a w.?, 342:2
Weehawken, 109:2
Well
'tis w., 270:2
Well done
a thing w.d., 2
WEST, THE, 527
West
ain't no law w. of St.
Louis, 527:7
definition of the term
"W.", 527:5
everything in the W.
is on a grander
scale, 529:4
go w., young man,
204:5, 527:8
history of the colo-
nization of the
Great W., 529:1
is hope's native home,
529:7
new states of the W.,
310:8
no law w. of St. Louis,
527:7
that's where the W.
begins, 529:2
to the W., to the W.,
528:5
WEST VIRGINIA, 529
West Virginia
mountain momma,
530:2
West Virginians,
529:10
Western
humor, 529:3
inventions, 529:8
settlements & democ-
racy, 310:7
thronged to the w.
wilds, 528:7
wilderness is the ge-
ography of hope,
531:6
youths, 204:6
Westerns
TV w., 529:5
Westward
I go free, 527:6
the course of empire,
15:2
the land is bright
(note), 15:2
Whale ship
was my Yale College,
454:11
What
hath God wrought!,
446:1
Price Glory?, 520:6
Wheat
first in w., 260:8
Wheel
that does the squeak-
ing, 119:6
Whipped
he is w. oftenest who
is w. easiest, 432:5
Whirlwind
precipitated upon the
moneyed men,
434:11
Whiskey
all the courses were
w., 12:2
gimme a w., 12:6

is taken into the com-
mittee rooms, 120:5
what brand of w.
Grant uses, 11:5
Whiskeys
seventeen w., 272:2
Whispering
into her mouth, 178:4
Whistle
and I'll come to you
(note), 458:1
and know how to w.,
don't you? 458:1
Whistling
girl (note), 458:1
White
among the thousand
w. persons, 422:6
and colored people of
this country, 419:3
danger of a conflict
between the w. and
black inhabitants,
418:1
it doesn't matter if it's
a w. snake or a
black snake, 425:8
life of w. men is slav-
ery, 420:5
man became very
large, 417:3
man will never be
alone, 418:7
Man's burden, 469:3
White Christmas, 84:2
White House
choose between the
penitentiary and
the W. H., 402:1
gone to the W.H., ha,
ha, ha (note), 384:2
in the W. H. the fu-
ture rapidly be-
comes the past,
404:4
is a bully pulpit, 427
is another world,
404:7
president has paid
dear for his W.H.,
401:4
White Way
the Great, 98:6
Whites
of their eyes, 38:4 &
note
Who
are we?, 414:1
do you know w. I
am?, 420:4
he?, 414:4
we? (note), 414:4
Wicked
I's w., I is, 176:3
Wife
how's your w.? (note),
300:10
I'll be no submissive
w., 298:11
if ever w. was happy
with a man, 289:1
she's my w., 299:7
take my w., 300:10
Wild
rank place, 530:9
w. and wooly, 64:1
WILDERNESS, 530
Wilderness
Bill of Rights, 531:5
God made the w.,
531:4
if we ever let the re-
maining w. be de-
stroyed, 531:3

into the universe
through a forest w.,
531:1
is the raw material,
531:2
western w. is the ge-
ography of hope,
531:6
Wildness
in God's w. lies the
hope of the world,
530:10
in w. is the preserva-
tion of the world,
530:8
WILL, 531
Will
and wisdom are both
mighty leaders,
531:10
fat kitchen, a lean w.,
531:7
free w., 531:11
not our w. but His,
271:6
springs from moral
sense and self-
interest, 531:8
Wilson
and his Fourteen
Points!, 195:7
Win
as if you were used to
it, 532:3
as quick as you can,
316:7
sometimes it's worse
to w., 533:4
this one for the Gip-
per, 472:2
you can't w. all the
time (note),
475:9–476
you can't w. them all,
533:3
Wind
has blown the rain
away, 345:9
what if a much of a
which of w., 349:4
where the w. is al-
ways north-north-
east, 352:9
W.'s politics, 534:5
Winds
like anthems, roll,
348:8
Wine
& Noah's health, 12:8
WINE. See FOOD, WINE,
& EATING, 190
Wings
she flies with her own
w., 365:3
Winner
can only be one w.,
532:9
declare the United
States the w., 510:3
Winners
never give up, 532:5
never quit, 149:3
WINNING & LOSING,
VICTORY & DEFEAT,
532
Winning
I can teach a lot more
character w., 474:6
is the only thing,
533:5
isn't worthwhile un-
less, 532:7
Winter
afternoons, 344:1

becomes an infinite alas, 342:3
is icumen in, 345:2
lies too long in country towns, 345:5
WISCONSIN, 534
Wisconsin
is the soul of a great people, 534:4
WISDOM, 534
Wisdom
comes by disillusionment, 535:2
his w. lags so far behind his ambition, 253:1
is of the soul, 534:8
is wealth, 65:14
justice, and moderation, 210:2
not to do desperate things, 534:7
privilege of w. to listen, 534:9
this is w., 535:5
WISDOM, WORDS OF, 535
Wise
art of being w., 535:1
being w. in time, 535:3
Man: One who sees the storm coming, 535:4
Wit
& satirist & humorist, 240:7
inspires more admiration than confidence, 239:8
is the only wall between us and the dark, 240:5
makes its own welcome, 239:7
Witch
I have gone out a possessed w., 358:3
Wives
absolute power over w., 540:11
Wobegon
Lake W., 319:1
Wolfe
if General W. is mad (note), 11:5
Woman
beautiful w. cooking dinner, 542:2
beautiful w. & homely w., 538:10
beautiful w. is a practical poet, 537:11
Christ [came] from God and a w., 537:8
first a w. [wants only] a husband, 539:2
first w. God ever made (note), 537:8
has her way, 541:4
I am, being w., hard beset, 539:1
I am w., 540:6
I'm a young w., 557:1
in every true w.'s heart, 537:4
Is a Sometime Thing, 539:8
is Lordess, 540:12
liberated w., 540:2
little w. who wrote the book that (note), 460:3
must be taught to protect herself, 538:4

never forgets her sex, 541:7
no slave like a loving w., 367:3
no w. has had a fair chance, 537:7
only a w. can understand, 5:1
should always challenge our respect, 537:6
so unto the man is the w., 541:3
some w. will wind up in the senate, 539:5
strong w., 540:8
takes a smart w. to love a good man, 542:7
waits for me, 289:6
wants what you're out of, 538:11
why can't a w. be more like a man?, 307:1
will always have to be better than a man, 542:1
w.'s best protection is a little money, 540:1
w.'s life is a history of the affections, 537:3
w.'s work is seldom done, 539:11
Womanhood
heroic w., 537:10
worth of a race & character of its w., 539:7
WOMEN, 537
Women
& idea that they ought to improve their minds, 538:8
all men and w. are created equal, 541:2
American w. are intelligent, 537:12
civilization & good w., 538:3
damned mob of scribbling w., 537:9
do not recognize themselves as discriminated against, 540:4
elegant w., 539:9
few grown w. like their lives, 540:7
have simple tastes, 539:12
married w. are kept w., 300:4
monogamous, 541:9
new races of perfect w., 538:5
prolonged slavery of w., 538:7
superiority of their w., 537:5
tell that to w. and children, 541:1
their rights and nothing less, 541:5
want mediocre men, 305:6
when w. kiss, 539:13
where w. cease from troubling, 541:12
would rather be right, 540:3
WOMEN & MEN, 540

Wood
splits his own w. (note), 130:6
Woodman
spare that tree!, 341:4
Woods
are lovely, dark and deep, 494:12
culture is no better than its w., 168:6
I went to the woods, 280:8
proximity of the w., 530:5
Wooing
if I am not worth the w. (note), 289:5
Woollcott
all W. and a yard wide (note), 457:9
Wooly
wild and w., 64:1
WORDS. See LANGUAGE & WORDS, 266
Word
almost-right w., 267:8
each w.—a stroke of genius, 267:3
every suppressed or expunged w., 77:8
every w. was once a poem, 267:1
is dead when it is said, 267:5
shorter and more ugly w., 268:4
to the wise, 483:3
Words
are a great trap, 269:10
are chameleons, 269:5
are slippery, 268:2
are weapons, 269:4
do not pay for my dead people (note), 483:5
for of all sad w. of tongue or pen, 428:3
hard w. bruise a child, 81:9
honeyed w. like bees, 269:1
man does not live by w. alone, 269:7
many w. won't fill a bushel, 483:5
omit needless w., 54:11
one look is worth 1,000 w. (note), 303:4
pretty w. like blades, 267:6
short w. are the best, 268:3
smooth w. like gold-enameled fish, 269:3
stroke people with w., 269:6
two w.—im possible, 269:9
weasel w., 268:5
WORK & WORKERS, 542
Work
& drudgery, 544:2
a lifetime to pay off a house, 545:5
as if you were to live a 100 years, 535:7
chance to w. hard at w. worth doing, 544:6

conquers all things, 360:1
hands to w., hearts to God, 514:3
hard, keep your mouth shut, 536:2
if w. was a good thing, 545:10
is a four-letter word, 545:11
loveliest of all four-letter words, 546:4
most wonderful work, 126:9
no substitute for hard w., 545:4
no w. with interest is hard, 545:2
noblest w. of our lives, 27:1
useful w. is worship, 544:5
when a lot of people are out of w. (note), 223:7
which is well done, 177:4
Workers
are invisible, 77:5
of the world unite (note), 163:9–164
Working
class is loyal to friends, 546:1
Heaven will protect the w. girl, 545:1
no prestige to actually w., 546:3
people have lot of bad habits, 545:3
WORLD, THE, 546
World
actual w. & fantastic w., 426:12
dung heap of this w., 546:5
each day the w. is born anew, 399:12
good-bye proud w.!, 546:9
I came into this w. to live in it, 546:10
I cannot hold thee close enough!, 546:12
I do not weep at the w., 547:3
I had a lover's quarrel with the w., 173:4
in a new world, 95:12
is a fine place, 547:4
is a force, not a presence, 547:8
is a hell, and a heaven, 546:8
is a severe schoolmaster, 546:6
is but thickened light, 444:4
is puddle-wonderful, 345:8
is so big, and I am so small, 546:11
is too much governed, 216:3
look on this beautiful w., 546:7
most incomprehensible thing about the w., 547:7
must be made safe for democracy, 548:3
my country is the w., 174:8

World (cont.)
of nuclear giants and
ethical infants,
175:3
one w. at a time,
270:10
only exists in your
eyes, 547:6
some say the w. will
end in fire, 547:1
this is the way the w.
ends, 547:1
Turned Upside Down,
40:6
what if the w. is a
kind of show?,
56:6
what the w. says of
someone, 210:3
will little note what
we say here, 210:3
(paragraph 3)
w.'s best hope (note),
461:5
WORLD WAR I, 547
WORLD WAR II, 550
World War III, 522:8
Worm
to tread by chance
upon a w., 139:7
Worms
going into the garden
to eat w., 501:5
WORRY. See ANXIETY &
WORRY, 43
Worry
never hurry and never
w.!, 43:3
we w. away our lives,
43:5
What, Me W.?, 43:4
Worshipping
protected in w. the
Deity, 429:1
Worse
and w., 364:9
Worst
is yet to come, 364:2
Worth,
well's dry—we know
the w. of water,
506:1
Wounded
better to be w., 286:10

deer leaps highest,
479:10
Wounded Knee
bury my heart at
W. K., 422:2
Wounds
love your w., 480:4
Writer
[needs a] shit detec-
tor, 58:10
being a great w., 58:14
face to face with a
revered w. (note),
181:7–182
if a w. has to rob his
mother, 58:9
no tears in the w.,
58:4
w.'s only responsibil-
ity is to his art, 58:8
Writing
—all you do is open a
vein, 58:13
be ruthless with one's
own w., 58:6
comes by the grace of
God, 57:7
is nobler when it is a
deed, 57:8
legal w., 278:4
never put anything in
w., 131:7
vigorous w. is con-
cise, 54:11
WRITING. See ART: STYLE
IN WRITING AND EX-
PRESSION, 54; ART:
WRITING, 57
Written
so much has already
been w., 263:11
Wrong
Constitutional right
to be w., 378:8
forever on the throne,
500:4
I know what's w., my
dear, 349:5
if anything can go w.,
it will, 496:3
war, at the w. place,
265:1
Wrongs
two w., 178:7

WYOMING, 554
Wyoming
cattleman, 554:7
—land of great open
spaces, 554:6
will be your new
home, 554:4

Yacht
annual upkeep of a y.,
455:6
Yankee
Doodle, 15:3
Doodle Dandy, 373:9
I am a Y. of the Y.s,
122:9
word Y. came to
mean Connecticut
Y., 123:3
you can always tell a
Y., 352:6
Yankees
damn Y. (note), 123:3
Year
plunges into night,
346:5
Years
adequate for choosing
a direction, 309:7
Yeats
William Y. is laid to
rest, 173:3
Yellow ribbon, 289:7
Yellowstone River,
554:5
Yesterday
a night-gone thing,
370:3
December 7, 1941,
550:6
mortgaged to y.,
369:10
You
ain't heard nothin'
yet, 206:1
know more than you
think you do,
367:11
never had it so good,
387:9
now that I am with-
out y., 290:2
You press the button,
5:3

Young
compliment him
about looking y.,
360:6
man & old man, 8:12
ready to give benefits
of their inexperi-
ence, 556:4
woman ain't done run-
nin' around, 557:1
Young, Brigham
has 200 wives, 299:5
Your
tired, your poor, 29:5
Yourself
nothing can bring you
peace but y., 451:4
YOUTH, 556
Youth
& middle age & old
age, 8:8
American ideal is y.,
557:4
cannot go back to his
y., 557:5
condemns, 8:11
in our y. our hearts
were touched with
fire, 369:6
is the pollen that
blows through the
sky, 557:5
our y. is our strength,
18:6
replies, I can, 556:3
secret of eternal y.,
557:5
that's now so bravely
spending, 556:7
Youths
O you y., Western y.,
204:6
Yukon
the law of the Y., 10:3

ZEAL. See ENTHUSIASM
& ZEAL, 166:7
Zeal
insidious encroach-
ment by men of z.,
166:7
Zigged
when I should have
zagged, 474:3